A Melville Encyclopedia:
The Novels

Second Edition

compiled by
Kathleen E. Kier

The Whitston Publishing Company
Troy, New York
1994

Copyright 1990, 1994
Kathleen E. Kier

Library of Congress Catalog Card Number 90-70385

ISBN 0-87875-453-9

Printed in the United States of America

In memory of Kenneth F. Kier,
another sailor who loved reading

Contents

Preface

When Herman Melville began writing in the 1840's, most American literary critics still carried the shield of eighteenth-century rationalism, judging a work in terms of its factuality. "Fact" was preferred to "fancy" in literature, and the two were most certainly never to be intermingled. Writers might even be called upon to prove the veracity of their works, and Melville was challenged by critics to demonstrate that his first novel, *Typee*, was "fact" and not "fancy" or some intolerable hybrid. He was "saved" by the serendipitous eye-witness testimony of Richard Tobias Greene, the novel's "Toby," and *Typee* found acceptability that carried over to the sequel, *Omoo*. But the critics and the readers they guided were dumbfounded by Melville's third novel, *Mardi*. That book's early chapters passed the credibility test, but later chapters soared off into flights of metaphysical and philosophical fancy; Melville had allowed his imagination to insinuate itself. Chastened and impoverished by *Mardi's* failure, a dutiful Melville produced two more relatively factual works: *Redburn* and *White-Jacket*. But the "something unmanageable" in him that had made *Mardi* tack from the empirical to the empyreal bolted again, and Melville next created the anomalous *Moby-Dick*, which simultaneously appeared to be a zoological study, a blasphemous philosophical tract, a ghost story, and an ordinary tale of the big fish that got away. What we now recognize as the great American epic novel met with utter rejection. And the work which followed it, *Pierre*, suggested some "facts" about Melville's family too horrifying to be credited—until twentieth-century biographers certified some skeletons in the family closet. Melville's growing reputation for mad intransigence probably precluded success for his last novels, the highly factual *Israel Potter* and the darkly truthful *The Confidence-Man*. He was sharply criticized in the New York *Literary World* (Vol. 9, 15 November and 22 November 1851), where a former friend, Evert Duyckinck, accused him of wanting to have it both ways in his books: "in one light they are romantic fictions, in another statements of absolute fact."

Melville's contemporaries seem to us very limited and literal-minded in their insistence on separating fact from fiction. We moderns like to think that we are fully mature readers who recognize "truth," whatever its disguise. We have outgrown a stodgy insistence on empiricism and indeed prefer the complex novel that mingles the landscape of the planet and the landscape of the mind. We have in fact done an about-face, finding less import in Melville's "facts" than in his "fictions," and increasingly focusing on the "little lower layer" of meaning beneath the surface of the novels—the very layer that most distressed his contemporaries. From the time when Melville's works were "rediscovered" in the early part of this century, much of our critical attention has sought ever *deeper* meaning. We have produced some rather fanciful flights of exegesis in the process, skimming over the very surface content which was previously privileged.

Our reversal of critical focus has caused an inconvenient gap in Melville scholarship, which the present work hopes to ameliorate. The journeyman work of identifying people and things mentioned throughout the canon has still not been fully accomplished, and indeed may never be. Several attempts have been made to provide a "standard edition," at least partly annotated. But the Constable Edition used British texts rather different from those published in America. The Hendricks House series was never completed, and the Library of America series emphasized text, rather than elucidation. The recently completed Northwestern-Newberry prose series provides much historical background and justification for text establishment but does not annotate. And notes for those novels which have been annotated tend as much toward interpretation as identification. At the time of this writing, there are no fully annotated editions of *Typee, Omoo, Redburn*, or *Israel Potter*. Furthermore, the vagaries of modern publishing have caused most annotated editions to go quickly out of print. So America's most allusive and undoubtedly greatest author remains to some extent still its greatest orphan, with little basic scholarship available despite pioneer efforts such as those of Jay Leyda (*The Melville Log*), Merton M. Sealts, Jr. (*Melville's Reading*), and Charles R. Anderson (*Melville in the South Seas*). There are recent concordances to some of the novels, and some other nonconjectural works, such as Gail Coffler's *Melville's Classical Allusions*, as well as other basic studies and biographies used in the composition of the *Encyclopedia* and mentioned in its bibliography.

When I first began reading Melville's novels, like many of my contemporaries I was swept away by an irresistible undertow of implication, attempting to dive beneath a surface upon which I had not yet learned to float. I was embarrassed to admit that I really did not know what Melville was referring to in many of his most direct allusions. My puzzlement over *White-Jacket*'s references led to a dissertation annotating that work—and it led to fuller enjoyment in my future readings of it. But my curiosity was fired regarding the other novels; my own education seemed paltry if I could not comprehend the allusions of a man whose "Yale College and Harvard" were a "whaleship." Aware of the hubris involved in writing an encyclopedia about an encyclopedic writer, I compiled the present work, utilizing previous scholarship, standard reference works, and nineteenth-century sources. In doing so, I was perhaps signing on with those antiquated empiricists, but I was more comfortable in my readings. I think that I am rather a "common reader," and I hope that *The Melville Encyclopedia* will provide bearings for other "common" readers, as well as "uncommon" ones.

The *Encyclopedia* is a reference work for twentieth-century readers, yet in some ways a throwback to the "time before steamships." I have attempted to identify specific things (people, places, events, ideas) mentioned in the novels—not from our modern perspective but from that of Melville and his contemporaries—in order to give a frame of reference. I have aimed for a book of facts, although I confess to allowing other, more fanciful, kinds of truth to slip in occasionally and to editorializing where it was irresistible to do so. Yet although my emphasis has been on the literal, there is little in Melville's works that should be taken merely literally. He spoke literal and figurative truth, to the consternation of his contemporaries and modern readers, as well. The clearest example of this legerdemain is perhaps the "Cetology" chapter (32) of *Moby-Dick*. While many readers still flip past the seemingly arcane (and seemingly endless) pages of cetacean lore, more imaginative readers dote on every word, hoping to extract the *real* meaning behind all of the Latinate diction. Melville undoubtedly knew precisely what he was doing in "Cetology"; he was aware of the seeming dichotomy between "realism" and "metaphysics" and must have enjoyed undercutting scientific taxonomies while simultaneously milking them for symbolic content. In our modern-day emphasis on symbols, we might bear in mind his overt praise of the "realism" of Richard Henry Dana and J. Ross Browne, in a *Literary World* review (1 March 1847). His own target in literature was probably located somewhere between poetry and pamphleteering, and in our latter-day preference for the one, we should not totally neglect the other.

"What did Melville know?" we might ask. If his formal schooling was all but over when he was thirteen years old, where did he learn what he knew? That he was an autodidact and a voracious reader with a formidable memory is well established. But the present reader should remember that "common knowledge" was more commonly possessed in the nineteenth century, when people knew more about their pasts and their presents than modern people know, even given a "Yale College and Harvard." We have much to learn for mere survival in the twentieth century, and we cite that truism as an excuse for our ignorance of the past. But nineteenth-century people, certainly including Melville and his family, appear to have had more of a love of learning for its own sake than we do. In those days, primary school education was often the basis for a lifetime of learning. Instead of watching electronic "talking heads," people read aloud to each other in leisure time, discussing books, journals, and newspapers at length, and exchanging them. They wrote long, well-composed letters, reading, re-reading, and discussing those they received (and, when we are lucky, saving them for posterity). I do not wish to claim that Melville's generation knew all of the facts in this *Encyclopedia*, but I do believe that most middle- and upper-class people, and probably many laborers, knew the gist of many of my entries. If they had not, our best western literature would have meant little to them, as it often means little to present-day college freshman reading without guidance. As his contexts show, Melville had an even broader frame of reference than most of his contemporaries with a college education. He knew the implications of Plato's philosophy for nineteenth-century America, but he also knew who was the current champion prize-fighter and who the challengers were (probably via his subscription to the popular New York *Herald*). He knew as well the lessons of a laboring man and those of a father, brother, orphaned son, and friend. His works have endured because they speak to us on many levels. And if we are willing to confront the surface of his text and then dive into it, we undergo a sea-change, perceiving truths above and below the surface, much as Thoreau did when his fishing line simultaneously reached the muddy bottom of Walden Pond and the sparkling stars above. Melville read Shakespeare *and* the *Penny Cyclopedia*, Hawthorne's works *and* pulp sailor magazines. His densely allusive novels reflect the "anatomies" of Burton and Sir Thomas Browne and anticipate those of James Joyce and others in our century. Surely he did not learn all that he knew in social settings; he had to have print "sources," as well. And when these sources seem clear, I mention them in my entries. But my major concern has not been source-study but identification, which I see as placing a horse before the elegant scholarly cart we have constructed. My own sources, and some of Melville's, are listed in the bibliography of the present work.

In *White-Jacket* 76, Melville speaks of "concocting information into wisdom." His novels are rich and elaborate tapestries, and the literary scholar may find significance beyond more informed understanding of particular references, in the patterns of allusions which Howard Vincent said in *White-Jacket* constitute a "patch-work" or "tesselation." The types of allusions in particular works speak to Melville's preferences, to his biography, to contemporary history. The allusions relate the works to one another and to the canon, often allowing one work to gloss others. The allusions in *White-Jacket*, for example, are similar to those in the short story, *Billy Budd, Sailor*, written some forty years later. (Short works will be treated in a projected third volume of the *Encyclopedia*.) Identification can help us to study broad fields such as Melville and Literature; Melville and Politics, Art, Music, Popular Culture. (Yet we do this at our own risk; Melville often referred only covertly to things most important to his work. *Penny Cyclopedia*, which he regularly raided, goes unnamed in the novels, as do Emerson, Dickens, Poe, and others to whom he responds. Such "hidden" allusions are discussed in the present work, despite their being unnamed.) Melville's bending or coloring of the facts bespeaks much about his biases, or even a hidden agenda. Elsewhere, I have suggested that he was a "geophobe," evincing distaste for many nations (his own included) in stereotypical references throughout the canon. Was he a "man without a country"? He has been called an Anglophile, but examination of his British allusions and their contexts disproves that charge. The largest number of allusions *are* geographic references, and there is much room in scholarship for an examination of Melville's physical, political, and imaginary geography, especially in *Moby-Dick*, a most densely allusive novel.

"What did Melville believe?" is an even harder question than those posed earlier. Lionel Trilling might have had Melville in mind when he spoke of certain American artists as "repositories of the dialectic of their times," containing "both the yes and the no of their culture" (*The Liberal Imagination*, Chapter 1). The United States was in social and cultural turmoil during Melville's lifetime, its growing-pains exacerbating problems simultaneously experienced in other nations, as well. Melville's allusions reflect the fact that Americans had no firmly received epistemology by which to steer a course, as those other nations did. By the time of his birth, Americans had cherished and discarded "isms" great and small, to many of which he refers in his novels. Early Puritanism had yielded a good deal to eighteenth-century secular rationalism. By the time of his adulthood, transcendentalism had taken as much root as it was ever to do, and by the time of his death Social Darwinism had sharpened the idea of the strong, self-reliant individual into a weapon by which weaklings might be subjugated. From the time of Andrew Jackson's Presidency (1829-37), the American political system was in throes; Melville's highly placed Dutch patroon forebears had watched the paternalistic system by which they had prospered in New York yield to machine party politics, while small-town agrarianism gave way to urban industrialism. Federalism had caved in to Democratic Republicanism, and during Melville's lifetime only two Presidents (Jackson and Grant) were reelected, reflecting the inate instability. With no permanent aristocratic class, no ruling church, no long-term precedents in arts or philosophies, Americans turned to reliance on "the Law" as authority, to "Freedom" as justification for bending that law, and to "Wealth" as evidence of moral progress. Before Melville's birth, the War of 1812 had badly split north and south, making the United States seem more like two nations than one. By the time of his maturity, the idea of manifest destiny had validated the war with Mexico. By his middle years, the evil of slavery, simmering from the time of the earliest settlements, had boiled over into the Civil War. His old age found America an imperialistic nation casting an eye southward for territory, while its individual citizens seemed to replicate their homeland's ethos in increasing acquisitiveness. During such a lifetime, to what consistent belief might any "pondering" man cling?

Artists and writers were witness to the failure of idealism in the nineteenth century but were powerless to change the nation's course, given clear evidence of a standard of living and potential for individual advancement better than had been seen before. Emerson's charge that "things" were in the saddle and rode mankind seemed precisely the route modern people approved. And artists were forced to seek "things" as well, because the system did nothing to support them. In Melville's case, distaste for orthodoxy of any kind probably suggested that there was indeed no epistemology for Americans other than belief in a full stomach: a powerful notion that he could share. As Trilling suggested, not only are we unable to posit a consistent political stance for such artists, but we encounter inconsistencies so disturbing as to suggest roots for the "alienated" outlook of the twentieth century. Given a world in turmoil, the artist can but record what he sees, as he sees it, at a given moment; by next year (or next book), his vantage point may be different. We see Melville's vacillation, for example, in his apparent embrace of manifest destiny in *White-Jacket* 36, and his apparent condemnation of

it in *Moby-Dick* 89. Melville's allusions are not heavily
weighted toward things American, and his especial difficulty
in getting a fix on local matters or holding them up as positive
examples may reflect his turning elsewhere in an effort to
locate stability. In our desire to solve the riddle of Melville's
beliefs, we might also bear in mind a comment he made in a
letter (1 June 1851?) to Hawthorne, explaining his wavering
appraisal of chronically optimistic writers: "the thing that
plays the mischief with the truth is that men will insist upon
the universal application of a temporary feeling or opinion." I
should like the *Melville Encyclopedia* to be read with this pro-
nouncement in mind.

Any reference work invariably has errors and
omissions. I shall be grateful for information regarding the
former; I am already painfully aware of the latter. Who *was*
"Pinzella" (of *White-Jacket* 44), his name invoked in a passage
suggesting sado-masochism? Was Melville one of the "other"
Victorians who hypocritically led secret lives or indulged
secret appetites? Much of *White-Jacket*'s nautical language
was double-entendre for sailors, enabling Melville to be quite
naughty without fear of censorship. I believe that he tried to
appeal simultaneously to various readerships, with all of
whom he identified: sailors, the American literati, the British
elite, the "common" reader of novels. His broad aim adds to
the richness of his works for us, but it perhaps added only
confusion for critics such as Duyckinck, whose literary fodder
had to be either fish *or* fowl.

I have compiled what seems a rather disproportionate
book. How much should one say about an allusion? Although
the reader will find much more space given to things most
important in Melville scholarship, he will also find lengthy
entries on minor things that a modern reader might struggle
to decipher. I have short-changed items that have had major
treatments elsewhere and perhaps overemphasized some that
have been justly neglected. Melville study has been called the
"endless, winding way," and even a book of "facts" merely
beckons us on to further detective work. "Oh, Time, Strength,
Cash, and Patience!"

In a list of persons whom one thanks, typists traditionally come last, but I should like to chart my own course here,
as well. I am grateful to Diane Menna, who entered this work
onto computer disks: a scholar herself, she caught me in some
blatant errors, untangled my syntax, and counseled me wisely
when the need was great. Patricia Zaccardo also entered
much material. This research was supported in part by a
grant from the City University of New York PSC-CUNY Research Award Program and a Faculty-in-Residence grant
from Queens College. The Benjamin Rosenthal Library

(Matthew J. Simon, Chief Librarian) provided work space; that library, as well as Paul Klapper Library (Queens College), Butler Library (Columbia University), and the New York Public Library, have been my major resources. I have been kept afloat emotionally and otherwise aided by the Melville Society and Melville scholars including Joyce S. Adler, John Bryant, Allan Moore Emery, Stanton Garner, Thomas Heffernan, George Monteiro, Donald Yannella, and the late Jay Leyda. My colleagues in the Queens College Department of English (Charles H. Molesworth, Chairman), and Department secretaries Dolores G. Beckerman and Evelyn Diaz, deserve mention, as does Jean Goode, of The Whitston Publishing Company. My children, David, Peter, and Linda Hamm and Jane Hendricks, bore too often with my insufferable interjection: "It's in my book." The sweet baby demands of my grandson, Matthew Hendricks, kept me from becoming a solemn drone of a "Sub-Sub librarian."

I have presumed that nothing is "too familiar" for inclusion in this work and have attempted to arrange material in an accessible but not redundant manner. For rubrics, I have usually used Melville's often idiosyncratic spelling (found in most circulating editions) even when newer texts correct that spelling; I silently correct within entries. My standard in other respects has been the Northwestern-Newberry editions where possible; Volumes VI and IX, *Moby-Dick* and *The Piazza Tales*, were published too late for me to make full use of their findings, but I have referred to them when it was feasible to do so. The revised edition of Sealts's *Melville's Reading* was likewise too late; "Sealts numbers" referred to in the *Encyclopedia* are limited to those from the first edition of the work that lists print sources known to have been accessible to Melville.

Because my references are to chapter rather than page number, the reader should have little difficulty using most editions (the commonest of which are listed in the bibliography). Beneath each entry is a list of allusion locations; I have tried to avoid the use of "passim," but it has been necessary sometimes to resort to it. I have added "and elsewhere" when I deal with only the most significant locations for a given allusion. Asterisks indicate the presence of a separate entry elsewhere in the *Encyclopedia*. In some places, the reader's follow-up unearths merely a chapter citation, but I have presumed an interest even in location of allusions, despite my own distaste for cul-de-sacs. Some very brief entries are included on the presumption that the reader would rather know a little than know nothing. Full documentation of works mentioned in the entries is found in the bibliography. Throughout the text, "M." means "Melville." Abbreviations for the novels are as follows:

T.	*Typee*
O.	*Omoo*
M.	*Mardi*
R.	*Redburn*
W.	*White-Jacket*
M.D.	*Moby-Dick*
P.	*Pierre*
I.P.	*Israel Potter*
C.M.	*The Confidence-Man*

A "Chronology" of the events of Melville's life precedes the main alphabet, which locates and defines allusions. The "Cetology" section contained within the main alphabet is a layman's guide to the system Melville undercuts in *Moby-Dick* 32. There are appendices at the end of the main alphabet: the "Extracts" appendix, with "Extracts" numbered here for ease of reference, contains probable sources for the "Extracts" of *Moby-Dick*. The "Nautical Language" appendix defines many maritime expressions but does not locate them in Melville's texts, except when they have special significance or are also treated in the main alphabet. The "Quotations" appendix identifies originals for some of the myriad overt and covert quoted allusions in the novels. The "Bibliography" lists sources consulted and works mentioned in my text, as well as many works alluded to by Melville.

Chronology

1819   1 August: M. born at 6 Pearl Street, New York
City. Parents: Allan Melvill (7 April 1782 - 28
January 1832), Maria Gansevoort Melvill (6 April
1791 - 1 April 1872). Previous children:
Gansevoort (6 December 1815 - 12 May 1846);
Helen Maria (4 August 1817 - 14 December 1888).
Later children: Augusta (24 April 1821 - 4 April
1876); Allan (7 April 1823 - 9 February 1872);
Catherine (21 May 1825 - 17 January 1905);
Frances Priscilla (26 August 1827 - 9 July 1885);
Thomas (24 January 1830 - 5 March 1884).

1820   Family moves to 55 Courtlandt Street.

1824   Family moves to 33 Bleeker Street.

1825   M. enters New York Male High School.

1826   M. is sent to visit the Gansevoorts, in Albany.

1828   Family moves to 675 Broadway.

1830   Father's business fails; family moves to Albany.
M. attends Albany Academy.

1832   Father dies; M. is taken out of school, works as
clerk at New York State Bank.

1833   M. vacations at his Uncle Thomas Melville's farm
            (later "Broadhall") in Pittsfield, Massachusetts.

1834   M. works at Uncle Thomas's farm.   Brother
            Gansevoort's business is destroyed by fire.

1835   M. clerks in fur store, joins Albany Young Men's
            Association, enters Albany Classical School.

1836   M. joins the Ciceronian Debating Society;   with
            family debts mounting, mother mortgages in-
            herited property.

1837   Gansevoort's business fails in financial panic;   M.
            teaches at Sikes District School, Pittsfield.

1838   M. becomes president of Albany's Philo Logos
            Debating Society; family moves to Lansingburgh;
            M. takes course in surveying and engineering, at
            Lansingburgh Academy.

1839   May: *The Democratic Press & Lansingburgh
            Advertiser* publishes M.'s "Fragments from a
            Writing Desk"; June: M. sails for Liverpool on *St.
            Lawrence*, a trader; fall: M. teaches in a
            Greenbush school.

1840   M. visits Uncle Thomas in Galena, Illinois;   un-
            employed, in December M. signs on whaling ship
            Acushnet.

1841   3 January: *Acushnet* leaves Fairhaven for Pacific
            Ocean;   stops at Rio de Janeiro;   rounds Cape
            Horn, visits Santa, Peru;   cruises through
            Galapagos Islands.

1842   June: *Acushnet* arrives at Marquesas Islands; 9
            July: M. and Richard Greene desert, escaping to
            interior of Nukahiva; 9 August: M. signs on

Australian whaler *Lucy Ann*; September 24: M. and others imprisoned by British Consul at Tahiti for refusing duty; October: M. escapes to Eimeo, signs on as boat-steerer on Nantucket whaler *Charles & Henry*.

1843   April: *Charles & Henry* reaches Lahaina, Hawaiian Islands; May: M. is discharged and sent to Honolulu where he works at odd jobs including store clerk and setter of pins in a bowling alley; August: M. signs on as ordinary seaman on frigate *United States*, which visits Marquesas, Tahiti, Valparaiso, Callao, Lima, Rio Harbor.

1844   14 October: M. is discharged, returns to Lansingburgh and begins writing (*Typee*).

1845   *Typee* is rejected by Harper & Bros., accepted by British publisher John Murray.

1846   Gansevoort's political career blossoms; February and March: London publication of *Narrative of a Four Months' Residence Among the Natives of a Valley of the Marquesas Islands*; March: Wiley & Putnam publish *Typee*; 12 May: Gansevoort dies in London;   July: Greene verifies *Typee* experience; M. composes a "Sequel" for revised edition; *Omoo* is accepted by Murray and Harpers.

1847   M. writes for Duyckinck's *The Literary World*, seeks government position in Washington; March: *Omoo* published in England; May: *Omoo* published in U.S.; M. writes political satires for *Yankee Doodle*; 4 August: M. marries Elizabeth Shaw (13 June 1822 - 31 July 1906), daughter of Massachusetts Chief Justice Lemuel Shaw (1781 - 30 March 1861); they set up housekeeping at 103 Fourth Avenue, New York City, along with brother Allan and his wife, plus M.'s mother and unmarried sisters.

1849   16 February: son Malcolm born (died 11
            September 1867); Murray rejects *Mardi*; March
            and April: Richard Bentley in England and
            Harpers publish *Mardi*; M. writes *Redburn* and
            White-Jacket;   September and November:
            *Redburn: His First Voyage. Being the Sailor-boy
            Confessions and Reminiscences of the Son-of-a-
            Gentleman, in the Merchant Service* is published
            by Bentley and Harpers; October 11: M. sails for
            England with proofs of *White-Jacket*, visits Paris,
            Brussels, Cologne, the Rhineland, leaves for New
            York on Christmas morning.

1850   February and March: *White-Jacket* published by
            Bentley and Harpers;   M. and family spend
            summer in Pittsfield; Evert Duyckinck (1816-1878)
            visits and attends excursion to Monument
            Mountain and Icy Glen where M. meets
            Nathaniel Hawthorne, then living in Lenox; *The
            Literary World* publishes "Hawthorne and His
            Mosses"; September: M. buys a farm adjoining
            Broadhall, calling it "Arrowhead" and moving his
            family there; M. begins writing "The Whale."

1851   22 October: son Stanwix is born (died 23 February
            1886); October: Bentley publishes *The Whale*;
            November: Harpers publishes it as *Moby-Dick*.

1852   Spring: Bentley refuses publication of *Pierre*
            unless it is expurgated;   August: Harpers
            publishes *Pierre*; M. visits New Bedford,
            Nantucket, and the islands and seeks a consular
            post abroad.

1853   11 May: daughter Elizabeth is born (died 26 May
            1908); M. contributes to Putnam's and Harper's
            monthly magazines.

1854   *Putnam's* begins serial publication of *Israel Potter*
            (at first subtitled "or, Fifty Years of Exile. A
            Fourth of July Story").

1855   2 March;   daughter Frances is born (died 15
            January 1938);   *Israel Potter* is published in
            March by Putnam's (Dix & Edwards) and in May
            by Putnam's (Sampson Low, Son & Co.) in
            England;   the book is pirated, as were earlier
            works;   Dr. Oliver Wendell Holmes (1809-1894)
            examines M., at his family's request.

1856   *The Piazza Tales* is published in March by
            Putnam's and later in England; "The Bell Tower"
            is rejected for publication; October 11: M. sails for
            Europe and the east, visiting Scotland, England,
            Malta,   Syra,   Salonica,   Constantinople,
            Alexandria, Cairo, the Holy Land.

1857   M. visits Greece, Sicily-Naples, Rome, Florence,
            Pisa, Padua, Venice, Milan, Turin, Genoa,
            Switzerland,   Germany,   the   Netherlands,
            England. April and March: *The Confidence-Man*
            is published by Longman in England, Dix &
            Edwards in U.S.

1858   M. gives lectures, traveling as far as Tennessee
            and Ohio.

1859   M. lectures continue as far as Milwaukee;   he
            writes poetry to be offered for publication.

1860   M. sails on *Meteor* to San Francisco, returning on
            North Star.

1861   M. seeks a Civil War naval appointment.

1862   M., ill with rheumatism, is seriously injured in a
            road accident.

1863   M. sells Arrowhead to brother Allan, moves
            family to 104 East 26 Street, New York.

1864   M. visits the Virginia front, has severe attack of neuralgia.

1865   M. protests reissue of *Israel Potter* as *The Refugee*.

1866   *Harper's Monthly* publishes four of M.'s poems from the forthcoming *Battle-Pieces*; December: M. is sworn in as Inspector of Customs at the Port of New York.

1867   M. discovers son Malcolm dead of self-inflicted pistol shot.

1869   Son Stanwix goes to sea.

1870   Stanwix returns; M. begins *Clarel*; his portrait is painted by Joseph Oriel Eaton (1829-1875). In the 1870's, Stanwix regularly appeared and disappeared, and many deaths occurred of M.'s close relatives and friends.

1872   M.'s brother Allan and his mother die; Elizabeth Melville's property is destroyed in a Boston fire.

1873   Customs House threatens dismissal.

1875   M. projects a volume of prose and poetry, "Parthenope"; his uncle Peter Gansevoort (1788-1876) offers to pay for publication of *Clarel*.

1876   *Clarel* is published; Uncle Peter and sister Augusta die.

1877   Customs House again threatens dismissal.

1878   Elizabeth Melville inherits a substantial sum.

1879 M.'s daughter Elizabeth stricken with severe arthritis; M.'s son Stanwix stricken with tuberculosis, in California.

1880 M.'s daughter Frances marries Henry B. Thomas (1855-1934).

1882 M.'s first grandchild, Eleanor Thomas, is born.

1884 M.'s brother Thomas dies.

1885 M.'s sister Frances Priscilla dies; M.'s poem, "The Admiral of the White," is published in New York and Boston newspapers; 31 December: M. resigns as Customs Inspector.

1886 M. writes his will; son Stanwix dies in San Francisco.

1888 M. voyages to Bermuda, returning via Florida; *John Marr and Other Sailors* is privately printed; composition begins on *Billy Budd, Sailor*.

1890 M. suffers an attack of erysipelas.

1891 *Timoleon* is submitted for private printing; 28 September, M. dies.

AARON

In *Exodus 6, 7, and 8, and Ezra 7, Aaron is the elder brother of *Moses, his helper in freeing the *Israelites from *Egyptian bondage, his spokesman to *Pharaoh. Anointed by his brother as "the priest," Aaron is the ancestor of lawful priests and the founder of the priesthood, from which his two sons, Nadab and Abihu are removed. The rod of Aaron brings about the first three plagues upon the Egyptians. (Biblical scholars disagree as to whether the *Bible speaks of two different Aarons.)
M. 40

ABANA

The *Bible's Abana River is the Barada of southwestern *Syria, the site of *Damascus and a source of irrigation from ancient times.
O. 7

ABBA THULE

See "Spenser."
W. 50

ABBE-BELLEGARDE

Jean Baptiste Morvan de Bellegarde wrote *Politeness of Manners and Behavior in Fashionable Society*. Sealts #57 is the 1817 edition owned by M.'s father.

As William H. Gilman points out (*Melville's Early Life and Redburn*, Chapter 1), M.'s early education included instruction in etiquette, dancing school, and other lessons designed to make him a proper upper-middle-class gentleman.
I.P. 22

ABBEYS

Monasteries, homes of religious communities (called Abbeys when ruled by an abbot) originated as groups of cells surrounding the dwellings of hermitic holy persons. Monks of various types have existed since before the second century B.C. and developed in most religions that encouraged withdrawal (Buddhist, Taoist, *Hindu, Islamic, etc.). At the peak of its popularity, the monastic life was probably chosen for reasons other than religion.

The first real *Christian monastery appeared in *Egypt in the fourth century A.D., but the elaborate structure we associate with it came about only as need for defense arose: strong walls surrounding cloistered courts and chapels. Not until the seventh century was monasticism widely followed, when St. *Benedict of Nursia organized the structure to suit the structured life he prescribed. By the eleventh century, massive cathedrals became the central concern; by the fourteenth century, libraries became important. The monastic life was later assumed by women, whose domiciles are properly called convents.

M.'s comments on hermits are generally negative (see "Charles V").
R. 31

ABEDNEGO

See "Shadrach, Meshach, and Abednego."
M.D. 97

ABEL

In *Genesis 4, the second son of *Adam and Eve. A keeper of sheep, Abel is the first martyr, murdered by his brother, *Cain, when Yahweh (see "Jehovah") accepts Abel's sacrifice but not his brother's.
R. 38; M.D. 40

ABELARD

Petrus Abaelardus (1079-1142), a *French theologian and philosopher, was castrated (c.1118) for having impregnated his pupil, Heloise. Separated, they conducted a famous correspondence and, when Heloise died in 1163, she was buried in his tomb.

Abelard's *Sic et Non* is considered the first text in scholastic theology; his brilliance as a teacher brought pre-eminence to the University of *Paris.
W. 44

ABOLITIONISM
     The radical nineteenth-century anti-slavery movement
demanded immediate abolition of slavery in the United States,
regardless of consequences. From before the 1820's, Abolitionist sentiments had been expressed in newspapers, periodicals,
sermons and other addresses, correspondence, and slave
memoirs, but the word "Abolitionist" did not arise until the
mid-1830's. Slavery had enriched the *American South, and
Abolitionists were mostly Northerners whose aims were not
always idealistic. The *Missouri Compromise of 1820 had provided that new states be admitted in pairs: one slave state and
one free, stimulating political organization by Abolitionists. In
1833, William Lloyd Garrison formed the American Anti-Slavery Society in *Philadelphia, reflecting the views of his *Liberator* weekly publication. Other prominent Abolitionists, including Wendell Phillips, Charles Sumner, Gerrit Smith, and Lu-
cretia Mott, assisted the "Underground Railroad," which
helped slaves escape to the North. By 1840, political splits
within the movement had weakened it somewhat, but Abolitionists were active into the time of the *Civil War, which
*Lincoln suggested was caused by the influence of Abolitionist
Harriet Beecher Stowe's *Uncle Tom's Cabin* (1852).
     There can be little doubt of M.'s anti-slavery position,
although he probably never engaged in Abolitionist (or any
other political) activism. The anti-slavery movement was related to other causes that touched M., as well (Abolitionists
were against *flogging, for example), but the question was a
thorny one throughout M.'s family, as Rogin shows in *Subversive Genealogy*. M.'s father-in-law, *Massachusetts Chief Justice *Lemuel Shaw, declared the Fugitive Slave Law constitutional in 1851, making it the obligation of citizens to assist slave
owners in reclaiming their "property." Shaw's general policy
of conciliating the South aimed at saving the Union, but he was
severely criticized by Garrison and others.
     M.'s poem, "The Portent," is about Abolitionist John
Brown.
C.M. 21

ABORD
     Fr.: Approach, arrival, or attack.
C.M. 25

ABRAHAM
     The progenitor of the Jewish (see "Hebrew") people, in
*Genesis, Abraham becomes *Israel's first great patriarch.
The birth of the son of Terah marks the start of the Judaeo-

*Christian era, with *God's blessing extended to those who bless Abraham and His curse to those who curse him. Abraham is called by God to *Palestine, where his descendents are to become a great nation, *Canaan. His wife, *Sarah, appears to be barren, and Abraham, momentarily lacking faith, begets a son, *Ishmael, upon the servant *Hagar

The two are banished, and Sarah bears a son, *Isaac, conceived in Abraham's old age. God tests Abraham, commanding him to sacrifice his only son, and Abraham's willingness to comply brings God's forgiveness, the safety of Isaac, and Abraham's becoming the father of many peoples.
W. 7; W. 68; M.D. 42; M.D 70; M.D. 111; P. 2:3; I.P. 4; C.M. 7

ABRANTES, DUCHESS D'
    See "D'Abrantes."
I.P. 12

ABSTRACT NOUMENONS
    Noumenons are objects of intution apprehendable by intellect alone.
M. 170

ABYSSINIAN, --S
    See "Ethiopian."
M. 14; M. 98

ACADEME, GROVES OF
    *Horace: "seek for truth in the groves of Academe" (*Epistles*, bk. II [14 B.C.], epistle ii, l.45).
    Sealts #147: *Classical Library*. Harper (18--). 37 vol. Vols. 18 and 19, contains Horace's works.
C.M. 39

ACADEMY OF ARTS AND SCIENCES
    M. was familiar with the works of members of the great academies (*French Académie des Sciences, *British *Royal Society and others) and recognized in W. the official sanction membership brought to one's least valuable performances and publications. In the *United States, the most influential scientific society was The American Philosophical Society Held at *Philadelphia for Promoting Useful Knowledge (founded by *Benjamin Franklin in 1743). Its rival, the American Academy of Arts and Sciences, was incorporated at *Boston in

1780. Although France had its Academie Française and even
*Spain and *Russia had literary academies, there was no seri-
ous counterpart in the United States.

M.'s *lecture tours of the late 1850's were sponsored by
such minor associations as the Clarksville [*Tennessee] Literary Association, the Boston Mercantile Library Association,
the Pennacook [Concord, *Massachusetts] Lyceum, and the
Young Men's Associations of New Haven, *Detroit, Yonkers,
and Flushing, N.Y.
W. 22

ACADEMY OF SCIENCES
    See "Academy of Arts and Sciences."
M.D. 105

ACAPULCO
    The *Mexican *Pacific port (16°49' N., 99°57' W.) was a
main depot for *Spanish fleets because of its superior harbor,
with deep natural anchorages and accessibility to land.
Galleons left Acapulco loaded with gold taken as tribute.
R. 61; W. 50

ACARTY, MARQUIS D'
    See "D'Acarty."
W. 56

ACE-OF-TRUMPS
    The ace is the highest ranking card, in most card
games; the trump is the winning card (Fr. *triomphe*,
"triumph").
I.P. 14

ACEPHALI
    Acephalites were originally various schismatical early
*Christian sects, especially the Monophysites and Nestorians.
The term also refers to priests who reject episcopal authority
and to the *Levellers, under Henry I. The name, also given to
various headless legendary monsters, is from the Greek
akephale, "without a head."
M. 60

ACETABULUM
    See "*os innominatum.*"
W. 63

ACHATES
    Achates is the loyal friend of Aeneas throughout the
Aeneid of *Virgil. "Fidus" refers to fidelity.
M. 3; M. 174

ACHILLES
    Legendary *Greek son of Peleus, King of Myrmidon in
*Thessaly, and *Thetis. Hero of Homer's *Iliad*, brave
Achilles refused to fight after a quarrel with *Agamemnon,
sent Patroclus to oppose the *Trojans and, when he was killed,
rushed into battle himself to kill *Hector. He was slain by
Paris, before the taking of Troy, by an arrow in his heel, the
heel becoming the proverbial vulnerable spot.
    Homer describes his shield in *Iliad* XVIII as huge and
heavy, five-fold, with a triple rim and elaborate decoration,
showing the earth and heavens.
R. 28; M.D. 57

ACTIUM
    A promontory in Acarnania, *Greece (modern Akra
Nikolaos), Actium was the site of Octavian's victory over
*Mark Antony (31 B.C.). *Cleopatra's squadron, in the rear of
Mark Antony's, contained her treasure. When it became clear
that Antony's fleet of some 500 ships would be bested by Octavian's 400, Antony and Cleopatra managed to escape, and the
rest of their fleet was surrendered. The battle made Octavian
undisputed ruler of *Roman territories.
    *Shakespeare's version of the battle appears in *Antony
and Cleopatra* III, x. M.'s copy (Sealts #46) contains a note referring to *Plutarch's claim that Cleopatra's *barge was called
Antoniad. See "Augustus Caesar," for "Octavian."
W. 50; M.D. 83

ACTS
    Acts of the *Apostles is the fifth book of the *New Testa-
ment. It continues the story of the four *Gospels, covering
early Church episodes, early martyrs and conversions, the
story of Peter's conversions, and *St. Paul's conversions and
travels.

(The *Apocryphal Acts are adventure tales of no authority that attempt to fill in the gaps in Acts of the Apostles.)
W. 65

ACUSHNET RIVER
The Acushnet, of southeastern *Massachusetts, rises in southwestern Plymouth County and flows c. fifteen miles past Acushnet to Buzzards Bay, between Fairhaven and *New Bedford, forming a wide estuary. (The town of Acushnet, north of New Bedford, was settled in 1660 and incorporated in 1860.)
See also "Pequod."
M.D. 13

A.D. 1839
The publication date of M.'s copy of "Surgeon *Beale's" *Natural History of the Sperm Whale*: the second edition.
M.D. 32

ADAM
The first man, according to *Genesis (I-IV). The *Talmudists believed Adam to be in *Paradise only twelve hours.
A *Mohammedan legend says that *God sent *Gabriel, *Michael, *Israfel to fetch various colored earth samples for Adam's creation (accounting for the different races), but they failed because a creature thus created would rebel against God. Azreal was sent and accomplished the task, becoming the Angel of Death because he had to separate souls from bodies. The earth was taken near *Mecca, *Arabia, where it was fashioned by God and left to dry for forty days (or forty years). Adam was buried on an Arabian mountain.
The date of the Creation of earth and the first man, Adam, was argued by various schools. James Usher (1581-1656), Archbishop of Armagh, fixed it as 4004 B.C.; nineteenth-century scholars argued for 5411 B.C. Both schools claimed that Adam lived for 930 years.
When "Ahab" asks that the "old Adam" be driven away, he refers to the flesh, in contrast to the "new Adam," or *Christian spirit.
O. 73; M. 3; R. 30; R. 33; R. 38; W. 7; W. 42; W. 68; M.D. 7; M.D. 41; M.D. 42; M.D. 104; M.D. 105; M.D. 108; M.D. 132; P. 2:2; P. 7:8; C.M. 17; C.M. 22

ADAMO
       See "Adam."
O. 73

ADAM'S ALE
       Water.
P. 22:1

ADAM'S APPLE
       See *"pomum Adami."*
W. 63

ADDISON, --IAN
       Joseph Addison (1672-1719), *English essayist and critic,
is best remembered for his work on the periodicals, *The Tatler*
(1709-11) and *The Spectator*, with *Sir Richard Steele. The two
were friends from school years, although a quarrel estranged
them in Addison's last year. The son of a clergyman, Addison
became a classical scholar at Queens College, *Oxford, and
his early skill at *Latin verse was encouraged by such authors
as *John Dryden, *William Congreve, and Jonathan Swift, enabling him to reject ordination in favor of the literary life. As a
member of the Kit-cat club, he made important *Whig connections, leading to a political career (member of *Parliament
from 1708 until death) and a commission to write *The Campaign* (1705), a celebration of *Marlborough's victory at
*Blenheim. He also wrote a successful tragedy (*Cato*) and an
unsuccessful comedy (*The Drummer*).
       His prose style, acclaimed by *Samuel Johnson, was a
model of clarity and grace, and his essays developed new standards of judgment, especially in recognition of women as potential audience. A political disagreement with *Alexander
Pope led to his being satirized as "Atticus" in *An Epistle to Dr.
Arbuthnot.*
       In 1883, M. presented his daughter, Bessie, with a copy
of "Sir Roger De Coverley."
R. 43; R. 58

*"A DESCRIPTION OF BLENHEIM, THE SEAT OF HIS
GRACE THE DUKE OF MARLBOROUGH . . ."*
       Thorp supplies the full title of this volume, in
"Redburn's Prosy Old Guidebook": *New Description of
*Blenheim. The Seat of His Grace The Duke of *Marlborough.
Containing a full and accurate Account of the Paintings,*

Tapestry, and Furniture. A Picturesque Tour of the Gardens and Park; And every other Circumstance connected with the Subject, that can afford either Information or Entertainment . . . A New and Improved Edition. Embellished with an elegant Plan of the Park, &c. London, 1793. Thorp adds that the frontispiece is labeled, "North, or Grand Front of Blenheim, in Oxfordshire."
R. 30

"A DESCRIPTION OF YORK, ITS ANTIQUITIES AND PUBLIC BUILDINGS,..."

Thorp supplies the full title of this text, in "Redburn's Prosy Old Guidebook": *A Description of York, Containing Some Account of its Antiquities, Public Buildings, &c Particularly The Cathedral. "Semper honos, nomenque tuum, laudesque manebunt." . . . Compiled from the most Authentic Records and Authorities.* York-London, 1809.
R. 30

ADMIRAL OF THE BLUE

The *British Admiralty was formerly a hierarchy ranked, Red, White, Blue, with corresponding squadrons, Red being highest.
W. 4

ADMIRAL'S "CORRESPONDENCE"

The "editor" of *Collingwood's "Correspondence" is G.L. Newnham Collingwood: *Selections from the Correspondence of Lord Collingwood, With Memoirs of His Life* (1828). For full text of material quoted in *Edinburgh Review*, see "Quotations" section: "This young gentleman . . . . "
W. 51

ADMIRALTY, THE

Until the early eighteenth century, the British Navy was governed by a *Lord High Admiral, who had great powers. The office was replaced by a Board of Admiralty directly responsible to the Crown and immune to *Parliamentary control except in matters of discipline regulated by law. It had power to issue direct orders to ships, control shipbuilding, and govern research operations. By the second half of the nineteenth century, the First Lord of the Admiralty (a member of *Parliament) had been vested with overriding power. He was attended by Sea Lords and other commissioners.

*London's Admiralty Building was erected 1722-26 (the Arch was built later). *Nelson's body lay in state here in 1806. R. 30; W. 27; W. 75

ADONDO
A prototype handsome man or fop. "Adon" is another form of *Adonis.
M. 142

ADONIS
A beautiful youth in *Greek mythology, of mysterious incestuous *Asiatic origins; loved by Aphrodite (see "Venus") and Persephone (*Proserpine). A hunter, he was killed by a boar while very young. Followers of his cult planted "gardens of Adonis," which sprang up and withered quickly.
"Adonais" is a song about Adonis.
M. 142 (Implication);   W. 6

ADRIAN, EMPEROR
Publius Aelius Hadrianus (A.D. 76-138) became the *Roman Emperor (117-138) Hadrian (whose name M. appears to confuse with those of the Popes Adrian/Hadrian) as a result of kinship with *Trajan. His reign was marked from its inception by problems relative to his abandonment of Trajan's conquests beyond the *Euphrates, his execution of suspected conspirators, and other acts.
Hadrian was an inveterate traveler within the Roman world, absent for twelve of his twenty years on the throne. He built Hadrian's Wall defending the *British frontier, stabilized the Roman population in *Africa, established a league to unite *Greece, and built the Temple of Zeus (see "Jove" and "Jupiter") at *Athens. His *Egyptian city, Antinoopolis, honored his drowned lover, Antinous. In Rome, he developed the *Pantheon and built a splendid villa at *Tivoli. His mausoleum is now the Castel Sant'Angelo.
M. praises the rule of Hadrian, his immediate predecessors and successors, in his poem, "The Age of the Antonines." But Hadrian was so unpopular at his death that repeal of his acts and denial of his choice of successor were possible. History has painted him as a highly cultured and efficient bureaucrat whose acts reflected natural and inevitable changes in the Roman Empire of the time.

In *Naples in 1857, M. undoubtedly saw the bust of
Hadrian in the Museo Borbonico, repository of royal art treasures. The bust reveals an elaborately curled and groomed
*beard, as noted in *W*. 85. But M. copies an error from *Penny
Cyclopaedia* in his assertion that *Plutarch says Adrian wore
a beard to hide scars on his face; William Dillingham suggests
that the reference comes from *Historia Augusta* (The *Scrip-
tores Historia Augusta*), I, 79.

ADRIATIC

The arm of the *Mediterranean between *Italy and the
Balkan peninsula has always been an important trade route.
It is notorious for its dangerous storms, suggested in *M*. 149,
and famous for its clarity and freshness, like the blue eyes of
"Lucy" in *P*. 2:5.

M.'s 1856-57 excursion to the *Holy Land and *Italy did
not bring him into the Adriatic.

M. 149; P. 2:5

ADULLAM, CAVE OF

In *Genesis 38, a fortified *Canaanite royal city. In
*Joshua 12:15, the king of Adullam is defeated by Joshua. In I
*Samuel 22:1-2, *David, his family, and followers take shelter
in the Cave of Adullam, making it a headquarters. In
Nehemiah 11:30, *Hebrew returnees from exile occupy
Adullam.

I.P. 21

ADULTERESS

P.'s Mr. Falsgrave refers to *John 8:11: *Jesus says to
the adulteress: "Neither do I condemn thee: go, and sin no
more."

P. 5:4

"ADVANCEMENT OF LEARNING"

See "Bacon" ("Advancement of Knowledge").

M.D. 55

ADVENT

A term designating the coming or second coming of
*Christ; in church calendars, the weeks before *Christmas.

In 1843, the Adventist prophecies of William Miller started the spread of Adventist sects that predicted the Second Coming or the end of the world during M.'s time.
C.M. 1

ADVOCATE, THE
M. derived the facts for his mock two-person argument from *Beale (Chapter 11), *Scoresby (II, 117, 119), and *J.R. Browne (Appendix, 539).

Perhaps the form of a theoretical discourse between opponents comes from *Bunyan's *The Pilgrim's Progress*, Part II, wherein "Objection" and "Answer" counter one another.
M.D. 24

ADYTA
Gr.: *aduton* "not to be entered." In ancient *Greek and *Roman architecture, the adyta (or adytum) was the innermost sanctuary of a temple: the forbidden "holy of holies."
M. 110; M. 170

AENEAS
See "Aeniad."
M. 149; M. 174; C.M. 16

AENIAD, THE
The national epic poem of the *Romans is *Virgil's rendering of the adventures of the *Trojan *Aeneas (in mythology, son of the goddess Aphrodite [*Venus] and Anchises; in *Homer, a warrior second in command to his cousin, *Hector). *The Aeniad* became the model for medieval and Renaissance epics.

Virgil's picture of Aeneas has established our view of him as symbolic of early Roman *Caesars. The heroic Aeneas journeys from Troy to *Sicily, *Carthage, and the *Tiber in *Italy—strong, self-denying, and obedient to the gods. Enroute in his ship, *Bis Taurus, to fulfill his destined founding of Rome, he is widowed and shipwrecked, tarries with *Dido, fights bravely to marry Lavinia, and founds Lavinium, the parent city of Rome.

Sealts #147, *Harper Classical Library*, Vols. 11, 12, contains *The Aeniad* and other works by Virgil.
R. 30; W. 11; P. 15:2

AEOLIAN; EOLEAN

The Aeolian Islands, north of eastern *Sicily, are important in several *Greek myths or legends as the home of Aeolus, god of the winds. An Aeolian harp is one which gives forth music when the wind plays over it; it was a popular item in many nineteenth-century homes and a trope for romantic writers such as *Emerson.
W. 12; P. 2:7 ("Eolean")

AEORAI SOCIETY

See "Arioi."
O. 32

AESCHYLUS

The earliest and greatest *Greek tragic poet, some of whose complete plays (perhaps originally totaling ninety) survive. Aeschylus (525-456 B.C.) was a pioneer in the writing and staging of the classic tragic play. Born at *Eleusis, Attica, of an aristocratic family, his early experience of war led to his stressing its horrors rather than its glories. His interests lay in the lives and fates of individuals and communities, and with man's religious problems, rather than with an afterlife.

Seven of his plays have survived, the most famous forming the *Oresteia* trilogy (*Agamemnon, Choephoroe, Eumenides*). *Prometheus Bound*, the story of defiance of Zeus (see "Jupiter"), has influenced literature since the early nineteenth century. *Persae* centers on the importance of *Darius as expounder of the moral order of Zeus.

Sealts #147, *Harper's Classical Library*, Vol. 13, is the works of Aeschylus. See also "Prometheus."
C.M. 5

AESCULAPIUS

Lat. form of *Asclepius.
T. 11

AESON

In *Greek myth, the father of *Jason, Aeson, born rightful heir to the throne of Iolcus, shields his son from Aeson's usurping half-brother, Pelias. The *Medea myth has Aeson restored to youth by his sorceress daughter-in-law, but some versions say that Pelias forced Aeson to commit suicide while Jason was young.

Aeson is cited by "Jessica," "*Shylock's" daughter, in
*Shakespeare's *The Merchant of Venice* V, i, 12-14:

> In such a night
> Medea gather'd the enchanted herbs
> That did renew old Aeson.

C.M. 16

AESOP'S

Aesop was perhaps legendary, perhaps a comic *Greek
fabulist who died in 564 B.C. *Herodotus and others supply
some biography: he was a contemporary of *Sappho, was
originally from *Thrace, was a slave on the island of Samos,
died at *Delphi. Other versions make him a Phrygian;
various claims are made in the multitude of myths and
legends about him, which include a *Life of Aesop.*

The fables, which use animals as metaphors to
illustrate a moral, were first collected at the end of the fourth
century B.C. They were not popular literature but were told in
a learned context, as wisdom literature.

Sealts #6 is *Fabulae Aesopi Selectae, or, Select Fables of
Aesop,* originally owned by Allan Melvill. (See "Walter
Redburn.")
C.M. 39

AFFGHANISTAN

M.D. reference to a "bloody battle" recalls the 1841
massacre of the British Army at Kabul, or the Sikh War of
1848.
M.D. 1

AFREHITOO

M.'s "Afrehitoo" is Afareaitu, a settlement on the
southwestern coast of *Moreea, directly across from *Tahiti.
*Charles Stewart describes it as a lovely town with a chapel,
cottages, and South Sea Academy; *Ellis praises the honesty of
its people.
O. 49; O. 58; O. 61

AFRICA, --N; AFRIC; AFRIKY

The name Africa was given by the *Romans to the area
around *Carthage. In M.'s time, much more was known
about northern Africa than about southern because of devel-

opment of the *Barbary Coast. Northern Africa had originally
been divided among barbarian tribes; it was united under the
*Arabs from the seventh to the eleventh century, adopting Is-
lam. The *Moors invaded next and were not expelled until the
fifteenth century, at a time when *Portuguese explorers were
first examining the western coast of the continent. (*Diaz
rounded the Cape of *Good Hope in 1488; Da*Gama sailed
around Africa to *India in 1499.) The Portuguese soon established *slave stations, but *Dutch, *British, and *French
slavers gave competition until the seventeenth century. The
Dutch established a colony at the Cape in the seventeenth century.

Penetration of the "dark continent" began in the eighteenth century. By 1808 the British had established Sierra
Leone. The nineteenth century saw the "scramble for empire,"
with most major powers overrunning Africa. Discovery of
Lake Victoria in 1852 solved the puzzle of the *Nile's source.
By the twentieth century, the entire continent had been partitioned, with only *Ethiopia and Liberia (founded for slaves returned from the *United States) retaining nominal independence.

M.'s fascination (in W. 56) with the *Brazilian rowing
style associated with African slaves is shared by Reverend
Stewart, who says that the emperor's boat was pulled by "four
stout, muscular negroes," and that the manner of rowing was
different from any he had seen:

> After every stroke, which is long and slow, the
> rowers rise entirely from their seats, and throw
> themselves forward as they lift the oar from the
> water;   and then in a measured and uniform
> motion, accompanied with a monstrous cry, drop
> again into their seats; and as they pull, brace
> themselves almost at full length against a
> footboard at the bottom. They then rise again, and
> repeat the same movement. The manner seems
> both indolent and laborious;   but the motion
> produced is as rapid apparently as that by our
> method.

In *M.D.* 108, the reference is to traditional legend that
when *Prometheus made man out of clay he used soot to make
Africans.

See also "Abyssinian"; "African Colonization Society";
"Algiers"; "Berbers"; "Caffraria"; "Congo"; "Egypt"; "Gold
Coast"; "Guinea"; "Leo, John"; "Libya"; "Morocco"; "Niger";
"Nubia"; "Ptolemy Philophater"; "Sahara"; "Senegal";
"Tunisia."
Passim

AFRICAN COLONIZATION SOCIETY

The *American Colonization Society was officially founded in 1816 by Robert Finley, a *Presbyterian minister of *New Jersey. The aim was to aid the emigration of former *slaves to *Africa, to land bought by the Society which was to become the nation of Liberia. It was supported by many anti-slavery groups (see "Abolitionism"), but its early efforts ended tragically. The first 114 settlers (1820-21) were almost all wiped out by disease. In 1822, thirty-seven emigrants established a settlement at Cape Mesurado (near modern Monrovia, Liberia). Branches of the organization arose in many American states, and between 1821 and 1867, about 6,000 people were moved to Africa.

See also "Stockton, Commodore."
W. 38

AGAMEMNON

Probably a historical figure, Agamemnon is celebrated as the King of *Argos or Mycenae and leader of the *Greeks in the *Trojan War, by *Aeschylus, *Homer, Euripides, *Sophocles, *Horace, *Byron, *Spenser, and others. The son of Atreus and brother of Menelaus, Agamemnon was the father of *Orestes, Iphigenia, Electra, and others. At Troy, he loved King Priam's daughter *Cassandra, and Homer has him killed with her at a feast. In Aeschylus, Sophocles, and Euripides, he is killed by his wife, Clytemnestra, an adulteress; Orestes avenges his death by killing his mother and her lover.
C.M. 42

AGASSIZ

(Jean) Louis (Rodolphe) Agassiz (1807-1873) was a *Swiss/*American naturalist, geologist, and teacher. He was educated in Europe and focused on icthyology, publishing *Selecta Genera et Species Piscium* and *History of the Fresh Water Fishes of Central Europe* while still in his twenties. With the help of *Baron Cuvier, he secured a professorship in *Paris and studied at the Jardin des Plantes. His *Recherches sur les Poissons Fossiles* (1833-1844) revolutionized icthyology. In Neuchatel, he published *Etudes Critiques sur les Mollusques Fossiles* (1840-45), began *Nomenclator Zoologicus*, and started research leading to *Etudes sur les glaciers* (1840).

By 1848, Agassiz had accepted a professorship at *Harvard, where he eventually published *Lake *Superior* (1850), *Contributions to the Natural History of the United States*

(1857-63), and *Essay on Classification*. He made trips to
*California and *Brazil during this time.

At Harvard, Agassiz revolutionized study, discouraging
the reading of books in favor of direct and practical reading of
nature. Modern scholars tend to disvalue his work because it
opposed *Darwin's, seeing species as separate creations of
*God. (The wife of Agassiz, Elizabeth Cabot Cary Agassiz
[1822-1907] was a founder and president of Radcliffe College;
she published a biography of him in 1885.)
M.D. 68

AGNELLO

In Canto 25 of *Dante's *Inferno*, Agnello de'
Brunelleschi's human form is merged with that of Cianta de'
Donati, previously transformed into a six-legged serpent, the
two noble *Florentine thieves becoming one. The others look
on, exlaiming, "Ah! how dost thou change, Agnello." M.'s
quotation follows that of H.F. Cary, with the exception of Cary's
"nor double now."
P. 4:5

AHAB

M.'s name for his most compelling fictional character
was not common in early *New England, although there was
much nineteenth-century interest in the *Bible story
surrounding him, chiefly for its demonstration that prophecy
should be heeded.

There are two Ahabs in the Bible—a false prophet in
*Jeremiah 29:21-22, and M.'s model, the seventh king of
*Israel after its division, discussed chiefly in 1 *Kings 16:28 to
22:40. The proud son of Omri married the pagan *Jezebel and
with her worshipped *Baal, identified with the *Babylonian
sun god. Thus, Ahab defied the prophets: *Elijah the Tishbite,
who had warned him three times, and Micaiah, who also
prophesied disaster. But Ahab, encouraged by Jezebel, killed
his neighbor, Naboth, and seized his vineyards. The prophecy
that dogs would lick his blood was fulfilled after Ahab's death
at the hands of *Syrian enemies.

A full examination of other possible prototypes for M.'s
character is found in Howard P. Vincent's notes to the Hendricks House edition of *M.D.*
M.D. Passim

"A HARREE TA FOW ... "
As Anderson shows (Chapter 10, p. 282), this is an ancient *Tahitian folk song, a version of which was given in *Ellis I, 91-92.
M. probably invented the chant as nonsense verse in past tense ("A"). It is not proper Tahitian language.
O. 49

AHASUERUS
See "Xerxes."
M. 117; M. 181; M.D. 27

AHAZ DIAL
In *Isaiah 38:8, Hezehiah, son of Ahaz, is given a sign that he will be healed and live another fifteen years: "Behold, I will bring again the shadow of the degrees, which is gone down in the sundial of Ahaz, ten degrees backward. So the sun returned ten degrees, by which degrees it was gone down."
M.D. 32

AHITHOPELS
A proverbial sagacious royal counselor to *David, Ahithopel hangs himself when his advice to Absalom, the son of David, is rejected, in I *Chronicles 27:33-34. He is the grandfather of Bathsheba (the wife of Uriah the *Hittite), who becomes David's second wife, then wife to *Solomon.
M. 138

AIKEN, DR.
John Aikin (1747-1822) was a *British physician who wrote a six-volume work for children, *Evenings at Home* (1792-6), in collaboration with his sister, *Anna Laetitia Barbauld. He was first literary editor of the *Monthly Magazine*, a journal of radical dissent, and collaborated on several biographical works.
Sealts #7 is Aikin's *Letters to a Young Lady on a Course of English Poetry*.
R. 30

AILSA, CRAG OF; --CRAIG OF
The isolated mountainous isle of Ailsa Craig, in the mouth of the *Firth of *Clyde, rises sheer from the water. M.

passed it on a steamship bound for *Glasgow, commenting in his journal (November 1856) on its "looming up in the mist." I.P. 15

AIX LA CHAPELLE
     After the Franco-Spanish War of 1667-68, peace was concluded at Aix la Chapelle (the German "Aachen") in April of 1668, with Louis XIV (see "Bourbon") regaining much *French territory from the *Spanish.
     It is the burial place of *Charlemagne.
W. 71

AKENSIDE
     Mark Akenside (1721-70) was an erudite *British poet and physician satirized as the Doctor in *Smollett's *Peregrine Pickle*. His most famous work is "Pleasures of Imagination" (1744), a long didactic blank verse poem that ranks sorrow among the greatest of human pleasures.
C.M. 5

ALABAMA; ALABAMIAN
     "The Cotton State" was the twenty-second admitted to the Union (in 1819). It is approximately 280 miles long (N.-S.) and 200 miles wide (E.-W.) and is bordered by *Tennessee (N.), *Georgia (E.), Mississippi (W.), *Florida (S.), and the *Gulf of Mexico (S.W.). *Spaniards had explored the area, but the *French first settled (in the Mobile area) in 1702. By 1763, it was under *British control (ceded to the *United States in 1783). *Andrew Jackson drove out the *Indians in 1814, and Alabama assumed its present dimensions in 1817. If *M.D.*'s "*Pip" *is* an "Alabama boy" (*M.D.* 27), he is from a slave state.
     See also "Creagh, Judge."
R. 13; M.D. 27; M.D. 93; M.D. 104; M.D. 105; C.M. 30

ALADDIN'S LAMP
     "Aladdin and the Wonderful Lamp" is an oriental tale of the *Arabian Nights*. Aladdin, son of a poor tailor, is employed by a sorcerer to obtain a magical lamp hidden in a cave. He keeps the lamp, by means of which he becomes wealthy and successful. The sorcerer tricks him by offering "New lamps for old," then using the lamp to move all of Aladdin's wealth (including his wife and palace) to *Africa. Aladdin follows, killing him and regaining his lamp and his possessions.
M.D. 97

ALADDIN'S PALACE; PALACE OF ALADDIN

Critics disagree about the historicity of the opulent *London gambling den of *R*. M. had used details of the interior in the very early (1839) "Fragment No. 2," composed before he had ever been abroad. Gilman's *Melville's Early Life and Redburn* argues that M. himself did not make the trip to *London from *Liverpool assigned to "Wellingborough Redburn," supporting the claim that Aladdin's Palace is a fiction.

See also "London: Club Houses"; "Corinth."
R. 46; R. 47

A-LA-MODE

Fr.: fashionable.
I.P. 10

ALANNO

M.'s fictional portrait of Senator William Allen of *Ohio.
M. 158

ALBATROSS, --'S

The albatross, of the genus *Diomedea*, is a large web-footed sea-going bird with a hooked beak, related to the petrel. *Coleridge gave it great significance as a mystical burden (especially for sailors), in "The Rime of The Ancient Mariner" (1798).

(In *M.D.* 52, "Goney.")
O. 9; M. 122; W. 2; W. 7; W. 28; M.D. 42; M.D. 52; M.D. 123; M.D. 133 and elsewhere

ALBE BELLGARDE

See "Abbé Bellegarde."
I.P. 22

ALBERT, PRINCE

Albert of Saxe-Coburg-Gotha (1819-1861) was Prince Consort to *Britain's Queen *Victoria. He was born in Coburg, *Germany, the second son of the local duke, and baptized Francis Charles Augustus Albert Emmanuel. He married Victoria, his first cousin, in 1840 and, despite lack of official political status, immediately became involved in politics, especially in alliance with Sir Robert Peel. He improved the Queen's properties and the Crown's status in government, performing many other admirable services, but he was unpopular with almost everyone except Victoria, especially just before the *Crimean War (1846-47).

The marriage was a prolific (nine children) and a happily domestic one, with Albert's German thoroughness and efficiency a model for the family. After his death from typhoid fever, his contribution to the nation was reassessed and many memorials were erected, including Albert Memorial (1863-72) and Royal Albert Hall (1867-72).

His influence with Victoria remained strong even after his death, especially as regards the conspicuous decorum with which we habitually endow our images of the Queen.
W. 42

ALBICORE, --S
    Large food fish of the family *Scomberidae*, found in shoals. Up to six feet long and 100 pounds. Familiarly called "tunny."
T. 2; O. 3; M. 13; M.D. 132

ALBINO
    Lat. *albus*, white. Albinism denotes the congenital absence of yellow, red, brown, or black pigments in living things, caused in humans by the absence of melanin. There are localized areas of high incidence where intermarriage is common.
    Oliver Wendell Holmes, in *The Autocrat of the Breakfast Table*, uses "albino" figuratively to suggest a lack of virility. William and Robert Chambers, eds. of *Information for the People. A Popular Encyclopedia* (Philadelphia, 1847), concur with popular opinion: albinos are "scarcely to be called a variety of mankind, being a race whose peculiarities depend on *defects*."
    See also "Kingsmill . . . . "
M. 42; M. 49; M.D. 42

ALBION
    The 434-ton *Albion* was wrecked and many lives lost in a gale off the southwestern coast of *Ireland, in 1822. She was an *American packet of the Black Ball Line. As Huntress points out, M. probably read about the wreck in R. Thomas, *Interesting and Authentic Narratives of the most Remarkable Shipwrecks . . .* (299-306).
    In mythology, Albion is the son of *Neptune by *Amphitrite; he established a kingdom in *England, which adopted his name.
R. 27

ALBUMS

In the nineteenth century, young ladies kept books of memorabilia—autographs, sketches, etc.—upon which to feed romantic fancy. The *Album Amicorum*, popular from the sixteenth century in *Britain, was probably the progenitor; carried by students and scholars, it housed mottoes and uplifting inscriptions. "Album" derives from Lat. *albus* ("white"), used to designate blank spaces to be filled with writing.
P. 17:2

ALDEBARAN, --S

A reddish giant star, one of the twenty brightest, located in the *constellation *Taurus: the eye of the bull.
M. 75; M. 136; M. 161; M. 184

ALDROVANDI; ALDROVANDUS

Ulisse Aldrovandi (1522-1605) was an *Italian naturalist who turned from medicine and pharmacology to botany, setting up *Rome's first botanical garden. He labored with a large staff for thirty years on an unfinished illustrated compilation of natural history, of which fourteen volumes were eventually printed. The museum he founded in *Bologna is still in existence.
M.D. 32; M.D. 105

ALE

Ale is an inexpensive alcoholic beverage originally made (fifth century B.C.) from barley. In *Britain, ale was made (from before *Roman times) from pale malt, without hops, which was introduced from *Holland in 1524 and almost immediately prohibited from use by act of *Parliament. Old English ale was the very potent beverage of choice until replaced by lighter beers in the early seventeenth century.

Beers of the *German Lager type have been more popular than ales in the *United States. Beers are made with bottom-fermenting yeasts and ales with top-fermenting, accounting, along with differing aging processes, for differences in taste.

In M.'s time, ales were often combined with other ingredients to produce such beverages as Wassail, or flavored with spicy mixtures or butter. To encourage the poor to drink ale instead of gin or other spirits, the British government remitted the beer tax in 1836.

See also "Pale Ale"; "Stout."
R. 43; W. 68

ALEMBERT, D'
        See "D'Alembert."
R. 1

ALEWIVES
        Clupea alosa: food fish of herring family.
R. 52; M.D. 32

ALEXANDER, --'S; ALEXANDER THE GREAT
        The son of Philip II of *Macedon and Olympias, Alexan-
der (356-325 B.C.) was born at Pella and educated by *Aristotle.
He became King Alexander III in 336 and with the sanction of
the *Greek people entered upon the series of conquests that furthered Greek expansion and inspired a large body of romances
and legends. Alexander's empire eventually extended on the
south from northern *Egypt and the *Indian Ocean, on the
north from *Thrace and *Bactria, on the east from *India, on
the west from Macedonia. He established several cities called
*Alexandria, as well as a Bucephala, in honor of his horse,
Bucephalus (*M*. 29), who died there. Alexander died in
*Babylon of a fever incurred after one of his numerous drink-
ing bouts (as suggested in *M*. 84). The Indian elephant (*M.D.*
92) presented to Alexander might be any one of many such
gifts.
        See also "Antipater"; "Athos, Mount"; "beards";
"Darius"; "Hephestion"; "Porus, King."
M. 29; M. 33; M. 75; M. 84; R. 33; R. 46; W. 85; M.D. 14;
M.D. 87; M.D. 92

ALEXANDER, HERR
        A *German magician who played engagements in *New
York from 1845 to 1849.
M. 6

ALEXANDRIA
        Alexandria, *Egypt, was founded by *Alexander the
Great in the fourth century B.C., as a naval base and *Greek
center. It was soon larger than *Carthage and close to *Rome
in its importance as a *Hellenic and Semitic center. The
*Ptolemies developed a great university and library there be-
fore official *Roman aegis brought *Julius Caesar to court
*Cleopatra. The home of the *Septuagint, it is traditionally
thought the site of *St. Mark's introduction of *Christianity, as
well as the home of *Arianism. It fell to *Persian, then *Arab

rule, losing importance until *Napoléon's 1798 conquest, three years after which it fell to the *British.

In M.'s time, Alexandria had been much reduced in size, but the mid-century exertions of Mohammed Ali were to restore some of its importance. Homesickness in 1849-50 had cancelled M.'s original plans to visit, so that it was not until December and January of 1856-57 that his dream was realized. His journal notations of the trip seem impulsively jotted down, displaying the uneasiness he felt throughout the journey (perhaps a manifestation of the agitated state at home that had prompted the trip):

> Seems Mcadamed (see "Macadamized") with the ruins of thousand cities. Every shovel full of earth dug over . . . . The sea is the principal point. Catacombs by it. R.R. extension driven right through. Acres. Wonderful appearance of the sea at noon . . . . Sighing of the waves. Cries of watchmen at night. Lanterns. Assassins. Sun strokes.

See also "Pompey's Pillar."
W. 18

ALFRED, KING

Alfred (Aelfred) the Great (848 or 849-899), *Anglo-Saxon King of Wessex, *England from 871-899. Son of King Aethelwulf, he traveled early to *Rome for education and official entry into the Roman *Catholic Church. Before ascending the throne, he fought many *Danish invaders and, upon becoming King, made the temporary peace necessary to strengthen England's defenses against inevitable future invasions. Ultimately, he prevented a *Scandinavian takeover of Britain, insuring its remaining *Christian. His rule spread to *London, where he organized a standing army and established the burghal system of defense, with widespread fortifications.

He aided the Welsh (see "Wales . . . . "), and opened his court to many other foreigners. Among his achievements were a new code of laws, based on the laws of *Exodus and on successful contemporary codes. He raised the level of learning, promoting the use of *Latin for scholars and vernacular literacy for others; he translated Boethius, *St. Augustine, parts of the *Bible, and other Church works. He composed an Old English version of Orosius's *History of the World*, containing Octhere's voyage and reference to the *Norwegian whale fishery. (See "Other.")

Our knowledge of Alfred is flawed by the errata of the *Anglo-Saxon Chronicles* and by legend spread in the oral tradition.

(See also "Extracts" 9.)

M. 3; R. 33; M.D. Extracts 9; M.D. 24.

ALFRED THE GREAT
   See "Alfred, King."
M.D. 24

"ALGERINE"
   In *W.*, "Algerine" represents the sloop, *Cyane*.
   In *M.* 13, "Algerines" are sharks. See also "Cetology."
M. 13; W. 62

ALGIERS
   The seaport site of Algiers was occupied by *Phoenicians and *Romans before *Moslems founded a city there in the tenth century. It was subsequently occupied by the Spanish and had a large population increase upon *Spain's expulsion of the *Moors. The Spanish were expelled by Khair ed-Din (Barbarossa) in 1529, whereupon the Algerian capital city was built. It became residence of the last two *deys and by the eighteenth century was home to many *pirates. *French rule began in 1830 after a struggle instigated by the dey Hussein's striking the French consul in 1827.
   M. probably read *Morgan's *History of Algiers*, listed in the catalogue of the Albany *Young Men's Association, as was one volume of a *History of Algiers* by J.W. Stevens (Brooklyn, 1800). He sailed close to the coast of Algiers in 1857, commenting in his journal (26 November) on memories of *Don Quixote's "Story of the Morisco" invoked by the beautiful white Moorish-style hillside residences, as well as on the "wild looking" villages and "piratical corsair look" of the area.
   See also "Barbary coast; - pirates."
W. 71; W. 88; M.D. 102

ALHAMBRA
   *Granada's Alhambra was built by Mohammed II about the year 675 of the *Hegira (1273 A.D.). Its name (from kal'-at al hamra) means "red castle." The palace and fortress of the *Moorish monarchs of southern *Spain is enclosed by a wall and thirteen towers made from local red clay and gravel bricks, covering some thirty-five acres. By M.'s time, restora-

tion work had ameliorated the ravages of time and war, and
the Alhambra was a beautiful tourist attraction; but M. expressed disappointment about it in his journal, calling it
"overdone" and too large (29, 30 April, 1 May 1857).

The Court of the Lions is a 116- by 66-foot patio
surrounded by white marble columns, containing the
Fountain of Lions, an alabaster basin surrounded by twelve
stone lions. M.'s "Moorish pillar" refers to the elaborately
carved colonnades supporting the traditionally filagreed
arches of the buildings.
M. l; M. 75; W. 20; R. 49

ALL, THE

In a June 1 (?) 1851 letter to *Hawthorne, M. examined
the sublime but dangerous *Transcendental sense of the "All":

> This "all" feeling . . . there is some truth in.
> You must often have felt it, lying on the grass on a
> warm summer's day. Your legs seem to send out
> shoots into the earth. Your hair feels like leaves
> upon your head. This is the *all* feeling. But what
> plays the mischief with the truth is that men will
> insist upon the universal application of a
> temporary feeling or opinion.

W. 19

ALLAH

The Arabic word for *God, since pre-Islamic times. In
the *Koran, Allah is the unique creator and omnipotent judge
who always was and always will be. He is a mysterious and
inaccessible deity who demands man's complete submission
and in return performs good works.

M.'s model for his many appellations for God may be the
Koran, which lists Allah's "most beautiful names": the One
and Only; the Living One; the Real Truth; the Sublime All-
high; the Wise; the Omnipotent; the Absolute and Unceasing
Creator; the One who is unlike all else; the Benefactor and the
Merciful, etc.
W. 75

ALLEGHANIES; ALLEGHANIAN

The Allegheny Mountains are part of the
*Appalachians, running c. 500 miles from north-central
*Pennsylvania into southern West Virginia and southwestern

*Virginia. Their maximum altitude (c. 4800 feet) occurs in West Virginia, where they are particularly scenic. ("Alleghany" is a former spelling.)
M.D. 3; M.D. 42; C.M. 30

ALLEN, ETHAN; ETHAN TICONDEROGA ALLEN

Allen (1738-89), *American Revolutionary War hero, had become a folk hero as leader of the *Green Mountain Boys, an irregular militia that defended *Vermont's *New Hampshire Grants against *New York interference. He was with *Benedict Arnold at the capture of Fort *Ticonderoga, claiming that on 10 May 1775 he had called for *British surrender "in the name of great *Jehovah and the *Continental Congress." He described his imprisonment by the British (1775-1778) in *Narrative of Colonel Ethan Allen's Captivity* (1779) and claimed authorship of a deistic book, *Reason the Only Oracle of Man* (1784). Frustrated in 1778 by rejection of Vermont's claim to statehood, he briefly attempted to re-ally Vermont with the British as a province.
P. 5:6; I.P. 21; I.P. 22.

ALLIANCE, THE

The thirty-two gun *American frigate *Alliance* was the only remaining American ship after the *Revolutionary War. She was never defeated in battle, but was in ill repair and sold at auction in 1785 to a private syndicate (for $26,000) that used her thereafter to ferry tobacco to Europe.
I.P. 19

ALLUMETTES

Fire-lighting devices.
P. 18:2

ALP ARSLAN'S

Alp is the hero of *Byron's tale, "The Siege of *Corinth" (1815?). A renegade from *Christianity, Alp becomes a *Turkish commander. When he is shot during the siege, the daughter of the governor of Corinth dies of a broken heart because of his apostasy.

(Gilman's *Melville's Early Life and Redburn* makes explicit M.'s debt to "The Siege of Corinth.")
M. 149

ALPS

South central Europe's great mountain system extends (SW-NE) c. 680 miles from the *Mediterranean coast of southeast *France and northwest *Italy into southern *Germany. *Mont Blanc is the highest peak, at 15,781 feet.

M. was in the Italian Alps in April of 1857, sailing across Lake Maggiore into *Switzerland. He commented in his journal (15 April) on the beauty and loneliness of the area and suffered the violent storms of the San Gotthard Pass. He took a steamer across Lake Lucerne, traveling on to Bern for the "noble views" (19 April). In the French province of Jura, he viewed the "whole Alps" (20 April) through the defile.
M. 12; M. 119; W. 50; W. 85; M.D. 14; M.D. 35; M.D. 104; P. 21:1

ALTON

Alton is in southwestern *Illinois, on bluffs above the *Mississippi River, four miles above the mouth of the *Missouri, and seventeen miles north of central *St. Louis. Marquette and Jolliet had explored the area in 1673. Alton was laid out in 1817 and incorporated in 1821. (It was the scene of the last *Lincoln-Douglas debate in 1858.)
C.M. 22

AMARANTH; AMARANTHINESS

In the *Massachusetts area, several flowers are referred to as Amaranths: *Antennaria neglecta, Antennaria Canadensis, Antennaria plantaginifolia, Anaphilis margaritacea.* Their beauty is said to be unfading.

M.'s neologism, "amaranthiness," suggests fadelessness. Following *Pliny, *Milton addresses the "immortal amarant" (*Paradise Lost* III, 353), and *Spenser recalls sad lovers turned to Amaranthus (*Faerie Queene*, III, vi, 45).
P. 1:2; P. 25:4

AMAZON, AMAZONIAN

A Greek word meaning "without breast." *Herodotus tells of a race of female warriors living in *Scythia without men; other Greek stories attest to a similar race in Africa. The girls had their right breasts removed to facilitate use of the bow.

Modern use refers to any physically strong woman who does not behave in the traditionally "feminine" (i.e. weak) way.
M. 28; R. 28

AMAZON
    The river which drains almost half of *South America is
the world's largest in volume and area of drainage. As M.
notes in *R*. 33, it is really the confluence of numerous rivers
with sources in an area of glacial lakes in the *Peruvian
*Andes. Its principal mouth was discovered in 1500 by Vicente
Yáñez Pinzón (see "Pinzella"); it was descended from the Andes in 1541 and ascended to *Quito in 1638.
    *Dom Pedro II authorized steam navigation in 1850 and
opened the river to world traffic in 1866. Exploration by naturalists such as *Agassiz and early nineteenth-century
*American and *British military expeditions contributed to
scientific knowledge of the river's rich terrain, but it was still
relatively mysterious in M.'s time.
M. 119; R. 33

AMBERGRIS
    The waxy, aromatic substance is marbled ashy gray. It
was originally called "amber," suggesting yellow.   The Fr.
amber gris, gray amber, clarified the misnomer. M.'s sources
for *M.D.*'s chapter are *Beale (Chapter 10) and *Cheever (pp.
115, 116), as Vincent shows in his 1962 edition.
M.D. 92

AMELIA
    See "Enderby, Samuel . . . . "
M.D. 101

AMELIA!
    See "Smollett."
O. 77

AMENS
    In the *Old and *New Testaments, "Amen," from a
*Hebrew word meaning "to take care, or support," is an exla-
mation supporting or approving an oath, blessing, curse,
prayer, or *doxology.
M. 187

AMERICA, --N; AMERICANISM; AMERIKY; THE UNION;
UNITED STATES; COLUMBIA
    The name "America" is a misnomer especially when
applied only to "United States of America"; the "Americas,"

north and south, were named for Amerigo Vespucci (1454-
1512), who reached the continents in 1497. The name
"Columbia" is perhaps also misapplied, referring to
*Columbus, the supposed "discoverer" in 1492. It is now
known that the *Vikings and perhaps others were here centuries before.

The United States of M.'s time consisted of nineteen
states in 1819 and forty-one states by 1891. The original thirteen "colonies" which became states between 1787 and 1790
were *Connecticut, *Delaware, *Georgia, *Maryland,
*Massachusetts, *New Jersey, North and South *Carolina,
*New York, *Pennsylvania, *New Hampshire, *Virginia,
*Rhode Island.

A close examination needs to be made of M.'s relation to
his native land. His allusions suggest that many of the stereotypical views now current were already in place in the nineteenth century. "Ameriky" (R. 21) is an attempt to portray the
rather corrupt English spoken by many Americans.
"Americanism" (I.P. 22), an anomaly for many peoples of the
world (who do not believe they practice, for example,
"Frenchism," or "Germanism"), was a touchy issue even in
the nineteenth century, when there was even less agreement
about what it was. The reference in M.D. 89 (and elsewhere) to
the *Mexican War is a case in point; M's own family was divided on the subject, with M.'s brother *Gansevoort a "hawk"
and M. himself probably a rather secret "dove." *Slavery had
been an issue from the nation's inception, when *Jefferson
wished to refer to it in the *Constitution but was voted down, allowing the practice to flourish.

M.'s reference to regional characteristics portray the
standard differences between "north," "west," and "south":
the "Northman" (of M.D. 41, for example) is a rugged
"*Yankee" laborer; the *New Englander is a "*Brahman" or a
"*Puritan"; the westerner has a pioneer "spirit" (I.P. 22) the
"southerner" has an aristocratic and slightly decadent
"temperament" (W. 83). M. played with the idea of sectional
differences in "Hawthorne and His Mosses," disguising himself as a "Virginian Spending July in Vermont."

Much has been made of M.'s seeming embrace of
"Manifest Destiny" in W. 36 and elsewhere; the W. 36 reference I believe a sop thrown to the reader who has just been told
that his most cherished national documents are "lies" and that
he should mutiny (W. 35). Certainly, chapters such as M.D.
89, "*Fast-Fish and Loose-Fish," lump the United States with
other aggressively imperialistic nations.   America is
"demogoguical" in P. 1:3, worshiping the *President and
other national figures (especially the military), despite a
*Constitution that makes *Congress at least equally important.

"Middle American States" of *M.D.* 42 are probably New Jersey, Delaware, Maryland, and Virginia.

The American flag (*M.D.* 41) was suggested 14 June 1777 by the *Continental Congress: thirteen red and white stripes and thirteen white stars on a blue field. By the time of Francis Scott Key's (1814) writing of what would become in the twentieth century the national anthem, the flag was popularly referred to as the "Star-Spangled Banner."

Rogin's *Subversive Genealogy* examines M.'s politics and those of his family.

See also "Democrat," "Federalism," and references to individuals and states.
Passim

AMERICAN CONGRESS
        See "Congress."
R. 29; R. 43.

AMERICAN CONSTITUTION
        See "Constitution."
W. 35; W. 38.

AMERICAN REVOLUTION
        The Revolution (1775-1781) of the American colonies against *Britain (also called the American War of Independence) began with a skirmish at Lexington, *Massachusetts, 19 April 1775 (celebrated in Massachusetts today as "Patriot's Day"). The last major confrontation ended in the Yorktown, *Virginia surrender of Cornwallis. M.'s maternal grandfather, Peter *Gansevoort, was the Revolutionary War hero of Fort *Stanwix (covertly referred to in *P.* 1:2 and elsewhere in *P.*), and his paternal grandfather, Thomas Melvill, had participated in the *Boston "Tea Party." The war was officially ended by the Treaty of *Paris.

        Among related allusions, the reader of the present work will find: "Allen, Ethan"; "Arnold, Benedict"; "Brandywine"; "Bunker Hill"; "Burgoyne"; "d'Estaing"; "de Grasse"; "Howe"; "Jones, John Paul"; "LaFayette"; "Long Island"; "Navy"; "Parker, Sir Peter"; "Quebec"; "Saratoga"; "Ticonderoga"; "Vincennes"; "Washington, George."
Passim

AMERICAN STATUTE-BOOK
        See "United States Statute Book . . . . "
W. 34

AMERICAN WHISKY
    Distilling of alcoholic beverages had a long history in
*America even before founding fathers such as *Washington
and *Jefferson became distillers of rye whiskey, developed in
*Pennsylvania in the mid-eighteenth century.   Bourbon
whiskey was first produced in 1789 in Bourbon County,
*Kentucky, when a local minister placed distillate of corn
mash into charred oak barrels, resulting in typical color and
flavor sweeter then that of rye. *Irish and *Scottish immigrants developed and perfected both products.
    The "Whiskey Rebellion" (1794) against an excise tax on
distilled liquors resulted when Pennsylvania farmers who
commonly distilled surplus grain revolted against a tax imposed by Secretary of the *Treasury Alexander Hamilton, who
forcefully suppressed the revolt.
    In the nineteenth century, Americans were great
drinkers of whiskey (which cost approximately twenty cents
per gallon), as Mrs. Trollope and Dickens (see "Hard Times")
noted, to the horror of the latter. M. himself confessed disbelief
in a "*Temperance Heaven," in a letter to *Hawthorne (1? June
1851).
    (The spelling "whisky" is *English and Scottish usage:
M. alternates between that spelling and the American
"whiskey.")
W. 44 and elsewhere

AMITTAI
    See "Jonah."
M.D. 9

AMMONITE
    The *Bible's "sons of Ammon," Ammonites were a
Semitic people of Transjordan from the thirteenth to the
sixteenth century B.C. Little is known of them except for their
denunciation by the *Hebrew prophets, their defeat by
Jephthah and *Saul, and their subduing by *David.
M. 47; I.P. 8.

AMONTILLADO
    Apéritif *sherry wine of Jerez de la Frontera province,
*Spain.
C.M. 24

AMOREE
    M.'s fictionalized form of "Amoret," meaning sweet-
heart. In *Spenser's *Faerie Queene* (Book III), Amoret is the
type of female loveliness, loving and loved by everyone, having
been brought up by *Venus at the Courts of Love.
M. 183

AMPHITRITE
    In *Roman mythology, granddaughter of the *Titan,
*Ocean; sea-goddess/wife of *Poseidon; mother of a son,
*Triton; and daughters, Rhode, and Benthesicyme. Tradi-
tionally, Amphitrite accompanies Poseidon (or Neptune) on his
ceremonial visit to ships crossing the *Equator.
W. 19; I.P. 10

AMPHITRITE
    In April 1777, the *Navy ordered *John Paul Jones to
travel from *Portsmouth, *New Hampshire to *France on the
French armed merchant ship which had delivered munitions
and was to pick up rice in *Charleston for delivery to France.
Jones's strange orders were to travel as a passenger and seize
command "on suitable occasions." The French Captain
Fautrel refused these conditions, and Jones left on *Ranger*.
Not only is M. in error in *I.P.* 10; adding to the confusion is the
fact that the *British Navy's HMS *Amphitrite* made part of the
squadron sent in pursuit of Jones in 1779.
I.P. 10

A.M.'s
    A.M. is used when one wishes to refer to the *Latin
Artium Magister, *Master of Arts (M.A.).
R. 12

AMSTERDAM
    The capital of the *Netherlands, at the mouth of the Am-
stel River, thirty miles northeast of The Hague, is a major port
dotted by canals that connect to the *Rhine system. It was me-
thodically erected on piles over swampy ground in the seventeenth century, preserving many thirteenth- and fourteenth-
century buildings erected after the building of the first dam.
Chartered in 1300, Amsterdam has always been an important
trade center: a member of the *Hanseatic League from 1369.
It was occupied by the *Prussians and the *French in the late
eighteenth century and incorporated into the French Empire

in 1810 but proclaimed independence in 1813. Separation of *Holland from *Belgium occurred in 1830.

M. visited in 1857, commenting wryly in his journal (24 April: error for 23) on his residence at the "Old Bible" Hotel (on the Warmoesstraat, near the center of town). On the following day, he "got a queer little old Dutchman for guide" and saw works of Rembrandt, *Teniers, and other *Dutch and *Flemish masters at the Trippenhuis collection. He observed: "Streets of Amsterdam like long lines of old fashioned frontispieces in old *folios and old *quartoes. Canals and drawbridges. Greasy looking old fellows . . . . Shape of Amsterdam like ampitheater, water all round it . . . . place of cheese, butter, & tidiness" (24 April). He also visited the Plantaadje (public garden) and inspected an old *galliot containing a "chest of drawers" such as "White-Jacket" had longed for.
M.D. 40; M.D. 101; I.P. 10

ANACONDAS
    See "Brazil . . . ."
M. 121; M. 144

ANACREON
    A sixth-century B.C. *Greek lyric poet whose main topics for his sweet odes were love and wine. Only a few genuine poems survive, but Anacreon has been much imitated. *Thomas Moore published a translation of the *Odes of Anacreon* in 1800.
M. 119; P. 2:2; P. 17:2; C.M. 5.

ANAK
    In the *Old Testament, Anak and his sons were giants who terrified scouts sent from Kadesh. *Joshua (11) destroyed most of them, and Caleb (Josh. 15) killed the three remaining sons of Anak: Sheshai, Ahiman, and Talmai.
M. 159; M.D. 59

ANATOMICAL MUSEUMS OF EUROPE
    The history of the study of anatomy properly begins as late as the sixteenth century, when the first thorough scientific dissection was clandestinely performed by Andreas [Witing] Vesalius (in 1543). Vesalius, who invited the public to his dissections at *Padua, demonstrated skeletons and made many illustrations. He destroyed these when he gave up anatomy, but his *Italian successors produced many others, as did

anatomists of other countries. *England's *College of Physicians built an anatomical theatre, but scientific and philosophical societies, texts, atlases, and museums did not appear until
the late eighteenth century. The first serious collection of specimens was probably *William Hunter's at the *London school
he established in 1770. By his death in 1783, he had spent
£100,000 on specimens studied by *Benjamin Franklin and
other scientists. The Hunter Museum was bequeathed to
*Glasgow, and William's brother, John, amassed probably the
world's best collection at the *Royal College of Surgeons in
London. Specimens were collected clandestinely until 1831,
when the *Massachusetts state legislature legalized the use of
unclaimed human bodies. The British anatomy act followed in
1831, but dissection was focussed on more extensively in the
*United States than in Europe. By the early 1830's Pennsylva-
nia College (later the University of Pennsylvania) had founded
a museum.
        See also "Horn."
W. 61

ANCHOR BUTTON
        The symbolic importance of the official U.S. *Navy
button is not original with that institution. Buttons have had
significance at least from *Shakespeare's time. In *China, a
first-grade literary honor was rewarded by the privilege of
adding a gold button to the cap, a practice adopted by some
collegiate schools in *England. *Mandarins were
distinguished by the color of the button on their caps.
        The incident described in W. may well have happened to
M. himself, the "brother" being his cousin, *Stanwix
*Gansevoort, officer-of-the-deck on the supply ship *Erie,
anchored beside *United States in *Callao during the week of
14 February 1844.
W. 59

ANDALUSIAN
        Andalusia (Sp. Andalucía) is a region of south-
ern/southwestern *Spain on the *Mediterranean and Strait of
*Gibraltar as well as on the *Atlantic, bordering west on
*Portugal. There are eight provinces named for their chief ci-
ties: south of the *Guadalquiver are *Cádiz, Málaga,
*Granada, and Almería. North of the river are Huelva,
Seville, Córdoba, and Jaén. The most populous area of Spain,
it is a productive region of vegetation, animal life, fisheries,
and mining, and famous for such wines as *Amontillado
(from Montilla). The *Phoenicians settled the area and were

followed by the *Greeks, Ligurians, *Carthaginians, and
*Romans, who brought the region to a high cultural level. The
*Moors entered in 711 but were conquered by *Castile by the
thirteenth century. The *Alhambra and other architectural
marvels reveal the Moorish influence, also manifested in the
character, language, and customs of the Andalusian peoples.
M. 116; R. 49

ANDES
      The Andes mountains of *South America run parallel to
the *Pacific coast from *Tierra del Fuego north to the
*Caribbean coasts of *Colombia and *Venezuela (4,000 miles).
They connect with the Sierra Madre (see "Sierras") and *Rocky
Mountain chains. Highest volcanos include *Chimborazo.
M. 36; M. 116; M. 119; M. 152; M. 165; W. 50; M.D. 42; M.D.
99; M.D. 104; M.D. 119; M.D. 132; P. 21:1; I.P. 11

ANDREA FERRARA
      From *Elizabethan times, a common referent for a
sword, after a famous sixteenth-century sword maker (also
"Andrea" or "Ferrara").
M. 32

ANDREW MILLER
      A sobriquet for the *Navy, after a press gang member
who shanghaied so many men into the navy that he seemed to
own it. A well-known naval catch phrase is "You shouldn't
have joined Andrew if you couldn't take a joke." An ironic
variant is "Merry Andrew."
W. 4; W. 90

ANDROMEDA
      A northern *constellation, named for the Andromeda of
*Greek legend. It contains the Great Andromeda Nebula, the
brightest of the spiral nebulae and is a source of meteor showers, a remarkable example of which occurred in 1872—the de-
bris of Biela's comet, previously seen in 1852.
      See "Medusa" and "Guido."
M. 151; M.D. 55; M.D. 82

ANGEL-HILL
      See "Bury St. Edmunds."
R. 44

ANGELO
        Michelangelo Di Lodovico Buonarroti-Simoni (1475-1564),
the greatest Renaissance painter, sculptor, and architect, left
*Florence for *Rome in 1496, after the death of his patron,
Lorenzo Di*Medici. He completed several major sculptures,
including the "Pieta" of *St. Peter's, in the late 1490's. Back in
Florence in the early 1500's, he did the giant statue of *David
and several frescoes before returning to Rome in 1505 under
the patronage of Julius II. He worked on the Pope's tomb and
on the ceiling of the Sistine Chapel (1508-12), which represents
the *Creation, the *Deluge, and other biblical events in a
*Christian/classical style relecting the gloom of the post-
*Reformation period. "*The Last Judgement" in the Chapel is
considered his finest painting.
        Michelangelo worked on the re-building of St. Peter's,
did spiritual drawings and paintings, and left many unfinished works as well as many which are now lost.
        Despite Michelangelo's tremendous influence on art, M.
seems not to have been inordinately impressed, preferring
gentler and more voluptuous art. He saw the Sistine Chapel
twice in March of 1857, at a time when the work had been injured by dampness and an explosion and had been retouched to
cover the nudity of the figures. In that month he also visited
Michelangelo's elaborate tomb at the church of Santa Croce
and saw "The Three *Fates" in the hall of *Jupiter. His journal (27 March) records his great interest in the expressions of
the faces of the Fates. In his *lecture, "Statues in Rome"
(delivered in 1857), M. discussed the statue of *Moses done by
Michelangelo in 1515 and considered the artist's finest sculpture. M. commented on the figure (probably seen in March
1857) of a "stern, bullying genius of druidical superstition"
(Sealts, *Melville as Lecturer*, 146).
M.D. 86; P. 26:1

ANGEL OF DOOM
        *Revelation 8-9 tells of angelic destroyers.
M.D. 2

ANGELS THAT FELL FROM HEAVEN
        In *Paradise Lost*, angels who followed *Satan. (See
"Milton.")
M.D. 135

ANGLESEA

Henry William Paget, First Marquess of Anglesey (1768-1854), commanded the *British cavalry at *Waterloo, where he suffered amputation of one leg. He is also famous for an enforced toast to the despised wife of *George IV, Queen Caroline: "May all your wives be like her."
M. 22; M. 24; M. 121

ANGLESEA

The Welsh island of Anglesea, or Anglesey, largest island of the *British Empire, is the site of Holyhead mountain. The name probably means "island of the Angles." It has been since pre-historic times an important sea route site and has many ancient ruins, including evidence of *Celtic *Druidism. By M.'s time Holyhead was a packet mail station, with a road that was to become part of the main route to *London. The railroad and harbor were also active. M. would have seen the island from shipboard, enroute to *Liverpool, as "Wellingborough" does in *R*. 27.
R. 27

ANGLO-SAXON

The expression originally designated *English Saxons, as distinguished from Old Saxons of the continent. By M.'s time it was used rhetorically to refer to all persons of Teutonic descent, especially the English and, therefore, during M.'s time, the *Americans.
T. 26; M. 3

ANGUS

A nobleman of *Scotland who (along with "Rosse") addresses "Macbeth" as the "*Thane of Cawdor," in *Shakespeare's *Macbeth* I, iii.
W. 51

ANKERS

Cask or keg measures of spirits, of differing capacity in various countries. The *Rotterdam anker, formerly used in *England, was 8 1/2 imperial gallons (about ten U.S. gallons).
M.D. 101

ANNALS OF EUROPE
      The 1739-44 yearbook, *The Annals of Europe*, covered major domestic and foreign events.
C.M. 26

ANNAWON
      In 1676, in *Rhode Island, a remarkable Indian warrior in *King Philip's War, Annawon, was captured by Captain Benjamin Church, commissioned by the Plymouth Colony. In *M.D.*, M. is in error in ascribing the capture to Lieutenant William Butler (See "Captain Butler"). Annawon is praised by *Cooper in *The Wept of Wish-ton-Wish*.
M.D. 45

ANNO MARDIS
      A play on Anno Domini, "in the year of our lord," used to signify dates since *Christ's birth, the date of which was fixed in the Sixth Century.
M. 177

ANNUS MIRABILIS
      See "Dryden, John"; "Extracts " 26.
M.D. Extracts 26

A. No. 1
      In Lloyd's Register of Shipping, a ship's hull is rated by a letter, her anchors, cables, and stores by a figure. A1 means all first rate. Inferior vessels are classified AE, E, and I.
      The *London-based Lloyd's is a surveying and classifying society of merchant shipping whose standards for construction and maintenance are accepted throughout the world. The company originated in the coffeehouse of Edward Lloyd in the seventeenth century. In 1764 the first register was published. By 1834 the (then) Lloyd's Register of British and Foreign Shipping had developed standard rules for shipbuilding. The modern Lloyd's has committees worldwide and publishes comprehensive rules for shipbuilding standards. The modern "excellent" rating for steel ocean-going ships is 100A1. Lloyd's does not rate ships' messes, such as *W.*'s "Forty-two-pounder Club."
W. 44

ANSON, LORD
    Baron George Anson Anson (1697-1762) earned the title
"father of the navy" in *Britain. He entered service at fifteen,
was promoted to captain by twenty-six, and performed seventeen years of service on the British *Admiralty Board.
    Accounts of Anson's 1740-44 expedition (M.'s date erro-
neous), popular though they were, were a seat of controversy
regarding timing, sales, and authorship. They are: *A Voyage
to the South Seas in the year 1740-1 containing a faithful narrative of the Loss of the *Wager Man of War, one of Lord Anson's
Squadron*, by *John Byron, grandfather of the poet (Sealts
#113), and *A Voyage Round the World in the Years MDCCXL,
I, II, III,IV by George Anson, Esq., Now Lord Anson . . .
Compiled by Richard Walter, M.A., Chaplain of His Majesty's
Ship the *Centurion, 1748.* This last was an eighteenth-century best-seller, despite its authorship by a professional pamphleteer.
    M. invokes Anson's adventures as much for their social
import as for their art.   Anson was not only a brilliant
militarist and administrator who reformed the Admiralty, he
also revised the *Articles of War, created the permanent corps
of marines, and inspired his crews by his justice and
democracy on board, despite tremendous losses due to battle,
accident, and illness.
    The *Centurion* circumnavigation was his most
memorable act. As a result of his earlier voyage at the outbreak
of the War of Jenkins' Ear (against *Spain in 1739), the need
for scurvy prevention was demonstrated, as well as the need
for the *chronometer to fix longitudes. As a third account
points out, the *Centurion* was manifestly deficient in
equipment, and it was only through Anson's efforts that the
practice of under-equipping was halted (Leo Heaps, *Log of the
Centurion: Based on the Original Papers of Captain Philip
Saumarez on Board HMS Centurion, Lord Anson's flagship
during his circumnavigation 1740-44*).
W. 24

ANTARCTIC
    The Antarctic continent surrounding the South *Pole
was unknown in M.'s time, as a result of its having the sever-
est climate on Earth. *Cook had sailed into Antarctic waters
in 1774, but the continent itself was not discovered until 1820,
when the *American Captain Nathaniel Palmer was seeking
new whaling grounds. *Wilkes visited, but little exploration
was done in the late nineteenth century, when interest turned
to the *Arctic region.
M. 119; M. 145; M. 181; W. 70; M.D. 27; M.D. 42

ANTEMOSAIC
        Before the time of *Moses.
M.D. 104

ANTHONY
        See "St. Anthony."
M. 94

ANTHONY ABSOLUTE, SIR
        In *Sheridan's play, The Rivals, "Captain Absolute" is
a bold and boorish despot.
M. 2

ANTICHRONICAL
        Defying temporal measurement.
M.D. 104

ANTIGONUS
        Antigonus I (*Cyclops, or Monophthalmus: "The One-
Eyed"; 382-301 B.C.) was a *Macedonian General under
*Alexander the Great. After Alexander's death (323), he at-
tempted to gain authority over all of *Asia. He took the title of
king in 305 but was killed in the battle of Ipsis, in *Phrygia.
        (*Shakespeare borrowed the name for a *Sicilian lord in
The Winter's Tale who exits "pursued by a bear" [III.iii. 58].
*Beaumont and *Fletcher also use the name in The Humorous
Lieutenant, performed 1619.)
M. 181

ANTIGUA
        The Antigua from which "Israel Potter" sails for Puerto
Rico (see "Porto Rico") is one of the volcanic Leeward Islands
(17°5' N., 61°50' W.) discovered by *Columbus in 1493 and colonized by *Englishmen from St. Kitts in 1632. Antigua was
briefly occupied by the *French, but by 1667 it was British
again. *Nelson served at Antigua's English Harbour from
1784 to 1787.
        (There are also Antiguas on the *Canary Islands and in
Guatemala, as well as an Argentine desert by the name.)
I.P. 2

ANTILLES

The main island group of the *West Indies, extending 2,500 miles from *Florida to the northern coast of *Venezuela, the Antilles form a natural breakwater separating the *Atlantic from the *Gulf of Mexico and the *Caribbean. They include all major West Indies islands except the Bahamas. The Greater Antilles include *Cuba, *Jamaica, Hispaniola (modern Haiti and the Dominican Republic), and Puerto Rico (see "Porto Rico"). The Lesser Antilles include the Virgin Islands, the Leeward Islands, the Windward Islands, Barbados, Trinidad, and Tobago.
M.D. 110

ANTIOCHUS, KING; ANTIOCHUS'S ELEPHANTS

M. appears to have his Antiochuses confused, which is not surprising, considering that there were thirteen kings or princes of the name who ruled in the Seleucid *satrapy of *Syria. The reference in M. 181 is probably to Antiochus III the Great (c. 242-187 B.C.), who rebuilt the Syrian Empire, gaining control of Armenia, *Parthia, *Bactria, and parts of *Palestine and *Phoenicia. He was defeated by the *Romans at *Thermopylae, losing control of Asia. The horrible death mentioned in R. 12 might be his: Antiochus III was killed in *Elam while plundering a temple. However, his predecessor, Antiochus II (Theos), was poisoned by his wife in 246 B.C., and several others of the satraps also died horribly.

"Antiochus's elephants" of M.D. 133 refers to Antiochus V (Eupator), who reigned 164-162 B.C. In the *Apocryphal I *Maccabees 6:34, the forces of the child-king make war on Judas Maccabaeus and the *Hebrews, using elephants stimulated to drunkenness by the "blood of grapes and mulberies." Elephants had been forbidden in battle by *Roman treaty with Antiochus IV (Epiphanes), ruler from c. 175 to 164. He had plundered the temple in *Jerusalem, bringing about the revolt of the Maccabees. Antiochus V was murdered by official order.
M. 181; R. 12; M.D. 133

ANTIPAROS

A thirteen-square-mile Aegean Island of the *Cyclades, noted for a remarkable stalactite cave.
M. 75

ANTIPATER

Antipater (c. 397-319 B.C.) was a *Macedonian general under *Alexander the Great, who made him regent of Mace-

donia in 334. He was an unpopular ruler, and after his death
regional governors denied such central authority as he represented.
M. 181

ANTONINA; DAME ANTONINA
      See "Belisarius."
M. 23; M. 25; M. 26; M. 35

ANTONY, MARK
      Marcus Antonius (c. 82-30 B.C.) came from an old
*plebeian *Roman family. He served *Julius Caesar in vari-
ous roles but had broken with him repeatedly when he was
questioned by the senate in 44 as regards Caesar's assassination. His later funeral oration won him huge popularity and
power. But the rise of Octavian, Caesar's nephew and heir
(later *Augustus Caesar), led to his flight. In a ceremony un-
recognized in Rome, he took *Cleopatra as his fourth wife, replacing Octavian's sister.
      Financially and politically supported by her, he amassed
a fleet in the last Roman civil war but was defeated by Octavian's force at *Actium, in 31 B.C.
      Given false news of Cleopatra's death, he committed
suicide in 30 B.C. Among his descendents were the emperors
Gaius, *Claudius, and *Nero.
      M.'s knowledge of Antony, despite his derogatory tone,
seems derived mainly from *Shakespeare's plays (themselves
derived from *Plutarch). Antony and Cleopatra is a romantic
vision of Antony's budding romance with the queen, his defeat
by Octavian, and the suicides of the lovers; Julius Caesar covers the events surrounding the assassination, with Antony
painted as Caesar's bereaved friend.
M. 22; M. 149; W. 47

ANTWERP
      The province and city of north *Belgium is a leading port
and center of the diamond trade. Settled from the seventh century, it has many *Gothic churches and other ancient landmarks. The center of *Flemish painting, Antwerp (Fr. Anvers) was the birthplace of Van Dyck and the center of
*Rubens's activity.
M.D. 104

AORAI

Mount Aoraï, near Mount *Orohena, is a central peak of *Tahiti (6,788 feet).
O. 18

AOTOOROO

Aotooroo was taken to *Paris in 1769.
O. 18

APEMANTUS' DOG

In *The Life of Timon of Athens*, *Shakespeare plays a word game throughout. The philosopher "Apemantus" the Cynic (i.e. "dog") has only himself or *Timon the Cynic as "dog."
C.M. 23

APHRODITE; APHRODITEAN

See "Venus"; "Corinth."
R. 46; P. 15:1

APOCALYPSE

The most important apocalyptic book of the *Bible is the Book of *Revelation, or the Apocalypse of *John. Apocalypticism originated in *Zoroastrianism; basically, it refers to belief in two opposing cosmic powers, *God and *Satan, and in two ages: a present imperfect time under Satan, and a perfect future under God's blessings forever. Secondary features include the occurrence of visions; pseudonymity; messiah and an anti-messiah; angelology and demonology; animal symbolism; numerology; predicted woes; astral influences, all of which can be seen in M.'s works.

Other apocalyptic works are the Revelation of *Daniel, which contains four "beasts" from the sea; Baruch, with *Behemoth and *Leviathan; the Song of *Solomon, with a dragon; the Book of Enoch.
M. 168; P. 19:2; C.M. 45

APOCRYPHA

The word means "things that are hidden"; in the *Old Testament Septuagint and Vulgate, books not written in *Hebrew and therefore discounted by Jews and, later, by *Protestants. The books include historical, novelistic, didactic, devotional, epistolary, and apocalyptic genres, but not

prophecy. In most versions they are: 1 and 2 Esdras, Tobit, *Judith, Additions to Esther, the Wisdom of *Solomon, Ecclesiasticus, Baruch (with the Epistle of *Jeremiah), The Prayer of Azariah and the Song of the Three Young Men, the History of Susanna, *Bel and the Dragon, The Prayer of Manasses, 1 and 2 *Maccabees.
W. 82; C.M. 45

APOLLO

In *Greek and *Roman mythology, the son of Zeus (see "Jupiter" and "Jove") and Leto (Latona) and a great god of *Olympus, identified with the sun, music, poetry and the healing art. His son was Aesculapius (see "Asclepius"). He is represented as a model of manly beauty.
T. 18; R. 46; M.D. 6; P. 15:1; P. 21:3; C.M. 29

APOLLO GREEN

I have been unable to locate an "Apollo Green" in *Bombay. Perhaps it is, like "Booble Alley," a nickname for a sailor hang-out.
M.D. 6

APOLLYON

The *Greek name (from a root referring to destruction, death, loss) for Abaddon, king of the devils of hell and angel of the bottomless pit in *Revelation 9:11. M. probably comes to the name through *Bunyan's use in Pilgrim's Progress: "The Destroyer."
M. refers to "Abaddon" in Clarel II. xxv. 184.
I.P. 19

APOLOGY FOR RAIMOND SEBOND

See "Montaigne"; "Extracts" 10.
M.D. Extracts 10

APOSTLE, THE

Both references are to *St. Paul.
W. 34; W. 65

APOSTLES; APOSTOLIC; THE CHURCH OF THE APOSTLES

Although in *P. M.* seems to have borrowed the name of the (Episcopal) Church of the Holy Apostles, built in 1848 at 28th Street and 9th Avenue in *Manhattan, his description of the edifice corresponds more to a church at 82 Nassau Street. Murray's notes to *P.* give full particulars, including its conversion to an office building. The "Apostles" living near the building are among the anti-*Christian "rascalities" discussed by Thompson (*Melville's Quarrel With God*, 8:11).

The original Apostles ("persons sent") of *Christ were his twelve most intimate disciples (*Luke 6:13). The list has some variation in *Mark 3, *Matthew 10, and Luke 6: *Peter, James and *John the sons of Zebedee, Andrew, Philip, Bartholomew, *Matthew, *Thomas, James the son of Alphaeus, Thaddaeus or Judas the son of James, Simon the Cananaean or the zealot, and *Judas Iscariot, replaced after his death by Matthias (*Acts 1). The word "apostle" came to signify "missionary," and there are biblical citations of *Paul and Barnabas as Apostles. Paul's writings speak of the inclusiveness of the designation (I *Corinthians 15:5-7) and of "false apostles" (II Corinthians 11:13). In artistic representations of the twelve, Paul usually takes the place of Judas. Legends tell that the original group dispersed to separate territories to evangelize (see "Evangelists").

P. 19; P. 20; P. 21; P. 22; P. 23; P. 24

APOTHEOSIS

The term literally means "deification" (Gr. *apotheoun*, "to make a god"), especially in polytheistic systems. *Greek tradition apotheosized even living persons (such as Philip II of *Macedonia), and later whole dynasties (the Seleucids and the *Ptolemies) were deified. The apotheosized *Julius Caesar presented the first departure from traditional *Roman belief only in the god, Quirinus, and later Roman emperors were granted similar status. The Christian expression, "consecrate," follows the Roman *consecratio*, the equivalent of the Greek *apotheosis*.

In M.'s works, along with *M.D.*'s "Bulkington," the title character of *Billy Budd, Sailor* is apotheosized by his shipmates.

M.D. 32

APPALACHIAN

Eastern North America's Appalachian chain of mountains runs parallel to the coast for 1,600 miles (from St.

Lawrence in *Quebec to the Gulf Coast plain in *Alabama). Its highest peak (6,684 feet) is Mount Mitchell, in North *Carolina's Black Mountains. The chain includes New York's *Catskills and *Allegheny plateaus, the *Blue Ridge and Cumberland chains, the *White Mountains of *New Hampshire, *Green Mountains of *Vermont, *Taconics and *Berkshires.
W. 50

APPLE, CINDERED
      See "Sodom."
M.D. 132

APPLES OF SODOM
      See "Sodom."
T. 8

APRIL, FIRST OF
      April Fool's Day throughout the Northern Hemisphere, commemorated at the Vernal Equinox, when the day has equal amounts of light and darkness. Its origin remains a mystery. Its traditional pranks are associated with the Hilaria of ancient *Rome, on March 25, *New Year's Day (April 1 being its octave) and with the Huli festival of *India, on March 31. In *France, the butt of a joke is the *poissson d'Avril*; in *Scotland, he is the *gowk* (cuckoo).
      (M.'s mother, Maria *Gansevoort Melville, died on 1 April 1872.)
C.M. 1

APRIL MAN
      A newly married man.
R. 58

APSLEY HOUSE
      An eighteenth-century *Greek-style *London mansion designed by the (four) Adam brothers, highly successful *Scottish architects.
M. 121; R. 46

AQUARIUS
      See "Zodiac."
M. 169; M.D. 99; M.D. 121

AQUILA
In astronomy, a northern *constellation: The Eagle.
Named after the favorite bird of *Jupiter, and the symbol of
*Rome.
M. 136; M. 151

AQUOVI
This fictional character's name is a play on aquavit,
*Scandinavian spirits flavored with caroway.
M. 121

ARAB, --S; ARABIA, --N; ARABY
The word "Arab," originally referring to the Semitic
people of the Arabian peninsula (bounded by the Red Sea, Gulf
of Aden, Arabian Sea, Gulf of Oman, *Persian Gulf), and in
modern times to speakers of the Arabic language, was used by
M. and contemporaries in a rather general and romantic
sense. "Arab" invoked visions of the curious Islamic religion;
the exotic oriental *Moorish culture; a certain wildness lost in
the western world but preserved by a people for whom time
stands still; extremes of wealth and poverty and extremes of
violence, gentility, and sensuality. As Finkelstein (*Melville's
Orienda*) and others show, M.'s position on Arabs and Arabia
was influenced by romantic fiction of *Byron, Irving, and the
Arabian Nights, as well as by *Biblical and historical references to Arabs and by a mass of contemporary travel literature.
T. 27's reference to Arab hospitality reinforces that
book's skepticism about western charity. All the great Eastern
philosophies stress duty toward the unfortunate (in contrast
expecially to *Emerson's position). One of Islam's obligatory
duties is payment of the Zahat tax to support the needy, in addition to Sadagat, the voluntary charitable contribution. The
early *caliphs established a structured system assisting wid-
ows, orphans, students, the ill, and the indigent. Thus even
the "wild" Arab tends toward compassion for the helpless.
R. 1's "arid-looking book in a pale yellow cover" perhaps
refers to Carsten Niebuhr, *Travels through Arabia and Other
Countries of the East* (1792), a skeptical work by the sole sur-
vivor of the *Danish expedition of 1760-67. In the same place,
"Stony Arabia" refers to *Ptolemy's distinction between *Arabia
Petroea* ("Stony Arabia"), *Arabia Felix* ("Fertile Arabia," Yemen or the south-west coast), and *Arabia Deserta* ("Desert
Arabia").
M.'s 1856-57 excursion to the middle east did not take in
the Arabian peninsula, but it brought him into direct contact

with many Arabs, as shown in *Clarel* and in his journal. The
Arab "paupers" of *C.M.* 36 are shown to be reality in the 7
February entry, when M. is approached by an "Arab holy man
. . . almost naked . . . solemn idiocy--lunatic--opium-eater--
dreamer--yet treated with profoundest respect & reverence."
     See also "Algiers"; "Bedouins"; "Holy Land"; "Koran";
"Lebanon, cedar of"; "Libya"; "Mecca"; "Medina";
"Mohammed"; "Petra"; "Sinai."
T. 27; M. 158; R. 1; R. 15; W. 20; W. 44; P. 2:2; C.M. 36

ARABIAN NIGHTS
     Arabian Nights Entertainments, or *The Thousand and
One Nights*, was translated into *English in part by the early
eighteenth century and available in an expurgated annotated
scholarly edition of 1839-41 (editor Edward William Lane, 1801-
76). Sir Richard Francis Burton's (1821-90) daring complete
edition did not appear until 1885-8. *Indian, *Persian, and
*Arabic sources of the ninth and tenth centuries supplied plots
for many of the tales told by Scheherazade, the clever wife who
preserves her existence by recounting to her murderous husband, the king, all but the conclusion of adventurous tales,
thus forcing his forebearance until the following day, when
she would begin another tale.
R. 8

ARABIAN ROMANCE
     As Bruce Franklin shows in his edition of *The Con-
fidence Man*, *Emerson tells such a tale in his "Heroism"
(*Essays*, 1841; Sealts #204).
C.M. 36

ARARAT
     An extinct volcanic massif located at the convergence of
present-day *Turkey, Iran, and Soviet Armenia (39°50' N.,
44°20' E.). Mount Ararat rises some 17,000 feet above sea level,
on the elevated Armenian plateau. Like *Greylock, it consists
of two peaks separated by a saddle, but both peaks are in perpetual snow. In *Genesis 7, 4, it is the *Hebrew equivalent of
Urardhu (or Urartu), meaning "highlands."
     Ararat is venerated as the "Mother of the World" by Ar-
menians, following the legend that *Noah's Ark landed nearby
and Noah here located his altar and his vineyard. Despite a local taboo against climbing it, Mount Ararat was scaled in 1829
and 1845.
M. 161; W. 50

ARAUCANIANS
Indians of southern *Chile and Argentina who speak dialects of a common language. They resisted the *Incas in the
fifteenth century, were mostly victorious against the *Spanish
for two centuries thereafter, and successfully defended their
independence from Chile in the mid-nineteenth century.
Chilean Araucanians belonged to three geographical and cultural divisions: *Picunche, Mapuche,* and *Huilliche.* Except
for the *Picunche,* they survive until the present, culturally and
socially distinct from neighboring peoples and maintaining
most traditional tribal customs.
C.M. 25

ARBELA
Arbela (also known as Irbil, Arbil, or Erbil) is located in
northeast Iraq (36°15' N, 44° E.) and has been an important city
since at least the third millenium B.C. (then as Urbillum, later
Arba'ilu), when it was a principal city of *Assyria. It is most
noted for the Battle of Gaugamela, where *Alexander the
Great (M.'s "son of Olympia by *Jupiter himself") defeated
Darius III of *Persia. The city was a center of communica-
tions in a fertile area; it also contained an important shrine of
Ishtar and Sennacherib.
The famous battle took place on 1 October 331 B.C. The
Persians outnumbered the *Macedonians and had superior
equipment, but Alexander's brilliant use of penetration tactics
helped him overthrow the Persian empire.
M. 181

ARCADIA
The original Arcadia was a dreary mountainous area in
*Greece's *Peloponnesus. *Virgil's *Eclogues* made it the tra-
ditional ideal pastoral world. *Sidney and other Renaissance
writers who revived the ideal were apparently unaware of Vir-
gil's re-working of the truth; they passed along the false ideal
to later writers such as *Wordsworth (and M., who admires
"Arcadian unaffectedness" in *I.P.* 8 and seeks a "new Arca-
dia" in *C.M.* 27).
M. also wrote a poem, "Suggested by the Ruins of a
Mountain-Temple in Arcadia, One Built by the Architect of the
*Parthenon."
(There are numerous "Arcadias" in the United States.)
I.P. 8; C.M. 27

ARCHANGEL
In religious belief, angels are spiritual beings, messengers of *God. The *Bible speaks variously of three, four, or seven Archangels: the top of a hierarchy of angels.
M. 11

ARCHANGEL
Archangel (*Arkhangelsk*, in *Russian) is a port at the northern Dvina delta mouth, twenty-five miles from the *White Sea and 700 miles north-northeast of Moscow (see "Muscovite"). It was named for the Cathedral of the Archangel *Michael (built 1645-89). The only Russian port in the sixteenth and seventeenth centuries, Archangel's prosperity declined after the founding of *St. Petersburg, in 1703. During M.'s time, it continued to be a center of shipbuilding and maritime supplies, with a nearby naval base (until 1863).
Archangel is connected in *M*. 11 to two other rich ports: *Savannah and *Surat.
M. 11; R. 7

ARCHBISHOP
An archbishop in the *Christian church presides over his own diocese and over other local bishops. The title began in the fourth century as an honorary appellation in Eastern churches; it spread to the Western church by the seventh century, and was common during Carolingian times. By M.'s day, archbishops had little disciplinary power left and, among *Protestant denominations, survived only in the Anglican and *Episcopalian branches.
A See is the diocese or jurisdiction of a bishop or archbishop (Lat. *sedes*, a seat). The Holy See is the domain of the *Pope.
W. 87

ARCHBISHOPRICK
Properly, "archbishopric," but M. is being "improper" here.
M.D. 95

ARCHER, THE
See "Zodiac."
M. 69; M.D. 99

ARCHIMEDES; ARCHIMEDEAN

The *Greek mathematician/inventor was born at *Syracuse, *Sicily, about 287 B.C., the son of an astronomer. After study at *Alexandria, he returned home to do mathematical research, preferring pure scientific pursuit to contrivance of the machines for which he is best remembered. There are many legends: he shouted "eureka" in the bath tub and ran outdoors without clothing, having solved a mental puzzle; he said "Give me a place to stand and I will move the earth"; he constructed a burning mirror which set *Roman ships on fire.

Archimedes was killed by accident when *Marcellus captured Syracuse (212 B.C.). His tomb was embellished by a geometrical figure he himself had devised.

Among extant treatises are: *On the Sphere and Cylinder; The Measurement of the Circle; On Conoids and Spheroids; On Plane Equilibria or Centres of Gravity of Planes; The Quadrature of the Parabola; On Floating Bodies; The Sand Reckoner; The Method; A Collection of Lemmas.* There are also many works presumed lost.

The "Archimedes (or Archimedean) screw" is a spiral within a cylinder for raising water to a height, especially from the hold of a ship. It can also move grain from a low to a high level. Although it would seem an unlikely device in surgery (in *W.* 63), *Penny Cyclopaedia's* article on "Tourniquets" says it is a component of a device to replace the tourniquet.

C.M.'s reference to "Archimedean money power" (7) probably relates to the arithmetical procedure of multiplying a number or amount by its own value, increasing it geometrically.

M. 48; W. 63; C.M. 7

ARCHIPELAGOES

Chains or groups of islands, or the seas in which they are found.

Passim

ARCHON

In the ancient *Greek city-states, the noble chief magistrates holding executive power and members of the Areopagus, or council, named for a hill near the acropolis.

ARCOS DE CARICO

Carioca Aqueduct, M.'s "arch-over-arch" structure, dates from colonial times and is still in use in modern *Rio de Janeiro.

W. 39

ARCTIC
See "Pole . . . . "
M. 45; M. 161; M. 192; M.D. 27; M.D. 32; M.D. 68; P. 2:4; P. 2:5; P. 9:1; I.P. 16 (and elsewhere)

ARCTURION, THE
See "Arcturus"; "Leviathan."
M. Passim

ARCTURUS
One of the brightest northern stars, Arcturus is in the *constellation *Bootes; in *M.* 100 the "blood-red star" for which the fictional ship "Arcturion" is named.

"Arcturion," M.'s fictional ship in *M.*, is seen by Mills ("The Significance of 'Arcturus' in *Mardi*") as embodying negative connotations about mankind connected with the giant star. The *Duyckincks published a magazine, *Arcturus* (1840-42), noting in their first issue that Arcturus "looks down with a keen glance on the errors, follies, and malpractices of men."
M. 136; M. 146; M. 175; M. 195

ARDAIR
Finkelstein (6) suggests an explanation for the name of this fictional place, based on Edward William Lane's (1801-76) notes to *Arabian Nights* (a series on which was running in *Duyckinck's *Literary World* in 1848). The Arabic word "*Ard*" means "country, earth, and world." Thus M. might have wished to express "the country of air."
M. 84

AREOPAGITICAS
*Areopagitica: a speech of Mr. John Milton for the liberty of the unlicenc'd printing, to the *Parliament of *England,* *John Milton's 1644 response to Parliament's 1643 attempted suppression of his pamphlet on divorce. *Areopagitica* showed in brilliant exhortative language that censorious "licensing" of printed matter was a) a *Papal-style pursuit, b) morally stultifying and educationally unsound, c) useless. (The title derives from Areopagus, hills of *Athens near the Acropolis.)
M. 161

ARETHUSA

In legend, Arethusa was a nymph of Elis and attendant to *Diana. The river/river god, Alpheus, son of Oceanus, pursued her until, turned into an underground stream, she rose as a fountain at Ortygia, near *Syracuse. Traditionally, an object in the Alpheus eventually rises at Syracuse. There is some confusion about the site of Arethusa's transformation, which may have occurred in *Greece, arranged by *Artemis. The story receives various treatments: *Ovid (*Metamorphoses*, Book 5), Keats (*Endymion* Part 2), *Shelley ("Arethusa"), and *Cervantes (*Don Quixote*, Part 2, Book 3, Chap. 23).
M.D. 41

ARETHUSAS

H.M.S. *Arethusa*, the last ship in battle entirely under sail, was launched in 1849, as M. was racing to complete *R*. She burned in 1855, all of her decks catching fire from explosions of *Russian shore guns, at the bombardment of Sevastopol, in the Crimean War.
R. 41

ARGO-NAVIS

In astronomy, a southern *constellation: The Ship.
M.D. 57

ARGOS

See "Jason."
M. 149

ARGOSY

See "Jason."
M.D. 133

ARGUS

In mythology, Argus was a one-hundred-eyed watchman who could sleep with some of his eyes while guarding with the rest. He was finally defeated while guarding Io (see "Hera"), when Hermes appeared as a reed pipe musician who played and then told stories until one story finally put all of Argus's eyes to sleep. Hermes killed him but Io collected the eyes for the tail of her favorite bird, the peacock.

His name, Argus, is the genus of Asiatic pheasants.

M. defended the historicity of *T.* in a letter (21 April 1846) to the Albany *Argus*.
M. 31

"ARHEEA"
Ahia is the *Tahitian fruit referred to.
O. 61

ARIAN HERESY
Arianism, first propounded by Arius (d. c. A.D. 335), an *Alexandrian priest who saw himself in *Origen's tradition, holds that *Christ is not divine but a created being; *God's uniqueness precludes his being shared. Arius was condemned at the Council of Nicaea, but his polytheistic teachings had widespread repercussions throughout history, especially in the Germanic tribes. He influenced nineteenth-century *Unitarians, as well as modern-day Jehovah's Witnesses.

ARIEL
Ariel was the (twenty-gun) warship borrowed from the *French government for *John Paul Jones's return to the *United States in 1779; it was returned the same year.
("Ariel" is the airy sprite in *Shakespeare's *The Tempest*, who carries out the schemes of "Prospero," the usurped duke. Ariel became symbolic of the poetic imagination.)
(Another *Ariel* was with *Oliver Hazard Perry's squadron at Lake *Erie in 1812. She had a crew of thirty-six and four twelve-pound guns.)
I.P. 20

ARIES
See "Zodiac."
M.D. 99

ARIMANIUS
See "Zoroastrianism."
C.M. 9

ARIMATHEA
In the four *Gospels, a city connected with Joseph of Arimathea, who retrieved the body of *Jesus and interred it in

his own tomb. It is believed to have been located about twenty miles east of *Joppa.
P. 4:1

ARIOI

Arioi was a large (mostly male) *Tahitian sect dedicated to worship of *Oro. They are discussed in full in Oliver's Volume II. Ariois were variously painted by contemporary observers as warriors, affluent libertines, or native *freemasons. *Ellis likened them to "strolling players" (Chapter III). They were denounced as "wicked" demonic libertines, or praised as talented "comedians"; *Tyerman and Bennet castigated them, as did most other missionaries.

Originally, Ariois were probably of the race of chiefs. They were usually young, attractive people, who traveled by the hundreds from place to place. They performed religious ceremonies and entertainments, and were honored and feted. Ariois dressed themselves and their canoes lavishly, scrupulously performed dedicatory services, made precisely specified offerings, and exchanged gifts with their hosts. Especially prepared foods were ritually eaten for the several days of the visit. Ariois sat in specified postures, painted their bodies red and white, and decorated themselves with feathers. They held athletic contests and exhibitions, danced and sang, and performed sexually explicit comedy acts. They were often nude, but any ritual clothing used was disposed of in a bonfire.

Their entertainments, like their private lives, were a mixture of pious religious acts and sexual ones; wildly uninhibited love-making was part of their entertainment, and while Europeans saw them as lascivious, Ariois held celebration of sexuality as sacred. Female Ariosis served as sexual partners during the entertainments and at other times walked about announcing their availability (on the spot, for a fee).

*Cook and many other visitors witnessed their festivals. Ariois presided at post-childbirth rituals, weddings, and inaugurations, and served as warriors for chiefs. Their secret rites involved dances, music, poetry, and gymnastics. Hierarchies within groups were distinguishable by tattoos, cosmetics, and loin cloth colors, red marking a high-caste Arioi. There were tests for admission into this privileged group, which might demand food or gifts from any islander. Inept Arioi (poor dancers, singers, or cooks) were banished.

Europeans were much offended by the Arioi practice of infanticide. Ariois sometimes sacrificed only first-born infants, but usually they sacrificed all; parenthood disqualified them from active membership because it marked age and maturity in a group where youthfulness was most valued. The practice might have sprung from the celibacy required of early chiefs; it served as a means of birth control and caste control.

M.'s two allusions reveal his own hedging about the sect; in *T*. 26, Ariois are spreaders of "licentiousness"; in *O*. 32, they are merely "celebrated" gourmets who cook better than the *French. M.'s inconsistant orthography in his two references is probably not in this case attributable to his own failing (despite the intrusive "r" that suggests a *New England accent). the word is variously spelled "Arii oi," "Erreoy" (by *Bligh), "Areoi" (by Ellis).
T. 26 ("Arreory"); O. 32 ("Aeorai")

ARION
    A *Greek poet and musician of the seventh century B.C. who was cast into the sea or jumped to avoid robbers. His music summoned a dolphin, who carried him safely ashore at Taenaros.
    *Shelley alludes to him in "The Witch of Atlas" (lv).
M.D. 83

ARISTOTLE
    The great philosopher and scientist Aristotle (384-322 B.C.) was born at Stagira, *Macedon. In *Athens, he was *Plato's student for twenty-seven years, after which he tutored the future *Alexander the Great. He opened his own school in the *Lyceum grove outside of Athens and wrote on philosophy, physics, zoology, politics, and rhetoric, affecting thought until the late seventeenth century, after which his *Poetics* continued to influence neo-classicists.
    The surviving body of some forty-seven works includes the *Politics* (*De Republica*, or *Politica*), mentioned in *C.M.* 29. As Franklin's notes point out, nowhere in the work does Aristotle refer to hatred of humor and love of puns as attributes of the "least loveable" men.
    "De Coelo" (alt. "*De Caelo*," W. 38), "On the Heavens," posits the existence of a fifth element. In addition to the basic earth, air, fire, and water, Aristotle spoke of aether, a circular-moving substance in contrast to the others, which moved up and down. *De Coelo* was disputed by *Simplicius.
    Sealts #s 14a and 14b are an 1889-90 edition of *The Organon or Logical Treatises* and an annotated 1872 edition of the *Treatise on Rhetoric* and *The Poetics*.
R. 40; W. 38; M.D. 32; C.M. 29

ARK, THE

*Noah's ark, in *Genesis 6:14-16, is a vessel ordered by *God before the *Deluge (Genesis 6:14-8:19). The *Bible describes it as a floating house approximately 450 feet long, 75 feet wide, 45 feet high, with three decks, one door, and one window. Noah's family of eight is placed aboard, along with animals: either one pair of all living creatures, or one pair of unclean and seven pairs of clean animals, with no "creeping things" or insects.

W. 65 reference to the "little boat" which "according to *Rabbinical tradition, pushed after" Noah's ark is unclear. One nineteenth century source (John Gill's *Exposition of the Old Testament*) annotates *Genesis 7:23 regarding Og's surviving the Deluge on a piece of wood that trailed after the ark, being fed each day by Noah.

W. 7; W. 65; M.D. 104

ARKANSAS

The "Bear State," or "*Bowie State," was the twenty-fifth admitted to the Union (1836). It is c. 275 miles from east to west and 245 miles north to south, and is bounded by *Missouri (N.), *Tennessee and Mississippi (E.), *Louisiana (S.), *Texas (S.W.), and Oklahoma (W.). Arkansas had a rugged history, right up to M.'s time, when it was still very much frontier land. DeSoto found the Quapaw or Arkansas Indians there in the 1540's, and Marquette and Jolliet explored in the 1670's: LaSalle in 1682 claimed the area as part of *France's "Louisiana." The French quickly settled the area, only to lose it to the *Spanish in 1763. They regained the territory in 1800, but it was ceded in 1803 as part of the Louisiana Purchase. It made part of the Louisiana Territory from 1804 to 1812 and part of Missouri Territory from 1812 to 1819, when it became separate. A *slave state, Arkansas seceded in 1861.

M. 13; M. 119; M.D. 41; C.M. 3

ARKANSAS RIVER

The Arkansas runs c. 1,450 miles east-southeast, from the *Rocky Mountains of central Colorado, through Kansas, Oklahoma, and *Arkansas, to the *Mississippi River north of Greenville, Mississippi. It was probably descended by DeSoto and was explored in 1806 by Zebulon Pike. Despite some limitations on navigability, it became important to trade and travel in the nineteenth century.

W. 75

ARKITE
        The Arkites were a *Phoenician tribe of ancient *Syria.
M.D. 82

ARMAGEDDONS
        Armageddon is possibly derived from a *Hebrew word
designating the scene of the final struggles of the forces of good
against the forces of evil. The original of the site was perhaps
a Mount Megiddo, on *Mount Carmel.
I.P. 24

ARMS HOTEL
        When M. first visited *Liverpool, in 1839, the Queen's
Arms Hotel (formerly the Liverpool Arms) was still in existence on *Castle Street, near the *Merchant's Exchange and
the *Customs House. Gilman suggests (*Melville's Early Life
and Redburn*, VI, 189) that Allan Melvill (see "Walter
Redburn") stayed here in 1811.
R. 29

ARNOLD, BENEDICT
        The name of Benedict Arnold (1741-1801), *American
Revolutionary War officer, has come to signify the
quintessential deserter, for his defection to the *British.
Arnold came from a distinguished *New England family and,
after serving with militia in the French and Indian Wars, he
settled at New Haven, *Connecticut, a prosperous druggist.
        Elected captain of a militia company in 1774, he went to
war immediately after the Battle of Lexington. As a colonel, he
proposed the seizure of Fort *Ticonderoga but found himself
second to *Ethan Allen. Appointed by *Washington to attack
*Quebec, he was severely wounded in the failed campaign but
continued the siege, for which he was made a Brigadier General. He returned home a hero, but unpopular for his rash-
ness. He was passed over for promotion but continued to fight
in Connecticut, only to be bypassed a second time.
        Considering resignation, he half-heartedly fought in the
siege of Fort *Stanwix and then at *Saratoga. Wounds received
there crippled him, and he was sent to *Philadelphia, where
his financial dealings brought accusations referred to
*Congress. A second marriage, to a Loyalist's daughter, ap-
parently convinced him to spy for the British. Found guilty of
financial crimes at Court Martial, Arnold increased his spying activity, finally abusing even the enemy, in allowing the
hanging death of Major John André. He was now in disfavor

from both sides. He retired on half pay in England, but later dealings in the *West India Trade and personal skirmishes with the *French brought increasing grief and inactivity. He died in England, where his wife received a small pension for her collaboration.
M. 24; M.D. 87; P. 19:2

AROOSTOOK
     Aroostock is the largest county of *Maine, bordering on *Quebec and *New Brunswick, *Canada. The Aroostook War of 1838-39 was the result of a lingering border dispute with *Britain, resulting in establishment of permanent boundaries in 1841.
     The Aroostook River rises in north *Penobscot County, Maine, flowing c. 140 miles to the St. John River, in New Brunswick.
     ("Aroostoock Hemlock," of *M.D.* 126 grows in the thickly forested county.)
R. 27; M.D. 126

ARRACK
     Strong alcoholic drink of eastern countries, usually made from rice, molasses, or *cocoanut milk. The word "arrack" is derived from Arabic and *French words for "sweat."
M. 84

ARRAS
     In *Shakespeare, a wall hanging or curtain.
O. 81

ARREORY SOCIETY
     See "Arioi."
T. 26

ARRIAN
     Flavius Arrianus (c.96-c.180), *Greek philosopher/historian, received honors early: in an appointment unheard of for a Greek, he was made governor of Cappadocia by *Hadrian, then became archon at *Athens. A friend of the *Stoic *Epictetus, he wrote the eight-book *Diatribai* (*The Dissertations*), the chief authority for Stoic ethics. His most important work is the *Anabasis* ("Expedition") *of Alexander*, a biog-

raphy from *Alexander's accession to his death. He also wrote
many other works and fragments, some of which are lost.
C.M. 36

ARSACIDES

The small group of islands just south of the *Solomon
group was probably discovered by *Bougainville about 1768.
Because their inhabitants resisted civilized incursions, the
islands were named after a fierce *Parthian dynasty which
endured from the third century B.C. to the third century A.D.
M.D. 102

ARSENIC

The widely available chemical element (As.) has been
used as a poison since at least the fourth century B.C. It appears in two basic forms (common metallic gray and unstable
yellow) and varies in toxicity, so it has been used as a medication. Thus *Benjamin Franklin's comment in *I.P.* 9 about its
being "sweeter than sugar." Arsenic acts as a poison by interfering with particular cellular enzymes essential to
metabolism. Accidental poisoning in industry was common
during M.'s time.
I.P. 9

ARTAXERXES

Son of *Xerxes, and King of *Persia (465-425 B.C.). His
Persian name is Artakhshatra; he is called the long handed
(Longimanus) because his right arm was longer than his left.
In Ezra 4, 6, 7 and Nehemiah 2, 5, 8, he is mentioned in con-
nection with the restoration of *Jerusalem after the Captivity.
M. 75

ARTEDI

The Swiss naturalist Peter Artedi (1705-1735) was a
friend and associate of *Linnaeus who studied fossils and
quadrupeds. Artedi drowned in a canal at *Leyden. His works
were completed by friends and published as *Bibliotheca ichthyologica* and *Philosophia ichthyologica*. (Linnaeus and Artedi
were mutual heirs.)
M.D. 32

"ARTICLES OF WAR"

An act of 2 March 1799, for the government of the *Navy, was followed by the act of 3 April 1800, for the *better* government of the navy, usually known as the *Articles of War*. John Adams gave the order to draw up articles based on the raw materials of the *British Act of 1661 (under *Charles II), as amended by the Act of 1749 (which provided for *flogging). This 1775 version provided that "no commander shall inflict any punishment upon a seaman beyond twelve lashes upon his back" without a court-martial. The act of 1799 authorized flogging for "oppression, cruelty, fraud, profane swearing, drunkenness, or any other scandalous conduct, tending to the destruction of good morals." Sleeping on watch called for the death penalty, if ordered by court-martial. This act allowed the court-martial to order up to 100 lashes; it was not revised again until 1862.

M.'s expertise in the Articles probably comes from *Democratic Review* (XXV, 99).
W. Passim

ARTINGALL

See "Spenser."
W. 50

ART OF WAR

See "Machiavelli."
W. 41

ARVA-ROOT

M. misrenders "kava" (*Piper methysticum*), a plant of the pepper family, the roots of which are commonly used in the south sea islands to prepare a narcotic beverage. *Porter mentions *vie kava*, spring of water already affected by the roots.
M. 81

ASCLEPIUS

Asclepius is the *Greek hero and god of healing, sometimes invoked to protect from shipwreck. In *Iliad* he is the mortal "blameless physician" taught by Chiron. To *Hesiod and Pindar (Pyth. 3), he was son of *Apollo and the nymph Coronis, daughter of Phlegyas; Apollo saved the boy from his faithless mother's funeral pyre, entrusting him to Chiron. Zeus (see "Jupiter" and "Jove") slew him with a thunderbolt for daring to restore Hippolytus to life.

Probably he was both a mortal and a god, to whom a cult erected shrines and temples, recording miracle cures. Some were actually sanatoria, with theaters, gymnasia, and baths, where secular physicians (Asclepiadae) prescribed diets, baths, exercise, and faith healing based on Asclepius's methods. Patients sometimes slept in the temples, seeking dream cures. The cult came to *Rome from Epidaurus, its most famous seat, after a plague in 293 B.C., thriving in Dacia and *Spain and yielding late to *Christianity.

In art, Asclepius is usually represented as a mature, bearded, bare-breasted man with a kingly expression. He holds a club-like staff with a snake coiled about it, a symbol of rejuvenessence because it sheds its skin. He sometimes carries a scroll or tablet, representing medical learning, and is pictured with his daughters, Hygieia (goddess of Health) and Panacea, and sometimes with a dog. (The Caduceus with winged staff used in the *United States mixes in the magic wand of Hermes or *Mercury, messenger of the gods and patron of trade.) Legend tells that after death he was turned into the *constellation Ophiuchus, the snake-holder.

Aesculapius is the *Latin form.
T. 11

ASHANTEE

The Ashanti people of Ghana, *Africa, descend from the last and greatest of the Akan states, established about 1600, north of the *Gold Coast. They are noted for their bravery and fierceness and for their elaborate costumes and crafts. The king was elected by the matrilineal clans, who worshipped ancestors and took slaves, who might be sacrificed. Leaders had special stools, which were kept as objects of veneration after their deaths. The powerful nation was subdued by the *British early in the nineteenth century and kept in a humiliated state until hostility re-erupted in the 1860s.
M.D. 54

ASIA, --N; ASIATIC

Asia is the world's largest continent, with one-third of its land area. Among its ancient civilizations were the *Sumerian, *Babylonian, *Assyrian, *Median, *Persian, *Greek, *Roman, *Arabian, as well as the cultures of *China, *India, and *Japan. The *Huns, Tatars (see "Tartar"), and *Turks made westward migrations; the *Mongols visited by *Marco Polo prevailed in the thirteenth and fourteenth centuries, and in the seventeenth the *Cossacks crossed *Siberia to the *Pacific. By that time, *Dutch, *Portuguese, and

*English companies were beginning to trade with Asian countries, leading to increased European control (especially in India); China and Japan began trade with the west in the nineteenth century.

　　　　See also "Orient . . . . "
Passim

ASIATIC CHOLERA
　　　See "Cholera."
R. 58

ASIATIC STYLE
　　　In seventeenth-century *England, a split developed between proponents of two distinct prose styles. The "Attic" or "plaine" (*Ciceronian) style, which has heavily influenced modern prose, aimed for plain, direct, clear expression in relatively short simple declarative sentences, composed of relatively common words. Previously, the prevailing "Asian" or "loose" (*Senecan) style had featured lengthy, ambling, digressive, grammatical constructions with much subordination in sentences, much use of coordinating conjunctions, absolute participial constructions, and parentheses.
　　　M.'s prose utilizes both styles, and in *I.P.* he puns on the term "Asiatic," suggesting it is a slow but luxurious way to "travel."
I.P.1

ASMODEUS
　　　In Jewish (see "Hebrew") tradition, the giant demon of vanity, the *Talmud's "king of the devils." In *Le Diable Boiteux* (1707) (the lame devil), Alain René Le Sage (1668-1747) has Asmodeus fly through the air, lifting off the roofs of houses to show his benefactor what is happening inside.
C.M. 18

ASPASIA
　　　In the fifth century B.C., Aspasia was mistress of *Pericles for twenty years, bearing him a son who gained recognition after the death of the legitimate heirs. A controversial character, she was accused of provoking the *Peloponnesian War. As one of the *heterae* (independent, wealthy courtesans), she was respected by philosophers such

as *Socrates and lent her name to a philosophic dialogue by
Aeschines, a Socratic orator.
M. 80

ASPHALTITES
*Thomas Browne used this name for the *Dead Sea,
*Palestine (*Pseudodoxia Epidemica*, Book 7, Chap. 15: Sealts
#89 and #90). *Milton referred to "the Asphaltic pool" in *Paradise Lost* I, 411.
M.D. 117

ASSES' EARS
Handles so shaped.
M.D. 15

ASSUMPTION
See "Sumption," for discussion of M.'s playful syllogism.
M. 171

ASSYRIA, --N
The ancient empire of western *Asia developed around
the city of Ashur (or Assur) in *Mesopotamia, on the upper
*Tigris, south of *Nineveh: a locale settled from the sixth millenium B.C. Early development began c. 1300 B.C. with an aggressive outward reach taking *Babylonia and moving forces
as far as the *Mediterranean. Conquests continued through
the ninth century, and in the eighth century B.C. Sennacherib's actions led to the eventual (seventh century) defeat
of the *Chaldeans and entry into *Egypt. Assyria reached its
zenith under Ashurbanipal, or "Assurbanipal" (669?--626?
B.C.), who created the library that became one of the chief historical sources of antiquity. The nation fell after his death;
Babylonia renewed its power, and *Cyrus the Great established
the *Persian Empire (which owed much to the Assyrian).
As Finkelstein (4) suggests, much of M.'s knowledge resulted from contemporary reaction to archaelogical discoveries
(as shown in the *W.* 86 reference to "Assyrian kings").
Knickerbocker, *Duyckinck's *Literary World*, and other popular peridicals were full of aritcles on the subject.
Remains of the rulers of *Nineveh, the most populous
and oldest city in Assyria, were unearthed starting in the nineteenth century. *Layard discovered the palace of Sennacherib
and collected bas-reliefs from the library of Ashurbanipal II.
In the twentieth century, Campbell Thompson unearthed the

palace of Ashurnasirpal. Later excavations revealed the remarkable art and architecture of numerous Assyrian and Neo-
Assyrian monarchs dating from the 6th millenium B.C. in
modern Iraq. (See also "Beards.")
M. 75; M. 181; W. 86; M.D. 91; P. 1:5

ASTOR HOUSE
      *Manhattan's Astor House hotel and restaurant was
built by John Jacob Astor (1763-1848), on the site of his resi-
dence-office on *Broadway, at the junction of Park Row and
Vesey Streets, across from *St. Paul's Church. Astor had to
purchase all of the property on the block in order to build his
hotel in what was at that time the "uptown" area. The Astor
House opened in 1836 and soon became the most famous tavern
in the United States (displacing the *City Hotel), favored by distinguished visitors and prominent locals, especially high-
standing *Whig politicians. Its architecture was English style,
with a rather plain granite front, but it was lavishly appointed
within. Its 300 rooms were among the first to boast gas lighting, interior plumbing, and steam heat.
      Proprietors *Robert B. Coleman and *Charles Augustus
Stetson became famed hotelliers as a result of their distinguished clientele, which included *Andrew Jackson, *Daniel
Webster, *Abraham Lincoln, *Hawthorne, Dickens (see "Hard
Times"), and others. Walt Whitman is said to have habitually
lounged on the front steps, watching the passing parade.
Although M.'s frequent citation of Astor House suggests his
approval as a gourmand, he complained in a letter to
*Duyckinck (1847) that the building itself was only another part
of the mortar that was rapidly covering Manhattan's greenery.
      The image of the Astor House faded in the 1850's, despite
attempts at innovations such as forced air cooling. It was torn
down at the end of the century.
R. 33; R. 60; W. 15; I.P. 16

ASTORIA
      At inlet of *Columbia River, *Oregon, U.S.: 46°11' N.,
123°51' W.
W. 29

ASTRAL
      M.'s references throughout M. to stars as astral crosses,
crowns, cups, and hosts probably reflect his experience of some
contemporary public events in astronomy. In December of
1847, the New York *Daily Tribune* announced the January pub-

lication of lectures by a Professor Mitchell, of the *Cincinnati Observatory; in January and February of 1848, John P. Nichol, of the University of *Glasgow published a pamphlet containing his seven lectures on space; in February of that same year, *Edgar Allan Poe gave a lecture (reported in the *Tribune*): "The Cosmogony of the Universe."

M. was familiar with at least three highly accessible works on astronomy (two of which were for children): Sealts #s 68a, 75a, 214.

M. Passim (especially M. 188)

ASTREA
The daughter of Zeus (see "Jupiter" and "Jove") and Themis, Astrea was the last of the gods to leave men, her departure marking the transition from the bronze to the iron age. She is the Goddess of Justice. As the *constellation *Virgo, she holds *Libra, the scales or balance.

C.M. 5

ATAHALPA'S
Atahualpa (or Atabalipa; from *atahu*, "virile," and *allpa*, "sweet") (c. 1502-1533) was last ruler of the *Inca empire in *Peru. Lacking descent from both sides of the royal line, Atahualpa was officially only ruler of *Quito and, at the time of *Pizarro's invasion, had only recently wrested control from his half-brother to become Inca. Atahualpa received the *Spaniards hospitably, only to be deceived. With hundreds of Peruvians dead in battle, the Inca himself was seized. He offered as ransom a roomful of treasure, which was received by the Spaniards. Kept in captivity and accused of plotting, Atahualpa was tried and put to death by strangulation.

C.M. 30

ATHANASIUS
Saint Athanasius, the Great (c. 295-373), an *Egyptian, was Bishop of *Alexandria who disputed the *Gnostics in the *Arian heresy regarding the Trinity. Although there are many authentic published works, he is wrongly credited with the so-called Athanasian Creed, the *Quicumque vult*, which represents orthodox Trinitarian doctrine of a later period. Athanasius helped develop the Nicene Creed.

The wrongly-named Athanasian Creed expounds the doctrine of one *God in trinity and trinity in unity, the full humanity and full divinity of *Christ, the indispensability of adherence to the *Catholic Church.

M. 97

ATHEISM; ATHEIST, --S

An atheist is one who denies the existence of, or refuses moral obligation to, a *god. Thompson's *Melville's Quarrel with God* suggests that M. qualifies under the secondary part of the definition.

Earliest use of the term appears to be the sixteenth-century *French *atheiste*, which M. invokes in the name of the ship which conquers that of "Captain Vere," in *Billy Budd, Sailor*. *Holland's *Plutarch's Morals* (1603) talks of "beastly cogitations and Athisticall discourses."
M.D. 42; P. 25:3; P. 26:4

ATHENIAN

Athens is the political, economic, and cultural center of modern-day *Greece. It was named for the goddess Athena (Minerva), and was originally ruled by Ionian kings. It rose to prominence during the *Persian Wars (500-449 B.C.), with a powerful military force. Its apogee, the time of *Socrates, *Aeschylus, Sophocles, and Euripides, occurred under *Pericles (443-429 B.C.). Rivalry with *Sparta led to the *Peloponnesian War of 431-404, in which Athens was defeated; it rose against Sparta and was victorious, with Sparta defeated at the battle of Leuctra (371). Philip II of *Macedonia conquered Athens in 338 B.C., and the high Athenian culture spread throughout the world. It was taken by the *Turks and by the *Venetians (who destroyed the *Parthenon, 1687-8). It changed hands several times during the Greek war of independence (1822-30) and from 1834 was the capital of Greece.

M. visited February 8-11, 1857.
W. 85; C.M. 24; C.M. 36

ATHOS, MOUNT

The contemporary Holy Mountain (ancient Acte), Mount Athos (6,667 feet), on the peninsula of Chalcidice, *Greece, is the site of an orthodox monks' republic. It has been the home of hermits since ancient times. Although it is dedicated to the *Virgin Mary, no women have been allowed on the mountain since the eleventh century.

M. saw Mount Athos on 6 and 9 December 1856, noting in his journal (6 December) its "rather conical" shape.
M. 75; M. 147

ATLANTIC

The ocean bordered by North and *South America in the Western Hemisphere and Europe and *Africa in the Eastern is

divided by the *Equator into the North Atlantic and the South
Atlantic. It covers c. 31,530,000 square miles: with connecting
seas c. 41,000,000 square miles. M. crossed the Atlantic east to
west and north to south, as a passenger and as a sailor before
the mast. But when M. speaks of "ocean," he usually means
the *Pacific.
Passim

ATMOSPHERE
The air pressure at sea level is an "atmosphere."
M.D. 81

ATROPOS
See "Fates."
I.P. 19

ATTILA
The *Huns were a barbaric tribe who invaded the East
*Roman Empire in the fourth and fifth centuries, gaining a
reputation as uncivilized brutes. Attila (or Etzel; d. 453) was
King of the Huns in *German heroic legend. The "Scourge of
*God," as he was known, ruled an empire that reached from
the *Alps and the *Baltic in the west to near the Caspian Sea in
the east. Among his other acts: he murdered the brother with
which he shared his throne, demanded heavy tribute from
those he conquered, sacked cities, force-married a woman who
had asked his intervention to save her honor, and demanded a
large dowry. Priscus describes him as a short, squat man
with a large head, of irritable temper but not pitiless.
M. 36; W. 16; I.P. 19

AUBURN
Seat of Cayuga County, *New York, Auburn is 25 miles
southwest of Syracuse in the Finger Lakes district. Its main
attractions are Auburn Theological Seminary, a monument to
the Cayuga chief, *Logan, and Auburn State Prison (W. 58).
While on the *lecture circuit, M. visited the prison (6
January 1857). It was innovative from its opening in 1816. By
1825, it was much admired around the world for introduction
of the "Silent System," which replaced the current "Separate
System" in which prisoners lived in large solitary cells, saw no
one, and (initially) had no employment. Auburn's system introduced small back-to-back individual cells in the center of a
narrow cellblock, the only light and air from cell windows

opening on to the windowed corridors. Prisoners worked together, forbidden to speak. They marched to work in lockstep line, hands on shoulders of leaders, on pursuits for private industries interested in cheap labor. The private sector was finally barred in 1882 from exploiting prison labor.

Mount Auburn Cemetery, in Cambridge and Watertown, *Massachusetts, was the first *American cemetery detached from church or private property. It was established in 1832.

W. 58; C.M. 5

AUGUSTUS CAESAR'S
    See "Caesar . . . . "
I.P. 8; C.M. 7

AURELIAN
    Lucius Domitius Aurelianus (d. A.D. 275) was *Roman emperor from 270 to 275. An army officer who succeeded *Claudius II by virtue of his military success and clever politics, Aurelian reunited the Roman Empire, began the twelve-mile city wall, and reformed the coinage. Seeing himself as appointee of the god of the Unconquered Sun, he alienated his associates and was finally murdered on his way to the *Persian campaign by officers who believed he would execute them.
    See also "Beards."
M. 97; W. 84; P. 18:1

AURORA, --S
    *Roman goddess of the dawn; *Greek "Eos."
    In astronomy, a light-bringing phenomenon, such as the *Northern Lights.
M. 38; M. 164; M. 165; M. 187; W. 65; W. 74; P. 7:6

AURORA BOREALIS
    See "Northern Lights."
M. 38

AUSTRALIA, --N
    Australia (Lat. "southern") is the smallest continent: approximately the same size as the continental *United States.
    Early explorers found two general groups of natives: northern negroid people similar to western *Papuans, and

southerners like the Dravidians of *India. The *Portuguese sighted the continent in 1601; the *Spanish followed in 1605. The seventeenth- and eighteenth-century *Dutch called the land New Holland. *Dampier landed on the northwestern coast in 1688, and in 1770 *Cook landed at *Botany Bay and sailed northward, claiming the entire coast for *England as *New South Wales. By 1788, a penal colony (Port Jackson) had been established on the site of *Sydney, and in 1829 the entire continent became a British dependency, with an economy based on sheep-raising and wheat production. Gold was discovered at Victoria in 1851, contributing to a lawless and unstable life for many squatters and drifters.
O. 2; O. 14; M.D. 24; M.D. 87; C.M. 14

AUSTRIAN, --EMPIRE
    The Austrian Empire began in the tenth century with *Bavarian settlements in lower Austria, designated *Ostarichi*. The Babenbergs and Habsburgs governed under the feudal title *österreich*, the *Latin form of which, Austria, came into use in the twelfth century. Lands ruled by Habsburgs came to be called Austrian after the *Thirty Years' War, but the constitutional empire proper was not created until 1804, as a result of the *Napoleonic Wars. *Holy Roman Emperor Francis I assumed the title of Austrian Emperor, giving Napoléon his first defeat in 1809, but losing land and prestige as a *German leader. Metternich's mediation by 1813 ended the struggle against the *French (bringing about restoration of the *Bourbons), regained some lost provinces, and brought Austria into the German Confederacy.
    In M.'s time, the Austrian Empire was an arbitrary, bureaucratic, and conservative police state that censored literature, discouraged education, and focused on dangers from without rather than within. The revolutions of 1848 came about under the rule of the feeble-minded Ferdinand I, in *Hungary (under *Kossuth), *Bohemia, and *Lombardy. "Treaty breaker" of *C.M.* 26 refers to Austria's 1849 reneging on promises made about the revolutions. After Ferdinand's abdication, Francis Joseph ruled, becoming Emperor of the Austro-Hungarian Empire in 1867. (Hungarian territories of the Empire were not considered part of Austria from 1867 to 1918.)
    In *M.D.* 42, the reference to the Empire as "heir to overlording *Rome" alludes to the fact that after the fifteenth century all *Holy Roman Emperors were from the Austrian house of Habsburg.
    See also "Charles V."
M.D. 42; C.M. 26

AUTO-DA-FE, --S
    Auto-de-Fé, or "act of faith," was the ceremony during which sentences of the *Spanish Inquisition were read upon faithful penitents. It encompassed a procession, solemn mass, oath of obedience to the Inquisition by the king and laymen, sermon of the grand inquisitor, and reading of the sentence.
    Despite some confusion, Auto-de-Fé (which was not granted to impenitents) does *not* include execution (usually burning at the stake) but precedes it.
M.D. 54; C.M. 45

AUTOLYCUS
    In *Shakespeare's *The Winter's Tale*, a charming but dishonest peddlar. In *Greek mythology, Autolycus was a thieving son of Hermes.
C.M. 30

AVATAR
    Incarnation of a god, from the *Sanskrit *avatara*, descent. In *Hindu mythology an avatar is a god on earth in visible form. Most famous are the ten avatars of Vishnu (see "Vishnoo"):   l. the fish (Matsya); 2. the tortoise (Kurma); 3. the boar (Varaha); 4. half man/half lion (Nrisinha); 5. the dwarf (Vamana); 6. Rama with an axe (Parasurama); 7. Rama again (Ramachandra); 8. Krishna (of the *Bhagavad-Gita*); 9. Buddha (Prince Siddhartha, founder of Buddhism); 10. yet to come: a winged white horse.
    Metaphorically, the word is used to represent the embodiment of some idea or phrase.
M. 53; P. 20:2

"AVEC PRIVILEGE DU SOUVERAIN PONTIFE"
    Fr.: licensed or permitted by the *Pope.
R. 30

AVENEL, WHITE LADY OF
    A mischievous, frightening spirit that has power over benighted *Catholics in *Sir Walter Scott's *The Monastery*. "Mary Avenal" marries the hero,"Herbert Glendinning," the family name M. assigns to the mother, in *P*. The White Lady calls herself the "mystery of mysteries" (See "Quotations" section).
W. 1

AVERNUS

The reference in *I.P.* 25 is metaphoric. In *Aeneid* VI, *Virgil says "Facilis descensus Averni," "Easy is the descent to Avernus," the opening to *Hades. In February 1857, M. visited Virgil's original, Lake Averno, west of *Naples, *Italy. Since ancient times the volcanic crater lake had exuded noxious fumes. Its *Greek name, *"Aornos,"* refers to the fact that no bird could fly above it and live.
I.P. 25

"A VISIT TO THE SOUTH SEAS"

See "Stewart."
T. 1

"A VOYAGE AMONG THE ICEBERGS ... "

A parody. See "Scoresby."
M.D. 35

"A VOYAGE ROUND CAPE HORN INTO THE SOUTH SEAS ... "

See "Colnett, Captain."
M.D. 55

"A WHALING VOYAGE ... "

See "Extracts 30."
M.D. 55

AYACUCHO, BATTLE OF

The Battle was won by the "patriots" of *Peru on 9 December 1824, freeing the country from Spanish rule and breaking *Spain's hold on the new world. The revolutionary forces numbered about 6,000 yet all but annihilated 9,000 enemy troops.
W. 63

AYRSHIRE

A county of southwestern *Scotland, east of the Firth of *Clyde, Ayrshire is dotted with lochs and is the county of *Ailsa Craig. It has been inhabited for about 6,000 years and has been invaded by *Romans, *Normans, *Norwegians, and *Englishmen. Its eleventh-century King Duncan became the first king of all Scotland; it is also associated with *William Wallace, *Robert Burns, and other important Scots.

M. wrote little about Scotland in his journal, but he is known to have been in Ayrshire in early November, 1856.
I.P. 15

AZIMUTH COMPASS

Webster's New World Dictionary of the American Language (1984) defines "azimuth" (used in astronomy, surveying, etc.): "distance in angular degrees in a clockwise direction from the north point or, in the Southern Hemisphere, south point; arc of the horizon measured clockwise from such a point to a vertical circle passing from the zenith through the center of a star." *Bowditch adds that in navigation it is employed for taking bearings; he describes its form.
O. 60; M.D. 35

AZORES

The Azores (properly "Açores") archipelago in the North *Atlantic (c. 37°44' N., 29°52' W.) is 300 miles long, with nine main active-volcanic islands, geysers and mineral springs. Mt. *Pico, on Pico Island, is the highest peak (7,611 feet). The islands are known to have been settled by the *Carthaginians by the fourth century B.C. They were visited by *Portuguese navigators early in the fifteenth century and became an important exile place. Politically part of Portugal, the Azores were important in resisting the accession attempts of Philip II of Spain, and as the site of an important naval battle between *Revenge* (under Grenville) and the *Spanish fleet, in 1591.
M.D. 29; M.D. 40; M.D. 45; M.D. 51; P. 14:3

AZTEC

The important *Mexican Indian groups derive their name from Aztlán, an area of Mexico. The Aztec Empire, second only to that of the *Incas, rose to prominence in the twelfth and thirteenth centuries. Aztecs were originally farmers, and irrigation and other technologies helped their culture to thrive. The powerful city of Tenochtitlán (on the site of the modern Mexico City) was the culmination of much wandering and expansionist warfare. It became the center of dynasties that ruled much of Mexico by the time of the ninth Aztec king *Montezuma's defeat by Cortés (see "Cortez"). Ritual worship of the sun god, Tonatiuh, involved much mutilation of human sacrificial victims, so contemporary writers such as Prescott tended to focus on the "Moral corruption" of the Aztecs rather than on their predominantly agrarian characteristics, in the process justifying the actions of the conquistadors.

(In *M*. 169, M. is in error about "*Balboa's band," which did not rove through "Aztec" glades.)
M. 169

B

BAAL
   *Phoenician word for "Lord." (M. does not use the name "Baal"; see "Bel"; "Belial"; "Belus.")

BABEL
   The word is the *Hebrew form for *"Babylon." In *Genesis 11:1-9, after the *Deluge, men decide to build a tower to heaven; God punishes them by mixing up their language, and they disperse, unable to finish.
   Historically, the Tower of Babel was probably a ziggarut or stage tower known to be in Babylon at this time, and still in existence in *Hellenic times.
R. 33; R. 34; W. 25; M.D. 35

BABYLON, --IAN, --ISH
   Babylon, the ancient *Mesopotamian city on the *Euphrates (modern southern Iraq), is mentioned as early as the third millenium B.C. About 2100, Hammurabi made it the capital of his kingdom of Babylonia, which extended from the Euphrates to the *Tigris (modern central Iraq).
   Babylon's wealth was derived from commerce; it is known to have had elaborate and colorful buildings, a brick palace, and the famous Hanging Gardens, and to have worshipped Marduk, a god identified with *Bel.
   The city was destroyed in the seventh century B.C. by *Assyrians under Sennacherib. It was rebuilt, then ruled by Nebuchadrezzar (see "Nebuchadnezzar"), who died in 562 B.C. It was captured by *Persians under *Cyrus the Great in 538 B.C., becoming only an unimportant part of the Persian Empire.
   Interest in Babylon was high in the nineteenth century, stimulated by *Layard's work. As Finkelstein shows (*Melville's Orienda*), M. saw the Babylonian kings' experience as prophetic and the Babylonian *Ninevah as a prototype of

modern large cities. Probably he knew James B. Fraser's popular histories of Mesopotamia, *Assyria, and Persia, which had been included in Harper's Family Library of 1845.

Murray's notes to *P.* suggest that the "Babylonian City of the Day" (*P.* 2:5) might refer to Baalbec, *Syrian City of the Sun (Heliopolis), which had famous ruins, or it may simply suggest that Babylon had so many cities that developed rapidly that "Pierre" finds himself in a contemporary one.

See also "Chaldean."

M. 60; M. 181; R. 46; R. 56; M.D. 124; P. 2:5; P. 19:2

BACCHUS

The *Roman god of wine, equivalent to *Greek Dionysus, and son of Zeus (see "Jupiter" and "Jove") and Semele. The name comes from the Greek word *iacchus*, to shout, and Bacchus is usually thought of as a rowdy god. He is represented as a youth with flowing hair, crowned by vines and ivy. In the *Lusiad*, he is an evil demon, but he is the guardian power of *Mohammedanism.

M. 119; M. 181; W. 37

BACHELOR; BACHELORS' HALL

The designation "bachelor" would appear to have special meaning for M., other than its usual classification as 1) inferior grade ecclesiastic; 2) low-ranking knight; 3) holder of preliminary university degree; 4) inferior guild member; 5) unmarried man. Most clearly seen in the short story, "The Paradise of Bachelors and the Tartarus of Maids," M.'s use suggests a self-centered sybarite free of responsibility (especially to women), a role he probably never enacted in his early years, having little money and large obligation to family, even before his marriage.

The "Ti" (*T.* Passim) is the *Polynesian equivalent of the bachelor's hideway.

In his *London journal (December 1849), M. expressed guilt at living the life of a "bachelor" while his wife and infant son remained at home, adding, "Yet here I have before me an open prospect to get some curious ideas of a style of life, which in all probability I shall never have again." The sketch "The Paradise of Bachelors" reflects on his temporary sybaritic existence; at the time of its publication in 1855, Elizabeth Melville was expecting her fourth child.

Passim

BACHELOR
    M.D.'s ship "Bachelor" is probably fictional. Perhaps M.
means some association with the *pirate John Cook's (d. 1684?)
Batchelor's Delight (piloted by *Cowley), which plagued the
*Panama coast. ("Bachelor's Delight" is the name of the
*American Captain Delano's ship in "Benito Cereno." It is not
the name of the historical Delano's ship.)
M.D. 115

BACON, FRIAR
    *English Franciscan friar, Roger Bacon   (c. 1220-c.
1292), was a philosopher and scientist of great learning. The
early part of his career was predictable, but his interest in
what were known as the "new sciences" (including alchemy)
caused him to begin secret experimental research, which he
hoped would lead to a vast encyclopedia of all knowledge,
backed by Pope Clement IV. He attacked theologians and
scholars of his day but was superstitious and credulous about
alchemy and astrology, so that eventually he was imprisoned
by his fellow Franciscans.   As legend grew about his
wonderful and dangerous experiments (possibly including
necromancy), he earned the sobriquet "Doctor Mirabilis," and
posterity has retained his image as the classic brilliant but
dangerous (and possibly mad) scientist.
    He is parodied in a comedy by R. Greene (acted in 1594):
The Honorable Historie of Frier Bacon and Frier Bungay.
I.P. 8

BACON, LORD; BACONIAN
    Sir Francis Bacon, first baron of Verulam, viscount St.
Albans (1561-1626), was born into a family whose high rank
might have furthered his career but did not. Born in *London,
son of the Lord Keeper of *Elizabeth's reign, he attended Trinity College, *Cambridge, became a barrister at Gray's Inn in
1582, and served in *Parliament for the first time in 1584.
Sometime friend to the Earl of Essex and longtime rival of *Sir
Edward Coke, Bacon rose with difficulty through a series of
high posts to the Lord Chancellorship of England. His career
ended after a bribery scandal, for which he was fined, imprisoned in the *Tower, disqualified from Parliament, and excluded from the Court. Thereafter he did the writing that was
to be his real contribution to the world. His major pursuit was
the incompleted "Great Instauration," written in English and
in *Latin (*The Advancement of Knowledge,* 1605; *De Augmen-
tis Scientarum,* 1623). Bacon projected five volumes, aiming at:
l) systematic classification of all branches of knowledge;

2) regularization of scientific study; 3) recording of "histories" of natural phenomena; 4) and 5) (unfinished) illustration of the new method in use, and "anticipations of the new philosophy."

Bacon's belief that man's knowledge was not serving him led to his distinguishing between natural world knowledge and spiritual knowledge, to his condemnation of "idols" or habits of mind that hampered progress, and to the use of the inductive ("scientific") method. He criticized scholastics, humanists, and occultists who placed obstacles in man's path to knowledge. His work gave impetus to the founding of the *Royal Society.

His most important literary works are *New Atlantis* (1627), about a Utopian community; *Essays* (1597-1625), a potpourri of pungent aphoristic comments on a wide range of subjects; and *The History of Henry VII* (1622). Among his other works are *Maxims of the Law* (1597), *De Sapientia Veterum* (1609); *Apophthegms,* and *The Translation of Certain Psalms into English Verse* (1625).

"Baconian fulling mills," in *P.* 12:3 suggests that M. anticipated the effects on individuals of industries run by efficiency experts.

(See also "Extracts" 13, 14.)

R. 50; M.D. Extracts 13; M.D. Extracts 14; P. 12:3; P. 14:3; C.M. 9; C.M. 24; C.M. 37

BACONIAN FULLING-MILLS
      See "Bacon, Lord . . . . "
P. 12:3

BACTRIA, --N
      Bactria was a central *Asian *satrapy of the *Persian Empire (corresponding to modern Afghan Turkestan). The many Stone Age remains reveal its ancient origins; references in the *Avesta (see"Zend Avesta") suggest its part in the history of *Zoroastrianism and prophecy. Part of the Achaemenid satrapy, Bactria was conquered by *Cyrus the Great and by *Alexander the Great. In 246 B.C., independence was declared, and it became a powerful Greco-Bactrian state, which fell c. 130 B.C.
M. 60; M. 119

BAD ANGEL
      See "Quotations": "Bad Angel shall tend the Good."
P. 26:6

BADEN-BADEN
        The most popular spa of *Germany's *Black Forest,
Baden-Baden, on the Oos River, has mineral springs known to
have been used by the ancient *Romans. Until the eighteenth
century the residence of the margraves princes, it has many
castles.
M.D. 55

BAFFIN'S BAY
        Baffin Bay is an arm of the North *Atlantic between the
Northwest Territories and *Greenland, 700 miles long and
from 70 to 400 miles wide. It opens on the Atlantic via Davis
Strait and on the *Arctic via Smith Sound and Lancaster and
Jones sounds, providing a water route through the Arctic
archipelago (in summer months only). The *Labrador current
passes through the bay, bringing many icebergs.
        The bay was explored in 1616 by *English navigator
William Baffin (1584?-1622). Baffin Island, on the western
shore, had originally been visited by *Martin Frobisher; it is
the largest island of the *Canadian Arctic Archipelago.
R. 40

BAGDAD
        Bagdad (alt. Baghdad) is the capital of modern Iraq, in
the center of the country on both banks of the *Tigris, twenty
miles from the *Euphrates; it is enclosed on three sides by ancient walls and was from Sumerian times important in desert
travel and trade. The present city dates from A.D. 762.
        The Islamic "Abode of Peace" under Caliph Harun-al-
Rashid, Bagdad became a center for the arts and scholarship,
as painted in the *Arabian Nights. It was weakened when the
caliphate was moved, and fell to various conquerors: the
*Mongols in 1258: *Tamerlane in 1400; Shah Ismail of *Persia
in 1524: the *Ottoman Empire in 1638. In the nineteenth century, Bagdad was controlled by *Mameluke governors until it
fell under *British influence after the first third of the century.
        "Bagdads" are pipes, in M. 4.
M. 4; W. 93

BAHIA; BAHIA DE TODOS OS SANTOS
        A coastal state of *Brazil (the capital of which is Sal-
vador: see "Salvator"), Bahia de Todos os Santos consists of a
coastal plain and the diamond-rich Chapada Diamantina
range, which produces mostly black industrial diamonds, rock
crystal and semi-precious stones, gold, and other metals. It

was first sighted in 1500 and became the center of seventeenth-
and eighteenth-century colonization, with plantations based on
negro *slave labor. In 1823 it became a province of the Brazilian Empire (and in 1889 a state of the federal republic).
    Todos os Santos Bay is a sheltered inlet twenty-five miles
long and twenty miles wide, at Salvador. It was investigated in
1501 by Amerigo Vespucci.
W. 50; W. 63

BAINBRIDGE
    William Bainbridge (1774-1833), of Princeton, *New Jer-
sey, started his career in the American Merchant Service,
which he left in 1798 to become a strictly disciplinarian officer
in the newly organized U.S. *Navy. He was commander of the
frigate *Philadelphia* in the Tripolitan (or *Barbary) wars and
was recommissioned, after a return to civilian ships, during
the *War of 1812. As Commander of the frigate *Constitution*,
he captured the *British frigate *Java* in the South *Atlantic.
After retiring, he served on the *Board of Naval Commissioners.
W. 3: W. 50

BAJAZET
    Bajazet or Bayezid I, *Ottoman Sultan (1389-1403). A
famous warrior, Bajazet was finally defeated by Timur and
imprisoned at Ankara from 1402 until his death.
M. 119

BAKER-KNEED
    Baker- or knock-knee is the inward inclining of the knee
joint. Bakers are particularly subject to the deformity because
of the position in which they stand to knead bread, putting an
undue burden on one side of the body.
C.M. 22

BALAENE
    Common early synonym for "whale." See "Cetology
section."
M.D. "Extracts" 9

BALANCE ROCK; TERROR STONE; STONE
    The original of the remarkable stone in *P.* is Balance
Rock, a 165-ton limestone boulder (25 x 15 x 10 feet), located

north of *Pittsfield, *Massachusetts, in the *Pontoosuc Lake district. A favorite visiting place, it is called "Rolling Rock" in *Taghconic* (1852) by Godfrey *Greylock (Joseph E.A. Smith), Sealts #s 478 and 479.

(The stationary Balance Rock is unlike *British "Logan Stones," which rock. The best example is found at Lands End, England.)

See also "Memnon."
P. 7:4; P. 7:5; P. 7:6

BALBOA'S

Vasco Nuñez de Balboa (c. 1475-1519), *Spanish conquistador, was an empoverished descendent of nobility. In 1501, he sailed west, settling at Hispaniola, where he accumulated debts that eventually caused his covert departure. In 1513, in command of a small, badly equipped expedition unsanctioned by King Ferdinand V, he crossed the hostile isthmus of *Darién and first saw the fabled *Pacific Ocean from a hill near the Gulf of San Miguel. Taking possession of the "South Sea" for the kings of *Castile, he was appointed governor by Ferdinand. But rivalry with Pedro Arias de Avila led to his trial for treason and his eventual beheading.
M. 169

BALEEN

See "Cetology" section.
M.D. Passim

BALIENE ORDINAIRE

Fr. *baleine ordinaire*: the common whale.
M.D. 32

BALLY

Bali Island is located in the Lesser *Sundas between the Java Sea (N.), and the *Indian Ocean (S.), east of *Java across Bali Strait (two- to fifteen-miles wide). Highest peak of the mountainous island is Mount Agung (Peak of Bali), 10,308 feet. Bali is known for its exotic woods (including *teak and waringen trees, sacred to the Balinese) and for fauna including deer and tigers.

The Balinese are *Malayans related to the Javanese and renowned for their physical beauty and high culture. Hindus (see "Hindoo") entered Bali in the seventh century, and the *Japanese migrated in the ninth and tenth centuries. Trade

with the *Dutch began early in the seventeenth century, with
brief incursions by the *British (who ruled from 1811 to 1816.
Dutch rule was established from 1980.)
M.D. 87

BALM OF COLUMBIA; "BALM OF PARADISE, OR THE
ELIXIR OF THE BATTLE OF COPENHAGEN"
     Perhaps mythological hair oils used like *Macassar oil.
R. 18; W. 6

BALSAMIC
     The family *Balsaminaceae* includes plants that yield oily
or gummy aromatic resins. (They are related to impatiens:
balsamina.) Although balsam is usually thought of as a soothing, healing plant, and its aroma is used to scent closets, in
"flower language," it signifies Impatience.
M. 116

BALTIC
     The northern European arm of the *Atlantic linked to
the North Sea by the Danish Straits, Kattegut (see "Cattegat"),
the Skagerrak, and *Germany's Kiel Canal, the Baltic is shallow and low in salinity, making for easy freezing: thus M.'s
frequent references to its coldness. In the *Middle Ages, the
Baltic was dominated by the Hanseatic League (see "Hanse
Towns").
M. 3; R. 30; M.D. 40; M.D. 87; M.D. 86

BALTIMORE
     The capital city and major seaport of *Maryland is lo-
cated at the head of the Patapso River estuary, fifteen miles
above *Chesapeake Bay, to which it is connected by the Chesapeake and Delaware Canal (1829). With forty miles of water
frontage, Baltimore has always been a busy shipbuilding and
repair facility; *Constellation* (sister ship to "*Old Ironsides"
and to *United States*) was built here in 1797; clipper ships
were a major focus in the nineteenth century.
     The area was first settled in the mid-seventeenth cen-
tury, but the town was not established until 1729, thereafter becoming a colonial shipping center for grain and tobacco.
     The *Continental Congress met in Baltimore (1776-77);
Francis Scott Key's "Star-Spangled Banner" (not the official
anthem in M.'s time), composed in 1814, was inspired by the
defense of Fort McHenry in the *War of 1812.

Its many historical sites make Baltimore the
"Monumental City." The memorial to *Washington (*M.D.* 35)
is a *Doric column topped by a statue (1809-1829) by Robert
Mills.
M. *lectured in Baltimore, 8 February 1859.
O. 11 ("Baltimore," a character); M.D. 35; C.M. 16

BANCROFT

George Bancroft (1800-1891), *Harvard-educated *Massachusetts scholar, orator and *Jacksonian Democratic statesman, wrote the nationalistic *History of the United States* (10
vols, 1834-76), celebrating *God's plan made visible in democratic virtues. As *Secretary of the Navy under *Polk, he
helped abolish flogging, instigate merit promotion, and in general cut through traditional *Navy policies that hampered
progress and damaged morale among sailors.
As Secretary of War *pro tem,* in 1845 he ordered
*General Zachary Taylor across the *Texas border, starting
the *Mexican War. He later served as Minister to *Britain and
then to *Germany.
W. 34

BANIAN

The banian, or banyan, an East Indian fig tree (*Ficus
benghalensis*), has branches which grow shoots that set out
tangles of new trunks.
M. 91; M. 174

BANK OF ENGLAND; BANKS OF ENGLAND

The *London institution was established in 1694 as a private enterprise paying a large percentage to the *British government, then waging a costly war against *France. The
Threadneedle Street site was acquired in 1724; the original
structure had been accumulating for a long time before Sir
John Soane's gradual (1788 to 1833) addition and rebuilding to
what M. would have seen when he strolled in the area in
November of 1849. (That early Greek revival style building was
rebuilt in the twentieth century.)
Despite its status as a private institution, the Bank became the sole note-issuing facility for England and *Wales.
The "specie vaults" (*W.* 13), guarded by military personnel
since the *Gordon riots of 1780, hold the complete gold and
cash reserve not in circulation of England and Wales.
W. 13; P. 25:1

BANKS

Sir Joseph Banks (1743-1820), *English explorer and naturalist, used his large fortune to further scientific discovery. He went to *Newfoundland and *Labrador in 1766; circumnavigated the globe (along with his friend, *Daniel Solander) on *Cook's expedition of 1768-71, and traveled to *Iceland in 1772. He was President of the *Royal Society, Knight Commander of the Bath, member of the Privy Council. His important herbarium is at the *British Museum.
M.D. 105

BANKS

See "Newfoundland."
R. Passim; M.D. 58

BANNOCKBURN

Bannockburn, *Scotland (near Stirling) was the scene of *Robert Bruce's defeat of Edward II's *English forces in 1314, described in *Scott's Lord of the Isles (vi, 1815). M. might also have known John Barbour's 13,000-line poem of the fourteenth century, The Bruce, which gives a graphic account of the battle.

Bruce's victory at Bannockburn is regarded by Scotsmen as the culmination of Scotland's war of independence, whereby the nation was permanently lost to England. English losses amounted to perhaps 20,000 men, including many nobles and knights; the Scots lost far fewer, at least partly through familiarity with the forested area of the Bannock.
M. 119; R. 40

BANYAN DAY

M.'s definition in W. is slightly different from the customary one: "day on which sailors eat no flesh," or on which makeshift meals are eaten. The name derives from the Banians, a Hindu (see "Hindoo") caste who eat no meat.
W. 15; W. 82

BAPTIST, --S

The Baptist faith is an offshoot of Congregationalism, in the English *Puritan movement. In the nineteenth century, Baptists were perhaps the fastest-growing *Protestant denomination, with much missionary activity. "Hard-shell" Baptist (C.M. 2) probably refers to those Baptists who remained very close to the teachings of *Calvin. The split between Southern

and Northern Baptist conventions occurred in 1845, in disagreement over *slavery.

Baptists profess the supreme authority of the *Bible; believer's baptism; churches composed of believers only; equality
of all Christians in Church matters; independence of the local
church; separation of *Church and State.
W. 38; W. 76; P. 25:4; C.M. 2

BARBARY COAST; --PIRATES
The coast of northern *Africa, including Tripoli,
Tunisia, *Algeria, and *Morocco, tolerated and even organized
*piracy as early as the fifteenth century. By the seventeenth
and eighteenth centuries, Morocco was the center of an efficiently organized network in which *pirate captains (reises),
sailing ships built specifically for the purpose at Bougie, were
financed by wealthy agas, *deys, or *beys, who received ten
percent of the profit. Captured persons were enslaved if not
wealthy enough to ransom themselves.

The Barbary pirate countries plagued ships in the
*Mediterranean. Their harassments made clear the need for
the U.S. *Navy provided by the *Constitution but hitherto un-
acted upon. After the *American Revolution, only one rotting
warship was left (*Alliance), but the Barbary crisis, involving
the loss by 1793 of some thirteen American ships and crews,
brought about the order in 1794 for six ships, sufficient to force
a treaty in 1796 with the dey of Algiers which cost the U.S. one
million dollars.

In 1800 the frigate George Washington was comman-
deered to carry an ambassadorial party of 200 people and fifty
animals (including lions and tigers), and the *Bashaw of
Tripoli had plundered a U.S. brig, leading to the creation of the
enlarged Mediterranean squadron to blockade the port.

Morocco ratified a treaty of 1786, but other problems persisted: relations with the British were strained; ships went
aground; bombs exploded prematurely; men deserted, "going
*Turk," and finally Tripoli declared war on the U.S. Rein-
forcements brought about a surrender, but U.S. support of a
Tripolitan pretender, and the payment of $60,000 ransom
money, made the conclusion less a victory than a sellout. Poor
performance by ships stationed at *Gibralter, ransoming of an
American captain held by the bey of Tunis, an accidental explosion, and the wounding of *Porter brought further difficulty
until negotiations with Tunis. War with Algiers was declared
in 1815, but *Decatur's force coerced a treaty. Port *Mahon
was leased as a permanent naval base. The French conquest
of Algiers brought some relief, but piracy was not finally eradi-
cated until steam ships outsped Barbary vessels.
R. 51; W. 50; M.D. 45; M.D. 104

BARBAULD, MRS.

Anna Laetitia Barbauld (1743-1825) was an *English poet and editor who collaborated with her brother, *Dr. John Aikin, on a prose work for children (*Evenings at Home*). After the death of her husband, the Reverend Rochemont Barbauld, she focussed on literary activity and the support of radical causes. Her idealistic poem, *Corsica* (1768), and her editions of *The British Novelists* (fifty volumes; 1810) were perhaps her finest works, but she is remembered also as an editor of *Akenside and Richardson, and as author of "Life! I know not what thou art," much admired by *Wordsworth.
R. 30

BARBICAN

An outpost protecting a castle, fort, or moat drawbridge. *London's Barbican Street was built on the site of a barbican at an old city gate. M. walked in the area on 10 November 1849.
I.P. 25

BARBON, PRAISE-GOD

Praise-God Barbon (Barebon, or Barebones; c. 1596-1679) was a wealthy *English leather salesman and sectarian preacher (*Baptist or Anabaptist) whose preaching attracted riotous mobs. *Cromwell summoned him to *Parliament in 1653, in an assembly later named after him. A strong opponent of the Restoration, he published pamphlets against *Charles II and was eventually imprisoned in the *Tower.
C.M. 22

BARDIANNA'S WILL

Perhaps M. had in mind connections with the widely publicized 1848 will of John Jacob Astor.
M. 177

BARGE

See "Commodore's Barge; --bargeman."
T. 6; M. Passim; W. Passim

BARLOW

Joel Barlow (1754-1812), was one of the Connecticut Wit poets, an eighteenth-century Hartford group connected to *Yale. His most ambitious literary project was *The Columbiad* (1807), orginally published in 1787 as *The Vision of Columbus*, a nationalistic *American epic in heroic couplets, envisioning a final world union devoted to the aims of a noble *Columbus. He earned *French citizenship after seventeen years abroad which liberalized his politics. He published several political pamphlets. His most famous work, *Hasty Pudding* (1796), was a mock epic poem in heroic couplets, advancing the claim that such simple food as boiled Indian meal increased one's virtue. After a consulship in *Algiers, he was appointed U.S. minister to France. He died in Poland enroute to a meeting with *Napoléon. R. 52

BARONS
The lowest order of *English nobility. Formerly, barons were vassals of a great noble (Late Lat.: *baro*, a free man, especially a "king's man"). Eventually, "greater barons" became peerage. The first was Baron De Ros (1264). A baron is addressed as "Lord"; the Sovereign addresses him as "Our right trusty and well beloved ___."
In *M.D.*, "baron" refers to *Cuvier.
W. 56; W. 68; M.D. 41; M.D. 54

BARTHOLOMEW MASSACRE
See "Bartholomew's Day."
W. 87

BARTHOLOMEW'S DAY
Commemoration of the Massacre of St. Bartholomew keeps this saint's day important in *France. On 24 August 1572, at the instigation of Catherine de' *Medici, mother of Charles IX, slaughter of the *Protestant Huguenots began. It is estimated that as many as 50,000 were killed in *Paris and the provinces.
St. Bartholomew was reputedly flayed alive in A.D. 44 in Armenia. Little is known about the *Apostle except his missionary work. His symbol is the knife.
W. 85; W. 87

BASHAW
Bashaw in common usage means an arrogant, domineering person; a corruption of *Turkish "pasha," an important governor.
A Three-Tailed Bashaw, a beglerbeg or Turkish Prince of Princes, has a three horse-tail standard borne before him.

Next in rank is the Bashaw with two tails; last is the *bey, with only one.
O. 61; M. 121; M. 181; M.D. 88

BASHEE ISLES

The Bashi Islands of the *Philippines are the modern Batan Islands, in Luzon Strait (20°N., 121°53' E.). There are fourteen very flat islands in the group.
M.D. 109; M.D. 111

BASILISK

*Browne's *Pseudodoxia Epidemica* devotes a chapter to the "little king of Serpents": "men still affirm, that it killeth at a distance, that it poisoneth by the eye" (chapter 7).

Penny Cyclopaedia also discusses the Cockatrice, or basilisk, which is always pictured with a king's crown on. The more important legends connected to it are detailed there:

1. It burns up whatever it approaches.

2. It is a "wandering *Medusa's head" that causes an "instant horror . . .immediately followed by death."

3. Its touch causes the flesh to fall from the bones of any animal it contacts.

4. There is a "concentration of evil" produced from it; it is produced from the eggs of very old cocks hatched under toads or serpents.

P.C. also notes Psalm XCI. 13: "super aspidem et basiliscum ambulabis," which translates as "thou shalt walk upon the lion and asp." A basilisk carcass was suspended in the Temple of *Apollo, so that no one would dare enter.

M. was much taken with the idea of the "evil" gaze; in *C.M.* 43 he discusses the "Cosmopolitan's" "power of persuasive fascination"; in *Billy Budd, Sailor*, the evil Master-at-Arms, "Claggart," has a mesmeric glance.
W. 61

BASILOSAURUS

The family Basilosauridae of the *Eocene and Oligocene periods were progenitors of whales (see "Cetology" section). Of the extinct Archaeoceti suborder, they had skulls, nostrils, and dentition similar to that of recent Cetacea. Basilosaurus is commonly called "King Lizard."

See also "Creagh, Judge."
M.D. 104

BASTILES
The *French Bastille was a *Paris fortress built by
Charles V and used as a state prison until it was stormed by
the French Revolutionary mob on 14 July 1789 (a date now cele-
brated as Bastille Day, similar in spirit to the American
*Fourth of July); it was demolished one year later.
The word bastille means "fortress," from the Old French
bastir, to build.
In Paris, stones mark the outline of the old fortress.
M. 24; W. 20; W. 31; M.D. 115

BATAVIA
The Batavia of *R*. 12, where sailors get fever, is probably
Djakarta, Indonesia. (There are many Batavias; the ancient
one was between the arms of the *Rhine River and the North
Sea, peopled by Germanic Batavi. The Batavian Republic was
the name given in 1795 to the area *Napoléon was to declare in
1806 the Kingdom of *Holland.)
R. 12

BATTAS
See "Sumatra."
M. 94

BATTERY, THE
The Battery, at *Manhattan's southern tip, was named
for a 1693 *British fort which was replaced by an 1807 U.S. fort,
after the *War of 1812 called *Castle Clinton. City property
after 1822, it was renamed Castle Garden, hosting official
functions and special occasions. "The Battery" today refers
more to the park surrounding the fort than to the building itself.
In M.'s time the Battery was as carefully landscaped as
*Napoléon's garden at the "end of *Venice," as M. notes in the
journal of 5 April 1857.
R. 7; R. 60; R. 62; M.D. 1; M.D. 3

BATTLE OF NEW ORLEANS
See "New Orleans . . . . "
R. 12

BATTLE OF THE BRANDYWINE
See "Brandywine."
W. 42

BATTLE OF THE SUMMER ISLANDS
See "Waller, Edmund," and "Extracts" 20.
M.D. Extracts 20

BAYARD
Probably Chevalier de Bayard, Pierre du Terrail (1475-1524), a *French knight distinguished in battle service of Charles VIII, Louis XII, Francis I. (See "Valois.")
M. 32; I.P. 22

BAY OF ALL SAINTS
See "Bahia de Todos os Santos."
W. 50

BAY OF ISLANDS
*New Zealand's Bay of Islands is a five-mile-wide inlet of the *Pacific Ocean on the northeast coast of the north extension of North Island, W. of Cape Brett. It was visited by *Darwin in 1835, when it was the scene of much whaling activity, which eventually yielded to deep sea fishing.
O. 19; O. 25; O. 76; R. 23

BAY OF NAPLES
See "Naples . . . . "
R. 21; W. 88

BAY OF VALPARAISO
See "Valparaiso."
W. 74

BEACH-DE-MER
Bêche-de-mer, or sea cucumber.
O. 60

BEACH OF THE FLAMINGOES
See "Prays do Flamingo."
W. 60; W. 63

BEACHY HEAD
England: 50°40'N.; 0°25'E.
W. 3

BEADLE

A minor *British official who cites persons to appear in court or church, from Old High Ger. *Bitel*, "one who asks," through Old Fr. *badel*, " a herald."
M.D. 79

BEALE, --'S; SURGEON BEALE

Vincent's *The Trying-Out of Moby-Dick* makes explicit M.'s debt to Beale (Sealts #52): *The Natural History of the Sperm Whale . . . to which is added a Sketch of a South-Sea Whaling Voyage . . . in Which the Author Was Personally Engaged* 2nd ed. London: Van Voorst, 1839. M. went to great lengths to secure a copy, marking the date (July 10th 1850) and noting: "Imported by Putnam for me $3.38."

Beale was M.'s major source for *cetology and history, as well as for tangential concerns such as *ambergris and amputation. The copy is heavily annotated and marked.

See also "Extracts" 42, 47, 48, 61.
M.D. Extracts 61; M.D. 32; M.D. 59

BEARDS

M. was a lifelong wearer of a beard (to the chagrin of some of his relatives). As such, he probably took the subject seriously, seeing the beard as an important symbol of manhood and indeed "personhood." But as my *Melville Society Extracts* article, "'A Thing Most Momentous'? . . . " shows, much of M.'s "expertise" on the subject of beards came from an unintentionally amusing article in *Penny Cyclopaedia*: "Beards." The article starts out with a solemn definition of the facial hair growth found "rarely" on women, and proceeds to examine prominent hirsute individuals and groups throughout the world, in war and peace, in religion, literature, and fashion, from ancient times to modern. Among M.'s allusions "borrowed" from *P.C.* for the "beards" chapters of *W.* are those to *Socrates, *Persius, *Aurelian, *Merovingians, *Lombards, *Plutarch, *Adrian, *Alexander the Great, the *Macedonians, *Mathew Paris, and *William the Conqueror. The language of the "catalog" of *W.* 86 is from a poem by "Taylor, The Water Poet," in "Whip of Pride," in the same article.

Apparently, M. undercuts *P.C.*'s article because he could not beard total solemnity, as Jane Mushabac's *Melville's Humor* shows.
Passim (especially important in W. 84; W. 85; W. 86; W. 87)

BEAST
    See "Beauty."
M. 47

BEAST OF THE APOCALYPSE
    See "Apocalypse."
M. 168

BEAUMONT
    Sir Francis Beaumont (1584-1616) was born in Leicester-
shire, *England, of an ancient family. He attended *Oxford
and entered the Inner *Temple in 1600. He is best remembered
as the collaborator of *John Fletcher in the production of some
fifteen dramatic works from 1606 to 1613. Which plays, portions, or aspects of the works are Beaumont's is unclear, but
*Ben Jonson regularly submitted his works for Beaumont's
scrutiny.
    Sealts #53 is *Fifty Comedies and Tragedies.* Written by
Francis Beaumont and John Fletcher . . . . *London, 1679.
The annotated *folio is inscribed as having been purchased in
London in 1849.
    See "Fletcher" for names of individual works.
M. 174; W. 41

BEAUTIFUL GATE
    The "cripple" of the Beautiful Gate appears in *Acts 3.
The *Apostles *Peter and *John are approached for alms outside the temple, and Peter cures the crippled beggar by using
the name of *Jesus. The crowd marvels at the restored health
of "he which sat for alms at the Beautiful gate of the temple"
(3:10).
    M. visited *Jerusalem in January of 1857; he com-
mented at length on the Beautiful Gate in his journal: "The
Beautiful, or Golden, Gate—two arches, highly ornamental
sculpture, undoubtedly old, Herod's time—the gate from
which *Christ would go to *Bethany & Olivet—& also that in
which he made is [sic] entry (with palms) into the city. *Turks
walled it up because of tradition that through this Gate the city
would be taken.—One of the most interesting things in
*Jerusalem—seems expressive of the finality of Christianity,
as if this was the last religion of the world,--no other, possible."
I.P. Dedication

BEAUTY
Beauty and the Beast are the heroine and hero of the fairy tale of that name. Beauty saves her father's life by marrying the ugly Beast, who then turns into a handsome prince. The story is of great antiquity but was popularized by Mme. le Prince de Beaumont's 1757 version.
M. 47

BEAVER, DRIVE DOWN A
Put on a beaver hat.
M.D. 121

BECKET; BECKETT; THOMAS-A-BECKET
Thomas à Becket (1118-1170) became a clerk in the household of the *Archbishop of *Canterbury, c. 1142. He studied law briefly and became Archdeacon after ordination in 1154, then became chancellor to Henry II. His acts were not in perfect accord with expectations, but he became an intimate friend of the king, which led to his appointment as Archbishop in 1162.

Difficulties arose when Thomas refused full cooperation with the king regarding payments to the throne and other customs of the realm. Under the Constitution of Clarendon, the king sought to reinforce the boundaries between royal and ecclesiastical jurisdiction, wishing to regulate excommunication, relations with *Rome, and episcopal elections. Thomas escaped to *France in 1164, living an austere abbey life and studying canon law for two years. Upon his return, the Pope granted him power to excommunicate many of Henry's allies, and Henry responded by having the heir apparent crowned outside of *Canterbury, by bishops whom Thomas then excommunicated. This act provoked Henry to send four knights who murdered Thomas in his cathedral, causing a shock to Christendom and stimulating a cult of the martyr. Becket's biography was rewritten within the next decade to include vast numbers of miracles leading to his canonization in 1173. Becket remains a subject for modern speculation; was he an eccentric and intransigent seeker after power, or a saintly martyr who placed *God above even royalty?

The shrine at Canterbury soon became a resort for pilgrims, including *Chaucer's.

In 1174, Henry performed a famous penance, walking barefoot into the shrine to be flogged. The simultaneous capture of the invading King of *Scotland was laid to a miracle, further stimulating pilgrimages. Inns were erected and the area developed to accommodate them. *Henry VIII attempted to destroy the shrine in 1538, hoping to obliterate the cult.

M.'s *Journal* for 5 November 1849 comments on the "ugly place where they killed him."
R. 31; M.D. 16

BEETHOVEN, --'S
Ludwig van Beethoven (1770-1827), the most important nineteenth-century composer, was born in Bonn, *Germany. Despite heavy family responsibilities which interrupted his career and deafness which began before he was thirty years old, he became a highly successful freelance concert pianist and composer of masterpieces in all the main musical genres. By the time of his death, his nine symphonies, masses, religious and secular cantatas, and the opera *Fidelio* had transformed music, ushering in the Romantic Age and inspiring a freedom in music that had previously been discouraged.

The "wild, Beethoven sounds" of *P.* 3:2 are the startling *forte* outbursts (compared with rockets, even in M.'s time) and arpeggio figures which became a trademark, in opposition to the more "sedate" mathematically precise earlier music of the Classical Age.

In February of 1858, *The Life of Beethoven* . . . , by Anton Felix Schindler (London, 1841) was charged to the *Boston library membership of M.'s father-in-law, at a time when M. was visiting (Sealts #442). In M.'s copy of William Rounseville Alger's *The Solitudes of Nature and of Man*; or, *The Loneliness of Human Life* (Boston, 1867; Sealts #11), M. underscored a passage attributed to Beethoven: "I was nigh taking my life with my own hands. *But Art held me back. I could not leave the world until I had revealed what lay within me.*"
R. 49; P. 3:2

BEDLAM
The word (a contraction of "Bethlehem") has become the generic term for madhouse. St. Mary of Bethlehem, in *London, was a lunatic asylum, dating from 1377. By the seventeenth century, it had taken on the character of a public spectacle, as a seedy lovers' lane where people might look at and tease inmates for a fee. By M.'s time, it had moved to St. George's Fields, Lambeth. (Since 1931, the building has housed the Imperial War Museum.)
W. 25

BEECHEY, CAPTAIN

Frederick William Beechey (1796-1856), *British Rear-Admiral and geographer, entered the navy in 1806, seeing little action as a *Midshipman. Appointed to HMS *Tonnant* (under Sir Alexander Cochrane, commander-in-chief in North America), he participated in the 1815 boat operation on the *Mississippi River, for which he was promoted to Lieutenant. On *Trent* in 1818, under Lieutenant (later Sir John) Franklin, he participated in the *Artic expedition described in *Voyage of Discovery Towards the North Pole, performed in his Majesty's Ships Dorothea and Trent* (1843), also served off the north coast of *Africa, on *Adventure*, providing material for his 1828 book with his brother, Henry William Beechey: *Proceedings of the Expedition to Explore the Northern Coast of Africa from Tripoli Eastward, in 1821-2*. In 1822, he was appointed Commander of *Blossom* for the *polar expeditions described in the text to which M. refers: *Narrative of a Voyage to the Pacific and Bherring's Straits, under the Command of Captain F.W. Beechey, R.N.* (London: 1831). His health failed in 1835 while he was surveying the *South American coast on *Sulphur*, and he was reassigned to the coast of *Ireland. In 1850 he became superintendent of the Marine Department of the Board of Trade, and in 1855 President of the Royal Geographical Society.
O. 48

BEEF-STEAK CLUB OF KINGS

Although the connection with Kings is tenuous, *England has had steak societies since 1709, when the first Beef-Steak Club was formed in *London, its badge the gridiron. In 1735 the Sublime Society of Steaks was formed; it lasted until 1867. The modern Beefsteak Club was formed in 1876.
M. 84

BEELZEBUB

The name derives from *Greek, *Latin, and *Assyrian words for "fly-lord." In the *Old Testament (2 *Kings I, 2, 6, 16), Baalzebub is a pagan god, "Prince of Flies." In the *New Testament (*Matthew 10:25), he is "Prince of the Devils." In *Milton's *Paradise Lost*, he ranks second only to *Satan in evil.
M. 122; M.D. 50; M.D. 73;

BEGUM
     *Indian lady, princess, or woman of high rank; wife of
a nawab (corruption—nabob), a wealthy governor during the
*Mogul Empire.
M. 128

BEHEMOTHS
     *Job 40:15-24 describes this probably mythological beast
whose "bones are as strong pieces of brass" or "bars of iron."
(Precedes *leviathan description). Behemoth has been associated with the rhinoceros or the hippopotamus.
M. 121

BEHRING'S STRAITS
     See "Bhering's Straits."
M.D. 105

BEL
     See "Belial."
W. 91; M.D. 18

BELAYING PIN
     A favorite weapon of sailors, the belaying pin, used to
coil ropes, gave rise to the expression, "Belaying-pin soup":
the rough treatment given recalcitrant merchant seaman by
bullying officers.
W. 42 and elsewhere

BELFAST
     The name of the modern capital of Northern *Ireland is
from the late twelfth-century *Beal Feirste* ("mouth of the sandbank," of the Lagan River). By the eighteenth century, shipbuilding was a central industry, and by the 1840's harbor activities had gained great importance. Thus the unskilled Belfast
"Able" seaman of *R*. 12 seems an aspersion. (As Gilman
shows in *Melville's Early Life and Redburn*, 4, Irish sailors on
St. Lawrence were far more experienced than the "boy" M.)
Perhaps the Belfast sailor's appeal to the *Virgin in *M.D.* 40 is
another stereotypical slur. (See "Ireland . . . " regarding anti-
Irish sentiment.)
R. 12; M.D. 40

BELGIAN
        Belgium is bordered by forty-two miles of North Sea
coastline, the *Netherlands (N.), *Germany (E.), *Luxembourg
(S.E.), and *France (S. and S.E.). One of the "Low Countries"
(a political and historical rather than geographical designation), it has many canals and shipyards, diamond-cutting centers, art museums, and Medieval-to-Renaissance architecture.
        Belgians speak *Flemish (low German, akin to Dutch)
and French dialects, reflecting the nation's history. It was
conquered by Franks in the third century, a division of
*Charlemagne's empire in the ninth. By the fifteenth century
it had feudal states of the Burgundy duchy, followed by those of
the Hapsburgs. Belgium was awarded to France in 1797, but
the 1815 Treaty of *Paris gave it to the Netherlands. The revolt
of 1830 led to independence; in 1831 Leopold I of Saxe-Coburg
Gotha became king, and peace with the Dutch guaranteed neutrality, in 1839.
        M. visited *Brussels 7 December 1849, confessing in his
journal: "A more dull humdrum place I never saw--though it
seems a fine built place. *Waterloo is some 8 miles off. Cannot
visit it--& care not about it." He returned 12 December, complaining that the laundry he had left five days before was not
yet ready.
        See also "Antwerp"; "Flanders."
        ("Belgian giants" of *I.P.* 22 has not been traced.)
I.P. 22

BELIAL
        *Milton's fallen angel in *Paradise Lost*:

                Belial came last, than whom a Spirit more lewd
                Fell not from Heaven, or more gross to love
                Vice for itself (I, 490-92).

        The name originally referred to abstract qualities of
worthlessness or destruction.
        In ancient times, Ba'al was a generic term for god, ex-
cept for *Jehovah. Scholarship of M.'s time confused the Tyrian Baal of *Jezebel with the *Babylonian Bel. "Sons of Belial"
throughout the *Bible refers to idolaters.
W. 91; M.D. 18

BELISARIUS
        A *Byzantine general under *Justinian I, Belisarius (c.
505-565) saved the throne from a revolt in 532. He defeated the
*Vandals of North *Africa and was awarded *Rome, and

*Ravenna from the *Goths, whose admiration of his cavalry tactics brought Justinian's displeasure. In 562, he was imprisoned on conspiracy charges but restored before his death. (In M.'s time, it was believed that he had died a blind beggar.) His career was recorded (rather unsympathetically) by *Procopius.

M. may have seen the May, 1847 issue of *Blackwood's Edinburgh Magazine*, containing an article entitled "Belisarius,—Was he Blind?" The article decries the profligacy of Antonina, wife of Belisarius and a favorite of the Empress Theodora, and compares her, as M. does, to Sarah, Dutchess of *Marlborough.

The reference in *M*. 35 to Antonina's affair with a "youth Theodosius" is probably an error which may have originated in any source but Procopius, who does not mention Antonina. The confusion with the name of Theodora may be found in one of the spurious legends promulgated by *Byron, Lord Mahon, or Gibbon.
M. 23; M. 25; M. 26; M. 30; M. 35; M.D. 45

BELL
Sir Charles Bell (1774-1842) was a *Scottish physician in military surgery, a professor of anatomy at the *London *College of Surgeons.

M. could have read about him in *Penny Cyclopaedia*, in the article on Bell, or in one on "Gun-Shot Wounds."

"Bell on Bones" would be Volume I of Bell's *Anatomy*, a description of the bones, muscles, and joints.
W. 63

BELL, MR.; BELL, MRS.
As Charles R. Anderson discovered, Mr. and Mrs. Bell were real persons, commented on by several later visitors who sought out M.'s *Eimeo associates. According to Lieutenant Henry A. Wise, Mrs. Bell was a heavy drinker; Edward T. Perkins claimed she eventually drowned.
O. 78

BELLATRIX
Lat. adj.: "warlike."
Bellatrix is the third brightest star in the *Constellation of *Orion.

(It is the name of a modern-day U.S. *Navy attack cargo ship.)
M. 175

BELLES-LETTRES
A vague term for unscientific or non-technical literature such as poetry and prose fiction; sometimes what we now think of as "the humanities" or even "literature" or the aesthetics of literary study. M. seems to suggest the latter in his derogatory use of the term for something effete.
M. 3

"BELL ON BONES"
See "Bell" [Sir Charles].
W. 63

BELMONT
Home of "Portia," in *Shakespeare's *The Merchant of Venice*. The residence is so named in Shakespeare's source, *Il Pecorone* (1558), by Ser Giovanni Fiorentino.
R. 46

BELSHAZZAR
The historical Belshazzar (Bel-shar-usur), perhaps a descendent of *Nebuchadnezzar, was coregent of *Babylon at a time of famine and economic hardship. He died in 539 B.C., just before *Cyrus entered the city.
Until the mid-1850's, Belshazzar was known only from the *Old Testament. *Daniel 5 describes his great feast, at which mysterious Aramaic words appear, written on the wall by a disembodied hand, while the feasters drink wine and praise the gods of riches. The prophet Daniel is brought in to interpret "Mene, Mene, Tekel Upharsin," which he reads as a prophecy of the downfall of Belshazzar: "God has numbered the days of your kingdom and brought it to an end; . . . you have been weighed in the balances and found wanting; . . . your kingdom is divided and given to the *Medes and *Persians." Belshazzar is slain that night and his throne taken by *Darius the Mede.
M. 20; M. 60; M.D. 34; M.D. 99

BELTS OF JUPITER
See "Jupiter, Belts of."
M. 175

BELUS, TEMPLE OF

Belus was an *Egyptian king, son of *Poseidon and Libya, ancestor of the *Persian kings and of *Dido, queen of *Carthage. His name is a *Greek form of the *Phoenician *Baal (Lord). His great temple at *Babylon was built for purposes of astronomy.
M. 75; M. 181

BELZONI

Giovanni Baptista Belzoni (1778-1823) was born in Padua. An actor and an engineer, he turned his huge stature to advantage in exhibitions of strength at street fairs and theaters in *England. His early study of hydraulics led to improvements in water engines and, after delivering one to Mohammed Aly, Pasha of *Egypt, he was employed by the British to remove the colossal granite bust of Ramesis II from *Thebes to the British Museum. Continuing excavations at Karnah, he opened the supulchre of Seti I, in the Valley of the Tombs of the Kings, Libya (called "Belzoni's Tomb"), removing the sarcophogus. He found the entrance to the second pyramid of Gizeh, as well as a room eventually named for him. He was honored by Padua and by England, where facsimiles of his discoveries were shown.

Belzoni was not a scholar but paved the way for later exploration. The gentle, eccentric giant set out in 1823 for Timbuktu, hoping to trace the source of the *Niger, but he died of dysentery at Bato, in Benin.

In 1820, Murray published the "Narrative of the Operations and Recent Discoveries within the Pyramids, Temples, Tombs, and Excavations in Egypt and *Nubia," the first published English research. Belzoni also wrote a "Preface to the Narrative of Operations" for a life of Henry Salt, Consul General who had provided funds for his work.

In 1854, M. purchased a copy of The Life of Benjamin Robert Haydon, Historical Painter, from His Autobiography and Journals. Edited and Compiled by Tom Taylor . . . New York, Harper, 1853. 2 vol. (Sealts #262). Haydon extols Belzoni's "singleness of aim" and "energy of intention," decrying those who called him insane.

The "big arm & foot" recorded in M.'s 16 November 1849 journal had been found by Belzoni at Karnak in 1817 and placed in the British Museum.
T. 9; M. 123

BENBOW, ADMIRAL

John Benbow (1653-1702) was an *English admiral whose exploits made him a popular hero. In 1702, as commander in chief of the *West Indies squadron engaged with the *French near St. Martha, his right leg was shattered by shot, but he continued on the quarter deck rather than leave his fleet of seven ships in the charge of insubordinate captains, some of whom were later court-martialed and shot. Benbow died of his wounds.

M.'s admiration may be based on Benbow's having "come in at the *hawse holes." George Bernard Shaw was to have the snob Hotchkiss (*Getting Married*) admire "martyrs" who despise rising from the ranks: "The navy boasts two such martyrs in Captains Kirby and Wade, who were shot for refusing to fight under Admiral Benbow, a promoted cabin boy. I have always envied them their glory."
W. 71; W. 86

BENCH OF BISHOPS

The collective mass of prelates who sit in *England's *House of Lords. "Bench" originally referred to long wooden seats which were the official places of judges in courts, government officials, and bishops.
W. 75

BENDIGOES

William "Bendigo" Thompson (1811-80) was *English prizefighting champion, 1839-1845. In 1847, M. wrote to an ill friend (Augustus Van Schaick), hoping he would soon be well enough to "fight Bendigo for the Champion's belt of all England." Bendigo had gained the title from Benjamin Gaunt, winning a 93-round match on 9 September 1846.
M. D. 37

BENEDICT, --S

A sworn *bachelor, from St. Benedict, who preached celibacy; the term was popularized via *Shakespeare's *Much Ado About Nothing*.
M. 181; C.M. 6

BENEDICTINE

The Roman *Catholic order of St. Benedict of Nursia, "Black Monks," was well established throughout western Europe by the year 800. Benedictines became the chief educators and preservers of literature, with many wealthy monasteries and abbeys. Their austere life style was tempered by the eleventh century, and they became great propagators of the faith throughout the world. They remained separate from politics and from schools of theology. Monasticism declined starting in the twelfth century, and although there was a revival during the *Protestant Reformation, by the nineteenth century their numbers were few.

(The Benedictine convent at *Rio do Janeiro, close to *Gloria Hill, is probably the Convent of Santo Antonio, with many famous tombs.)
W. 39

BENGAL, --ESE
Bengal is now a region of modern northeastern *India and eastern Pakistan, in the common delta of the Brahmaputra and *Ganges Rivers. Its boundaries have fluctuated throughout history. The *British *East India Company made its first settlement in 1700, but there were also *French, *Dutch, and *Portuguese interests. *Calcutta became India's capital in 1833 (moved to *Delhi in 1912).

In M.'s time, "Bengal" denoted British military control in India, or else evoked visions of dense mangrove swamps, impossible-to-navigate rivers, forests of the *Himalayan foothills, replete with man-eating tigers. But the racially mixed Bengal area produced many important scientists, spiritual leaders, social reformers, and poets, as we now know.
M. 68; M.D. 119

BENGAL BAY
An arm of the *Indian Ocean on the south coast of *Asia between *India and Ceylon on the west, and Andaman and Nicobar Islands on the east. One thousand miles wide, it is the site of *Calcutta and the deltas of the *Ganges-Brahmuputra and other rivers; very shallow and very stormy.
M.D. 44

BENJAMIN
In *Genesis, full brother and favorite brother of *Joseph.
I.P. 25

BENNET
     The only information I have been able to unearth about
George Bennet, (--t), with *Tyerman a deputy of the *London
Missionary Society, is that he was from *Sheffield, England.
     See also "Extracts" 65.
O. 49; M.D. Extracts 65

BEN NEVIS
     The highest mountain in the British Isles, Ben Nevis, in
the *Scottish Highlands, is 4,406 feet in altitude.
P. 1:3

BENTHAM'S, JEREMY
     The great proponent of *Utilitarianism, Jeremy Ben-
tham (1748-1832) left instructions at his death that his skeleton
be donated to the University of *London. There it was used in
discussion and study and exhibited--clothed in ordinary vestments.
M.D. 55

BERENICE'S LOCKS
     The *Coma Berenices* is composed of seven stars near the
tail of *Leo. Legend of its origin: the sister/wife of Ptolemy II
Eurgetes (246-221 B.C.) vowed to sacrifice her hair to the gods
in exchange for her husband's victory. The hair was stolen
from the temple where she had placed it and carried to heaven
on the wind.
M. 188

BERKELEY, BISHOP; BERKELEYAN
     George Berkeley (1685-1753), *Irish-born philosopher,
was Anglican Bishop of Cloyne from 1734 until retirement to
*Oxford in 1752. An associate of *Pope, Swift, *Addison, and
*Steele, he wrote philosophical works stressing "passive obe-
dience," especially in response to *Whig free-thinking and the
teachings of *Hobbes, *Locke, and *Descartes. For Berkeley,
spirit is the only cause or power, and *God speaks to us
through nature. He also wrote on vision, economics, and social reform in Ireland. *"Esse est percipi"* ("to be is to be perceived") is his most famous dictum. His often-quoted line,
"Westward the course of empire takes its way," was written before a trip to *America in 1728.
     His chief philosophical works are *Treatise Concerning
the Principles of Human Knowledge* (1710) and *Three Dia-*

logues Between Hylas and Philonous (1713). Although his philosophy was not popular in his own day, it was admired by *Kant, *Coleridge, and Mill.
M. 20; P. 19:1

BERKS
     English county west of *London.
I.P. 24

BERKSHIRE
     Berkshire County, in western *Massachusetts, bordering on *Vermont, *New York, and *Connecticut, was formed in 1761. It was the setting for much of M.'s life, including visits to relatives and summer holidays spent in the area even before M. purchased the *Pittsfield home he called "Arrowhead" in honor of his finding of Indian arrowheads on the property. The M. nuclear family lived at Arrowhead from September 1850 to November 1862, during which time various relatives made it their residence, as well.
     M.'s works are sprinkled with allusions to Berkshire County and its attractions. *Hawthorne lived for two years at nearby *Lenox, and M. often rode his horse some seven miles to visit there. *"Balance Rock" is located in Lanesboro (originally called "Berkshire"), five miles north of Pittsfield, near *Pontoosuc Lake. Mount *Greylock is fifteen miles north of Pittsfield; M. often climbed it, probably using what is now the *Appalachian Trail, which crosses the county's state forests. The *Housatonic and Hoosic rivers flow through the Berkshire Hills, the granite and marble highlands which are part of the *Taconics and of the Hoosac extension of the *Green Mountains.
     Berkshire County is the setting for much of *P.*, as well as for short stories. "The Piazza" relates to the view of Greylock from the large porch M. constructed on the northern side of Arrowhead. "I and My Chimney" was inspired by the large curving chimney which cuts through the center of the house and opens to a huge dining room hearth. "The Tartarus of Maids" has as its setting the site of the present-day Crane Paper Company complex and Museum, at Dalton: just north of Pittsfield.
M.D. 94; P. Dedication; I.P. 1; I.P. 3

BERLIN
     Berlin, *Germany, Brandenburg, is an inland port on the Spree River, 100 miles from the *Baltic Sea, 150 miles east-

southeast of *Hamburg. The core of the city began development in the thirteenth century, with frequent occupations, becoming one of the largest cities of the world (much destroyed in
World War II). In 1871, it became the capital city of the
German Empire.

(The *Berlin Gazette*, mentioned in *Eckermann's *Conversations With Goethe*, has not been traced.)
M.D. Extracts 57

BETELGEUSE
A bright, yellowish-red supergiant star in the
*constellation *Orion.
M. 169

BETHEL FLAG
The first organized prayer assemblies for sailors occurred in 1814 on *Friendship*, a collier brig on the *Thames. A
shoemaker named Zebulon Rogers and *Friendship's* Captain
Simpson began shipboard Bethel meetings, taking their name
from the *Old Testament meeting place of *Jacob with *God.
Other *London ships expressed the desire for similar meetings, and it became necessary to identify host ships. By 1817 a
lantern on the top-gallant mast had been replaced by a special
blue flag with the word "Bethel" in white letters. Later a red
star in a corner (representing the star in the east) and a dove
bearing an olive branch were added. These flags were forerunners of the chaplain's pennant.
*Floating chapels were established in many ports, and
the first Bethel flag was delivered to the *United States by 1820.
In 1826 more than seventy Bethel societies in the United States
united as The American Seaman's Friend Society, publishing
reform journals of varying quality and effectiveness, running
sailors' residences, and opening savings banks. By 1847, there
were Bethels in many major cities, on inland waterways, and
in foreign lands; gifts of Bethel flags furthered the cause.
See also "Missions"; "Temperance Society"; "Whaleman's Chapel."
R. 35

BETHESDA, POOL OF
The word Bethesda comes from the *Chaldaic root for
"house of kindness." In *John 5, it is a pool by a sheep market
where cripples come for the comfort of the soothing waves.
*Jesus cures a crippled man on the *Sabbath, commanding
him to "Rise, take up thy bed, and walk" (5:8), incurring the

wrath of the *Hebrews, who begin his persecution. M. visited the Pool in January 1857, commenting in his journal: "full of rubbish--sooty look & smell."
R. 38

BETTER ANGEL
See "Quotations": "Bad Angel shall tend the Good."
P. 5:4

BETTY
Betty and Molly are low-world nicknames. When applied to men, the names cast doubt on their sexual proclivities.
O. 14; M.D. 17

BEY
See "Bashaw."

BHERING'S STRAITS
Bering Strait separates Chukchi Peninsula (of northeast *Siberia) from Seward Peninsula (of Alaska). The fifty-five mile wide waterway is frozen from October until June. The International Date Line passes through the Diomede Islands, in the center. The Strait was discovered in 1648 by the *Russian explorer Semen Ivanov Dezhnev (c. 1605-73), who sailed through it to demonstrate the lack of connection between Asia and North America. It was named for the Danish-Russian Vitus Jonassen Bering (1681-1741), who repeated the feat in 1728.
M.D. 14

BIBLE
M.'s copy: *St. James version: *The Holy Bible . . . Together with the Apocrypha* . . . (Philadelphia, Butler, 1846.) Sealts #62 (annotated).
M. variously refers to the Bible as Holy Bible, Holy Guide-Book (*R*. 31), the Book (*M.D.* 9), Holy Book (*M.D.* 54), True Book (*C.M.* 43), and Scripture.
Wright's *Melville's Use of the Bible* is an exhaustive study.
Passim

BILDAD, CAPTAIN
Bildad the Shuhite was a sanctimonious comforter of *Job whose warnings of disaster were rejected finally (Job 8; 18; 25; 19, 2).
M.D. 16; C.M. 40

BILL OF RIGHTS
The first ten amendments to the *Constitution of the *United States were adopted in 1791 to extend citizens' rights seemingly limited in the Constitution.
Amendment 1 deals with citizen liberties including freedom of religion, speech (W. 91), the press, association, assembly, and petition.
Amendment 2 allows states armed militias through the "right to keep and bear arms."
Amendment 3 limits the quartering of troops in private homes.
Amendment 4 limits searches and seizures.
Amendment 5 guarantees due process of the law to the accused, including Grand Jury indictment; it prohibits double jeopardy and self-incrimination.
Amendment 6 confirms the rights to a speedy public trial by an impartial local jury, information regarding charges, the confrontation of hostile witnesses, and time to prepare a defense.
Amendment 7 provides for a jury trial, except when waived, in cases involving the sum of $20.00 or more.
Amendment 8 prohibits excessive bail and fines, as well as "cruel and unusual" punishments.
Amendment 9 guarantees that rights are not limited to those enumerated.
Amendment 10 limits the powers of the Federal government to those specified in the Constitution.
W. 91

BIOGRAPHIA LITERARIA
See "Coleridge."
W. 38

BIOGRAPHICO-SOLICITO CIRCULARS
Probably a neologism for the pretentiously pedantic forms circulated to literary figures in order to publicize them. On M's second trip to *England, he wondered at the marvels of publicity: "English earth after the lapse of ten years--*then* a sailor, *now* H.M. author of 'Peedee' 'Hullabaloo' & 'Pog-Dog'"

(journal 4 November 1849). In a letter to James Billson (1858-1932), an admirer, M. spoke of the cheapness of fame, which was "manufactured to order" by professionals (20 December 1885). In *Billy Budd, Sailor* (Chapter 1), he openly decries "that manufacturable thing known as respectability."
P. 17:3

BIRKENHEAD
Birkenhead is a seaport of *Cheshire, *England, on a peninsula opposite *Liverpool. The "abbey" of *R.* 31 is a *Benedictine monastery constructed about 1150. Many ruins remain of the structure, which drew revenue from *Mersey ferry tolls. Docks were completed in 1847, transforming what had been a resort area into an industrial center.
(H.M.S. *Birkenhead*, wrecked in 1852, inspired Rudyard Kipling's tribute to the Royal Marines, in "Soldier an' Sailor Too.")
R. 31

BIRMAH
See "Burmese."
M.D. 87

BIS TAURUS
The ship of *Aeneas; "bis" means "twice." See also "Taurus."
M. 149

BLACK-ART
Sorcery or necromancy, practised by wizards and others dealing with the *Devil. "Necromancy" derives from Lat. *niger*, "black" (and from Gr. *nekros*, "the dead").
I.P. 8

BLACK FOREST
The heavily forested mountain range of southern *Germany extends some ninety miles from the *Rhine River to the *Swiss border, with peaks up to 4,900 feet. The Danube, Neckar, and other rivers run through the resort area famous for natural beauty, cuckoo clocks, music boxes, and elaborate toys.
(By the late twentieth century, the forest was severely damaged by man-made pollution.)
M. 33

BLACK FRIAR; BLACKFRIARS
*London's Blackfriars area is named for the *Dominican monks (important symbols of "the old order," in "Benito Cereno") whose monastery was located on the site. Blackfriars Bridge was opened in 1769, extending the area to both sides of the *Thames. In the mid-nineteenth century, excavation was uncovering portions of the old priory and other historical sites.
P. 19:1

BLACK GUINEA
As H. Bruce Franklin points out in his edition of *C.M.*, this fictional character has an interesting name. Guinea is short for "Guinea Negro" and *guinea pig. A gold guinea is a coin: a black guinea is a brass (?) counterfeit.
C.M. 3

BLACKHEATH
Blackheath, six miles southeast of *London's center, was long a haunt of highwaymen and such historical personages as *Wat Tyler and *Jack Cade. M.'s comment about its being a "nursery for seamen" (*R*. 26) is a reference to the presence of *crimps in the Blackheath/*Greenwich area.
R. 26

BLACK HOLE OF CALCUTTA
See "Calcutta."
I.P. 25

BLACK KNIGHT
Reference may be to *Ivanhoe* of *Sir Walter Scott, in which Richard I, the Lion-Hearted, appears thus disguised at a tournament, or to the son of Oriana and Amadis de Gaula, in *Spanish romance. *Chaucer's allegorical *Book of the Duchess* has a lamenting Black Knight, said to represent *John of Gaunt.
P. 3:6

BLACKLEGS
Swindlers: from game cocks, whose legs are always black.
W. 18; W. 44

BLACK LETTER
Black Letter was a *Gothic or *German type used in the early days of printing, so called from about 1600 because of its dark appearance as compared with that of roman type.
See also "Sir Martin Frobisher."
M.D. 32

BLACK PARLIAMENT
See "Tophet."
M.D. 2

BLACK PRINCE
Edward, *England's Black Prince (1330-1376), son of *Edward III (1312-1377) and Philippa, daughter of the Count of Hainaut, earned his nickname from his enemies, whom he constantly defeated in the Hundred Years War. His greatest coup led to the capture of the *French king, John II, forcing a French truce. His health was poor from about 1371; presumably he died of plague ("the Black Death"). Four of his seven brothers are important historically: Lionel of *Antwerp, Duke of Clarence; *John of Gaunt, Duke of *Lancaster; Edmund of Langley, later Duke of *York; Thomas of Woodstock, later Duke of *Gloucester.
Edward's tomb at *Canterbury Cathedral has a portrait effigy, his helmet, shield, scabbard, and surcoat. The effigy shows Edward lying so stiffly that he seems standing at attention, hands touching, with a suggestion of supplication, not of rest.
See also "Plantagenets."
M. 32; W. 14

BLACK RAPIDS
Although M.'s "Black Rapids Coal Company" may be fictional, he might have taken its name from Black Rapids Glacier, at the foot of Mount Hayes, in Alaska. The glacier has had several dangerous slides.
C.M. 4; C.M. 9

BLACK SEA
An inland sea between Europe and *Asia, connected with the *Mediterranean by the *Bosporus, the Sea of *Marmara, and the *Dardanelles, the Black Sea is bounded by the modern U.S.S.R., *Turkey, Bulgaria, and Rumania. It is 750 miles long and 350 miles wide, with two layers of water, the

deeper of which is so highly saline as to support no marine life. An important but difficult navigation route, the sea has had colonized banks since ancient times.

M.'s comment on its color (*M.D.* 3) is an error. The sea was originally given a Turkish name expressing both danger-ous difficulty and blackness; it is not black.

On 16 December 1856, M. voyaged up the Bosporus outlet of the Black Sea, commenting in his journal on "The water clear as *Ontario."
M.D. 3

BLACKSTONE
    Sir William Blackstone (1723-1780) became the most fa-mous *English jurist despite his vague grasp of the concep-tions of law. His most famous work, *Commentaries*, is more admirable for literary merit than for its treatment of the law, a handbook for laymen, rather than a legal treatise. Its fame was greater in the *United States than in Britain, and a new edition was advertised on the front page of the 6 March 1847 *Literary World*: "*Mr. Sergeant Stephen's New Commentaries . . . on the Laws of England, in which are interwoven, under a new and original arrangement of the general subject, all such parts of the work of Blackstone as are applicable to the present time; together with full but compendious expositions of the modern improvements of the law up to the present time . . .* by Henry John Stephen, Serjeant at Law."
    (See also "Extracts" 44.)
R. 54; W. 35; W. 72; M.D. Extracts 44; M.D. 90

BLACK SWAN INN; "BLACK SWAN"
    The famous *English (*Tudor) Black Swan Inn of Helmsley, on the edge of the North *Yorkshire moors, was the local center for wool collection. It was being rebuilt between 1849 and 1868, perhaps inspiring M.'s borrowing of its name for *P*.
    Dickens (see "Hard Times") is known to have stayed at the Black Swan Inn of *York.
    Notes to the Hendricks House edition of *P*. suggest a lo-cal model in the *Berkshire Hotel (1827-1866), *Pittsfield's cen-ter for stage routes before completion of the Western Railroad, in 1845.
P. 11:4; P. 12:3; P. 13:1; P.20:1

BLACK VOMIT
    Yellow fever.
M.D. 134

BLACKWELL'S ISLAND

The present Roosevelt Island in *New York's East River, was the site of Corporation Hospital, opened 1853. (See "East River" for more of its history.)
C.M. 19

BLACK WHALE

See "Cetology" section.
M.D. 32

BLACKWOOD

William Blackwood (1776-1834), *Edinburgh publisher, founded *Blackwood's Edinburgh Magazine* (originally *Edinburgh Monthly Magazine*, a *Tory response to the *Whig *Edinburgh Review*. By M.'s time, the firm was conducted by Blackwood's sons, Alexander (1806-45), Robert (1808-52), and John (1818-79).
W. 90

BLAIR'S LECTURES

The Reverend Hugh Blair's *Lectures on Rhetoric and Belles Lettres*, which went through fifty-three editions, had vast influence in the *United States, especially at *Yale and *Harvard. The lectures encouraged stiff correctness and discouraged native idiom, literary enthusiasm being undesirable. *Penny Cyclopaedia* (IV, 1835) calls the lectures "Exceedingly feeble productions" that "show no intimate acquaintance with the best writers antient and modern; nor do they develope and illustrate, as a general rule, any sound practical principles."

The *Lectures* were contained in the 72-volume *Harper's Family Library* known to make part of the library of *United States* when M. was aboard.

Blair (1718-1800) was professor of rhetoric at *Edinburgh and an associate of *Hume, Carlyle, and *Adam Smith.

(By 1987, Blair was back in style, in E.D.Hirsch's *Cultural Literacy*.)
W. 41

BLAKE, ROBERT

Blake (1599-1657), an *English admiral, fought on the parliamentary side in the English Civil War, reorganizing the navy into a crack fighting force. In command in the English *Channel at the outbreak of the first Dutch War (1652), he defeated the forty-two ship Dutch fleet commanded by *Martin

Van Tromp, with only twenty ships of his own. He eventually
lost in the Dungeness engagement against Tromp, retreating
to the *Thames, in the action that originated the legend of
Tromp's lashing a broom to his mast-head as a sign he would
sweep the English from the sea.
    Blake was author of the *Fighting Instructions* that in-
troduced tactics that became standard; he also introduced the
*Articles of War, the basis of naval discipline.
W. 36; W. 55; W. 71

BLANC, LOUIS
    Louis Jean Joseph Charles Blanc (1811-1882) was a
*French political leader and historian who greatly influenced
the development of socialism.   His most famous essay,
"L'Organisation du travail," attributed all social evils to competition. He had a stormy career in the 1840's and was forced
to flee to *England, from which he did not return until 1870.
His works total some twenty-five volumes, exclusive of his
speeches.
M.D. 35

BLANCHARD
    Jean Pierre Blanchard (1753-1809), pioneer aviationist
who made the first balloon ascents in *England and in
*America, crossed the English *Channel in a balloon in 1785
with an American physician, Dr. John Jeffries, studying avia-
tion medicine. The flight carried the first international air
mail and escaped disaster by the jettisoning of all ballast, including much clothing.   Blanchard was also the first
parachutist and in 1793 ballooned near *Philadelphia, observed
by President *George Washington. He died in *Paris, after a
fall from his balloon at The Hague, *Netherlands.
M. 4

BLANCO, CAPE OF
    There are at least six Cape (or Cabo) Blancos; that of
northwestern *Peru north of Payta is probably meant in *M.D.*
M.D. 3

BLENHEIM CASTLE
    The castle and estate at Oxfordshire, *England were
voted by *Parliament as a grant to the Duke of *Marlborough,
victor of the battle of Blenheim. The castle was designed by Sir
John Vanbrugh (1664-1726), dramatist/architect. Construction

was plagued by difficulty: financial problems, clashes with
*Queen Anne and with Sarah, Duchess of Marlborough.
R. 28; R. 30; W. 20

BLESSINGTON, LADY
      Marguerite, Countess of Blessington (1789-1849) was an
*Irish writer remembered chiefly for her *Conversations with
Lord Byron*. Born into a shabby family, she was sold into marriage at an early age. Despite her more-than-humble early
life, she rose to marry Charles Gardiner, Viscount Mountjoy
and Earl of Blessington. She developed a fashionable salon attended by Comte *d'Orsay, who became her son-in-law by marriage to Blessington's daughter. With d'Orsay, she traveled to
*Genoa to visit *Byron, exhausting the Blessington fortune.
She was forced to write for a living but despite great popular
success she fled with d'Orsay to *Paris in 1849 to avoid ruin.
      (M.'s grouping of Lady Blessington with the fictional
"Lord Lovely" [perhaps a covert reference to d'Orsay] indicates
his opinion of the falsely refined "upper" class.)
R. 56

BLIGH
      William Bligh (1754-1817), commander of the ill-fated
Bounty, was born at Plymouth (?), *England, into an old family. He entered the Navy early, was with *Cook on his second
voyage (1772-74), and was Sailing Master on *Resolution* when
breadfruit was discovered at Otaheite (*Tahiti) in 1776, earning
the sobriquet, "Bread-fruit Bligh." He made some important
hydrographic surveys, was present at the Battle of the Dogger-
bank (1781) and at *Gibralter (1782).
      Commander of the 220-ton *Bounty*, in 1787, Bligh sailed
to Otaheite, where his crew become demoralized because of the
heat and native misbehavior. Bread-fruit specimens were secured for acclimatization in the British *West Indies, despite
West Indian preference for plantains, and Bligh sailed there.
      Historians have blamed Bligh's irascibility for the
mutiny that occurred under the leadership of Master's Mate,
Fletcher Christian, but Bligh was probably no harsher than
Cook, his role model, and was a courageous and skillful navigator.
      On 28 April 1789, as punishment, Christian and eigh-
teen crew members were cast adrift in a twenty-three foot-long
boat, with no chart, and few provisions. They sailed for three
months, a distance of 3,618 miles, reaching *Timor, off Java,
on 14 June 1789. The mutineers settled on *Pitcairn Island;
three had been captured at Otaheite and hanged, but the Pit-

cairn Islanders were not discovered until 1808, by then in firmly established families whose descendents still reside there.

Bligh became Post-Captain, and in 1791 sailed *Providence* to the *Society Islands, earning the Gold Medal of the Society of Arts in 1794, at which time he became Captain of *Warrior*. As Captain of *Director* in 1797, he distinguished himself at the *Nore when his crew joined the mutiny. In 1801, Commander of *Glatton* at *Copenhagen, he was appointed Fellow of the *Royal Society. When Captain General and Governor of *New South Wales (starting in 1805), his harshness again caused unpopularity, and in 1808 he was deposed and imprisoned for two years by Deputy Governor George Johnson, who was later punished. Bligh became *Rear-Admiral of the Blue in 1811 and Vice-Admiral of the Blue in 1814.

He was married to Elizabeth Betham and was the father of six daughters.
O. 49; W. 8

BLOCKSBERG'S; BLOCKSBURG
Blocksberg, or Brocken, is the highest peak (3,747 feet) in central *Germany's Harz (see "Hartz") forest. It is the site of a meteorological observatory but is even more famous for the Blocksberg "Specter." The phenomenon occurs in foggy weather, when the spectator's shadow is magnified and reflected by the setting sun. *Goethe sets part of *Faust* on the mountain, which is associated with Walpurgis Night, or Witches' Sabbath.
R. 49; M.D. 42

BLOODY GROUND
See "Kentucky, Kentuckian."
C.M. 26

BLOODY TOWER
See "Tower of London."
M.D. 42

BLOOM, WIDOW
An "appellation" hearkening back to Restoration or eighteenth-century drama, perhaps suggested to M. by Carlyle's imperious "Blumine," in *Sartor Resartus* (Bk. 2, Ch. 5).
P. 1:2

BLUCHER

Gebhard Leberecht Von Blücher (1742-1819) was a rough, ill-educated, but courageous *Prussian field marshall who gained fame in his seventies in the *Napoleonic Wars, especially in the battle of *Waterloo. The name "Blucher" became attached to many things in addition to a dog in *R.* Bluchers are low boots, subordinate prefects at some *British colleges, non-privileged cabs at British railway stations. Legend says that Blücher arrived late at Waterloo.
R. 43

BLUE BEARD

Prototype of the powerful, wealthy, repulsive villain, Bluebeard is a central figure in Charles Perrault's *Contes de ma mère l'Oye (Mother Goose's Tales*; 1697), although he has many parallels in other folklores. Perrault's story line: a curious new wife forbidden by her husband to unlock a certain castle door disobeys, finding the bodies of former wives. Her husband threatens to cut off her hand as punishment, but she is rescued by her brothers at the last moment.

Perrault probably based his tale on the career of Gilles de Rais, or Comorre the Cursed, a fifth-century Breton chief (1404-1440) who became marshal of *France. The wealthy and influential de Rais was made guard of Joan of Arc, but was later barred from service. A patron of the arts, he wasted his fortune and turned to alchemists, becoming involved in necromancy, Satanism, and ritual murder of children. Tried for heresy, he was hanged 26 October 1440.
T. 27; M. 94

BLUE DEVILS

Depression; took the name "blues" when indigo dyers were found to be especially subject to melancholy.
See also "Burton, Robert."
M. 1

BLUE FLUJIN

"Blue Flujin" is an imaginary cold place, where such mariners as Nathaniel Ames say "fire freezes."
W. 25

BLUE MONDAY

Originally, "Blue Monday" referred to the Monday before *Lent, which was spent in the drunkenness that gave every-

thing a blue tinge. By M.'s time, the expression had acquired
the more general interpretation of modern times; *I.P.*'s "Blue
Monday" occurs in November, on *Guy Fawkes Day.
I.P. 24

BLUE PETERS
     Signal flags hoisted on the foremast by merchant vessels
to indicate that the vessel is ready to sail: blue with a white
square in the center.
W. 91

BLUE WHALE
     See "Cetology" section.
M.D. 32

BOARD OF COMMODORES AND NAVY COMMISSIONERS
     In 1815, *Congress authorized a board of *Navy commis-
sioners under the superintendence of the *Secretary of the
Navy. It supervised the procuring of supplies and stores, materials and construction, armament and employment of all
navy vessels. It was abolished in 1842.
W. 44; W. 52; W. 53

BOAT PLUG
     A plug in the bottom of a boat to let water out when in
drydock.
W. 52

BOBADIL
     "Bobadil," whose name was probably suggested by
Bobadilla, first governor of *Cuba, who sent *Columbus home
a prisoner, is a character in *Ben Jonson's *Every Man in His
Humor*; he characterizes the epitome of military braggadocio.
     Finkelstein's *Melville's Orienda* suggests an original in
"Boabdil," King of *Granada, hero of *Irving's *Alhambra*.
W. 52

BOERHAAVE
     Hermann Boerhaave (1668-1738) was a *Dutch clinical
physician and professor of medicine whose raising of the University of Leiden to fame rested on his theories of the teaching
of medicine, which revolutionized medical education. His

principal works are *Institutiones medicae* (1708), *Aphorismi de Cognoscendis et Curandis Morbis* (1709); in neither is there advice such as "White-Jacket" imparts about keeping the feet dry. M.'s usage may be ironic; Boerhaave was well known for his theories of the "acrimony of the fluids" and for his hydraulic theories, making possible a frivolous analogy to wet feet.
W. 22

BOHEMIA
An historic province of modern Czechoslovakia (adjoining *Moravia and *Silesia), Bohemia is bounded by *Austria, *Germany, and *Poland; it has been sought after throughout history for its mineral springs and dense forests. Slavonics replaced the original settlers by the first century A.D., and by the ninth Bohemia was a part of the Great Moravian Empire. The Magyars arrived in the tenth century, before Bohemia became part of the *Holy Roman Empire. (Its first great ruler was St. Wenceslaus.) There was increasing German settlement, and the city of Prague became an important cultural center. Habsburg domination began with the election of Ferdinand I of *Austria to the thrones of Bohemia and Hungary in 1526 (and continued until 1918). The *Thirty Years' War expressed the conflicting claims of *Catholics and *Protestants, and by the nineteenth century there was a strong movement for independence (not achieved until 1918), with Bohemia part of the new republic (only to lose its political identity in 1849).
I.P. 1

BOLD-STREET
*Liverpool's Bold Street, running between Hanover and Berry Streets, was the site of a fine concert hall constructed in the early nineteenth century.
R. 30; R. 42

BOLIVIA
The area which became Bolivia is the west-central *South American region bordering on *Peru (sharing Lake *Titicaca), Chile (across the *Andes), *Brazil (across *Amazon system rivers), Paraguay and Argentina. Rural Indians still speak native languages in the region, which has many ruins showing evidence of high pre-*Inca civilization. Seeking silver, *Pizarro took control for *Spain in 1538. The silver mines

of *Potósi were discovered seven years later, making it a boom town.

Peru dominated the area until 1809, when uprisings against Spain began. Liberation (*M.D.* 24) was achieved in 1824, after the expeditions of José de San Martín (1778-1850) and the victory of Simón Bolivar (1783-1830) at *Ayacucho, which broke Spain's hold on the new world.

At the 1825 proclamation of independence, the new nation was called Bolivia, after its liberator. There was a brief (1836-39) confederation with Peru, but the new government fell into autocratic oligarchy and military errors that lost much Bolivian territory by the end of the nineteenth century.

Bolivian gold "*doubloons" of *M.D.* 99 would probably be silver.
M.D. 24; M.D. 99

BOLOGNA
Bologna is in north-central *Italy, at the foot of the *Etruscan Appennines, fifty miles north of *Florence. Of pre-*Roman origin, the city belonged to the *Byzantines in the sixth century and to the *Papacy in the eighth. It was much disputed by the *Guelphs and Ghibellines. By M.'s time it was under Papal rule again (until 1860). Bologna is among Europe's greatest learning centers, with a university dating from the eleventh century. It has many medieval buildings, two leaning towers, and arcaded streets dating from the thirteenth to the sixteenth centuries.

M. visited Bologna on 30 March 1857, commenting in his journal on the "leaning tower," on the artworks of the Accademia delle Belle Arti, and on his first taste of Bologna sausage (*M.* 123), sampled because "at Rome you first go to St. Peters."
M. 123; R. 52

BOMBAY
The western *Indian port city of Bombay state is on the *Arabian Sea, at the south end of Salsette Island (converted, along with other islands, into a peninsula). It was acquired from the *Mogul Empire by the *Portuguese in the 1530's, its excellent harbor making it an ideal missionary and trading port. Bombay was ceded to *England in 1661 by the marriage treaty of *Charles II and the Infanta Catherine of Portugal.

The combined Hindu (see "Hindoo"), *Moslem, *Christian, and *Parsee population saw much expansion during the *American *Civil War, when the Indian cotton crop gained new importance.

*Elephanta Island is located in Bombay Harbor.
R. 9; R. 34; R. 44; R. 50; M.D. 6; C.M. 22

BOMBAZINE
Twilled material: usually silk, and usually dyed black.
M.D. 6

BONA FIDE
In good faith or sincerity; without fraud; in *C.M.*, used
ironically, as are most of the *Latin expressions in that book.
C.M. 9

BONAPARTE, --AN
See "Napoléon . . . ."
T. 17; R. 18; W. 49; W. 87; W. 90; M.D. 32

BOND-STREET
Especially in M.'s time, the location of fine jewelry stores
and shops: a fashionable place to walk in *London.
M. 13

BONEETAS; BONETAS; BONETTAS
Thynnus pelamys: "Bonito"; of the scomber (fish) fam-
ily. Two feet long, with a sharp head and "semi-lunar" tail.
T. 4; O. 3; M. 48

BON HOMME RICHARD
The old *French East Indiaman *Duc de *Duras*, fitted
with forty-two guns, was re-named by her commander, *John
Paul Jones, in honor of *Benjamin Franklin's "Poor Richard."
In one of the most famous battles in naval history, off
*Flamborough Head on 23 September 1779, Jones's small
squadron by moonlight intercepted the *Baltic merchant fleet
led by HMS *Serapis* and *Countess of Scarborough*. Losses
were severe on both sides, with Jones incurring perhaps 300
wounded or killed, and *Bon Homme Richard* sinking. He
transferred his crew to *Serapis*, extinguishing fires and taking
command of *Alliance*.
Jones was later to comment on the "defiant waving of
her unconquered and unstrucken flag" as *Bon Homme
Richard* went down: perhaps a suggestion for M.'s sinking of
*"Pequod."

(Maritime tradition holds it bad luck to re-name a ship.)
I.P. 18; I.P. 19

BOOBLE ALLEY, --S
    M. glosses in *R*. 39 "pestilent lanes and alleys . . . putrid
with vice and crime; to which, perhaps, the round world does
not furnish a parallel."
R. 39; M.D. 22

BOODLE HYDRANTS
    I have not been able to trace this reference. Partridge's
"Underworld Dictionary" discusses "boodle," which refers to
fake or counterfeit money or property. A "boodle game" is a
cheating procedure or trick; a "boodler" is a crooked politician
or grafter. The "Boodle Hydrant" of *R*. 37 actually produces
water and cannot be a fake.
R. 37

BOOKBINDER'S WHALE
    On the spines of M.'s copies of *Shakespeare and
*Milton (both Hilliard, Gray, and Company) is the Aldine
printer's mark of a dolphin encircling an anchor.
M.D. 60

BOOK OF MORMON
    See "Mormon . . . . "
P. 21:3

BOOK OF NATURE
    See "Mason Good's Book of Nature."
W. 41

BOONE, DANIEL
    Boone (1734-1820), the legendary hunter/trapper/pioneer,
was a wanderer throughout his life. Born in *Pennsylvania,
he had little schooling and soon moved with his family to North
*Carolina. His most famous feat in *Kentucky is misunder-
stood. Kentucky had already been examined by many white
men before Boone led a group of settlers, including his own
family, to the site of Boonesborough, where a fort was erected
in 1775. He should be credited, therefore, with the first permanent settling of the area, where he held several local offices.

He next moved to Point Pleasant (now West *Virginia) and then to the Femme Osage Valley in *Missouri. During his life, he traveled as far south as *Florida and as far west as the Yellowstone River, was captured several times by Indians, and became a legend even before his death. Some of the legends arose from John Filson's spurious biography, as well as from *Byron's *Don Juan* (1823; eighth canto), and from various tall tales.

The question of his relatives murdered by Indians is unclear; one son appears to have been murdered in the Cumberland Gap; the Filson biography claims rather two sons and one brother killed, as noted in *C.M.*

M.D. 88; C.M. 26

BOOTES

In astronomy, a northern *constellation: the oxen-driver. It is said to represent Icarius, a follower of *Bacchus, whose daughter Erigone was killed by shepherds who believed she gave them poisoned wine. Erigone perhaps became *Virgo.

M. 100; M. 175; I.P. 1

"BOOTS"

The demeaning appellation for the youngest officer in a ship's mess (late eighteenth to twentieth century) is shared with the shoe-polishing servant of Dickens's (see "Hard Times") *The Boots of the Holly-tree Inn*, and with the *House of Lords bishop who reads prayers: walking in the boots of his predecessor.

R. 15

BORABORA

Bora-Bora, one of the (volcanic) Leeward group of the *Society Islands, twenty-five miles northwest of Raiatea (see "Raiatair") is four miles long and two and a half miles wide. The mountainous Bora-Bora's tallest peak is Mount Taimanu (2,379 feet). It has a large lagoon with a good harbor; its chief town is Vaitape.

O. 76

BORDEAUX

The Bordeaux region of southwestern *France produces the world's finest wines. Its thirty-six winemaking districts have been controlled since 1855 by a classification system which maintains quality and distinctiveness. Bordeaux wines may range from rich, dry white Graves and fruity Sauterne to full-bodied dark Médoc and St. Emilion.

The port city of Bordeaux was joined to *England for three hundred years, when Eleanor of Aquitaine married Henry *Plantagenet in the twelfth century. Even then it was known as "la région de bien boire et de bien manger" (region of fine drinking and dining).
M.D. 91

BOREAS; BOREAL

Boreas is the north wind and, in *Greek mythology, the god of that wind.
W. 3; M.D. 54; P. 2:5; I.P. 20

BORGIA, CAESAR

Cesare Borgia (1475-1507), who held the *French title, duc de Valentinois, was *Machiavelli's model for *Il principe*. Following the rapacious pattern of the Borgia family, Cesare terrorized his subjects in brutal attempt to conquer all of central *Italy, with the cooperation of his father, Pope Alexander VI, whose death in 1503 was his downfall. The Borgias' greatest enemy became Pope Julius II, and Cesare was imprisoned for two years and killed after his escape. Machiavelli's praise of his statesmanship, military prowess, and patronage of the arts is without any basis in history.
C.M. 26

BORNEO

The third largest island of the world (after *Greenland and *New Guinea) and the largest of the Greater *Sundas and *Malay Archipelago, Borneo lies between the Sulu Sea and *Java Sea, South China Sea and *Macassar Strait (7°2' N. - 4°10' S., 108°52' - 119°16' E.). It is an 800-mile-long island, from 160 to 690 miles wide, containing many rivers, jungles, and swamps, as well as a mountainous interior, the highest peak of which is Mount Kinabalu (13,455 feet). There are valuable woods and much large wild life on the island, but in M.'s time Borneo was most remarked upon for its principal native group, the *Dyaks: headhunters.

The *Portuguese visited Borneo in 1521, the *Dutch in 1600, the *English in 1665.
M. 94; M.D. 68; I.P. 11; C.M. 7

"BORN UNDER A GUN AND EDUCATED ON THE BOWSPRIT"
Lovett's *Naval Customs, Traditions and Usage* gives the old definition of the man-of-war's man: "Begotten in the galley and born under a gun. Every hair a rope yarn, every tooth a marline spike; every finger a fish hook and in his blood right good *Stockholm tar."
M.'s version may also be a *double entendre*.
W. 90

BOSTON
The capital of *Massachusetts is located on an arm (Boston Bay) of Massachusetts Bay, c. 180 miles northeast of *New York City. It was settled in 1630 as the main colony of the Massachusetts Bay Company. Its cultural importance began at once, with *Harvard founded in 1636.
Boston was central to *Revolutionary War hostilities, including the Boston Massacre of 1770 and the Boston Tea Party of 1773, in which M.'s paternal grandfather had participated in full Indian regalia (earning the family sobriquet, "the last *Mohawk"). The battle of *Bunker Hill (1775) was a turning point for colonist morale, and the British withdrew from Boston in 1776.
The "Athens of America" was the nation's intellectual center for much of the nineteenth century. Here *Puritanism had yielded to Unitarianism and then to *Transcendentalism as the prevailing ethos. The "*Brahmins" who made Boston at least a sometime residence included *Emerson, *Hawthorne, Longfellow, Whittier, Lowell, Holmes, and Thoreau. *Abolitionism made its center here, as well.
Boston was also a commercial and judicial center for the nation. M.'s father-in-law, Massachusetts Chief Justice *Lemuel Shaw, was a permanent resident, so M. was a frequent visitor throughout his life.
Upon M.'s 1844 arrival, the city was ending the commercial trade era and beginning the industrial period with a large immigrant population. The Log and Pay Roll of *United States* verify his 14 October *Navy discharge. The *T.* reply to American reaction against British Hawaiian activity may be a response to his brother *Gansevoort's anti-British speech in Boston (17 October): "She is insidiously attempting to check our territorial extension, and to increase her colonial possessions in America" (quoted in Leyda *Log*, from *The Schenectady Reporter*).
See also "Charles River," "Dorchester."
Passim

BOTANY BAY
The circular inlet five miles south of *Sydney, *Australia between Cape Banks and Cape *Solander is one mile wide and five miles in diameter. It was the scene of *Cook's first landing on Australian soil in 1770. It became a famous penal colony, but sources differ as to whether Botany Bay or Sydney was the site of the first such establishment.
I.P. 22

BOTOFOGO, BAY OF
Botafogo Bay, *Rio de Janeiro, is a semi-circular inlet of Guanabara Bay, overlooked by *Corcovado.
W. 39

BOTTLE CONJUROR, THE
In the *Arabian Nights, a genie imprisoned in a bottle, who attains normal or giant size on his release and then exercises his powers.
M.D. 112

BOTTLE-NOSE WHALE
See "Cetology" section.
M.D. 32

BOUGAINVILLE, DE
Louis Antoine de Bougainville (1729-1811), *French navigator/commander, colonial explorer and organizer, made important *Pacific discoveries. He colonized the East *Falkland Islands at his own expense (1764). On his 1766 voyage in the frigate La Boudeuse, he traversed the *Straits of Magellan, later sailed northwest to the Tuamotus, visited *Tahiti (where he contracted venereal disease), naming it La Nouvelle Cythère, went west to *Samoa (Archipel des Navigateurs) and the New Hebrides (Les Grandes *Cyclades), farther west into unnavigated waters, and turned north at Great Barrier Reef, missing *Australia. He passed through the Louisiade Archipelago (named by him for Louis XV) and the *Solomon Islands to New Britain. With scurvy on board, he put in for supplies in the *Moluccas and went on to *Batavia, arriving in France in 1769 having lost few men. After attaining high court government position, he was court-martialed after the French defeat at the *Battle of the Saints (off Martinique, April 12, 1782). Banished, he joined the army. When he retired in 1792, *Napoléon I made him a senator, Count of the Empire, and

member of the Legion of Honor. The largest of the Solomons, and the strait between Malekula and Espiritu Santo islands of the New Hebrides were named after him, as well as the climbing plant, Bougainvillea.

In 1848, M. borrowed his book: *A Voyage round the World. Performed . . . in the Years 1766, 1767, 1768, 1769. . .* Translated from the French by John Reinhold Forster, F.A.S. London, Nourse [etc], 1772 (Sealts #85).
T. 26; O. 18

BOUNTY

The 23-ton H.M.S. *Bounty* (originally *Bethia*, and a good example of the hard luck that follows changing a ship's name) was the scene of the famous mutiny against Captain William *Bligh. *Bounty* had been sent to the South Seas to collect *breadfruit plants for possible cultivation in Europe. Her forty-seven-member crew occupied the small area of the ship that was not taken up by greenhouse facilities. Poor conditions, and problems between the crew and the captain, who was the only commissioned officer on board, brought about seizure of *Bounty* off Tofua Island, 28 April 1789. The mutineers who escaped to *Pitcairn Island set her afire on 15 January 1790.

See also "Pandora."
O. 18; O. 33; O. 80; M. 1; M. 28

BOURBON, --S

The royal house of Bourbon, a branch of the house of Capet, was certainly "broad-flung," as M. says in *P.* 25:4: kings of *France, *Navarre, *Spain, *Naples, the *Two Sicilies, and *Etruria, and nobles in Parma and Lucca, one branch even pretending to the throne of *Brazil.

French Bourbons descended from Louis IX (1214-70; reigned from 1226). But French Bourbon kings properly begin with extinction of the *Valois line and coronation of Henry IV, "le Grand" (1553-1610; reigned from 1589), husband of Marie de *Médicis, of the house of *Orléans. He was succeeded in 1610 by his son, Louis XIII, "le Juste" (1610-43), who married the *Spanish Anne of *Austria. Louis XIV, "le Roi Soleil" (1638-1715) ruled from 1643 and was married to the Spanish Marie Thérèse of Austria. (Louis XIV, whom M. calls "*Louis le Grand," would not have used the *Oriflamme at his coronation, as claimed in *M.* 60, the *Fleur de Lis having replaced it in 1415.) Louis XV "le Bien Aimé" (1710-74), was king from 1715; regent until he reached majority was Philippe Egalité d'Orléans. He was succeeded by *Louis XVI (1754-92), king from 1774, and husband of the detested Marie Antoinette of

Austria. (M.'s memoir of his uncle *Thomas Melvill, Jr.
refers to his appearance during farm chores as that of a
"courtier of Louis XVI, reduced as a refugee, to humble employment, in a region far from the gilded *Versailles" [Leyda
Log I, Summer? 1834]).

Titular king from 1792-95 was Louis XVII (1785-95); his
uncle, Louis XVIII (1755-1824), reigned from 1814, succeeded
by his brother, Charles X (1757-1836) from 1824-30. After the
July Revolution, the side of the family descended from the
brother of Louis XIV (Philippe, duc d'Orléans, 1640-1701)
claimed the throne of the "July Monarchy" in the person of
*Louis Philippe (1773-1850), son of Philippe Egalité d'Orléans.
Last of the Bourbon kings of France, the "citizen-king" was
overthrown in the elections of 1848, when French citizens
"burned Ludwig's throne," as M. says in *M.* 168. His descendents are *de jure* pretenders to the crowns of France, Spain,
*Naples, Sicily, and Parma.

The Spanish line of the family descends from the Habsburg wives of Louis XIII and Louis XIV. In Brazil, descendents make up the houses of Orléans-*Braganza and Bourbon-
Brazil.

A far-flung family in other respects, illegitimate Bour-
bon descendents, some long ago legitimized, form the houses of
Bourbon-Busset and *Vendôme.
M.D. 101; P. 25:4

BOURSE, PARIS
Reference may be to either of two *Paris exchanges. The
Bourse des Valeurs (stock exchange), near the Bibliotheque
Nationale, was constructed in 1808-27, to resemble the Temple
of *Vespasian in *Rome. The Bourse du Commerce (former
corn exchange) was built in the mid-eighteenth century, near
Les Halles.
C.M. 18

BOUTON DE ROSE
Although "bouton de rose" is *French for "rose-bud," in
vulgar French usage it refers to the clitoris. In light of M.'s
fanciful description of this "romantic" ship (*M.D.* 91), one may
presume that he is using double-entendre, as he does for ship's
parts throughout *W.*
M.D. 91

BOW BELLS
The bells of St. Mary-le-Bow, in *London's *Cheapside, have had important official functions since the church's construction c. 1090. To be "born within the sound of Bow Bells" is to be a true *cockney. M.'s journal for 18 November 1849 records: "at last entered Bow Church, Cheapside. Was shown to a seat like a pit & sat out the entire service. Curious old church indeed."
See also "Whittington."
O. 17; R. 36

BOWDITCH; BOWDITCH'S NAVIGATOR; EPITOME; NAVIGATOR
Nathaniel Bowditch (1773-1838), navigator, mathematician, and astronomer, was born in *Salem, *Massachusetts. He made four long sea voyages between 1795 and 1799, including one command. In 1802 he published *The New American Practical *Navigator: Being an *Epitome of Navigation,* which corrected J.H Moore's *The Practical Navigator.* Adopted by the U.S. *Navy Department, the work has had some sixty editions since the first. Bowditch, who translated *Mécanique céleste,* by P.S. Laplace, refused several academic appointments.
M. 1; R. 18; W. 68; M.D. 35; M.D. 99

BOWERY, THE; BOWERYS; BOWERY-BOY
The *Manhattan area called the Bowery was originally an enclave (centering on Bowery Lane) of fashionable residences owned by wealthy *Dutch gentlemen farmers such as Peter Stuyvesant. (The word "Bowery" is a corruption of a Dutch expression designating "farm," or "country seat.") By the early nineteenth century, it had utterly changed character, becoming an area of theaters that variously presented culture of the highest and lowest types. A popular haunt, it was a center of beer halls, oyster saloons, and minstrel shows. The *Astor Place Riots took place at the Bowery's Astor Place Opera House, in 1847. (Bowery Lane splits at this point into Third Avenue and Fourth Avenue—later "Park Avenue South.")
By the 1850's Bowery Lane had been extended from *Chatham Square to ease the press of traffic on *Broadway, and M.'s last permanent address was just north of the upper reach of the Bowery, at 124 E. 26 Street. (This is noted in an excellent chapter on the Bowery, in Wilson's *New York: Old and New,* II.)
The "Bowery-boy" (W. 16) became the characteristic nineteenth-century denizen. As Wilson describes "Bowery Boys," they were mostly *Irish working class young men

whose weekends were devoted to the volunteer fighting of fires
and to a species of contentious dandyism. Great patrons of the
theatre and of the ladies, Bowery boys became an increasingly
pugnacious lot whose street brawls over insults (real or imag-
ined, to themselves or to women) led to the development of
prize-fighting in the United States. The dandy Bowery boy
would wear a polished black broad-brim hat over artfully arranged bear-greased curls. His shirt collar (on a heavily embroidered shirt) was turned down to reveal his manly upper
chest, the lower part of which was adorned with a brilliantly
colored satin or velvet vest. His trousers resembled a sailor's
"bell-bottoms," and were topped by a long black frock coat
which partially concealed his heavily perfumed and bejewelled
person.
R. 9; R. 30; W. 16

BOWLING-GREEN
*New York City's small Bowling Green Park has been in
common use since the *Dutch of New Amsterdam set aside
(for parades and fairs) the tiny triangle at the southern end of
*Broadway just above the *Battery, bounded by Whitehall and
State Streets. Bowling was the preferred diversion in the park
until the 1730's; thereafter it was a place for congregation and
conspicious perambulation, of increasing importance in the
nineteenth century. Until Central Park was developed (late
1850's), the Green and City Hall, Washington, Union, and
Madison Squares were among the few public parks in a dramatically developing city.
R. 25

BOWIE-KNIVES
The Bowie hunting knife was said to be the invention of
James Bowie (1796-1836). The first such knife, made by the
blacksmith to Bowie's order, was up to fifteen inches long, with
one sharp edge curving to a point. Sent to *Philadelphia for
reproduction, it was marketed as the Bowie knife.
Bowie (pron. Boo--ee) was born in *Kentucky and grew
up on the frontier. From 1818 he smuggled *slaves with Jean
Lafitte, then speculated in land. The famous knife first appeared in 1827, at a duel that ended in a mêlée with many par-
ticipants and spectators dead or wounded, and during which
Bowie killed an army major with the weapon.
He was with *Davy Crockett at the Alamo, where he was
found dead on his cot after the defeat.
M.D. 54

BOX COAT
A heavy, loose overcoat, fitted only at the shoulders: formerly worn by coachmen.
M.D. 3

BRACTON
Henry de Bracton (Bratton, or Bretton; d. 1268), *English judge/priest, and writer on law, is famous for a *Note-Book*, a collection of cases, and a *Treatise on the Laws of England* (*De Legibus et Consuetudinibus Angliae*), which was unfinished at his death and printed for the first time in 1569. A commemorative stone at Exeter Cathedral, his burial place, makes him "Author of the first systematic treatise on the Laws of England," as noted in *M.D.*
M.D. 90

BRAGANZA
The house of Braganza ruled *Portugal from 1640 to 1910 and *Brazil from 1822 to 1889. For lack of legitimate issue, illegitimate offspring and claimants by marriage were repeatedly placed on the throne.
See also "John VI, King of Portugal," and "Don Pedro II."
W. 56

BRAHIM
See "Brahma."
W. 87

BRAHMA; BRAHMINS
Brahma is the first member of the Hindu (see "Hindoo") trinity, with *Vishnu (see "Vishnoo") and *Shiva. He is the creator-god usually pictured as four-faced and four-armed (for the four *Vedas), bearded, and sitting on a lotus above a swan, holding a sacrificial spoon, a string of beads, and a manuscipt, as the god of wisdom and piety.
Brahma refers to the supreme reality supporting the universe, its original meaning "prayer" or "speech." In *Indian philosophy, there are two conceptions, the personal god Brahma and the impersonal Absolute Brahman.
"*Brahim" is M.'s idiosyncratic spelling of Brahman, highest ranking in the Hindu hierarchy of hereditary castes since the first millenium B.C. Among the "twice-born" castes, Brahmins have traditionally been privileged and venerated,

well-educated and influential. They are subject to complex rituals of purity relating to diet and contact with other castes, and are observers of many taboos. They are found in India, Nepal, and Ceylon. The Brahmanas, M.'s "books of the Brahmins," are prose treatises on the specific Vedas studied by Brahmans.

During M.'s time writers associated with *Harvard and Cambridge, *Massachusetts (especially Lowell, Holmes, and Longfellow) were called *New England Brahmins.
M. 3; M. 181; W. 87; M.D. 40, M.D. 55; M.D. 82

BRANDRETH'S PILLS

A laxative.

For *M.D.* 92 ("*Ambergris"), M. borrowed heavily from *Beale and *Cheever. The latter suggests (115, 116) that "a peck of Morrison's or Brandreth's pills, or the *homeopathic dose of a pound of calomel and jalop" would probably irrigate a constipated whale. He then goes on to lament the ensuing loss to the world of precious ambergris.

(Among the objectionable advertisements carried in the *New York *Herald, those for "Dr. Brandeth's" patent medicine drew the most fire. When at last they were discontinued, the editor, James Gordon Bennett, remarked: "without a doubt Brandeth is the most superlative quack that ever appeared in the world" (29 March 1837).
M.D. 92

BRANDT

Joseph Brant, or Thayendanegea (c. 1742-1807), was a *Mohawk war chief allied with the *British. A spokesman for Christianity, he translated parts of the *Bible into Mohawk.

W.L. Stone's *Life of Joseph Brant* (1838) shows that he dined with General *Gansevoort. M. used this book (Sealts #491a) and should not have confused the expedition in 1778 of Lt. Col. William Butler with that of Captain Benjamin Church in King Philip's War (See "Philip of Mount Hope.") in 1676. Brant had led Indian raids on Herkimer and German Flats, *New York, leading to Butler's vain pursuit.
P. 1:2

BRANDY

A spirit distilled from wine or fermented fruit mash, then aged in wood. *Cogniac of France is the best.
O. 37 (and elsewhere)

BRANDY-NAN
History's *Brandy-Nan* was *England's *Queen Anne, who liked *brandy so much that even her statue in *St. Paul's Churchyard was once marked with the nickname by a graffitist.
R. 37

BRANDYWINE, BATTLE OF THE
An engagement of the *American Revolution, the battle was fought on 11 September 1777 in southeastern *Pennsylvania. Rather a serious comedy of errors, the victory went to General *Washington, no forebear of W.'s "Captain *Claret," whose relation to the battle is in name only.
W. 37; W. 42

BRAZEN-NOSE
Brazen *head* was a legendary brass head that knew all and spoke, in early romances. *Friar Roger Bacon is supposed to have tested the head, which spoke while he slept and then smashed to pieces.
M. may be confusing with Brasenose College, *Oxford, where a brass nose on the gate is the college arms.
M. 3

BRAZIL, --IAN; THE BRAZILS
In M.'s time the fourth largest country of the world, Brazil was much discussed during the nineteenth century. The Brazilian coast had been visited by the Spaniard Yáñez Pinzón (see "Pinzella") before the *Portuguese represented by Pedro Alvares Cabral claimed it in 1500. Portuguese claims were always tenuous and under challenge by the *French, the *Dutch, and others.
With the *Napoleonic invasion of *Portugal, King *John VI was forced to flee to Brazil in 1807-08, where he made *Rio de Janeiro the capital (moved to Brasilia in 1960). His son Dom *Pedro became Emperor of Brazil when John returned. With Lord *Cochrane's help, Pedro declared independence in 1822. (The United States was first to recognize Brazil, in 1824.) Pedro was forced to abdicate in 1831, in favor of his son, Pedro II. This was a time of large-scale European immigration. The *slave trade was abolished in 1850 and slavery ended in 1888. Indigenous Tupi Indian population was decimated by European disease.
Brazilian diamonds (*M*. 19) were first discovered in the early eighteenth century at Mato Grosso.

Anacondas (*M*. 121, *M*. 144) are arboreal constrictors of the rain forests: up to thirty feet in length.

Brazilian wood (*W*. 44) may be as light as cork or as dense as that of the Brazilian Pepper Tree (one and one-half times as dense as water). The hardwood trees of the *Amazon forest were much sought after and highly priced because of their inaccessibility. The Paraná Pine, a conifer, was most in demand. Also valued were rubber trees, hard Brazilwood, and trees yielding Carnauba wax and certain dyes.

The Brazilian flag (*W*. 56) has a green field with a large yellow diamond twice as wide as it is high. In the diamond is a blue globe showing the *constellations of the southern skies, dominated by the *Southern Cross. A banner reading *Ordem e Progresso* surrounds the globe.

Although M.'s "White-Jacket" visits Rio for two days of dissipation (*W*. 56), the Log Book of *United States* indicates no shore leave granted to M. or anyone else during its week-long harboring in 1844. The visit of the Emperor to "*Neversink" is likewise a fiction.

See also "African slaves" (for the "Brazilian manner of rowing" of *W*. 56); "Bahia de Todos os Santos"; "Brazil Banks"; "Organ Mountains"; "Rio Belmonte"; "Toucan," as well as entries under "Rio de Janeiro."
M. 19; M. 121; R. 62; W. 44; W. 56; M.D. 32; M.D. 58; C.M. 24

BRAZIL BANKS
M. glosses in *M.D.* 58, citing the designation "Banks" as expressive of the "meadow-like appearance, caused by the vast drifts of brit continually floating in those latitudes, where the Right whale is often chased."
R. 62; M.D. 32; M.D. 58

BREAD-BARGE
See "Commodore's Barge . . . . "
T. 6; M. 20

BREAD-FRUIT, --TREE
The tropical breadfruit tree is *Artocarpus altilis*, a member of the mulberry family. It produces a large round (usually seedless) fruit with starchy pulp that can be baked like bread. Breadfruit (and *cocoanut) trees were carefully culti-vated on South Sea islands, as many visitors of M.'s time noted. Breadfruit was also stored in pits against times of famine. It makes a great variety of dishes (as M. notes in *T*.), including the pasty poi ("poee-poee"), which can also be made

from *taro, and which was served at feasts and harvest festivals.
T. 15; O. 27; M. Passim and elsewhere

BREMEN
     The modern designation "Bremen" refers to two
*German cities (Bremen and Bremerhaven), thirty-three miles
apart, which constitute a major trade port on the North Sea.
In M.'s time, Bremen referred to the city on the Weser River,
an important member of the *Hanseatic League in the thirteenth century, with an archbishopric established since 845,
the see of which encompassed large parts of *Scandinavia,
*Iceland, and *Greenland. At the time of "Wellingborough
Redburn's" (and M.'s) first cruise, there was much traffic and
commerce between Bremen (and *Hamburg) and the *United
States.
R. 1; M.D. 81

BRENTFORD
     In *Middlesex County, *England, Brentford was a major
polling place and site of the county court where the sheriff proclaimed the election of knights of the shire. Its proximity to
*London prevented its growing to greater importance after the
eighteenth century.
     ("Brintford" in the original of *Israel Potter's adventures.)
I.P. 4; I.P. 6; I.P. 12; I.P. 13; I.P. 24

BREST
     The seaport of western *France (315 miles west of
*Paris) has a land-locked harbor around which Richelieu developed the city in 1631. The French defeated the *British here
in 1694, but *Lord Howe defeated the French fleet here in 1794.
T. 3; I.P. 10; I.P. 15; I.P. 18

BRIDEGROOM
     A traditional *Biblical designation for *Christ, especially
in *Matthew 9:15, *Mark 2:19-20, *Luke 5:34-35, Matthew 25:1-
13.
C.M. 45

BRIDEWELL

An area in *London's *Blackfriars between Fleet Street and the *Thames, Bridewell was named for the miraculous well of St. Bride (or St. Bridget). *Henry VIII built a palace on the site, which Edward VI turned into a school for homeless children. It had become a prison by M.'s time, so that "bridewell" was taken to mean "prison." "Molly Bridges of Bridewell" (*I.P.* 13) would probably be a young prostitute or pickpocket. Most of the complex of school-hospital-prison was demolished in 1863.

M. visited St. Bride's Church on 18 November 1856, commenting in his journal: "Woman showed me to a big pew—almost unasked—blushed a good deal, what with Stout, jam, heat, & modesty. Excited vast deal of gazing somehow. Good sermon—a charity one. Gave Sixpence."

(*New York City's "Bridewell" was located west of the present *City Hall.)

"Mr. Bridewell," of *W.* is appropriately named.
I.P. 13

BRIDGE OF SIGHS

The *Ponte dei Sospiri,* in *Venice (rebuilt 1595-1605), derives its name from its original use. The Bridge, which connects the Palace of the *Doges to the state prison, conveyed prisoners from the judgement hall to the place of execution. M. visited 5 April 1857, noting in his journal that the building was still blackened by fires (of 1574 and 1577).

(There is another "Bridge of Sighs" at *Cambridge, *England.)
I.P. 19

BRIDGEWATER CANAL

Between *Liverpool and *Manchester, *England. The first cross-country canal in England, it was constructed 1758-72 for the Duke of Bridgewater.
P. 1:3

BRIDPORT, LORD

Alexander Hood Bridport, First Viscount (1726-1814), *British admiral, was called "father and friend" by the *Spithead mutineers.

(In sailor slang, to be "stabbed with a Bridport dagger" is to be hanged: after Bridport, Dorsetshire's monopoly on ropes and cables for the British Navy.)
W. 85

BRIGHGGIANS
Unidentified: probably an invention (or perhaps such a corrupt phonetic spelling as to be unidentifiable).
M.D. 6

BRIGHT FUTURE
See "Bunyan; Bunyanish."
C.M. 40

BRINVILLIERSES
Marie Madeleine Marguerite D'Aubray, Marquise de Brinvilliers (c. 1630-1676), was a *French poisoner whose crime career avenged the *Bastille emprisonment of her lover by her father, a *Parisian civil officer. She tested her poisons in hospitals before using them on her father, two brothers, and perhaps a sister. Having failed at poisoning her husband, she was betrayed by documents found after her lover's death. She escaped from France but was returned and tortured. She confessed and received the sacraments, then was beheaded after refusing to name other poisoners, who were later apprehended.
C.M. 29

BRISTOL, MOST NOBLE MARQUIS OF
The first earls of Bristol (1622-1698) were the Royalist Digby family. The title was revived in 1714 for the family of John Hervey (1665-1751), which has borne it since. Since 1826, earls of Bristol have also been called marquesses of Bristol and Earls Jermyn. At the time of "Redburn's" experience, the Marquess of Bristol would have been Frederick William Hervey (1769-1859).
R. 44

BRIT
See "Cetology" section.
M.D. Passim

BRITAIN; BRITANNIC; BRITISH; BRITON
See "England . . . . "
Passim

BRITISH OAK
British ships.
W. 71

BRITANNIA
On the *British pence, Britannia is a female figure sitting on a globe with one arm on a shield and a spear in the
other hand. The original was a *Roman coin of the 2nd Century A.D.

*Charles II produced the coin in 1665. His model was
the celebrated beauty, Frances Teresa Stewart, wife of Charles
Stewart (1639-72), a gentleman of the bedchamber to Charles.
She became the Duchess of *Richmond. In light of Charles's
reputation, Pepys was to snicker in his *Diary* that the face was
a "pretty thing" to represent Britannia. It is possible that *R.*'s
"Carlo" has some lewd message in claiming that he is paid in
this coin.
R. 51

BROAD-STREET
Southern *Manhattan's Broad Street runs from a point
on *South Street (east of the *Battery) to *Wall Street, where it
becomes Nassau Street. One of New York's original thoroughfares, Broad Street originated at wet docks, running north
through swampy terrain; it was lined by canals. By the time
of M.'s youth, it was in the heart of *New York's business
district, and intersected by *Pearl Street and other thriving
"Midtown" routes.
R. 1; R. 9

BROADWAY, --S
The contemporary fashionable *New York City street, in
the mid-nineteenth century.
R. 4; R. 30; R. 32; R. 41; R. 44; W. 13; W. 28; M.D. 6; M.D. 53;
C.M. 2

BROADWAY TABERNACLE
One of *New York City's largest buildings of the mid-
nineteenth century, the edifice that served as the Broadway
Tabernacle was built on *Broadway between Worth and
Catherine Streets, in 1836. It was originally a Congregational-
ist Church, but the *Abolitionists who followed used its great
acoustics to further their cause. It later became a concert hall.
R. 41

BRODIE
Sir Benjamin Collins Brodie (1783-1862) was a physician to William IV and *Victoria, President of *England's *Royal Society, and a leading surgeon and medical writer.
W. 63

BROOK KEDRON
See "Kedron, Brook."
W. 63; M.D. 95

BROOM ROAD
This beautiful *Tahitian thoroughfare, which extends completely across the island from *Matavai to *Papeete, is described by *Stewart (II, 19) and *Wilkes (II, 33-34). Convicts had constructed it of gravel, with wooden plank bridges over waterways. (Derivation of the name is unclear.)
O. Passim

BROTHER JONATHAN
See "Jonathan."
M.D. 89

BROWNE, J. ROSS
*Irish immigrant John Ross Browne, (1821-75) moved to *Kentucky at an early age, the son of an outspoken journalist father. He traveled for much of his life and based his graphic writings on actual experience. As a journalist, he covered *Senate debates and attended the first Constitutional Convention. He was, variously, a deckhand, customs inspector, Indian affairs inspector, commissioner of mines, *United States minister to *China. He held many minor government posts, which supplied materials for his exposés of current shams, corruption, and favoritism.

After contributing regularly to southern literary periodicals, he composed his most famous work, *Etchings of a Whaling Cruise* (Sealts #88), based on the manuscript journal he had kept during the cruise involved. The book was well-received in the U.S.; M,'s favorable review (*Literary World*, 1 March 1847) showed appreciation of the brutally graphic detail which was to influence his writing of *M.D.* Browne, by now married to Lucy Anna Mitchell, of *Washington, decided that the literary life was less rewarding than government service and *California development schemes, for which he lectured and wrote pamphlets, becoming one of California's most noted residents.

His literary reputation now rests on his influence on M. and on Samuel Clemens's *Roughing It* and *Innocents Abroad.* (See also "Extracts" 63.)

M.D. Extracts 63; M.D. 32; M.D. 56

BROWNE; SIR T. BROWN; SIR THOMAS BROWN

Sir Thomas Browne (1605-1682), *English physician, was an outstanding seventeenth century prose writer. His works are seen as highly influential on M., who referred to Browne as a "crack'd archangel"—an appellation parallel to those settled upon M. himself, by his contemporaries.

Browne was born in *London and educated at Winchester and Pembroke College, *Oxford, with medical studies at Padua and Leiden. His first great work, *Religio Medici*, was published (1642) without his permission and gained wide success throughout Europe for its original latitudinarian position on religion, its paradoxical humor, its scientific spirit, and its concern for the individual.

While practicing medicine in Norwich, Browne accumulated notebook jottings which were published (1646) as *Pseudodoxia Epidemica, or Enquiries Into Very Many Received Tenents, and Commonly Presumed Truths* (M.'s "*Vulgar Errors"). The work, frequently reprinted during Browne's lifetime, corrected many superstitious popular beliefs. Browne also wrote *Hydriotaphia, Urne-Buriall, or a Discourse of the Sepulchrall Urnes Lately Found in Norfolk*, a reflection on death and the transitory nature of human glory, and *The Garden of Cyrus, or the Quincunciall, Lozenge, or Network Plantations of the Ancients* (both 1658), a history of horticulture written in a highly stylized latinate prose. *A Letter to a Friend, Upon Occasion of the Death of His Intimate Friend*, a clinical history, was published posthumously (in 1690). Browne was knighted for his work and for his Royalist politics by *Charles II (1671).

M. borrowed some of Browne's works from *Duyckinck in 1848 (Sealts #89) and purchased his own set of *The Works, Including His Life and Correspondence* (London, 1686: Sealts #89) in 1849. Reviewers of *M.* saw emulation of Browne's manner in that book, and M. confessed in a letter to Duyckinck (5 April 1849) to a summer "with the *Phaedon in one hand and Tom Brown in the other, " anticipating "*Ishmael's" exhortatory remarks in *M.D.* 35 ("The Mast-Head"): "Beware of . . . any lad . . . who offers to ship with the Phaedon instead of *Bowditch in his head."

After the publication of *P.*, reviewers saw Browne as a negative influence on M. He was warned to "diet himself for a year or two on *Addison, and avoid Sir Thomas Browne" (Fitz-James O'Brien, "Our Young Authors," *Putnams Monthly*, February 1853).

See also "Extracts" 19.

M. 13; M.D. Extracts 19; M.D. 32; M.D. 91

BRUCE

James Bruce (1730-94), *British explorer, reached the source of the *Ethiopian Blue *Nile in 1770. Bruce was a poet and *Arabic scholar with some medical skill. His *African stories were thought apocryphal by many people, which accounts for M.'s comparison (*W.* 36) with Baron *Munchausen.
W. 36

BRUCE, --'S

Robert I, the Bruce (1274-1329), was king of *Scotland from 1306 to 1329. Descendent of a *Norman family related to the *British royal family, the young eighth Robert de Bruce may have supported *William Wallace, but his overt opposition to English rule was not clearly demonstrated until he had himself crowned at *Scone. Thereafter, he waged constant war against the forces of Edward I of England and his successor, Edward II, whose army was vanquished by the Bruce's at *Bannockburn in 1314. This was the decisive battle in the war for Scottish independence.

The Bruce's subsequent reign over the new nation was administratively difficult, especially complicated by the power of families such as the Douglases. At his death, his heart was taken by Sir James Douglas on a pilgrimage to the *Holy Land. Douglas was killed, but legend says the heart was recovered and placed in Melrose Abbey.

A host of sentimental tales were fostered by John Barbour, a fourteenth century poet who wrote the 13,000-line *The Actes and Life of the Most Victorious Conquerour, Robert Bruce King of Scotland*, and by *Sir Walter Scott, especially in *Tales of a Grandfather* (Sealts #454).
M. 98; M. 119; R. 40

BRUMMEL, BEAU

The *English George Bryan Brummell (1778-1840) was leader of fashion in the early nineteenth century, a favorite of the *Prince of Wales (later George IV). Beau (or "Buck") Brummell was a popular wit at *Oxford and was early com-

missioned in the prince's regiment. When he inherited a
large fortune, he set up an elaborate and fashionable Mayfair
residence, eventually going into such great debt that he fled to
*Calais, was imprisoned there, and never regained his inter-
est in fashion. He died in a charitable asylum.
M. 60

BRUNSWICK [DOCK]
*Liverpool: originally twelve and two-thirds acres water
area; opened 1832, for timber trade.
R. 32; R. 40

BRUTUS
The idealistic friend of Caesar in *Shakespeare's
*Julius Caesar, who joins the conspiracy against the ruler and
fatally stabs him as Caesar asks disbelievingly, "Et tu,
Brute?—Then fall, Caesar'" (III, i, 76). The episode prompts
Mark *Antony's "tribute" to Brutus as "the noblest *Roman of
them all" (V,v, 68).
See also "Quotations" section for M.'s citation of "Et tu
Brute" in *M.D.* 65.
R. 14

BRYNHILDAS
In *Scandinavian myth, Bryhild had herself ritually
burned on a funeral pyre so that she might join Sigurd the
Volsung as his wife in *Valhalla: a role not granted her in her
mortal existence. Thus, she became the prototype brave and
devoted woman.
Brynhild (or Brunhild) is a principal character in the
Niebelungenlied and in various *sagas.
M. 3

BUBBLE
A bubble may be a dupe or cheated person; to bubble may
be to swindle, in underworld parlance.
C.M. 15

"BUCCANEER"
In *W.*, "Buccaneer" represents the frigate, *Raritan*.
W. 62

BUCCLEUGH
First Duke of Buccleuch was the *Scottish James Scott, Duke of Monmouth, (1649-1685) who married Countess Anne Scott (1651-1732), of the border family Scott of Buccleuch, which gained wealth from its support of *James II of Scotland against the Douglas rebels. After Monmouth's execution, Anne's grandson, Francis Scott, inherited the title, and the family fortunes continued to rise through important marriages. M. sees the Buccleuchs as social climbers.
P. 1:3

BUCEPHALUS
See "Alexander . . . . "
The "fiery" Bucephalus is referred to also in *Billy Budd, Sailor,* 1.
M. 29

BUENA VISTA
A village eight miles south of Saltillo, *Mexico, where about 5,000 U.S. troops fought in 1847 under Major General Zachary Taylor, against a Mexican force of about 20,000, under General Antonio L. de Santa Anna. There were many casualties on both sides; neither was clearly victorious.
C.M. 19

BUFFALO
In M.'s time, Buffalo (*New York) was a new city, incorporated in 1832 as a result of expansion following the opening of the *Erie Canal. It is located at the eastern end of Lake *Erie, at the *Niagara River outlet, on the U.S.-Canadian border. It was laid out as a town in 1803 to become a *Great Lakes port and eventually serve barge canal shipping.
M. visited in 1840 when, as Howard (I,2) notes, he would have seen, on *macadamized streets, "Indians in deerskin trousers, platoons of soldiers, backwoodsmen, *German emigrants, wild-looking *Irishmen, dainty lady tourists, squaws with papooses on their backs, an occasional British officer in a red coat or an *English farmer in gaiters, *Frenchmen and *Canadians from across the river." Just above the city was "unbroken primeval forest."
(Among M.'s *Lecture expenses was a bath in Buffalo: cost—37 cents.)
R. 30; M.D. 54

BUFFON, COUNT

Georges Louis Leclerc, Comte de Buffon (1707-1788) was born into wealth in Montbard (Côte d'Or), *France. *Jesuit-educated, he became a fellow of the *British *Royal Society, eventually keeper of the French Jardin du Roi, his work on forests and timber being of importance to French shipbuilding. When a catalogue of the king's museum was ordered, Buffon transformed it into his account of the whole of nature: *Histoire naturelle, générale et particulière.* Published in illustrated editions in various languages, it ran to forty-four *quarto volumes, from 1749 to 1804 (English translation by W. Smellie, with *Life of Buffon* by M. Wood: *Natural History* 1781-1812).

Buffon's was the first modern attempt to synthesize all scientific knowledge. In cosmogony, he suggested the planets formed when the sun collided with another star. In evolution, he promulgated the environment's molding influence, perpetuated by heredity. His derogatory comments on nature in the Americas prompted *Jefferson's challenge in *Notes on the State of Virginia*. Two particular quibbles (*Histoire* XVIII): Buffon's suggesting the puniness of *American animals countered by Jefferson's noting the skeletal remains of the North American mammoth; Buffon's charges about the poor character and physiognomy of American aborigines, Jefferson's response including the famous speech of *Logan, the Mingo chief, to Lord Dunmore.
T. 29; M. 13

BUGGERY ISLAND

The Oxford English Dictionary defines "buggery" as originally meaning abominable heresy, later describing "unnatural intercourse of a human being with a beast, or of men with one another, sodomy" (earliest use: R. Brunne Chron., 1330).

M. utilized the sailor's designation for an island where licentiousness reigns;   publisher Arthur Stedman demanded it be changed to "Desolate Island" for his 1892 edition of *T.*
T. 4

BULL; JOHN BULL

A nickname for an *Englishman and caricature of England or the English, popularized by (but not originated in) Dr. John Arbuthnot's *The History of John Bull* (1712), renamed from *Law is a Bottomless Pit*. John Bull is usually portrayed as a stout, good-natured farmer in a red waistcoat and leather breeches, bearing an oaken cudgel. *Charles Dibdin wrote a prologue for the play:

JOHN BULL is--*British Character* at large; . . .
Plain, blunt, his heart with feeling, justice full,
That is a Briton, that's (thank heaven!) JOHN
BULL.

Although Arbuthnot's Bull is a clothier, caricatures have varied to suit the age; nineteenth-century *Punch* cartoons often showed him as a Royal Navy seaman.

John Bull was a popular periodical. Another John Bull, organist at Antwerp Cathedral from 1617-28, is the author of "*God Save the King."
M. 161; W. 65; M.D. 89

BULL, THE
    See "zodiac."
M.D. 99

BUM-BOATS
    A bum-boat is a scavenger's boat, or one carrying provisions or merchandise to ships in port. The expression is a corruption of "boom-boat," a floating stall filled with goods lying around ships' booms in an anchorage. A secondary profession arises when one speaks of "bum boat woman."
W.43

"BUNG UP, AND BILGE FREE"
    Said of a barrel that has been floating in sea water. The "bung" is the tapping place; if no salt water has contaminated the contents, it is "bilge free," the bilge water being the dirty water in a ship's hold.
W. 37

BUNKER HILL; BUNKER'S HILL
    The Battle of Bunker (or Breed's) Hill, in the Charlestown area of *Boston, took place on 17 June 1775. The first severe engagement of the *Revolutionary War occurred when the *British attacked a newly constructed *American fort on the hill. After charging twice, they ran out of powder, lending a massive boost to American morale and creating a symbol that has been celebrated throughout American history.
    M.'s grandfather, Major Thomas Melvill (1751-1832), had participated in the battle and was present at the 1825

ground-breaking ceremonies for the obelisk-monument (along
with *Lafayette and *Daniel Webster). The 221-foot monument
was completed in 1843 (again in the presence of Webster).

The *I.P.* dedication "To His Highness The Bunker Hill
Monument" is a (punning) continuation of the pattern begun
with *P.*, which is dedicated to another inanimate object, Mount
*Greylock. (The dark humor continues, but the pattern is bro-
ken somewhat in the dedication of *C.M.* to "victims of *Auto da
Fe.")

The equally dark humorist, Mrs. Trollope, comments (p.
205, n. 1) on the Bunker Hill Monument as recording "some
victory; I forget which."
R. 27; W. 35; W. 57; I.P. Passim

BUNYAN, --ISH
The greatest writer of the early *Puritan movement,
John Bunyan (1628-1688) was born near Bedford, *England.
Converted by his first wife, he became a *Non-conformist
preacher/writer and was imprisoned almost continuously
from 1660 to 1672, for preaching without the license necessary
during the Restoration period. Among works done in prison
were *Grace Abounding to the Chief of Sinners* (1666) and the
masterpiece, *The Pilgrim's Progress* (1678 and 1684). Other
writings include *The Life and Death of Mr. Badman* (1680),
and *The Holy War* (1682).

Part I of *The Pilgrim's Progress* is the hero
"Christian's" dream-allegory of the Puritan soul's journey to
salvation at the Celestial City, incorporating a symbolic picture
of the human condition and a portrayal of English country life
during the reign of *Charles II. Part II follows Christian's
wife "Christiana" and her children on a similar quest.

M. was certainly influenced by Bunyan's most important work, even to citation of "The Delectable Mountain" (in *P.*
25:4), "Christian's" place of refreshment near the Celestial
City. "The Despairer" of *M.* 40 and "Doleful Dumps" of *C.M.* 40
are like Bunyan's "Giant Despair," and names such as
"Bright Future," "Old Plain Tale," and "Old Prudence" (*C.M.*
40), as well as personifications of abstractions (such as "Sin,"
"Virtue," and "Vice," in *W.* 94) are "Bunyanish." "The
*Advocate" chapter (24) of *M.D.* sets up a theoretical discourse
between adversaries much like that between "Objection" and
"Answer," in Bunyan's Part II, and M.'s tributes to
*Leviathan must have been reinforced by Bunyan's words
about the creature, derived from *Job. Even "Great Heart,"
M.'s salute to *Jack Chase, in the dedication of *Billy Budd,
Sailor*, comes from *The Pilgrim's Progress*.

Sealts #95 is an unknown edition.

See also "Extracts" 22 and "Fidele."
M.D. Extracts 22; M.D. 26; P. 25:4

BURDOCK HUT; BURDOCKS
The reference is probably a joke. A burdock is a course
weed with burrs which grows on waste land.
C.M. 25

BURGOO
"Wellingborough Redburn" glosses (*R*. 11): The oatmeal
and water eaten by *Irish emigrants was called by them
"mush." The *Dutch called it "supaan," *New Englanders referred to it as "hasty pudding." But to sailors, it was "burgoo."
R. 11; W. 32

BURGOYNE
British General John Burgoyne (1722-1792) had had
some battle experience before being sent with *British forces to
the *New England colonies in 1775. He was much criticized for
his actions relative to the battle of *Saratoga (1777) and left the
army in 1783 to become a playwright. (His *The Heiress* was
produced in *London in 1786.) "Gentleman Johnny" was a
rather unorthodox and boastful person, as M. points out in *P*.
2:3. At twenty-one, he had eloped with a daughter of the
eleventh Earl of *Derby. He later sired four children by a
mistress, the singer Ellen Caulfield. Thus a flamboyant personal life might account for M.'s referring to him as a
"bragging boy" at Saratoga.
M.'s grandfather, Peter *Gansevoort, was instrumental
in Burgoyne's defeat at Saratoga. The then-Colonel Gansevoort stopped the British and *Indian force enroute from Lake
Ontario in summer of 1777, preventing its supporting
Burgoyne in September and October.
P. 2:3

BURGUNDY
True Burgundy wines come only from *France, where
they have been produced since *Roman times in the area corresponding to the modern départements of Côte-d'Or, Saône-et-
Loire, and Yonne. Wine-making in the area was greatly expanded in the eighteenth century, when many types were developed, from dry white Chablis to the more characteristic full-
bodied reds including Chambertin and Beaujolais.
M. 181

BURKE; EDMUND BURKE'S REFERENCE IN PARLIA-
MENT TO THE NANTUCKET WHALE-FISHERY
     Edmund Burke (1729-97), *British statesman, orator,
and political thinker, was born in *Dublin, *Ireland, to a
*Protestant father and a *Catholic mother. After attending
Trinity College, he entered London's Middle *Temple briefly
and then traveled for some years before beginning publishing
anonymously. Although none of his own writings were fiction,
Burke's closest ties were with the most famous artists of his
day, including *Samuel Johnson, *Goldsmith, Garrick, Sir
Joshua Reynolds.
     Burke played an important part in all of the political is-
sues of late eighteenth-century England: he favored emancipation of the *American colonies and Ireland; cessation of
*George III's control over the *House of Commons; emancipa-
tion of *India from the *East India company. He opposed the
atheistical Jacobinism of the *French Revolution, becoming
subject to much criticism from liberal thinkers such as Paine,
*Bentham, and Mill.
     Burke's most important speeches and essays include:
On American Taxation (1774); *On Moving His Resolutions for
Conciliation With America* (1775); *A Letter . . . to the Sheriffs of
Bristol* (1777); *Reflections on the Revolution in France (1790)*;
*Observations on a late Publication on the Present State of the
Nation* (1769); *On the Nabob of Arcot's Private Debts (1785); A
Letter to a Noble Lord* (1796).
     Burke's comment (*W.* 44) on the moral condition of *an-
cien-regime* society decries what had been lost after the French
Revolution:

          It is gone--that sensibility of principle, that
          charity of honor which felt a stain like a wound,
          which inspired courage whilst it mitigated
          ferocity, which ennobled whatever it touched, and
          under which vice itself lost half its evil by losing
          its grossness (*Reflections on the Revolution in
          France*, V., "A Critical Analysis of the French
          Revolution," 2).

     In his copy of Matthew Arnold's *Essays in Criticism*
(Boston, 1865), M. underscored a quotation from Burke: "Our
antagonist is our helper. This amicable conflict with difficulty
obliges us to an intimate acquaintance with our object, and
compels us to consider it in all its relations. It will not suffer
us to be superficial."
     See also "Extracts" 42, 43.
M. 24; W. 44; M.D. Extracts 42; M. D. Extracts 43; M.D. 24

BURKERS

Figuratively, body-snatchers, or smotherers: from William Burke (1792-1829), an *Irishman who smothered his victims and sold their bodies to *Edinburgh surgeons for use in medical schools. With the aid of William Hare and their respective wives, Burke received between £8 and £14 for fifteen bodies before his accomplice turned him in. He was hanged in 1829, but Hare went free, only to become a pariah.

To burke a question is to smother or suppress it.
R. 39; W. 90

BURKES

Jem "Deaf" Burke was *English Prizefighting champion in 1833.
M.D. 37

BURMESE

Burma is on the Indochinese peninsula, bounded by the Bay of *Bengal, modern east Pakistan and *India (W.), *China, and modern Laos and Thailand (E.), and by the Andaman Sea (S.). It extends c. 1,200 miles from north to south, between the eastern *Himalayas and the Isthmus of Kra, cut off by a horseshoe of mountains. The Burmese are a *Mongoloid race of *Buddhists. Burma was unified between 1044 and 1097. In 1289 the invasion of Kubla *Khan split it, but by the sixteenth century it was unified again, and trading began with major European nations. The eighteenth century saw Burma politically split agian, and the nineteenth brought the Anglo-Burmese wars (1824-26, 1852, 1862, 1886). (Burma did not become fully autonomous until the twentieth century.)

See also "Tibet."
R. 34

BURNET

Gilbert Burnet (1643-1715), author of *Exposition of the *Thirty-Nine Articles, and Vindication of the Authority, Constitution, and Laws of the Church and State of *Scotland*, was a defender of the doctrine of passive obedience: in M.'s terms in *P.* (14:3), a "horologe."
W. 76

BURTON

Robert Burton ("Democritus Junior," 1577-1640) was an *English *Anglican clergyman, whose patron, Lord *Berkeley, helped him to become a life fellow of Christ Church, *Oxford, and focus on scholarship. He accumulated much property and gained the vicarage of St. Thomas's Church, Oxford. He is most noted for his *Anatomy of Melancholy* (Sealts #s 102 and 103), begun to continue the study of the philosopher, *Democritus, of what we call depression. Burton's encyclopedic work on *"blue devils" is a valuable assessment of seventeenth-century philosophical and psychological ideas, anticipating today's psychosomatic medicine. It is a mixture of colloquial and classical allusion, replete with lists and humorous asides.

M. mentioned Burton in "Fragment #1." Sealts #s 102 and 103 are editions of the *Anatomy*.
M. 1

BURTON CONSTABLE
See "Constable, Sir Clifford."
M.D. 102

BURY
See "Bury St. Edmunds."
R. 44; R. 50

BURY ST. EDMUNDS
The borough and market town in West *Suffolk, *England, is on the Lark River, a tributary of the Great Ouse. About 630, a monastery was founded in the area by Sigebert, King of the East Angles. In the *Danish invasions of the late ninth century, St. Edmund, then East Anglian king, was martyred, and the area became a shrine by the eleventh century, with a *Benedictine abbey founded by *Canute. In 1214, English barons met at Bury St. Edmunds to agree on demands of *King John, an event connected by historians with *Magna Carta.

"Angels," probably derived from "Angles," are prominent in the area; there is an Angel Hotel, which was visited by Dickens (mentioned in *The Pickwick Papers*), as well as a building called "Angel Corner."

The "old Church of St. Mary's" (*R*. 44) dates from the early fifteenth century. It is the site of Mary Tudor's (see "Bloody Mary") tomb. The nave roof shows a procession of angels moving toward the altar.
R. 44; R. 45

BUSHMEN
A catchall expression referring to *African or *Australian peoples who live in the "bush," away from developed areas (from the *Dutch *Boschjesman*).
R. 50

BUSKS
Corsets.
M.D. 57

BUTLER, CAPTAIN
Lieutenant Colonel William Butler pursued *Joseph Brant, not Annawon (as M. has it), in an expedition in 1778.
The reference in *M.D.* 45, corrected in some editions, should be to Benjamin Church, in 1676.
M.D. 45

BUTTER-BOX GALLIOT
Long, slim light-draft Dutch merchant vessel.
"Butter-box" is also used as a contemptuous name for a Dutchman (see also "Dutch).
M.D. 16; M.D. 81.

BUTTONS; "BUTTONS"
All of the originals of the sobriquet "Buttons" are pejorative. It is the derogatory appellation of the decoy in an auction room who "buttons" customers to purchases they do not want; the warden or superintendent of a work-house; the stock character page of pantomime theater whose jacket is buttoned from chin to waist.
R. 6; R. 15

BUXTON, JEDEDIAH
Buxton (1707-72) was a lightning calculator who performed amazing mathematical feats. His mental faculties were otherwise so meager that he is said to have seen David Garrick play *Richard III* and missed all of the action while tabulating the numbers of words each actor spoke.
W. 3

BYRON

John Byron (1723-86), grandfather of the poet George Gordon *Byron, was a midshipman on *Wager, in *Anson's squadron, when it was wrecked on an island off *Chile in 1741. The poet used his grandfather's "Narrative" in composing *Don Juan*. M. owned the second edition (Sealts #113): *The Narrative of the Honourable John Byron . . . containing an Account of the Great Distresses Suffered by Himself and His Companions on the Coast of Patagonia, from the Year 1740, till Their Arrival in England, 1746. With a Description of St. Jago de Chili, and the Manners and Customs of the Inhabitants. Also a Relation of the Loss of the Wager, Man of War, One of Admiral Anson's Squadron. Written by Himself.* London: Baker and Leigh, 1768.

"Foul Weather Jack" became a vice-admiral and commander in chief of the *West Indies Squadron. He was also known as *"Mad Jack."
T. 24; O. 18; O. 54; W. 8; W. 24

BYRON; LORD BYRON

George Gordon, sixth Baron Byron (1788-1824), was the son of Captain John (*"Mad Jack") Byron and the *Scottish Catherine Gordon. The handsome romantic poet and political libertarian led a life of wild adventure colored by constant debt, affliction with a club foot, scandalous love affairs (including one with his half-sister Augusta which resulted in the birth of a daughter). He is known to have swum the *Hellespont, addressed the House of *Lords, and been lionized in *England for his literary works, before debt and charges of incest and insanity led to his permanent departure from England, despite encouragement from *Goethe and others. Byron lived in *Geneva with the *Shelleys, as well as in *Rome, *Venice, *Ravenna, *Pisa, and *Genoa. He died of fever after having formed the "Byron Brigade" on the side of the *Greeks against *Turkey.

Among his highly acclaimed but widely condemned works are *Childe Harold's Pilgrimage* (referred to in *M.D.* 35): an autobiographical metaphysical poem, fourth canto of which contains the "address to the ocean" of *R.* 26 and the third the paean to *Lake Leman of *W.* 50), and *Don Juan* (a wildly romantic unfinished epic satire on hypocritical and sentimental social conventions as practiced by *Wordsworth, *Wellington, and *Southey).

Many of M.'s works are "Byronesque" in their melancholy tone, their allusions, and their extravagant language and actions. Gilman makes M's early debt to Byron explicit in *Melville's Early Life and Redburn*. The reference in *W.* 52 is to

Elegaic Stanzas (1814), written by Byron on the death of his cousin, *Sir Peter Parker, who was killed while navigating near *Chesapeake Bay. In *W.* 65, M. refers to Byron's participation (with *Trelawney) in the 1822 cremation of Shelley's body. The accusation in *P.* 23:4 ("Plus head, minus heart") probably refers to Byron's abandonment of his wives, lovers, and children, in contrast to "Pierre's" attempt to juggle all.

There were many copies of Byron's works known to the Melville family. Sealts #s 107-112 are various editions of *The Complete Works, The Bride of Abydos, Don Juan, Dramas, Miscellanies, Tales*: read by M.'s brother *Gansevoort, sister Augusta, and wife Elizabeth Shaw Melville. M.'s copy (Sealts #112) is: *The Poetical Works* . . . Boston: Little, Brown, 1853?. 10 v. M.'s annotations suggest that he studied Byron as late as the late 1850's and beyond. His journal for 7 December 1849, composed in Brussels, shows M.'s ability to quote from *Childe Harold* verbatim:

> There was a sound of revelry by night,
> And Belgium's capital had gathered then her
> beauty and her chivalry
>
> . . .

Byron is mentioned also in the journals for 10 December 1856 (at the Hellespont), 24 January 1857 (at *Joppa), 3 and 5 April 1857 (at *Venice). His name appears also in a list of perhaps especially important impressions at the conclusion of M.'s trip (5 May 1857).

See also "Alp Arslan's warhorse"; "Manfred . . . . "; "Roll on, thou deep . . . " ("Quotations" section).
R. 26; R. 56; W. 4; W. 50; W. 52; W. 65; P. 23:4

BYWARD TOWER
    See "Tower of London."
M.D. 42

BYZANTIUM
    The ancient city on the site of M.'s "*Constantinople" (modern Istanbul, *Turkey) was founded by the *Greeks in 658 B.C. because of its position on the *Bosporus. It was repeatedly captured and rewon in the *Peloponnesian Wars and was taken by the *Romans in A.D. 196. In A.D. 330, the Emperor Constantine I ordered a new city, Constantinople, to become the capital of the Byzantine Empire, which succeeded the *Roman. That empire lasted until 1453, when the *Ottoman

Sultan Muhammad I besieged Constantinople (not *Solyman the Magnificent, as M. has it in *T.* 17).

(M. visited Constantinople in December of 1856.)
T. 17

C

CABALISTICAL; CABALISTICALLY
The Cabbala (Kabbalah, Qabbala) is a *Jewish tradition of mystical Scripture interpretation (especially of the prophecies of *Elijah), in which the letters of the text, converted into numbers, reveal secret truths: a second revelation of *God to *Moses. The name for the essentially oral system came to indicate the entire esoteric doctrine of Judaism. It emerged fully c. A.D. 1200 and prevailed well into the eighteenth century. Practical application as white magic (in use of God's powers, as opposed to black magic's use of the *Devil) has always been forbidden, but the Cabbala has often been related to necromancy, astrology, alchemy.

(Viola Sachs, in *The Game of Creation*, tries to show that M. used a similar system of hidden meanings in *M.D.*).
M.D. 91; M.D. 118

"CABOOSE"
A caboose in M.'s time was not part of a train but in maritime usage an office, small cabin, or compartment.
O. 16

CACHALOT BLANCHE
Fr.: White spermaceti whale.
M.D. 91

CACIQUES
Chiefs of *Mexican and *West Indian tribes.
M. 181

CADE, JACK
The historical Cade was a *Yorkist peasant who led a popular revolt against England's King Henry VI, in 1450. Abandoned by his followers near *London Bridge, Cade re-

treated to Sussex, where he was killed. M.'s reference in *C.M.*
29 is to the cynical character given Cade in *Shakespeare's
King Henry VI, Part 2.
C.M. 29

CADELL
　　　*Londoner Robert Cadell, publisher of works of *Sir Wal-
ter Scott, took over Scott's liabilities and copyrights in 1848,
making a fortune.
W. 90

CADI
　　　Arabic name for town magistrate or inferior *Moslem
judge whose justice is based on religious law (Span. *alcade* or
alcalde: mayor, or peace officer).
M. 60

CADIZ
　　　Cádiz province of *Spain's *Andalusia has many inlets,
rivers, and fine harbors and is famous for its *sherry. The city
of Cádiz is a major *Atlantic port sixty miles west-northwest of
*Gibralter on a small spit of land on the Bay of Cádiz. It was
the leading maritime city of the colonial era, with fine harbor
installations and a landmark watch tower: Torre de Vigía.
Cádiz was founded c. 1100 B.C. by *Phoenicians who called it
Gadir. It passed to the *Carthaginians, the *Romans (as
Gades), the Barbarians, and the *Moors. *Columbus sailed
from nearby *Palos enroute to *America. After the colonial
period the city's fortunes fell, and by the late eighteenth century Cádiz was forced to fend off attacks by *Nelson,
*Wellington, and the *French. In the Bay of Cádiz, the revolu-
tion removing Isabel II from the throne began, in 1868.
R. 21; R. 39; W. 8; M.D. 9

CADMUS
　　　In *Ovid's *Metamorphoses* III (1-137), Cadmus, founder
of *Thebes and brother to *Europa, killed a sacred dragon
guarding the fountain of *Mars in Boeotia. He sowed the
dragon's teeth, which grew into armed warriors. Burdened
with troubles thereafter, he was changed into a serpent (IV,
563-603), along with his wife, Hermione.
C.M. 32

CAESAR, --S; CAESARIAN; JULIUS CAESAR; AUGUSTUS CAESAR'S

Because it is not always clear to which "Caesar" M. refers, I have elected to deal with the generic reference (signifying for M. absolute power), along with the two most important Caesars mentioned by him. Originator of the title was Gaius Julius Caesar (100/2--44 B.C.), referred to directly in *M.* 1; *M.* 22; *M.* 181; *R.* 31; *W.* 16; *W.* 47; *W.* 77. He was a *Roman patrician who rose through public office to consulship, generalship of the army, and final dictatorship that set a pattern for six centuries. The title "Caesar" was passed to male members of his dynasty and to successive emperors of all or part of the Roman Empire. (After *Hadrian, the title was assigned to successors nominated by the emperors.) Julius Caesar's autocratic policies and military prowess kept Rome from barbarian invasion and prolonged the life of the Greco-Roman culture which was to color almost all of the western hemisphere. He was assassinated in a plot enlisting sixty men.

Among relevant persons cited by M.: *Sulla, *Pompey, *Marius, *Crassus, *Antony, *Cleopatra, *Brutus, *Cicero. Many of the geographical sites mentioned by M. (notably *Gaul) became parts of the Roman Empire (which eventually extended north to *Scotland, south to *Africa, and east to the *Holy Land) through the conquests of this Caesar. M.'s knowledge of him probably comes through *Shakespeare, *Plutarch, and *Suetonius.

(The operation known as Caesarian Section, in which a fetus is surgically removed from the uterus, was supposedly performed to deliver Julius Caesar. "Caesar" is from *caedere*: "to cut." Derivations are "*Tsar" and "Kaiser.")

Augustus Caesar (63 B.C.--A.D. 14), referred to in *I.P.* 8 and *C.M.* 7, was born Gaius Octavius but changed his name to that of his adoptive father, Julius Caesar, in 44 B.C. He is conventionally referred to as "Octavian." Early military victories brought him into Julius's favor (there being no natural son), and he was made heir, ascending to power at the age of eighteen. Antony was his rival in politics, but Octavian was elected to rule in 43. The First Triumvirate (in 38; expired in five years) consisted of these two men and Marcus Aemilius Lepidus, governor of Gaul. Brutus and Cassius were crushed, new conquests were made, and Antony married Octavian's sister. But friction continued as Octavian gained power in the west and Antony struggled in the east. Octavian defeated Antony, who was heading *Cleopatra's forces at *Actium, in 31, becoming undisputed master, repeatedly elected consul. His resignation in 27 forced conference of the title "Augustus" and other honorifics. Despite territorial gains, he was forced for political reasons to renounce consulship in 23 but was re-peatedly given new titles and new power, which he directed away from the republic he claimed to support.

Octavian established a standing army that advanced the Roman frontier to the Danube and added several provinces. He attempted political and moral reform and encouraged the arts of *Mecaenas, *Virgil, *Horace, and *Ovid--products of what has come to be known as the "Augustan Age." He was suc-ceeded by his wife Livia's son, *Tiberius.

Other "Caesars" mentioned by M. include *Caligula, *Claudius I, *Nero, *Vespasian, *Titus, *Domitian, *Trajan, *Aurelian, *Diocletian, *Alexander the Great, Constantine (see "Constantinople"), and *Valens.
M. 57; M. 161; R. 33; R. 55; W. 46; W. 85; M.D. 34; M.D. 43; M.D. 45; P. 1:3; I.P. 14

CAFFRARIA, --N
Kaffraria (Arabic "land of Kafirs" or "unbelievers") is in South *Africa's present day East Cape Province, between the Great Fish River (S.) and Basutoland and Natal borders (N.), on the *Indian Ocean (E.). In was settled by *Germans in the 1850's and annexed to *Britain's Cape Colony in 1865.

(The modern area is Cape of Good Hope Province, with borders extended south beyond the Great Fish. The present-day Mountain Zebra National Park marks the center of the ze-bra colony which M. refers to in *M. 1*.)
M. 1; R. 50

CAFFRE
Caffre (or *Kafir*) is Arabic for "infidel," applied by *Mohammedans to *Christian and *Pagan negroes. It even-tually designated certain Bantus who strenuously resisted conversion.
O. 2; C.M. 45

CAIN, --S
Cain, the prototype wicked man, is the eldest son of *Adam, in *Genesis 4:1-16. The meaning of his name is un-clear. In 4:2-8, his younger brother, *Abel, makes an accept-able offering to *God, but Cain's is rejected. He slays his brother and becomes alienated from the land, the family, and God. Instead of banishing Cain to the "Land of Wandering," God mercifully sets a mark upon him, "lest any finding him should kill him" (4:14-15).

In Genesis 4:16-17, "Cain went out . . . and builded a city." M. refers to this city negatively in *C.M.* 24 and in the poem, "The Armies of the Wilderness" (in *Battle-Pieces and Aspects of the War*), he associates it with the evil of war.
O. 7; R. 22; M.D. 32; M.D. 40; C.M. 24; C.M. 27

CAIN, MARK OF
   *Genesis 4:14-15: "The Lord set a mark upon Cain, lest any finding him should kill him."
M.D. 32

CAIRO
   The southernmost city of *Illinois, at the confluence of the *Ohio and *Mississippi Rivers, Cairo had lain undeveloped from its founding in 1818. In 1837, the Cairo City and Canal Company attempted to settle the swampy, disease-ridden town, but it was not until 1846 that eastern investors identified with the Illinois Central Railroad succeeded in a settlement that resulted in government's being established in 1855. The site resembled that of its *Egyptian counterpart, inspiring the southern Illinois nickname of "Little Egypt."
   Charles Dickens (see "Hard Times") visited in 1842, collecting the negative impressions for his ironically named "*Eden," in *Martin Chuzzlewit*.
C.M. 22; C.M. 23

CALABOOZA;   CALABOOZA BERETANEE;   HOTEL DE CALABOOZA
   "Calabooza Beretanee" was a veritable confinement place for unruly sailors, near *Papeete. As Anderson shows (*Melville in the South Seas*, 214, 215), it had recently been established when M. was confined there in 1842, with ten to fourteen others who had mutinied aboard *Lucy Ann* (see "Julia"). Other writers of the time refer to a "caliboose" (or "calliboose") complete with stocks, where punishment was apparently just as gentle and confinement just as lax as M. pictures it in *O.*: more like a hotel than a prison.
   (The word "calaboose" is from the *Spanish *calabozo*, "dungeon," through New Orleans French *calabouse*. *O.E.D.* records first written use in 1837, but this may be an error. "Beretanee" is, of course, a corruption of "*Britain" or "British.")
O. Passim

CALABRIA, --N

Southern *Italy's mountainous peninsula, forming the "toe" of the "boot," is separated from *Sicily by the Strait of *Messina. Calabria was settled by *Greeks in the eighth century and conquered by the *Romans in the third century B.C. The ancient "Bruttium," it was named Calabria in the *Middle Ages, becoming part of the *Norman kingdom of Sicily, then part of the kingdom of *Naples. It was conquered by Garibaldi in 1860.

Calabria evokes images of feudalism, malaria, earthquakes, and droughts, but its picturesque bleak scenery was such as nineteenth-century "Hudson River School" painters were depicting in the *United States. M.'s journal of his visit (15 February 1857) records his (correct) vision of Calabria's mountains as reminiscent of the paintings of Salvator Rosa.

R. 55; I.P. 19

CALAIS

The *French seaport in the Strait of *Dover has had a stormy history because it is the closest French soil to *England. Originally a fishing village, Calais was developed by the end of the tenth century A.D. and fortified by the end of the thirteenth. *Edward III of England besieged Calais for a year starting in 1346, at the end of which time famine had reduced it crucially. The famous six burghers, with halters around their necks, then surrendered themselves as hostages, to save their fellow citizens. They are memoralized in an elaborate piece of statuary by Auguste Rodin (first exhibited in *Paris in 1889). The French regained control of Calais in the mid-sixteenth century and, except for a brief *Spanish occupation, retained it during M.'s lifetime. In 1805, a large *Napoleonic force was camped there.

M. 4; W. 68; M.D. 60; I.P. 6; I.P. 7; I.P. 12

CALCULATING MACHINE

Man's earliest attempt to simplify calculation was probably the abacus. It was not replaced until the seventeenth century, when new physical science theories suggested more sophistication. John Napier simplified multiplication by inventing logarithms, the mechanization of which led to analog or measurement machines. In 1642, *Blaise Pascal invented the forerunner of digital machines which count integers, and in 1671, Gottfried Wilhelm *Leibniz invented a multiplying machine. The late nineteenth century saw the development of

compact machines that performed all basic arithmetical procedures and stored results.
M. 161

CALCUTTA
*India's largest city and chief commercial port, Calcutta
is the capital of West *Bengal, in the *Ganges Delta on the left
bank of the Hooghly River, seventy miles north of the Bay of
Bengal. It was the capital of *British India from 1773 to 1912
(replaced by *Delhi.)
The "Black Hole of Calcutta" was located at the original
Fort William (built in 1696; replaced in 1773). It was a notorious guardroom eighteen feet long by not quite fifteen feet wide.
On 20 June 1756, Siraj-ud-daula, the nawab of Bengal, captured the fort, including almost an entire British garrison. It
is traditionally claimed that 146 British soldiers were placed
under arrest in the "Black Hole," only twenty-three emerging
alive the following morning. (Some authorities believe that
some of the British died during the storming of the fort, rather
than in the notorious guardroom.) "Black Hole of Calcutta"
became the popular name for the punishment cell in British
military barracks.
The "Cheroots" of *R*. 9 are the famous square-ended cigars or cigarettes of Calcutta.
R. 1; R. 9; R. 12; R. 39; I.P. 25

CALEDONIAN
Caledonia was the *Roman name for the area of *Britain
north of the Firths of *Clyde and *Forth. It is used rhetorically
to refer to *Scotland, especially in poetry.
O. 61

CALENDS
From Lat. *calare*, to call: first day of *Roman month,
from practice of calling people together on this day to inform
them of data relative to the heavens and the festivals of the
month. By A.U.C. (*ab urbe condita or anno urbis conditae*:
founding of the city of Rome) in 450 (753 B.C.), the *fasti* (list of
events) or *calendar* was posted in writing, in public.
M. 80

CALENTURE
Franklin's notes to *C.M.*: "delirium characterized by
delusions; sailors, from heat or fatique, are sometimes seized

by a calenture which makes the sea seem an inviting meadow with fatal results."
C.M. 26

CALIBANS
     *Shakespeare's "Caliban" (in *The Tempest*) is "*Prospero's" slave: a deformed, half-human son of a devil and a witch. In colloquial usage, a rude, uncouth, anomalous person is a "Caliban."
M. 174

CALIF OF BAGDAD
     Penny Cyclopaedia (III, 1835) wrote of the then-current Caliph: "Ali Pash . . . brought to *Bagdad a very high reputation for talent and energy of character; but from mistaking his position, and from his ignorance of the character of the people with whom he has to deal, he has become highly unpopular."
W. 93

CALIFORNIA
     The thirty-first state was admitted to the Union in 1850. The "Golden State," or "Eldorado," is 770 miles long (N.-S.) and from 150 to 375 miles wide, with 1,200 miles of coastline. Its varied topography includes the active volcano Lassen Peak; Mount Whitney, 14,495 feet in altitude; Death Valley, 280 feet below sea level.
     Juan Rodríguez Cabrillo called the area "Alta California" in 1542, and *Drake visited in 1579, but California was not colonized until 1769—in the San Francisco area, where missionaries and traders lived a spartan and isolated existence. By 1845, the last *Mexican governor had been driven out, and in 1846 California became the Bear Flag Republic. After the *Mexican War (1848), it was ceded to the *United States. Gold was discovered that year, and by 1849 the rush was on to stake a claim. The transcontinental railroad reached California in 1869, but massive immigration did not begin until the 1880's.
     So California was still mostly undeveloped in 1860, when M. made his sole visit. He had sailed on 12 May, on *Meteor*, commanded by his brother Thomas Melville (1830-1884). They sailed around Cape *Horn and up the coast of three continents to San Francisco, arriving 12 October. M. remained only eight days, despite moderate "lionizing" by newspapers in the culturally starved city. He returned on *Cortes*, connecting with the (Vanderbilt) steamship *North Star*, which arrived in New York 12 November.
O. 54; O. 61; M.D. 111; C.M. 22

CALIFORNIA-SHELL
Probably a flat mollusc of the *Anomidiae* family, commonly known as a "Jingle Shell," which fixes itself to underwater objects as a barnacle does, growing quite large in the process.
W. 37

CALIGULA
Gaius Caesar (A.D. 12-41) succeeded *Tiberius as *Roman Emperor, in a reign so unpopular that historians cannot accurately portray it. The son of Germanicus and Agrippina and brother of *Nero and *Germanicus, he was called Caligula ("little boot") from infancy but later adopted his father's name, Gaius Caesar Germanicus.

As Emperor, he squandered funds, restored treason trials, and was despised for his capricious cruelty and licentious sexuality, shocking Rome by his relations with his sister, Drusilla. He was presumed mad as a result of illness early in his reign. He declared himself and his sister gods, but many acts ascribed to his madness are now presumed untrue, including the deification of his horse, mentioned in *M*. At the Palatine Games, he was murdered by a tribune participating in a conspiracy.
M. 149

CALLAO
A major *Pacific port, Callao is located at the base of a low peninsula seven miles west of *Lima, *Peru. It was founded in 1537 and attacked by *Drake (1578) and other *pirates; *Spain abandoned the port in 1826.

Callao was headquarters of the *United States *Navy Pacific *Squadron. M. arrived on *United States* on 28 December 1843 and departed on 3 January 1844, probably having had a forty-eight-hour shore liberty that took him to Lima. The ship returned to Callao on 6 June 1844, remaining until 6 July, with another twenty-four-hour shore leave. Thus M.'s specificities about the city, such as the road from Callao to Lima, are probably first-hand. The two cities are now connected by several wide boulevards and a railroad line.

*Stewart comments at length (I, Letter 1, 200-203) on the burial practices alluded to in *W*. 42, noting that of local inhabitants the bodies of the wealthy were cemented into a wall, while the poor were tossed over rear walls into a mass of earthquake ruins: "Heaps of skulls and broken skeletons . . . entire bodies, shrivelled and dried like a mummy . . . lie scattered abroad in sickening confusion and deformity!" *Wilkes

(I, p. 235) confirms this vision, having discussed the toleration of *Protestantism in Chile, and the interesting burying ground of "English men and Americans." (See also "Rio de Janeiro" for M.'s *W*. 63 reference to a cemetery there.)
O. 59; M. 32; R. 62; W. Passim; M.D. 54

CALMUC
    Calmucks (Kalmucks, Kalmyks) are a *Tartar tribe of *Mongolia. They are western nomads who in M.'s time had a complex hierarchical structure and a history of isolationism and war with Mongols to the east.
    Finkelstein suggests in *Melville's Orienda* (Chapter 5; "Tamerlane and the Tartars") that M. cites Calmucks (as well as *Scythians, *Huns, and Tartars) "to convey opulence, despotism, and unbridled wildness." She suggests that M. learned about the tribe from Jonas Hanway's *Journal of Travels* (4 vols., London, 1753), which includes details about Tartar idols similar to "*Yojo" in *M.D.*
    The Calmucks have a strictly patrilineal society, so M.'s using the epithet for the female "Annatoo" is not particularly apt.
M. 23; M. 28; M. 34

CALVINIST, BLUE LIGHT; CALVINISTIC
    M.'s expression in *W*. relates or equates religion and politics. "Blue-light" is a general term of abuse for those who are sneaky and sanctimonious, so called for the use of blue-flamed pyrotechnic lights (ordinarily to summon a pilot) by *Americans friendly to the *British in the *War of 1812.
    Calvinists, followers of the reformer, Jean Calvin (1509-1564), had developed rather a poor reputation by M.'s time, for their insistence upon strict adherence to some unpopular tenets: among them the total depravity of natural man; *predestination or particular election; scriptural authority; enforcement of the Church's discipline by the community.
R. 48; W. 12; P. 16:1

CAMBRIDGE
    The *English city (in the county and borough of the same name) is located c. fifty miles north of *London; it was the site of a *Roman fort, *Camboritum* (Lat. *Cantabrigia*), as well as the site of a castle of the *Norman *William the Conqueror. The university for which it is famed was established in the twelfth century. Among its most remarkable colleges are Peterhouse (1284), *Pembroke (1347), Trinity Hall (1350), Cor-

pus Christi (1352), King's (1441), Queens' (1448), Jesus (1496), Christ's (1505), St. John's (1511), Magdalene (1542), Trinity (1546), Emmanuel (John *Harvard's college, 1584), and two women's colleges established during M.'s lifetime: Girton (1869) and Newnham (1871).

"The Cambridge Guide . . . " of *R.* 30 has not been identified.   Thorp ("Redburn's Prosy Old Guidebook") discovered one possible candidate, with a rather different title: *The Cambridge Guide: Including Historical and Architectural Notices of the Public Buildings, and A Concise Account of the Customs and Ceremonies of The University. With a Sketch of the Places Most Worthy of Remark in the County* . . . Cambridge: . . . MDCCCXLV.
R. 30

CAMBRIDGE

The *American Cambridge is in Middlesex County, *Massachusetts, on the *Charles River, just north of *Boston. Settled in 1630, it was incorporated as a town in 1636 and as a city in 1846. *Washington took command here in 1775. Cambridge is the site of *Harvard, as well as of *Mount Auburn Cemetery. The reference to "Israel's" hospitalization here occurs in "*Israel Potter's autobiographical story."
I.P. 3

CAMBYSES

Two kings of ancient *Persia were named Cambyses. Most famous is Cambyses II, who reigned from 530 to 522 B.C. *Herodotus wrote of his invasion of *Egypt, accusing him of atrocities and madness, but later scholarship disproves this. A 1570 tragedy by Thomas Preston presents him as a loud and pompous character, but *Shakespeare probably originated his reputation as a drinker in *I Henry IV* (II, iv, 378-81), with "Falstaff": "Give me a cup of sack to make my eyes look red, that it may be thought I have wept; for I must speak in passion, and I will do it in King Cambyses' vein."
M. 84; M. 119; M.D. 45

CAMDEN

William Camden (1551-1623), *English antiquarian and historian, wrote *Britannia* (1586, 1607), the first topographical survey of England. After graduation from *Oxford, he became a headmaster in *London (and *Ben Jonson's teacher), but devoted himself to literature after publishing a Greek grammar (1595). After publishing various miscellaneous chronicles, he

abandoned plans for a general history of England for a history of the reign of *Queen Elizabeth I, two volumes of which were published. Camden wrote principally in *Latin, but there are many translations into English. He was the first to study the relation of place names to ancient languages. The Camden Society (1838; merged with the Royal Historical Society in 1897) was named after him.
M. 29

CAMOENS

Luis de Camöens (or Camões; 1524-80) was a *Portuguese poet whose widest fame rests on his (ten-canto, eight-line stanza) epic poem *Os Lusiades* (1572), which traces the history of Portugal and her heroes, including Vasco de *Gama. Camöens led an adventurous but unfortunate life; he was imprisoned, suffered shipwreck, and lost an eye in service against the *Moors. He died penniless in *Lisbon. M. probably indentified closely with Camöens; both men started life with all the bright optimism of youth and ended in dark *Solomonic wisdom. Like M.'s works, Camöens's epic is at once deeply symbolic and startlingly realistic in its portrayal of vicious Nature at work at sea. Among the scored lines in M.'s copy of Camöens's Sonnet VI is:

My senses lost, misjudging men declare,
And Reason banish'd from her mental throne,
Because I shun the crowd, and dwell alone.

There are numerous translations of the *Lusiad*, including *Mickle's 1776 (heroic couplet) version, mentioned in *W.* 65. M.'s early reading of Camöens remains a mystery. It is not known whether a copy was on board *United States* (*W.*), but *Blair's *Lectures*, which was highly critical (along with *Voltaire and others), made part of the ship's library. M.'s annotated copy (Sealts #116), in the *Strangford translation (1824 edition), was acquired in 1867. But there is much internal evidence throughout the canon to suggest that M. knew the work well, early on. He was still thinking of the Portuguese poet late in life; in *Billy Budd, Sailor* (Chapter 8) he refers to Camöens's "*Spirit of the Cape." M. also wrote a poem, "Camoens."

(A useful list of articles on M. and Camöens is in Monteiro's "Melville and Camões: A Working Bibliography."
W. 4; W. 65; W. 74; W. 93

CAMPAGNA

The Campagna di Roma, the lowland surrounding *Rome, is an area of volcanic sediments, traversed by the *Tiber River. The once-fertile lowland deteriorated because of over-grazing of sheep. It was "accursed," as M. says in *M.D.* 96, as a malarial swamp and was abandoned until the late nineteenth century, when restoration began.

M. arrived in Rome (24? February 1857) via the Alban Hills boundary on the southeast of Rome: the most notorious section of the Campagna. On 20 March, he traveled across it on the northeast, passing Lake *Tartarus and the Villa of *Hadrian, enroute to *Tivoli. He left Rome the following day, crossing again on the northwest.

M.D. 96

CAMPANELLA

Tommaso Campanella (1568-1639) was an *Italian utopian philosopher. Born Giovan Domenico Campanella, he assumed the name of Tommaso upon entering the Dominican Order. An upstart in theology, he encountered lifelong difficulty: trial, imprisonment and tortures resulted from charges of heresy, sodomy, disputation with *Jews. Imprisoned for life for political sedition, he reverted to acceptance of *Catholic dogma, producing his *La Città del Sole*, a utopian work, as well as madrigal lyrics and sonnets. His most important work is the *Metafisica*, an eighteen-book treatise, followed by the *Theologia* of thirty books. Released from prison, Campanella fled to *France, welcomed by Louis XIII (see "Bourbon") and Richelieu; he died in *Paris.

R. 49

CAMPBELL CLAN OF EDITORS

The "Campbell clan" of *P.* 17:1 is perhaps symbolic of *Scots in general. But the allusion to Campbells as "editors" probably has other significance, given "Pierre's" literary aspirations. Thomas Campbell (1777-1844) was an immensely popular writer of sentimental and martial lyrics—all rather derivative of *Pope and others, and all an attempt at perfection of form, with content of less interest. His ballads include "Lord Ullin's Daughter," and "Lochiel's Warning." His most famous war songs are "Ye Mariners of England," "The Battle of Hohenlinden," and "The Battle of the *Baltic."

Or M. is perhaps alluding to the vastly influential "Scottish School" of rhetoricians that stressed correctness—best represented by *Blair's Lectures, derided in *W.* 41.

A last but still strong possibility, given "Pierre's" religious problems, is that the allusion refers to the Campbellites—a Scottish cult following John McLeod Campbell (1800-72), which accepted the universality of the atonement. In the *United States, the Disciples of *Christ, founded in *Pennsylvania in 1809 by Thomas and Alexander Campbell, were called Campbellites (or New Lights). They rejected creeds, practiced immersion, and focused closely on the *Bible.
P. 17:1

CAMPEACHY
The state of Campeche, on the western Yucatan peninsula of *Mexico, is a collection center for mahogany and other woods, including cedar, logwood, dyewood, and *lignum vitae* (important in maritime uses). It ships these by river to Carmen, which exports them. The old (1540) colonial town of Campeche is also famous for trade in hides, cigars, and cigarettes.
R. 33

CANAAN
Canaan is the ancestor of the Canaanites (*Genesis 10:15-19, I *Chronicles 1:13-16). He was perhaps the son of Ham (therefore grandfather of *Noah), or perhaps the youngest son of Noah and brother to *Shem and Japheth. The nation of Canaan in pre-Israelite times contained the area of *Palestine west of the *Jordan and the part of *Syria called *Phoenicia by the *Greeks. The Canaanites occupying the area at the time of the Israelite invasion were Bronze-Age worshippers of *Baal and their king was Baal's representative. ("Canaan" probably means "merchant.")
M.D. 6; M.D. 22; P. 2:4; I.P. 25

CANADA; CANADIAN
The area to the north of the mainland *United States (and east of Alaska) was visited by the *Vikings c. A.D. 1000. The *British explorer John Cabot made a brief stop in 1497, but the *French (including Jacques Cartier in 1546) fully explored the territory, planting the French culture that continues to the present day in much of Canada. Champlain began the first European settlement in 1604, at Port Royal (now Annapolis, *Nova Scotia); *Quebec was founded in 1608. France established Royal Government in 1663, but by the eighteenth century the British were holding the *St. Lawrence valley, and in 1759

Quebec fell to the forces of James Wolfe, defeating those of Montcalm. *Montreal fell in 1760, and British rule was established in 1763.

British loyalists fled to Canada during the *American Revolution, exacerbating boundary disputes in the *Great Lakes area which were not settled until the *War of 1812. Thereafter, Canada was plagued by internal struggle between the North West Company and Hudson's Bay Company. The amalgamation of the two in 1821 contributed to the unification (c. 1849) of what had been in effect two Canadas: Lower (present-day Quebec area) and Upper (present-day *Ontario area). *Newfoundland and *Labrador became provinces at this time, making a total of ten very distinct provinces by 1864. (The others are *New Brunswick, Prince Edward Island, Quebec, Ontario, Manitoba, Saskatchewan, Alberta, and British Columbia.) North of the provinces are Yukon and Northwest Territories. Canada gained autonomy in 1867, although the British sovereign remains nominal head of government.

Throughout Canada, native Indian culture has had much influence (along with French and British) because Canadian settlers did not follow the drastic policies which in the United States amounted to extermination. *M.D.* 14 alludes to the fact that from c. 1837 (MacKenzie insurrections) to 1846 (Oregon treaty with Britain), Americans talked of annexing Canada.

The newlywed Melvilles traveled to Montreal and Quebec on their honeymoon in August of 1847. M. *lectured in Montreal 10 December 1857.

M. 19; R. 33; R. 34; R. 43; M.D. 14; M.D. 105; P. 5:1; I.P. 2; I.P. 16; C.M. 3 (and elsewhere)

CANALLERS
    See "Erie Canal."
M.D. 54

CANARIES, THE
    The volcanic Islas Canarias, a *Spanish-ruled *Atlantic Ocean archipelago 67 miles from the *African coast (29°09' N.; 17°30' W.), were visited by the *Romans about 40 B.C., as noted by *Plutarch and *Pliny. In 1833 and 1834, the Canary Islands were linked by cable to Europe and the Americas.
M. 181

CANARIS

In the war of Greek independence (1821-29), the *Greeks used fire ships against the *Turks. Constantine Kanaris, stationed at Hydra, destroyed the Turkish flagship by this means in 1822.
M.D. 96

CANCER
See "Zodiac."
M. 169; M.D. 99

CANT LANGUAGE

In underworld parlance, cant may simply mean "talk." It can refer to secret underworld language or to empty, meaningless speech. A seondary meaning is "portion," or "share."
See "Flash."
P. 16:3; C.M. 15

CANTERBURY; CANTERBURY CATHEDRAL

Canterbury is a city and county borough and an archdiocese of the *Church of England, in *Kent. It was occupied long before the *Roman period and is most famous for the Cathedral, originally built between 1070 and 1089. The tombs of many historical figures are contained in the richly-decorated 522-foot-long, 235-foot-high cathedral.

The inside of the church is different from most British cathedrals in that the choir and nave are separated not merely by a screen but by a flight of steps, the two being on different levels.

M. called the church "the most remarkable in England" (*Journal*, 5 November 1849).
W. 14; M.D. 16; C.M. 2

CANTERBURY PILGRIMS
See "Chaucer" and "Canterbury Cathedral."
C.M. 2

CANTERBURY TALES
See "Chaucer" and "Canterbury Cathedral."
W. 86

CANTON

Canton, *China (Kwangchow, or Kuangchou) is a port in the southern part of the nation, on the *Canton River. A part of China since the third century B.C., Canton was the first Chinese port regularly visited by European traders, in the tenth century; the name became corrupted at that time. By the eighteenth century, there were *British, *Dutch, and *French factories. Chinese-British incidents of 1841 and 1856 led to the first and second Opium Wars; Canton was occupied by the British and French, 1856-61. It was surpassed as a port by *Hong Kong, in the second half of the nineteenth century.
R. 9; R. 12; R. 50; W. 26

CANTON RIVER

The Canton (Yueh Kiang, or Yueh Chiang) River of *China flows for 110 miles, becoming the Pearl River at the east side of the Canton River delta. It is the main navigational link of *Canton to *Hong Kong and the sea.
W. 8

CANUTE, KING

Son of Sweyn, king of *Denmark, Canute (Cnut, or Knut) accompanied his father on the successful expedition to gain control of *Britain (1013). For many years Canute struggled with England's king *Aethelred and his son, Edmond Ironside, losing control rapidly, and regaining it in 1015. By 1017, he was accepted as king of all England and, to solidify his power, married Emma of *Normandy, Aethelred's widow, and raised Aethelred's children. Despite constant internal strife between England's counties, Canute's rule was good. He did not impose Danish culture, supported the Church, and made a pilgrimage to *Rome at least once. At his death (1035), he was king of Denmark, *Norway, and England (including *Scotland) and held in universal esteem.

Legend tells that Canute one day in public commanded the sea not to wet him, so as to demonstrate to admirers the futility of human pretense to power.
M. 119; W. 46

CAPE BLANCO

Northwest *Peru's Cabo Blanco is located on the *Pacific Ocean, north of Restin, twenty-three miles north of Talara (4°15'S., 81°15'W.). Its port is a village called Cabo Blanco, Piura Department.
O. 52

CAPE CLEAR

Cape Clear is at the most southerly point of *Ireland, on the *Atlantic Ocean (51°24' N., 9°15' W.). Although there is no record of M.'s first voyage (on *St. Lawrence*, probable prototype of *R*.'s "*Highlander"), we may presume that he sailed past the Cape enroute to *Liverpool in 1839.
R. 23; R. 51; R. 58

CAPE COD

The Cape Cod peninsula (broken by a canal completed in 1914) is an arm-shaped sandy headland of glacial origin, sixty-five miles long and from one- to twenty-miles wide. At the arm's "elbow" is Chatham; at the northern tip is Province-town (Race Point). Cape Cod is bounded by Cape Cod Bay (N. and W.), Buzzards Bay (S.W.), *Vineyard and *Nantucket Sounds (S.), and the *Atlantic (E.). The *Puritan settlers dropped anchor here in 1620.

In July of 1852, M. traveled with his father-in-law, *Lemuel Shaw, from Falmouth to Sandwich (both on the western edge), via the Cape Cod Railroad.
R. 59; W. 29; M.D. 16

CAPE COD MAN

*R.H. Dana claimed in *Two Years Before the Mast* that a "Cape-Cod man" might be from any part of the *Massachusetts coast south of *Boston.
M.D. 27; M.D. 28

CAPE DE VERDES; CAPE DE VERD ISLANDS

See "Cape Verde . . . . "
O. 12; W. 12; M.D. 51

CAPE GIRARDEAU; CAPE GIRADEAU

Cape Girardeau, *Missouri, is c. 140 miles down the *Mississippi from *St. Louis, and c. 50 miles upriver from *Cairo, *Illinois.
C.M. 21; C.M. 22

CAPE HORN

References to Cape *Horn in the first third of *M.D.* should be read figuratively. The "*Pequod" actually sails around the Cape of *Good Hope.
M.D. Passim

"CAPE HORN FEVER"
A malingerer's imaginary disease, most prevalent in bad weather.
W. 77

CAPELLA
The sixth brightest star, in the *constellation Auriga.
M. 136

CAPES
In *M.D.*, Cape *Horn and the Cape of *Good Hope.
M.D. 22

CAPE TORMENTOTO
*Bartholomew Diaz discovered what he called *Cabo tormentoso* (Tempestuous Cape) in 1486. The *Portuguese *King John renamed it the Cape of *Good Hope, anticipating its role in trade with the Indies.
In the *Lusiad*, *Camöens called it *Cabo Torment rio*.
M.D. 51

CAPE VERDE; CAPE DE VERDES; CAPE DE VERD ISLANDS
The crescent-shaped Ilhas do Cabo Verde archipelago, owned by *Portugal, is from 300 to 450 miles west of West *Africa's Cape Verde. It is approximately 170 miles long (N-S) and 180 miles wide (E-W), at 14°48'-17°12' N., 22°52'-25°22' W. There is one active volcano (on Fogo Island) and some earthquake activity (including a severe disturbance in 1847). The partially inhabited islands, probably discovered in the 1450's, are an important stopping-off point between Africa and *South America. They were central to the Portuguese West Africa *slave trade, which was administered from the islands until 1879.
O. 12; R. 12; W. 12; M.D. 51

CAPRAEAE
The rocky island of Capri, in southern *Italy opposite the Sorrento peninsula and near the southeast entrance to the Bay of *Naples, is a mere three and three-quarters miles long and one-half to one-and three-quarters miles wide. It has a tall peak (Monte Solaro, 1,932 feet) which is the center of its picturesque scenery. The Blue Grotto, rediscovered in 1826, is its

most famous wave-cut cave. An important tourist lure since ancient times, Capri has ruins of villas constructed by *Augustus and *Tiberius, the latter of which used it as a hideaway for sexual misconduct, according to *Suetonius.
R. 46; R. 55

CAPRICORN SOLSTICE
    See "Zodiac."
M. 108

CAPRICORNUS
    See "Zodiac."
M. 95; M.D. 99

CAPTAIN CLARET
    The name suggests M.'s intention to portray a type rather than an individual. Captain of *United States for part of the cruise covered in W. was James Armstrong, whose reputation did not include charges of alcoholism. Admiral Franklin (p. 18) remembers Armstrong as a "stalwart *Kentuckian, about six feet tall and large in proportion . . . the grotesqueness of his whole appearance made an impression upon my youthful mind which has never been effaced." Franklin further notes (p. 65) Armstrong's "very red face."
W. Passim

CAPTAIN EZEKIEL HARDY
    See "Whaleman's Chapel."
M.D. 7

CAPTAIN PORTER
    See "Porter."
T. 4

CAPTAIN SLEET
    M.'s parodic name for Captain William Scoresby, Sr. (father of the author of An Account of the Arctic Regions, an important source for M.D.), who made thirty successful *Arctic voyages without losing a ship. He invented numerous devices to improve nautical life and improved the "crow's nest," inspiring much levity on M.'s part, especially in M.D. 35.

See also "Scoresby."
M.D. 35

CAPULET
    In *Shakespeare's *Romeo and Juliet*, the noble family
(Cappelletti) of "Juliet": opposed to the *Montagues.
P. 1:6

CARAMBA!
    *Spanish interjection of surprise or annoyance.
M.D. 43

CARA-SPOSA
    It.: "dear wife."
O. 80

CARDAN
    Geronimo (or Girolamo) Cardano (1501-1576), or
"Jerome Cardan," was an *Italian physician, mathematician,
and astrologer. His fame as a teacher and physician grew
through the support of prominent friends (such as *Leonardo
da Vinci) and through his cures and discoveries in mathematics and medicine. He published many works, achieving stature
in his profession and with the public, but he was arrested for
heresy in 1570 for his claim to have a familiar spirit who revealed to him the secrets of nature.
P. 21:3

CARDAN, CAPTAIN
    See "*Macedonian*, the."
W. 74

CARDINAL VIRTUES
    The "natural" virtues of justice, prudence, temperance,
and fortitude, upon which all other virtues depend, as distinguished from the "theological" virtues: faith, hope, and charity.
P. 15:1

CARDS

Playing cards were known in *China as early as A.D. 969 and in Europe by the thirteenth century. The earliest European elaborately hand-painted cards were too costly for general use, but when they became more accessible, what had been for *Catholics a superstitious but harmless pastime was deemed by *Puritans "the devil's picture books" and forbidden. (M. was a devotee of whist.)
W. 46

CARET

Father François d'Assisi Caret was the superior of *Father Murphy in the South Seas. Forsythe's "Herman Melville's Father Murphy" examines his missionary career in the south seas in the 1830's. Caret is known to have worked for the Roman *Catholic missions at *Valparaiso, the *Gambier Islands, and *Tahiti (where he was arrested and expelled in 1836). Caret's station was at Vapou (*Society Islands); he died in the Gambier Islands in 1844.
O. 32

CARIBBEAN

The Caribbean Sea of the *Atlantic Ocean lies between the northern coast of *South America (S.), the archipelago of the *West Indies (N. and E.), and Central America (W.). It is c. 1,800 miles long and c. 900 miles wide at its maximum. The low-salinity transparently blue sea was named for the Carib Indians (who drove the Arawaks out of the Lesser *Antilles). *Columbus sailed it in 1492 (as well as in 1502), and it eventually became a haven for smugglers and *pirates.
Passim

CARMELITES

See "White Friar."
M. 83

CAROLINA, THE

Carolina was a small *American schooner that participated in the attack that destroyed Barataria, the lair of *pirate Jean Lafitte, in 1814 at *New Orleans. She was blown up by the *British in December of that year.
See also "North Carolina, The."
M. 28

CAROLINA; CAROLINA-MOSS

M. does not distinguish between the states of North and South Carolina, both of which were part of the original thirteen-state Union and both of which were important in the *slavery question. North Carolina (503 miles east-to-west and 188 miles north-to-south) was explored by Verrazano in 1524; by the 1650's *Virginia colonials had permanently settled the area. The Indians were pushed out in the eighteenth century. South Carolina (250 miles northwest-to-southeast and 100-200 miles in width) was unsuccessfully colonized by the *Spanish in 1526. DeSoto explored it in 1540. The *English gained control and by 1680 had founded *Charleston. South Carolina was the center of the nullification (see "Nulli") controversy of 1832, when secession was avoided, but it was the first state to secede in 1860. The attack on Fort Sumter opened the *Civil War; Sherman laid waste to South Carolina in 1865.

"Carolina-moss" is *pogonatum pensilvanicum*, which produces felt-like mats; it slows erosion in the Great Smoky and Blue Ridge *Appalachian mountains.

See also "Catawba"; "Dismal Swamp."
R. 31; C.M. 17

CAROLUS DOLLARS

Gold coins issued during the reign of *Charles I; worth 20-30 shillings. Carolus dollars are not likely to turn "green," as M. claims.
M. 19

CARRICKFERGUS

The seaport of *Ireland nine and one half miles north of *Belfast derives its name from "rock of Fergus"; he was a king shipwrecked off the coast in the fourth century A.D. Carrick-fergus Castle had had a stormy public history as a refuge for *Protestants, even before *John Paul Jones on *Ranger* defeated the *British *Drake* off its shores in 1778, adding to its fame.
I.P. 16; I.P. 17

CARRISBROOK WELL

The 160-foot deep well of Carisbrooke Castle, Isle of Wight.
P. 9:2

CARROL GROUND
    Feidelson's map in the 1964 edition of *M.D.* locates the Carroll Ground off the coast of southwestern *Africa (c. 25°S., 15°E.).
    (There is a Carrol Inlet of Bellinghausen Sea, *Antarctica, at 73°15' S., 79° W.)
M.D. 51

CARRON
    Scotland: 57°25' N.; 5°25' W.
W. 16

CARSON, KIT
    Christopher (Kit) Carson (1809-68), frontiersman, U.S. Indian Agent, and soldier, was born in *Kentucky and raised on the *Missouri frontier, remaining illiterate until late in life. At fifteen, he ran away from an apprenticeship to become a *Santa Fe Trail guide. He made his most permanent home in Taos, New Mexico, where he hunted to supply a trading post. Carson become the guide for Frémont's Western expeditions. He aided the U.S. in the *Mexican War and the Union forces in the *Civil War, becoming brevet Brigadier General of New Mexican volunteers.
    Legends about him have continued to grow, even in the 20th century, in such works as Willa Cather's *Death Comes for the Archbishop*. His former home in Taos has become a popular museum.
M.D. 82

CARTHAGE
    Tradition makes *Dido the Founder of Carthage. In the ninth century B.C., *Phoenicians from *Tyre formed a city/state on the north shore of *Africa, on the Gulf of Tunis. The name "Carthage" is from the *Latin *Carthago* (or *Cartago*), derived from the Phoenician word for "new city."
    By the sixth century, Carthage had great seapower and control over much of the *Mediterranean. Rivalry with *Rome led to the *Punic Wars, in the first of which (264-241 B.C.), Carthage lost *Sicily but won part of *Spain. In the second (218-201 B.C.), *Hannibal was defeated by the Roman generals *Fabius and Scipio Africanus Major. In the third (149-146 B.C.), the Romans achieved cessation of Carthaginian power and razing of the city.
    *Julius Caesar founded a colony on the site which was further developed by *Augustus. From A.D. 439 to 533, it was

the capital of the *Vandals. *Belisarius captured it for the
*Byzantine Empire in 533 but immediately lost it again.
Carthage was finally destroyed by *Arabs in 698. There are
few remains of the ancient city in what is now merely a mod-
ern suburb of Tunis.
M.D. 2

CARYATIDE, --S
     Figures of *Greek-costumed women, used in architec-
ture to support entablatures. The custom began when Praxite-
les used them to perpetuate the memory of the women cast into
slavery at *Thermopylae when Caryae in Laconia sided with
the *Persians.
     Similar figures of men are called Atlantes, after Atlas,
or Telamones, after Telamon, the father of Ajax and a hero of
the Calydonian hunt and expedition of the Argonauts (See
"Jason").
     It is presumed that M. saw the Caryatid of the British
Museum's *Elgin collection when he visited in 1849.
O. 29; R. 46; M.D. 41

CASE, THE
     *Beale provides a gloss (pp. 25-26) on the whale's
"Case":

> In the right side of the nose, and upper surface of
> the head, is a large, almost triangular-shaped
> cavity. . . lined with a beautiful glistening mem-
> brane, and covered by a thick layer of muscular fi-
> bres and small tendons, running in various
> directions, and finally united by common
> integuments . . . . secreting and containing an oily
> fluid, which, after death, concretes into a
> granulated substance of a yellowish colour, the
> spermaceti . . . . it not infrequently contains a ton,
> or more than ten large barrels.

M.D. 77

CASKS
     "Old Casks," the innkeeper of *P.* 11:4, is appropriately
named. The barrels in which alcoholic beverages were stored
had evolved by M.'s time from their original purpose into important features of pub decor. Constructed of somewhat porous
woods suitable for the liquors contained, and sometimes

charred on the inside to flavor the contents, casks were elaborately painted, varnished, and labeled with beverage names or advertisements as well as gallon capacity, and arranged in long rows, as shown in *Cruikshanks's "Gin Shop" series. Champion of the large casks was probably the *Heidelburgh Tun, but large numbers of smaller casks were probably just as inspirational to the serous drinker.
P. 11:4

CASSANDRA
      In *Shakespeare's *Troilus and Cressida*, a prophetess and daughter of King *Priam of *Troy. In the *Greek mythological original, she is the daughter of *Hecuba and Priam who spurns the advances of *Apollo. Apollo punishes her by preventing belief in her invariably correct prophecies.
C.M. 17

CASSIOPEIA
      In astronomy, a northern *constellation recognized by five stars forming the letter "W"; source of the most brilliant nova on record (observed by Tycho Brahe in 1572). It is named for the vain mother of *Andromeda, in the *Perseus story.
M. 151; M. 175

CASSOWARIES
      See "Sandwiches"; "Casuarinas."
M. 132

CASTILIAN
      Castile is a region and former kingdom in north and central *Spain extending from the *Bay of Biscay south to Sierra Morena, *Andalusia: elevated plains flanked by mountain ranges. The name probably derives from the castles erected by *Christians against the *Moors. The Sierra de Guadarrama mountains separate its two portions: "Old Castile," referring to the original kingdom of Castile proper, and "New Castile" referring to the area added from the Moorish kingdom of *Toledo after the eleventh century. Old Castile was originally part of the kingdom of Leon and was autonomous until 1029 when Sancho III of Navarre subsumed it, passing it on to his son Ferdinand I in 1035. The two areas officially merged in 1230 under Ferdinand III, evolving under Ferdinand and *Isabella, representing the union of Aragon and Castile.

Philip II moved the capital to *Madrid, and Castile be-
came the center of the monarchy. The highly traditional
Castilian people thought of themselves as the true representa-
tives of Spain, and their martial spirit assured the spread of
Castilian culture. The Castilian dialect became the official
Spanish language, and by the *Middle Ages Castile meant
"Hispania." M. uses the word to signify pure Spanish blood or
royalty.
W. 83; W. 85

CASTLE GARDEN
        The circular Castle Garden was constructed from the
incomplete and abandoned foundations of an old fort (Castle
Clinton; begun c. 1790) at the *Battery, the extreme southern
end of *Manhattan. The land was extended to accommodate
the structure. In 1820 it was converted into an assembly room
and opera house seating from six to eight thousand persons. It
became a fashionable center of "high" and "popular" culture
(*Lafayette was feted at Castle Garden in 1824; Jenny Lind
sang here in 1850: under the sponsorship of Barnum).
        The 1854 opening of the Academy of Music (Fourteenth
Street) ended Castle Garden's use as an entertainment center,
and it thereafter served as a landing place for immigrants
(until 1890. Under the *New York Department of Parks it has
survived as an aquarium, a cultural center, etc.). The Castle
Garden area became a dangerous locale, with cheap lodging-
houses and low taverns by the mid-nineteenth century.
R. 60

CASTLE GREEN
        At *Pendennis Castle.
I.P. 22

CASTLE STREET
        A principal *Liverpool street from early times, Castle
was wide at the northernmost point and narrow at its southern
terminus at Castle moat. St. George's Castle had been torn
down in 1786 and *St. George's Church erected on the site. By
M.'s time, Castle Street's medieval houses had been supplanted by commercial establishments.
R. 31

CASTOR AND POLLUX

Types of inseparable identical twin-ship: In *Roman mythology, the twin sons of *Jupiter and *Leda. (Accounts are contradictory; the most commonly accepted are given here.) When Jupiter visited in the form of a swan, two of Leda's eggs were fertilized, the one yielding Castor and Clytemnestra and the other Pollux and Helen.

Known as the Dioscuri ("stripplings of Zeus"), Castor and Pollux had many adventures, including sailing with *Jason for the Golden Fleece. They were worshipped as gods and finally placed among the constellations as the *Gemini. Pollux proved his devotion upon Castor's death; when he prayed to die himself, Zeus allowed Castor to share Pollux's life, so that both lived. They were never separate again, whether living in *Hades or on *Olympus.

The two are special protectors of sailors, associated with St. Elmos's fire (*corpusants); when there are two or more flames the twins are present and the storm will soon end.

In astronomy, they are the brightest stars in the *constellation Gemini; Castor is a system of at least six stars; Pollux is a reddish giant.
M. 149; R. 53

CASUARINAS

The casuarina derives its name from the *Malay *Kasuari*: cassowary (see "Sandwiches"). It has twigs similar to the bird's feathers and is found especially in *Australia.

(In "flower language" it signifies Death, Mourning, Extinguished Hope.)
M. 116

CATACOMBS

Subterranean burial vaults, especially in *Rome. Although they were in use in the third and fourth Centuries, the word was not used until about the fifth Century, in connection with St. Sebastian's cemetery on the Appian Way: the *Coemeterium Catacumbas*. The *Christians used them also for meetings; they were mostly destroyed by the *Goths and *Lombards, were rediscovered in 1578, revealed by a landslide.
M. 123; R. 31; P. 12:3; C.M. 36

CATACOMBS, PARIS

The labyrinthine catacombs of *Paris extend for several miles, from the Jardin des Plantes on the eastern Left Bank to Porte de *Versailles and into the suburbs on the western. They

are a tourist attraction, with an entrance near the Observatoire.
R. 46

CATAWBA
Longfellow's poem, "Catawba Wine," celebrates the wine produced in the picturesque Catawba River area of North and South *Carolina, home of the Catawba Indians.
C.M. 30

CATEGUT
The Kattegat Straits connect the *Baltic with the North Sea between *Sweden and *Jutland, a *Danish province; whaling has occurred here since ancient times.
M.D. 16 (Categut); M.D. 40 (Cattegut)

CATHARINE MARKET
Catherine Market was located at the intersection of Catherine and Cherry Streets, in *Manhattan. (Catherine Street runs E.-W. from the *East River to *Chatham Square: the present-day Cherry Street runs N.-S. from Catherine to Montgomery Street, picking up again briefly at *Corlaers Hook Park. It originally ran south to the *Battery area.)
R. 5; R. 18

CATHAY, --S
Cathay was the medieval name for *China, derived from *Kitan (Khitan), or Kitai: founders of the Liao dynasty (937-1125) of northern China. The name remained in poetic usage.
M. 13; M. 173; W. 76

CATHEDRAL OF PAPOAR
The Royal Mission Chapel of Papaoa (*Papoar).
O. 44

CATHOLIC, --S; CATHOLIC CHURCH; ROMAN CATHOLIC, --S
Like most *Americans of his time, M. rather feared the Catholic Church and what it appeared to stand for. Along with "Nativists" who were openly against admission into the country of any more *foreigners, M. identified the Catholic Church with more than those problems that had brought about

*Luther's defection and the *Protestant Reformation. Exami-
nation of his allusions shows much concern about things
"Romish" (*M.D.* 54); Catholics were believed to be superstitious "vassals" (*M.* 114) of a hypocritical and secretive hierarchy headed by a *Pope descended from a long line of military
men (such as the *Holy Roman Emperors), or corrupt and
greedy "princes" exempt from the rules they imposed. Convents were brothels serving decadent priests: Bishops and
*Archbishops were political climbers.

In M.'s view, "The Church" (in *O.* 80) or "Mother
Church" (*W.* 42) denied the very principles of liberty and
democracy upon which America was founded. It worshipped
statues and relics and cherished impossible beliefs such as
transubstantiation and the virginity of Mary, the mother of
*Jesus ("the Virgin" in *O.* 45; "Holy Mary" in *R.* 35; "Mary
Queen of Heaven" in *P.* 2:2). The Catholic Church was responsible for the actions of the Conquistadors and for conversion of
peoples through fear. Catholic countries such as *France
*Spain, and *Ireland come in for their share of contempt
throughout the works, perhaps for their association with the
Church.

(Billington's *The Protestant Crusade* enlarges upon
nineteenth-century America's view of Roman Catholicism.)
See also "Jesuit."
Passim

CATNIP

Nepeta cataria: a member of the mint family with
downy leaves and bluish flowers. It has a narcotic effect on
cats.
P. 25:4

CATO

Cato the Younger, in *Plutarch's *Lives*, read *Plato's
Phaedo, about immortality, before killing himself to avoid capture by *Caesar; he was not depressed, as *M.D.*'s "*Ishmael"
is.
M.D. 1

CATSKILL

The Catskill (or, in *R.* 27, "Kaatskill") Mountains are a
range of the *Appalachians in southeastern *New York,
mainly in Greene and Ulster Counties. They are for the most
part rolling wooded hills averaging 3,000 feet in altitude, with
some deep gorges and picturesque waterfalls. Highest is Slide

Mountain (4,204 feet), eighteen miles west of Kingston. Hunter
Mountain (4,025 feet) is nineteen miles west of Catskill village
on the *Hudson, and thirty miles south of *Albany. Catskill
reservoirs supply some of *New York City's water. Irving's
"Rip Van Winkle" is set in the Catskills, which, in M.'s time,
were still relatively undeveloped and safe for the "Catskill eagle" of *M.D.* 96.
M.D. 96

CATTEGUT
     Kattegat Strait is an arm of the *North Sea between
*Sweden and *Jutland, *Denmark. It is 137 miles long, from
thirty-seven to 100 miles wide, and has several islands.
("Categut" in *M.D.* 16.)
M.D. 40

CATULLUS
     Gaius Valerius Catullus (c. 84- c. 54 B.C.) wrote love po-
ems, elegies, and satires which were unknown until the four-
teenth century. His work influenced that of *Jonson, Herrick,
Lovelace, and Tennyson, and was translated in part by Leigh
Hunt.
P. 17:2

CAUCASIAN
     In general, white-skinned. See also "foreigners"; "Cau-
casus."
W. 90; C.M. 22

CAUCASUS
     Caucasus (Kavkaz) refers to the mountain chain or to
the area in which it is found in what is now the Soviet Union
(43°20' N.; 42°00' E.), an extensive area ranging from Kuban
and Terek on the north, to the frontiers of *Turkey and Iran on
the south, and from the *Black Sea on the west, to the Caspian
Sea on the east. Inhabited from ancient times, it is an area of
rich mixed culture, with some fine early architecture. It has
traditionally been the route of nomads and a gateway of migration, so that today one finds the area inhabited by at least fifty
different peoples. During M.'s time, the Caucasus was still
resisting *Russian rule (not fully in place until 1864). In legend, the Caucasus mountains are the setting for the punishment of *Prometheus and the voyage of the Argonauts (see
"Jason" and "Colchis.")
M. 168

CAUL
A membrane surrounding the heads of some infants at birth: from early antiquity esteemed a good omen and a preservative against drowning.
W. 8

CAVALIERS
The original cavaliers (Fr. *chevaliers*) were the equestrian body guard of *Charles I: horse-soldiers, knights, and gentlemen *Tories, politically opposed to *Whig "Roundheads."
They were known, as M. notes in W. 84, for their long ringleted hair and their ornate costumes: full breeches, lace-collared jerkins, buckle-topped cuffed boots, and large-brimmed hats with sizable feathers.
W. 84; W. 87

CAYENNE
The capital of French Guiana (4°56' N., 52°18' W.) was founded in 1643. A poor port, located at the estuaries of the Cayenne and Mahoury rivers, Cayenne was long used by the French as a penal colony.
M. 40

CELLINI
Benvenuto Cellini (1500-1571) was an *Italian sculptor, goldsmith, and autobiographer who led an adventurous and sometimes violent life between commissions by important rulers: Clement VII in *Rome, Cosimo de' Medici in *Florence, François I in *France. Cellini's best known work, unveiled in 1554, was a bronze statue of *Perseus holding the head of *Medusa. The statue, in the Loggia dei Lanzi, Florence, was allegedly made for the *Medici, who claimed descent from Perseus. M. saw it on 24 March 1857. In his *lecture, "Statues in Rome," he called the statue an "astonishing conception, conceived in the fiery brain of the intense artist and brought to perfection as a bronze cast in the midst of flames which had overshot their aim." As Merton Sealts points out (*Melville as Lecturer*, 147), M. refers in *M.D.* 27 to Cellini's account of creating the statue while he had a high fever.
M.D. 27

CELSUS

Aurelius [Aulus] Cornelius Celcus (fl. c. 14-37), "the *Cicero of physicians," wrote treatises of many kinds, especially on medicine and surgery, most notably *De Medicina*, among the earliest works of its kind in *Roman literature.
W. 63

CENCI

See "Guido."
P. 26:1

CENTURION

See "Anson, Lord."
W. 24

CEPHALASPIS

See "Sandwiches."
M. 132

CEPHIORIS

A fictional lake, the name probably derived from Cephisis, mentioned in Chambers, in connection with *amber.
M. 121

CERES

*Roman Mother Earth (*Greek Demeter), goddess of agriculture, fruits, corn. Daughter of Cronus and Rhea; her daughter by *Jupiter was *Proserpine (Greek Persephone). Ceres was mankind's friend but withheld her gifts when Proserpine died; Proserpine was eventually restored to her mother, but only for eight months of the year, during which time Ceres rewards mankind again.
M. 181

CEREUS, NIGHT-BLOWING

A species of cactus, the cereus sometimes has flowers shaped like wax candles (*cera*: wax) that bloom at night. It is native to the southwestern *United States and *Mexico.

(In "flower language," it signifies Transient Beauty.)
M. 190

CERRO-GORDO

Arroyo de Cerro Gordo (26°12' N.; 104°06' W.), about 60 miles northwest of Veracruz, *Mexico, was the site of the first serious resistance (in 1847) against the United States Army under Gen. Winfield *Scott, the Mexicans being led by Santa Anna.
M. 14

CERVANTES

Miguel de Cervantes Saavedra (1547-1616), *Spanish novelist, playwright, and poet best known for his creation of *Don Quixote, was born in Alcalá, of an old but impoverished family that moved frequently. He may have had *Jesuit schooling, but little is known of his life until 1569, when he published his first poetry and was sought by the police for a violent infraction of the law.

As a common soldier aboard *Marquesa* in the battle of *Lepanto against the *Turks (7 October 1571), he received wounds that permanently maimed his left hand. (It was not amputated, as M. claims in *M.D.* 26.) In a later battle, he was taken into *slavery by *Moors in *Algiers. Despite frequent severe punishment for misbehavior, he became personal servant to the Pasha, who spared his life after escape attempts. His freedom was purchased after five years, and he returned to Madrid in 1581, where he became a popular playwright. His literary career was interrupted again from 1587 to 1605, during which time he was excommunicated, jailed, and otherwise chastised for various offenses. The first part of Don Quixote appeared in 1605 and was frequently reprinted, but despite his success, Cervantes and his wife were frequently involved in criminal and legal infractions. The second part of his masterpiece was produced in 1610, and short stories (*Novelas ejamplares*) and poetry soon followed, under the patronage of the cardinal-archbishop of Toledo. At his death, his wife had become a nun; his only daughter died in 1652, leaving no progeny.

Sealts #s 124 and 125 are editions of *Don Quixote*.
M.D. 26

CETOLOGY SECTION

M.'s expertise (mingled with playfulness), in *M.D.*'s "Cetology" chapter (32) and elsewhere, derived from several sources: *Beale; *Bennett; *J.R. Browne; *Cheever; *Olmstead; *Scoresby, Jr.; *Penny Cyclopaedia*. For explicit discussion of M.'s debt, the reader is directed to Vincent's *The Trying-Out of Moby-Dick* and to two articles in *Melville Society*

Extracts: Deborah C. Andrews, "Attacks of Whales on Ships:
A Checklist" (Number 18; May 1974), one of an on-going series
on the subject; Kendra H. Gaines, "A Consideration of an Additional Source for Melville's *Moby-Dick*" (29; January 1977),
which explicates M.'s use of the article "Whales" in *Penny Cyclopaedia*.

Cetology remains an imprecise science, and it is not
within the scope of the present work to supply full-scale treatment of M.'s references to whales and whaling, nor to examine full particulars of any given species. What follows is intended to clarify or correct specific references in *M.D.* and
elsewhere and to demonstrate to some extent the cetacean
classification system undercut in *M.D.* 32. Particular
cetaceans are discussed here under their usual, rather than
their Melvillean classification.

The aquatic mammals known as cetaceans form three
suborders:

ARCHAEOCETI are extinct species known only from
fossil evidence; they had differentiated teeth.

MYSTICETI are baleen, or whalebone whales (*M.D.* 32);
they have a double set of some 300 triangular horny plates,
narrowest where attached to the palate, forming a fringed
strainer through which plankton is collected. "Whalebone" is
a misnomer; baleen is of the material of hair, not of bone.
"Under-jawed whales" (*M.D.* 32) have a protruding lower jaw;
they are *balaenopteridae*, such as the finback and the blue.

The blue whale (*balaenoptera musculus*), M.'s *Sulphur
Bottom Whale* (*R.* 21; *M.D.* 32) is the largest animal that ever
existed. It grows as long as 100 feet and may weigh over 150
tons, yielding 70,000 pounds of blubber and 100,000 pounds of
meat. Blue whales are slate blue and have a furrowed throat.
They travel singly and eat krill (see "Brit," below); the most
hunted species, there are few left at the present time.

Fin-backs (*R.* 21; *M.D.* 32), or rorquals (*balaenoptera
physalus*) are M.'s "Long-John," "*Razor Back Whale*," and
"Tall-Spout" of *M.D.* 32. Finbacks may reach seventy-five feet
in length and weigh fifty tons. They are grayish black, with
white undersides. They travel in schools of up to 100 individuals, feeding on plankton, crustaceans, and small fish. (The
species is now perhaps 90% destroyed.)

The *Grampus* (*T.* 2; *M.* 13; *M.* 84; *M.* 95; *M.* 132; *M.D.*
3; *M.D.* 32) is properly the *gran pisce*: suborder *delphinidae*.
It grows to twenty-five feet in length, has a high dorsal fin and
large, pointed teeth.

Hump-backs (*R.* 21; *M.D.* 31; *M.D.* 32) are of the suborder *megaptera novaeangliae*. Up to forty feet long, they have
black backs with white throats and chests. Their large white
flippers are perhaps one-third the length of their bodies. They

eat crustaceans. Hump-backs are M.'s "bunched whales" of *M.D.* 32, as well as "reydan-siskur," of *M.D.* 105. M. calls them "Wrinkled Bellies" because of the multiple furrows on their necks and undersides.

Mysticetus (*M.D.* 55) has many appellations. It is the *Greenland (*R.* 21; *M.D.* 32; *M.D.* 55); the Right (*M.* 1; *M.* 13; *M.D.* 32; *M.D.* 55); the True (*M.D.* Extracts 18); the Black, or Great, Whale (*M.D.* 32). *Balaena mysticetus*, up to sixty feet in length, has black skin, with a cream-colored throat and chin. It has no back or dorsal fin. It eats much krill (see "Brit," below), with a mouth one-third as wide as the whale's length. (The Greenland whale is no longer found between Greenland and the Barents Sea.)

ODONTOCETI: whales with simplified teeth.

The *Albino whale of *M.D.* 42 might of course be an aberration within a species (or Moby-Dick himself!), or a beluga whale, of the family *monodontidae*, genus *delphinapterus*. It is without a dorsal fin and grows up to fourteen feet in length. The beluga is born gray; the color lightens to white at maturity. ("Beluga" is from *bieluha*, Russian for "white.")

The *Black Fish* (*M.* 13; *M.D.* 32; *M.D.* 115) is the "Hyena Whale" of *M.D.* 32. *Delphinidae globicephala* is the pilot whale or perhaps pilot fish (*M.* 18; *M.* 32): up to twenty-eight feet long, with a rounded head projecting over the upper jaw. Black fish travel in schools of up to 1,000 individuals, eating mostly squid (see below). They are *Newfoundland's principal whale resource.

The Cachalot (*M.* 1; *M.* 38; *M.* 68; *M.D.* Extracts 18; *M.D.* 32; *M.D.* 105), also known as the physeter (*M.D.* 32; *M.D.* 55) is the sperm, spermaceti (or parmacetti) whale (*O.* passim; *M.* 1; *M.* 121; *R.* 21; *R.* 23; *W.* 4; *W.* 44; *W.* 86; *M.D.* passim). (The "Trumpa" and "Anvil-Headed" whales, and the "Pottsfich," of *M.D.* 32). *Physeter catadon* has a square-snouted head extending perhaps one-third of its sixty-foot length; there are teeth, up to ten inches long, located only in the lower jaw. The thirty-five-ton sperm whale lives in groups of up to fifty individuals. Gestation lasts for sixteen months. Cachalot Blanche (*M.D.* 91) is the French name for the white sperm whale.

The *Killer* whale (*M.D.* 32), of the order *delphinidae*, is *orcinus orca*, largest of the dolphin family: up to thirty feet in length and up to one ton in weight. It is black with distinctive white underside markings extending from the lower jaw to the mid-stomach; it often has smaller white spots, especially above the eyes. The killer whale eats seals, dolphins, and baleen whales. It is perhaps the "*Thrasher*" whale of *M.D.* 32.

The Narwhale (*M.D.* 32), *monodon monoceros*, is a denizen of the *Arctic; up to seventeen feet in length, with a characteristic spiral twisted tusk up to nine feet in length, slightly to the right of the spout (in males only). Narwhales travel in groups of about ten individuals, eating cuttlefish (see below), crustaceans, and fish. In *M.D.* 32, the narwhale is one of the "rostrated" whales: the "Horned," the "Nostril," the "Tusked," the "Unicorn" whale.

Porpoises (*O.* 5; *O.* 9; *O.* 16; *M.* 13; *M.* 93; *M.* 121; *M.* 165; *R.* 18; *R.* 20; *R.* 40; *R.* 51; *M.D.* passim) are also of the order *odontoceti*: family *phocaenidae*. The common porpoise (*phocaena phocaena*) is probably the "Huzza" porpoise of *M.D.* 32: brown or black with a white underside and a dark streak extending from eye to snout. It is up to nine feet in length and eats fish, crustaceans, and cuttlefish.

M. appears to confuse porpoises with dolphins (which are mostly found in American waters). His Right-Whale Porpoise (and "Mealy-mouthed" porpoise, of *M.D.* 32) is probably the right whale dolphin (*lissodelphinae*) or southern right whale dolphin (*lissodelphis peroni*). His River Whale (*M.D.* 102) is probably *physeleridae platanistidae*, a dolphin found in rivers from the *Amazon, to the *Ganges, to the *Yangtze. (Another possible candidate is the Irawadi dolphin: *orcaella brevirostris*.)

The whale's blowhole (especially important in *M.D.* 51) is the working nostril of a pair. It is controlled by muscles, air pockets, and lip- and tongue-like structures, the articulation of which regulates breathing and modulates sound.

Yokes (*M.D.* 105) are pairs of whales.

Among non-cetacean creatures which M. connects to whales are the following:

Cuttlefish (*M.D.* 45): the mollusk *decapoda*, with ten suction-cup legs.

Dugongs, or Sow-fish (*M.D.* 32): *halicoridae*, of the order *sirenia*: eight feet long and up to 450 pounds, feeding on algae in the Indo-Pacific, *Red Sea, and *Australian waters.

Elephant whale (*M.D.* 32): the elephant seal: *mirounga angustirostris*. Found on the *Pacific coast, it grows up to twenty feet long; its name derives from its trunklike snout. (The elephant whale was hunted almost to extinction in the nienteenth century.)

Lamatins, or Pig-fish (*M.D.* 32) is the porkfish, *anisotremus virginicus*: a perch-like fish related to the grunt (which makes a grunting sound by grating its teeth). It has a huge mouth.

Brit (*M.D.* 58), krill: *euphasia superba*: a small, shrimp-like crustacean with an orange head and green underside produced by eating algae. A layer of two-to three-inch-long krill can be up to 3,000 feet deep.

Maccaroni (*M.D.* 56): *cirripedia*: small barnacle-like crustacean parasites that drop off the whale in cold water.

Squid (*M.D.* 59): cephalopod sea mollusks, having ten arms; the variety (calamari) eaten by humans is *loligo*. A giant squid has been thought the original of many sea-monster legends.

In *M.D.* 32, M. includes a list of what he says may be "half-fabulous" whales. Rather, his *list* is probably "half-fabulous," or half-fabricated. The following creatures (perhaps half of that list which contains genuine cetaceans) are probably inventions: "Cannon whale," "Cape whale," "Coppered whale," "Iceberg whale," "Junk whale," "Leading whale," "Pudding-Headed whale," "Quog whale " "Scragg whale." The "*Algerine Porpoise*," in the same chapter, may also be a playful fiction. "Algerine" refers to Algerians, *Berbers, *Moors, and *Arabs of the *Mediterranean area: known in M.'s time for *piracy—as is his porpoise.

"Does the Whale's Magnitude Diminish?—Will He Perish?" (*M.D.* 105): the answer in the twentieth century appears to be, "Unfortunately, yes."

CETUS
In astronomy, a southern *constellation: The Whale, said by the *Greeks to be the monster slain by *Perseus when it was sent by *Neptune to devour *Andromeda.
M.D. 24; M.D. 57

CHACE, MR.; CHASE, OWEN
Owen Chase (1797-1869), author (probably with help) of *Narrative of the Most Extraordinary and Distressing Shipwreck of the Whale-ship Essex. . .* (New York: W.B. Gilley 1821), was born in *Nantucket and was First Mate of *Essex* when she was stove by a whale and sank, 20 November 1820. He later became captain of *Charles Carroll*. He had a stormy personal life, with four marriages, the third of which was terminated by divorce granted by M.'s father-in-law, Judge *Lemuel Shaw. M. is probably mistaken in his claim to have seen Chase, although he may have met his son. The *Narrative* was heavily drawn upon by M., especially for the concluding chapters of *M.D.* Sealts #133 is M.'s edition, to which he made elaborate notes.
M.D. 45; M.D. Extracts 58 (as "Chase"); M.D. Extracts 17

"THE CHAINS"

"Billy Budd" (Chapter 14) is approached about the mutiny while at the chains:

> A narrow platform, one of six, outside of the high bulwarks and screened by the great deadeyes and multiple columned lanyards of the shrouds and backstays; and, in a great warship of that time, of dimensions commensurate to the hull's magnitude; a tarry balcony, in short, over-hanging the sea, and so secluded that one mariner of the *Bellipotent*, a Nonconformist old tar of a serious turn, made it even in daytime his private oratory.

W. 76

CHALDAIC; CHALDEAN; CHALDEE

The earliest historic nation, in the South *Babylonia area, the Chaldeans (Assyrian *Kaldu*; Babylonian *Kasdu*; *Hebrew *Kasdim*), were semi-nomads from *Arabia who occupied Ur from about the nine-hundreth to the seven-hundredth centuries B.C. They were doubtless navigators of the *Persian Gulf, and held the sea sacred.

Believers in unalterable divine predestination, the Chaldeans came to be associated with occult science or magic. Their priests, M.'s "*Magi," were schooled in astronomy and astrology. But many imposters called themselves magi. The Book of *Daniel (1,4) lists King *Nebuchadnezzar's demands of Jewish children brought before him as candidates:

> children in whom was no blemish, but well favoured and skilful in all wisdom, and cunning in knowledge, and understanding science, and such as had ability in them to stand in the king's palace, and whom they might teach the learning and the tongue of the Chaldeans.

The *Bible calls Aramaic (the language of *Jesus) "Chaldee." But Babylonia's cuneiform inscriptions were often referred to as "Chaldea."

In *M.D.* the term "Child-magian" refers to the innocence and naïveté of the magi.

(See also "Cologne, three kings of.)
W. 19; M.D. 79; M.D. 110; M.D. 111; P. 1:4; P. 2:3; P. 2:5; P. 3:2; P. 17:1; I.P. 8; C.M. 36

CHALK, OR CORAL SANDWICH
     See "Sandwiches."
M. 132

CHAMOIS
     A goatlike *Alpine antelope, *rupicapra rupicapra*. It
has black and white facial markings, straight horns with distinctive back-turned tips, a black tail and dorsal stripe.
W. 85

CHAMOIS
     See "Russia."
P. 17:1

CHAMPAGNE
     The sparkling wine takes its name from the Champagne
district of *France (the historically important area bounded on
the north by Liège and Luxembourg, on the east by Lorraine,
on the south by *Burgundy, and on the west by Ile de France
and Picardy). Said to have been first created by the seventeenth-century *Benedictine monk Dom Pierre Pérignon, it is
the product of black Pinot (or Meunier) or white chardonnay
grapes. It is blended after a first fermentation and then fermented in bottles a second time and reopened to discard
residue. Vintage champagne is made only from wines of the
vintage year. *Brut* champagne is unsweetened; *sec* has some
sweetening; *demi-sec* or *doux* has more.
W. 93; M.D. 94

CHAMPOLLION
     Jean François Champollion (1790-1832), *French
founder of scientific Egyptology, was called *Le Jeune*, distinguishing him from his brother, Jacques Joseph Champollion-
Figeac, an archaeologist. He began deciphering hieroglyphics
as a professor of history at Grenoble and, as director of the
*Egyptian museum at the *Louvre, was commisssioned to
conduct the expedition to Egypt for which he was rewarded
with a chair at the Collège de France.
     He deciphered the *Rosetta Stone, found in 1799 at
Rosetta (or Rashid), continuing work begun by the
*Englishman, Thomas Young. Champollion was the first to
realize that the signs were variously alphabetic, syllabic, or de-
terminative, standing for a thing previously expressed.
M. 40; M. 157; M.D. 79

CHAMPS ELYSEES

The park-and monument-lined *Paris boulevard runs from Arc de Triomphe (1836) on the west to the *Tuileries gardens on the east, on the right bank of the *Seine. The thoroughfare was begun in 1670, becoming surrounded by museums, government buildings (including the Palais de l'Elysées, 1718), and embassies (along with commercial establishments on the western end). The area offers incomparable views—to the *Place du Carrousel and the Palais du *Louvre on the east; Ste. Madeleine on the north and Hôtel des Invalides on the south (from Place de la Concorde—in itself a marvel).

The Arch is centered on Place de l' Etoile (officially now Place Charles-de-Gaulle, but never referred to thus), with twelve scenic avenues radiating from it.

M. strolled along the Champs Elysées on 3 December 1849 (undoubtedly surrounded by other *American tourists).
T. 3

CHANCE, FREE WILL, AND NECESSITY

See "Fixed fate and Free Will."
M.D. 47

CHANCERY

In the *United States, "chancery" refers to a court of equity, as opposed to a common-law court; that is, one having jurisdiction in cases where a plain adequate remedy cannot be obtained in courts of common law. Because material possessions are not highly regarded in "Typee Valley," there is no need for a court to adjudicate divorce cases there.
T. 26

CHANNEL

The English Channel, an arm of the *Atlantic Ocean between *England and *France, is 350 miles long and 112 miles wide at the entrance between Land's End and *Ushant, narrowing to twenty-one miles near *Dover. It contains many British Navy landmarks and lighthouses mentioned by M., including *Eddystone Rocks, *Beachy Head, *Dungeness.

M.'s 1849 journal records his sense of the Channel's importance in history (1 November), its rough seas (27 November), and his own sense of importance at encountering England again after ten years: "*then* a sailor, now H.M. author of 'Pedee' 'Hullabaloo' & 'Pog-Dog'" (4 November).

As M. notes in *M.* 4, *Blanchard and Jeffries crossed the Channel in a balloon in 1745.
Passim

CHAPEAUX-DE-BRAS
A soft three-cornered flat silk hat, folded and carried under the arm in the *French eighteenth-century court.
W. 56

CHAPEL-OF-EASE
A worship place for distant-resident-members of a parish church.
R. 36

CHAPEL-STREET
*Liverpool's Chapel Street runs east-west from Old Hall Street to the water. It adjoins *Launcelot's-Hey and is the site of *St. Nicholas Church. At one time the locale of a salt works, by M.'s time it was a commercial area and site of the old Fish House.
R. 31; R. 36

CHAPMAN'S HOMER
George Chapman (1559-1634), famed for *Homeric translations, has a sketchy early biography: born in Hertfordshire, *England; perhaps *Oxford-educated; perhaps a soldier. He began translating while a prolific playwright; *Seven Books of the Iliads* appeared in 1598, followed by another twelve in 1608. In 1616 he published *The Whole Works of Homer; Prince of Poets*. His translations are now superseded, and despite praise by *Jonson, *Marlowe, and others, his fame rests mainly on Keat's tribute: "On First Looking Into Chapman's Homer."
Sealts numbers 276, 277 and 278 (annotated or marked) are Chapman's translations of Homer.
W. 75

CHARING CROSS
The center of *London, from which mileage was measured, Charing Cross was the site of public hangings, royal proclamations, etc. A statue of Queen Eleanore, erected there by Edward I, was replaced by one of *Charles II.
R. 30; M.D. 32; I.P. 6; I.P. 25

CHARLEMAGNE
King of the Franks from 768 and *Holy Roman Emperor of the West from 800, Charlemagne (742-814) was the elder son

of Pepin the Short and was baptized Charles. He and his brother, Carloman, ruled two vast kingdoms stretching from the *Alps to the *Netherlands and *Germany, but at Carloman's death, Charlemagne annexed his brother's portions, bringing the wrath of the *Lombards and Charlemagne's subsequent incursions into the *Italian peninsula. He eventually assumed the title "King of the Lombards," despite de facto independence of Lombard duchies.

His victories in Bavaria and *Saxony and south of the Pyrenees brought increasing official *Catholic Church recognition by several *Popes, leading to a cult of beatification after his death.

German and French legends grew apace, spread by such works as the *Chanson de Roland* and other epics. *English literature honored him for the learning established at his court during the "Carolingian Renaissance."

His tomb is in the church he built at Aachen (Fr. *Aix-la-Chapelle), marked by a stone slab engraved *Carlo Magno* and lighted by a bronze chandelier presented by Barbarossa (Frederick I).
M. 63; W. 46; M.D. 54

CHARLEMONT
        Karcher discusses the function of this fictional character, in "The Story of Charlemont . . . ," showing how M.'s introduction and undercutting of Christology is a confidence game played on the reader.
C.M. 32; C.M. 33; C.M. 34; C.M. 35

CHARLES ARNOLD NOBLE; CHARLIE
        In the navy, to "shoot Charlie Noble" is to clean the galley smokepipe of dirt and soot by firing a pistol in it. The original Charlie Noble was a Commander in the *Mediterranean fleet about 1840 who made a fetish of a shiny galley funnel.
C.M. Passim

CHARLES EDWARD THE PRETENDER
        Charles Edward, the Young Pretender, or Young Chevalier (1720-1788), was the last *Stuart seriously to claim the *British throne. The grandson of *James II of England, he was created *Prince of Wales by his father, James III. In 1744, after scheming in *France for support, Charles Edward reentered Britain, proclaimed himself James VIII, and occupied Holyrood. He invaded England in 1746 but was defeated,

ending Stuart hopes. Escaping to France again, he was imprisoned at *Vincennes as a result of the treaty of *Aix-la-
Chapelle and thereafter wandered incognito about Europe,
drinking heavily, in ill health, abandoned by his friends. He
died in *Rome, nursed by his daughter, Charlotte Stuart.
M. 3

CHARLES, THE ELDER
     See "Charles The First, King of England."
P. 20:1

CHARLES THE FIRST, KING OF ENGLAND
     Charles I of *England (1600-1649), son of James VI of
*Scotland and Anne of *Denmark, ruled from 1625 to 1649, his
reign instigating the English Civil War. Charles was shy and
reserved and spoke in a Scots accent with a stammer. A patron of the arts, he began a fastidious, proper, religious
(Anglican) court, with the help of his wife, Henrietta Maria,
sister of the *French Louis XIII (see "Bourbon").
     Charles had no respect for commoners, particularly
those in the *Puritan House of *Commons, causing early conflict. With the advice of his favorite, George Villiers, First
Duke of Buckingham, he waged war with France and *Spain,
dissolving Parliament when it disagreed, imposing forced
loans and arresting non-compliers. By the Third Parliament
(1628), his government was completely discredited. Buckingham was assassinated, and by the Fourth Parliament, Charles
was being accused of "Popish practices" and other ills. He
ruled without a Parliament in the "Eleven Years' Tyranny,"
citing the Divine Right of Kings. He alienated the
*Presbyterian Scots by enforced liturgy, and lost the "Bishops'
War," in 1639. Charles called the "Short Parliament," dissolving it when it refused money to renew the Scottish conflict. He
convened a Council of Peers, then the Long Parliament of 1640,
which frustrated his efforts again. When a *London mob harassed the House of *Lords, Charles began a series of concessions, but by 1641, the "Grand Remonstrance" of Parliament
detailed the abuses of his reign. The Queen sold the crown
jewels when it became manifestly clear that England was split
between Royalists and Parliamentarians. Issued an ultima-
tum, "the Nineteen Propositions," Charles rejected it, and the
Civil War began in 1642.
     The Royalists appeared successful for the first year, but
by 1648, Charles was imprisoned for treason, at the army's
demand. He refused to plead at what he considered his illegal

trial, and was executed as a "tyrant, traitor, murderer, and public enemy." He is buried at *Windsor.
M. 31; R. 36

CHARLES II, KING OF ENGLAND

Britain's King Charles (1630-85), son of *Charles I (1600-1649) and Henrietta Maria (1609-69), Roman *Catholic daughter of Henry IV of *France and Marie de Medici, reigned from 1660 to 1685. Raised an Anglican, Charles was exiled from the start of the Civil War (1642) until he was nineteen, while his father remained a Scottish prisoner. Proclaimed king at his father's execution, he was defeated in 1651 by *Oliver Cromwell, spent forty days of hiding in the "royal oak" at Boscobel, then escaped to France. Upon Cromwell's death (1658), negotiations with the *Presbyterians changed public opinion, and he was restored by the 1660 *Parliament. He generally pardoned revolutionaries, executing few.

History paints him as lazy, self-indulgent, and romantically charming, with many mistresses and fourteen illegitimate children. He married the Roman Catholic Catherine of *Braganza. He ruled mainly through Edward Hyde, First Earl of *Clarendon, who restored the Anglican Church, exacerbating problems with harassment of Noncomformists, appointment of *Judge Jeffreys, and formation of the Cabal. Charles's reign produced chronic fear of popery and of France during the *Titus Oates intrigues, his policies arousing opposition that was to plague *James II. His major achievements were creation of traditional Parliamentary opposition and passage of the *Habeas Corpus Act, but during his time the British Navy was all but devastated through careless lack of concern. He died of a stroke, having become a Catholic on his deathbed and was succeeded by his brother, *James II.

Some of Charles's mistresses ("Beauties"): Villiers, Barbara; Countess of Castlemaine and Duchess of Cleveland (1641-1709). She was mistress for seven years, bearing Charles at least five children, and becoming very wealthy. She was called the "lewd Imperial Whore."

*Gwynne, Nell (1650-87): bore a son (later Duke of St. Albans) in 1670, another in 1671. Charles on his deathbed commanded: "Let not poor Nelly starve."

DeKeroualle, Louise: Duchess of Portsmouth (1649-1734). Her son (b. 1672) became Duke of Richmond; in 1674, she became Duchess of Portsmouth and was given a large annuity. Unpopular, as a greedy French Catholic, she was called "Madam Carewell" by the English.

Charles II was nicknamed "Old Rowley" (M. 84), for his favorite stallion, whose name also graces a portion of the

Newmarket race course in England (Rowley Mile) and an important race (The Rowley Stakes). *Scott used the sobriquet in *Peveril of the Peak* (Ch. xxxi). In 1769, Thomas Chatterton hoaxed the British public with *The Rowley Poems*, reputedly by a fifteenth-century cleric.
O. 81 M. 75; R. 46; W. 71; P. 1:3; P. 5:1

CHARLES V, HOLY ROMAN EMPEROR; CHARLES THE FIFTH

Son of Philip the Handsome of Habsburg and the mad Joan of *Castile, Charles (1500-1558) became Charles I of *Spain in 1516. As last *Holy Roman Emperor (1519-1556), he made his period one of international strife, European expansion, and contests between kings and emperors. The last Holy Roman Emperor to pursue the idea of a universal empire led by Emperor and *Pope, and a firm believer in *Catholicism, he fought continuously against *Protestantism in *Germany and Islam in Spain. Francophilic espouser of chivalric pomp and ceremony, he spoke little Spanish or German. M.'s reference to his facility with languages may have come from Prescott's *History of Philip the Second* or *Bayle's *Dictionary*.

Charles alienated much of Europe, appointing arrogant foreigners in Spain, attempting to "rescue" Germany from *Luther's ideas, struggling with invading *Turks and with *Italians represented by the Pope. He quarreled with *Henry VIII of England and finally challenged France's François I to personal combat (which did not occur). In addition, his reign was marked by arranged political marriages (notably his son Philip's to "Bloody" *Mary of England), bribery, and debts incurred to finance mercenary armies with which he waged war for at least half of his tenure.

After a series of humiliating defeats and ill with gout, in 1556 he abdicated to Philip in Spain, Italy, and the colonies. He abdicated the Imperial title in 1558, having taken up residence at the Hieronymite monastery of Yuste, Spain. He thereafter remained, despite M.'s suggestion, active adviser to Philip II.

Penny Cyclopaedia discusses Charles's fascination with "works of ingenious mechanism," which may have inspired M.'s remark about his watching clocks (*W*. 46). Titian's portrait probably supplied M.'s knowledge of his physical appearance.

(See also "Beards.")
M. 97; W. 4; W. 46; W. 84

CHARLES LAMB'S TRIUMPH OF THE WHALE
See "Lamb, Charles"; "Extracts" 52.
M.D. Extracts 52

CHARLES RIVER
The Charles of eastern *Massachusetts rises in southwestern Norfolk County, winding c. sixty miles past *Cambridge and *Boston, to the western side of Boston Harbor. A twentieth-century dam with locks near the mouth now limits navigability; only the lower half-mile has a channel and wharves.
(Certifying to the existence of the despised garment of W., M. claimed that he had thrown the white jacket into the Charles River at the conclusion of his cruise on *United States.)
I.P. 13

CHARLESTON
Charleston, South *Carolina, is located on a low, narrow peninsula of Charleston Harbor. The 1670 English settlement of Albemarle Point in 1680 moved to Oyster Point, which became Charles Town, soon developing into a center of wealth and culture.
*Slavery was strongly ensconced here, and in 1860 the convention to proclaim secession was held at Charleston. With firing on Fort Sumter, the first battle of the *Civil War began at Charleston, 12 April 1861. Union forces besieged the city, 1863-65.
I.P. 14

CHARLESTOWN
Charlestown, in *New Hampshire's Sullivan County, is located on the *Connecticut River, ten miles south of Claremont. It was settled in 1740 as "Township No. 4," mentioned in *I.P. 2.
I.P. 2; I.P. 3

CHARLEY COFFIN
Vincent believes this another pseudonym for *Scoresby (*The Trying-Out of Moby-Dick*, IV, 2). "Coffin" being a common *Nantucket name, "Charley" is probably a fictional representative of Nantucketers in general.
M.D. 32

CHARLIE MILLTHORPE
     The name may suggest M.'s position regarding this fictional character (usually seen as representing James [Eli] Murdock Fly, a chum of M. through young adulthood). "Charlie" (or "Charley") was a pejorative in the nineteenth century, especially in connection with the police. A "thorpe" is a tiny village or hamlet, so "Charlie Millthorpe" suggests the watchman of a small (mill) town.
P. 20:1

"CHARLIES"
     Alt. "Charleys." Before 1829, an organization of the *English police force, night watchmen appointed by townships (since the Thirteenth Century) were Charlies, probably after *Charles I, who reorganized the Watch system in 1640. The Watch Committee joined the County Police in 1697.
R. 40

CHARLOTTE
     See "Goethe."
C.M. 4

"CHARLOTTE TEMPLE"
     Charlotte Temple: A Tale of Truth, the *English-born Susanna [Haswell] Rowson's (c. 1762-1824) sentimental romance, was published in England (1791) and in the U.S. It was followed by a sequel, the 1828 *Charlotte's Daughter* (or, *Lucy Temple*). It is a moralistic tale of seduction, desertion, and poverty, aimed at credulous young girls. The prolific Rowson was variously an actress, editor, and boarding-school director. She became a great sympathizer with *America, her adopted home.
R. 17

CHARLTON, CAPTAIN
     The only information I have secured about Charlton is that he was the *British Consul at the *Sandwich Islands who left *Honolulu in 1842 to complain to *London about personal and official grievances against the native king, Kamehameha III (see "Kammahammaha . . . ."), after which *Lord George Paulet arrived with the means to enforce British demands.
T. Appendix

CHARON
In mythology, the ferryman of *Hades who transports the dead across the river Styx or *Acheron. Earlier writers represented him as a less malign creature than those after *Virgil.
P. 16:1

CHARTIST
A member of the (1837) *English working class movement, with demands expressed in the 1838 *People's Charter*; among them: manhood suffrage, ballot vote, annual parliaments, emendation of other rules for Members of *Parliament. A petition to Parliament (1848) failed, and the movement collapsed by 1849.
R. 41

CHARTRES, DUKE DE
Duc de Chartres during *I.P.*'s time period was Louis Philippe Joseph de Bourbon (1747-1793), father of Louis Philippe (1773-1850; see "Bourbon"), king of France from 1830-48. The son of Louis Philippe, and duc d'Orléans from 1752, he was at first duc de Monpensier, then duc de *Chartres, later duc d'Orléans (at which point his son, the future king, became duc de Chartres). He had four children with Adélaide de Bourbon-Penthièvre and was always in debt. He built the shops surrounding the Palais-Royal in *Paris. Hostile to Marie Antoinette, he travelled much away from the court at *Versailles. He was grand master of the *Freemasons and a member of the Jacobin club. His pseudonym, "Philippe Egalité," was bestowed at his request by the Commune. He sat on the extreme left of the Constituent Assembly and died on the guillotine.
I.P. 10; I.P. 15

CHASE, JACK
John J. Chase, to whom M. was to dedicate *Billy Budd, Sailor*, was a veritable shipmate, details of whose life may be found in Vincent's *The Tailoring of Melville's White-Jacket*. Rear-Admiral S.R. Franklin says of him:

> I have a very distinct recollection. He was about as fine a specimen of a seaman as I have ever seen in all my cruising. He was not only that, but he was a man of intelligence and a born leader. His topmates adored him although he kept them

up to the mark, and made every man do his share
of work.

Although M. makes Chase sound young and hale, he
was about fifty-three years old at the time of M.'s cruise on
*United States.

*Navy Department records show that Chase deserted the
St. Louis 18 November 1840, at *Callao, Peru. A year and a
half later, *United States, at anchor at Callao, recorded in her
Log Book:

> May 29, Received on board John J. Chase, a de-
> serter from the U.S.S. St. Louis, with a particular
> request to Como. Jones, from the Peruvian Admi-
> ral (in whose service he had shipped) that he
> might be pardoned, which was complied with by
> Com. Jones.

Six weeks later, Chase was promoted to Captain of the
*maintop, an important petty office.
W. Passim

CHASE, OWEN
    See "Chace, Owen."
M.D. Extracts 58

CHASSEE
    Chassé: a rapid, gliding dance-step.
M.D. 40

CHATHAM-STREET
    *New York City's Chatham Street no longer exists, hav-
ing been replaced by Park Row. Chatham connected *Broad-
way to east-side arteries and made part of the Boston Post
Road. It was adjacent to the *Bowery and the notorious Five
Points: factors in its obliteration. The name survives in
"Chatham Square."
R. 4

CHAUCER, --'S
    The biography of Geoffrey Chaucer (c. 1343-1400) is
clouded. The son of a *London vintner, he is known to have
served in the army of *Edward III, been taken prisoner in the
invasion of *France, and ransomed. He married into the fam-

ily of *John of Gaunt, who became his patron. Chaucer traveled much on diplomatic missions and other service to the king. In 1374, he became controller of London *customs. The latter part of his life was spent in *Kent in high political office. In addition to *The Canterbury Tales* (c. 1387), he is known for *The Book of the Duchess* (c. 1370), *Troilus and Criseyde* (c. 1385), and numerous other works.

The Canterbury Tales, a 17,000-line humorous prose and verse work, tells the stories of twenty-three (of thirty) travelers of varying backgrounds on a pilgrimage to *Canterbury Cathedral. The satirical work which became a major document of *English literature was never completed and was "retracted" by its author for its vulgarity.

The "shipman" of W. 86 speaks in the Prologue II, 392-406:

> A daggere hangynge on a laas hadde he
> About his nekke, under his arm adoun.
> The hoote somer hadde maad his hewe al broun;
> And certeinly he was a good felawe.
> Ful many a draughte of wyn had he ydrawe
> Fro Burdeux-ward, whil that the chapman sleep.
> Of nyce conscience took he no keep.
> If that he faught, and hadde the hyer hond,
> By water he sente hem hoom to every lond.
> But of his craft to rekene wel his tydes,
> His stremes, and his daungers hym bisides,
> His herberwe, and his mone, his lodemenage,
> Ther was noon swich from Hulle to Cartage.
> Hardy he was and wys to undertake;
> With many a tempest hadde his berd been shake.

M.'s Chaucer library included two eight-volume sets of the *Poetical Works* edited by Robert Bell (1854-56), an unknown edition he purchased in 1876, and *The Riches of Chaucer*, by C. C. Clarke (2v., rebound in 1, 1835). (Sealts numbers 138-141.) In an 1876 letter to his cousin, Catherine *Gansevoort Lansing, M. referred to Chaucer as the "old poet who didn't know how to spell, as Artemus Ward said."
W. 86; C.M. 2

CHEEVER, REV. HENRY T.; THE REV. T. CHEEVER

Henry Theodore Cheever (1814-1886) graduated from Bowdoin and studied theology at Bangor, *Maine. After traveling the South Seas, he became a Congregationalist Pastor. Cheever was a worldly man with many interests. He was an editor of the New York "Evangelist" from 1843 to 1844 and

headed his church's anti-*slavery society from 1859 to 1864.
Cheever wrote many popular books in addition to *The Whale
and His Captors* (first published 1849), including works on the
sea, slavery, the ministery, and several memoirs. He was a
great proponent of *Sabbath observance in the American
Sperm Whale Fishery. (Vincent makes M.'s debt to Cheever
explicit in *The Trying-Out of Moby-Dick*.)
   See also "Extracts" 67.
M.D. Extracts 67; M.D. 32

CHEF D'ESCADRE
   French Commodore (Chief, or Commander, of Squad-
ron).
W. 6

CHELTENHAM
   The medicinal saline springs of the Pittville, Montpellier
and Central spas have attracted tourists to this borough of
*England, about 96 miles W.N.W. of *London, since their dis-
covery in 1716. The fashionable pump room attracted such
guests as *George III and his family, and the borough was reconstructed suitably at this time. Among Cheltenham's other
claims to fame, it is an educational center of long standing, as
well as a cultural haven and National Hunt race meeting
place. (Gustav Holst was to be born at Cheltenham in 1874.)
T. 21

CHEOPS, PYRAMID OF; CHEOPIAN
   Cheops is the *Greek name for Khufu (or Khufwey), second *Pharaoh of the *Egyptian fourth dynasty (reigned c. 2590-
2567 B.C.), and builder of the Great Pyramid and other monuments at Giza. There are conflicting reports of his reign; despite later claims of his having ruled wisely, earlier writers
such as *Herodotus said that Egyptians lived in misery and
oppression during his reign and that of his son.
   The great limestone pyramid a few miles southwest of
Cairo is the largest and oldest of Egyptian pyramids, called
"Horizon of Khofu" by the ancient Egyptians. An engineering
marvel, its original base was 230 meters long, so that it covered
an area of more than thirteen acres. It was 146.59 meters
high, with sides rising at an angle of 51°52', oriented to the
four cardinal points.
   M. visited in 1856, confessing "a feeling of awe and terror" when he attempted to enter the pyramid.
T. 21; M. 75; R. 31; R. 32; P. 25:4; I.P. 15

CHERUB, THE
H.B.M. *Cherub*, a sloop of war carrying up to 28 guns, was consort to H.M.S. *Phoebe* in the *British Pacific squadron in 1813, part of the force that brought about U.S. loss of *Essex* to the Royal Navy.
W. 74

CHESAPEAKE BAY
The deep, fertile arm of the *Atlantic Ocean penetrating into the North American Coast is 195 miles long (N.-S.) and from three to thirty miles wide. It is an extension of the lower valley of the Susquehanna River, providing approaches to *Baltimore, Annapolis, and *Washington (via the *Potomac River). It has innumerable inlets, including the James River inlet to *Virginia's Hampton Roads anchorage and *Norfolk. The Chesapeake and Delaware Canal connects it with the Delaware River; the Chesapeake and Albemarle and *Dismal Swamp Canals connect with Albemarle Sound.
The *English anchored in the bay in 1607; Captain John Smith explored it in 1608. The first permanent settlement was made at Kent Island (*Maryland) in 1631. The Chesapeake was the route of British invasion in the *War of 1812.
(M. has "Neversink" anchor in the Chesapeake at the conclusion of *W.* to avoid perfect identification with *United States*; his cruise on that ship ended in *Boston.)
W. 51

CHESHIRE
*England's northwest maritime county is mostly a low-land plain which produces coal, rock-salt, peat, cotton, and dairy products. The area has not always been settled but shows evidence of *Roman, *Celtic, *Anglo-Saxon, *Norse, and *Norman civilizations. It is famous as the headquarters of Hotspur (see "Percy") and as a site of shipbuilding (see "Birkenhead") and other industries along the *Mersey River.
See also "Liverpool."
O. 14; M. 123; R. 31

CHESS-PLAYER, AUTOMATON
The "automatic" chess player invented by Wolfgang von Kempelen (1734-1804) and exhibited from 1826 in the *United States concealed a human player.
I.P. 19

CHESTERFIELD, LORD; CHESTERFIELDIAN

Philip Dormer Stanhope, fourth earl of Chesterfield (1694-1773), courtier, statesman, and diplomatist, is famous for his book of letters to his illegitimate son, Philip Stanhope (1732-68), published in 1774 by the son's widow. The book of etiquette was widely praised and widely criticized, especially by *Samuel Johnson, who said Chesterfield's maxims "teach the morals of a whore and the manners of a dancing-master."

Sealts #142 was originally Allan Melvill's property: Chesterfield, Philip Dormer Stanhope, 4th Earl of. *Principles of Politeness, and of Knowing the World ... Methodized and Digested under Distinct Heads, with Additions, by the Rev. Dr. John Trusler ... To Which Is Now First Annexed a Father's Legacy to His Daughters: By the Late Dr. Gregory, of Edinburgh* ... Portsmouth, N.H., Printed by Melcher and Osborne, 1786.

M. 3; P. 15:2; I.P. 22; C.M. 22; C.M. 30

CHESTNUT STREETS

Chestnut Street is a residential thoroughfare of northwest *Philadelphia.

M.D. 6

CHEVALIERS

In M.'s time, taken to mean adventurers or swindlers who live by their wits. The word is the *French version of *cavalier.

M. 32; M. 48; C.M. 1

CHEVIOT HILLS

A stretch of highlands marking the boundary between *Scotland and *England: in bygone times the scene of much border warfare and cattle thievery.

I.P. 18

CHICHA'S

Chicha is a fermented liquor made from corn or sugar cane.

M.D. 54

CHIEF HARPOONEER

*Scoresby supplied data for M. The office of *Specksynder had changed since its inception and was now oc-

cupied by the "principal harpooneer," who was answerable to the commander. As Vincent points out (*The Trying-Out of Moby-Dick*, IV, 4), such a seemingly petty detail bears heavily on "*Ahab's" supremacy on "*Pequod."
M.D. 33

CHILDE HAROLD
        See "Byron; Lord Byron."
M.D. 35

CHILD-MAGIAN
        See "Chaldee . . . . "
M.D. 79

CHILE; CHILIAN
        Chile occupies an area on the southwest coast of *South America approximately 2,600 miles long and from 110 to 250 miles wide. Its great length makes for a climate ranging from hot to frigid, with snow-capped volcanoes, earthquakes, and tidal waves. The original inhabitants were the *Araucanian (or Mapuches) Indians, who resisted incursions by the *Incas and *Spain and were still hostile in the nineteenth century. Diego de Almagro, an aide of *Pizarro, had been resisted by the Araucanians in 1536, but in 1540 Pedro de Valdivia founded *Santiago (the present capital) and other towns, some of which the Indians destroyed. By 1778 Chile was part of the Viceroyalty of *Peru, frequently attacked by *pirates such as *Drake.
        The move to independence was begun in 1810 by Juan Martínez and Bernardo O'Higgins. With the assistance of *Lord Cochrane, it was won in 1818. But O'Higgins fell in 1823, and the constitution was abolished in 1833. There was war against the confederation of Peru and *Bolivia from 1836 to 1839 and again from 1879 to 1884 (the War of the Pacific).
        "Don Miguel," the "Chilian" whale referred to in *M.D.* 45 is presumed fictional.
        See also "Coquimbo"; "Diegoes"; "Juan Fernández"; "Tierra del Fuego"; "Valparaiso."
T. 4; O. 30; O. 73; M. 1; W. 24; M.D. 24; M.D. 36; M.D. 45

CHIMBORAZO
        The province east of Bolivar, Ecuador (1°35' S.; 78°45' W.), is the site of the highest mountain in the nation: Mount Chimborazo (20,561 foot elevation).
M. 36

CHIMNEY HAG
     Old witch in the chimney corner, as in fairy tales.
M.D. 31

CHINA; CHINAMAN; CHINESE
     In the nineteenth century, there was much interest in
China and *Japan as these countries were (forcibly) opened up
to western intercourse. As Finkelstein points out, *Orientalists such as *Emerson shifted their attention from the Near
to the Far East for spiritual focus.
     China (*Chung-Kuo*, or *Hua-Kuo*) remains the most pop-
ulous country of the world and is among the oldest known to
have had human denizens, and the oldest with recognizable
polities (including dynasties which emerged in the third millenium B.C.). The *Romans called China "Serica"; in Medieval times, it was called "*Cathay," a name which remained
in poetic use in M.'s time. The Opium Wars (1839-42) with
*Britain ended with opening of some ports and establishment
of *Hong Kong; China made further concessions after war
with Britain and *France from 1856-60.
     Many of M.'s references show his interest in the then-
exotic traditional Chinese garb (the black cotton jacket of *M.D.*
48; the tasseled cap of *R*. 25), as well as in Chinese silk (the
handkerchief of *M*. 40) and Chinese slippers (*O*. 76) too small to
be useful: a reference to the ancient practice of foot-binding of
females. His allusions also reflect increasing importation of
Chinese articles such as chessmen, puzzles, and carved boxes.
Although the parasol or umbrella (*O*. 78, *R*. 23) had been used
in China since the eleventh century, it was not commonly used
in western countries such as England until the late eighteenth
century and in M.'s time was apparently still a rather rare article. The "*Chinese Society for the Suppression of Meddling
with other People's Business" (*M.D.* 89) perhaps represents
M.'s sympathy for peoples who did not wish to be "saved" by
"civilization" as represented by traders and missionaries.
     See also "Canton"; "Canton River"; "Cathay"; "Great
Wall of China"; "Hang-ho"; "Joss"; "Mandarin."
Passim

CHINA ASTER
     An invented name. H. Bruce Franklin's notes to *C.M.*
suggest a flower allegory, the suffix, -aster, meaning "star," in
biology.
C.M. 39; C.M. 40; C.M. 41

CHINESE DRAWING

From the second millenium B.C., Chinese porcelain has been elaborately decorated with standard subjects and stories illustrated using techniques so much in favor that by the seventeenth century "china" was a standard synonym for porcelain and other dishes. By M.'s time, "Chinese" porcelain was much in vogue. It was emulated and produced on a large scale throughout Europe, with many poor copies on tables there and in the *United States.

Among the drawings M. calls "queer" in *M.D.* 55 were correct and incorrect representations: five bats representing blessings; storks, pines, tortoises, fungi, and bamboo, representing long life; "Buddha's hand," a fruit with fingerlike appendages, representing wealth; *Pa Kua* lines representing natural forces; *yang-yin*, the male/female symbol appearing like two interlocked tadpoles; beneficent dragons and phoenixlike creatures representing emperors and empresses; religious symbols such as *Lao Tzu* (with a large forehead), Lions of Buddha, and composite animals
M.D. 55

CHINESE SOCIETY FOR THE SUPPRESSION OF MEDDLING WITH OTHER PEOPLE'S BUSINESS

See "Humane Society."
M.D. 89

CHLOROFORM

Chloroform, used by Dr. John Snow on Queen *Victoria, became a common childbirth anaesthetic in the nineteenth century, despite the first recorded death from the inhalant in the 1840's. It is a fast-acting and potent nonflammable halogenated hydrocarbon which fell into disuse in the twentieth century for its adverse effects on the heart, liver, and other vital organs.
C.M. 23

CHOCK A'BLOCK

Crammed, or crowded.
W.78

CHOLERA

Technically, "cholera" refers to various diarrheal diseases of short duration, ranging from the mild to the fatal, spread through food or water infection by enteric bacilli. A common water supply, such as that on a ship, is the most frequent cause of contagion. The fatal strain, *Vibrio cholerae*, or what is commonly called Asiatic cholera, is now most often meant by the word.

*Thucydides reported a form of cholera in Athens as early as the fifth century B.C., but fatal epidemics were not described until the fifteenth century, with *India the endemic center. Western pandemics began in the early 1830's; there was cholera in *New York City in 1832, and from 1836-38 it was present in most of the United States. The greatest wave occurred from 1840 to 1849, while M. was a sailor.

The causal agent was isolated by the German bacteriologist, Robert Koch, in 1883.

The Melville family fled to *Pittsfield in 1832 to escape an outbreak of cholera in Albany.
R. 58; W. 14

CHOLULA
Cholula de Rivadavia, in central *Mexico, is the site of an ancient (pre-Colombian) pyramid with a church built on top: the original site of *Aztec human sacrifices. Cholula was devoted to worship of Quetzalcoatl. It was destroyed by Cortés (see "Cortez") in 1519.
R. 46

CHRIST; CHRISTIAN
Jesus Christ, founder of Christianity, is believed by Christians to be the savior of the world and the Son of *God: with God the Father, and the Holy Spirit, the "Trinity." He is thought to have been a historical person living in *Palestine during the reigns of *Augustus Caesar and *Tiberius, but what we call his "history" comes from the *New Testament *Gospels, which are works of faith. In M.'s novels, the name of Jesus Christ is treated with dignity (see "God"), suggesting that M. was a believer. Lawrance Thompson's *Melville's Quarrel With God*, and other works, suggest that despite his seemingly reverent treatment of the name, he was not a true Christian. Wright's *Melville's Use of the Bible* suggests that M. identified with the *Old rather than the New Testament.
Passim

CHRISTIAN; -S; CHRISTENDOM; CHRISTIANIZE; -ED; CHRISTIANIZATION
M. uses these expressions in several senses: the state or condition of being Christian; the Christian faith or religious

system; the sacraments and other ordinances of Christianity; the body or community of Christians—all of which have long traditional use in English.

In context, however, M.'s usage often appears to be ironic or derogatory, especially when he pairs the root with adjectives such as "practical" or "confident," or when he attributes skills such as "spying out" heresy (in *C.M.*), or specifying a *Tahitian "Christian *Sabbath" (in *O.*). The reader may infer a meaning other than the standard literal one for usage of the verb "Christianize," which often asperses missionaries.

Relatively recent discoveries in M. scholarship reveal his membership in The Unitarian Church of All Souls, New York City (Park Avenue and 20th Street) and in other Christian churches from the time of his marriage in 1849 until his death in 1891 (see especially *The Endless, Winding Way in Melville: New Charts by Kring and Carey*).
Passim

CHRISTMAS, --DAY
Commemoration of the traditional day of *Christ's birth (25 December, in the western calendar) was suppressed in the *United States until at least the mid-nineteenth century, probably because the *Puritan *Protestant tradition recognized the *Pagan origins of such phenomena as the Christmas Tree, and limited observation to religious services. At this time, children received gifts on St. Nicholas's day, 6 December, and adults received gifts on *New Year's Day. During much of M.'s lifetime, and especially in his *Dutch-tradition family, New Year's Day was the more important holiday. Yet, emerging American recognition of Christmas is seen in M.'s works, in the expression "Merry Christmas," in *M.D.* 22 and *P.* 22:4, the "Christmas turkey" of *W.* 25, the "Christmas sleigh" of *P.* 25:4. The giving of gifts at Christmas was not a tradition until the later part of the century, when commercialism began coloring every aspect of American life.

As Anderson shows in *Melville in the South Seas* (Chapter 13), the only custom observed for ships' crews of the time was doubling of the *grog ration. M. was often at sea on Christmas: in 1842 on *Acushnet* (see "Pequod"); in 1843 on *Charles and Henry*; in 1844 on *United States* (at *Lima); in 1849 as a passenger in *Portsmouth, England, preparatory to sailing back to the United States: his journal commemorates his viewing of *Nelson's *Victory* on the occasion. The journal for 25 December 1856 finds him in *Syra Harbor: "Today appears to be no holyday among the Greeks. Or theirs is the old style of almanack; people are so busy here I cannot learn which."

Various Christmas books appeared in the Melville family (Sealts #s 143a and 143b): of one (unidentified) item, M. wrote to a relative: "I liked that Christmas Story you sent me, especially in the opening portion—the good old Dutch Saint's [Nicholas's] lamentation over these 'degenerate days' which we account such an 'advance'." The comment may refer to creeping commercialism, or indeed to the whole panoply of practices which Professor Donald D. Stone of Queens College says Dickens (see "Hard times") practically *invented*.
     M.D.'s ill-fated "Pequod" sails on Christmas Day.
W. 23; W. 25; M.D. 17; M.D. 22; M.D. 28; M.D. 81; P. 2:3; P. 3:3; P. 21:2; P. 22:4; P. 25:4; C.M. 3; C.M. 24 and elsewhere

CHRONIC RHEUMATICS
     Chronic-rheumatics were probably victims of Rheumatoid Arthritis, a crippling progressive disease of the joints.
     M. was much afflicted by rheumatism, and in March 1862 was too much in pain to attend the funeral of his uncle, Herman *Gansevoort. In 1876, he contributed $100.00 to the New York Society for the Relief of the Ruptured & Crippled.
P. 21:3

CHRONICLES, BOOK OF
     The *Old Testament's Chronicles I and II cover history from *Adam to *Cyrus, king of *Persia, running parallel to *Genesis through II *Kings, concluded with Ezra-Nehemiah.
R. 17

"CHRONOMETRICALS AND HOROLOGICALS"
     M. acts as his own gloss on the pamphlet in succeeding pages of *P*. The chronometer, aside from its use at sea, is an ancient symbol of Absolute Time, eternity, heavenly wisdom. The "Horologe" is a symbol of earthly local time and practical wisdom and morality in *Sir Thomas Browne's "Horologie," in *Pseudodoxia Epidemica* 5 and is also referred to by Carlyle (*Sartor Resartus* 9) and Longfellow (*Hyperion* 1, 6).
     As Murray points out in his notes to *P*., M.'s analogy is not apt, given the twenty-four conventionally accepted earthly horological times: "according to Melville's figure the godliness of a society depends on its closeness to the *Greenwich meridian" (p. 477).
P. 14:1; P. 21:3

"CHRONOMETRICS"
        See "Chronometricals and Horologicals."
P. 21:3

CHRYSTOSTOM
        Saint John Chrystostom (c. 347-407), Archbishop of
*Constantinople from 398, was a lawyer, scriptural exegete,
and orator. (His surname is from the Greek for "golden-
mouthed.") A model of Christian abnegation, plain speech,
and orthodox thinking, he incurred many enemies but was
supported by the people, even to applause during his sermons.
Eventually exiled, he wrote many treatises and scriptural
commentaries and is honored on his feast day by both the
Roman Catholic and Greek Orthodox Churches.
M. 3

CHURCH, THE
        The word "church" comes from Middle English *chirche*,
through the Anglo-Saxon *circe*, from the Greek *kyriakon*,
meaning "the Lord's house." (Although sacred writers used
the Greek *Ekklesia*, that word originally referred to an assembly of legislating citizens.) *New Testament writers used it to
refer to a single community of Christians, or to the whole body
of Christians, or to an ideal perfect church membership
independent of time, related to the "kingdom of God."
        M.'s use in *T.* seems to refer to Church as a governing
body with orthodox dogma and perhaps bureaucratic personnel, more in keeping with the Greek *Ekklesia* than with *kyriakon*.
T. 26; C.M. 8 and elsewhere

CHURCH OF ENGLAND
        The conservative *Protestant Anglo-Catholic faith which
considers itself successors to the pre-Reformation Church in
*Britain. The Church of England differs from the Roman
*Catholic Church in, among other things, its refusal of the
*Pope as head, intolerance of Monasticism, inclusion of new
texts and creeds, including the *Thirty-Nine Articles. The
*American branch is the Episcopal Church, mentioned in *W.*
38 and *C.M.* 3.
R. 34; R. 35; W. 38

CHURCH OF THE APOSTLES
M.'s name for a church in *P.* may have been suggested by the Episcopal Church of the Holy Apostles, at Twenty-eighth Street and Ninth Avenue, New York City.
P. 19:1

CHURCH OF THE COCOA-NUTS
The Royal Mission Chapel of Papaoa (*Papoar), according to *Ellis (Chapter 15) constructed with and decorated by local materials.
O. 44

CHURCH AND STATE
The First Amendment to the *United States *Constitution has two clauses referring to religion.   The less problematical, the "free exercise" clause, grants citizens the right to practice chosen religions.   The difficult one, "no law respecting an establishment of religion," was made intentionally ambiguous by the Founders.   During the *Revolutionary era, eight of the thirteen states had official, state-supported churches. *Jefferson was firmly opposed to official support of the *Church of England in *Virginia;   he interpreted the clause as constituting a "wall of separation" between Church and State, and the *Supreme Court has thus interpreted it since its adoption.
But the ambiguous clause has consistently been a problem, especially in the nineteenth century as regards the *Mormon, Roman *Catholic, and other churches (and by extension the *"Apostles" of *P.*).
In modern times, the problem is exacerbated.   Among other objections, free-thinkers point to the fact that both houses of *Congress have since 1789 opened their sessions with a prayer by a chaplain.
P. 19:1

CHURCH DE CANDELARIA
Our Lady of Candeléria, built in 1635, is located in the present-day commercial section of *Rio de Janeiro, overlooking *Ilha das Cobras. It is an ornate domed and gilded example of *Portuguese baroque architecture.
W. 39

CHURCH OF NOSSA SENORA DE GLORIA

The favorite church of *Dom Pedro, on *Gloria Hill, overlooking Gloria Bay; it was built in the late eighteenth century with blue-faced tiling and a famous carved wood altar. From the church grounds one sees what is reputedly the best view of *Rio.
W. 39

CICERO, MARCUS TULLIUS

Cicero (or, Tully, 106-43 B.C.), *Roman statesman, scholar, orator, and writer, was the son of a Roman knight, whose early study of philosophy, rhetoric, and law led to a successful career. He was put to death after *Julius Caesar's assassination, for speaking against Mark *Antony, but the importance of his writings has lingered throughout history, especially in words contributed to the language and in theorizing of the *Stoics, sceptics, and republicans in general.

Among the most important works: *De inventione*, a textbook; *De republica*, on Roman history; *Academica*, on judgement; *De finibus*. on the Supreme Good; *Tusculanae Disputationes*, on pain, evil, distress, and virtue; *De natura deorum*, on a Supreme Being; *De officiis*, on moral obligation.

Sealts # 147, *Harper's Classical Library*, vols. 8-10, contain Cicero's orations; vol. 37 is *Dialogues on the Orator*.
C.M. 22

CID, THE

The most famous Spanish epic hero, Rodrigo Diaz de Bivar, el Cid Campeador (*Seyd*, lord; *campeador*, champion) was a nobleman (1030-99) whose invincibility in war and prowess as sword-wielding soldier of fortune led to his portrayal as a near-saint, said to have died of grief after a defeat. His major victories were in the war between Sancho of *Castile and Sancho of Navarre, but he became a soldier of fortune against the *Moors (and sometimes against the *Christians).

Literature portrays him as a type of patriotic Christian knight, especially in the *Poema del Cid*, a long Spanish poem of the twelfth century. Somewhat more historical are the *Historia Roderici*, a contemporary Latin chronicle, and a narrative of his conquest of Valencia.
M. 21

CINCINNATI

The city of southwestern *Ohio was laid out as Losantiville in 1788, settled in 1789, renamed in 1790. It was an early

transshipment point for settlers and a station of the
"Underground Railroad" before the *Civil War. The nineteenth century saw an influx of *German and *Irish emigrants.

M. *lectured (rather poorly) in Cincinnati, 2 February
1858. He attended the National Theatre, where he saw
"*Mazeppa; or the Wild Horses of *Tartary," and "Karmel, the
Scout; or, The Rebel of the Jerseys." The subject matter of
these plays is probably indicative of Cincinnati's cultural level
of the time, at least if Mrs. Trollope is to be believed.
C.M. 22; C.M. 45

CINCINNATUS
        Lucius Quinctius Cincinnatus (b. c. 519 B.C.), early
*Roman patrician hero/farmer, became a dictator after oppos-
ing codes of laws applicable to *plebians and to his own class.
*Livy tells of his twice emerging from private life to take con-
trol, the first time rescuing the consular army, and the second
checking the success of Spurius Maelius, who sought kingship.
R. 56

CINGALESE
        See "Senegal."
R. 34

CINQUE PORTS
        In the thirteenth century, *Sandwich, *Dover, Hythe,
Romney, and Hastings formed an association that furnished
ships and men for the *British Navy, protected against invasion, and enjoyed special privileges.
        M.'s journal for 5 November 1849 incorrectly assumes
that Deal, his location of the moment, made up one of the five
ports.
M.D. 90

CIRCASSIA
        In the northern *Caucasus near the Black Sea of the
modern Union of the Soviet Socialist Republics, Circassia
(Cherkessia) derives its name from its people, who were finally
subjugated to the *Russians by 1864, causing a mass immigration into *Turkey. The area is known for its many distinct
dialects and for its great antiquity (pre-classical origins).

*Byron (in *Circassia; or, A Tour to the Caucasus*) and other poets marvelled at the blond beauty of Circassian women, who held a low place in the society and were often sent to harems of oriental potentates.
M.D. 60; P. 2:4

CIRCE-FLOWERS; CIRCEA FLOWERS
     Circaea, of the *Onagraceae* family (myrtle order) is "Enchanter's nightshade." It has beautiful flowers but bears fruit with hooked bristles. In "flower language," it signifies Fascination, or a Spell.
     Circe is the sorceress and temptress of *Homer's *Odyssey*. Odysseus (*Ulysses) resists her, using a protective herb to avoid her changing him into a swine.
M. Passim

CITIES OF THE PLAIN
     In the *Old Testament, the "Cities of the Valley": *Sodom, *Gomorrah, Admah, Zeboiim, and Zoar, in the valley of the *Jordan and the *Dead Sea. They are located in the Valley of Siddim in *Genesis 14:3, 8, 10 (now under Dead Sea waters). They are destroyed for "wickedness" (usually taken to mean sexual excess) in Genesis 19:24-29. (The "Five Cities" of the Wisdom of *Solomon 10:6.)
     (In *Melville's Use of the Bible*, Wright says: "With the names of . . . places the association is one of condition rather than topography . . . Cities of the Plain mean doomed societies.")
W. 89; I.P. 24

CITY DIRECTORY
     See "Directory."
R. 61; P. 17:2

CITY HALL
     *New York City's City Hall evolved from the original *Dutch *Stadt Huys of 1641, which overlooked the harbor at *Pearl Street and *Coenties Slip. By the eighteenth century, it was located on *Wall Street (on the site of the present-day Federal Hall). The building M. cites in *I.P.* 16, on a "triangular Park" near *St. Paul's and the *Astor House, is the present structure (having been submitted to various changes, including enlargement of the park). It was built in 1811, with a marble facade (and an inexpensive brownstone exterior facing the

less fashionable neighborhood to the north). The Park was bounded by the Bloomingdale Road (now *Broadway), and the Boston Post Road (now Park Row and *Bowery), and "Newspaper Row" grew up around it in the 1840's. The French Renaissance/Federal-style building was the scene of innumerable receptions and prestigious official functions (including the display of Lincoln's corpse in the Rotunda). It was damaged by a blaze (started by fireworks) in 1858 and thereafter degenerated rather badly, with only minor reconstruction work performed until the twentieth century.
I.P. 16

CITY HOTEL
     The City Hotel (from c. 1792) was the most highly favored domicile and watering-place of the city of *New York until construction of the *Astor House. Located opposite *Trinity Church on the *Broadway block bounded by Thames and Cedar Street, its plain (four-storey) exterior belied its elegant interior, where important visitors might stay in lavishly decorated rooms and be feted (as was *Lafayette, in 1824) in large and ornate dining rooms. In December of 1812, five hundred *Navy dignitaries attend a banquet honoring *Hull, *Decatur, and *Jones (who was not present), amid massive flag-draped depictions of naval scenes. They listened to elegant and lengthy toasts and readings by fashionable poets praising the glories of the U.S. Navy.
     The City Hotel was torn down in 1850, but at the time depicted in R. it was still the most chic gathering place, as evinced in the pawnbroker's slur in R. 4 and in "Captain Riga's" owning a "City Hotel suit" (R. 61).
R. 4; R. 14; R. 61

CIVIL LIST
     An annual grant by the *English *Parliament, paying the Sovereign's personal and household expenses and Royal pensions; a fixed sum since 1952.
     The name derives from the Eighteenth Century, when civil servants were paid from it (until 1831). *George III had given up most hereditary revenues in exchange for it (1760).
     The modern Civil List includes the Royal Bounty, for charity and official subscriptions.
O. 65

CIVIL WAR
        Although the American Civil War postdates M.'s novels, the conflict (1861-65) between the Union represented by the Northern states and the Confederacy represented by the southern is anticipated by many of M.'s allusions. See in particular: "America"; "Democrat"; "Randolph"; "slavery"; "Webster."
        At the age of forty-two, M. attempted to enlist in the Union *Navy but was rejected. He visited the *Virginia front in 1864. M.'s *Battle-Pieces* record his reaction to the tragic war in which finally none of the victims seemed deserving of punishment.

CLAM
        The edible bivalve *venus mercenaria*: important to the *New England economy and diet.
M. 174; W. 91; M.D. 3; M.D. 14; M.D. 15

CLARENCE
        George *Plantagenet, Duke of Clarence (1449-1478), was born in *Dublin, the sixth son of Richard, Duke of *York (1412-1460). Brother Edward IV's accession brought the *Percy properties, knighthoods of Bath and Garter, Lord Lieutenancy of *Ireland. As heir presumptive, he became involved in *Warwick's schemes, including marriage to Warwick's eldest daughter, to which Edward objected. Working with Warwick against Edward, Clarence finally fled when he discovered he had been duped; Warwick restored the Lancasters, making it unlikely Clarence would ever reign. He then joined Edward's forces, and possibly murdered his brother-in-law, Prince Edward, after the battle of Tewkesbury. Strife began anew when his brother Gloucester resolved to marry the widowed Anne *Neville, gaining her custody despite Clarence's efforts at her concealment. Edward then vetoed a good second match for Clarence after his wife's death, and he avenged himself by charging one of the late wife's attendants with poisoning her, finally executing the attendant. After numerous offenses involving necromancers, etc., Edward committed Clarence to the *Tower for various slanders, condemning him to death. The secrecy of the execution on 17 or 18 February 1478 led to rumors, among them his having been drowned in the butt of *malmsey wine. An idol of the people for his revolutionary zeal, Clarence is buried in Tewkesbury Abbey; he was survived by two children.
        *Shakespeare's *The Tragedy of King Richard III*, based on Holinshed, has the executioner stab his victim, threatening

to drown him in the nearby malmsey-butt if that does not kill him (I, iv, 259-260).
O. 10

CLARENCE [DOCK]
      *Liverpool: originally, six acres of water area; opened 1830, for the berthing of steamships.
R. 32

CLARENDON
      Edward Hyde, First Earl of Clarendon (1609-1674), *English statesman and historian, became *Charles II's lord chancellor during the Restoration settlement. Although his influence on history was profound, he made some unpopular decisions that caused his eventual downfall and exile. In 1660, Anne Hyde, his daughter, became pregnant by the duke of *York and secretly married him, to the disapproval of the court and of her father. He writes of his rage in his six-volume *History of the Great Rebellion and Civil Wars in England* (pub. 1888), a work of much autobiographical bias. Anne's marriage did Clarendon no good at court, but her daughters were to become Queen *Mary and *Queen Anne.
W. 55

CLARET
      The traditional *English name for *French wine of *Bordeaux. During the twelfth-century English occupation of the area, claret was made by mixing red and white wines, the dilution perhaps explaining *Samuel Johnson's saying: "Port for men, claret for boys" ("Quotations" section).
P. 22:1

CLAUDE'S
      Claude Gelleé, or Claude Lorraine (1600-82), *French painter of ideal landscapes, visited *Naples early in life, acquiring a taste for coastal scenes. He spent most of his life in *Rome, developing an extraordinary sensitivity to the effects of light. Eventually he became more classical and monumental in his style, painting *Biblical or mythological scenes, especially from *Virgil. He was enormously influential in art, and his works were avidly collected in *England and even emulated in garden landscaping there.
      M. saw Claude's paintings at the Dulwich Gallery in England in 1849. At the Sciarra Palace on the Corso in Rome,

he probably saw Claude's "The Sunset" and "Flight into Egypt," commenting in his journal (7 March 1857): "he paints the air." Three days later two large landscapes at the Doria Pamfili Gallery had an opposite effect: "did not touch me."

Sealts #192 is Owen John Dullea's *Claude Geleé le Lorrain* (1887).
M. 13

CLAVICLE
See "Ulna."
M. 139

"CLAW-HAMMER-JACKET"
Tail coat of full evening dress, colloquial since mid-nineteenth century. "Coat" or "jacket" is generally omitted: "a claw-hammer."
O. 21

CLAY-EATERS
Like modern-day "Starch-eaters," "clay-eaters" were those with bizarre appetites for unusual substances: in the nineteenth century especially southern low-class whites. (Clays such as bentonite and fuller's earth are used in refining edible oils and fats, in medicines, and in cosmetics.)
C.M. 2

CLEOPATRA, --'S
The Cleopatra to whom M. refers was the daughter of Ptolemy XII Auletes. Upon his death in 51 B.C., she succeeded him, ruling *Egypt successively with her brothers Ptolemy XIII (51-47) and Ptolemy XIV (47-44) and her son Ptolemy XV *Caesar (44-30). The highly educated and popular *Greek/*Macedonian queen is best remembered for her desire to share Rome's central power and for her liasons with *Julius Caesar and Mark *Antony, by both of whom she bore children. Caesar helped Cleopatra to consolidate her Egyptian power and established her in a Roman villa. After Caesar's death (44), Mark Antony married Cleopatra and attempted to expand her realm. She was present at *Actium when Antony was defeated by *Octavian's forces. The two committed suicide the following year. Cleopatra chose death by snake bite, for the snake's position as minister to the sun-god Amon-Ra.
M.'s knowledge about Cleopatra probably derives mainly from the plays of *Shakespeare. Cleopatra's "barges" (*M.D.*

83) refers to the queen's fleeing the sea fight at Actium, in *Antony and Cleopatra* III, viii.

Cleopatra's barge (*M.* 149) was an elaborately outfitted vessel that became the paradigm for sumptuous yachts, many of which were named after her. In 1817 a fast sailing yacht (hermaphrodite brig) called *Cleopatra* raced *United States* off the *Spanish coast. She was taken into the service of Kamehameha (see "Kammahammaha . . .") II and wrecked in 1824.

M. 22; M. 29; M. 149; R. 49; M.D. 54; M.D. 83

CLERK, JOHN, ESQ.

Penny Cyclopaedia (VII, 1837) says Clerk was "inventor of one of the most important parts of the modern *British system of naval tactics . . . what is technically called 'breaking the line,' a manoeuvre employed by "*Sir George (later Lord) Rodney, leading to his 'decisive victory' over the *French, under *DeGrasse, in the *West Indies." Clerk is responsible not only for *An Essay on Naval Tactics, systematic and historical*, but also an article in *Edinburgh Review*, vol. vi.

W. 83

CLEVELAND

The northern *Ohio city is a harbor of Lake *Erie, at the mouth of the Cuyahoga River. The city was laid out by Moses Cleaveland in 1796 and was chartered in 1836. Development was bolstered by the opening of the Ohio and *Erie Canal in 1832 and by extension of the railroad in 1851.

M. visited Cleveland and was surprised by its development in 1840; he *lectured there 11 January 1858.

M.D. 54

CLOOTZ, ANARCHARSIS

Jean Baptiste du Val-de-Grace, Baron de Cloots (1755-1794), born into a noble *Prussian family, changed his name to Anarcharsis at the outbreak of the *French Revolution. A member of the Jacobin Club and a founder of the cult of reason, he presented himself to the Assembly at the head of thirty-six silent foreigners of many nations and races, whom he called "ambassadors of the human race" eager for a universal republic. Thereafter, he was called "the orator of the human race," dropping his hereditary title. He was elected to the Convention in 1792 but guillotined as an Hébertist in 1794.

His pseudonym was taken from Jean Jacques Barthelemy's (1716-1795) romance, *Voyage du jeune Anarcharsis en Grèce*, widely read in France.

Clootz is also referred to in *Billy Budd, Sailor*.
M.D. 27; C.M. 2

CLOTHES-PRESSES
Shelved recesses, chests, or cases in which clothes are kept folded.
W. 9

CLUNY, HOTEL DE
M. visited *Paris's famous fourteenth- and fifteenth-century museum in 1849, commenting in his journal (5 December 1849) on its "glorious" appointments and artifacts: "just the house I should like to live in." He descended into the *Palais des Thermes* beneath, inspecting the remains of *Roman baths presumably built under Constantius Chlorus (292-306) and sometimes known as the *Palais de Julien* because *Julian the Apostate is said to have been crowned emperor there in 360. *Hôtel de Cluny* is "spiked" with gargoyle water spouts.
M.D. 41

CLYDE
*Scotland's most important river, the Clyde, is 106 miles long. It begins at Queensberry Hill, Dumfriesshire and empties at Greenoch, where the firth (seacoast indention) begins. In November 1856, M. traveled up the Clyde on a steamship, stopping at *Glasgow and Loch Lomond.
I.P. 15

COAST-OF-GUINEA-MAN
See "Guinea . . . . "
R. 35

COCHIN CHINA
An area of modern-day South Vietnam, including the fertile Mekong delta and Saigon, Cochin China had no clear boundaries before being part of *French Indochina, from 1862-1948.
W. 5

COCHITUATE

Lake Cochituate, in eastern *Massachusetts, sixteen miles west of *Boston, is the three-mile-long reservoir for the Boston area.
P. 22:1

COCHRANE, LORD

Thomas Cochrane, Tenth Earl of Dundonald (1775-1860), a hero of the *Napoleonic Wars, commanded the fleets of *Chile and *Brazil against *Portugal, assisting in attainment of Chile's independence.

The colorful Cochrane was the author of *Autobiography of a Seaman* (2 vols., 1860-61) and *Narrative of Services in the Liberation of Chili, Peru and Brazil* (1959), which M. could not have seen.

See also "King's Bench."
W. 63

COCKATOO POINT

Cockatoo Island, in Port Jackson, *New South Wales, *Australia, is just west-northwest of *Sydney. Although a tiny island (three-quarters of a mile by one-half of a mile), it has long been the site of shipyards.
M.D. 87

COCK LANE

The *Smithfield, *England, Cock Lane ghost of 1762 was proved an imposture by *Samuel Johnson and others, after all *London became captivated by stories of rappings supposedly made by a spirit at the home of one Mr. Parsons. He was condemned to the pillory when it was discovered that his eleven-year-old daughter was the rapper. M.'s journal records a visit to the site (10 November 1849).
M.D. 69; C.M. 17

COCKNEY

M.E. *cokeney* refers to a "cock's egg," a malformed egg. Originally the epithet referred to misbehaving children, or simpletons. *Shakespeare uses it in *King Lear* to describe a squeamish woman. Later it referred to country folk, the majority of the population, or to townsfolk for their ignorance of country life. Still later it was restricted to *Londoners born within the sound of the bells of St. Mary-le-Bow (see "Bow Bells"), then finally to denote the peculiar London speech.
O. 53; R. 51

COCK-ROBIN
A soft, easy fellow, from the nursery rhyme, "Who killed Cock Robin?"; probable origination Balder (Baldur), or other *Scandinavian myth-maker. The nickname was applied to *Britain's Robert Walpole when he fell from power in 1742.
R. 20

COCOA-NUT TREE
The coconut *palm (*Cocos nucifera*) bears the fibrous-husked nut containing white meat and sweet milky fluid which are mainstays of South Sea island diets. *Ellis (I, 53-59) goes into even more detail than M. (*T.* 29) on the uses of the tree: wood for spears, house-building materials, canoe-rollers, fences, fuel; leaves for thatch, baskets, hats, symbols of authority; shell fiber (M.'s *kayar*, in *R.* 34) for ropes and clothing; shells for eating and drinking vessels. He goes on to provide instructions for cultivation.
Passim

COD
Gadus morrhua, an important food fish found off banks, expecially in the north *Atlantic.
M.D. 15

CODRINGTON, ADMIRAL
Sir Edward Codrington (1770-1851) entered the *British Navy in 1783. After serving with *Howe, he was given command of *Orion* off *Cádiz in 1805 and was *Nelson's Squadron Leader at *Trafalgar. After serving with *Collingwood, he was sent to the North American Station in 1814 as Captain of the Fleet to Sir Alexander Cochrane at *Chesapeake Bay and *New Orleans. He was Commander in Chief at the *Mediterranean station in 1826 and at *Navarino in 1827, where he was questioned regarding the firing of the first shots.
W. 75

COELUS
In mythology, Coelus (Gr. Uranus) was the son and husband of Tithea (or *Terra, or Gaea, or Ge—the Earth), father of the *Titans and the *Cyclops. His son, *Saturn (Gr. Kronos), castrated him with a sickle.
P. 25:5

COENTIES SLIP
     *New York City's Coenties slip was a busy *East River
inlet and chief shipping center until it burned in 1835 and 1845.
The slip, northeast of *Broad Street extending from the water
to *Pearl Street, had been the site of the first *American tavern, in 1642.   The present-day "Coenties Alley" marks the
slip's location before landfilling.
R. 1; M.D. 1

COEUR DE LION'S
     Richard I (1157-1199), King of *England from 1189 to
1199, was called "Coeur de Lion" ("Lionhearted"). Third son of
Henry II and Eleanor of Aquitaine, he rebelled against his father early but was pardoned and went on to great military
glory as Duke of Poitiers. He led the Third *Crusade against
*Saladin in 1190, conquering *Sicily and *Cyprus enroute, but
international quarrels among crusaders weakened the drive,
and Richard was forced to sign a three-year truce with Saladin
in 1192. Imprisoned and ransomed on the trip back to England,
he had himself recrowned in 1194, fearing a compromised
reign. The rest of his life was spent in *Normandy, making
war against Philipe II; killed in battle, he was buried in
Fontevrault, France, having spent only six months of his reign
in England.
     Historians paint him as an energetic, hot-tempered, but
accomplished man: a splendid soldier, skilled politician, and
excellent troubadour poet, probably homosexual.
I.P. 22

COFFINS OF NANTUCKET
     See "Charley Coffin."
M.D. 32; M.D. 82

COGNIAC
     The unprepossessing town of Cognac, in the *Burgundy
region of *France (c. 70 miles southeast of La Rochelle), is best
known for its amber *brandy, double-distilled from local white
grapes and aged in Limousin oak casks. François I was born
in Cognac.
M.D. 72

COKE, EDWARD; COKES
     Sir Edward Coke (1552-1634), a distinguished lawyer and
legal writer, in conflict with *James I, maintained that the

king could not disobey laws or make laws without
*Parliament's consent. His work on the (1628) Petition of
Rights and his "Bill of Liberties" were sources for the
*American *Bill of Rights. Among his publications are the
four-volume *Institutes*, of which vol. I is known as *Coke Upon
Littleton*.

A member of the *Star Chamber, Coke was a just judge
but a fierce prosecutor. He conducted the great treason trials
of his time, prosecuting the earls of Essex and Southhampton
in 1601, *Sir Walter Raleigh in 1603, and the *Gunpowder Plot
conspirators in 1605; he was also involved in inquisatorial proceedings regarding *Catholics. His strength and incorrupt-
ability made him enemies, including *Francis Bacon.
O. 19; W. 72; M.D. 89; P. 17:2

"COKE UPON LYTTLETON"
        See "Coke, Edward; Cokes."
M.D. 89; P. 17:2

COLCHIS
        In mythology, Colchis is an *Asian country at the east-
ern end of the black sea, to which *Jason sailed in quest of the
golden fleece. Home to *Medea, it was the site of the oracle of
Artemis/*Diana, and very hostile to strangers.
M. 149

COLCHURCH
        St. Mary Colechurch, *Southwark, *London, home
parish of *Peter of Colchurch, was destroyed in the *Great
Fire. *Thomas à Becket had been baptized in the church. (The
church name referred to a family named Cole.)
I.P. 24

COLD-STREAM GUARDS
        The Guards, which play a prominent part throughout
*Scottish history, were created in 1659-60, by General Monk,
Duke of Albemarle, for the march into *England which re-
sulted in the restoration of *Charles II to the throne. They are
one of the guard regiments of the royal household in Britain.
        See "Horse Guards."
W. 42

COLD WATER CUSTOMER
    A tea-totaler, who does not drink alcoholic beverages.
W. 91

COLEMAN (AND STETSON)
    See "Astor House."
W. 15

COLERIDGE, --'S
    Samuel Taylor Coleridge (1772-1834), Romantic poet, lecturer, journalist, philosopher, and critic of literature, theology, and society, was himself partly responsible for his somewhat clouded biography. Plans for the ministry were put aside before his brilliance in classical reading and discussion attracted the friendsip of Leigh Hunt and *Lamb. Inspired by *French Revolutionary politics, Coleridge left Jesus College, *Cambridge, when debts and heavy drinking became a problem. In 1793, he enlisted under the name "Comerbache," in the Fifteenth Light Dragoons but was either discharged for unfitness or bought out of the service by his brother.
    By 1794, he was working with Southey on Pantisocracy, a *Utopian plan to set up a small *New England commune, and writing poetry praising such radicals as Godwin and *Priestley. He named his son by wife, Sara Fricker, after *David Hartley.
    Intimate friendship with the *Wordsworths focussed Coleridge's poetic efforts; during years at Dorset, he produced "The Rime of the Ancient Mariner" (to which W. was likened in *The Athenaeum* [Feb. 1850] and *M.D.* was likened in *The Contemporary Review* [Sept. 1884]). His work in *Lyrical Ballads* (1798) helped create a permanent change in literary sensibility.
    In *Germany, Coleridge studied or translated *Kant, *Schiller, and other "*German mystics." A return to the Wordsworths, now in the Lake District, brought personal problems exacerbated by opium addiction. He returned to the Continent, breaking with his wife, and then settling with the Wordsworths and Sara Hutchinson to lecture and work on the philosophy that came to fruition after a break with the circle. *Biographia Literaria* (1817), which M. purchased in 1848 (Sealts #154), is his major autobiographical work of Romantic metaphysics and philosophy. It examines the creative principle, poetic language and form, the nature of inspiration, as well as specific works, justifying literary Romanticism, which M. appeared to see as a link in the overly optimistic chain of thinking that started with *Plato, continued in the German

mystics, and culminated in *American *Transcendentalists such as *Emerson.

In *London, Coleridge published poetry and prose under the influence of *Byron and Carlyle, as well as radical *Christian treatises on morals and reform and dialectical pieces on poetics.

Among his major poems are "Christabel" and "Frost at Midnight" (1798), "Dejection: an Ode" (1802), and "Kubla *Khan" (1816).

In M.'s time, Coleridge was called a political turncoat, a drug addict, adulterer, and humbug. But tributes from writers such as *Hazlett and *Shelley and autopsy evidence of lifelong illness have gone far toward explaining his moodiness, apparent hypochondria, and drug reliance.

M. also knew (Sealts #155) *Notes and Lectures upon *Shakespeare and some of the Old Poets and Dramatists; with Other Literary Remains* (2 vols., 1849).
W. 13; W. 38; M.D. 42

COLERIDGE'S "HIGH GERMAN HORSE"
Coleridge's *American reputation was as a *Kantian metaphysician, not as a poet. *New York intellectuals despised German *transcendentalist ideas, and indeed most things German. Coleridge boasted in *Biographia Literaria* of his ease with the German language. *Penny Cyclopaedia* dismisses Coleridge as a parrot or a plagiarist, typical of Germans.
W. 41

COLIC
A general term for paroxysmal pain usually seated in the lower digestive system near the colon (hence the name). It is common in human infants and in animals.
O. 50

COLLEGE OF PHYSICIANS AND SURGEONS
See "College of Surgeons."
M. 24

COLLEGE OF SURGEONS
*London's *Royal College of Surgeons is probably exemplary of the species as is *Philadelphia's College of Physicians and Surgeons (1787).
W. 61

COLLEGE OF THE SORBONNE
See "Sorbonne."
I.P. 8

COLLINGWOOD
Cuthbert Collingwood, Baron Collingwood (1748-1810), *Nelson's second-in-command at *Trafalgar and later *Mediterranean commander, went to sea at the age of twelve. He won lieutenancy in 1774 at the battle of *Bunker Hill, then served on the sloop *Hornet in the *West Indies. He followed Nelson in command of several ships, developing a close friendship. He participated in the *French Revolutionary wars and as captain of Excellent took part in the victory of *St. Vincent. In 1799 he became Rear-Admiral. When his squadron appeared at *Cádiz, he became second-in-command at Trafalgar and was first to engage the enemy. Command passed to him on Nelson's death. He was created Baron Collingwood and given a pension but was unable to retire for lack of admirals to replace him. He died at sea, remembered as a humane commander.
See also "Admiral's 'Correspondence'" and "Quotations" section: "This young gentleman . . . . "
W. 17; W. 27; W. 36; W. 51

COLNETT, CAPTAIN
The James Colnett book referred to in M.D., A Voyage to the South *Atlantic and Round Cape *Horn into the *Pacific Ocean for the Purpose of Extending the Spermaceti Whale Fisheries and Other Objects of Commerce (London, 1798), contained an illustration of a "Physeter or Spermaceti Whale," hoisted on deck in 1793, off the coast of *Mexico. The picture was sketched in *Beale's work.
In "The Encantadas," Sketch Fifth, M. refers to "Colnet, the whaling-ground explorer," one of "three eye-witness authorities" on the *Galapagos Islands.
See also "Extracts" 49.
M.D. Extracts 49; M.D. 55; M.D. 56

COLNETT'S VOYAGE FOR THE PURPOSE OF EXTENDING THE SPERMACETI WHALE FISHERY
See "Colnett, Captain"; "Extracts" 49.
M.D. Extracts 49

COLOGNE

The *German port on the *Rhine River (295 miles west-south-west of *Berlin) was created as the Roman *Colonia Agrippinensis* by *Claudius in A.D. 50. *Charlemagne created an archdiocese here of princes and electors of the *Holy Roman Empire, but feuds caused their removal by the thirteenth century. The famous Cathedral was begun in 1248 on the site of a ninth-century church (but was not completed until 1880). The city was a member of the *Hanse League, becoming a free imperial city in 1474.

In M.'s time, it was a chief transit port and depot of western Germany, as well as a focal point of Lower Rhenish culture. M. visited twice (1849 and 1857), commenting in his journal on the first occasion (9 December) on the "everlasting 'crane'" atop the Cathedral (*M.D.* 32) and continuing expansively: "I had to spend the day in Cologne. But it was not altogether unpleasant . . . . In this antiquated gable-ended old town—full of *Middle Age, *Charlemagne associations—where *Rubens was born and Mary De *Medici died—there is much to interest a pondering man like me." He goes on to mention the "Three Kings" (see "Chaldee") who supposedly brought gifts to the infant *Jesus, said to be entombed at Cologne Cathedral, their skulls on view, crowned and decorated with precious gems, and their names on display: Gaspar, Melchior, and Balthazar. M.'s journal of 8-11 December 1849 reports his visit.

The three kings are known as patrons of travelers and pilgrims, not of barbers, as is claimed in *C.M.*
M.D. 16; M.D. 32; M.D. 85; I.P. 9; C.M. 43

COLOSSUS

A statue of Helios, the sun-god, is said to have bestrode the entrance to the harbor of *Rhodes in the third century B.C., falling in an earthquake in 224 B.C. (Modern engineers tend to doubt that such a construction could have existed.)
M.D. 35

COLT'S REVOLVER; COLT'S PATENT REVOLVERS

Colonel Samuel Colt (1814-1862), born in Hartford, *Connecticut, ran away to sea when he was sixteen. Starting in 1831, he marketed a metal revolver the prototype of which he had whittled in wood while at sea. The single-barreled, multichambered revolver had a rotating breech which was turned, locked, and unlocked by cocking. A first attempt at widespread manufacture failed, but Colt became wealthy after the U.S. Army purchased large numbers for use in the *Mexican War

(1846-48). He set up his factory in Connecticut, where he also amassed the world's largest private armory.

Colt was also an inventor of mines and owner of a telegraph business. He promulgated the ideas of interchangeable parts and production lines three quarters of a century before they became standard procedure. His revolver became "patented" in 1835.

W. 30; C.M. 29

COLUMBIA

The Columbia River of the northwestern *United States and southwestern *Canada, is second to the *Mississippi in volume. It rises in the *Rocky Mountains of British Columbia, eighty miles north of the American line, flowing c. 1,200 miles to the *Pacific southwest of Tacoma. Captain Robert Gray discovered the mouth in 1792, naming the river after his ship. Lewis and Clark began exploration in 1805, and the entire course was examined between 1807 and 1811. The Columbia is the legendary "River of the West," or "Oregon."

W. 64

COLUMBIA, --AN

Synonym for "*America," or *United States," from the name of its putative "discoverer," *Columbus.

W. 47; P. 19:1 and elsewhere

COLUMBUS, CHRISTOPHER; COLUMBUS'

Christopher Columbus (c. 1446-1506; It. Cristoforo Colombo, Sp. Cristóbal Colón) was probably Genoese. He was supported in his explorations by Ferdinand and *Isabella of *Spain, setting sail along with Martin Pinzón 3 August 1492, with the small ships Nina, Pinta, and Santa Maria. He landed in the Bahamas (calling the landing place San Salvador), discovered *Cuba and Hispaniola. On his second voyage (1493), he discovered the Leeward Islands, St. Christopher, and Puerto Rico (see "Porto Rico"). On the third voyage (1498), he discovered Trinidad and the mouth of the Orinoco (see "Oronoco"). His fourth voyage (1502) was so difficult that he was forced to return to Spain, ending his life in ignominy.

M.'s "Benito Cereno" suggests that American adulation of Columbus is misplaced.

See also "Columbia."

M. 97; R. 24; R. 33; W. 38; W. 65; M.D. 58; M.D. 89; P. 7:4

COME-OUTERS
Members of a nineteenth-century *New Englanders'
movement, originating in *Cape Cod, who denied the need for
ministers and creeds, claiming direct Divine guidance. They
were violently opposed to most religious institutions.
C.M. 40

COMMENTARIES
See "Blackstone."
W. 35

COMMITTEE OF SAFETY
Franklin's notes to *C.M.* suggest that M.'s Committee is
like the Committees of Public Safety of the *French Revolution:
Danton's, formed in April, 1793, directing a Reign of Terror;
Robespierre's more powerful one; a weak one which followed
Robespierre's; a brief one in *Vienna during the revolutions of
1848.
C.M. 45

COMMITTEE ON LECTURES
See "Lecture."
P. 17:2

COMMODORE; COMMODORE J__
Thomas Ap Catesby Jones (1790-1858) is the *Virginia-
born original of the "Commodore" in *T.* and *W.* and
"Commodore J__" in *M.D.* He began a colorful career as
*midshipman under *Hull and *Decatur at *Norfolk, then
served seven years under *Porter, Shaw, and Patterson, suppressing the *slave trade, smuggling, and *piracy, and enforc-
ing neutrality laws. He was wounded at Lake Borgne, opposing *Cochrane's fleet, then spent three years in the
*Mediterranean *Squadron and five years at the Washington
Navy Yard. Commanding the *Pacific Squadron in *Peacock* in
1825, Jones visited the *Sandwich Islands to collect debts and to
pick up deserters from *American merchantmen; he supported American missionaries there against *British
sovereignty claims. In 1836 he resigned command of the South
Seas Surveying and Exploring Expedition, after disagreeing
with the *Secretary of the Navy, spending four inactive years.
By 1842 he was again in command of the Pacific Squadron, but
was relieved after a serious blunder: assuming the United
States and Mexico were at war, he asked for and received the

surrender of the governor of Monterey. In 1844, he was again
Commander of the Pacific Squadron, but was court-martialed
and given five years' suspension in 1850 for using military
funds to transport refugees from Lower *California after the
*Mexican War. Fillmore remanded the suspension in 1853,
placing Jones on reserve until 1855.

A director of the Seaman's *Bethel movement, Jones
considered rum the "jailer" in a man-of-war "prison," circulated abstinence pledges and gave speeches to that effect. As
Charles R. Anderson notes, Jones left *United States before
the time M. has him aboard "*Neversink." A stickler for discipline, Jones would not have tolerated the whiskers acclaimed
in that book.

Married to Mary Walker Carter, of Virginia, Jones had
four children.
T. 1; W. 6; W. 21; W. 51; W. 54; M.D. 45

COMMODORE DAVID PORTER
        See "Porter."
T. 25

COMMODORE PREBLE
        The real name of the original ship of a dynasty of
"Commodore Prebles" was *Preble*. She was a sloop purchased
on Lake Champlain and commissioned in 1813 (with a Lieutenant Charles Budd in command). After the battle, which
gave control of the waterway to the Americans, she was sold
(1815).

The second *Preble*, to which M. refers in *M.D.* 67, was a
sloop-of-war launched at *Portsmouth in 1839 and commissioned the following year, serving at *Labrador (1840), the
*Mediterranean (1841-43), the *African coast (1844-45), with the
Pacific *Squadron in the *Mexican War (1847), the East Indies
(1849), and *Japan (1849). This *Preble* served as a practice ship
for *Midshipmen (1851-58) before going back into active service
in the *Civil War (1860-63), with the Gulf Blockading Squadron
and then at *Pensacola, where she was destroyed by accidental
fire.

(There were three other U.S. *Navy *Prebles* after this
veteran ship, all of them affectionately called "Commodore
Preble," in honor of the veteran officer Edward *Preble.)
M.D. Extracts 67

COMMODORE'S BARGE, --BARGEMAN
A barge is a long, slight, spacious craft which is carvel-built (as opposed to clinker-built), double-banked, often with a large sprit-sail on a hinge for low bridges. Next in strength to a launch, it is often a sumptuously furnished vessel of state, as was *Cleopatra's or the *Lord Mayor's. The Commodore's Barge (of the *Navy) is for that dignitary's use exclusively.
(Barges are heavily used for transport of sand, coal, etc. Early *men-or-war were barges of about 100 tons. The "bread-barge" of *T*. 6 is a serving utensil shaped similarly.)
W. 39; W. 43

COMMONS IN BLUE
See "Parliament; Parliamentary."
W. 54

COMO, LAKE
Lago di Como (or Lario) is *Italy's third largest lake, located in *Lombardy, twenty-five miles north of *Milan. The lake is some thirty miles long and up to two and one-half miles wide, with a maximum depth of 1,345 feet. The mountain-surrounded two-armed lake formed by the Adda River is famous for its beauty and its elegant resorts and villas.
The "*Yankee" M. took a steamer ride on the lake (8 April 1857), comparing it in his journal to Lake George, *New York.
M. 84

COMPARATIVE ANATOMISTS
Comparative anatomy, the zoology branch dealing with the structure of related animals, began in the sixteenth century, with Pierre Belon's study of human and bird skeletons. But until *Darwin's time, homology was not taken very seriously. The publication of *M*. in 1849 precedes any of Darwin's public announcements by nine years, and *The Origin of Species* by eleven years, so M.'s light treatment of Comparative Anatomists was appropriate at the time.
M. 174

"COMPENSATION"
See " 'Optimist' school."
P. 20:1

COMSTOCK, SAMUEL

Major characters in the saga of the whaleship *Globe* were sons of the *Quaker Nathan Comstock, a whale outfitter. Samuel was twenty years old when he led the *Globe* mutiny (January 1824). His younger brother, George, was at the helm when the uprising began, and he is the one threatened by the remarks M. relates in *M.D.* "Extracts" 68. A ballad sprang up about Samuel, whose skull may have been exhibited in Barnum's museum (according to survivors Lay and Hussey).

William Comstock (1804-1822) was the putative author of an 1840 work: *The Life of Samuel Comstock*. An 1845 edition was a thirty-six page summary: *The Life of Samuel Comstock, the Bloody Mutineer*. Full title of the original is *The Life of Samuel Comstock, the Terrible Whaleman. Containing an Account of the Mutiny, and Massacre of the Officers of the Ship Globe, of Nantucket; with His Subsequent Adventures, and His Being Shot at the Mulgrave Islands. Also, Lieutenant Percival's Voyage in Search of the Survivors.* By His Brother, William Comstock. Boston: James Fisher, Publisher, No. 71 Court Street. Turner & Fisher, New York and Philadelphia, 1840. William later wrote at least part of a work entitled *Whaling in the Pacific*. An excerpt published (7 August 1843) in the *Daily Telegraph* is an account of a captain's chasing a white whale despite objections of his first mate.

(William's son, Augustus [1837--?] was the pseudonymous writer of popular sea tales by "Roger Starbuck.")

See also "Extracts" 68.

M.D. Extracts 68

CONDORCET

The *philosophe* Marie Jean Antoine Nicolas de Caritat, Marquis de Condorcet (1743-1794), *French mathematician and philosopher, greatly influenced nineteenth-century thought. Born into an ancient family, Condorcet was educated by *Jesuits and became the friend of most of the distinguished men of the time. One of the first to declare for the Republic, he was a leader of French revolutionary thought, his independence in the Legislative Assembly causing his condemnation and imprisonment. He died in prison under mysterious circumstances.

Among Condorcet's most important publications are a work on the doctrine of probability (1785, 1805), a life of Turgot (1786) and one of *Voltaire (1789). After his death his wife, Sophie de Grouchy (1764-1822), whose salon attracted the greatest of revolutionary thinkers, helped edit the complete works (21 vols.).

P. 21:3

CONEY ISLAND
The *New York City beach and amusement area is in Brooklyn, on the peninsula between Gravesend Bay (N.) and Lower Bay (S.). It became a popular resort, famed for its boardwalk, in the 1840's. The *P*. 17:3 reference to a publication called "A Week at Coney Island" is ironic, given its proximity and its mundane attractions.
P. 17:3

CONGO
Although Congo is the proper name of various *African areas, M.'s references seem to be to people, and much influenced by *phrenology (as in *M*. 140, where he refers to hard heads; *M.D*. 3, where he refers to black skin; *I.P*. 11, where he speaks of wooly hair).
M. 140; M.D. 3; I.P. 11

CONGRESS
The Congress of the *United States, the Legislative branch provided for in Article I of the *Constitution, consists of the Senate and the House of Representatives (although the tendency even for M. has been to refer to the House as "Congress.")
Congress at first had great power over the nation, but by the time *Jackson was elected *President (1828), the "Imperial Presidency" was emerging, and rivalry between the Executive and Legislative branches became intense. Not until *Lincoln's tenure did the President wrest great control.
Passim

CONGRESS OF VIENNA
See "Vienna."
P. Dedication

CONGREVE
Sir William Congreve (1772-1828) was the son of a baronet Lieutenant General, comptroller of the Royal Laboratory at Woolwich, and superintendent of military machines, a fortuitous start for study in gunnery science. Congreve became a Fellow of the *Royal Society and eventually succeeded his father at the Laboratory. He wrote numerous works in the sciences and in economics and was active in politics, as M.P. for Gatton, then for Plymouth from 1818 until his death. In 1805, Congreve made the first serious modern

suggestion about armored warships (carried out in 1841 by the John Stevens family of Hoboken, N.J.). He foresaw an armored floating mortar battery as proof against artillery fire. Among his rocketry works: "A Concise Account of the Origin and Progress of the Rocket System" (1807); "A Treatise on the General Principles, Powers, and Facility of Application of the Congreve Rocket System, as Compared with Artillery" (1827).

The rockets which bear Sir William Congreve's name were developed as a result of *Indian use of rockets against Britain in 1792 and 1799. Congreve experimented privately until his rockets could exceed the range of the Indians'. In 1806, rockets caused great fires in Boulogne, and in 1807 a massed attack of 25,000 rockets burned most of *Copenhagen. In the *War of 1812, at the Battle of Fort McHenry, *Baltimore, Francis Scott Key had Congreve rockets in mind when he wrote of the "rockets' red glare" and "the bombs bursting in air."

Their success relied on Congreve's standard specifications and design refinements. They weighed from 25 to 60 pounds, had incendiary heads or steel ball charges, with a range up to three miles. A twelve- to sixteen-foot-long guidestick made possible their firing from small craft. Eventually most of the armies of Europe had Congreve rockets, and one version was used by *Scoresby in whaling—with a parachute to keep the flare visible.
T. 3

CONNECTICUT

One of the original thirteen states of the Union, Connecticut derives its name from a Mohegan dialect word, *Quonaughicut*, meaning "long tidal river." The "Nutmeg State" is ninety miles in width (E.-W.) and fifty-five miles in length (N.-S.). The *Connecticut River was discovered in 1614 by the *Dutch, who established a trading post on the site of Hartford (the present capital); it was abandoned in 1654. Permanent *English settlements began in the 1630's. The Pequot (see "Pequod") Indians were driven out of the Mystic area in 1637. Congregationalism was declared the official religion of the constitutional commonwealth in 1708, giving rise to "Blue Laws" designed to enforce morality. (See entry which follows.)

In the nineteenth century, Connecticut's shipping industry gradually yielded to focus on agriculture. Advent of the railroad brought a large influx of European laborers, leading to increasing urbanization.

M. *lectured in New Haven (see "Yale"), 30 December 1857.

See also "Litchfield Hills"; "Tolland County."
T. Appendix; R. 27; M.D. 93; I.P. 2

CONNECTICUT BLUE LAWS

Restrictions on *Christian Sunday behavior were late enactments, although Constantine I (see "Constantinople") introduced civil legislation (321) compelling recognition of the day of Christ's resurrection. Connecticut Blue Laws were strict enactments of the New Haven *Puritan government in the 17th century, modeled upon *Old Testament regulations. There are forty-five listed in Rev. Samuel A. Peters's *General Historv of Connecticut* (1781), many of which spread throughout the colonies, mostly disappearing after the *Revolution. Among them (and possibly spurious): "No woman shall kiss her child on the *Sabbath or fasting day," and "No one shall travel, cook victuals, make beds, sweep house, cut hair or shave on the Sabbath."

Charles R. Anderson notes (*Melville in the South Seas*, X, "Tahiti in 1842," p. 265) that *Tahiti visitors such as *Darwin and Fitzroy noted the severity of the Sunday laws but did not find them damaging, corroborating words of the *Rev. Daniel Tyerman (*Journal of Vovages and Travels* I, 50):

> Not a fire is lighted, neither flesh nor fruit is baked, not a tree is climbed, nor a canoe seen on the water, nor a journey by land performed, on *God's holy day; religion—religion alone—is the business and delight of these simple-minded people on the Sabbath.

T. Appendix

CONNECTICUT RIVER

The longest river of *New England rises in the Connecticut Lakes in northern *New Hampshire, flowing 345 miles south to Long Island Sound at Old Saybrook. The lower Connecticut River valley is agriculturally rich, especially in Tobacco crops.
I.P. 2

CONQUEROR

W. 87's reference to the "Conqueror" does not allude to any specific individual but reverberates with symbolic meaning in celebration of "*Ushant's" victory over: *Washington; the *Navy; the *Commodore; the *Captain; the scourge; the prison cell; indeed over the "Man-of-War world" and its "*Lord High Admiral," *God, as manifested perhaps in *Poe's "Conqueror Worm" (in "Ligeia," first published in *Baltimore American Museum*, 1838).
W. 87

CONQUEST, THE
     Accession of *William I to crown of *England (1066),
after conquest of Harold II.
M. 84

CONSTABLE, SIR CLIFFORD
     As Howard Vincent pointed out, M.'s knowledge of Sir
Clifford Constable and his whale is derived from *Beale, p. 76.
Sir Clifford, lord of the seignories of Holderness, whose seat
was at Burton-Constable, in *Yorkshire, claimed the body of a
sperm whale that washed onto the coast on 28 April 1825. The
whale measured fifty-eight and one-half feet long, and its di-
mensions were later compared with those of its surprisingly
small skeleton, details of which were painstakingly recorded.
M.D. 102

CONSTANTINE'S BATH
     Perhaps a reference to an ancient baptismal font in the
Baptistery of San Giovanni in Laterano, *Rome.
M.D. 94

CONSTANTINOPLE
     The former capital of the *Byzantine and *Ottoman Em-
pires, and the largest and most splendid of Middle Ages cities,
Constantinople ("Istanbul" since 1930) was created in A.D. 330
by the Emperor Constantine, on the site of *Byzantium. It was
built on seven hills (like *Rome), on both sides of the Golden
Horn, an inlet of the *Bosporus, and was surrounded by
moated and turreted triple walls. It was destroyed by
earthquake in 1509 and rebuilt by Sultan *Bajazet II.
*Suleiman I erected an important mosque. Other interesting
remains (now mostly museums) include the Hagia Sophia
(first a church, then a mosque) and the *Seraglio (palace) of
the Sultans, who moved their residence just before M. visited
in 1856.
     Constantinople was besieged innumerable times and
taken by *Crusaders in 1204, 1261, and 1453. Its greatest period
was the tenth century, when there were one million residents,
representing every race in the world. Its artistic and literary
treasures, sacked by Crusaders, were among the finest. It fell
to the *Turks in 1453 but was revived by the Sultans.
     M. kept a very specific and inclusive journal of his visit
(12-18 December 1856), noting the beauty and mystery as well
as the pervading danger of assassins and thieves in the fire-
prone labyrinthine unmapped streets. The Hagia Sophia had

just been renovated, and such attractions on his walks and cruises brought forth a burst of writing fervor necessitating purchase of another notebook in which to record his observations (some twenty-eight pages in Horsford's *Journal of a Visit to Europe and the Levant: October 11, 1856-May 6, 1857*). As Horsford points out, M. was perhaps aided in his observations by Thomas Hope's (1819) *Anastasius*, which contains much description of the area.

The "Grande Porte" of *W*. 39 is the "Sublime Porte": the court of the Sultans.

M. 149; W. 39; W. 50; W. 68; M.D. 44; M.D. 45; C.M. 1

CONSTELLATIONS

In astronomy, constellations are apparent groupings of stars (Lat. *con*: "with"; *stella*: "star"), named by pre-Semitic, Semitic, or ancient *Greek peoples. The three major designations are northern, *zodiacal (16 degrees centered on the *ecliptic), and southern constellations. By M.'s time there were thought to be over 80. Modern astronomers accept twenty-eight northern, twelve zodiacal, and forty-eight southern constellations.

It is not known whether M. owned an adult-level astronomy book. He mentions only constellations on *Ptolemy's list of forty-eight. See entries under the following [northern]: Andromeda; Aquila; Boötes; Casseopeia; Corona Borealis; Cygnus; Draco; Hercules; Lyra; Pegasus; Perseus; Great Bear (Ursa Major); [zodiacal]: Aquarius; Aries; Cancer; Capricornus; Gemini; Leo; Libra; Pisces; Sagittarius; Scorpio; Taurus; Virgo; [southern]: Argo (as Argo-Navis); Cetus; Southern Cross (Corona Austrina); Crux (as Crux Australis); Hydra (as Hydrus); Orion.

Passim

CONSTITUTION

The Constitution of the *United States is the oldest written constitution continuously in force. The fifty-five delegates to the Constitutional Convention of 1787 met in *Philadelphia from May to September, ostensibly to revise the *Articles of Confederation then in force; they were instead discarded, and amid much contention between *Federalists and "states' righters," the new document was created. A major underlying issue was *slavery, and despite serious objections, the question of *abolition was officially disregarded, permitting continuance. *Delaware was the first state to ratify, on 7 December 1787 (unanimous); *New York ratified 26 July 1788, by a thirty-to-twenty-seven vote, and *Massachusetts on 6 February 1788, by 187-168.

The reference in *M*. 18 to *Webster's being "close" to the Constitution alludes to his mid-nineteenth-century support of slave-holders' rights based on the document: the first dramatic example of the continuing dispute between "strict constructionists" and those who favor flexibility. Article I, Section 8, the "elastic clause," had been deliberately left ambiguous to allow for new laws, but opponents found it insufficient. The *Bill of Rights (1791), the first ten amendments, went far toward making the document acceptable to opponents such as *Thomas Jefferson, who believed that it had been composed to support economic interests, rather than as a "living Constitution" adaptable to changing temporal needs of all the population.

The only other amendments affecting M.'s generation were number 11 (1795), protecting states from certain lawsuits; 12 (1804), changing the electoral system; 13 (1865), abolishing slavery; 14 (1868), granting citizenship to former slaves; 15 (1870), granting suffrage to former slaves. (At the present time there have been twenty-six amendments.)

M.'s fondness for the expression "*the people" (especially in *W*.) probably derives from the Constitution's Preamble, which begins, "We the People of the United States . . . . "
Passim

CONSTITUTION

The most celebrated ship in the annals of *American maritime history, the frigate *Constitution* was designed by Joshua Humphreys and launched in 1797 in *Boston—a sister ship to *Constellation* and to M.'s "Neversink," *United States*. *Constitution* is 204 feet long, 43 and one-half feet in beam, with over a 14 feet displacement. She was constructed of live oak, red cedar, and hard pine, with bolts made by Paul Revere. Although officially carrying 44 guns, she usually bore more with 32-pounder carronades, instead of 44-pounders: her gun range 1,200 yards. *Constitution* traveled at up to 14 knots, carrying a crew of 450 into some of the *Navy's most stunning victories: she was *Preble's flagship in the *Barbary Wars; victor over the *British frigate *Guerriere* (gaining her nickname, "Old Ironsides") and over HMS *Java*, in the War of 1812.

Constitution had a severe disciplinary code and was on several occasions the scene of near-mutinies because of punishment of men whose terms had expired and the practice of *Flogging Through the Fleet. She was saved from scrapping in 1828, perhaps as a result of Oliver Wendell Holmes's popu-

lar poem, "Old Ironsides," and, restored to nearly original condition, is on display in Boston Harbor.
W. 87

CONSUL
    In *O.* 21--*O.* 43, "Consul" refers to Charles B. *Wilson.
Passim

CONSULATE OF THE SEA, THE
    The proper title of the collection of maritime law and custom, in the Catalan language, is *Lo Libre de Consolat, The Book of the Consulate.* It consists of matters decided upon by commercial judges, or consuls, holding office in *Mediterranean ports during the Middle Ages. First published around 1494, the "Consulate" was thought to have first been translated into *English in 1874, but M.'s knowledge of its contents suggests otherwise.
W. 72

CONTINENTAL CONGRESS
    The thirteen *American colonies sent delegates to the first Continental Congress in *Philadelphia, in 1774. The second Continental Congress, which instigated the *Revolution by adopting the *Declaration of Independence in 1776, functioned as a (shaky) governing body until creation of the Articles of Confederation, in 1781 (replaced by the *Constitution).
    See also "Allen, Ethan."
I.P. 21

CONTRARIA CONTRARIIS CURANTUR
    See "Hahneman."
W. 54

CONTRERAS
    In the *Mexican War, the battle of Contreras followed *General Winfield Scott's march on Mexico City.
C.M. 19

CONVOLVULUS
    Convulvulus, or "bindweed," has trailing, twining, or erect funnel-shaped flowers and triangular leaves; it resembles the morning-glory plant.

(In "flower language," convulva signify Bonds, Repose, or Worth sustained by affection; the half-closed convolvulus signifies extinguished hopes.)
M. 116

COOK; CAPTAIN COOK; CAPTAIN JAMES COOK; COOKE; CAPIN TOOTEE; *COOK'S VOYAGES*

James Cook (1728-1779), circumnavigator, was born at Marton in Cleveland, *England, son of a laborer. With some village schooling, he was bound at twelve to Whitby shipowners, serving for several years. In 1755 he volunteered to the king's service, as able seaman on *Eagle*; as master of *Mercury*, he was employed in North America in surveying the *St. Lawrence. Returning to England, he became master of his own ship. *Northumberland*, and continued studies in mathematics and astromonical navigation. In 1762 he was appointed "marine surveyor of the coast of *Newfoundland and *Labrador," aboard *Grenville*.

In 1768, as commander of *Endeavor*, he led the expedition to the Pacific to observe the *transit of Venus at *Tahiti; homeward bound, he first charted *New Zealand's coast. Promoted to commander, on *Resolution* and *Adventure*, with a staff of astronomers, naturalists, and artists, he reversed the order of previous circumnavations. The main aim was confirmation of a great southern continent, but disappointment in its non-existence was tempered by increase in knowledge of the South Pacific, as well as means of keeping crews alive and well. Promoted to captain on his 1775 return, Cook's next venture was search for a *Northwest passage around America. Again in *Resolution*, with *Discovery* under command of Captain Charles Clerke, Cook first sighted *Oahu on 18 January 1778, anchoring 20 January; he sighted Maui (*Mowee) on 25 November and *Hawaii 30 November of that year, naming the chain the *Sandwich Islands, after his patron, John Montagu, Fourth Earl of Sandwich. He dropped anchor at Kaawaloa Village, *Kealakekua Bay, 18 January 1779, at the time of a religious festival in honor of the god Lono, with whom he seemed identified, and was honored by priests and treated with respect, leaving on 4 February. *Resolution* having a damaged foremast, he returned 11 February, and at this point accounts differ.

Some historians claim that the previously welcoming natives had turned sour, robbing and generally misbehaving; after the thievery of an important piece of ship's equipment, one of Cook's officers seized a native canoe, and Cook himself went ashore to take the friendly native king as hostage. The people objected and attacked Cook with daggers and clubs in a frenzy of hatred. This version has Clerke a coward in failing to come to his aid, and Cook's body partly burned by the natives but later given up for burial.

Hiram Bingham's account is different: Cook had encouraged idolatry of himself; had offended by using wooden deities to repair the ship and by abusing native women. Cook fired, killing a native first, then was himself killed by a chief, Kalaimanohoowaha; his body was stripped of flesh, but his bones, palms, and entrails were preserved for ceremonies. After the English burnt the village, the bones were returned and buried at sea.

In either event, *Byron set up a stone cairn and wooden pillar with a plate in Cook's honor, in 1825. Cook was survived by a wife and six children.

"Cook's Voyages" (*O*. 80) is *A Collection of Voyages round the World, . . . Containing a Complete Historical Account of Captain Cook's Voyages*. 2 vols. London: 1790.

"Capin Tootee" in *O*. 31.

See also "Extracts" 39.

T. 1; T. 12; T. 24; T. 25; T. 26; T. 32; O. 18; O. 31; O. 41; O. 49; O. 54; O. 61; O. 65; O. 80; M.D. Extracts 39; M.D. 24; M.D. 105 and elsewhere

COOPER, JAMES FENIMORE

*America's first highly popular novelist, Cooper (1789-1851) lived his early life at Otsego Hall, Cooperstown, *New York, among other landed gentry. Expelled from *Yale for pranks in 1806, he spent five years at sea as a foremast hand and was a *Navy *midshipman for three years. He married the wealthy Susan Augusta DeLancey and became a Mamaroneck country gentleman involved in agriculture, politics, finance, and Westchester society.

Cooper began writing professionally in response to his wife's challenge about an *Edinburgh Review* question: "Who reads American books?" He became an extremely popular writer of novels (33), a social commentator, historian, and travel writer, best known for his "Leatherstocking" books. Cooper inaugurated use of American topics, settings and characters in high quality literature.

A rather patrician democrat in the age of *Jackson, Cooper returned in 1828 from a European trip expressing concern about American tendencies to mediocrity, especially in the arts. He was castigated widely until the end of his life for his rather cranky expressions of displeasure that *Jefferson's hoped-for "uncommon" common man had not risen to the fore in an age of greed for power and money.

Cooper was a close friend of General Peter *Gansevoort, M's maternal grandfather. M.'s comments about Cooper's works were almost certainly colored by that fact. He had never met Cooper, and their works were frequently compared—not necessarily to M.'s advantage. M. reviewed *The Sea Lions* (Sealts #160) for *Duyckinck and did an anonymous review of *Red Rover* (Sealts #159) in *Literary World* (16 March 1850): "A Thought on Book-Binding," in which he suggests the book should have "flame-colored," "jet black," or "blood-colored" cover.

It is not clear at what stage in his youth M. read the "Leatherstocking" tales (*The Pioneers* [1823], *The Last of the Mohicans* [1826], *The Prairie* [1827; Sealts #158a], *The Pathfinder* [1840], *The Deerslayer* [1841]), or *The Pilot* (see "Extracts" 56). He was invited to Rufus Griswold's memorial service after Cooper's death, but instead contributed a letter (19 December 1851) which was read at the service and published in February 1852. The letter recalls M.'s "boyhood" readings and calls Cooper "a great, robust-souled man."

(As late as 1917, M. was regarded as an inferior Cooper. Carl Van Doren's *Cambridge History of American Literature* lumps him with other "Contemporaries of Cooper.")
M.D. Extracts 56

COOPER'S PILOT
See "Cooper, James Fenimore," and "Extracts" 56.
M.D. Extracts 56

COPENHAGEN
The name of *Denmark's largest and capital city derives from "merchants' haven." In 1043 it was called Hafnia; it was chartered in 1254 and became the capital in 1443. Between the thirteenth and sixteenth centuries it suffered attacks from the *Hanse Towns; in the sixteenth century the problem was religious wars, and in the seventeenth siege by *Sweden (ended by the Treaty of Copenhagen, 1660). The *British, *Dutch, and *Swedish fleets attacked in 1700, and there were serious fires throughout the eighteenth century.

The Battle of Copenhagen (*W.* 50) took place in 1801. The British fleet under Sir Hyde Parker, with *Nelson second in command, was sent in March to the *Baltic, in response to the league of *Russia, *Prussia, *Denmark, and Sweden, formed to resist British claims of the right of search at sea. Nelson refused to retreat against nearly impossible odds posed by unknown shallow waters and unfavorable winds. His persistence forced negotiations, and Nelson replaced Parker in May.
O. 15; R. 8; R. 18; R. 29; W. 50; M.D. 99

COPERNICUS; COPERNICAN
Nicolaus Copernicus (Mikolaj Kopernik) (1473-1543), *Polish astronomer, revolutionized planetary astronomy by his heliocentric theory contradicting *Ptolemy's geocentric theory. Copernicus studied (in *Cracow, *Bologna, and Padua) mathematics, philosophy, law, medicine, astronomy, and theology. His astronomical observations made him dissatisfied with the Ptolemaic system, which was virtually an article of religious faith. In his readings of early *Greek philosophers, he found the heliocentric theory he was to expound after conquering his own initial resistance. The theory met with debate and condemnation for almost a century after the publication of *De Revolutionibus orbium coelestium* (1543), the six parts of which discuss the earth's shape and movement, the ecliptic, the moon, the planets, and the apparent motion of the sun.
M. 6; P. 14:2

COPTIC
Coptic language has been dead since the sixteenth or seventeenth centuries except for its use in religious services by descendents of the Copts, Jacobite *Christians of *Egypt and patriarchs of *Alexandria since 451.
M. 94

COQUIMBO
A province and town of north-central *Chile between the *Pacific and the *Andes. The town, on the southwestern shore of Coquimbo Bay, is an important port and headquarters of the Chilean navy. ("*Jack Chase" errs in *W*. 85 in locating Coquimbo "on the *Spanish Main," or perhaps is adding color to a tall tale in doing so.)
W. 85

CORAL ISLANDS
See "Pomotu."
O. 17

CORAL SANDWICH
See "Sandwiches."
M. 132

CORCOVADO

Corcovado (*Portuguese: "hunchback") is a jagged granitic peak (2,310 feet) overlooking *Rio de Janeiro: a landmark (which in 1931 was topped with a floodlit statue of Christ). Its range is not M.'s "Corcovado mountains," but the Cariocas.
C.M. 2

CORFU

Modern Kérkira Island, *Greece, on the Ionian sea across from Epirus (39°33' N., 19°36' E.), traditional *Homeric island of *Scheria*, the home of the Phaeacians, and in M.'s time a *British protectorate and seat of the British high commissioner (until 1864 cession to Greece).
M. 28

CORINTH, --IAN

A chief city of *Greece's northeastern *Peloponnesus, Corinth is a port on the Gulf of Corinth, forty miles west of *Athens. In ancient times, it was a wealthy Greek intellectual center, home of the Dorians from as early as *Homeric times. By the eighth and seventh senturies B.C., it was already a maritime power and shipbuilding center. The natural rival of Athens, Corinth was allied with *Sparta, leading directly to the Peloponnesian War. A *Macedonian center, it was destroyed by *Rome in 146 B.C. and refounded as "Achaea" by *Julius Caesar in 44 B.C. Corinth was conquered in the 1204 *Crusade, held by Latin princes, taken by the *Turks in 1458 and by *Venice in 1687. The Turks regained it in 1715, losing it to Greek insurgents in 1822.

It was the site of the preaching of *St. Paul, who wrote two epistles to the Corinthians. There are many *Roman ruins, including a Temple of *Apollo. The Temple of *Aphrodite (*R*. 46) was the center of a cult of religious prostitution designed to promote fertility. Thus the "pictures" at "*Aladdin's Palace" are such as one finds in a house of prostitution. The bisexual goddess was called "Urania" at Corinth and was worshipped also by a cult of Aphrodite the Dark, an earth goddess.

Corinth was destroyed by earthquake and rebuilt in 1858. (That new city was destroyed in another quake in 1928.) Near the conclusion of his essay "Hawthorne and His Mosses," M. alludes to the discovery of bronze by the "melting of the iron and brass in the burning of Corinth."
R. 29; R. 46; W. 92

CORIOLANUS, CAIUS MARCIUS

Gaius Marcius Coriolanus was a legendary fifth-century B.C. patrician *Roman hero who supposedly gained his name at the siege of Corioli (493 B.C.), in war against the Volsci. The legend, built on by *Shakespeare, tells that he advised the Roman people during a famine not to use corn from *Sicily unless they abolished their tribunes. Driven into exile, he led the Volscian army against Rome. He died either murdered as a traitor or by his own hand.

Given confirmed history of the times, the story is probably untrue except for the famine and enmity of Romans and Volsci.
W. 16; I.P. 15

CORLEAR'S HOOK; CORLAER'S HOOK

Now a public park, south of the east end of Grand Street, below the Williamsburg Bridge, in *Manhattan, it was the residence of Peter Stuyvesant's trumpeter, Antony Van Corlear.
M.D. 1; M.D. 99

CORNWALL

*England's southwesternmost county is a rocky peninsula settled from prehistoric times and showing evidence of *Roman, *Saxon, *Celtic, and *Norman civilizations. Fisheries and mining of tin were early occupations; by M.'s time, the "Cornwall miner" might be extracting copper, iron, china stone, granite, slate, other rocks.
W. 3; W. 16; P. 2:4

COROMANDEL

Coromandel, or the Carnatic Coast, is the east coast of Madras, *India. It is said to be named for the *mandal* (region) of the *Cholas*: a sea-going dynasty from the early Christian era to the mid-eleventh century.

The Coromandel battle "Israel" escapes in *I.P.* 13 involved at least five bloody indecisive encounters (February 1782-June 1783) between the *British and the famous *French admiral Pierre André de *Suffren.
I.P. 13

CORONA BOREALIS

In astronomy, a northern *constellation: the northern crown. It represents a wedding gift to Ariadne, who tried to

help Theseus escape the *Cretan labyrinth, in mythology. It
was placed in the sky by Dionysus after her death.
M. 84

CORPORATION HOSPITAL
　　　See "Blackwell's Island."
C.M. 19

CORPOSANTS
　　　The balls of electrical luminosity playing around ship
masts in a storm get their name from the *Spanish *corpo
santo*, holy body. They are also called Comazants or St. Elmo's
fire. "Elmo" is Italian corruption of *Erasmus, fourth century
bishop who became patron saint of seamen. Another name for
the phenomenon is Helen's Fire, after the beautiful sister of
*Castor and Pollux.
　　　M.'s journal for 13 October 1849 recounts his witnessing
of the phenomenon.
M. 162; M.D. 119

CORSICA, --N
　　　The ancient Cyrnus island of the *Mediterranean, south
of the Gulf of *Genoa, is separated from *Sardinia by the Strait
of Bonifacio. It is leaf-shaped, with short mountain chains
(ranging in altitude up to 9,000 feet) which, in combination
with its impenetrable shrubbery, made it an excellent hideout
for bandits: the scene of the first vendettas. The *Romans held
it from the third century B.C. to the fifth century A.D.; the
*Vandals from the fifth to ninth centuries; *Arabs from the
ninth to the eleventh; *Pisans from the twelfth to the fourteenth; *Genoese from the fourteenth to the eighteenth. Corsica was ceded to *France in 1768, temporarily joined the
*British in 1794, and was recovered by France in 1796.
*Napoléon Bonaparte was born in Corsica in 1769.
O. 7; M. 30

CORTEZ
　　　Hernán (or Hernando) Cortés (1485-1547), *Spanish con-
queror of *Mexico, had been a farmer and notary at Santo
Domingo (Hispaniola) before he sailed for *Cuba with Diego
Velázquez. Sent by Velázquez to explore the Yucatan, he
headed a large, well-armed flotilla. He founded the city of
Veracruz in 1519 and, dismantling his ships, headed inland,
gathering allies against *Montezuma, who received him at

Tenochtitlán (later Mexico City) as an incarnation of the
*Aztec god, Quetzalcoatl. Cortez seized the emperor, who was
later killed, and then conquered Tlaxcala, last stronghold of
the Aztec empire.

On his return to Spain, he was honored and rewarded by
*Charles V but resisted by his many powerful enemies, so that
he returned to Mexico denied the viceroyship. He explored
Lower *California and the Gulf, but on his final return to
Spain, was kept from power again. He died an ignominious
death in retirement.
R. 46

CORUNNA
        La Coruña (M.'s spelling an alternative) city in north-
western *Spain's mountainous *Atlantic province of the same
name was fortified from ancient times to protect its deep-har-
bor facilities and shipbuilding. It is the site of the *Roman
Tower of *Hercules, a 157-foot high lighthouse. The *Spanish
Armada sailed from La Coruña in 1588 and *Drake sacked the
city in 1598. It became really prosperous in the eighteenth century and was the scene of an important British/French battle of
1809. (La Coruña was formerly called The Groyne.)
I.P. 25

COSSACKS; COSSACS
        The *Turkish word "Cossack" ("Adventurer," "rebel")
applied in the Middle Ages to a nomadic people of *Asian
*Turkey who were fleeing serfdom; it passed to Ukrainian
peasants escaping Polish control and thereafter to a large
number of Ukrainians. Bellicose Cossacks were organized in
the sixteenth century to ward off Tatar (see "Tartar") invaders
and in the seventeenth to further the conquests of the *tsar.
Military service was compulsory, so there were many rebels.
Cossacks were organized into partly autonomous communes
subject to central control. M.'s allusions suggest that they are
rapacious (M. 59) and unwashed (W. 15), inhuman creatures
of the cold (C.M. 3).
        See also "Hetman"; "Russia . . . . "
M. 59; W. 15; C.M. 3

COUNCIL OF TEN
        A powerful unit established in *Venice in 1310 to re-
strain the patrician class and maintain the policy denying personal rule by influential wealthy families.
M. 181; W. 72

COUNT, --S
        L. *comitem*, accusative of *comes*, a companion: a
*Roman military title. A count is the Continental equivalent of
a *British *Earl, of which Countess is the feminine. It is a title
of honor.
W. 56; P. 15:2; P. 21:3

COUNT CENCI
        See "Shelley," and "Guido."
W. 89

COUNT D'ESTANG
        See "Estaing, Charles Hector, Comte D'."
I.P. 10; I.P. 15

COUNT D'ORSAYS
        See "D'Orsay, Count."
R. 28

"COUNTERFEIT DETECTOR"
        Ted N. Weissbuch shows in "A Note on the Confidence-
Man's Counterfeit Detector" that numerous counterfeit-
detectors were published during the nineteenth century, in
addition to counterfeit counterfeit-detectors.
C.M. 45

COUNTESS OF SCARBOROUGH
        The twenty-gun *British *Countess of Scarborough* was
leading the *Baltic merchant fleet with *Serapis* off
*Flamborough Head 3 September 1779 when *John Paul Jones
on *Bon Homme Richard* attacked and captured the two. *Scarborough* was taken by the *French ship *Pallas* and sailed for
the *Texel.
        (In informal military parlance, "Scarborough" means
"strike first and warn afterwards.")
I.P. 19

COUNTER-JUMPING SON OF A GUN
        Counter-jumpers were drapers' assistants who jumped
over the counter to move from one part of the shop to another.
W. 56

COUNT FATHOM!
     See "Smollett."
O. 77

COUROUPITA GUIANENSIS
     The "Cannonball Tree" of Guiana, *South America, and
*Australia, which produces spherical woody fruits with seeds
similar to *Brazil nuts. It has large, showy orange flowers
and valuable hard wood. As "pills" for "King Bello" (M. 152),
the seeds would be boluses.
M. 152

COURT OF COMMON PLEAS
     *Britain's Common Pleas court of law for contests be-
tween private individuals originated during Henry II's reign
(in 1178), its councilors assigned by the king. It separated from
the King's court about one hundred years later, convening at
*Westminster Hall, *London. During the Middle Ages, it was
the busiest of the three common-law courts, in an increasingly
complex system. Not until 1873 were the three replaced by a
single supreme court of judicature.
C.M. 36

COURT OF THE BRAZILS
     In 1808, the *Portuguese regent, John (Dom João; see
John VI . . . "), took refuge in *Rio de Janeiro. After his return
to *Portugal (1822), his son *Dom Pedro I was Emperor of an
independent *Brazil, establishing a court and making Rio the
capital of his empire.
W. 69

COURT OF THE LIONS
     See "Alhambra."
W. 20

"COVE"
     Old thieves' cant meaning an individual; usually used
with an adjective: a "flash cove" is a swell; a "rum cove" one
whose character or position is not quite obvious. Also used for
"fellow" or "sailor."
O. 20; M.D. 40

COVENT GARDEN

*London's main produce market, north of the *Strand, was originally a "convent garden" owned by *Westminster Abbey. In the late seventeenth century, Inigo Jones redesigned it as the square of *St. Paul's Church, surrounded by vaulted loggias, some of which still stand. The market, established in 1671, was rebuilt from 1829 to 1830. The Royal Opera House (1858) stands to the northeast.
R. 51; I.P. 25; C.M. 24

COWPER

A presager of literary Romanticism, William Cowper (1731-1800), wrote melancholy memoirs (pub. 1816), poetry, hymns, and satire. The manuscript for his "Verses supposed to be written by *Alexander Selkirk" ("I am monarch of all I survey") was seen by M. at the British Museum in 1849.

Cowper's best known long poem is *The Task* (1785); "The Castaway" (1803) is based on an incident from *Anson's *Voyage Round the World*.

Sealts #161 is an unidentified edition of *Poems*, purchased in 1846.

See also "Extracts" 46.
M.D. Extracts 46; M.D. 96

COWPER, ON THE QUEEN'S VISIT TO LONDON

See "Cowper, William"; "Extracts" 46.
M.D. Extracts 46

COWRIES

Shells of the cowrie (*Cypraea moneta*) have, along with other objects, long been exchange media of fixed value, especially in *Africa, where they have been used also as small change for European currency.
M. 68

COZZENING

Cheating, deceitful, fraudulent.
M.D. 132

CRAB, THE

See "Zodiac."
M.D. 99

CRACOW

Cracow (or Krakow), in southern *Poland, is located on both banks of the Vistula, 155 miles south-southwest of Warsaw. It was founded c. 700 and by the fourteenth century was the residence place of Polish kings. Cracow passed to *Austria in 1795 and was in the grand duchy of Warsaw by 1809. The *Congress of Vienna (1815) created the republic of Cracow, a *protectorate of *Russia, *Prussia, and *Austria. It was absorbed into Austria by 1846 and was the center of revolution in 1848.

There are major salt mines at nearby Wieliczka and Bochnia.
M. 14

CRANMER, --'S

Thomas Cranmer (1489-1556), Archbishop of *Canterbury from 1533, supported the divorce of *King Henry VIII and his claim to be head of the *Church of England. He wrote many prayer and sermon books and promulgated the forty-two articles of religion that were to become the *Thirty-Nine Articles. Condemned for heresy during the reign of Queen *Mary, he attempted to recant in favor of the Roman Catholic Church but was burned at the stake. To demonstrate his rejection of his earlier recantation, Cranmer first submitted to the fire the right hand with which he had written the recantation.

M.'s dubbing him "*pantheistic" is undoubtedly playful, based on the scattering of Cranmer's ashes into a river that flowed far and wide.

The reference to Cranmer in *M.D.* 35 is an error in the first American edition. The English edition referred, correctly, to Wickliffe.
M. 9; M.D. 35

CRAPPOES

Corruption of *crapauds*: Fr. for "toads," thus a concealed insult, "frogs" being a derogatory sobriquet for "*Frenchmen."
M.D. 91

CRASSUS

There are several important members of the distinguished *plebian Roman family, Crassus. The "Nabob" Crassus in *M.* is probably the prominent and wealthy politician Marcus Licinius Crassus Dives (c. 115-53 B.C.), whose dispro-

portionate influence on senators and businessmen helped him
rise to a political alliance with *Pompey and *Caesar: the
"first triumvirate." He was killed in battle, in an invasion of
*Parthia.
M. 181

CREAGH, JUDGE
        The "almost complete vast skeleton of an extinct mon-
ster" found in *Alabama was a hoax. Some bones found on
Judge Creagh's plantation were first identified in
*Philadelphia as those of a reptile, *Basilosaurus* (king lizard).
Later examination in *London by *Sir Richard Owen led scientists to say it was a sea-going mammal, "Zeuglodon" (strap
tooth). Back in the *United States, a charlatan, Albert Koch,
formed some of these bones into a 114- foot skeleton, along with
other bones. He exhibited the whole in *Boston and *New York
in 1845, to the chagrin of experts who realized the fraud. Un-
deterred, Koch took his show to Europe.
M.D. 104

CREATION
        In both the *Old and *New Testaments, *God created all
things. In *Genesis, Yahweh ("Lord"; modern "*Jehovah"),
the God of *Israel, is the creator, as opposed to the creators of
other contemporary civilizations. Although Yahweh is all-
powerful, the Old Testament mentions primordial battles with
creatures such as *Leviathan, but the creation myth reaffirms
God's sovereignty, showing harmony and goodness, and man
in a position of honor. The creation is seen as the beginning of
history, with divine purpose in the division into a heaven, an
earth, and an underworld.
        In Genesis 1 and 2, God gives form to the dark primor-
dial void: on the first day he creates light and separates day
from night; on the second he creates the firmament heaven;
on the third he creates Earth and seas; on the fourth he creates the sun and the moon; on the fifth he adds living creatures in the sea and on the earth; on the sixth he makes men
in his own image; *Adam and Eve, who are commanded to "be
fruitful and multiply," "have dominion over" beasts, and eat
plants for food. On the seventh day, God rests, establishing the
*Sabbath.
        During M.'s time, the historicity of the creation myth
was widely challenged.
W. 94

CREMONA

The city in *Lombardy, *Italy, was founded by the *Romans on the north bank of the Po River c. 219 B.C., but the area had been settled earlier by *Gallic peoples. It is known as *Virgil's schoolplace, but Cremona's greatest fame springs from the "fiddles" of *R*. 49: violins produced in the city from the sixteenth to the eighteenth centuries by the Amati family and their pupils, Antonio Stradivari and Giuseppe Guarneri. Examples of their work can be seen in a museum in Cremona's Palazzo dell' Arte.
R. 49

CREOLE

(Fr. *créole*, from Span. *criollo*; *West Indian corruption of *criadillo*, from *criado*: "bred," or "brought up.") The term originated in the sixteenth century, denoting *Spanish descendants born in the West Indies, as distinct from immigrants, Negroes, and Indians. It then was used to designate descendants of non-Indians born or settled in the West Indies and descendants of Spanish, *Portuguese, and *French colonists of the *American continents. (Modern use usually refers to French-speakers in *Louisiana, where the patois derives from French and Spanish.) It is wrongly used to designate persons of mixed blood, but its usage still varies from place to place.
C.M. 17; C.M. 23

CRETAN LABYRINTH

In myth, a structure designed by *Daedalus and built at *Crete to imprison the half-human, half-bull Minotaur. Once inside the Labyrinth, there was no escape for the victims sacrificed to the monster. But Theseus used a string to enter, slay the Minotaur, and return.
M.D. 4; M.D. 85; P. 10:1

CRETE

The fourth largest island of the *Mediterranean, Crete is at the southern limit of the *Aegean Sea (35°15' N., 23°30'--26°20' E.). It is 160 miles long and from seven to thirty-five miles wide: the rugged mountainous site of *Mt. Ida (8,058 feet).

Many civilizations have flourished on Crete, including the *Minoan (one of the world's earliest), early *Cretan (c. 1500 B.C.), Dorian Greek (C. 1000 B.C.). Always an important station of Mediterranean trade routes, Crete was by the third century A.D. a *Macedonian *pirate haunt. Conquered by *Rome

(c. 68 B.C.), it fell to *Byzantium in A.D. 395. The *Saracens controlled it in the ninth and tenth centuries, and it was taken in the *Crusade of 1204, passing to *Venice as "Candia." The *Turks invaded successfully in 1669, and by the nineteenth century it was the scene of anti-Turkish revolts leading to the 1897 Greco-Turkish war, won by the Turks. Crete then became autonomous.

See also "Cretan labyrinth."
M.D. 133

CRIM. CON CASE
Criminal conversation: adultery.

The case referred to in *M.D.* 89, involving *Lord Ellenborough and *Mr. Erskine, was elaborated upon in *Scoresby's Vol. 2 Appendix, containing "An Account of a Trial Respecting the Right of the Ship Experiment, to a Whale Struck by One of the Crew of the Neptune."
M.D. 89

CRIMPS
Illegal procurers of seamen, crimps originally impressed men into the Royal Navy—often getting them drunk and then physically abducting them. *Edinburgh Review* (October 1824) decried the relation of crimps to impressment: along with the necessity of keeping marines aboard to maintain order among impressed men, crimps added to the high cost of the "machinery of impressment," which *ER* opposed.
W. 23

CRINKUM-CRANKUM WHALES
A joke. See "Cetology" section.
R. 21

CROCKETT, --'S
Davy (David) Crockett (1786-1836), *Tennessee-born frontiersman/politician, became an *American legend noted for his pioneer spirit, backwoods eccentricities and humor. Although without formal schooling, he was twice elected to the state legislature and then served in *Congress from 1827 to 1831 and 1833 to 1835. An opponent of *Jackson, he was adopted by the *Whigs, who encouraged the frontier hero image. Numerous books were written under his name, promulgating the myth, but at the height of his renown he was not returned to Congress. He left Tennessee to join the *Texas war

and was killed at the Alamo. His "autobiography," *A Narrative of the Life of David Crockett, of the State of Tennessee* (1834), was probably only partly his own work. "Crocket almanacs," collections of tall tales of frontier heroes, also added greatly to the myth and continued publication until the late 1850's.
M. 32; M.D. 82

CROCODILE
    M. calls the crocodile "tongueless," following an old tradition that its tongue was not movable.
M.D. 79

CROKARKY, LAIRD OF
    This is perhaps a joke. Cromarty is a tiny burgh on Black Isle, Cromarty Firth, *Scotland, sixteen miles north-northeast of Inverness (57°42' N., 4° W.). It has a small port and naval station. The "Laird" cannot be a very important one. If there is a "Crokarky," its Laird must be even less important.
I.P. 18

CROMWELL'S
    Oliver Cromwell (1599-1658), Lord Protector of the *British Commonwealth from 1653 to 1658, came from a respectable old British family (surname Williams), attended *Cambridge briefly, and in his late twenties became a dedicated *Puritan. He served in minor civil posts until election to *Charles I's Parliaments of 1640, in which he outspokenly denounced the "innovative" practices of the *Church of England and helped pass the Grand Remonstrance (1641) against the king.
    "Cromwell's Wars" (*R*.36) were planned, supervised, and fought by him between 1642 and 1648, at the end of which time the king was executed with Cromwell's full assent. He then subdued *Ireland and *Scotland and became Lord Protector, official ruler of the "Puritan Republic" (*W*. 71), with a "freely elected" unicameral republican *Parliament and a constitution created by the military (the "Parliamentary Army" of *W*. 55). When this system failed, Cromwell instituted regional government with military supervision by Major Generals. A second Parliament was hand-selected in 1656 to support war with *Spain, but government through the military was not accepted. It was briefly proposed that Cromwell become king, but opposition to destruction of the republic led instead to a proposed new constitution with a bicameral Parlia-

ment. When republicans of the lower house refused to recognize an upper, Cromwell dissolved Parliament in 1658 and
thereafter ruled without one.

Cromwell subdued the *Dutch and the *Spanish but
failed in a projected European *Protestant alliance. He made
many legal reforms including a union of England, *Scotland,
and *Ireland (repealed, along with other acts, at the Restoration). Despite early Puritan fanaticism, he later granted a
measure of freedom to sects persecuted by Parliament
(including *Quakers, Unitarians, and Roman *Catholics).

He died of malaria and was buried in *Westminster
Abbey, but at the Restoration his remains were disinterred and
exhibited at *Tyburn gallows and elsewhere, piece by piece.
Although he is much praised in the literature of *Milton, Carlyle, and others, for M. he seems a symbol of militaristic Puritan severity.

See also "Blake, Robert."
R. 36; W. 36; W. 71

CROSSBONES
See "Skull and Crossbones."
C.M. 23

CROSS, THE
The *New Testament word for the structure on which
*Jesus Christ died, it became the prime symbol of
*Christianity, with several meanings: symbol for Christ him-
self, whereby one could be an "enemy of the cross," or "crucify
Christ again" through sinning; in *St. Paul's metaphorical
use as the type of renunciation of the world—true Christianity;
in general use signifying suffering or death; in Jesus' words,
a willing acceptance of hardship: "If any man would come
after me, let him deny himself, and take up his cross and follow me" (*Matthew 16:24; *Mark 8:34; *Luke 9:23). Jesus'
cross is mentioned in all four gospels.

Crucifixion was a common execution method, using a
cross of strong, cheap wood (perhaps olive or oak), 7 1/2 to 9 feet
high, sunk vertically into the ground, sometimes with a horizontal piece forming a "T" or as the familiar Christian symbolism form. It was frequently inscribed to indicate the nature of
the crime, as was Christ's: "This is Christ, the King of the
Jews."

In *Clarel* II. vi. 7, M. refers to a tradition that the true
cross was made of three (cypress, pine, cedar) or four (cedar,
cypress, palm, olive) woods.

Two of M.'s characters ("*Jarl" in *M*. 47, and the hero of the poem "Daniel Orme") are tattoed with images of the cross.

As M. notes in *W*. 65, the oldest European flags displayed the cross.

T. 26; M. 47; W. 3; W. 65; M.D. 14

CROTON

Croton Lake, thirty miles north of *New York City, became a reservoir in 1842, when an aqueduct connected it with the city. Although planned earlier, its construction was hastened after the great *fire of 1835.

P. 22:1

CROW

When, in *M.D.*, "Pip" calls himself a "crow," he may be referring to the stock minstrel figure, Jim Crow.

M.D. 99

CROWN-PIECES

Very large silver coins with a likeness of the sovereign, who had exclusive coinage rights. They disappeared during the reign of Queen *Victoria, when smaller coins gained in popularity.

I.P. 13

CROZETTS

The Crozet Islands are a small archipelago in the subantarctic south *Indian Ocean, 1,500 miles off the southeastern coast of *Africa (46° S., 51° E.). There have been many wrecks on the steep cliffs, submarine reefs, and wild seas of the volcanic Crozets (still visited by whalers).

M.D. 52; M.D. 58; M.D. 73

CRUIKSHANK

George Cruikshank (1792-1878) illustrated the work of Grimm, *Burns, Defoe, Dickens (see "Hard Times"), *Scott, Thackeray, and Stowe. He edited *The Comic Almanack* and did much political caricature.

(Sealts #489 is: Stephens, Frederic George. *A Memoir of George Cruikshank... and an Essay on the Genius of George Cruikshank by William Makepeace Thackeray*. New York: Scribner and Welford, 1891.)

W. 91

CRUSADES; CRUSADERS

In the Middle Ages, wars of *Christians to recover the *Holy Land from *Mohammedan *Turks and *Saracens. There were eight principal crusades.

1. 1095-1099; capture of *Jerusalem
2. 1147-1149; unsuccessful
3. 1188; stalemate
4. 1202; attack on *Constantinople
5. 1217; recovery of Jerusalem
6. 1222-1229; Nazareth, Bethlehem, Jerusalem regained by negotiation
7. 1248-1254; against *Egypt
8. 1270-1272; fall of last strongholds.

These classic "holy wars" had lasting results: destruction of the *Byzantine Empire and civilization; establishment of *Moslem supremacy; spread of Islamic faith; transfer of intellectual supremacy to Europe; stimulation of trade; increase in geographical and navigational knowledge; development of chivalry and its art forms; transfer of fortunes and property.
M. 170; M.D. 46

CRUSOE

See "Robinson Crusoe."
R. 34

CRUX-AUSTRALIS

In astronomy, the most famous *constellation of the southern hemisphere: the Southern Cross (discovered in 1679).
M. 168

CUBA

The *West Indies' and Creater *Antilles' largest island (c. 700 miles long, 50 miles wide), Cuba is located on major sea routes at the entrance of the *Gulf of Mexico. It is mountainous, with many bays, coral islands, and keys. The Arawak Indians were the inhabitants when *Columbus discovered Cuba in 1492. The Spanish called it "Juana," and "Santiago," but the original Arawak name was eventually restored. Spain was well established by 1511; Havana became the center for viceroyalty treasure fleets of the "Pearl of the Antilles," and a prime *pirate target, as well. Sugar was the main crop, raised by the Indians and then by black slave labor when the Arawaks died off. *Britain briefly held Cuba (1762-63), but in M.'s time it was a Spanish possession.

Tobacco has been a major crop since pre-Colombian times, chiefly in Pinar del Río province, in the west (see "Havanna"). On 17 December 1849, before departure from London, M. bought "3/4 pound of very fine Cuba cigars at about 2 cents & a half (our money) a piece."

The reference in *M.D.* 14 alludes to the United States's ambition to acquire Cuba, given its success in the *Mexican War. Many Americans favored annexing Cuba in the late 1840's. *President Polk offered *Spain one hundred million dollars for the island.

Penny Cyclopaedia (V, 1836) gives a gloss for "Cuba blood-hound" (*W.* 73):

> The reputation which this variety has obtained for sagacity and fierceness, and the share that the terror of its name had in extinguishing the last Maroon War in Jamaica, render it an object of some interest . . . . It is mournfully true . . . that dogs were used by . . . Christian barbarians against the peaceful and inoffensive Americans, and the just indignation of all mankind has ever since branded . . . the Spanish nation with infamy for such atrocities.

Among the dog's achievements, *PC* notes its ability to tear apart the stocks of guns. The article describes an attack on a woman in which a dog seized her throat and would not let go until his head was cut off.
W. 73; M.D. 14; M.D. 119

"CULPRIT FAY"
         See "Drake's 'Culprit Fay'."
P. 20:1

CUMBERLAND
         The mountain lake area in the extreme northwestern corner of *England, settled since at least 2500 B.C., shows traces of Bronze Age, *Roman, early *Christian, *Scandinavian, and *Scottish civilizations. The area identified formally with England only after the Jacobite rebellion of 1745. It was to become home to *Wordsworth, *Coleridge, Southey, *Walpole, and other literary artists and painters, for its picturesque natural beauty, ancient castles, churches, bridges,

abbeys, and houses. Fisheries and mining have been major occupations since ancient times.
I.P. 15

CURRAN
John Philpot Curran (1750-1817): *Irish lawyer, orator, and statesman, proponent of *Catholic emancipation, associate of *London wits Sheridan, *Lord Byron, etc.
R. 27

CURTIS'S "TREATISE . . . "
Sir Roger Curtis (1746-1816) became an Admiral in 1804, after an active naval career. In 1805 he served on the commission for revising the civil affairs of the *British navy, which produced a new edition of *Admiralty Instructions* in 1809. The reference to Curtis's "Treatise on the Rights and Duties of Merchant-Seamen, according to the General Maritime Law" (*W.* 71) has not been traced.
W. 71

CURTIUS
Marcus Curtius was a legendary *Roman hero who supposedly saved his nation in 362 B.C. A chasm had opened in the Forum, and seers predicted that it would close only if Rome's most valuable possession were thrown in. Curtius, believing that Rome's finest possession was a brave citizen, leaped, fully armed and on his horse, into the gulf, which closed over him, later forming a pond called the *Lacus Curtius*.
P. 20:2

CUSTOM-HOUSE [LIVERPOOL]
*Liverpool had its own *Customs House after 1700, having wrested control from Lord Molyneaux. By M.'s time, it was located at the east end of *Water Street Dock.
R. 31

CUSTOMS
The Bureau of Customs (replaced in 1973 by the United States Customs Service) was instituted in 1797, and like *Hawthorne at *Salem before him, M. became Inspector of Customs: at the Port of *New York on 5 December 1866, earning $4.00 per day at the North (*Hudson) River office, 207 West

Street, *Manhattan. His experience as an honest Customs Inspector during a time of corruption and political upheaval is discussed in Garner's "Melville in the Customhouse . . . . " In 1877 he was transferred to an office at 76th Street and the East River. He retired 31 December 1885.
Passim

CUSTOMS HOUSE, DORIC
     *New York City's Custom House (which became Federal Hall and then the Subtreasury Building) was located on *Wall Street between William and Nassau Streets. Designed by Alexander Jackson Davis (1803-92), it was completed in 1842 and soon became known as "The *Parthenon of New York City Public Buildings." It was built of Westchester marble in Greek Revival style, with a multitude of columns and a large dome. Much history had occurred on the site before M.'s time. Here Peter Zenger had been tried in 1735 for sedition; the Stamp Act Congress met and the *Declaration of Independence was read on the site, which housed the capital of the *United States in 1789. In the same year, *Congress met and *Washington was inaugurated on the spot. (The statue of Washington was added in 1883.)
     (Although the Custom House is certainly *Doric in style, its columns have been called Ionic and Corinthian in some sources, and I have not been able to verify.)
R. 30

CUTTLEFISH
     Decapoda: a mollusk with ten suction-cupped legs.
M.D. 45

CUVIER, BARON
     Cuvier, Georges Léopold Chrétien Frédéric Dagobert, Baron (1769-1832). Born in Montbéliard, *France, Cuvier was inspired from childhood by *Buffon. Founder of the studies of comparative anatomy and paleontology, he was educated at the Academy of Stuttgart and later studied marine fauna and fossils as professor at Muséum National d'Histoire Naturelle. Early publications include *Tableaus élémentaire de l'histoire naturelle des animaux*, the first general statement of his classification of the animal kingdom, and *Leçons d'anatomie comparée*, expounding his theory of the "correlation of parts," the interdependence of structure and function. His most famous publication is *La Règne animal distribué d'après son organisation*. M. owned Volume 10 (Sealts #171: The class

Pisces) of the English translation: *The Animal Kingdom Arranged in Conformity with Its Organization, by the Baron Cuvier . . . With Additional Descriptions of All the Species Hitherto Named, and of Many Not Before Noticed*, by Edward Griffith . . . and Others . . . London, 1827-43.

Cuvier believed that each species and each organ was created for one special and specific function and that local catastrophes caused extinction. Promoted by *Napoléon as well as his restoration successor, Louis Philippe, Cuvier became a peer of France.

Lines quoted in *M.D.* 41 are not Cuvier's. They are quoted from *Beale (790), from *The Animal Kingdom*, by Edward Griffith et. al. (vol. 4, 1827).

(See also "Extracts" 49.)

T. 29; M.D. Extracts 49; M.D. 32; M.D. 41; M.D. 54; M.D. 56; M.D. 104

CYCLADES, GRAND

The Cyclades (Greek *Kikladhes*) are a group of twenty-four picturesque islands that circle around Delos, *Greece (35-32° N., 25° E.). With *Crete and later Mycenae, they were from c. 2500 to 1100 B.C. a center of Bronze Age Aegean civilization. *Hellenic and *Roman remains have been uncovered on the mountainous volcanic islands which produce minerals, wine, and tobacco, and have medicinal hot springs.

M. links them erroneously with the "Islands of *King Solomon."

M. Visited Syra, in the Cyclades group, in 1856, commenting at length in his journal (2 December) on its picturesqueness.

W. 75; M.D. 52

CYCLES AND EPICYCLES

See "Milton . . . ."

M. 143

CYCLOID

A cycloid curve is traced by a point on a circle running along a straight line.

M.D. 96

CYCLOPS

Giant cannibal monsters, each with one eye in the middle of his forehead, the Cyclop(e)s are represented in *Greek

mythology as three sons (Arges, Brontes, and Stereopes or Pyracmon) born to *Uranus and Ge after the *Titans. They forged thunderbolts for Zeus (see "Jupiter" and "Jove"). In the *Odyssey*, Polyphemus and others are rather more untameable Cyclops who eat companions of Odysseus (*Ulysses).
P. 12:3

CYGNUS
    In astronomy, a northern *constellation: The Swan, named by the *Greeks for the form in which Zeus (see "Jupiter") seduced *Leda.
M. 136

CYNTHIA
    The moon. Cynthia is a surname of Artemis (see "Diana"), from *Mount Cynthus, on *Delos.
M. 6; M. 136

CYRUS; CYRUS THE GREAT
    Cyrus II (559-530), *Persian King, conquered most of Asia Minor and perhaps detached parts of *Syria and *Palestine from the *Babylonian Empire, raising what was an obscure tribe to the powerful Achaemenid Empire and clearing the way for the conquest of *Egypt by his successor, *Cambyses II.
    M.'s "epitaph" for him ("I could drink a great deal of wine") is probably fictional, biographers (*Cicero, *Herodotus) stressing his temperance.
M. 152; P. 22:1

CZAR, --S
    See "Tsar."
M. 75; M. 181; M.D. 12; M.D. 24; M.D. 89

D

DABOLL'S ARITHMETIC
    Nathan Daboll (1750-1818), *New England almanac maker and navigation teacher, wrote the widely used *Daboll's Complete Schoolmaster's Assistant* (1799).
M.D. 99

D'ABRANTES, DUCHESS

Laure Junot, Duchesse d'Abrantès (1784-1838), born to a socially influential *Parisian mother (Julie Comnène, Madame Permon), was early accustomed to entertaining prominent people, including *Napoléon Bonaparte. She married Andoche Junot, Duc d'Abrantès (1771-1813), who became Commandant of Paris, and set up her own lavish salon, where guests were mostly *Bourbon sympathizers, to Napoléon's chagrin. He called her "la petite peste," and her personal fortune diminished rapidly, especially after the second restoration. In retirement at a Paris abbey, she wrote her famous *Mémoires historiques sur Napoléon la Revolution, le Consulat, l' Empire et la Restauration* (1831-35), a lively personalized account of her times.
I.P. 12

D'ACARTY, MARQUIS

*Rev. Charles Stewart (Vol. I) was "particularly pleased" with "the Marquis de Aracaty, the minister for foreign affairs" in Brazil, whom he called the "most highly educated, and most intelligent nobleman in the empire; perfectly accessible in his manners, and free and winning in conversation."
W. 56

DAEDAL

In mythology, Daedalus was an *Athenian artist, craftsman, and inventor of the *Cretan labyrinth. He is best remembered for his creation of wax and feather wings for himself and his son, Icarus, who flew too near to the sun and plummeted into the sea (now called the Icarian), when his wings melted.

"Daedal" means "displaying artistic cunning or fertility of invention; mazelike" (NED).
C.M. 16

DAGON

A *Philistine idol, in 1 *Samuel 5:2-4 and *Judges 16, 23.
M.D. 82

DAGUERROTYPE

A *French painter and physicist, Louis Jacques Mandé Daguerre (c. 1789-1851), invented the photographic process which was perfected by the late 1830's and by the 1840's had be-

come more popular in the *United States than in any other nation. M. refused *Evert Duyckinck's request for a daguerro-
type in 1851, on the grounds that the practice had become so
common as to add distinction to those who refused.
P. 17:3

D'ALEMBERT
        Jean le Rond D'Alembert (Dalembert, 1717-83), one of the
*French *Philosophes*, was *Diderot's chief assistant on
L'Encyclopédie (1751-1776), a dictionary of universal knowledge
and symbol of the rationalist Enlightenment.
        The illegitimate son of a highly placed family,
D'Alembert studied law but never practiced, turned to
medicine, and finally to mathematics, making numerous contributions to science, notably "D'Alembert's Principle" on equilibrium and motion of fluids in *Traité de dynamique*. As a
member of the Academy of Science, he published much, in
addition to literary works for *L'Encyclopédie*.
R. 1

DAMASCUS
        Damascus (Dimaskq), longtime capital of *Syria, is
called "the pearl of the east," for its beauty, and "the gate of
*Mecca," for its role as transportation center for pilgrimages.
It is located at the foot of Mt. Qasyun, fifty-seven miles southeast of Beirut, *Lebanon, and is divided into "old" and "new"
sectors. It is a holy city for *Moslems and *Christians, as
burial place for *Saladin and site of conversion of *St. Paul.
Bronze Age artifacts show its existence from ancient times;
there is a First Century AD Great Mosque and *Roman citadel.
Under the *Persian Empire, Syria was the fifth *satrapy;
Damascus has been variously claimed by *Greeks, *Egyptians,
*Seleucids, *Romans, and changed hands often even after the
establishment of Islam (Seventh century) and the prosperous
dynasty of Saladin, occupied by *Mongols, *Mamelukes,
Timurians, and *Turks. In M.'s time, tremendous expansion
occurred after incorporation into the empire of Mohammed Ali
of Egypt. In 1840 and 1860, it was the site of great massacres of
Christians and *Jews by the Turks. (Modern-day union of
Syria and Egypt made it part of the United Arab Republic.)
        Damascus sword blades are known for extraordinarily
keen edges and flexibility. A superior smelting process was
followed by innovative molding: wrought iron bars were repeatedly hammered fine, then folded back and forge-welded.
Toughness depended on multiple repetitions, insuring that
original metal flaws ended longitudinal. Early blades were

straight; they were curved after 1500. They are distinguished
by flecky grain and peculiar odor when subjected to friction.
(Notice also "White-Jacket's" pun on blades).
(See also "Abana"; "Pharpar.")
O. 7; M. 32; W. 39

DAME ANTONINA
See "Belisarius."
M. 23

DAME ISABELLA'S INQUISITION
See "Isabella" and "Spanish Inquisition."
M.D. 54

DAMOCLES
According to *Cicero, Damocles was a courtier of the
Syracusan tyrant *Dionysius the Elder. When the syncophan-
tic Damocles overly praised the happy life of the tyrant, he was
invited to try the position at a sumptuous banquet. Having
accepted, Damocles found himself dining under a sword suspended by a hair. "The sword of Damocles" has come to mean
impending evil or danger.
M.D. 102

DAMON AND PYTHIAS
The type of inseparable friends; the originals were
Fourth Century Syracusans. *Dionysius the Tyrant con-
demned Pythias to death; Damon volunteered to take his place
as captive while Pythias went home to arrange his affairs.
Pythius arrived back just as Damon was to be executed; Diony-
sius was so touched he pardoned both.
Pythias is correctly *Phintias*.
O. 39; W. 41; I.P. 22

DAMPIER
William Dampier (1652-1715) was an *English *pirate
and in 1688 explorer of parts of *Australia, *New Guinea, and
New Britain, described in his 1697 *New Voyage round the
World* and "A Discourse of the Winds." Dampier Archipelago
(20°15' S., 116°25' E.) is named for him. His admiralty-sub-
sidized 1699 voyage of discovery ended in severe deterioration of
ship and crew, so on his subsequent voyages he returned to

buccaneering, which he had pursued between 1678 and 1691.
His late piracies were highly lucrative.
M. 1; M.D. 45

DANAE'S SHOWER

In *Greek mythology, Danaë was daughter to King
Acrisius of Argos. The oracle predicted to him that he would
have no son, but that Danaë's son would kill him. He shut her
up in an underground house with part of the roof open to the
sky. In the form of a shower of gold, Zeus (see "Jove" and
"Jupiter") came into the house and she later bore his son,
*Perseus. Acrisius had mother and son cast into the sea in a
great chest, but they landed on an island and were rescued.
After Perseus slew *Medusa, both returned to Greece, where
Perseus accidentally killed Acrisius with a discus, proving the
oracle true.
M. 119; P. 2:2

DANA'S

Richard Henry Dana, Jr. (1815-82) was born in *Cambridge, Massachusetts of a wealthy and respected *New
England "*Brahmin" family. He left *Harvard at the age of
nineteen to serve as a common sailor and laborer, completing
a law degree later. Non-traditional experience left him with
life-long devotion to the cause of the "common man." Even before publication of *Two Years Before the Mast* (1840), he had
written about cruelty to seamen. Following his popular novel
in 1841 was *The Seaman's Friend* (in England *The Seaman's
Manual*), a reference book of naval law for sailors.

Dana assisted Fugitive Slave Law victims and served in
local government but never rose high in *American politics.
He was the object of a plagiarism suit for his edition of *Elements of International Law by Wheaton* (1866) and ended his
life in regret that his greatest claim to fame had been what he
called "a boy's work."

M. And Dana expressed admiration for each other's
work, although M.'s regard appears to have been more earnest
than Dana's. M. read *Two Years* in 1840 and wrote to Dana
(May 1850) of the "*Siamese link of affectionate sympathy" he
had felt from that time. Dana incurred the gratitude of Guert
*Gansevoort for his account of the *Somers* trial. But he refused
to help M. secure a consulship in 1861, and correspondence
between the two appears to have stopped from that time.
Reviewers compared M.'s early work to Dana's, with *Two
Years* usually preferred.

Sealts #173 is *Two Years before the Mast. A Personal Narrative of Life at Sea . . . .* New York, 1840.
W. 24

DANE, --S; DANISH

The lowland kingdom of Denmark (capital, *Copenhagen) was central in early *Viking raids and invasion of *England. Its most famous king, *Canute (r. 1018-35), united Denmark, England, and Norway. *Sweden was in Danish hands until 1658 and Norway until 1814. In the twelfth century King Valdemar I had achieved control of much of northern Europe, and from the sixteenth to the eighteenth centuries, Denmark was at war almost continually (especially against Sweden). In the *Napoleonic Wars, it was attacked by England (1801 and 1807). The 1849 Constitution of Frederick VII led to the Prusso-Danish War of 1849.

The "Dansker" of *Billy Budd, Sailor* derives his name from Danskë, the early name for Denmark. (*Shakespeare had "Polonius" use the expression in *Hamlet* II, 1.) Most of M.'s references to Danes suggest an appraisal of them as cool, tough, mysterious, and canny.

See also "Jutland."
O. 15; O. 38; M. 3; M. 149; R. 28; R. 35; W. 50; M.D. 30; M.D. 40; M.D. 87; M.D. 101; M.D. 105; C.M. 2

DANIEL, --S

In the *apocalyptic Book of Daniel, the fourth prophetic book of the *Old Testament, the central figure is perhaps the wise King Dnil (meaning "God has judged") or perhaps a wise and loyal young *Hebrew. The Book divides into two parts. There are stories of Daniel: with his three friends, *Shadrach, Meshach, and Abednego; foreseeing *Nebuchadnezzar's madness; the writing on the wall at *Belshazzar's feast; Daniel in the lion's den for refusing to recognize one *Darius the Mede as a god. The visions are of the four beasts from the sea (representing the nations of mankind), and three other symbolic visions of a ram and a he-goat, the seventy weeks, and the revelation of the Angel. The visions are said to symbolize the history of *Israel from the time of the *Persian Empire to the *Greek Empire under *Alexander. They were composed during a time of persecutions under *Antiochus (IV) Epiphanes, model for the Anti-Christ.
M. 20; I.P. 12

DANTE; DANTE ALIGHIERI; DANTEAN

Dante Alighieri (1265-1321) was born into a *Guelph family of *Florence. He is known in his youth to have participated in military operations, married, and fallen in love with the unattainable woman he celebrates as "Beatrice" in the *Vita Nuova* and the *Divina Commedia* (*Divine Comedy*). He became politically active and was banished after a split in the Guelph party, becoming a wanderer. He died and was buried at Ravenna. His masterpiece, the *Commedia*, was completed just before his death. Dante's literary reputation had faded somewhat, but in the nineteenth century his works were newly acclaimed by *Byron, *Shelley, Carlyle, and other Romantics.

The *Inferno* (*M.* 3; *M.* 98; *P.* 9:2; *P.* 25:5) is the first of the three parts of the *terza rima Commedia* (along with the *Purgatorio* and the *Paradiso*). M.'s references are all to Dante's description of Hell, painted as a conical funnel the circles of which punish sinners in accordance with their sins.

On 22 June 1848, M. purchased a copy of the highly praised H.F. Cary (1772-1844) blank verse translation (1805): *The Vision; or Hell, Purgatory, and Paradise* .... Translated by the Rev. Henry Francis Cary, M.A. From the Last Corrected London Edition. New York, Appleton 1845; or, *A New Edition, Corrected. With Life of Dante, Chronological View of His Age, Additional Notes, and Index.* London, Bohn, 1847 (Sealts #174).

M. visited what he called Dante's "tomb" (actually a memorial monument of 1829) at *Florence's Santa Croce church, 25 March 1857. He had referred to *London as a city of *Dis in his journal of 9 November 1849. And he entitled *I.P.* 24 in honor of Dante's abode of *Lucifer.

M.'s heavily annotated and marked edition of Dante came up for sale in 1985, enabling examination by scholars. *Paradiso* is the most heavily marked book, followed by *Inferno* and *Purgatorio*. (Reported in *Melville Society Extracts* 63, September 1985).

See also "Agnello"; "Francesca, --'s,"; "Paolo"; "Quotations" section: "Through me you pass into the city of woe. . . . " M. 3; M. 98; W. 24; M.D. 85; M.D. 86; P. 2:7; P. 3:3; P. 4:5; P. 9:2; P. 9:3; P. 23:4

DARBIES; DOUBLE-DARBIES

Old colloquial term for irons or handcuffs. The poem which concludes *Billy Budd, Sailor* is "Billy in the Darbies." W. 56; W. 58

DARBY AND JOAN
Darby and Joan are the type of loving, virtuous couples.
The originals are not certain; they were either John Darby of
Bartholomew Close, *England (d. 1730) and his wife, or a cou-
ple of West Riding of *Yorkshire. They were immortalized by
Henry Woodfall, once apprenticed to John Darby, in a ballad
published in *Gentleman's Magazine* in 1735.
O. 67; M. 23

DARDANELLES
The strait between Europe and Asia Minor which con-
nects the *Mediterranean to the Sea of Marmara.
M.D. 45; M.D. 87

DARIEN, ISTHMUS OF
Serrania del Darien, *Panama: 8°13' N., 77°28' W.
W. 24; W. 29; M.D. 76

DARIUS
Darius I the Great, of *Persia's Achaemenid dynasty
(reigned 522-486 B.C.), was the son of Hystaspes, *satrap of
*Parthia. His history is clouded by autobiography and legend.
Ambitious from youth, he perhaps plotted against *Cyrus the
Great and perhaps secured the throne by murdering rivals.
He imposed his rule by force outside Persia, subduing rebels in
*Babylonia, *Egypt, and Susiana. He enlarged his empire by
military might as far west as *Scythia, controlled approaches
to and repeatedly attempted invasion of Greece.
He reorganized the Persian Empire into satrapies, pro-
moted trade, and attempted to unite diverse peoples. As M.
notes in *M.*, he was considered a great lawgiver, especially by
the Egyptians and the Jews (see "Hebrews"), consistently respecting religion and custom. In Persia, he is credited with
establishing *Zoroastrianism as the state religion. He fortified
*Susa and erected many important buildings.
(Darius II Ochus reigned ineffectually from 423 to 404
B.C. Darius III Codommanas reigned from 336-330 B.C., losing Persia to *Alexander the Great. There were others of the
name in later dynasties, up to 40 B.C.)
M. 60

DARK AGES
The historical Dark Ages were the early centuries of the
Middle Ages, thought to be in intellectual darkness after the

collapse of the classical civilizations of *Greece and *Rome: roughly from the death of *Charlemagne to the end of the Carlovingian dynasty (c. 476-1200).
M. 75

DARMONODES' ELEPHANT

Although the story M. tells in *M.D.* about the elephant who loves women is found in sources from *Pliny to the contemporary *Harper's Family Library* (*The Elephant*, Vol. 164, 1842), the name, Darmonodes, is probably an invented one.
M.D. 86

DARWIN

Charles Robert Darwin (1809-82) was born in Shrewsbury, *England, and educated at *Edinburgh University and Christ's Church College, *Cambridge. Although his major fame was to rest on two later works (*On the Origin of Species by means of Natural Selection*, 1859, and *The Descent of Man*, 1871), M. was familiar with the 1839 work, originally entitled *Narrative of the Surveying Voyages of His Majesty's Ships Adventure and Beagle . . . 1826 and 1836 . . . and the Beagle's Circumnavigation . . . 1832-1836*. M. acquired a two-volume 1846 edition in 1847: *Journal of Researches into the Natural History and Geology of the Countries Visited during the Voyage of H.M.S. Beagle round the World, under the Command of Capt. Fitz Roy, R.N.* (Sealts #175; hereafter cited as *Journal*).

The *Beagle Journal* resulted from Darwin's four-year cruise on the small warship refitted to survey the *South American coast and measure longitudes around the world. Although Darwin himself was a partial invalid and imperfectly trained in science, and despite initial objections of Captain Robert Fitzroy (a mercurial religious fundamentalist), *Beagle*'s voyage provided the raw materials that facilitated Darwin's fleshing-out of the evolutionary theories of Alfred Russell Wallace (1823-1913) in the two later works. The *Journal*, constructed from Darwin's diaries, was an instant but controversial success, yielding important data on coral formations and introducing the nascent theory of evolution bolstered by Darwin's observations of acquired characteristics of *Galapagos Islands creatures. (M.'s "The Encantadas" sketches are thought to respond to Darwin's observations on the same sites.) Although Darwin began the cruise a putative believer in *Creation theory, he became a professed agnostic afterwards, devoting the rest of his life to developing and illustrating his theories though various editions of his works.

The *Civil War interrupted *American attention to *The Origin of Species*. Afterwards, the somewhat misleading interpretations of Herbert Spencer (1820-1903) became the focus of American Darwinian lore.

(An edition of Darwin's *Journal* is known to have been in the library of *United States* during the time of M.'s cruise.)

See also "Extracts" 77.

M.D. Extracts 77

DAUPHINS

Title of heirs to the *French crown, eldest sons of Kings from 1349-1830. The first dauphin, Guy IX, Count of Viene, was so designated because of his emblem, the dolphin (see "Cetology" section), and the title continued.

M.181

DAVENANT, SIR WILLIAM

Sir William Davenant (D'Avenant, or D'avenant, 1606-1668), *English poet laureate and playwright, producer of the first English opera (in 1656), was godson to *Shakespeare. Tutored briefly at *Oxford, he began writing plays in *London, under the patronage of Fulke Greville and of Queen Henrietta Maria. His popular comedies, tragedies, and masques gained him the laureate in 1638, but his career was repeatedly interrupted by military service. Knighted in 1643, he joined the exiled court in *Paris after the Civil War and there began the uncompleted *Gondibert* (1651). Imprisoned in the *Tower of London after the execution of *Charles I, he later returned to the theatre to revive the drama banned by *Cromwell. Until his death, he operated the Duke of York's Playhouse, presenting his own innovative plays (the first to include female actors), operas, and works of Shakespeare.

M. owned Davenant's *Works* (Sealts #176). His annotations proclaim: "Ah Will was a trump."

(See also "Extracts" 18.)

M.D. Extracts 18

DAVID

The *Old Testament's David (?1000-962 B.C.) is the second king of *Israel, chosen by the Lord. The main sources of information are the Book of *Samuel and I *Kings 1-2, paralleled in I *Chronicles 11-29; these are among the most authentic of Old Testament historical writings.

The stories about David reveal an honorable and diplomatic but shrewd politician, a fierce warrior and military or-

ganizer, a skilled poet and musician, a religious man. He is
known to have been a member of the *Bethlehem family of
Jesse, and Samuel discusses his life: anointing by Samuel;
musicianship at the court of *Saul; struggle with Goliath (see
"Gath"); friendship with *Jonathan, the son of Saul; fugitive
years at *Adullam; Kingship of *Judah, then of Israel at
*Jerusalem; conquests of the *Philistines, Moabites,
*Ammonites, Edomites; revolt of his son, Absalom; marriage
with Bathsheba and her arranging that his son, *Solomon,
succeed him as King.
R. 27; W. 39; I.P. 15; I.P. 21

DA VINCI
        See "Leonardo."
    P. 26:1

DAVIS, CAPTAIN
        Edward Davis (fl. 1683-1702) was a *pirate. He sailed
with *Cook in 1683 and then ranged the coasts of *Peru and
Central America on his own ship, on which *Wafer served as
surgeon. He was apprehended and tried but pardoned by
*James II, and then temporarily retired near Point Comfort,
*Virginia. He was active again by 1702. Davis is mentioned in
*Dampier.
        The second edition (1704) of Wafer's *New Voyage and
Description of the Isthmus of America* (originally published
1699) has a supplement: "Davis, His Expedition to the Gold
Mines."
    M.D. 45

DAVIS, COMMODORE
        This is perhaps a reference to John Davis, or Davys
(1550?-1605?), English navigator who first (1585, -86, -87) sought
a *northwest passage through the *Arctic to the *Pacific. In
1588, he fought against the *Spanish Armada. He later explored the south *Atlantic (discovering the *Falkland Islands),
sailed with *Raleigh to *Cádiz and the *Azores, and piloted a
*Dutch expedition to the *East Indies. He was killed by
*Japanese *pirates near *Sumatra. M. would have read about
Davis in *Purchas.
    M.D. 45

DAVY, SIR HUMPHREY, --S

Sir Humphrey Davy (1778-1829) was a brilliant *English chemist and exponent of the scientific method, discoverer of sodium and potassium, and would-be poet. He founded the Society for Preventing Accidents in Coal Mines and studied the conditions under which mixtures of fire-damp and air explode, eventually leading to the invention of the safety lamp. His publications are many and various, ranging from highly specialized scientific tracts to a book on fishing illustrated by himself.
M. 19; W. 31; C.M. 13

DAVY JONES

Davy Jones is the evil spirit of the sea, with a locker at the bottom of the sea where drowned sailors go. He is seen in various shapes and is often associated with *pirates and smugglers, who are said to be his children. His name perhaps derives from that of *Jonah, the prophet thrown into the sea, and from a corruption of the *West Indian word for devil: "duppy."
O. 76; W. 43; M.D. 18; M.D. 81 and elsewhere

DAYALIZED

A neologism meaning "fixed at a certain day in time," as M. believed a *Daguerreotype did.
P. 17:3

DEACON DEUTERONOMY COLEMAN

The fictional deacon (layman, or minister's assistant) derives his name from the *Old Testament last book of the Pentateuch. Deuteromony consists largely of supposed speeches of *Moses just before his death, with a description of that death and burial. "Coleman" is perhaps a poor pun on "coal man," the deacon being black.
M.D. 18

DEAD-HOUSE

A morgue, or a low drinking dive.
R. 36

"DEAD RECKONING"

The calculation of a ship's position without observation of the heavenly bodies: approximation from log, compass, chronometer readings, direction and speed of wind, or plotting

from the last fix or trustworthy observed position and speed
along the compass course steered. M.'s use of the term is often
metaphoric.
O. 17; M. 34; M.D. 118

DEAD SEA

The salt lake of south *Palestine, on the border of modern Jordan and *Israel, fourteen miles east of *Jerusalem, is
forty miles long and ten miles wide. It receives the *Jordan
River but has no outlet. The Sea is about twenty-five percent
saline (several times the salinity of the ocean); it has an
oily/frothy texture due to the presence of calcium chloride
(among other salts). In the *Bible, it is the "Salt Sea," "Sea of
the Plain," or "East Sea." For the *Romans it was *Lacus
Asphaltites. The surrounding land is absolutely sterile.

M.'s visit in January of 1857 utterly depressed him. He
took the customary three-day tour of the *Holy Land (including
visits to Jerusalem, Bethany, Jericho, and the Jordan), but as
his journal shows, his mental stress was exacerbated: "Valley
of *Jehosaphat . . . grows more diabolical as approaches Dead
Sea . . . foam on beach & pebbles like slaver of mad dog—
smarting bitter of the water,—carried the bitter in my mouth
all day—bitterness of life—thought of all bitter things . . .
nought to eat but bitumen & ashes with desert of *Sodom
apples washed down with water of Dead Sea . . . all is barren"
(26 January).
R. 31

DEAF AND DUMB INSTITUTION

Although attempts at education of the deaf had previously been made elsewhere in the *United States (notably near
Hartford, *Connecticut), the *New York Institute for the Deaf,
founded in 1818, was the largest scale such school of the time.
Its sixty-two pupils followed methods of sign language developed by Thomas Hopkins Gallaudet (1787-1851), himself not
deaf. Early success led to state funding enabling expansion, so
that the physical structure had been outgrown several times
before it settled in 1856 into a large, elaborate building with extensive grounds, in Washington Heights (west of Fort Washington Avenue at 164th Street). At the time referred to in *R*. 23,
it was probably in a structure on Fiftieth Street, into which it
had moved in 1829. M.'s pun on the "signs of the times" lectured upon by the "deputy" probably refers to the constant intercourse between the *United States, *Paris, and *London by
Gallaudet and his associates.
R. 23

DEAN
Ecclesiastical dignitary, especially in *British usage. The reference to *Rabelais as dean is tenuous. Rabelais was *curé* of Meudon for two years without officiating or residing there.
I.P. 13

DEBONNAIRE, THE
See "Louis I, King of France."
M. 181

DECALOGUE
The Ten Commandments.
W. 10; P. 5:4

DECATUR
Stephen Decatur (1779-1820) entered the U.S. *Navy as *midshipman in 1798, was promoted to lieutenant in the same year and served until 1800 in the "Quasi-War" against the *French. By 1803, he was with *Commodore Preble's *Mediterranean squadron and in 1804 he personally led the burning at Tripoli of the captured U.S. frigate *Philadelphia* (once commanded by his father), earning captaincy. In the *War of 1812, commanding *United States*, he captured *Macedonian* and was soon appointed commodore. He returned to the Mediterranean and in 1815 became a Navy Commissioner (see "Board of Commodores and Navy Commissioners). He was killed in a duel with Commodore James Barron, in *Maryland.
He is remembered as well for having said in a toast at *Norfolk (April 1816): "Our country! In her intercourse with foreign nations may she always be in the right; but our country, right or wrong." Cities in *Alabama, *Georgia, and *Illinois are named for him, as was the U.S. sloop-or-war upon which M.'s cousin, Guert *Gansevoort, lost command in 1856, charged with drunkenness.
See also "Barbary."
W. 3; W. 74

DECLARATION OF INDEPENDENCE
The *American Declaration of Independence was created in response to a motion at the Second *Continental Congress, by Richard Henry Lee (1732-1794) of *Virginia, who claimed that "these United Colonies are, and of right ought to

be, free and independent states." It was drafted by a committee of five headed by *Thomas Jefferson, and was approved 4 July 1776 (see "Fourth of July"). It became perhaps the most influential secular document ever known, its phrases entering the lexicons of philosophy, law, and politics, and its power as a manifesto making it a model for revolutionary cries in *France and other European countries in the nineteenth century.

The Declaration begins with a philosophic discussion of the nature of law and the rights of men (inspired by *Locke's thinking), continues with a list like a legal brief containing twenty-seven complaints against King *George III, and concludes with a declaration of independence and mutual loyalty pledge by the fifty-six "Representatives of the United States." (These came from the thirteen colonies of *New Hampshire, *Massachusetts, *Delaware, *New York, *New Jersey, North *Carolina, *Maryland, South Carolina, *Rhode Island, *Connecticut, *Pennsylvania, *Virginia, and *Georgia. Signers alluded to by M. include *Stockton, *Franklin, and Jefferson.)

Despite widespread embrace of the Declaration's tenets, there has always been disagreement about its language and content, so M.'s suggestion (*W.* 35) that for some people it is a lie was not received as blasphemy in all quarters. The document's language had been much toned-down from Jefferson's original draft, and there were serious questions about its real meaning. "The pursuit of happiness" to which all men are entitled was, and has been, interpreted as "pursuit of property"; an explicit twenty-eighth reference, to the evils of *slavery, was expunged, permitting continuance of this form of "property."

The Declaration was a bold and illegal step by a group of disaffected colonists who by no means represented all Americans. Its adoption might have amounted to support of a meaningless tirade, with severe punishment for signers; instead, it swayed colonists from their belief in unquestioning loyalty to a king and brought about the *American Revolution.

In a (3 March 1849) letter to *Duyckinck, M. admitted that "the Declaration of Independence makes a difference"; it removes the "muzzle which all men wore on their souls" in previous ages. As a member of *Young America in Literature, Duyckinck would probably have had a more tempered view of the extent to which souls ought to be unmuzzled. The young and hopeful M. of 1849 became increasingly skeptical about the Declaration's worth in later statements, as such practices as *flogging, slavery, the *Mexican War, and domination of *"the people" by tyrants continued. As Rogin dramatically suggests in *Subversive Genealogy*, "Melville's Declaration of Independence went down with the *Pequod*" (Chapter 4, x, p. 151).
R. 32; R. 41; W. 35; W. 71 and elsewhere

DEFENDER OF THE FAITH
      See "England . . . ."
C.M. 29

DE GRASSE
      See "Grasse, Count de."
W. 83

DELECTABLE MOUNTAIN, THE
      See "Bunyan; Bunyanish."
P. 25:4

DELHI
      The capital city of *India's Delhi state was the capital of
India briefly in the twentieth century. It is located on the western bank of the Jumna River, 740 miles north-northeast of
*Bombay and 800 miles northwest of *Calcutta. It is the site of
the Red Fort, a *Mogul palace of the seventeenth century
which contains the Peacock Throne. (It is now a shrine; the
site of Mohatma Gandhi`s cremation.) There is a famous
mosque and a bazaar where gold- and silversmiths sell their
wares.
      Delhi was not important to western nations until the
seventeenth century. The *British took it in 1803; there was a
brief rebellion (Sepoy Rebellion) in 1857, but by 1877, Queen
*Victoria declared herself Empress of India at Delhi.
M. 3

DELIGHT
      *Father Mapple's artful repetition of the word "delight,"
in contrast to his repetition of "woe," has precedent in the *Old
Testament. In a section of an 1844 edition of New Testament
and Psalms (Sealts #65) obtained in 1846, M. sidelined *Psalm
37. The word appears in verses 4, 11, and 23, and M. especially
marked: "But the meek shall inherit the earth, and shall delight themselves in the abundance of peace" (11).
      There are similar precedents in *Milton and in other fa-
vorite authors of M.
M.D. 9

DELILAH
      The (probably *Philistine) woman beloved by the strong
man, *Samson, in the *Old Testament Book of *Judges (16:4-

22) seduces him and learns that his hair is the secret of his strength. She cuts off the hair, betrays him to the Philistines, and he is imprisoned.
W. 38; I.P. 21

DELIRIUM TREMENS

In "A Note on Melville's *Redburn*," Huntress suggests an original book of that title written by Andrew Blake, published in England by Burgess in 1830. Another possible original is *The Horrors of Delirium Tremens* (N.Y. 1844), written by James Root: a temperance tract within a theological disquisition.
R. 18; W. 43

DELMONICO'S

One of *New York City's finest (and most enduring) restaurants, Delmonico's was founded in 1827 by *Italian immigrants Peter and John Delmonico. The restaurant went through numerous incarnations. By the time of M.'s writing of R., it was located on Beaver Street. By the 1850's it had moved to the more fashionable *Fifth Avenue and Twenty-Sixth Street site (near Madison Square). From the 1880's until 1923 it inhabited a grandly elegant Beaux-Arts building with ballrooms and bachelor apartments, at Fifth Avenue and Forty-Fourth Street.
R. 8; R. 33

DELPHI; DELPHIC

In classical times, the supreme oracle of *Greece, Delphi was presumed the center of the earth, marked by the sacred navel-stone: omphalos. *Sir Thomas Browne presumed the oracle of *Apollo to be the work of *Satan and referred to "The devil of Delphos," but Delphi is associated with the *Hellenic ideal of manhood.
W. 4; P. 3:2

DELTA

The deposit of sand and soil at the mouth of rivers such as the *Nile and *Mississippi; usually triangular in shape.
Passim

DELUGE, THE
The Flood in *Genesis derives from many previous flood legends. With some discrepancies, the Genesis story is of *God's judgement on a corrupt world. He saves only *Noah and the creatures on the *Ark from the flood that engulfs the world, in order to begin it again. The rainbow is given afterwards as a sign of God's covenant that the world will not be destroyed by water again. The event is no longer considered historical, although there is evidence of severe local floods at the time of the story's setting.
M. 97; W. 25

DEMIGORGON
See "Medusa."
M.D. 38

DEMIJOHN
A large glass vessel with a small neck, enclosed in wicker.
M.D. 110

DEMOCRAT, --IC
The word "democrat" written in lower-case letters of course designates an espouser of the principle that a state's power derives from the will of the people. However, M.'s use with the capital letter (in P. 1:4, for example) is more complex. "Democratic" with the capital refers to the political party springing from *Thomas Jefferson's (basically anti-*Federalist) Democratic-Republican Party, which became the Democratic Party when *Andrew Jackson ran for the *Presidency (serving 1828-36). Theoretically, this party stood for greater egalitarianism than the *Whig Party, as well as for abolition of special privilege. The fact was, however, that *slavery was tolerated or even practiced by Party members (especially in the *South), which led to splitting of the Party and eventual creation of (former Whig) *Lincoln's Republican Party.
In P. 1:4, the reference to "Pierre's" grandfather, the *Major-General, personalizes M.'s comments and their implications. M.'s maternal grandfather, Peter *Gansevoort (1749-1812; see also "Fort Stanwix") had been active in Democratic politics, and M.'s uncle Peter Gansevoort (1789-1876) served in very high offices, becoming a Van Buren Democrat, as did M.'s politically ambitious brother Gansevoort Melville (1815-1846), who straddled factions and eventually became a *Polk

Democrat.   *P*. 1:4's brief mention of the subject, citing
"Pierre's" "Radical" actions, hearkens back to Gansevoort
family connections: although the Gansevoorts (and Gansevoort Melville) were "paper" liberals, the more radical principles of the Democratic Party worked against them. Heirs of
the "proud, elated" *Dutch *Patroon tradition, they lost power
(and political office) as a result of extensions of suffrage; they
had freed their own slaves in the eighteenth century not out of
high-minded objection to a foul institution but out of preference
for poor *Irish immigrants as servants.

Gansevoort Melville apparently swayed his convictions
in order to secure the main chance. M. himself was, of course,
the "Radical" who never tried very hard to play the political
game (one would like to think, out of superiority to the moral
compromises it compelled), although he did eventually seek politically tied appointments in the *Treasury Department and as
*Consul, probably at the urging of family members attempting
to lure him away from writing. M.'s *Custom House appointment was essentially political (as *Hawthorne makes
clear of his own tenure, in the introduction to *The Scarlet Letter*).

In M.'s short story, "Bartleby the Scrivener," the narrator is permanently piqued by his removal from a political plum
job similar to one lost by M.'s uncle Peter Gansevoort: Peter
had been Secretary to *New York State Governor DeWitt Clinton but lost his lucrative and prestigious office to politics.

Thus, the political history of "Pierre's" family is the political history of the Gansevoort family and the history of the
Democratic Party, writ small. (The reader is directed to Kenney's *The Gansevoorts of Albany* and to Rogin's *Subversive
Genealogy* for complete discussion of Gansevoort and Melville
family politics.)
P. 1:4 and elsewhere

DEMOCRITUS
Little is known of the early life of the great *Greek physical philosopher. He was probably born in *Thrace in the fifth
century B.C. and studied in *Egypt, perhaps influenced by the
*Magi. His many written works made him as influential in
philosophy as *Plato or *Aristotle. His major theories on the
similarity, motion, and permanence of atoms anticipate later
findings and exclude the idea of an intelligent first cause. He
placed great emphasis on the existence of a material soul and
considered perception and knowledge as physical functions.
He explained the origin of religion as arising from man's fear
of unexplainable phenomena and caused by physical particles,
eidola. His was perhaps the first system of morals, once again

based on the physical; he counseled prudence and moderation, which would in turn make for a "cheerful" soul.
M. 119; M. 184

DENDERAH
The temple of Dendera (Dandarah) at Tentyra, an *Egyptian village on the *Nile some four hundred miles north of *Cairo, was built in the *Ptolemaic period (completed by *Caesar Augustus) and dedicated to *Isis. The 260 foot-long sandstone structure has north columns fifty feet high. It was elaborately decorated, inside and out, and contained many sacred chambers, the function of which is unknown. The planisphere ceiling, representing the arched heavens, showed representations of whale-like fish. It had a *Zodiac which was removed to the Bibliothèque Royale (now Nationale) in *Paris; M. visited in December, 1849. He might have read an elaborate discussion of the temple in Vivant Denon's *Travels in Upper and Lower Egypt*, a translation from the French, available from 1803.
M. 132; M.D. 104

DENEBOLA
Perhaps a reference to Deneb, the brightest star in the *constellation *Cygnus.
M. 136

DENIQUE COELUM
The Melville family motto: "Heaven at last!" (according to Robert Douglas, *The Baronage of *Scotland*, 1798).
W. 93

DERBY
The *English Derby (pronounced Darby) races or Derby Stakes were begun in 1780 by Edward Stanley (the twelfth Early of Derby), for three year old colts and fillies, so that no horse might win twice. One of the classic races, it is called "The Blue Ribbon of the Turf." Derby Day occurs during the great Epsom Summer Meeting, usually near Whit Sunday (the seventh Sunday after Easter; see "Whitsuntide").
R. 28; R. 44; W. 66

DERBY, EARL OF

The Earl of Derby referred to in *R.* was Henry Stanley, fourth Earl of Derby (c. 1531-93), one of the commissioners who tried Mary, Queen of Scots (see "Stuart, Mary.") just prior to the honor mentioned in *R.* His younger brothers, Sir Thomas (d. 1576) and Sir Edward (d. 1609) had participated in a plot to free the Queen, and his father, Edward, third Earl, had also been suspected of disloyalty to Queen *Elizabeth, by virtue of his fidelity to Roman *Catholicism.
R. 31; R. 36

DERBYSHIRE

The anciently settled (from the Late Paleolithic Age) north midland *English county is noted for its strong geological contrasts between highland and lowland terrain and for its warm mineral springs at Matlock, Buxton, and Bakewell. Matlock was long famous for hydropathic treatment and for its "petrifying wells." Its waters remain at a constant 20°C. (68° F.) temperature, and it is still much used as a vacation resort.
P. 4:1

DESCARTES; DESCARTIAN

René Descartes (1596-1650), *French philosopher/mathematician, was a *Jesuit-educated graduate of University of Poitiers law school. He traveled widely before settling into studious retirement in *Paris and *Holland. His early focus was on mathematics, especially geometry. Following *Copernicus and *Galileo, he developed in *Le Monde* (1633) the theory that all motion was circular, or in vortices. The displacement of one body sets up continuous circular motion among others, creating a universe of innumerable vortices. His mathematical work was widely influential until disproved by *Newton.

Perhaps as an extension of his belief that mathematical reasoning was applicable to all science, and in negative reaction to *Montaigne's radical scepticism, Descartes later began to focus on philosophy. He sought a reliable philosophical method based on self-evident intuition, especially about the existence of *God. His philosophical works include *Discours de la méthode. . .* (1637), *Méditations philosophique* (Lat. 1641; Fr. 1642), *Principia philosophiae* (1644), and *Traité des passions de l'âme* (1649). He is generally considered the founder of modern philosophy.

M.'s interest in the work of Descartes probably centers on its suggestion of a mechanized universe—a comfort, perhaps, to a believer, but as much a threat to a sceptic as a disorderly one.
M.D. 35; P. 19:1

DESMAREST
Anselme Gäetan Desmarest (1784-1838) added notes to a work by *Lacépède. M.'s derogatory comment on his picture of a whale probably came from *Beale, who accuses Desmarest of emulating a "*Chinese drawing," that is, a fanciful one.
M.D. 32; M.D. 55

DESPAIRER, THE
See "Bunyan, --ish."
M. 140

DETROIT
*Michigan's historic city (240 miles east-northeast of *Chicago) is a port on the Detroit River, connecting with Lake *Erie. The *French built a fort (Pontchartrain) on the site in 1701, and the area remained a French fur trading center until *British control in 1760. Detroit became an *American city in 1796, only to be seized by the British again during the *War of 1812 (restored 1813). It was the state capital from 1805 to 1847 (incorporated as a city in 1806). Destroyed by fire in 1805, Detroit was rebuilt and was rapidly developing as a railway center for immigrants when M. visited in 1840. He *lectured in Detroit 12 January 1858.
C.M. 27 refers to *Hull's surrender to the British without a fight, during the *War of 1812.
C.M. 27

DEVIL
The *Old Testament word "devil" is related to the *Hebrew word for "slanderer," "calumniator," or "adversary." The Old Testament devil does not represent metaphysical dualism. For example, in *Job (1:6-12), the devil is Job's accuser before *God rather than a demonic power; he becames the bringer of misfortune to Job. Later Jewish writings brought more pejorative connotations of evil desire, fallen angels, the angel of death: one who destroy's God's relationship to man, leading him to sin, accusing him before God, and seeking to interfere with God's plan. In the *New Testament, the devil is the supernatural adversary of God and the tempter and seducer of man. Early hermits probably developed the modern picture of the devil as a bizarre corporeal visitant. The *Gnostics attached special importance to the devil in their dualistic universe. The *Manichaean Luciferians actually worshipped the devil under the name of *Satan (or *Lucifer). Most Christian creeds, especially those of *Calvinist or *Lutheran

derivation, stressed the idea of the devil as active opponent. The Knights *Templar were accused of diabolism; by the Middle Ages, exorcism was an important ritual.

From early times, the devil was represented in art as a horned, tailed, and hoofed (*M.D.* 36) creature. He might be represented as a buffoon or, as in *Dante, a tragic outcast. *Goethe's "*Mephistopheles" develops the idea of an infernal agreement, and *Milton's "Satan" is so powerfully depicted as to dominate *Paradise Lost*, as "*Ahab" does *M.D.* Certainly, M.'s painting of the "Cosmopolitan's" transformation in *C.M.* 35 owes much to Milton's Satan.

Among the devil's other traditional manifestations are: *Abaddon, *Apollyon, Beelzebul (see "Beelzebub"), *Belial, the Serpent, the Dragon, the Evil One, the Lion.
M. 104; W. 8; W. 44; M.D. 18; M.D. 36; M.D. 85 and elsewhere

DEVIL'S BLUE
        Tattoo marks.
M.D. 18

DEVIL'S JOKE, THE; DEVIL'S-TAIL PEAK
        These probably fictitious places follow the trend of local inhabitants to associate particular sites with the *Devil. Among (actual) places in the *United States, one finds the Devil's Elbow, Devil's Head, Devil's Paw, Devil's Punch Bowl, Devil's Thumb, and Devil's Woodyard.
T. 4; C.M. 22

DEVIL'S REGIMENT
        This is probably a figurative, rather than a specific, reference. A big question in *C.M.* is the possible presence on board "*Fidele" of the *Devil and his legions.
C.M. 19

DEVIL'S-TAIL PEAK
        See "Devil's Joke, the; Devil's-Tail Peak."
T. 4

DE WITT, --'S
        Johan de Witt (1625-1672), leading *Dutch statesman of his time, was Grand Pensionary (legal and estates administrator) of *Holland from 1653-1672. His years of office were trou-

bled by the Anglo-Dutch war and the strained relations which followed. De Witt went to sea with his large fleet and was as instrumental in Dutch victories as the officers. Forced by *Charles II to sign the Triple Alliance with *England and *Sweden, his doom was sealed when Louis XIV (see "Bourbon") of France joined with Charles in war on the United Provinces of the *Netherlands. De Witt was overthrown and resigned, but while visiting his brother, Cornelis, in prison, he was set upon by a mob who seized the two men and tore their bodies into pieces.
M.D. 24

DEY

Title of *Mohammedan governors in *Algiers from 1710 until the *French conquest in 1830, at other times in Tripoli and Tunis. From *Turkish *dai*: maternal uncle.
M. 60; W. 41; M.D. 102

DIANA

In mythology, Diana, known to the *Greeks as Artemis, or *Cynthia, for her birthplace, Mount Cynthus, is perhaps the clearest example of the contradictions of good and bad in the gods. She was the daughter of Zeus (see "Jupiter" and "Jove"), who abandoned her mother, Leto, fearing Hera's jealousy. The island of Dêlos magically received Leto, and there Artemis and her twin brother, *Apollo, were born. He was to be honored by a great temple on the site.

Among her many names, in addition to "Artemis" on Earth, she is also identified with *Phoebe and Selene (Lat. "Luna") in the sky and with *Hecate, who is present in the underworld and on Earth's moonless nights. With Vesta and Athena, she is a maiden goddess of *Olympus.

*Ovid and Euripides wrote of both her light and dark deeds. Among the positive aspects: she was sometimes goddess of childbirth and protector of young maidens, as well as the Lady of Wild Things (especially cypress trees and deer). She was rescuer of *Arethusa and Iphigenia and helper to the *Trojans against the *Greeks. On the other hand, especially as Hecate, Goddess of the Crossways, she was associated with dark magic deeds, and as Artemis performed many fierce or vengeful acts: she demanded sacrifice of *Agamemnon's daughter during the Trojan war, when his Greek army killed a wild hare; she tricked the twin giants Otus and Ephialtes into killing each other; killed *Orion in a jealous rage; sent the Calydonian boar to ravage Calydon, punishing the king, who had forgotten to sacrifice to her. When *Acteon acciden-

tally saw her bathing naked, she changed him into a stag to be devoured by his own hounds, and when Niobe hubristically demanded sacrifice, she killed all of Niobe's children.
M. 75; M. 81; R. 56

DIAZ, BARTHOLOMEW

Bartholomeu Dias de Novais (fl. 1478-1500), *Portuguese navigator, discovered the Cape of *Good Hope (see also "Cape Tormentoto") in 1486, confirming a sea route around the south coast of *Africa. Despite his achievement, Diaz was bypassed in favor of Vasco da *Gama as commander of the *Indian expedition of 1497. He died in a storm off the Cape of Good Hope.
M.D. 83

DIBDIN

Charles Dibdin (1745-1814), *British actor, dramatist, and song writer, is best remembered for his sea chanteys. He is said to have composed about 1,000 popular songs, some of them inspired by the death of a brother who was a naval captain.

Perhaps his most popular song was "Tom Bowling," which describes a sailor much like "Billy Budd":

> The darling of our crew;
> No more he'll hear the tempest howling,
> For death has broached him to.
> His form was of the manliest beauty,
> His heart was kind and soft;
> Faithful below he did his duty,
> But now he's gone aloft.

M.'s lengthy quotations from "The King, God Bless Him," "The True English Sailor," and other songs, are from *Scenes from Old Ironsides*, rather than from memory. "The True Yankee Sailor," as M. notes, is deducible from the paean to the British tar.

"No mean auxiliary to the British government," Dibdin was pensioned, as M. notes in *Billy Budd, Sailor*, his music . . . "subserving the discipline and purposes of war" (Chap. 27).
T. 29; R. 30; W. 90

DIDDLER

See "Jeremy Diddler."
C.M. 24

DIDO

Dido is the legendary founder of *Carthage and its first queen. Her greater fame rests on her part in *Virgil's *Aeneïd*. When her suitor, Aeneas, abandons her to perform his destined duties in *Italy, she commits suicide.
T. 6

DIEGOES

Islas Diego Ramirez, *Chile: 56°15' S.; 70°15' W.
W. 24

DIGITAL FOSSA

See "*femur*."
W. 62

DIOCLETIAN

Gaius Aurelius Valerius Diocletianus was *Roman Emperor from A.D. 284 to 305. Of humble birth, he rose through military service to dominate Rome in a twenty-year reign that saw the reorganization of the Empire and the last persecution of the *Christians. He called himself "Jovius," *Jupiter's representative on earth, and entitled his friend Maximian, "Herculius," as emulator of *Hercules's enactment of Jupiter's will.

He redesigned rule of the Empire, creating four *Caesars, which lent stability to the Empire but caused confusion in division of power, mostly vested in Diocletian. His reorganization doubled the number of Roman provinces and separated military and civil rule. He reformed the currency and made economic reforms. Although a religious man himself, he undertook systematic persecution of Christians. He abdicated, after a long illness, on 1 May 305.
M. 97

DIODORUS

Diodorus Cronus, fourth century B.C. *Greek philosopher, a formal logician of the Megarian school. It is said that he died of shame when he failed to solve a logical problem.
M. 144

DIOGENES

Originator of the Cynics, a group of ascetic *Greek philosophers, Diogenes (c. 400-320 B.C.) is the center of many

legends, mostly attributable to Menippus or *Seneca: all he asked of *Alexander the Great was that he should stand out of his light; sold into slavery, he became tutor to his master's son; he lived in a tub; he searched for an honest man; asked who he would like to be if not himself, Alexander the Great answered "Diogenes." The historical Diogenes was a wandering beggar, "citizen of the world." Authenticity of his (lost) writings on living "the natural life" is disputed; they are said to have defended cannibalism and incest. His *Republic* posits an anarchist *Utopia.
R. 57; C.M. 24

DIONYSIUS
It is unclear which of the many men named Dionysius is referred to in *M.* as the tyrant who impels the torturous labor of writing. Most likely is Dionysius Thrax (fl. c. 120 B.C.), author of the first *Greek grammar (the model for most subsequent grammars), as well as commentaries on *Homer and Hesiod and a work on *Rhodes. Another likely candidate is the fifth-century Neo-platonic writer, now called Pseudo-Dionysius, whose works influenced the medieval mystical tradition and who claimed to be Dionysius the Areopagite (see "Areopagiticas"), a disciple of *St. Paul referred to in *Acts 17:34.
Other possibilities are Dionysius Exiguus (Denis the Little, c. 500-560), a monk in *Rome who wrote canonical works and translations and who introduced the modern chronology (with a misdating of the birth of *Christ); Dionysius of Halicarnassus (fl. c. 20 B.C.), Greek historian and teacher of rhetoric; Dionysius the Carthusian (1402-1471), writer of dogmatic and mystical theology who called for a *crusade against the *Turks; Saint Dionysius the Great, of *Alexandria (c. 200-c. 265), a student of *Origen whose work survives mainly in quotation. Less likely models are two tyrants of Syracuse, the Elder and the Younger, of the fifth and fourth centuries B.C. The Elder was the notorious torturer of *Damocles.
M. 119

DIRECTORY
City directories, alphabetical lists of a given locality's inhabitants, were standard features in the nineteenth century. *The Trow Business Directory of *New York City for 1848/49* is a curiously intimate listing by profession, supposedly of all the then-residents of New York City. The forword proclaims that any omissions are the fault of those omitted, since the city was carefully canvassed. There is no listing for "Melville," nor a

listing for "writer" or "private citizen," although the range of occupations includes lines from "spar-maker" to "carpet shaker." The Melville clan may be represented in an earlier *Trow Metropolitan Directory of Select Names*, or in *Social Elite*.
R. 61; W. 31; P. 17:2

DIS, CITY OF

Dis was the god of the *Roman underworld (also called "Orcus"), identified with the *Greek *Pluto, or *Hades. *Dante makes the City of Dis the Lower Hell, the red city of *Lucifer, the abiding place of those who commit the most heinous sins. In *Milton (*Paradise Lost* IV, 270), Dis is the one who "gathered" the "flower," *Proserpine.

The reference to *London as the City of Dis is M.'s addition, not found in the original of *Israel Potter*.
I.P. 24

DISCOUNT

Interest deducted in advance.
M.D. 89

DISCOVERY EXPEDITION

See "Krusenstern."
M.D. 45

DISJUNCTIVE

In logic, having the property of disjoining, disconnecting, distinguishing, or separating: involving an alternative between two or more things or statements. A disjunctive axiom or proposition is one in which we assume that one statement of two or more is true.

Subdisjunctive means partly disjunctive. *OED* offers an example (1656): "Contraries are either disjunctive or subdisjunctive . . . . Subdisjunctives are of two kinds, either in whole, betwixt Universals, . . . or in part, betwixt particulars. Of subdisjunctives in whole, both cannot be true, both may be false; both cannot be affirmative, both cannot be negative. Of subdisjunctives in part, both may be true because they are taken in part."

The *Stoics built an entire deductive theory upon disjunction. At the time of composition of *M.*, M. was reading *Seneca. Much of the language of Doxodox and Babbalanja is satire of pedants.
M. 171

DISMAL SWAMP
The heavily wooded coastal swamp is now c. twenty miles long, extending between *Norfolk, *Virginia (N.) and Elizabeth City, North *Carolina (S.); it includes the three-mile-long Lake Drummond. The swamp was much larger and almost impenetrable in M.'s time. It had been surveyed by *George Washington in 1763 and crossed by a canal in 1828, connecting it to *Chesapeake Bay.
R. 11; M.D. 96; I.P. 23

DISPENSATION, NEW
"Dispensation" is the biblical term for the system of relations between *God and man, from the *Latin dispensatio (dis- and pendere—to dispense, distribute, arrange). By Roman *Catholic Church law, the *Pope bestows God's dispensations in the form of special permissions and omissions.
The reference in M. is to the early abuse of Papal dispensation during the time of *Louis I, accused of excessive deference to the Church.
M. 168

"DIVERSIONS OF PURLEY"
See "Horne Tooke."
I.P. 6

DIVES
See "Lazarus."
M.D. 2; C.M. 2; C.M. 15

DIVINATION
Various species are alluded to in the *Bible; among them: Astrology (*Daniel 2:2); Witchcraft (1 *Samuel, 28); Enchantment (2 *Kings 21:6); Dreams and their interpretation (*Genesis, 37:10); Casting lots (Joshua, 18:6).
R. 18

DOBS AND HODNOSE
These burlesque names for fictional characters seem to refer to physical characteristics rather than to actions. "Dobs" are animals inhabiting the razor clam, used as fishing bait. "Hod" is a hole under a rock forming a retreat for fish. "Hod" is also a verb describing riding a horse lobbing up and down.
W. 32

DOC
         Colloquial for "doctor" since c. 1850.
P. 16:2

DOCK GATE
         See "Prince's Dock."
R. 34

DOCK POLICE
         In the late 1830's, along with other reforms, *Liverpool's
police force of 170 aged "Old *Charlies" was replaced and the
new force built up to almost 600 young and hale men. Dock police were part of this new force, but were paid out of corporate
revenues. As M. suggests in R. 37, division of labor must have
been a serious issue.
R. 37

DOCTORS COMMONS
         The area and buildings near *St. Paul's Church,
*London, where in the sixteenth century practitioners of canon
and civil law held court. The buildings (demolished in 1867)
were the site of compulsory dinners of the Association of Doctors of Civil Law. To "common" means to dine together, after a
*Cambridge University tradition.
M. 2

DODONA
         See "Jupiter."
W. 2

DOGE
         The greatly powerful chief elected magistrate in the old
Venetian Republic. First doge was Paolo Anafesto (Paoluccio)
in 697; last was Luigi Mann in 1789. From the fourteenth to
the eighteenth centuries, *Genoa also had a doge.
M. 149; M. 181

DOG'S BODY
         Pease pudding, or peas boiled in a cloth.
         "Dogsbody" is also a colloquialism for a junior officer,
especially a *midshipman.
W. 32

DOG-STAR, THE
    See "Sirius."
M. 183

DOG TO IT!
    Give chase and persist!
M.D. 81

DOG-WATCHES
    The two short watches from four to six and six to eight
P.M., originated to stagger the manning of a ship.
W.66

DOLEFUL DUMPS
    See "Bunyan, --ish."
C.M. 40

DOLLAR
    It has been taken as an error in arithmetic by which
"*Flask" makes the *doubloon equal nine hundred and sixty
dollars, but *American seamen might take "dollar" to mean
"*Spanish dollar," then worth $1.20, as was the *British
*crown piece.
M.D. 99

"DOLLY"
    Probably a sobriquet, with *"Pequod," for *Acushnet*, the
whaleship M. deserted in July of 1842.
T. Passim

DOMENICHINO
    Domenico Zampieri (1581-1641), Bolognese painter called
Domenichino, was the leading painter in *Rome in the early
seventeenth century. His frescos, altarpieces, portraits, and
ideal landscapes influenced Poussin and *Claude, but his popularity diminished after the 1620's, along with that of other
Bolognese artists.
    M. saw either "St. John the Evangelist" or "The
Guardian Angel Defending Innocence," at *Naples, 21 February 1857. In Bologna the following month, he saw "Madonna
of the Rosary" (30 March).
P. 26:1

DOMINICA;
   One of the Lesser *Antilles, approximately twenty-five
miles south of Guadeloupe and twenty-five miles north of Martinique (15° N, 61°30' W.), Dominica is thirty-one miles long,
with an area of 290 square miles. A volcanic mountain forest
with hot springs, it produces chiefly vegetable matter. Its port
capital is Roseau. *Christopher Columbus named Dominica
in honor of the day of its discovery: Sunday, November 3, 1493.
It was first colonized by the *French, eventually passed to the
*British.
W. 83

DOMINORA
   M.'s fictional equivalent of *England.
M. 145 and elsewhere

DOMITIAN
   Titus Flavius Domitianus, *Roman emperor from A.D.
81 to 96, whose reign of terror led to his murder. His rise to the
throne was marked by political rivalry and family jealousy. As
second son of Vespasian, Domitian expected to rise into positions of power, as his brother *Titus had. He did not, and may
have hastened Titus's death to secure the throne.
   Domitian was hated by the aristocracy not alone for his
cruelty but for unpopular actions he ordered: strict control of
magistrates; severe legislation over vices he himself practiced;
excessive pomp and demand for veneration; executions
(including his own cousin's); treason charges; persecution of
*Stoics; confiscation of properties. The conspiracy to murder
him was joined by prefects, palace officials, and his wife,
Domitia Longina. Perpetrators were punished, but the Roman
senate was pleased by his death.
M. 97

DON, --S
   A Don is an aristocrtic gentleman, especially *Spanish
(Lat. *dominus*, lord; same title of honor as *Portuguese
"Dom," Middle English "dan"). Also a *British university tu-
tor or fellow.
M. 28; M. 138; M.D. 54; I.P. 13

DON JUAN
   *Mozart's opera, *Don Giovanni*, was based on a
*Spanish story by Gabriel Téllez ("Tirso da Molina") about the

Sevillian, Don Juan Tenorio. Having killed the father of the
woman he has attempted to rape, Don Juan visits the man's
statue-bedecked tomb. The statue moves and eventually kills
Don Juan and delivers him to Hell.

(The story is also treated in plays by Molière, Goldoni,
Pushkin, Browning, Shaw, and others, and in *Byron's unfinished poem.)

See "Byron; Lord Byron."
M. 15; W. 4; W. 90

DON MIGUEL
This whale is presumed fictional, no other reference be-
ing located.
M.D. 45

DONNYBROOK
Donnybrook's riotous Fair existed from *King John's
time until 1855, in the village near *Dublin, *Ireland. Donnybrook has become the proverbial name for any disorderly social
gathering.

The Donnybrook-jig (W. 25) is a wildly energetic dance to
six-eight or twelve-eight time music. *Gigue* originally referred
to the music, rather than the dance. The Donnybrook shillelah
(shillelagh) of R. 40 is an oak or blackthorn club, from the oak-
forested village in Ireland.
R. 40; W. 25

DON OF GERMANY
See "Charles V. . . . "
W. 46

DO-NOTHING, THE
Louis V of *France (967-987) was called *le Fainéant,* or
Do-Nothing. The last Carolingian king of France, he was
frivolous and disregardful of political advice. His neglect of his
wife, Adelaide (of Aquitaine), who abandoned him, increased
his unpopularity. He died in a hunting accident after one year
on the throne.
M. 181

DON QUIXOTE
Don Quixote de la Mancha, world famous satirical romance by Miguel de *Cervantes Saavedra (1574-1616), was pub-

lished in 1605, with a second part added in 1615. Originally designed as a burlesque of the literature of chivalry, the work developed into a profound study of man and his institutions. "Don Quixote," influenced by tales of chivalry, sets out to face the world on his horse, "Rosinante," accompanied by squire "Sancho Panza." He chooses a beautiful girl, dubbed "Dulcinea del Tobosco," to whom to dedicate his feats (tilting at windmills, etc.). A friend, "Samson Carrasco," tricks him into returning home, where he dies immediately.

Sealts #s 124 and 125 are editions of the work.

A Quixotic person is one with foolish, impractical ideas of honor or schemes for doing good.

O. 65; W. 13; W. 54; C.M. 44

DON SATURNINUS TYPHUS

Typhus fever, now recognized as a group of diseases transmitted by lice, fleas, mites, or ticks, was prevalent long before the *Middle Ages but had reached its height of infection in *Ireland about 1846, as the potato crop failed. It was introduced into the U.S. by immigrant ships but did not get a permanent foothold.

As Bruce Franklin's notes to *C.M.* show, M.'s designation links etymologically two beings overthrown by Zeus (see "Jupiter" and "Jove"): typhus ("smoke") representing the monster Typhoëus, and *Saturn, saturnine" meaning born under Saturn.

C.M. 23

DOOMS-DAY BOOK

*William the Conqueror's Domesday Book, as it has been known since the twelfth century, the record of his 1086 survey of *English lands, reflects ownership, tenancy, and value of holdings of the time.

M. 127; R. 30

DORCHESTER

A district of south *Boston, *Massachusetts: fortification of Dorchester Heights by the Continental Army in 1776 prevented *British occupation of Boston.

"Ishmael's" uncle, in *M.D.* 45 is probably M.'s uncle, Captain John DeWolf (see "D'Wolf"), a resident of Dorchester.

M.D. 45

DORIC

In the Doric order of *Greek architecture, a base with steps serves as the foundation of an edifice, from which rise columns, in turn supporting a crowning entablature. Doric columns taper toward the top, are grooved, and terminate in a capital supporting fluted necking, a cushion-like molding, and a square block. The most famous example is the *Parthenon; another is, as M. notes in *R*. 30, the *New York City *Custom House.
R. 30

D'ORSAY, COUNT

Alfred de Grimod, Comte D'Orsay (1801-1852), *French dandy and sportsman, was a bodyguard to Louis XVIII (see "Bourbon") when he met the Earl of *Blessington and his wife, Marguerite the Countess, a famous beauty and popular writer. While traveling through *Italy with the pair, Alfred's appearance and wit brought much admiration, including that of *Byron (subject of the Countess's *Conversations with Lord Byron*, 1834). Alfred set standards in hair style and fashion, and his clean-shaven face was considered a model of epicene beauty. He may have introduced the "imperials" (tuft of chin hair on an otherwise shaven face) worn by *Napoléon III.

He married Blessington's daughter by a previous marriage but was separated from her after the earl's death because of scandal about his relation to her stepmother. In 1849, he fled to *Paris, followed by the Countess, to escape creditors. He was protected by Louis Napoléon for his work for French exiles and was faithfully dedicated to the Countess until her death that same year. The two are buried together at Chambourcy.
W. 85

DOUBLE-SHUFFLE

The shuffle is a clog dance, in which the feet are dragged; the double-shuffle is performed by a pair of people.
M.D. 40

DOUBLOON

The model for M.'s richly symbolic gold coin was probably the "onza" (ounce) of *Ecuador. Curiously, the symbolic images on the coin were seen by M. rather differently from what others saw. His "flame" is really a vulture; his "crowing cock" is really a condor; there were no volcanoes on coins of

Ecuador. The coin in question could have been minted no earlier than 1836, when Ecuador separated from Colombia.

The *Spanish gold doubloon was worth sixteen Spanish
silver dollars; the silver dollar was a half *escudo*, or an *escud-
ito*. The *escudo* (M.'s "Joe, in *M.D.* 99) by M.'s time contained
c. 3.38 grams of gold. Thus the doubloon would contain c. 27
grams, or about one ounce of gold (one ounce equals c. 28
grams).

Spanish and *Portuguese colonial coins were in wide
circulation in the *United States. See also "Joes," "Moidores,"
"Pistareens," "Pistoles," "Crown-Pieces."
M. 19; M.D. 99

DOUGH-BOYS
      Boiled floor dumplings.
W. 32

DOVER
      The *Kent seaport on the Straits of Dover, between
*England and *France, was settled before the *Roman inva-
sion and was a major area of *Saxon defense. It contains ruins dating from the fourth century, was one of the original
*Cinque Ports, and has always been a principal passenger
port.

M.'s memories of Dover were not pleasant. His journal
for 12 and 13 December 1849 records his arrival at 5 A.M., after
a cold and bumpy all-night journey. At Dover, *Customs officials seized his "fine copy" of *Anastasius*, recently purchased
in *Paris. The book (subtitled *Memoirs of a *Greek*), written by
Thomas Hope, was a Paris 1831 edition (Sealts #281). M. replaced the confiscated one with an 1836 *London edition (Sealts
#282), thought to have influenced his writing of *M.D.*
M. 4; M.D. 90; I.P. 6; I.P. 12; I.P. 13

DOWAGER, --S
      The rather unpopular title originally designated widows
of medieval barons or landed gentry, living in a "dower" house.
The title was meant to distinguish such a woman from the
wife of the head.

"Queen Dowager" has rather an air of fallen glory—
probably M.'s point in using it.
M. 181; P. 1:5

DOWN-EASTER
An *American from *New England.
R. 26; W. 32; W. 84

DOXOLOGY
A formulaic expression of praise to *God which evolved from early *Hebrew blessings into the modern "God the Father, the Son, and the Holy Spirit," in response to the *Arian heresy.

In early Jewish services, blessings such as "ascribe the Lord glory," "the glory of his name," "for ever and ever," were proclaimed at the ends of hymns, longer prayers, or even after the mention of God's name. Sometimes they were proclaimed at the beginnings of prayers to protect the speakers.
M.D. 89; M.D. 119

DRAGON, THE
In astronomy, the Dragon is Draco, a northern *constellation in the *Polar region, site of Gamma Draconis, a third-magnitude star. It was perhaps named for Draco, a severe *Athenian lawgiver.
M. 151

DRAKE, --S; SIR FRANCIS DRAKE
The most famous Elizabethan admiral, Sir Francis Drake (c. 1543-1596), first sailed on *Guinea slaving voyages and as a *pirate on the *Spanish Main. His circumnavigation (1577-1580), the first by an *Englishman, took place on the *Golden Hind* (originally *Pelican*). Drake sailed down the east coast of *South America and through the *Strait of Magellan, demonstrating that *Tierra del Fuego was an island. He went up the west coast, possibly to San Francisco, crossed the *Pacific to the *Moluccas and returned to Plymouth, to be knighted by *Elizabeth in 1581.

By the late 1580's he was harassing Spanish possessions in the *Caribbean and played an important role in the sinking of the *Spanish Armada. Returning to the Caribbean, he was killed off *Portobello.

The "shallow gossip" M. mentions in *M*. may refer to Drake's constant booty-taking, his execution of a respected opponent for "conjuring," his "excommunication" of his chaplain, his playing "bowls" at the onset of engagement with the Armada, or his overall ruthless ambition. His exploits fired many legends; they are recorded in *Hakluyt and *Purchas.
M. 3; W. 19; W. 24; I.P. 16; I.P. 17

DRAKE'S "CULPRIT FAY"
    "The Culprit Fay" was a widely popular 600-line poem with a background of *Hudson River scenery, about a fairy who loves a mortal. The author, Joseph Rodman Drake (1795-1820), was a druggist and sometime-author castigated by *Edgar Allan Poe. The poem was the title piece of a posthumously published collection (1835). Drake was memorialized by Fitz-Greene Halleck in an important elegy, "On the Death of Joseph Rodman Drake."
P. 20:1

DREADNAUGHT, THE
    H.B.M. *Dreadnaught* was blockading the harbor off *Cádiz in 1805 when U.S. Gunboat No. 6, commanded by Lieutenant James Lawrence, was enroute to the *Mediterranean. An impressment incident occurred of such clear insult to the *United States and such personal humiliation to Lawrence, that Commander John Rodgers issued a general order to navy captains, the gist of which was "you are not to be detained by force."
M. 28

DR. GREEN
    A fiction, punning on the appropriate "green" for an herb doctor.
C.M. 21

DR. HUTTON'S TRACTS
    Charles Hutton (1737-1823), *British mathematician, was the author of many miscellaneous scholarly writings and a member of the *Royal Society. His papers include "Force of Exploded Gunpowder and the Velocities of Balls" (1776-78).
W. 83

DR. SNODHEAD
    A fictional character, probably based on George J. Adler, M.'s friend, who taught *German at New York University.
M.D. 101

DRUID
    Little is known about Druidism—the religion of the Celts of ancient *Gaul and the *British Isles. The earliest reliable evidence, *Julius Caesar's, shows them established in Gaul as

early as 100 B.C.   Most traditional belief about them stems
from the work of the *Stoic philosopher Poseidonius (c. 135-c.
50 B.C.) and his followers, who saw the Druids as *God-
endowed philosophers and theologians in charge of divination
and sacrifice and as students of theology, ethics, and natural
science, including physics.

   We now know that the Celts divined by human sacrifice
and that probably the Druids had no body of coherent religious
doctrine.

   The word *drui* (pl. *druid*) in Old *Irish is probably a
combination of "he who knows" and the word meaning "oak."
Irish folklore shows Druids as malignant magicians opposed
to *Christianity. No evidence supports M.'s contention that the
Druids built *Stonehenge.
T. 21

DRUMMOND LIGHT

   Captain Thomas Drummond (1797-1840) invented the
calcium or "lime" light around 1820. He adapted it by 1825 for
use in lighthouses and by the mid 1830's for use in the theatre.
The intense and focusable but soft illumination results from
heating of calcium in burning oxygen and hydrogen jets. In
the 1840's P.T. Barnum introduced Drummond lights to *New
York, installed on the top of his museum, flooding a large
expanse of *Broadway.
C.M. 44

DRURY-LANE

   The Drury Lane Theatre, situated in *London on the
street of the same name, was named for Drury House, built by
Sir William Drury during the reign of *Henry VIII. First
opened in 1663, the theatre has burned and been replaced several times. The present structure, built in 1812, has housed
the world's most famous plays with casts of great actors (in
M.'s time, Garrick, Kemble, etc.).
W. 23

DRYADS

   Gr. *drus*, oak tree.

   In *Greek mythology, Dryads were lesser gods of earth,
nymphs of trees, who died when their respective trees died.
*Orpheus's wife, *Eurydice, was a dryad.

   Also called Hamadryad.
M. 77

DRYDEN, JOHN
      *English poet, dramatist, and critic John Dryden (1631-
1700) was born into a moderately well-off *Puritan family.
After graduation from Trinity College, *Cambridge, he moved
to *London to write rather political verse. His first major work
was *Annus Mirabilis . . . 1666. An Historical Poem* (1667), referred to in *"Extracts" 26: a *Virgilian heroic treatment of the
Anglo-Dutch war and the *fire of London, with deeper implications about England's splendid present and future achievement.
      The versatile Dryden wrote numerous verse and blank-
verse plays, satires, lives, and translations. He became Poet
Laureate in 1668 and Historiographer Royal in 1670. His politically expedient principles and his conversion to Roman
*Catholicism, as well as his flexible critical stances, made him
a controversial figure, but he is generally considered the father
of English literary criticism.
      Sealts #191 is *The Poetical Works* (1854), presented by M.
to Mrs. J.R. Morewood. Sealts #147, the *Harper Classical Library*, v. 12, contains Dryden's translation of the *Aeneid*.
M.D. Extracts 26

DRY-DOCK
      Although M.'s note explains (*R.* 32) that the "Dry" dock
is used for ship-bottom repair, in *Liverpool "dry dock" referred locally to the reconstructed tidal basin: with no flood
gates, it was empty at low water (in 1829 converted into a wet
dock: Canning Dock).
R. 32

DUBLIN
      The capital of the modern Republic of *Ireland is on a
bay of the *Irish Sea at the mouth of the river Liffey, which divides the city into two parts. The name derives from *Dubh
Linn*: "Black Pool," the character of the Liffey. *St. Patrick introduced *Christianity here in the fifth century; the *Norse invaded in the ninth and were replaced by the Anglo-Normans in
the twelfth. Dublin was a center of *British royal proceedings
and often at odds with the rest of Ireland, as well as the scene
of much disturbance during the Irish Revolution, led by
*Daniel O'Connell and *Robert Emmet.
      Had "Wellingborough Redburn" fulfilled his desire (*R.*
27) to visit Dublin, he would have done more than his creator
did; he might have seen the thirteenth-century castle, the
eleventh-century Christ Church Cathedral, the sixteenth-

century Trinity College, and the Guinness Brewery, established in the nineteenth century.
R. 27; I.P. 15

DUFF

The *British ship *Duff*, commanded by Captain James Wilson, arrived at *Tahiti on 4 March 1797, carrying eighteen missionaries and five of their wives, to establish a *Protestant mission. She delivered eleven other missionaries to the *Marquesas and *Tonga Islands and departed for England in August of the same year.
O. 42

"DUFF," "--DAY"

A corruption of "dough." It was a mixture of flour and water, with raisins or prunes added (plum duff)—a baked delicacy. It was sometimes called "figgy duff," or "lum duff." Duff Day was the day, usually Thursday, when "duff" was served, instead of meat.
O. 41; M. 3; M. 8; W. 68; W. 82; M.D. 81 and elsewhere

DUGONGS

See "Cetology" section.
M.D. 32

DUKE, THE

The Duke referred to in *M.D.* 90 is *Wellington.
M.D. 90

DUKE OF DUNDER

A fiction; a "dunderhead" is a "blockhead."
M.D. 89

DUKE OF YORK

See "York."
W. 71

DUKE-STREET

*Liverpool's Duke Street was in the nineteenth century an affluent thoroughfare of Georgian houses, the Liverpool Free Public Library (1852), the Unitarian Church where Har-

riet Martineau's father preached (and which M. visited 14
November 1856), and the fashionable St. James Cemetery. It
runs roughly northwest to southeast, from Hanover Street to
St. James Walk.
R. 30

DUMBARTON
        A shipbuilding burgh of western *Scotland on the *Clyde
at the mouth of the Leven River, fourteen miles west-northwest
of *Glasgow, Dumbarton was the ancient *British Alcluith,
capital of the kingdom of Strathclyde. *Wallace was imprisoned here in 1305; *Mary Queen of Scots was removed to
*France from here in 1548.
        M. is known to have visited Dumbarton on 28 October
1856, but the visit occurred during the period for which there is
no journal.
O. 53

DUNFERMLINE
        Dunfermline is fourteen miles northwest of *Edinburgh,
*Scotland, three miles from the Firth of *Forth. *Robert the
Bruce chartered the town in 1322. Early Celtic monks had settled on the site upon which *Benedictine monks built in the late
eleventh century. Several important kings were born there,
and most of Scotland's royal dead are buried at the abbey, mentioned in the ballad "*Sir Patrick Spens." M. may have visited
in October or November 1856.
M.D. 65

DUNKER; DOWAGER DUNKER
        This fictional character's name in P. suggests connec-
tion with the Dunkers (*German Baptist Brethren: Tunkers,
Dunkards [Ger., "dippers"], Taufers, Donkelaars), members of
the Church of the Brethren, a forerunner of modern Seventh-
Day Baptism. Their theology, evolved from that of the
*Lutheran *Pietists, prescribes adult baptism, literal *Bible in-
terpretation, rituals modeled after the Bible, nonresistance, refusal of oaths, total abstinence from alcohol and tobacco, and
avoidance of places of amusement.
        Many members of the church, founded in Germany in
1708, emigrated to *Pennsylvania and *Canada shortly
thereafter.
P. 17:2; I.P. 9

DUNKIRK

Dunkirk (Fr. "Dunquerque") is from the *Flemish "dunkerk": "church of the Dunes." Like the rest of Flanders, it often changed hands after its foundation in the tenth century (near the modern *Belgian border, twenty-four miles east-northeast of *Calais). Louis XIV (see "Bourbon") acquired it for *France in 1662. Dunkirk became a key French stronghold: the northernmost port and one of the most important, especially in shipbuilding.
M.D. 24

DUODECIMO

A printer's term referring to the size of a book, based on the number of leaves made from a standard-sized piece of paper. Duodecimo books are small, with twelve leaves made from a sheet.
M.D. 32

DU PETIT THOUARS, REAR-ADMIRAL

*French Admiral Abel Dupetit-Thouars had brought *Catholic missionaries (including *Father Murphy) to the *Marquesas in 1838, assisting them in propagation of an unpopular religion. Commanding the frigate *La Reine Blanche and a squadron of men of war, he took possession of the Marquesas for France, 1 May 1842, beginning at Tauata and ending at Anna Maria Bay (Taiohaë), *Nukuheva by 2 June. Dupetit-Thouars made a puppet of King Moana (*Mowanna), dressing him in lavish military ceremonial garb, bedecking his wife luxuriously, and furnishing his home with *European goods. A fact omitted by M. in his T. castigation is Dupetit-Thouars's rescue of Moana's *Typee wife from the Taioas (*Tiors) at the bay of Acaui.

In *Tahiti, Dupetit-Thouars proclaimed Queen *Pomaree's "request" for French protection 9 September 1842, at the time of M.'s arrival at *Papeete on Lucy Ann. He appointed the detested Moerenhout (see "Merenhout") a member of the provisional governing council under the *protectorate.

Secretary to the état-major général was Max Radiguet, author of Les Derniers Sauvages: la vie et les moeurs aux Iles Marquises (1842-1859). Paris: 1929. This study of life among "the last savages" was first published in part as "La Reine-Blanche aux Iles Marquises: souvenirs et paysages de l'Océanie," in Revue des deux Mondes (XXII, 431-479; XXIII, 607-644, 1859). Radiguet verifies many of M.'s observations about Dupetit-Thouars's actions and about local culture, albeit from a different perspective.
T. 2; T. 3; O. 19; O. 32

DURAS
     See *"Bon Homme Richard."*
I.P. 18

DURER, ALBERT
     Albrecht Dürer (1471-1528), *German painter and
printmaker, was the son of a Nuremberg goldsmith, with
whom he apprenticed. He spent much of his early adulthood in
*Venice, studying contemporary artists and in 1498 published
an innovative album of woodcuts, including *The *Apocalypse*,
achieving a *Gothic quality and a subtlety not previously seen
in woodcuts.   Among later woodcuts, produced in the
*Netherlands or in Germany, are *Melancholia I* (1514), and
The Triumph (1526).   Paintings include several self-portraits,
*Four *Apostles* (1526), *A Young Hare* (1502), *The Piece of Turf*
(1503).   His work was enormously influential, and he is now
considered perhaps the greatest Renaissance artist.
     M.'s journal for 4 December 1849 shows that he saw
Dürer's plates at the Bibliothèque Royale in *Paris. The journal for 1857 shows some confusion about works he saw in
*Rome. As Howard Horsford notes (*Journal of a Visit to Europe and the Levant*), he was sometimes looking at Dürer's
works unknowingly.   On 7 March he accurately records seeing
The Holy Family at Sciarra Palace, and on 26 March a self-
portrait at the Uffizi.
M.D. 57

DUTCH; DUTCHMAN
     Many of M.'s references to things Dutch are facetious.
Among the more serious: the "Dutch Admiral" of *W*. 71 is
*Von Tromp; the "Dutchman" of *M.D*. 24 is one of the explorers who sighted *Australia in 1606; the "Dutch settlements"
on the *Hudson of *I.P*. 2 are those *patroon-descended societies
discussed in such works as *Cooper's *Satanstoe* and *Home As
Found*.
     In colloquial usage, "Dutch" has been a belittling adjec-
tive since the seventeenth-century Anglo-Dutch wars. For example, "Dutch gold" is an alloy of copper and zinc used in imitation gold leaf ("Dutch leaf"), easily tarnished. The "Dutch
looking-glass" of *O*. 45 will probably reflect poorly and break
soon; the "Dutch tankard" of *W*. 12 is probably a joke based on
the notion of heavy Dutch drinking, which brings "Dutch
courage"; the "Dutch dogger" of *M.D*. 81 is a clumsy fishing
vessel and he who sails on it; the "Dutch volume" of *M.D*. 101
is probably a derogatory reference to *Scoresby's work, which
is parodied in the same chapter.

See also "Holland . . . . "; "Holland Gin"; "Low Dutch."
Passim

DUTCH MANORS
See "New York, --State"; "Gansevoort."
P. 1:3

DUYCKINCK, EVERT AUGUSTUS
Although Duyckinck is not mentioned in M.'s novels,
his dealings with M. (see especially "Young America in Literature') necessitate this entry. Duyckinck and his brother George (1823-63), editors of the influential New York *Literary
World* (1847-53), at first encouraged the young M., assigning
him book reviews, introducing him to their important circle of
friends, and giving him full use of their voluminous libraries.
However, the very growth that may have sprung from
"education" by the Duyckincks helped lead to dark, complex
and metaphysical works such as those following *W.* (1850).
The Duyckincks disapproved of M.'s abandonment of
"simpler" works such as *T.*, *O.*, and *R.* and were shocked by
his seeming rejection of orthodox "civilization" and its dogma.
The "blasphemous" *M.D.* was apparently the last straw, and
the Duyckincks quietly withdrew their previously generous
support.

D'WOLF, CAPTAIN
Captain John DeWolf II (1779-1872), who was married to
M.'s father's oldest sister, Mary, sailed with *Langsdorff and
is mentioned in Langsdorff's account of his voyages. In 1861,
De Wolf published *A Voyage to the North Pacific and a Journey
through Siberia More than Half a Century Ago.*
M. spent the summer of 1828 at DeWolf's home in Bris-
tol, *Rhode Island.
M.D. 45

DYAK, --S
The Dyaks (Dayaks, or Dajaks) of *Borneo are not a uniform physical or cultural type or strongly grouped tribes.
Rather the term refers to non-muslim peoples of Borneo,
although in M.'s time one spoke of Dyaks as a group with similar characteristics. Their origins are clouded; many ancient
hunting agricultural tribes migrated from the mainland, several of them composed of headhunters. Dwellings were long
houses sheltering many people, with heads of enemies decorat-

ing the entrance. Religious beliefs prescribed protection of the people's well-being, along with appropriate behavior toward friendly and unfriendly spirits, interpretation of omens, and propitiation of powers. Favored individuals were prophets, and the existence of multiple souls led to soul-stealing. Head-hunting was practiced for revenge and for appeasement of spirits, as well as for prestige but was almost completely obliterated during eighteenth-century *Dutch rule.
M. 94; I.P. 22; C.M. 7

DYING GLADIATOR
       M. saw *The Dying Gaul* at the Capitoline Museum in *Rome, in 1857. The marble Pergamene sculpture, dating from c. 225 B.C., gives an impression of great physical prowess, courage, and endurance: the figure's hair is matted; his feet are cut and calloused, and gore drips from his wound. M.'s journal for 26 February includes a comment: "shows that humanity existed amid the barbarians of the Roman time, as it [sic] now among *Christian barbarians." In his 1859 *lecture, "Statues in Rome," M. also contrasts the *Dying Gaul* with the *Fighting Gladiator* which he saw in the *Louvre in 1849, and quotes from *Byron's *Childe Harold's Pilgrimage*, which describes the *Dying Gaul* at length.
W. 87

18 MO
       "Eighteenmo" or octodecimo is a printer's term referring to the size of a book, based on the number of leaves made from a standard-sized piece of paper. An eighteenmo is made from eighteen leaves per sheet, a small book.
R. 30

EAGLE, AMERICAN
       Eagles have symbolized prowess since ancient times. The white-headed (not "bald") American eagle, *Haliaetus leucocephalus*, was chosen symbol of the *United States despite *Benjamin Franklin's preference for the turkey. A highly efficient predator on land or water, the American eagle often had a near-devastating effect on northern fisheries before becoming nearly extinct in the twentieth century.

M. playfully reverses the natures of the "*British Unicorn and American Eagle," portraying them as "the lion and the lamb," in *R.* 28.
R. 28

EARL
A *British peer ranked below *Marquise; in *Anglo-Saxon times, of the highest eminence in politics. The wife of an Earl is a Countess.
From A.S. *eorl*, a man of position, as opposed to *ceorl*, a churl (*Danish *jarl*).
M. Passim; W. 68; M.D. 29 and elsewhere

EARTH
Many Christians of M.'s time still held to *Creation theory, which made Earth 6,000 years old. Nineteenth-century scientists were still in accord with the thinking of such eighteenth-century minds as *Kant and Laplace regarding the age and origins of Earth. (Modern theory makes the planet about 4,500,000,000 years old.)
M. 75 and elsewhere

EARTH'S PARADISE
From *Medieval times, an Earthly *Paradise was believed to exist: a perfect land or island on earth where all things were immortal. Believers (including *Mandeville) placed it in the east, in *China or off the coast of *India.
R. 33

EAST, THE
See "Orient . . . "
Passim

EASTERN PHILOSOPHERS
As Bruce Franklin points out, *Franklin, *Cooper, *Poe, *Emerson, Thoreau, *Socrates, Krishna, all may be counted as "Eastern philosophers."
C.M. 2

EASTERN TITLE
See "Bashaw."
O. 74

EAST INDIA COMPANY
        *London's East India Company was formed in 1600 to
compete with the *Dutch East India Company monopoly of the
spice trade. With government support, it became the greatest of
such companies, with factories and trade connections
throughout the *Malay Archipelago and *India. Ships built
for the company stimulated progress in British shipbuilding
and navigation. By the late eighteenth century, the company
ruled over rich and extensive territories and some Britons
were becoming "nabobs" of great wealth and political influence
under Governor-General Warren Hastings. William Pitt's India Bill of 1784 established controls, and by 1833 the company
was no longer autonomous or powerful. In 1858 it was forced
to transfer its possessions to the crown.
        East India House (demolished 1862) was in Leadenhall
Street, *London. *Charles Lamb, who was a clerk there for
thirty-three years, claimed that his "true works" were on the
shelves in Leadenhall Street.
        There was still much prestige about the East India
Company in M.'s time. It had spawned generations of
Englishmen committed to *noblesse oblige* as regards India;
there were even special educational establishments that
trained Britons in "handling" Indians. M. "wandered about"
Leadenhall Street on 25 November 1849 and had social dealings
that year and in 1857 with at least one person connected with
the company, a resident of the East India United Service Club.
W. 50

EAST INDIANS
        The expression usually refers to the inhabitants of In-
donesia (former *Netherlands Indies, or Dutch East Indies), or
of the *Malay Archipelago. Probably, in *C.M.* 43, M. uses the
expression to distinguish between inhabitants of *India and
*American Indians, who do not charm snakes.
C.M. 43

EAST INDIES
        "East Indies" first referred to *India, then to southeast
*Asia, and finally to the *Malay Archipelago. It was often
used in a political sense to refer to the Netherlands East Indies
(which became Indonesia after World War II).
R. 51

EAST RIVER
       *New York City's navigable tidal strait on the eastern
shore of *Manhattan is c. sixteen miles long and up to 600 feet
wide. It connects Upper New York Bay and Long Island
Sound, separates *Manhattan and the Bronx from the *Long
Island boroughs, and is connected with the *Hudson by the
*Harlem River and Spuyten Duyvil Creek, at the north end of
Manhattan. Flushing Bay indents the Queens shore.
       The East River "thicket of masts" (of *R*. 32) was densest
in M.'s day in the *South Street area.
       The "island barracks" with boys in prison (*C.M*. 22) were
probably those of the present-day Roosevelt Island:
"*Blackwell's Island" in M.'s time, and in a later incarnation
"Welfare Island." (The Indians had called it "Minnahan-
nonck" and the *Dutch "The Long Island.") It was named by
an eighteenth-century owner, Robert Blackwell, and passed to
the city in 1828. Blackwell's thereafter housed a penitentiary, a
charity hospital, and almshouse, a work-house, and an
asylum for the pauper insane. Randall's Island (variously
named "Little Barent's," "Belle Isle," "Talbot's Island," and
"Montresor's Island"), was named by Jonathan Randel, an
eighteenth-century farmer; it passed to the city in 1835 and
eventually housed a refuge for juvenile delinquents. (The
neighboring Ward's Island housed a city hospital and asylum.) Also in the East River in the nineteenth century was the
prison ship *Jersey*, housing 1,000 prisoners and referred to as
"hell afloat." (Not much appears to have changed in our twentieth century, when the East River's Rikers Island holds an
unconscionable number of prisoners, and the city plans to
move some of them to floating barges in, among other places,
the East River.)
R. 9; R. 32; R. 60

EBLIS, HALL OF
       In *Arabian mythology, Eblis is the angel who refused to
worship *God and became ruler of the evil genii, or devils. His
name as an angel was Azazel, and in *Leviticus 16:7-8, he is
the scapegoat. In *Paradise Lost* (I, 534) he is standard-bearer
for lost angels. Traditionally, he is pictured as one hundred
feet tall, with scaly red-striped skin, long haired, with ears like
an elephant's, a ringed nose, and a sixty-foot-long clawed tail.
In 1849 M. acquired a copy of William Beckford's *Vathek*
(Sealts #54), in which Eblis's hall is described as torch lit,
heavily curtained, deeply vaulted.
W. 73

EBONY
Various trees producing hard, dark, heavy, durable wood are called "ebony," especially a persimmon group of *Africa, *Asia, and *Ceylon: *Diospyros*. *Ebenaceae* is the family of trees and shrubs yielding calamander and persimmon.

It has been valued since ancient times, when it was used for ceremonial articles and for drinking cups (as an antagonist of poisons). Robert Southey's *Thalaba, the Destroyer* (1801) spread the traditional belief that the tree was leafless, fruitless, and never seen in sun.
M.D. 64; C.M. 3

ECCLESIASTES
The *Old Testament Book of Ecclesiastes is wisdom literature which was by courtesy ascribed to *Solomon, as M. does in *M.D.* The word evolved from the *Hebrew for "participant in a popular assembly." Probably it was not written by one person, for it lacks a clear-cut ethical system and has many contradictions.

The content of Ecclesiastes is now thought to have been heavily colored by *Greek philosophies; its ambiguous ethics seem related to M.'s ideas of virtuous expediency, especially in the *"Chronometricals and Horologicals" pamphlet in *P*.: heterodox piety. Ecclesiastes counsels man to "eat, drink, and be merry," as *God wishes, but it also warns of a not-particularly-accessible God. Its ironic and grim humor, like M.'s, is not finally anarchic but reflects a sense of right and wrong, as well as pity for the human condition.
M.D. 96; P. 7:4

ECKERMAN; ECKERMANN, JOHANN PETER; *ECKERMANN'S CONVERSATIONS WITH GOETHE*
Eckermann (1792-1854), born into poverty at Winsen, Hanover, *Germany, was studying at Göttingen when he sent a manuscript for *Goethe's examination. He became Goethe's assistant at Weimar and was appointed to various court positions. Goethe's confidante, he is best known for his three-volume *Gespräche mit Goethe in den letzten Jahren seines Lebens, 1823-1832*, an important source of material on the life, translated into many languages. He also prepared the first complete edition of the *Works*.

M.D.'s reference to Eckerman's inspecting Goethe's dead body has its original in Eckermann's *Conversations*, 23 March 1832.

See also "Extracts" 57.
M.D. Extracts 57; M.D. 86

ECLIPTIC, --S

The sun's track in the heavens—an imaginary line produced by earth's motion around the sun; it lies in the middle of
the *zodiac.
M. 143; M. 169; M.D. 99

EDDYSTONE, --LIGHTHOUSE

The first rock tower lighthouse was constructed in 1698
on Eddystone Rocks, in the English *Channel thirteen miles off
*Plymouth. It was destroyed in a 1703 storm and replaced sev-
eral times. A stone tower completed in 1759 was extant during
M.'s time. It was removed and set up as a memorial in Plymouth when it began to break up; a new one replaced it in
1881.
M.D. 14; M.D. 133

EDEN; GARDEN OF EDEN

First mentioned in *Genesis 2:8 ("and *Jehovah *God
planted a garden eastward, in Eden; and there he put the man
whom he had formed"). The word "Eden" probably comes
from the *Hebrew word meaning "delight"; the Sumerian
name of the plain of *Babylonia was "Edin." Although its site
has never been definitely located, the plain in the depression
between the *Tigris and the *Euphrates rivers is presumed the
locale (Babylonia: from 30°-33° N., 45°-49° E. bounded on the
west by the Arabian desert, on the north by *Mesopotamia, on
the east by the plain at the foot of the Elamite Mountains, on
the south by the *Persian Gulf); Shinar or *Chaldea are also
considered possible locales.
The "garb of Eden" is nudity; after eating of the forbidden fruit, *Adam and *Eve "knew that they were naked; and
they sewed fig leaves together, and made themselves aprons"
(Genesis 3:7).
O. 18; M. 167; R. 43; W. 68; P. 2:4; C.M. 22

EDESSA

The ancient city said to have been founded by *Nimrod
was located at the extreme north of the *Syrian plateau, on the
site of the present city of Urfa, *Turkey. It was refounded in
the third century B.C. by Seleucus I. Among the remains are
a castle, a tower, parts of city walls, and a dam built by
*Justinian. Edessa was continually involved in *Roman/
*Parthian conflicts, was captured in the first *crusade and
returned to the *Moslems 150 years later, then captured by the
Turks in 1637.

The persecutions mentioned in *M*. 9 occurred under Roman aegis, in the third and fourth centuries, when Decius, Valerian, and *Valens ruled. (I have been unable to trace the heroic "lorn widow" of Edessa.)
M. 9

EDINBURGH
*Scotland's capital city is a seaport on the Firth of *Forth, in Midlothian. It was settled as early as the sixth century, and chartered in the thirteenth by *Robert the Bruce. It was destroyed shortly thereafter, in the Wars of Independence, and once again in the latter part of the century by Richard II. *James II made Edinburgh the political and cultural center of Scotland. Parts of the castle date from the twelfth century. Holyrood Abbey, of the same period, became the site of Holyroodhouse Palace, begun by Mary, Queen of Scots (see "Stuart, Mary"). The University was founded in 1582. By M.'s time, Greek and Gothic revival buildings were under construction.
It is presumed that M. visited Edinburgh in late October or early November 1856. There are no journal entries for the period, but he mentions Edinburgh in retrospect in the later (1857) entries of the same journal. Among the monuments he would have seen is a *Trojan column topped by a figure of Henry Dundas, First Viscount of Melville (1742-1811), probably a distant relative. Forty miles north of the city, in Fifeshire, is Melville House, known to have been visited by M.'s father, Allan Melvill (see "Walter Redburn").
W. 90; I.P. 17; I.P. 18

EDINBURGH REVIEW
The highly successful *Edinburgh Review, or Critical Journal* (1802-1929) was founded by Sydney Smith and Francis Jeffrey, for the expression of liberal *Whig thinking in a city predominantly *Tory. The quarterly, which aimed for more balanced political expression than its rival, *Quarterly Review*, published influential reviews and articles on literature by contributors such as Carlyle and Macaulay. In contrast to *QR*, it was critical of *Wordsworth, *Coleridge, and other "Lake School" writers.
In *W*. 36, the reference to *Hermione and Danae probably springs from *Edinburgh Review* LXXXI (October 1824) on mutineers: "It is a fact . . . that they have taken away even ships,—as, for example, the Hermione and Danae,—putting to death without mercy the officers and marines, who were the means of carrying into execution this tyrannical system."

The reference to *Edinburgh Review* of "a still later period" is to the same issue, in an article which is a digest of five others:

1. Letters on the Evils of Impressment, with the outline of a Plan for doing them away; on which depends the Wealth, Prosperity, and Consequence of Great Britain. By Thomas Urquhart.
2. Basis of a Plan for Manning the Navy at the Commencement of a War, &c. By the Same.
3. Impressment: An Attempt to prove why it should and how it could be Abolished. By Lieutenant R. Standish Haly, R.N.
4. Suggestions for the Abolition of the Present System of Impressment in the Naval Service. By Captain *Marryat, R.N.
5. Cursory suggestions on Naval Subjects; with the Outline of a Plan for raising Seamen for His Majesty's Fleets in a Future War, by Ballot.

Thomas Philbrick attributes the article to Thomas Hodgeskin.

(Sealts #200 shows M.'s borrowing of V. 41 [1824-25] and V. 47 [1828], the latter erroneously cited [as 1824] in *W.*
W. 36

EDMUND BURKE'S REFERENCE IN PARLIAMENT TO THE NANTUCKET WHALE-FISHERY

See "Burke, Edmund," and "Extracts" 42.
M.D. Extracts 42

EDSON

Calvin Edson was the thinnest man on record at M.'s time. By 1830, Edson weighed only fifty-four pounds but lived what appears to have been a normal life with a wife and three children. He was exhibited at P.T. Barnum's American Museum as a "living skeleton."
W. 1; C.M. 16; C.M. 23

EDWARD III, KING OF ENGLAND

Edward III of *England (1312-1377) reigned from 1327-77 after the forced resignation of his father, Edward II. His mother, Isabella of *France, ruled in his name for four years, along with her lover, Roger Mortimer. After his marriage to

Philippa, daughter of William III, count of *Holland, he forcibly seized his throne, executed Mortimer, and set about restoring England to glory. Among his aims were restoration of King Arthur's Round Table. He rebuilt *Windsor Castle, inaugurated the Order of the Garter, and conducted a brilliant but extravagant court, reflecting the rather frivolous romantic nature that kept him from great glory.

His attempt to claim the French throne began the Hundred Years' War. He laid siege to *Calais in 1346, colonized the surrendered town, but forfeited his advantage for lack of funds. His son, Edward, the *Black Prince, captured the French John II, and Edward unsuccessfully entered France again, forced to settle for the treaty of Calais, renouncing his French claims except for Aquitaine. The treaty was repudiated later by the French Charles V, enabling Edward to claim the crown again. The plague years notwithstanding, Edward and his sons Edward and *John of Gaunt waged war until, the king's mind failing, family quarrels and the death of the Black Prince enabled John of Gaunt to seize power.
W. 68; M.D. 60

EDWARD THE CONFESSOR
Saint Edward (Eadweard), the Confessor (c. 1003-1066), was *English king from 1042 until his death. After living in *Normandy for most of his life, he succeeded his brother, *Hardicanute. He immediately seized the goods of his mother, Emma (daughter of *Richard I, Duke of Normandy), suspecting collusion with his *Norwegian enemy, Magnus. In 1051, his introduction of foreigners brought him into conflict with Godwin, Earl of the West Saxons, whose daughter was his queen. He dismissed her, but Godwin's forces and their successors became England's chief powers. Conflict with the *Danes, the *Welsh, and the *Scots, and continental political skirmishes occupied the remaining years of his reign. Because of his reputation for piety, after his death he was called the "Confessor." He was buried in a church he had built at Westminster, which was almost completely pulled down in 1245, to be replaced by *Westminster Abbey. He was canonized in 1161.
R. 44

EGBERT
An invention, generally accepted as a caricature of Henry David Thoreau.
C.M. 37

"EGO NON BAPTIZO TE IN NOMINE PATRIS, SED IN NOMINE DIABOLI."
"I baptize thee not in the name of the father, but in the name of the devil."
This *Latin sentence is written in an expanded form in M.'s edition of *Shakespeare (Sealts #460).
In a letter to *Hawthorne (29 June 1851), M. said that the sentence was the "book's motto (the secret one)."
M.D. 113

EGYPT, --IAN, --S
The *Bible's "Mizraim," Egypt is located in the northeastern corner of *Africa and on the Sinai Peninsula of southwestern *Asia; it has a 1,300-mile coastline. Egypt's history is as old as that of *Mesopotamia; its culture was well advanced by the fifth millenium B.C. There were thirty dynasties of *Pharoahs before *Alexander the Great brought *Hellenism. The culture had peaked c. 2900 B.C., when the Pyramids and other structures appeared. Egypt became an Arab *Moslem nation from A.D. 639. By M.'s time, it was ruled by the royal line of Mohamed Ali, who became Pasha in 1805; he massacred the *Mamelukes and modernized the country. Finkelstein's *Melville's Orienda* discusses M.'s relation to Egypt. He visited *Alexandria and Cairo in January of 1857.
The "fate of the first-born of Egypt" (*C.M.* 39) refers to *Exodus 12:29.
See also "Abukir"; "Cheops"; "Cleopatra"; "Crusades"; "Luxor"; "Memnon"; "Nile"; "Ptolemy"; "Red Sea"; "Sais"; "Sesostris"; "Thebes"; "Trajan."
T. 9; T. 21; M. 97; M. 117; R. 32; W. 22; W. 36; W. 50; M.D. Passim; P. 2:4; P. 7:6; P. 21:1; P. 25:4; I.P. 23; C.M. 16; C.M. 36; C.M. 39 and elsewhere

EGYPTIAN FORTUNE-TELLER
Fortune-telling dates from at least 4000 B.C., when it was practiced in *Egypt, *China, *Chaldea, and *Babylonia. Palmistry (Chiromancy, or Chirosophy) dates from 3000 B.C. China. It involves prognostication as suggested by the structure of the hand: its shape, texture, moisture content. As in *phrenology, relative parts are associated with human characteristics and emotions. Although there is no scientific evidence of its value, much can be told from examination of the hand.
R. 56

EGYPTIAN SARCOPHAGUS

The earliest stone coffins of the Fifth Dynasty Egyptians were designed to represent palaces—with ornate false doors and windows (such as the coffin of Ra'wer in the Cairo Museum). By the Eighteenth Dynasty, these were replaced by mummiform anthropoid wooden coffins, sometimes gold-plated, with carved portrait heads and elaborate inscriptions.
T. 1

EHRENBREITSTEIN

The *German fortress on the right bank of the *Rhine opposite Coblenz was built in the twelfth century and rebuilt between 1816 and 1826. M. visited Coblenz in 1849, commenting in his journal (10 December) on the fact that the "finest wine of all the Rhine is grown right under the guns of Ehrenbreitstein." He crossed the river several times and spent a whole day inspecting the fortress and musing expansively on wines, fortresses, and home, to which he would head in the morning. A Rhine cruise took him to the area again in 1857.
M.D. 8; P. 4:2

"EI"

EI is "if," in *Greek.
P. 14:3

EIGHT BELLS

Twelve o'clock midnight. Ship's bells ring every half hour, with the cycle repeated after eight.
M. 6; R. 26; M.D. 40 and elsewhere

ELBA

Elba is the largest island of the *Tuscan archipelago, in the Tyrrhenian Sea, in *Italy's Livorno province, seven miles southwest of Piombino (42°47' N., 10°17' E.). It is a mountainous island eighteen miles long by eleven miles wide, the source of iron ore since ancient times and under many foreign rulers. *Napoléon's 1814-15 exile on Elba made it a sovereign principality.
W. 49

ELBE, THE

The major European river flows through modern Czechoslovakia and central *Germany to the North Sea at

Cuxhaven (fifty-five miles northwest of *Hamburg), cutting through *Switzerland. It is linked with the Weser and *Rhine rivers via canal. The *Roman *Albis*, the Elbe marked the limit of the Roman advance into Germany and later that of *Charlemagne's conquests.
M.D. Extracts 13

ELDER CHARLES; THE
See "Charles the First, King of England."
P. 20:1

ELDIN
I suspect that "Eldin" is a confusion of "Eidin," an early name for *Edinburgh.
W. 83

ELEPHANTA
Elephanta Island (Hindi *Gharapuri*), on the east side of *Bombay harbor, *India, is famous for its cave temples (*lenen*), made by men in the eighth century A.D. The eight trap-rock caves are dedicated to Siva (See "Shiva"), whose history is shown on wall panels in the Main Cave. It has a main hall approximately 123 feet long, 55 feet wide, and 16 feet high, large columned atriums and side aisles, and various richly decorated shrine rooms, all damaged by natural catastrophes and by seventeenth-century *Portuguese canon. The island was named for a large stone elephant, removed to Bombay in 1864.
There was no painted representaton of the Matse Avatar of *Vishnu, as claimed in *M.D.*
M. 75; M.D. 7; M.D. 55

ELEPHANT AND CASTLE
In *England, a popular motif for inn signs and decorative carvings was the fighting elephant of the East, with a huge "castle" on its back to carry warriors. It was a common illustration in medieval manuscripts. The "elephant and castle" whale is a joke.
M. visited the old hub, the "Elephant and Castle Borough" Pub in *Southwark *London, in November of 1849.
M.D. 32

ELEPHANTIASIS
In *O.*, "Fa-Fa," or elephantiasis, is any of several chronic diseases of lymphatic obstruction causing enormous enlargement of infected parts. It is caused by parasitic infestation. Ancient writings show some confusion of the condition with leprosy, which was called *elephantiasis graecorum.* O.33

ELEPHANT WHALE
See "Cetology" section.
M.D. 32

ELEUSINIAN
Performed originally by an agrarian cult at *Eleusis, Attica, and later at *Athens, the rites in honor of *Ceres, or Demeter, were held in hope of a happy life after death. The Greater Eleusinia occurred after harvest; the Lesser in early spring. Little is known except that they included sea bathing, processions, dramas. They were abolished at the end of the fourth century A.D. by Emperor Theodosius and are the type of the deeply mysterious.
M. 41; P. 26:2

ELGIN MARBLES
A collection of classical sculptures from *Athens, including statuary, works of *Phidias, and the frieze from the *Parthenon, assembled in the British Museum, which purchased them for about £35,000 in 1816 from the Scottish Seventh Earl of Elgin (1766-1841). The Earl, Thomas, son of Charles Bruce, removed the treasures with the permission of the *Turks, arousing a violent controversy in which he was publically denounced by *Lord Byron. In 1810 he published a *Memorandum* defending his actions; *Parliament vindicated him, but the controversy continues to the present time; in the 1980's *Greece began serious efforts to restore the works to their place of origin.
M. 20

ELIJAH, --'S
The *Old Testament prophet Elijah, master of Elisha (his disciple and successor), was a ninth-century B.C. leader in the struggle of *Jehovists against worshippers of *Baal. He was from Tishbe of *Gilead, in the northern kingdom. To Elijah are attributed many miracles: revival of a dead child;

feeding from a never-ending source;   crossing the *Jordan
River while remaining dry; ascending to heaven in a chariot
of fire with horses of fire (II *Kings 2:11), as M. mentions in
M.D. 64. Elijah is seen as the eschatological precursor of the
*New Testament *John, who is Elijah reborn, or heir to his
powers.

Elijah's major symbolic importance to M. lies in his role
in the story of *Ahab. In I Kings, King Ahab is warned by Elijah of a drought (17:1), witnesses fire sent from heaven to
demonstrate Jehovah's superiority over Baal (18), hears Elijah's prophecy that dogs will lick his blood (21:17-29). The
great denouncer of kings, Elijah warns Ahab against taking
Naboth's vineyard (21,22). He is the great enemy of Ahab's
wife, *Jezebel, in her worship of Baal.
M.D. 19; M.D. 21; M.D. 28; M.D. 48; M.D. 64

ELIPHAZ
One of the mistaken counsellors in the book of *Job.
C.M. 40

ELIZA
Eliza is probably a fictional ship. M. might have bor-
rowed the name from that of a sixty-ton armed fishing
schooner chartered in the *American Revolution and renamed
Franklin. (*Eliza Anne* was a fast *Hudson River sloop.)
M.D. 7

ELIZABETH, QUEEN; ELIZABETHAN
The *Tudor Elizabeth (1533-1603) was daughter of
*Henry VIII by Anne Boleyn. She was queen of *England and
*Ireland from 1558 to 1603. Her father's execution of her
mother had made Elizabeth illegitimate and had altered her
position as heir presumptive. She was classically educated,
and when her Roman *Catholic sister, "Bloody" *Mary lost
popularity, whe became a dangerous possible candidate for the
throne (along with Mary *Stuart), and was imprisoned in the
*Tower.

She acceded with the help of King Philip of *Spain and
became a strong and intelligent monarch, courted by
*Leicester and many royal suitors. But she maintained her
status as "Virgin Queen." Her reign endured threats from
*Scotland, *France, and Spain (see "Spanish Armada"), the
Catholic Church, and from the *Puritans, who wished self-
government. She was active in making foreign policy and for
the most part avoided war. The Spanish conflict darkened the

last seventeen years of her reign, but she was victorious in securing French and *Dutch independence, in uniting England,
and in securing a successor (James I; see "Stuart").

Considered one of Britain's greatest monarchs, Elizabeth, a poet herself, was celebrated by the most important poets
of her time and is the subject of works right up to the present
time. "Elizabethan" became a designation for works of art, literature, architecture, costume, and music, as well as for historical references.

See also "Queen Bess."
O. 74; R. 30; W. 7; I.P. 12

ELLENBOROUGH, LORD
Edward Law, First Baron Ellenborough (1750-1818), Lord
Chief Justice of *England, counseled Warren Hastings during
his impeachment trial (1788-1795) and had a lucrative mercantile practice. His reputation for harshness and bias, his holding simultaneous political and judiciary offices, and his flout-
ing of *Parliament's decorum eventually brought much criticism.

See also "Crim. Con. Case"; "East India Company."
M.D. 89

ELLICE'S
The nine coral Ellice Islands are today commonly
grouped with the Gilbert Islands, although the former are
peopled by *Polynesians and the latter by Micronesians. The
Ellice (or Lagoon) Islands lie between 5° and 11° S. and 176°
and 180° E. They are thought to have been sighted by *Mendaña
in 1568 and 1595; they are clearly shown on the maps of
*Wilkes.
M. 3

ELLIS, --'S
William Ellis (1794-1872) was ordained a minister in
1815. He was sent by the *London Missionary Society to the
South Seas, arriving at the *Tahiti mission in 1817, where he
built a church and set up a printing press at Afareaitu (see
"Afrehitoo"). He returned to *England in 1825, visiting
*America on the way.

Ellis's most important publication, the 1833 *Polynesian
Researches* (*T*. 1; *O*. Preface; *O*. 48) was much used by M. for
details of *T*. and *O*. But Ellis, one of the chief defenders of
*Polynesian missions, cast them in too positive a light, as
*Beechey complained.

"Ellis's Journal of a Visit to the Sandwich Islands" (*O.* 54) is his Tour *Through *Hawaii.* He also published a *History of *Madagascar* (2 vols., 1838), which he later visited and lectured upon. His *History of the London Missionary Society* was published in 1844.
T. 1; O. Preface; O. 48; O. 54

ELYSIAN; ELYSIUM
Elysium, or Elysian Fields, is variously represented in mythology as the earthly dwelling place of mortals made immortal by the gods, who engage in all the mortal pleasures on the "Islands of the Blessed"; or as a section of *Hades isolated from the area for ordinary ghosts; or as a place of eternal springtime.
R. 49

EMERSON, RALPH WALDO
Ralph Waldo Emerson (1803-82) is not mentioned by name in M.'s novels, in keeping perhaps with a policy of avoidance (extending to *Poe and Dickens; see "Hard Times"). Emerson's ideas were probably the most important focus of serious American literature in the nineteenth century and were highly influential in the development of an American "character." It has become convenient (if simplistic) to see writers such as Whitman and Thoreau (also blackballed in the novels) as "Yay-sayers," on Emerson's side; in opposition are "Nay-sayers" such as M. and *Hawthorne. But as much as M. disagreed with Emerson's seemingly rosy view of the universe, he respected the philosopher as a "diver."
Emerson studied at *Harvard Divinity School to be a Unitarian minister but soon resigned a pastorate in *Boston when even the liberal tenets of that faith would force him into hypocrisy. After meeting Carlyle (another important M. omission), *Wordsworth, and *Coleridge in Europe (1832-33) and studying *German idealism, he returned to Concord, *Massachusetts to formulate his own American version of *Transcendentalism, lecturing and writing essays that were to stimulate and irritate contemporaries and were to become classics of the American canon. His book, *Nature* (1836), is the fundamental document; its ideas about man's natural place in his environment are built upon in the essays and lectures.
"The American Scholar" (1837) advised disposal of books (written for the most part by "ancients" or by *Europeans), in favor of direct study of nature. "The Divinity School Address" (1838) attacked formal religion (and made Emerson *persona non grata* at Harvard for c. thirty years). In *Essays: First*

Series (1841), "Self-Reliance" posited an ideal independent human being; "The Over-Soul" saw man and the physical world as integral parts of a unifying god-head. *Essays* (1844) solidified his reputation, and he went on to write intellectual and metaphysical poetry, full-length books, and numerous letters and sketches, especially biographical. His call for an American bard (in "The Poet") emboldened Whitman. Emerson was instrumental in publication of *The Dial* (1840-44) and helped found the Brook Farm commune (in which he did not participate). Emerson's life of personal tragedy (deaths of his first wife, his son, and other close persons) darkened his philosophy as he aged, but the instinctual optimistic independent faith and joy in nature of the early works came to be his hallmark.

M.'s response to Emerson is too complex to be examined in the present work, but we can posit a personal response as demonstrated in M.'s annotations to the works and elsewhere. M. was favorably impressed with Emerson's *Boston lecture, "Mind & Manners in the Nineteenth Century," which he heard in February of 1849. But by 3 March he was correcting his position in a letter to *Duyckinck: "I do not oscillate in Emerson's rainbow . . . . Yet I think Emerson is more than a brilliant fellow . . . . I love all men who *dive*. Any fish can swim near the surface, but it takes a great whale to go down stairs five miles or more; & if he dont attain the bottom, why, all the lead in Galena can't fashion the plummet that will." Yet M. vented positive wrath in his 1862 annotations of *Essays: First Series*, especially regarding Emerson's refusal to see evil when even *Christ had seen it; his counseling men to trust one another (especially important to *C.M.*'s "*No Trust"); his vision of nature as man's friend ("To one who has weathered Cape *Horn as a common sailor what stuff all this is."). M.'s final assessment of Emerson's philosophy admits of some "admirable" thoughts but adds, "His gross and astonishing errors & illusions spring from a self-conceit so intensely intellectual and calm that at first one hesitates to call it by its right name. Another species of Mr. Emerson's errors, or rather blindness, proceeds from a defect in the region of the heart." (Quotations reproduced from Leyda *Log*.)

M. is thought to have caricatured Emerson as "Mark Winsome," in *C.M.* 36. My personal sense is that aspects of Emerson surface as well in "Captain Delano" (in "Benito Cereno"), and in M.D.'s "*Ahab." Scholarship on Emerson's effect on M.'s work is voluminous.

Sealts numbers 203, 204, 205, 206 are various editions, including *Essays* in 1844 and 1847 editions.

EMIO
        See "Moreea."
T. 3

EMIR, --S, --'S
        Emir (or Amir) is a common title in the *Moslem world.
Originally it designated a military commander, but it was later
applied to governors of provinces. Omar, second *Caliph of
*Baghdad, called himself *amir al-mu'minin*: "commander of
the faithful." The title passed on to most other dynasties and
later signified a descendent of the Prophet. It has been used to
identify office, in combination with other terms, and has been
assumed by various leaders of other nations. Amir is the origin of the *English "admiral."
M. 39; W. 39; M.D. 34; C.M. 24

EMMET, ROBERT
        Emmet (1778-1803) was the great hero of the *Irish Revo-
lution. Tried for treason and hanged, he became the legendary
Irish hero of lost causes.
R. 27

EMPEROR OF ALL THE RUSSIAS
        See "Tsar."
C.M. 36

EMPERORS
        The Latin title *Imperator* was originally used in the
*Roman Empire. During the Republic it applied to magis-
trates with the highest power;   later military commanders
were so termed temporarily. *Julius Caesar was first Emperor of Rome and the title for monarch eventually spread
worldwide. Last Roman emperor was Constantine Palaeolo-
gus, defeated in the 1453 siege of *Constantinople.
M.181 and elsewhere

EN BON POINT
        Fr. *embonpoint*: "plumpness," or "obesity."
M.D. 88

ENCELADUS
In mythology, the *Titan *Terra (Gaea) created the mu-
tilated Enceladus (with Coelus, or Uranus) to avenge herself
against *Jupiter (Jove), who had seized power from her son,
*Saturn. In the war between gods and giants, Enceladus
fought against Jupiter and in the process had the mass of Mt.
Aetna (see "Etna") piled on his head, from which he still
breathes flames.
P. 25:1; P. 25:4; P. 25:5

ENCHANTED ISLANDS
See "Gallipagoes."
M. 1

EN CONFIANCE
Fr.: in (or with) trust, or confidence
C.M. 24

EN COSTUME
Fr.: in costume.
C.M. 24

ENDERBY; SAMUEL ENDERBY; ENDERBY & SONS
*Poe had alluded to Samuel Enderby in *The Narrative of
Arthur Gordon Pym* (1838), but M.'s knowledge about Samuel
and Charles Enderby probably comes from *Beale (pp. 148-150),
with minor changes. Beale says that in 1788 the *London merchant and shipowner Samuel Enderby had fitted out *Amelia,
which returned a year and one-half later with a huge cargo of
sperm oil. In 1793, Enderby had cooperated in the *British
goverment's South Seas expedition under *Colnett. In 1819, he
fitted out the 500-ton-burthen *Syren with a crew of thirty-six,
to open the whale fishery in *Japan.
Charles Enderby wrote *Proposals for Re-establishing the
British Southern Whale Fishery, through the Medium of a
Chartered Company, and in Combination with the Colonization of the Auckland Islands, as the Site of the Company's
Whaling Station* (London, 1847, 3rd ed.).
Samuel Enderby was a veritable whale-ship (built 1834)
which may actually have gammed with M.'s ship, *Acushnet*
(see "Pequod").
As Poe points out in *Pym* (16), the Enderbys had also
sponsored an *Antarctic exposition. Enderby Land is at 72° S,
52° E.
M.D. 100; M.D. 101; M.D. 106

ENDOR
     In ancient *Palestine, six miles east of Nazareth, home
to part of the tribe of Manasseh. In I *Samuel 28, *Saul con-
sults the resident witch before the battle of Bilboa. Legend tells
that Saul wished to communicate with the dead Samuel Nabal
and went with his adjutants, Abner and Amasa, to Abner's
mother, the witch of Endor. The witch saw the ghost but could
not hear his message, whereas Saul could hear but not see. A
number of other spirits arose, and Samuel, believing it to be
*Judgement Day, summoned *Moses. Saul prevailed upon
him to prophecy *God's will, and Samuel cautioned him to flee
rather than fight. Saul lied to his companions about the
prophecy, went into war, and was killed, along with his three
sons.
M. 68; R. 49

ENDYMION
     A four-book poem (pub. 1818) by the Romantic poet John
Keats (1795-1821). *Endymion* is an obscurely allegorical rendering of the dream love of a "shepherd-prince" for *Cynthia
(the Moon) and "*Phoebe," her human alter ego, with allusions to other figures of classical mythology. Book I contains
the "Hymn to *Pan."
     The prolific Keats published two volumes of important
odes, sonnets, and long poems in his brief life. His letters to
Fanny Brawne, *Shelley, Leigh Hunt, and others have come to
be equally admired. Among Keats's most important works
are: "On First Looking into *Chapman's *Homer"; "Ode on a
Grecian Urn" and "Ode on Melancholy"; odes to *Apollo,
*Psyche, and The Nightingale; "La Belle Dame Sans Merci";
The Eve of St. Agnes (of which Sealts #305 is an illustrated annotated edition).
     (The reference in *C.M.* 2 contrasts day-dreaming with
the night-dreaming of Endymion.)
C.M. 2

ENGLAND; ENGLISH; ENGLISHMAN; ENGLISHWOMAN;
BRITAIN; BRITANNIC; BRITISH; BRITON
     M. has been called an Anglophile by virtue of his fre-
quent references to things British. But if his position about
England is taken as the sum of its parts, examination of many
of his allusions suggests otherwise. The survey which follows
is of course skewed to reveal the negative side of M.'s Angli-
cism, the positive of which is manifestly clear.
     As the ironic "Appendix" to *T.* shows, M. believed that
the British acted as badly in the South Seas as the *French did.

Stern brute force was used by the boorish *Lord George Paulet
to achieve submission of the *Sandwich Islands. In *T*. 3, M.
admires the spirit of Mrs. *Pritchard, the English missionary's wife, but there was much for British *Christians to object
to in *T*. , and it was thoroughly Bowdlerized before publication
in England. In *T*. 17, M. defends cannibalism by invoking the
torturous execution in "enlightened England" of the guerilla
"convicted traitor" *William Wallace. The sights of *Typee valley remind him of *Cheltenham, *Stonehenge, and the
*Druids (*T*. 21); the Typee women are like those at coronations
at *Westminster Abbey; the local king (*T*. 23) is like *Warwick;
one native (*T*. 24) is a "Knight *Templar"; a characteristic souvenir left by English visitors is a *Tower Hill musket (*T*. 25);
the "Anglo-Saxon hive" (*T*. 26) have extirpated entire races,
along with their *Pagan beliefs, forcing upon them a creed at
variance with their prevailing ethos.

Although the *French in *Tahiti are a major target in
O., *Protestant delegates of the *London Missionary Society
come under fire in *O*. 45: they teach the natives useless things
about "steamboats, *lord mayors' coaches, and the way fires
are put out in *London" (gunpowder). The *Calabooza Beretanee" (*O*. 31) makes a mockery of punitive incarceration, and
the alcoholic British "Doctor Long Ghost" makes a mockery of
medicine; the loose-moraled Tahitian belles are no worse than
*King Charles's "Beauties."

In *M*., England is "Dominora," the domain of "King
Bello," the officious, choleric, and rapacious king against
whom "Vivenza" (the *American colonies) must rebel. Like
British monarchs, Bello rewards those "who to do him a service, for hire betray their kith and kin" (*M*. 148). His most
shameful acts involve the domination of "Verdanna"
(*Ireland).

The England of *R*. is the progenitor of *Launcelott's Hay,
where *Liverpool's indigent die in ignominy.

Although the English Navy is praised in *W*. 34, in *W*. 36
"British press-gangs" are invoked, along with the spectre of
the *Nore mutiny, which resulted from blatant injustice in
that navy. "Sink, burn, and Destroy" (*W*. 75) are standing
*Admiralty orders; the *Articles of War" (*W*. 70, 71) are the
despotic code that drafts "tyranny upon freedom" when
adopted by the United States *Navy. We emulate the wrong
things about the British.

In *M.D*. 89, *John Bull is included in the list of imperialist nations: guilty of injustice to Ireland and *India. The
"English sailor" of *M.D*. 40 is the *Dibdin-trained follower of
his leader who will blindly take even mad "*Ahab's" mission
as his own.

Among other questions in *P.* are the central notions of royalty, chivalry, and family blood lines. The "Millthorpe" family (*P.* 20:1) sprang from an "English Knight who had crossed the sea in the time of the elder Charles"—presumably during the Civil War; his nobility is soon dissipated in the "howling wilderness." The exalted British names of *P.* 1:3 (*Richmond, *St. Albans, *Grafton, *Portland, and *Buccleugh) are all besmirched by scandal.

The hero of *I.P.* wanders an exile in England for forty-five years, at first seeing much British "decency." But he struggles for a lifetime in the slums to feed his family and find a way home.

The swindlers of England people *C.M.*, along with villains of all nations. The "World's Fair in London" (*C.M.* 7) is the perfect place to advertise the "World's Charity" society; that 1851 exposition was a shamelessly chauvinistic phenomenon in a London where poverty, hunger, and early death were endemic. The British *Wordsworth is mocked in *C.M.* 10's "Ode on the Intimations of Distrust in Man." *Sir Humphrey Davy is a "Jackanapes" (*C.M.* 13). The *Missourian (*C.M.* 21) muses, "Nature is good Queen Bess; but who's responsible for the *cholera?" A "*Chesterfieldian exterior" hides "strong destructive propensities" (*C.M.* 22). *Hume and *Bacon are challenged in *C.M.* 24; *Judge Jeffries and the *Newgate Calendar are dangled in *C.M.* 26. "*St. Shakespeare" is maculate in *C.M.* 30, as is *Bunyan in *C.M.* 40. *Jack Ketch (*C.M.* 30), the executioner, is the paradigmatic British craftsman. The oily "Mark Winsome" (*C.M.* 36) is "Saxon-looking." London may be among the world's great cities, but it is all "fog" and "mud" (*C.M.* 45). The *Yankee in M. proves dominant at last.

M. refers frequently to "broken" or imperfect use of English (as in *M.* 21); his eccentric orthography suggests that his own speech must have had a broad New England accent, replete with intrusive "r's" and absent "r's." British English by M.'s time was probably not so distant from American English as it was to become in the early twentieth century, but it had already gone through distinct phases. A derivative of a West Germanic branch of a Germanic or Teutonic division of the Indo-European or Aryan family of languages, it passed from Old English or Anglo-Saxon to Middle English (c. 1100-c. 1500), and thence to Modern or New English. The *New England colonists probably spoke (as Shakespeare and *Queen Elizabeth did) with an accent akin to Irish brogue or to *cockney. Two hundred years of cultural isolation in the American "colonies" made such difference in diction and spelling that *Webster saw the need for the American dictionary that became M.'s (theoretical) standard (see Sealts #s 550-552).

M.'s second and third visits to England (1849, 1856-57) were in sharp contrast to his (1839) stay as a poor sailor in *Liverpool. Now he was lionized by the British, who received his books more generously than the American public did (perhaps because of the toning-down by publishers there). His journal for 4 November 1849 anticipates his reception, given good reviews for *T.*, *O.*, and *M.*: "*then* a sailor, *now* H.M. author of 'Pedee' 'Hullabaloo' & 'Pog-Dog.'"

Like all well-bred Americans of his time, M. knew much about British history, politics, culture, and tradition, as entries throughout the present work show. The "lion" of *I.P.* 5 is of course England's symbol since the twelfth century. The "British Arms" (*R.* 30, etc.) reflect the practice of heraldry in armor, wherein the lion and other British symbols appear along with particulars of a given family of nobles. The "old tattered British banner" (*P.* 1:4) handed down by "Pierre's" grandfather is like one that M.'s grandfather, General *Gansevoort, captured (a photo of which is in the New York Public Library's Gansevoort-Lansing Collection). Its pattern is an earlier version of the Union Jack, the final version (1801) of which had evolved from early renderings of the cross of *St. George. M.'s forebears were rather like English squires (passim), landed country gentlemen with local political power.

"Defender of the Faith" (*C.M.* 29), *Fidei Defensor*, was a title conferred on *Henry VIII by *Pope *Leo X, in 1521. The title was challenged by Pope Paul III when Henry broke with the *Catholic Church but it was confirmed to him and his successors by *Parliament, in 1544.

The "English Moralist" who said he liked a good hater (*C.M.* 27) was *Samuel Johnson (quoted by Hestor L. Piozzi, in *Anecdotes of the Late Samuel Johnson*, 1786).

For "English statutory law" (*M.D.* 24), see "Royal Fish."

See also "Britannia"; "Cambridge"; "Oxford"; "War of 1812," as well as entries for particular Britons and particular places.
Passim

ENGLISH ADMIRALTY
        See "Admiralty, The."
W. 27

ENGLISH ALE
        See "Ale."
R. 43

ENNAS
The mythological vale of Enna was a flowery springtime meadow in which *Proserpine found the most beautiful flower, the *narcissus—planted as a lure by Zeus (see "Jupiter" and "Jove") to help his brother, the lord of the underworld. When Proserpine found the narcissus, Zeus's brother arose from under the earth, driving a chariot drawn by coal-black horses and taking her away to the world of the dead.
M. 167

ENTHUSIAST TO DUTY
As Murray points out in his notes to *P*., in the "Phaedrus" *Socrates makes an "Enthusiast" one possessed by Eros, or passionate love, an early step on the soul's journey back to the *God who created it. "Duty," for moral philosophers, is the conscience's definition of the obligation to benevolent action. Thus M. would seem to be defending his hero, "Pierre," in calling him an "Enthusiast to Duty."
P. 5:5

EOCENE
The name bestowed on the earliest group of fossils by Sir Charles Lyell (1797-1875), along with *Miocene, and *Pliocene representing the later periods. All three names were universally adapted. The Eocene was the second and longest of the *Tertiary Period of the Cenozoic Era (c. 65 million years ago), when mammals began to dominate.
See also "Sandwiches."
M. 132

EOLEAN
See "Aeolian."
P. 2:7

EPAMINONDAS
The *Theban general, Epaminondas (c. 418-362 B.C.), was the central figure of the Battle of Leuctra, as commander of the Boeotians against the *Peloponnesian army. His strategy and tactical innovations brought glory, but he was eventually tried, for reasons that are unclear, and had to work his way up from the ranks again. His reputation as a statesman sprang from his representation of Thebes at the congress at *Sparta in 371, where his prevention of an unsatisfactory peace

led to the Battle of Leuctra and to the final overthrow of
Sparta's predominance in the Peloponnese.
M. 9

EPHESIAN; EPHESUS

An ancient (mid-seventh-century B.C.) trade route city of
Ionia, Ephesus is the traditional home of the *Amazons and
site of the great temple of Artemis (or *Diana), not as huntress
but as productive mother. Ephesus was famous for coinage;
and coins of c. 40 B.C. show a cult statue of the goddess with
many breasts. The temple itself was rebuilt with columns (*M.*
75) donated by the Lydian conqueror Croesus; it was destroyed
by the *Goths, along with the rest of the city, in A.D. 262, rebuilt numerous times, and then deserted by the fourteenth century.

Ephesus is connected with many of M.'s other allusions:
it was the home of *Heraclitus; conquered by *Cyrus the
Great; visited by *Xerxes; conquered by *Alexander the Great;
moved by *Mithradates to revolution against *Rome; the first
*Asian province of Rome under *Augustus; mentioned in
connection with *St. Paul, the *Virgin, *St. Luke, *Revelation;
reconstructed by Constantine (see "Constantinople") and
*Justinian. *Erostratus burned its temple.

By the late 1860's, the British Museum was excavating
sites and clarifying traditional stories about Ephesus.

M.'s source for the fable about the Ephesian soil undu-
lating over the grave of the "sleeping" *St. John (*M.D.* 111) is
probably *Bayle's *Dictionary* (Sealts #51), Vol. 3. *Hawthorne
had used the passage as a filler in *The American Magazine of
Useful and Entertaining Knowledge* (April 1836), and Robert
Southey referred to it in *The Doctor*, Vol. 7 (1847). *Sir Thomas
Browne had crusaded against the story in *Pseudodoxia Epidemica*, Book 7 (Sealts #89 and 90).

The Ephesian matron of *P.* 14:3 is in the *Satyricon* of
*Petronius, where Eunolpus tells a popular fable: When a
chaste Ephesian woman is widowed, she attempts to sacrifice
herself by refusing nourishment in her husband's burial
vault. A man guarding robbers' bodies brings her food and
wins her sexual favors. Subject to the death penalty because of
the disappearance of one of the robbers' bodies, the guard is
saved when the woman offers to substitute the body of her dead
husband on the criminal's *cross.

See also "Erostratus."
M. 75; M.D. 111; P. 14:3

EPICTETUS
The *Greek *Stoic philosopher (c. A.D. 50--c. A.D. 100)
was much valued by early *Christian thinkers. Born into slavery, the weak Epictetus was lamed by his master and remained poor even after being freed. He wrote nothing himself;
his disciple, *Arrian, compiled his teachings in *Discourses*
and the *Manual*, or *Encheiridion*. For Epictetus, health, pleasure, and possessions had no value; we own only our *God-
given will or purpose and should direct actions toward the
general welfare even though only God's will governs events.
"Bear and forebear" was his favorite motto. But perhaps M.
reacted most to *Discourses* bk. 1, ch. 27:

> Appearances to the mind are of four kinds.
> Things either are what they appear to be; or they
> neither are, nor appear to be; or they are, and do
> not appear to be; or they are not, and yet appear to
> be. Rightly to aim in all these cases is the wise
> man's task.

P. 21:3; C.M. 19

EPITOME
See "Bowditch."
M.D. 99

EPISCOPAL, --IAN
See "Church of England."
W. 38; C.M. 3

EQUATOR, --IAL
The imaginary circle (the *Line, or *Equinoctial Line) at
Latitude 00-00, equally distant from the North and South
*Poles, has long been endowed with heavy symbolic signifi-
cance based on its actual characteristics. Not only does it
mark the place where the Sun's rays decree the difference in
seasons, it is also a differentiation point in Earth's gravity,
producing some wondrous anomalies. As M. suggests in *M.*
34, equatorial currents are mystifyingly treacherous; whirlpools and *tornadoes circle in opposite directions, dependent
upon their location relative to the Equator.
Little wonder then that from ancient times maritime
custom has decreed special initiation ceremonies for those
"Crossing the Line" for the first time. There is no record of
M.'s having been so initiated; he first "crossed the line" on

Acushnet (see "Pequod"), probably in early March of 1841. His *Meteor* journal ("Journal of Melville's Voyage in a Clipper Ship") records his crossing on 29 June 1860. *Acushnet's* Log Book for the period is missing, and because some captains forbade the procedure, we may interpret M.'s silence as indicative of his not having been ceremoniously inducted into the fraternity of the initiate. Potential initiates suffer indignities such as mast-head searches for a physical "line" for days before the actual ceremony, which varies in its character from ship to ship and from time to time. (Modern initiates might suffer electrical shock as part of the hazing!) But most rites are picturesque and include the traditional visit from "Neptunus Rex," portrayed by the oldest seaman on board. *Neptune is attended by his wife, *Amphitrite, as well as by *Davy Jones. His "court" might include the *Devil, a Royal Scribe, Royal Doctor, Royal Dentist, Royal Baby, Royal Chaplain, Royal Navigator, Neptune's Officer of the Day, Judges, Attorneys, Barbers, and Policemen, all portrayed by previously initiated "shellbacks." "Bears" round up the initiates. Neptune is often received aboard the night before, and the ship's officers participate in "The Ritual for the Ancient Order of the Deep," in which, despite their pleas to the contrary, Neptune vows to "be as severe as I can." Until Neptune is appeased, homage must be paid by novices who salaam and praise him. Actual initiation can range from simple tricks to demean or mortify (especially young officers), to *keel-hauling, a dangerous procedure in which the victim is dragged underwater from one side (or end) of the ship to the other. But all ceremonies include ducking of some kind—usually on the safety of the deck. Ear-piercing is another common practice (accounting for the pride with which old-time sailors wore their earrings). Ritual shaving such as that of W. 85 (for quite another purpose) is also common.

Even today, seamen may receive a cherished certificate, usually addressed to "all Mermaids, Sea Serpents, Whales, Sharks, Porpoises, Dolphins, Skates, Eels, Suckers, Lobsters, Crabs, Pollywogs, and other living things of the sea." It testifies that in "Latitude 00-00 and Longitude ___" the initiate "has been found worthy to be numbered as one of our trusty shellbacks, has been gathered to our fold and duly initiated into the solemn mysteries of the ancient order of the deep."
Passim

EQUINOCTIAL LINE
    The celestial *equator, or in common usage, the earth's.
M. 94 and elsewhere

EREBUS
In *Greek mythology, Erebus is a lower world deity born of Chaos and perhaps the father of *Charon. Erebus is a general synonym for the underworld, or *Hades. Thus the "Erebus arches" of the *Thames River are its dark bridges.

Mt. Erebus is the only active volcano in *Antarctica; H.M.S *Erebus* explored the area on an expedition of 1839-43.
I.P. 24

ERIE CANAL
The inland waterway connecting Lake *Erie at *Buffalo with Albany and Troy on the *Hudson River, in *New York, was begun in 1817 and completed in 1825. The eighty-two-lock canal was 363 miles long, forty feet wide, and four feet deep. It was built by horse- and man-power through thick swamp and immediately became a major traffic artery. Enlargement began in 1835, doubling the width and depth by the 1860's.

The canal was much written and sung about, especially by sailors who made ironic jokes about its "storms." M. traveled on the canal en route to *Illinois in 1840.
R. 41; W. 91; M.D. 54; M.D. 85; C.M. 36

ERIE; LAKE ERIE
The fourth largest of the *Great Lakes is c. 241 miles long, c. 30-57 miles wide. Its many outlets and ports touch on *New York, *Pennsylvania, *Ohio, and *Michigan. It was probably sighted by Louis Jolliet in 1669 and was soon ringed by forts and trading posts. The French and Indian wars brought *British control, which was maintained even after the *Revolution. But in the *War of 1812, Oliver H. *Perry's victory at the battle of Lake Erie brought *American control of the southern half. (The United States/*Canada boundary runs through the center of all Great Lakes except Lake *Michigan.)

Erie is ice-bound from mid-December until the end of March. It is noted for its violent storms. M. took a (woodburning) steamer trip on Lake Erie in June or July of 1840. If, as Howard points out (Chap. 2, p. 34), he crossed on the evening of 1 July, he survived a storm that made even horses seasick, warranting his (*M.D.* 54) comments on the toughness of professional "Lakemen."
M. 95; R. 32; R. 44; W. 50; M.D. 54 and elsewhere

EROSTRATUS
The *Ephesian Erostratus set fire to the temple of *Diana in order to make his name immortal, causing the Ephesians to

forbid mention of his name for all time. The fire occurred in 356 B.C., on the birth day of *Alexander the Great.
M. 119

ERROMANGA; ERROMANGGOANS

Erromanga, or Eromanga, is in the southern group of the *New Hebrides Islands. It is thirty-five miles long and twenty five miles wide, with several mountain ranges and extinct volcanic peaks up to 2,600 feet. Among the good anchorage bays are Dillon Bay on the west coast, *Cook Bay on the east. There is a famous Martyrs' Memorial Church honoring missionaries killed by the natives.

The entry in *M.D.* Etymology is not in the Erromangoan language.
O. 48; M.D. Etymology; M.D. 6

ERSKINE, MR.

Thomas Erskine, First Baron Erskine (1750-1823), was a *British lawyer who had been born into poverty and educated himself during four years' service in the Navy. He published an unsigned pamphlet, *Abuses in the British Army* (1772) and, encouraged by *Lord Mansfield, entered Lincoln's Inn. He defended *Lord George Gordon successfully and *Thomas Paine unsuccessfully, becoming England's preeminent defender of personal liberties and advocate in adultery cases. His reputation was dimmed by undistinguished service in the *House of Commons and in the Lord Chancellorship, but his defense of Queen Caroline (wife of George I) brought him once again into public regard. Erskine was a vigorous speaker of cogent argument and successful pamphleteer on political and literary topics.

See also "Crim. Con. Case"; "Fast Fish."
M.D. 89

ESAU

In *Genesis, the twin son (with *Jacob) of *Isaac and Rebekah, and the traditional ancestor of the Edomites. The name means "hairy," as Esau was born: at birth, Jacob is said to have grabbed his heel, symbolically showing the relation of the *Israelites of Jacob to the Edomites of Esau: Jacob is prophesied to be master over Esau. Esau becomes a hunter, rather than a shepherd like his twin, and after an unsuccessful hunt bargains away his birthright for Jacob's food. He is cursed by Isaac instead of blessed to share in fertile *Palestine.

Esau's plan to kill his twin is thwarted by his mother, and the twins reconcile.
M.D. 87

ESCHYLUS
       See "Aeschylus."
C.M. 5

ESCURIAL
       The palace of the *Spanish soverigns, about fifteen miles north-west of *Madrid: convent, palace, cathedral, and mausoleum in one. It was built by Philip II to commemorate the 1557 victory of St. Quentin. *Penny Cyclopaedia* (X, 1838) describes the edifice, built on rocks:

> A convent with cloisters, two colleges, one for the clergy and one for seculars, the royal palace, three chapter houses, three libraries with about 30,000 volumes and some valuable Mss., five great halls, six dormitories, three halls in the hospital, with twenty seven other halls for various purposes, nine refectories, and five infirmaries, with apartments for artisans and mechanics. There are no less than eighty staircases.

M. 75; W. 93

ESQUIMAUX
       The prehistoric origins of the Eskimo peoples are unknown. The word "Eskimo" is a misnomer derived from an Indian word meaning "eater of raw meat"; Eskimos have traditionally cooked their meat. They refer to themselves as *inuit*, which means "people." American Eskimos inhabit the 6,000 miles of coastline from south Alaska to East *Greenland and *Labrador. In M.'s time, they were a relatively pure-blooded group living a stationary existence on a diet of sea-mammal and other meat, and fish. Canadian Eskimos were builders of ice-block igloos. (Eskimo peoples of the *Asian *Arctic are physically *Mongoloid; they are of differing cultures and speak different languages from American Eskimos.)
       Their numbers diminished as a result of famines, blood feuds, infanticide, and the introduction of European diseases. The complex Eskimo language did not become debased by the jargon used by Europeans, but much of their culture was lost, except in rare cases of isolated groups.
M.D. 65; M.D. 101 and elsewhere

ESSAY ON FRIENDSHIP
Probably *Emerson's "Friendship" (*Essays*, 1841).
Sealts #204 is the fourth (1847) edition.
C.M. 39

ESSEX
The frigate *Essex* was the first *American man-of-war
to double the Cape of *Good Hope and Cape *Horn and to fight
in the *Pacific. She was rather a hard-luck ship, for all her
accomplishments, beginning with her behind-schedule
launching in 1799. She was fast but not properly armed, having only carronades which were useless for long distance engagements. *Captain David Porter trained his crew in close
battle, even to swordplay. But *Essex* was captured by the
*British in the South Pacific in 1813, in an engagement with
Phoebe, and served the Royal Navy for twenty years thereafter.
T. 4; T. 25; W. 74

ESSEX
The whaleship *Essex* left *Nantucket in August of 1819.
She was stove by a whale and sank on 20 November 1820. The
dramatic details of the sinking and its aftermath were published in several works, but the ones most important to M. are
probably *Owen Chase's *Narrative of the Most Extraordinary
and Distressing Shipwreck of the Whale-Ship Essex . . .* (New
York, 1821) and the account of *Captain George Pollard, in
*Tyerman and Bennett, *Journal of Voyages and Travels* (2
vols., 1831).
There is some discrepancy between the two accounts, but
the basic outline is that the 238-ton whaleship was
"deliberately" rammed by a large sperm whale on 20 November. The crew of twenty struggled for three months to survive
in open boats. Eight of them lived, including Chase and two
others who were picked up on 18 February 1821, and five who
were picked up five days later. Six men died of natural causes;
their bodies were eaten by the survivors. A seventh lost a lot-
tery and was shot to be eaten. Several others remained on Hen-
derson's Island and faced starvation.
Chase's narrative, from which M. drew much for the
conclusion of *M.D.*, is Sealts #133.
See also "Extracts" 17.
M. 13; M.D. Extracts 17; M.D. 45

ESTAING, CHARLES HECTOR, COMTE D'

Count D'Estaing (1729-1794) was a *French admiral supporting the *American colonies in 1778. With little knowledge of sea warfare, he had been made admiral shortly before, and most actions under his aegis failed: he had limited success against *Admiral Richard Howe, failed to destroy the *English division at St. Lucia, fought indecisively against *Admiral John Byron, made an unsuccessful attack on *Savannah, *Georgia. He is probably the prime source of M's claim that the French were poor sailors.

D'Estaing's liberal ideas led him to the guillotine in *Paris, during the Terror.
I.P. 10; I.P. 15

ESTERHAZY

Esterházy of Galántha was a noble Magyar family originating in early thirteenth-century Hungary (see "Hungarian"). They were important in history and in court life and were patrons of *Haydn, who was *Kapellmeister* of the Esterházy court orchestra. For M. they are symbols of the self assurance derived from success.
M. 29; R. 46; W. 54

ETHIOPIA, --N

"Abyssinia" is Ethiopia, on the Red Sea in eastern *Africa. The terms "Abyssinia" and "Abyssinian" refer to *Arabic tribal groups and are not used in Ethiopia. The nation has been important since ancient times because of its location on the sea route from the *Mediterranean to *India. *Christianity, introduced in the fourth century, began to be supplanted by Islam by the seventh, and for many years (especially during the *Crusades) Ethiopia separated itself from the western world. By the early nineteenth century, Christian missionaries had been expelled and the nation struggled violently until the end of that century, when *Italy recognized its independence in the treaty of Addis Ababa.

Conventional nineteenth-century thinking saw Ethiopia as an enclave of ignorant violence between peoples of "Ethiopian hue" (*M.D.* 61): brownish black. The reference (*M.* 98) to "Abyssinians" cutting live steaks from their cattle is from James Bruce (1730-94), *Interesting Narrative of the Travels of James Bruce, Esq. into Abyssinia, to Discover the Source of the Nile* (1798). The work of the poet Bruce was considered by some apocryphal, but Finkelstein (*Melville's Orienda*, p. 50) verifies the practice. She also notes that the *Edinburgh Re-

view issue referred to in *W.* 36 discussed *Journal of a Visit to some Parts of Ethiopia*, by two Englishmen.
M. 98; M.D. 61

ETNA, THE
   Etna brig was with *Perry's forces in June of 1847 at Tabasco River, *Mexico.
M. 28

ETNAS
   Mount Etna is the highest volcano in Europe and the highest peak in *Italy south of the Alps. Its height tends to decrease: approximately 10,500 feet today, down from close to 10,900 feet in M.'s time. It covers about 500 square miles, with a base circumference of some ninety miles, in Catania province on the East coast of *Sicily. Etna has been prominent in literature since the time of *Hesiod; the *Greeks believed it the workshop of Hephaestus and the *Cyclops, or a column supporting the sky. Its 200 cones have caused over 135 recorded eruptions: sixteen in the eighteenth century; nineteen in the nineteenth.
   Enroute from Sicily to *Naples (17 February 1857), M. saw Etna from Reggio.
T. 21; P. 25:4

ETRURIA; ETRUSCAN
   The ancient country of west-central *Italy occupied what is now *Tuscan and Umbrian territory. Etruscans were artistic people thought to have emigrated from Asia Minor c. 800 B.C. By the sixth century, their civilization had spread through much of Italy. It was finally absorbed by the Roman. In 1801, *Napoléon restored the name, setting up the kingdom of Etruria.
   Massive arched sewers (*M.* 75) and tombs unearthed in the area show that the Etruscans mastered the use of the arch and vault long before the *Romans, enabling them to erect larger structures than the contemporary *Greeks.
   Etruscan pottery was a cheap imitation of Greek work, with much carelessly done elaborate decoration, especially on the red-figure objects.
M. 75; M. 121

"ET TU BRUTE!"
   *Shakespeare: *Julius Caesar* III, i, 77.

*Suetonius (*Lives of the Caesars*) claims that Caesar said this in *Greek, not in *Latin.
M.D. 65

EUCHARIST
See "Holy Sacrament, --s."
O. 46

EUCLID, --EAN
The *Greek Eukleides was a mathematician and founder of a school at *Alexandria, c. 300 B.C. His *Elements* (13 vols.), a geometry text incorporating original and derived material, has been in use almost in its original form for over 2,000 years. By M.'s time, an "away from Euclid" movement had begun which ended in widescale confusion in texts and in teaching. M.'s praise in *R.* of Euclid's "undeniable demonstrations" may be a comment on the situation.
Other extant Euclid works include *Data, On Divisions, Optics, Phaenomena, Elements of Music.* Several lost works are presumed to deal with geometry.
R. 35; M.D. 74; M.D. 77

EUPHRATES
Southwest *Asia's Euphrates River (c. 1,700 miles long) forms in east central *Turkey, swings south into *Syria and modern Iraq to join the *Tigris and flow with it 120 miles to the head of the *Persian Gulf (ancient *Mesopotamia, past *Babylon and other cities). Not very navigable, the Euphrates is mostly used for irrigation.
M. 48

EUROCLYDON
*Acts 27, 14: a south, north- or south-east wind that shipwrecks *St. Paul.
M.D. 2

EUROPA
In classical mythology, the daughter of the king of *Tyre or Sidon. Zeus (see "Jupiter" and "Jove") fell in love with her and seduced her by appearing as a beautiful white bull who carried her away to *Crete to be his mistress. She bore him three sons (Minos, Rhadamanthus, and Sarpedon) and was

eventually married to Asterius, king of Crete, by whom she had a daughter.
M.D. 42; M.D. 133

EUROPE; EUROPEAN; EUROPEANISM; EUROPEANIZED
There can be little doubt of *Yankee M.'s disparaging intent in most of his references to Europe. Especially in *P.*, "Europeanism" (26:1) and "Europeanized" (15:1) suggest an overlayer of sophistication that is at once effete and immoral. (M.'s position can perhaps be compared with that of another world-traveler, Henry James, whose naive but wholesome American characters are simultaneously educated and corrupted by his European characters.)
European countries visited by M. include: *England; *France; *Belgium; *Germany (1849); *Scotland; *Italy; *Switzerland; *Holland (1856-57).
Passim

EUROPEAN SEAMEN IN AMERICAN SHIPS
See "Foreigners."
R. 16

EURYDICE
The Eurydice referred to in *P.* is the beautiful *Thracian nymph of mythology who married *Orpheus. She died of a snakebite and went to hell. Orpheus's music charmed *Hades into releasing her, but he disobeyed the warning not to look at her until daybreak, thus losing her forever.
P. 3:3

EUSTON SQUARE
The Square is one block southwest of *London's Euston Railroad Station, opened in 1838 and remarkable for its massive *doric-arched front entryway.
R. 25

EVANGELISTS
Evangelists were early *Christian missionaries and preachers of the *Gospels; in *Acts 21:8 and *Ephesians 4:11, third in the *Christian ministerial hierarchy, following "*Apostles" and "Prophets." Their activities were similar to the Apostles'. After the third century, "Evangelist" came to

indicate an author of the canonical Gospel, as M. does. In
later liturgies, Evangelists were readers of lections.
M.D. 54

EVE

The traditional "first woman" in *Genesis, created after
*Adam. The name is connected in Genesis 3:20 to the verb "to
live," but rabbinical exegetists linked it to the Aramaic word
for "serpent." The Genesis story is used throughout the *Bible
to show the vulnerability of women and the need for their silence and submissiveness. *Paul uses the name of Eve in II
*Corinthians 11:3 to show women's tendency to be led astray.
M. 3; M. 167; R. 38; W. 7; P. 2:2

EVIL ONE, THE

*Satan is thus designated in the *New Testament, espe-
cially in *Matthew, *John, and *Ephesians.
M.D. 78; P. 7:7; P. 14:1

EXCHANGE, THE

*London's Royal (Stock) Exchange was the world's
greatest in the nineteenth century. London brokers had
formed an association in the eighteenth century, meeting in
coffeehouses and spare rooms, one of which became the Stock
Exchange Coffeehouse or Tavern. The new building for 500
members opened in Capel Court, Bartholomew Lane, in 1802.
A second large room was added in 1823, and in 1854 the whole
was rebuilt in the form of a dome. (The second dome was not
added until 1885.) The London Exchange was not open to the
public, as M. found in 1849: "Went down to the Exchange in an
omnibus & tried to thrust my way in 'Lloyd's'—but it was no
go" (Journal, 14 November).
R. 45

EXETER HALL

Exeter (Originally Burghley, then Cecil) house, *Strand,
*London, was built in the time of Edward VI and was much
visited by British royalty. After its demolition, Exeter Hall
arose on the site (1831) as the scene of "May Meetings" of religious and charitable institutions and later as headquarters of
the Young Men's Christian Association.
R. 23

EXHILARATING GAS
The anaesthetic Nitrous Oxide, or "laughing gas," was introduced at *Harvard Medical School in 1845 by a dentist, Horace Wells. *Sir Humphrey Davy had published papers on its use in 1800. Nitrous Oxide is an odorless, nonflammable inorganic compound that acts rapidly but relatively feebly. It is limited to short-term use because of its adverse effects on white blood cells and bone marrow.
(See also "chloroform.")
W. 25

"EX LEGE NATURAE JURE MERITOQUE"
Lat.: "Justly and deservedly because of the law of nature."
M.D. 32

EXODUS
The second book of the *Bible's *Pentateuch, Exodus tells of the *Hebrews' enslavement in *Egypt and the deliverance that led to the tribes' thinking of themselves as a nation. It is a relatively trustworthy history of events surrounding *Moses and the sojourn at Mount *Sinai (c. 1290 to 1225 B.C.).
C.M. 26

EXPLORING EXPEDITIONS
Among M.'s numerous references to such expeditions, probably most important was the United States Exploring Expedition led by *Wilkes.
M.D. 24

EZEKIEL
A prophet of the *Babylonian exile and author of the *Apocalyptic *Old Testament book, he is known to have been a priest captured by Nebuchadrezzar (see "Nebuchadnezzar") in 598 B.C. From his youth, Ezekiel had symbolic visions: *God in a chariot with wheels within wheels; God with four faces—a man, a lion, an ox, an eagle. His prophecies include the fall of *Jerusalem and the reappearance of God after destruction, and his work heavily influenced the *New Testament's *Revelation and the *Gospel of *John
In M.D. 82 the reference is to Ezekiel's words to *Egypt's *Pharaoh: "Thou art like a young lion of the nations, and thou art as a whale in the seas" (32:2).
M.D. 82

FABIAN
Fabius Maximus Verrucosus, Cunctator, Quintus, Consul I. Fabius, The Cunctator ("the Delayer") earned his sobriquet, which began as an epithet and became an honor, in the Punic Wars. Dogging *Hannibal's heels, refusing engagement, cutting off his supplies, and otherwise harassing, Fabius wore down Hannibal's strength, making possible Scipio's victory over *Carthage.

A courageous but cautious patrician, Fabius was elected dictator of *Rome in 217 B.C. There is a life of him by *Plutarch. In the words of Ennius: *unus homo nobis cunctando restituit rem*: "One man by delaying restored our fortunes." Fabius died in 203 B.C.
T. 17

"FACE DIVINE"
*Charles Lamb (1775-1834) used the expression in *Letter to Mrs. Wordsworth* (1818), in reference to Fanny Kelly's face. The expression had also appeared in *Pope's "Eloisa to Abelard," 1. 147; *Milton's *Paradise Lost* III, 44 and 140-41; *Spenser's *The Faerie Queene* I, ix, 15, 5.
T. 30

FAIR
In *C.M.*, "fair" may refer to Vanity Fair, in *Bunyan's *The Pilgrim's Progress*. (Sealts' #95 is an unidentified edition.)
C.M. 24

FAIR, THE
See "World's Fair."
C.M. 7

FAIR BREEZES, GOD OF
In mythology, Aeolus, King of the Winds, lived on the earthly island of Aeolia. The four chief winds were *Boreas—North (*Latin Aquilo); Zephyr—West (Latin Favonius); Notus—South (Latin Auster); Eurus—East (same in Latin). There was no god of Fair Breezes; all were whimsical.
See also "Aeolian; Eolean."
M. 170

FAIRMOUNT

The Mount Pleasant reservoir in Fairmont Park, on the eastern bank of the Schuylkill River in *Philadelphia, was a common subject for verbal landscapers such as Mrs. Frances Trollope (*Domestic Manners of the Americans*, XXIV). who quite fell in love with its spacious lake, gardened grounds, ornate fountains, elaborate buildings and statuary. As "Pierre" notes, the drinking water supplied was of excellent quality.
W. 30; P. 22:1; P. 22:2

FAIRY BOWER

The sylvan home of legendary tiny magical beings in human shape, such as elves, gnomes, goblins, pixies, leprechauns, etc.
M. 64

FALCONER; *FALCONER'S SHIPWRECK*

William Falconer (1732-69), *Scottish poet and seaman, survived the foundering of a merchant ship off *Greece, becoming famous for the three-canto poem he wrote about the experience: *The Shipwreck* (1762). He published a *Marine Dictionary* in 1769 but drowned that year in the wreck of the *Aurora*. He had rejected a partnership offer from publisher John Murray to take the more lucrative position of *Aurora*'s *purser.

Although M. was fond enough of the poem to quote from it in *M.D.*'s *Extracts (#45), it is alluded to negatively in *R.*, along with his father's "useless" guide book.
R. 30; W. 65; M.D. Extracts 45

FALERNIAN

Falernian is a choice *Italian wine which was much used by the ancient *Romans. "Falernian foliage" on a vase (*R.* 49) is probably grape leaves.

(Falernum, a liqueur of Barbados, is white, with a lime-almond flavor. It owes its name to Falernian, which comes in sweet and dry varieties.)
R. 49

FALKLAND ISLANDS

The Falklands (Spanish Malvinas) lie 250 miles off the southeastern coast of Argentina, east of the Strait of *Magellan (51°-53° S., 57°-62° W.). There are two large islands (East and West Falklands) and some 200 small ones. They are for the most part cold, bleak, treeless regions dedicated to sheep farming; in light of this ambiance and M.'s suggestion in *R.* 19 that they are at the end of the world, it is difficult to understand why they have been lusted after throughout their relatively brief history. British claims are based on probable discovery by John Davis (c. 1550-1605, see "Davis, Commodore") in 1592. *Bougainville established a *French colony in 1764 which was transferred to *Spain in 1766. Britain was soon back but abandoned its claim in 1774, only to be in occupation by 1832-33. Both Argentina and *Chile have actively disputed Britain's claim. When a sealing vessel was seized at Soledad in 1832, the *United States sent a punitive expedition.

(Further complicating the problem is the twentieth-century question of what are called the Falkland Island Dependencies—South Georgia and South Sandwich Islands—and British Antarctic Territory—South Shetland, South Orkney, and *Antarctic Peninsula regions.)
R. 19

FALL, THE
        Refers to *Adam's transgression in the garden of *Eden. In *Genesis, *God had put a curse on the serpent, causing a war between it and man; Adam and *Eve's succumbing to its invitation to the forbidden fruit subjected them to God's curse of painful childbearing for Eve and lifelong labor for Adam, as well as expulsion from the garden, with cherubim guarding against their re-entry, amounting to a death sentence in place of immortality. There are parallel stories throughout Semitic legends: *Zoroastrian, *Babylonian and *Assyrian, *Chaldean, *Mesopotamian. These have been accepted: 1: literally; 2. allegorically, as types; 3. as legend with truth in mythological disguise.
        The story's major impact is in its changing of the basic beliefs about man's nature, from the *Greek notion of man as healthy and normal (shared by M.'s Typees), to the *Hebraic one of man possessed by depravity traceable to Adam's fall from God's favor. Although there are few overt references to the Fall in either book, the New Testament supports the Hebraic Old Testament position vis-a-vis depravity, especially in the *Pauline Epistles: Adam fell from a high state by breaking his covenant with God, revealing man's bias towards evil. Later interpretations suggest our guilt only if we willfully err (seen in the work of John of *Damascus).
        M.'s works are much preoccupied with the implications of the Fall. His copy of Schopenhauer (Sealts #s 443-48)

marks the philosopher's comment that the story of the Fall
was "the sole thing that reconciles me to the *Old Testament"
(*Studies in Pessimism*).
T. 26; M. 167

FALMOUTH
An ancient seaport and borough in *Cornwall,
*England: site of *Pendennis Castle and a *Tudor fortress:
center of the Royalist cause in the British Civil War.
I.P. 20

FANCY-MEN
In common nineteenth-century use, describing kept
men or gigolos.
W. 73

FANNING
Edmund Fanning (1769-1841) was born in Stonington,
*Connecticut and shipped as a cabin boy at fourteen. Having
risen to mate's rank in 1790, he married Sarah Sheffield, of
Stonington, by whom he later had two children. By 1792, he
was first mate on a sealing voyage to the South *Shetlands,
and in 1793 received his first command, a *West Indian brig.
Declining a British Navy commission as well as command of
a new *American frigate, he sailed on the sealer *Betsey* from
1797-98, and rescued a missionary in the *Marquesas. In
1798 he discovered the Line Island which bears his name, as
well as *Washington and Christmas Islands (between 1° and
5° N. and 157° and 161° W.). After this profitable voyage he
devoted his life to promoting the South Sea trade. His 1833
memoirs, *Voyage Around the World* . . . (which had little to
do with the Marquesas), helped secure authority for the 1838-
42 *Wilkes expedition, after Fanning was turned down for an
expedition of his own. In 1838 he published *Voyages to the
South Seas, Indian and Pacific Oceans* . . ., issued in an ab-
breviated version in 1924: *Voyages and Discoveries in the
South Seas.*
T. 25

FANNING'S ISLAND
See "Fanning."
0. 51; M.D. 53

FARARER
     Probably Fa'a'a (Tettaha), *Tahiti.
O. 32

"FAREWELL . . ."
     See "Spanish Ladies."
M.D. 40

FARNOOPOO
     Phonetic spelling of *Tahitian "Fanaupo."
O. 67

FARNOW
     "Faa nau," in *Tahitian.
O. 46

FARNOWAR
     Phonetic spelling of *Tahitian "Fanauao."
O. 67

FARTHINGALE
     From *Elizabethan times, a hooped underskirt framed
by whalebone.
M.D. 75

FASCES
     A bundle of rods with projecting axe blade, carried by
ancient *Roman Magistrates, as symbol of power.
M.D. 57

"FAST-FISH AND LOOSE-FISH"
     Vincent's notes to his 1952 edition of *M.D.* (p. 791) and
his *Trying-Out of Moby-Dick* (IV, 19) discuss the use of
*Scoresby's material in M.'s treatment of "Fast-Fish and
Loose-Fish." M. uses the "tag end" of Scoresby's discussion
(Vol. 2, pp. 312-332), or his "fundamental articles":

          First, That a fast-fish, or a fish in any way in
          possession, whether alive or dead, is the sole and
          unquestionable property of the persons so main-
          taining the connection or possession; and, sec-

ondly, That a loose fish, alive or dead, is fair game.

The example of *Erskine's "*crim. con case" comes from Scoresby's Appendix (Vol. 2, pp. 518-521). As Vincent points out, the rather dry Scoresby probably did not notice Erskine's playful use of the word "loose" in connection with an accused adulteress. Nor would he have understood M.'s expansive analogizing of the expressions into questions of morality, ethics, politics, and economics, or his final challenge to the "Loose-Fish/Fast-Fish" reader," who may at this stage be "hooked" by the book or may escape unmarked by putting it down.
M.D. 89; M.D. 90

FASTING AND HUMILIATION
The practice of ritualistic fasting is so ancient that its origins are unknown. Long before *Old Testament *Hebrews incorporated fasting into their Day of Atonement, fasting was used as a sign of mourning, a preparation for eating sacramental food in a ritual meal, a means of inducing visions and dreams. In the *New Testament, private fasting is a work of merit. Humiliation to show the opposite of pride, arrogance, and violence became a most important characteristic of the *Christian life.
M.D. 17

FATALISTS
See "Necessitarians."
M. 135; W. 31

FATA MORGANA
The name of Morgan Le Fay ("fairy"), King Arthur's sister, is given to a phenomenon often seen in the Strait of *Messina, between *Sicily and the *Italian mainland: in certain atmospheric conditions, objects on or near the water are reflected up-side down. An inverted ship reflection was considered ominous.
M.D. 135

FATE; THE FATES: THREE FATES
The *Greeks and *Romans believed in three arbitrary and uncaring *Parcae or Fates who controlled every man's life and destiny: Clotho holds the distaff; Lachesis spins the

thread of life; Atropos cuts the thread to end life (From the Greek *klotho*—to draw thread from a distaff; *lagchano*—to assign by lot; *atropos*—inflexible).
M. 28; M. 180; M.D. 1; M.D. 47; M.D. 113; M.D. 124; M.D. 132; P. 25:3; C.M. 41 and elsewhere

FATHER MAPPLE

M.D.'s fictional "Father Mapple" is thought by some scholars to have an original in the famous *Boston minister Father Edward Taylor (1793-1871), whose preaching in the 1830's and 40's had impressed *Emerson, Dickens (see "Hard Times") and others. His Boston church contained a painting similar to the one in "Father Mapple's" church. *Dana (*Two Years Before the Mast*, Chaper 12) notes his direct addresses to seamen based on his having been a sailor himself before entering the clergy. M. undoubtedly heard him preach in Boston in 1849.

A second likely condidate is the Reverend Enoch Mudge (1776-1850), pastor of the *New Bedford Seaman's *Bethel (see "Whaleman's Chapel") from 1832 to 1844 and therefore at the time of M.'s visit. His preaching is known to have relied on nautical metaphors.
M.D. 8; M.D. 9

FATHER MURPHY

There is some disagreement about Murphy's biography in the many contemporary works that discuss him. Columba Murphy was a native of Dundalk, County Meath, *Ireland. Although some sources claim his early ordination in *France, Forsyth's "Herman Melville's Father Murphy" says he was probably a Brother when he arrived in the South Seas in 1833 and was (secretly) ordained at Taravai in 1837. Murphy is known to have worked for the Roman *Catholic Church, officially or otherwise, at *Valparaiso, the *Gambier Islands, *Tahiti, the *Sandwich Islands, Monterey (then in *Mexico), and the *Marquesas (before M.'s arrival).

Murphy was well regarded by natives, who gave him nicknames relative to his many skills. He was apparently the worldly, genial, practical man painted by M., albeit one not above practicing deception to further missionary activities countered by those of the much stronger *Protestant *London Missionary Society. In 1842, when M. was in Tahiti, Murphy and others ran the *Mission de Notre Dame de Foi*. M. makes him about fifty years old at the time. According to Wise, Murphy was dead perhaps as early as 1843. As Forsythe points out, the *Annales de la Propagation de la Foi* do not mention him after this time. Forsythe's articles include information about Murphy garnered from Bingham, *Ellis, *Wheeler, and others.

See also "Caret"; "Laval"; "Merenhout."
O. 37

FAUST, DOCTOR
See "Goethe."
M. 13; R. 40

FAUST'S
See "Fust, Johann."
C.M. 30

FAWKES, GUY
Guy Fawkes (1570-1606), infamous conspirator, was born in *York, *England, to an eminently respectable family, and attended school there with some of his co-conspirators in the "Gunpowder Plot" to blow up the buildings of *Parliament. A zealous *Catholic, in 1593 he became a soldier of fortune in the *Spanish army, where he impressed eminent Catholic Sir William Stanley, who accompanied him to Philip III, hoping to secure Catholic relief from oppressive *British laws. Fawkes had no part in devising the plot hatched upon the ascension of *James I, but was soon enlisted. On 24 May 1604, a house adjoining the Parliament building was rented, in which he lived disguised as a servant, while a tunnel was dug. Rental of an adjoining house, directly beneath the *House of Lords, obviated need for the tunnel, and its cellar was filled with concealed barrels of gunpowder and iron bars. The courageous Fawkes was to fire it with a slow match, facilitating his escape. Preparations were finally completed, and Parliament was to meet on 5 November 1605, after many postponements. Efforts began to warn Catholics in the House, and the plot was revealed. Fawkes determined to continue when his fellows fled and was found on 4 November with a watch, matches and tinder, and a lighted lantern.

Interrogated in the king's bedchamber, he refused to name his co-conspirators or admit remorse but finally broke down on 8 November under torture on the rack; he signed the confession "Guido Fawkes." Parliament had met on schedule on 5 November, and that was designated a permanent day of Thanksgiving, although ironically it is still called "Guy Fawkes Day." Fawkes was executed 31 January

1606. The lantern M. mentions in *O.* is in the Ashmolean Museum, *Oxford, inscribed from Robert Heywood, late proctor, 4 April 1641.

M.'s first full day in England, on his trip to publish *W.* was Monday, 5 November 1849, Guy Fawkes day, which is celebrated, similarly to our Halloween, with frightening effigies ("guys"), pranks, and bonfires. Because of Fawkes, Parliament's cellars are still formally searched every day.

See also "Monteagle."
0. 9; W. 31; I.P. 24

FEDALLAH

M. perhaps derived the name for this satanic fictitious character from the recounting in *The Spectator*, No. 578, 9 August 1714, of a *Persian tale about Fadlallah and Zemroude, in which a demon soul inhabits a body not its own.
M.D. 48

FEDERALISM

*American Federalists were originally the supporters of the *Constitution before its ratification; they became members of the Federalist political party (which included *Washington, Adams, and Hamilton). With assistance from Hamilton's, Madison's, and Jay's *Federalist Papers*, aims for a strong central government came to pass, with the Constitution providing for divided powers, levels of government over citizens, and distribution of powers that cannot be altered unilaterally by any level of government or by the ordinary process of legislation. The Federalist Party promulgated strict adherence to a relatively unchangeable Constitution, as well as a large degree of control over citizens by a relatively aristocratic class of leaders. With the emergence of *Jefferson's Democratic-Republican Party (see "Democrat. . . . "), the Federalist Party lost influence and had completely disappeared by 1816, remembered mostly as the "bigoted" group M. cites in *P.* 15:1.
P. 15:1

FEEGEE, -S, --ANS; FEEJEE, --S; FEJEE

However he spells it, M. means "cannibal" when he mentions the people of Fiji. The Melanesian island group of the southwest *Pacific is 2,000 miles northeast of *Sydney: 16°35'-20°40' S., 178°44'-179°17' E. Fiji consists of some 250 islands, eighty of which are inhabited today. The volcanic, coral, and limestone islands were discovered by the *Dutch navigator Abel Janszoon Tasman (c. 1603- c. 1659) in 1643. They were ceded by native chiefs to *Britain in 1874. Arrival of missionaries in 1835 lessened the practice of cannibalism. T. 4; T. 25; M. 14; M. 27; W. 61; W. 74; W. 75; W. 91; M.D. 3; M.D. 6; M.D. 32; M.D. 65

FEEGEE FISH
Like "Algerine Porpoise" (see "Cetology"), an invention for political purposes, Feegees being known for fierceness.
M.D. 32

FEEJEE, --S
See "Feegee . . . ."
T. 4; W. 74; M.D. 65

FELIX
An archdeacon Felix became the Antipope Felix II (355-365), imposed on the *Catholic Church by the *Arian Emperor Constantius, after he had exiled the orthodox Pope Liberius. Popular opinion forced Felix to flee, and he died in retirement.
In *Acts 24, 1-25, Antonius Felix, *Roman procurator of *Judea, married Drusilla, wife of King Azizus of Emesa, after inducing her to leave her husband. *St. Paul, summoned to appear before the pair to expound the Christian faith, caused Felix to tremble.
W. 38

FEMUR
The *femur*, or thigh bone, is the "longest, largest, and strongest bone in the skeleton," according to *Gray's*. It is almost perfectly cylindrical and is slightly inclined from the vertical in the erect posture. The upper shaft forms a head, a neck, and *great* and *lesser trochanters*, prominent growths facilitating muscle movement. The *digital fossa* is a deep depression for tendon attachment, found in the *great trochanter*. The *anterior* and *posterior intertrochanteric lines* wind around the shaft of the *femur*; the *linea aspera* is a longitudinal ridge on the middle third of the bone.
W. 62

FENNEL

The tall herb *Foeniculum vulgare* is a member of the parsley family, bearing yellow flowers and aromatic seeds used in seasoning and medicine. It is among the plants "Ophelia" offers in *Hamlet* IV, v, 173. In "flower language" it stands for Strength, or Restorer of strength.
P. 4:4

FERDINAND, COUNT FATHOM

The hero of *Smollett's novel of that name is conceived and born in gin, his camp-follower mother selling that commodity.
W. 8

FETCH

Steal.
C.M. 15

FEVER & AGUE; *FEVER NAGUR*

A form of malaria. "White-Jacket's" *fever-nagur* is a corruption of the term.
W. 47; C.M. 23

FIDELE

M.'s fictional riverboat in *C.M.* probably takes its name from *Shakespeare's *Cymbeline*, a drama of faith, trust, and their opposites. The faithful heroine, "Imogen," disguised as the boy "Fidele," is told: "With fairest flowers / Whilst summer lasts, and I live here, Fidele, / I'll sweeten thy sad grave" (IV, ii, 218-220). M. used the first two lines as a preface to his short story, "The Piazza."

The name ("Faithful") derives from Lat. *fides*: "faith."

M. may also have had in mind a covert reference to *Bunyan's "Faithful," who is executed by the people of Vanity-Fair, in *The Pilgrim's Progress*.
C.M. Passim

FIDUS-ACHATES

See "Achates."
M. 3

FIERY DESERT
See "Sahara."
O. 73

FIERY YOUTH
In *M*. 161, a reference to John Van Buren, son of
*President Martin Van Buren.
M. 161

FIESOLE
In central *Italy's *Tuscany, three miles northeast of
*Florence, Fiesole is a hill resort overlooking the Arno valley.
Along with *Etruscan and *Roman ruins, there is a Ro-
manesque cathedral of 1028 (restored 1878-83) and a Francis-
can convent on the site of the former Roman acropolis.
M. visited on 28 March 1857, commenting in his
journal on Villa dei tri Visi, the locus of Boccaccio's
Decameron story-tellers, as well as the Villa Mozzi of Lorenzo
*Medici, and the Etruscan wall ruins to the north.
I.P. 18

FIFE
The *Scottish county of Fife makes up the northern
boundary of the Firth of *Forth. The ancient Pictavia, Fife
was settled by the Picts long before *Roman times, visited by
early *Christian missionaries, invaded by the *Danes.
*Dunfermline and other towns were traditionally scenes of
royal festivities, despite lack of support for the *Stuarts. M.
may have visited the area in late October or early November
1856.
M.D. Extracts 13; I.P. 18

FIFTH AVENUE
*New York City's Fifth Avenue (begun in 1824) was cut
through and opened in 1837, facilitating the progress of fashionable life northward. By the late 1840's, development of
mansions for such magnates as Astor and Vanderbilt sent
real-estate prices soaring on the avenue, which extended
from Waverly Place (formerly Art Street) at Washington
Square (archless, until 1889), to the forties. The topography of
*Manhattan Island was responsible for the avenue's late de-
velopment. An alternate thoroughfare to *Broadway was
much needed, but high hills and bodies of water had to be cir-
cumvented in order to pave the roadway; large private lots

had to be acquired, including one lot containing a four-block-long botanical garden.

The southern terminus of the avenue was land originally earmarked for *Sailor's Snug Harbor, but it was soon realized that the plot was too valuable to waste on such charitable endeavors. The allusion to Fifth Avenue in *R.* 30 is a sardonic suggestion that today's most fashionable residence is tomorrow's ruin.

In the 1850's, a reservoir still stood (opposite a farm) at the southwest corner of Fifth Avenue and Forty-Second Street (since 1911 the site of the New York Public Library). It was not until after the *Civil War that Fifth Avenue began to acquire its chic commercial aspect.

In a letter of 1857 (quoted in Sealts's *Melville as Lecturer*, p. 7), M. playfully suggested as a *lecture topic, "Daily progress of man towards a state of intellectual & moral perfection, as evidenced in history of 5th Avenue & 5 Points." Fifth Avenue at that time represented for many people the zenith of human achievement, and Five Points the nadir. Five Points was the notorious slum area at an intersection of Orange, Cross, and Anthony Streets (no longer in existence; the area was northeast of *City Hall, slightly northwest of present-day *Chatham Square.) The wonder for M. is that the two could coexist.
R. 30

FIFTH MONARCHY ELDER
The Fifth-Monarchy Men were a fanatic *English *leveller/reformer sect during *Cromwell's time (c. 1554-1560) who believed that *Jesus Christ was about to return to earth (following *Daniel 2), to establish the Fifth Monarchy after those of *Assyria, *Persia, *Macedonia, *Rome.

Their last futile attempt was the 1661 "Venner's Rising," with eighty men led by Thomas Venner, who was executed with sixteen others.
M. 33

FIFTH OF NOVEMBER
See "Guy Fawkes."
I.P. 24

FIGHTING GLADIATOR
See "Dying Gladiator."
P. 16:2

FINE ARTS
Arts which depend upon fine imagination: music, painting, poetry, sculpture, dance, etc., as opposed to useful arts such as weaving, metalworking, etc.
T. 18; O. 8

FINLANDERS; FINNISH; FINNS
A central part of *Lapland, Finland is known to have been settled 5,000 years ago. It was conquered before the eighth century A.D. by the Finns, who replaced the Lapps. Much of its history has been intertwined with that of *Sweden, which controlled Finland from the twelfth century, but there has been constant battle over it with *Russia, as well. By the late eighteenth century, there was a strong separatist movement, so that when Russia took charge in 1809, it was forced to permit a constitutional democracy separate from the Russian system. The nineteenth century saw a revival of Finnish nationalism and culture (along with increasing industrialism). Finland had long had two official languages, Swedish and Finnish, and the latter language had been little used in literature until the middle of that century, despite a richness of folklore and orally transmitted epic poetry.
O. 12; M. 20

FIRE OF 1835
The great New York fire of 1835 began at the foot of Maiden Lane and destroyed some 600 buildings valued at 20 million dollars. It demolished the South (Dutch Reformed) Church on Garden Street, where M. had been baptized. M.'s aunt, Mrs. Herman *Gansevoort, lost all of her property, but M.'s immediate family was living in Albany at the time.
P. 22:1

FIRKINS
Small casks for food storage, holding about fifty-five pounds.
M.D. 101

FIRST LORD IN WAITING
Lords and Ladies in Waiting are highly-placed functionaries in a Royal household, for personal attendance upon the sovereign and other royal persons. First Lord in Waiting would be most important of these.
O. 65

FISHES, THE
See "Zodiac."
M.D. 99

FISTIANA
The art of boxing, and that which pertains thereto.
W. 66

FIVE NATIONS
The Five Nations of the *Iroquois League, the Seneca, Cayuga, Onandaga, Oneida, and Mohawk tribes (in 1715, with the addition of the Tuscarora, the Six Nations), formed a confederation (c. 1570) that became the most powerful native political entity in North America. Longfellow's "Hiawatha" original was supposedly among the chiefs who formed the warlike league which, after securing firearms from the *Dutch, controlled land from the Ottawa River to the Tennessee and from the Kennebec to the Illinois. Despite their bellicose nature, the Iroquois Confederacy tribes were highly cultured agriculturists with elaborate religion and highly structured political administration. For the most part, they were allied with the *English against the *French and, with the exception of the Oneida and the Tuscarora, were against the *American Revolutionaries. They take important parts in *Cooper's "Leatherstocking" tales.
W. 46; C.M. 25

FIVE THOUSAND YEARS AGO
A nineteenth-century *Biblical chronology dated the *Deluge from that time.
See also "Creation."
M.D. 135

FIXED FATE AND FREE WILL
During the 1850's, M. was obsessed with metaphysical questions regarding free will, but even before that time he tended to enlist kindred spirits in such discussion. His Journal for 13 October 1849 records his talk with *German philologist George J. Adler (1821-1868) while crossing the *Atlantic: "Walked the deck . . . till a late hour, talking of 'Fixed Fate, Free will, foreknowledge absolute'."
His tendency toward determinism (see "necessitarian") was fed by readings in *Bayle, *Spinoza, *Thomas

Browne, *Goethe, Jonathan Edwards, *Hartley, Godwin, and
*Shelley.
        The combination of words he probably found in *Milton
(*Paradise Lost* II, 557-561). The poet speaks of those who

>   ... sat on a hill retired
> In thoughts more elevate and reasoned high
> Of Providence, Foreknowledge, Will, and Fate--
> Fixed fate, free will, foreknowledge absolute,
> And found no end, in wandering mazes lost.

        M. visited *Hawthorne in *Liverpool in 1857.
Hawthorne recorded in his journal that they had reasoned
together of "Providence and futurity, and of everything that
lies beyond human ken." M. was in a "morbid state of mind,"
and Hawthorne added, "he will never rest until he gets hold
of a definite belief . . . . He can neither believe, nor be
comfortable in his unbelief."
        The question of "chance, free will, and necessity" is the
focus of *M.D.* 47, "The Mat-Maker." The theme, if not the
words, is present in many of the works.
P. 11:1

FLAG OF CAPTURE
        Pennoned "waif" pole, marking ownership of a
captured whale.
M.D. 56

FLAG-STAFF
        To "call upon the Flag-staff" is to swear by the flag.
W. 54

FLAMBOROUGH HEAD
        A 450 foot-high promontory of *Yorkshire, *England's
Chalk Hills, from which spectators watched *Bon Homme
Richard*, under *John Paul Jones, defeat H.M.S. *Serapis* in
1779.
        In 1886, Peter Toft gave M. a water-color, *Flamboro'
Head*, painted in 1883.
I.P. 19

FLASH; "THE FLASHES"

Although M.'s "Flashes" tavern is in *New York, a flash-house pub in *England is one frequented by thieves and prostitutes. Flash language is their argot.

"Flash" is also an *Australian term for a proud, showy, vulgar, vain, superficially brilliant person.
0. 12; 0. 34; R. 61; M.D. 27; P. 16:3

FLAXMAN"S

John Flaxman (1755-1826), *English sculptor, draftsman, book illustrator, and colleague of William Blake, did neoclassical illustrations for *Pope's translation of the *Iliad and Odyssey, published in 1793. Among his other works are illustrations for *Aeschylus (1795) and the *Divine Comedy (1802), funerary sculptures at *Westminster Abbey, the *Nelson monument at *St. Paul's Cathedral. His work is not considered sentimental.

Sealts #147, Harper Classical Library Vols. 32-34, contain Pope's Homer.
P. 2:7

FLEMISH

The medieval county of Flanders extended along the North Sea from the Strait of *Dover to the mouth of the Scheldt River: modern West *Belgium, adjacent parts of northern *France, and the southwest *Netherlands. In the fourteenth and fifteenth centuries, painting developed in competition with Early Renaissance *Italian art. Flemish painters, moving away from religious subjects, focussed on the accurate representation of people and things in fore- and background, becoming superb craftsmen and colorists of miniscule objects and harsh realities (such as wrinkled faces). Their oil technique produced enamel-like smoothness. The Van Eyck brothers (Jan, c. 1385-1440, and Hubert, c. 1366-1426), creators of the *Ghent altarpiece, are credited with popularizing the style, of which M. saw many examples on his European tour of 1857.

(See also "Teniers.")
W. 91; P. 1:16; P. 2:7

FLETCHER

John Fletcher (1579-1625) was born in Rye (Sussex), *England, the son of the subsequent chaplain at the execution of Mary Queen of Scots (see "Stuart"). He was educated at *Cambridge but was left destitute at his father's death. For-

tuitous collaboration with *Sir Francis Beaumont and others
(including *Shakespeare and *Ben Jonson) gained his liveli-
hood and lasting fame. Fletcher died of *plague.

The Beaumont affiliation lasted from about 1606 to 1613.
Attempted attribution of plays, portions, and aspects of the
works has yielded many theories but little surety. Among
plays known to be Fletcher's alone are *The Faithful Shep-
herdess, Valentinian, The Humorous Lieutenant, The Wilde
Goose Chase, The Woman's Prize, Rule a Wife and Have a
Wife, The Chances.*

Plays by Beaumont and Fletcher include *Philaster*
(1609), *The Maid's Tragedy* (1610-11), *A King and No King*
(perf. 1611), *Arcadis* (perf. 1612), *Bonduca* (perf. 1613-14),
Thierry King of France (printed 1621).

Sealts #53 is Beaumont, Francis. *Fifty Comedies and
Tragedies.* Written by Francis Beaumont and John Fletcher.
. . . London, 1679. The annotated *folio is inscribed as having
been purchased in London in 1849.
M. 174; W. 41

FLIP
The popular *Victorian Flip was made of spiced rum,
*ale, or wine, with whisked eggs, sometimes given a burnt
taste by the insertion of a hot poker. Dickens (see "Hard
Times") gives his own recipe in *Little Dorrit*: "the yolk of a
new-laid egg, beaten up . . . with a glass of sound sherry,
nutmeg and powdered sugar."
M.D. 101

FLOATING CHAPEL
The first floating chapel was established in 1818 on the
*Thames River; an old frigate's interior was altered to pro-
vide a large meeting space. The idea quickly spread; by 1821
the *Bethel flag flew over a *New York-bound ship when the
*Tennessee *Presbyterian minister John Allen conducted
services.

M. probably heard the Reverend Doctor *William
Scoresby preach at *Liverpool's Floating Chapel in 1839.
R. 9; R. 35

FLOGGED THROUGH THE FLEET
Where there was more than one ship or an entire
squadron in a harbor, a prisoner might be "flogged 'round
the fleet." He would be transported in a boat to each of the

ships in turn and his lashes inflicted in front of each crew, as an example.
W. 88

FLOGGING

The practice of punishment by flogging aboard ship had been standard procedure for many centuries. In the nineteenth century, *Navy specifications existed regarding the weapons used (heavy cat o' nine tails, or lighter "colt"), the number of stripes, and the manner of administering them. But there was much disregard of the "rules," as M. demonstrates especially in W. 33-36. Flogging was abolished in the U.S. Navy in 1850; popular belief credited W.'s chapters with its discontinuance, one legend claiming that a copy of the book had been placed on each Senator's desk so as to influence him.

Some sample U.S. Navy offenses and their punishments: drunkenness, fighting, or mutinous conduct, 12 lashes with the cats; smuggling cigars from ship to shore, twelve lashes with the cats; smoking after 10 P.M., eight lashes with the "colt"; filthiness, eight lashes with the cats; missing muster, eight lashes with the cats; taking indecent liberties with boy in hammock, twelve lashes with cats. Many of these offenses were regular occurrences, and those men punished were, or felt that they were, unfairly or arbitrarily singled out.

M. witnessed a flogging on his second day aboard *United States.
W. 33; W. 34; W. 35; W. 36 and elsewhere

FLORA

Flowers generally. Flora was *Roman goddess of flowers.
T. 11; T. 17

FLORENCE; FLORENTINE

The capital of Tuscany and Firenza province of central *Italy is located at the foot of the *Etruscan Apennines, on both banks of the Arno River, 145 miles north-northwest of *Rome. The cradle of the Italian Renaissance (see "Revival of Learning"), Florence contains many works by and monuments to *Michelangelo, *Leonardo, *Raphael, *Dante, *Machiavelli, and the *Medicis, as well as cathedrals and palaces. Important since *Roman times, Florence was the center of the thirteenth- and fourteenth-century struggle of the *Guelphs and the Ghibellines, in which Dante (the "blistered Florentine" of *P.* 2:7) was caught up. It was the capital of the kingdom of Italy from 1865 to 1870.

M. visited 23-29 March 1857. He comments in his journal on the sixteenth-century Uffizi and fifteenth-century *Pitti palaces. The former had the richest collection of art in the world, including Cellini's *Perseus, and the latter, at this time still the Grand Ducal residence, the best collection of paintings. M. saw tombs of the Medici, Michelangelo, Machiavelli and others, as well as the memorial to Dante which is called his "tomb," at the Church of Santa Croce: the pantheon of Florence. Despite much rain, he appears to have enjoyed his stay, the only low point occurring at the Museum of Natural History adjoining the Pitti, where the Medici anatomical collection's focus on horror and decay brought back the depressed state he suffered before and during his long tour. His journal entry for 27 March focuses on "horrible humiliation . . . . Roman sarcophagus . . . putrid corpse thrown over it . . . rats, vampires--insects. slime & ooze of corruption."
R. 30; P. 2:7; P. 16:2

FLORIDA; THE FLORIDAS
The twenty-seventh state (admitted 1845), at the extreme southeastern portion of the continent, is a peninsula with a "panhandle," c. 400 miles long from its northern boundary with *Georgia to Cape Sable (S.); the Florida Keys have as their southern neighbor *Cuba, ninety miles away. The panhandle is c. 475 miles wide, the peninsula c. 125 miles.

Florida was named by the discoverer, *Ponce de Léon, who arrived at the Easter season in 1513 and called the land *Pascua florida* in honor of the season. Saint Augustine, established in 1565, is the oldest city of the *United States. The *British controlled Florida from 1763 to 1783; it was peopled by many *Tories fleeing the mainland before it was returned to *Spanish control in 1783. Florida was purchased by the United States in 1821. The *Seminole Wars (1818, 1835-42) forced removeal of the Indians to Oklahoma, but some took refuge in Florida's Everglades, the site of modern Reservations.
See also "Gulf Stream"; "Pensacola."
M. 28; R. 20; R. 21; R. 61; W. 15; W. 64; P. 22:1

FLOWERY KINGDOM
See "Hang-Ho."
C.M. 2

FLUKES
The whale's horizontal tail, which is visible as it descends into the sea.
M.D. Passim

FLYING DUTCHMAN
This legendary ill omen is a ghostly ship seen in stormy weather off the Cape of *Good Hope. It lures other ships to destruction. The legend is of a *Dutch captain who tried to round Cape Horn in a storm, persisting despite the protests of his passengers and crew. He even defied *God when he appeared on deck, cursing and blaspheming (as "*Ahab" does), until God condemned him to sail the Cape until *Judgement Day.
*Marryat retells the story in *The Phantom Ship*.
0. 26

FLYING FISH, THE
In astronomy, a southern *constellation: Piscis Volans.
M.D. 57

FLYING FORE-TOPSAIL
Flying sails are floating loosely, fluttering, waving, hanging from only one place. To pay one's creditor's with a flying fore-top sail is to give an IOU with no real tie between creditor and debtor.
W. 2

FOBBING
Stealing; pocketing.
M.D. 90

FOLDER
Paper knife.
M.D. 32

FOLGER, MARY
See "Franklin, Benjamin . . . . "
M.D. 24

FOLIO

A printers' term referring to the size of a book, based on the number of leaves made from a standard-sized piece of paper. A folio is made from two leaves per sheet: a large book.
M.D. 32

FONTENOY

A *Belgian village, site of a famous battle in the War of the *Austrian Succession, in which the *French defeated an Anglo-*Hanoverian force. A granite cross marks the area where some 14,000 men were killed.

(M. was in Belgium in December of 1849 but did no sightseeing.)
I.P. 3

FOOT-PADS

Pedestrian highwaymen.
W. 10

FOREIGNERS

Admiral Franklin verifies M.'s claim that an *American man-of-war was staffed largely by foreigners. In W., M. seems to side with the then-popular Nativist position: immigrants were a threat to the American economic, political, and social structure. Yet in M.D., the "*Anarcharsis Clootz deputation" merits no similar diatribe.
W. 90

FORMOSA

The *modern Taiwan is off the coast of southeastern *China, separated by the Formosa Strait. The earliest settlement occurred in the seventh century. In 1590, the *Portuguese arrived, bestowing the European name. By 1624, there were *Dutch and *Spanish fortifications. Taiwan became an independent kingdom in 1662 but was lost to the Manchus in 1683. By M.'s time, the aboriginal population had been completely crowded out by the Chinese.
M.D. 109

FORT

If "Pierre's" biography is modeled after M.'s, the Fort his grandfather defended is Fort *Stanwix.
P. 1:2; P. 19:2

FORTH, FIRTH OF
*Scotland's Forth River flows west from Ben Lomond mountain, emptying into the North Sea at Kincardine. The Firth is a major fishing port. M. probably visited the area in October or November 1856.
I.P. 18: I.P. 19

FORTUNATE ISLES OF THE FREE
Fortunate Islands, an ancient name for the *Canary Islands, came to mean any imaginary distant land such as *Byron's "Islands of the Blest" ("The Isles of Greece," *Don Juan* iii). The Fortunate Isles "of the Free" in *I.P.* are of course, the *United States.
I.P. 25

FORTY-TWO POUNDER
Charles R. Anderson expressed doubt that *United States* carried guns over thirty-two pounds, but Admiral S.R. Franklin remembered forty-two pounder carronades on the spar deck, higher calibre guns not being in use yet.
The "Forty-two-pounder Club" is the kind of "strongman" nickname that messes and other cliques assumed in the *Navy.
W. 15; W. 44

FOURIER
François Marie Charles Fourier (1772-1837), *French socialist, advocated collectivist communities, or *phalanges*, of about 1,600 members, subsisting harmoniously because of common economic goals, variety of occupation, and sexual freedom. Fourierism had temporary popularity in mid-nineteenth century America, notably at Brook Farm and in colonies in New Jersey, *Wisconsin, and *Texas. But the teachings of an increasingly eccentric Fourier made it difficult for *Utopists to remain associated. His six or more volumes of writings center on his claim that he alone comprehended *God's plan for the universe.
In 1859, a *New York newspaper playfully suggested that M. had been approached by a Fourier disciple about emigration of a party to the *Marquesas.
C.M. 7

FOUR-IN-HAND; FOUR-IN-HAND WHIP

M.'s use of the term is rather obtuse. "Hand," proceded by a numeral, denotes a number of horses driven by one person. To drive the hours "four-in-hand" is to make them go faster, as happens when one drives a carriage pulled by four horses, as opposed to one or two. A "four-in-hand whip is a whip for a four-horse wagon.
W. 42; P. 16:1

FOURTEENTH-STREET

By the time of M.'s writing of *R*., *New York City's Fourteenth Street had passed from a lightly developed and undesirable area to a demarcation point in the continuing press of fashionable life uptown. The implication in *R*. 30 is that Fourteenth Street would also lose its cachet in the inexorable drive for the new which was concomitant with the rise of fortunes in business. Opening in 1854 of the Academy of Business (replacing the by-now shabby *Castle Garden) confirmed Fourteenth Street's chic. (M. would probably be unsurprised to learn that his prediction came true in the twentieth century, when Fourteenth Street had lost its preeeminence, only to have the process begin all over again with the late-twentieth century gentrification of downtown areas of the island.)
R. 30

FOURTH OF JULY; JULY'S IMMORTAL FOURTH

Independence Day in the *United States commemorates the adoption of the *Declaration of Independence, July 4, 1776. The holiday was first celebrated in *Philadelphia in 1777, with adjournment of *Congress, a ceremonial dinner, bonfires, bell-ringing, and fireworks. By M.'s time, it had become the nation's most important secular holiday, marked by picnics, parades, speeches, and military displays. July 4 became the appropriate starting date for important occasions: the *Erie Canal (1817) and the first American railroad (Baltimore and Ohio, 1828), as well as cornerstone-laying of the *Washington monument (1850), and private commencements such as Henry David Throeau's at Walden, 1845 (although Thoreau proclaimed the timing but an accident).
W. 23; W. 39; M.D. 32; M.D. 83; M.D. 93 and elsewhere

FOXES

An Algonkian Indian tribe of Iowa and Oklahoma. They call themselves "Mesquakie" ("Red-earth people").
W. 64

FOY

The British twenty-gun ship *Foy* is mentioned in *"Israel Potter's Autobiographical Story" as having captured Israel and others at *Boston and transferred the *Americans to *Tartar* for shipment to *England, December 1775.
I.P. 3

FRANCE; FRENCH; FRENCHMAN; FRENCHWOMAN

A review of M.'s allusions to France reveals a distinct Francophobia. Although it is not within the province of this work to examine that phobia, it should be pointed out that M. was of French descent on his father's side and that Allan Melvill (see "Walter Redburn") was an importer of French goods, a collector of French artifacts, and a fluent speaker of French, as M. was *not*. The reader is invited to ponder the problem, especially given M.'s evident distaste for the *Dutch, the *Scots, and the *Irish, with whom his genes were also probably mixed.

M.'s complaints in fiction about the French are of several kinds and are the more difficult to explain given the quality of his visit to France, as revealed in his journal (27 November-7 December 1849), and given his admiration for French philosophers and artists. In general, he seems to have thought the French effete and mean-spirited, perhaps following the *British view: thus the derogatory reference in *W*. 39 to navy officers "scraping and bowing, as if they had just graduated at a French dancing-school," and in *P*. 2:2 to the "heathen" *Salique law which denies French females the right to rule. The first chapter of *R*. perhaps encapsulates M.'s resentment of French "cultivation" as represented by his own father.

Throughout the works are references to the poor quality of French mariners: despite their prowess as shipbuilders, they win few sea battles (*O*. 29); yet they are imperialistic invaders througout *T*. and *O*. (Anderson's *Melville in the South Seas* gives an overview of Rear-Admiral *Dupetit-Thouars and the seizing of *Tahiti and the *Marquesas in 1842.) Frenchwomen are dangerous seductresses, like "Isabel," in *P*.; French men are fugitive politicians like the "*Apostles" of *P*. 19:1, or they are liable to melancholy, like "*Charlemont," in *C.M.* 34. *Bourbon and *Valois rulers of France come in for much criticism, as does *Napoléon Bonaparte.

The "King of France" (*I.P.* 10) who in 1777 bought the large frigate *Indien* built in *Amsterdam to be commanded by *John Paul Jones was the Bourbon Louis XVI. The ship had to be sold to prevent British seizure, although M.'s petulant Jones does not admit that.

The "French rolls" of *P.* 1:6 are *petits pains.*

See also "Bordeaux"; "Brest"; "Burgundy"; "Champagne"; "Cogniac"; "Havre"; "Marseilles"; "Norman . . ."; "Paris"; "Passy"; "Rhenish"; "Rhine"; "Seine"; "Versailles."
Passim

FRANCESCA, -'S

In Canto Five of *Dante's *Inferno*, Francesca, daughter of Guido da Polenta, Lord of Ravenna, was the wife of the deformed Giovanni Malatesta of Rimini. She fell in love with *Paolo while reading about *Launcelot and Guinevere, was killed with her lover by her husband, and is now confined in the Second Circle of Hell forever flying with Paolo before the wind.
P. 2:7

FRANCIS GOODMAN; FRANK GOODMAN

"Goodman" means a husband or master, as in *Matthew 24:43. It became the *Puritan title of address but has various slang meanings: the devil; a thief, or *Don Juan.

As Bruce Franklin's notes point out, "Francis" is only one of many surreptitious references to *France and the French, in *C.M.* But perhaps "Frank" is also used ironically, as a synonym for "honest." ("Goodman" is a fictitious character.)
C.M. 29; C.M. 43

FRANKFURT

The reference in *M.D.* 34 is to Frankfurt am Main (not Frankfurt), Hesse, *Germany, a port on the canalized Main River, 100 miles southeast of *Cologne (50°6' N., 8°40' E.). The city is an important center: the birthplace of *Goethe; ancestral home of the *Rothschilds; site of *Holy Roman Emperor elections from 1356 (at the thirteenth-century *Gothic Church of *St. Bartholomew).

Frankfurt am Main had been a *Roman settlement captured by the *Franks c. A.D. 500. It was the site of *Charlemagne's residence, one-time capital of the East-Frankish Empire, and locus of important trade fairs starting in the thirteenth century. It was the site of the Diet of the German Confederacy from 1816 to 1866, thus at the time of M.'s visit in 1857. His journal records visits to "Goethe's statue" (actually *Faust's, recently set up in the Ross Market), *Luther's preaching place" (actually Luther's residence), and the Rothschilds' home (22-23 April).

The reference in *M.D.* 34 is to Goethe's posing as a waiter at the Palatine buffet honoring the coronation of Joseph II in 1764 (*Truth and Poetry: From My Own Life*, Sealts #228).
M.D. 34

FRANKLIN, BENJAMIN; DR. FRANKLIN; THE DOCTOR
The most famous *American Enlightenment sage, Benjamin Franklin (1706-90) was born in *Boston into a hardy family. His maternal grandfather, Peter Folger (1617-90) had migrated from *England in 1645, settling in *Nantucket in 1664. He was (according to Labaree), a "weaver, schoolmaster, miller, public official," and author of an appeal for religious freedom, *A Looking-Glass for the Times* (1676). Benjamin's grandmother, Mary Morrel (Morrill, or Morriel), mentioned in *M.D.* 24, was an indentured servant when she married Folger; she died in Nantucket in 1704. (Among later prominent Folgers was whaling Captain Mayhew Folger, who found the *Bounty* mutineers on *Pitcairn's Island, in February of 1808.) Benjamin's father Josiah Franklin (1657-1745; Franklin's *Autobiography* makes it 1655-1744), a tallow chandler in *Boston, had seventeen children by two wives; the second, Abiah Folger (1667-1752), was Benjamin's mother.

The *Autobiography* (American edition 1818) provides details about the Horatio-Alger-style rise of the poor young Boston apprentice to his role as world-renouned *savant*, and M.'s references make clear that he not only read Franklin's works but perceived the full implications of his personality: a "tanned *Machiavelli in tents," "everything but a poet," in *I.P.* 8. Franklin was at once a generous homely wit and an archetypal shrewd cynic, in the apothegms of *Poor Richard's Almanac* (1733-58), as noted in *I.P.* 7. "The Way to Wealth" (*I.P.* 9) is the 1758 Preface to *Poor Richard Improved*, for which Franklin probably wrote only the Preface.

Franklin the scholar founded numerous *Philadelphia-based organizations, including the forerunner of the University of *Pennsylvania; Franklin the scientist experimented with the control of electricity; Franklin the inventor produced the flexible catheter, the Franklin Stove, and the lightning rod (*M.* 28). He often eschewed personal profit-taking from such pursuits (despite what is suggested in his writings and those of M.). Franklin the statesman became America's most effective spokesman in Europe,

especially in *Paris, as we see throughout *I.P.* Having
secured an important treaty with France in 1778, he was
appointed plenipotentiary to the French court, where he
furthered his nation's interests and became a local pet by
virtue of his liberality and sly humor. At the time of her
death, his wife, Deborah Read Rogers Franklin (1708-1774)
had not seen him in ten years and had lived in relative
poverty during that time.

Franklin appears in M.'s source, *Israel Potter's autobiographical story, but Potter's contact is brief, general, and
all-approving, so the coloration of him in *I.P.* is M.'s, as
Devil's Advocate against a secular saint.

M. saw a letter of Franklin's in the Paris Bibliotheque
Royale, 4 December 1849.

M. 28; W. 7; M.D. 24; I.P. 6; I.P. 7; I.P. 8; I.P. 9; I.P. 10;
I.P. 11; I.P. 12

FRANKLINS

In the *Middle Ages, non-noble middle-class freeholders.
W. 87

FRANKLIN-SQUARE

I have been unable to trace this reference to a *New
York City site. Franklin Square may have been on the tiny
triangle at the convergence of Franklin and *Varick Street
with *West Broadway: the present-day Finn Square.

The printing facility of Harper's publishers fronted on
Franklin Square.
R. 7

FRANKLIN-WARRANTED

*Benjamin Franklin's *Autobiography* (Part II) offers a
"Scheme of Employment for the Twenty-four Hours of a natural Day," alloting the hour of 12 noon to 1 P.M. to "Read, or
overlook my Accounts, and dine."
W. 7

"FREE AMERIKY"

Perhaps a covert reference to the anti-*slavery Free Soil
Party.
C.M. 19

"FREE COMPANIONS"

After the *Crusades, roving companies of free-lance knights wandered about selling their services. In *Italy they were called Condottieri. In 14th century *France, "free companies" roamed about, terrorizing the people.
W. 90

FREEMASON; FREEMASONS

Curiosity about and distrust of Masons is characteristic of the *American nineteenth century. Overt anti-masonism came to the fore on 6 December 1833, when the *New England Palladium and Advertiser* informed its *Boston and *Salem readership that masonic organizations constituted a secret menace to government. Ray Allen Billington's *The Protestant Crusade: 1800-1860: A Study of the Origins of American Nativism* gives a full account of the development of the Anti-Masonic Party and its contribution to antiforeign Nativism. Probably Masonry frightened the common man because its secrecy resembled that of the hierarchies of governments, courts, and businesses.

In an April 16 (?) 1851 letter to *Hawthorne (*Letters*, p. 125). M. was still whistling in the dark about the subject: "We incline to think that the Problem of the Universe is like the Freemason's mighty secret, so terrible to all children. It turns out, at last, to consist in a triangle, a mallet, and an apron—nothing more!"

"Free-mason" as an adjective has several meanings, all of them connected with secrecy or covert action. It may be equated with "Freeman," meaning to cuckold. In *English public schools of the time, upper classmen spit on a new boy's penis, "freemaning" him.

The Anti-Masonic Party held the first political convention (as opposed to caucus selection) in American history, in 1831.

See also "Foreigners."
T. 24; W. 69; M.D. 86

"FREE STATES"

See "Slave . . . . "
R. 41

FRENCH IMPORTER

See "Walter Redburn."
R. 9; R. 61

FRENCH LEAVE

Taking French leave is leaving without permission or slipping away unnoticed and announced from a social event.

Many objectionable practices have been labeled "French" (or "*Dutch") but the equivalent is "S'en aller à l'anglaise," depart like the *English.

R. 44

FRIAR TUCKS

Steward and Chaplain to the legendary "Robin Hood," "Friar Tuck" is a Falstaffian, combative, self-indulgent "monk" clothed in a red Franciscan habit.

"Robin's" band has been legendary since about the Twelfth Century; the Friar is a late addition to the group of outlaws who rob the rich, help the poor, and honor women.

0. 37

FRIESLAND

The ancient Frisia, Friesland is a very lowlying northern province of the *Netherlands which passed to stadholder Prince William IV of Orange in 1748. Frisians have their own language and literature. The only large town is the capital, Leewarden: a port in M.'s time. (The modern port is Harlingen, with facilities built in the 1870's.) As suggested in *M.D.* 101, the processing of cattle is a major focus. There was serious flooding throughout Friesland in 1825.

(An imaginary country called Friesland appears on some sixteenth century maps, between *Iceland and *Greenland. This caused some confusion for explorers until the nineteenth century.)

M.D. 55; M.D. 101

FROBISHER, SIR MARTIN

The English navigator/explorer Sir Martin Frobisher (c. 1539-1594) went to sea at the age of fourteen and was privateering by the 1560's. In Queen *Elizabeth's service in the 1570's, he sighted the coast of *Labrador, while searching for a *northwest passage. A second expedition in 1577, inspired by the possibility of gold mining, further explored the area, and a third in 1578 reached the south of *Greenland.

In 1585, Frobisher was *Drake's vice-admiral on a *West Indies expedition. He later visited the *Azores area; he died in battle against the *Spanish at *Brest.

His exploits are recorded in *Hakluyt's *Principal Navigations* and in *The Three Voyages of Martin Frobisher* (1867).

M.'s sobriquet, "*Black Letter," may have some connection with the "black earth" thought to be gold ore, which Frobisher brought back from his first voyage in the Queen's service.
M.D. 32

FROISSART
Jean Froissart (c. 1337-c. 1404), the greatest *French fourteenth-century author, rose from a bourgeois background to the company of high royalty. He traveled extensively with various patrons, including *Edward III and the *Black Prince, and as an ordained priest became personal counselor to others. His most imporant work, *Chroniques*, was designed to commemorate the courtly tradition as much as to record history. He also produced didactic pieces, romantic love poems, and an important romance, *Meliador*, about an imaginary golden age of courtly and brave knights. *Chroniques* was translated into *English by John Bourchier in the sixteenth century.
M. ordered "Froissarts Ballads" from publisher John Wiley, 2 December 1847.
M. 24; R. 1; M.D. 42

FRY, MRS.
Elizabeth Gurney Fry (1780-1845), of *Quaker descent, made early visits to *Newgate Prison, where her observations led to her life's work in prison reform, in her native *England and other European countries.
C.M. 19

FULLER; FULLER'S "GOOD SEA CAPTAIN"
Thomas Fuller (1608-1661) was a witty scholar and preacher who loved word play. His most imporant works are *The Holy War* (1639), *The History of the Worthies of England* (1662), and *The Holy (and Profane) State* (1642), which M. acquired in 1841 (Sealts #221) and from which he drew the dedicatory sentence for *W.* and a paradoxical "extract" for *M.D.*
A sample from "The Good Sea Captain"; "The sea is the stable of horse-fishes, the stall of kine-fishes, the stye of hog-fishes, the kennel of dog fishes, and in all things the sea the ape of the land."
See also "Extracts 25."
W. Dedication; W. 90; M.D. Extracts 25

FULL FIG

Full dress: from the *Italian *in fiocchi* (in festive costume). Partridge ties the expression to the priapistic "fig," referring to the *pudendum muliebre*, linking with the contemptuous gesture made by thrusting the thumb forth from between the first two fingers.

Although such connotations may seem tenuous, allusions to *Jack Chase throughout W. suggest sexual or phallic meaning, not the least representative Chase's stage-name, "Percy Royal-Mast." Only one early reviewer noted W.'s double entendres: "A vein of sly humor percolates through the book; and a sort of unctuous toying with verbal double meanings" (Attributed to Frederick S. Cozzens in *The Knickerbocker*, Vol. 35, May 1850, by Hershel Parker, in *The Recognition of Herman Melville*).
R. 24; W. 23

FULTON MARKET

See "Fulton Street."
R. 18; R. 41; W. 41

FULTON-STREET

*Manhattan's Fulton Street, which now runs from the *East River as far west as Church Street (where it meets the World Trade Center), had gone through several incarnations before M.'s time. Originally a short stretch called "Old Ferry Road," it became "Fair Street" (with a name change to "Partition Street," where it meets *Broadway), as late as an 1803 Plan of the City. I have not been able to determine the date of the next name change, but a street guide of 1850 calls it "Fulton Street," running clear across the island.

Fulton Street's greatest claim to fame remains the Fulton Market (R. 18; R. 41; W. 41) on the north side of the street between *South and Front Streets (present-day South Street Seaport area). Built in 1821, it has been replaced several times since and is now an example of latter-day "gentrification" of many areas mentioned by M. In his day, the Market sold many items in addition to fish. (Fourteen wholesale firms running 111 ships sold up to two million dollars' worth of salt- and fresh-water-fish per year.) There were stands that sold beer, watermelon, and oysters (as large as nine or ten inches in diameter in those days), as well as the "sailor books" of R. 18.

The Patent Office was located at 128 Fulton in the 1850's; Duncan Phyfe's furniture warehouse/store/workshop was on Fulton west of Broadway, as was *St. Paul's. (From

1866 to 1868, a footbridge crossed Broadway on Fulton, but it was removed at the request of local merchants, leaving pedestrians once again at the mercy of heavy traffic.)
R. 61

FURLONGS
One furlong is 220 yards.
M.D. 59

FURY
The Furies (Lat. *Furiae*) were the *Greek *Erinyes*.
*Hesiod says they were daughters of Gaea (Earth), sprung from the blood of Uranus; others call them daughters of Night or Earth and darkness. The three are: Tisiphone (avenger of blood); Alecto (the implacable); Magaera (the jealous one), goddesses of vengeance whose punishments continued after death. *Virgil places them in the underworld, where they punish evildoers. The Greeks placed them on earth, with writhing snakes for hair, and eyes that wept blood. They could not be banished from Earth, as other monstrous creatures were.
M. 13; M. 33; W. 91

FUST, JOHANN
A goldsmith and burgher of Mainz, *Germany, Fust (c. 1400-1466) founded the first commercially successful printing firm. He financially backed Gutenberg until he foreclosed on Gutenberg's debt, winning rights to the press Gutenberg had invented. The firm of Fust and Schoeffer published a 1457 *Latin psalter, seven other major works, and numerous minor ones.
C.M. 30

G

GABRIEL
The *archangel Gabriel's *Bible role is a confused one. The name is from *Hebrew words for "man" or "strong," plus the word for "*God," so that it may mean "Man of God," or "God has shown himself mighty."

In *Genesis 37:15, Gabriel leads *Joseph to his brothers; in *Deuteronomy 34:6, he helps bury *Moses. In *apocalyptic books, he is a man revealing what the *Day of Judgement will be (*Daniel 8:16) or, throughout the Book of *Enoch, one of four archangels at the left hand of God in heaven: the primary intercessor for man, who casts the wicked into the furnace. In I *Chronicles 32:21, he destroys the armies of Sennacherib.

In the *New Testament, he announces the birth of *John the Baptist (*Luke 1:11-20) and the birth of a son to *Mary (26-38): thus his "messenger" role.

Further confusion arises from his grouping with *Michael and *Raphael in secular literature, especially in *Dante's *Paradise*, *Paradise Lost*, and *Faust*. Of the three archangels, only Gabriel is important in the Bible, which does not often mention angels by name; there are presumed allusions to him in *Revelation

Tradition makes him the trumpet-blower on Judgement Day. M. seems to see him as all-obedient believer (in *M.*, *M.D.* Extracts and *M.D.* 1), or as prophet of doom (*M.D.* 71).
M. 60; M. 97; M. 168; M.D. Extracts; M.D. 1; M.D. 71

GAINSBOROUGH
Thomas Gainsborough (1727-88), *British portrait and landscape painter, trained in *London in the Rococo style of Watteau and in seventeenth-century *Dutch landscape style. Despite his professed preference for landscapes, Gainsborough earned a confortable living from 1748 to 1759 painting portraits that endow his subjects with all the social graces (as in *Mr. and Mrs. Andrews* [1748]). His work is also remarkable for the texture of the paint, as shown in *The Blue Boy* (1770).

Gainsborough was not attracted to historical or literary subjects, so his work is often seen as lacking in intellectual value and bearing an excess of "charm." M. clearly recognized these flaws, as seen in his sardonic reference in *P.* to the "povertiresque"; Gainsborough made run-down shanties with damaged thatch roofs seem appealingly romantic.

Sealts #87 is George Moss Brock-Arnold's *Gainsborough and Constable* (1881).
P. 20:1

GALAPAGOS
See "Gallipagoes."

GALILEO

Galileo Galilei (1564-1642), *Italian mathematician, astronomer, and physicist, was a *Florentine whose discoveries contributed greatly to modern science. He began his studies in physics by observing a swinging lamp (such as those in *M.D.* 44 and *C.M.* 45), suggesting the principle of the pendulum for clock regulation. Dropping weights from the leaning tower of *Pisa, he supposedly demonstrated that unequal weights drop with equal velocity.

Galileo was the first to study the skies by telescope, first to combine mathematical analysis with experimentation, and, countering *Aristotle's teachings, the founder of the modern experimental method. Forced by the Inquisition (see "Spanish Inquisition") in 1633 to repudiate *Copernicus's theory, he is said afterward to have muttered a denial that condemned him to house arrest for the rest of his life.
I.P. 18

GALL

Franz Joseph Gall (1758-1828), *German anatomist and physiologist, was the founder of *phrenology. His popular lectures in *Vienna were eventually interdicted by the government, and after 1805 he practiced, lectured, and wrote in *Paris.
M. 158; M.D. 79

GALLEY

Early long ship of the *English and the *Vikings, known from before the fifth century B.C. Length was about four times breadth, and the number of rowers greatly exceeded the number of warriors: archers, javelin throwers, etc. It was also used to ram and sink other ships.
Passim

GALLIA; GAUL

Gaul (Lat. *Gallia*) is the ancient designation for the area south and west of the *Rhine, west of the *Alps, and north of the Pyrenees—roughly equivalent to modern *France. The *Romans eventually included in the term *Italy from Lucca and Rimini northwards, excluding Liguria. Invading *Celts were called Gauls by the Romans, but the area was inhabited as well by Franks, *Germans, *Burgundians. "Gaul" has come to signify France or the French, as M. does in *O.* 29.

Cisalpine Gaul was the Italian portion "on this side of the Alps" (south and east, as opposed to Transalpine Gaul to

the north and northwest) and was divided into Cispadane Gaul ("on this side of the Po") and Transpadane Gaul, the southern part of which was called *Provincia* (hence the modern Provence). *Julius Caesar conquered Gaul in the Gallic Wars (58 B.C.-51 B.C.). Ethnic divisions were characterized by Caesar as Aquitania (south of the Garonne), Gaul proper (modern central France), and Belgica (roughly, modern *Belgium).
T. 1 (Gaul); O. 29 (Gaul); R. 30 (Gallia); W. 64 (Gaul); C.M. 26 (Gaul)

GALLIPAGOES
        Ecuador's Galápagos (Archipiélago de Colón), M.'s "Encantadas," near the "Off-Shore" whaling ground of *M.D.*, are fourteen main volcanic islands and numerous smaller ones, on the *Equator near 90° W. They cover an area of approximately 23,000 square miles, 3,075 square miles of it in land. Largest of the group is Albemarle (Island Isabela). Bishop of *Panama Tomás de Berlanga discovered and named them Las Encantadas ("the bewitched") in 1535, but they were occupied before the many sixteenth century *Spanish arrivals. An important *pirate hideout in the seventeenth century, they were afterwards a center for whaling and sealing. Colonization began on Charles Island in 1832, with resources of coffee, fish, and sulfur.
        As M. notes in "The Encantadas" (borrowing from *Darwin, *Porter, and *Colnett), the curious flora and fauna are the islands' chief interest, especially the birds, lizards and tortoises ("galapago" is the old Spanish word for "tortoise."); after several species had been hunted to extinction, part of the area was made a wildlife sanctuary.
        See also "Isle of Albemarle."
T. 2; T. 29; M. 1; M. 3; M.D. 54; M.D. 127; I.P. 24

GALLOW
        See "*gally* or *gallow*."
M.D. 87

GALLY OR *GALLOW*
        O.E.D.: *gally* or *gallow* is from Old English *gaelwan*, "to alarm": in use as late as the end of the nineteenth century, especially in whaling.
        M. would have seen the words in some of his favorite authors:

*Shakespeare, *King Lear* (1605), III, ii, 44: "The wrathful skies Gallow the very wanderers of the darke And make them keep their Causes."
*Sir Thomas Browne, *Works* (1708) III: people look as though they were "gallied."
*Marryat, *Poor Jack* (1840), vi: bull whales are "easily 'gallied', that is, frightened."
"Gally" is also used by *Cheever.
(The politically aggressive "note" appeared only in the English first edition.)
M.D. 87

GAMA
Vasco Da Gama (c. 1460-1524), *Portuguese navigator, was first to double the Cape of *Good Hope, and the discoverer of a sea route to *India, completing the work of Bartolomew Dias (*Diaz). His exploits are celebrated in the *Lusiads* of *Camöens.
When Portugal's desire to occupy Indian lands conflicted with *Arab monopolies, Da Gama and others conquered them (c. 1500) to found Portugal's hegemony in India.
W. 50; W. 65

GAMBOGE
A reddish-yellow pigment derived from resin from a tree in Cambodia, for which "gamboge" is a corruption.
O. 28; M.D. 73

GAMMON
Gammon may mean "nonsense," or "pretense," or "cheat," or it may refer to a thief's accomplice, in underworld parlance.
W. 65; C.M. 15

GANGES, THE
The sacred river of the *Hindus in northern *India and parts of modern Pakistan, the Ganges (*Ganga*) is formed in the *Himalayas. It bifurcates into the Padma and Bhagirathi rivers (the lower course of the latter becoming the Hooghly River), flowing into the Bay of *Bengal through the vast (220 miles wide) Ganges Delta. The sacred cities of Allahabad and Varanasi are situated on its shores.
M. 136; M.D. 40

GANSEVOORT

The town of Gansevoort, *New York, is located in *Saratoga County, c. ten miles northeast of Saratoga Springs and c. seventeen miles south of *Lake George. Its history is closely tied to that of M.'s maternal ancestors, the Gansevoorts, who were, successively, prototypical energetic immigrants eager to rise in the world, prototypical wealthy *Dutch patroons, prototypical politicians, and prototypical "failures," whose name died out except in New York monuments. The first American "Gansevoorts" arrived c. 1660; they were (*French- and *Dutch-speaking) *Lutheran plebian soldiers and farmers from *Westphalia. They struggled against the *Mohawk Indians, along with the *Van Rensselaers, Ten Eycks, and Douws, with whom they were in competition. Their European values traveled with them, and for over a century the area from Albany southward to *New York City was somewhat like a chunk of the old country implanted along the *Hudson River. Those who became patroons were family- and community-oriented; they spoke Dutch at home and English in business; they joined the Dutch Reformed Church and were public models of "*Christian" success (both morally and financially); they intermarried "sensibly" to unite fortunes but were publically faithful and loving to their spouses; they produced multitudes of children (mostly females, in the case of the Gansevoorts); they were shrewd business men practicing *noblesse oblige* for the good of the community while working assiduously at such mercantile pursuits as brewing, farming, and accumulation of real estate; they formally educated their male children to become doctors and lawyers and their female children to become scrupulous housekeepers, excellent cooks and hostesses, *and* sensible business counselors to their husbands.

By the mid 1700's, the Gansevoorts had become full-fledged patricians of the type portrayed in *James Fenimore Cooper's *Home as Found*, and *Satanstoe*. M.'s great-grandfather, Peter Gansevoort (1749-1812), was the *Revolutionary War hero of Fort *Stanwix; he retired from the military (which paid poorly) as Brigadier-General, establishing a sawmill business and rising in local government. His brother (M.'s great-uncle) Leonard (1751-1810) was the living embodiment of "trade plus public service"; he served in the *Continental Congress (1788, as a *Federalist), but made some enemies (who probably set his house on fire in 1793). Leonard had daughters who married well, but the Gansevoort name was lost for that branch.

Peter's children included M.'s mother, Maria Gansevoort (1791-1872). Three of his sons were highly successful, at a time when the family fortunes were reaching a peak. One son, Wessel (1781-1863) was perhaps mentally unstable: an alcoholic black sheep whose actions brought the family to court several times. (There are examples of mental or character instability on both sides of M.'s lineage.) Leonard H. (1783-1821) was a judge and State Senator (1799-1803). Herman (1779-1862; see below), for whom M. was named and to whom *O.* is dedicated, became a wealthy lumberman, building a mansion for his family although childless himself, and holding local public offices. Peter (1789-1876) was a founder of the New York State Bank, and military agent for the Northern District (supplying army posts in what was still essentially wilderness in the early 1800's). He rose to Brigadier General of the Army, at one time in command of one-third of the entire U.S. Army (in an area extending from *New England to the *Great Lakes and from the *St. Lawrence Valley to *Pennsylvania). The only one of his generation with a formal education (Williams and Princeton), he was a lawyer who became Secretary to Governor De-Witt Clinton and then Judge Advocate General of New York State.

The Gansevoort family was at its zenith when overconfidence in the economy and changes in American politics began working against them. Peter was removed from his secretaryship for political reasons (like "Bartleby" and his employer, in M.'s short story, "Bartleby the Scrivener"). He became a Van Buren *Democrat, uneasily assenting to the "machine" politics that put party ahead of community. Despite the fact that *New England "*Yankees" and the *Irish were taking New York politics out of the hands of the Dutch, he rose to service in the Assembly and Senate. But Peter found himself rather the patriarch at a time when his elder brother Herman's fortunes were suffering from overextension. His sister's husband, who had made similar business errors, died suddenly (and rather unaccountably), leaving her destitute with eight young children to support, including the twelve-year-old M. During M.'s youth, Leonard's five children and Maria's eight were an increasing drain on Peter and on the Gansevoort fortune, which was simultaneously suffering the effects of business panics and recessions.

The town of Gansevoort grew up around Herman Gansevoort's house, on the east side of Snock Kill, on the *Hudson. It was originally called "Gansevoort's Mills," and was on the railroad routes to Saratoga and Fort Edward. A triangular green was bounded by the railroad depot, the Empire Hotel, and Herman's mansion. A *Post Office, churches, and other houses soon followed, and prosperity seemed eternal. The mansion was the scene of many local celebrations and of summer visits for M. In nearby Albany, a pet project of Herman and Peter was the $100,000 Stanwix Hall, an elaborate four-storey complex containing business space, a restaurant, public meeting rooms, and a ball room. But the Panic of 1837 stopped development, and Stanwix Hall became a hotel in 1844, another symbol of a fallen dynasty. Herman's need to settle an estate necessitated Peter's selling of many properties, as the gamble of an ever-developing fortune was lost.

The Gansevoorts and their town stand as an example of the vagaries of human life; health problems, poor character, failure to marry or to produce sons, family estrangements, and alcoholism, even in relatively small "doses," all conjoined to bring down an American family, and the town they created reached stasis when the "founding fathers" fell.

(Almost all of the material in this entry is derived from Kenney's *The Gansevoorts of Albany*; the reader is directed to that source for fuller, and therefore fairer, treatment.)
O. Dedication

GANSEVOORT, HERMAN
Herman Gansevoort (1779-1862), of *Gansevoort, N.Y., was eldest son to General Peter Gansevoort (1749-1812) and Catherine Van Schaick (1752-1830), M.'s maternal grandparents. He married Catherine S. Quackenboss (1774-1855), who felt antipathy for his sister, M.'s mother, Maria Gansevoort Melvill (1791-1872). Gansevoort had connections in the Albany branch New York State Bank where his namesake clerked in 1832, and provided some scant support for the widowed Maria and her children, despite his wife's objections and financial problems of his own. Leon Howard (*Herman Melville: A Biography*) feels the O. dedication was an attempt to cheer up Gansevoort, with whom M. appears to have remained friendly despite family awkwardness.
0. Dedication

GARDEN OF EDEN
See "Eden."
0. 18; W. 68

GARNERY
*French engravings of whales by Ambroise-Louis Garneray (1783-1857), South Sea traveler and painter of marine scenes, are rare and valuable. They were reproduced in George F. Dow's *Whale Ships and Whaling* (Salem, 1925).
M.D. 56

GASPAR, STRAITS OF
The modern Kelasa Strait, between Bangka and Belitung islands, Indonesia, east of south *Sumatra. It is forty-five miles wide.
R. 12

GATH: GIANT OF GATH
The braggart of Gath was *Goliath (or Goliah), the giant *Philistine slain by King *David when he threatened Saul the Benjamite (I *Samuel 17). Gath's precise location is unknown. It was one of the five royal Philistine cities, heavily walled, flourishing before 700 B.C.
M. 39; I.P. 15

GAUDENTIO DI LUCCA
Focus of Simon Berington's fictional *Memoirs of Sigr. Gaudentio di Lucca* (1737).
M. 75

GAUL
See "Gallia; Gaul."
T. 1; O. 29; W. 64; C.M. 26

GAYHEAD, --ER
M. glosses in *M.D.* 27: "the most westerly promontory of *Martha's Vineyard." It was still inhabited by the original Indian population at M.'s time. Gayhead was reputedly the first place in *New England to be visited by *Norsemen (1006). Its name derives from the many-colored clays found mixed with the sand.
M.D. 16; M.D. 27; M.D. 28; M.D. 36; M.D. 47

... GEESE SAVED THE CAPITOL
Traditionally, sacred geese saved *Rome from *Gallic invasion in 390 B.C. by cackling warning of an intruder that awakened the Roman garrison. In commemoration, the Romans carried a golden goose in procession to the capitol every year.
In modern *Scotland, whiskey storehouses are sometimes guarded by geese.
R. 20

GEHENNAS
    Places for the ritual sacrifice of children in *Kings II,
23:10. Figuratively, hells.
M. 98; W. 90

GEMINI
    See "Zodiac."
M.D. 99

GENERAL HOWE
    See "Howe; General Howe; Lord Howe."
I.P. 21

GENESEE
    Genesee County, in western *New York State, was
formed in 1802. It became a leading agricultural area, with
farming in dairy and poultry products, as well as fruit, wheat,
potatoes, and hay. Part of the Tonawanda Indian Reservation
is in this county, which M. probably traversed in 1840.
R. 43

GENESEE [RIVER]
    *New York: 42°45' N., 78°10' W.
M. 136

GENESIS
    The fifty-five-chapter Book of Genesis is the first of the
*Bible's five books of *Moses (with *Exodus, *Leviticus,
*Numbers, and *Deuteronomy), who cannot have been the au-
thor of the *Pentateuch. Genesis is named after its first word,
which translates "in the beginning." It relates the primitive
pre-history of *Israel, from the *creation to the dispersion of
mankind at the tower of *Babel: a span thought to represent
about 2,400 years.
    Genesis is more mythological poetry than history. Its
various genres include: semi-historical lists of nations, tribes,
and men: semi-historical folk notes and cult legends within
saga narratives; songs and proverbs; cosmological anthropological myths such as the creation and the *Deluge; legends of
foreign lands, such as *Babylon and *Egypt, and of *Canaan;
fairy tales and novelle.

By M.'s time the historicity of Genesis was much in question, but its interplay of fact and fiction made difficult drawing a line between empirical and symbolic truth.
M.D. Extracts 1; M.D. 50; C.M. 44

GENEVA
An alternative name for the very strong *Holland gin.
M.D. 101

GENIUS OF COMMERCE
In *Roman mythology, genii are men's governing tutelary spirits, controlling their fortunes like the *Christian Guardian Angels. Some versions tell of one genius for good and one for evil in each man, attending us until death. Roman women had *Juno instead of a Genius.
Eastern genii were the Jinn, fallen angels dwelling in Djinnestan, under *Eblis.
The genius loci is the tutelary deity of a place, and M.'s Genius of Commerce is an appropriate spirit for commercial nineteenth-century *Liverpool, in R.
R. 33

GENOA; GENOESE
The capital of Liguria and Genova province of northern *Italy, Genoa is a fortified port at the head of the Gulf of Genoa at the center of the *Italian Riviera, eighty miles south of *Milan. It was the chief port of the Ligurians, and under the *Romans from the third century B.C., invaded by the *Lombards in the eighth century and the *Saracens in the tenth. Genoa became a great maritime republic, in rivalry with *Venice in the fourteenth century. Part of the Ligurian Republic, it was annexed to *Napoléon's French Empire in 1805 and by 1815 was in the kingdom of Sardinia.
M. visited Genoa (11-15? April 1857), commenting at length in his journal on the many tourist attractions, as well as on the forts which seemed to "make Genoa rather the capital and fortified camp of *Satan: fortified against the *Archangels" (12 April).
W. 50; P. 2:1; P. 12:1

GENTILE
In the *Old Testament, the word is related to "heathen"; in the *New, it refers to non-*Hebrew nations. "Gentiles" is synonymous with "peoples" in the Old Testament and syn-

onymous with "nations" in the New. By M.'s time it commonly
referred to non-Jewish people, but the reference in *M*. 3 to Gentiles' joining hands with *Christians and Jews suggests that
M. does not use the word thus.
M. 3; W. 84

GEORGE'S [DOCK]
        *Liverpool: originally, three acres of water area; opened
1771, center for the *West India trade, ferry boats, and packet
ships.
R. 32

GEORGE III; GEORGE THE THIRD; KING GEORGE
        George III (1738-1820), king of *Britain from 1760 to 1820,
is most remembered as the addressee of *Jefferson's complaints in the *Declaration of Independence—the loser of the
first British Empire. The son of Frederick Louis, *Prince of
Wales, and Princess Augusta of Saxe-Gotha, and grandson of
*George II, George was a slow-learning child, heir to the
throne from his twelfth year. He married out of duty in 1761
(Charlotte Sophia of Mecklenburg-Strelitz), but was closer emotionally to his first mentor, John Stuart, Earl of Bute. Through
Bute's influence, George (in effect) dismissed William Pitt (the
Elder) and others, and was forced to deal with less able and
even corrupt politicians, permanently damaging Britain's internal political stability. Because the Indian trade brought little revenue, George agreed to have American colonists further
taxed, passing the Stamp Act (1765), Townshend duties, and
other tariffs, only to repeal them rapidly. The remaining tax
on tea, of course, led to the *Boston Tea Party. Under the later
guidance of Lord North, George became slightly more
malleable and less imperious, but North's insistence on coerc-
ing the American Colonies led to George's prolonging the war
and to his eventually being blamed for it, by Americans and
Britons, as well. North's fall in the early 1780's, after charges
of corruption, left George so powerless as to consider abdication. But the emergence of William Pitt (the Younger) calmed
matters by transferring much power to Pitt.
        George's seeming insanity began to evince itself as early
as 1765, and conflict with his sons seems to have triggered a
period of madness from 1788-89. George then concerned himself with minor matters rather than actual leadership of the
nation, until disagreement with Pitt over *Irish emancipation
(1801). Pitt yielded, but after his death in 1806, a second crisis
in the *Catholic issue led to *Whig defeat. George's physical
decline, exacerbated by the death in 1810 of his youngest and

closest child, Princess Amelia, coincided with the onset of insanity which lasted until his death.

During his long reign, Britain's population doubled and changed from the stability of bucolic squiredoms to the unrest of an industrial nation discontented with the Constitution. M.'s complaint in *P*. about George's appointment of peers is historical; George became notorious for making appointments and then undermining them, causing constant traffic in government officials. Historians now generally see George as a well-intentioned man of limited mentality, responsible not only for the American war, but for the beginning of party politics as we know it—all but divorced from statesmanship, focussed on power struggles, and seemingly privileging expediency over ethics.

In *R*. 41, M. mistakenly refers to a *Liverpool equestrian statue in *St. George's Square as a likeness of George IV; it is of George III.

(See also "Hanover.")
O. 80; R. 32; P. 1:3; I.P. 5; I.P. 13; I.P. 14; I.P. 25

GEORGE THE FOURTH, KING OF ENGLAND

*Britain's George IV (1762-1830), eldest son of *George III, reigned as regent from 1811, when his father was declared insane, and as king from 1820 to 1830. It is difficult to find any positive comment about him other than his cleverness in art and literature and his dislike of violence. He was a self-indulgent, dissipated, extravagant, and inefficient ruler, influenced by unfit advisors rather than appropriate ministers. He had much power, and the only real good that came from his reign was the backlash that followed it. He is remembered for his many amours, an illegal marriage, and illegitimate children. He was succeeded by his brother, William IV.

M. himself undoubtedly saw the equestrian statue of George III—not IV—at *Liverpool, at the base of which a young *Chartist holds forth in *R*. 41.
R. 41; O. 68

GEORGE THE SECOND, KING OF ENGLAND

*England's George II (1683-1760) reigned from 1727-1760. The son of George I and Sophia Dorothea of Celle, George never pleased his father, who created the title "guardian of the realm" so as to avoid conferring on him the regency. Constant personal misunderstandings with his family caused some rash actions when he did accede to the throne. His major interest was in military matters, particularly discipline, which helps explain British success in the *American colonies.

His low intellect led to his yielding more and more authority to his ministers, strengthening such positions permanently. During his reign, such men as Robert Walpole, Lord Carteret, and William Pitt achieved great power.

He was succeeded by his grandson, *George III.
W. 71

GEORGIA

One of the thirteen original states of the Union, Georgia is 320 miles long (N.-S.) and 254 miles wide (E.-W.). It was crossed by Hernando DeSoto in 1540. The *English founded *Savannah in 1733, and the battle of Bloody Marsh in 1742 ended rivalry with *Spain. The present boundaries were finally established in 1802; the Creek and Cherokee Indians were moved out in the 1830's.

Georgia was a *slave state; it was devastated by Sherman's march in 1865.
C.M. 21

GERMAIN, BERNARD

See "Lacépède."
M.D. 55

GERMAN COMMENTATOR

See "Coleridge."
W. 3

GERMAN CONCEIT

The "German conceit" advanced in *M.D.* regarding the vertebrae as "undeveloped skulls" was first proposed by Lorenz Oken (1779-1851).
M.D. 80

GERMAN DOCTOR

See "Preissnitz."
C.M. 16

GERMAN EMPERORS

German emperors with "golden seals" on their "decrees" were *Holy Roman Emperors.
M.D. 79

GERMANICUS

Son of Nero Claudius Drusus and Antonia, niece of the *Roman Emperor *Augustus, Germanicus Caesar (15 B.C.- A.D. 19) was adopted by his uncle, the Emperor *Tiberius. In military action and in consulship, he became famous for prudence, morality, and acumen.   After incurring the displeasure of Tiberius by unsanctioned entry into *Egypt, he died at Antioch, probably poisoned by Gnaeus Calpurnius Piso, Tiberius's governor of Syria, who was envious and violent of temper. Piso committed suicide, and the ashes of Germanicus were placed in the tomb of Augustus, with great honor.

The father of nine children by Agrippina, grand-daughter of Augustus, including *Caligula and Agrippina, mother of *Nero, Germanicus was also brother to the Emperor *Claudius.

His reputation as republican hero rests much on the writings of *Tacitus, who is also responsible for our grim view of Tiberius.
W. 85

GERMAN MYSTICS

See "Coleridge."
W. 90

GERMAN NEOPLATONICAL ORIGINALS

See "Coleridge."
P. 14:2

GERMANY; GERMAN, --S

The modern-day north central European nation on the North Sea and the *Baltic had larger boundaries in M.'s day and was divided into separate regions until the 1870's. To a large extent, "German" meant for M. the metaphysics of *Goethe and *Coleridge, and others who ushered in the Ro-mantic Age, as well as militarism and the *Holy Roman Em-pire. He visited Germany in April of 1857.

See entry under "Phrenology" (for the "high German forehead" of W. 62), as well as entries under "Aachen"; "Bavaria"; "Berlin"; "Black Forest"; "Blücher"; "Bremen"; "Cologne"; "Ehrenbreitstein"; "Frankfurt"; "Friesland"; "Hamburg"; "Hanoverian"; "Harz Forest"; "Heidelberg"; "Luther"; "Prussia . . . ."; "Rhenish"; "Rhine"; "Thuringi-an"; "Westphalia."

M. 3; M. 13; R. 33; W. 38; W. 62; M.D. 32; M.D. 34; M.D. 83;
P. 2:2; P. 17:2; P. 19:1; I.P. 2; C.M. 2; C.M. 22 and elsewhere.

GESNER

Konrad Von Gesner (1516-1565), *German/*Swiss naturalist, wrote *Historia animalium* (4 vols., on quadrupeds,
birds, fishes; 1551-58), the first major work of zoology. (A fifth
volume, on snakes, was published in 1587.) Gesner also wrote
on bibliography, theology, languages, the *Roman writer
Aelian, and mountaineering.
M.D. 32

GEYSER

The generic name for any spring from which regularly
burst columns of boiling water and steam is from *Geysir*, a
particular hot spring in *Iceland.
M. 88

GHENT

The capital city of East Flanders (see "Flemish")
province of *Belgium, thirty-one miles northwest of *Brussels,
has been a center of art and culture since ancient times, with
many important works housed in its castles, seventh-century
abbeys, and churches dating from the thirteenth century.
Ghent was built on the site of two monasteries and around a
fortress. The sixteenth century brought religious struggles,
with *Spain in control almost continuously until the *French
Revolution. The 1814 Treaty of Ghent officially ended the *War
of 1812.

"White hoods of Ghent" (*M.D.* 42) is a reference to the
White Hoods (or White Hats) band led by Johan Lyon, who
killed Roger Dauterve, bailiff of the Earl of Flanders, in a local
war over franchises, in 1379. (Details appear in Sir John
*Froissart's *Chronicles of England, France, and Spain*,
translated by Sir John Bourchier, Lord Berners [1523-1525],
Part I, Chapter 350.)
M.D. 42

GHIBELLINES

See "Guelphs and Ghibellines."
I.P. 19

GIANT'S CAUSEWAY, THE
On the North coast of *Ireland, a formation of thousands of prismatic basalt columns projecting into the sea. Legend says it is the beginning of a road constructed by giants that was to reach to *Scotland.
M. 75; R. 27

GIBRALTER, --S; ROCK OF GIBRALTER; STRAIT(S) OF GIBRALTER
The two-and-three-quarter-mile by three-quarter-mile *British crown colony at the southern tip of *Spain is linked to *Cádiz province by a low isthmus c. one mile long and one-half-mile wide. The strategically important area is crowned by the 1,396 foot Rock, a Jurassic limestone mountain with many natural and artificial caves and tunnels. The ancient Calpe, Gibralter was occupied by the *Phoenicians, *Carthaginians, *Romans, and Visigoths before being taken by the *Moors in 711. Its name derives from the Arabic *Jebel-al-Tarik*, "Mount of Tarik," the conqueror. The Moors first fortified Gibralter, and it has been a fortress ever since, with artificial harbors at the low-lying portion. Spain held it in parts of the fourteenth century, and from 1462 to 1704, when it was taken by a combined English/Dutch fleet in the War of the Spanish Succession. It was officially transferred to Britain in 1713 but was later besieged by the Spanish and the French. The "siege of Gibralter" (*W.* 6) was probably the longest and most successful coast defense in history, with the British defending from June 1779 to February 1783. French and Spanish losses totalled 2,000, as compared with sixteen British dead.
The Strait of Gibralter (*M.* 94; *M.D.* 9) is the thirty-six-mile-long connection between the *Atlantic and the *Mediterranean. The two promontories at the east entrance are the Pillars of *Hercules. M. entered the Strait on 24 November 1856, enroute to the *Holy Land. He commented in his journal on the prospects from the Strait, with the Rock and therefore England "throwing the rest of the [world] in shade."
M. 94; R. 9; R. 21; R. 24; W. 6; W. 39; W. 50; W. 51; M.D. 9; M.D. 79; I.P. 14

GIL BLAS
*French dramatist and novelist, Alain René Le Sage (or Lesage; 1668-1747), published *L'Histoire de Gil Blas de Santillane* in three installments (1715, 1724, 1735). He achieved only sporadic fame, but his picaresque novel highly influenced the *English comic fiction of *Smollett and others. *Gil Blas*,

adapted from *Spanish materials, is the story of a scheming
valet who moves in a world of comic social types.
W. 12

GILDER
        The Dutch *Gulden*, or *guilder*: divided into 100 cents.
M.D. 114

GILLES DE RAIS
        See "Bluebeard."
T. 27

GILLIES, ROBERT PEARSE
        Robert Pearse Gillies (1788-1858), active in *Edinburgh
literary pursuits, was a friend of *Scott, *Wordsworth, and
*Byron. His was an exciting existence, involving the loss of a
fortune, and imposition of lawsuits and imprisonment. He
worked on *Blackwood's Magazine* and founded *Foreign
Quarterly Review*. Among his publications is *Tales of a Voyager to the Arctic Ocean*, 6 vols, 1826, 1829.
        See also "Extracts" 72.
M.D. Extracts 72

GIPSYS; GYPSYS; GYPSIES
        A nomadic race originally presumed to have come from
*Egypt (hence the name). Probably they came from *India and
were in *Germany and *France by the fifteenth century. They
call themselves "Romanies" (*rom*: a man or husband);
Romani is the name of their language, a mixture of Hindi,
Persian, Armenian, and European languages. They have
often been persecuted for their reputation as fortune-tellers,
swindlers, etc, most recently in the twentieth century when
large numbers were exterminated by the Nazis.
0. 75

GLACIER
        Probably another joke on *Scoresby, whose ship was
Resolution, not "Glacier."
M.D. 35

GLADIATOR, MARBLE
        See "Dying Gladiator."
M. 135

GLASGOW

The largest city in *Scotland, Glasgow, on the *Clyde River, is the industrial and commercial center. Many of its ancient buildings were replaced in the nineteenth century, but in 1856 M. would have seen many which dated from the fifteenth. The Cathedral (Officially St. Mungo's High Church), standing on the reputed grave of St. Mungo (Celtic for "my dear friend"), was in severe disrepair at the time, with two towers removed. The adjoining Necropolis is terraced, rising 300 feet to a *Doric column topped by a statue of *Calvinist minister John Knox (c. 1513-72), erected by public subscription in 1824.

M.'s visit to Scotland was not carefully recorded. It is known that he visited Glasgow from 26 to 28 October 1856, but the journal gives few details and there is a gap of ten days before it recommences on 8 November. M. does note the "defaced" state of the Cathedral, the "Acropolis" with its statue of Knox, the "miserable poverty" of the area. He visited the University (founded c. 1450), then situated on High Street.
R. 33

GLASS RETORTS

Vessels with long necks bent downward: used for distilling. In W., a rather far-fetched pun on "retort" of a gun.
W. 11

GLAUBER SALTS

A *German alchemist, Johannn Rudolph Glauber (1604-68) discovered the purgative (sodium sulphate, crystallized below 34°), presumably strong enough for a horse.
R. 18

GLENDINNING STANLY; GLEN STANLY

Murray's notes to P. suggest that an original for this fictional character is *Stanwix *Gansevoort (1821-1901), M.'s cousin. The two had been boyhood friends but broke relations as adults.

In *Poe's "William Wilson," a tale of the *Doppelgänger*, "Lord Glendinning" is a "young *parvenu* nobleman" at *Oxford who is tricked by the protagonist into a card game that brings about his "total ruin." The castigated Wilson flees Oxford and falls into utter villainy on the Continent, the victim of his own "other self."
P. Passim

GLOBE
    See "Comstock."
M.D. Extracts 64; M.D. Extracts 68

GLORIA HILL
    At the eastern foot of the *Organ Mountains, *Rio de
Janeiro, overlooking the present-day Praca Paris.
W. 39

GLOSTER RICHARD
    See "King Richard."
M. 84

GLUEPOTS
    A slang expression for a clergyman or parson: perhaps
"Ahab's" assessment of *"Starbuck," in *M.D.* 120.
M.D. 120

GLYTOLEPIS
    See "Sandwiches."
M. 132

GNOMON
    The column that casts a shadow on a sun dial.
M.D. 32

GNOSTIC
    Gnostic is a general term for some widely influential
second-century A.D. mythological systems of belief which developed from *apocalyptic Judaism. Among them are the
*Syrian gnosis, and those of *Marcion, Valentinus, Basilides,
the *Ophites, the Sethians. "Gnosis" means "knowledge," and
in Gnostic systems, knowledge, rather than behavior, brings
redemption from a world made evil by hostile powers. (Gnostic
ideas are prevalent in the *New Testament, especially in the
*Gospel of John, and the letters of *Paul.)
    Basic belief of the early Gnostics, who rejected the *Old
Testament as an authentic interpretation of human existence,
is the dualistic visible universe controlled by evil spirits.
Knowledge is to be brought by a descending redeemer to those
related to him by origin, who would intuit the unlearnable
truth of the self. An immortal divine spark (M.'s "psychical

essence," in *M*. 170), separate from both body and soul, must escape from the wicked world back to its consubstantial source, an unknown god.

Gnosticism was a real threat to the early Christian church because it saw Christ as but a revealer; atonement was not possible; the creation was flawed and the world was disintegrating; the creator was not the redeemer. Church fathers such as *Origen were swayed by such beliefs; *Tertullian and others refuted them. Some Gnostic groups claimed an already existing "savior"; some included antinomian and libertarian ideas such as the good "female principle"; others saw that principle as the thing to be destroyed. Marcionites believed in two gods: the good Father of *Jesus and the Old Testament Creator. By the third and fourth century, Manicheanism, which had originated in *Persia, had spread throughout the *Roman Empire, the sole existing form of Gnosticism. It was extinct before the fifth century. But by the sixteenth century, Gnostic works had become available; they greatly influenced later romantic thinkers such as Hegel and *Goethe (and in the twentieth century, Carl Jung).

Much of M.'s knowledge of Gnosticism must have come from the widely popular *The Evidences of the Genuineness of the Gospels* (1844), Andrews Norton's work which includes much material on the subject. Certainly the characterization of *M.D.*'s *"Ahab" owes much to Gnostic ideas.

M. perhaps bemoaned the systematic obliteration of Gnostic materials; he wrote a few lines called "Fragments of a Lost Gnostic Poem of the Twelfth Century." (In our own century, the availability of material discovered at Naj Hammadi, the Gnostic gospels, has clarified our view of Gnosticism and of the essentially political struggle it waged with "orthodox" Christianity.)
M. 170; W. 38

GOA

Goa is on the western coast of *India on the *Arabian Sea, 250 miles south of *Bombay. It was a *Portuguese possession in M.'s time. The Old Goa seaport, with sixty-two miles of coastline, had been founded in 1440 under the Bahmani dynasty. Taken by the Portuguese in 1510, it was made the capital of Portuguese India, gaining the height of its importance between 1575 and 1625. The original site was abandoned early in the eighteenth century because of *cholera epidemics.

Goa is also famous as the place of origin of St. Francis Xavier's missionary work: 1542-1552.
M.D. 105

GOAT, THE
      See "Zodiac."
M.D. 99

GOBBLER, THE
      See "Heliogabalus."
M. 181

GOBELIN TAPESTRY
      The famed *French Gobelin tapestries have been pro-
duced and avidly sought after since the fifteenth century. The
modern state-owned manufactory occupies the site where Jean
Gobelin (d. 1476), head of a family of dyers, produced a scarlet
dye for tapestries said to result only from the waters of the
adjacent Bièvre River (now defunct). The family-owned
business was rescued from mismanagement by the French
government in the seventeenth century and has remained a
French treasure.
      The tapestries utilize a special weaving technique which
creates a dense and precise pattern. They are still produced by
hand, using the original method, and in very limited
quantities—mostly for official government use.
      At the Quirinale Palace in *Rome in 1857, M. saw Gob-
elins depicting the marriage of Louis XIV (see "Bourbon"),
*Christ washing the feet of the *Apostles, the expulsion of the
money-changers, etc. He may also have seen Gobelin work at
*Versailles in 1849.
R. 46

GOD
      God is the most frequently mentioned personage in M.'s
works, despite or perhaps because of his ambivalent feelings
about the deity. This entry does not attempt to explicate those
feelings, nor does it include every reference to God in the
works. Rather, it agglomerates a host of honorific titles for the
godhead as well as miscellaneous expressions pertaining
thereto. (I have omitted most expletives and expressions
calling on God's name, as well as plural and lower-case
usage.)
      M.'s appellations follow sacred traditions of Islamics
(see "Allah"), and Jews (see "Hebrews") whose designations
for Yahweh (see "Jehovah") complied with proscriptions regarding the use of God's personal name. Thus, for ancient
people of *Palestine, the following appellations refer to God: El
was Semitic for "God" or "deity"; El Shaddai perhaps meant

"God, the one of the mountains"; El Elyon meant "Exalted One," or "most High," to *Canaanites; El Olam was "God the Everlasting One"; El Bethel was God revealed in a shrine named *Bethel; El Roi was perhaps "God who sees me"; El Berith was "God of the *Covenant"; El Elohe was "El, the God of Israel"; Elohim and Eloah were sometimes used by polytheists; Baal (see "Belial") meant "lord" or "owner" to Canaanites and was a god of storm and fertility confused at first with El, which was synonymous with Yahweh; Adon, "lord," was a Canaanite designation for God, who is also called "Father," "Brother," "Kinsman," "King," "Judge," "Shepherd," and descriptively, "the living God," "The First and the Last," "The Ancient of Days."

That M. understood the importance of holy designations is a given; his intention in using them can only be conjectured. In a letter to *Hawthorne (1? June 1851), he confessed to "flunkeyism" in using the capital letter in references to God. Presuming pre-emptive official Christian affiliations, I have included references to *Jesus Christ. The reader is directed also to entries on "Hebrew" and "Jehovah" in the present work.

M.'s references include: Providence (passim); Admiral of the Fleet—God Almighty (W. 75); the All (W. 19); All-Plastic Power (M. 75); The Almighty (M.D. 9); Almighty goodness (C.M. 19); Captain and Lord (P. 1:4): the Creator (O. 18; W. 34; C.M. 14; C.M. 45); the Deity (M.D. 79; P. 22:1); the Divine Inert (M.D. 33); Father of all (R. 29); Giver of all feasts (M.D. 13); God Almighty (W. 33); God Omnipotent (P. 12:3); God the Father (M.D. 86); Him (W. 74); Himself (M. 75); Holy One (M.D. 42); the Immeasureable (M. 75); the Eneffable Silence (M. 75); the Infinite (M. 75); Keel of the Ages (M.D. 9); Lord (I.P. 21); Lord High Admiral (W. 50; W. 94); Lord the God of Heaven (M.D. 9); Maker (M. 75; M. 109; M. 158; W. 38); Master (W. 38); divine Master (R. 35); Messiah (M. 146; W. 36); Power (C.M. 45); power of the Most High (O. 45); Searcher of the cores of all hearts (M. 135); Spirit of Equality (M.D. 26); Supreme Disposer (I.P. 13).

Jesus is referred to in M. 3; R. 35; W. 76; M.D. 134 and as Jesu in M.D. 54. Christ is mentioned in M.D. 40; P. 2:5; P. 5:6; P. 14:3. He is called our Lord (O. 9); Master (W. 38); Messiah (M. 146); a chronometer (P. 14:3); Prince of Peace (W. 50); our blessed Redeemer (W. 54); blessed Savior (W. 76); Saviour (M. 3; M. 47); the Son (M.D. 86).

Among miscellaneous references are: race accursed of God (W. 71); appointed of God (P. 21:1); better than to gaze upon God (M.D. 132); big white God (M.D. 40); condition in which God placed man (M.D. 57); Deliverer God (M.D. 9); ever-encroaching appetite for God (P. 25:4); The Finger of God

(P. 7:8); fit image of his God (P. 2:3); God forbid (C.M. 28); God bless you (W. 4); God's burning finger (M.D. 119); God's creatures (M. 13); God's diadem (M. 58); God-Fugitive (M.D. 9); God's natural air (C.M. 16); great God himself at work in me (M. 163); God is against thee (M.D. 119); God is my Lord (M. 119); God keep me!—keep us all (M.D. 36); God keep thee! (M.D. 58); God of breezes (M.D. 8); God of Gods (M.D. 82); God of the blessed Bible (W. 75); God's great, unflattering laureate, Nature (M.D. 42); God's quick wrath (M.D. 8); God's wrath (M.D. 35); God's sunlight (P. 16:3); God's true princes of the Empire (M.D. 33); God's worm-hole (I.P. 21); God that made *Napoléon or *Byron (P. 23:4); The great God Absolute! (M.D. 26); Great God, where art thou? (M.D. 123); Hand of God a hollow, truly! (P. 7:8); I believe to God (P. 12:1); I disobey my God in obeying him (M.D. 135); indefinite as God (M.D. 23); inscrutable tides of God (M.D. 35); insufferable splenders of God's throne (M.D. 118); Is it I, God, or who, that lifts this arm? (M.D. 132); judgement(s) of God (M.D. 54; P. 24:4); magnanimous God of heaven and earth (M.D. 10); man of God (M.D. 8); men of God (R. 35); My God, stand by me now (M.D. 135); the partial God (P. 15:2); sapphire throne of God (P. 6:1); sons of God wed our mothers (M. 3); temple of God (P. 24:4); thou great democratic God (M.D. 26); to Himself His own universe is He (M. 75); trade that God intended him for (P. 22:2); uncompromised, indifferent as his God (M.D. 93); University of God (P. 18:1); Would God it were tomorrow (I.P. 25).

Lord only knows (Passim) the origins of these expressions.
Passim

GOD OF WAR
See "Mars."
W. 85

"GOD SAVE THE KING"
The fervently loyal *British National Anthem has been attributed to Dr. *John Bull (d. 1628), organist at *Antwerp Cathedral from 1617-28. Bull's manuscript is preserved there.Whatever its origin, its title comes from I *Samuel 10:24:

> "And all the people shouted, and said, God save the king."

Various lyrics suggest origins other than Bull: even possibly the Roman *Catholic Domine Salvum. Politics have influ-

enced the evolving words, as well: "frustrate their knavish tricks" was possibly added in reference to the *Gunpowder Plot. In 1740, Henry Carey reset the words and music for the birthday of *George II, and the song became highly popular as opposition to the Jacobites: "confound their politics."
W. 23; W. 39

GOD'S TOKEN
The oldest European flags displayed the *Christian *cross.
W. 65

GOD'S TRUE PRINCES OF THE EMPIRE
In the *Holy Roman Empire, princes who elected the Emperor.
M.D. 33

GOETHE
Johann Wolfgang von Goethe (1749-1832) was born at *Frankfurt am Main, *Germany. He trained for the law and spent much of his life in government positions and as director of the court theatre at Weimar. A painter and art critic, scientist and dramatist of great importance, Goethe achieved his most famous work in the two-part *Faust* (1808, 1832). Based on the story of a late fifteenth/early sixteenth-century conjuror in Germany, the first part tells of "Faust's" pact with "*Mephistopheles" and his mistreatment of "Gretchen" (Margaret). The second finds "Faust" pursuing the beautiful "Helen" and losing their son, "Euphorion," who symbolizes the union of classical and romantic poetry as did *Byron. "Faust" thereafter attempts to serve mankind and at his death is saved from *Hell. *The Sorrows of Young Werther (Die Leiden des jungen Werthers*, 1774) is a semi-autobiographical novel in which the artist/hero commits suicide for love of the already-promised "*Charlotte." *Iphigenia in Tauris (Iphigenie auf Tauris*, 1787) is based on Euripedes. The prototype *bildungsroman, Wilhelm Meister's Apprenticeship and Travels* (written 1777-1829) examines fate and chance in the education of a young man.
Goethe's prose, poetry, and songs were widely celebrated and emulated, partly as a result of *Conversations with Goethe* (1823-32), by his secretary, *Johann Peter Eckermann. But Goethe's greatest proponent was Thomas Carlyle, who translated his work, wrote essays in praise, and extolled him as the greatest genius, in *Sartor Resartus*.

M.'s Goethe library is heavily annotated, especially in those sections dealing with solitude, fame, genius, madness. Yet in a letter to *Hawthorne (1 June? 1851), he mentions the "immense deal of flummery" in the more *transcendental pronouncings such as "Live in the All!" M. visited Frankfurt am Main on 21 and 22 April 1857, commenting in his journal on the statue of "Faust."

Sealts #227 is one volume in German. #228 is an 1848-49 edition of the *Autobiography* which M. purchased in London. #229 is *Iphigenia in Tauris*, translated by M.'s friend, G.J. Adler. #230 is *Wilhelm Meister's Apprenticeship and Travels*. M. is also known to have read *Elective Affinities* (1809), a novel dealing with a married couple's affections for two other persons.
M. 57; W. 44; M.D. 86; P. 14:2; P. 22:3

GOFFE
William Goffe (or Gough; c. 1605-79), *English soldier and regicide, participated in the army's decision to try *Charles I in 1648, acted as a judge, and signed the death warrant, along with his father-in-law, *Edward Whalley. By 1654, he was a Major General and member of *Parliament. At the Restoration, he was excepted from the Royalist Act of Indemnity but escaped with Whalley to *New England, living much of the rest of his life in seclusion in Hadley, *Massachusetts.

He is said to have helped repel an Indian attack during *King Philip's War, and his story is told in *Cooper's *The Wept of Wish-ton-Wish*, *Hawthorne's "The Gray Champion" (in *Twice-Told Tales*, Sealts #260), and *Scott's *Peveril of the Peak* (Sealts #452).
M. 97

GOG AND MAGOG
In the *Bible:

*Genesis 10, 2: Magog is the son of Japhet.
*Revelation:Gog and Magog are symbols of future enemies of God's kingdom.
*Ezekiel: Gog is prince of Magog.

Seventh-century A.D. rabbinical writers identified Gog with the Antichrist.
In *British legend: Gog and Magog were the surviving monsters of the destroyed brood of demonic offspring of the daughters of the Emperor *Diocletian. They were pris-

oner/servants on the site of London's *Guildhall, where effigies have stood since the time of Henry V. Destroyed several
times, they have always been replaced, the last time in 1953.
Effigies were also carried in the *Lord Mayor's shows.
M. 56

GOLCONDAS

Golconda, a ruined ancient fortress city in *India (near
Hyderabad), is famed for its great wealth and diamond cutting
in the sixteenth and seventeenth centuries. The Qutb Shahi
tombs are located near the site of the famous diamond mines
that gave *English literature a synonym for the precious
stones.

Golconda was annexed to the *Mogul empire in 1687,
after a long history of *Moslem sultanate rule.
M. 43; M. 58; M. 194; R. 46; W. 6; M.D. 99

GOLD-BEATER'S SKIN

Ox intestine membrane separating sheets of gold during
beating into gold leaf.
M.D. 93

GOLDEN HILLS

In *M.*, perhaps metaphoric. There is a Gold Mountain
in the state of Washington (47°33' N., 122°48' W.).
M. 166

GOLDEN NUMBER, THE

The number of the year in the Metonic Cycle of nineteen
years at the end of which the new moons fall on the same days
of the year (after Meton, *Greek astronomer). On ancient
*Roman and Alexandrian calendars, the number was marked
in gold.

The number is found by adding one to the number of
years and dividing by nineteen; the quotient gives the number
of cycles since B.C. 1 and the remainder is the Golden
Number.

It is used to determine the Epact (excess of solar over
lunar year) and the date of Easter.
M. 166

GOLDEN RULE
Familiarly: "Do unto others as you would have others do unto you."

*Matthew 7:12: "Whatsoever ye would that men should do to you, do ye even so to them; for this is the law and the prophets."

Philip Dormer Stanhope, Earl of *Chesterfield: "Do as you would be done by, is the surest method of pleasing."

In mathematics, the *Rule of Three.
M. 166

GOLDEN VERSES
*Greek verses containing the moral rules of *Pythagoras, probably composed by his followers, the Golden Verses enjoin obedience to *God and rulers, deliberation before action, daily critical view of one's behavior, among other aims.
P. 2:5

GOLD SHERRY
Golden *sherry is a heavy, sweet dessert wine, produced in Jerez de la Frontera province, *Spain.
M. 40

GOLDSMITH, OLIVER; GOLDSMITH'S; 'GOLDSMITH'S ANIMATED NATURE'; GOLDSMITH, NAT. HIS.; GOLDSMITH TO JOHNSON
Oliver Goldsmith (?1730-74), son of an Anglo-Irish clergyman, graduated from Trinity College, *Dublin, but was rejected for ordination. After two years of wandering through Europe, he was rejected for a medical post. He began a literary career as reviewer, becoming friend to *Burke, *Samuel Johnson, and others. Close to arrest for debt after years of struggle as a writer, he was rescued when Johnson sold *The Vicar of Wakefield* (Sealts #232) in 1762. Other successes were the play, *She Stoops to Conquer* (1768) and the poem *The Deserted Village* (1770; Sealts #231). His imaginative eight-volume fantastic reconstruction of the work of *Buffon, *Linnaeus, et al, *An History of the Earth and Animated Nature*, was published posthumously (1774). M. probably saw the abridged *London edition of 1807.

There are many anecdotes about Goldsmith in Boswell's *Life*, and several biographies were published, including one by John Forster in 1848.

I have not been able to trace the "suppressed maxim: whatever is new is false" (*P.* 17:1). In *She Stoops to Conquer*

(Act 1), is the statement "I love everything that's old: old
friends, old times, old manners, old books, old wines."
(Henry Peter, Lord Brougham [1778-1868], *Edinburgh
Review, The Work of Thomas Young*, said, "What is valuable
is not new and what is new is not valuable" [1802]. *Daniel
Webster quoted him in a speech at Marshfield, *Massachusetts
[1 September 1848].)
See "Extracts" 37, 38.
T. 11; W. 12; M.D. Extracts 37; M.D. Extracts 38; M.D. 55; P.
17:1

GOLDSMITH'S HALL
Livery halls in *Britain are owned by craft guilds. The
goldsmiths, who hallmark gold and silver, were among the
earliest guilds to have their own hall, perhaps as early as 1400.
C.M. 30

GOLGOTHA
Aramaic for *Calvary, where *Jesus was crucified. Calvary is from the *Latin *calvaria*, translated from the *Greek
kranion, meaning "skull." It was located outside *Jerusalem,
the precise site unknown.
W. 88

GOLIATH
See "Gath."
M. 9; W. 2

GOMORRAH, --S
Cities of legendary wickedness in *Genesis. Like Cities
of the Plain, doomed societies in general, rather than
particular cities.
Sodom and Gomorrah are destroyed in Gen. 19, 24, 27,
28, passages marked in M.'s *Bible (Sealts #62).
M. 97; R. 31; W. 89; M.D. 2; M.D. 9; M.D. 117; I.P. 19

GONERIL
One of "*Lear's" perfidious daughters, in *Shakespeare's *King Lear*; she poisons her sister "Regan" and then
kills herself.
C.M. 12

GONEY; *GONEY*
    Nickname for the *albatross.
M.D. 52; M.D. 54 and elsewhere

GONFALON
    (Earlier Gonfanon). In ecclesiastical processions, a standard or banner with streamers, often suspended from a cross bar. *Gonfalonier* was a chief magistrate in the old *Italian republics.
M. 121

GOOD ANGEL
    See "Quotations": "Bad Angel shall tend the Good."
P. 26:6

GOOD-ENOUGH MORGAN
    See "Morgan, Good-Enough."
C.M. 9

GOOD HOPE; CAPE OF GOOD HOPE; CAPE OF DOOD HOPE
    The Cape of Good Hope is located at the extremity of Cape Peninsula, southwestern South *Africa on the west side of the entrance of False Bay, thirty miles south of present-day Cape Town (34°21' S., 18°29' E.). Cape Point rises to a sheer cliff 840 feet high: Vasco da *Gama Peak. It was first rounded in 1486 by *Bartholomew Diaz, who erected a commemorative pillar (traces of which remain); de Gama rounded it in 1497.
    See also "Cape Tormentoto."
O. 42; R. 22; W. 24; M.D. 36; M.D. 51; M.D. 119; and elsewhere

"GOOD SEA CAPTAIN"
    See "Fuller."
W. Dedication

GOODWIN SANDS
    Shoals off the *Kentish coast at the mouth of *England's *Thames River; the scene of many shipwrecks. Legend says that they were originally Earl Godwin's Island, inundated in 1099.
M.D. 7

GOR
     *Cockney or other dialectical usage for "*God."
M.D. 64

GORDON, LORD GEORGE
     The instigator of the 1780 Gordon Riots was born into a
royal *British family in 1751, educated at Eton, and was briefly
in the navy. The riots were intended to compel the *House of
Commons to repeal the 1778 relief bill for Roman *Catholics.
The city of *London was virtually at the mercy of the mob for
several days, during which *Lord Mansfield's home and
library were destroyed.   Mansfield so fairly conducted
Gordon's trial that he was acquitted. *Edmund Burke likewise
pleaded for Gordon, the rest of whose life was a series of weird
or unpredictable actions, such as his conversion to Judaism.
Gordon died in *Newgate Prison in 1793.
W. 3

GORGON, --S; DEMIGORGON
     See "Medusa."
M. 63; R. 39; M.D. 38; M.D. 169; P. 3:2; P. 3:6; P. 12:1

GOSHEN
     Goshen is an *Old Testament place name, its location
disputed and meaning unknown. Because the *Bible makes it
a fertile land, safe from plagues, many towns have been
named Goshen for its aura of safety and plenty. The town
appears in *Genesis 40:10, *Exodus 7-9, and elsewhere
(Septuagint "Gesem").
     Also, a district of southern *Palestine, southwest of He-
bron, in *Joshua 10:41 and 11:16. (Septuagint "Gosom").
     Goshen is frequently the key rhyming word in limericks.
C.M. 24

GOSPEL, --S
     Gospel is the modern form of the *Anglo-Saxon "god-
spell"—a story from or about a god (Lat. *evangelium*). The
popular meaning, starting from *Luke 2:10, is "good tidings,"
or "good news." Gospel is also understood as a process of
preaching or proclaiming, as in its use by missionaries:
"gospelizing."
     The *New Testament Gospels were a new genre, the
only literary form peculiar to *Christianity. They are a holy

history of the ministery of *Jesus and of the *Church, as well as a proclamation of *God's message regarding salvation.

It is now known that the Gospel According to *St. Mark was the earliest of the four canonical gospels, upon which the others are based. It is a Christian folk book, rather artlessly compiling ninety unconnected anecdotes, without a first person narrator. The historical Mark (probably the person mentioned in *Acts and the *Pauline letters) was an associate of *Peter who probably collected material from many other people, writing the book in *Rome c. A.D. 64 or 65. Mark wrote narratives and sayings material in simple everyday speech, with much emphasis on the passion of Jesus.

The Gospel of *St. Matthew, an expanded version of Mark, is a more dramatic and personal piece of prose, with a tangible author, a Church-centered *apocalyptic vision with many *Old Testament quotations. The historical Matthew, an *Apostle (called "Levi" in Mark 2:14), is thought to have been a tax collector. His was traditionally considered the first written Gospel, and the ordering of the New Testament reflects that misunderstanding, making Matthew's Gospel the first book of the New Testament.

The Gospel According to *St. Luke is a very polished version of Mark's story, albeit a vaguer one. Luke is presumed to have been a *Gentile, a physician who was companion to *Paul.

The Gospel According to *St. John deviates most from Mark's original and was certainly the last written. The most influential New Testament book in early Christian dogma, St. John's Gospel, which contains long meditative discourses and dialogues, reorders Mark's version and differs in its inclusiveness. Many incidents are added (the Cana miracle; baptism by Jesus, his visiting and preaching in *Jerusalem; the raising of *Lazarus). It omits the birth and baptism, the temptations, exorcisms, transfiguration, and blessing and distribution of bread and wine at the *Last Supper. The presumed author is John the son of Zebedee in *Ephesus (not *John the Baptist), an Apostle, brother to James, a fisherman by trade. He is presumed also the author of *Revelation.
M.D. 9; P. 1:4 and elsewhere

GOTH, --S; GOTHIC
The history of the Goth people is clouded because their own literature was for the most part systematically destroyed by their enemies and because contemporary *Roman writers probably falsified in their efforts to excoriate them. The Goths were a Teutonic people who probably originated in *Scandinavia, migrated to the mouth of the Vistula River (in

modern *Poland), and drove southward during the third century A.D. to invade Roman territories. Those settling in the general area of modern *Germany and westward were known as Visigoths; those settling in the area of the modern Ukraine and southwestward through modern *Italy were known as Ostrogoths. Goths eventually migrated throughout the continental Roman Empire, sacking Rome in 410. They apparently became *Arians and remained separate from other peoples through a ban on intermarriage. They were destroyed by the *Moslems in 711.

The expressions "Goth" and "Gothic" seem to have been used by M. in the conventional sense of anything antiquated, crude, and destructive (as in R. 30's allusion to one who vandalizes books), or as alluding to "Gothic" sculpture or architecture. *Middle Ages architecture (from the mid-twelfth to the sixteenth century) was characterized by the use of pointed arches (as in M.D. Extracts 54) and gargoyle figures which frequently caricatured contemporary people. Thus, the "Gothic" nose of M. 30 is probably meant to suggest the proboscis of a gargoyle. The "Gothic genealogies" of M.D. 54 and the "Gothic Knight" of M.D. 27 refer to the grim, closely clustered figures of Gothic statuary.

The reference to the "chief of the Goths" in W. 86 is an error. It was not the Goths but the *Gauls who *Livy says entered the Roman Senate in 385 and massacred the Roman officials when one whose long *beard was touched by a Gaul struck the offender with an ivory staff, infuriating his fellows.
M. 30; R. 30; R. 49; W. 86; M.D. Extracts 17; M.D. 27; M.D. 54

GOTHLAND
The *Swedish island of Gotland (Gothland, or Gottland), in the *Baltic Sea (56°54'-57°56' N., 18°6'-19°7' E.), is seventy-five miles long and from two to twenty-eight miles wide. It has been inhabited since the Stone Age and in ancient times became an important center of commercial activity. Its chief town, Visby (M.'s "Wisbury," in W. 72), was an important *Hanse town. Conquered by the *Swedes in 1280, the island suffered from plagues and fires before being taken by the *Danes in 1362. It returned to the Hanse League in 1370 and was taken again by the Danes in 1570 and the Swedes in 1645. Gothland was also an important *pirate base.
W. 72

GOUGE
Swindle, in underworld parlance.
C.M. 15

GOVERNOR'S ISLAND
The 173-acre island of Upper *New York Bay is just south of the *Battery. Purchased from the Indians in 1637 as a residence for *British colonial governors, it was taken by the *Americans in 1776 and reinforced, but the British under *Howe retook it. By 1794 it was part of New York, and Governor Clinton had installed a race-course and hotel on the island; by 1790, Columbia College was located there.
The island took on its permanent character starting in 1794, when it was heavily fortified (in anticipation of renewed British hostilities). It was ceded by New York to the U.S. Government in 1800; by 1821 it was Federal Military Headquarters. Castle Williams (1807) became a military prison, and other forts and an arsenal were added. (Governor's Island was used as a prison again during the *Civil War.)
R. 7; R. 60

GRACCHI
Gaius Sempronius Gracchus (154-121 B.C.) was a radical *Roman statesman who became Tribune in 123. He attacked the powers of the senate, proposed citizenship extension for Latins, enacted agrarian laws and guaranteed a monthly grain ration, increased court efficiency, reordered external relations, and reorganized tax collection. Denied the Tribuneship in 121, he and his supporters revolted and were killed when the senate proclaimed *martial law for the first time in history.
M. 60

GRACES
In classical mythology, the three Graces, daughters of Zeus (see "Jupiter" and "Jove") and Eurynome, are goddesses of beauty and charm. Aglaia represents splendor; Thalia is good cheer; Euphrosyne is mirth. They are not usually treated as separate personalities. *Spenser mentions them (*Faerie Queene* VI, X, 22).
R. 46

GRAFTON
The *English dukes of Grafton descend from an illegitimate son of *Charles II, Henry Fitzroy (1663-90). They have held high military and court appointments and have created controversy in matters such as *American colonial policy and religion.
P. 1:3

GRAMPIANS

In *R*. 33, the reference is to the *Australian mountain range in southwest-central Victoria, a forty-mile-long spur of the Great Dividing Range. There is gold in the chain, the tallest peak of which is Mount Williams (3,828 feet).

(There is also a Grampian range in *Scotland, of which *Ben Nevis is a part.)

M. 75; R. 33; I.P. 15

GRAMPUS, --'S

A common name for a whaleship; Peleg Folger of *Nantucket sailed on a 1751 *Grampus*; the ship in **Miriam Coffin; or, The Whale Fisherman* (by Joseph C. Hart) is the *Grampus*, as is Pym's stowaway craft in *Edgar Allan Poe's *The Narrative of Arthur Gordon Pym, of Nantucket*.

Another *Grampus* was a war-schooner launched in the *Washington Navy Yard around 1819; it was designed by Henry Steers (or Steer), an *English shipwright.

M.D. 3

GRANADA'S

Granada is the capital city of Granada province, in southern *Spain's *Andalusia. The Darro River divides the city into three major areas; on its left bank is *Alhambra Hill, with a *Moorish fort, towers, and palaces including that of *Charles V. The old *Roman colony rose to prominence under the *Moors, whose last stronghold was conquered in 1492 by Ferdinand and *Isabella.

W. 20

GRAND BANKS

See "Newfoundland."

R. Passim

GRAND CANAL

The major traffic artery of *Venice is two miles long and eighteen feet deep, an average of 228 feet wide. It runs from the Piazza San Marco to the railway station connecting Venice with mainland *Italy. M. visited Venice in April of 1857, traveling much on the Grand Canal, portions of which were "compulsory" tourist attractions.

M.D. 54

GRAND CONTESTED ELECTION FOR THE PRESIDENCY OF THE UNITED STATES

M. may here have in mind one of three exciting Presidential elections. In 1840, just prior to M.'s shipping on *Acushnet*, Whig *William Henry Harrison defeated incumbent Democrat Martin Van Buren, after a campaign famous for "Tippecanoe and Tyler too." In 1844, James Knox *Polk gained a close victory over Henry Clay, and M.'s brother, *Gansevoort, gained a political appointment for his part in the victory. In 1848, Zachary Taylor won an electoral vote over Free Soil Party's Van Buren and the Wilmot Proviso.

See also "President."

M.D. 1

GRAND JURY

In *M.D.* 21, a playful reference to the *Last Judgement.

M.D. 21

GRANDE PORTE

See "Constantinople."

W. 39

GRAND LAMA

The Grand, or Dalai (Sacred) Lama ruled Tibet (see "Thibet") before *Chinese suzerainty. "Lama" is from the Tibetan *blama* (b is silent), meaning spiritual teacher or lord. Lamaism is a modified form of Buddhism.

O. 50; M. 181; W. 68; M.D. 106

GRAND NATIONAL MUSEUM ON THE PRACA D'ACCLAMACAO

*Rev. Stewart discusses this *Rio de Janeiro museum, in a large building housing "many valuable specimens in natural history, and the various departments of science—with some tolerable paintings—numerous articles of curiosity," and a collection of "Ramphastos Tucanus," the *toucan (I, p. 84).

W. 61

GRAND RUSSIAN

An ironic title for "Captain Riga," whose name is that of a chief *Russian port (in Latvia), and whose character does not really suggest comparison with the *tsar.

R. 57

GRAND TOWER
Grand Tower is a seventy-five-foot-high rock in the *Mississippi River on the *Missouri shore.
C.M. 27

GRAND TURK
See "Turk; Turkish."
M. 5; M. 20; M. 80; W. 6; M.D. 34; M.D. 88; P. 2:2

GRANVILLE, DR.
Augustus Bozzi Granville (1783-1872), physician and *Italian patriot (through relatedness to the *Bonapartes), was in the *Turkish service before joining the *British Navy. From 1813, as Surgeon to the Fleet, he survived shipwreck and was seriously injured, serving in the *West Indies, *Quiberon Bay, and at the bombardment of *Cádiz.

Retiring to private practice, he became eminent in medical and diplomatic circles, publishing works on *French science of the Revolutionary period. He edited the *Medical Intelligencer* and the *London Medical and Physical Journal*, introduced new medications, and advanced midwifery and childcare. His (1831) *Catechism of Health* addressed the *cholera problem. Granville wrote on the spas of several countries, on mummies, on sewage, on medical reform, and on politics. He published an autobiography, as well as the work alluded to in W. 88, which reflected on his 1827 visit to *Russia: *St. Petersburg: A Journal of Travel* (1828).
W. 88

GRASSE, COUNT DE
Comte François Joseph Paul Grasse, Marquis de Grasse-Tilly (1722-1788) was a *French naval commander against the *British in the *American Revolutionary War. He became admiral as a result of his service in the *West Indies. In April 1782, he was defeated by *Rodney and taken prisoner. A French courtmartial (1784) acquitted him of any malfeasance, after his publication of *Mémoire justificatif*.
W. 83

GRATTAN
Henry Grattan (1746-1820), *Irish statesman and orator. His five-volume *Memoirs and Speeches* was published by his son, Henry, 1839-46.
R. 27

GRAVE-DIGGER
"The grave digger in the play" is in *Hamlet* (See "Shakespeare") V.i.
M.D. 127

GREASY BALLYHOO OF BLAZES
"Grease" often refers to whaling, as in wishing a whaler "greasy" (that is, good) luck. The "ballyhoo of blazes" is simply confusion.
W. 4

GREAT BEAR
In astronomy, the northern *constellation Ursa Major. In *Greek mythology, the Great Bear Arctos (*Roman *Ursa Major*) was said to have been a nymph transformed into a bear.
M. 151; W. 65

GREAT CHIEF
In *M.* 160, a reference to President *Polk.
M. 160

GREAT GEORGE'S
*Liverpool's Great George Street runs from *Duke Street to St. James Street, roughly northeast to southwest.
R. 31

GREAT KHANS
See "Khan."
M. 181

GREAT LAKES
The largest group of fresh water lakes in the world marks the *United States/*Canada border in the central part of the continent. Lakes *Superior, *Huron, *Michigan (entirely in the United States), *Erie, and *Ontario are interconnected by navigation straits and canals, some of which M. sailed in 1840. Crossing Lake Erie to the connecting lake *St. Clair and St. Clair River, he crossed Lake Huron to *Mackinac Straits, descending Lake Michigan as far as *Chicago.
The lakes were discovered by the *French in 1612; they were explored by Champlain (1615) and LaSalle (1679). Control

of the lakes was important to the fur trading competition with the *British, who lost power in the *War of 1812.
See also "Erie Canal."
R. 61

GREAT MOGUL
See "Mogul."
M. 75

GREAT MORAI
See "Morai, --s."
M. 109

GREAT POMPEY
See "Pompey."
M. 181

GREAT SPIRIT
Manitou: either the Great Good or the Great Evil Spirit. From an Algonquin word meaning mysterious or supernatural.
M. 181; W. 46; M.D. 42

GREAT TOM OF OXFORD
The bell of Christ Church, *Oxford, weighed almost eight tons.
W. 49

GREAT WALL OF CHINA
The Great Wall of *China was built by Shih Hwangti (246-209 B.C.) of the Ch'in dynasty, to defend his people against the *Huns. The Great Wall runs 1,500 miles from Kansu (W.) to the Gulf of Chihli of the *Yellow Sea at Shanhaikwan. Twenty feet wide at the base, it tapers to twelve feet wide at the top, and is from fifteen to thirty feet high, with forty-foot high towers at 200-yard intervals. It is composed of earth, stone, and some brick.
The wall was restored in the fifteenth century. It forms a boundary between Chinese and *Mongol settlements but has never been very effective militarily.
R. 58

GREAT WHALE
See "Cetology" section.
M.D. 32

GREECE
The ancient "Hellas," Greece occupies the southernmost part of the Balkan peninsula, as well as islands in the Ionian and Aegean seas of the *Mediterranean. Some of the world's oldest civilizations arose here in the second millenium B.C. There were colonies scattered in many places by the eighth century; the first Olympic Games took place in 776 B.C.

Greece was the scene of the *Persian War of 499 and was at its peak in the age of *Pericles, fifth century B.C. *Alexander the Great spread Greek culture around the world, and when the *Romans conquered in 146 B.C., it was their culture which was rejected, rather than *Hellenism. Greece made part of the *Byzantine Empire until the fifteenth century A.D. The Greek war of independence (1822-30) ended with *Athens the capital.

M. visited in December of 1856 and January of 1857.

See also "Achaeans"; "Aeolians"; "Cyclades"; "Epirus": "Lesbos"; "Mount Olympus"; "Navarino"; "Parnassus"; "Rhodes"; "Salamis"; "Samos"; "Thessaly"; "Thrace."
O. 18; M. 119; R. 49; W. 3; W. 38; W. 41; W. 50; W. 51; W. 75; M.D. 42; M.D. 57; M.D. 82; M.D. 89; M.D. 108; M.D. 110; P. 2:6; P. 10:3; P. 12:3; P. 14:2; P. 17:1; P. 20:1; C.M. 5; C.M. 28; C.M. 38 and elsewhere

GREEK
In *M.D.*, the Greek who made *Africans of soot is *Prometheus.
M.D. 108

GREEK
The epithet "you Greek" has had negative connotations since before *Shakespeare's reference to "Helen" as a "Greek" (meaning woman of pleasure) in *Troilus and Cressida*. The epithet can imply not only hedonism regarding sex and alcohol, but also is used to designate a gambler or card-sharper, roisterer, or highwayman. *Irishmen and *Australians were often referred to as "Greeks."
R. 22

GREEK DUAL NUMBER

In ancient *Greek, a grammatical number indicating two, or a pair, distinguished from singular and plural by inflection; the form disappeared as the language became modernized.
R. 53

GREEK FIRE

The Greeks used fire ships to win their war of independence (1821-29).
M.D. 96

GREEKS

The ancient Greeks called their sea god Poseidon, later associated with the *Roman *Neptune.
See also "Beards."
W. 85; M.D. 1

GREEK SAVAGE

A reference to *Achilles, with his elaborately decorated shield.
M.D. 57

GREEK TO ME

Unintelligible, like an unknown foreign language.
*Shakespeare: *Julius Caesar*, I, ii, "Casca" says, "For mine own part, it was all Greek to me."
R. 6; I.P. 7

GREEN HILLS

See "Green Mountains; Green Hills"
W. 50

GREENLAND, --ER

The largest island in the world (1,660 miles long, up to 750 miles wide) is the northernmost point of land: 440 miles from the *North Pole, c. 175 miles from *Iceland, bounded on the north by the *Arctic, east by Greenland Sea, southeast by *Denmark Strait, south by the *Atlantic, west by Davis Strait and *Baffin Bay.

The Danish crown colony (with mostly *Eskimo/Danish population) is 85% icecap over 7,000 feet thick. It is a basin surrounded by coastal mountains up to 12,000 feet high, with numerous fjords and glaciers which shed massive icebergs; it is a good site for observation of the *Northern Lights.

Greenland was discovered in 982 by Eric the Red. Leif Ericson sailed from here to North America. It was a whaling center, as well as a port for searchers for a *Northwest Passage (including *Frobisher, *Davis, and *Hudson) and for exploring expeditions including *Scoresby's.
M. 1; M. 32; R. Passim; W. 80; M.D. Passim

GREENLAND WHALES
    See "Cetology" section.
R. 21; M.D. 32

GREEN MOUNTAINS; GREEN HILLS
    *Vermont's *Appalachian range mountains run north-south through the center of Vermont from *Quebec to *Massachusetts (where they become the Hoosacs). Average height of peaks is between 2,000 and 3,000 feet; Mount Mansfield is highest, at 4,393 feet. The Long Trail of the Appalachian Trail runs for 260 miles through the Green Mountains, which are noted for their scenic beauty and for production of marble and granite.
    For "Green-Mountain boys," see "Allen, Ethan."
W. 50; M.D. 5; M.D. 6; I.P. 1; I.P. 21

GREEN RIVER COUNTRY
    The Green River commences in north western Colorado and flows through Utah, joining the Colorado River just before it flows into what is now Powell Reservoir, thus helping create the Grand Canyon.
    In the early nineteenth century, bandits such as *Samuel Meason and the *Harpe brothers made life in the area precarious.
C.M. 1

GREEN ROOM
    Performers' waiting room in a theatre: so called because originally walls in such a room were colored green to relieve eyestrain caused by stage lights.
W. 23

GREENWICH

One of the boroughs constituting Greater *London, England; on the south bank of the *Thames, bounded on the east by Bexley, south by Bromley, and west by Lewisham: notable as the past home of the Royal Observatory, where the prime meridian mark is still visible (since 1884 the mark from which all countries have reckoned longitude). The clipper *Cutty Sark* is in dry dock near Greenwich pier, a memorial to the merchant navy of the days of sail.

Greenwich is also remarkable for its architecture, including that of the former Greenwich Hospital for retired naval men—M.'s "Pensioners." *Charles II commissioned a palace to replace Placentia (home to *Tudor monarchs), but only the present King Charles block was built. William and Mary instructed *Sir Christopher Wren (1632-1723) to complete it as a naval hospital to commemorate the naval victory of La Hogue, patterned after the *Chelsea Hospital for soldiers. 2,700 pensioners were accommodated in Wren's large twin-domed baroque edifice. The building included the Painted Hall, with frescoes by Sir James Thornhill (1675-1734) and a chapel later redecorated by James ("Athenian") Stuart (1713-1788) and William Newton (1735-1790). In 1873 the hospital was closed, and the building became the home of the Royal Naval College.

Greenwich Hospital was Greenwich Palace (*M.D.* 32) in the time of Charles II. William III and Queen Mary gave it to the Navy.

M. commented at length on the Greenwich facilities in his journal for 21 November 1849.

(See also "Chronometricals and Horologicals.")
T. 4; M. 139; M.D. 32; P. 14:3

GREENWICH-STREET

*New York City's Greenwich Street dates from the 1730's. It commences on *Manhattan's lower west side at *Battery Place, running north to *Gansevoort street (in modern times with a gap for the World Trade Center between Liberty and Vesey Streets). The area surrounding the street became known as Greenwich Village. In the early nineteenth century, its low buildings, verdant gardens, and fresh *Hudson River air made it a refuge from the more developed and disease-ridden east side, and many New Yorkers "escaped" to it during times of epidemic. Artists and writers including *Poe began claiming the area as their own in the first third of the century. (Poe lived on Greenwich Street at Rector.) By the 1860's, even the formerly bucolic "Greenwich"

was yielding its open spaces and breaking up its fine private homes into tenements.
R. 1

GREENWICH TIME
The mean time for the meridian of *Greenwich, or time at which noon occurs at the moment of passage of the mean sun over the meridian. It is Standard Time, adapted by astronomers, from which all civilized nations compute time.

Greenwich time was Standard in *Britain until 1968, when British clocks were advanced one hour, making Summer Time permanent—now called British Standard Time.
0. 17; 0. 42

GREENWOOD
One of the earliest (1842) *American cemeteries detached from church or private property, in Brooklyn, *New York.
C.M. 5

GREGO
*Turkish name for a hooded jacket.
M.D. 3

GRENADIER'S STEAK
Grenadiers being the tallest strongest, toughest, and bravest of soldiers, their steak is probably raw.
M.D. 61

GREYLOCK, --'S
Mount Greylock, fifteen miles north of *Pittsfield, *Massachusetts, is the highest mountain in the state, at c. 3,500 feet. There are two roads to the summit, and the mountain is crossed by the *Appalachian Trail.

Greylock, or Saddleback, as it is called because of its double-humped shape, held great significance for M., whose desk faced window views of the mountain at both of his Massachusetts residences. *P.* was dedicated to Greylock probably because M. had lost faith in human dedicatees (such as *Hawthorne) by the time of its publication (1852). Greylock is thought by some to be the original of that novel's "*Mount of the

Titans," and it has a role in several of the short stories (most importantly in "The Piazza").

M. and his friends often climbed the mountain for all-night picnics in the wooden observatory on its summit. If women were in attendance (as they were on an August 1851 excursion), wagons were taken to within three miles of the summit and the remainder of the climb covered on foot, despite the encumbering clothing of the "ladies" and the heavy provisions (often including *champagne) carried by the men.
P. Dedication

GRIFFIN
Legendary creature: half lion and half eagle.
M.D. 82

GROG
Grog was the sailor's name for the daily spirit ration (usually 1/2 pint of rum, or the equivalent in beer or ale) to which he was entitled. If a man were scheduled to be punished, he might instead forego his grog to avoid *flogging. Thus, grog was a bargaining chip for the sailor; it benefited the officers as well to have the tie because grog was frequently a cause for infractions. The U.S. *Navy began working against the practice of tying the two in the 1830's, and *temperance and religious organizations of the time crusaded against grog. But it was not until 1862 that the grog ration was abolished, with an appropriate pay raise taking its place.
W. Passim and elsewhere

GROIX
Groix Island, in the *Bay of Biscay, off *France's Brittany coast eight miles south-southwest of Lorient, is five miles long, two miles wide. It is remarkable for its sea caves and megalithic monuments. M. may be in error in *I.P.*'s reference to *John Paul Jones's sailing on *Bon Homme Richard* from Groix; most sources say he sailed from Lorient.
I.P. 18

GROWLANDS WALFISH
Grönlands Valfisk: *Greenland whale.
M.D. 32

GRUMMET
Modern Grommet. A ring of rope used as a substitute for an oarlock or to secure the upper edge of a sail to a stay.
Also, a ship's boy or cabin boy.
W. 47

GUADALQUIVER
The chief river of southern *Spain, the Guadalquiver originates at over 4,000 feet elevation and rapidly descends in small streams until it joins the Guadalmena, traveling through large swamps to the *Atlantic, a 348-mile journey.
M. 32

GUARDO
A military boat for harbor-watch, used to collect and impress seamen from the streets.
W. 73; W. 91 and elsewhere

GUAYAQUIL
Guayaquil is a *Pacific port of western *Ecuador, on the right bank of the Guayas River, forty-five miles from the Gulf of Guayaquil, and 170 miles southwest of *Quito. Guayaquil was founded in 1536 and is today the largest city of Ecuador. In the seventeenth century, it was attacked by *pirates, destroyed by fires, and wracked by plagues (including yellow fever). It gained independence from *Spain in the 1820's.
One of its major exports remains the high-crowned, immensely brimmed straw hat, often worn decorated with a huge ribbon bow on one side of the brim: worn by men and women in the tropics.
O. 78; M. 15; M. 59

GUDGEONS; SEA-GUDGEON
Gudgeons are killifish: *Gobio fluviatilis*, a freshwater fish used as bait. Sea-gudgeons are small sucking ocean fish.
M.D. Extracts; M.D. 48 and elsewhere

GUELPHS AND GHIBELLINES
The medieval *Italian political parties of the Guelphs and the Ghibellines arose in thirteenth-century *Florence. The names are corruptions of the family name of the *German house of Welf and the local name of Waiblingen, in Swabia, indicating adherents of the Welf Otto IV and the Hohenstaufen

Frederick II, *Holy Roman Empire rivals. The *parte Guelfa* became identified with the papal party; the *Ghibellina* with the imperial. Both parties survived the initial period of struggle from which they emerged, spreading across Italy and lasting into the fifteenth century, with rather altered allegiances.

See also "Dante."

I.P. 19

GUERNSEY

The ancient Sarnia is the second largest (eight miles long, five miles wide) of the *Channel Islands. It is sixteen miles west of *Normandy. The inhabitants of Guernsey, which is famous for its cattle, are *French-speaking, although the island belongs to *Britain. Its capital is Saint Peter Port.

R. 15; R. 44; R. 45; R. 50; W. 25; W. 75; M.D. 91

GUERRIERE, THE

The *British frigate *Guerriere* (thirty-eight guns) had been captured from the *French. It was commanded by Captain James Dacres at *Portsmouth in 1812 when it engaged with *Constitution*, commanded by Captain *Isaac Hull. In short order, *Constitution* dismasted the British prize, earning her nickname, "Old Ironsides," when *Guerriere* sank. The American victory was psychologically important, along with victories over *Java* and *Phoebe*, in the same year.

M.'s father, Allan Melvill (see "Walter Redburn"), had been aboard a ship captured by *Guerriere* in 1811.

R. 18; W. 87

GUICCIARDINI

Francesco Guicciardini (1483-1540), *Florentine historian/statesman, wrote *Storia d'Italia*, a history of *Italy from 1492 to 1534. His aristocratic origins led to early relations with the *Medicis and with the *Papacy, as governor of a recently acquired papal state and counsel in the *Vatican. His fortunes suffered finally as a result of both associations, and he retired to write the uncompleted *Storia*, political treatises, and a collection of maxims and observations, the *Ricordi* (1528, 1530).

R. 30

GUIDE TO PARIS

It is presumed that the book referred to in *I.P.* is that mentioned in *R. 30*: Louis Marie Prudhomme, *Voyage

descriptif et philosophique de l'ancien et du nouveau Paris. Miroir fidèle . . . *Paris, Chez l'auteur, 1815 (Sealts #538; originally published in 1814). The book was owned by M.'s father, Allan Melvill. (See "Walter Redburn.")
I.P. 7; I.P. 9

GUIDO'S
Guido Reni (1575-1642) was a self-taught Bolognese painter and engraver who gained fame in *Rome, especially for his *Vatican frescoes. His best work, however, was done after his permanent return to *Bologna in 1630. His "Academist" painting was praised by pre-neo-classicists, especially in *France, but Ruskin and the romanticists disagreed, faulting his nostalgia-coated invoking of classical standards of beauty.

The painting of Beatrici *Cenci mentioned in *P.* was one of many copies. It was regarded as an almost sacred object at the time, in light of the subject's presumed innocence, a sentiment furthered by *Shelley's *Cenci* and later by *Hawthorne's *The Marble Faun.* Later data suggested that Beatrici was probably not a victim of incest; her reputation, furthermore, became rather maculate with the discovery that she had plotted to assassinate her father. M. saw the original at the Palazzo Barbarini in February 1857; he owned an engraving.

The picture of *Perseus rescuing *Andromeda was in *London's National Gallery, which M. visited in 1849. He commented in his journal on "Guido's Murder of the Innocents" (17 December).

"Guido's Apollo" is a fresco in the Palazzo Rospigliosi, Rome: "Phoebus and the Hours, Preceded by Aurora."
R. 46; M.D. 55; P. 26:1

GUILDHALL
*London's Guildhall was built in 1411 by the merchant guilds, which had become allied with the municipal government. It has been used as a town hall, law court, and most recently a museum dedicated to the history, architecture, and daily life of London. The basement has underground crypt vaults with intricately ribbed architecture.
M. 149

GUINEA; COAST-OF-GUINEA; GUINEA COAST
Guinea is the former designation for the west coast of Central *Africa along the Gulf of Guinea and northward (c.

15° N.-16° S.). It was the major source of African slaves from
colonial times and has been called variously Slave Coast, Ivory
Coast, Gold Goast, Grain Coast.
        See also "Black Guinea"; "West Indian Trade."
R. 35; W. 90; M.D. 132; C.M. 6

"GUINEA-PIG"
        In *England, originally used in finance, designating a
figurehead company director, paid a fee for use of his name.
        *Captain Marryat uses it to designate a *midshipman (like
"Harry Bolton" in R.): neither a sailor nor an officer, as a
guinea pig is neither from *Guinea nor a pig.
        Other English uses: a special juryman paid a guinea a
day, a clergyman without a parish who gives sermons for a
guinea; anyone used in an experiment, as guineapigs are.
        An actual guinea pig is a *South American rodent:
"cavy."
R. 44

GULF STREAM
        The largest of the oceanic warm current systems in the
North *Atlantic, the Gulf Stream is formed by junction of the
*Antilles and *Gulf of Mexico currents. It runs through the
Straits of *Florida, northeast along the continent's southeast
coast, veering east at 40° to merge with the North Atlantic
current. Technically, the term only applies to the middle section of the current, between *Cape Hatteras and the *Grand
Banks southeast of *Newfoundland. Surface temperature of
the water is between 65 and 70°. The deep-blue highly saline
stream moves at speeds up to four miles per hour; it is slowest
in its most southerly portions, where the water is deepest:
averaging perhaps the one and one-half miles per hour off
*Florida noted in R. 20. The Gulf Stream was first observed by
*Ponce de Léon.
R. 14; R. 20

GULF-WEED
        Of the genus *Sargassum*, gulf-weed is a greenish-brown
seaweed with berrylike air vessels keeping it afloat: found
mainly in the *Gulf Stream and Sargasso Sea.
R. 20; M.D. 87

GUTHRIE

G.J. Guthrie is author of *A Treatise on Gun-Shot Wounds, on Injuries of Nerves, and on Wounds of the Extremities Requiring the Different Operations of Amputation, in which the Various Methods of performing these Operations are shown, together with their After-treatment; and Containing an Account of the Author's successful Use of Amputation at the Hip-joint* (Second Edition, 1820).
W. 63

GUY, CAPTAIN

Little is known of the prototype of "Captain Guy" of the "*Julia." The journal of the *French ship *La Reine Blanche confirms that at the time the *Lucy Ann*, the broken-down whaler presumed the model for the "Julia," arrived at *Tahiti, it was captained by one Vinton (or Venton, or Ventom), a weak man whose mate ran his ship. The mutiny in *O.* is also confirmed in this journal.
0. Passim

GWYNNE, NELL

Eleanor Gwyn (Gwynne, or Gwynn;   1650-1687), *English actress, was a popular mistress of *Charles II. Her putative father is said to have died in debtor's prison, and her mother kept a brothel. As a refreshment-purveyor in the King's Theatre, *London, Nell attracted the attention of an actor who sponsored a stage debut leading to a successful career and a series of highly placed lovers, including the king. Retiring in 1670 to bear the king's son, she was established in a fine house, where she entertained the King and his circle. Charles eventually made her son, Charles Beauclerk, Duke of St. Albans. Nell was the king's favorite, preferred as well by the public, despite her illiteracy and humble origins. She did not interfere in politics and remained faithful to the King, whose brother, *James II supported her after his death. She is buried in the Church of St. Martin's-in-the-Fields.

M. sees her as a social climber.
P. 1:3

HAARLEM; HARLEM

Haarlem (formerly Harlem), a city of the west *Netherlands eleven miles west of *Amsterdam, is famous for its medieval gabled houses, including the Stadhuis (the Stadt House of *R.* 30), begun in 1250. The city was chartered in 1245 and has been famous for its bulb-growing industry, and its seventeenth century artists (Frans Hals and Jacob von Ruisdael, among others).

The "Haarlem organ" of *M.D.* 75, for many years the largest organ in the world, was the Groote Kerk (St. Bavo) organ. Constructed 1735-38, it had 5,000 pipes.
M.D. 75; P. 26:5

HABEAS CORPUS

Lat.: "have the body." *Habeas corpus* provides for the right of a person in custody to appear in court rather than be detained on suspicion or detained for a long period. The idea originated about the time of *Magna Carta (1215), and has been interpreted and tested frequently. It has also been suspended often; *Lincoln suspended *habeas corpus* during the *Civil War.
W. 35

HABISCUS

Hibiscus, of the lobe-leaved mallow family, is a shrub or small tree with large colorful flowers, often used as hairdecorations.
T. 14; O. 36

HACKLUYT

Richard Hakluyt, *The Principal Navigations* (1598), I. p. 568—Arngrimus Ionas of Island, Part I, sec. 14, is M.'s etymology source.

The "third old gentleman in Hackluyt" of *M.D.* 75 is *Thomas Edge. M.'s quotation paraphrases a comment in *Purchas His Pilgrimes* (1625), not in Hackluyt.
M. 75; M.D. Etymology; M.D. 56; M.D. 75

HADES

In *Greek mythology, kingdom of the dead, ruled over by *Pluto (or Hades) and Queen Persephone (see "Proserpine"). In the *Odyssey*, it is located across the Ocean, off the edge of the world. Later writers locate entrances in caverns beside deep lakes.

Hades was not necessarily like Hell but has been used as a euphemism for Hell. It was a gloomy place, corresponding to *Hebrew *Sheol*.
M. 140; I.P. 15; I.P. 24

HAFIZ

Shams ud-din Muhammad Hafiz (c. 1325-c. 1389 or 90), was a *Persian poet and philosopher. He is most noted for his *Divan*, short lyric poems called "*ghazals*" or "*ghasels*," which operate, despite their simple colloquial language, on three levels of meaning: they are tributes to a patron, potent images of love and wine, and philosophical mysteries. Hafiz was born, lived, died, and was buried in Shiraz, where he was a lecturer on Koranic and other theological subjects. (Hafiz refers to "one who knows the *Koran by heart.")

He was a court poet with many patrons, during the stormy era of Timur (*Tamerlane). The first *English translation of *Divan* was J. Richardson's 1774 *Odes of Hafez*, superseded many times since then.
M. 33; M. 119; P. 17:2; C.M. 36

HAGAR

See "Ishmael."
M. 13; P. 5:1

HAHNEMAN, MR. SIMILIA SIMILIBUS CURANTUR

Playful *Latinate name for Dr. Samuel Christian Friederich Hahneman (1755-1843), describing an important facet of his methodology, homeopathy: "like cures like."

"*Contraria contrariis curantur*" is M.'s idea of an opposite method: "contraries cure contraries."

Homeopathy revolutionized medicine in the nineteenth century. It has three major principles: 1. diseases are cured by medicines that produce the disease in healthy bodies; 2. medicine should be simple, not compounded; 3. doses should be minute. These principles have had great effect on modern medicine; most important was the cessation of administration of massive doses.

Like *phrenology, homeopathy had adherents and opponents in the United States. *Hawthorne's father-in-law was a physician interested in it; Oliver Wendell Holmes believed patients cured by the methods may have been psychosomatically afflicted, responding to the idea of a cure, rather than to the treatment itself.
W. 54

HAIRY ORSON

A character in the fifteenth-century *French romance, *Valentin et Orson*, about twins: Valentin is reared at court, while Orson is reared in the woods by a bear who has carried him off. (Fr. *ourson* means "bear-cub.") There are later versions, including one in *English: "History of two Valyannte Brethren, Valentyne and Orson," by Henry Watson (1550).
C.M. 26

HALE, MATTHEW

Sir Matthew Hale (1609-1676) was lord chief justice of *England under *Charles II, a distinguished lawyer and legal writer who played an important role in political trials. Steering a middle course between the *Puritans and Charles's court, he held a secure position in the unsteady political world of the time. Despite his reputation for fairness and moderation, he is known to have convicted two women of witchcraft and to have rapidly condemned a soldier accused of murder, for fear of his being reprieved. His most famous works are *History of the Common Law of England* (1713) and *History of the Pleas of the Crown* (1685).
W. 72

HALF JOES

See "Joes."
M.D. 99

HALL, JAMES

The writings of Hall (1793-1868), circuit judge and editor in *Illinois, comprise a valuable record of the nineteenth-century *American West. Hall edited two newspapers and a magazine and wrote many books, the most important of which for M. was *Sketches of History, Life, and Manners, in the West* (1834 or -35), used, sometimes verbatim, in the writing of *C.M.* Hall also wrote *The Wilderness and the War Path* (1846), a valuable sourcebook for *Indian traditions.
C.M. 25

HALLOWELL, CAPTAIN

Sir Benjamin Hallowell Carey (1760-1834) was in command of the *Scorpion* sloop in the *Mediterranean when he first caught the attention of *Nelson. Accused of possible negligence in the loss of *Courageux*, Hallowell waited on *Victory* to return to *England (where he was eventually cleared) and was thus present at the battle of Cape *St. Vincent (1797). He was on *Swiftsure* against the *French in Aboukir Bay and helped destroy *L'Orient*. When he rejoined Nelson two years later, the Admiral was surprised to receive a coffin certified made of *L'Orient*'s wood and iron. A note from Hallowell explained that the gift was intended "that when you are tired of this life you may be buried in one of your own trophies." (DNB ascribes the grimness of Hallowell's humor to his early education in *America.)

Hallowell's career continued with capture by the French, court-martialing, and service in the *West Indies and at the *Nore, where he was noted for strict discipline, warding off repetition of the mutinies of the past.
W. 74

HAMAN

In the *Old Testament Book of Esther, the perhaps historical prime minister of the *Persian king Ahasuerus (see "Xerxes") is the son of Hammedatha. An enemy of the *Hebrews, Haman plots to destroy them because *Mordecai, the uncle of Esther, refuses to bow before him. Haman is hanged on the gallows he prepares for Mordecai, and his ten sons are killed in a subsequent purge of the Jews by their enemies.
M. 24

HAMBURG; HAMBURGH

The northwestern *German city is on an *Elbe River estuary, fifty-five miles southeast of the North Sea and 150 miles northwest of *Berlin. Hamburg dates from the ninth century, when *Charlemagne captured a local castle. The town developed in the twelfth to thirteenth centuries and was one of the originators of the *Hanse League. Its fortifications were razed in the early nineteenth century, and a fire in 1842 destroyed one-third of its buildings, but Hamburg remained Germany's largest port, joining the German Empire in the 1870's.
R. 1; R. 9; R. 15

HAMILTON, LADY

Lady Emma Hamilton (c. 1765-1815), neé Amy Lyon, was the daughter of a blacksmith. Changing her name to Emma Hart, she rose in the world with the help of a protector who taught her the social graces and introduced her to such society as *Admiral Romney and his own uncle, Sir William Hamilton (1730-1803), diplomat, archaeologist, and collector. She became a favorite in European society, especially for her *poses plastiques*, or *tableaux vivants*, and Hamilton married her to justify her reception at court.

She is said to have spied for the *British fleet during the *Nile campaign, during which she met her most famous lover, *Admiral Nelson. After traveling across Europe with the two men, she bore Nelson's child, and after her husband's death lived with him, eventually inheriting fortunes from both, which she gambled away. After a year in debtor's prison, she died in comparative poverty in *Calais.

M. owned an engraving of Lady Hamilton as a Bacchante.
W. 6

HAMLET; *HAMLET*; HAMLETISM

*Shakespeare's tragic play about the melancholy *Danish prince had great influence on M., especially for *P*. Shakespeare's violent plot focuses on the mores of traditional royalty, revenge of a relative's honor, misguided heroics, madness and sanity, and possible incest, all of which also afflict M.'s "Hamlet"-like hero, "Pierre."

In his own copy of the play (Sealts #460), M. scored "Hamlet's" observation in II, 2, 259-61: ". . . there is nothing either good or bad, but thinking makes it so; to me it is a prison." He commented in the margin: "Here is forcibly shown the great *Montaignism of Hamlet."

See also "Extracts" 16; "gravedigger"; "Laertes"; "Polonius"; and "Quotations" Section: "to consider the thing too curiously"; "the friends thou has . . . "; "The time is out of joint . . . . "
W. 39; M.D. Extracts 16; (Covertly: "the play," M.D. 127); P. 7:6; P. 9:2; P. 9:4; C.M. 18; C.M. 44

HAMO; HAMORA

In *M*., a fictional term relative to *Noah's son, Ham (*Genesis 9:22-25), cursed by his father. The curse was popularly taken to refer to black skin. In *M*. 157 and 162, black slaves are said to belong to the tribe of "Hamo"; in *M*. 168, "Hamora" alludes to *Africa.
M. 157; M. 162; M. 168

HAMPDENS

M.'s "*English farmer" Hampdens are a line of Buck-inghamshire country gentlemen, the most famous of which, John Hampden (1594-1643), was a cousin of *Oliver Cromwell. He opposed *Charles I in matters of the nonparliamentary ship-building tax, property tax, and *Puritan settlements. He was tried and imprisoned in the *Tower and died of wounds incurred in battle against Royal forces.
P. 1:4

HAMPTON COURT

The *Tudor palace in *London's *Richmond-upon-Thames was built by Cardinal Wolsey, who gave it to *Henry VIII as a residence. In the palace, Jane Seymour died, and Henry married Catherine Howard and Catherine Parr. It was the scene of the 1604 Hampton Court Conference, which led to the translation for the "Authorized Version" of the *Bible in 1611.

The palace, which had been used by monarchs up to *George II, was newly opened to the public by *Queen Victoria when M. visited on 11 November 1849.
M.D. Extracts 7

HAND-BOOK OF THE NEVERSINK

City directories, alphabetical lists of the inhabitants of a given locality, were standard features of large cities. *Dana (p. 312) mentions the *Boston directory; Smalley's notes to Mrs. Trollope cite the *Cincinnati Directory for 1829.

The Trow Business Directory of New York City for 1848/49 is the first edition of that series. It is a curiously inti-mate listing by profession, supposedly of all the then-residents of *New York City. The foreword proclaims that any omis-sions are the fault of those omitted, because a "thorough can-vass of the whole city was made by careful canvassers." A brief scan revealed no Melvilles. There is no listing for "writer," nor for "private citizen," although the range of occu-pations includes lines from "sparmaker" to "carpet shaker." The Melville clan may be represented in an earlier Trow Metropolitan Directory of Selected Names, or in Social Elite.

(M. should have remembered the uselessness of guide-books from his comments on them in R.)
W. 31

HANDEL

George Frederick Handel (1658-1759), German/English composer, wrote operas; cantatas and other vocal music with Italian words, as well as vocal music in English; church music; instrumental, and chamber music. His greatest work, *The Messiah* (1742), is mentioned in *W*. 50, along with *Israel in Egypt* (1739), *Judas Maccabeus* (1747), *Samson* (1741), *Saul* (1739), *Solomon* (*and Susanna*, 1748). This section of *W*. 50 is unclear; the composer mentioned is *Haydn, but the "anthems" cited are Handel's.
R. 51

HANDSOME MARY

Although Partridge does not include the sobriquet "Handsome Mary," we may infer that she is the female equivalent of his "Handsome Harry," who is a *Lothario.
R. 28; R. 31; R. 37

HANG-HO

One section of *China's Grand Canal (Chah ho, or Yun ho), in the Shantung province, was named Hwang-ho. The 650-mile-long Canal was begun in the seventh century (Tang dynasty), and completed under the thirteenth-century *Mongols and fourteenth-century Ming dynasty. The earliest section followed a former river bed of the Yellow River, called the Hwang-ho. Presumably, this is also M.'s "canal of Ving-King-Ching, in the Flowery Kingdom," in *C.M.* 2.
M.D. 64

HANNAMANOO

A bay on Hivaoa (La Dominica), *Marquesas. Correct spelling is Hanamenu.
O. 7; O. 8

HANNIBAL

The most famous Hannibal (247-183 or 182 B.C.), son of Hamilcar Barca, was a great military leader said at an early age to have sworn eternal hostility to *Rome. He was Commander in Chief of the Carthaginian army at the age of twenty-six. Among his more picturesque military feats in the Second *Punic War was his crossing of the *Alps from *Gaul into *Italy with large numbers of infantry and cavalry drawn from several nations, and with thirty-eight elephants, few of which survived the constant guerilla attacks and snowstorms.

After a treaty was made between Rome and *Carthage, Hannibal became unpopular and, after a series of defeats, he poisoned himself rather than surrender to Rome. Biographies were written by Polybius, *Livy, and others. (Sealts #147, *Harper's Classical Library*, Volumes 24-28, are Livy's works.) M. 24; W. 91; M.D. 105; C.M. 26

HANOVER, HOUSE OF

*Britain's House of Hanover, rulers from before M.'s time to the present, secured succession to the throne as a result of the 1701 Act of Settlement. First Hanover king was George I (reigned 1714-27); he was succeeded by *George II (1727-60), and the (in the *American colonies) infamous *George III (1760-1820). Hanover rule ended the possibility of *Stuart recovery of the throne, especially after quelling of the Jacobite Rebellion (1715), which all but disintegrated the *Tory party and established *Whig supremacy. Hanover rule brought few reforms, but it stabilized Britain, bringing it to world supremacy, despite loss of the colonies and charges of corruption.

Other Hanoverians were *George IV (1820-30), William IV (1830-37), and *Victoria (1837-1901). Present-day Windsors are Hanoverians whose name was changed when George V decreed in 1917 that all male descendents of Victoria would adopt the name. Elizabeth II chose to name her offspring Windsor.
M. 3; M.D. 42

HANOVERIAN

Hanover was a former province of the *Prussian province of northwestern *Germany. The House of Hanover ruled in union with *Britain from 1692 until the time of *Victoria, when enforcement of the Salic (see "Salique") law placed a male on the Hanover throne and the union was terminated.
M.D. 42

HANSE TOWNS

From the thirteenth to the seventeenth centuries, the Hanseatic League (including the Hanse Towns and *Wisbury, or "Wisbuy") dominated Northern European commerce. Formed as a defense against robbers and *pirates, the League of Northern *German towns developed into a powerful, tightly-knit organization with increasingly stringent and parochial laws.
W. 72

HAPPAR; HAPPARS; VALLEY OF HAPPARS
Properly, "Hapa." See "Marquesas; Marquesans."
T. Passim

HAPPAR MOUNTAIN
See "Marquesans; Marquesas!"
T. 13; T. 20

"HAPPY VALLEY"
The Abyssinian (see "Ethiopian") valley in which the
hero grows up, in *Samuel Johnson's *Rasselas* (1759).
T. 17

HARARPARPI
Ha'apape district of *Tahiti, of which *Matavai is a divi-
sion.
O. 32

HARDICANUTES
King of *Denmark from 1028, Hardicanute (c. 1019-1042)
was also king of the *English from 1040. He was an unpopular
ruler who defiled his buried predecessor's remains, collected
large taxes to support his navy, and burned and ravaged
Worcester, England.
M.D. 1

HARD-SCRABBLE
Strenuous effort under stress, such as that of a cultiva-
tor of barren soil.
M.D. 72

"HARD TIMES"
The reference in *O*. 34 cannot be to the 1854 Charles
Dickens novel, *O*. making its appearance in 1847. But the
inevitable comparisons of M. and Dickens (who is not mentioned by name in M.'s novels) suggest that one treat "hard
times" as a starting-off point.
It is not surprising that M. does not allude more frequently to the works of Charles John Huffham Dickens (1812-
70), the most popular writer of the time. The publicly optimistic Dickens was considered a "healthy" writer; his sentimental portraits and stories represented the "happy ending"

desired by the reading public. The *Duyckincks wished M. more inclined to "Dickensianism," and reviewers praised such elements in *O.* and *R.* in particular.

Among Dickens's most important works: *Sketches by "Boz"* (1836-7); *The Posthumous Papers of the Pickwick Club* (1837; Sealts #182); *Oliver Twist* (1837); *American Notes* (1842); *A Christmas Carol* (1843; Sealts #143a); *David Copperfield* (1849-50; Sealts #181); *Bleak House* (1852-3); *A Tale of Two Cities* (1859); *Great Expectations* (1860-1).

M. read *Pickwick Papers* on his trip to *England, October 1849; he heard Dickens read in *New York in March of 1868. M. was an acquaintance of Thomas Powell (*The Living Authors of England*, 1850), whom Dickens publicly accused of plagiarism and insanity (New York *Herald*). Powell also turned on *American writers, including Irving and M. The "Historical Note" to the Northwestern-Newberry edition of *M.D.* gives particulars.

M.'s relation to the work of Dickens is examined in Solomon's *Dickens and Melville in Their Times*.
O. 34

HARLEM RIVER
        In *New York City, a navigable tidal channel separating the northern tip of *Manhattan from the Bronx, joining the *East River at Hell Gate Channel. It is eight miles long, with Spuyten Duyvil Creek, which joins the western end of the Harlem River with the *Hudson River. As the *R.* 30 allusion suggests, the area was undeveloped in M.'s time.
R. 30

HARMATTANS
        Dust-laden winds on the *Atlantic coast of *Africa.
M.D. 44

HARPE, THE BROTHERS
        Bloodthirsty criminals in the southwest. Big Harpe was captured and beheaded; Little Harpe joined the gang of *Samuel Measan, whose head he cut off and tried to sell. He was seized and beheaded also.
C.M. 1

HARRIS; HARRIS COLL.; HARRIS'S COLLECTION OF VOYAGES; HARRIS'S VOYAGES

John Harris (c. 1666-1719) edited the earliest *English encyclopaedia, *Lexicon technicum*, or *Universal Dictionary of the Arts and Sciences* (1704). His *Navigantium atque Itinerantium Bibliotheca*, or *Collection of Voyages and Travels* (1705; 1748) was an important source for *M.D.*

An ordained minister at Trinity College, *Oxford, Harris was a mathematician and member of the *Royal Society; his ardent support of government led to his being parodied in *The Picture of a High-Flying Clergyman* (1716), by his enemy, the Rev. Charles Humphreys.

M. is in error in "Extracts 30." Friedrich Martens's *Voyage into Spitzenbergen* was not in the Harris collection but in one by Tancred Robinson (1694).

See also "Extracts" 12, 28, 29, 30.

M.D. Extracts 28; M.D. Extracts 29; M.D. Extracts 30; M.D. 55; M.D. 56; M.D. 83

HARRISON, GENERAL

William Henry Harrison (1773-1841), ninth *President of the *United States and the first to die in office, came from an important political family; his father was a signer of the *Declaration of Independence and Governor of *Virginia. Harrison left medical school for the army in 1791 and married Anna Symmes (1775-1864), daughter of Judge John Cleves Symmes; their grandson, Benjamin Harrison, became the twenty-third President. Resigning a captaincy in 1797. Harrison became secretary of the Northwest Territory, then Governor of Indian Territory. As special commissioner to the Indians, he enforced several treaties that agitated them into the 1811 Tippecanoe River incident. His victory gained him much prestige, as did his action as Brigadier General commanding northwest troops in the *War of 1812. After his defeat of the British at the Battle of the *Thames, he turned to politics, serving in both houses of *Congress. Defeated by Martin Van Buren in his 1836 run for the Presidency, he was nominated to run again in 1840, with anti-*Jacksonian running mate, John Tyler.

In a loud and colorful campaign, the slogan "Tippecanoe and Tyler too" gained Harrison an overwhelming victory over Van Buren. He died one month after taking office, succeeded by Tyler.

Harrison had planned to reorganize the *Navy, thus the W. sailor flogged for voting for him had trod on sensitive toes.
W. 88

HARRY HALYARD
The author of "dime novel" thrillers including *The Doom of the Dolphin: or, The Sorceress of the Sea. A Tale of Love, Intrigue, and Mystery* (Boston 1848), as well as *Wharton's the Killer! or, The Pride of the Pacific; a Tale of the Ocean* (1848).
See also "Extracts" 78.
M.D. Extracts 78

HARRY THE EIGHTH
See "Henry VIII's."
R. 41; W. 6

HART, JOSEPH C.
Colonel Hart (1798-1855), lawyer, journalist, eventual U.S. consul in the *Canary Islands, was a *New Yorker who spent much time in *Nantucket. His *Miriam Coffin; or The Whale Fishermen* (1834) was the first *American whaling novel and an important source for *M.D.* (a debt made explicit in Anderson's *Melville in the South Seas*). M. refused to review the 1848 *The Romance of Yachting*, a collection of essays (Sealts #242).
(See also "Extracts" 75.)
M.D. Extracts 75

HARTFORD, CHARTER IN THE OLD OAK
Legend says that the charter of *Connecticut was hidden in an oak at Hartford when Sir Edmund Andros sought its surrender in 1687.
M. 97

HARTO
*Sir Thomas Browne says in *Pseudodoxia Epidemica* (Sealts #s 89 and 90), Book 6, Chapter 6, that Garcias ab Horto was physician to the Viceroy at Goa, *India, and claimed that the King of Siam had captured 4,000 elephants at a time.
M.D. 105

HARTSHORN
In alchemy, spirits of ammonia (from the Middle Ages practice of obtaining an aqueous solution by distilling the horns and hoofs of oxen).
M.D. 32; M.D 107

HARTZ FOREST

The Harz Mountains, in *Germany (51°42' N; 10°50' E.) are densely forested and famous for demons and ghosts.
M. 1; R. 60; M.D. 42

HARVARD

Harvard University was founded at Newe Towne (Cambridge), in 1636, under a *Massachusetts Bay Colony grant. In 1639, it was named for John Harvard, a colonist who contributed his library and half of his estate. *Emerson was a graduate of the Divinity School (1819) of the Unitarian-affiliated college. Other schools extant in M.'s time were those of medicine (1782), law (1817), Lawrence Scientific (1847-1907), Radcliffe College for women (1879). Most of the American "*Brahmins" were graduates.
M.D. 24; M.D. 88

HATTERAS

North Carolina, U.S.: 35°15' N; 75°24' W.: called "the graveyard of the Atlantic," for its many shipwrecks.
W. 3; W. 8

HAUSER, CASPER

Casper (or Kaspar; 1812?-1833) was a celebrated "wild boy" who mysteriously appeared in Nürnberg, Germany, 26 May 1828, bearing letters supplying a putative birth date and a request that the unspeaking boy be educated. He later claimed that he had spent his early years confined in a hole and only late taught to stand and walk by a rescuer who then abandoned him. At Nürnberg he was taken in by several prominent persons, educated, and eventually given a clerkship in the President's office at the Ansbach Court of Appeals. He died of a mysterious knife wound which he claimed had been inflicted by his early rescuer. The case received much publicity, especially regarding Hauser's forebears, who may have been heirs to the German throne. In 1838 the first of several fictionalized versions of the story appeared, a play by Anicet Bourgeois and Adolphe Philippe Dennery (D'Ennery): *Gaspard Hauser.*

(See also "Peter the Wild Boy," and "Hairy Orson." Hauser is also alluded to in *Billy Budd, Sailor.*)
P. 18:1; C.M. 2

HAVANNA, --S

Havana (La Habana), capital city of *Cuba, is on Havana Bay, Gulf of *Mexico, 100 miles south-southwest of Key West, *Florida. It was founded in 1519 by Diego de Velázquez. The Cathedral (1704) contained until 1898 the supposed remains of *Christopher Columbus, European discoverer of Cuba.

As M.'s references suggest, the city's greatest fame has been for the manufacture of cigars. Columbus had discovered the Indians smoking a primitive cigar—twisted tobacco leaves wrapped in a palm or maize leaf. The *Spanish word *cigarro* was probably derived from an Indian word for "smoking." By the early seventeenth century, smoking and tobacco-growing were widespread, but the Havana cigar, with tobacco grown from special seed-leaf varieties and raised in certain moist Cuban soils (especially in the Pinar del Río province) remained the most favored. M. was an inveterate cigar-smoker.
R. 1; R. 9; R. 25; R. 50; P. 18:1

HAVRE FROCKS, --SHIRTS

The sailor's favorite heavy woolen work shirt takes its name from Le Havre, on the English *Channel in northern *France, at the mouth of the *Seine, 110 miles west-northwest of *Paris. It was founded in 1516 as Havre-de-Grâce, by François I. Although three-quarters destroyed during World War II, it is still famous for the manufacture of work clothes.
T. 6; R. 1; R. 8; R. 9; R. 29; W. 25

HAWAII; HAWAIIAN, --S; HAWAIIAN ISLANDS

The chain of volcanic and coral islands near the center of the north *Pacific is 1,578 miles long from east-southeast to west-northwest (between 18°55' and 28°25' N. and 154°48' and 178°25' W.; not surveyed until 1871-1900). The principal islands are Hawaii (ninety miles long, seventy-five miles wide), Maui (M.'s *Mowee), Molakai, Lanai, Kahoolawe, *Oahu (capital since 1850 is *Honolulu), Kauai, Niihau; the Northwestern Islands are tiny islets.

The islands were populated about A.D. 400 by *Polynesians presumed mostly of *Caucasian stock who had traveled to Polynesia from *Asia via the *Malay Peninsula and *Java. There was early inter-marriage of Hawaiians with *Tahitians and *Marquesans, then a period of isolation after 1300. At the time of *Cook's discovery (1778) of what he called the *Sandwich Islands, Hawaiians were an attractive strong and healthy brown people with straight or wavy black hair; they resembled the *New Zealand Maoris(see "Mowree"). After the death of Cook (1779), no western ship put in again for several years, and the isolated islands pursued a system of "Kapu," by which men ruled in order of their closeness to the gods and with the assistance of royal inbreeding: a system of oppressive taboos enforced by an administration full of favoritism and arbitrariness. Renewed Western contact brought active trade because of the Hawaiian need for firearms. During this pre-missionary western contact period, most powerful king was the great Kamehameha I (see "Kammahammaha"), uniter and ruler of all the islands from 1790; he reigned until 1819, when he was in his sixties (died 1827). Kamehameha II, Liholiho, reigned from 1819 to 1822; he and his queen died of measles during a visit to *London, and their bodies were brought back to Hawaii by Captain *Byron. Kamehameha III, Kauikeaouli, who ruled from 1824 to 1854 (with Queen *Kaahumanu regent until 1833), was the most liberal-minded of the three because of increased western contact and urbanization due to whaling and missionary activity.

M.'s complaint that the Hawaiians of his time were starving, diseased, and dying is not exaggerated. At the time of Cook's discovery, population was estimated at from 200,000 to 300,000 full-blooded Hawaiians. An 1804 epidemic decimated the population, so that missionaries estimated the 1823 population at 142,050. The first census (1832) showed a total of 130,300; by 1853 that was down to 73,100; by the late nineteenth century it was 60,000. As early as the 1850's, it became necessary to import labor for westernized sugar plantations; thousands of *Chinese (and later, *Japanese) workers were contracted for, adding eastern stock to the bloodlines during the process of cultural westernization.

M. arrived at *Lahaina on *Charles and Henry* on 27 April 1843; went to Honolulu on 10 May; returned to Lahaina on 18 May and was sent back to Honolulu on the schooner *Star*; on 17 August he joined the U.S. *Navy at Oahu, shipping on *United States* on 18 August and leaving Hawaii the following day. His claim of a "four months' residence at Honolulu" is false.

The 1820's had brought missionaries mainly from *New England, although *France pushed its powers from the 1820's to the 1850's and the *British actually annexed the islands for six months in 1843 (see "Lord George Paulet"). Most influential were *Protestants, although French Roman *Catholics (arriving from 1827) and *Mormons (from 1850) later developed strength. *Ellis's *Journal of a Tour Around Hawaii* (1825) was the first book-length treatment of the Hawaiian mission, but *Stewart's *Residence in the Sandwich Islands* (1828) was more popular. The religious "awakening" of the 1830's made thousands of nominal converts, despite backsliding into licentious paganism. Instrumental in *Christianizing was Hiram

Bingham, who responded directly to M.'s charges in *Residence of Twenty-One Years in the Sandwich Islands* (Second Ed. 1848): "I have not altered my views of heathenism or Christianity since the uncivilized 'Tipee' has sought, through the presses of civilization in England and America, to apologize for cannibalism, and to commend savage life to the sons and daughters of Christendom, instead of teaching the principles of science and virtue, or the worship of our Maker, among idolaters, man-eaters, and infidels" (XIX, 466). He boasts of the rapid advancement of the Hawaiians in Christianity and civilization by 1842. Bingham reprints the pledge of the Hawaiian Temperance Society (*T.* 26): 1. We will not drink ardent spirits for pleasure. 2. We will not traffic in ardent spirits for gain. 3. We will not engage in distilling ardent spirits. 4. We will not treat our relatives, acquaintances, or strangers, with ardent spirits, except with the consent of a temperate physician. 5. We will not give ardent spirits to workmen on account of their labor. The Society held a meeting in the chapel at Maui on 27 April 1843, the day M. arrived. *Blue Laws were in effect for the *Sabbath—so much a day of prayer and rest that even cooking was forbidden. The system of Christian taboos stressed chastity, temperance, loyalty, and Sabbath consecration, with major emphasis on the first two. Bingham also reprints "An Act of Grace," July 31, 1843, signed by Kamehamehas II and III. The paragraph which M. interprets as an invitation to licentious lawbreaking reads: "All Government business will be suspended for ten days after this date, that all persons may be free to enjoy themselves in the festivities and rejoicings appropriate to the occasion."

With the continuing interweaving of religion and politics, missionaries became influential unofficial advisers to chiefs, aiming for a literate, westernized, Protestant people and as much American republicanism as might coexist with the monarchy. Bingham's mission was such a technical success that by the 1850's and 60's it was phased out in favor of an independent Hawaiian Church. In the 1840's, the Protestant influence was already so great that as the kingdom became modernized along constitutional lines, many missionaries left for cabinet or judicial posts. Among them was *Gerrit P. Judd, pre-eminent in policy-making until the mid 50's.

The native Hawaiian religion had had four principal gods and innumerable lesser ones; human sacrifice and infanticide had been widespread, and native priests had been powerful figures. In addition to theology and music, *New England missionaries brought church steeples to replace family cult temples; Kapus were overthrown, and art was channeled into western forms. Arts such as the Hula dance (M.'s "*Hoolah-Hoolah") had been religious in association; the chant and stylized gestures for description and narration were condemned by missionaries as much for their pagan connections as for indecency.

The complexity of the Hawaiian verb "conjugated through all its mood and tenses" (*T*. 30) at the Lahainaluna College may be deduced from the following: prior to white incursions, there was no written language, so transliterations of local pronunciation were used (accounting, to some extent, for M.'s eccentric spellings). Hawaiian is a member of the Polynesian branch of the Malayo-Polynesian family of languages which has been corrupted by foreign influence, so that the modern languages today may be any or all of the following: 1. English-based Hawaiian pidgin; 2. English-based Hawaiian creole; 3. Nonstandard Hawaiian English; 4. Standard Hawaiian English.

Bingham's *Residence* provides useful "explanations" for important names, as well as a section of Hawaiian orthography and pronunciation, and a lengthy discussion of orthographical problems which explains M.'s usage: The old form "Tamaahamaah" became corrected in English to Kâh-ma-hâh-ma-hâh, thence to the New or Hawaiian Ka-mé-ha-mé-ha; *Owhyhee is the old form of Hawaii; Hanaroorah is Honolulu.

See also "Hilo"; "Kohala"; "Mauna Kea"; "Mauna Loa." See "Commodore; Commodore J." for material on Thomas ap Catesby Jones's connections with Hawaii.
T. Passim; O. Passim; M. Passim; M.D. 57 and elsewhere

HAWKE, ADMIRAL
Edward Hawke, Baron Hawke (1705-1781), *British admiral who defeated the *French at *Quiberon Bay, inspiring David Garrick to write *"Hearts of Oak."
W. 50

HAWSE HOLES, COME IN AT THE
A "hawse-holer," like an army "ranker" is one who rises from a low position; in maritime usage, from the forecastle. Technically, hawse holes are holes in a ship's fore-part through which cables pass. The term originated to describe one who started to sea such a small boy that he might have passed through the hawse holes.
W. 6

HAWTHORNE, NATHANIEL; *HAWTHORNE'S TWICE TOLD TALES*

Nathaniel Hawthorne (1804-64) was born into a prominent *Salem, *Massachusetts family, the *Puritan forebears of which included a persecutor of *Quakers and a witchcraft trial judge. This fact, along with the early death of his sea-captain father and subsequent rearing by a reclusive widow-mother, appear to have marked him as a solitary and introspective man, even after marriage to Sophia Peabody (1809-1871), member of an important family of *Transcendentalists. Hawthorne lived a secluded life after graduation from Bowdoin College, developing his art in an immature novel (*Fanshawe*, 1828) and allegorical short stories (including "The Maypole of Merrymount," "The Minister's Black Veil," "A Rill From the Town Pump" [*W.* 68], and others later reprinted in *Twice-Told Tales* [*M.D.* Extracts 54]).

Hawthorne emerged from seclusion in 1836, doing hack writing and editing *The American Magazine of Useful and Entertaining Knowledge.* He worked in the *Boston *Custom House from 1839 until 1841, when he participated briefly in the Brook Farm commune (see "Fourier"). Settling in Concord after his marriage, Hawthorne wrote the stories to be published in the 1846 *Mosses From an Old Manse* ("Young Goodman Brown," "The Celestial Railroad," "Rapaccini's Daughter," etc.), which so impressed M. that he paid anonymous tribute in the essay "Hawthorne and His Mosses" (published in *The Literary World*, 17 and 24 August 1850).

Hawthorne was living in *Lenox in 1850 when M. was visiting *Pittsfield. The two appear to have formed an instantaneous bond, visiting and corresponding regularly. Hawthorne's letters to M. are not available, but M.'s to Hawthorne demonstrate his profound attachment for the older man, who appears to have pulled away from M. within a few years. This rather fell conclusion to an intimate friendship has given rise to much imaginative speculation as to its cause. But the solitary Hawthorne might simply have found it impossible to maintain close ties with anyone beyond his own nuclear family, which was to include three children Una (1844), Julian (1846), Rose (1851).

Hawthorne's greatest work, *The Scarlet Letter*, appeared in 1850; it was followed by *The House of the Seven Gables* and *The Snow-Image and Other Twice-Told Tales* (including "Ethan Brand"), in 1851, and by *The Blithedale Romance* and *A Wonder Book* (1852), and *Tanglewood Tales* (1853), the latter two works for children. A campaign biography of Franklin Pierce (1852) brought the kind of political regard M. (perhaps half-heartedly) sought: Consulship in *Liverpool (1853-57). M. visited the Hawthornes in that city for several days in November of 1856. Hawthorne spent two years in *Italy and returned to Concord in 1860, producing *The Marble Faun* (1860), a book of essays on *England (*Our Old Home*, 1863), and several unfinished works and notebooks.

Much has been written about Hawthorne's influence on M.'s works, especially on *M.D.* (dedicated to Hawthorne), which may have evolved from a relatively direct whaling story into a complex and profound work as a result of M.'s "shock of recognition" ("Hawthorne and His Mosses") about shared concerns—morality, ontology, epistemology—and shared rejection of the easy optimism of Transcendentalist thinkers. The relative paucity of specific references to Hawthorne in M.'s canon belies Hawthorne's importance to M. scholarship and may indeed demonstrate the reticence M. practised when most moved by another writer's work.

Sealts #s 245-261 are works by Hawthorne. Sealts #387 is *An Analytical Index to the Works of Nathaniel Hawthorne, with a Sketch of His Life* (Boston: Houghton, Mifflin, 1882), by Evangeline Maria (Johnson) O'Connor. Sealts #244 is Julian Hawthorne's two-volume *Nathaniel Hawthorne and His Wife; a Biography* (Boston: Osgood, 1885), presented to M. by his wife in 1885. M.'s poem, "Monody," probably composed immediately after Hawthorne's death, illustrates M.'s sense of loss and his use of poetry as therapy: "Ease me, a little ease, my song!"

See also "Extracts" 54, 55.
W. 68; M.D. Dedication; M.D. Extracts 54; M.D. Extracts 55

HAYDN

Franz Joseph Haydn (1732-1809), born into a family of laborers in *Austria, was a boy soprano whose early compositions were unremarkable. His first successes occurred after his twenty-fifth year, when a series of minor appointments led to his becoming assistant Kapellmeister of the *Esterházy court orchestra. He remained in the family's service until his death.

During the 1760's, his church music was played throughout Europe, and his instrumental works began to be published, but acclaim in Austria eluded him. The Esterházy commitment kept him from much traveling, but trips to *England (1791, 1794) finally brought the great fame which in turn stimulated his composing. Haydn perfected the early symphonic form (107 symphonies), devised the modern string quartet (84 quartets), wrote masses, concerti, sonatas, songs, and operas, developing the Viennese classical school.

His last years of depression and illness were exacerbated by the *Napoleonic Wars. When *Napoléon besieged *Vienna,

Haydn refused to escape, and Napoléon placed a guard of honor at his home, but he died within the month. *Penny Cyclopaedia* (XII, 1838) may be the source of M.'s claim (*W.* 50) that "nervous" Haydn could not endure the "crashing commotion" of the bombardment: Haydn's death was "supposed to have been accelerated by the bombardment of Vienna, which powerfully agitated his weakened frame."

See also "Oratorio of the Creation."

(M.'s writing in *W.* 50 does not make clear that the compositions referred to immediately after the reference to Haydn are those of *Handel.)
W. 50

HAY-SEED
A country bumpkin, or rustic.
M.D. 6

H. DURAND
For *French engravers and woodcarvers, "une signature de convention": pseudonym.
M.D. 56

HEAD, --S
A "Head" is the projecting point of a coast: a cape, handland, promontory, point of rock, or sandbank.
Passim

HEAD OFF
Begin.
M.D. 82

HEADS
"Heads" and "Tails" refer to objects (such as coins) that have an "up" and a "down" side. The ancient *Romans said, "Heads or ships." It is unclear what kind of dice in *M.* have an "up" and a "down," since dice (cubes) are usually marked on all six of their sides.
M. 142

"HEARTS OF OAK"
This famous song was written in 1759 to celebrate *Hawke's victory at *Quiberon Bay. It had words by the

actor/producer/dramatist/poet, David Garrick (1717-1779) and music by the church music composer, William Boyce (1710-1779).
W. 16

HEATHENDOM

Heathen were originally literally dwellers on a heath—far from *Christianized towns. In modern use, unconverted individuals who do not acknowledge the *God of the *Bible; gentiles or pagans, irreligious persons.
R. 33

HEAVEN; THE HEAVENS

Several words are translated as "Heaven," among them the *Hebrew *shamayim* and *Greek *ouranos*; both are used as plurals, with no great difference from singular usage.

Heaven is considered the abode of *God and those associated with him, as well as the ultimate destination of good people on earth; it is also used as a periphrasis for God. The Bible writers might have thought of Heaven as a solid geographical place; some ancient peoples believed in a multiplicity of Heavens, as in the rabbinic idea of seven Heavens.

The "bounty of Heaven" is that which God gives man freely; the fruits of the earth as well as abstract commodities.

Missionary Hiram Bingham (Chapter XXV) discusses King Kamehameha (see "Kammahammaha") III's difficulties with his subjects' notions about Heaven's bounty and his efforts to write laws in carefully chosen words: "Care was taken to instruct   . . . as to the basis of personal rights, i.e., the *gift by God* and the *earnings of personal labor*, physical and mental. Every man derives his right to life and liberty directly from God; but the right to anything else of which he can justly claim possession must be the result of human effort." He goes on to compare the King's generosity in limiting his own powers to *George Washington's, which pale by comparison.

M. also refers to the firmament as "heaven, or "the heavens." Among his exclamations: "Heaven knows," "would to Heaven," "Pray Heaven," "Thanks be to Heaven," "Heaven forefend!" His references are too numerous to list in accordance with the rest of these volumes.
Passim

HEAVENS, SEVEN-STORIED
Ancient astronomy's seven concentric spheres, or seven planetary heavens, in *Dante's *Paradiso* (Sealts # 174).
M.D. Extracts

HEBE
*Greek goddess of Youth, daughter to Zeus (see "Jupiter" and "Jove") and Hera (*Juno), sometimes cupbearer to the gods. The only story about her is marriage to *Hercules. She was supposedly able to restore youth and beauty to aged gods and men.
M. 167; C.M. 29

HEBREW, --S
The word comes from the name of Eber, son of the *Old Testament's *Shem. From Eber and Shem descend *Abraham, ancester of the Hebrews; Nahor, ancestor of the Aramaens; *Lot, ancestor of the Moabites, *Ammonites, and others. The word is used interchangeably in the *Bible (and in M.'s work, along with "Jew") with "*Israelite."

The Hebrew religion, dating from the second millenium B.C., was unique in the ancient world and has remained relatively unchanged. The Patriarchs before *Moses who migrated to *Palestine saw their deity as god of the clan, the personal god of the clan chief. Ideas about this supreme but not exclusive god, El, led to the concept of the *Jehovah (Yahweh) of *Moses, founder of the monotheistic religion of normalized traditions for *Israel. It was centered on the memory of the *Exodus from *Egypt and other marvelous happenings in history. Israel was the elected nation of Jehovah, with prescribed prohibitions and obligations, divine blessings (as in *P.* 1:4) and curses, rituals, and symbols, as well as a covenant with God that he would bless Israel and punish her enemies, if the Israelites were faithful and observant.

The name "Yahweh" is a form of the verb "to be." The Israelites' God was anthropomorphic, but no images were to be made of him. Yahweh manifested himself throughout nature, but he was not to be identified with heavenly bodies or any one aspect of nature, nor was he to perform magic.

The Israelites were originally a league of twelve independent tribes, with a tent shrine covering the Ark of the Covenant, with sacrifices, feasts, and covenant law that was both casuistic ("If a man . . . ") and apodictic ("Thou shalt/shalt not . . . "). The eleventh-century *Philistine destruction of the tribes led to the image of the "Wandering Jew" (of *M.* 3; *W.* 6; *I.P.* 25). A political monarchy followed, with

*Saul popularly acclaimed first king. By the time of *David, cults evolving from outside influences were a problem. In an effort at centralization, David made *Jerusalem the location of the Ark, with the state as patron and protector of the religious heritage. King *Solomon's building of a great temple caused the breaking off of Judah (see "Judea"). By the time represented in *Kings I and II, political instability, pagan influence, and social disintegration prevailed. Judah's independence ended with its destruction by *Babylon in 587, leading to spiritual crisis and the Exile. The temple was rebuilt between 520 and 516, and one hundred years later, Judaism rose again. *Roman governors replaced kings, among them (*C.M.* 7) *Pontius Pilate, said in *Matthew 27:24 to have washed his hands of the decision to declare *Christ guilty.

The Hebrew language, a Canaanitish branch of the Northwestern Semitic group of languages associated with the Arameans, probably developed around the tenth century B.C., using the old Canaanitish twenty-two-letter alphabet to make nouns, verbs, and particles, written from right to left, and including a wide range of sounds. There was no standard grammar or punctuation until after the time of Solomon. Standard *Rabbinical Hebrew, a literary medium formulated at a time of many spoken vernaculars, was only established after many borrowings (especially from Arabic).

If it is impossible to summarize the history of the Hebrews in the present space, it is likewise daunting to explicate M.'s paradoxical position in his references to "Hebrews," "Israelites," and "Jews." His writings manifest all of the conventional biases of the time. The "illiterate" (*M*. 19) "clothesman" (*P*. 1:3 and *P*. 21:3) with a sharp eye (*R*. 40), and a prominent nose (*M.D.* 92), who abhors pork (*M*. 122) and tricks strangers (*C.M.* 26), was a picture that sprang from the unique reality of Jews in ancient times. M. and others probably called Jews "bigoted" (*R*. 33) because, like *Calvinists, they saw themselves as "chosen" by God. Contemporary visions of Jews were also no doubt colored by "Nativist" sentiments (see "foreign"), regarding all but native-born white *American *Protestants as dangerous interlopers.

But if imitation is flattery, the obverse of M.'s unattractive prejudice should also be a focus of Melvilleans' studies. As Nathalia Wright shows in *Melville's Use of the Bible*, M. identified more closely with the *Old Testament of the Jews than he did with the *New Testament of the Christians. M.'s vision of a vague and dreadful world with an impersonal deity is a perspective more closely allied with Hebrew tradition than with either Greek or Christian thought. His very prose style is like that of the Old Testament, with its subjectivity, antiphonalism, parallelism, apocalypses, catalogues, poetry, idioms, imagery, and proverbs. As the present volume shows, his citations of Old Testament allusions greatly outnumber his references to the New. Allusions such as that to the tortured Middle Ages money-lenders beset by mobs (*O*. 14; *W*. 31; *C.M.* 22) also demonstrate a sympathy belying M.'s anti-Semitism.

The "Jew rustics" of *C.M.* 42 appear in *Matthew 8:28-34 and *Mark 5:2-18, wherein two men (or a man) possessed by devils "run amuk amidst the tombs."

In *M*. 97, the reference to the Israelites who fainted in the wilderness comes from *Exodus 14:10.

The Israelites who remained "dry shod" (in *W*. 22) appear in Exodus 14:21.

The Israelites reference in *M.D.* 73 comes from Exodus 17, in which *Moses smites a rock, bringing forth a fountain from which they drank.

The "Hebrew captives" of *R*. 56 "hung their harps on the willows" in Psalms 137:2.

The "Hebrew spies" of *T*. 14 appear in Numbers 13:17-26.

The "Hebrew Governor" who "knew how to keep his hands clean" in *C.M.* 7 is Pontius Pilate, a Roman.

For "Hebrew cripples" of *R*. 38, see "Bethesda, Pool of."

The "Hebrew spies on their return to Moses with the goodly bunch of grapes" of *T*. 14 occur in Deuteronomy I:22-25. Yahweh has led the Israelites out of Egyptian slavery and is about to give them the land of Canaan as their inheritance. Moses speaks to the Israelites:

> And ye came near unto me every one of you, and said, We will send men before us, and they shall search us out the land, and bring us word again by what way we must go up, and into what cities we shall come. And the saying pleased me well: and I took twelve men of you, one of a tribe: And they turned and went up into the mountain, and came unto the valley of Eshcol, and searched it out. And they took of the fruit of the land in their hands, and brought it down unto us, and brought us word again, and said, It is a good land which the Lord our God doth give us.

T. 14; R. 33; R. 38; R. 56; W. 3; M.D. 9; M.D. 58; M.D. 83; P. 1:4; P. 17:1; I.P. 25; C.M. 7 and elsewhere

HEBREW STORY OF JONAH
    See "Jonah."
M.D. 82

HEBRIDES

Of the c. 500 Hebrides, or Western, Islands off the west coast of *Scotland, some 100 are inhabited. The Inner and Outer Hebrides are separated by the straits of The Minch, the Little Minch, and the Sea of Hebrides. The Inner group includes: *Skye, *Jura, Islay, *Mull, Eigg, Coll, Iona, Staffa, Colonsay, Oronsay, Rum, Tyree, Ulva, and Scarba. The Outers include Lewis with Harris (or Lewis), North Uist, Benbecula, South Uist, Barra, Flannan Isles, and Saint Kilda.

In the eighth century the Celtic inhabitants came under *Norwegian rule, and the Islands were ceded to Scotland in 1266. By the fourteenth century, they were united under John Macdonald of Islay, "Lord of the Isles." The Hebrides are famous for their beautiful scenery, their hand-woven Harris tweeds, and visitors such as *Scott and Boswell, who acclaimed them in literature.
M. 3

HECATE; HECATIC SPHERULA

Hecate was *Greek Goddess of the Dark of the Moon, associated with deeds of darkness; also Goddess of the Crossways, places of evil magic where black offerings were made to her. She identified with Artemis (see "Diana"), showing the uncertainty between good and evil, and also with Persephone (see "Proserpine"). She was daughter to the *Titan Perses and to Asteria, with powers over Heaven, Hell, Earth, and Sea: represented as a triple goddess, sometimes with three heads (horse, dog, bear), sometimes with three bodies standing back to back.

A "spherule" is a small sphere, although M. seems to intend it as a rule, possibly mocking ecclesiatic language, especially *Papal decrees. A "Hecatic Spherula" sounds like an orbit of grim natural laws understood by skeptics and others with a pessimistic outlook on the world.
M. 170; R. 49

HECATOMBS

A large number: from the ancient *Greek slaughter of 100 oxen.
M. 27

HECLA, MT.

Probably the volcanic Mt. Hekla (5,108 ft.) in *Iceland, which erupted in 1845. There is also a Mt. Hecla in the *Hebrides.
M.D. 3

HECTORS
    In the *Iliad*, Hector is leader and most valiant of the
*Trojan warriors. The son of King *Priam, he is killed by
*Achilles, and his body is held for ransom, then buried at
*Thebes in obedience to an oracle.
M. 32

HEEVA-HEEVA
    O. 62 and 63 describe the "hevar," or *Tahitian reel as a
"genuine pagan fandango." The double form "heeva-heeva"
indicates a special ceremonial dance.
M.D. 40

HEGIRA, THE
    The flight of *Mohammed from *Mecca to then Jathrib
—now Medina: City of the Prophet—after he was expelled by
the magistrates. The date was 16 July 622, from which the Mohammedan calendar starts (From Arab. *hejira*—departure).
O. 65; O. 67; O. 72; O. 81

HEIDELBERG; HEIDELBURGH
    The city in North Baden, *Germany, on the canalized
Neckar River, was celebrated in the nineteenth century as a
center of romantic University of Heidelberg student life, involving much singing, drinking, and dueling. Its red sandstone
castle dates from the fifteenth century (completed seventeenth).
In the cellar is the famous wine cask, the "Great Heidelburgh
Tun" (*M.D.* 77, 94), holding 49,000 gallons. M. visited in 1857,
commenting in his journal (22 April) on the (1386) University
and the "charming old ruin" of a castle. He probably saw the
much-decorated tun. Thirty-one feet long and twenty-one feet
high, it is topped by a platform mounted by visitors to the (now
restored) castle. He might also have seen a picture
(reproduced in the hard-cover edition of Vincent's *The Trying-
Out of Moby-Dick*) and read a description in the revised edition
of *John Harris, ed., *Navigantium Itinerantium Bibliotheca.
Or, a Complete Collection of Voyages and Travels.* (1748), Vol.
2: "The travels of Mr. Maximilian Mission, through part of
*Holland, etc."
M. 3; M.D. 77; M.D. 94

HELIOGABALUS
    Heliogabalus or Elagabalus: Syro-*Phoenician *sun
god/emperor of *Rome. The original was Varius Avitus Bas-

sanius (205-222), Roman Emperor as Marcus Aurelius Anton-
inus (from 218 to 222), who had been a child high priest of the
sun god at Emesa. A most cruel and debauched Roman Emperor (thus M.'s designation), he is said to have smothered a
group of important Romans in a shower of roses at a banquet.
He was slain by *Praetorian Guards.
      The God is represented by a huge cone-shaped stone.
M. 181

HELLENIC
      The word which (along with "Hellenistic") came to sig-
nify pure and high *Greek culture originated from the *Old
Testament expression "Hellenes," which stood for uncircum-
cized Greek-speaking peoples. Ancient Greeks called their nation "Hellas"; the *Romans later referred to it as Graecia,
which for the Greeks signified *Epirus. "Hellenic" came to refer to the Attic-based language and culture of Greece from the
late eighth century B.C. to the death of *Alexander, as well as
to the common dialect that followed.
      Nineteenth-century historians appropriated the expres-
sions to label the period from the death of Alexander to the incorporation of *Egypt into the *Roman Empire, marking the
transition from classical Greece to the *Christian age. But M.
appears to use "Hellenic" in the commonest sense of a catchall
referent to pure Greek high culture suggesting a "Golden
Age."
R. 30

HELLESPONT, THE
      Ancient name for the Dardanelles. The Hellespont, or
"sea of Helle" was named after the sister of Phrixus (in myth,
cousin to *Jason), who drowned there, fleeing to *Colchis on
the ram of the *Golden Fleece to escape her cruel stepmother,
the Princess Ino.
      The Hellespont was the river Leander swam to visit
*Hero. M.'s reference in *M.* is to *Xerxes's crossing of the
river on a double floating bridge supported by nearly 700 vessels
anchored with their keels in the direction of the current.
M. 164

HELOTS
      Serfs to ancient *Spartans, helots came from many
races after the Dorian conquest. Messenian helots were state
agricultural *slaves with individual masters; they had limited
property rights when masters' claims were satisfied.

Helots are archetypal threatening slaves. Because there were many more of them than Spartan masters, Spartans lived in constant fear of revolution and executed large numbers as a precaution. Some helots were forced into military service in the *Peloponnesian War. By 370 B.C., *Epaminondas liberated Messenia, but the system continued elsewhere.
M. 3; M. 63

HEMP
The hemp rope which kills "*Ahab," as prophesied, is made from *Cannabis sativa*, the herbaceous plant also known as the source of marijuana. The fiber used for rope since the third millenium B.C. comes from the part of the hollow stem commonly called bark. Hemp has been grown in North America since the seventeenth century. Manilla, sisal, *New Zealand, and Mauritius hemps are false hemps which have no botanical relationship to *Cannabis sativa*.
M.D. Passim

HENLE
Friedrich Gustav Jakob Henle (1809-1885), *German physician, anatomist, histologist, and naturalist, publisher of monographs on human and animal sciences, wrote about new species of animals, especially sharks and rays (in conjunction with *Müller). The major focus of his work was human research. His *Manual of Rational Pathology* (1846-53) revolutionized pathological study.
M. 13

HENNER
This is a misprint or misspelling for John Hennen (1779-1828), *British surgeon in the *Napoleonic Wars who wrote *Principles of Military Surgery, Comprising Observations on the Arrangement, Police and Practice of Hospitals, and on the History, Treatment, and Anomalies Variola and Syphilis. Illustrated with Cases and Dissections* (Third Edition, 1829). *Penny Cyclopaedia* (XI) credits him also with *Observations on some important Points of Military Surgery* (1818); its discussion is reminiscent of a passage in W.:

> Some most remarkable cases of circuitous passages are recorded. Dr. Hennen mentions one in which a ball entered at the *pomum Adami, ran completely round the neck, and was found close by the aperture at which it had penetrated . . . .

Sometimes the portion of clothing carried before the ball is not perforated, but driven inwards in the form of a cul-de-sac, which may be drawn out again with the ball in it. Such a case is related where in an attempt at suicide a man fired a pistol close by the side of his head; the ball passed some depth into the brain, carrying the side of his night-cap before it, so that on taking it off the portion forced into the skull drew out the ball.

W. 63

HENRY I

Henry I (1068-1135), king of *England from 1100, was the youngest son of *William the Conqueror, and grandfather of Henry II (the first *Plantagenet king). He was an exception-ally well-educated man, referred to in later centuries as "Beauclerk." He protected the Church, maintained close ties to *Normandy, and ruled systematically, efficiently, and somewhat oppressively.

See also "Beards."

W. 87

HENRY IV STATUE

The statue of Henri IV (see "Bourbon") seen from *Pont Neuf in *Paris is located at Square du Vert-Galant ("Gay Old Blade"), named for the amorous king. The sculptor Lemot's work of 1818, (which M. would have seen in 1849) replaced the original which "*Israel Potter" would have seen. That statue stood from 1635 to 1792; sculptors were Giambologna and Tacca.

I.P. 7

HENRY VIII'S; HARRY THE EIGHTH

The *Tudor Henry VIII of *England (1491-1547) ruled from 1509. Second son of Henry VII (1457-1509) and Elizabeth of *York, he was an accomplished scholar, musician, and ath-lete, and eventually the perfect *Machiavellian monarch.

Henry married six times and fathered three English rulers. He first married his brother's widow, Catherine of Aragon (m. 1509), who failed to produce a son but whose daughter became *Mary I. By second wife, *Anne Boleyn (m. 1533), he sired another future queen, *Elizabeth I. His third wife, Jane Seymour (m. 1536) was mother of Edward VI. Henry's breach with the *Catholic Church which he had pre-

viously served, started with the succession problem. No
woman had ruled England, and Catherine's failure to produce
a son led to his divorcing her in order to marry Anne Boleyn;
in the process, he caused the fall of the powerful Cardinal
Thomas Wolsey (c. 1473-1530), executed Sir Thomas More and
a number of high and low-ranking Catholic clergymen. This
marriage also produced no sons, so Henry had Anne executed
on charges of adultery and then married Jane Seymour, who
died immediately after giving birth to a son. She was followed
by Anne of Cleves (m. 1539), Catherine Howard (m. 1540), and
Catherine Parr (m. 1543).

Henry's reign was marked by his violent and despotic
methods in breaking with the Catholic Church. But the coincidence of his egotistical desires and the good of the state
worked to the advantage of a nation that had been on the verge
of civil war, as well as in power struggles with Catholic countries. Henry's centralized government and developed parliamentary system, his control of *Wales, breaking up of feudal
franchises, building of a navy, all paved the way for England's
rise under Elizabeth's rule. Although his attempted control of
*Scotland failed, it demonstrated the need for a union of the
two nations.

His colorful life and rich court inspired portrayals by
*Shakespeare, *Fletcher, and numerous others.
R. 41; W. 6; M.D. 65

HENRY, PATRICK
The orator and statesman, Patrick Henry (1736-1799)
was born into a *Scottish/*English family of Hanover County,
*Virginia. Becoming a lawyer after failure at other pursuits,
he was soon famed for his eloquence as a member of the colonial House of Burgesses and of the *Continental Congresses of
1774 and '75. A leader of radical opposition to British government, he delivered speeches that brought him the governorship of Virginia, in which capacity he authorized George
Rogers Clark's *Illinois expedition.

He later served in the state legislature, but broke with
*Jefferson and declined attending the Constitutional Conven-
tion of 1787, focussing instead on states-rights issues. Finally
reconciled with the Federal government, he was primary
drafter of the *Bill of Rights.

In 1828, M. was elected best speaker in the "introductory
department at the New-York Male *High School, so
"Wellingborough Redburn's" reference to Henry's speeches is
probably biographical. Among favorite examples of Henry's
utterances (preserved in a biography by William Wirt, in 1817)
was the speech at the Virginia Convention, 23 March 1775, in

which he said: "I know not what course others may take, but
as for me, give me liberty or give me death!" In opposition to
the Stamp Act, he said (29 May 1765): "*Tarquin and *Caesar
each had his *Brutus, *Charles the First his *Cromwell, and
*George the Third may profit by their example . . . . If this be
treason, make the most of it!"
R. 7; P. 20:1

HEPHESTION
        Hephaestion, oldest friend of *Alexander the Great,
*Macedonian general, Commander of Alexander's Compan-
ion cavalry through *India, Grand *Vizier, or chiliarch. Like
Alexander, he married a daughter of *Darius: Barsine, or
Stateira. He died in 324 B.C. in Ecbatana. Alexander went into
deep mourning and provided a royal funeral in *Babylon, with
a huge and expensive pyre.
M. 181

HEPTADS
        The sum or number of seven, or a group of seven. In use
in matters of worship, as in heptads of petition to *God. Hep-
tad itself was once considered worthy of veneration.
M. 171

HERACLITUSES
        Heraclitus of *Ephesus (c. 540-475 B.C.) declined his
rightful place in royalty and became a violent critic of mankind
in general. He held that all was etenal flux, scorning the limited mental capacity of man. He earned the sobriguet "the
Dark, or Weeping Philosopher," and his biographers painted
his life and work even more darkly than was true.
P. 20:1; C.M. 9

HERALD, THE; NEW YORK HERALD
        James Gordon Bennett (1795-1872) founded the *New
York Herald in 1835. It started as a "penny" paper (later two
cents) which proclaimed political independence and aimed for
the widest possible audience, in contrast to more "serious"
"six-penny" dailies. Bennett called his paper "lively, saucy,
and spicy." A fore-runner of modern tabloids, it shocked the
journalistic establishment in its punchy treatment of world
news, its printing of coarse and sensational stories, its curt
dramatic headlines, its acceptance of questionable advertisements (such as those for "*Brandreth's pills"), its high-speed

gathering of data by telegraph and utilization of other technological advances. When Bennett turned the *Herald* over to his
son in 1866, it had attained wide circulation and had revolutionized American journalism.

M. was a subscriber.
R. 61; W. 59

HERCULANEUM
The ancient city of Campania, *Italy, traditionally connected with the *Greek hero, Heracles, was destroyed (along
with *Pompeii) when *Vesuvius erupted in A.D. 79. It had
recently been severely damaged by earthquakes. Rediscovered
and excavated in the early eighteenth century, it was visited
and commented upon by *Goethe. Excavations continued sporadically, even in M.'s time.
M.D. 119; I.P. 24

HERCULES; HERCULEAN
In *Greek myth, Hercules is the greatest hero of Greece
(except for the *Athenians, who prefer the more intellectual
*Theseus, "The Attic Hercules"). The brawny, simple-minded
possessor of super-human strength and energy appears in the
works of *Ovid, Apollodoros, Euripides, *Sophocles, Pindar,
*Theocritus, and others.
He was born in *Thebes and was early called Alcides
after the family of Amphitryon, at first thought to be his father.
He was really the son of Zeus (see "Jupiter" and "Jove") by
Amphitryon's wife, Alcmena, thereby incurring throughout
his life the wrath of Hera (*Juno). Prophets predicted his
greatness when, as an infant in his crib, he killed two huge attacking snakes. Also in his youth, he accidentally killed his
music teacher and at age eighteen killed the Thespian lion and
wore its skin forever.
Hercules's life was tragic because of an unfortunate
mixture of attributes. His emotional nature and simple mind
often led him into murderous rages for which he later was
sorry. He began to consider himself equal to the gods when he
helped them conquer the brute sons of earth, the Giants, and
quarreled with *Apollo over the oracle, expressing complete
confidence in his own powers. He deserted *Argo* and *Jason to
search for his lost armor-bearer and suffered many outbursts
of rage followed by punishments he willingly endured or even
inflicted upon himself.
Among his other feats: he conquered the Minyans, winning the Princess Megara as wife from the grateful Thebans.
In an insane rage, despite his love, he killed Megara and his

three sons. His friend, Theseus, talked him out of suicide, and he submitted himself to the king of Mycenae, who devised a series of twelve penitential acts: "The Labors of Hercules": 1. Kill the lion of Nemea; 2. Kill the nine-headed *Hydra at Lerna; 3. Capture the golden-horned stag sacred to Artemis (see "Diana") in the forest of Cerynitia; 4. Capture the great boar of Mount Frymanthus; 5. Clean the Augean stables in a day (he diverted rivers to do this); 6. Drive away the Stymphalian cannibal birds (Athena helped in this); 7. Capture the *Cretan bull that Poseidon had given Minos; 8. Capture the *Thracian man-eating horses of King Diomedes; 9. Secure the girdle of Hippolyta, queen of the *Amazons. (Trouble from Hera made him kill Hippolyta despite her cooperation); 10. Secure the cattle of Geryon, a three-bodied monster of Erythia. (He set up the *Pillars of Hercules [at *Gibralter and Ceuta] and got the oxen); 11. (Most difficult) Get the Golden Apples of the Hesperides (He asked for Atlas's help and had to use intelligence when Atlas tried to trick him); 12. (Worst) Free Theseus from the Chair of Forgetfulness and bring the three-headed dog, Cerberus, from *Hades. (*Pluto agreed to help, provided Hercules used no weapons. Eurystheus decided he did not want Cerberus, so Hercules had to carry him back to Hades.)

Hercules was awarded immortality for performing these tasks, but despite his expiation was never at rest: he conquered the Giant Antaeus, then fought the river-god Achelous, winning Deianira as his wife; he rescued a maiden in *Troy, freed *Prometheus, but felt guilt at the many accidental deaths he had caused. He finally had himself immolated and went to heaven, where he reconciled with Hera and married her daughter, *Hebe.

Seventeenth-century writers such as *Browne associated Hercules with *Jonah, probably following a lesser legend that Hercules had destroyed a sea monster from inside, having been swallowed by it.

Two famous "carved" Hercules artworks of the time were the Belvedere in the *Vatican and the Farnese in *Naples. M. saw the Farnese, commenting in his journal (21 February 1857) on its size and "gravely benevolent face." In his *lecture, "Statues in Rome," he commented on its benign aura.

A northern *constellation is named for Hercules.

M. 132; W. 50; M.D. 35; M.D. 82; M.D. 83; M.D. 86; I.P. 1; I.P. 22; C.M. 28

HERCULES' PILLARS
    See "Hercules" and "Gibralter."
W. 50; M.D. 35

HERD'S-GRASS
Common North American pasteurage and hay plants include Redtop (*Agrostis alba*) and Timothy (*Phleum pratense*), a perennial European grass introduced in the *Carolinas c. 1720 by Timothy Hansen, from whence comes its familiar name.
P. 2:5

HER MAJESTY THE QUEEN
In *R*. 41, a reference to *Victoria.
R. 41

HER MAJESTY'S NAVY
*Henry VIII first referred to the British Navy as "His Majesty's Navy"; the expression became popular with the *Stuarts. In M.'s day, *Her* Majesty's Navy was *Queen Victoria's Navy.
R. 40

HERMETIC
"Sealed," or "closed off." The word honors Hermes Trismegistus, an *Egyptian philosopher/priest equated with the *Greek god Hermes (see "Mercury"). He invented an airtight seal for vessels.
T. 31; O. 55; R. 58; W. 77; M.D. 98

HERMIONE, THE
In 1797, the *British frigate *Hermione* was the scene of a famous mutiny. In the waters off Puerto Rico (see "Porto Rico"), the rebellious crew, incensed by excessive *flogging, killed the captain and nine others. Twenty four of those apprehended were hanged, but at least 100 mutineers were never caught, and among these several later served on U.S. merchant ships.
W. 36

HERMIT ISLAND
*New Guinea: 1°48' S., 144°55' E.
W. 8

HERMON

Mount Hermon is on the modern border of *Syria and *Lebanon, twenty-five miles west-southwest of *Damascus. It is 9,232 feet in altitude and has been held as a sacred landmark throughout history. The *Biblical "Hermon," "Sion," "Senir," and "Shenir" was also revered by the *Romans. The mountain is the Arabic *Jebel esh Sheikh* ("mountain of the chief") or *Jebel eth Thelj* ("snowy mountain").
R. 56

HERO (AND LEANDER)

In myth, Leander lived in Abydus, on one side of the *Hellespont, and his love, the Priestess of *Aphrodite, Hero, lived in Sestus, on the other side. Leander swam to her every night, guided by a mysterious light until one stormy night the light blew out and Leander was drowned. When Hero found his body on the shore, she killed herself. The story is oft repeated in poetry, and *Lord Byron repeated Leander's feat in 1810—a four-mile swim in about one hour—and spoke of it in *Don Juan* (II, cv).
M. 38; W. 43

HERODOTUS

Called "the father of history" for his systematic arrangement of events of his time, the *Greek historian Herodotus (c. 480-c. 425 B.C.) is most famed for his account of the *Persian wars, the first masterpiece of Greek prose.

His biography is confused, but he is known to have lived in or visited *Athens, *Egypt, *Libya, *Syria, *Babylonia, *Susa, Lydia, *Phrygia, *Byzantium, *Thrace, and *Macedonia, to most of which places M. refers. His references to historical personages are also duplicated in M.'s works, suggesting that M. was very familiar with vols. 29-31 of *Harper's Classical Library* (Sealts #147). Like M., Herodotus was a story-teller who mixed fantasy and fact, a travel writer of exquisite detail, and a historically-oriented chronicler of his times.
M. 89

HEROD'S MURDERED INNOCENTS

In *Matthew 2:16:18, Herod, King of *Israel, slaughters children in hope of destroying the *Christ Child.
M.D. 126

HERSCHEL'S GREAT TELESCOPE
Sir William (originally Friedrich Wilhelm) Herschel (1738-1822), *German-born astronomer, went to *England as a young musician but soon educated himself in astronomy. He built his own microscope, grinding and polishing hundreds of specula so as to observe the entire heavens. In 1780, he began publishing with the *Royal Society on distant stars, the mountains of the moon, and the rotation of the planets. In 1781, he discovered the planet Uranus, and in 1782 was finally able to give up music to become private astronomer to *George III. His work on the positions of the stars was furthered by completion in 1789 of a great reflecting telescope (forty-foot focal length, four-foot aperture), through which he discovered *Saturn's seventh ring. His publications include "Motion of the Solar System in Space" (1783) and sequels (1784-1818) speculating on the *Milky Way and the formation of the universe.
M.D. 74

HESPERUS
The *Greeks called the evening star after the sun (or brother) of Atlas. Its *Latin name was *Vesper. As a morning star it was called Phosphoros (or Heosphoros) after the son of Astraeus (or Cephalus) and Eos, *Titans.
M. 58

HESSIANS
Hessian cloth is a strong fabric made from jute or hemp, originally in Hesse, *Germany. In the nineteenth century, German troops' boots were fashionable: the "Hessians" of *M.* 114, *R.* 31, and *I.P.* 21.
M. 114; R. 31; I.P. 21

HETMAN
*German *hauptmann*—chief. A commander-in-chief, especially in *Poland, later chief of *Cossacks of the Ukraine (*ataman*). The hetman was elected when followers declared allegiance to their candidate by throwing their fur hats at his feet.
M. 59; M. 181

HEVAR, --S
The *Tahitian reel described in *O.* 62 and 63 is referred to in *M.D.* 40, where the double form "heeva-heeva" indicates a special ceremonial dance.
O. 62; O. 63

HEXADS

The number six, in *Pythagorean theory, which held it (like three) a perfect number; a series of six numbers, mostly in use in science and mathematics.
M. 171

HIBERNIA

The steamship *Hibernia* carried a copyright agreement and proof sheets of M.'s *O.* to publisher John Romeyn Brodhead, 1 February 1847, and returned Brodhead's response on 3 March 1847.
R. 29

HIBERNIAN, --S

From the Lat. name for *Ireland: Hibernia (a variant of Celtic *Erin*).
T. 7; O. 37; R. 27

HIC JACET

A tombstone: after the Latin words for "Here lies . . . . "
P. 23:1

HIGH GERMAN

There is no such language; this is probably a joke, such as *"Coleridge's High German Horse."
M.D. 101

HIGHLAND, --S

See "Scotland."
R. 24; W. 50; M.D. 79 and elsewhere

HIGHLANDER

The ship is probably patterned on *St. Lawrence*, on which M. sailed to and from *Liverpool in June of 1839. An advertisement in the (New York) *Evening Post* proclaimed the trader a "splendid fast sailing" ship under Captain Oliver P. Brown. She was a medium-sized coppered and copper-fastened vessel of 356 tons burthen, with a crew of sixteen (of which five deserted) and room for cabin and steerage passengers. She probably carried a cargo of cotton.

"No. 12" on the crew-list was "Norman Melville," of the city of *New York: nineteen years old, five-foot eight and one-

half inches tall, with light complexion and brown hair. How much of "Highlander's" action actually occurred on *St. Lawrence* cannot be determined. Undoubtedly the itinerary was similar, but it is doubtful that M. had time to visit *London (as "Wellingborough" does) during *St. Lawrence's* stay in *England. She returned to New York in September, carrying two cabin and thirty-two steerage passengers (probably not in the dire predicament of "Highlander's" "four or five hundred" *Irish emigrants).
R. Passim

HIGHLAND GORGE
    Some gorge of the *Catskill mountains, through which the *Hudson River flows.
M.D. 41

HIGHLANDS
    In *R*. 1, the *Hudson Highlands portion of the *Appalachian system, with rugged banks along the Hudson River south of Newburgh.
R. 1

"HIGH-LOW-JACK-AND-THE-GAME"
    In card games, announcement of the final winner or highest possible hand. Origination is from the game All Fours, or Seven Up, or Old-Sledge, or High-Low-Jack.
R. 54

HIGH PONTIFF
    A Pontiff was formerly any bishop; the term now refers only to the *Pope (Bishop of *Rome—Sovereign Pontiff).
    In ancient Rome, literally one in charge of bridges (Lat. *pons, pontis*—bridge); head of the college of priests was Pontifex Maximus.
M. 105

HIGH SCHOOL
    In M.'s time, "high school" did not refer to the age level of attending students. Thus, M. entered New York Male High School in September 1825, at the age of six. Before leaving the school in January 1830, he had become a "monitor" and "best speaker" in the introductory department.

After the move to Albany necessitated by family financial problems, M. entered the "fourth department" of Albany Academy (in October 1830). Although it claimed otherwise, Albany Academy catered to the needs of the wealthy. In an atmosphere of rigid traditional discipline, the school offered a curriculum in which almost every subject was focused on *Calvinist *Christianity: geography; reading; spelling; penmanship; arithmetic; English grammar; natural history; classical biography, and *Jewish antiquities. At Albany, M.'s scholarship was no match for his brother *Gansevoort's. M. won a "first best" in "Ciphering Books," leading his father to envision for him a career in business. But M.'s copy of the awarded book (now in the *Yale Library) shows that a childish hand tried to scratch out "Ciphering Books." He left the school in March 1832, after his father's death, to become a bank clerk at the age of thirteen.

Despite M.'s undistinguished performance at Albany Academy, in 1863 he was asked to serve on a committee commemorating the school's fiftieth anniversary.
R. 26

HILO
    The city of Hilo, on the crescent-shaped Hilo Bay, is the only anchorage on the eastern coast of the island of *Hawaii. It is the site of Rainbow Falls (and of the modern Lyman Museum of Hawaiiana) and was much threatened by lava flows in the nineteenth century.
O. 54

HIMALAYAS; HIMMALAHS; HIMMALEH, --S; HIMMALEHAN
    The ancient Imaus mountain system between central *Asia and the *Indian subcontinent is c. 1,500 miles long and from 100 to 150 miles wide and contains some of the world's highest peaks. The Great Himalayas include the world's highest mountain, Mount Everest (29,000 feet). Other portions are the Lesser and Outer Himalayas, sites of *Tibetan monks' retreats associated with many legends of Hindu (see "Hindoo") mythology.

    In the nineteenth century, "Himalaya" was a common expression meaning the highest possible peak.
M. 119; M. 181; R. 40; W. 50; M.D. 14; M.D. 104; M.D. 119

HINDOO, --S; HINDOOISH
Hinduism is a way of life promulgated by peoples of several eastern religions, especially in *India, *Ceylon, and present-day Pakistan. Practitioners believe in the transmigration of souls, polytheism subsumed under fundamental monotheism, mystic and monastic philosophy, and the caste system.

There was much modernization of Hindu life in the nineteenth century, when such practices as widow sacrifice (*M*. 68) were discontinued.

Franklin's *The Wake of the Gods* examines M.'s relation to Hinduism.

See also "Brahma"; "Pariah"; "Shiva"; "Vishnu."
M. 68; M. 116; M. 181; W. 76; M.D. 55; M.D. 82; M.D. 96; M.D. 116; P. 1:3

HINDOSTAN; HINDOSTANEE
Hindustan is a term applied to the *Ganges Plain of northern *India. The name derives from Indus (Sanskrit *Sindhu*), a river; it came to apply to the whole of northern India, from the Punjab to Assam, to the whole Indian subcontinent, or to the small part of the Ganges plain where Hindi is spoken.
R. 34; M.D. 81; P. 2:2

"HIO-HIO'
M.'s fictional equivalent of *Ohio.
M. 158

HIPPOCRATES
The great *Greek physician was born c. 460 B.C. on the island of Cos, died c. 400 B.C. at Larissa. What little we know of his life is supplied by Soranus, a physician of the second century A.D. But he is also mentioned by *Plato and *Aristotle. He is pictured as the perfect type of the physician: learned and moral. One of the Asclepiadae (See "Asclepius"), he is credited with some seventy works that reflect the teachings of that school: the "Hippocratic Collection" includes the famous oath and Aphorisms, among them, "Life is short, but the art is long, the opportunity fleeting, the experiment perilous, the judgement difficult."
T. 11

HIPPOGRIFF
A legendary animal, half horse and half griffin
(combination lion and eagle); a winged horse used as a symbol
of love in Ariosto's *Orlando Furioso*.
M.D. 55

HIS IMPERIAL MAJESTY
See " Pedro II."
W. 39

HIS MAJESTY
In *I.P.*, *George III.
I.P. 4

HISTORIA MAJOR
See "Paris, Matthew."
W. 87

HISTORIAN OF THE REBELLION
See "Clarendon."
W. 71

"HISTORY OF LIFE AND DEATH"
See "Bacon, Francis," and see "Extracts" 14.
M.D. Extracts 14

HITTITE, --S
Scholars rediscovered these powerful second century
B.C. people in the late nineteenth and early twentieth centuries. M.'s knowledge of them was probably *Bible-based,
although explorers started unearthing their ruins in 1834.
The Bible variously tells that they were a tribe inhabiting
*Palestine, or were foreigners who stocked the royal harem, or
were allied with *Israel against the *Syrians ("Hittim," in
*Genesis, *Joshua, *Ezekiel, I *Kings, II *Chronicles). The
mountain-dwelling children of Heth sold to *Abraham the cave
of Macpelah as a tomb, but were defeated by the Israelites and
became symbols of the dispossessed.
Historically, they lived in small city-states in northern
Syria and the Cilician region, north-central Anatolia, and
elsewhere: a powerful dynastic military empire, feudally
structured, with flexible laws, a complex written language, a

multitude of gods, divination and magic, barbarous but power-ful plastic arts.

In *Clarel* I, xvii, 308, Hittites are "foes pestilent to *God."
M. 62; M.D. 18

HIVARHOO
M.'s "Hivarhoo" is Hivaoa, La Dominica, *Marquesas, famous for its warlike people and cannibals. John M. Coulter, *Adventures in the Pacific* (*Dublin, 1845) told of his captivity there; he was treated like a god and then forced into being tat-tooed.
O. 6; O. 18

HOBBES
Thomas Hobbes (1588-1679), political philosopher, was born in *Malmesbury, in Wiltshire, *England—a parson's son. After *Oxford he became tutor to William Cavendish (later Earl of Devonshire), remaining with the family on and off for some thirty years. He was one-time amanuensis for *Lord Bacon, left England for *Paris from 1640-52, to avoid civil turmoil, but returned, accepting the republican government. Having tutored *Charles in his youth, he also accepted the Restoration.

His *Leviathan* was published in 1651. An eccentric scholar who loved geometry but read few books, Hobbes was condemned for his idiosyncratic views of monarchists and re-publicans, but especially by *Catholic, Anglican, and *Puritan churchmen. *Leviathan* defends absolutism, and explains hu-man nature and behavior mechanistically. Hobbes saw politi-cal society as controlled by expediency, with religion of little use except to reinforce secular arguments—an unpopular stance in the seventeenth century.

See also "Extracts 21."
0. 2; M.D. Extracts 21; P. 19:1; I.P. 8

HOBOMACK; HOBOMAK
See "Extracts" 73.
T. 4; M.D. Extracts 73

HOCK
A catch-all name for *Rhenish wine, some of which is produced in Hockheim, *Germany, on the Maine River. Hock was formerly called hocamore.

The reference to "green glasses" (*M*. 14) is a joke; the wine is bottled in green glass to prevent deterioration—not quite so rapid as to require green drinking glasses.

M.'s journal for 22 April 1857 records his passing through "Hockland."
M. 14

HODNOSE
    See "Dobs."
W. 32

HOGARTH, --IAN
    William Hogarth (1697-1764), highly original and influential *English painter and engraver, rose from a seamy *London background to become famous for his unsentimental realistic satires on the social customs of his day and on their consequences. His six- or eight-scene narrative paintings exposed follies and vices. Among the more famous: *The Rake's Progress* (1733-35), and *Marriage à la Mode* (1743-45). *Perseus Descending* was an illustration for Lewis Theobold's *Perseus and Andromeda, as it is Perform'd at the Theatre Royal in Lincoln's-Inn Fields* (1730). It is reproduced in Willard Thorp's edition of *M.D.* (1947). A fine portraitist, Hogarth did *Captain Coram* (1740).

    (The "old quarto Hogarth" of *R*. 30 has not been located.)
O. 81; R. 30; W. 90; M.D. 55

HOLBORN
    A thoroughfare and district of *London; originally the name of the northern part of the Fleet River, spelled Holeburne (the *burne* or stream in the *hole* or hollow).

    The old route to *Tyburn from *Newgate was Holborn. To "ride backwards up Holborn" is to be taken for execution; prisoners sat facing the rear in carts bringing them to their deaths. "Holborn Bars" refers to the law offices there.
0. 14; I.P. 25

HOLLAND, PHILEMON; *HOLLAND'S*
    *English scholar Philemon Holland (1552-1637) was renowned for clear and informal translations of *Livy (1600); *Plutarch *Morals* (1603); *Pliny *Natural History* (1604); *Suetonius *History of Twelve Caesars* (1606); Ammianus Marcellinus (1609); *Xenophon *Cyropaedia* (1632).

In 1573, Holland became a Fellow of Trinity College,
*Cambridge; he received an *Oxford M.S. in 1583 and an M.D.
in 1597. He practiced medicine and taught at Coventry, War-
wickshire, from 1595.
See also "Extracts" 6, 7.
M.D. Extracts 6; M.D. Extracts 7

HOLLAND; HOLLANDER, --S
The *Netherlands, popularly called Holland, is the
largest of the Low Countries (a political and historical, rather
than geographical designation). It is bounded by the North Sea
(W. and N.), *Belgium (S.), and *Germany (E.). Nominal capital is *Amsterdam; The Hague is the seat of *Dutch government. Although Holland is but 190 miles long (N.-S.) and 120
miles wide, it is transversed by 4,817 miles of intersecting
canals which, with dikes, control the constantly threatening
sea.
Holland had no unified political history before the sixteenth century; to the left of the *Rhine was the *Roman
province of Lower Germany, residence of the Batavi people; to
the right were Germanic Friscians. It made part of
*Charlemagne's domain and then the *Holy Roman Empire's
in the eighth and ninth centuries. The counts of Holland ruled
after the tenth century, the dukes of *Burgundy by the fifteenth. *Charles V gave the area to his son Philip II of *Spain
in 1555, but a strong independence movement began, culminat-
ing in the 1579 Union of Utrecht, representing the seven northern provinces of Holland, Zeeland, Utrecht, Gelderland, Overi-
jssel, *Friesland, and Groningen. After thirty years of war,
independence was recognized in 1648; the nation encompassed
southern provinces, including Belgium.
The Dutch were highly prosperous in the seventeenth
century. The Dutch East India Company (1602) and Dutch
West India Company (1621) made the Netherlands master of
the seas, establishing such important outposts as New Amsterdam (1626), the modern-day *New York. Wars with
*England and *France were almost continuous until late in
that century, as were internal struggles between pro-Orange
monarchists and republicans. (King William III of Orange
became ruler of England in 1689.)
The *Batavian Republic was set up after the French Revolution, and *Napoléon put Louis Bonaparte in charge. The
*Congress of Vienna united the nation under William I, but in
1830 the Belgians rebelled and declared independence
(recognized in 1839).
M. visited Holland in 1857, commenting in his journal:
"Entering Holland, began to look a great heath—passed much

waste, brown, muddy looking land—immense pastures, light green" (23 April). He "got a queer old Dutchman for a guide" (24 April) in Amsterdam and enjoyed the art museums, quaint streets and houses: "a place of cheese, butter, & tidiness." In *Rotterdam he went to a "Dance House" (public ballroom), and visited the birthplace of *Erasmus, taking his leave 25 April.

Information in *M.D.* 89 about the "formal whaling code" of the Holland "States-General in A.D. 1695" was drawn from *Scoresby's extended discussion of whale-fishery laws (Vol. 2, pp. 312-332), as Vincent's edition shows.

Despite being of Dutch descent on his mother's side (or perhaps *because* of that), M. had to a large extent a stereotyped picture of the Dutch. The reader is directed to "Dutch; Dutchmen," for examples. See also "Gansevoort"; "Haarlem"; "Leyden"; "VonTromp."
M. 74; R. 15; R. 31; W. 23; W. 44; W. 71; M.D. 89; P. 19:1

HOLLAND GIN
Gin drinking was considered a low pursuit in the nineteenth century, but strong gin such as Schiedam was smuggled into *England from Holland—to be taken as an after-dinner drink. "British Hollands" were gins made in England by the Dutch method, but British "Gin Palaces" served cheap neutral spirit that could be distilled even from garbage, flavored with juniper, and sold, even to children.
W. 44

HOLLAND, --SHEETS
The unbleached or dull-finish linen called Holland was usually used in furniture covering or other homely situation. It was sometimes glazed or otherwise refined for use in clothing, as M. suggests in *M.D.* 98. (But then the fastidious *Hawthorne was to complain that his friend M. was "a little heterodox in the matter of clean linen" [Hawthorne's journal, 11 November 1856, quoted in Leyda *Log* II]).
T. 8; M.D. 98

HOLOFERNES
See "Judith."
M.D. 70

HOLY EVANGELISTS
See "Evangelists."
M.D. 54

HOLY-HEAD
See "Anglesea."
R. 27

HOLY ISLAND
"Holy Island" of *M*. 187 may have an original in Lindisfarne, or Holy Island, six miles off *Berwick, in the northeast-
ernmost part of *England. A little-inhabited area consistently
claimed by *Scotland before the late fifteenth century, the island is reachable at low tide. St. Cuthbert resided on Lindisfarne (685-687) in the early days of British *Christianity, and
the Lindisfarne Gospels were written and illuminated there.
The *Danes burned the island's settlement and killed many
monks in 793, which perhaps explains M.'s references to oppression and murder.
M. visited North Berwick in November of 1856, but no
complete journal remains of the time; see "Scotland."
M. 187

HOLY LAND, THE
In *M.D.* 41 and throughout M.'s works, the Holy land
refers to *Palestine, where *Christ was born, ministered, and
died. (For *Mohammedans, *Mecca is the Holy land, as the
birthplace of Mahomet; for *Chinese *Buddhists, *India is the
Holy land; for ancient *Greeks Elis, site of the temple of Zeus
[see "Jupiter" and "Jove"], was the Holy Land.)
M.D. 41

HOLY MARY
See "Catholic . . . . "
R. 35

HOLY ROMAN EMPIRE; HOLY ROMAN EMPEROR
Holy Roman Empire is a general designation for the
complexity of lands ruled over by Frankish and German kings
from at least the ninth to the early nineteenth century.
*Charlemagne was first Holy Roman Emperor (crowned 800).
The Emperor was crowned by the *Pope and closely allied to
the politics of the Roman *Catholic Church. Last Emperor
was Francis I of *Austria (1806).
M. could not miss what Brewer notes is a prime contra-
diction in terms, the phenomenon being not "holy," "Roman,"
or an "empire."
See also "Charles V."
Passim

HOLY SACRAMENT, --S

In *Christian usage, sacraments are ritual signs of sacred mystery inaugurated by *Jesus, as suggested by the *New Testament. The Council of Trent specified seven sacraments still promulgated by Roman *Catholics and believed by them to demonstrate the efficacious presence of *God: Baptism, Confirmation, the Eucharist, Penance, Orders, Matrimony, and Extreme Unction. *Protestant usage as promulgated by the *Thirty-Nine Articles reflected controversy about the sacramental nature of baptism and the Lord's Supper (Eucharist): in *P*. 14:1, "The Holy Sacrament of the Supper." While Catholics believe in consubstantiation, Protestant sects vary in their attitudes toward the supper, some seeing it only as a symbol of union with Christ.

M. was baptized (19 August 1819) in *New York's South Reformed Dutch Church, which followed *Calvin's teachings against belief in transubstantiation. After his marriage in 1847, he belonged to the Church of the Divine Unity in New York, apparently continuing Unitarian affiliation in *Pittsfield from 1850 to 1863. By 1865, he is known to have attended All Souls Church (which had changed its name from Church of the Divine Unity and had moved uptown). As a bona fide member of the Unitarian Church until his death (28 September 1891), he was entitled to take communion under its rules granting freedom of interpretation. Central to Unitarianism is nonsubscription to human creeds such as those of the orthodox church. Thus, we cannot clearly establish M.'s belief regarding the "Holy Sacrament of the Supper," if, indeed, he partook of it.

P. 1:2; P. 14:1

HOMER

Little is known about the supposed auther of the two early *Greek hexameter epics, *The Iliad*, and The Odyssey, and what are called the Homeric poems. It is now presumed that he was a blind bard or rhapsode of 7th and 8th century (B.C.) Ionia whose stories were put in written form by others. His work was studied closely in ancient Greece, but by the fourteenth century, interest had flagged. *Chapman's seventeenth-century work revived interest, and *Hobbes and *Dryden also attempted translations. Admiration peaked in the eighteenth century, when *Pope translated The Iliad, and *Victorians Tennyson, Arnold, and Kingsley emulated the Homeric manner.

Sealts #s 276, 277, 278 are Chapman's translations; #147, *Harper's Classical Library*, vols. 32-34, is Pope's.

The "cameo-head" of Homer in *P.* would have to be a highly imaginative rendering of a person not certain even to have existed.

M. 3; M. 75; M. 119; M. 180; R. 33; W. 45; W. 65; W. 75; P. 2:7; P. 18:1; P. 18:2

HOMEWARD BOUND

In addition to obvious connotations, "homeward bound" may refer to the last stitches taken in a navy shroud: "homeward-bound stitches." These last may also indicate temporary clothing repairs designed to last only until one can buy more clothing.

W. 2; W. The End

HOMEWARD-BOUNDERS

See "Beards."

W. 84

HONDURAS

The Central American country's c. 350-mile coastline runs along the *Caribbean and along the Gulf of Fonseca, on the *Pacific. Honduras borders Guatemala, Salvador, and Nicaragua. It is a mountainous country which was visited by *Columbus on his fourth voyage (1502). It gained independence from Spain in 1821 and was part of the Central American Foundation from 1823 to 1838 but thereafter was immersed in bloody wars. The (mainly Mestizo and *Jamaican) population produces gold, silver, bananas, *Manilla hemp, and valuable woods, including the *Mahogany of *R.* 33.

R. 33

HONG KONG

Hong Kong (Hsiang-chiang, or Hsiang Kang), in southern *China, was a desolate fishing island until 1841, when the *British created a colony. Hong Kong is eleven miles long and from two to five miles wide and has one of the world's best deepwater anchorages. Ceded in 1842, it gained its greatest development c. 1850 as an emigration station for poor Chinese leaving for *Australia, where gold had been found (thus *C.M.* 7's reference to pauper pagans dying in the streets.).

C.M. 7

HONG MERCHANTS
*Chinese merchants licensed by the Imperial Government of China in a trade monopoly with Europeans, restricted to *Canton. The 1842 Treaty of Nanking, after the Opium Wars, abolished the practice. "Hong" means "row," a word used for foreign warehouses in Canton.
0. 3

HONOLULU
The city on the southeastern shore of *Oahu, *Hawaiian Islands, M.'s "Honolula," eclipsed *Lahaina in the 1870's.
*Ruschenberger, who had visited the city a few years before M., gives a full and impartial description. He estimates the population at 7,000, with about 200 whites, and mentions the presence of a "seaman's chapel" and "reading room," as well as "billiard tables, bowling allies, grog shops, livery stables, and restaurants . . . because the vices are more aptly acquired than the virtues of civilized life" (457).
Although the "*American connection" to an elegant chapel is not clear (other than in donations of money and materials for construction), M. probably refers in *T*. 26 to the large structure described by missionary Hiram Bingham (*Residence of Twenty-One Years in the Sandwich Islands*, XXV); an illustration shows a rather austere *New-England style edifice of several stories. Bingham describes *Kamehameha (see "Kammahammaha") III's desire for such a church, the raising of funds ranging from the King's initial $3000.00 behest, down to $1.00 gifts from his subjects. Lesser rulers donated stone, lime, and timber; Americans apparently donated timber from *California, shingles from the northwest coast, miscellany from *Boston, a large exterior timepiece from Charlestown. Generous donations of money came from New York, Brooklyn, and New London, as well as a pulpit and communion table from New Haven.
The church, with stone and coral walls thirty-three inches thick and front ornamental pillars twenty-six feet high and four feet in diameter, opened on July 21, 1842, at the end of Bingham's twenty-year stay in the islands, and some six months before M.'s presumed arrival in February of 1843. Bingham's judgement was that it might "stand centuries as a monument of the favor of God to the nation, and of the rapid advancement of the people in Christianity and civilization" (p. 573), especially in its cost in money (probably $30,000) and labor to the *Sandwich Islanders.
T. Passim; O. 49; O. 54; O. 65

HONOLULU COURT JOURNAL

Bingham mentions the 1835 inauguration of the *Hawaiian Almanac* and *The Hawaiian Teacher*, aims of which were educational and salvational.
T. 26

HONORABLE BOARD OF COMMODORES

See "Board of Commodores and Navy Commissioners."
W. 7

HOOK, THE

R. 8's "Greenlander" probably refers to Hoek van Holland, a port town in the south west *Netherlands on the North Sea, ten miles southwest of the Hague: the terminus of cross-channel boats from Harwich, *England.

(Other "Hooks" include a town of northeast Hampshire, England, six miles east of Basingstoke; Hook Head or Hook Point, a cape in southwest county Wexford, *Ireland, at the entrance to Waterford Harbor, twelve miles southeast of Waterford; Hook Norton, a village of Oxfordshire, England, eight miles southwest of Banbury.)
R. 8

HOOLAH-HOOLAH GROUND

As Charles R. Anderson pointed out, M.'s description of the *Tohua*, or festival grounds, is accurate. The "hoolah-hoolah" (or, "hula") is best known as a sacred dance and chant celebrating the prediscovery of the *Sandwich Islands, rather than the *Marquesas.
T. 12

HOOSIER

Hoosier is a colloquial term of uncertain origin; it refers to a rustic or frontiersman, or to a native of the state of Indiana.
C.M. 21

HOPE PLACE

Hope Street is part of a semi-circular belt of Georgian streets built in *Liverpool in the 1820's and 1830's (not dating from 1803, as M. has it): on the northeastern limit of the old city.
R. 30

HOP-POLES

Hops, the dried ripe flowers of which are used to flavor beer and ale, grow long, twining vines (up to twenty-five feet long), necessitating the support of poles or (usually, in the *United States) trellises. Commonest hop is *Humulus lupulus.*
M.D. 108

HORACE

Quintus Horatius Flaccus (65-8 B.C.), perhaps the best-loved *Roman poet, was friend to *Virgil and *Caesar Augustus, supported by Maecenas (see "Mecaenas"). The son of a freed slave, Horace was well educated in Greek culture early in life, at a time of constant civil war. With *Brutus's armies in Greece, he returned in poverty to Rome under an amnesty and took an administrative post, during which time he began writing poetry. He became a popular and influential figure of the time, eventually drawing closer to Augustus than to Maecenas, from whom the Emperor was estranged.

His work is moralistic and epigrammatic. The early *Epodes* and *Odes* were imitations of Greek lyric poetry. The *Satires* (or *Sermones*) and *Epistles* are realistic anecdotal satires, sometimes autobiographical, including vignettes about troublesome *slaves. The *Ars poetica* is a survey of the history and theory of poetry. In all, there are extant 121 lyric poems and 41 verse essays.

(Sealts #147, *Harper's Classical Library* vols. 18 and 19, contain the works.)
C.M. 5; C.M. 22

HORATII

In *Roman legend, the Horatii triplet brothers were matched against the Curiatii triplet brothers of Alba to defend the honor of Rome. Two Horatii were killed, but the third defeated the opponent triplets. On his return home, he killed his sister, who was mourning the death of the Curiatus she was to marry, her sorrow seeming unpatriotic.
R. 53; M.D. 119

HORICON

Horicon is *James Fenimore Cooper's name for *New York's beautiful Lake George. The lake, in the foothills of the *Adirondack Mountains, is thirty-three miles long and from three-quarters to three-miles-wide, with an outlet to Lake Champlain. It was the scene of engagements of the "French

and Indian Wars" which are the background of Cooper's
"*Leatherstocking" novels.
M. 165

HORN

W.'s horned woman had an original in Baron de Maine,
"The Sunday Widow," or "The Horned Mother," described in
Magazin pittoresque for 1841 (pp. 394-396). A portrait was
made in wax by Monsieur Guy the Elder, a maker of anatomical casts for medical pathology museums. The horn was removed when the woman was eighty-four years old, eight
months before her death.
W. 61

HORN, CAPE; CAPE-HORNER; THE CAPE; THE HORN

"The Cape" in M.'s works almost always refers to Cape
Horn, which is more difficult of passage than the Cape of
*Good Hope or other capes. It is marked by a steep rocky head-
land (1,391 feet) at the southernmost point of *South America:
the five-mile long Horn Island of *Tierra del Fuego, *Chile. It
was sighted by Schouten in 1616 and named for Hoorn,
*Netherlands. (There is a False Cape Horn thirty-five miles
northwest.)
M.'s fictional accounts of rounding the Cape are drama-
tized renderings of his own less terrifying roundings on board
Acushnet (see "Pequod") in 1841, on *United States* in 1844, and
on *Meteor* (captained by his brother Thomas: 1830-84) in 1860.
Even his claim in *R*. 41 that the Cape's latitude "very nearly"
corresponds" to *Liverpool's (53°25' N.) is a bit overdrawn; the
Cape is at 55°59' S., 67°16' W.
The "Cape-Horner" of *M.D.* 3 is a ship capable of round-
ing the Cape or in the process of doing so.
See also "Staten Land."
Passim

HORNET, --S

Hornet was an eighteen-gun brig built in 1805 in
*Baltimore: sister-ship to *Wasp. Re-rigged as a ship-sloop
(1810-11), she became a bomb vessel with the *Mediterranean
*squadron. *Hornet* was with *Essex (under *Porter) and
*Constitution on an 1814 mission to destroy the *British whal-
ing industry in the *Indian Ocean. She disappeared in a
storm off Tampico, *Mexico, September 1825.
(*Hornet's finest hour had been her sinking of the British
brig *Peacock off British Guiana, in 1813.)
M. 7; M. 28

HORNE TOOKE

John Horne (1736-1812), *English radical and philologist, assumed the name Tooke in honor of a wealthy benefactor, William Tooke. He became a political activist/minister, supporting parliamentary reform and self-government for the *American colonies, for which activities he was frequently arrested and imprisoned. His friendships touched on many circles, including those of Boswell, *Bentham, Godwin, *Paine, and *Coleridge.

His two-volume book, *The Diversions of Purley* (1786, 1805), projected as three volumes, was the first philological work to regard languages as changing historical developments. It was much admired by the *Utilitarians, but its eccentricities precluded real recognition until later in philological study.
I.P. 6; I.P. 13

HORNPIPES

The hornpipe is a dance originally performed to music of the *pib-corn*, or hornpipe, an instrument with both ends made of horn.
W. 25

HORSE GUARDS

The traditional *English Royal Horse Guards were begun as body guards to *Charles I. The group was thereafter expanded and eventually separated into two groups: "Tins" (body guards in scarlet tunics) and "Blues." Their title was officially changed to Royal Horse Guards in 1819. M. watched the changing of the guard at *St. James on 25 November 1849.
R. 30

HORSE-MARINE, --S

Horse-marines were theoretical awkward, out-of-place persons, a nuisance like the standard *marines of the time, who were excess baggage except in times of battle. By 1868, "Bryant's Minstrels" were to popularize a comic ditty about "Captain Jinks of the Horse Marines," who fed his horse on "corn and beans": a rather explosive diet.
W. 29; W. 53

HORSE SALTS

See "Glauber salts."
R. 18

HORSE-SHOE SIGN
See "Zodiac."
M.D. 99

HOSANNAHS
The expression appears for the first time in *Psalms 118, when a pilgrim recognized as virtuous commemorates with the expression translated in the later Vulgate as, "Save us, we beseech thee." Believers would sometimes wave branches of myrtle, willow, or palm, which were also called hosannahs, as they are in the *New Testament's description of the entry of *Jesus into *Jerusalem (*Matthew 21:9).
P. 2:4

HOSPITAL, THE
Old sailors' hospital-retirement homes include *Chelsea and *Greenwich in *England, and *Sailors' Snug Harbor in the *United States. M.'s brother Thomas Melville (1830-1884) became Governor of the *Staten Island institution in 1867. M. regularly visited and attended the annual Trustees' dinner there.
R. 9

HOT COPPERS
Parched mouth and throat caused by excessive drinking; relief is obtained when one cools one's coppers (from cooking utensils: coppers).
W. 54

HOTSPUR
Sir Henry *Percy (1364-1403), eldest son of Henry, first earl of Northumberland, is depicted in *Shakespeare's Richard II and 1 Henry IV, as well as in other literature. He saw active service from the age of fourteen and participated, with his father, in the usurpation of Henry of Lancaster (*Henry IV), after which the family was enriched with positions and land grants in northern *Wales. With the young prince Henry (later Henry V), he led the Welsh campaign. Relations with the king broke down, however, and with an eye to replacing him, Hotspur attempted to occupy Shrewsbury. He was killed in battle and his head displayed on one of the gates of *York.
M. 36

HOTTENTOT

A general designation for nomadic herder/hunter/gatherer peoples of several areas of South West *Africa. In M.'s time, a catch-all expression for an outlandishly uncivilized or semi-civilized dark-skinned foreigner; in these terms, "Queequeg" might be called a "Hottentot."
R. 50

HOUNDSDITCH

The Houndsditch area in the East End of *London largely developed in the nineteenth century to house dock and construction workers. It was a crowded pocket of poverty, with no drainage as late as 1850.
I.P. 25

HOURIS

Perpetually youthful beautiful damsels in *Mohammedan *Paradise, with renewable virginity; every believer will have seventy two of them in heaven and produce offspring with them that mature instantly.
        The word came to refer to any dark-eyed beauty.
R. 43

HOUSATONIC

The Housatonic River rises in the *Berkshires of northwestern *Massachusetts and flows c. 130 miles to join the Naugatuck River at Derby, *Connecticut, emptying into Long Island Sound at Milford. The "Housatonic mountains" of *I.P.* 25 are the Berkshires, or Hoosacs: part of the *Appalachian chain.
        (The village of Housatonic is located in Great Barrington, eighteen miles south-southwest of *Pittsfield, Massachusetts.)
I.P. 1; I.P. 2; I.P. 25

HOUSE OF COMMONS

See "Parliament . . . . "
Passim

HOUSE OF LORDS

See "Parliament . . . . "
Passim

HOWARD, --S
John Howard (1726-1790) spent much of his wealth on prison reform and other philanthropy. As High Sheriff of Bedfordshire, *England, he observed abuses in Bedford jail and dedicated much of his life to prison reform in legislation and practice. He died of camp fever contracted while visiting hospitals to study the prevention of *plague and other diseases.
R. 36; R. 58; M.D. 87

HOWDAHED
A howdah is the railed and canopied seat used on an elephant's back.
M.D. 42

HOWE; GENERAL HOWE; LORD HOWE
William Howe, Fifth Viscount Howe (1729-1814), a *Whig, was commander in chief of the *British army in *America from 1776 to 1778. Brother to Admiral Lord Richard Howe (1726-1799), he did not become "Lord" Howe until his brother's death—an anachronism in *I.P.* General Howe was second-in-command to General Thomas Gage at *Boston and a leader in assaults on *Bunker Hill. He captured *New York in 1776 and claimed victory at the battle of the *Brandywine and at Germantown, after which he resigned his command.
As Walter E. Bezanson shows in the "Historical Note" to the Northwestern-Newberry edition of *I.P.*, M.'s source for Howe's attempted bribery of *Ethan Allen was *A Narrative of Colonel Ethan Allen's Captivity* (Philadelphia: Robert Bell); the claim is therefore suspect.
Howe figures in a fanciful short story by *Hawthorne: "Howe's Masquerade" (*Twice-Told Tales*, 1842).
I.P. 21

HUDIBRAS
Samuel Butler's three-part, nine-canto poem (pub. 1663-78); a humorous mock-epic political satire of the *Puritans, with outrageous rhymes, satiric epigrams, written in octosyllabic couplets. Hudibras himself is probably a caricature of Butler's patron.
M.'s 17 November 1849 journal records purchase of "a little copy of Hudibras" (Sealts #104) dated 1710. He presented the copy to *Evert Duyckinck, along with a suitable message about the book's ownership, and followed up with a message mentioning the "fine old spicy *duodecimo mouthful." M.'s

own edition of *Hudibras* (Sealts #105) was apparently lost in the 1938 *New England hurricane.
0. 2

HUDSON, GEOFFREY

Sir Jeffrey Hudson (1619-82) was a dwarf who was eighteen inches tall at the age of thirty; he later grew to three feet, six inches or so.

He made his debut at an entertainment given *Charles I, when he was served to guests in a pie, then given as page to Queen Henrietta Maria. He was Captain of horse in the Civil War, captured by *pirates and sold into *slavery in *Barbary, from whence he escaped. He was imprisoned for complicity in the *Popish Plot, and is immortalized in literature in *Scott's *Peveril of the Peak*, and in painting by Vandyke.
M. 9

HUDSON; HUDSON RIVER

The Hudson rises as the Opalescent River in tiny Lake Tear of the Clouds, near Mount Marcy, in the *Adirondacks, *New York. It flows c. 315 miles south to Upper New York Bay (where it is called the North River). It is tidal to Albany and is linked there to the *Great Lakes by the *Erie Canal. The two-to three-mile-wide section between Westchester and Rockland counties is called *Tappan Zee.

When Hendrick Hudson discovered the river in 1609, it was already an important Indian route; it played an important role also in the American *Revolution.

As a longtime resident of the New York City-Albany-Pittsfield triangle, M. traveled much on the river (which was not bridged until 1889, near Albany).

The "Hudson Highlands" of *P*. 7:4 are a rugged part of the Appalachian system along both banks of the river south of Newburgh.
O. 27; R. 1; R. 2; R. 10; R. 27; R. 30; R. 60; M.D. 41; M.D. 87; P. 1:3; P. 7:4; P. 18:1; I.P. 2

HUGGINS'S

One "Huggins" is mentioned in *Beale's book; probably the reference is to marine painter William John Huggins (1781-1845).
M.D. 56

HULL

Isaac Hull (1773-1843), one of *America's legendary naval heroes, gained his greatest glory in the *War of 1812. Hull had "come in at the *hawse holes" as a fourteen year-old cabin boy, was master by the age of nineteen, and had twice been captured by privateers by twenty-one. As fourth lieutenant on *Constitution, he served in the Quasi-War with *France and afterwards commanded *Argus during the *Barbary wars. As captain of Constitution in her action with *Guerrière, he gained the greatest American victory in the *War of 1812 without the loss of one man or one piece of equipment, earning from the government $50,000 in prize money to be shared with his crew.

Relinquishing active command, he became one of the first members of the *Board of Naval Commissioners and later was commodore of the U.S. *Pacific and *Mediterranean *squadrons.

Among the many Hull exploits that sailors in W. might recount: he ordered *Porter's daring destruction of Tripolitan craft and on Argus watched marines land on "the shores of Tripoli."
W. 3

HULL, GENERAL

In the *War of 1812, Brigadier General William Hull (1753-1825) surrendered *Detroit to the *British without a battle.
C.M. 27

HULL

The ancient port city of Hull, *England (properly Kingston upon Hull) is in Yorkshire, at the junction of the Hull and *Humber rivers. Among its several fine museums is the Maritime Museum (M.'s "Leviathanic Museum" in M.D. 102) in Pickering Park, reflecting the city's pioneering efforts in the whaling industry.
M.D. 27; M.D. 102

HUMANE SOCIETY; HUMANE AND MAGNANIMOUS SOCIETIES

By M.'s time, there was excessive uncoordinated private *American effort at social relief and reform, probably reflecting obsessive fear of pauperism as much as desire to help one's fellow man. The first public American social zealot was Cotton Mather (1663-1718), whose Essays to Do Good stressed voluntary individual charity, including the making of lists of the physically and spiritually needy. The Great Awakening of the 1740's went far toward increasing interest in organized charity, as did *Benjamin Franklin's efforts in stimulating self-help through free education. The *American Revolution dramatically increased the need for social relief, which was insufficiently supplied by the government.

Lack of coordination and concomitant excess of fervor in the nineteenth century resulted from the specialized nature of each of the nearly 500 known "humane societies" of the time. Many of them were connected with specific religious denominations and focussed on saving souls through saving bodies; some stressed *Abolition, medical service, prison reform, capital or other punishment, orphan relief, free education, *temperance, tobacco prohibition, asylums for the blind and the insane, Sunday Schools. Although some of these societies actually achieved progress, many of them represented pious busybodies, and M. sided with *Transcendentalists such as Thoreau and *Emerson (especially in "Self-Reliance") in his condemnation of the impulse toward privately organized charity.

His fictional "Seminole Widow and Orphan Asylum" (*C.M.* 6; *C.M.* 8) and "Chinese Society for the Suppression of Meddling with other People's Business" (*M.D.* 89) sound not so farfetched when one peruses the names of some of the actual organizations of the time. A sampling of "Humane Societies": American Temperance Society; Sunday School Union; Association for the Relief of Respectable Aged and Indigent Females (Astor's project); American Colonization Society (founders of the colony in Liberia); American Anti-Slavery Society; Society for Promoting the Observance of the Seventh Commandment; Society for Promoting Manual Training in Literary Institutions; Society for Promotion of Collegiate and Theological Education in the West; *Bunker Hill Monument Association; Children's Aid Society of *New York (in addition to "New York Children's Aid Society"); New York Association for Improving the condition of the Poor; New York Society for Prevention of Pauperism; Society for Alleviating the Miseries of Public Prisons.

If only to curb redundancy, efforts at coordination began in the 1830's. But it was not until the *Civil War's United States Sanitary Commission that a scientific approach began to disentangle relief programs. (The Sanitary commission was led by Henry Whitney Bellows, pastor of M.'s All Souls Unitarian Church in New York City, whose intervention was sought during M.'s psychological difficulties of the late 1860's.) By the end of M.'s life, massive foundations of Carnegie, Rockefeller, and other millionaires were turning philanthropy into big

business, and Social *Darwinism was deflecting the ordinary
individual's impulse to tamper with nature—a secular stance
suggesting an ironic return to the early *Puritan settlers'
notion that one should not interfere with "God's plan."
     See also "*No Trust*."
W. 17; M.D. 13

HUMBER
     Western *England's Humber River is the outlet of the
Ouse and Trent Rivers separating the counties of *Yorkshire
and Lincolnshire, with important docks and maritime science
institutions.
     See also "Hull" and "Spurm."
I.P. 19

HUME, --S
     David Hume (1711-1776), radical philosopher, historian,
economist, and prolific essayist, attracted controversy
throughout his career, with several suppressed works, including "Of Suicide," in which he defends the act as a human right
and even an occasional act of wisdom.
     Born and educated in *Edinburgh, he studied privately
for three years in *France, returning to publish the 1739-40
Treatise on Human Nature, which influenced *Adam Smith.
More popular was his 1741-2 *Essays Moral and Political*. After
further travels, he published *An Enquiry concerning Human
Understanding* (originally *Philosophical Essays...*), containing
the notorious "Of Miracles." Controversy grew after his 1751
Enquiry concerning the Principles of Morals, but the 1752 *Political Discourses* brought success on the Continent. His *History
of Great *Britain* (1754, -57, -59, -62) was initially rejected, then
greatly influenced Gibbon and *Voltaire. Suppressed essays
on suicide and on immortality preceded his 1757 *Four Dissertations*. A diplomatic post in *Paris (1763-65) brought temporary
friendship with *Rousseau, whom he introduced to *England.
An autobiography preceded the posthumous *Dialogues
concerning Natural Religion* (1779).
     Hume incurred enmity from a wide spectrum of politi-
cians and religionists for his seeming skepticism and was rejected for chairs at Edinburgh and *Glasgow; appointment as
keeper of the Advocates' Library at Edinburgh (1752) enabled
completion of his *History*. In 1761, all of his works were put on
the *Index* at *Rome, amid charges of heresy and atheism
stemming from Hume's claims that belief in a supreme being
results from our imaginative faculty, that religion had degenerated from polytheism, and that humans created the seeming

order of the universe. He believed in most civil liberties and envisioned a world in which happiness of self would not conflict with happiness of others.

Among his supporters were Boswell, who called him "the greatest writer in Britain," *Kant, *Comte, *Bentham, and Mill.

M. scored a footnote revealing Hume's feelings about writing for money in *The Literary Character; or the History of Men of Genius* (Chapter XVI).
R. 58; C.M. 24

HUNGARIAN

Modern day Hungary (the 1949 Hungarian People's Republic) is bounded by Czechoslovakia (N.), the Transcarpathian oblast of the Ukraine (N.E.), Rumania (E.), Yugoslavia (S.), and *Austria (W.). It is bisected by the Danube River.

Hungary's history is a violent one. *Romans, *Huns, Ostogoths, Avars, and *Magyars, all had controlled it before eleventh-century *Christianization by *St. Stephen. Slavic, *German, Latin, and other elements were absorbed into a feudal system leading to the (1100-1500) *Croatian Union. Despite a Hungarian magna carta of 1222, *Mongols invaded in 1241, leading to anarchy. The Angevins appeared in 1308, and Hungary was joined to *Poland in 1370. The *Turks entered in 1526, and in 1686 the Austrian Hapsburgs acquired much Hungarian territory, contested in the 1848 *Kossuth revolution. A republic of 1849 was almost immediately suppressed by Austria. In 1867 the Austro-Hungarian dual monarchy was formed.

The "Hungarian *gypsies" of *M*. 128 and *M*. 177 are descendents of dark-skinned nomads called Romanies, themselves descended from low-cast *Indians who migrated to *Persia and Europe by the fifteenth century. They were first called "*Egyptians," and the name was corrupted to its present form. In Hungary, they are *Czigany*. The literature of many nations paints them as romantic (if larcenous) fortune-tellers, craftmen, and musicians who sit around fires (*M*. 177) a good deal.

See also "Transylvania."
M. 128; M. 177

HUNS

A catchall expression signifying uncivilized and untidy brutes. The barbarian tribe of Huns invaded the East *Roman Empire in the fourth and fifth centuries.

See "Attila."
M. 36; W. 84

HUNTER, JOHN; JOHN HUNTER'S ACCOUNT OF THE
DISSECTION OF A WHOLE. (*A SMALL SIZED ONE.*)
     See "Hunter, William and John . . . . "
M.D. Extracts 47

HUNTER, WILLIAM AND JOHN; HUNTERIAN DEPART-
MENT OF THE ROYAL COLLEGE OF SURGEONS
     The Hunter brothers were influential *British medical
teachers and practitioners. The elder, William (1718-1783),
had more formal education than John, eventually graduating
from the University of *Glasgow as a doctor of medicine. He
taught anatomy, practiced obstetrics, and brought obstetrics
from a field dominated by midwives and forceps to an accepted
branch of medicine. He amassed a large collection of specimens which was acquired by the University of Glasgow. A
scholarly and ascetic man, William published works including
Two Introductory Lectures, Medical Commentaries, and his
most famous *Anatomy of the Human Gravid Uterus, Exhibited
in Figures.*
     John Hunter (1728-1793), a surgeon, natural historian,
and originator of many important experiments, was his
brother's best pupil but never completed university study or attempted to become a doctor of medicine. Early on, he assisted
in William's dissecting rooms and learned surgery at
*Chelsea Hospital. He was admitted to the Corporation of Sur-
geons in 1768 and as a teacher gave private and public lectures.
His collection of over 10,000 anatomical, pathological, and biological specimens became the Hunterian collection at
*London's *Royal College of Surgeons. M.'s knowledge of the
Hunterian collection comes from *Penny Cyclopaedia,* which
says the collection of monstrosities proves that Hunter "knew
the fact that they are, as it were, represention of the natural
form of animals lower in the scale of creation, and possess the
form natural to themselves at an earlier period of development." Much of the collection was destroyed by bombing in
World War II. Earlier, many of John's papers had been destroyed after his death by his brother-in-law, Edward Home,
later accused of having plagiarized them. John's published
works were on human teeth, venereal disease, gun-shot
wounds. John was a more open and vivid and less bookish
person than William. He studied *in situ* where possible, experimented with his own body (injecting himself with syphilis, for
example), and kept an extensive menagerie. He married the
poet, Anne Home, and had four children. John's works of
most importance to Melvilleans are probably the 1787
"Structure and Economy of Whales," and the 1791 "Horny Ex-

cresences of the Human Body." M.'s acquaintance with these
works was probably also at second hand.
See also "Extracts 47" and "Horn."
W. 63; M.D. Extracts 47; M.D. 32; M.D. 55

HURON
Lake Huron, second largest of the *Great Lakes (206
miles long, 183 miles wide), was probably the first to be visited
by Europeans: *Frenchmen in 1612 and 1615. It is subject to
violent storms and is ice-bound from mid-December to early
April. M. sailed across it in July (?) of 1840.
R. 32; M.D. 54

HURRA'S NEST
*Dana defines a hurrah's nest as "everything on top,
and nothing at hand." Other definitions suggest it refers to any
disorderly mess or state of confusion. W.'s *Jack Chase uses
the word in the sense that my father, Kenneth F. Kier, a World
War I tar, did: to describe a noisy argument or scuffle.
W. 56

HUSSEY
See "Comstock"; "Extracts" 64.
M.D. Extracts 64

HUWYENEE
Huahine, *Society Islands.
O. 76

HYADES
In astronomy, stars in the *constellation *Taurus,
named for seven nymphs of *Greek mythology who wept over
the death of their brother Hyas. As stars, they threaten rain
when whey rise with the sun.
M. 126

HYDE-PARK, --CORNER
The site of *London's Hyde Park (with adjoining
*Kensington Gardens, a 615-acre expanse) was acquired by
*Henry VIII on the dissolution of the monasteries of
*Westminster Abbey. It was opened to the public by *James I
and has been noted as a dueling site, a horse-riders' paradise

("Rotten Row"), a haven at "Speakers' Corner" for orators, a spot in which to gaze upon the large lake, the *Serpentine. The Crystal Palace of London's 1850-51 exhibition was first created here.

M. visited in late April 1857, admiring the "Fine & Bold riding of the ladies."
R. 30; R. 43; R. 44; P. 1:3

HYDRA
In *Greek mythology, a many-headed water-snake killed by *Hercules as one of his twelve labors.
(See also "Hydrus.")
M. 121; R. 39

HYDRIOTE
One from Hydra (Idhra, Idra, or Ydra), in the Aegean Sea off East *Peloponnesus, *Greece. The Island is thirteen miles long and two miles wide and is mostly barren rock. But under the *Turks in the nineteenth century, it was a thriving trade and commercial center. The allusion in *M.D.* 96 refers to the important role played by Hydriotes in the Greek War of Independence (1821-29).
M.D. 96

HYDRUS
In astronomy, a southern *constellation: *Hydra, the Water Snake, said by the *Greeks to be the one killed by *Hercules as one of his twelve labors.
M.D. 57

HYER, TOM
Hyer was the son of pioneer *American boxer Jacob Hyer, who had declared himself heavyweight champion in 1816. Tom Hyer became the first fighter recognized as heavyweight champion of the United States after defeating George McChester ("Country McCloskey") in a one-hundred-and-one-round, two hour and fifty-five-minute fight at Caldwell's Landing, *New York, in 1841.
I.P. 22

HYPARXES
Hyparxis is a rare philosophical term for existence, subsistence.
M. 170

HYPERBOREAN

In *Greek mythology, the Hyperboreans were a race of *Apollo-worshippers living in perpetual bliss, warmth, and sunshine, above the source of the North Wind. The Greeks probably misinterpreted the name Hyperboreioi as "beyond the North Wind," and M. certainly seems to have misunderstood the word, identifying it with cold.
M.D. 3; M.D. 68

HYTYHOO

M.'s "Hytyhoo" is Vaitahu, *St. Christina Island, *Marquesas.
O. 3

I

IBERIA

The ancient Hispania, given a name derived by the *Greeks from the Ebro River, is the peninsula comprising *Spain and *Portugal, separated from the rest of Europe by the Pyrenees and bordered by the Strait of *Gibralter, the *Mediterranean and the *Atlantic.

(A second Iberia, in the modern South Georgian U.S.S.R., was allied with Mithradates VI and defeated by *Pompey.)
R. 30

ICELAND

The island between the North *Atlantic and *Arctic Oceans 155 miles southeast of *Greenland is 290 miles long and 190 miles wide. Because of its climate and topography, Iceland is mostly uninhabited. In addition to the great snow-field of Vatnajoküll (3,247 square miles in area), there are about 120 glaciers and 100 volcanoes (mostly active), the largest of which is Mount Hekla (see "Hecla").

Iceland, settled by *Norwegians in the ninth century, may have been the legendary Thule, considered the northern-most extremity of the world. The late eighteenth century was a most difficult time for Iceland; volcanoes erupted regularly, and privateers plagued the coast. Although M. appears to think of Iceland in terms of the world's most extreme cold, the average temperatures range from 30° f. in January to 52° in

July. Until 1918 the *Danes possessed Iceland, the capital of
which is Reykjavik.
R. 33; W. 93; M.D. 40

ICKWORTH
    A rotunda-crowned *Suffolk seat built c. 1794-1830 by the
fourth Earl of *Bristol, bishop of Derry (owned since 1956 by the
English National Trust).
R. 44

ICY GLEN
    Icy Glen, near *Stockbridge, *Massachusetts, is a hill of
huge rocks under which there is ice all year round. On 5 August 1850, after dinner in Stockbridge, M. visited Icy Glen,
along with *Hawthorne, Oliver Wendell Holmes, *Evert Duyckinck, and others, for a much-discussed scramble on the rocks.
M.D. 102

ICY SEA
    Undoubtedly one of the *polar seas. In Alaska, there are
an Icy Bay and an Icy Strait.
M.D. 113

IDES
    Ancient *Roman calendar: the fifteenth day of March,
May, July, and October; the thirteenth of other months; eight
days after the nones. Interest, debts, and tuition were paid on
this day. *Julius Caesar was warned to beware the Ides of
March, on which day he was assassinated in B.C. 44 (b. B.C.
100).
    See also "Calends" and "Nones."
M. 80

ILHA DAS COBRAS
    Cobras Island, in Guanabara Bay, near the eastern end
of *Rio de Janeiro, is M.'s "Isle of the Snakes." Even in the
nineteenth century, it had many wharves, naval establishments, an arsenal, and dry docks. It was to be the scene of a
large-scale naval revolt in 1893. (The island is today connected
by a bridge to the mainland.)
W. 39

ILIAD
*Homer's epic poem deals with the events of a few days at the end of the *Trojan war, focussing on the wrath of *Achilles. In 1860, M. underscored lines in his *Chapman translation:

> But Gods at all times give not all their gifts to
>   mortal men.
> *If then I had the strength of youth, I miss'd the*
>   *counsels then*
> *That years now give me; and now years want that*
>   *main strength of youth.* (Book IV)

M. 75

ILLINOIS
The twenty-first state, admitted to the Union in 1818, is bounded by *Wisconsin (N.), Iowa and *Missouri (W.), *Kentucky (S.), and Indiana (E.), with natural boundaries at the *Mississippi River, Lake *Michigan, the *Wabash and *Ohio Rivers. Elevation of the "Prairie State" slopes gently southward from c. 1,220 feet to 280 feet above sea level, with the "Illinois Mounds" (*M*. 75) the highest point. The mounds are composed of fossil-rich soil deposited by glacial winds in the last Ice Age. (Charles Mound is the highest, on the Wisconsin border.)

Illinois was the domain of the *Kaskaskia, Sac, and *Fox Indians when Marquette and Jolliet went up the Illinois River in 1673. LaSalle visited in 1680, and until the 1720's Illinois was part of *French *Louisiana. It was ceded to *Britain in 1763 and was part of the Northwest Territory or Indian Territory until 1809. The *War of 1812 spurred development, especially at Fort Dearborn, on the site of modern Chicago. Nauvoo was the site of Joseph Smith's *Mormon settlement; his murder there drove the Mormons westward to *Utah.

M. visited his uncle Thomas Melville in Galena, in 1840. Thomas was struggling to support his family during depression times in what was still a wildly rugged area. There was no occupation to detain M. there, but he collected impressions that were to color later works, especially the poem, "Trophies of Peace," which uses the fertile Illinois prairies to show nature's (post-*Civil War) healing power. The steamboat ride enroute home supplied impressions for *C.M.* M. *lectured in Chicago, Rockford, and Quincy, Illinois, in February and March of 1858.

See also "Prairies."

M. 75; R. 43; M.D. 14; M.D. 105; C.M. 25; C.M. 27

IMEEO; IMEEOSE
     See "Moreea."
     The "chief of Imeeo" whom M. makes out to be husband
to *Pomaree Vahinee I was actually chief of Huaheine and Raiatea (see "Raiatair"), according to *Ellis. *Olmsted wrote at
some length about him.
O. Preface; O. 25; O. 55; O. 69; O. 80

IMPERIALS
     The *beard style of *Napoléon III: a tuft of chin hair on
an otherwise clean-shaven face.
W. 85

INCAS
     Although the word Inca refers to an *Andean people, as
well as to their chief, M. uses the word most often in the latter
sense. The great Inca empire, preceded in the *Peruvian area
by other sophisticated civilizations, dates from about A.D. 1200,
when the legendary *Manco Capac became emperor. The thirteenth and last emperor was Atahualpa (1532-33; see
"Atahalpa"), deposed when *Pizarro arrived at the end of a
century of Inca expansion.
     Inca religion was highly organized and included sacri-
fices (seldom of humans), divination, and elaborate ceremony
in adoration of the Sun and many minor deities. There was no
system of writing, but a numbering system and medi-
cal/surgical science was highly developed.
     The emperors, or "Incas," were divine descendents of
the sun. Although endowed with great power, they were not
tyrants, but nepotism was the rule in the highly structured
and bellicose society.
     The "Inca's crown" of *C.M.* 30 would have been made of
the gold which lured the conquistadors.
M.181; C.M. 30

INDIA; INDIAN, --S; INDIAMAN
     The word "India" was derived through *Greek corrup-
tion of the *Sanskrit word for "river": *sindhu* (specifically, the
Indus). The idea of an Indian subcontinent defined geographically by the *Himalayas and the oceans was a western political expedient. The area is actually a multitude of ancient discrete cultural entities delineated by geography. *Portugal was
the first large western European nation to make claims on India, at the end of the fifteenth century. By the seventeenth,
powerful *British and *Dutch fleets brought an end to Por-

tuguese domination. The British gained ascendency over the Dutch and the *French by the late eighteenth century, and the powerful English *East India company firmly established British governance by the early nineteenth. During M.'s time, the British struggled to Briticize India socially, religiously (as suggested in *C.M.* 7), and linguistically; to establish law and order; to found an administrative system making India the "*Fast-fish" of *M.D.* 89.

Conflicts arose in Britain between "Orientalists" and "Anglicists." At the same time (early 1840's), Lord *Ellenborough as Governor-General fought off influence of the *Russians in *Afganistan. Sikh wars, *Burmese wars, and myriad other battles continued, providing in England the "war news" of *R.* 46. By the late 1850's, the Indians were mutinying in protest against the acceleration of enforced westernization and its demonstration of utter disrespect for traditional Indian values. Wars, famines, and disease exacerbated Britian's Indian problems throughout M.'s lifetime, and the Indian nationalist movement was becoming more powerful and more virulently anti-British by the time of his death. M.'s political references to India show sympathy for the subjugated peoples and distaste for British imperialism. (India did not become a sovereign republic until after World War II.)

M.'s knowledge of India was probably heavily based on readings. He knew the work of *Sir William Jones, who had helped organize the *Royal Society of *Bengal and *Calcutta; he published *Asiatick Researches* thoughout the 1780's. The Reverend Thomas Maurice's *Indian Antiquities*: (1794) is known to have been a source for M., and his *History of Hindostan* (1820) might have been, as well. Material of Leo Africanus (see "John Leo") was contained in *Harris's "Collection." Finkelstein suggests in *Melville's Orienda* that M.'s knowledge of fire-worshipping *Parsees of *Bombay came to him through Carsten Niebuhr's *Travels through Arabia and Other countries of the East* (1792).

An "Indiaman" (*R.* 12; *R.* 50; *M.D.* 81; *I.P.* 18; *I.P.* 19) is an Indian ship or one trading with India. The "Indian isles" of *M.D.* 1 are probably the *Laccadives, *Maldives, and *Ceylon.

See also "Apollo Green"; "Delhi"; "Elephanta"; "Gama"; "Ganges"; "Goa"; "Hindostan"; "Hindu"; "Lascar"; "Mogul"; "Thugs"; "Vedas"; "Vishu"; "Wellington."
Passim

INDIAN CHARACTERS CHISELLED ON THE . . . PAL-
ISADES . . . OF THE UPPER MISSISSIPPI
    Before it was destroyed by quarrying about 1845, the fig-
ure of a large bird was visible on the Piasa Rocks, north of Al-
ton, *Illinois, where the Piasa stream enters the *Mississippi.
"Piasa" is "bird that devours men," in local Indian language.
M.D. 68

INDIAN CORN
    In the nineteenth century (and to some extent in the
twentieth), in *Britain expecially, "corn" referred to grains
such as wheat, rye, barley, etc. "Indian corn" referred to
maize (*Zeamays*), common North American eared, husk-
covered corn.
C.M. 22

INDIAN EYES
    "Indian eyes" represent the kind of sentimental passion
expressed by a lovelorn East Indian youth in *Shelley's "The
Indian Serenade."
M.D. 32

INDIAN HUG
    A style of wrestling in which the opponents begin by fac-
ing each other, grasping each other with both arms around the
opponent's body.
W. 25

INDIAN OCEAN
    The smallest (28,350,000 square miles) of the three great
oceans, the Indian is bounded by *Asia (N.), *Australia (E.),
*Antarctica (S.) and *Africa (W.), and lies mostly south of the
*Equator. It has two major indentations, the Arabian Sea and
the Bay of *Bengal, and is separated from the *Pacific by the
*Sunda Islands. Its greatest depth (24,440 feet) occurs off
*Java. *Gama sailed the Indian Ocean in 1498; in 1869 the
Suez Canal connected it with the *Atlantic Ocean.
R. 21; R. 27; W. 65; M.D. 6; M.D. 7; M.D. 44; M.D. 133

INDIAN SEA
    See "Indian Ocean."
M.D. Extracts 7

INDIAN TOWN (GIFT OF ELEPHANT)
One *Indian town reputed to have given a decorated elephant to *Alexander the Great was Taxila. Various other towns did likewise after the defeat of *Porus in 327 B.C.
M.D. 92

INDIAN TRADITIONS (WHITE STEED)
The American Indian White Steed of the Prairies is discussed in *The Wilderness and the War Path* (1846), wherein *James Hall perhaps confuses the legend with that of the "Black Steed of the Prairies," a remarkable horse coveted by Western Plains Indians.
M.D. 42

INDIA-RUBBER
Ficus elastica, the India rubber tree, was the chief source of world rubber before *Brazilian products replaced it. It is a large (unedible) fig tree with roots contorted like a mangrove's, sometimes used as a house-plant. The rubber yielded is especially resilient and bouncing.
W. 90

INDIEN
The large frigate *Indien*, built in *Amsterdam, was to be commanded by *John Paul Jones. But to prevent *British seizure, it was sold in 1777 to the *French.
I.P. 10

INDIES
"Indies" is a vague term. "East Indies" at first referred to *India, then southeast *Asia, finally to the *Malay Archipelago (the *Netherlands East Indies islands of which became modern Indonesia). "West Indies" refers to the *Antilles crescent off Central America from *Florida to *Venezuela, separating the *Atlantic from the *Caribbean: discovered by *Columbus in 1492. These islands became a pawn among *England, *France, *Spain, and *Holland, and, late in the nineteenth century, the *United States.
M. 75; M.D. 7; M.D. 26 and elsewhere

INDOMITABLE, THE
The *French warship *Indomptable* was driven onshore and wrecked with her entire crew after the battle of *Trafalgar.
M. 28

INFANTAS
Formerly, in *Spain and *Portugal, any princess of the royal blood except heiress to the crown.
M. 181

INFERNO, --S, THE INFERNO
See "Dante . . . ."
M. 3; M. 98; P. 9:2; P. 25:5

INGRAHAM, CAPTAIN
Joseph Ingraham (1762-1800). Biographical data is rare: born in *Boston, *Massachusetts, he married Jane Salter of Boston, had three sons. A surviving manuscript journal suggests he was in the *Navy during the *Revolution, then traveled to *Asiatic waters. In 1787 he was second mate of *Columbia* on the Boston trade to the northwest coast. As chief officer he wrote an account (since lost) of a trip to the *Cape Verde Islands. As commander of *Hope* brigantine in 1790, he discovered the northern group of the *Marquesas, naming them the *Washington Islands. This voyage was a financial loss, and he returned to Boston in 1793. As Navy Lieutenant on the U.S. brig, *Pickering*, he was lost with the ship, probably in gales.
T. 2

INQUISITION
See "Spanish Inquisition."
W. 31; M.D. 54

IN SKINS
Wine was commonly stored in skins until the late seventeenth century, when the use of corked bottles resulted from the work of Dom Pierre Perignon, a *Benedictine Monk who also produced the first *Champagne. Skins continued to be useful for special purposes, such as the smuggling in W. 43.
W. 43

INTEGRAL CALCULUS
A branch of mathematics based on the concept of the limit. Two limits are fundamental: the derivative, in differential calculus; the definite integral, in integral calculus.
In the seventeenth century, Kepler, *Descartes, *Pascal, and *Newton were theoreticians of the study, which developed

further in the eighteenth century, despite attacks from, among others, *Bishop Berkeley. Only after the first quarter of the nineteenth century was calculus accepted as legitimate.
M. 136

INTELLIGENCE OFFICE, --S
    See "Philosophical Intelligence Office."
C.M. 22; C.M. 24

IN TERROREM
    To inspire terror.
M.D. 33

INTERTROCHANTERIC
    See *"femur."*
W. 62

INVINCIBLE
    L'Invincible was an ornately decorated *French three-decker ship of the eighteenth century.
M. 28

INVULNERABLE KNIGHT
    See "Black Knight."
P. 18:1

IO
    See "Juno."
M.D. Extracts 52

IRELAND; IRISH; IRISHMAN; IRISHMEN
    The Gaelic "Eire," *Latin "*Hibernia," poetic "Erin" is the second largest of the British Isles, separated from Great *Britain by the North Channel, the *Irish Sea, and St. George's Channel. Celts were the original inhabitants, but Ireland was regularly invaded (except by the *Romans). The *Milesians became forerunners of the modern Irish people. *St. Patrick converted them to *Christianity in the fifth century. The *Norse raided in the eighth, founding *Dublin, Waterford, and Limerick. The English conquered for Henry II in

the twelfth century, beginning a struggle that continues until the present.

During the potato blight of the 1840's, one million Irish people starved to death. One and one-half million emigrated, mostly to the *United States, where they became the focus of much animosity against foreigners, ostensibly for their willingness to work cheaply, their abundant reproduction, their unfamiliar style of living, and their alcoholic brawls. Probably a central cause for objection was their Roman *Catholicism, which was painted by Nativists and others as ignorant and superstituous support of a licentious and rapacious ecclesiastical hierarchy, a backsliding into pre-Reformation ways.

M.'s paternal heritage probably included Irish blood. For the most part, his allusions to the Irish partake of stereotypical contemporary distaste (as in *M.D.* 40's *Belfast sailor's praising the *Virgin for a violent fight). Yet the chapters of *R.* focussed on Irish emigrants rise above popular prejudice to show liberal sympathy for their plight. "Wellingborough" expresses a desire to see Ireland (*R.* 27), but M. never visited. He saw the coastline from shipboard in 1839 and 1857.

"Irish" had been used as a derogatory adjective since the late seventeenth century. *Edinburgh Review* (May 1828) suggested that young Irish boys be raised on board ship, so that the "ignorant paupers" in Ireland would not "continue the breed of paupers, as ignorant and wretched as themselves."

See also "Cape Clear"; "Carrickfergus"; "Donnybrook"; "Emmet, Robert"; "foreigners"; "Irish Sea"; "Kilkenny"; "Meath"; "Mull of Galloway"; "O'Connell, Daniel."
O. 37; R. 12; R. 27; R. 40; R. 51; W. 23; W. 39; W. 68; W. 73; W. 89; M.D. 32; M.D. 40; M.D. 89; I.P. 15; C.M. 2; C.M. 5; C.M. 22 and elsewhere

IRIS

The perennial iris, of the family *Iridaceae* (with crocuses and gladiolas), has sword-shaped leaves. It bears elaborate flowers of varying colors with three petals and three drooping sepals.

(In "flower language," iris stands for "Message.")
M. 64; M. 70; M. 101; M. 190 and elsewhere

IRISH COCKNEY

As a "graduate" of *Radcliffe Highway, *R.*'s "Jack Blunt" has learned about ale houses and murders, becoming a "*cockney" by adoption, despite his being of *Irish extraction. However, M. might also refer covertly to the so-called "Cockney School" of writers such as Leigh Hunt, Hazlitt, and Keats,

*Londoners of humble origin with penchants like "Jack's" for overly romantic literature.
R. 18

IRISH REBELLION
Of the many *Irish rebellions since the sixteenth century, the one most likely in M.'s mind in *C.M.* is the "Young Ireland" rebellion of 1848, led by Charles Gavan Duffy and Thomas Osborne Davis, in opposition to the cautious policies of *Daniel O'Connell.
C.M. 13

IRISH SEA
Separating *Ireland from Great *Britain, at 53°55' N., 5°25' W. M. sailed it, enroute to *Liverpool in 1839, and departed through it from the same city in 1857.
R. 22; R. 27; R. 47; I.P. 15

IRISH, WILD; "WILD IRISH" EMIGRANTS
"The Wild Irishman" was a mail train between *London and *Holyhead in the middle of the nineteenth century. See "Irish . . . " regarding emigrants.
R. 47

IRON CROWN OF LOMBARDY
See "Lombardy, Iron Crown of."
M.D. 37

IRON MASK, MAN IN THE
The Man in the Iron Mask, by Alexandre Dumas, is the story of a man imprisoned for over forty years by Louis XIV (see "Bourbon") who might have been the king's twin brother.
M. 97

IRON-WOOD
Several kinds of very hard wood are called "Ironwood," especially hornbeam (*Carpinas*), a polishable white wood, and hop hornbeam (*Ostrya*): both of the birch family.
M.D. 13

IROQUOIS
See "Five Nations"; "White belt of wampum."
M.D. 42; M.D. 57

ISABELLA
Isabella I the *Catholic (1451-1504) was queen of *Castile from 1474. Her marriage to the Catholic Ferdinand II of Aragon unified *Spain politically but not culturally. Among their most famous actions, in 1478 Isabella and Ferdinand obtained the papal bull establishing the *Spanish Inquisition; in 1492, they expelled the *Jews; by the end of the century they attempted to force conversion on the *Moors.

Isabella's agreement to finance the expedition of *Christopher Colombus has been much romanticized; it was a shrewd political move. Some of the blame for the whitewashing must go to W.H. Prescott's immensely popular *History of the Reign of Ferdinand and Isabella* (3 vols, 1838), which was probably in the library of *United States* during M.'s cruise.
M. 97

ISABELLA, LADY
See "Mendanna."
W. 76

ISABEY
Louis Gabriel Eugène Isabey (1803-86), *French painter and lithographer, was highly influenced by the romanticism of Delacroix. His early work in historical painting and costume genre scenes was highly popular, but late in life he turned to marine painting.
M. 13

ISAIAH
The first of the three *Old Testament "major" or "latter" prophets, with *Jeremiah and *Ezekiel (and *Daniel, in the English *Bible), Isaiah is thought to have been born in *Jerusalem c. 760 and to have had a ministery of forty years. The name in *Hebrew means "Yahweh is salvation," and Isaiah preached that faith in *Jehovah, a holy and sovereign god, would save sinners.

Isaiah was not the author of the sixty-six chapter Book of Isaiah, which covers the time before, during and after the *Babylonian exile (597-537 B.C.). The most quoted book in the *New Testament (especially in the *Gospels), Isaiah looks to a messianic age and to a savior who will suffer, die, and be exalted, as the New Testament tells of *Jesus. The book contains poems, song adaptations, enumerations of kings, biography, and historical background; it sees Zion as a pilgrimage center for all nations, predicts the destruction of Babylon, warns other foreign nations, and sees *Egyptians as future worshippers of Jehovah; it contains *Apocalyptic material and much long-range prophecy.

See also "Extracts" 5.
M.D. Extracts 5; M.D. 86

ISHMAEL
*Biblical Ishmael (*Genesis 16:1-16; 17:18-25; 21:6-21; 25:9-17) is firstborn son of *Abraham by the *Egyptian slave, Hagar, sent into the wilderness because of the jealousy of Sarah, Abraham's wife, mother of *Isaac. An angel prophesies: "And he will be a wild man; his hand will be against every man, and every man's hand against him."

There are five Ishmaels in the *Old Testament. The name became infamous after *Mohammed claimed descent as a result of the angel's further prophecy that Ishmael would be the ancestor of a large nation.

(M.'s cousin, Thomas Wilson Melvill, may have been the model for M.D.'s "Ishmael": a family black sheep, ex-midshipman, whaleman, alcoholic; buried at *Lahaina, 1844.)
M. 13; R. 12; M.D. Passim; P. 5:1; C.M. 24

ISINGLASS
Isinglass, or mica, is a transparent or translucent form of gelatin, often derived from the air bladders of fish (especially sturgeon). It was used as transparent or translucent sheet plastics would be in the next century.
M.D. 68

ISLANDS OF KING SOLOMON
See "Cyclades."
M.D. 52

ISLE OF ALBEMARLE
Albemarle, or Isabela Island, largest of the *Gallipagoes, is crossed at the north end by the *Equator, not the center, as M. has it in M.D. 127.
M.D. 127

ISLE OF DESOLATION
The Isle of Desolation is one of the Kerguelen Islands, a dependency of *Madagascar, in the subantarctic *Indian Ocean (49-50° S., 69-30° E.). Desolation is a one-hundred mile-long volcanic island with a deeply indented coast of peninsulas, capes, and fjords. Cook Glacier covers one-third of the island, which is noted for whaling and sealing activity. It was discovered, along with some 300 other islands in the group, by the French explorer Kerguélen-Trémarec, in 1772.
(*Chile's Desolación is at 53°05' S, 74°00' W.)
M.D. 7

ISLE OF MAN; MANX; MANXMAN
The rocky Isle of Man, in the *Irish Sea, equi-distant from *England, *Ireland, *Scotland, and *Wales (54°26' N., 4°21' W.), is about thirty miles long and ten miles wide. Although it has little in the way of wildlife or vegetation, it is known to have been settled since c. 2000 B.C. The *Scandinavian invasions of c. 800 A.D. permanently marked the island's culture, as did ensuing Scottish rule. Britain controlled Man from the fifteenth to the seventeenth centuries, when there was no male heir to the Stanley family, traditional rulers who refused kingship. The Isle of Man was long a center of the contraband trade, and in M.'s time home rule was hotly contested. (The Manx-Gaelic name of the island is Ellan Vannin, Eilan Mhannin, or Mannin—from Old Celtic *man*: a place.)
R. 36; M.D. 125; I.P. 15

ISLE OF ST. MARY'S
See "St. Mary's Isle."
I.P. 17

ISLE OF THE SNAKES
See "Ilha das Cobras."
W. 39

ISLES OF MYRRH
See "Isles of Palms."
M. 167

ISLES OF PALMS
    Although Merrill Davis takes these, along with the
"Isles of Myrrh," as fictionalized versions of South Sea Is-
lands, (*Melville's Mardi: A Chartless Voyage*), the *Canary
Islands (Islas Canarias, *Spain: 29°09' N.; 17°30' W.) have
been called "Las Palmas."
M. 167

"ISLES OF THE SEA!"
    *Cyprus, *Rhodes, and *Crete.
T. 26

ISRAEL
    The capital city is *Jerusalem. Present-day boundaries
are on the Gulf of Aqaba of the *Red Sea: Sinai Peninsula and
*Egypt (S.W.), Jordan (E.), Syria (N.E.), *Lebanon (N.).
    See "Palestine," for general history; see also "Carmel";
"Dead Sea"; "Galilee"; "Jaffa"; "Jezreel"; "Jordan";"Judea";
"Nazareth."
W. 36

ISRAEL IN EGYPT
    See "Handel."
W. 50

ISRAELITES
    See "Hebrew."
M. 97; W. 22; M.D. 73

ISRAEL POTTER'S AUTOBIOGRAPHICAL STORY
    The basic source for *I.P.* (reprinted in photographic re-
production in the Northwestern University/Newberry Library
edition of 1982) is Henry Trumbull, *Life and Remarkable Adventures of Israel R. Potter (A Native of Cranston, Rhode-
Island.) Who was a Soldier in the American Revolution . . .*
(Providence: 1824).
    Little is known of Trumbull; he was born in
*Connecticut in 1781, was a busy printer in *Providence who
also published a life of *Daniel Boone, and who died in Brooklyn, N.Y. in 1842.
    Potter was an historical personage (1744?-1826) the facts
of whose experience are more or less accurately portrayed by
Trumbull. An orphan, he was raised by paternal grandpar-

ents, *Quaker preachers. After his European exile, he went to
Providence in 1823 to tell his story to Trumbull, who compiled it
to sell at "28 Cents." Three editions were published in 1824,
perhaps not all by Trumbull. It is not clear which edition was
used by M.
I.P. Dedication

ITALIAN LIVES
     Probably those of *Suetonius.
R. 30

ITALIAN PICTURES
     M. saw "hermaphroditical" Italian Renaissance paint-
ings in 1849, at the National Gallery in *London and the
*Louvre in *Paris.
M.D. 86

ITALIAN PUBLISHER, OLD
     A book M. borrowed, *Browne's *Pseudodoxia Epidemica*
(Sealts #89), is a clue toward identification. An annotation (not
M.'s) comments on Browne's analogy to a "dolphin clasping
an anchor": "The device of the family of Manutius, celebrated
as learned printers at *Venice and *Rome." The firm was
established in Venice in 1495.
M.D. 55

*"ITINERAIRE INSTRUCTIF DE ROME, OU DESCRIPTION
GENERALE DES MONUMENS ANTIQUES ET MODERNES
ET DES OUVRAGES LES PLUS REMARQUABLES DE PEIN-
TURE, DE SCULPTURE, ET DE ARCHITECTURE DE CETTE
CELEBRE VILLE*
     By Mariano Vasi, 1815.
     Thorp supplies the full title, in "Redburn's Prosy Old
Guidebook." M. omits *Et De Ses Environs, Par Le Chevalier M.
Vasi, Membre De L'Académie Etrusque De Cortone. Corrigé
et augmentée par le même Auteur . . . . A Rome MDCCCXX.
Avec Privilège du Souverain Pontife.* Chez l'Auteur, rue du
Babouin, pré de la place de'Espagne, num. 122. Prix, deux
écus, broché. Thorpe adds that M. invented the vignette about
*Romulus and Remus.
R. 30

IXION

In mythology, the treacherous *Thessalian king Ixion attempted to seduce Hera, wife of Zeus (see "Jupiter" and "Jove"), who put a phantom image of her in Ixion's bed, catching him in the act. Ixion was punished by being chained forever to a fiery winged wheel revolving in the sky (or in the Underworld, according to later writers). The phantom he impregnated gave birth to the first of the *Centaurs.
R. 25; M.D. Epilogue

J

JACK, --ISH

The universal name for a sailor: short for Jack tar (-pot), from the tar smeared on clothes to waterproof them.

"Jolly Jack" is nautical usage for civilian illusions about *Navy life.
R. 28; R. 54; W. 27 and elsewhere

JACK JEWBOY

See "Hebrew."
I.P. 20

JACK KETCH

Traditional sobriquet for a hangman. The original may have been Richard Jaquett, to whom the manor of *Tyburn in *England once belonged, or Edward Dennis, who was jailed in the *Gordon Riots but pardoned to hang the other conspirators.
W. 70; C.M. 30

JACK OF ALL TRADES

"A Jack of all trades is master of none." Refers to a dilettante, ordinarily, although as M. points out, a sailor must be a Jack of all trades to master his own. Modern use of the term is increasingly meliorative.
R. 26; I.P. 8

JACK, OR JILL
      Jack is a common male name for a prototype, often
contemptuous. Paired with "Jill," the generic names for men
and women. In the familiar nursery rhyme:

> Jack and Jill went up the hill
> To fetch a pail of water.
> Jack feel down and broke his crown,
> And Jill came tumbling after.

      Calling a man "Jill" reflects on his sexuality.
R. 6

JACKSON
      A fellow-sailor on board the *St. Lawrence* in 1839 was
Robert Jackson, perhaps a partial model for the fictional sailor
who claims kinship with *Andrew Jackson.
R. Passim

JACKSON, ANDREW; -- GENERAL
      Andrew Jackson (1767-1845), seventh *President of the
*United States (1829-37) was a South *Carolina-born
backwoodsman who participated in the *Revolutionary War at
the age of thirteen, became a *Tennessee lawyer at twenty, was
sent to *Congress at thirty-one and to the *Senate at thirty-two.
(He was later a Supreme Court Justice and Major-General of
the state militia in *Florida.) After several years in retirement
he led the militia against the Creek Indians, driving the tribe
westward. His victory at the Battle of *New Orleans, fought
after the peace was signed, made him the hero of the *War of
1812, celebrated in song, story, drama, and everyday conversation.
      Jackson's 1818 devastation of the *Seminoles (performed
against orders) brought him the military governorship of
Florida, but by 1825 he had returned to the Senate. He was
defeated for the Presidency by John Quincy Adams in 1824, but
by the 1828 and 1832 elections, his personal popularity, support
of expansionism and the tariff, opposition to states' rights and
to centralization of power in such institutions as the Bank of
the United States made him an overwhelming favorite, despite
his introduction of the spoils system and a financial policy that
split his political party.
      Jackson's name became a synonym first for government
by all the people and then for the power of the unbridled mob.
Among events for which he was famous was opening Federal
buildings for his inauguration ceremony, by the end of which

much government property was lost to unruly crowds of souvenir hunters.

Jackson's spoils system removed M.'s grandfather, Major Thomas Melvill, from high *Naval office. *Gansevoort Melville much admired Jackson and visited him at his plantation, "The Hermitage" in 1844. M.'s feelings about "Old Hickory" were undoubtedly mixed. Although he appears to extol Jackson as a democratic hero in *M.D.* 26, the implied anti-expansionist position of *M.D.* 89 ("*Fast-Fish and Loose-Fish") undercuts the impression. Although he seems to praise the idea of "Manifest Destiny" in *W.* 36, elsewhere in that work he parodies the spoils system (32) and examines the implications of "*leveling" (40).
R. 12; M.D. 26

JACK THE GIANT-KILLER

There are two equally gory versions of the story in Katherine M. Brigg's *A Dictionary of British Folk Tales* (Bloomington, Indiana: 1970), of which the following summaries suggest the extravagance of the action. In Version I: a nameless, cattle-eating giant eighteen feet high and three yards around is first of Jack's conquests—a pickaxe the weapon. Giant 2, Blunderbore, gets a friend (#3) to help imprison Jack, but he catches them in a noose and dispatches them with his sword. The innkeeeper Giant #4 threatens to dash Jack's brains out with a club, then plans to poison him. But Jack tricks him, pretending to stab himself while actually protected by a padded leather pudding bag; #4 emulates the self-stabbing and dies. #5, tricked into cooperation, gives Jack magic implements with which he kills #s 6 and 7, sending their heads to King Arthur. #8, a two-headed relative of previous dead giants, is the best known, reciter of:

> Fee, fi, fo, fum!
> I smell the blood of an Englishman!
> Be he alive or be he dead
> I'll grind his bones to make me bread.

Jack tricks the literary #8, cutting off his two heads and encounters #9, Galligantus, who lures victims to his castle. At the sound of a magic trumpet, Jack cuts off his head, which he sends to the King, who marries him to a Duke's daughter, giving him a great estate.

Version II incorporates some first-person narration by Jack, as well as background detail suggesting the perils of traveling in England. Traveler Jack first encounters a lady with a nose as long as an arm; she threatens him, so he kills

her and frees some of her prisoner ladies hanging by their
hair. Giant #2 unfortunately kills Jack, but three dogs dig him
up and restore him to life. In a "cloak of darkness," "shoes of
swiftness," and a "cap of knowledge," he returns to kill #2,
freeing more ladies hanging by their hair. He travels on to the
house of Giant 3, where the wife hides him in the oven.
Suspecting ill will, he escapes to the giant's bedroom, only to
hear:

> Fee, fi, fum
> I smell the blood of an Englishman.
> Let him be alive or let him be dead.
> I'll have his flesh to eat for my bread,
> And his blood to drink for my drink.

Jack mocks the giant's attempts to kill him, pulls his old
leather pudding bag trick, and the giant stabs himself. Jack
frees lady prisoners.
T. 27

JACOB

In *Genesis, Jacob is the clever son of Isaac and
Rebekah, husband of Leah and *Rachel. His name refers to
his holding the heel of his twin brother *Esau at birth. In
*Exodus 1:1 and I *Chronicles 2:1, his twelve sons become the
sons of *Israel.

There are many oral tradition legends about Jacob's life
of conflict and family quarrel. In Genesis 25:29-34, he is the
shepherd who obtains the birthright of his unsuccessful
hunter-brother. In 27, he "steals" the blessing of the aged
Esau. In 28:19, *Jehovah appears to him at *Luz. In 28:12-15,
he dreams of a ladder reaching from earth to heaven, with
angels ascending and descending and *God standing above,
promising that Jacob will be the ancestor of the nation of
Israel. In 32:1-2, he wrestles until daybreak with a man
presumed to be an angel of *God, or God himself.
M. 165; R. 16; M.D. 87; I.P. 8; C.M. 2

JAFFA

See "Joppa."
M.D. 9; M.D. 82; I.P. 3

JAMAICA

The *West Indies *British colony is the third largest
island of the Greater *Antilles. *Columbus discovered it in

1494, calling it St. Jago, but the Indian name, *Xaymaca*, prevailed. The first *Spanish settlement of 1509 led repidly to the extinction of the natives, so *Africans were imported as *slaves to work in the (still important) sugar industry. The British captured the island in 1655; it was ceded in 1670.

"Jamaica spirits" is of course rum: the original distilled spirit, made from the time when *Alexander the Great introduced sugar-cane into Europe, and perfected by *Arab distilling methods in the *Middle Ages. In the nineteenth century it was often served hot, with water and pineapple.

The importation of rich, pungent Jamican rum, made from molasses, was an important component of the slave trade in the seventeenth and eighteenth centuries. The slave trade was stopped in 1807 and slavery abolished in Jamaica in 1833.
R. 8

JAMES II

First ruler of the parlous union between *Scotland and *England, James is frequently M.'s symbol of paranoid terror, as he is in "Benito Cereno."
See "Stuart."
W. 71

JANE

The bark *Jane* referred to in *O.* 25 may be the ship chartered by the U.S. *Navy which in 1822 captured four *pirate schooners off *Cuba.
O. 25

JANIZARY

Janissary: in the *Ottoman Empire from 1330, a celebrated militia originally conscripted from the *Sultan's *Christian subjects. Their tyrannical militaristic power became excessive, and they were totally massacred in 1826.
M. 5

JANUS-FACE

Janus is the *Roman deity: heaven's gatekeeper, guardian of gates and doors. He is shown with two faces, one in front, one behind. The doors of his temple were open in times of war, closed in peace. His name is used as a metaphor for two-faced, especially in reference to war. *Milton mentions him (*Paradise Lost* xi, 129) as does *Dante (*Paradiso*).

In modern usage, Janus stands for arbitrary reversals, unpredictability, untrustworthiness, as when M.'s captain in *W.* "ships" his "quarter-deck face," turning sour in the midst of jollity.
R. 44

JAPAN, --ESE
     Japan ("Nippon," "*Niphon," or the "Nihon Empire") was a relatively unknown and exotic place before *Perry forced the opening of trade in 1854. The crescent-shaped volcanic archipelago (31°-45° N., 128°30'-146° E.) had an empire founded c. 660 B.C. (which continues into the present dynasty). There was Korean and perhaps *Chinese influence before sixth century A.D. introduction of Buddhism; the main island of Honshu was not occupied until the tenth century. There was much civil war in the twelfth, and under the rule of the *shoguns* (1192-1867), the imperial court was in seclusion. Kublai *Khan led *Mongol invasions and *Marco Polo visited in the thirteenth century. *Columbus sought Japan as "Zipangu," and the *Portuguese entered by 1542. St. Francis Xavier visited in 1549.
     In the seventeenth century, only the *Dutch were permitted to trade, at Nagasaki. Yedo ("Edo," "Yeddo," or M.'s "*Jeddo"), which became the modern Tokyo, was the capital city of the Samurai overlords. Perry's entry brought about a political, economic, cultural, and technological revolution, with the *shoguns* put out of power and the royal family reinstated by 1868. Japan soon became a great naval power, with large merchant and whaling fleets. Feudalism was abolished in 1871, and the constitution of 1889 was modeled on *Prussia's, leading Japan to much expansionist action.
     The whaleship *Acushnet* (see "Pequod") traveled to Japan's seas after M.'s desertion in July of 1842, so M.'s multitudinous references to Japan in *M.D.* must have been derived from print sources. The sea of Japan is an arm of the *Pacific between the *Asian mainland and Japan, 1,000 miles long, 500 miles wide, and up to 13,000 feet deep: a rich source of cetacean life, as were the open seas to the east: the "Japanese Cruising Ground" of *M.D.* 114.
     "Japanese-looking Mississippi cotton-planters" (*C.M.* 2) is an unclear allusion. The Japanese are a homogeneous race of *Mongoloid, Indonesian, and Malayo-*Polynesian origin, with the exception of the Ainus, a minority people of *Indian appearance. Perhaps the allusion refers to costume.
     See also "Kumbo-Sama"; "Matsmai"; "Sikoke."
T. 4; M. 94; M. 149; W. 4; M.D. Passim; C.M. 2

JAPAN, KING OF
In *M.D.* this reference is to a whale presumed fictional: "Morquan."
M.D. 45

JAPONICAS
Japonicas (originally from *Japan) are members of the tea family: evergreen, with glossy leaves and waxy flowers (Camelias, or Japanese quince).
M.D. 42

JAPUS
In *Roman mythology, Iapis is a *Trojan who learned herbal medicine from *Apollo.
C.M. 16

JARL
See "Earl."
M. 3 and elsewhere

JASON
The myth of Jason and the Golden Fleece has evolved from versions by Apollonius of *Rhodes, Euripides, and Pindar.

The most famous sea story of travels, trials, and faithless love begins with the loss of Jason's father's *Greek throne to Jason's cousin (?), Pelias. At Jason's return to Greece, Pelias announces he will yield the throne if Jason will secure for him the Golden Fleece of a wondrous ram which had saved Greek people in the past. Jason sails on the ship "Argo" with a crew including *Hercules, *Orpheus, *Castor and Pollux, *Achilles's father, Peleus, and the helpful Hera (see "Juno"). The Argonauts face perils in the form of killer women, Harpies, Clashing Rocks, *Amazons, and finally the King of *Colchis, possessor of the Fleece. Through Hera's help, *Medea, the magical daughter of the King, falls in love with Jason and helps him perform the impossible tasks set by her father. She finally kills her own brother, Apsyrtus, when his army threatens.

Back in Greece, Jason marries Medea after she has arranged the death of the usurper, Pelias, and she bears him two sons. But the faithless Jason forgets all she has done for him and arranges to marry the daughter of the King of *Corinth. Medea kills the girl and slays her own two sons

rather than see them tortured by those who would punish her.
As Jason arrives and sees his dead sons, Medea is carried into
the air in a dragon-drawn chariot. Some accounts say Jason
then kills himself; others claim he is crushed to death by the
stern of "Argo," under which he is resting.

"Argosy" came to mean any large, richly laden ship.
M. 149

JAVA
H.B.M. *Java*, a thirty-eight-gun frigate captured by the
*British from the *French, was under the command of
Captain Henry Lambert on the coast of *Brazil when it
engaged in action against *Constitution*, under *William
Bainbridge, in 1812. Although *Java* did great damage to
Constitution, Lambert's daring decision to close caused *Java's*
bowsprit to become entangled with the enemy, leaving her at
such a disadvantage that the ship was a floating wreck and
her captain dead by the time Bainbridge transferred the crew
to his ship. *Java* was then blown up rather than remain a
danger to other ships, her defeat a psychological boon to the
*United States.
W. 48

JAVA, --S; JAVA HEAD; JAVAN
The island of Java is in the Greater *Sundas (modern
Indonesia), between the Java Sea and the *Indian Ocean,
twenty miles southeast of *Sumatra, west of *Bali across the
Bali Strait, 220 miles south of *Borneo across the Java Sea
(6°5'-8°52' S., 105°18'-114°36' E.). The *Dutch arrived in 1596,
establishing *Batavia as the capital. The luxuriant vegetation
(yielding pepper, tea, coffee, cinchona tobacco, precious woods,
and exotic tropical fruits) made for valuable trade. The
*British occupied Java from 1811 to 1816, and in the 1820's
there was much threat of revolt against the reestablished
Dutch.

Java Head (*M.D.* 3; *M.D.* 59; *M.D.* 87), or Gede Point, is
a cape at the westernmost point of Java in the Indian Ocean,
opposite Prinsen Island (6°46' S., 105°12' E.).
M.D. 3; M.D. 59; M.D. 87; P. 5:4

JEBUSITES
Jebus, a southern portion of *Jerusalem, was separated
by a physical wall and by differing tradition which led to the
emergence of the two kingdoms of Judah (see "Judea") and
Jerusalem. Capture by *David led to the combining of the two.

David erected an altar on the site of the threshing floor of
Araunah the Jebusite, where *Solomon later was to build his
Temple (II *Samuel 24:18-25; II *Chronicles 3:1).
M. 62

JEDDO

Jeddo (Edo, Yeddo, or Yedo) is the name ("Estuary
Gate") by which Tokyo was known until 1868, when it was
proclaimed the residence of the emperor and capital city of
*Japan. A small fishing village in the sixteenth century,
within one hundred years, under *shogun* Tokugawa Ieyasu,
the population had grown to one million.

M.'s vision of sending a grandson on a vacation to Japan
has come full circle by the 1980's, with Japanese grandsons
visiting *America more often than the reverse.
W. 29

JEFFERSON, THOMAS; THOMAS JEFFERSON'S

Thomas Jefferson (1743-1826), primary author of the
*Declaration of Independence, was *Washington's Secretary of
State, John Adams's Vice-President, and *President of the
United States from 1801 to 1809. Although his anti-*Federalist
notion of strong states' rights and his aim for a population of
agriculturalists rather than manufacturers did not completely
prevail, Jefferson's political philosophy colored the thinking of
both modern major political parties. His Democratic-
Republican Party (established to oppose Federalists, in 1791)
evolved into the *Democratic Party by 1828; a splinter group
formed the *Whig Party in 1834; *Lincoln's *Republican Party
arose from a coalition of *Whigs and Democrats in 1856.

Jefferson's ideals included a limited government over an
agrarian society; freedom of religion, speech, and the press; a
"naturally aristocratic" governing class; laissez-faire economic policies, and strong states united by a relatively weak
national constitutional government.

Jefferson was born into a prominent *Virginia family;
he practiced law (1767-74) after graduation from William and
Mary, and was an early proponent of revolution. He served in
the (second) *Continental Congress (1775-76) and almost
single-handedly created the Declaration (although his
denunciation of the British, was much toned down to become
the document we know). He was Governor of Virginia from
1779 to 1781, during which time he promulgated many liberal
policies, including abolition of *slavery. In local government,
he collected data for his *Notes on the State of Virginia*
(privately published in *Paris in 1784, but dated 1782). It was a

response to challenging questions of the Marquis de Barbé-Marbois, Secretary of the *French legation in *Philadelphia, containing a (rather chauvinistic) compendium of statistical information on the geography, natives, flora and fauna, social and political life of the territory of Virginia (a much larger area than the state). *"Thomas Jefferson's Whale Memorial to the French Minister in 1778"* (*M.D.* "Extracts" 41) is the memorandum of October 1788 (M.'s date in error) to Armand Marc Comte de Montmarin-Saint-Herem, French Minister of Foreign Affairs; it protests French cessation of foreign whale oil imports. (Jefferson was Minister to France, 1784-89.)

He opposed the *Constitution until adoption of the *Bill of Rights (1791); he opposed the Bank of the United States, the protective tariff, and indeed most of the policies of Secretary of the *Treasury Hamilton. Yet Hamilton gained him the Presidency in 1800 by casting the vote that broke a tie with Aaron Burr.

As President, Jefferson made the *Louisiana Purchase, commissioned the expedition of Lewis and Clark, and sent *Decatur's forces to *Tripoli. He retaliated against foreign trade interference by passing the Embargo Act, which lost him much popularity, especially in *New England.

After "retirement," he founded the University of Virginia; completed his home, Monticello; designed the Virginia State Capitol and various parts of *Washington, stimulating a revival of classical architecture in the United States. An extraordinarily talented man, Jefferson had expertise in mathematics, science, philosophy, languages, music, and the arts.

M. owned a copy of a Jefferson speech of 4 March 1801. He scored this passage:

> And let us reflect that having banished from our land that religious intolerance, under which mankind so long bled and suffered, we have yet gained litte, if we countenance a political intolerance, as despotic, as wicked, and capable of as bitter and bloody persecutions.

See also "Extracts" 41; "Logan."
W. 71; M.D. "Extracts" 41

JEFFRIES; JEFFREYS, JUDGE

The prototype of the brutal *English judge, George Jeffreys Jeffreys (1645-1689), First Baron of Wem, was deeply involved in the dangerous politics of *Charles II and James II (see "Stuart"). He was prosecutor of *Titus Oates, but his

major infamy rests on his role in the "bloody assizes" of 1685,
when many hundreds were executed or deported in *slavery.
As Lord Chief Justice, he was responsible for the conviction,
torture, or execution of some three hundred people, including
*Algernon Sidney (1622-83), a republican political thinker
accused of treason. Sidney's attainder was reversed after his
death, when it became clear that he had been unjustly
incriminated. The brave and learned Sidney gained
posthumous fame in the English-speaking world as a
champion of constitutional liberties and leader of popular
opposition.
W. 71; C.M. 26

JEHOSHAPHAT
      The King of *Judea, Jehosaphat (or Josaphat) was a 9th-
century B.C. in-law of *Ahab (II *Chronicles, I *Kings). In
the Book of Joel (3), the valley of Jehosaphat is the bed of the
*Kedron River, the literal or figurative valley of *Jehovah's
judgement. M. commented on the tomb-filled area in his
journal (26 January 1857).
P. 23:3

JEHOVAH
      The word is an artificial written form which sprang up
about A.D. 1500. It resulted from the tetragrammaton
"YHWH," with vowels substituted from the word "Adonai"
("Lord"), used after the sixth century B.C., when the name
Yahweh was withdrawn for fear of profanation. For the
*Israelites, *God's self was concentrated in his personal
name, which expressed his authority, power, and holiness.
Rules were instituted to invoke reverence for the name. In
*Exodus 20:7 and *Deuteronymy 5:11, it is proscribed to take
the name in vain; in Deuteronomy 18:19 and *Jeremiah 26:20,
44:16, prophets are inspired when they speak in the name; in
*Numbers 23-24, blessings and curses are potent if given in the
name; in Deuteronomy 6:13, oaths are binding when taken in
the name; in *Psalms 20:7, and 44:5, battles in the name are
victorious; in *Leviticus 18:21 and 24:11, Israelites are warned
against defiling or blaspheming the name.
      Yahweh is the *Covenant name disclosed to *Moses at
the time of the *Exodus, but it was probably used before that
time. The meaning is not clear; it is perhaps related to the
verb "to be"; "I am."
      The invisible God of the Israelites was believed to have
entered into relations with the people and revealed himself
through history, which was composed of his deeds, recorded in

the *Old Testament (of which the books of *Job and *Ecclesiastes, two favorites of M.'s, are probably the least historical). All the Earth was to serve God's purpose; man was not autonomous; ethics consisted of obedience to God. Although there was no doubt of God's existence, the Old Testament writers expressed doubt when he did not fulfill his promises. This is evident in the Israelites' questioning of his presence with them (*Exodus 17:7), in Jeremiah's calling him deceitful (Jeremiah 15:18), and in *Job's tormented separation from him. God was known by what he had done, was doing, and would do, and man was dependent upon him for everyday things. The Ark of the Covenant was a wooden chest regarded as the throne of the invisible God.

Jehovah's traits, as expressed in the Old Testament, include holiness, beneficence, love, righteousness, jealousy, wrath, and uniqueness.

In his *Bible, M. marked many references to Jehovah, as Nathalia Wright shows in *Melville's Use of the Bible*. He appeared to envision Jehovah as a hard, arbitrary, and vindictive deity. Lawrance Thompson's *Melville's Quarrel with God* suggests that, for M., God was more like Jehovah than like *Jesus Christ. In his frightening visit to the Egyptian pyramids M. pondered the "idea of Jehovah. Terrible mixture of the cunning and awful" (journal 3 January 1857).

See also "God," for appellations of Jehovah, and see "Hebrew."
M. 3; W. 67; I.P. 21; C.M. 45

JENNY
"Israel Potter's" lost love is named for the quintessential down-to-earth homespun girl: probably from the nursery tale of Robin Redbreast and his simple sweetheart.
I.P. 22

"JENNY! HEY, HEY, HEY, HEY, HEY, JENNY, JENNY! AND GET YOUR HOE-CAKE DONE!"
Adapted from the refrain of "Old King Crow," a minstrel song.
M.D. 99

"JE PENSE"
Fr. "I think."
In *M.*, a playful motto for a philosophical tract ("Book X. of the Ponderings, 'Zermalmende'"). "I think" in this sense

reflects either an ingenuous literal rendering of the philosopher's pursuit, or an admission of uncertainty.
M. 175

JEREMIAHS
The authenticity of the *Old Testament Epistle of *Jeremy (commonly added to the Book of Baruch, but sometimes printed separately) was much questioned in the nineteenth century. The first- or second-century B.C. author who calls himself Jeremiah addresses idolatrous *Babylonian exiles, denouncing present sins and warning of seven generations of captivity to come.
M.'s journal of *Jerusalem (January 1857) records his nearness to the "Cave of Jeremiah"; "In its lamentable recesses he composed his lamentable lamentations."
C.M. 9

JEREMY
See "Jeremiahs."
C.M. 24

JEREMY DIDDLER
Chief character of *Raising the Wind* (1803), popular farce about a charming swindler who became a stock character. His name gave rise to the verb "to diddle," to cheat or deceive.
C.M. 3; C.M. 24

JEROBOAM
In I and II *Kings and II *Chronicles, there are two Jeroboams who are kings of *Israel. Jeroboam I (10th century B.C.), first king of Israel after the division, was an impious idolater regarded as responsible for Israel's disasters. Jeroboam II (8th century B.C.) was the last of the great kings of Israel, who brought the nation to prosperity despite its corruption, as prophesied by *Jonah.
M.D. 71

JERSEY
The ancient *Caesarea*, Jersey is the largest and southernmost of the *Channel Islands: fifteen miles west of *Normandy, *France, and eighteen miles southeast of *Guernsey. The island is eleven miles long and five miles

wide; its capital is St. Helier. In the eighteenth and nine-
teenth centuries, Jersey was a center for privateering. (See
"Pirate.")
I.P. 10

JERUSALEM
        The city in central *Palestine is located on a rocky ridge
in the Judaean Hills. The "*Zion" of the *Bible, it dates from
before the fifteenth century B.C. and is a holy city for *Jews,
*Christians, and *Moslems, with many shrines.
        The old city (E.) wall was built by *Suleiman; it has
eight gates. *David made Jerusalem his capital in 1048 B.C.,
and *Solomon built his temple here. *Alexander the Great
captured it in 333 B.C., and in 168 B.C. *Antiochus Epiphanes
razed the city and massacred its citizens. The *Maccabees and
Herods left their marks, and *Titus destroyed Jerusalem again
in A.D. 70. *Hadrian established a new city, which became a
shrine under Constantine I (see "Constantinople"). It fell to
the Moslems in 637, to the *Crusaders in 1099, and to *Saladin
in 1187.
        M. visited Jerusalem 7-18? January 1857.
        See also "Gethsemane"; "Jebusite"; "Kedron"; "Mount
of Olives"; "New Jerusalem."
P. 14:3; C.M. 9

JESSICA
        In *Shakespeare's *The Merchant of Venice*, the
daughter of "*Shylock": a Jewess courted surreptitiously and
then married to "*Lorenzo."
R. 46

JESUIT
        The Society of Jesus (popularly, the Jesuits) was founded
by Ignatius Loyola (see "Spanish Inquisition") c. 1533 to
perform charitable and educational functions and to combat
the *Protestant Reformation. It was a highly organized and
disciplined secret society that chose members on the basis of
intelligence as well as character and that achieved great
political power. The Jesuits were driven from *France and
*England in the sixteenth century, from *Venice in the
seventeenth, and from *Spain and *Naples in the eighteenth,
at which point they were suppressed by Pope Clement XIV,
only to revive in 1814.
        In M.'s day, *Americans were being warned by both
*Catholic and *Protestant publications of pernicious Jesuits

roaming the country disguised as pedlars, musicians, and
showmen: thus the "masques" of *C.M.* 18.
C.M. 18

JESUS; JESUS CHRIST
        See "Christ"; "Christian"; "God."
Passim (see "God" for a selection of allusions)

JETS D'EAU
        Fountains (Fr.).
M.D. 55

JEW, --S, --'S; JEWISH
        See "Hebrew."
O. 14; M. 3; M. 19; M. 57; M. 122; M. 181; R. 40; R. 49; W. 6;
W. 31; W. 84; M.D. 92; M.D. 22; P. 14:3; P. 21:3; I.P. 20; I.P.
24; I.P. 25; C.M. 22; C.M. 26; C.M. 42 and elsewhere

JEWS, GREAT TEMPLE OF THE
        The great Temple of *Solomon on Mount Moriah,
*Jerusalem, was built about 1006 B.C. and destroyed at
*Nebudchadnezzar's siege, 588 B.C. Some seventy years later
the Temple of Zerubbabel was built on the site, and in 20 B.C.
Herod the Great began building the last Temple, destroyed by
the *Roman siege of 70 B.C., under *Titus. One of the chief
emblems of Herod's temple was the Holy of Holies, wherein
Jews were portrayed as God's only chosen people. When the
veil separating it from the temple was "rent in twain," it
signified that both Jews and Gentiles were now one people of
God (*Exodus 25, 30-32; *Revelation 1, 12-20).
        The site is now covered by a *Moslem mosque, *Haram
esh Sherif.*
O. 44

JEW'S HARP
        Since the 16th Century, a small musical instrument
held between the teeth and twanged with the hand to play.
There is no demonstrable connection with *Jews, and it does
not look like a harp. *Lord Bacon called it *jeutrompe*;
*Beaumont and Fletcher called it jew-trump; *Hakluyt
(*Voyages* 1595) called it jew's harp. (Fr. *jeu* refers to a game;
trompe is "trick.")
R. 49

JEZEBEL
Likening of the *Sandwich Island's *dowager queen to the *Old Testament's Jezebel is apter than modern use for a "shameless" woman. In I *Kings, the daughter of Ethbaal, King of the Sidonians, marries *Ahab, the king of *Israel, offending Israel politics and religion. In I Kings 21:1-29, she arranges Naboth be stoned to death, so that Ahab can claim his vineyard, thus bringing down *Jehovah's curse on the family. In I Kings 18:4-13, she persecutes the prophets of Yahweh, causing the prophet *Elijah's challenge to *Baal's authority, resulting in the *Tyrian prophets' destruction in I Kings 20:20-46. She is put to death by Jehu, Ahab's revolutionary general and later king (II Kings 9:33-37):

> And he said, Throw her down. So they threw her down, and some of her blood was sprinkled on the wall, and on the horses; and he trod her under foot. And when he was come in, he did eat and drink; and he said, See now to this cursed woman and bury her; for she is a king's daughter. And they went to bury her; but they found no more of her than the skull, and the feet, and the palms of her hands. Wherefore they came back and told him. And he said, This is the word of Jehovah, which he spake by his servant *Elijah, the Tishbite, saying In the portion of Jezreel shall the dogs eat the flesh of Jezebel: and the body of Jezebel shall be as dung upon the face of the field in the portion of Jezreel, so that they shall not say, This is Jezebel.

T. 25; O. 80; W. 24

JIMINI!; JIMMINI
An exclamation, perhaps derived from "Gemini" (see "Zodiac").
M.D. 40; M.D. 99

JIMMY DUXES
This derogatory sobriquet originally referred to the ship's poulterer.
R. 9; W. 3

JIM THE PILOT
James Mitchell was locally famous in *Tahiti in the early nineteenth century, praised for his interpreting and his ability to pilot large ships (in Tahiti's harbor only). He is exclaimed over by *Beechey, *Bennett, Admiral S.R. Franklin, Fitzroy (see "Darwin"), and *Wilkes.
O. 26

JINGLING JOE
The sobriquet is probably related to the epithet "Jingle-brains," meaning a wild harum-scarum fellow.
A Jingling Johnnie was a *Turkish noise-making instrument in military bands—bells on a stick hanging from a crescent-shaped attachment.
O. 35

JOAN
See "Darby."
O. 67

JOB
The book of Job was one of the *Bible's most compelling works for M., and his most heavily annotated in his own copy. It is the story of *Satan's challenging the Lord (see "God") regarding the faith of Job (which means "the persecuted one," in Hebrew). The Lord sends multiple afflictions and losses to Job, whose "advisers" (*Bildad, *Eliphaz, and *Zophar) counsel him wrongly. Job is finally saved from further affliction and a new family provided for the one the Lord has destroyed. M. was to conclude *M.D.* with the Epilogue, "And I only am escaped alone to tell thee," an antiphon in Job.
M.'s multitudinous indirect references to and quotations from the book of Job are examined in Vincent's edition of *M.D.* and in Wright's *Melville's Use of the Bible*.
What is called in *M.D.* "the first account" of *Leviathan is *Job* 41.
See also "Extracts" 2.
R. 59; W. 7; M.D. Extracts 2; M.D. 24; M.D. 32; M.D. 41; M.D. Epilogue; P. 2:1; C.M. 40

JOB-SHOP
A piecework shop where a jobber does small jobs, often acting as a middle-man.
M.D. 126

JOES

M.'s "joes" are Spanish *escudos*. The *escudo* in the nineteenth century contained c. 3.38 grams of gold. "Half joes" were half-*escudos* (or "*escuditos*"), containing half as much. "Quarter joes" were perhaps non-existent, but in silver coinage there was a quarter-*reale* or *cuartillo*. (A *reale* was worth c. 3.4 grams of silver, having half the value of a like amount of gold.)

See also "Doubloon."
M.D. 99

JOHN VI, KING OF PORTUGAL

John VI of *Portugal (1767-1826), acting as regent for his insane mother, Maria I, sided with *England against *Napoléon. As a result, in 1807 he was forced to move his entire court to *Brazil to avoid capture, returning only in 1820, when the Portuguese revolution proclaimed a constitutional monarchy. He was the father of *Pedro I, emperor of Brazil.
W. 56

JOHN BULL

See "Bull."
M. 161

"JOHN FERDINANDO"

See "Juan Fernandes; Juan Fernandez, Isle of."
M.D. 45

"JOHN NICHOL, MARINER"

John Nicol's *The Life and Adventures of John Nicol, Mariner* (Edinburgh: 1822) is a source for M. in W. 75, W. 90, and in data fleshing out the character of *Jack Chase.
W. 90

JOHN OF GAUNT

The Duke of Lancaster, *England (1340-1399), was the son of *Edward II, influential uncle of *King Richard II, father of *Henry IV. Immortalized in *Shakespeare's plays, John has not been so admired by historians, who see him as a mediocre force at best. His undeniable forte was making peace, representing a moderating voice between opponents. His military feats are of secondary importance compared with the political prestige and power he held as a result of great

landholdings. After his second marriage, he unsuccessfully claimed the throne of *Castile and Leon. Throughout his life, his accomplishments were less picturesque than those of his brother, Edward, the *Black Prince.
R. 31; P. 19:2

JOHN O'GROATS

The traditional northernmost point of mainland *Britain, so called from Jan Groot, a *Dutch immigrant.

Also, groat is an epithet: worthless like the devalued groats (fourpence) of *Henry VIII's reign.

Since about 1800, groat is a coat, in playful British rhyming speech.
R. 24

JOHN RINGMAN

The character is fictional. "Ring-man" is old slang for a "sporting man," as well as for the ring (middle) finger.
C.M. 4; C.M. 10

JOHN, SIR

See "Mandeville's Travels."
M. 98

JOHNSON, COLONEL GUY

Guy Johnson (c. 1740-1788) was a loyalist who served in the French and Indian wars. He was made Colonel as a result and later became Adjutant General of the New York Militia. He served in the New York Assembly from 1773 to 1775 and was named Superintendent of Indian Affairs in 1774.

Like many other loyalists, Johnson returned to *London after the Revolution, where he died while attempting to secure recompense for confiscation of his estates.
I.P. 22

JOHNSON, DOCTOR

A Doctor Johnston living at *Tahiti in 1842 became family physician to the *Pritchards, as noted in W.T. Pritchard's *Polynesian Reminiscences*. In *Los Gringos*, Henry A. Wise claims that Johnston thought of suing the publishers of *O.* for libel, so incensed was he about M.'s derogatory comments. Edward Lucett attempted to disprove

M.'s contentions of Johnston's greed and incompetence, in *Rovings in the Pacific*, a work highly critical of M.
O. 20; O. 35

JOHNSON, SAMUEL

Samuel Johnson (1709-84) attended Pembroke College, *Oxford, married (Mrs. Elizabeth Porter, who died 1752), and opened an unsuccessful private school at Lichfield, in which David Garrick was a student. Finding teaching "intolerable," he moved to *London in 1737, where he contributed to *The Gentleman's Magazine*, wrote essays, poems, *Latin verses, and *Parliamentary Debates*, which purported to be speeches by famous contemporaries. *The Vanity of Human Wishes* (1749) was the first publication under his name. In the 1750's he began writing biography, including material for *The Lives of the English Poets* (1779-81). *His Dictionary of the English Language* (1755) was the first of its kind in English, fixing the spelling, pronunciation, and usage of some 40,000 words; it brought him financial relief and an Oxford degree. Johnson founded the periodical *The Rambler* in 1750 (continuing with it until 1752), wrote *The Idler* papers (1758-60), and *Rasselas, Prince of *Abyssinia* (1759), as well as fiction and non-fiction works concerned with the theatre, politics, the "*American question," and personal philosophy in an overly optimistic Age of Reason.

Johnson met his biographer, James Boswell (1740-95), in 1762. *The Life of Samuel Johnson* (1791) and journals of tours the two men made together give in meticulous detail a picture of Johnson's life and times. In 1765, Johnson met Hester Lynch Thrale (1741-1821), later Mrs. Piozzi, who published *Anecdotes of the Late Samuel Johnson* in 1786. As these works alone show, Johnson was one of the most brilliant conversationalists of all time. His learning was staggeringly wide-spread; his eccentricities, wit, and humane skepticism continue to endear him to readers, despite the overarching opinionation which made M. refer to him (in the margin of his copy of *Shakespeare's *Coriolanus*, an edition for which Johnson had written notes) as "the old codger." Much of Johnson's life was spent in poverty and illness (scrofula), and in support of dependent people.

M. visited the Mitre Tavern, *Fleet Street, *London, on 26 November 1849, sitting near Johnson's favorite corner. He bought a copy of Boswell's *The Life of Samuel Johnson, L.L.D.* (Sealts #84; London: Murray, 1839? or London: Bohn, 1848) on 19 December and commented at length (before February 1850) in his journal on Johnson's incapacity as a teacher. M. notes the paradox that "the greatest abilities are not only required for

this office, but render a man less fit for it." Along with
*Rousseau and M. himself, Johnson may have inspired the
"pale Usher," of *M.D.* "Etymology."

M. borrowed volumes of essays from *Duyckinck in 1860,
commenting on their inferiority to those of Johnson, who did
not "hesitate to use the word *malignity*" (Duyckinck's diary, 26,
31 January).

The reference in *C.M.* 28 to the *Lisbon earthquake
alludes to Hester Lynch Piozzi's quoting Johnson on the
subject. Asked if he believed the stories of disaster, Johnson
replied, "Oh! not for six months . . . at least. I *did* think that
story too dreadful to be credited." As Franklin points out in his
notes to *C.M.*, the earthquake, on All Saints' Day, 1775, was a
turning point in belief. Religious people saw it as *God's
visitation upon an irreligous people who had conducted the
Inquisition (see "Spanish Inquisition"); optimists saw the
quake as part of God's great design (a position countered by
*Voltaire). Johnson proves himself (at least at first)
independent of the dichotomy in his disbelief even in the
phenomenon until proven by sensory evidence.

See also "Cock Lane" (for Johnson's investigation of a
ghost); *M.D.* "Extracts" 14; *M.D.* "Extracts" 38.
W. 54; M.D. Extracts 14; M.D. Extracts 38; M.D. 53; M.D. 69;
M.D. 104

JOHN TALBOT
       See "Whaleman's Chapel."
M.D. 7

JOHN TRUMAN
       A fiction, ironically playing with "true man."
C.M. 20

JONAH
       The *Old Testament Book of Jonah (or prophecy of
Jonas) is the story of the fifth of the twelve minor prophets: his
prophecy, the rise of *Israel's fortunes under *Jeroboam II (II
*Kings 14:25).
       Jonah, the son of Amittai, disobeys *God's order to
prophecy disaster at *Nineveh and instead sails from *Joppa
in a ship plagued with storms because of his disobedience. At
his own request, he is thrown overboard, and the storm
subsides. A great fish swallows him and deposits him back on
land (chapters 1 and 2). God again directs him to Nineveh,
and the city repents (3). *M.D.*'s "Father Mapple" omits the rest

of the story wherein Jonah hopes for the city's destruction, while he is sheltered by a plant that grows for a night and dies, to his regret. God points out his lack of pity for the people of Nineveh, and Jonah's lesson is complete (4).

Biblical scholars interpret the book as a protest against Judaism's pure-race policy; as a trope for the *Babylonian exile; as a parable of God's fight against evil enemies; as a prototype for the Resurrection. A Jonah is a proverbial pariah.

See also "Tigris"; "Extracts 3"; "Jehovah."
M. 94; R. 20; W. 3; W. 78; M.D. Extracts 3; M.D. 3; M.D. 9; M.D. 55; M.D. 75; M.D. 81; M.D. 83; I.P. 3

JONAS IN THE WHALE
See "Extracts 30," and "Jonah."
M.D. Extracts 30; M.D. 55

JONATHAN
In *M*. 174, M. appears to confuse the *Old Testament story of Jonathan. He was the loving son of *Saul (I *Samuel 13 and II Samuel 1) but is most celebrated for his friendship with *David.
M. 174

JONATHAN; BROTHER JONATHAN
"Brother Jonathan," or "Jonathan" was a sobriquet for an *American, until replaced by "Uncle Sam." The nickname is said to have originated when *General George Washington, having run out of ammunition, decided, "We must consult brother Jonathan," referring to Jonathan Trumbull, then governor of *Connecticut.
W. 56; M.D. 89

JONES, JOHN PAUL; CAPTAIN PAUL
The adventurer/naval hero of the *American Revolution, John Paul Jones (1747-92), was born in *Scotland as John Paul, taking the name "Jones" perhaps to avoid legal difficulties. He served in the *West Indies *slave trade before earning fame for his skill in destroying or capturing *British ships and harassing the North American coastline fisheries.

On *Bonhomme Richard*, he captured *Serapis* (23 September 1779), replying to British Captain *Pearson's query regarding surrender: "I have not yet begun to fight." Jones was briefly in the *Russian marine before moving permanently to *Paris, where he was buried. (His body was removed to the United States one hundred years later.)

On *Ranger, Jones had successfully raided *Whitehaven and *St. Mary's Isle, where he participated in the fiasco involving the Countess of Selkirk (mentioned in I.P. 17). Unaware of the Earl's absence, Jones had sent a party to take him prisoner. His agents had to settle for stealing the Selkirk family silverware, and Jones later wrote a distastefully personal letter to the Countess, praising her poise and breeding and promising to return her possessions.

M.'s portrait of Jones in I.P. builds upon a mere mention of him in "*Israel Potter's Autobiographical Story." He probably used the Robert C. Sands Life and Correspondence of John Paul Jones (New York: 1830) as a source, adding his own coloring, perhaps via *Fanning's Narrative, of the lowborn adventurer who behaved like a ruffian *pirate while seeking the respectability that would come long after his death in adulatory literature such as *Cooper's The Pilot. John Adams, who had been a passenger on Jones's ship *Alliance, wrote of him: "the most ambitious and intriguing officer in the American Navy, Jones has Art and Secrecy . . . . Eccentricities and Irregularities are to be expected from him."

See also "Ariel"; "Countess of Scarborough"; "Maxwell, Mungo."

I.P. 10; I.P. 11; I.P. 12; I.P. 14; I.P. 17; I.P. 20

JONES, SIR WILLIAM

Sir William Jones (1746-1794) was the son of mathematician William Jones (1675-1749), who died when his son was three years old, leaving early education to Jones's mother and scientific friends. Born at Beaufort Buildings, *Westminster, *England, he was early marked as a genius, studying the classics, French, Italian, Arabic, and Hebrew in early years, later Persian, Chinese, German, Spanish, Portuguese. After taking an M.A. at *Oxford in 1773, Jones wrote a translation into French of a Persian biography, works on Oriental and Hebrew poetry and literature, and a grammar of the Persian language. He became a member of the *Royal Society in 1772 and was admitted into *Samuel Johnson's Literary Club in 1773.

Unable to earn a living at Oriental literature, he studied law and became an excellent jurist. Among his law texts: "An Inquiry into the Legal Mode of Suppressing Riots" (1780), and "On the Law of Bailments" (1781), which has had great influence on American jurisprudence. A liberal in politics, Jones's open disapproval of the American war kept him from success. He sailed for *India in 1783, with his wife, Anna

Maria Shipley, daughter of the Bishop of St. Asaph, and there produced his most important literary works, in the study of Indian language, literature, and philosophy. Some important titles (in *Asiatic Researches*, vols. i-iv): "On the Orthography of Asiatick Words" (1784); "On the Gods of *Greece, *Italy, and India" (1785); "On the Hindus" (1786); "On the *Arabs" (1787); "On the *Tartars" (1788); "On the *Persians" (1789); "On the *Chinese" (1790); "On the Borderers, Mountaineers, and Islanders of *Asia" (1791); "On the Origins and Families of Nations (!792); "On Asiatick History, Civil and Natural" (1793); "On the Philosophy of the Asiaticks" (1794). In a lighter vein, he wrote on Hindu (see "Hindoo") chronology, music, chess, botany, and zoology. His works are collected in a thirteen-volume 1807 edition.

Jones was the first English scholar to master *Sanskrit and was instrumental in the development of comparative philology. He died before completion of a digest of Hindu and *Mohammedan law as observed in India, his chief claim to fame his mastery of Sanskrit and twenty-seven other languages. There is a portrait of him by Sir Joshua Reynolds and a monument in *St. Paul's Cathedral.
T. 30; M.D. 79

JONSON; BEN JONSON

Ben[jamin] Jonson (1572/3-1637), dramatist, poet, and scholar, was educated at Westminster School and worked at bricklaying and soldiering before becoming an actor/playwright (along with *Shakespeare) c. 1601. His seditious satire and his responsibility for a dueling death sent him to prison, where he (temporarily) became a Roman *Catholic. Among his first important plays were *Every Man in his Humour* (performed 1599) and *Sejanus* (performed by Shakespeare's company, 1603). Jonson presided over illustrious literary circles at the Mermaid Tavern and The Devil and *St. Dunstan Tavern. He was incapacitated by a stroke in 1628. Upon his death, he was entombed in *Westminster Abbey, his tombstone reading "O rare Ben Jonson."

Jonson plays mentioned by M. (in *W.* 41) are *Volpone, or The Fox* (performed 1605-6), a dark comedy about a rich *Venetian whose friends have the natures of the fly, the vulture, the crow, and the raven, and *The Alchemist* (performed 1610), a burlesque glance at a charlatan who plays on human appetites for gold, knowledge, and love.

Sealts #302 is a 1692 folio edition of *The Works* which M. purchased in *London in 1849. It is annotated by M.
R. 29; W. 41

JOPPA

The port of *Jerusalem (modern *Jaffa) was founded by the *Canaanites (15th century B.C.), later becoming an *Egyptian capital (as Yapu, 13th century). The *Philistines controlled it early, as did the *Old Testament tribe of Daniel. *David and *Solomon occupied it, and Sennacherib captured it in 701. It was conquered by *Alexander the Great and others, including *Ptolemy IV Philopator, and the *Syrians. *St. Peter is known to have lived there, and in A.D. 68, *Vespasian captured it, as did the *Crusaders (1126), who lost it to *Saladin (1187). Richard I *Coeur-de-Lion reclaimed it in 1191, losing it in 1196. In the 14th century, a threatened new Crusade caused its razing by the *Mameluke sultan of Egypt.

M.'s journal for 24 January 1857 records his visit to "*Jonah's pier," in a city he found depressing and upsetting.
M.D. 9; M.D. 82

JORDAN

The River Jordan (*Nahr al Urdunn*) is the *Holy Land's "river of Dan," emptying into the *Dead Sea. Its revered waters are important in the *Bible's stories of *Elijah, Elisha, *John, *Lot, and *Jesus. The crossing of the Jordan marked the *Hebrew's entry into the *Promised Land of *Canaan after the *Exodus. It came to symbolize the purification marking the passage to blessedness.
M.D. 22

JOSEPH

In *Genesis, Joseph is the eleventh son of *Jacob and the first-born of his favorite wife, *Rachel. He was probably born in Haran in the first half of the second millenium B.C. There are many stories about him: a shepherd boy in *Hebron, he was sent forth to seek his brothers; he was the favored son, born in Jacob's old age; his father made him a strange and colorful long robe with sleeves; his dreams were symbolic and prophetic; he was sold by his brothers to the *Israelites (Medianites), then sold to the *Egyptian, *Potiphar, in whose house he was promoted; accused of seducing Potiphar's wife, he was imprisoned; his wisdom pleased *Pharaoh, to whom he became adviser; given wide powers, he became an important administrator in Egypt; when his family fled *Canaan to avoid famine, he was reconciled with them and they settled in *Goshen; he was then blessed by his father; on his deathbed he predicted the *Exodus from Egypt and settlement in the *promised land of *Abraham, *Isaac, and Jacob.
R. 17

JOSH [JOSS]
Joss is probably a Pidgin-English corruption of *deos*
(Port.) or *deus* (Lat.), meaning god. A joss came to mean a
*Chinese god or idol; a temple is called a joss-house.
P. 2:3

JOSH; JOLLY JOSH
Josh, or Joss, is a countryman or rustic: a rube.
M. 56

'JOURNAL OF THE CRUISE OF THE U.S. FRIGATE ESSEX, IN THE PACIFIC, DURING THE LATE WAR'
See "Porter; Captain Porter; Commodore Porter";
"Essex."
T. 1

JOVE
Also known as *Jupiter (or Zeus). In *Phäeton*, the son
of the sun and an earth mother, Phaeton seeks to replace his
father as chariot driver of the heavens, for one day. Despite his
father's warnings, the foolish youth takes the chariot, loses
control of it, and only Jove can save the day. He hurls a
thunderbolt that kills Phaeton but brings the horses under
control and saves the earth.
*Milton (*Paradise Lost* I, 512) makes Jove one of the
fallen angels.
In the *Europa myth, the god takes the form of a
beautiful white bull munching on flowers who appears so
innocent that the girl climbs upon his back and is abducted to
*Crete, where she becomes his mistress.
See also "Danae" and "Phidias."
(Excludes use as expletive.) M. 5; M. 181; W. 91; M.D. 1; M.D.
7; M.D. 42; M.D. 79; M.D. 133; P. 2:2

J. ROSS BROWNE'S ETCHINGS OF A WHALING CRUISE. 1846
See "Browne, J. Ross," and see "Extracts" 63.
M.D. Extracts 63

JUAN FERNANDES; JUAN FERNANDEZ, ISLE OF
The Juan Fernández Islands are a *Chilean group in
the South *Pacific, four-hundred miles west of *Valparaiso
(33°36'-33°48' S., 78°45'-80°47' W.). There are two main islands

and one islet in the rugged volcanic ridge: Más a Tierra (see "Massafuero; Massfuero") and Más Afuera. They were discovered by Fernández c. 1563, and their major fame has resulted from Defoe's novel *Robinson Crusoe*, inspired by *Alexander Selkirk's stay on Más a Tierra.

Juan Fernandez (1536?-1604) was a *Spanish navigator whose many discoveries earned him the nickname of "Brujo" ("wizard").
M.D. 45; I.P. 15; I.P. 17

JUBA, KING
There were two *African kings named Juba. M.'s reference (probably by way of *Plutarch) is to Juba II (c. 50 B.C. - c. A.D. 24), king of Numidia and Mauretania and husband to Cleopatra Selene, daughter of *Cleopatra and *Mark Antony.

He was a *Roman citizen, an idealistic king on the *Greek model, a prolific writer, and was much praised by historians. He was son to Juba I (c. 85-46 B.C.), castigated by ancient writers as an arrogant and cruel enemy of *Caesar.
M.D. 86

JUDAS; JUDAS ISCARIOT
There are several important Judases in the *Bible; M.'s reference in *W.* 38 is to Judas Iscariot, the *Apostle who betrayed *Jesus. "Iscariot" may mean in *Hebrew "man from Kerioth" (*Judea), or in Aramaic, "assassin," "liar," or "hypocrite." In *John 6:71 and 13:26, he is the son of Simon Iscariot.

An important Apostle, Judas came from a wealthy family and may have been the group's treasurer. Motivation for his betrayal for thirty pieces of silver (a small sum of money) is unclear, but the *Gospels increasingly blackened his reputation. In *John 6:70 and 17:12, he is identified with *Satan and the *Antichrist. In *Matthew, Judas hangs himself after attempting to return the money, and priests purchase with it a potter's field, the "Field of Blood." In *Acts 1:18, he dies by accident. *Moslem tradition claims that Judas defended Jesus or was hanged in his place.
R. 4; W. 38

JUDAS MACCABEUS
See "Handel."
W. 50

JUDD, DR.

Gerrit Parmele Judd (1803-1873) was born in Oneida County, N.Y., graduated from medical school in 1825, converted in 1826, and by 1827 had been appointed physician to the *Sandwich Island Mission of the American Board of Commissioners for Foreign Missions. He was with *Wilkes in 1840, and in 1842 separated from the mission to work for the Sandwich Islands government. His perfect command of the language made for wide input in councils through interpretation and translation. He was at various times a member of the treasury board, recorder and translator, secretary of state for foreign affairs, minister for foreign affairs, minister of interior, minister of finance, and Prime Minister in all but name. A controversial figure, he was often violently criticized, expecially by other foreign residents. In 1849, he represented Kamehameha (see "Kammahammaha") III in new treaties with the U.S. and *Britain, but was forced out in 1853 when the monarchy was threatened by overthrow. A member of the Legislature in 1858, he attended the constitutional convention in 1864, opposing Kamehameha V's efforts to increase the crown's power. An original member of the board of the Hawaiian Evangelical Association, he served until death in *Honolulu, survived by his wife, Laura Fish, and nine children.
T. Appendix

JUDEA

The *Hebrew state after the *Exile, Judea (formerly called Judah, after the tribes which settled there) was the southern part of western *Palestine. It achieved independence and expanded under the *Maccabees, assimilating Galilee, Samaria, and Idumea. Its boundaries always shifted under various rules, so that in modern times part of Judea is in Jordan.

The Maccabees revolted in Judea in 168 B.C. The *Romans established Herod the Great as king in 40 B.C., and the kingdom was divided under his sons' rule, so that Palestine's three main divisions became Judea, Samaria, and Galilee. Rome then established governors to replace the kings, the best known of which was *Pontius Pilate (A.D. 26-36). Revolts in A.D. 66 and 135 resulted in the downfall of Jerusalem and the Jewish state, with *Jews forbidden to live in Judea. In 451 the Council of Chalcedon created the Patriarchate of Jerusalem, with Judea as Diocese 1. *Moslems seized it in 637, and *Crusaders held it from 1099 to 1187.

M. visited Judea in January of 1857, commenting in his journal on its "barrenness" of "bleached . . . crunched, knawed, & mumbled" rocks, the "mere refuse & rubbish of creation . . . . compares with ordinary regions as skeletons with living & rosy man" (n.d.).
M. 3; M.D. 95

JUDGEMENT, DAY OF

Judgement Day, the end of earthly things: "We shall not all sleep, but we shall all be changed, in a moment, in the twinkling of an eye, at the last trump" (I *Corinthians 15:51, 52).

In *Matthew 25, those condemned stand at the left hand of *God. M. also calls the day: "Last Trump," "Last Day," "Last Judgement."
M. 3; M. 71; R. 18; W. 33; W. 34; W. 44; W. 50; M.D. 18; M.D. 96

JUDITH

In the *Apocryphal book of Judith, the widow smuggles herself into the camp of Holofernes, the *Assyrian enemy. She gets him drunk, cuts off his head with his own sword, places it in her food bag, and carries it home to Bethulia, where her daring inspires the *Hebrews to fight and conquer the Assyrians.
M.D. 70

JUGGERNAUT

In common use, the car of Juggernaut designates customs or institutions beneath which people are crushed.

Juggernaut (Jagannath) is the form under which the Indian Hindu (see "Hindoo") god *Vishnu is worshipped. In *Sanscrit, *Jagannatha* means "Lord of the world." An elaborate twelfth-century temple at Puri (Orissa) is the site of a yearly festival honoring "the remover of sin." His image is venerated for three days and then retired for ten, after which it is pulled back to the temple in a huge car dragged by hundreds of people. Among the festival's legends, it is said that fanatical pilgrims threw themselves under the car's wheels so as to gain immediate entrance into *Paradise.
M. 149; P. 1:6

JUGGLARIUS
No definition or original has been found for this expression, which Murray's notes to *P.* suggest refers to a "Great Juggler, *God." (In Murray's edition spelled "Juggularius.") Carlyle's *Sartor Resartus* employs the word "juggle" throughout.
P. 14:2; P. 18:1

JUGGLING
Deceiving. See also "Jugglarius."
M.D. 124

JULIA
"Julia," the "British Colonial Barque" in *O.* has its original in the *Sydney whaler, *Lucy Ann*, which picked M. up at *Typee Bay in 1842, her crew having been depleted by desertions. *Lucy Ann*'s commander was named Vinton, or Venton, not *"Guy," and despite the absence of a ship's journal, records suggest that M.'s details about her are accurate except for her service in the *War of 1812 (*Lucy Ann* was built in 1819). Her cruise of 1842 was as unproductive as M. paints "Julia's," and daily conditions as poor. Twelve of the original crew of thirty-two had deserted, and those left were in poor health. On her next voyage, *Lucy Ann* had a different commander and different owners, suggesting a previous unsuccessful venture.
"Julia" may also spring from *Charles & Henry*, the whaler on which M. shipped in 1842. See "Leviathan."
T. 34; O. 2; O. 14; O. 36

JULIAN, EMPEROR; JULIAN THE APOSTATE
Flavius Claudius Julianus, *Roman Emperor (322, 361-363) and nephew of Constantine the Great (see "Constantinople"), attempted to restore paganism, discriminating against *Christians, though not persecuting them. He led an ascetic life centered on public welfare, literature, and philosphy.
M. 119; C.M. 26

JULIAN YEARS
The average year of 365 1/4 days, according to Julian Calendar instituted by *Julius Caesar in B.C. 46. It divided the months into the present number of days (with July named in

Caesar's honor) allowing for an extra day every four years, after the sixth of the *calends of March.
M. 75

JULIUS CAESAR
    See "Caesar . . . . "
M. 1; M. 22; M. 181; R. 31; W. 16; W. 47; W. 77

JULY'S IMMORTAL FOURTH
    See "Fourth of July . . . . "
M.D. 83

JUNGFRAU
    Ger.: "virgin."
M.D. 81; M.D. 84

JUNGFRAU, THE
    A peak in southern *Switzerland, above Interlaken (46° N., 7°59' E.). The 13,642 foot high Jungfrau was first ascended in 1811.
M. 84

JUNIUS
    The Letters of Junius appeared anonymously in the *London *Public Advertiser* from late 1768 to early 1772, directed against William Draper, The Duke of *Grafton, and the Ministers. Authorship of the polished vitriolic letters has variously been ascribed to *Edmund Burke, or Edward Gibbon, among others.
M. 97; R. 26

JUNO
    In mythology, Juno, or Hera, was wife and sister to Zeus (*Jupiter, or *Jove), raised by the *Titans Ocean and Tethys. She was mother to several important gods: Ares, or *Mars, god of war; *Hephaestus, or Vulcan, god of Fire; *Hebe, goddess of Youth, who married *Hercules; Ilithyia (or Eileithyia), who helped women in childbirth. Although Hera herself is sometimes called the goddess of childbirth, she was mainly the protector of marriage, especially of married women whom her own husband, Zeus, fell in love with: among them, Semele, Echo, Aegina, and *Io.

The "white oxen" M. mentions is probably the white heifer in the Io story. At the time when Io assisted *Prometheus, she was in the plagued animal state Hera kept her in. Zeus had fallen in love with Io and, to hide her from Hera's jealousy, changed her into a white heifer. The suspicious Hera was not deceived and asked for the heifer as a gift. If Zeus refused, he would reveal his latest adultery, so he complied and Hera turned Io over to the care of the one-hundred-eyed watchman, *Argus. When Io escaped, Hero sent a stinging gadfly to torment her. Eventually restored to original form, Io gave Zeus a son who was the forebear of Hercules, whom Hera also plagued but later reconciled with. The Ionian Sea and the *Bosphorus (Ford of the Cow) are named for Io.

Probably Hera's grandest mischief occurred when the *Trojan Paris declared Helen more beautiful than she. Hera thereafter had a great hatred of Trojans and helped the *Greeks defeat them in the Trojan War. She especially hated *Aeneas becuase his descendents would found *Rome, conquering *Carthage, her favorite city. Carthage had been founded by a woman, *Dido. When Hera attempted to trick Aeneas into lingering with Dido instead of traveling to *Italy, only the intervention of Hera's brother, *Neptune, prevented her drowning Aeneas.

Among her few positive actions: assistance to *Jason in securing the Golden Fleece.
M. 136

JUPITER

In classical mythology, chief of the gods; also called *Jove, or Zeus. The exact position of the statue in *Dodona has not been ascertained. Dodona was originally the site of the oracle but was later eclipsed by *Delphi.

In a June 1(?) 1851 letter to *Hawthorne, M. said: "I stand for the heart. To the dogs with the head! I had rather be a fool with a heart, than Jupiter Olympus with his head."
M. 60; M. 84; M. 175; M. 181; W. 2; M.D. 82; M.D. 85; M.D. 133

JUPITER, BELTS OF

The largest planet, Jupiter has 1,300 times the volume of Earth and appears as the second brightest object in the sky (after *Venus). Through its cloudy atmosphere, it is marked by parallel dark streaks (belts) and bright spaces (zones). The belts vary in color from red to brown to gray, depending on the planet's position in its 12.08-year cycle. Jupiter appeared very

red in the mid 1850's; its reddest spot was described in the 1830's and officially reported in 1857. The four largest of its twelve known satellites were observed by *Galileo, but the smaller were not pinpointed until after M.'s death.
See also entry on the god, "Jupiter."
M. 175

JUSTICE OF THE PEACE
In the *United States, Justices of the Peace have strictly limited and inferior jurisdiction in civil and criminal cases. They are elected, and in M.'s time were often small-time opportunists paid on a fee basis to decide misdemeanors, perform hasty marriages, etc. The *British "J.P." is a magistrate appointed on recommendation of a local populace; he is generally unpaid, and dependent for legal advice upon an experienced barrister/clerk. The hypothetical "*Greenland Justice of the Peace" in *M.D.*, who will verify the authenticity of a picture, sounds more like the nineteenth-century American in his legal right to arbitrate despite a lack of expertise.
M.D. 56

JUSTINIAN; JUSTINIAN'S PANDECTS
Justinian (483-565) ruled the Eastern *Roman Empire from 527. He is famous for codifying Roman laws, his *Code*, *Digest*, *Institutes*, and *Novellae* forming the basis of European codes of law for centuries.
W. 35; M.D. 45; M.D. 89

JUTLAND
The Danish Jylland (or Cimbric) Peninsula projects north from *Germany between the North Sea and the *Kattegat. It consists of the *Danish mainland and part of the Schleswig-Holstein state. Politically, "Jutland" applies to mainland Denmark, including the islands north of Lim Fjord.
M. 3

JUVENAL
The *Roman Decimus Junius Juvenalis (c. A.D. 60- c. 136) wrote sixteen vivid satires on public, literary, and private life during the reign of *Domitian (not published until *Trajan's reign). They contain many pungent and memorable expressions ("Bread and circuses," "A sound mind in a sound body," etc.) and were much emulated by satirists, especially in

the eighteenth century, despite their status as superb
rhetorical exercises, rather than major documents, and
despite their pervading ill will toward almost everything.
    Sealts #147, *Harper's Classical Library*, vol 35, is
Charles Badham's translation; #276 contains *Chapman's
translation of the Fifth Satire.
C.M. 5

JUVENILE, THE
    The Capetian, Louis VII *le Jeune*, or the young (c. 1120-
1180), ruled the *French from 1137. Married to Eleanor of
Aquitaine, he later had the marriage annulled.
    Early in his reign, he broke with Pope Innocent II but
made peace with the Church by 1144. After participating in
the unsuccessful *Crusade of 1147-49, he continued the kind of
reform begun by his father, Louis VI (see "Ludwig the Fat").
    *Plantagenet conquest of *Normandy made for almost
constant warfare, but Louis succeeded in resisting further
incursions from the forces of Henry II of England, second
husband to Eleanor and by then possessor of Aquitaine.
M. 181

JUVENILE TEMPERANCE SOCIETY
    See "Temperance Society."
R. 46

JUVENILE TOTAL ABSTINENCE ASSOCIATION
    See "Temperance Society."
R. 8

K

KAAHUMANU
    Kaahumanu, born about 1773, ruled as Regent of Maui
(see "Mowee"), *Hawaii. The favorite of King Kamehameha
(see "Kammahammaha") converted to *Christianity in 1825
and was thereafter known as the "New Kaahumanu." She
died in 1839 of mumps and ensuing paralysis and could not
have been living at the time to which M. refers in *T.* 25.
T. 25

KAATSKILL MOUNTAINS
A former spelling of Catskill: derived from the *Dutch.
R. 27

KALEEDONI
M.'s fictional equivalent of *Scotland.
M. 152

KAMMAHAMMAHA; KAMMEHAMAHA; TAMMAHAMA-HA; TAMMAHAMMAHA
M.'s references to famous early kings of *Hawaii vary in their spelling because of variations in pre-literate Hawaiian language, M.'s idiosyncratic usage, and the vagaries of editors. Thus, allusions to "Tammahamaha," "Tammahammaha," "Kammahammaha," and Kammehamaha," refer to one of the rulers now commonly known as "Kamehameha." Adding to the confusion is M.'s tendency to confuse their biographies.

Kamehameha I (The Great) became ruler of one of Hawaii's then-four kingdoms in 1782. By 1810 he had consolidated all into one realm, driving away would-be intruders, and developing trade. He died in 1827.

Kamehameha II (Liholiho) acceded to the throne in 1819. Missionaries began arriving soon afterwards, and Kamehameha II cooperated in westernization. His wives Keopuolani and *Kaahumanu converted to *Christianity, as did many chiefs. Kamehameha II and Keopuolani died of measles in *London in 1824. Their bodies were returned by *Byron. Kaahumanu acted as Regent until her death in 1839.

Kamehameha III, Kaahumanu's son Kauikeaouli, was on the throne from 1824 to 1854. He was the most liberal of the three kings because of western-style urbanization brought by missionaries and whalers.

Although there were succeeding Kamehamehas, they do not figure in M.'s works.

See also "Judd, Dr." for material relative to the reign of Kamehameha III.
T. Passim; O. 54 ("T" spelling); M. 68 ("T" spelling); W. 50 ("T" spelling)

KAMSCHATKA, BAY OF
Kamchatka Peninsula of north-eastern *Siberia separates the Sea of Okhotsk (W.) from the Bering Sea and the *Pacific Ocean (E.). Linked to the mainland by a sixty-three mile-wide isthmus, the peninsula is 750 miles long and 300

miles wide. It has two active volcanic ranges, with peaks up to 15,666 feet high, and its severe climate makes it suitable for little more than fishing industries. It was discovered by *Russian explorers in 1697 and conquered by 1732. The "Bay of Kamschatsk" is probably Kamchatsk Gulf, on the eastern coast between Kronotski Cape (S.) and Ust-Kamchatsk (N.), which receives the Kamchatka River.
M. 1

KANDY
Kandy (or Candy). in central *Ceylon (7° 18' N., 80° 42' E.) has been since the fifteenth century the capital of the island and an important commercial, cultural, education, and tourist center. The Sinhalese occupants call the city Senkadagala Mahanuwara, and it is known for its natural beauty and important Buddhist temples with sacred relics, the center of an annual torchlight procession of richly decorated dancers and elephants. It was occupied by the *Portuguese in the sixteenth century, the *Dutch in the eighteenth, and the *British in the nineteenth.
M. 194

KANNAKIPPERS
The word is a *Tahitian corruption of "constables." These were, as M. says, police officials appointed to coerce natives into such odious duties as church attendance. They were enforcers of many abusive laws, using fines and other punishments. *Wheeler corroborates M.'s picture, as do others. *Kotzebue speaks of special police officers armed with bamboo canes, driving natives to church. *Olmsted mentions night patrols seeking out sexual corruption.
O. 46

KANT, --'S; KANTIAN; KANTIST
Philosopher Immanuel Kant (1724-1804) was born into a *Pietist family and educated in provincial Königsberg, *Prussia, and aside from his work led an uneventful life. Kant began publishing in 1747, but his philosophy was fully developed only after appointment as professor of logic and metaphysics at Königsberg in 1770. Among his most important publications are *Critique of Pure Reason* (1781 and 1787), *Prolegomena to any Future Metaphysics* (1783), *Fundamental Principles of the Metaphysics of Ethics* (1785), *Metaphysical Rudiments of Natural Philosophy* (1786), *Critique of Pure Reason* (1788), *Critique of Judgement* (1790), and *Religion Within*

the Boundries of Pure Reason (1793), which brought much criticism.

Kant saw man as caught in a central dilemma of interpretation: one side holding events to be the product of Necessity, the other calling attention to man's apparent freedom. He described his position as one of *transcendental, critical, or formal idealism and redirected philosophy away from focus on a Supreme Being. In contrast with *Locke (with whom he is compared in *M.D.* 73), Kant emphasized the innate order of the human mind, with sensory perceptions secondary and conditioned by that mind; the external world was the product of that conditioning, leading to insoluble contradictions. He posited twelve principles or laws of thought: the "categories" derided in *P.* 19:1 and 22:1.

M.'s references to Kant suggest that he placed the philosopher with *Plato, *Emerson, and other optimists, in direct contrast with more skeptical philosophers (such as *Hume). In actuality, Kant's work attempted mediation between the two extremes. M.'s journal entries for 12 and 22 October 1849 record his lengthy metaphysical discussions of Kant and others with Dr. George Adler, enroute to England.

See also "Fixed Fate and Free Will," and "Necessitarian."
M. 3; R. 40; M.D. 73; P. 19:1; P. 20:2; P. 21:3; P. 22:1

KARAKIKOVA

M.'s "Karakikova" is Kealakekue Bay, off the island of *Hawaii. It is the site of Kaawaloa village, where *Cook was killed 2 February 1779.
T. 32

KASKASIA

The Kaskasia River of central and southwestern *Illinois rises near Urbana, flowing 320 miles southwest to the *Mississippi northwest of Kaskasia village. The village (swept away in a late nineteenth-century flood) was located on a six-mile-long island in the Mississippi. By 1703, *Jesuits had established a trade center there. Nearby bluffs held Fort Kaskasia (now a State Park).
C.M. 27

KATHERINE

Probably a fictional ship. M. might have borrowed the name from a *British ship captured at Lake Champlain in 1775 and re-named *Liberty*.
T. 4

KAYAR
See "Cocoa-nut tree."
R. 34

KEDGER
A cadger is a scrounging beggar or other person who tries to obtain money or things from others. Originally, the word referred to itinerant dairy dealers in *England. M.'s "kedger" showing a whaling scene is probably derived from an illustration in *Uncle Philip's Conversations with Young People about the Whale Fishery, and Polar Regions* (London, 1837).
M.D. 57

KEDRON, BROOK
M.D. provides a gloss: "Queequeg's" idol, "Yojo," is like "that found in the secret groves of Queen Maachah in *Judea; and for worshipping which, King Asa, her son, did depose her, and destroyed the idol and burnt it for an abomination at the Brook Kedron, as darkly set forth in the 15th chapter of the first book of *Kings."
The word "Kedron" means "black." The dark river flows from near Gethsemane to Mar Saba and the *Dead Sea.
W. 63; M.D. 95

KEEL-HAULING
One of the most drastic forms of punishment at sea, wherein the victim was hoisted by a whip or light tackle to a fore yardarm and dropped overboard weighted so as to sink, pass under the keel, and be dragged up again to the yardarm on the ship's opposite side. It was commonly used by *pirates in the sixteenth century and then adapted by the *English and the *Dutch navies.
W. 88

KEKUANOA, GENERAL
Rev. Hiram Bingham's chart of *Sandwich Island chiefs, 1747-1847 (*Residence of Twenty-One Years in the Sandwich Islands*) shows Kekuanoa's descent as a "child-in-law" of Kamehameha I (see "Kammahammaha").
T. Appendix

KENILWORTH

The ancient town in Warwickshire, *England, is famous for the ruins of its twelfth-century castle. Built by the *Norman Geoffrey de Clinton on land granted by *Henry I, the castle was passed on to *King John and used by many succeeding monarchs, the *Leicesters, *John of Gaunt, Robert Dudley, and the Hydes. It was abandoned after dismantling by *Oliver Cromwell's forces. *Sir Walter Scott's *Kenilworth (1821) is set in *Elizabethan times.
R. 28

KENILWORTH

See "Scott, Sir Walter."
M. 139; W. 65

KENNEBEC

Kennebec County, in southern *Maine, has long been known for its farms, dairies and orchards. (Modern-day Kennebec is also a center for textiles, wood, and paper production, as well as lake resorts.)
M. 22

KENT, --ISH

The county of Kent is southeast of *London and extends to the chalk cliffs over the English *Channel. Throughout history it has been the site of settlement, invasion and departure for the continent and has yielded many artifacts, especially evidence of *Roman occupation. Agriculture (especially *hops farming), sheep-rearing, papermaking, pottery/brick/tile manufacture, and fishing remain major pursuits, as they were when M. visited in early November of 1849. Landing at *Deal, he walked six miles to *Sandwich for breakfast, then took a train to *Canterbury.

See also "Cinque Ports"; "Colchester"; "Cymbeline"; "Dover'; "Dungeness"; "Goodwin Sands."
I.P. 22; I.P. 25

KENTUCKY; KENTUCKIAN

Kentucky was admitted to the Union as the fifteenth state, in 1792. The "Bluegrass State" is bounded by *Ohio and Indiana (N.), *Tennessee (S.), West Virginia (E.), *Virginia (S.E.), *Illinois (W.), and *Missouri (S.W.) The Ohio and *Mississippi Rivers flow through the area, which was first explored in 1750. Settlement began a year before *Daniel Boone created Boonesborough in 1775. The Indians were driven out by 1794, by which time Kentucky had been awarded the Indian name for "Dark and Bloody Ground" (*C.M.* 26).

"Kentucky bites" (*W.* 25) alludes to notoriously fierce Kentucky brawls. It was not unusual for noses and ears to be bitten off and eyes to be put out by thumbs thrust into sockets.

Kentucky was a *slave state.

O. 82; M. 75; M. 121; R. 41; W. 25; M.D. 95; M.D. 105; P. 2:2; C.M. 1; C.M. 2; C.M. 4; C.M. 17; C.M. 26

KEW; KEW GARDENS

The Royal Botanic gardens at Kew, in *London's Richmond upon *Thames was begun in the 1600's and officially established in 1759. By M.'s time, it encompassed 288 acres and housed a wide variety of plants and buildings. M. visited on 11 November 1849, commenting in his journal on the "splendid" place, "justly renowned for its beauty." He especially noted Sir William Chambers's pagoda orangery and the lovely view from Richmond Hill.

I.P. 5; I.P. 13; I.P. 14

KHAN; GENGHIS KHAN

A title of respect in *Moslem countries, Khan is a contracted form of *kaghan*, a *Mongolian word meaning "sovereign." Its use eventually included reference to property owners.

Genghis (Chinghiz, Chinggis, Jenghis, etc.) Khan (1167?-1227), Mongol conqueror, was not the mere barbarian popular history has painted him, but a shrewd politician and diplomat, skilled in psychological warfare.

The Mongols were a small group of separate clans surrounded by *Turks and Tatars (see "Tartar"), among other enemies, in what is now the Mongolian People's Republic. Until his father's death from poisoning, Genghis grew up as "Temujin" (the name of a great warrior his father had killed) in the camp of his betrothed's father. Earning honor for recovering stolen horses, he became a warrior and married at fifteen, giving his wife's dowry to a powerful estranged ally, the first of many clever acts augmenting his prestige and power. The complexities of kinship were also used skillfully in his oath of blood kinship with his powerful "brother," Jamukha, later his enemy. The two formed Mongol groups into an efficient army. Several brilliant tacticians swore "companionship," further solidifying his power. Having settled local feuds and conquered the Tatars, in about 1206 he was proclaimed Genghis Khan, "chief" of the nomads against civi-

lized tribes, rather than "emperor." He pursued a policy of generous reward to allies and severe punishment to enemies, massacring for effect when necessary. His descendents (one of them Kubla Khan) lost control of what was in essence a temporary association of the discrete nomadic groups in his domain, and his later dynasties fell. (The Mongols and Tatars have frequently been confused, as M. appears to do in calling Genghis the "Khan of Tartary.")
M. 63; M. 84; M. 119; M. 181; M.D. 30

KIDD, CAPTAIN

William Kidd (c. 1645-1701), the *pirate, was born in *Scotland, the son of a *Calvinist minister. From 1689 he sailed as a legitimate privateer against the *French in the *West Indies and on the North American coast. Commissioned to capture pirates in the ship *Adventure Galley*, he instead became a pirate himself, sailing to *New England on the *Antonio*, only to be returned to England for trial. Found guilty of murder and piracy, he was executed at *Wapping on 23 May, 1701, and his body exhibited in chains. His booty was given to *Greenwich Hospital. The story of his ship's scuttling in the *Hudson River is a legend.
R. 1; P. 7:4

KILKENNY

Kilkenny, in south central *Ireland, is probably best known for fights between Kilkenny cats, which were tied together to battle to the finish. A Kilkenny grin is a somewhat diabolical smirk. A Kilkenny ring is a penny; a Kilkenny coat is made at tanneries there.
R.27

KING ALFRED

See "Alfred, King."
M.D. Extracts 10

KING CHARLES

See "Charles the First."
R. 36

KING CHARLES' OAKS

See "Charles the Second."
R. 46

KING EDWARD
    See "Edward III, King of England."
M.D. 60

KING HENRY
    The reference in *M.D*. Extracts is to *Shakespeare's *I
Henry IV* (I, iii, 57-58). The play is about the rebellion of the
*Percys and the rise of "Prince Hal" from a life of riotous
carousing to the character of a future king. Its greatest popularity has probably resulted from the character of "Falstaff,"
"Hal's" obese and boastful comic companion, who plays an
even larger role in *II Henry IV*, only to be finally scorned by
the now fully regal King Henry V.
    See also "Extracts" 15.
M.D. Extracts 15

KING JAMES, --'S
    First ruler of the parlous union between *Scotland and
*England. See "Stuart."
M. 57; W. 1; W. 3; P. 1:3

KING JOHN
    King John (1167-1216) was one of the most unpopular
monarchs in *English history (from 1199 to 1216), eventually
facing a baronial rebellion that ended his reign.
    Youngest son of the *Plantagenet Henry II and Eleanor
of Aquitaine, John was much favored by his father but deserted
him when his brother, Richard, rebelled in favor of the
*French, acceding as *Richard I. John was made the wealthy
Count of Mortain but attempted to seize the throne when
Richard recognized his three-year-old nephew, Arthur, as
heir. Later reconciled, Arthur passed the throne to John. As
king, he lost *Normandy (1204) and other French territory,
then imposed heavy revenues and questioned feudal tenures,
hoping to pay for the losses. He quarreled with Pope Innocent
III, who reversed his excommunication when John surrendered the kingdom to the Papal nuncio, receiving it back as a
paying vassal.
    By 1212, the barons were plotting against him, and his
failure to regain French territory led to civil war in 1215.
Prince Louis (later Louis VIII of France) entered England, receiving the homage of the barons, and John died unable to re-
trieve his throne.
    See also "Magna Charta."
0. 80

KING LEO'S SHARE
Lat. *leo, leonis*, lion.

The lion's share is all, or the larger part. In *Aesop's Fables*, the lion hunts with other beasts, then claims one quarter of the spoils as his prerogative, one quarter for his courage, one quarter for his family, and the last quarter to be disputed for with the claimant. He is King of the Forest.
M. 114

KING-MAKERS
See "Nevil, Richard."
M. 160

KING OF CUPS AND TOKAY
See "Ludwig the Fat."
M. 181

KING OF MACEDON
King Philip II (382-336 B.C.) brought *Macedonia to prominence in Europe. Father to *Alexander III (the Great), Philip lost his right eye to the arrow of a *Thracian at Methone; he was murdered by a courtier, Pausanias, at the wedding feast of his daughter Cleopatra to the king of *Epirus.
W. 16

KING OF PORTUGAL
See "John VI, King of Portugal."
W. 56

KING OF THE TWO SICILIES.
See "Two Sicilies."
W. 4

KING PHILIP, INDIAN
See "Philip of Mount Hope."
M.D. 45

KING PLUTO
See "Pluto."
M. 181

KING PORUS
        See "Porus, King."
M.D. 87

KING RICHARD
        Richard II (1367-1400), King of *England from 1377 to
1399, was the younger son of Edward the *Black Prince, and
succeeded to the throne as a minor. In 1381, he attempted to
appease rebellious peasants led by *Wat Tyler but otherwise
had little influence, government being mainly in the hands of
his uncle, *John of Gaunt.
        As actual ruler, Richard disliked war and chivalry and
was sensitive to the hostility of lords such as *Gloucester,
whose efforts had Richard's supporters put to death by the
"Merciless Parliament" of 1388. When come of age, he surrounded himself with strong royalists, made a successful expedition to *Ireland, and made peace with *France. He had
the earl of Arundel executed, *Warwick banished, and
Gloucester murdered, and exiled Henry Bolingbroke (John of
Gaunt's son) and Thomas Mowbray, duke of Norfolk, for
which historians have painted him a despot. His confiscation
of John of Gaunt's estates brought back Bolingbroke (the future
*Henry IV), and he was forced to abdicate, dying of starvation
in prison (rather than murdered, as *Shakespeare's play has
it).
R.24

KINGS
        The *Old Testament's Kings I and II report the events of
the *Solomonic monarchy and the divided kingdoms of
*Palestine, following events of the Book of *Samuel. Origi-
nally, they were one book, ascribed (probably falsely) by
*Talmudic tradition to *Jeremiah. I Kings 1-11 deals with
Solomon's ascension to the throne and his reign; I Kings 12--
II Kings 17 describes the vicissitudes of the two kingdoms; II
Kings 18-25 covers the surviving kingdom of Judah (see
"Judea").
        M.'s *Bible is heavily marked in the section of I dealing
with King *Ahab and in sections dealing with the wealth and
wisdom of Solomon. The prophet *Elijah appears in both I and
II Kings.
M.D. 95

KING SAUL

The first king of *Israel (reigned c. 1020-1000 B.C.) was secretly anointed by *Samuel (I Samuel 9), following the Lord's command. Saul's crushing of the enemies of Israel (*Ammonites, *Philistines, and others) placated *Hebrews who had previously believed that only *Jehovah could be "king." Israel thrived during his reign, but Saul's concern about *David's increasing influence and his break with Samuel after failure to destroy the Amalekites, denying a prophecy (*Exodus 17:14), led to fits of suspicion and melancholy. Brutal acts, consultation with the witch of *Endor, and visions of Samuel's ghost (*M.* 68) preceded Saul's defeat at Gilboa, where his three sons were killed and Saul either died by his own hand (31:4) or at the hands of an Amalekite obliging his wish (II Samuel 1:10).

The account of Saul's burial (*R.* 49) is in I Samuel 31:9-13: the Philistines cut off the corpse's head and fasten the body to a wall. The people of Jahesh-gilead remove the body, burn it, bury the bones under a tree at Jahesh, and fast for seven days.

M. errs in *M.* 174; the friend of *Jonathan was *David, not Saul.

M. 68; M. 174; R. 49; P. 1:3

KING'S BENCH

King's Bench Prison, in *London's *Southwark area, is first mentioned (1381) in connection with *Wat Tyler's rebellion. A later building held *Smollet, the father of Leigh Hunt, *Lord Cochrane (for stock exchange fraud), and Dickens's "Mr. Micawber" (see "Hard Times"). The large prison had 224 rooms, a courtyard, tap-room, wine-room, and market and was the most comfortable debtors' prison in *England. Leaves might be arranged for a fee, and one's wife might reside there. Later a military prison, King's Bench was demolished in 1880.

M.D. 90

KING'S DOCK

*Liverpool: originally, seven and three-quarter acre water area; opened 1788, it became the center for tobacco trade with *Virginia.

R. 32

KINGSMILL CHAIN, --ISLES; KING'S MILLS

The Kingsmill Islands are today part of the (British) Gilbert group, north of the *Ellices (c. 3-4° S., 176° E.). *Wilkes wrote at length on the "Manners and Customs of the Kingsmill

Islanders" (V, 37-110), as well as on the tropical cross currents that confound "Taji's" proposed itinerary in *M*. Wilkes's comments on *albinos (V., 41) on the chain's Tracy's Island perhaps influenced M.'s comments on *whiteness in *M.D.* and his picture of "Yillah," the pale maiden of *M*.
M. 3; M. 12; M. 30; M.D. 53

KING'S PLATE

Colloquial or low usage for fetters or manacles (along with "darbies"): obsolete by 1880, according to Partridge.
I.P. 21

KING WILLIAM'S

William III (1650-1702), king of *England (II of *Scotland, and I of *Ireland), was son of King William II, prince of Orange, and Mary, daughter of *Charles I of England. Raised in *Holland, he commanded *Dutch armies in the war of 1672-78.

Marriage to his cousin Mary, daughter of the duke of *York (later James II of England; see "Stuart"), advanced his chances of succession to the throne of England, despite his tie to the house of Orange. When James produced a son, and it appeared that there would be a Roman *Catholic succession, popular opinion rallied around William. When James fled to *France, William and Mary were proclaimed rulers of England and Scotland. Despite internal problems with Ireland and Scotland, William spent much time campaigning on the continent in the War of the Grand Alliance (see "King William's War").

In England, William was a rather unpopular, alien king, despite his status as a *Protestant hero. But historians paint him as the first great stabilizer of British politics.
R. 32

KING WILLIAM'S WAR

This prolonged struggle (1689-97), part of what is referred to as the French and Indian Wars, was the *American counterpart of the European War of the Grand Alliance, fought by *England, *Holland, the *Holy Roman Emperor, and others, in colonial rivalry with *France. As a result of King William's war, Port Royal (Annapolis, *Nova Scotia) was captured, and *Quebec was lost. The Treaty of Rijswijk (1697) restored all captured territory, bringing the War of the Grand Alliance to an inconclusive end. See also preceding entry.
R. 32

KIRKALDY
Kirkcaldy is located on the north of the Firth of *Forth, county of *Fife, *Scotland.
I.P. 18

KITOTI
The name is a corruption or perhaps a deliberate distortion of "Hitoti," mentioned by *Wilkes (II, 18,19) as a descendant of the ancient *Tahitian kings dethroned by *Pomare I. Along with others, Hitoti constantly sought to augment his own power and diminish the royal ruler's.
O. 32

KNADIJA
See "Mohammed."
W. 65

KNIGHT TEMPLAR
See "Templar."
T. 24

KNOX, GENERAL
Henry Knox (1750-1806), *Federalist *American Revolutionary War General, participated in most of the major engagements of the war. Among his more colorful actions, he transported the cannon that *Ethan Allen captured, enabling the taking of *Boston; he supervised *Washington's troops crossing the *Delaware on *Christmas night of 1776; he served at the court-martial of Major John André (see "Arnold, Benedict"); he was appointed Major General in charge of *West Point in 1782. Under the Articles of Confederation, in 1785 he was officially appointed Secretary of War, after having acted unofficially in that capacity for Washington.
M . is correct in calling Knox an amputee (*M*. 24); he is incorrect in designating the digit. Knox lost not a thumb but the third and fourth fingers of his left hand on a hunting expedition in 1770.
M. 24

KOAR-WOOD
Koa is the *Hawaiian acacia tree (of the legume family); its wood is used in building and cabinet-making, and its bark in tanning. (M.'s sentence structure is confusing in *O*. 74,

making it seem that the "Koar" provides the cord, rather than the *cocoanut.)
O. 74

KOHALA
The peninsula on the north of the island of *Hawaii was the birthplace of Kamehameha (see "Kammaham-maha. . . . "). It contains many relics of ancient times. The Kohala mountains range up to 5,489 feet in altitude.
O. 49

KOKOVOCO
In some editions, "Rokovoco." Not the name of any country, but similar to many.
M.D. 11

KONNO
The fictional equivalent of the *Irish patriot *Daniel O'Connell.
M. 152

KOOLOO
Not a *Tahitian name; it may be "Puru," or "Uru."
O. 40

KORAH
In Numbers 16, Korah, the son of Levi, is destroyed, along with Dathan, Abiram, and On, for rising up against *Moses and *Aaron. Korah illustrates the letter K in the *New England Primer (Sealts #384).
M.D. 58

KORAN
See "Mohammed."
W. 72; C.M. 24

KORIESH
See "Mohammed."
W. 65

KOSSUTH

Lajos Kossuth (1802-1894), *Hungarian patriot and leader of the revolution of 1848-48, came from a poor but noble *Lutheran family. Early experience in the diets, as agent for magnates, led to his radical nationalism, especially in opposition to *Vienna's power over the Hungarian people. Provocative pamphlet-writing led to his imprisonment, after which he emerged a popular hero, persuasive speaker, and leader of the Reform Party. The Hungarian Prime Minister put him into an office in which he had power to provoke a crisis with Vienna. He became *de facto* dictator as Governor of Hungary after the Viennese invasion but was forced to flee when *Russian troops were brought in for support. He escaped to *Turkey, *England, and the *United States, but was unable to gain official support for Hungary. In 1880 he published *Memoir of My Life*. He died in *Italy, still in touch with Hungarian nationalists.
C.M. 29

KOTZEBUE

Otto Von Kotzebue (1787-1846), *Russian navigator who sailed with *Krusenstern (1803-06), led an expedition (1815-18) to *Easter Island and the *Tuomotu archipelago, discovering many islands, charting much of the coast of Alaska, and, lacking a route to the *Atlantic through the *Arctic, visiting the Marshall Islands, where he acquired much data on botany and ethnology. His second voyage (1823-26) made valuable oceanographic discoveries.

Kotzebue was an even more serious critic of the *Christianization of native populations than M. paints him, and was much rebuked by Christian writers such as *Ellis. His narratives are *A Voyage of Discovery into the South Sea and Bering's Straits for the purpose of exploring a Northeast Passage* . . . 1815-18, 3 vols. (1821), and *A New Voyage round the World, in the Years 1823-26*, 2 vols. (English trans. 1830), which M. charged out of a Boston library in 1846 (Sealts #313).
T. 24; O. 48

KRAKEN

In *Norwegian folklore, a vast sea monster seen off Norway and later along North American coasts. In *History of Norway* (1752), *Bishop Pontoppidan describes a dark excretion surrouding it, suggesting that the original was a cuttlefish. *Pliny also speaks of a sea monster, commemorated by Tennyson in "The Kraken" (1830). In *English tradition, Kraken

is a giant spider at Shambles Shoal, at the entrance of Portland
Roads, and is responsible for shipwrecks.
M.D. 59

KREMLIN

*Moscow's famous triangular citadel was begun in the
fifteenth century. Its one and one-half mile long crenelated
wall encloses, in every style of architecture, fortresses, arse-
nals, palaces, cathedrals, churches, museums, barracks and
shops. The Great Palace (nineteenth century) was the domain
of the *tsars, with many treasures, throne room, etc.; what
survives of the collection is a museum. The *Russian word
kreml means citadel, and there are less important kremlins in
many cities in the U.S.S.R.
M.D. 105

KRILL

See "Cetology" section.
M.D. 58

KRUSENSTERNS; ADMIRAL KRUSENSTERN'S

*Russian navigator Adam Ivan Von Krusenstern (1770-
1846) circumnavigated the globe, 1803-1806, visiting the
*Marquesas, *Kamchatka, and Sakhalin. His three-volume
Voyage Round the World (1809-13) was published in *England
in 1813 (2 vols.). He also wrote *Atlas de l'Océan Pacifique* (1824-
27) and *Recueil de mémoires hydrographiques* (1824-35).
Krusenstern's naturalist on the circumnavigation was
*Langsdorff, a close associate of Captain John De Wolf II, M.'s
boyhood adviser (see "D'Wolf").
M.D. 24; M.D. 45

L

LABRADOR

The bleak Canadian *Atlantic coast strip of land which
is now a dependency of *Newfoundland remains settled only on
the coast: a deeply indented rugged mountainous area of
many lakes (including Lake Melville). "Labrador" formerly referred to the whole peninsula known as Ungava, in modern
*Quebec province.

Labrador may have been visited by *Norsemen in the eleventh century, John Cabot in 1498, and Corte Read in 1500. It is certain that Sebastian Cabot (1508) and Jacques Cartier (1534) sailed along the coast. The *Treaty of Paris assigned the area to *Britain in 1763, and it was transferred to Canada in 1774. Continuing boundary disputes returned it to Newfoundland in 1809. By M.'s time, settling was beginning, primarily by fisherman and *Moravian missionaries.

The Labrador Current is formed off the coast by currents from *Baffin's Bay and west *Greenland currents. It meets the *Gulf Stream off the *Grand Banks, resulting in dense fogs. The current brings much dangerous ice into main shipping lanes between North America and Europe.
R. 40; W. 75; M.D. 3; M.D. 6

LACEDEMONIAN
Lacedaemon was ancient *Sparta, where life and death struggles against enemies were frequent. Education aimed at preservation of Spartan dominance through military efficiency. Physical fitness was paramount, so infanticide was common. Seven-year-old male children were taken from their mothers for an eleven-year training period where endurance was the keynote, developed through boxing and other violent body contact sports. At eighteen years, boys served on active duty, and their military education continued until they were too old to fight. Females were taught physical fitness, although they were not removed from their homes, since motherhood and child-rearing were their objectives.

By contrast, although the *Athenians were also concerned about defense, their system aimed for development of well-balanced individuals. Although gymnastics and other physical training was given, the Athenian motto was "nothing in excess."

The city was founded about 900 B.C. by Dorians and soon became *Greece's strongest city by virtue of its bellicosity. Among Spartan victories: defense of *Thermopylae (480 B.C.); the *Persian *Wars (500-449); battle of *Salamis (48); victory of Plataea (479), under Pausanias. The Spartan *Peloponnesian League defeated *Athens in the Peloponnesian War (431-404). After *Thebes won the victory of *Epanimondas at Leuctra (371), Sparta fell to *King Philip II of *Macedon and rapidly declined.

M.'s C.M. 21 reference to the leisure, manners, and philosophy of the Spartans is of course ironic. The Spartans contributed little to the art, literature, or philosophy of Greece.
T. 29

LACEPEDE

Bernard Germain Etienne Delaville, Comte De Lacépède (1756-1825), *French naturalist, wrote also on music, physics, and electricity. His major early works were *Histoire des quadrupèdes ovipares et des serpents* (2 vols., 1788-89) and *Histoire naturelle des reptiles* (1789). His *Histoire des cétacès* (1804) was probably known only at second hand to M., who could not have read much French.
M.D. 32; M.D. 55; M.D. 105

LACKADAY ISLANDS

Probably a frivolous reference to the Laccadive Islands, in the Arabian Sea southwest of *India. The "Hundred Thousand Islands," as they were called, were visited by da *Gama in 1498.
M.D. 110

LA DOMINICA

See "Hivarhoo."
0. 6; 0.8

LADRONE

The modern Marianas Islands were discovered c. 1521 by *Magellan, who named them the Ladrones (Sp. "thieves") for the habits of the natives. They were renamed by *Spanish *Jesuits in 1668. Spain ruled until 1898, when the *United States, *Germany, and *Japan divided the islands. The Marianas are in the western *Pacific, 1,500 miles east of the *Philippines (13°25'--20°32' N., 144°45'--144°54' E.): a 500 mile-long volcanic chain which became important during World War II, especially for the island of Guam (United States territory).

(There are also Ladrone Islands in the south China Sea, Kwangtuag province of *China, off the *Canton River estuary, eighteen miles southeast of *Macao: the *Wanshan* Islands.)
C.M. 24

LADY, MY

Courtesy title in *Britain (corresponding to Lord) for wife of a nobleman or peer of the realm. Corruption of Anglo-Saxon words for "knead" and "loaf," literally "bread-maker," as opposed to male "bread-guarder." Used for female head of the family.
M. 129

LAERTES

In *Shakespeare's *Hamlet*, the brother of "Ophelia," son of "*Polonius," killer of "Hamlet" in a duel. The "advice" mentioned in *C.M.* 30 occurs in I, iii, 55-81. The "few precepts" of the loquacious Polonius extend to almost a full life-plan for the son and include some of the most familiar of Shakespeare's words ("neither a borrower nor a lender be," "to thine own self be true," etc.).
C.M. 30

LA FAYETTE

Marie Joseph Paul Yves Roch Gilbert Du Motier, Marquis de Lafayette (1757-1834), hero of the *American Revolution, was born into a wealthy and noble old *French family. Finding court life unsatisfying, he sought commission in the American continental army but was required to serve as an unpaid volunteer. Taking *George Washington as his model, he gained respect for his gallant action at the *Brandywine (where he was wounded) and in later action brought French sympathy to the American cause. He returned from a 1779 diplomatic mission to France, able to assure the dispirited American army that French support was forthcoming and was soon celebrated as "the friend of Washington" and "the hero of two worlds." He was made a citizen of several American states and on his return to France became a social and political reformer, especially advocating the abolition of *slavery. With *Thomas Jefferson's help, he drafted a Declaration of the Rights of Man and the Citizen; one year after *Bastille day his popularity was at its peak. He was imprisoned by the *Prussians in the Napoleonic wars and refused French honors because of his disapproval of *Napoléon.

"Guest of the nation" in the United States from 1824 to 1825, he was lionized in every state, a symbol of human freedom; the acerbic Mrs. Trollope noted that "the reception of General Lafayette is the one single instance in which the national pride has overcome the national thrift" (p. 329). Lafayette returned to France to continue his human rights crusade. He was married to Adrienne de Noailles (1759-1807), daughter of the duc D'Ayen. His *Memoires, correspondences et manuscrits* was published posthumously.
W. 69

LAHAINALUNA

Lahaina ("Lahina," in *M.* 22 and *M.* 28), the coastal city of western Maui (*Mowee) was the site of the first white settlement in *Hawaii and an early (1810-1845) capital of the

*Sandwich Islands. Auau Channel, known as Lahaina Road-
stead, was the anchorage of the *United States Pacific fleet, the
residence of Hawaiian kings, and the rival of *Honolulu as
most important city until the 1870's. It was an important place
for whalers.

When the United States Exploring Expedition visited Lahainaluna Missionary College (*T.* 30) in 1841, *Wilkes found it
"badly conducted and perhaps doomed to failure, since manual
training and vocational education had been abandoned for the
pursuit of higher abstract studies" (Wilkes *Narrative* IV).

Bingham claims rather more success for the institution,
established in 1831; of the 144 graduates alive in 1840, he
claimed 105 were teachers, thirty-five of whom were government officers, seven were in "other useful employments," and
only ten "openly immoral." The course of study included
Arithmetic, Geometry, Trigonometry, Sacred Geography,
Hawaiian Grammar, Language, Navigation and Surveying,
History, Natural Philosophy, Moral Philosophy, Church History, Bible Study.
T. 25; T. 30

LAHINA; LAHINNEESE
    See "Lahainaluna."
M. 22; M. 28

LAIS
    See "Sais."
M.D. 76

LAKE LEMANS
    Lake Geneva, on the *Swiss/*French border, is the
largest *Alpine lake in Europe: forty-five miles long and 224
1/2 square miles in area, with a maximum depth of 1,017 feet.
The name "Lac Léman" had revived in the eighteenth century
and was commonly used in M.'s time to signify the crescent-
shaped lake formed by the Rhône River.

    Penny Cyclopaedia mentions the lake's violent east and
north-east winds, causing such agitation that it seldom
freezes.
W. 26; W. 50

LAKEMAN
    "Steelkilt's" type is discussed at length in Vincent's edi-
tion of *M.D.* (p. 740, n. 242.29). M.'s portrait apparently sprang

from his own observation of the larger-than-life sailors of the
*Great Lakes, which he sailed (as a passenger) in 1840. The vi-
olent weather of the Lakes, the rugged surrounding terrain,
the western pioneering spirit, the independence and basic
straightness of character, all combined to produce a heroic
type worthy of "one insular *Tahiti" (*M.D.* 58).
M.D. 54

LAMA
     See "Grand Lama"; "Thibet."
O. 50; M. 181; W. 68; M.D. 106

LAMATINS
     See "Cetology" section.
M.D. 32

LAMB, CHARLES
     The *London-born Lamb (1775-1834), who became most
celebrated as author of *Essays of Elia*, wrote pseudonymously
to spare his family embarrassment. His essays, poems, and
dramas were never very successful financially, although
Lamb became one of the best-loved *British authors—especially
by M., who admired the wit of "Old Honesty" and perhaps em-
pathized with Lamb's bouts of mental derangement and protection of a sister (who had killed their mother).
     M.'s 1849 journey to London brought acquaintance with
Edward Moxon (1801-1858), publisher of Lamb and many other
prestigious writers. Moxon was Lamb's close friend, and M.'s
journal (20 November) marks the meeting. A letter to
*Richard Dana (1 May 1850) elaborates on Moxon's comments
on Lamb: he was "the best fellow in the world to 'get drunk
with.'" Moxon gave M. a copy of Lamb's works (Sealts #316).
M. also owned and annotated Thomas Noon Talfourd's 1848
Final Memorials of Charles Lamb (Sealts #317). Sealts #318 is
Lamb's *Specimens of English Dramatic Poets, Who Lived
about the Time of Shakespeare* (1845).
     See also "Extracts" 52.
M.D. Extracts 52

LAMBERT
     Daniel Lambert (1770-1809) was the most corpulent man
on record, measuring three feet one inch around the leg, nine
feet four inches around the body, and weighing well over 700

pounds. Lambert was a jail keeper in Leicester, *England, who later put himself on exhibition in *London.
M. 94; M. 95; M. 158; W. 1

LAMP-FEEDER
A can with a spout, for filling oil lamps.
M.D. 81

LANCASHIRE
R.'s "Lancashire lad" is from the scenic northwestern *English county on the *Irish Sea, along the southern edge of which flows the *Mersey River. The anciently settled area contains picturesque abbey ruins and quaint villages, as well as mining sites and industrial cities such as *Liverpool and *Manchester. The area was granted to the Lancaster family in the thirteenth century, becoming home to *John of Gaunt in the fourteenth. *Black Death, the Wars of the Roses, and the Civil War, all ravaged the area. Wool and cotton industries were principal pursuits until the eighteenth century when maritime industries and *slave trade developed at Liverpool. Canal construction and England's then-largest railway line (Liverpool to London, opened 1830) finally began linking Lancashire to the rest of England.
M.'s first voyage took him to Lancashire in July of 1839, but poverty limited his sightseeing to the very seamy Liverpool. He apparently explored the area a bit more in November of 1856, traveling from *Glasgow through *York, to Lancaster and Liverpool, calling it an "interesting country of manufactures" (journal, 8 November).
R. 5; R. 23; R. 26; R. 27; R. 31

LANDGRAVE
*German title of nobility, originated in the twelfth century when kings wished to undermine the power of dukes by creating "provincial counts" (*Landgrafen*) equal to them. First landgraviate was Thuringia.
M. 181

LANDLESS
Edinburgh Review (May 1828) noted the promotion of a Lieutenant Landless to Captain, by *Collingwood.
W. 90

LAND OF PROMISE

*God promised *Abraham, *Isaac, and *Jacob that their offspring would possess *Canaan, the Land of Promise—a type of heaven (*Exodus 12:25; *Deuteronomy 60:28, etc.).

The reference to *Australia as a Land of Promise is ironic. O. 14

LANDSEERS

Sir Edwin Landseer (1802-73), *English painter, sculptor, and engraver, is best remembered for his sentimental animal allegories, such as *The Old Shepherd's Chief Mourner* (1837) and *The Monarch of the Glen* (1850). Highly admired by Queen *Victoria, Landseers was sculptor of the lions at *Trafalgar Square, *London (1867).
M. 29

LANGSDORFF, CAPTAIN; LANGSDORFF'S VOYAGES

George Heinrich von Langsdorff, *German naturalist and travel writer (1774-1852), wrote *Voyages and Travels in Various Parts of the World . . . 1803-1807.* An English translation appeared in 1813-14.

*Krusenstern's naturalist on his circumnavigation, Langsdorff was a close associate of Captain John DeWolf II (see "D'Wolf").
R. 7; M.D. 45

LAOCOON

In *Greek mythology, the priest Laocoön warned his fellow *Trojans to destroy the large wooden horse the Greeks offered as a gift, and indeed all gifts from Greeks. Sinon, a Greek, barely finished telling a false story about the horse's purpose to Laocoön, when two huge sea serpents came out from the ocean and wrapped their coils about Laocoön and his two sons, crushing them to death. Credulous onlookers believed that Laocoön had been punished for opposing acceptance of the horse. They dragged it through the gate to the Temple of Athena, where that night the Greeks hidden inside opened the Trojan gates to the invading Greek Army.

There is a *Vatican statue, discovered in 1506 on *Rome's Esquiline Hill: a solid piece of marble attributed to Agesandrus, Athenodorus, and Polydorus, of the School of *Rhodes (Second Century B.C.). It depicts the son of *Priam, priest of *Apollo of *Troy, crushed to death with his two sons by serpents during his sacrifice to Poseidon, after an offense to Apollo.

In his *lecture, "Statuary in Rome," M. spoke at length about the statue, calling it "the very semblance of a great and powerful man writhing with the inevitable destiny which he cannot throw off . . . . the tragic side of humanity . . . the symbol of human misfortune."
M. 107; R. 46; P. 11:3

LAPIS LAZULI

A polishable opaque deep blue mineral of great decorative value, lapis lazuli occurs in crystalline limestone, especially in Afghanistan, the modern U.S.S.R., the *Andes, and *Italy.

Ultramarine is the color principle of the mineral, formerly equal in value to gold. It was first artificially produced in the 1820's, for use in paints, paper, and decorative construction material.

M. saw a large collection of Lapis lazuli objects at the *Florence Museum of Natural History (27 March 1857).
P. 2:5

LAPLAND, --ER, --ISH

Lapland is a region of northern Europe on the Barents Sea of the *Arctic Ocean, mostly within the Arctic Circle; the southern limit of Lapp settlement is c. 65° N. The Lapps (*Swedish for "nomads") are believed to have come originally from *Mongolian *Asia to *Finland and northern *Russia. They were continually pushed north by Finnish, *Scandinavian, and Slavic migration, causing much trouble over their traditional migrations: a problem not settled until the end of the nineteenth century.

The Lapps were *Christianized by the eighteenth century, but pagan and Shamanistic rites continued during M.'s time, including belief in witches and magicians, divination and spells. O. 12's reference to occult powers of the Finns is related to M.'s suggestions about Laplanders in M.D. 73; probably he confused the two peoples.
M.D. 14; M.D. 42; M.D. 73

LARANGIEROS

Laranjeiras, or the Valley of the Oranges, is a suburb of *Rio de Janeiro, nestled at the base of the Serra da Carioca mountains.
W. 39

LA REINE
The glass ship *"Walter Redburn" brings to "Welling-borough's" great-uncle is probably patterned after one that was owned by M.'s grandfather, Thomas Melvill; it was a gift from M.'s father, Allan. None of "Wellingborough's" biographical facts about "La Reine" fit a pattern in M.'s life.
R. 1

LARKE
See "Bury St. Edmunds."
R. 44

LA ROCHEFOUCAULD, FRANCOIS
The Duc de Rochefoucauld (1613-1680) was a classical author before publishing his famous *Maximes*. As prince de Marcillac, he participated in court intrigues resulting in a brief imprisonment in the *Bastille in 1637. He regained influence during the Fronde but retired with severe wounds received in 1652. At various fashionable households, La Rochefoucauld participated in moral and intellectual debates resulting in concise pungent epigrams fashionable with cynics during the Fronde. A disavowed edition of his work appeared in Holland (1664), as *Sentences et maximes de morale*. He published five editions of his own *Réflexions ou sentences et maximes morales* (1665, -66, -71, -75, -78).
Sealts #321: *Reflections and Moral Maxims . . . With an Introductory Essay by Sainte-Beuve and Explanatory Notes* (187-), annotated.
C.M. 29; C.M. 45

LARREY
Baron Dominique Jean Larrey (1766-1842) was surgeon-in-chief to *Napoléon's Grande Armée, famous for reforms in army medicine and for his *Mémoires de Chirurgie Militaire* (1812).
W. 63

LASCAR
Native of Lashkar (see entry which follows), *India, or *Afghanistan.
M.D. 6; M.D. 40; C.M. 22

LASCAR

Lashkar is a town of Gwalior, in north central *India, 175 miles south-southeast of New Delhi. It was founded in 1810 as the military camp of the maharajah's army. "Lashkar" means "camp" in Hindostani. "Lascar" is a popularized spelling.

M. 3; M. 19; R. 34; M.D. 40

LAST DAY

See "Judgement, Day of."

R. 18; W. 34

LAST JUDGEMENT

See "Judgement, Day of."

M. 71

LAST STITCH, THE

I have not discovered reference to this practice in sources other than those that cite M. as authority; it is mentioned in Vice-Admiral Leland P. Lovette's *Naval Customs, Traditions and Usage* (4th ed, 1959), but not elucidated. Granville's 1962 *A Dictionary of Sailor's Slang* calls stitches taken through the nose of a corpse* "homeward-bound stitches." Rear-Admiral Daniel Ammen (*The Old Navy and the New*, 1891) says the corpse was "sewed in canvas weighted with shot."

W. 80

LAST TRUMP

See "Judgement, day of."

W. 33

LAST WAR WITH ENGLAND

See "War of 1812."

W. 64 and elsewhere

LATE WAR WITH ENGLAND; LATE WAR BETWEEN ENGLAND AND THE UNITED STATES

See "War of 1812."

T. 2; W. 6; W. 27; W. 39; W. 64 and elsewhere

LATIN

M. is known to have studied the Latin language at Albany Academy from 1 September 1836 to 1 March 1837 and perhaps earlier, as well, at Albany or at Columbia Grammar School in *New York City, where his brother *Gansevoort Melville is known to have thrived on the Classical Curriculum. The rigorous course of Latin study at Albany is described in David K. Titus, "Herman Melville at the Albany Academy," *Melville Society Extracts* 42 (May 1980). What "Latin lexicon" (*M.D.* 57) he used is not clear.

See also "High School."
Passim

LATIN QUARTER

On the left bank of the *Seine in *Paris, the area which surrounds the Boulevard St.-Michel is called the Latin Quarter because, in times past, scholars of the *Sorbonne congregated in the area, speaking in *Latin. University students still frequent the area of picturesque bookstores, cafes, parks, and monuments. M. took rooms nearby in December of 1849 (Nos. 12-14 Rue de Bussy: untraced—perhaps destroyed in the landfill operations that demolished many structures or perhaps "Buci"). He used details of his chamber for *I.P.*

See "Rue Dauphine."
I.P. 8

LATIN WORD FOR WHITE

Album, albi.
M.D. 42

LATIUM

In ancient *Italy, a region in the area south of *Rome. The *Aeneïd* makes it the "place of concealment" to which *Saturn fled when overthrown by *Jupiter. His descendant, Latinus, married *Aeneas, whose descendants are said to have founded Rome.
M. 149

LA TRAPPE

Soligny-la-Trappe village is in the Orne département of northwestern *France, seven miles north of Mortagne. Two miles northeast of the village is the Monastery of La Trappe (founded c. 1140), parent house of the Trappist order of Roman *Catholic monks, an extremely austere order related to the

Cistercians. The "founder" referred to in *C.M.* 22 was Rotron, Count de Perche, but M. probably wishes to allude to the courtier Armand de Rancé (1626-1700), who transformed the community into one of strictest observance.
C.M. 22

LAUDANUM
Originally, laudanum referred to a medical concoction of *Paracelsus containing precious substances. By the nineteenth century, it was the popular name for an alcoholic tincture of opium, the habitual use of which was discussed in Thomas De Quincey's *Confessions of an English Opium Eater* (1822, 1856). The prescription of laudanum by physicians was widespread during M.'s time, despite evidence about addiction and psychological counterindications.
O. 35

LAUNCELOT
Sir Launcelot of the Lake is the most romantic of the knights of King Arthur's Round Table, father to Galahad, and lover of Queen Guinevere. His love story is found as early as the 1170's, in Chrétien de Troyes's *Lancelot*; other elements of his life are found in romances of the *French prose cycle (*Lancelot, Queste del Saint Graal, Mort Artu*).
Malory's treatment in *Morte D'Arthur* is the most lavish, carrying Launcelot past the affairs with Guinevere and Elaine the Fair Maid of Astolot, through strife with Gawain, and other battles, into the priesthood and a life after death. The reference in *P.* is to *Dante's Francesca and Paolo, who fall in love while reading about the love of Launcelot and Guinevere.
P. 2:7

LAUNCELOTT'S-HEY
Among the *Liverpool streets listed in the 1677 survey was Lancelot's Hay, a north/south block running from the *Mersey waterfront to *St. Nicholas's Church. M.'s story of the widow is probably a fictional anti-Nativist (see "Foreigners") variation on a similar rendering by Carlyle. But his characterization of this and surrounding streets as overcrowded dens of vice and disease is accurate. Furthermore, such streets as Lancelot's Hay, being close to the waterfront, were the first scenes beheld by visitors to the city.
A "Hay" ("Hagh," or "Haugh") was originally an enclosed estate of rich pasture land or royal park.
R. 37

LAURAS
"Laura" is *Petrarch's name for the Avignon woman who inspired his love poetry. Her true identity is unknown.
W. 8

LAVAL
Father Honore Laval was an associate of *Father Murphy and Father *Caret in Roman *Catholic south seas missions in the 1830's. He was arrested and expelled with the other priests in *Tahiti in 1836.
O. 32

LAVATER, JOHN CASPER
Johann Caspar Lavater (1741-1801), *Swiss founder of physiognomics, or *phrenology, was a *Protestant pastor who became interested in physiognomy while searching for proof of the Divine in human life. His *Essays on Physiognomy* (1789-98), originally published in German from 1775 to 1778, won European favor, especially with *Goethe and *Fuseli. Other works are *Secret Journal of a Self Observer* (1795), *Pontius Pilate* (1782-85), *Nathanael* (1786). The patriot Lavater was deported for opposition to the French Directory and killed by a plunderer when the French took Zurich.
Two weeks before M. bought a copy of Lavater's essays (Nov., 1849), he had seen a play in *London, J.R. Planche's *Not a Bad Judge*, in which the scientist is presented as a detective/hero. Lavater's head was analysed according to the rules of phrenology in the *Home Journal* for 16 February 1850.
M. 84; M. 158; R. 54; M.D. 79

LAW OF GRAVITATION
As *Sir Isaac Newton showed, bodies tend to fall toward the earth because they have weight caused by the attraction of bodies for one another. M.'s suggestion in W. 16 that military victories are attributable less to skill than to gravity is rather a liberal interpretation of Newton's law.
W. 16

LAW OF NATIONS
See "Vattel."
W. 5

LAW OF NATURE
Generally taken to denote a system of right or justice common to mankind and independent of positive law. *W.* 35's reference is to the Law of Nature according to *Blackstone: either the revealed or the inferred word of *God. Blackstone's work suffered from his mixing of God's and men's laws, but *Americans such as M. valued his thinking.
W. 35

LAY
*J. Ross Browne (Appendix): "The adventure is divided into *lays* or shares, of which the captain's lay is generally one seventeenth of the whole; the first officer's, one twentieth; the second officer's, one forty-fifth; the third officer's, one sixtieth; the boat steerer's, from one eightieth to 120th; and the common sailor's, from 120th to 150th."
M. received an $84.00 advance before sailing on *Acushnet*, as Jay Leyda notes (*Log* I, 113).
O. 13; M.D. 16 and elsewhere

LAY
See "Comstock"; "Extracts" 64.
M.D. Extracts 64

LAYARD
Sir Austin Henry Layard (1817-1894) explored the ruins of *Assyria 1845-47, and published *Nineveh and its Remains* in 1849, after which the splendor of *Nineveh's architecture became widely known. M. saw some of the bas-reliefs unearthed by Layard at the British Museum in 1849.
Layard was also a diplomatist, liberal politician, and collector of *Italian art.
W. 86

LAZARUS
Luke 16:19-31: the beggar, Lazarus, is saved, while a rich man, *Dives, is damned, for his lack of charity.
R. 32; R. 37; W. 77; M.D. 2; M.D. 49; C.M. 2; C.M. 9; C.M. 19

LAZARUS, THE *OTHER*
In *John 11-12, Lazarus of Bethany is resurrected by *Christ after burial for four days. M. side-lined John 12:2-6 in his *Bible (Sealts #65).
M.D. 49; C.M. 19

LEANDER
See "Hero."
M. 38; W. 43

LEANING TOWER OF PISA
See "Pisa."
W. 50

LEAR
The much-beleaguered and betrayed blind ruler of
*Britain, in *Shakespeare's tragedy, *King Lear*. M. was much
affected by this story of villainy and violence. He commented in
the margin of his own copy (Sealts #460): "The infernal nature
has a valor often denied to innocence." M. borrowed the name
of "Lear's" craftily wicked daughter "*Goneril" for a similarly
"dark" lady in *C.M.* 12.
See also "Samphire."
I.P. 25

LEATHER-STOCKING
See "Cooper, James Fenimore."
C.M. 26

LEBANON, CEDAR OF
The word "Lebanon," originally referring to a frequently
snow-capped mountain range in *Syria along the
*Mediterranean coast, derives from the *Hebrew for "white."
In the pre-*Christian era, the area was covered with cedar
woods and olive groves. Cedar, a symbol of strength, was used
for ship masts and buildings such as *Solomon's House of the
Forest of Lebanon. II *Samuel, I *Kings, and I, II
*Chronicles show that *David and Solomon imported huge
quantities.
C.M. 16

LECTURE
M.'s experience as a lecturer for *lyceums, church
halls, and young men's and civic associations says much
about the contemporary lecture "circuit," *American taste,
economics, and institutions. Having made the conscious decision to stop writing, given the poor reception of *C.M.* and *The
Piazza Tales*, the loss of his publishing contacts, and continuing failure to secure a *Customs House position, M. wanted to

utilize material in his travel journals. He set about becoming a lecturer in 1857, despite his own previous rejection of the possibility and the disapproval of influential contemporaries. Sealts's *Melville as Lecturer*, which gives a complete view of M.'s three seasons on the circuit, quotes Oliver Wendell Holmes's definition of a lecturer, pronounced at a dinner party (27 May 1857) which M. attended: "a literary strumpet subject for a greater than whore's fee to prostitute himself." Despite such protests, M. believed that lecturing might be a practical occupation, even lacking any professional lecture bureau or agent to set up dates, arrange fees, and advertise.

He drew on his journals, on guide-books, and on his own published works, to construct his three lectures, which were sometimes poorly attended because of competition from other cultural events or other (better) lecturers. He collected fees ranging from $20.00 to $100.00 (in one instance), sometimes also receiving housing and other perquisites. (In Flushing, N.Y., M. received $30.00, room and board, and a bouquet of flowers.) Reviews of his performances were very mixed; those of the second season do not show much improvement over the first, and the third, abortive, season brought but one review. In *New York, *Boston, and *Pittsfield, local connections perhaps inspired reviewers' praise. But a range of complaints garnered from other areas suggests that he was a mediocre lecturer at best: the first season's topic was poor, given M.'s lack of art background and his attempt to blend the empirical with the metaphysical (an echo from reviews of his writings); his voice was too low, and he did not know how to project it; he was too formal and inanimated; his delivery was monotonous, sing-song, a "painful bore"; his remarks were not "practical." Regional biases affected reception; in some places he was considered too "chaste"; in one he was too controversial a figure, given his prose comments on missionaries and contemporary society. Some reviewers noted sleepers in the audiences.

The three lectures are reconstructed in *Melville as Lecturer* from contemporary newpaper accounts, some of which quoted at length. They were entitled: "Statues in Rome" (or "Roman Statuary"), "The South Seas," and "Traveling." What follows here is an overview of the three seasons, from which we may draw inferences about American audiences, local reviewers, association managers, financial matters, M.'s speaking talents, and the pace of his daily life for three winters.

First Season (1857-58): "Statues in Rome"
 23 November: Lawrence, *Massachusetts—Provident Association.
 24 November: Concord, *New Hampshire (Phenix Hall)—Pennacook Lyceum

2 December: *Boston, Massachusetts (Tremont Temple)—Mercantile Library Association

10 December: *Montreal, *Canada—Mercantile Library Association

21 December: *Saratoga Springs, New York

30 December: New Haven, *Connecticut (College Street Church)—Young Men's Institute

5 January: *Auburn, New York (Corning Hall)— Young Men's Association

7 January: Ithaca (Town Hall)

11 January: *Cleveland, *Ohio: Library Association

12 January: *Detroit, *Michigan—Young Men's Society

22 January: Clarksville, *Tennessee (Fowler's Hall)—Clarksville Literary Association

2 February: *Cincinnati, Ohio (Smith and Nixon's Hall)—Young Men's Mercantile Library Association

3 February: Chillicothe, Ohio—Second Presbyterian Church

10 February: *Charlestown, Massachusetts— Mishawum Literary Association

18 February: Rochester, New York (Corinthian Hall)—Athenaeum and Mechanics' Association

23 February: *New Bedford, Massachusetts (Liberty Hall)

Gross receipts for this first season, in the middle of which M. was ill with a severe cold, were $645.00. His travel expenses were $221.30, leaving a net gain of $423.70 for sixteen performances.

Second Season (1858-59): "The South Seas"

6 December: Yonkers, New York (Getty House)

14 December: *Pittsfield, Massachusetts (Burbank's Hall)

31 January: Boston (Tremont Temple)— Mechanic Apprentices Library Association

7 February: *New York City (New-York Historical Society, 2 Avenue and 11 Street)

8 February: *Baltimore, *Maryland (Universalist Church)—Mercantile Library

24 February: Chicago (Metropolitan Hall)— Young Men's Association

25 February: Milwaukee, *Wisconsin (Albany Hall)—Young Men's Association

28 February: Rockford, Wisconsin (Warner's Hall)—Young Men's Association
2 March: Quincy, *Illinois (City Hall)
16 March: Lynn, Massachusetts

The gross for the second season was $518.50 (including one fee of $23.50), a higher profit for fewer (ten) lectures than the first season had yielded, despite reviews that bore many of the same complaints.

Third Season (1859-60): "Traveling"
7 November: Flushing, *Long Island—Young Men's Association
14 February: South Danvers, Massachusetts (Peabody Institute)
21 February: Cambridgeport, Massachusetts (Dowse Institute)

This short third season yielded a gross income of $110.00. Despite a topic that promised much, the lectures failed, perhaps because of M.'s poor health. There were no further invitations. Thus, "Pierre" may be thought wiser than his creator, in his rejection of the lecture circuit (*P.* 17:2).
See also "Literary and Scientific Societies," and "Young Men's Associations."
Passim

LEDA
The ship in *R.* is named for the mythological mother of *Castor and Pollux, who perhaps conceived the twins or other children when Zeus (See "Jupiter" and "Jove") visited her in the form of a swan. She also bore Helen, Clytemnestra, and *Phoebe. A daughter of Aetolian king Thestius, Leda was the wife of Tyndareüs, a king of *Sparta.
R. 1

LEDYARD
John Ledyard (1751-1789) was born in Groton, *Connecticut. He toured the *Pacific with *Captain Cook from 1776 to 1780, traveled extensively in *Russia and *Siberia in 1787, and died in the early stages of an *African expedition along the *Nile.
R. 43; M.D. 5

LEE

The lee is the side of the ship away from the wind, as opposed to the weather side, where the wind is striking. As M. suggests, paradoxically the "lee shore," being stationary, is a danger to the ship.
Passim

LEECH

Of the class *Hirudinea*, leeches, or bloodsuckers, are predatory parasitic worms, primarily aquatic. In the early nineteenth century, the medicinal leech, *Hirudo medicinalis*, was cultivated for use in bleeding human beings to relieve symptoms of various maladies. Its use has been reviving in the twentieth century.
M. 18

LEEDS CANAL

The Leeds and *Liverpool canal was opened in 1774; locks were added in the early 1840's.
R. 41

LEGHORN

Livorno, *Italy, south of *Pisa (43°32' N., 11°18' E.), where *Shelley drowned.
W. 65

LEICESTER, EARL OF

Robert Dudley, Earl of Leicester (1532?-1588), son of John Dudley, Duke of Northumberland, was imprisoned in the *Tower in 1553 after his father's attempt to place Lady Jane Grey on the throne of *Henry VIII. The son's reputation restored before the accession of *Elizabeth I, he soon became her favorite, rewarded with honors, posts, and possessions, which caused scandalous jealous rumors, especially after the mysterious death of his wife, Amy Robsart, heroine of *Scott's *Kenilworth.

Any idea Elizabeth had of marrying Dudley was stilled, and she created him Earl of Leicester, suggesting in 1564 that he marry *Mary Stuart. Although Dudley continued hoping for a match with the Queen, in 1573 he made a secret second marriage, and several years later a third.

Despite some diplomatic achievements and strong anti-*Catholic leanings, Leicester remained suspect in the eyes of highly placed nobles. When he was general of troops against

*Spain in 1583, his military performance was satisfactory, but his political gaffes finally brought his recall to a lesser post.

Dudley was a handsome, personable man, a patron of arts and letters. The "horn" M. says he presented to the Queen (*M.D.* 32) is, of course, a phallus.
M. 139; M.D. 32

LEIPSIC
Leipzig (or Leipsic), in east-central modern *Germany (sixty-five miles west-northwest of Dresden, ninety miles southwest of *Berlin) is the largest city of *Saxony and a chief commercial and cultural center, renowned (until the Second World War) for book and music publishing. An ancient *Slav settlement, it was founded around a fort and chartered in 1174, becoming famous for fairs in the early *Middle Ages. The printing industry made it a publishing center from the late fifteenth century. Modern museums and scholarly institutions testify to the accomplishments of its residents: J.S. Bach is buried here; *Goethe studied here and set part of *Faust* in a local *keller*; Mendelssohn, Schumann, and Wagner lived here; *Schiller and others made it a literary center.
R. 1

LEITH
*Edinburgh's Port of Leith was a fashionable beach and horse-racing resort in the eighteenth century, until bypassed by Portobello, *Scotland. In *I.P.*, perhaps another reference to fallen glory.
I.P. 18; I.P. 19

LE MAIR, STRAITS OF
Estrecho de Le Maire, Argentina: 55° 15' S., 65° 30' W.
W. 24

LEMSFORD
This fictional character may be based on one or both of two originals. George W. Wallace was Ship's Scribe on *United States*; he probably wrote the ship's journal used by Charles R. Anderson for *Melville in the South Seas*. Another likely candidate is Ephraim Curtiss Hine, who published *The Haunted Barque, and Other Poems*, as well as *Orlando Melville*, a story based on the frigate's history.
W. Passim

LENOX

The town of Lenox, *Massachusetts, is in *Berkshire County, seven miles south of *Pittsfield. It was settled c. 1750. M. had many occasions to visit Lenox, the site of *Hawthorne's "Red Cottage" (which burned in 1890 and was rebuilt; now used in conjunction with the Tanglewood Music Festival), as well as a court at which his father-in-law, Chief Justice *Lemuel Shaw, sometimes presided.
I.P. 3

LENT, --S

The *Christian period of pre-Easter fasting and mortification starting with Ash Wednesday falls for the most part in the month of March (for which it is named through Anglo-Saxon derivation).
See also "Ramadan."
M.D. 16; M.D. 17

LEO, JOHN

Leo Africanus (c. 1485-c. 1554), as he is known in Europe, was a *Spanish-born *Arab traveler/scholar: *Al-Hasan Ibn Muhammad al-Wazzan al-Zaiyati* (or *al-Fasi*). He traveled much in northern *Africa and was kept in *slavery by Pope *Leo X, having been captured by *pirates. He adopted *Christianity, taking the name Johannes Leo but returned as a *Moslem to Africa. His greatest work, *Descrittione dell'Africa* (1526) was translated into English in 1600 (*A Geographical Historie of Africa*). It contributed much to learning about Africa and Islam.

The quotation in *M.D.* 104 is from the *Harris collection, not from Leo.

Material of Africanus relative to *India was also available to M. in *Harris's "Collection."
M.D. 104

LEONARDO

Leonardo de Vinci (1452-1519), the classic Renaissance genius, was a painter, mathematician, hydrologist, aviationist, physicist, astronomer, engineer, anatomist, naturalist, and philosopher. In 1481, he left his native *Florence, where his work had astonished instructors, to live in Milan, where his *Madonna of the Rocks* (1483) and his Cathedral mural, *The Last Supper* (1495) showed his interest in the relation of psychology and science to painting. The *Mona Lisa* was completed in Florence between 1500 and 1506. After another period in Milan, he went to *Rome, where it is presumed he painted *The Madonna and St. Anne*. At the invitation of Francis I, he spent his last three years in *France, focusing mainly on science and making numerous drawings.

Leonardo conducted dissections to discover the structure of the human body, prepared architectural plans that were widely emulated, and left many unfinished works, testifying to the breadth of his interests.

In 1857, M. saw a self-portrait in Rome and other works in Milan. He commented at length in his journal (7 April) on *The Last Supper* (which was already badly deteriorated). Dwelling upon Leonardo's capturing of the human implications of the event, M. says: "The joys of the banquet soon depart . . . . the glow of sociability is so evanescent, selfishness so lasting."
P. 5:4; P. 26:1

LEO, POPE
There have been thirteen *Popes named Leo. The one referred to in *M.* is Leo X (Giovanni de'Medici, 1475-1521), Pope from 1513 to 1521. The second son of Lorenzo de'*Medici, he was placed in *Church service at the age of seven and rose constantly to higher positions. At the death of Julius II, as the younger Cardinals' candidate, he was ordained to the priesthood, consecrated a Cardinal, and enthroned as Pope within four days' time. His tenure was marked by continuing problems with foreign influence, schisms, a *French invasion, and internal crises including a plot to poison him.

The schism with *Germany, brought about by Leo's accumulation of political power, nepotism, and granting of indulgences, came to a head when *Martin Luther published his ninety-five theses, instigating widespread revolt and ultimately the *Protestant Reformation.

Leo is remembered as a patron of arts and letters, bestower upon *Henry VIII of the title "*Defender of the Faith," and excommunicator of Luther. (The reference in *M.* 3 to a talk with Luther is an ironic one.)
M. 3

LEO
See "Zodiac."
M. 169; M.D. 99

LEPANTO

The site of the last great galley battle (1571) in the straits between the Gulf of Patras and the Gulf of *Corinth in *Greece, where united *Christian naval forces destroyed the *Turkish fleet. It is memoralized in many paintings and poems.
W. 50

LESSON

René-Primivère Lesson (1794-1849), *French traveler and zoologist.
M.D. 32

LETHE, --AN

In myth, one of the five rivers of the underworld, *Hades: Acheron (river of woe) and Cocytus (river of lamentation), which separate the underworld from that above, and Styx (river of the unbreakable oath taken by gods), and *Phlegethon (the river of fire).

Lethe is the river of forgetfulness (from the Greek *letho*, to cause not to know). After the descent into the underworld in the *Aeneid*, the Sibyl Anchises leads Aeneas to the obligatory drink from Lethe before returning to the world above. Aeneas sees those who are to be his descendants waiting to lose the memory of previous lives and learns what will be his future path.
M. 6; I.P. 19

LETTERS OF MART

Commissions or licenses issued by a government to a private armed vessel, authorizing reprisals on an enemy, the first letters of mart were issued about the middle of the thirteenth century, during the reign of *England's Edward I. Vessels carrying such commissions, also called "letters of marque," continue into the present, sometimes constituting a license for crime.

During the *Revolution, the *Continental Congress had issued letters of marque to 1,697 *American vessels manned by 58,400 men (and mounting 14,872 guns). Despite armaments on *British merchantmen, American privateers seized prizes worth $18 million, as well as munitions and supplies from 2,980 merchant vessels.

In the *War of 1812, few British prizes were taken, despite American hopes that privateers would again be a decisive element in a victory.

See also "pirates."
W. Dedication

LEUWENHOECK

Anton Van Leeuwenhoek (or Leuwenhoek; 1632-1723) was a *Dutch microscopist who made many improvements in lenses and furthered examination of blood corpuscles, muscles, teeth, dog spermatozoa, and plants. He made the first drawing of bacteria (1683) and greatly increased knowledge of lower animals, especially ants, parasites such as the flea, and destructive pests such as the weevil. He demonstrated that shellfish were not generated from sand nor eels from dew. A member of the *Royal Society, he published much in *Philosophical Transactions* and *Memoirs of the *Paris Academy of Sciences*.
M.D. 56

LEVANT

A general reference to countries on the *Mediterranean's eastern shores: *Greece, *Turkey, *Syria, *Lebanon, *Egypt, modern *Palestine (or to non-European coastlands in the near east; the former French mandate over Syria and Lebanon was referred to as the Levant States).

M.'s *Journal of a Visit to Europe and the Levant: October 11, 1856--May 6, 1857* records his impressions of Greece, Turkey, Lebanon, Egypt, and the *Holy Land. Despite some pleasant moments in the area, M.'s holiday was somewhat marred by recurrent depression, especially in the Levant.
R. 35; W. 71; W. 75

LEVANTER

Local name for a mistral-type easterly wind in the *Mediterranean, often bringing cool weather from the mountain gaps.
M.D. 44

LEVELERS; LEVELLERS

In *England, during the reign of *Charles I and the Commonwealth, a group of radical republicans who wanted all men to be politically on a level respecting the franchise and eligibility for office. *Cromwell suppressed them after mutinies in 1647 and 1649.

*Irish eighteenth-century agrarian agitators, the Whiteboys, were likewise called Levellers, as were various schismatical *Christian bodies (See "Acephali").

M. was called a Leveller, especially after publication of *W*.
M. 60

LEVIATHAN
Old Testament sea monster, especially in *Job 41:1-34.
See also "Hobbes."
0. 76; 0. 78; 0. 79; 0. 82; M. 10; M. 13; M. 38; M. 94; R. 21; M.D.
Passim

LEVIATHAN
See "Hobbes, Thomas," and see "Extracts" 21.
M.D. Extracts 21

"LEVIATHAN"
M.'s fictional ship is probably partly based on *Charles &*
Henry, a whaler on which he shipped from *Eimeo, serving
from November 1842 until April 1843. Captain was John
Brown Coleman, Jr. (1800-?), who married into the *Coffin
family of shipowners. *Charles & Henry* was registered at
*Nantucket in 1835.
Charles & Henry may also be the original for
"*Arcturion" of *M*. and *"Julia" of *T*. and *O*.
O. Passim

LEVIATHANIC MUSEUM
See "Hull."
M.D. 102

LEVITICUS
The third book of the *Bible, Leviticus deals with the duties and legislation of the priests of the Tribe of Levi, descendants of the third son of *Jacob and Leah, who were located in
forty-eight cities of *Palestine in ancient times.
The book contains codes of laws addressed to *Israelite
worshipers and priests through *Moses. There are rules about
sacrificial worship, offerings, prohibitions, purification and
other rituals, the Day of Atonement, the Law of Holiness.
The reference to beards in *W*. 85 comes from Leviticus
19:27 and 21:5.
W. 85

LEXICON
Sealts #s 550, 551, 552 are editions of *Noah Webster, *An
American Dictionary of the English Language* (N.Y.: Harper,
1846 or later editions).
See also "Johnson, Samuel."
M.D. 53

LEXINGTON

Lexington, Middlesex County, *Massachusetts, is ten miles northwest of *Boston. It was settled in 1640, and incorporated in 1713. Lexington was the scene of the 19 April 1775 battle that began the *American *Revolution. The skirmish began when *England's General Thomas Gage, Royal Governor of Massachusetts, sent a detachment to Concord to seize military stores; colonists responded with what *Emerson was to call "the shot heard 'round the world," at nearby Concord.
I.P. 3

LEY

Lye.
M.D. 98

LEYDEN

Leyden (or Leiden) is a city of the west *Netherlands ten miles northeast of The Hague, on the Old Rhine River. Among its claims to fame: *Boerhaave taught at the University (founded 1575); the Leyden Jar was invented here; it was the home of the Pilgrims for eleven years before their embarkation to *America; it has been famous for textiles (fourteenth to eighteenth centuries), printing (sixteenth century) and for the cheese mentioned in *M.D.* 101, its market among the largest in the Netherlands.
M.D. 101

LIBRA

See "Zodiac."
M.D. 99

LIBYA, --N

In M.'s time, the *Greek name "Libya" referred not only to the modern nation of that name (so called by the *Italians in the twentieth century) but to much of northern *Africa. The *Romans had divided the area into Marmarica, or Lower Libya, and Cyrenaica, or Upper Libya, an area which came to comprise three historical regions: Tripolitania, Cyrenaica, and Fezzan. The 1,000 mile-long coastline, deeply indented by the Gulf of Sidra, borders the *Sahara Desert. In the nineteenth century, it was almost completely undeveloped and unknown, inhabited only by nomadic Berbers and *Arabs who could withstand the extremely hot, dry, and windy climate.

M.'s excursions of 1856 (-1857) brought him along the coastline. He passed *Algiers and was struck by the "Piratical corsair look" (26 November) of the territory of the *Barbary *pirates.

The allusion in *R*. 46 to *Alexander's "white temple in the Libyan oasis" refers to the Libyans' granting of a complimentary embassy to that conqueror.
M. 75; R. 46

"LICK HIS BLOOD"
    See "Ahab."
M.D. 16

LIFE INSURANCE COMPANIES; MARINE INSURANCE COMPANIES
    Scientific life insurance, using mortality statistics, started in the *United States in the early nineteenth century. The mutual companies arose in the 1840's, advertising heavily to convince the public of the need for life insurance; endowment insurance began in the 1850's. Premiums were extra in the case of unhealthful residence areas, military service, frontier travel, or hazardous occupation (such as whaling).
    The older "Marine Insurance Companies" (*M.D.* 121) insured shipowners, merchants, bankers, and mortgagees. Policies were individually drawn up using ratings of Lloyd's Register of Shipping (see "A. No. 1) and taking into account special risks involving cargo and facilities such as Try-works. "*Flask" may be correct in assuming that any ship of "*Ahab's" costs extra to insure, given his reputation.
M.D. 7; M.D. 121

LIFE-PRESERVER
    In addition to common name for buoyant ring or vest used to give flotation, a life preserver is a short stick loaded with lead, used by burglars, or a set of brass knuckles.
C.M. 45

LIGNUM-VITAE
    Guaiacum officinale: wood of life, representing the *New Jerusalem's *tree of life, in *Revelation 22:2.
C.M. 9

LIKE CURES LIKE
      See "Homeopathy" and "Hahneman."
M.D. 129

LIMA; LIMEEAN; LIMEESE
      Lima, *Peru (12° 06' S., 77° 03' W.) was founded in 1535
by *Francisco Pizarro. It was extensively damaged by
earthquakes in 1687, 1746, and 1828, but much elaborate architecture remained intact in M.'s time. He visited on forty-eight
hours' leave from *United States sometime around *New
Year's day, 1844. Contemporary visitors noticed the city's decay, but failed to substantiate M.'s claim of bleached pallor.
They remarked on the Cathedral (1625), the bull ring (1768), the
frescoed and gilded houses with latticed verandas, and the
colonnaded grand square of colorful shops. It would seem that
M. arbitrarily tied what he saw as Lima's iniquity and corrupt
*Catholicism to the whiteness he connected with evil.
      M. may have been influenced after the publication of
M.D. by an article in Harper's New Monthly Magazine
(October 1851): "Lima and the Limanians." (This article bore
greatly on M.'s composition of "Benito Cereno," as Allan
Moore Emery points out in "'Benito Cereno' and Manifest Des-
tiny": Nineteenth-Century Fiction 39 [1], June 1984, 48-68.)
T. 11; O. 59; M. 61; M. 165; R. 56; W. 42; W. 76; W. 85; M.D. 42;
M.D. 54; M.D. 100; P. 8:2

LINCOLN, ABRAHAM
      Abraham Lincoln (1809-65) did not become prominent
until M. had finished novel-writing and is not alluded to by
name in the novels. He served in *Congress (1847-49) in opposition to the *Mexican War and campaigned unsuccessfully for
the Senate in 1855. Lincoln was one of the founders of the
*Republican Party (1856) and served as the sixteenth
*President (1860-65). His opposition to *slavery culminated in
the *Civil War and the Emancipation Proclamation (1862)
which intensified it. He was reelected (1864) and was assassinated the following year by John Wilkes Booth.
      M. was recommended to Lincoln for a Consulship (1861)
but was not appointed. He met the President 22 March 1861,
shaking his hand along with other well-wishers and commenting in a letter to his wife that "Old Abe" was "much better
looking" and "younger looking" than he had expected: "He
shook hands like a good fellow." M.'s poem, "The Martyr,"
bemoans Lincoln's death.

LINDEN

Linden trees, of the genus *Tilia*, have dense heart-shaped leaves. The *American variety is familiarly called basswood. Tropical varieties of lindens and jutes are *Tiliaceae*.
(In "flower language," linden signifies Conjugal Love.)
M. 193

LINE, THE

The equinoctial line or *equator has been called the Line since the sixteenth century. *The Oxford English Dictionary* cites use in 1588, Parke's translation of *Mendoza's History of* *China*.
Passim

LINEAR ASPERA

See *"femur."*
W. 62

LINGUA-FRANCA

Any jumble of languages by which different people communicate: i.e. Pidgin English used in the Far East, or the species of *Italian spoken on the *Mediterranean coast.
M. 3

LINNAEUS

Carolus Linnaeus (Carl Von Linné;   1707-1778), *Swedish botanist, founded the binomial system of plant and animal names. As lecturer in botany (with medical degree) at Uppsala, he began publishing works leading to his *Species plantarum* (1753) and *Genera plantarum* (1754), the starting points for plant nomenclature. His most important work was the *Systema naturae* (1758). A delight in classification also led to work in mineral and disease classification, and after his death his collections were bought by the founder of the Linnean Society, *Britain's oldest biological society.
M.D. 32

LION, THE

See "Zodiac."
M.D. 99

LION'S DEN
>See "Daniel; -s."
I.P. 5

LIPOGRAPHS
>A fanciful name for kisses, along with the then-current "lip-clap," "lip-favor," "lip-labor," etc.
P. 17:2

LISBON
>The capital of *Portugal is a seaport on the right bank of the *Tagus estuary; Lisbon Bay is a narrow (two miles wide) channel to the *Atlantic. The city was built on the terraced-hill site of *Phoenician and *Roman settlements. The *Crusaders helped liberate the city from the *Moors in 1147, and it reached its greatest prosperity in the sixteenth century. *Camöens was born in Lisbon in 1524. The *Spanish Armada sailed from the Bay between 1580 and 1640. The earthquake of 1755 (referred to in *M.* 165) destroyed most of the city, but there are still remains of Moorish castles, a Hieronymite convent, and the tombs of the *Braganza kings.
M. 165; I.P. 16

LITERARY AND SCIENTIFIC SOCIETIES
>See "Academy of Arts and Sciences," "lecture," "Young America in Literature."
P. 17:2

"LITTLE JULE"
>See "Julia."
0. 2

"LIVER"
>The bird which M. represents as "extinct" and imaginatively represented on the *Liverpool city arms is, rather, an imaginary bird derived by seventeenth century antiquarians from the heraldic bird on the city arms: the eagle of *St. John the Evangelist.
R. 30

LIVERPOOL

England's second largest seaport (after *London, 200 miles southeast) is in *Lancashire, on the right bank of the *Mersey estuary, with the city center three miles from open sea. The name may derive from that of a mythical bird (see "Liver") or may be derived from the *Norse *Hlithar-pollr* ("pool of the slopes"), bestowed by Norse visitors of the eighth century.

Liverpool was chartered by *King John in 1208. Its development is connected to the "Pool," a river inlet originally of curving, shifting channels and sandbanks leading from a boggy inland sandstone ridge. Clearing of the Pool, dredging of rivers, and cutting of canals opened up public access to the borough and surroundings in the 1700's. Until the time of *Elizabeth I, Liverpool's economy had been based on agriculture. A struggle between the town Corporation and private owners of water rights kept it in a feudalistic bind. The turning point in development was breaking of this private ownership system and success in salt trade, which led to dealing in other commodities. The *slave trade was most productive, but local coal and iron and imported tobacco and sugar were also lucrative. The diversity of commodities led to specialization in docks and other facilities, which is turn led to shipbuilding as an additional endeavor.

By the time of Defoe's glowing comments in *A Tour through the Whole Island of Great Britain* (1724-26), Liverpool was a highly prosperous city, but with dramatic disparity between the lives of the rich and the poor and with much inefficiency caused by the vestment of authority in multiple agencies or, indeed, in no agencies. Reforms of the Municipal Corporations Act of 1835 set about curing many of Liverpool's ills, but by the time the nineteen year-old M. arrived (on his first voyage), there had not been much visible improvement. The docks were becoming the wonders of the maritime world, handling some 1,500 vessels per year, and there were many wealthy residents and new buildings, but the contrast between opulence and squalor was overt. M. arrived on *St. Lawrence* (see "Julia") on 2 July 1839 and left on 13 August, having confessed in a letter to his mother (9 July) that he would gladly exchange the sights of Liverpool for home. He had a $3.00 wages advance and was boarded ashore (near *St. Nicholas Church), but he was in no position to partake of local amenities, much less travel to London, as "Wellingborough" does in *R*. In many other respects, however, M.'s details about Liverpool in that book are accurate reportage on the city at that time. Unemployment was exacerbated by the presence of numerous emigrants from *Ireland, *Wales, and the English Midlands. Some 20,000 people lived in cellars, some 40,000 in slums, representing perhaps one-third of the population. Smog, ashpits, and privies that overflowed into the streets brought typhus and consumption; the average death age in the 1830's was seventeen. Prior to the reform act, there had been no police force beyond fifteen elderly night watchmen (see "Dock Police"), and with one pub for each 150 inhabitants, and 2,900 prostitutes (according to an 1840 survey), violent crime was rampant.

M. returned to Liverpool in 1856, remaining in the general area from 8 to 18 November. Despite a visit to *Hawthorne, the marvel of two miles of docks that set the pattern for the world, the wherewithal to enjoy things previously denied, and the prospect of the long tour of Europe and the *Levant of which he had always dreamed, his mood was grim. His journal entry for 17 November reads: "Tired of Liverpool."

As Gilman and others have shown, much of M's material on Liverpool was probably drawn from print sources. The seedier aspects of the city were commonly described in readily available materials (*Sailor's Magazine, Penny Magazine, Penny Cyclopaedia*). Allan Melvill's (see "Walter Redburn") putative guidebook *The Picture of Liverpool* ... (London, 1818) was almost certainly consulted. (A copy of the Liverpool, 1808 edition [*R*. 30, cited as 1803] in which the young "Wellingborough" scrawled pictures has not been located.) If indeed the young M. consulted this work, it could not have been an accurate guide for him because by 1839 much of old Liverpool had been torn down or was in the process, the medieval structures being replaced by modern commercial buildings.

M.'s (*R*. 41) claim that the latitude of Liverpool (53°25' N.) "very nearly" corresponds to that of Cape *Horn (55°59' S.) is a bit overdrawn.

See also entries for individual locations and structures, as well as "Manchester" (for Liverpool-Manchester Railway), "Bridgewater Canal."
O. 1; R. Passim; W. 73

LIVY
Titus Livius (59 B.C. - ? A.D. 17), *Roman historian of the city from its beginnings to 9 B.C., is our major source of legend about Rome and the second *Punic War. There are many errors of fact in the thirty-five (of 142) surviving books, but Livy is still considered important, especially for his encouragement of other historians. He wrote in the rhetorical tradition of *Cicero, aiming at pure Latinity, and inspiring much patriotism.

The quotation in *R*. 53 is from Livy's "Combat of the *Horatii and Curiatii."
R. 31; R. 53

LIZARD

Lizard was a small *British warship on patrol off the
*American coast in 1776: on the Gulf of *Maine and the line
between *Cape Cod and Cape Sable, *Canada.
I.P. 20

LOAD-STONE ROCK; LOADSTONE

Magnetite, magnetic iron ore, or lodestone, is a strongly
magnetic lustrous black opaque mineral found in igneous
rocks. *Middle-Ages pilots were called "lodesmen" for their
use of the stone in navigation.
M. 28; M.D. 124

LOB-DOMINION

Nathaniel Ames characterizes this substance as tea or
coffee tasting as though it were made from "two buckets of water and an old shoe" (p. 125).
W. 32

LOB-SCOUSE

Mentioned by *Smollett and *Cooper, this is a stew made
of meat, vegetables, and ship's biscuit.
W. 32

LOCHIEL'S

Sir Ewan Cameron of Lochiel (1629-1719),
hunter/warrior and ruler of the Cameron Clan, is memorialized as "the Ulysses of the Highlands," in *Macaulay's *History
of England*. He is supposed to have killed the last wolf in
*Scotland.
C.M. 25

LOCH KATRINES

Some twenty-five miles northeast of *Glasgow,
*Scotland, Loch Katrine is considered one of the world's most
picturesque lakes, surrounded by wild woods and lofty mountains of the Scottish Highlands.
*Rev. Charles Stewart had earlier made the connection
between *Botafogo and Scotland which M. makes in *W*.
W. 50

LOCK-AND-SIN

Lock hospitals were originally used in *England for lepers, who were secluded. They were later used for treatment of venereal disease, as was the Lock lazar-house in Southwark, England. The Lock hospital at Kingsland had a sundial inscribed: "*Post voluptatem misericordia*," roughly "Compassion after pleasure."
P. 16:3

LOCKE'S; LOCKE'S ESSAYS

John Locke (1632-1704), Enlightenment philosopher/exponent of liberal ideas, was born into a traditional middle-class *English Anglican family. At Christ Church, *Oxford, he became dissatisfied with prevailing scholastic philosophy and, starting with *Descartes, pursued his own broad reading plan, leading to *Essays on the Law of Nature* (1662-63; first English transl. 1954). Refusing holy orders and the practice of medicine, he continued study when in 1667 he joined the household of the liberal Lord Ashley (Sir Anthony Ashley Cooper), by 1672 Earl of Shaftesbury, as physician, adviser, and secretary focusing on the colonies. In 1667 he wrote an essay revealing increasingly liberal views on religious liberty and toleration, Divine Right, and judicial power.

He was made fellow of the *Royal Society in 1668 and in 1671 began drafts of the *Essay Concerning Human Understanding*, which he worked on in *France for several years. By 1679, Shaftesbury was leading *Whig opposition to *Charles II, and Locke fled to Holland, becoming further liberalized. In 1687, he published an abridged *Human Understanding* and anonymous works supporting separation of the sacred and the secular while maintaining safeguards against religious incursions by "foreign powers," James II (see "Stuart") and *Louis XIV (see "Bourbon"), representing Roman Catholic threats.

Locke returned to England when James was displaced by * King William III and in 1689 anonymously published *Two Treatises on Government*, vindicating the Revolution of 1688-89, and *A Letter Concerning Toleration*. In 1690, the complete *Human Understanding* was published and had wide influence on the search for "ultimate truth." It was republished throughout his life. In 1693, he published *Some Thoughts Concerning Education*, and in 1695 (anonymously), *The Reasonableness of Christianity*, which appealed to Unitarians and Deists. Essays on economics preceded work on the Epistles of *St. Paul and *The Conduct of the Understanding* (published posthumously).

The canon shows the increasing liberalization of Locke's thought, which began close to *Hobbe's authoritarianism. Views most discussed were on: the child's mind as *tabula rasa*; distinction between wit and judgement, rejection of metaphysics in favor of empirical experience as teacher; the workings of the mind and use of language; refutation of absolutism in government, in favor of "government as trust"; individual rights and sovereignty of the people; division of power; rejection of *determinism ; education of body and mind by parents and institutions; support of *Latitudinarists, Cambridge Platonists, and Dutch Remonstrants in religion, despite his lifelong fidelity to Anglicanism.

In *M.D.* (Chapter 73), "Locke's head" represents Locke's emphasis on sense data in the accumulation of knowledge.
W. 41; M.D. 73

LOCKJAW
An acute infectious disease (tetanus) caused by a common bacillus. Symptoms are muscular rigidity (especially of the jaw) and spasms. Tetanus has been known since the fifth century B.C. Although Joseph Lister studied it in the nineteenth century, isolation of the bacillus and understanding of its nature did not occur until the mid-1880's. At M.'s time, death from tetanus was common.
M. 11

LOCOFOCOS
The reference in *I.P.* 16 is to friction matches which replaced sulphur matches (*lucifers) in the 1830's. The name is from the Latin *locus in quo*, referring to the "place of fire," and at first referred to a self-lighting cigar (patented in 1834).

But M.'s allusion covertly applies to the radical *Jacksonian branch of the *Democratic party. A schism had been developing when at a Tammany Hall meeting in 1835 the conservatives then in power shut off the gas lights in response to the radicals' threatened insurrection. The radicals were prepared, lighting candles with pocket locofoco matches, thus gaining their sobriquet. The mostly Eastern movement represented what was to become the pervading political stance of the party: they opposed monopolies and corporations and favored free trade and hard (rather than paper) money. For rather complex economic reasons, they opposed *abolition, while theoretically standing against *slavery.

M.'s brother, *Gansevoort, was a Locofoco Democrat who campaigned for *Polk in *Tennessee, *Kentucky, *Ohio, *New York, and *Massachusetts, in 1844.
I.P. 16

LOGAN

Shawnee Indian Chief (James, or John) Logan (1725-1780), whose peaceful family was murdered at Yellow Creek, on the *Ohio River, thereafter waged war on *Pennsylvania/Ohio border settlements. He is quoted and defended in *Thomas Jefferson's *Notes on the State of Virginia* (1781).
M. 127; M.D. 34; C.M. 25

LOGARITHM TABLES

Before the invention of the *calculating machine, logarithms (invented in the seventeenth century) were basic tools to speed up tedious large-scale computations. Values in a logarithm table show numerical correspondences that can replace multiplication by addition. A logarithm is the exponent of that power to which a fixed number (the base) must be raised in order to produce a given number (the antilogarithm): 3 is the logarithm of 8 to the base 2.

By M.'s time, modern theory, extending to negative and complex numbers, had been completed and accepted, so that *Bowditch and other astronomers could provide reliable tables for navigation.
R. 18

LOGGERHEAD TURTLES

A very large species of turtle, shaped like the loggerheads or clogs put on the feet of grazing horses in *England. The turtles are found mainly in the *Indian and *Pacific Oceans.
W. 37

L'OLLONAIS

An early seventeenth-century *pirate.
M. 89

LOMBARDS; LONGOBARDI

In northern *Italy, a kingdom of Germanic people, flourishing from 568 to 774. Traces of Lombard civilization in *Germany date from the first century A.D.; Lombards led a pastoral life until their fourth century migration south. Their tribal name was Langobardas (classical Lat., *Langobardi*; Medieval Lat., *Longobardi*). Traces of Lombard civilization still exist in the Italian language and in judicial institutions.

See also "Beards."
W. 84

LOMBARDY

The northern *Italian region is bordered by *Switzerland on the north. The richest lake region in Italy became part of the *Roman Empire in the third century B.C., suffering many barbaric invasions and becoming in the sixth century A.D. the center of the kingdom of the Lombards before passing to *Charlemagne. Under the rule of *Spain, *Austria, and *France from 1796 to 1814, Lombardy was liberated in 1859, becoming part of Italy. M. visited 6-9 April 1857, stopping at *Milan and *Lake Como, which he compared to Lake George (journal, 8 April).
M. 168; M.D. 37; M.D. 104

LOMBARDY, IRON CROWN OF

The bejewelled gold diadem of Constantine (see "Constantinople") was traditionally used to crown *Holy Roman Emperors. *Charlemagne (774) and *Charles V (1530) were crowned with it; *Napoléon placed it on his own head in 1805; Ferdinand I of *Austria used it at his coronation in 1838.

The Iron Crown had been discovered in *Jerusalem in 326 by Helena, mother of Constantine, and was said to contain a nail from the cross of *Jesus. In 1866, the Emperor of Austria restored the crown to Italy, where it was placed in the cathedral of Monza.
M.D. 37

LONDON

The capital city of *England (and of the modern United Kingdom) is a port located on both banks of the *Thames near the North Sea estuary. It is one of the world's most populated and industrialized cities (although inner-city population has declined since the mid-nineteenth century). Even in M.'s time, London extended far into suburban areas centered around the ancient *Roman City on the north bank. Londinium is thought to have been created c. A.D. 43 and abandoned by the Romans in the early fifth century. The *Saxons were established by the sixth century, and *Christianity was introduced by the seventh. By. M.'s time, construction and concurrent over-population had made London the quintessential large city, with affluence existing side by side with extreme poverty. Although improved police, education, and hospital services had been introduced, along with better transport and amenities such as gas street lighting, such basics as sanitation remained primitive or, in some areas, non-existent. Apparently attitudes toward the poor were like those expressed in *C.M.* 7: "To that mob of misery, what is a joint here and a loaf there?"

Although M.'s "Wellingborough" visits London in *R.*, M. could not have done so when he was in England as a sailor in 1839. So his first personal experience of the city occurred in 1849 (6-27 November, 13-24 December). In November, he played the tourist, visiting all of the appropriate (and some "inappropriate") sites, but he was in London primarily to arrange publication of *W*. His energies were directed to finding the best offer for that book, with a publisher's advance, if possible. He stayed at 25 Craven Street, *Strand, and walked the city's streets daily, buying books, and attempting to use his letters of introduction. His journal entry for 25 November reads, "'Oh Solitude! where are the charms' &c. --." He returned from the Continent on 13 December, quite homesick while reading accumulated mail, and increasingly worried about finances. By 15 December, he had a £200 advance and debated with himself about lingering to gather material. Home ties prevailed, and M. booked passage on *Independence*, to depart from *Portsmouth. His introduction letters paid off in his remaining four days; material for "The Paradise of Bachelors" and "Poor Man's Pudding and Rich man's Crumbs" presented itself at dinners at the *Temple and the Erechtheum Club, *St. James. Here M. also met the publisher Charles Knight, whose *London* he had purchased on 15 December (Sealts #312), and whose *Penny Magazine and Penny Cyclopaedia* he often used as sources. He hurriedly purchased gifts and said goodbyes on 24 December.

M.'s second visit (26 April--3 May 1857) occurred at the conclusion of six months of travel in a depressed mood; London did not cheer him.

London materials M. might have used, in addition to Knight's include George Frederick *Cruchley's Picture of London* (1847; Sealts #166); 'Old Map of London' (1766; Sealts #330a); *The London Carcanet* (a children's book of 1831; Sealts #331); John *Murray's Handbook for Modern London* (1851; Sealts #379); *The Picture of London for 1818* (his father's book; Sealts #402); Angus Bethune Reach, *London on the Thames* (184?; Sealts #418); Thomas Sherlock, *A Letter from the Lord Bishop of London* (1750; his father's book; Sealts #472).

London club-houses (*R.* 61) have existed since at least the time of *Henry IV, and their meeting places have often gained much fame: the Mermaid Tavern housed the Friday Street Club (perhaps founded by *Raleigh); Devil Tavern at *Temple Bar was host to *Ben Jonson's Apollo Club. By the eighteenth century their numbers had increased remarkably. The Sublime Society of *Beefsteaks, and Boodles, were forerunners of literary clubs such as *Johnson's Ivy Lane Club at Turk's Head Coffee House, and the Kit-Cat Club. By the nineteenth century, Picadilly was the heart of club territory, and most clubs had become gambling dens, such as M.'s *Aladdin's Palace, or fraternity-like groups designed to foster special interests. M. dined at several exclusive London clubs in 1849, including the Erechtheum and the Reform.

"London Dock" (*W.* 37) and "London dock vault" (*C.M.* 24) refer to the wine in wine cellars beneath London dock warehouses. Visits might be made and samples purchased in M.'s time.

The fire of London (*I.P.* 19) began on 2 September 1666, according to the diary of Samuel Pepys (Sealts #398), raging for five days and destroying perhaps four-fifths of the city (including *St. Paul's Church). Gunpowder was used to stop the spread of the flames; this perhaps explains the *O.* 45 reference to "the way fires are put out in London." (Or M. may allude to Pepys's suggestion that they be extinguished by the method Swift invented for "Gulliver": urination.) Setting of the fire was attributed to Roman *Catholics. (The *plague epidemic followed extinguishing of the flames.)

Fog (*I.P.* 25) was apparently not a serious London problem until the seventeenth century, when authorities told *Charles II that the impurity of the air caused more Londoners to take medication than any other people on earth; the city could be smelled from miles away; even palaces were dark and smoky. *Fumifugium: or the aer and smoak of London dissipated. Together with some Remedies humbly proposed* was published in 1661 (and reissued in 1933). The 1667 fog, which extended some sixteen miles to the east, was so great that coach accidents were common, visibility being only a few feet; robberies were rampant, and ships were guided into port by drums. In 1758, *Benjamin Franklin complained: "the whole town is one great smoky house, and every street a chimney, the air full of floating sea-coal soot." In 1806, deaths occurred when people lost their way. M's London journal for 24 November 1849 says: "Upon sallying out this morning encountered the oldfashioned pea soup London fog—of a *gamboge color. It was lifted, however, from the ground & floated in mid air. When lower, it is worse. Lamps lighted   . . . . "

See related entries which follow, as well as: "Apsley House"; "Bank of England"; "Barbican"; "Blackfriars, Black Friar"; "Blackheath"; "Bondstreet"; "Bow Bells"; "Bridewell"; "Colchurch"; "Covent Garden"; "East India Company"; "Elephant and Castle"; "Euston Square"; "Exchange, the"; "Exeter Hall"; "Hampton Court"; "Holborn"; "Horse Guards"; "Houndsditch"; "Hyde-Park"; "King's Bench"; "Middlesex"; "Moorfields"; "Parliament"; "Peter of Colchurch"; "Radcliffe Highway"; "Red-Cross street"; "Regent Street"; "Royal College of Surgeons"; "Royal Society"; "St.

Giles'"; "Serpentine"; "Southwark"; "Surrey"; "Tower of London"; "Trafalgar Square"; "Wapping"; "West-End."
Passim

LONDON BRIDGE

M. first saw London Bridge on 9 November 1849, but his impressions were vivid enough to become the focus of an entire chapter of *I.P.* (24: "In the City of *Dis"), wherein he meditates on the construction, history, and vantage point of the bridge, using analogies to the grimmest natural and cultural phenomena.

From *Roman times London Bridge had been the only one in the area. The span M. saw in 1849, designed by John Rennie, had been built between 1824 and 1831. (It was removed to the *United States in the twentieth century.)
M.D. Extracts 15; I.P. 24

LONDON GEOGRAPHICAL SOCIETY

The Geographical Society of London was founded in 1830 and chartered as the Royal Geographical Society in 1859. It supported or promoted many important exploratory expeditions in *Africa and the *Arctic in the nineteenth century.
M.D. 104

LONDON MISSIONARY SOCIETY

The interdenominational *Protestant London Missionary Society was founded in 1795. The nineteenth century was to become the "Great Century" of *Christian expansion (and colonial growth). Evangelical Congregationalists were most active in the London Missionary Society which, in M.'s time was liberal in its overall aim of charitable voluntarism but often conservative in its intolerance of disbelief and indeed intolerance of other Christian sects (as in *O.* 32, wherein Roman *Catholic priests are banished).

As Anderson shows in *Melville in the South Seas*, the London Missionary Society had little success in converting the docile *Marquesans.
See also "Ellis"; "Lahainaluna"; "Sandwich Islands" ("Great Revival"); "Tyerman."
O. 45; O. 49

LONDON ROAD
*Liverpool's London Road was the main thoroughfare leading east out of the city. M. was there on 14 November 1857, perhaps revisiting scenes he had viewed on his first European trip in 1839.
R. 43

LONDON TIMES
See "Times; London Times."
R. 42; R. 51

LONG GHOST; DOCTOR LONG GHOST; THE LONG DOCTOR
Anderson (*Melville in the South Seas*, 285, 286) suggests that one mysterious John Troy is the original of *O.*'s erudite alcoholic adventurer.
O. Passim

LONG-HAIRED KINGS
See "Merovingians," and "Beards."
W.84

LONG-ISLAND
Southeastern *New York's Long Island is 118 miles long, from twelve to twenty miles wide. It extends east-northeast from the mouth of the *Hudson, separated from *Connecticut by Long Island Sound, from *Manhattan by the *East River. Long Island, created from glacial ridges and moraines, has a shoreline indented by many bays, harbors, and wooded peninsulas called "necks." A south shore barrier beach extends from present-day Brooklyn's *Coney Island to Fire Island, which M. visited regularly in summer in the last decade of his life.

Long Island was occupied by white settlers in 1636. The Battle of Long Island, 27 August 1776, was won by the *British. The nineteenth century saw much whaling activity, as well as agriculture, as the "Long-Island sailor" of *M.D.* 40 shows.

M. *lectured at Flushing, N.Y. (present-day Queens borough), 7 November 1859.
M.D. 40; M.D. 110; M.D. 115

LONGOBARDI
See "Lombards," and "Beards."
W. 84

LONG WHARF TRUCK HORSE
R. 40 provides a gloss for the famous work animals of
*London's Long Wharf:

> Among all the sights of the docks, the noble truck-
> horses are not the least striking to a stranger.
> They are large and powerful brutes, with such
> sleek and glossy coats, that they look as if brushed
> and put on by a valet every morning. They march
> with a slow and stately step, lifting their ponder-
> ous hoofs like royal *Siam elephants.

R. 40; W. 56

LONG WORDS
In *M.D.*, jibes at pretentious scientific terminology,
especially regarding "the classification of the constituents of a
chaos," in the "*Cetology" chapter. "Long Words" is a sobriquet.
M.D. 32

LOOHOOLOO
This hamlet on *Moreea remains unidentified, although
Charles R. Anderson (*Melville in the South Seas*) believes it an
actual place. Natives of Moreea deny its existence.
O. 67; O. 70

LOOM OF TIME
In *Sartor Resartus* (Sealts #123) I, 8, Carlyle translates
the Earth Spirit's words in *Goethe's *Faust* (I, 1):

> In Being's floods, in Action's storm,
> I walk and work, above, beneath,
> Work and weave in endless motion!
>> Birth and Death,
>> An infinite ocean;
>> A seizing and giving
>> The fire of living:
> 'Tis thus at the roaring Loom
>> of Time I ply,
> And weave for God the Garment
>> thou seest Him by.

M.D. 47

"LOOSE-FISH"
    See "Fast-Fish and Loose-Fish."
M.D. 89; M.D. 90

"LORA TATTOO"
    I have not been able to trace a *Tahitian "Lora Tattoo."
Perhaps M. misunderstood because by his time the *French
language was infiltrating Tahitian speech; he might have
heard "l'heure tattoo": "hour or time of tattooing."
    Tahitians were tattooed almost everywhere but on the
face; completely blackened buttocks were a popular pattern, but
tattoos were mainly an individual marking chosen by those
marked. Lamp black from the smoke of oily nuts (*Aleurites
moluccana*) was moistened as ink for instruments made from
bone or shell or teeth (such as the shark's teeth of *O*. 8). The
inked instrument was driven in by sharp blows from a ham-
mer-like stick, drawing blood. The tattoo would be painful for
about a month; it might become infected and sometimes ended
in the death of the subject.
O. 8

LORD ARCHBISHOP
    The title "Lord" refers to a nobleman or peer of the
realm, a ruler, master, or holder of a manor in *England. All
members of the *House of Lords are Lords; *Archbishops are
Lords Spiritual; lay peers are Lords Temporal. M.'s usage is
usually ironic.
T. 24

LORD BYRON
    See "Byron; Lord Byron."
R. 26; W. 51

LORD GEORGE FLAGSTAFF
    Ships were ranked according to the importance of their
commanders. "Lord George Flagstaff" is a theoretical royal
patriot commander whose identification with a ship would
bring much esteem. His theoretical ship "*Thetis" is named
for the mother of *Achilles.
R. 40

LORD HIGH ADMIRAL; LORD-HIGH -ADMIRALS
    See "Admiralty, the," and "God."
R. 61; W. 6; W. 71 and elsewhere

LORD HOWE
See "Howe; General Howe; Lord Howe."
I.P. 21

LORD MAYOR'S
Lord Mayor is chief magistrate of aldermen (seniors and elders) in *British corporate towns. Originally, the Lord Mayor of *London was elected on the Feast of St. Simon and St. Jude (28 October), but Lord Mayor's Day changed to 9 November after adoption of the Gregorian calendar in 1752. He is now sworn in at *Guildhall on the second Friday in November, presented to the Lord Chief Justice on the following Saturday. After the Lord Mayor's Show, a procession goes to the Royal Courts of Justice, and a few days later the Lord Mayor's Banquet takes place at Guildhall, where the Prime Minister speaks. The Lord Mayor and the Sheriffs pay the bills. The "Banquet of Kings" in "Poor Man's Pudding and Rich Man's Crumbs" is a satirical treatment of the banquet, pronounced in M's journal (8 November 1849) "A most bloated pomp, to be sure."
O. 45; R. 46

LORD OF CREATION
The "Lord of Creation" is not *God, but man.

LORD PRIMATE
Title of the Bishop of the "First" or chief see of a state (Lat. *prima sedes*); originally the metropolitan area of a province. In *England the *Archbishop of *York is Primate of England, the Archbishop of *Canterbury is Primate of All England.
"Lord Primo" in *M.* is probably a play on the title.
T. 24

LORD PRIMO
See "Lord Primate."
M. 148

LORD'S DAY, THE
See "Sabbath."
Passim

LORD STORMONT

"Redburn's" pseudonym is probably taken from the seat of the Northern *Ireland government, a few miles east of the center of *Belfast. The public buildings and estate containing Stormont House, official residence of the chief of government, are among the most beautiful in Ireland.
R. 46

LORD-STREET

*Liverpool's fashionably commercial Lord Street was developed in the 1670's by Lord Molyneux, who was improving his land running down to the Pool at a time when his rights as lord of the manor were being contested.
R. 31

LORD WARDEN

*Britain's office of Lord Warden was a sinecure and a holdover from medieval days: power over a "ward" of a certain size, replete with all the dignity implied in the title "Lord."
M.'s source for his Lord Warden story in *M.D.* 90 is a *Literary World* anecdote of 29 June 1850 (Vol. 6, p. 642). M. greatly expands on the very brief story of *Wellington's power as Lord Warden of the *Cinque Ports. Wellington was entitled to all local "royal fish," and when a poor fisherman captured a whale in Margate Bay, Dr. Wallingford, of the *College of Surgeons, pleaded for the poor man's ownership of what was not a "fish." Wellington paid the fisherman £28 and said he "did not see what any fellow of the College of Surgery had to do with the Warden of the Cinque Ports," in effect telling the doctor to mind his business and his position.
M.D. 90

LORENZO

In *Shakespeare's *The Merchant of Venice*, the *Christian artist who surreptitiously courts and then marries "*Jessica," daughter of the *Jewish "*Shylock."
R. 46

L'ORIENT

At the battle of the *Nile, between the *British and the *French near *Alexandria (1 August 1798), *Nelson had fourteen ships of the line and one brig with which to face seventeen French ships. The French *L'Orient*, much the largest ship in the battle, with 120 guns, blew up with most of her crew and an admiral. Nelson's coffin was later to be constructed of wood from *L'Orient*'s mainmast. It was rather poetic justice, in light of Nelson's own *Vanguard*'s having been dismasted in a storm not long before the battle.

See also "Hallowell."
W. 74

LOTHARIO: -S

A libertine and seducer of women, from Nicholas Rowe's (1640-1718) *The Fair Penitent* (1703); the name probably from *Sir William Davenant's (1606-1668) *The Cruel Brother* (1630), in which a similar character has the same name. Lothario is prototype for Samuel Richardson's (1689-1761) "Lovelace" in *Clarissa* (1747-48).
R. 44; M.D. 88; P. 2:4

LOT'S HOUSE, --WIFE

In *Genesis 19, the nephew of *Abraham, Lot, is a farmer in the *Jordan valley near *Sodom and *Gomorrah, wicked cities to be destroyed by *God. Two divine messengers, the "angels" of *C.M.* 42, spend the night in Lot's house and then lead him and his wife and daughters out of the city. Lot's wife disobeys the injunction not to look back and is changed into a pillar of salt, thereby becoming the proverbial warning against the curiosity which leads to disobedience. In *Luke 17:32, *Jesus says, "Remember Lot's wife."

Lot's subsequent incest with his daughters makes him the ancestor of the Moabs (which means "from the father") and the *Ammonites ("kinsmen").
W. 36; C.M. 42

LOUIS I, KING OF FRANCE

Louis I of *France, (778-840), *Le Debonnaire*, son of *Charlemagne and his successor as *Holy Roman Emperor (813-33 and 834-40). His character is unclear; he appears to have been a foppish and lethargic ruler, a sensualist, yet an intellect rather than a warrior king. Also called *The Pious*, he is regarded as having been excessively deferential to the *Church, responsible for dispensations that were penal, rather than permissive.
M. 181

LOUIS XVI OF FRANCE

See "Bourbon."
M.D. 24

LOUISBERGH

Louisbourg (or Louisburg), in Cape Breton, *Nova Scotia, was fortified by the *French after *Newfoundland and *Arcadia were lost to the *British in 1713. *New England volunteers captured it in 1745; it returned to the French in 1748, only to be retaken by the British in 1758. *John Paul Jones, on *Alfred*, took valuable prizes including *Mellish* off the coast of Louisbourg in 1776, escaping *Milford* and other British vessels and returning in triumph to *Boston.
I.P. 10

LOUISIANA

The eighteenth state, admitted to the Union in 1812, is bounded by the *Gulf of Mexico (S.), *Arkansas (N.), Mississippi (E.) and *Texas (W.). The *Spanish had entered the larger area extending to the *Rocky (then "Stony") Mountains before LaSalle descended the *Mississippi River to its mouth in 1682, claiming the entire drainage basin for *France and naming it after Louis XIV (see "Bourbon"). The oldest remaining settlement is *Natchitoches (1714): *New Orleans was founded in 1718.

The French and Indian Wars split Louisiana, giving the area west of the Mississippi to Spain and east to Britain. In 1800, the first of 5,000 deportees arrived from *Arcadia, giving rise to a "Cajun" population to join the "Creole" (French-Spanish). The French regained the territory, but *Napoléon sold it (as the "Louisiana Purchase") to the United States for fifteen million dollars, in 1803.

In the nineteenth century, *slavery, sugar, and cotton enriched the state, with the port of New Orleans ranking second only to *New York.
M.D. 104; C.M. 17

LOUIS LE GRAND

See "Bourbon."
M. 60; W. 38; W. 71

LOUIS LE GROS

Louis VI *le Gros*, or the Fat (1081-1137), was king of the *French from 1108. A popular and efficient king, Louis brought internal calm early in the Capetian dynasty. He protected the poor from preying lords, led his army against the invading *Holy Roman Emperor, Henry V (allied with the English), pleased the clergy, and created peaceful agrarian enclaves for peasants on his own property.
M.D. 94

LOUIS PHILIPPE
See "Bourbon."
O. 32; M.D. 35

LOUIS THE DEVIL
M.'s derisive name for *Louis Napoléon Bonaparte, President from 1848 to 1852 and later Emperor of *France.
M. D. 35

LOUISVILLE
Louisville, *Kentucky is located on the left bank of the *Ohio River, ninety miles southwest of *Cincinnati. It was settled in 1778 and in 1780 was named in honor of *France's Louis XVI (see "Bourbon"). It became noted for its tobacco and *bourbon whiskey production.

M. passed through Louisville enroute to his *lecture in Cincinnati in February of 1858. The steamship on which he traveled undoubtedly entered the two-mile Louisville and Portland Canal (1830), built for navigation around the Ohio's falls.
C.M. 16

LOUVRE
The Louvre Museum collection in *Paris has been accumulating on the site of the Palais du Louvre since perhaps the seventh century A.D., when the original building was a fortress (from whence perhaps the name: "blockhouse." "Louvre" may also refer to an early wolf-hunters' rendezvous.) The palace was a private residence of *French kings until 1793, when it became the Musée de la République. François I probably first amassed an official royal collection in the sixteenth century, and by M.'s time it had grown vast, mainly through spoils of war. Louis XVIII (M.'s "Louis the Devil"; see "Bourbon") had acquired the Venus de Milo and other attractions by the time of M.'s visit in 1849. *Leonardo's La Giaconda ("Mona Lisa") had been displayed from 1804. The Museum became the property of the state by 1848, and the physical area was rather different then, with the *Tuileries palace still standing and forming the western enclosing part of the rectangular complex.

The Louvre collection elicited M.'s rare praise for things French. He visited for three hours on 30 November 1849, commenting in his journal: "Heaps of treasures of art of all sorts. Admirable collection of antique statuary. Beats the British Museum." That he vividly recollected particular Louvre treasures is demonstrated in his comparing the *Dying Gladiators

of that museum and of the Capitol Museum of *Rome, in a
*lecture of 1859.
P. 16:2

"LOVE IN A COTTAGE" PRINCIPLE
The expression originally meant marriage for love,
without the means to maintain social status.
Keats *Lamia* (Pt. II, i):

> Love in a hut, with water and a crust,
> Is--Love, forgive us!--cinders, ashes, dust.
> Love in a palace is, perhaps, at last
> More grievous torment than a hermit's fast.

M. uses the expression to signify an adulterous couple.
O. 46

"LOVES OF THE ANGELS"
See "Moore, Thomas."
W. 41

"LOVE WAS ONCE A LITTLE BOY"
A song by J.A. Wade. (See J.L. Hatton, and E. Faning,
Songs of England 3:112.)
P. 2:2

LOW DUTCH
Popular *English usage applies the term *"Dutch" to the
Netherlandic language of *Holland, which descends from the
language of the Franks and is sometimes called "Low Frankish." Netherlandic was the (unofficial) language of the northern *Netherlands, with French (spoken mainly amoung the
upper classes in the south) the official language during the
nineteenth century. (Netherlandic did not gain "official" status until 1938.)
M.D. 101

LOWELL
Lowell is in northeastern *Massachusetts, on the Merrimack River at the mouth of the Concord, twenty-four miles
northwest of *Boston. Settled in 1653, it was incorporated as a
city in 1836. Lowell became world famous as the "Spindle City,"
or "*Manchester of America," for its textile mills, begun in

1822. The mills became a model for European visitors including Dickens (see "hard times"), who commented favorably upon them. For the reader of "The Tartarus of Maids," however, the "Lowell girls" of *I.P.* 19 invoke an unpleasant picture of the effects of industrialization.
I.P. 19

LOW GROUP
        See "Pomotu."
O. 17

LOWLANDS
        See "Scotland."
R. 24

LOYOLA
        See "Spanish Inquisition."
W. 70; C.M. 22

LUBBER-LIKE
        Awkward, ungainly, inexperienced: from "land-lover."
M.D. 13

LUCIAN
        Prolific satirist (c. 125- c. 190), born in Samosata, Syria (Samsat, *Turkey), who wrote in elegant Attic Greek prose. As a rhetorician, Lucian traveled to *Greece, *Italy, and *Gaul. In his forties, he moved to *Athens to become a dialoguist, and in old age he went to *Egypt.
        Eighty prose works are attributed to him. Most famous are the dialogues: biting satire on human vanity, credulity, and hypocrisy, as well as on imposters, religion, philosophy, and history. *Alethes historia* ("True History") is, despite a disclaimer, directed to the credulous; it describes a journey starting under the sea (including a visit into a whale's belly), proceeding into the sky and to the *Elysian fields. The highly amusing Lucian heavily influenced the work of Erasmus, *Rabelais, *Voltaire, and Swift.
        (See also "Extracts" 8.)
M.D. Extracts 8; P. 26:4; I.P. 13; C.M. 5

LUCIFER

The name, Lat. for "light bringer," was originally applied to *Venus as a morning star. In *Isaiah (14:4, 12), "Daystar" applies to the king of *Babylon who boasted he would make himself equal to *God but was instead cast into the pit: "How art thou fallen, from heaven, 0 Lucifer, son of the morning!" St. Jerome and other Church Fathers applied the name to *Satan, and *Milton (*Paradise Lost* X, 425) gives the name to the demon of "Sinful Pride," hence "Proud as Lucifer."
0. 72; W. 46; M.D. 99; P. 12:4

LUCIFERS

*Lucifer matches were early friction matches that were bad smelling, difficult to ignite, and dangerously prone to sparking. Some boxes carried the warning that those with delicate lungs "should by no means use Lucifers." They were replaced in the 1830's by less hazardous "*locofoco" matches.
W. 61; M.D. 113; M.D. 121

LUDWIG'S THRONE

See "Bourbon."
M. 168

LUDWIG THE FAT

See "Louis le Gros."
M. 181

LUFF UP INTO THE WIND

Talk hot air: if *President Tyler does it, it is political hot air. (See also "luff" in nautical appendix.)
W. 91

LUNAR MOUNTAINS

In the nineteenth century, people generally disbelieved in *Ptolemy's Lunae Montes Finis Oriental (Mountains of the Moon, which he thought the source of the *Nile). They have since been identified as Uganda's Ruwenzori Mountains.
C.M. 24

LUNNUN

See "London."
I.P. 3; I.P. 13

LUSIAD, THE
     See "Camöens."
W. 4; W. 65

LUTHER
     Martin Luther (1483-1546) was the *German Roman
*Catholic priest who began the *Protestant Reformation.
Luther joined the eremitical mendicant order of *St. Augustine after being educated for the law. He was selected for advanced theological studies at the University of Wittenberg, taking his D.D. in 1512. On a trip to *Rome, he was shocked by the
hypocrisy and corruption of Roman clergy. His continuing
studies in humanist philosophy and theology deepened doubts
about *God's righteousness, bringing about a crisis of faith
and of conscience. He found an answer in the importance of
man's faith. He explicated technical vocabulary and *Bible
language, and became a preacher speaking to the common
people about the relation of Scripture to their individual lives.
He wrote treatises countering scholastic theologians and was
finally driven by Church sale of indulgences to affix to the door
of All Saints Church, Wittenberg, the "95 Theses," on 31 October 1517 (the eve of All Saints Day).
     Luther was excommunicated (1520) and banned at the
Diet of Worms (1521). He left the order, married, and began
formation of the League of Protestantism. He translated into
German the *Old and *New Testaments (the *Lutheran Bible*,
1531), and composed numerous hymns which retain their
popularity.
     Lutheran doctrine is opposed to that of the Catholic and
Anglican Churches, as well as to *Calvinism. The Lutheran
Church, largest of the Protestant churches, has been strongest
in northern and western Europe (especially in Germany). It
has been active in missionary work and became important in
the *United States in the nineteenth century, when German
and *Scandinavian immigration was at a peak. M.'s forebears, the *Gansevoorts, were Lutherans when they arrived in
America in the seventeenth century.
     A talk between Luther and Pope *Leo (M. 3) would be the
height of human *caritas*; it was Leo X who excommunicated
Luther in 1520.
M. 3; R. 33

LUXEMBOURG, GARDEN OF THE
     The large *Paris park, with gardens, statues, fountains
and a pond, was laid out surrounding the Palais du Luxembourg, residence of Marie de *Médicis. The widow of Henri IV

had had the palace designed to remind her of her *Pitti Palace,
in *Florence. It was turned to government use, and the
gardens made public. M. visited and strolled in the park, 2
December 1849.
I.P. 8

LUXOR

    Luxor is in Upper *Egypt, on the eastern bank of the
*Nile, 450 miles south of Cairo: part of the site of the ancient
*Thebes. Its chief ruin is the Temple of Luxor, built by Amen-
hotep III, of the eighteenth dynasty.
    One of the "obelisks of Luxor" (R. 32) stands at Place de
le Concorde, *Paris, which M. visited on 29 November 1849. It
originally stood before a temple at Thebes, its hieroglyphical
"Luxor marks" (M. 132) commemorating the deeds of Ramesis
II (13 c. B.C.).
M. 132; R. 32

LUZ

    A *Canaanite city renamed *Bethel by *Jacob in
*Genesis 28:19 and 36:6, after *Jehovah appeared to him there.
M. 165; C.M. 2

L_____, VILLAGE OF

    "Wellingborough's" home town (R. 32) is undoubtedly
Lansingburgh, in *New York's Rensselaer County, to which
M.'s mother removed from Albany in 1838. Lansingburgh was
what is now northern Troy, New York (into which it was incorporated in 1900). It was located on the eastern bank of the
*Hudson (navigable by locks at this point), just below the
*Mohawk River juncture at Cohoes Falls, directly across from
Waterford: c. ten miles north of Albany and c. thirty miles
northwest of *Pittsfield, *Massachusetts.
    Maria Melville was forced for financial reasons to re-
move to Lansingburgh with her eight children after the death
of M's father, and after son *Gansevoort's business problems
in the Panic of 1837. As Gilman shows in *Melville's Early Life
and Redburn* (Chaper 3), Lansingburgh was a respectable but
dull town of some 3,000 business-oriented inhabitants who apparently thrived in an environment where the church choir
was perhaps the highest form of culture. They called their
town of c. 500 houses and fifteen factories "The Garden of
America." There is no evidence to suggest that the nineteen-
year-old M. was the church-going, tea-totaling youth painted
in *R*. In fact, his first published (anonymous) works, the

"Fragments from a Writing Desk" (reproduced in Gilman's "Appendix") reveal the overly romantic yearnings of a young man confined in a boring environment. M. studied engineering at Lansingburgh Academy, in hope of employment on the *Erie Canal. When this failed to materialize, he went to sea for the first time, in 1839.

(The Melville home, located on the bank of the Hudson at what was then River Street at the corner of North Street, is still in existence as #2 114 Street, Troy, under the care of the Lansingburgh Historical Society.)
R. 32

LYCEUMS
The first *American Lyceum for literary and scientific education was founded in 1826 by educational reformer, Josiah Holbrook (1788-1854), at Millbury, *Massachusetts. The concept rapidly spread, so that by 1839 the American Lyceum Union boasted thousands of units. The movement flourished until the end of the century, attracting the most noted guest speakers and debaters, contributing to reform movements, and stimulating the move toward public schools. After 1890, Chautauqua societies used a parallel system to provide entertainment to the nation. The word "Lyceum" honors the place where *Aristotle lectured the ancient *Greeks.
See also "lecture."
P. 17:2

LYCEUM, THE
The Lyceum, like other "public" facilities in *Liverpool, charged a fee or required appropriate introduction for admittance. But my sources locate it on *Ranelagh Street, not *Bold Street, as M. has it in R. 39 and R. 42. So perhaps "Wellingborough" is ejected from the Bold Street establishment because it is a private club and not the public Lyceum after all.
R. 30; R. 42

LYING-IN HOSPITAL
A hospital specializing in childbirth.
M.D. 92

LYRE
In astronomy, Lyra is a northern *constellation commemorating the lyre of *Orpheus.
M. 151

LYSANDER
Lover of "Hermia," in *Shakespeare's *A Midsummer-Night's Dream.*
C.M. 3

M

MACADAMIZED
Macadamizing was the road-making method introduced in the very early nineteenth century, in which layers of graded uniform broken stones were separately crushed into position, at first by traffic and later by a weighted roller. It was invented by John Loudon McAdam (1756-1836), a *Scottish engineer who was the first to suggest raising roads above adjacent surfaces and covering with stones. He became the general surveyor of roads in Great *Britain.
R. 56

MACAO
A *Portuguese colony off southern *China, on the south China Sea at the *Canton River delta (sixty-five miles south of Canton, forty miles west of *Hong Kong across the Pearl River estuary). The city of Macao is on Chungshan, or Macao island, the largest of four islands comprising the colony which is the oldest permanent European outpost in the Far East (leased from China in 1557). *Camöens wrote part of the *Lusiads here, 1558-59. *Portugal proclaimed Macao's separation from China in 1848-49 (confirmed by China in 1887), as Macao was losing its important position to Hong Kong. (There are also villages in Portugal and *Brazil called Macao.)
M. 22; W. 65

MACASSAR OIL
Many sailors affected elaborate coiffures necessitating the use of oils and unguents. *OED* says that Macassar Oil was "grandiloquently advertised in the early part of the nineteenth century, and represented by the makers . . . to consist of ingredients obtained from Macassar." *Byron's *Don Juan* (I, xvii) calls it "incomparable." Captain Ringbolt's "Charley Brail's True Story" (in Codman's *Sailors' Life and Sailors' Yarns, by Captain Ringbolt*) mentions a precious cargo of oil from

Macassar. Ammen (p. 30) describes a midshipman who used it on his side whiskers, as well as on his hair.

Macassar (or Makassar) is the largest town of *Celebes, Indonesia. It was first settled by the *Portuguese, but the *Dutch took over by 1668. Macassar Strait is the wide connection (230 miles) that runs for 600 miles between the Celebes Sea and the *Java and Flores seas, between *Borneo and Celebes.
M. 1; W. 6; M.D. 25; C.M. 43

MACBETH, --S

*Shakespeare's tragedy, *Macbeth*, is a story of ambition exacerbated by witchcraft. Three witches prophesy that the heroic General "Macbeth" will become King of *Scotland. Spurred on by his blood-thirsty wife, "Lady Macbeth," he facilitates the prophecy's fulfillment by killing "King Duncan," as well as his friend "Banquo," whose ghost then haunts him. The witches make another prediction which seems to guarantee good fortune, but the chain of slaughter continues, and "Lady Macbeth" goes mad and dies. The seemingly impossible conditions of "Macbeth's" fall comes to pass, and he is killed.

Critics such as Charles Olson point out M.'s debt to "Macbeth" for the character of "*Ahab," whose end is predicted by the wizard-like "*Fedallah," following a series of conditions that seem as unlikely as those that fell "Macbeth."

M. saw Fanny Kemble play "Lady Macbeth" in February of 1849 and heard Verdi's operatic version in *Messina, in February of 1857.

See also "Angus"; "Rosse"; "Thane"; and "I turn the leaf to read . . . . ," in the "Quotations" Section.
M. 60; R. 49; W. 4; W. 51

MACCABEES

The four *Apocryphal books of the Maccabees trace the history of the *Hebrew tribe from background conquests of *Alexander the Great and establishment of the Seleucids, and the attacks of *Antiochus IV Epiphanes ("God Manifest") in the second century B.C. *Judas Maccabaeus was an early leader in the revolt against the king and his successors, and his family of priest-kings continued the struggle. In addition to history, the books contain ahistorical episodes in the struggle to protect Hebrew tradition, and philosophical discourses, all much admired by *Christian preachers, who saw the works as lessons in steadfastness and bravery. After their successful revolt, the Maccabees ruled *Palestine for a century.

(The festival of Chanukah commemorates the Maccabees' eight-day dedication of the new altar of the temple destroyed by Antiochus.)
M.D. 133

MACCARONI
        See "Cetology" section.
M.D. 56

MACEDONIAN
        The Macedonian area of the Balkan peninsula (between
*Epirus and *Thrace) has been strategically important since
ancient times. It was said to have been founded c. 2600 B.C. by
a descendent of *Hercules, its boundaries thereafter shifting
and cultures mixing. Late arrivals, ancestors of the historical
Macedonians, established Early Bronze Age culture. By the
third century B.C., the Macedonians were expanding their
power, with *Greek assistance, under bellicose kings placed by
primogeniture and acclamation of the military. Brought to
great military power by *King Philip II's use of the Macedonian phalanx (shoulder-to-shoulder infantrymen in multiple
rows), it remained the heart of the Greek Empire until the
death of *Alexander the Great in 322 B.C. Clashes with
*Rome, beginning in the second century B.C., culminated in
Roman dominance and splitting of Macedonia into four independent republics. When the Roman Empire split into eastern
and western parts (fourth century A.D.), Macedonia became
part of the *Byzantine Empire. Thereafter, there were incursions by Slavs, Bulgars, *Turks, *Normans, *Crusaders,
Serbs. In M.'s time, *Russia attempted to compel Turkey to
liberate Bulgaria, into which Macedonia was to be subsumed.
British intervention prevented this, and the area remained a
bone of contention with its mixture of religions, languages,
and cultures. (Boundaries established in World War I were
temporary; modern Macedonia remains part of Bulgaria and
Yugoslavia.)
        See also "King of Macedon" and "*Macedonian*."
M. 147; W. 16; W. 58; W. 64; W. 74; W. 85

MACEDONIAN, THE
        H.B.M. *Macedonian*, a forty-nine-gun *British frigate in
excellent condition, was captained by John S. Cardan,
*Decatur's traditional adversary. In 1812, south of the
*Azores, the two engaged, with Decatur on *United States*. His
vessel reduced to a rolling hulk, Cardan surrendered, with 104

casualties, compared to Decatur's twelve. *Macedonian* was the first British ship ever brought back to an *American port. She was repaired and thereafter used by the Americans in the *Mediterranean against the *Barbary *pirates. Her capture was a great psychological boost for the U.S. in the first year of the *War of 1812.

W. 58; W. 64; W. 74

MACHIAVELLI; MACHIAVEL, --'S

Niccolò Machiavelli (1469-1527), *Italian statesman, political theorist, and sometime adviser to the *Medici, is best known for *Il Principe*, written in 1513. The treatise, taking *Roman history as a model, advocates use of unethical methods by rulers, given the low nature of most human beings, to secure and administer power.

Machiavelli rose from an empoverished branch of an important *Florentine family and was to a large degree self-educated. His first government position (1498) led to broadening travel in *France. On his return to Italy, he studied the methods of *Cesare Borgia, adopting them for his ideal "new prince." Borgia's downfall did not halt his progress. Missions to *Switzerland and *Germany increased his military expertise, but he lost influence, never to be regained, when the *Medici gained power. Machiavelli's shocking maxims do not represent his moral character, except in his sense of evil.

The Arte della guerra (*Art of War*) is closely linked to the *Principe*, taking Rome as its model and omitting technical advances, especially artillery, from deep consideration.

M. visited Machiavelli's tomb at Santa Croce, 25 March 1857. He was reminded when looking at buildings and architectural paintings in Italy of Machiavelli's "saying that the appearance of a virtue may be advantageous, when the reality would be otherwise" (journal, 11 April 1857).

M. 138; W. 41; I.P. 8; C.M. 23; C.M. 45

MACK

If not fictional, perhaps one James McDonnel, who shipped on *United States at *Tahiti (Log Book, October 19-20; Anderson, *Journal*, p. 61), according to Anderson (*Melville in the South Seas*, p. 352).

O. 38

MACKINAW

The straits of Mackinac connect Lakes *Huron and *Michigan. The small island they contain passed from the In-

dians to the *French and then the *British before the *Treaty of
Paris (1796) awarded it to *America. The British retook it in
1812, but it was returned in 1815. The island, some 300 feet
high, with perpendicular cliffs, is ideal for a fortress. Its original name was Michilamachinac, Indian for "great turtle."
M. passed through the straits enroute to *Illinois in 1840.
M.D. 54; M.D. 75

MACKINTOSH
     The waterproof double-textured cloak was first made in
*Glasgow, *Scotland in 1823, when chemist Charles Mackin-
tosh (1766-1843) and inventor Thomas Hancock (1786-1865) succeeded in rubber manipulation experiments far greater than
previous efforts had accomplished. Coaltar naptha was discovered to be a better solvent than the previously utilized tur-
pentine or camphene, which yielded imperfect (and expensive)
results.
W. 1; W. 19

MACPHERSON'S ANNALS OF COMMERCE
     David *MacPherson's Annals of Commerce, Manufac-
tures, Fisheries, and Navigation . . . containing the commercial transactions of the British Empire and other countries
from the earliest accounts to . . . January 1801* was published
in four volumes, in 1805.
W. 90

MACROCEPHALUS
     Having a large head.
M.D. 32

MACY, OBED
     Obed Macy, a pacifist *Quaker of *Nantucket, wrote *The
History of Nantucket* (1835), a major source for material on
that island, in *M.D.* It contains a short survey of the whaling
industry, decrying its violence.
     See also "Extracts" 30 and 53.
M.D. 35

MADAGASCAR
     The modern Malagasy Republic occupies a large
*Indian Ocean island off the coast of *Africa, crossed by the
Tropic of Capricorn. There is varied volcanic topography, from

swamp to savannah, and a large central plateau some 6,500 feet in height. The people are an ancient mix of Indonesians and Africans, with much differentiation from area to area. Traditional culture (Patriarchy, caste system, polygamy, religious taboos, and ancestor worship) has slowly yielded to *Moslem or *Christian influence.

There were Muslim settlements as early as the ninth century, but the island was not sighted by Europeans until 1500, when the *Portuguese Diogo Dias arrived. Britain's *Charles I attempted settlements, and the *French had a colony from 1642-74, retaining sovereignty claims even after colonists were massacred. In the seventeenth and eighteenth century, Madagascar was a *pirate base, but by 1803 the French had established an agency, replaced in 1811 by the British. By this time, kingdoms had developed, largely through slave and arms trade. King Radama I (r. 1810-28) cooperated with the British to educate and westernize, stopping the slave trade in exchange for arms and military training. The *London Missionary Society aided in development of a written language. Radama's wife, Queen Ranavalona I, seized power at his death, overturning his policies, excluding all Europeans, making Christianity illegal, imposing penalties, executions, and slavery. During her reign there were constant wars and rebellions, but after her death in 1861, her son, Radama II, attempted to reopen the island to European influence, only to be assassinated in 1863. His wife, Queen Rasoherina, made treaties that finally ended Madagascar's isolation.
R. 21; R. 27

MAD AS A MARCH HARE
John Skelton (c. 1460-1529), *Replication Against Certain Young Scholars*: "I say, thou mad March hare."
John Heywood (c. 1497- c. 1580), *Proverbs* I:5: "Mad as a March hare."
(Lewis Carroll's *Alice's Adventures in Wonderland*, the most famous "source," was not published until 1865).
I.P. 20

MADEIRA
Madeira (*Portuguese for "wood") is a small volcanic archipelago in the north *Atlantic, 600 miles southwest of *Lisbon and 400 miles west of *Morocco. With Porto Santo, Madeira is one of the two inhabited islands of the chain: a mountainous resort area of exotic trees, known to the Romans as *Insulae Purpurariae*. Madeira was rediscovered (1418-20)

by agents of Prince Henry the Navigator. It was occupied by the *British in the early nineteenth century.

"Madeira vines" (*P.* 6:1) refers to the grape vines of the Câmara de Lôbos area which produce the strong Madeira wine popular in the nineteenth century. It was aged by transporting to the *West Indies and back. Madeira wine was served (at room temperature) with the main dinner course and after the meal, as well.

M. 95; M. 181; W. 30; W. 37; W. 42; P. 6:1; P. 22:1

MAD JACK

The original for this fictional character is probably Lieutenant Latham B. Avery, whom Admiral Franklin calls: "The best sea-officer I have ever seen on the deck of a man-of-war. . . . The men jumped at his call . . . when we were buffeting about off Cape *Horn, when he was officer of the watch 'all hands' were never called for getting the ship under short canvas, for he, with the watch on deck, was sufficient of himself." Franklin confirms that "drunkenness was very common" among officers on *United States*, the Log Book for which records two occasions when Avery was reprimanded "for being drunk and leaving his post while Officer of the Deck."

M. could have borrowed the name from "Mad Jack" *Byron, father of *George Gordon Byron.

W. Passim

MADONNA, ROMISH-PAINTED
See "Raphael."
P. 3:2; C.M. 17

MADRAS

The state and city of Madras, in southern *India on *Coromandel Bay of the Bay of *Bengal, is known worldwide for its cotton (and other textile) industry and for local handweaving. The area was Buddhist from the third to the first century B.C., in the hands of Cholas by the eleventh century A.D., Hindus (see "Hindoo") by the fourteenth, and *Moslems by the sixteenth. *Portuguese, *Dutch, and English traders entered from the early fifteenth century. The city was founded in the seventeenth, at a time of warring *Mogul Empire dynasties.

P. 16:3

MADRE DE DIOS

Sp.: "Mother of God."
W. 5

MADRID

The capital of *Spain in New Castile, in the center of the Iberian peninsula. The name is *Moorish (*Majrit*), and there is evidence of the city's existence from 932 A.D. A large and wealthy city 2,373 feet above sea level, Madrid has had great historical importance in diplomacy and politics. It is M.'s symbol of excess ceremony and consumption.
W. 40; W. 87

MAELSTROM

Originally, the term referred to the Moskenström current running through a strait of the North Sea between various of the Lofoten Islands, off the west coast of *Norway. The strong tidal currents frequently reverse themselves, giving rise to the use of *Maelström to represent whirlpools as in *Poe's "A Descent into the Maelström," published in *Graham's Magazine* in 1841. (Sealts #404a is Poe's *Works*, presented by M. to his wife in 1861.)
R. 22; W. 90; W. 92; M.D. 36

MAGELLAN, STRAITS OF

Argentina: c. 53° S; 70° W. See "Magellans."
W. 24

MAGELLANS

The *Portuguese explorer Ferdinand Magellan (1480-1521) died before completion of the first circumnavigation. Of his early life little is known. He sailed in a *Portuguese expedition against the *Moslems in 1505, returning to *Indian waters in 1508. In 1511, he participated in the action off *Malacca which took key sea trade points from the *Arabs; he probably visited the *Moluccas that year.

As a result of charges of "irregular conduct," in 1512 he was ordered by the king to fight in *Morocco, after which he was told to choose another task which would remove him from *Lisbon.

He renounced his nationality and offered his services to Charles I of Spain (later *Charles V, Holy Roman Emperor), for an expedition to discover an all-Spanish route to the Moluccas that would avoid both Portuguese waters and the Cape. In

1517, he sailed down the east coast of *South America, discovering the Strait named for him, entering and crossing the *Pacific. He was killed in a confrontation with natives in the *Philippines. Two of the expedition's ships reached the Moluccas, but only *Victoria* returned to Spain in 1522. Juan Sebastián de Elcano, the Basque navigator who completed the voyage, was honored as first circumnavigator.

The "shallow gossip" M. mentions about Magellan in *M.* may concern his transfer of allegiance or the "irregularities" that brought about his break with the Portuguese throne.
M. 3

MAGI; MAGIAN, -S
    See "Chaldean."
M. 144; M. 147; W. 19; M.D. 79; M.D. 111; P. 1:4; P. 2:5; P. 3:2; P. 17:1; I.P. 8; C.M. 36; C.M. 41

MAGISTER BARBATUS
    See "Beards"; "Socrates"; "Persius."
W. 84

MAGNA CHARTA
    Magna Carta, the charter of *English liberties, was first grudgingly granted by *King John, in an effort to avoid civil war in 1215. This prototype was the forerunner of the Great Charter of 9 Henry III, the document of law and history, traditionally presented as a preamble and sixty-three clauses. It has been much emulated, even to its language use by various of the *United States.

    Magna Carta's basic provisions include free election to ecclesiastical office, reform in judicial and local administration, rights for freemen, regulation of taxes and commerce, regulation of the behavior of royal officials, forest use, maintenance of the charter, and particularities relevant to problems of John's reign.

    Four original copies still exist in England; M. saw one in the British Museum in 1849 (journal, 26 November).
W. 72

MAGNIFICENT, THE
    The *French seventy-four-gun *Magnifique* was wrecked in *Boston Harbor, in 1782. To compensate, the *United States gave to France the seventy-four-gun *America*, which had just slipped off the stocks and was to have been commanded by

*John Paul Jones. There is a famous painting of *Magnifique*
by J.D. Schetsky (1778-1874).
M. 28

MAGOG
　　　See "Gog and Magog."
M. 56

MAHANAR
　　　Mahaena, *Tahiti: ten miles east of Point Venus.
O. 32

MAHINEE
　　　The name remains untraced, but Mahinee is perhaps
one of the ambitious and covetous chiefs (along with *Kitoti) referred to by *Wilkes.
O. 39

MAHOGANY
　　　Among the world's most valuable woods, true mahogany is of the genus *Swietenia*, family *Meliacae*, first discovered in the *West Indies. *Honduras mahogany of Central
and *South America became even more commercially important. The hard wood is fine-textured, reddish-brown, often
with beautiful markings. It has been used in buildings and
shipbuilding, as well as for furniture. There are many similar
woods called "mahogany."
　　　See also "Brazil" and "Campeachy."
R. 33

MAHOMET, --'S
　　　See "Mohammed."
M.D. 104; C.M. 24

MAHON
　　　Port Mahon (modern Minorca) was headquarters for the
*American *Mediterranean *squadron. Most nineteenth-
century naval memoirists reminisce about its pleasures:
gaming, theater, parties, seafood, donkey rides, etc. A popular
ditty illustrated the contrasting characters of Cape de Gatt
(36°42' N., 2°00' W.) and Mahon:

Off Cape de Gatt I lost my hat,
And where do you think I found it?
In Port Mahon, behind a stone,
And all the girls around it.

W. 4

MAHRATTAS

Mahrattas are from the southern Maratha states of western *India (now part of Maharashtra). The Scytho-Dravidian race has been important throughout Indian history. Mahrattas asserted their independence upon the breakup of the *Mogul Empire and the sultanates, in the late seventeenth century. They became dominant in India until *British victory in 1818. Their principal centers are Poona and Satara.
R. 34

MAIN, THE

See "Spanish Main; the Main."
M. 22; W. 53

MAINE

The largest of the *New England states (315 miles N.N.E.-S.S.W., 205 miles E.-W.) is bounded by *New Brunswick (N.E. and E.), *Quebec (N. and W.), *New Hampshire (S.W.), and the *Atlantic (E.). In 1820, Maine was admitted to the Union as the twenty-third state, the non-slavery part of the *Missouri Compromise. The "Pine Tree State" has a deeply indented rugged rocky coastline with a fringe of c. 1,000 islands, a granite extension of New Hampshire's *White Mountains. Highest peak is Mount Katahdin, at 5,268 feet (described by Thoreau, in The Maine Woods). Its longest rivers include the *Penobscot, *Kennebec, *Saco, St. John, and St. Croix. Norse explorers navigated the coastline as early as the eleventh century, and the Cabots explored, 1497-99.
O. 53; M. 28; R. 61; W. 13; W. 64; W. 84; P. 22:1; C.M. 21

MAINTENON, MADAME DE

Françoise D'Aubigné, Marquise De Maintenon (1635-1719), rose from humble French Huguenot background to become the second, and secret, wife of Louis XIV (see "Bourbon"). Placed at an early age in the custody of a *Catholic countess who converted her, she was first married (in 1652) to a deformed invalid burlesque poet, Paul Scarron.

By the time of his death (1660), she had ingratiated noble ladies who made her governess to the illegitimate children of Louis XIV. When they were legitimized and appeared publicly at *Versailles, the king discreetly transferred his affections, marrying her soon after the death of the queen, Marie Thérèse (probably in 1684).

She became a powerful influence on domestic and religious affairs and sponsored several institutions for poor Catholic girls. Her years of power were marked by rather somber *Jesuit-dominated religious life, complete with colorless decorum in clothing and behavior (which accounts for M.'s comment in *M*.: "continence and calicoes").

Despite blackening of her reputation by *Mémoires* of the duc de Saint-Simon (1685), she was respected and supported by the government after the death of Louis (1715). Her correspondence was published in 1856 (and 1865-66).
M. 25

MAIN-TOP MAN
Topmen were young, active, relatively experienced seamen of acrobatic skills who did the hardest and most exacting work of a sailing ship.

Admiral Selfridge, among other complaints about *W*., claimed that M. was "stationed in the After-guard, & not in the Main top."
W. 3 and elsewhere

MALABAR
A district of southwestern *Madras, *India. The 450 mile-long coastline is indented by inlets with interconnecting canals and picturesque inland waterways for native craft. Malabar's Dravidian culture remains distinct. The *Apostle Thomas is said to have introduced *Christianity here in A.D. 52. *Gama and other *Portuguese explorers were attracted to the ancient kingdom of Kerala, renowned for its spices. The area came under *British control from the late eighteenth century.

M.'s reference to "mountains of Malabar" (*R*. 34) seems to be in error, given the relative flatness of the area. Perhaps he was confusing with Malabar Hill (3-4000 feet), in the mountainous *Bombay region.
R. 34

MALACCA
*Malay Malaka is the city on the Strait of Malacca, at the mouth of the Malacca River, 125 miles northwest of Singapore (2°12' N., 102°14' E.). It was settled about 1400 and became a rich trade center of southeastern *Asia. In the fifteenth century, the kings of Malacca ruled much of the Malay peninsula and part of *Sumatra. Islam was introduced to the Malay world here. The *Portuguese ruled from 1511 until the *Dutch entered in 1641. During the *Napoleonic Wars (1795-1814), it was held by the *British and was ceded by the Dutch in 1824.
M. 139; R. 41; M.D. 87; P. 4:3

MALACCA
A Malacca is a rattan walking-stick, mottled brown. A row of Malaccas makes a fence such as that of M. 139.
M. 139

MALAGAS
Málaga wine, from southern *Spain's *Andalusia region, is a very heavy, sweet fortified wine.
The city of Málaga is on the *Mediterranean's Costa del Sol, eighty-seven miles southwest of *Granada; it is a port second only to Barcelona. Málaga was founded by the *Phoenicians in the twelfth century and was conquered by the *Romans, Visigoths (see "Goths") and *Moors, and occupied by the *French from 1810 to 1812.
M. 181

MALAKOFF
On 8 September 1855, during the Crimean War, the so-called impregnable fortress, a principal defense of Sebastapol, *Russia, fell to the *French.
C.M. 13

"MALAY"
In W., "Malay" represents the frigate, Congress.
W. 62

MALAY
Malaya, on the Malay peninsula, is bounded on the north by present-day Thailand (N.), the Strait of *Malacca (W.), South China Sea (E.). It was divided into separate states until the twentieth century. The peninsula lies between the An-

daman Sea of the *Indian Ocean and the Malacca Strait on the
west and South China Sea and Gulf of *Siam on the east. It is
700 miles long and up to 200 miles wide: a jungle link between
the Asiatic mainland and the islands of Indonesia (M.'s
"Malay Archipelago"). Aboriginal proto-Malays populate the
jungle lowlands and hills. The islands were visited as early as
the first century A.D. by *Indian traders who founded a Hindu
(see "Hindoo") state. The *Portuguese traded in the sixteenth
century, the *Dutch in the seventeenth until the time of the
*Napoleonic wars. Malacca was ceded to Britain in 1824.
     For M., "Malay" is synonymous with treachery.
M. 178; R. 12; R. 22; R. 34; M.D. 6; M.D. 41; M.D. 87

MALDIVES
     A chain of several thousand coral islands (relatively few
of them inhabited) in the Indian Ocean (7°6' N., 0°42' E.),
southwest of *Ceylon. The capital island is Male. In the
twelfth century, Islamics traveled to the then-independent sultanate, followed by the *Portuguese in the sixteenth century,
the *Dutch in the seventeenth, the *British in the late nineteenth. Independence was re-achieved only after World War
II. Principal industry is fishing, especially tuna and bonito.
M. 66

MALIBRAN
     Malibran (1808-36) was a highly acclaimed opera singer.
The daughter of Manuel Garcia (1775-1832), *Sevillean tenor,
zarzuela composer, and teacher, Maria Felicitá Garcia married a *French merchant in *New York City, François Malibran. She took his name and then moved permanently to
*Paris. Her brief career was a brilliant one; she sang at New
York's Park Theatre in 1825 and at the opening of the *Bowery
Theatre in 1826. Her brother, Manuel Garcia (1805-1906), was
also a luminary in the worlds of performance, teaching, and
composing.
R. 51

MALMSBURY
     The market town of Malmesbury (in Wiltshire,
*England, twenty-two miles northeast of Bath) is the site of an
ancient (635) abbey and church (twelfth century). In M.'s time
these were unrestored ruins, and the town focused on silk and
cloth industries. Malmesbury was a seat of *Henry I, and
home of *George Washington's ancestors and of *Thomas
Hobbes, "the Philosopher of Malmesbury."
O. 2; I.P. 8

MALMSEY
The wine of Malvasia (also called Malvoisie), in the Morea, *Greece. A prize vintage.
See "Clarence."
0. 10

MALTA; MALTESE
Malta is a European island south of *Sicily (35°45' N., 13°55' E.). In *Acts 28:1, "Melita," the island of *Paul's temporary escape from the *Romans.
M. visited the island on 29 November 1856, recording in his journal only that he had been "ashore all day."
R. 21; R. 35; W. 23; W. 65; M.D. 40

MALTE BRUN
Conrad Malte-Brun (Malte Conrad Bruun), French geographer (1775-1826), was born in *Denmark but banished for his writings in support of the *French Revolution. A resident of *Paris, he published six volumes of the *Précis de la géographie universelle* (1810-29) and *Annales des voyages* (1808). He helped found the Société de Géographie in 1822 and was renowned for his liberal incorporation of geography study with naturalist and historical concerns.
M. 2

MALTHUSIAN
Thomas Robert Malthus (1766-1834), economist and demographer, was a curate in Surrey, *England, when he published *An Essay on the Principle of Population as it Affects the Future Improvement of Society, with Remarks on the Speculations of Mr. Godwin, M. *Condorcet, and Other Writers* (1798), arguing that because population grows geometrically, while foodstuffs increase arithmetically, checks on population growth such as war, disease, and starvation were desirable. The 1803 edition revised the argument, suggesting that greed and sexual practice could be preferable as checks on population increase. Malthus opposed poor laws, and favored workhouses, late marriage, and moral restraint. His ideas were in opposition to those of *Rousseau, Godwin, *Hazlitt and others, but they influenced *Darwin and the economist David Ricardo, and social policy in general. Less known works in economics tie the question of prices to "effective demand" and promote public and private works to increase demand, in opposition to thrift, anticipating the Keynesian economics of the twentieth century.
I.P. 25

MALVOLIOS

In *Shakespeare's *Twelfth Night*, "Malvolio" is the sour steward. His name has become synonymous with "ill will."
C.M. 30

MAMELUKES

Arabic *mamluk*, "owned." In the tenth and eleventh centuries, the *Caliphs of *Baghdad imported white male *Turks and *Circassians from *Russia to bolster their inadequate armies. *Saladin employed them in the *Moslem wars against the *Crusaders. They eventually formed a military ruling class that took over many states, becoming sultans in *Egypt and elsewhere. They were overthrown by the *Ottomans in the sixteenth century but regained power and were finally massacred in 1811 by Mohammed Ali Pasha, only a few remaining in power in Iraq until 1831.

Penny Cyclopaedia says the "Memlooks . . . presented one of the greatest obstacles to the consolidation of Mohammed Ali's power in Egypt, in the early 1800's." The illustration shows Ali gazing from his window, enjoying the spectacle of the 1811 slaughter. The article claims that "their morals were very depraved: they were rapacious and murderous, and their extinction has been rather an advantage than a loss to humanity."

(M. mentions Mamelukes in *Clarel* I and II. His journal for 3 January 1857 records a visit to the Cairo citadel of *Saladin, including "the spot where the Memlook saved himself by leaping his house.")
M. 36; W. 91

MAMMONISH

The word "mammon" is from a *Chaldaic root referring to confidence, wealth, and avarice. It is first encountered in the *Bible in *Matthew 6:24 (the *Sermon on the Mount). *Jesus says: "No man can serve two masters: for either he will hate the one, and love the other; or else he will hold to the one, and despise the other. Ye cannot serve God and mammon."
P. 14:2

MAMMOTH CAVE

*Kentucky's limestone caverns were discovered late in the eighteenth century. The complex totals more than 150 miles in length, with some rooms over 40 feet high. The caves were the only source of saltpetre for U.S. troops in the *War of

1812. In 1843, tubercular patients moved into the caves, seeking constant (54° F.) temperature and rich oxygen supply. The experiment failed.
M. 75; M.D. 74; C.M. 20

MANAVALINS
A term with various meanings relating to food: perhaps finger food or odds and ends of broken victuals.
W. 32

MANCHESTER
The port city (and county borough) of *Lancashire, *England, is 184 miles northwest of *London and thirty-five miles east of *Liverpool. The ancient *Celts settled the rocky area, followed by the *Romans, *Danes, and *Saxons. Textiles became important in the fourteenth century; by 1800, cotton had made Manchester an important city. M. was to say in his journal (22 December 1857) that the "people of Manchester imitate exactly every fabric in the world."
Manchester is connected to Liverpool by *Bridgewater Canal, and by the Liverpool and Manchester Railway (R. 41), which opened in 1830. Primarily instigated by Liverpool corn merchants, its completion opened trade and made Liverpool a far more important city, eventually creating a trade monopoly through the vast railway network terminating in that city.
R. 41

MANCHESTER
Manchester, in south-central *New Hampshire, is located on both sides of the Merrimack River, midway between Concord and Nashua. Now the state's largest city, it was settled c. 1722 by Scotch-Irish immigrants who developed it into an important industrial center. A textile mill of 1805 developed into the country's largest in the nineteenth century (Amosheag Mills). Among the many historically important buildings and collections are the Institute of Arts and Sciences, Currier Gallery of Arts, and Historic Association, one of which may hold the "perfect" whale specimen of *M.D.* 102.
M.D. 102

MANCO CAPAC
*Andean oral tradition says that the legendary Manco Capac (c. A.D. 1200) was the first of thirteen *Inca emperors. The Incas ruled a small, war-like tribe centered around Cuzco

when Manco Capac, an incarnation of the sun, mysteriously appeared at Lake *Titicaca.

"*Manko," in *M*. 113, is thought by H. Bruce Franklin (*The Wake of the Gods*) to represent Manco Capac.

C.M. 1

MANDARIN

From early *Chinese history, a hereditary ruling class of different religion, ethic, and political theory from those of the masses. Their emphasis on learning led to their becoming the administrators of imperial China, and they were still firmly ensconced during M.'s time. The body of twenty-seven mandarins was appointed for imperial birth, service, knowledge, or zeal. Their nine ranks were distinguished by a cap *button of precious gem or metal.

By M.'s time, a "mandarin" was a pompous official or scholar. ("Mandarin" is not a Chinese word but one descended through *Malay and Hindi words for "counsellor," from the *Sanskrit *mantra*, referring to thinking.)

I.P. 4

MANDEVILL'S; MANDEVILLE'S TRAVELS

Sir John Mandeville (fl. 1356), or "Johan Maundeville, chevaler," as he signed his greatest work, is famed for a fabulous traveler's guidebook, *The Voyage and Travels of Sir John Mandeville, Knight*. The work, treating of the fictitious as well as the actual locales of the world, earned Mandeville's later reputation as the greatest traveler and the greatest liar of the *Middle Ages. Among the exotic sites are: *Constantinople, *Palestine, *Egypt, *Turkey, *Tartary, *Persia, *Arabia, *Chaldea, and *China; among the marvelous are the Land of Darkness, the Valley of Devils, the land of the lost tribes of *Israel, and the fountain of youth, from which Mandeville claims to have drunk, to his great advantage.

The work is only partly spurious, and Mandeville's expertise seems derived from encyclopedias of the day. *Columbus took quite seriously Mandeville's claim that the world was round; *Chaucer and *Shakespeare were also influenced.

Because the work was tampered with in many translations, including a metrical version, it has become impossible to determine how much of the material was original with Mandeville.

M. 98

MANETHO
Probably a disguised reference to the *Gnostic, Mani.
M. 97

MANFRED-LIKE
*Byron's solitary *Count Manfred* (1817) sells himself to the Prince of Darkness and lives isolated in the *Alps without human sympathies.
M. 4; M. 11

MANHATTAN
M.'s "insular city of the Manhattoes" (*M.D.* 1) is Manhattan Island, and when he refers to *New York City, it is that island alone that he means. The island is twelve and one-half miles long and two and one-half miles wide, bounded by the *Hudson ("North") River and *New Jersey (W.), *Harlem River and Spuyten Duyvil and the Bronx (N. and E.), the *East River, Queens and Brooklyn (E.), and New York Bay (S.). Its territory includes Randalls, Wards, Roosevelt (see "Blackwell's), *Governors, Ellis, and Liberty (formerly "Bedloes") Islands. It comprised all of New York City until 1874, when Westchester County was added. Since 1898 it has been one of the five boroughs of New York City.
M. was a resident of Manhattan for much of his life (see "Chronology").
M.D. 1

MANHATTO, --ES
People of *Manhattan Island, after *Washington Irving's usage in *Knickerbocker History of *New York* and "The Legend of Sleepy Hollow."
M.D. 1; M.D. 2

MANIA-A-POTU
Delirium tremens.
W. 43

MANILLA
Manila has been the capital of the *Philippines since 1848; it is a port of southwest Luzon, on Manila Bay. Founded in 1571, Manila was developed by *Spanish missionaries; it was occupied by the *British from 1762 to 1764. (The "Pearl of the Orient," Manila was much destroyed in World War II.)

Manila Bay is a landlocked inlet of the South China Sea: one of the world's great harbors, thirty-five miles wide, c. thirty miles inland, with an entrance eleven miles wide.

(M.'s spelling "Manilla" is in error; Manilla is a town in east central *New South Wales, *Australia. He errs in *M*. 19 in referring to "Manilla-men" as *Lascars; Manila-men are Tagalog, Chinese, Spanish, or a mixture.)

"Manilla rope" (*M.D.* 60) is undoubtedly Manila hemprope, made from the leaf-stalks of the abacá.
T. Sequel; O. 37; M. 3; M. 19; M.D. 48; M.D. 54; M.D. 60; M.D. 100; M.D. 116

MAN-IN-THE-MOON

M.'s association in *I.P.* 19 of the Man-in-the-Moon with evil figures of the imagination is in a long tradition. One myth associates him with a man in *Numbers XV, 32-36 who violates the *Sabbath by gathering sticks (referred to in *Shakespeare's *A Midsummer Night's Dream*, Prologue). Another legend makes him *Cain, with a dog and a thorn bush, representing the fiend and the *Fall. Various poets have made him *Endymion, taken to the Moon by *Diana.

(*Man in the Moon* was also the title of a contemporary *London monthly humor magazine.)
I.P. 19

MANITOU

Manito, or Manitu, is a supernatural power used by Algonkian-speaking eastern North American Indians: sometimes personified as a supreme deity, a great good or great bad spirit (described at length in Longfellow's *Hiawatha*, 1855).
C.M. 26

MANKO

M.'s fictional prophet in *M*. 113 is thought to represent *Manco Capac (H. Bruce Franklin, *The Wake of the Gods*), or the *Manichean Manes (Merrell R. Davis, *Melville's Mardi: A Chartless Voyage*).
M. 113

MAN OF SORROWS

The Man of Sorrows in *Isaiah 53:3 is generally taken to be *Christ.
M.D. 96

MAN-OF-WAR; MEN-OF-WAR

*American ships were not built specifically for battle until 1775; before then commercial vessels were fitted with armament as make-shift "men-of-war." Most genuine wooden men-of-war were cumbersome in appearance, with full round bows, high freeboards, and massive bulwarks. Their heavy armament, which required large crews, caused great displacement and relative slowness of motion. As many muzzle-loading cannon as possible were crowded on to the ship's sides, making it impossible to fire ahead or astern without extra, lighter, guns at the bows and sterns. The hull was heavy and massive, with interior bracing to withstand damage; rigging was proportionately massive, to move the great weight.

No single man-of-war combined qualities of seaworthiness, weatherliness, and good steering, and all were compromises in design. Men-of-war were classified according to the number of guns, arrangement of battery, rank of commander, and size and rig of ship. The "ship-of-the-line" had from seventy to 140 guns on two or more armed decks, with armed forecastle and quarterdeck. The American *Navy had no ship-of-the-line until the *War of 1812. The "frigate" (such as *United States) was the most important American Navy ship, with twenty-four to forty-four guns on a single flush gundeck, forecastle, and quarterdeck. ("Double-banked" frigates appeared to have two gun-decks because of gangway arrangement.) Vessels of twenty-two guns or less were called "sloops" if ship-rigged (similar to *French corvettes and *British "post-ships"); they were single-decked. Armed vessels of brigantine rig were called "brigs"; others were classed according to rig as "schooner," "cutter," or "sloop." One-to four-gun ships were called "gunboats." "Galleys" were forty- to seventy-five feet long, carried up to twelve guns, and were fitted for rowing as well as for sail. Flat-bottomed "gondolas" (forty- to sixty-feet long) and square-ended "Radeaux" punts, and "bateaux" rowboats were men-of-war during *Revolutionary times. "Fireships" were superannuated vessels filled with combustibles to be ignited near the enemy.
Passim

MAN-OF-WAR BUTTON
    See "Anchor Button."
W. 59

MAN-OF-WAR LIBRARY
    Among books known to have been on *United States during M.'s service are: Prescott's Ferdinand and *Isabella, 3

vols.; *Bancroft's *History of the United States*; *Darwin's *Voyages of HBM "Adventure" and "Beagle,"* 4 vols.; Livingstone's *Atlas*; Hough's *Military Law Authorities and Courts Martial*; *Harper's Family Library*, 72 vols. (one of which was *Blair's *Lectures*).
W. 41

MANOR
   The *Norman *French introduced the term *manerium* into English to describe an institution headed by a territorial aristocracy dependent for its income on rented peasant agricultural holdings, which it dominated economically and politically.
P. 7:4 and elsewhere

MANSFIELD, LORD
   William Murray, first Earl of Mansfield (1705-93) was a reknowned *English chief justice and member of the cabinet through several administrations (a practice discontinued after his service). Mansfield's house and library were burned in the 1780 "No Popery" riots led by *Lord George Gordon, who was acquitted in the trial Mansfield conducted so fairly. Mansfield is credited inaccurately with the abolition of British *slavery but accurately with reform of international commercial law and *marine insurance law, then a new field.
W. 3

MANTUA-MAKER'S VOICE
   Dress-maker's voice.
W. 8

MANXMAN
   An inhabitant of the Isle of Man.
M.D.28; M.D. 40; M.D. 99; M.D. 125

MARAMMA
   Davis suggests (VII, "The Travelogue-Satire") originals for this satirical fictional representation of a land overrun by hypocritical priests who alone can guide one safely up the peak of "Ofo" to salvation: in *Dante's "Maremma" (*Inferno* xxix), in *Wilkes's word for *Mohammedan ceremonies, in *Bennett's *ofai marama* (moonstone) idol of *Tahiti, and in

*Ellis's *ao marama* (state of day or light) of the *Hawaiian
*Hades.
M. 108

MARCH 20, 1808
    Although "Wellingborough's" father, "*Walter Red-
burn," is said to have been in *Liverpool on this date, his original, Allan Melvill, was not. Either the date is arbitrary, or its
significance is lost.
R. 30

MARCIONITES
    Marcion was the leader of a second-century heretical
movement which posited two *Gods: the inferior Creator/
Judge and the God represented by *Jesus. His writings do not
survive, so our knowledge of him comes from orthodox writers
such as *Tertullian who opposed him. Marcion is thought to
have been a wealthy shipowner from Sinope, Bithynia-Pontus
(Galatia) and to have had great influence in *Rome, where he
was a follower of *St. Paul, a writer of new Scripture, and
gifted organizer/teacher. M. is correct in distinguishing in *W.*
38 between Marcionites and *Gnostics, who were not identical,
despite common belief in dualism.
    "*Ahab's" philosophy in *M.D.* 119 ("The Candles")
seems to owe much to Marcion.
W. 38

MARDI
    Davis ("The Writing of *Mardi*," III) offers an explana-
tion of the name of M.'s fictional locale. Anthon's *Classical
Dictionary* (793) defines "Mardi": "a people of *Asia, near the
northern frontiers of *Media, or rather of Matiene, which
formed part of Media." In the same place (807) it is explained
that "Media" is "a country of Upper Asia, the boundaries of
which are difficult to determine, as they differed at various
times."
    Finkelstein (6) suggests that M. might have seen por-
tions of Edward William Lane's (1801-76) notes to *Arabian
Nights* (a series on which was running in *Duyckinck's *Literary World* in 1848). The Arabic "*ard*" means "country, earth,
and world." M. might have wished in "Mardi" to express "my
earth, my world," based on a model construction found in
Lane's notes.
    The fictional "route" of the book suggests a voyage into
the archipelago comprising islands of *Ellice's group, the

*Kingsmill chain, *Radack and *Mulgrave clusters, all of which appear, as Davis shows, on *Wilkes's maps. The political allegory carries the characters westward into *France, *England, *Ireland, and across the *Atlantic to the *United States; around *South America via Cape *Horn; north to the west coast of the United States; westward across the *Pacific to the *Orient; through the *Indian Ocean, around the Cape of *Good Hope and northward back to Europe, where the political allegory ends and the characters cruise again through purely fictitious islands.
M. Passim

MARGARET
      *Goethe's heroine, "Gretchen," in *Faust*.
W. 44

MARHAR-RARRAR
      Phonetic spelling of *Tahitian "Mata ara."
O. 67

MARHARVAI
      An invented name, unknown in *Tahiti.
O. 67

MARIES, MARTHAS, ETC.
      Theoretical women. "The way of Martha" traditionally represents the active life, as opposed to "the way of Mary," the contemplative life.
P. 3:1

MARIES, RIGHTFUL QUEENS OF FRANCE
      See "Salique law" and "Valois."
P. 2:2

MARIETTA
      Marietta, *Ohio, at the confluence of the Muskingum and *Ohio Rivers, was *Ohio's first white settlement, Fort Harmar, 1778. It was named for the *Bourbon Marie Antoinette and developed from a center of flatboat trade to an important steamboat town.
C.M. 40

MARINE INSURANCE COMPANIES
See "Life Insurance Companies;   Marine Insurance Companies."
M.D. 121

MARINES
Groups functioning like modern marines have been in existence since ancient times.   The *Greeks and the *Phoenicians are known to have had both rowers and fighters on board their ships, and in this country the Marine force antedates the *Navy. Three *New York regiments were assembled in 1740, and the *Continental Congress instituted two official battalions of "American Marines" in November of 1775.
Serious problems first arose between marines and sailors in the *British Navy, where the Royal Marines came to be seen as land-lubbers afloat. Various slurs such as "tell it to the marines" and "for the benefit of the marines" (*M.D.* 55) came about to suggest their credulity in nautical matters. Empty bottles were called "marines," and an imaginary group called "Horse Marines" (*W.* 29) further suggested the ridiculous uselessness of their situation. (By 1868, "Bryant's Minstrels" were to popularize a comic ditty about "Captain Jinks of the Horse Marines," who fed his horse on "corn and beans.")
Edinburgh Review for October 1824 noted that enmity was exacerbated by the use of marines as jailors for impressed men. M. adds a further dimension to the strife by making his "Neversink" (see *"United States"*) marines "two-thirds *Irishmen."
W. Passim; M.D. 55 and elsewhere

MARIUS
Gaius Marius (157-87 B.C.), *Roman general and longtime Consul, was superior to Lucius Cornelius Sulla (see "Sylla") when Sulla's exploits brought acclaim. A jealous rivalry began that led to the first great Roman Civil War (in the 80's). Upon his death, his family became extinct, and his reputation suffered because of wide sympathy for Sulla. *Julius Caesar, his nephew, somewhat restored his glory, replacing his trophies in the Capitol in 65.
In "Bartleby the Scrivener," M. says that Bartleby is like a "sort of innocent and transformed Marius brooding among the ruins of *Carthage," referring to that general's discovery in 88 B.C. of the once-great city in ruins.
M.D. 45

MARK, --MARK ANTONY
See "Antony, Mark."
M. 22; M. 149; W. 47

MARK WINSOME; MARK
An invention; generally accepted as a caricature of *Ralph Waldo Emerson.
C.M.37; C.M. 38; C.M.41

MARLBOROUGH
*England's John Churchill, First Duke of Marlborough (1650-1722), gained fame for his victories against the *French in the War of the Spanish Succession. Well placed in the court of *Charles II, he temporarily left military life to court Sarah Jennings, attendant to the future *Queen Anne. They were secretly married in 1677, and Churchill rose in court and in service even under the Catholic *James II, until as a *Protestant he deserted to serve the future *King William III. In 1692, Queen *Mary attempted to force Anne to dismiss Sarah and (by then) Marlborough was excluded from court. He regained his position under Anne's rule, went on to further military glory, and helped secure Protestant succession in England.

His wife, Sarah, later Duchess of Marlborough (1660-1744), was a close friend of Anne, and the adored object of Marlborough's daring romantic activity, despite her reputation for bad temper. After her husband's death, she completed building of *Blenheim Palace.
M. 23; M. 26

MARLOW
Dramatist Christopher Marlowe (1564-93) showed signs of instability even at *Cambridge, where he excelled in classics. Involved in numerous violent quarrels, he was himself killed in a tavern brawl. Yet despite his temperament, he was an admired and influential figure, even for *Shakespeare and *Jonson.

His earliest written play was probably *The Tragedie of *Dido, Queene of *Carthage (pub. 1594). *Tamburlaine the Great (1590) was a milestone in the use of blank verse. It traces the violent rise to power of a ruthless *Scythian shepherd who conquers the *Turkish emperor *Bajazet (watching him die a cruel death in a cage) and comes to a violent end himself after conquering *Babylon. (The historical Tamburlaine was a fourteenth-century *Mongolian conqueror.)

M. also knew *Dr. Faustus* (1604); he checked lines quoted in his copy of *The Poetical Works of Thomas Chatterton* (Sealts #137; Vol. I, 1842):

> Cut was the branch that might have grown full
> straight,
> And burned was *Apollo's laurel bough.

Marlowe also wrote *The Jew of Malta* (1633; mentioned in *W.* 41), other plays, and much poetry (including the song, "Come Live With Me and Be My Love").

Sealts #348 is an unidentified edition of *Plays*, purchased in 1849.
W. 41

MARMORA, SEA OF

The ancient *Propontis, the Sea of Marmora (alt. Marmara), is the body of water between Europe (N.) and *Asia (S.) between European and Asiatic *Turkey. It is connected with the *Black Sea on the east through the *Bosporus, with the *Aegean Sea on the west by the *Dardanelles. The ancient *Constantinople (modern Istanbul) was on the shores of the sea, which is 170 miles by fifty miles in area.

M. sailed the foggy Sea of Marmora 10 December 1856, commenting in his journal on what a "sublime approach has the Sultan to his capital. Antichambers of seas & lakes, & corridors of glorious straits." He remained in the area until 19 December, observing the waterways from many points of view.
M.D. 45

MARQUESAS; MARQUESANS

Among the easternmost (09°00' S., 139°00' W.) of the *Polynesian archipelagos, the Marquesas is a chain of ten major islands of ancient volcanic origin some 230 miles in length from north to southeast and 385 square miles in area. They are 4,200 miles west of the *Peruvian coast, 850 miles northeast of *Tahiti, 220 miles southeast of *Hawaii, 2,000 miles east of *Samoa. The southern, or *Mendaña group, discovered in 1595, consists of Hiva Oa, Fatu Hiva, Tahuata, and Mohotani. The northern, or *Washington group, discovered in 1791 by *Captain Joseph Ingraham, are Nukahiva (see "Nukuheva"), Ua Pu, Ua Huka, Eiao, Hatatu, and Motu One. In 1813, Captain *David Porter, of the *Essex, annexed the Marquesas, but the annexation was never ratified. *French occupation followed, requested by the chief of Tahuata, but in 1842 the joint chiefs quarreled with the French and proclaimed cessation of French sovereignty.

Nukahiva, a flattened volcanic plain 2,600 feet in elevation, is the largest of the chain. M.'s "Tior," Taiohae (Hakapehi), on the west, is its central bay and major port. The eastern bay valley, home of the *Typees, is the richer, more fertile of the two major sides. With no spring water, the Marquesas rely on rains and suffered droughts and famines before western civilization decimated the population (in 1882, down to 4,865 from a height of 100,000).

Settled around the second century B.C. by voyagers from Samoa, the Marquesas are populated by peoples of Melanesian/Polynesian stock, who early spread their culture by voyages to Hawaii, Easter Island, and *New Zealand. Because the valley tribes (Haape, or Teiis, Typees, and others) have remained isolated from each other through much of their history, there has been much ritualistic intertribal hostility, but not really much bloodshed in the wars. Early western explorers discovered that cannibalism was tapering off and practiced only in the sacramental sense; to eat one's enemy was to pay tribute, ingesting his flesh so as to acquire his characteristics.

Much of early explorers' decrying of Marquesan ways arose because their civilization was so different from those of the west. Government as we know it was almost nonexistent at the time of M.'s visit (1842). This fact was dramatized by the absence of unity among the many tribes and subtribes on the islands. Even chiefs of individual tribes had little or no power. Yet each person had his own office to fulfill, with rather complex responsibilities. Early explorers noted that the Marquesans had no word for "law," nor, indeed, a word for "because." Yet an act such as theft was punishable by execution. Their religious practices were largely misunderstood because they ascribed no moral attributes to their gods (who might be nothing but small cloth dolls, or figures like M.'s "Moa Artua" in *T.*). Instructed in *Christianity by early missionaries, the friendly Marquesans feared the Christian god, seeing the Bible's *Jehovah as a vindictive hurler of thunder and lightning. Also difficult for westerners to comprehend was the importance of sexuality and fertility to the Marquesan life. Kinship structures were complex and frequently celebrated in ceremonial genealogical chants. Intermarriage was permitted within some boundaries and limited polygamy observed with strict hierarchical laws. Yet marriage did not have western sexual strictures attached; in fact, a Marquesan had not only sexual rights outside of marriage, but sexual obligations as well. Adolescent sexual initiations involved elaborate public display and examination of genitals, and eroticism and the fertility of life were so enmeshed that genitals were also displayed at funerals to show grief.

Much admired by Porter and other early visitors were the large Marquesan dwellings: thatch buildings with large stone porches, sometimes as long as sixty feet. Found in clusters, these "pae paes" formed small "estates" with a family's eating house, a cook house, and a sacred platform ("morai") for family rites, in addition to a public plaza for dancing and festivals: M.'s "tohua," the "*hoolah-hoolah" ground, or Taboo Groves, also remarked upon by Porter.

The Marquesan warrior's tapa house, part of the chief's estate, was a gathering place for men, especially at time of *tapu*, when association with women was interdicted. Similar men's halls are described by *F.D. Bennett, E.S.C. Handy, E.H. Lamont.

Porter's visit devastated the Typee valley, which recuperated after his departure. The voyage of the *Vincennes*, described by *Rev. Charles Stewart, was to conciliate the Typees damaged by Porter.

The word "Typee" is properly "Taipi." Anderson (*Melville in the South Seas*, 101) discusses the meaning of the word, in light of M.'s definition: "a lover of human flesh" (*T.* 4). Natives of the Marquesas who translated for European and American visitors cast words in accordance with their own political beliefs, with "Taipi" also rendered as "enemy," or "enemy people." Residents of Anna Maria Bay (see "Nukuheva") translated their own name, Teii, as "young man of noble condition." "Taioa" and "Hapa" were rendered as "fisherman" and "little fellow" or boaster."

The "certain work" treating of the "Washington, or Northern Marquesas" in *T.* is either the summary book of Pacific narratives: *Historical Account of the Circumnavigation of the Globe*, or *Georg H. von Langsdorff's *Voyages and Travels in Various Parts of the World* (1813).

See also "Hannamanoo"; "Hivarhoo"; "Hytyhoo"; "Protestant Missions"; "Santa Christina"; "Washington Group"; "Whitihoo."
T. Passim; O. Passim

MARQUISE
Marquise (or Marquess) is a courtesy title of nobility, with no legal status, ranked below *Duke. First was Robert de Vere, Earl of *Oxford, who became Marquess of *Dublin in 1385. A Marquis is addressed as "The most Honorable the Marquess of _"; the Sovereign calls him "Our right trusty and entirely beloved cousin," from the time when Henry IV was related to every earl in his kingdom.
W. 56

MARQUIS OF WATERFORD

Henry De La Poer (1811-1859) was Third Marquess of Waterford at the time referred to in *R.* 44. I have not been able to certify that he was a "madcap," but he did die in a fall from a horse, at Corbally, near Carrick-on Suir, where the Marquess of Waterford sits as Baron Tyrone.
R. 44

MARRYAT, CAPTAIN

Frederick Marryat (1792-1848): *English naval officer and novelist. Son of a *West Indian land owner who was a chairman of Lloyd's, Marryat entered the navy at fourteen, rising to captain's rank. Among his honors were a companionship of the Bath and membership in the *French Légion d'Honneur, awarded for a code of flag signals he devised. Retired from the navy in 1830, he became a prolific writer and editor of *Metropolitan Magazine*. Among his sea stories: *The Naval Officer: or Scenes and Adventures in the Life of Frank Mildmay* (1829); *The King's Own* (1830); *Peter Simple* (1834); *Jacob Faithful* (1834); *Japhet in Search of a Father* (1836); *Mr. Midshipman Easy* (his most popular, 1836); *Poor Jack* (1840). Other works are impressions of the *United States in 1839 and several children's books. Contemporary critics consistently held up Marryat's works as models for M. to emulate.

Marryat died a farmer in Norfolk; in 1872 his daughter published *The Life and Letters of Captain Marryat*.
T. 4; W. 90

MARS

The *Roman god of war (and agriculture), identified with the *Greek Ares, and second in power to *Jupiter. He was the father of *Romulus and Remus, whom he helped to survive.

In astronomy, the planet closest to Earth, about half its size, and fourth in order of distance from the Sun. Its bright red color caused ancient peoples to identify it with the god of war. In M.'s time, little was known about the planet. Its atmosphere had been observed in the late eighteenth century, and in the 1860's scientists began attempting to analyze it, discovering its two moons in the process. Its "canals" were described in the late 1870's, when confusion about the word led to much speculation about its hosting intelligent life. M.'s ascribing Mars a "constellated crown" (*M.* 168) may arise from occasional confusion with the stars Antares and *Aldebaran, or from its sometimes appearing brighter than Jupiter.
M. 168; W. 49; I.P. 17

MARSEILLES

*France's second largest city and chief *Mediterranean port is situated on a bay of the Gulf of Lions, surrounded by limestone hills. Although it is France's oldest city, few ancient buildings remain. Marseille (in French usage) was settled c. 600 B.C. by *Greeks from Asia Minor. The *Romans annexed "Massilia" in 49 B.C., and thereafter it was invaded by Visigoths (see "Goths"), *Burgundians, *Saracens, and *Normans. The city passed to France in 1486.

Marseille has always been known for its distinctive waterfront, crowded with an exotic mix of races, and sailors arriving at what Dumas called "the meeting place of the entire world." Even in the nineteenth century, Marseille was known to sailors as a dangerous and exciting city: one big "Booble Alley."
O. 32; R. 7; R. 18; R. 21; C.M. 34

MARSY

Balthazar Marsy (1624-74), sculptor of *Versailles gardens, created the *Basin d'Encelade* (see "Enceladus.") M. visited Versailles in December 1849.
P. 25:4

MARTAIR

M.'s "Martair" is Matea, a small, obscure settlement on *Moreea, near Afareaitu (see "Afrehitoo").
O. Passim

MARTHA, --S

See "Maries, Marthas, etc."
P. 3:1; P. 23:2; M.D. 132

MARTHA'S VINEYARD

The twenty-mile by ten-mile island is five miles south of the southwestern corner of *Cape Cod, across Vineyard Sound, and separated from its neighboring island to the east, *Nantucket, by Muskeget Sound. Gosnold visited the islands in 1602, and "the Vineyard" was settled by 1642. Its towns include Edgartown, Chilmark, *Gay Head, Oak Bluffs, *Tisbury (including Vineyard Haven village), and West Tisbury, some of which have developed since M.'s time. "Vineyarders" moved from the pursuit of whales in the nineteenth century to resort-keeping in the twentieth. The change was already in evidence

when M. and his father-in-law, *Lemuel Shaw, visited the island in July of 1852.

(M. errs in *M.D.* 54 in making "Radney" at first a
"Vineyarder" and then a "Nantucketer.")

O. 82; R. 23; W. 4; M.D. 16; M.D. 48

MARTIAL

Marcus Valerius Martialis (c. A.D. 40- c. A.D. 104) was
a *Roman historian of *Spanish descent whose 1,561 epigrams
are remarkable for wit and formal perfection and whose poems
accurately paint both Roman society and human foibles. He
was a friend to *Pliny, the *Senecas, and Quintilian, among
others, and his work has been faulted for its pervading flattery
of important people and for its obscenity. Martial dismissed
the latter charge: *"lasciva est nobis pagina, vita proba"*
(*Epigrams* I, 4): "My poems are lascivious, but my life is
pure."

R. 46

MARTIAL

Referring to *Mars, god of war.

M.D. 24 and elsewhere

MARTIAL LAW

The term is less significant in *England than in the U.S.
Definition is difficult owing to the question of the extent to
which "martial" means "military." Basically, it means temporary military rule of domestic areas at times during which
civil rule is impossible or undesirable. It may be proclaimed by
the *President or a state governor, but proclamation is not necessary, and it has been invoked illegally, along with revocation
of *habeas corpus.*

Under martial law, civilians may be tried by military
courts, and a military commander may later be called upon to
justify. *Washington invoked martial law during the 1794
Whiskey Rebellion (see "Monongahela"), and it was declared at
Pearl Harbor, Hawaii, in 1941.

(See also "Gracchi.")

W.70

MARY, BLOODY; MARY TUDOR

Mary I (1516-1558), queen of *England from 1553 to 1558,
was the daughter of *Henry VIII and Catherine of Aragon.
She was kept apart from her mother from 1531 and made to

acknowledge her own illegitimacy, living in constant fear of her father's second wife, *Anne Boleyn; upon the latter's beheading, Mary reconciled with her father and was restored to the succession. Under the reign of her brother, Edward VI, she was again persecuted, but personal popularity was restored to her when Edward died.

Her early acts as queen were charitable, but ill advisement and marriage to Philip of Spain, son of Charles V, crumbled her power. With reconcilement of the throne of England to the Vatican came enforcement of old heresy laws, which Mary might have gently enforced. Instead she chose fierce persecution of *Protestants. In four years, at least 300 persons were burned at the stake at *Smithfield, earning Mary's nickname of "Bloody," and deepening English hatred of Rome. Frequent illness, including false pregnancy, weakened her chronically frail constitution, and her death finally halted the executions.
M. 181; R. 44; W. 75

MARYLAND

One of the original thirteen states of the Union, Maryland is bounded by *Pennsylvania (N.), *Delaware and the *Atlantic (E.), *Virginia, *Washington D.C., and West Virginia (S. & W.), and West Virginia (W.). Measuring 195 miles (E.-W.) on its northern border, and from three to 125 miles north and south, the "Old Line State" is so-called because its northern boundary is the Mason-Dixon Line, which came to signify the separation of north and south in the *Civil War. (The line, which does not extend beyond the *Ohio River, was drawn and milestoned in 1763-68 by surveyors Charles Mason and Jeremiah Dixon to settle a dispute between the *Penns of Pennsylvania and the Baltimores of Maryland.)

Verrazano visited the area in 1524; Captain John Smith charted it, along with much of the *Chesapeake Bay, in 1608. Torn by feudal boundary disputes and religious conflicts, Maryland was further disturbed during the Civil War, when it remained in the Union despite sympathy to, and some practice of, *slavery. Thus, "Baltimore" in O. 11 is, paradoxically, a runaway slave from a Union state.

The United States Naval Academy is located in the capital city, Annapolis, as is St. John's College (established 1696).

M. *lectured in *Baltimore in February of 1859.
O. 11

MARY QUEEN OF HEAVEN

See "Catholic . . . . "
P. 2:2

MARY TUDOR
See "Mary, Bloody."
R. 44

MARZETTI, SIGNOR
Joseph Marzetti was an actor famous for his portrayals of apes; in 1848, he played in *The Brazilian Ape* at Burton's and in 1849 in *Jocko* at Niblo's Garden, *New York.
C.M. 24

MASON GOOD'S BOOK OF NATURE
Dr. John Mason Good (1764-1827), eminent *British scholar, philosopher, linguist, and physician, compiled a hubristic volume of essays, *The Book of Nature* (3 vols., 1826), discussing the nature of the material and animate worlds, as well as the nature of the mind. His tone and diction are sententious and smug, and his message rather too esoteric for most sailors. *The Book of Nature* took a strong stand against *phrenology. (Harper's published a Stereotype Edition in 1837.)
W. 41

MASONS; MASONIC
See "Freemason."
W. 39; W. 46; C.M. 4

MASQUES: MASQUERADE
The origins of this word's root are obscure. "Masque" may derive from Arab or Spanish (*máscara*)root, meaning "laughingstock," or "buffoon." Or it may come from the old Provençal verb, *masarer*: "to black the face."
The "masque" may have begun as an *Italian carnival amusement, like mumming. By the sixteenth century, the masque involved a band of colorfully masked persons who arrived at a social gathering in a politically symbolic procession or show, usually praising the host. The masquers would stop performing to mingle and revel with the guests, then rejoin their own pageant. In *France and *England, the masque became an important literary form. By the late sixteenth century, the word "masquerade" referred to a masque, or to a deceitful disguise.
See also "Jesuit."
C.M. 18; C.M. 45 and elsewhere

MASSA
OED lists the first printed use of the "negro corruption of *master*" as Samuel Foote's *The Cozeners* (1774) III (*Works* 1799 II, 190) and second in Stowe's *Uncle Tom's Cabin* (spelled "Mas'r").
M.D. 64

MASSACHUSETTS
The "Bay State" was one of the original thirteen states of the Union. It is bounded by the *Atlantic (E.), *Rhode Island and *Connecticut (S.), *New York (W.), *Vermont and *New Hampshire (N.). It extends 145 miles, east to west, and from forty-seven to ninety miles, north to south. The *Cape Cod peninsula (now cut by a canal) extends the state some sixty-five miles into the ocean, north of the islands of *Martha's Vineyard and *Nantucket.

M. was a longtime resident of the western part of the state, at *Pittsfield, in the *Berkshire Hills just south of *Mount Greylock, the highest peak. He frequently visited his in-laws at *Boston, the capital.

Massachusetts has many sites important to literature (especially M.'s), history, industry, and learning. The Norse explored the coastline in the eleventh century, leaving anchorage markings in granite boulders. John Cabot explored in 1497-98, and Gosnold examined Cape Cod in 1602. The *Puritans established the second *English colony on the continent at Plymouth, in 1620 (having landed first at Provincetown, Cape Cod). Among other important events in Massachusetts history are the *Salem Witch Trials of 1626, the founding of *Harvard University in 1636, the *Revolutionary battles of *Lexington, Concord, and *Bunker Hill. By M.'s time, Massachusetts was a center for *Abolitionism. The influx of *Irish immigrants turned the state increasingly industrial and urban, and brought about the fading of maritime interests in the nineteenth century.

See also entry on *Lemuel Shaw, M.'s father-in-law, who was Chief Justice of the state.
Passim

MASSACHUSETTS CALENDAR
An almanac, probably showing a picture of a man surrounded by *zodiac signs.
M.D. 99

MASSACHUSETTS INDIANS
In *M.D.*, M. mistakenly calls the *Pequods "Massachusetts Indians."
M.D. 16

MASSAFUERO; MASSFUERO
Más Afuera is one of the *Juan Fernándes Islands (Islas Juan Fernández), possessions of *Chile. Más Afuera (Spanish for "farther out") was named in contrast with Más Atierra ("nearer land"), the latter being 400 miles west of mainland *Santiago, and the former 500 miles. Más Afuera has a 5,415 foot-high volcanic mountain and is still uninhabited, although its waters are much used for fishing.
M. 1

MASSASOIT
Chief of the Wampanoag Indians, Massasoit (d. 1661), whose real name may have been Ousamequin or Wousamequin, made a peace treaty with the Plymouth (*Massachusetts) Colony in 1621. Winthrop, Williams, and Bradford mention his role in the peace which lasted until the rule of his son, *King Philip.
C.M. 25

MASSILON
Jean Baptiste Massilon (1663-1742), bishop of Clermont and preacher at the Court of *Versailles under Louis XIV and Louis XV (see "Bourbon"), was the most celebrated orator of the time. Popular with both the poor and the rich, Massilon gained his greatest stature in the funeral oration of the Roi Soleil with his opening words: *"Dieu seul est grand"* (Only *God is great).
R. 41; W. 38

MASTER OF FAITH
*Jesus, in the *Simeon story.
C.M. 45

MASTERS OF ARTS
Holders of the degree usually referred to as M.A. See A.M.'s
R. 12

MASTODONS
See "Sandwiches."
M. 132; M.D. 14

MATAVAI
United States arrived at Matavai Bay, southwest of
Point Venus, *Tahiti, on 12 October 1843. A dangerous dolphin
shoal precluded anchoring at night.
O. 38

MATCH-TUB
A match-tub was half-filled with sand or water, with
matches placed in notches in the rim so that burning ends
overhung safely. In W., match-tubs double as (dangerous)
furniture. Admiral Franklin identifies the original for the
"Gunner" in W. 31 as "a rare character," who had "no mercy
upon any delinquent subordinate, more especially if he sat
upon the match tubs." He would "place iron spikes on them so
that anyone sitting on them might receive an ugly wound, or if
he stepped upon them with bare feet, might be seriously injured" (p. 32). The gunner, Asa G. Curtis, was eventually
obliged to remove the spikes, lest the ship's crew be decimated.
W. 15; W. 84

MATERIALIST
*Epicurus and Lucretius were early exponents of Mate-
rialist anti-idealist philosophy, which maintains that nothing
exists but matter; mind is a phenomenon of matter, and there
is no spiritual first cause. The Post-*Darwinian era saw scientific applications, especially in Karl Marx's Dialectical Materialism.
M. 126

MATSE AVATAR
See "Vedas" and "Avatar."
M.D. 55

MATSMAI
The reference is probably to Matsumae (Matsumai, or
Fukuyama), a fishing town at the southwestern tip of
Hokkaido, *Japan, on Tsugaru Strait. Not an island, as M.
has it in *M.D.* 109, Matsumae is the oldest town on Hekkaido,
with a feudal era citadel built by the Matsumae family.

(M. probably saw "Matsmai" included in a list of "Islands and their provinces," in McCulloch's *Universal Gazeteer* [1804].)
M.D. 109

MATTOCK
An agricultural tool used from at least the eighth century, consisting of a curved and sharpened blade on a long sharpened pole; rather between a hoe, a pick, and a spade. It is used to loosen hard ground. "Mattock" is also used as a verb.
M. 19

MAUI
M.'s "*Mowee" (20°47' N., 156°22' W.) is the second largest of the *Hawaiian Islands, containing the largest extinct volcano crater, Haleakala ("House of the Sun"). Maui is shaped like the head and bust of a woman and consists of two mountains (East and West Maui) connected by a six-mile-wide low isthmus.
T. 25; T. 32

MAURY, LIEUTENANT
Matthew Fontaine Maury (1806-1873), of *Virginia, oceanographer and Director of the *Naval Observatory in *Washington, circumnavigated the globe in *Vincennes. Lamed in an accident, his subsequent shore duty led to development of the Observatory and to improvements in navigation and meteorology. After serving on the Confederate side in the *Civil War, he attempted to found a Virginian colony in *Mexico, then briefly resided in *England. Returning to Virginia, he became professor of meteorology at Virginia Military Institute. He published many works on astronomy, physical geography, sea lanes and coasts. M.'s *M.D.* reference is probably to pre-publication discussion of Maury's second edition of *Explanations and Sailing Directors to Accompany Lieut. Maury's Investigation of the Wind and Current Charts* (1851), which attempts to chart main whaling grounds.
M.D. 44

MAUSOLUS
*Persian King or *Satrap of Caria (part of modern *Turkey), whose widow, Artemisia, erected a sepulchral mon-

ument at Halicarnassus in 353 B.C., one of the Seven Wonders of the World. Source of "mausoleum."
M. 63; P. 4:1

MAXWELL, MUNGO
M. makes the commonly accepted error of claiming that Maxwell was killed by *John Paul Jones. In 1770, on the merchant man *John* in the *West Indies, Jones charged the carpenter with negligence and whipped him with a cat o'nine tails. Maxwell later died of malaria. Jones proved his innocence of the death but was widely criticized. Several years later, Jones did kill a mutineer who had swung a bludgeon at him. Jones escaped under an assumed name.
I.P. 14

MAY-DAY
In ancient times, *Roman youths spent the *Calends of May dancing and singing in praise of *Flora, goddess of fruits and flowers. Later, games and sports were added to the festivities. May-day in modern times is May 1.   In traditional *British celebrations, the chief personage is a *May Queen, who reigns over festivities such as "going-a-maying," bonfiremaking, dancing about a *Maypole, and bearing relics of nature-worship. *Hawthorne's "The Maypole of Merry Mount" focuses on the implications.
M.D. 79

MAY-POLES
See "May-day."
R. 28

MAY QUEEN
See "May-day."
P. 5:4; C.M. 17

MAZATLAN
San Juan, Mexico: 17°05' N., 95°26' W.
W. 53

MAZEPPA
*Byron's poem of that name (1819) was based on a passage in *Voltaire's *Charles XII*: a wild tale of Mazeppa's being bound naked onto a wild Ukrainian horse which carried him on a mad journey into the Ukraine and then fell dead, leaving the hero to be rescued by *Cossack peasants.
M.D. 60

MAZZINI
Giuseppe Mazzini (1805-1872), *Italian nationalist revolutionary and prophet of the Risorgimento, was born sickly and became studious. At *Genoa University, the religious but anticlerical Mazzini began a career in literature which was put aside in order to pursue the unification of Italy. From exile in *France and then *Switzerland, he formed the Giovine Italia ("Young Italy") group. Sentenced to death, along with *Garibaldi, as a result of his plotting, he was expelled from several European nations for urging insurrection. Settling in *England, he became the prophet of nationalism for all, inspiring Italian martyrs by his conviction that nationalism was *God's will.

In 1848 he returned to Italy, where he held office after the *Pope's flight. He helped defend Rome against the French, who were already victorious in the north, but after the Pope's restoration his teachings had less success, it becoming clear that outside assistance was needed. In *London in 1858, Mazzini continued writings aimed at the Italian people, as unification was brought about with the help of France and *Prussia. By 1861, when Italy had become a nation, he returned to raise controversy and eventually died a disguised fugitive in *Pisa.
C.M. 29

MCCULLOCH, JOHN RAMSAY
A *Scottish economist (1789-1864) who worked with James Mill to propagate the economic theory of David Ricardo. An influential contributor to *Edinburgh Review, McCulloch held a prestigious teaching position at University College, *London. He published *Principles of Political Economy* (1825), *The Dictionary of Commerce and Commercial Navigation* (1832), and *The Literature of Political Economy* (1837).

(See also "Extracts" 69.)
M.D. Extracts 69

M.D.

From Lat. *Medicinae Doctor*, one holding degree of Doctor of Medicine. When spoken, "em dee."
0. 35

MDCCCXLVIII

Davis suggests ("An Analysis of *Mardi*," VII) that the Roman Numeral reference to the year 1848 (during which M. was composing *M*.) is a covert slur on the Roman *Catholic Church. The chapter so titled is about a dreaded oracle, "Hivohitee," and the Church had elected a new *Pope, Pius IX, in 1846 (took office in 1847). By 1848, a schism developed in the Church, leading eventually to hostility on the part of other nations and negative public opinion regarding the Church in Rome.
M. 108

MEAD

In *Scandinavian mythology, the divinely intoxicating beverage of the gods and denizens of *Valhalla; thought to be hart's milk.
M.3

MEASON

Samuel Measan (or Mason) (c. 1750-1803) was leader of a gang of cutthroat bandits in the southwest *United States.

See also "Harpe, the brothers," for an account of Meason's death.
C.M. 1

MEATH

Meath is a pastoral county of what is now the Republic of *Ireland. It is famous for the Book of Kells, inscribed there in the eighth century, and for a huge Bronze Age burial mound, Newgrange tumulus.
O. 37

MECAENAS

Gaius Cilnius Maecenas, *Roman statesman, adviser to *Augustus Caesar, and patron of letters, died 8 B.C. He not only supported the work of *Virgil and *Horace; he preserved their lives. Thought the originator of shorthand writing, Maecenas spent his last years in the cultivation of the fine arts.
W. 11

MECCA

Mecca (Arabic *Makkah*) is the birthplace of *Mohammed and the most sacred city of Islam. The capital of the present-day Saudi Arabian province of Hejaz, it is a center for pilgrimages limited to Muslims, with pillars marking taboo territory. There is a large *mosque and reservoirs for ritual bathing. In the area of a small cube-shaped stone building (the Ka'ba), Muslims believe, several *Old Testament stories took place. Pilgrims follow elaborate ancient rules, and their numbers have remained constant despite power struggles over the city.
W. 69; M.D. 92; C.M. 2

MEDE, --S

Media, the fictional king in *M*. takes his name from an ancient west-Asian country bounded on the north by the Caspian Sea, on the west by present-day Armenia, on the south by *Persia, on the east by *Parthia. Originally called Aria, it took its name from Medus, the son of *Medea. The Medes overthrew the *Assyrian empire about 600 B.C. Conquered by *Cyrus, Media became part of the Persian Empire in 550 B.C., later part of Parthia, and then part of the *Roman Empire.
M. 3; M. 60; M.D. 16; C.M. 22

MEDEA

The sorceress-niece of *Circe and priestess of *Hecate, Princess Medea (or Medeia) of *Colchis figures in many *Greek myths, performing magic for both good and evil purposes in the works of Apollonius Rhodius, Pindar, Euripedes, *Ovid, and Pausanias.

In the *Jason story, Medea loves Jason and helps him perform the difficult feats imposed by her father, King Aeëtes, but she also helps him kill her brother, Apsyrtus. Married to Jason, she restores his father, *Aeson, to youth but has the children of king Pelias chop him to bits. In her most famous myth, rejected by her husband, Medea gets revenge by tricking his new fiance into burning herself alive; she then kills their two children, Mermerus and Pheres. There are no myths about her death; in one tale, she is exiled by her second husband, Aegeus; in another she or her son, Medus (or *Media, or Medeius), establishes the nation of the *Medes.
C.M. 16

MEDIA

See "Mede . . . . "
M. Passim

MEDICIS

The family that ruled *Florence, *Italy, from the fifteenth to the eighteenth century was notable as patrons of art, important *Popes, and the originals of *Machiavelli's *The Prince.*

See also "Leo, Pope."
M. 181

MEDITERRANEAN

The arm of the *Atlantic between Europe and *Africa extends from the Strait of *Gibralter to the coast of southwest Asia; it is 2,400 miles long and up to 1,000 miles wide. The Mediterranean has been since ancient times an important sea route, used by the *Phoenicians, *Carthaginians, *Greeks, and *Romans.
Passim

MEDITERRANEAN SQUADRON

See "Squadron"; "Barbary Coast . . . . "
W. Passim

MEDUSA

In *Greek mythology, Medusa and her sisters (Stheno and Euryale) are monstrous Gorgons (from *gorgos*, "terrible"), lesser earth gods whose glance turned men to stone. (Demogorgons were demon/gorgons whose names were not be be pronounced.) Their father was Phorcys, son of the Sea and Earth.

In the *Perseus story, the proud Perseus was tricked into promising King Polydectes the head of Medusa as a wedding gift. *Hermes and Pallas Athena helped him equip himself properly with the aid of the nymphs of the North, who could be found only through the three Gray Women living in a sunless land and sharing but one eye between them. With Hermes's magic sword and Athena's reflecting shield with which to avoid eye contact, Perseus found the Gray Women and went to the country of the *Hyperboreans, who gave him magic sandals and a cap to make him invisible. Perseus crossed the ocean to the sisters' island, where he found the three asleep—winged and scaled dragon-like creatures with hair of squirming snakes. Hermes and Athena pointed out Medusa (the other two were immortal), and Perseus cut her throat and put the head into a container, turning himself invisible to escape the other sisters. At his return, Perseus killed

the wicked Polydectes and gave Medusa's head to Athena, who carried it on Zeus's (see "Jupiter" and "Jove") shield forever.
M. 18; R. 49; W. 8; W. 91

MEDUSA, THE

Probably the most horrible shipwreck in history (and the subject of Theodore Gericault's painting, "The Raft of the Medusa"), the wreck of the *Medusa* in 1816 stands as an example of inefficiency and injustice. The forty-four-gun ship had headed to sea in a convoy, carrying 400 passengers, many of them drinking heavily, when the expedition turned into a tragedy of errors. The ship nearly grounded very soon after departure, probably because the captain had turned navigation over to a passenger. It grounded again tragically on the well-charted Arguin Banks north of *Cape Blanco, some sixty miles off the coast of *Africa, and some half-measures were taken to lighten the ship, which floated and then grounded again, badly damaged. There were only six boats, holding some 250 people, so a poorly constructed raft was built (65 x 23 feet) to hold 150 people and supplies. Important passengers were safe in the boats, which were to tow the raft. The lines were cut or broken, however, and the raft drifted helplessly for twelve days, during which time no attempt was made to send a rescue party. There was starvation, mutinous violence, and finally cannibalism before the brig *Argus arrived, taking off fifteen men and leaving more than that number, only a few of whom survived until the next attempt.

Abridged versions of J.B.H. Savigny and Alexandre Corréard's account of the sinking of *Medusa* and John McLeod's account of the *Alceste* tragedy (both 1817) appeared in one volume published in *Dublin in 1831.
W.8

MEGATHERIUMS

See "Sandwiches."
M. 132

MELANCTHON

Philipp Melanchthon (1497-1560) was a *German humanist theologian whose surname, the Greek form of Schwarzerd ("black earth"), was awarded for achievements in Greek classics. He questioned traditional scholastic theology as a student at *Heidelberg, Tübingen, and Wittenberg, and revolutionized study of the classics as Professor of Greek at Wittenberg. His revisions of *Luther's translations led him to become an Evangelist himself, as well as a leader of the *Reformation, continually embroiled in theological controversy.

Melanchthon's head was compared with that of a famous criminal in the article on *phrenology in William and Robert Chambers, eds., *Information for the People: A Popular Encyclopedia* (Philadelphia, 1847), where it was claimed that his moral superiority was revealed in his high forehead.
R. 33; M.D. 79

MELCHISEDEC

The name (variously Melchisedech, Melchizedek) is from the *Hebrew root for "king." Melchisedec is important in *Genesis, *Hebrews, and *Psalms; he is seen by *Christians as a foreshadower of *Jesus. He is first encountered in Genesis 14:18 as the *Canaanite "King of Salem" (*Jerusalem) and "priest of the most high God" who blesses and feeds *Abraham (in a ceremony seen as a type of the *Eucharist), after Abraham's defeat of a coalition of wicked kings. He is revered by Abraham, who *tithes to him. Melchisedec, in turn, calls Abraham "El Elyon," an honorific later applicable to *Jehovah (see also "God").

M. shows knowledge of Melchisedec's importance in *Clarel* I, iii.

(The Melchisedecians were third-century heretics who held that the king was a heavenly power, perhaps Christ himself.)
R. 33

MELITA

In *Acts 28:1, the island of *Paul's temporary escape from the *Romans. See "Malta."
W. 65

MELLISH

Mellish was a *British supply ship, with a valuable cargo, taken by *John Paul Jones off *Boston in 1776 (along with other prizes). A mistaken painting of 1777 has *Alfred* capturing *Mellish*; *Mellish* was actually the tender for the warship *Alfred*.
I.P. 10

MELVILLE, ALLAN

M.'s brother, Allan Cargill Melville (7 April 1823-9 Feb. 1872), appears to have been a problem child who did not become a reliable adult until after a stormy law apprenticeship led to an office at 10 *Wall Street. Allan married Sophia Thurston (1827-58) in 1847, the year M. married Elizabeth Knapp Shaw. The two young couples set up housekeeping together at 103 Fourth Avenue, New York—along with mother Maria Melville and her four daughters. A member of Tammany Hall, Allan ran for New York State Assembly, while keeping his brother's accounts. M. attempted to write at home while Allan was at his office, but the arrival of infants to both wives was probably the last straw in a daily life that must have been chaos. M. wrote M. (dedicated to Allan), R., and W. under these circumstances and was probably grateful to leave the household to Allan and sail for Europe to arrange publication of W. in 1850.

Early in the following year, Allan became a father again, creating what Leon Howard called "a household consisting of a widow, two wives, three babies, and four spinsters" (Chap. 7, i), and the Herman Melvilles soon moved to *Pittsfield, to a home M. called Arrowhead. As M.'s nervous problems increased and his financial resources decreased, Allan tried unsuccessfully to get political appointments for him. In later life, he helped with financial dealings, employed M.'s problem son, *Stanwix, corresponded with publishers and in general filled in whenever M.'s "hypos" would "get an upper hand."

After Sophia's death in 1858, when Allan had married Jane Dempsey (died 1890), he managed by creative accounting for Herman to purchase a house at 104 East 26 Street, N.Y., while he himself bought Arrowhead. Herman's family was later to vacation there often. Through Allan's influence, the brothers were able to visit *Civil War battlefields together, maintaining close ties despite the distance between their homes.

In 1871, a year filled with losses of ones dear to M., Allan died suddenly of consumption "in great agony." He left four dependent children and one brother who was dependent in his own way.
M. Dedication

MELVILLE, THOMAS

Thomas Melville, Herman's brother, was born on 24 January 1830, died 5 March 1884. He was married to Catherine Eliza Bogart. At the age of sixteen, he followed his brother's example and went to sea. M. dedicated a poem, "To Tom," in 1859 or 1860 and sailed with him on Meteor around

Cape *Horn in 1860, in hope of restoring his own health.
Thomas became governor of "*Sailors Snug Harbor" in 1867,
his presence in *New York much appreciated by his elder
brother.
R. Dedication

MEMENTO MORI
     A reminder of death (from the Roman *Catholic canoni-
cal prayer for the dead).
C.M. 26

MEMNON, --STATUE
     1.   In Greek mythology, a handsome king of the
*Ethiopians, Memnon was son of the goddess of dawn, Eos
(*Aurora) and of Tithonus, *Priam's brother. He was killed by
*Achilles at *Troy, and Zeus (see "Jupiter" and "Jove")
honored him with magic birds, *memnonides*, to sprinkle water
on his grave.   The statue of the pharaoh, Amenophis (or
Amenhotep III), at *Thebes, was mistakenly called the Colossus of Memnon; it was said to make mysterious musical
sounds at dawn, in honor of Memnon's mother.
     2.   A powerful *Rhodian sea commander who subdued
the islands of the Aegean.
     The mythical Memnon was a favorite figure of romantic
writers, especially *Byron, De Quincey, Keats, and Carlyle, as
well as of *Bacon and *Voltaire.
P. 7:4; P. 7:5; P. 7:6; C.M. 37

MEMNON STONE
     See "Balance Rock."
P. 7:4; P. 7:6

MEMOIRS OF VIDOCQ
     See "Vidocq."
W. 44

MENDANNA
     Alvaro de Mandaña de Negra (1541-1595), nephew of the
Viceroy of *Peru, discovered the *Solomon Islands in 1567. At
his death on his second voyage, his wife, Doña Isabel Berrete,
took command on the island of Santa Cruz.
     In his "South Seas" lectures (1858-9), M. paid tribute to
the bold captain, whose expeditions were joined by people of the

court hoping to find *Ophir, supposedly *King Solomon's
source for gold.
T. 1; T. 25; 0. 3; W. 76; M.D. 57;

MENDOZA, MARQUESS DE
     Antonio de Mendoza (1490-1552) was born in *Granada,
descendant of a distinguished family of warriors. *Charles V
made him a military commander and diplomat. He served fifteen successful years as first Viceroy of New Spain, moderating harsh treatment of Indians and improving cultural and
intellectual life. He introduced the printing press, built
schools and hospitals, improved agriculture and mining. He
was promoted to the Viceroyalty of *Peru in 1551 and died in
*Lima.
     (See also "Mendanna.")
T. 1

"MENE, MENE, TEKEL UPHARSIN"
     See "Belshazzar."
M.D. 119

MENTOR
     In *Homer's Odyssey, Mentor is a wise and faithful
counsellor whose form Minerva assumes, accompanying
Telemachus in search of his father.
M. 57

MEPHISTOPHELES; MEPHISTOPHELEAN
     Mephistopheles is the name of one of the seven chief me-
dieval devils in *Goethe's Faust, to whom the hero sells his
soul.
W. 44; M.D. 32; I.P. 19

MERCATOR, --'S
     Gerardus Mercator (Gerhard Kremer; 1512-1594),
*Flemish cartographer and geographer, is best known for the
map projection bearing his name. The complete collection of
107 maps, the result of a lifetime effort to correct maps such as
*Ptolemy's, was published in 1595, after his death, as Cosmo-
graphical meditationes de fabrica mundi et fabricati figura.
His Nova et aucta orbis terrae descriptio ad usum navigantium
accommodata (1569), a world chart drawn on his projection but

not his invention, was the first applied in a nautical chart, enabling seamen to lay off compass courses.

Mercator was a mathematician, astronomer, and cosmographer, and a maker of scientific instruments for *Charles V. His terrestrial globe was published in 1541, the celestial in 1551, the great map of Europe in 1554.
O. 60; M. 4

MERCHANT SERVICE (PAY)

As of 1820, the pay rates for merchant seamen were $12.00 (a month) for able seamen, $10.00 for ordinary seamen, and $7.00 for boys. The rate was unchanged until 1854, making it difficult to staff merchant ships.

M. was rated an ordinary seaman, despite his suggestion otherwise.
W. 90

MERCURY

The Roman god of commerce and patron of astronomy, after whom is named the planet nearest the sun. As winged-footed messenger of the god, he is identified with the Greek Hermes (the name M. uses for him in *Timoleon*; see also "hermetic").
M. 184

MERENHOUT

*American Consul at *Tahiti in the late 1830's was J.A. Moerenhout. He was dismissed by *President Van Buren upon complaint of Queen *Pomaree but became French Consul in the 1840's. By the time described in *O*, among his less attractive acts he had apparently cheated the Queen out of land upon which to build his house. *Father Murphy and others complained to the French government, which supported Moerenhout. By 1842 he was a member of the provisional council established by *Du Petit Thouars, with the title "commissaire du roi."

Moerenhout was the author of Voyages aux Iles du Grand Ocean. Contenant des Documents Nouveaux sur la Géographie Physique et Politique, la Langue, la Littérature . . . de leurs Habitans (Paris: A. Bertrand, 1837).
O. 17; O. 32

MEROVINGIANS

A Frankish dynasty presumed the first race of *French kings, so called from Merovech, who sired Childeric I in the fifth century A.D. Succeeding generations (more than thirty kings) expanded French boundaries until the last Merovingian, Childeric III, was deposed in 751, replaced by a Carolingian (see "Charlemagne").

(See also "Beards.")

M. 84; W. 84

MERRY ANDREW

The sobriquet refers to a buffoon or jester, sometimes the attendant of a quack doctor at fairs. It was supposedly inspired by Andrew Borde (d. 1549), *Henry VIII's eccentric learned physician.

0. 71

"MERRY CHRISTMAS"

See "Christmas."

M.D. 22; P. 22:4

MERSEY, THE

*England's Mersey River is formed at Stockport (*Cheshire) by the junction of the Goyt and Tame Rivers, which drain the *Derbyshire Pennines. It is canalized and artificial through much of its course through low-elevation terrain. By the time it reaches the *Liverpool area, it is an estuary of the *Irish Sea. it was improved for navigation starting in the early eighteenth century.

R. Passim

MESCHACH

See "Shadrach, Meshach, and Abednego."

M.D. 98

MESOPOTAMIAN

Mesopotamia (Greek for "between rivers") was the ancient *Asian country about the lower *Tigris and lower *Euphrates rivers (in modern-day Iraq), extending from the *Persian Gulf north to the mountains of Armenia, and from the Iranian plateau on the east, to the *Syrian desert.

Mesopotamia, which was developed before *Egypt, is rightly called the "cradle of civilization," for its cities of Ur,

*Babylon, and others. It was well settled by the fourth mille-
nium B.C., and kingdoms which arose in the area led to the
Babylonian, *Assyrian, and *Persian Empires. Mesopotamia
became part of the *Roman Empire and the *Byzantine, before
being taken by the *Arabs. The city of *Baghdad became a
caliphate in A.D. 762, but the *Mongols destroyed the area in
1298.

    *Layard's excavations made Mesopotamia a popular
topic in the early nineteenth century. M. probably also saw
J.B. Fraser's *Mesopotamia and Assyria* (N.Y.: 1845), which
was included in *Harper's Family Library*.
M.D. 33

MESSINA
    The city (and province) of *Sicily is on the Strait of
Messina, fifty miles north-northeast of Catania. It was
founded in the eighth century B.C. by the *Greeks and variously claimed by the *Carthaginians, *Romans, *Byzantines,
*Saracens, *Normans, and *Spanish. It was badly damaged
by an earthquake in 1783.

    M. visited Messina 13-15 February 1857, attending a per-
formance of Verdi's *Macbeth*, visiting American vessels picking up fruit, and walking about the city's suburbs along the
shore before taking the thirty-eight-hour steamer trip to
*Naples.
R. 21; R. 49

METHUSALEH
    The oldest man mentioned in the *Bible, Methusaleh (or
Mathusala) is said to have lived for 969 years (*Genesis 5:27).
His name is derived from *Hebrew words meaning "adult"
and "extend."

    Several interpretations have been offered regarding
Methusaleh's longevity: Biblical "years" may have been
shorter than ours; genealogies may have been written before
the time of precise chronology; the claim may be an exaggeration typical of national legends; ancient people *may* have lived
ten times as long as modern ones.

    In the *New Testament, Methusaleh is included in the
genealogy in *Luke 3:37.
R. 7; M.D. 104; P. 7:4

MEXICO, GULF OF
    The arm of the *Atlantic bounded on the north by the
*United States, and on the southwest by *Mexico is 1,000 miles

long (E.-W.) and 800 miles wide. The *equatorial current joins
the *Antilles current here to form the Florida current: the initial section of the *Gulf Stream.
R. 20

MEXICO; MEXICAN WAR
     The *Aztecs settled the area we know as Mexico in the
twelfth century. The Spaniard Fernández de Córdoba discovered the Yucatan in 1517, calling the area "New Spain."
*Cortés entered in 1519 and conquered in 1521. Subsequent
"westernization" occurred under the Viceroyalty of New Spain,
starting in 1535. A few wealthy landholders were favored and
the Indians exploited, giving rise to the poor and racially
mixed mestizo class.
     Mexico achieved independence in 1821, although revolu-
tionary activity had begun at least ten years earlier. Civil wars
and dictatorships followed, so that the *United States was able
to seize *Texas in 1845. The Mexican War (1846-48) ended in
cession of all territory north of the *Rio Grande (including
modern *California, Arizona, and New Mexico).
     Mexico City, the capital, is 200 miles west of the Gulf
port of Veracruz, in the shadow of *Popocatepetl volcano. The
Aztec capital, Tenochtitlán, was founded in 1176 on an island
in Lake Texcoco: now the heart of Mexico City. There was an
Aztec population of c. 300,000 before Cortés leveled the city. He
built the first *Christian church on the site of an Aztec temple,
in 1525. Mexico City was occupied in 1847 by forces under
*General (Winfield) Scott.
     M.D. 14 and *M.D.* 89 references to Mexico lump the
United States with other imperialist powers, despite the ardent
expansionism expressed by most Americans of the time, including the *Duyckincks and M.'s brother *Gansevoort
Melville. M.'s cousin, Guert Gansevoort, participated in the
bombardment of Veracruz. M.'s fears of world-wide disorder
to follow the Mexican War were soon realized in Europe and in
the United States, where the Democratic party of *Jackson
splintered into anti-slavery Free Soilers, secessionists,
expansionists, and pro-slavery factions.
     The War was on M.'s mind in a letter (29 May 1846) to
Gansevoort, in Europe (who, unknown to M., had died two
weeks before):

               People here are all in a state of delirium about the
               Mexican War. A military ardor pervades all
               ranks. . . . Nothing is talked of but the "Halls of
               Montezumas." . . . Who knows what else this
               might lead to—Will it breed a rupture with

England? Or any other great power? . . . Lord, the
day is at hand, when we will be able to talk of our
killed and wounded like some of the old Eastern
conquerors reckoning them up by thousands.

The *M*. 75 reference to a Mexican "House of the Sun"
may be an error. M. confused the Mexican Aztecs with the
*Andean *Incas, who were far more dedicated to sun-worship
than the highly polytheistic Aztecs.
        See also "Crockett"; "Manifest Destiny."
W. 36

MICHAEL, --S
        There are many Michaels in the *Bible. M.'s is the
*archangel standing beside the throne of *God, with *Gabriel
and *Raphael. The patron angel of *Israel, Michael is mentioned three times in the *Old Testament (especially in
*Daniel) and twice in the *New.
        His role is often confused with that of Gabriel. The Bible
has him leading the celestial hosts against the evil of *Belial,
*Gog and Magog, or the primordial dragon (see also
"Vikings"). Later Jewish writings represent him as the military leader against Edom (*Rome). His other tasks: interces-
sion before God; performance of charity; recording of the
names of the saved; mediating between God and *Moses at
Mount *Sinai.
W. 40; M.D. Extracts

MICHIGAN
        The twenty-sixth state was admitted to the Union in
1837. The "Wolverine State" or "Lake State" is cut by the four-
mile-wide Straits of Mackinac (see "MacKinaw") into two sections. The southern section, or Lower Peninsula, is 285 miles
wide (N.-S.) and 195 miles long. The Upper Peninsula is 320
miles wide (E.-W.) and 125 miles long. There are also Michi-
gan-owned islands in the adjacent Lake *Michigan and Lake
*Huron. The *French discovered the area in 1618; Marquette
established a mission in 1671; in 1679 LaSalle sailed *Griffon*,
the first sailing ship on the *Great Lakes. Michigan became
the center of the northern fur trade and was ceded to *Britain
at the conclusion of the French and Indian Wars (1754-63),
bringing about Indian rebellion. It was organized as a separate territory in 1805. Anti-*slavery sentiment led to the creation of the *Republican Party here in 1854.

M. sailed from Lake *Erie to Lake Huron in July of 1840, visiting *Detroit and Galena. He returned to *lecture in Detroit in January of 1858.
M. 121; M.D. 74

MICHIGAN, LAKE
The third largest of the *Great Lakes (207 miles long, 118 miles wide), Lake Michigan is the only one of the five totally in the *United States. It is bounded by *Michigan (E. and N.), *Illinois and *Wisconsin (W.), and Indiana (S.). The northeastern end is connected with Lake *Huron by the Straits of Mackinac (see "Mackinaw"). It was explored by the *French in 1634. Lake Michigan is iced over four months of the year and is subject to dangerous storms. M. sailed it enroute to Galena, *Ohio, in 1840.
R. 32; M.D. 54

MIDDLE-AGE; MIDDLE AGES
The Middle Ages are thought to date approximately from the fall of the ancient classical civilizations of *Rome and *Greece, when barbarians invaded, to the time of the Renaissance and Reformation (about the fifth to the fifteenth centuries: 476—fall of Roman Empire, to 1453—*Turkish capture of *Constantinople).
The *British date the period from the Heptarchy to the accession of Henry VII (409-1485), calling the period to 1200 the Dark Ages.
The *French date from the time of Clovis to that of Louis XI (481-1461).
The O. reference to mobs upon *Jews refers to their torture during the period to extort money; Jews were wealthy money lenders at the time.
Passim

MIDDLE AMERICAN STATES
See "America, --n."
M.D. 42

MIDDLESEX
The ancient *English county (now part of Greater *London), settled since the Stone Age, was much developed by the *Romans. Its name derives from its later positioning between the East and West *Saxons. It was the scene of *Danish invasions and later civil disturbance but was a favorite country

retreat of British royalty from the time of *Henry VIII until
that of *George II.

    See also "Hampton Court"; "Brentford"; "Staines."
I.P. 24 and elsewhere

MIDDLE-WATCH
    Midnight --4 AM.
M.D. 43

MIDNIGHT TREMELLA
    In "flower language," this blossom represents Resistance, or a challenge to "Resolve the Riddle."
M. 173

MIDSHIPMAN, --MEN; PASSED MIDSHIPMAN
    Midshipmen were not a highly regulated class of *Navy
personnel at the time of M.'s service on *United States. Admiral Franklin discusses their status (as had "Harry Bluff":
*Matthew F. Maury, crusader for Naval reform). Often in
their very early teen years, boys were appointed "Acting Midshipmen" by the *Secretary of the Navy or by *Congress and
warranted (not commissioned) after six months of acceptable
service aboard ship. Thus, as M. points out in W., the Navy
ship was a nursery for adolescents. Franklin estimates that
there were from 200 to 300 Acting Midshipmen serving in the
1840's. After six years of service, the Acting Midshipman
might apply to take the examination for "Passed Midshipman," instituted in 1819 and administered by a board of senior
captains at the Naval Asylum in *Philadelphia.
    Franklin had taken this route and decried the Asylum's
lack of organization and discipline (for which he himself was
no stickler). Commissioning as Lieutenant took place on board
ship, often many years after the young man had passed the examination. (The record for slow promotion is probably held by a
man who became a Lieutenant at the age of sixty-five!) Until
years after founding of the U.S. Naval Academy at Annapolis
in 1845 (at the urging of *Bancroft), there was little Government regard for the Service's need for officers, little screening-out of undesirables, and little effective training on shore or at
sea, where captains might have little time, skill, patience, or
interest in nurturing future officers. The despised "reefers" of
W. were also victims of a system that resisted the development
of efficient sea power, despite founding of West Point for the
Army, in 1802.
W. Passim; P. 2:3 and elsewhere

MILESIAN BROGUE

Milesian is a word for the ancient *Irish, based on a legend that the two sons of Milesius, king of *Spain, conquered and repeopled the country after exterminating the aborigines. (Properly the word refers to the inhabitants of Miletus.)

"Brogue" was the original Irish word for a stout, coarse, rough shoe; presumably brogue may be the speech of those who wear such shoes.

0. 37

MILFORD

H.M.S. *Milford* frigate in March of 1777 captured the Continental *Navy *Cabot* brig, the first Continental Navy ship to be captured in the *American Revolution.

I.P. 10

MILK-AND-WATER

This epithet has double meaning. It refers to a dull and insipid person but was in low colloquial usage with reference to ejaculation and urination.

W. 29

MILK-SOP

A lackluster and effeminate or woman-dominated man.

P. 1:6

MILKY WAY

In the late eighteenth and early nineteenth centuries, *Sir William Herschel and his son Sir John Herschel conducted star counts of the galaxy that has Earth on its periphery.

The *Greeks named the *galaxias kyklos* ("milky circle"): in one myth, it is named for Hera's (see "Juno") nursing of Heracles (or Hermes), a rival's child. When she tore her breast away, her milk squirted across the sky.

M. 3; M. 58; M. 119; M. 132; M. 175; M. 188; W. 19; W. 44; W. 50; W. 94; M.D. 99

MILLENIUM; MILLENIAL

A thousand years (Lat. *mille, annus*). *Revelation* 20:2 refers to an angel's binding *Satan for a thousand years. Verse 4 speaks of the resurrection of martyrs who "lived and

reigned with *Christ a thousand years," suggesting Christ's
return to earth for a thousand years.
P. 17:1; P. 19:1; C.M. 7

MILLER, JOE

Joseph (or Josiah) Miller (1684-1738) was a popular
*English comic actor whose fame spread as a result of the 1739
Joe Miller's Jests, or, the Wit's Vade-Mecum, the creator of
which was not Miller.
M. 33; W. 90; I.P. 22

MILTON, --'S; MILTONIC; JOHN MILTON

Milton was born in Cheapside, *London, in 1608 and attended Christ's College, *Cambridge, at the time of *Charles
I's accession to the throne. His "Nativity Ode," "L'Allegro"
and "Il Penseroso" were written before he took an M.S., rejected the ministry, and retired to private study. Masques including *Comus* were written before Milton traveled to *Italy in
1638-9. He began teaching in 1640, while composing early
sketches for *Paradise Lost* (*W.* 7, *M.D.* *Extracts 23, 24; hereafter cited as *P.L.*), his epic on the fall of man from *Paradise.
Areopagitica (1644), a defense of the liberty of the press, was
inspired partly by *Parliament's suppression of Milton's (1643)
pamphlet on divorce.

Before publication of his early poems in 1645, Milton had
written several anti-episcopal pamphlets, continuing to assist
the *Puritans politically, even to defense of the regicide of
Charles in 1649. He was totally blind (*M.* 119) by 1652. *P.L.* was
first published (in ten books) in 1667, *Paradise Regained* and
Samson Agonistes in 1671. Milton died in 1674, having published a final, twelve-book, version of *P.L.*

M.'s relation to Milton's works is detailed in Pommer's
Milton and Melville. M.'s familiarity with *P.L.* started as early
as his grammar school days, when Lindley Murray's *English
Reader* (see "Murray's Grammar") included hundreds of
lines, Milton's American reputation having been long established. M's own edition (acquired in 1844) was heavily annotated and marked: *The Poetical Works of John Milton with
Notes, and a Life of the Author. A New Edition.* 2 vols., 8 vo.,
Boston: Hillard, Gray, and Company, 1836.

Among the more resonant echoes of Milton in M.:
"Milton's Satan" (*R.* 55, *C.M.* 44): a drawing by John Martin,
Satan Exalted Sat (*P.L.* II, 5) decorated M.'s dining room in
*Pittsfield, testifying to compelling interest in Milton's fallen
angel, who became the prototype devil for M., as for the west-
ern world. Goldenhinged "gates of Milton's heaven" (*R.* 49) are

in *P.L.* V, 253-255 and VII, 206-207. "Milton's Invocation to the Sun" (*R.* 39) is the opening of *P.L.* III. "Miltonic contests of archangels" (*I.P.* 19) occur in *P.L.* V and VI. *Raphael (*C.M.* 37) is "heavenly meek" in *P.L.* VII, 217. "Cycles and Epicycles" (*M.* 143) refers to the movement of the stars in *P.L.* VIII, 84: "Cycle and epicycle, orb in orb."

Allusions probably indebted to Milton are too numerous to mention in the present volume, the influence of the earlier writer pervading M.'s dark philosophy regarding the indestructibility of evil, as well as his use of biblical and mythological references, especially in *Clarel*. The reader is directed particularly to "Beelzebub"; "Belial"; "Extracts" 23, 24"; "Fixed fate and free will"; "Genesis"; "Handel"; "Haydn"; "Pandemonium"; and to the "Quotations" section.
M. 97; M. 119; R. 39; R. 49; R. 55; P. 18:1; I.P. 19; C.M. 44

MINCER
       An effeminate man: preparing for M.'s phallic jokes about the "*Archbishoprick."
M.D. 95

MINNESOTA
       The thirty-second state was admitted to the Union in 1858. It is bounded by *Canada (N.), North Dakota and South Dakota (W.), Iowa (S.), and *Wisconsin (E.) and measures 405 miles from east to west. Its boundaries are mostly natural ones, including Lake *Superior (N.) and rivers. The *Mississippi rises here, joining the Minnesota River at the modern-day Twin Cities of Minneapolis and St. Paul.
       Fur traders and missionaries were active in the area in the mid-seventeenth century, and the *British entered in 1763, gaining Minnesota (along with all territory east of the Mississippi) in 1783. It came to the *United States as part of the *Louisiana Purchase, 1803, and began development as a result of John Jacob Astor's fur trading. Minnesota's history was stormy in the nineteenth century, with conflicts between railroad barons and poor farmers (leading to the late nineteenth-century Grange Movement and the Populist Party), and a Sioux rebellion in 1862.
C.M. 9

MIOCENE
       The name bestowed on the middle epoch of the *Tertiary Period, in the Cenozoic Era (c. 65 million years ago), by Sir Charles Lyell (1797-1875), along with *Eocene (earlier) and

*Pliocene (later). Fossils of this period include relatively modern mammals. See also "Sandwiches."
M. 132

MIRIAM
    In *Exodus 15:20, Miriam is the sister of *Aaron; she is a prophetess who rouses the people through song and dance. In *Numbers 12:1, she and Aaron speak out against *God's chosen leader, *Moses, for marrying a Cushite woman; Miriam becomes "leprous, white as snow" (12:10), punished by the Lord for challenging Moses's unique relation with Him and His leadership of the people. Moses pleads for Miriam, but she is shut outside the camp for seven days. In 20:1, she dies and is buried. Miriam's name is used as a warning about God's wrath in *Deuteronomy 24:9 and is also mentioned in 1 *Chronicles and Micah 6, grouped with Moses and Aaron.
    There may be no specific "Miriam" intended in M.D. 132, but the coupling with *Martha (representative of the active woman) suggests otherwise.
M.D. 132

MIRIAM COFFIN
    See "Hart, Joseph C."
M.D. 32

MISANTHROPE HALL
    The estate of *Moredock is probably an invention.
C.M. 25

MISERERES
    Various penitential prayers, especially the fifty-first psalm (opening words: *Miserere mei, Deus,*" "Have mercy upon me, 0 *God").
M. 175

MISS GUY
    See "Captain Guy."
0. 4

MISSIONS, PROTESTANT
The *Protestant Missionaries' despair of reclaiming the *Marquesas from heathenism is seen in Hiram Bingham's description of one experience with the Marquesans:

> Their rudeness, lasciviousness, shouts, and un-
> couth movements, were shocking in the extreme;
> and the insubordination, destitution, barbarism,
> cannibalism, love of war, and the awful moral
> darkness that covered the land.

These, coupled with other limitations, such as lack of respect for authority, account for the failure of Protestant efforts.
T. 1 and passim

MISSISSIPPI
The Mississippi River is, by some calculations, 2,350 miles long (second in length to the *Missouri River). It is 4,500 feet wide at Cairo.   The Mississippi rises in northern *Minnesota, flowing south to the *Gulf of Mexico in southeast-ern *Louisiana. It forms many state borders and is fed by many other rivers.   The upper course (1,170 miles above the Missouri confluence) is flanked by steep limestone bluffs (with the Indian hieroglyphs of *M.D.* 68). The lower course (below Cairo) flows more slowly, through many loops and oxbows.
The river was already much used for transport by the Indians when DeSoto explored it, 1541-42. In 1673, Marquette and Jolliet descended to the confluence of the *Arkansas River, and in 1682 LaSalle claimed the river for *France. It was un-der *Spanish control by 1762 but in 1803 made part of the *Louisiana Purchase.
The Mississippi was central to opening of the American west, at first by use of flatboats and then in the nineteenth cen-tury by steamboats. In autumn of 1840, M. returned east from Galena, *Illinois, via Mississippi steamer to the juncture of the *Ohio River at Cairo; details of the sights of his river trip appear in the first half of *C.M.*
M. 119; R. 20; W. 20; W. 47; W. 64; M.D. 48; M.D. 68; M.D. 104; C.M. Passim

MISSISSIPPI, PIRATE OF
See "Murrel."
C.M. 1

MISS NANCY
W. 59   A sobriquet for an effeminate or foppish young man.

MISSOURI, --AN
Missouri was admitted to the Union as the twenty-fourth state, in 1821. It is bordered by Iowa (N.), Nebraska, Kansas, Oklahoma (W.), *Arkansas (S.), *Tennessee, *Kentucky, *Illinois (E.). It is 305 miles wide (E.-W.) and 285 miles long. Marquette and Jolliet explored the area of the rugged Ozark Mountains in 1673, as did LaSalle in 1682. The first permanent settlement on the *Mississippi River was at Ste. Genevieve. Fur trade brought establishment of *St. Louis in 1764. The area had been ceded to *Spain in 1762 but it made part of the *Louisiana Purchase (1803). Lewis and Clark explored amid Indian hostilities in 1804. As part of the Compromise of 1820, Missouri was admitted to the union as a partial *slave state, causing much continuing conflict (and accounting for the "Herb Doctor's" questioning of "Pitch," the rugged backwoodsman, in *C.M.* 21). A Missourian is supposed to be a skeptic, whose motto is, "Show me," as seen in "Pitch's" words.
M. 119; W. 77; M.D. 34; M.D. 105; C.M. Passim

MISSOURI RIVER
The Missouri is the longest river of the *United States (2,714 miles), and the chief tributary of the *Mississippi. "The Big Muddy" forms at Three Forks, in western Montana, joining the Mississippi seventeen miles above *St. Louis after receiving many of its own tributaries. The Missouri was not explored until after 1762, but it was a regular route for Indians (and perhaps *French fur traders) long before. Lewis and Clark explored it, 1804-06, and it was used by the 1811 Astoria expedition as a route west. Steamboats made their appearance in 1819, and in the 1840's and 1850's it was the usual beginning route to the west coast. By the time of the *Civil War, traffic had boomed on the Missouri.
M. 119

MITYLENE
The reference to wine of Mitylene is to Mytilenoi (or Mitilino), a town on the *Greek island of Samos (not to the port town of Lesbos Island).
C.M. 30

MIVART'S

The elegant Mivart's Hotel, on Brook Street in *London, was owned by a Frenchman. About the time referred to in *R.*, it became Claridge's (not the present one). Mivart's is perhaps the hotel referred to in Dickens's (see "Hard Times") *Little Dorrit* II, xvi, although not named.

R. 33

MOBILE

*Alabama's only seaport is in the southwestern part of the state, on Mobile Bay, at the mouth of the Mobile River, 200 miles south-southwest of *Birmingham. The *French settled the area in 1702, yielding to the *British in 1763. The *United States gained possession after the *War of 1812; the city was incorporated in 1819. Ships to and from Mobile were able to elude the Federal blockade during the *Civil War, assuring continuance of the cotton trade.

R. 32; C.M. 21

MOBY-DICK

Among the many famous whales of M.'s time, the one thought to have most directly inspired *M.D.* was written about in Jeremiah N. Reynolds's "Mocha Dick: or the White Whale of the Pacific" (*Knickerbocker Magazine*, May 1839, Vol. 13, pp. 377-393), and elsewhere.

The whale's name had derived from the island of Mocha, off *Chile, where he was first sighted in 1810. Howard Vincent's notes to *M.D.* (Hendricks House, 1952) and his *The Trying-Out of Moby-Dick* make explicit the similarities between the veritable whale and M.'s fictional one.

After years of what was reported as willful destruction of men and ships, Mocha Dick was presumed still extant in the 1840's.

M.D. Passim

MOGUL; GREAT MOGUL; MOGULSHIP

The first Great Mogul, ruler of the *Mohammedan-*Tartar Empire in *India, was Babur (Zahir ud-Din Mohammed, 1483-1530): poet, diarist and military adventurer descended from Genghis *Khan and great grandson of *Timur (Tamerlane, 1336-1405), conqueror of *Persia and India. Other notable Moguls were Akbar, Jahangir, and Shah Jahan. Last Mogul was Aurangzeb (Mohi-ud-Din Mohammed, also called Alamgir I, 1618-1707), whose reign ended when the *British seized power.

The "Great Mogul" referred to in *M.* 75 is Kublai Khan, Grand Khan of *Tartary, who was host to *Marco Polo.
M. 75; M. 181; R. 49; W. 46; M.D. 39; M.D. 40; M.D. 99; M.D. 108; P. 2:2

MOHAMMED

The prophet Mohammed (c. 570-632), founder of Islam, the *Moslem religion, was born in *Mecca. The *Koran* (*C.M.* 24) is thought to be divine revelation given through Mohammed; it is the major source for the history of his life, written, like the *Bible, by the faithful.

Koreish (M.'s "Koriesh," in W. 65) is an earlier spelling of Quraish, a clan of which Mohammed's family were members.

Khadija (*W.* 65), an older widow, was his first wife; after her death he is said to have taken nine other wives, in addition to concubines.

The influence of Mohammed has been as great on the world as that of any other great religious leader. Finkelstein's *Melville's Orienda* discusses M.'s relation to Mohammed and to Islam. Much of his response might have come from *Penny Cyclopaedia*'s article, which points out the waging of war in the name of Allah and gives a laconic summary of the Koran.

See also "Arab"; "Moor."
W. 65; W. 72; W. 75; W. 90; P. 5:3; P. 21:3

"MOHAWK"

In *W.*, "Mohawk" represents *Constitution*.

(M.'s paternal grandfather, Major Thomas Melvill, was called "The Last Mohawk," for his participation at the *Boston Tea Party dressed in Mohawk regalia. See "Five Nations.")
M. 97; W. 62; M.D. 54

MOHAWK COUNTIES

In *New York State, Herkimer County, Utica, and the *Erie Canal area were most populated Mohawk counties. The Mohawk River flows 140 miles from Oneida County to the *Hudson falls at Cohoes. The Mohawk Trail runs from the Hudson into the *Great Lakes region, following the river through the *Appalachians; this was a major artery before construction of the canal, although part of *Iroquois Confederacy territory. See "Five Nations."
M.D. 54

MOIDORES
*Spanish or *Portuguese coins. The word is a corruption of the Portuguese *moeda d'ouro*: "coin of gold."
M. 19; M.D. 99

MOLINO DEL REY
A bloody battle in the *Mexican War, near Mexico City, in September, 1847.
C.M. 19

MOLLUSCA; MOLLUSKS
A soft animal lacking internal or external skeleton.
M. 38; M. 132; M. 163

MOLOCH
The god of the *Ammonites (variously Milchon, Malcham, Molech) came to represent any sacrifice of a thing held most dear. Moloch was the fire-god to whom Ammonites and others sacrificed their first-born children, by burning. The name of the god, mentioned throughout the *Old Testament, is *Hebrew, from a primitive root for the verb "to reign."
Strongest condemnations of Moloch appear in *Leviticus 20:2-5, in which the Lord cautions *Moses:

> Whosoever he be of the children of *Israel or of the strangers that sojourn in Israel, that giveth any of his seed unto Molech: he shall surely be put to death: the people of the land shall stone him . . . . And I will set my face against that man . . . . And if the people of the land do any ways hide their eyes . . . . when he giveth of his seed unto Molech, and kill him not . . . Then I will set my face against that man, and against his family, and will cut him off, and all that go a whoring after him, to commit whoredom with Molech, from among their people.

In I *Kings 11:5,7, *Solomon turns to Moloch and builds a place for his worship close to the Temple. In II Kings 23, Josiah includes in his reforms an end to the worship of Moloch.
*Milton's *Paradise Lost* (I, 392-93) makes Moloch first in abominations: "besmeared with blood/Of human sacrifice, and parents' tears."
M. 168

MOLUCCAS
The term Moluccas, or Spice Islands (*W*. 29), though properly only the Ternate group, refers to all the islands of the *Malay archipelago between *Celebes, *New Guinea, *Timor, and the open Pacific.
W. 50; M.D. 2; M.D. 6

MONADNOCK
The isolated, bald-domed Mt. (Pack) Monadnock (2,288 ft.), in southern *New Hampshire, was celebrated in *Emerson's poem, "Monadnoc" (*Poems*, 1847) as a "barren cone" and an "aerial isle."
M.D. 135

MONDO
Fictional.
It.: World, universe.
M. 91; M. 92

MONGOL
A separate division of central *Asiatic peoples, often used to refer to all Asiatic peoples, as in *C.M.* 22 reference to "Caucasian or Mongol." True Mongols originated in the area once called Outer Mongolia (modern Mongolian People's Republic—eastern *Siberia). They are a short-statured people of yellow to dark-brown skin, with characteristic high cheekbones. Nineteenth-century references usually conjured up the wild Mongol hordes of Genghis *Khan, who conferred the name during his thirteenth-century westward sweep.
See also "Calmuc"; "Mogul."
C.M. 22

MONONGAHELA
Monongahela county, on the Monongahela River south of Pittsburgh, *Pennsylvania, is most renowned for its whiskey-making. It was the scene of the Whiskey Rebellion of 1794-95, led by such notables as Hugh Henry Brackenridge, in opposition to Alexander Hamilton's excise tax on distilled liquors. The Federal government defeated this, its first rebellion.
M.D. 83

MONSIEUR, --S
Although also used as a generic name for a Frenchman, Monsieur refers to the eldest brother of the King of *France, since Louis XIV's (see "Bourbon") time (late seventeenth century), when it was given to his brother Philippe, *Duc d'Orleans. Thus, there is double significance in M. use in discussion of royalty.
T. Sequel; M. 28; I.P. 7 and elsewhere

MONSIEUR
M. uses this word in reference to a *French ship.
W. 64

MONSOONS
Periodic winds of the *Indian Ocean, *India, and *Asia: during the season, a continuous flow of air from the subtropical height of the ocean toward the low pressure over Asia.
M.D. 44

MONTAGUES
In *Shakespeare's *Romeo and Juliet*, the noble family (Montecchi) of "*Romeo": opposed to the "*Capulets."
P. 1:6

MONTAIGNE; MONTAIGNIZED
Michel Eyquem de Montaigne (1533-92), creator of the essay form, came from a family of wealthy *French merchants of mixed religious background. Learning *Latin as his native tongue even before starting school, he was a lawyer by the age of twenty-four but started writing in response to a friend's death ("On Friendship"). He translated Raimond Sebond's *Theologia naturalis* and in 1570 resigned a judicial office to begin *Essais* (in his tower-library) and fill miscellaneous roles including liaison of Henry de Navarre with the court (which briefly landed him in the *Bastille).
The first two books of his major work were published in 1580; a third appeared in 1588. All three were constantly emended, and the first English translation appeared after his death (1603). He conceived of the essay as making a "test" of his thoughts, rather than as definitive argument. Over the years, his philosophy appears to have moved from *Senecan Stoicism to scepticism to moderate *Epicurean acceptance of nature. At his death he accepted *Catholic Church rites. Montaigne's work is the forerunner of *Bacon's essays, the greatest

influence on *Descartes, and a seedbed for *Bayle and *Sir Thomas Browne; he was a negative force for *Pascal.

It is difficult to overestimate the similarity between M.'s thinking and Montaigne's. Throughout M.'s works (especially where Montaigne is *not* cited) one senses analogousness. Especially, M. seems to have admired the liberality of the thinking in the 107 essays. He often quoted phrases or ideas, or used the essayist's name as synecdoche, as he does in W. 13 and P. 7:6. T. is heavily influenced by "On Cannibals" (*Shakespeare's source for *The Tempest*), although M. does not cite that work, which compares European civilization to that of newly discovered societies. In his youth, M. apparently wrote a poem (now lost), "Montaigne and His Kitten." In 1849, he scored his copy of *Hamlet* (II,2), adding to Shakespeare's "nothing either good or bad, but thinking makes it so; to me it is a prison." M.'s comment in the margin is, "Here is forcibly shown the great Montaignism of Hamlet."

Sealts #366 is an unidentified volume of Montaigne's work, purchased in 1848.

See also "Extracts" 10.
M. 119; W. 13; M.D. Extracts 10; P. 7:6

MONT BLANC
Mont Blanc (15,781 feet) is in the highest *Alp massif, on the French/Italian and French/Swiss borders (in France). Its granite and crystalline schist mass extends some thirty miles north from the Little St. Bernard Pass to a point overlooking the *Rhone River valley at Martigny-Ville. It is a maximum of ten miles wide.
M. 40; M. 84; P. 21:1

MONTEAGLE
M. uses Monteagle as a symbol of one who is warned and saved. When *Guy Fawkes and others planned the "Gunpowder Plot" to blow up the buildings of *Parliament in 1605, one of the co-conspirators was Francis Tresham, the Roman *Catholic brother-in-law of William Parker, fourth Baron Monteagle (1575-1622), a sympathizer with Catholics. In a letter, Tresham warned Lord Monteagle about the plot so as to prevent his taking his usual seat in the *House of Lords and thus save him personally. Monteagle revealed the information to Secretary of State Robert Cecil (first Earl of Salisbury), and after some delay, the search was conducted which uncovered the explosives in the basement of Parliament buildings. Monteagle was pensioned and awarded large estates for his service to the Crown; Tresham died in prison.
R. 40

MONTEZUMA

Montezuma (or Moctezuma) II (1466-1520) was the last *Aztec emperor of *Mexico, displaced by *Cortès, the conquistador. He was a great military leader and a priest of the war god, and his conquests and despotic rule were of longstanding when Cortès was taken prisoner. The circumstances of his death are not clear. He is said to have been addressing his people, who attacked him with stones and bows and arrows, or to have died at the hands of the *Spaniards. M.'s knowledge of him probably derives from Prescott's *Conquest of Mexico* (1843), which subscribes to the former of the theories.

*Dryden's play, *The Indian Emperor* (1665), focuses on Montezuma.

M. 181

MONTGOMERY'S WORLD BEFORE THE FLOOD

James Montgomery (1771-1854), *Scottish poet, hymnist, and essayist, was the son of the-then only *Moravian minister in *Scotland (*Ayrshire), who took his family to Barbados in 1783. Back in Scotland, James Montgomery began writing poetry ("The World") in the manner of *Milton and by the 1790's was a contributor to newspapers and a publisher of the *Sheffield News. He was the object of several libel suits stemming from his ballad, "The Fall of the *Bastille," was imprisoned for political rioting, and began publishing pseudonymously, as "Gabriel Silvertongue." He also contributed poems to the *Eclectic Review* and in 1831 was the compiler of the South-Sea journals of *Tyerman and Bennet. His poems were collected in 1841 and his hymns in 1853.

Among his successes was the (1812) "The World before the Flood," a heroic verse epic on the wars of the giants and the patriarchs. (*M.D.* Extracts 51 is not from this poem but from the title poem of *The Pelican Island and Other Poems* [1827]. M. uses a reading similar to that of his source, *Cheever.)

DNB characterizes Montgomery as "something less than a genius and something more than a mediocrity."

See also "Extracts" 51.

M.D. Extracts 51

MONTREAL

Montreal, in southern *Quebec, on the *St. Lawrence and Lechine rapids, was the capital of *Canada 1844-49, and thus the capital when M. visited on his honeymoon trip with Elizabeth Shaw Melville (18? August 1847). It had been the site of an Indian village on the slopes of the extinct volcano Mount

Royal (900 feet) when Cartier visited in 1535. Champlain built the first fort in 1611 (replaced by the stone fort in 1725).

The honeymooners visited all of the local attractions, and "Lizzie" expressed a preference for Montreal over Quebec which M. shared. Ten years later (10 December), he *lectured at Montreal, apparently to the displeasure of local residents who objected to the strong anti-missionary bias of his works. I.P. 22

MONUMENT, THE

A 202-foot-high Portland stone Roman *Doric column designed by *Sir Christopher Wren to commemorate the *Great Fire of London of 1666. Located near the north end of *London Bridge, the Monument, completed in 1677, was inscribed in 1681 with a message that was erased in 1831:

> This Pillar was set up in perpetual remembrance of that most dreadful burning of this *Protestant city, begun and carried out by ye treachery and malice of ye popish faction, in ye beginning of Septem in ye year of Our Lord 1666, in order to carry out their horrid plot, for extirpating the Protestant religion and old English liberty, and the introducing Popery and slavery.

*Pope's *Moral Essays* refers to the column as a "tall bully" (III, 339). (See also "Catholic.")
0. 53; R. 30; W. 23

MOON, THE

*Earth's only satellite has since ancient times been utilized scientifically (to measure time), imaginatively (especially in mythology), and superstitiously (as influencing man's behavior). Its orbit was studied as early as the second century B.C.; *Galileo observed it with a telescope; Tycho Brahe made precise observations in the sixteenth century; *Newton, *d'Alembert, and others continued study, as did scientists of the 1860's, so a good deal was known in M.'s time.

The reference in W. 64 to *Christianizing the Moon may arise from the 1830's "Moon hoax," wherein Richard Adams Locke, of the *New York Sun*, wrote generally accepted reports of life on that body.

See also "Diana"; "Selene"; "Man in the Moon."
M. 64

MOONS OF SATURN
     See "Saturn."
M. 175

MOOR, --S, --ISH
     From the *Middle Ages, Europeans have called
*Mohammedans (of darker skin) Moors; *Camöens (*Lusiad*
Bk. viii) uses the expression for the *Indians. The word actually originates from Gr. and Lat. *Maurus*, an inhabitant of
Mauritania.
     M. often uses the adjective "Moorish" to describe Islamic
art or architecture. Muslim *mosques were originally highly
decorated conversions of churches or temples, especially of the
*Byzantine style; great Islamic architecture did not start until
the late 600's. The circle or curved design was preferred to the
right angle which, it is said, was reminiscent of the *Christian
*cross. Muslim buildings were often domes resting on sup-
ports but appearing free-floating, or multiple domes giving the
impression of a cluster of buds (the dome being preferred to cu-
bic space as a symbol of universal power). The pointed or
round arch (often in an arcade) was preferred to squared post-
and-lintel openings. A sense of rhythm was achieved in the
use of arabesques, spirals, and concentric spirals. Pierced
stone filagree and decoratively grilled windows were common,
in naturalist or geometric sculpture. After about 800, human
figures were not represented. After about 1600, Islamic buildings were less decorated than their originals.
     *Penny Magazine of the Society for the Diffusion of Useful
Knowledge* II (March 31-April 20, 1833) contained a print of the
Moorish-arched entrance of the Liverpool and Manchester
Railway which "Wellingborough" recognizes in *Liverpool (*R.*
41).
     See also "Alhambra"; "Saracen."
M. 1; R. 33; R. 41; R. 46; R. 49; W. 39; W. 50; C.M. 24 and
elsewhere

MOORE, SIR JOHN
     Charles Wolfe's elegy, "The Death of Sir John Moore,"
showing Moore laid out without coffin or shroud, "With his
martial cloak around him," has symbolic importance, regarding *England's misuse of Moore.
     Moore (1761-1809) was born into an influential family in
*Glasgow, went on to *Parliament and became an important
military officer (Lietenant General) despite frequent criticism
on the ground of political interference. He died of wounds incurred at the battle of La Coruña, on the *Spanish coast, and

was buried there. Although he was not given credit, *Wellington recognized that his actions had in effect ended *Bonaparte's interference in Spain.
W. 19

MOORE, THOMAS, --TOMMY; MOORE'S "LOVES OF THE
ANGELS," --MELODIES
    *Dublin-born Thomas Moore (1779-1852), *Irish poet,
lyricist, and satirist, showed dramatic flair even before attending Trinity College. After entering *London's Middle *Temple
in 1799, he published *Odes of Anacreon*, and *The Poetical
Works of the Late Thomas Little*, a much criticized collection of
love poems. After travels to Bermuda, the *United States, and
*Canada, he published *Epistles, Odes and Other Poems*. His
Irish Melodies (including "The Last Rose of Summer") supplied lyrics for traditional tunes; it was highly successful, as
was *Lalla Rookh* and the 1823 *The Loves of the Angels*, written
to avoid debtors' prison.
    His modern reputation as national bard of Ireland rests
on his song lyrics and his light satires on politics and manners
of his time. A close associate of *Byron, in 1830 he produced
The Letters and Journals of Lord Byron, including a biography. A pension in later years finally relieved the strain of lifelong impecuniousness.
    In 1862, M. acquired *The Poetical Works of Thomas
Moore* (Boston, 1856), underscoring in the Preface to "Lalla
Rookh" Moore's claim to be a more "slow and pains-taking
workman" than was guessed. Later in that same year, M. acquired Vol. II of the *Works* (Boston, 1854). Sealts #s 369 and
370 are the life of Byron and the *Works*.
R. 27; W. 41; P. 2:2; P. 17:2

MOORFIELDS, --'S
    An ancient marshy area in *London's East End, Moor-
fields is an archaeologist's delight. Although settled since the
*Middle Ages, it was consistantly sinking into a fen which res-
idents used as a junk yard. If "*Israel Potter's" children were
raised in Moorfields, they lived in great poverty. Continuous
efforts at filling finally succeeded in the early part of the nineteenth century.
    (Mentioned in the original of Israel Potter's adventures.)
I.P. 25

MOORISH ARCH, --ED, --PILLAR, --TURRET
    See "Alhambra"; "Moor."
M. 75; R. 41; W. 20; W. 44

MORAI, --S

Common spelling of the name for *Marquesan burial grounds is "me'ae." M.'s spelling probably reveals his debt to *Bennett, who describes "morais" in detail, particularly the "Great Morais" (*M*. 109) of Raiatea (see "Raiatair") and of Papaia, on *Tahiti (I, 134-5, 329-30, and II, 41-2).
M. 105; M. 109

MORAVIAN, --S

The *Christian Moravian Brethren were founded by followers of John Huss (or Hus, c. 1370-1415). After their near-extermination in the *Thirty Years' War, they rose again with renewed missionary zeal and piety.

M.'s reference to Moravians' Christianizing the *Moon may arise from an 1830's incident, the "Moon hoax," involving generally accepted newspaper reports in the *New York Sun* by Richard Adams Locke, concerning life on the moon. The need for missionaries was suggested by Harriet Martineau, who said that the effect of the Moon story on the ladies of Springfield, *Massachusetts was sufficient to induce them to start a subscription toward the cause.

*Thomas Melville was buried (1884) in the Moravian Cemetery at New Dorp, *Staten Island.
W. 64; P. 2:4

MORBID ANATOMY

Morbid Anatomy, the study of diseased organs and structures, is an appropriate field for W.'s "Dr. Cuticle," whose unwholesome mind and body reflect the *Latin root, *morbidus*: sickly.
W. 61

MORDECAI

Insulting generic name for a Jew, as well as a proper *Hebrew name. See "Xerxes" for *Bible original.
O. 65; M.D. 89

MOREDOCK, COLONEL JOHN; MOREDOCKS; MOREDOCK HALL

Moredock was a historical figure discussed in *James Hall's *Sketches of History, Life, and Manners, in the West*, Vol. II, Chapter 6: "Indian-hating—Some of the Sources of this Animosity—Brief Account of Col. Moredock."

Moredock Hall has not been identified.
C.M. 25; C.M. 27; C.M. 28

MOREEA

M.'s "Emio," "Imeeo," or "Moreea" is the island of
Moorea, (*Society Islands), c. twelve miles northwest of
*Tahiti. The mountainous island has several 2,500-foot peaks
and one that reaches 3,960 feet; it is roughly triangular in
shape, with two large bite-like bays scooped out of the northern
side: *Captain Cook Bay (Paopao) and *Taloo.
O. 25

MORE HOMINUM

Lat.: In the manner of men.
M.D.87

MORGAN, GOOD-ENOUGH-

An adequate substitute, especially a device to temporarily influence voters.

William Morgan (1774?-1826?) was kidnapped to prevent
his publishing a book of *Freemason secrets. When a corpse
was found in the *Niagara River, at election time, Thurlow
Weed, a prominent anti-*Mason is said to have called it " a
good enough Morgan until after the election."
C.M. 9

"MORGAN'S HISTORY OF ALGIERS"

John Morgan: *A Complete History of Algiers*, London,
1731.

The book was in the catalogue of the Albany *Young
Men's Association at the time M. was a member.
W. 41

MORGUE IN PARIS

The *Paris Morgue stood at the south end of Ile de la
Cité. M. rented a room nearby and visited the Morgue in December of 1849, confessing in his journal to being somewhat
spooked: "I don't like that mystic door (tapestry) leading out of
the closet" (2 December).
R. 36

MORMON, --S

The Church of *Jesus Christ of Latter-Day Saints, commonly miscalled the Mormon Church, was founded in western
*New York in the 1820's after Joseph Smith (1805-1844), having
received what he believed were messengers of *God, said he

had unearthed ancient gold plates containing the materials he later translated and published as *The Book of Mormon* (1830). Smith was shot to death by an anti-Mormon mob, and the Church split into factions. Adherents saw him as God's tool in guiding men to what would be the "dispensation of the fulness of times" (*New Testament, *Ephesians 1:10), or final conjunction of heaven and earth. Although the western-wandering evangelistic Church settled its center in what was to become the territory of *Utah, it became universal, despite much adversity. Exposes abounded, such as one by J.H. Beadle, editor of the *Salt Lake Reporter* and Utah correspondent for the *Cincinnati Commercial* (reproduced in McCabe's *Lights and Shadows* . . .). Beadle warns of "secret rites" surrounding the "multitude of gods" of the polygamous Mormons; he calls "Joe Smith" a criminal who cheated his following of "thieves, murderers and assassins." Mormons were said to conduct massacres and commit murder to gain property, outrage female modesty in intitiation ceremonies, teach licentiousness, and perform prostitution in the name of religion. Senior member Brigham Young (1801-1877) led the first Mormon pioneers of the Reorganized (1830) Church westward in 1846, and by 1860 the Utah population had grown to 40,000 despite the hostile environment and the hostile publicity. The Mormon movement was central to development of the American west despite its uneasy articulation with the Federal government.

Church doctrines include belief in the restored authority of the *Christian Church; a trinitarian Godhead with a fleshly as well as a Godly Jesus; the eternal nature of all things (including matter); a highly organized ministry of service by all worthy males; God-given free agency of human beings (see "Fixed Fate and Free Will"). Closely knit Mormon life is guided throughout by social institutions including education and welfare programs. Drugs, alcohol, and stimulants are forbidden. Plural marriage was practiced openly until its prohibition by laws starting in 1862. (Smith had perhaps fifty wives; Young had seventeen surviving wives and forty-seven children). By 1890, it was largely discontinued, paving the way to Utah's becoming the forty-fifth state, in 1896. Salt Lake City became the modern *New Jerusalem provided for in *The Book of Mormon* (440, 444, 503).

The reference in *M.D.* 18, "The Latter Day Coming; or No Time to Lose," is undoubtedly a parody of Mormon missionary workings: still a major function of the Church.

Among referents M. might have found in *The Book of Mormon* is "Alma" (*M.*): a convert who became a great missionary baptizer, judge, and leader of the people. His son, Alma, contributed "The Book of Alma."

The reference in *C.M.* 9 is either an error or a trick
(given its location). Fugitive Mormons did not establish a
"New Jerusalem" in *Minnesota, on the *Mississippi. Nau-
voo, *Illinois was founded in 1840 by Mormons driven from
*Missouri. They were expelled from Nauvoo in 1846.
P. 21:3; C.M. 2; C.M. 9

MORNING-GLORY
        See "Convulvulus."
M. 116

MOROCCO
        The sultanate of northwestern *Africa, along the
*Atlantic and *Mediterranean coasts, is situated in an area
visited by the *Phoenicians c. the twelfth century B.C. The
*Carthaginians later developed trading posts, and the
*Romans made it their province of Western Mauretania (A.D.
42). The area was ravaged by the *Vandals in the fifth century
and conquered by the *Arabs in the seventh. By the late eighth
century, Morocco was an independent Islamic state, with dynasties established. The *Portuguese invaded in 1415 and the
*Moors in 1578.
        Morocco was a center for *pirates from the seventeenth
to the nineteenth centuries. *France had conquered *Algiers
by 1847, and the *Spanish were to invade by 1859-60. Sultans in
place during M.'s time include Mulay Suleiman (1792-1822),
Mulay Abderrahman (1822-59), Sidi Mohammed (1859-73), Mulay el-Hassan I (1873-94).
        M.'s references in *R.* are to Moroccan book leather
(usually goatskin), which had become popular in medieval Europe because of its fine quality and beautiful color. Early or-
nately gilded Moroccan book bindings were reserved for
*Korans. By the fifteenth century, *Persian bookmaking had
superseded Moroccan.
R. 30; R. 31; R. 36

MORPHEUS
        See "Somnus."
C.M. 42

MORQUAN
        This whale is presumed fictional, no other reference be-
ing located.
M.D. 45

MORREL, MARY
    See "Franklin, Benjamin . . . . "
M.D. 24

MORVEN
    Morven is the invented realm of Fingal. (See "Ossian.")
    Also a mountain in Caithness, *Scotland: 2,313 feet.
I.P. 19

MOSELLE
    The Moselle River of northeastern *France and western *Germany rises in the central Vosges and flows 320 miles north and northeast, forming the Luxembourg-Saar border and passing through Germany to the *Rhine at Coblenz.
    Moselle white wine is grown on the slopes of the lower Moselle valley, in Germany. M. crossed the river to Coblenz, 10 December 1849. He "regaled" himself with Moselle wine, commenting in his journal: "The wine is bluish—at least *tinged* with blue—and seems a part of the river after which it is called." Thus the *R.* 56 comment on the "Banks of the Blue Moselle" was still on his mind.
R. 56

MOSES
    The founder of the *Hebrew nation of *Israel (thirteenth century B.C.) is the hero of the *Bible's book of the *Exodus and other *Old Testament books. He is called by Yahweh ("*Jehovah") to lead his people out of enslavement in *Egypt, to wanderings in the *Sinai, where he is given the *decalogue, to forty years of wandering in the wilderness, to the *Promised Land.
    M.D. 45 "history of the plagues of Egypt" refers to Exodus 7-12.
    Wright's *Melville's Use of the Bible* is a detailed study.
M. 28; R. 30; M.D. Extracts 10; M.D. 45; I.P. 25; C.M. 26

MOSLEM; MOSLEMISM
    See "Mohammed."
M. 87; M. 168; W. 72; W. 75; W. 84

MOSQUE
    A mosque is a *Moslem prayer place, from the Arabic *masjid*, "place of prostration" (the word is used in *Turkish,

*Persian, and Urdu).   Since ancient times, the mosque has had designated features; it is an open carpeted space (usually roofed), with: 1. mihrab (semicircular niche for *imam*, or prayer leader), facing *Mecca. 2. mimbar (seat at top of steps at right of mihrab, for *khatib* or preacher). 3. on top of structure a minaret (*mi'dhana*), usually a tower, used by the *muezzin (mu'adhdhin, or crier), who calls to worship five times a day via the *azan*. 4. a place for ritual washing.

The state- or privately subsidized mosque is for prayer, not ceremonies, with barefooted men separated from women. There are no decorations but koranic (see "Koran") verse inscriptions and names of *Mohammed and followers on the walls, no music but the Koran chanted by *muqri*, professional chanters.

Turkish mosques have occasionally attempted innovations, but these have not endured.

By the eighth century, Islamic mosques and palaces competed with *Christian cathedrals in size and splendor of decoration, with intricate surface decoration in mosaic, marble, metal, and wood. It is said that the architectural curve, rather than the straight line, was adopted so as to distinguish Islamic architecture from Christian architecture, with its heavy reliance on the use of the *cross form.

See also "Moorish."
R. 35 and elsewhere

MOST HOLY TRINITY, THE
    See "Santissima Trinidada."
M. 28

MOTHER CAREY'S CHICKENS
    The "stormy petrels": in the north *Atlantic and *Mediterranean, petrels are usually small black and white swallow-like birds: *Hydrobates pelagicus*. Mariners believe that they presage bad weather.
M.D. 113

MOTOO-OTOO
    Moto Utu, or Motu Uta, is an islet near the entrance to *Papeete harbor, *Tahiti. *Bennett discussed it at length, noting its surrounding by cannons mounted on coral and its residence of the Queen. *Wheeler explored it at length, calling it "Queen's Island."
O. 42

MOTOOS
These probably fictional "little tufts of verdure" on "Mardi" may be inspired by the Latin *motu proprio*, meaning "of one's own motion or accord." This would suggest that they are weeds.
M. 147

MOUNA KEA
Mauna Kea, in the center of the island of *Hawaii, is a dormant volcano with numerous cinder cones. Among the highest island mountains in the world at 13,825 feet, it is snow-capped in the winter.
O. 54

MOUNA ROA
Probably Mauna Loa, in the center of the island of *Hawaii. It is 13,675 feet in altitude and has numerous volcanic craters, including the second largest active crater in the world: Kilauea.
O. 54

MOUNT, THE
Probably not a particular mountain, the *Sermon on the Mount being a collection of teachings of *Jesus, rather than words spoken on any one occasion.
P. 2:3

MOUNT OF THE TITANS
Although M.'s description in *P*. 25 is partially applicable to Mount *Greylock, fifteen miles north of Broadhall, the mansion usually seen as the original of "*Pierre's house," the original of "Mount of the Titans" is more likely Monument Mountain, in Stockbridge, a similar distance south. The altitude of Monument is somewhat less, and the configuration of rocks on the north side more suggestive of the fictional "Mount."
    M. is known to have loved climbing the peaked rocks of Monument Mountain, scene of a famous picnic in August of 1850. Participants included *Hawthorne, *Duyckinck, Oliver Wendell Holmes, and other literati.
P. 25:4; P. 25:5

MOWANNA

Moana was a principal chief of *Nukuheva; he is mentioned by Max Radiguet, secretary to *DuPetit-Thouars. Moana's grandfather had been made king of the island by *Porter after his 1813 conquest of the *Typees. His son became Moana I. M.'s king is Moana II; he was an eight-year-old regent when *Stewart visited in 1829. By 1840, Moana had been to *England and returned. He was a moody and corrupted chief, fashioned by DuPetit-Thouars into a puppet.

His beautiful wife ("Queen of Nukuheva" or "Island Queen" in *T.* 1) was apparently dressed as M. describes. According to Radiquet, she was quite willing to display her elaborately tattooed body.
T. 1

MOWEE

See "Maui."
T. 25; T. 32

"*MOWREE*"

The Maori people are mostly associated with *New Zealand, although these *Polynesian sea-farers sailed their canoes to many places in the *Pacific. Separate Maori tribes descended from the canoers that landed on various islands, so that all Maori people in a given place traced their ancestry to the "chief." Maoris became communal agriculturists with strong military tradition, religions of many deities, and belief in multiple spirits in men.

Maoris settled New Zealand in the early *Christian era. European contact in the late eighteenth century was mostly peaceful, but by M.'s time Maoris had developed a reputation for formidable fierceness. Theirs was a rather typical story of the encroachment of "civilization," although M. seems to follow contemporary stereotypical belief in their villainy (unlike his position about *Marquesan and *Tahitian peoples).

By the eighteenth century, the Maori people of New Zealand had perfected their culture; they were master ship-builders, farmers, builders, and hand-to-hand warriors. Many sailors and convicts from *Sydney had taken refuge with tribes; trade with Europeans was established, and Maori chiefs had traveled as far as *England. These ambassadors brought guns back to new Zealand, where tribal wars intensified. Responding missionary colonies brought many conversions to *Christianity and to European life style, and Maori individuals began sale of (communal) lands in exchange for the "protection' of British guardians. Discovery of gold in the

1840's brought more forceful European intrusion, and the
Maori Nationalist Movement organized around kings who resisted "progress." These violent confrontations induced the
dark picture of "wild New Zealanders" (O. 2) accepted by M.
and most others. The Maori was seen as the purveyor of the
"'balmed New Zealand head" (*M.D.* 3) that "Queequeg" trades,
in. (There was a ready European market for "pickled heads,"
which Maoris dried and preserved so that features were recognizable. M. and others seem to miss the irony of this fact
and to forget that head-hunting and amputation of souvenir
anatomical parts had been widely practiced throughout Europe
until relatively recent times.)

Violent Maori resistance continued well into the 1860's;
by the 1870's, almost all the island was the relatively undisputed property of Europeans.
O. 2

MOYAMENSING
The Egyptian-style Moyamensing Prison, in
*Philadelphia, *Pennsylvania, was built in 1832.
C.M. 26

MOZART, --'S
Wolfgang Amadeus Mozart (1756-1791), thought to be the
greatest musical genius of all time, was born in Salzburg,
*Austria, and was composing by the age of five. His precocity
at composing and performing was soon made use of in tours
throughout Europe. He was engaged by Emperor Joseph II of
Austria in 1787 but spent the last years of his brief life in catastrophic debt, neglected by all but close friends and family.

The first collected *Works* appeared 1876-1905: masses
and other sacred music; cantatas; oratorios; operas, recital
pieces and other songs; orchestral works; chamber music,
and keyboard music. The Köchel catalog was first published in
1862 but was not definitive until the edition of 1937. It lists 626
separate compositions of Mozart. In M.'s time, many of the
major works were unknown, even in Europe, but the adulation
expressed for Mozart today was well established in the
Romantic Age that followed the "Classical" eighteenth century.

See also "Don Juan."
R. 51; W. 91

MR. FOREMAN
The Foreman is the chairman and spokesman for a jury; the first person chosen as a juror becomes Foreman.
C.M. 45

MR. MEGRIMS
Colloquially, a migraine headache: a corruption of the Greek hemi-crania: "half the skull" (the afflicted area in such headaches).
C.M. 24

MSS.
Manuscripts.
M. 123

MUFTI
In Islam, a consulting canon lawyer or official expounder of *Moslem law who gives *fatwas* (opinions) on sacred matters. The mufti had great power under the *Ottoman Empire, but modern legislation curtailed their influence, except regarding the field of Arab nationalism.

"In mufti," a colloquial expression meaning "in civilian clothes," as opposed to "in uniform," is probably traceable to the loose robes worn by the mufti.
M.D. 44

MUGGLETONIAN
The Muggletonians were followers of a sectarian *English tailor, Lodowicke Muggleton (1609-1698), who believed that he and his cousin, John Reeve (1608-1658) were the two witnesses mentioned in *Revelation 11:3. They denied the Trinity and preached that matter was eternal and reasoning power from the devil.
P. 14:2

MULATTO
Loosely applied to signify any person of mixed black and white parentage (from Span. *mulo*, a mule).
C.M.22

MULGRAVE

The Mulgrave cluster is the original name of Mili, the southernmost atoll of the Ratak chain, Marshall Islands (see "Radack"). Its thirty islets enclose a lagoon twenty-three miles long (6°08' N., 171°55' E.).
M. 3

MULL

Mull Island, *Scotland: 56°40' N.; 6°19' W.
M. 3

MULLER

Johannes Peter Müller (1801-1858) was a *German physiologist and comparative anatomist noted for his work in nerve and sense physiology. His later focus, with *Henle, was on ocean fauna. His important *Handbuch der Physiologie des Menschen* (1833-40) was first translated into English in 1842.

M. may also have had access to the untranslated but illustrated folio, *Systematische Beschreibung der Plagiostomen . . . mit sechzig Steindrucktafeln* (Berlin, 1841), which disagreed with *Cuvier's classification of sea creatures.
M. 13

MULL OF GALOWAY

The Mull of Galloway is the portion of the North Channel between Wigtown, *Scotland, and Antrim and Down countries, *Ireland.
I.P. 15

MULTUM IN PARVO

Ingeniously condensed or compressed, said especially of information: literally, "much in little."
M.D. 107

MUNCHAUSEN, BARON

Karl Friedrich Hieronymus, Baron Münchausen (1720-1797), told marvellous stories of his service in the *Russian army, which were collected by Rudolf Erich Raspe (1737-1794) and published in 1785 as *Baron Münchausen's Narrative of his Marvellous Travels and Campaigns in Russia*. Raspe's later edition adds adventures from other sources.

Several reviewers of *T.* called it a "Munchausenism," or tall tale.
M. 98

MURAT

Joachim Murat (1767-1815), *French cavalry leader whose participation in the Revolution brought honors from *Napoléon, was born the son of an innkeeper at Quercy. His career advanced through expeditions to *Egypt and *Italy and numerous victories in which his forces were irresistible.

Napoléon made him Marshal of the Empire (1804), Grand Admiral and Prince (1805), and finally King of *Naples (1808). But Murat's ambition and resentment of Napoléon's imperious rule brought a break with the Emperor before the latter's defeat. He made secret alliances with *Austria and *Britain in 1814 but reneged on these, aiming to unify Italy as an appropriately important kingdom. Defeated by the Austrians, he attempted to recover his kingdom but was court-martialed and shot by *Bourbon troops at Calabria.

Napoléon, who had given his youngest sister, Caroline, as bride to Murat, called him "incomparable on the battlefield, but a fool in his actions everywhere else."

There is a reference to Murat's "dandyism" in *Billy Budd, Sailor*.

M. visited the scene of Murat's death in February of 1857.
M. 36

MURILLO, --'S

Bartolomé Esteban Murillo (1618-82), *Spanish painter, gained fame in Seville for an eleven-painting series executed (1645-46) for the local Franciscan monastery. His best known works are sentimental scenes of peasant children and devotional works in the "vaporous style" of muted colors and fluid forms. He did several versions of *The Immaculate Conception, The Flight into Egypt* (1645), and a few portraits.

M. saw his paintings at the Dulwich Gallery, *London, in November 1849.
R. 49; C.M. 45

MURRAY'S GRAMMAR

The *Pennsylvania *Quaker Lindley Murray (1745-1826) was the author of the widely used *The English Grammar* (1795), as well as *The English Reader: From the Best Writers* (1819), which was owned by M. (Sealts #380).
M.D.99

MURRELL
    John A. Murrell (fl. 1804-44), folk hero outlaw, headed a
gang of *Mississippi Valley bandits supposedly numbering
1,000, Murrell's Mystic Clan, some members of which were
reputedly otherwise respectable citizens. The *Tennessean, in
a variety of disguises, led highway robberies that yielded
money, horses, and slaves, who would be resold so often that
eventually Murrell would have to murder them. Unsuspecting
travelers, charmed by the clever villain, would often end
murdered and disemboweled, their bodies weighted with
stones and cast in the river.
    Vigil A. Stewart captured Murrell in 1834 and published
*A History of the Detection, Conviction, Life, and Designs of
John A. Murel*, during the outlaw's ten-year imprisonment.
C.M. 1

MUSCAT
    The brandy of *Pisco, *Peru, produced from freshly fer-
mented muscat grape wines.
O. 2

MUSCAT, SULTAN OF
    Oman was the most powerful state of the Arabian
peninsula under Said Ibn Sultan of Muscat (1804-56). Senate
Documents No. 448, first session of the twenty-sixth Congress
(Vol. VII) details the Sultan's offer of horses, declined by the
*President, as well as the gift of a lion and a lioness.
W. 44

MUSCOVITE
    In Moscow (in M.'s "*Russia"), the average daily low
temperature in January is 9° F.; the average high is 21°.
    The "Czar's Ice Palace" (*M*. 75) was built not in Moscow
but in *St. Petersburg.
M. 75

MUSES, THE NINE
    In *Greek mythology, nine goddesses said to be daugh-
ters of Zeus (see "Jupiter" and "Jove") and Mnemosyne
(memory) who preside over music, literature, and the liberal
arts.   Three earlier muses (Melete, meditation; Mneme, remembrance; Aoide, song) are sometimes given, but the conventional list of muses includes the nine: Calliope (epic poetry), Clio (history), Erato (lyrics and love poetry), Euterpe

(music), Melpomene (tragedy), Polyhymnia (sacred poetry), Terpsichore (choral dance and song), Thalia (comedy), Urania (astronomy).
M. 180; W. 11; P. 9:3; P. 15:1

MUSH
See "Burgoo."
R. 52

MUSICAL GLASSES
Musical glasses are drinking glasses filled with varying amounts of water to produce different notes, placed atop a sounding board. Striking the glasses or running a moistened finger around the rims produces music of such high quality that *Mozart, *Beethoven, and Gluck wrote music for the instrument. In 1761, *Benjamin Franklin redeveloped it into a self-tuning treadle operation which later was given a keyboard.
M.D. 127

MUSSULMAN
See "Mohammedan."
W. 69

MUSTAPHA, VIZIER
The reference in *M*. 20 is to the militarily ambitious Kara Mustafa, in 1676 grand *vizier of *Turkey under "*Grand Turk" Sultan Mohammed IV. Mustafa brought about several unnecessary wars. In violation of a truce, he led a huge army against *Austria which took and then lost *Vienna, precipitating the decline of the *Ottoman Empire. The Sultan abdicated in 1687, and Kara Mustafa was replaced.
M. 20

MUTIUS SCAEROLA
C. Mucius Scaevola, *Roman hero, burned off his own right hand after being discovered infiltrating the camp of Porsenna, King of Clusium in *Etruria, who sided with *Tarquin in war against Rome.
M. 24

MUZZLE-LASHINGS
Literally, ropes confining lower-deck gun muzzles to housing bolts. Figuratively, beards, usually long and disheveled.
W. 87

MY FIRST VOYAGE
The working title of M.'s contract with Harper's (1849) for the book we know as *Redburn: His First Voyage* was "My First Voyage etc." The full title deposited for copyright was *Redburn: His First Voyage. Being the Sailor-boy Confessions and Reminiscences of the Son-of-a-Gentleman, in the Merchant Service.* An 1853 edition shortened the subtitle to "*Being the Confessions of a Sailor-Boy.*"
(See also "Son-of-a Gentleman.")
R. 62

"MY LORD"
*British courtesy address to noblemen, peers of the realm, rulers or masters, or husbands, younger sons of *dukes and *marquises, eldest sons of viscounts and *earls, important judges, *Lord Mayors, Judges of Supreme Court, bishops, Lord Provosts and Lord Advocates. A baron is called by his peerage title (surname or territorial designation), in informal use for Marquis, Earl, or Viscount, with "of" dropped. Members of the *House of Lords are "Lords."
R. 46

MYSTERIOUS MOTHER
See "Walpole, Horace,"
W. 89

"MYSTERY! MYSTERY!..."
See "Avenel, White Lady of"; "Quotations" section, "Mystery of Iniquity."
P. 6:6; P. 8:2

MYSTICETUS
See "Cetology" section.
M.D. 32

N

"NAHEE"

The *Tahitian fern referred to is "naehe."
O. 68

NANTUCKET

The fourteen-mile-long *Massachusetts island twenty-five miles south of *Cape Cod across Nantucket Sound is separated from its westerly neighboring island of *Martha's Vinyard by Muskeget Sound. The glacially formed islands were seen by Gosnold in 1602. Nantucket was privately bought in 1641 and settled by associates of Thomas Macy in 1659. The town of Nantucket was incorporated in 1687.

There were conflicts in the seventeenth century between Massachusetts and *New York, which technically owned Nantucket. A large *Quaker population (*M.D.* 16) developed concurrently with the whaling fishery in the early eighteenth century. The first sperm whale was caught off Nantucket in 1712. The island remained a chief whaling station until the mid-nineteenth century, so it is appropriate that M. makes so many of his fictional whalemen (including *"Ahab," and "Starbuck") Nantucketers. (One of the careless errors of *M.D.* occurs in Chapter 54; "Radney" is at first called a "Vineyarder," and later a "Nantucketer.")

M. visited both the Vineyard and Nantucket on an excursion with his father-in-law, *Lemuel Shaw, in July of 1852.
Passim

NAPLES; BAY OF NAPLES; NEOPOLITAN

The capital of Campania and Napoli province of southern Italy, Naples is now the second largest seaport and third largest city of Italy. The ancient *Greek colony known as Parthenope (Palaeopolis, Neopolis), it was conquered by Rome in the fourth century B.C., was under *Byzantine rule by the sixth century A.D., and was part of the kingdom of *Sicily by the twelfth century. After the *Sicilian Vespers of 1282, it became the Kingdom of Naples, eventually seized by *France, *Spain, and *Austria. In 1815, Ferdinand IV merged Sicily and Naples into the Kingdom of the *Two Sicilies (which fell to Garibaldi in 1860 and was incorporated into Italy in 1861).

M. visited the area for six days in February 1857, entering the Bay by steamer. Suffering from a sleepless night in a second class steamer cabin, he was in poor spirits. He complains in his journal of the industrial city's smell, and its ubiquitous police. Taking the train to *Pompeii, he visited *Vesuvius on horseback and was full of complaints about bureaucracy, railroads, guides, cold, and ashes. Strolling about crowded Naples on 19 February, he observed even more *Bourbon guards. He visited the tourist's "compulsory" landmarks, including those of Pozzuoli (the ancient Puteoli), locale of Greek and Roman myths of *Hades, *Elysium, and *Avernus, as well as the supposed tomb of *Virgil. He commented at length in his journal (21 February) on the Museo Borbonico (where he saw the *Hercules Farnese), but even the San Carlo Opera (1737; rebuilt 1816) had a sentinel on stage (19 February). Despite the beautiful scenery, his visit was marked by his own lingering depression. He left the area through "Neopolitan vineyards" (R. 49), eager to see Rome (120 miles northwest). The motto of the Neopolitans, famous for their songs and festivals, seemed to be: "Let us eat, drink & be merry, for tomorrow we die" (23 February).

M. recalls Naples in two poems: "Pausilippo," and "Naples in the Time of Bomba."
T. 28; M. 153; R. 21; R. 28; R. 49; W. 88

NAPOLEON, --'S; NAPOLEON BONAPARTE; BONAPARTEAN

Napoléon Buonoparte (1769-1821) was born into a *Corsican family of ancient nobility which had moved to cooperation with the *French occupation. He was educated in *France, where he began his military career and became convinced of the need for political change through readings in *Voltaire, *Rousseau, and other Enlightenment authors. Leader of a Jacobin group, he spoke against the ruling class of nobles (see "Bourbon") and ecclesiastics and against Corsican separatists. He fled to France with his family in 1793 and was rapidly promoted after early revolutionary activity in which he was wounded and imprisoned (at the fall of Robespierre). Defense of the Convention brought a rise in status. By the time of his becoming chief of the army of *Italy against *Austria, he had become romantically involved with Désirée Clary, married Joséphine Tascher de La Pagerie, and changed the spelling of his family name.

Military victories led to armistices with Italian rulers and with the *Pope, as well as to the reorganization of Italy. Napoléon marched on *Vienna in 1797 and waged sea war against the *British in 1798 in an effort to occupy *Egypt. But *Nelson's actions at the battle of the *Nile destroyed the French squadron, leading to Napoléon's retreat to Egypt in 1799, to an opposing coalition of Britain, Austria, *Russia, and *Turkey, and to defeat of French armies in Italy.

Back in France, he carried out the *coup d'état* (9-10 November 1799) which replaced the Directory, becoming dictator Consul of great popularity. He forced peace in Europe, and reorganized the French Republic's government, military force, and civil law, under the new Constitution becoming Consul for life with power to name a successor. Expansionist policies led to war with the British again in 1803. Becoming Emperor (crowned by the Pope at Notre-Dame) in 1804 and King of Italy in 1805, Napoléon restored many royalist traditions and built many of *Paris's monuments and bridges. His projected invasion of England with *Spanish assistance was frustrated by the battle of *Trafalgar, which brought British mastery of the seas and British alliance with Austria, *Russia, *Sweden, and *Naples against him. In 1805, he defeated the Austrians and Russians at Austerlitz, leading to the *Rhine Confederation, Franco-Russian peace, bestowal of the Kingdom of Naples to his brother Joseph, and creation of the *Polish Duchy of Warsaw.

His attempted 1810 blockade of English waters turned Spain and *Portugal against him, but marriage to Marie Louise, daughter of the Austrian Emperor Francis I brought almost complete control of continental Europe, which he reorganized disregarding geographical and ethnic considerations, exacerbating general discontent. Failure in attempted winter invasion of Russia decimated his forces as satellite nations rebelled against him. By 1814, France was under attack at every frontier, and *Talleyrand became President of a provisional government. At Marshall *Ney's suggestion, Napoléon abdicated at Fontainebleau. With the *Bourbons reinstated, he was banished to *Elba but returned to Paris in 1815, briefly restored to power, only to have the *Waterloo defeat lead to a forced second abdication on 22 June 1815 and his replacement by Louis XVIII. Exiled to *St. Helena, he died, of apparent natural causes. Entombment at Hôtel des Invalides followed an elaborate funeral in Paris.

The Napoleonic Wars had lasted from 1804 to 1815, at great cost in French lives but to France's advantage in institutional stability and human rights. A large body of romantic literature praising Napoléon's intelligence and military prowess made possible Louis Napoléon's becoming Emperor in 1852. But M.'s references, especially the association with "Tamerlane" (see "Marlow") in *M.* 181 suggest he sided with those who saw Napoléon only as a callous and egotistical despot, in keeping with his generally negative feelings about the French. M. was in Paris in December of 1849 and visited many of the monuments constructed by Napoléon, as well as the Hôtel des Invalides, where he was much impressed by the Austerlitz flags and other military display.

See also "Haydn"; "Vienna, Congress of."

T. 17; O. 7; M. 6; M. 30; M. 181; R. 18; R. 50; R. 55; W. 49; W. 50; W. 87; W. 90; M.D. 32; M.D. 35; M.D. 104; P. 15:1; P. 23:4; C.M. 45

NARCISSUS

A scorner of love, Narcissus of mythology died after falling in love with his own image reflected in a pool; he was transformed after death into a flower. *Ovid's *Metamorphoses*, Book 3 (Vol. 20 of *Harper's Classical Library*; Sealts #147) retells the ancient tale.

M.D. 1

NARII

The battle of Narii (near Bunaauïa, in the district of Atehuru), *Tahiti, took place on 12 November 1815. *Ellis (Chapter 7) describes the confrontation when 800 Sabbath observers from *Eimeo were attacked by local idolaters; *Pomare's forces were victorious.

O. 80

NARRAGANSETT, --BAY

Narragansett Bay, *Rhode Island's *Atlantic inlet, cuts c. thirty miles into the state. Its inlets and islands were important colonial shipping centers. The "Narragansett woods" of *M.D.* 45 are those of the area south of *Providence, settled in the mid-seventeenth century. The town of Narragansett is twenty-seven miles south of the capital. In *M.D.* 45, M. is in error regarding *Captain Butler's pursuit of *Annawon. Captain Benjamin Church captured the Indian during *King Philip's War.

M.D. 45; I.P. 25

"*NARRATIVE OF THE SHIPWRECK OF THE WHALE SHIP ESSEX OF NANTUCKET, WHICH WAS ATTACKED AND FINALLY DESTROYED BY A LARGE SPERM WHALE IN THE PACIFIC OCEAN.*"

See "Essex"; "Chace, Owen"; "Pollard, Captain"; "Extracts 58."

M.D. Extracts 58

NARRATIVE OF THE U.S. EXPLORING EXPEDITION
See "Wilkes."
0. 49; 0. 54

NARROWS, THE
The stretch of water between Brooklyn and *Staten Island connecting Upper *New York Bay to Lower Bay: c. one to
one and one-half miles wide, two and one-half miles long.
R. 7; R. 60

NARROW SEAS
There are many bodies of water called the "Narrows"
(*New York Bay, Leeward Islands, Virgin Islands, Vancou-
ver, *Dardanelles), but M.'s allusion to *Von Tromp on the
"Narrow Seas" (W. 71) seems to refer to the English *Channel,
which is not called by that name. In R. 40's reference to
*American ships negotiating the "Narrow Seas," he may be
punning. "Narrow Seas" to the sailor means drinking of alco-
holic beverages.
R. 40; W. 71

NATCHITOCHES
The oldest city of *Louisiana, located in the northwest-
central part of the state, sixty-five miles southeast of Shreve-
port, Natchitoches was founded as a *French military and
trading post on the Cane River, in 1714. It was incorporated in
1819 (reincorporated in 1872).
C.M. 24

NATHAN COLEMAN
Although this name appears to be invented, the legend
about the introduction of mosquitoes in O. 56 seems to have ex-
isted.
See "Whaleman's Chapel."
O. 56; M.D. 7

NATURAL HISTORY
See "Cuvier."
M.D. 41

NATURAL HISTORY OF WHALES
See "Cuvier."
M.D. 55

"NATURE IN DISEASE"

Jacob Bigelow, M.D., *Nature in Disease* (Boston 1854) discusses the history of medicine, including quackery and homeopathy, holding the thesis that some diseases cure themselves. As Franklin's notes to *C.M.* suggest, the book's title is ambiguous.
C.M. 16

NATURE'S NOBLEMAN

Martin Farquhar Tupper (1810-1889) wrote *Nature's Nobleman* (1844):

> Nature's own Nobleman, friendly and frank,
> Is a man with his heart in his hand.

T. 11

NAUTILUS

The paper nautilus is a tropical cephaloped mollusk with a many-chambered spiral shell and pearly interior. It was much fancied in the nineteenth century for the mystique spread by the ancient *Greeks. They believed that the nautilus extended two arms out of its shell to use as a sail in order to float on the ocean.
(Oliver Wendell Holmes's poem, "The Chambered Nautilus," was first published in 1858.)
M.D. 133

"NAVAL SUBJECTS"

As Philbrick shows, *Cursory Suggestions on Navel Subjects* (1822) was mentioned in M.'s source for *W.* 90 *British Navy lore: an article by Thomas Hodgeskin, "Abolition of Impressment," in *Edinburgh Review* XLI [1824], 154-181.
W. 90

NAVARINO

A decisive battle on 20 October 1827, in the War of *Greek Independence. The 6 July treaty of London had provided *British, *Russian, and *French intervention in the *Turkish/Greek conflict. A Turkish/*Egyptian force entered Navarino Bay (ancient Bay of Pylos) when the allied forces tried to block Turkish supply vessels. British Admiral Sir *Edward *Codrington, assuming a ceasefire, left the Bay with the allied forces, and a series of further misunderstandings caused the

four-hour battle which killed 8,000 *Moslems and 176 members
of the allied force.
W. 4; W. 75; W. 92

NAVIGATOR
See "Bowditch."
W. 68

NAVIGATOR ISLANDS; NAVIGATOR'S ISLANDS
See "Samoa; Samoan."
M. 3; M. 22; M. 30

NAVY [UNITED STATES]
The first "official" action of an "American" navy occurred in June of 1775, when two armed vessels chartered by
the government of *Rhode Island captured a *British vessel in
*Narrangansett Bay; this event instigated creation of the Con-
tinental Navy in October of that year. General *George Washington chartered eleven vessels which took many prizes, and
*Congress outfitted four vessels for temporary service before
funds were secured in November for purchase of eight merchant vessels to complete the small fleet. These were renamed
and armed: Alfred, twenty-four guns; Columbus (eighteen to
twenty); Andrew Doria (fourteen); Cabot (fourteen); Providence (twelve); *Hornet (ten); *Wasp (eight); Fly (eight). Two
battalions of "American *Marines" were organized as fighting
forces aboard the ships and on land.
John Adams composed the first set of regulations for the
Navy, and a permanent committee was established for ad hoc
decisions. Among first officers commissioned was *John Paul
Jones. Of thirteen heavily armed ships ordered by Congress in
1775, only seven were completed, and all were lost during the
*Revolution. The first operation of the Continental Navy oc-
curred in February and March of 1776; of the eight vessels assigned to the American coast, two went their separate ways before the commander set course for the Bahamas, where he
landed Marines, occupied territory, and captured munitions.
Privateering was authorized in late March, and in April the
first engagement with an enemy warship took place, off Block
Island.
Under commanders such as Jones, the little Navy had
surprising success, leading to the daring dispatch in November of 1776 of *Benjamin Franklin and other diplomats to
*France, where (after the battle of *Saratoga in October of 1777)

intervention was secured. The Continental Navy was terminated, and its last remaining vessel, *Alliance, sold in 1785.

The *Constitution, approved in 1788, provided for a navy, but none was established until 1794, after the *Barbary Wars and the French Revolution had begun: its only task was to be protection of American shipping in the *Mediterranean. *Jefferson opposed creation of a navy, as did most southerners, but Hamilton's *Federalists supported it, and the Navy was founded on compromised principles. Six frigates (of 44 or 36 guns) were ordered and three cancelled when peace was secured in the Mediterranean. *Constitution (44), *United States, and Constellation (36) were mothballed until the following year (1797) and not put into service until 1798.

It was not until 30 April 1798 that Congress created the *Navy Department and the office of *Secretary of the Navy, and the continuing saga of that force's development was written by the men who filled that office.

M.'s negative feelings about the navy are vividly expressed throughout W., which is a highly accurate portrayal of that service in the 1840's. As M. noted, in its development of a navy, the *United States was emulating the worst aspects of the British Navy, undoubtedly due to lack of wholehearted support for its existence.

Among M.'s other references to American Navy vessels, officers, encounters, and policies are the following: "Algerine"; "Amphitrite"; "Andrew Miller"; "Articles of War"; "Bainbridge"; "Bancroft"; "Board of Commodores"; "Bon Homme Richard"; "Buccaneer"; "Carolina, the"; "Chase, Jack"; "Commodore . . ."; *Commodore Preble*; "Countess of Scarborough"; "Decatur"; "Dreadnaught"; "Erie . . ."; "Essex"; "Flamborough Head"; "Foreigners"; "Great Lakes"; "Guerriere, the"; " Hornet"; "Hull"; "Indien"; "Jane"; "Java"; "Letters of Mart"; *Macedonian*"; "Magnificent, the"; "Mahon"; "Man of War"; "Mellish"; "Midshipman . . ."; "Milford"; "Mohawk"; "Navy Register"; "Ohio"; "Pallas"; *Peacock*"; "Pearson, Captain"; "Pennsylvania . . ."; "Pensacola"; "Perry's"; "Phoebe"; "Polk, President"; "Porter . . ."; "Preble"; "President, the"; "Ranger"; "Ruschenberger"; "Scorpions"; "Serapis"; "Soleby"; "Spitfire, the"; "Stockton, Commodore"; "The Old Wagon . . ."; *United States*"; "Vermont"; "Vincennes"; "Virginia"; "War of 1812"; "Wasps"; "Wilkes."

See also references in "Nautical Appendix."

W. Passim and elsewhere

NAVY DEPARTMENT
Founded 30 April 1798, along with the office of its govern-
ing force, *Secretary of the Navy.
W. 85; W. 87 and elsewhere

NAVY REGISTER
As of 1825, Register or Intelligence Offices were opened,
where seamen might enter their names and addresses, for application by ship-owners and masters.
By 1839, the Navy was officially registering seamen to
encourage permanent enlistment, and commanding officers
were issuing muster rolls of discharged seamen, with reports
on their deportment. Registered seamen had certain privileges: pay raises; right to resign after three years of service;
exemption from corporal punishment; furloughs for merchant service; possibility of promotion to petty officer rank.
W. 27

NEBUCHADNEZZAR
M.'s spelling is a misrendering also scattered throughout the *Old Testament, along with the correct
"Nebuchadrezzar" (closer to the *Hebrew rendering). Nebuchadrezzar II, the greatest *Babylonian king, reigned from c.
605 to c. 562 B.C. He defeated the *Egyptians, won *Syria and
*Palestine, sieged *Tyre, and punished Judah (see "Judea").
In Babylon, he restored property and rebuilt the city, restored
the Temple of Bel (see "Belial"), erected a palace, banked the
*Euphrates, and built the Hanging Gardens. Much of our
knowledge of him comes from the Old Testament, especially
from *Daniel and *Jeremiah, as well as from the *Apocrypha.
Nebuchadrezzar comes under Daniel's influence when the
seer can guess and interpret his dreams. In Daniel 3, he
attempts to punish *Shadrach, Meshach, and Abednego for
failing to worship his idol. There are many legends about
him, but references in *Judith are ahistorical.
"Nebuchadnezzar fare" (O. 1) is vegetarian.
O. 1; M. 60; R. 56; P. 19:2

NECESSITARIAN
Those who negatively answer the question, "Is man a
free agent?" as opposed to Libertarians, who answer positively.
The question is related to the discussion of "Chronometricals
and Horologicals," in P.: if God foreordains all our actions, we
are but clocks—mechanical creatures. If man on the other

hand is responsible for his actions, he must be free to perform them.

Fatalism is loosely synonymous with necessitarianism or determinism, but the latter accepts moral responsibility, whereas fatalism excludes responsibility except for submission to the course of events.

Among Christians, the *Quietists, who rely solely on inspiration, are more fatalistic than religious determinists such as *Calvinists, or Jansenists. Eastern religions such as Islam presume inexorable fate (kismet, nasib); submission to *God is resignation to fate.

M.'s tendency toward a deterministic view probably began with his Calvinistic upbringing and continued with his readings in such figures as *Bayle, *Spinoza, *Browne, Edwards, *Goethe, Godwin, *Shelley, and especially in David Hartley's 1801 Observations on Man, His Frame, His Duty, and His Expectations. See also "Fixed Fate. . . . "
M. 123; M. 135

NECESSITY
    See "Necessitarian."
M. 135; M. 180 and elsewhere

NED KNOWLES
    There is a *German joke about Fritz Knolls, meaning the head.
W. 75

NEGRO MOB
    This is probably a reference to the "Great Negro Plot" of 1741. The ensuing riots have been compared with the *Salem Witchcraft trials in the panicky reaction of local citizens, responding to a delusion with inhuman violence. In March 1741, rumor blamed a series of mysterious *New York City fires on discontented *slaves. A tavern-worker arrested for robbery sought to claim a large reward by falsely confessing herself a co-conspirator with slaves bent on wide-spread arson. A reign of terror followed in which scores of people were jailed and tortured; fourteen blacks were burned at the stake, eighteen were hanged, and seventy-one were transported; of twenty whites imprisoned, four were put to death (including an unpopular *Catholic school teacher whose faith was outlawed in New York at the time). Hangings occurred at the junction of *Pearl and Centre Streets; burnings were conducted at *City Hall Place, near Duane Street. The panic continued until

September, after which positive feeling about blacks grew.
Perhaps as a result of lingering shame, slavery was abolished
in New York City starting in 1758, with an act declaring free
all children born of slaves.

New York City had many riots during M.'s lifetime. Riots of 1834 centered on protest against *abolitionism, which
threatened to reduce cotton-trade business; 1837 riots followed
financial panic; 1849 saw the *Astor Place Opera-House riot;
in 1857, enmity between the *Bowery Boys and the *Irish fighting gang, the "Dead Rabbits," resulted in a very bloody riot; the
July Draft Riots of 1863 ended with 1,200 people slain.

The reference might also be to the riots mentioned in
Marie, by Gustave de Beaumont, to whom M. had sought an
introduction.

Cornelius Mathews, in *Big Abel and the Little Manhattan* (1845) recollects the "old Negro Plot, when all the blackness
of the city roused, and like an angry tempest rising from the
earth—not now, from heaven!—threatened every life."
W. 16

NELSON

Horatio Nelson (1758-1805), son of a Norfolk (*England)
parish rector, went to sea at the age of twelve, serving in the
*West and *East Indies. Sent home in depression in 1775, he
resolved to return and become a hero. Nelson was a lieutenant
by 1777 and was rapidly promoted, becoming post-captain in
1779. (Under complex British Navy promotion arrangements,
seniority would determine future promotions; had he lived, he
would not have become highest-ranking officer until his eight-
ies.) After service in Nicaragua, he was appointed in 1781 to
the frigate *Albemarle*, traveling to the *Baltic, *Newfoundland,
and the West Indies, where the Duke of Clarence (future
William IV) admired his spirit, his manners, and his appearance. After visiting *France in 1783, he was assigned to the
frigate *Boreas* in the West Indies, where he married (1787)
Frances Nisbet, a widow. While captain of *Agememnon*
against the French in the *Mediterranean, he met Sir William
Hamilton, minister at the court of Naples, and began the
intimate relationship with Emma (see "Hamilton, Lady") that
was to become a scandalous blot on his reputation.

Nelson's battle-blasted body probably fascinated M. as
much as his balanced attributes of "head and heart." (There
are amputees and references to amputation in *M.*, *W.*, *M.D.*,
and elsewhere.) Nelson lost his right arm in an unsuccessful
attack on Santa Cruz de *Tenerife (24 July 1797). At the battle
of the *Nile (1 August 1798), he was struck in the forehead by a
shot and briefly disabled. He was later blinded in one eye but

continued undiminished in fervor at the battle of *Saint Vincent (14 February 1797). Nelson became Rear-Admiral by virtue of seniority but gained numerous honors for his actions at the blockages of *Cádiz and *Naples, where his popularity dimmed somewhat because of his peculiar personal arrangements with the Hamiltons and his refusal to accept the treaty of peace. He was honored by the restored Neapolitan royal family but was returned to England on leave, officially separating from his wife after having traveled across Europe with the Hamiltons. Promoted to Vice-Admiral in 1801, he was second in command at the battle of *Copenhagen, where his disobedience of Sir Hyde Parker's orders brought victory and the title of Viscount, as well as Parker's recall.

As Mediterranean commander against the French from 1803, Nelson apparently felt personally goaded by *Napoléon. By 1805, the French ruler's threatened invasion of England was halted by Nelson's brilliant tactics at the battle of *Trafalgar (21 October): at the cost of Nelson's death from a French sharpshooter's bullet. Nelson had appeared a clear mark on the deck of *Victory, dressed, as usual, in his admiral's frock coat bedecked with four stars representing his honors. M. saw a collection of Nelson's elegant coats at *Greenwich Hospital, 21 November 1849.

Admiration of Nelson was inspired not only by his courage in battle. He was known for his courtesy to subordinates, even to dining with them (a fact which M. might have had in mind in *M.D.* 34 "The Cabin-Table," wherein "*Ahab" rules over an uncomfortable hierarchy of diners on "*Pequod"). Nelson was a teacher of officers and enlisted men, believing one must be a seaman to be a good officer, and a gentleman, as well. His concern for detail extended even to the more sensible painting of warships. His determination was undiminished by such plodding tasks as re-laying buoys to mark channels before the battle of Copenhagen. In disobeying Parker at Copenhagen, Nelson is said to have applied his telescope to his blind eye, so as to miss Parker's faulty orders. Throughout much of his career, he flew an ensign that read, "England expects every man to do his duty."

M. was obviously fascinated by Nelson. His journals show his awareness of sailing in waters traversed by the British hero. He saw *Victory* at *Portsmouth (25 December 1849), and the statuary dedicated to Nelson in *Liverpool (described in *R*. 31), some time in 1839 and again on 8 November 1856, at which time he wrote in his journal of his "peculiar emotion, mindful of 20 years ago." He owned an engraving of Lady Hamilton and saw Turner's *The Fighting Temeraire* in London (28 April 1857). "The Temeraire" (second ship to *Victory* at Trafalgar) is one of M.'s *Battle-Pieces*, decrying the end of the "navies old and oaken" (1.63). *Billy Budd, Sailor* evokes Nelson throughout. M. apparently pored over his copy of Robert Southey, *Life of Nelson* (New York, 1855) for *Billy Budd*, heavily marking and annotating it. In a twist on a reference to *Wellington in Tennyson's "Ode," M. apparently projected a chapter of *Billy Budd* praising Nelson, to be entitled: "Concerning 'the greatest sailor since the world began'."

The *W.* 74 reference to **L'Orient* is confirmed in John Fairburn's 1806 pamphlet describing Nelson's funeral. The body was "placed in the coffin made out of the main-mast of the *L'Orient* which blew up at the battle of the Nile . . . the outside was covered with black cloth, and the inside lined with white silk, stuffed with cotton. That coffin was put into a leaden one, soldered up and enclosed in an elm one." (See "Hallowell.")

The *Trafalgar Square monument of *M.D.* 35, constructed between 1840 and 1867, consists of a base like an elongated capstan, decorated with plaques made from captured French guns, and surrounded by *Landseer lions. The statue of battleclad Nelson (by E.H. Bailey) is not considered great art, but its position some 100 feet atop the base makes that unimportant.

The reference in *R.* 32 is to *Liverpool's street named for Admiral *Nelson. It bounds *St. George's Square on the north and runs east-west from *St. James Street to Berry Street.
O. 15; O. 29; M. 24; M. 30; R. 29; R. 31; R. 32; R. 38; R. 41; W. Passim; M.D. 8; M.D. 35

NEMESIS
    A *Greek goddess of retribution, who punishes the evil, the proud, and the undeservedly fortunate. A daughter of Night (Nyx), she is represented in some tales as being raped by Zeus (see "Jupiter" and "Jove") and persecuted by Aphrodite (see "Venus"). Taking the form of a goose, she lays an egg which hatches into Helen.
C.M. 26

NEOPOLITAN
    See "Naples; Bay of Naples; Neopolitan."
R. 49

N.E. PRIMER
    The New England Primer sold more than five million copies after publication (c. 1683) by its compiler, *Boston resident Benjamin Harris (fl. 1673-1716). The *Calvinist catechism for school children featured woodcut alphabet letters illustrat-

ing *Old Testament-type moral texts. "The Little Bible of New England" introduced the children's prayer, "Now I lay me down to sleep."

M. acquired a popular reprint in 1851 (Sealts #384).

See Also "Extracts" 33.

M.D. Extracts 33

NEPTUNE

In *Greek mythology, Poseidon (*Roman Neptune) is son of *Cronos and *Rhea, brother to Zeus (see "Jupiter" and "Jove"), and ruler of the sea and underground rivers. He has a palace beneath the sea but is mostly found on *Olympus. Also called "Earth-shaker," he gave men the first horse and is also connected with bulls. He is represented carrying a Trident (three-pronged spear). His wife *Amphitrite, is granddaughter of the *Titan, Ocean.

In none of M.'s allusions to Neptune does he refer to the planet discovered in 1846.

See also "Beards"; "Equator."

M. 9; M. 48; M. 149; R. 60; W. 8; W. 19; W. 37; W. 84

NEPTUNE

A very common name for a ship; the *Neptune* tied up at *Prince's Dock, *Liverpool, could not have been the warship *Neptune* at the battle of *Trafalgar.

R. 32

NERO, --'S

Nero Claudius Caesar (A.D. 37-68) was *Roman Emperor from 54 to 68. He was the son of Agrippina (great-granddaughter of *Augustus) and was adopted by her uncle (and second husband), *Claudius I. Agrippina persuaded Claudius to elevate the boy, who was to become Emperor at the age of seventeen.

Nero was at first an effective Emperor, but his instability and self-gratification were soon exacerbated by his grand position. His reign was marked by embarrassing public displays of his poetry, lyre-playing, and charioteering, so that by the time of the great fire (64), he was accused of setting the conflagration himself to facilitate replacement of existing structures with his "House of Gold" (*M.* 75). It was a massive , sumptuously decorated structure set amid gardens and fountains, with an artificial lake and a gilded bronze statue of Nero, 120 feet high. The Golden House was remodeled and built upon by later Emperors. Its remains were discovered during the time of *Raphael, who was said to be much influenced in his painting style by its decor.

A frequent murderer of political enemies, Nero conducted a reign of terror which removed *Thrasea and many other patriots. His extravagant personal expenditure, building program, and gift-giving left Rome devoid of a treasury at his death.

M.'s *lecture, "Statues in Rome," allowed him to editorialize on the emperor's appearance as represented by a statue he saw in *Naples in 1857. Reports of the lecture quote M. as finding "something repulsive, half-demoniac in the expression" of the "genteely dissipated youth" much like contemporary young men "who would scarce be guilty of excessive cruelties" (*Melville as Lecturer*, p. 133).
M. 75; R. 55; W. 91

NERVA
    In Huelva province, *Andalusia, *Spain: thirty-five miles northwest of *Seville.
M. 75

NESCIO QUID SIT
    Lat.: "I do not know what it is."
M.D. Extracts 11

NESKYEUNA SHAKERS
    See "Shaker."
M.D. 71

NESSUS
    M. errs about the mythological Nessus's "fatal shirt." When the centaur Nessus tried to violate Deianira, the wife of *Hercules, he was shot by a poisoned arrow. As he died, he gave Deianira some poisoned blood as a charm to keep her husband faithful. She smeared it on Hercules's robe, and the poison killed him.
    See also "Hercules" for another version of the death story.
W. 47

NESTOR
    In *Greek mythology, a wise and vigorous king of Pylus, renowned for his prowess in games, hunting, and war. Nestor

was king for three generations; he figures prominently throughout the *Iliad (Sealts #277) and in Book 3 of the Odyssey (Sealts #278).
W. 86

NETHERLANDS
     See "Holland . . . . "
M.D. 105 and elsewhere

NEVERSINK
     See "United States."
W. Passim

NEVERSINK HIGHLANDS
     As the context of M. 16 shows, this is not a reference to *New York's Neversink River (which rises in the Catskills and flows some sixty-five miles to Port Jervis), but to Nevesinje, present-day Yugoslavia, where highlands overlook the turbulent *Adriatic Sea.
M. 16

NEVIL, RICHARD
     Richard Nevil (d. 1471), the "King-Maker" was probably the most influential member of *English nobility's most extensively connected family. His most famous power plays deposed Henry IV and enthroned Edward IV in 1461 but then in 1470 deposed Edward and restored Henry.
     *Warwick, home of the Nevils, is a feudal castle, heavily fortified and artfully decorated, a major modern tourist attraction near the confluence of the Avon and Leam rivers in England.
     (See also "Clarence.")
W. 68

NEW BEDFORD
     Settled in 1764 on the west bank of *Massachusetts's *Acushnet River, New Bedford was first called by the Indian name, Acushnet. It was founded by *Nantucket *Quakers in the whaling business, and burned by the *British in 1778, but by the 1830's was the world's chief whaling port. A bridge connected New Bedford with its twin town, Fairhaven.

M. arrived in New Bedford on 26 December 1840 and
sailed on *Acushnet* from Fairhaven on 3 January 1841, which
left him much time to explore.
R. 23; M.D. Passim

NEW BRUNSWICK

The east *Canadian province is bordered in modern
times by *Maine (W.), *Quebec (N.E. and N.), Chaleur Bay
(N.), the Gulf of *St. Lawrence and Northumberland Strait
(E.), *Nova Scotia (S.E.), and the Bay of Fundy (S.). The Cabots
explored the area in 1497 and Cartier in 1534. Champlain
made the first settlement in 1604, and Acadia (see "Arcadia")
was established in 1633. The area passed to the British in 1713,
and many loyalists moved here at the time of the *Revolution.
New Brunswick became separate from Nova Scotia in 1784.
R. 22

NEWCASTLE

*England's Newscastle upon Tyne is famous for coal
mining. "Carrying coals to Newcastle" refers to any ridicu-
lously unnecessary labor, action, or journey. The "Newcastle
collier" of *R.* 26 is a ship (probably a brig) carrying coal on the
Tyne River from Newcastle, the word "collier" referring both to
a miner and a vessel.
R. 26

NEW CYTHEREA

The *French called *Tahiti "Nouvelle Cythere," the New
Cytherea. Cythera, *Greece (Kythnos), is a resort area of hot
springs.
O. 18

NEW ENGLAND, --ER

An unofficial name for the states of *Maine, *New
Hampshire, *Vermont, *Massachuseets, *Rhode Island, and
*Connecticut, bestowed when the *English made their second
settlement in 1620, at Plymouth, Massachusetts. When he was
not a "New Yorker," M. was a "New Englander."
Passim

NEW ENGLAND HAGS

Probably refers to the 1690's witchcraft trials, especially
in *Salem, *Massachusetts.
M.D.3

NEWFOUNDLAND
    The island of Newfoundland (which includes *Labrador)
is the easternmost province of modern *Canada, separated
from the mainland by Cabot Strait (S.W.), the Gulf of *St.
Lawrence (W.), and Strait of Belle Isle (N.W.). It has a deeply
indented steep and rocky coastline, with fjord-like inlets. The
*Grand Banks is the chief whaling, sealing and fishing
ground.
    Newfoundland was discovered by Cabot in 1497 and was
*Britain's first colony. The *French and British concurrently
developed parts of the island. The Treaty of Utrecht (1713) gave
the land to England, along with a fishing monopoly on the
western and northeastern coasts (not changed until the twentieth century).
M. 30; R. Passim; M.D. 58; C.M. 3

NEWFOUNDLAND DOG
    The large working dog of a breed originally developed in
the *Arctic appears to be a symbol for M. of good nature tri-
umphing over brute strength. M. owned a Newfoundland, as
*Hawthorne's son Julian notes in *Hawthorne and His Circle*
(N.Y., 1903) and in "Herman Melville and His Dog," in *The
Dearborn Independent* (24 September 1927).
    (The obtuse narrator of M.'s "Benito Cereno" mistakenly
likens rebellious black *slaves to Newfoundland dogs.)
M. 30; M.D. 4; M. 30

NEWGATE, --CALENDAR
    The famous *London prison was constructed in 1769 to
the specifications of architect George Dance the Younger (1741-
1825), combining classical, romantic, and mannerist elements
of architecture. New Gate was part of the original ancient
London Wall, used for confinement of felons of London and
Middlesex since the thirteenth century. Conditions were so
deplorable by 1780 that Newgate was almost burned down, but
the building survived until its demolition in 1902. In the eighteenth and nineteenth centuries, the prison gained a reputation
for squalor, with up to twenty prisoners confined in rooms
approximately 300 square feet in area. Felons were mixed in
with those who had committed minor offenses or with debtors
(by far the largest population); prisoners paid for food or
worked for it. The condemned were hanged in front of the
building.
    From the seventeenth to the nineteenth century, the
Newgate Calendar was published: a periodic chronological
series of lurid memoirs of prisoners, descriptions of their

crimes and their last moments alive. Among the more
renowned inmates were *Captain Kidd, Richard Turpin, and
Jenny Diver.
M. 1; R. 39; W. 43; W. 44; C.M. 26

NEW GUINEA
     The modern Indonesian island of New Guinea (or
*Papua) is the second largest island of the world (next to
*Greenland): 1,500 miles long and up to 400 miles wide. It is
separated from *Australia by *Torres Strait and the Arafura
Sea. New Guinea's mountains include the world's highest island peak: Mount Carstensz (16,400 feet). The swampy tropical jungle which is home to much exotic flora and fauna (as
well as to headhunters in the interior) was almost totally unexplored in M.'s time (and remains partly so). New Guinea
was first sighted by the *Portuguese in 1511; It became
separated into three political divisions: *Netherlands New
Guinea, Territory of New Guinea, Territory of Papua.
R. 33; M.D. 45

NEW HAMPSHIRE
     One of the original thirteen states of the Union, New
Hampshire is bordered by *Quebec (N.), *Maine (E.), the
*Atlantic (S.E.), *Massachusetts (S.) and *Vermont (W.). It is
180 miles long (N.-S.) and from fifteen to ninety miles wide.
The area was explored by Champlain in 1605 and by Captain
John Smith in 1614. The first *English settlement was made in
1623, and by 1679 it was a separate Royal Province. Portsmouth
was blockaded by the British in the *War of 1812.
     A major attraction of New Hampshire, for the Melville
family and many other nineteenth-century Americans, was
the ruggedly picturesque *White Mountain chain, which includes the often-painted Franconia Notch and Crawford Notch
(which *Hawthorne pictured in "The Ambitious Guest").
Mount Washington is the highest peak in the state, at 6,288
feet; Mount Monadnock is 3,165 feet. The Melvilles' honeymoon journey of 1847 included stops at Concord, Center Harbor, Conway, and Mount Washington. M. *lectured in Concord
in November of 1857, and the family vacationed in the White
Mountains in the 1870's and 80's.
W. 79; M.D. 6; M.D. 42; M.D. 102; I.P. 2

NEW HEBRIDES
     A group of (twelve principal) western *Pacific islands (c.
500 miles west of Fiji; see "Feejee"), 250 miles N.E. of New

Caledonia), of coral and volcanic origin. The group was discovered by the *Portuguese in 1606, rediscovered by de
*Bougainville in 1768, and charted by *Cook in 1774. Missionar-
ies settled in the bellicose islands in 1848. The *British monopolized trade until *French inroads in 1870.
        See also "Erromanga."
O. 25

NEW HOLLAND, --'S
        The *Dutch visited *Australia in the early eighteenth
century, calling it "New Holland."
R. 33; R. 40; M.D. 105; I.P. 10

NEW JERSEY
        New Jersey, one of the original thirteen states of the
Union, is bordered by *New York (N. and N.E.), Delaware Bay
(S.), *Delaware and *Pennsylvania (W.). In 1620 the *Dutch
settled the area along the *Hudson River; the *Swedes settled
along the Delaware River by 1640, and *British settlers were
permanently ensconced by 1664. New Jersey was an important
area during the *American *Revolution, with *Washington's
headquarters at Norristown and important battles at Trenton,
Princeton, and Monmouth.
        The "green heights of New Jersey" are probably the Pal-
isades: 350-500 foot cliffs along the southern Hudson. The New
Jersey Highlands are up to 1,200 feet, but the highest peak, Kit-
tatinny Mountain (1,801 feet) is in the northwest corner of the
state, overlooking the Delaware Water Gap.
R. 60; W. 42

NEW JERUSALEM
        *Revelation 3:12: "Him that overcometh will I make a
pillar in the temple of my *God, and he shall go no more out:
and I will write upon him the name of my God, and the name
of the city of my God, which is new *Jerusalem, which cometh
down out of heaven from my God: and I will write upon him
my new name." The city is described in Revelation 21-22 as a
magical, jewel-encrusted home for the saved.
        (See also "Mormons"; "Swedenborg.")
C.M. 9

NEW ORLEANS; ORLEANS
        The commercial metropolis of the south is in southeast-
ern *Louisiana, on the east bank of the *Mississippi River, 107

miles above the mouth. In 1722, it became the capital of the
*French colony of Louisiana, but the *Treaty of Paris trans-
ferred it to *Spain in 1763. France regained the city in 1803, in
time for it to make part of the Louisiana Purchase. It was incorporated in 1805 and until the late nineteenth century retained its Creole culture. The masked carnival parades which
developed into Mardi Gras began in the late 1820's, and by the
late 1830's float processions made their appearance; by 1857,
the full pageant was held (except during the *Civil War). The
"Queen City of the Mississippi" dealt heavily in *slaves and cotton; it fell to Farragut in the Civil War (1862).
     The "Battle of New Orleans" (R. 12) occurred against the
*British, 8 January 1815 (after the official close of the *War of
1812); it was an important victory for the *United States and
for the political reputation of *Andrew Jackson.
     Orleans (M.D. 83) is the parish of New Orleans.
R. 12; W. 16; M.D. 83; C.M. 1; C.M. 6; C.M. 21; C.M. 24

NEW SOUTH WALES
     Now a state in the southeastern part of the modern-day
commonwealth of *Australia, New South Wales originally included Tasmania, South Australia, Victoria, Queensland, the
Northern Territory and *New Zealand--in effect all of Australia and more. (The states separated between 1825 and 1863,
becoming separate colonies.) The chief port is *Sydney. *Cook
arrived in 1770, proclaiming *British sovereignty over the east
coast of the continent; the first settlement (1788) was Sydney
(perhaps as a penal colony; see also "Botany Bay").
O. 23; M. 28; R. 33; R. 40

NEW TESTAMENT
     The new Testament received by *Christians covers a his-
torical period over 300 years after that of the *Old Testament
(during which occurred the *Greek rule of *Palestine, period of
the *Maccabees, and *Roman rule before the birth of *Jesus
somewhere between 20 and 4 B.C.). It covers the period of Roman procurators (from A.D. 6), that of the crucifixion (30), the
work of *St. Paul (35--c. 65), rebellion against Rome (66--70),
and completion of the New Testment (70--150), in the *Gospels.
The canon was not settled until 367, when *Athanasius named
the twenty-seven books since considered authoritative.
M.D. 1; C.M. 45 and elsewhere

NEWTON, ISAAC; NEWTONIAN

Sir Isaac Newton (1642-1727), mathematician and physical scientist, was born in Lincolnshire, *England. He received a B.A. from *Cambridge and became a Fellow at the time of the Great *Plague (1664-67), during which time his private study formed the basis for much of his later work. His early study of mathematics greatly advanced the use of *calculus; it was followed by work with light and color and by discovery of the *moon's gravitation. Newton's work in optics greatly improved the telescope lens, and despite quarrels with Robert Hooke, he was elected to the *Royal Society (of which he later became President). His work in gravitation (which he claimed was inspired by observation of a dropping apple) explained planetary motion.

As M. notes in *O*. 27, Newton related his theory of universal gravitation (1687 *Principia*) to tides, giving a geometrical construction for tide-generating force and calculating the magnitude of the solar equilibrium tide, accounting for springs and neaps, priming and lagging, and diurnal and elliptic inequalities, leaving only the effect of earth's rotation unaccounted for. (The use of automatic tide gauges began about 1830.)

Newton served in *Parliament in 1689 and 1701, suffering nervous difficulties between the two terms. Recognition of his achievement came late in his life, when he was able to resign from Cambridge with government appointments. He was knighted in 1705 and shortly thereafter was quarreling with *Leibniz over invention of the calculus. The *Principia* went through many editions; it was first published in English (*Mathematical Principles of Natural Philosophy*) in 1729. The *Opticks* appeared starting in 1704. *Arithmetica universalis* came out in 1707. Newton's theories were widely popularized, making Newtonianism a dominant Enlightenment philosophy. Miscellaneous papers were not collected until the twentieth century (including those on alchemy), when it became apparent that Newton's theories anticipated the work of Einstein and others.

O. 27; R. 50

NEW WORLD

The Western Hemisphere; the Americas.   Eastern Hemisphere is the Old World.

R. 44

NEW YEAR'S DAY

Celebration of the first day of the year dates from 2000 B.C. *Mesopotamian practice, the year beginning with the new moon nearest the spring or autumn equinox. After 153 B.C., the *Romans designated 1 January as New Year's Day, confirmed by the *Julian calendar, 46 B.C. Medieval Europe designated other dates, but 1 January was restored by the Gregorian calendar (1582) in Roman *Catholic countries and confirmed in *England in 1752.

Nineteenth-century *American custom made much more of New Year's Day than of *Christmas (the *Pagan aspects of which were suppressed), especially among *Dutch-tradition families such as M.'s maternal forebears, the *Gansevoorts. Lavish gifts were exchanged and elaborate cakes and punches were prepared to serve the many callers who would appear briefly. (In the 1820's, M.'s uncle Peter Gansevoort made 150 calls on one New Year's Day!) This traditional observation faded away after the *Civil War.

M. was often at sea on New Year's Day: in 1843 on *Charles and Henry*; in 1844 on *United States*; in 1849 as a passenger returning from England. His journal for 1 January 1857 completely overlooks the holiday: "From *Cairo to *Alexandria. Put up at Victoria Hotel."
M.D. 93; P. 22:4 and elsewhere

NEW YORK [CITY]

The site of New York City, above *New York Harbor at the mouth of the *Hudson River, was probably visited by Giovanni da Verrazano in 1524. Henry Hudson's explorations of 1609 led the *Dutch to settle the tip of *Manhattan, and in 1624 Peter Minuit, of the Dutch West India Company (see "Holland") purchased the entire island from the Indians for $24.00 in trinkets. By 1625, the town of New Amsterdam had been established at the southernmost point. (Dutch buildings of this period were in evidence until the *Fire of 1835.) The *English gained control of the settlement and in 1664 named it for the Duke of *York, with the Dutch returning only briefly (1673-74). Surrounding settlements, not part of the city until late in the nineteenth century, sprang up in Queens (1635), Brooklyn (1636), the Bronx (1641), and *Staten Island (1661); M. usually means Manhattan, when he mentions New York City.

The City was capital of the state and capital of the nation (from 1789 to 1890); rapid development followed the *Revolution.

During M.'s lifetime, the city's center moved continuously north; M. complained of the covering of the island's greenery by pavement, but "Progress" was inevitable. He lived

most of his life in New York City, born (1 August 1819) at
Number 6 *Pearl Street. By fall of 1820 his socially climbing
(and seemingly affluent) family had moved to 55 Courtland
Street, and by 1824 to 33 Bleeker Street. M. entered the New
York Male *High School in 1825, and in 1828 the Melvills (the
"e" was added later) moved to 675 *Broadway. The family
moved to the Albany area in 1830, in an attempt to ameliorate
Allan Melvill's (see "Walter Redburn") financial woes. Except
for the periods at sea, M. lived in upstate New York until his
marriage in 1847, when he and Elizabeth Shaw Melville,
brother Allan and his wife, their mother and several sisters,
all set up housekeeping at 103 Fourth Avenue (present-day
Park Avenue South). M. purchased Arrowhead (*Pittsfield,
*Massachusetts) in 1850 and lived there until 1863, at which
point the family moved to their last New York City address, 104
East 26 Street. (In 1866, M. became Inspector of *Customs at
the Port of New York, resigning in 1885.) The Madison Square
area was a desirable neighborhood at this time, although the
Park itself had shrunk considerably from its early nineteenth-
century incarnation as The Parade. It had been the site of a
Potters' Field, which was replaced by an Arsenal when the
area became too fashionable around the turn of the century to
support the sight of pauper funerals. By the 1840's (through
the efforts of the Harper family of publishers), it had been developed into the center of fashion and amusement, and just
above the Park, Madison Avenue rivaled *Fifth Avenue for its
elegant dwellings, churches, and clubs. Many beautiful buildings surrounded the Park where Grandfather M. was to walk
his grandchildren in the 1880's. Starting in 1876, Madison
Square contained the arm of the Statue of Liberty, on display to
raise funds for completion of the statue (1886). In 1890, the
original Madison Square Garden was erected overlooking the
park. By this time, M.'s neighborhood had become almost his
total orbit, except for excursions to *Staten Island, Fire Island,
and other relatively close places.

New York City bore many mementoes of M.'s Dutch maternal forebears, among them *Gansevoort Street (Hudson
River to Thirteenth Street; originally Great Kiln, then Southhampton Road), and other namesakes. During M.'s lifetime,
Manhattan evolved from a relatively short stretch of dense development (far short of the modern-day Central Park), south of
farms and forests, to the fully settled center of the nation's
trade, immigration, and culture: evincing, perhaps, even less
regard for the preservation of tradition than it does today. M.
probably shared the mixed feelings of modern New Yorkers
about the city: it is crowded, noisy, expensive, and *Philistine,
but it is where life (and employment opportunities) settled, the

tumultuous "civilized" world surrounding the "one insular *Tahiti" (*M.D.* 58) of his dreams.

See also: "Astor House"; "Battery, the"; "Blackwell's Island"; "Bowery, the"; "Bowling-Green"; "Broad-Street"; "Broadway . . . "; "Broadway Tabernacle"; "Castle Garden"; "Catherine Market"; "Chatham Street"; "City Hall"; "City Hotel"; "Coenties Slip"; "Coney Island"; "Croton"; "Deaf and Dumb Institution"; "Delmonico's"; "East River"; "Fourteenth-Street";' "Franklin-square"; "Fulton Market"; "Fulton Street"; "Governor's Island"; "Greenwich Street"; "Harlem River"; "Herald, the"; "Long-Island"; "Narrows, the"; "Negro Mob"; "Olympic Theatre"; "Palmo's"; "Peck Slip"; "Rockaway Beach"; "`Sailors'-Snug-Harbor'"; "St. John's Park"; "St. Paul's"; "South Street"; "Tombs, the"; "Water Street"; "West-Broadway."
Passim

NEW YORK HARBOR
The *Atlantic seaport and port of entry at the mouth of the *Hudson River, on *New York Bay. The virtually land-locked harbor is almost never severely iced, and potential con-nection with the *Great Lakes and the *St. Lawrence via the *Erie Canal made New York eventually a more important port than *Philadelphia or *Baltimore. The Harbor is connected as well with Long Island Sound, via the *East River. The first ships traversing the *Atlantic under steam power did not reach New York Harbor until 1838.
R. 7

NEW YORK HERALD
See "Herald, the . . . . "
W. 59

NEW YORK, --STATE
New York was one of the original thirteen states of the Union. It is bordered by *Vermont (since 1791), Lake Cham-plain, *Massachusetts, *Connecticut (E.), Long Island Sound, *Atlantic Ocean (S.E.), *New Jersey, *Pennsylvania (S.), Lake *Erie, *Niagara River, Lake *Ontario (W.), *St. Lawrence River and *Quebec (N.).

Henry *Hudson and Champlain explored the area in 1609; a *Dutch fur-trading station was set up near Albany (the capital) in 1614, and permanent settlement began in 1625. In that year the Dutch West India Company purchased *Manhattan island and established the forerunner of *New

York City, New Amsterdam. Patroon grants stimulated settlement of the Hudson Valley, with its "Dutch Manors" (*P.* 1:3),
but by 1664 the *British forced surrender of Manhattan.
    The French and Indian Wars took place here, 1689-1763.
Many New Yorkers were loyalists during the *American Revolution, and the state was the site of many Revolutionary War
events mentioned by M.:   *Ethan Allen's actions at
*Ticonderoga; the battle of *Long Island; *Burgoyne's sur-
render after *Saratoga: *Benedict Arnold's attempted betrayal. In the *War of 1812, there were engagements along the
*Niagara and *St. Lawrence Rivers.
    Opening of the *Erie Canal in 1825 brought New York's
largest period of development through linking of waterways
from the *Atlantic to the *Great Lakes. This in turn stimulated much immigration of the *Germans, the *Irish, and
other nationalities in the nineteenth century.
    M. was a New York State resident for much of his life.
In addition to his years in New York City, he lived, or visited
extensively, in Albany, Lansingburgh (see "L_____"),
*Saratoga, *Gansevoort, and Long Island. As the scion of
Hudson Valley Dutch patricians on his mother's side, he knew
much about the state's development; during his lifetime, New
York State grew from a mostly agricultural and forested area
to the locale of many large industrial cities with thickly settled
suburbs.
    See also "Adirondacks"; "Allegheny"; "Buffalo";
"Catskills."
Passim

NEW ZEALAND, --ER
    The country 1,200 miles southeast of *Australia is a
1,000 mile-long island chain which includes North, South
(largest), Stewart, Wellington, and Chatham Islands. Cook
Strait separates North Island from South. Highest peak is
Mount Cook, on South Island, at 12,349 feet; highest volcano is
Ruapehu, on North, at 9,175 feet. The islands are picturesque
areas of glaciers, fjords, hot springs, giant trees, and exotic
fauna. New Zealand had been discovered by Tasman in 1642
and visited by *Cook in 1769; by M.'s time the islands had become provinces of *Britain. The colony established in 1840 as a
dependency of *New South Wales was British by 1841.
    The "wild New Zealander" of *T.* Sequel is the Maori (see
"*Mowree*"), who is also producer of the "'balmed New Zealand
heads" of *M.D.* 3. There were bloody wars between Maoris and
Europeans after establishment of the colony, which became
particularly intense from 1854 to 1864.

The *Bay of Islands or Bay of Plenty, on the northern coast of North Island, is probably the locus of the "Bay whale-men" of *M.D.* 35.
T. Sequel; O. 2; O. 3; O. 38; O. 76; O. 79; M. 3; M. 149; R. 1; R. 33; W. 61; M.D. 3; M.D. 35; M.D. 81; I.P. 11

NEW ZEALAND JACK
    *Beale's *Natural History of the Sperm Whale* (Sealts #52) discusses a particularly destructive whale with a "white hump," "New Zealand Tom."
M.D. 45

NEY, MARSHAL
    Michel Ney, Duc d'Elchingen and Prince de la Moskowa (1769-1815) was a hero/martyr of *French forces in the *Napoleonic Wars. Having distinguished himself in battles of the 1790's, he was received into Napoléon's Court (1801), where his marriage was arranged. As Marshal of the Empire (1804-10), he earned Napoléon's accolade: "the bravest of the brave." He became Prince de la Moskowa for his *Russian victory in 1812.
    Ney was among those demanding Napoléon's abdication in 1814 but back in the fold by 1815. He served ineffectively at *Waterloo and left the army. Captured by ultraroyalists, he was tried and convicted by court-martial and by peers and was shot to death in the *Luxembourg Gardens.
    Ney was not really a good commander of forces, but he was much decorated (M.'s "plumed"), and his execution granted him the status of martyr.
M. 121; I.P. 18

NIAGARA, --'S TABLE ROCK
    The famous Niagara Falls of southern Ontario, *Canada, and *New York State are located on the Niagara River at the international line. The American Falls are 167 feet high and 1,000 feet wide; the Canadian (Horseshoe) Falls are 160 feet high and 2,500 feet wide. La Salle discovered the falls in 1678.
    A piece of the famous Table Rock fell on 25 June 1850, just in time to be memorialized in *M.D.* 78.
T. 9; M. 90; R. 24; R. 30; R. 51; M.D. 1; M.D. 78

NICHOLAS THE CZAR
    See "Tsar."
M.D. 33

NIGER, --'S
*Africa's third largest river (after *Nile and *Congo) was surrounded by much mystery until the 1830's, when its source was established. The Niger rises in the outskirts of the Fouta Djallon, near Sierra Leone, on the *Guinea border, (c. 9° N., 10°45' W.) some 175 miles from the *Atlantic coast. It was long thought to be an arm of the Nile. *Mungo Park explored it 1795-96 and 1805-06, but the source was located during the explorations of others, from 1827 to 1834.
M. 84; M.D. 116; P. 23:4

NILE, --S
The longest river in *Africa flows north some 4,150 miles from Lake Victoria or Lake Tanganyika to the *Mediterranean, with many branches and name changes. The upper reaches were explored from the fifteenth to the seventeenth centuries, but the lower were in the process during M.'s time.
See also "Nile, Battle of the."
M. 149; M. 158; W. 63; M.D. 54

NILE, BATTLE OF THE
One of the *English navy's greatest victories, the Battle of the Nile took place at Abu Quir bay, near *Alexandria, on 1 August 1798. Blown up with most of her ship's company, the *French flagship *L'Orient later provided the wood for *Nelson's coffin. The effect of the battle was manifold: it stopped French expansion in Europe and provided a peerage for Nelson. Most important, it was a victory for social reformers, many changes being made afterwards that bettered the lot of the average sailor.
W. 16; W. 74; W. 87; W. 91

NIMROD
The *Bible gives little information about the *Assyrian King of what was to become *Babylon, who is the type of the daring hunter. Nimrod (or Nemrod) was the son of Cush (and grandson of *Noah), "a mighty one in the earth" (*Genesis 10:8), who was a "mighty hunter before the Lord" (9). He is said to have built *Nineveh. Among legends about him: his tomb in *Damascus remains dry when all is saturated with dew. He is said to have inspired the "Epic of Gilgamesh."
M. invokes him as a primitive hunter in *Clarel* II, 6.
M. 13; M. 60; M. 84; M. 145

NINE, --MUSES
      See "Muses."
W. 11; P. 15:1

NINEVEH
      The oldest and most populous city of ancient *Assyria,
Nineveh, on the Tigris, was probably inhabited as early as the
sixth millenium B.C. It began full development in the ninth
century, when *Semiramis ruled and attained high importance when Sennacherib (reigned 705-681 B.C.) rebuilt it as a
planned town with thoroughfares, canals, and a splendid
palace with gardens. The last great king, Ashurbanipal
(reigned 669-630) constructed a new palace and founded the
great library which still attracts scholars. Nineveh was
sacked and burned in 612 B.C. and thereafter lost importance.
      Nineveh is the city that repents in the *Old Testament's
Book of *Jonah.
      (See also "Nimrod.")
M. 1; M. 94; R. 30; M.D. 9; M.D. 83; M.D. 105; P. 3:2

NINON
      Anne de Lanclos (1620-1705), known as Ninon de Lenc-
los, was a *Parisian courtesan who chose her career when her
father, a murderer, fled *France, foreclosing her marriage
possibilities. She became the lover of numerous noblemen,
bearing a son who later committed suicide, upon learning that
the woman he admired was his mother. Ninon's irreligious
intellectuality brought many admirers to her salon, including
*La Rochefoucauld, Molière, and *Voltaire. She was protected
by *Mme. de Maintenon, and after her official retirement in
1671, attendance at her receptions became both fashionable and
respectable. At her death she left money to Voltaire for the
purchase of books.
P. 7:8

NIP AT THE CABLE
      A surreptitious drink.
W. 43

NIP-CHEESES
      In ordinary usage, misers; in nautical usage, ship's
*pursers.
W. 48

NIPHON

Niphon, or Nippon, is a Japanese general name for *Japan, not the name of an island, as M. has it in *M.D.* 109.
M.D. 109

NO. 4

See "Charlestown."
I.P. 2

NOAH

In *Genesis 6-10, Noah, a grandson of *Methusaleh and a just man, is selected by *God to survive the destruction of the earth by *Deluge. He builds an *Ark and fills it with pairs of animals, in accordance with God's commands. Noah's family and the animals survive "forty days and forty nights" (7:12) of rain which destroys all else. Upon its cessation, the Ark alights on "the mountains of *Ararat" (8:4); God promises not to destroy the earth by flood again (9:15).

"Noah's press" (*C.M.* 30) is a winepress. In Genesis 9:21, Noah has become a vineyarder and gets drunk.

Noah lives to be 950 years old (9:29), and his three sons become progenitors of all the peoples of the world: *Shem of the Semites: Ham of the African peoples; Japheth of the Indo-European or Aryans.

The name "Noah" derives from a primitive root meaning "rest." As "Noe," the *Greek form, it derives from the *Hebrew for "patriarch."
M. 3; M. 75; W. 7; W. 25; W. 50; W. 65; W. 68; M.D. 14; M.D. 58; M.D. 105; M.D. 107; M.D. 110; M.D. 135; C.M. 30

NOD, LAND OF

In *Genesis 4, 16, *Cain is exiled, after slaying his brother, to "the land of Nod," a place of wandering. Swift, in *A Complete Collection of Genteel and Ingenious Conversation*, first used the expression in its commonly accepted sense: going to the land of Nod is going to sleep, a pun.
M.D. 3

NONES

In ancient *Roman calendar, the ninth day before the *Ides (Lat. *nonus*, ninth.).
(See also "Calends.")
M. 80

NOOAR
    See "Noah."
O. 73

NORE, THE
    One of the gravest rebellions in *British naval history oc-
curred in 1797. Ringleader Richard Parker of the Nore was an
ex-convict who hoisted red flags on thirteen ships, blockading
the mouth of the *Thames. His charisma waning, Parker lost
control of his men, was court-martialed and hanged.
    Prime Minister William Pitt's Quota Act of 1795, along
with press gangs and poor conditions, had made for a navy
manned by misfits and criminals, and men like Parker, influenced by the ideas of Thomas Paine and caught up in the Quota
Act, were constantly threatening rebellion.
    M. experienced his own disruption at the Nore enroute
to the Continent, recording in his journal (27 November 1849):
"I am on board the steamer "Emerald" bound for Boulogne—
we are just in the Nore, and the jar & motion are so great that
writing is too hard work. I must defer bringing up my journal
till I reach terra firma."
W. 36; W. 85; W. 90

NORFOLK
    A county and city of southeastern *Virginia, on
*Chesapeake Bay, with an important harbor at *Hampton
Roads. The city was founded in 1682 (incorporated 1845), soon
becoming a leading seaport and port of entry, and later a major
yard and headquarters of the *United States *Navy. It was
burned by the *British during the *Revolution.
    (Although M. had "Neversink" finish her cruise at Nor-
folk, *United States ended her cruise of August 1843-44 at
*Boston. United States was scuttled at Norfolk, April 1861, to
save her from capture by Confederate forces.)
W. 53; W. 74; W. 93

NORMANDY; NORMAN
    The Normandy region of *France (capital Rouen) ex-
tends along the English *Channel from Brittany on the southwest to Picardy on the northeast. The area was conquered by
*Caesar and was *Christianized by the third century. The
Franks conquered the region in the fifth century, setting in
place the dominant culture. "Normans" in M.'s sense refers
to the peoples resulting after the eighth century invasion by
*pagan barbarian *Viking *pirates. They resettled the area,

eventually forming the Frankish Empire, which conquered and colonized the British Isles and areas as far away as *Sicily. These *Scandinavians adapted Christian Frankish culture and ceased roaming the seas, but they continued to some extent brutal and ruthless "thief knights," as M. calls them in *P.* 1:3. By the eleventh century, Normandy was a highly feudalized state with elaborate social and military arrangements (including fortified castles which the Normans perfected).

The "Norman Monarch" of *R.* 30 is *William the Conqueror, who invaded *England in 1066. Normandy passed to England in 1106, but in 1204 Philip II took it again for France. The area was devastated during the Hundred Years War, and repeatedly taken by the English.

Modern-day Normandy retains a distinctive culture and use of the French language.
M. 24; R. 30; R. 44; P. 1:3

NORSE CONCEITS
If "*Jarl," in *M.*, speaks in Norse conceits, he probably uses the kennings of the *Scalds.
M. 20

NORTHAMPTONSHIRE
The east-midland *English county is a rocky iron- and building stone-mining area, source of many English rivers. Settled since ancient times, Northampton was a meeting site for *Norman and *Plantagenet kings (including Henry II with *Thomas à Becket) and a center of noncomformity, home to *Thomas Fuller and, presumably, the *Moredocks of *C.M.*
C.M. 25

NORTH CAROLINA, THE
The *American *Navy line-of-battle ship *North Carolina* was a flagship under Commodore John Rodgers. In 1827, it received the first national salute, by the Regency of Tunis. It later became a school ship in *New York City.
R. 60; W. 91

NORTH CORNER
The expression "North Corner" is perhaps nautical jargon alluding to whatever area of a given port city sailors frequent, like "Rotten Row" (which is an ironic reference to a very exclusive part of *London's *Hyde Park). I have not been able

to pinpoint a "North Corner" in *Plymouth (*R.* 29), England, but M.'s journal for 25 December 1849 mentions the "North Corner" of *Portsmouth (probably the "Points," a sailor hangout). One rather prurient contemporary chronicler (Smith, in *Sunshine and Shadow in New York,* 1868) devotes a whole chapter (24) to the lot of "Sailors in New York." His sailors' stomping-grounds are probably like "North Corners" the world over: "Where the lanes are the darkest and filthiest, where the dens are the deepest and foulest, where the low bar-rooms, groggeries, and dance-houses are the most numerous, where the vilest women and men abide, in the black sea of drunkenness, lewdness, and sin, the sailor has his New York home."
R. 29

NORTHEASTERN BOUNDARY QUESTION

From 1783 to 1838, the *United States and Great *Britain had squabbled over the *Canadian border. The "*Aroostook War" in 1838 theoretically had settled the question, due to *Jackson's desire for "peace with honor."

The dispute over the *Maine/*New Brunswick boundary was settled in 1842 by the Webster-Ashburton Treaty.

The reference may really be to the Northwestern boundary problem of *Oregon, an issue in 1843 and 1844.
W. 49

NORTHERN LIGHTS

The aurora polaris, or polar light, is seen in high latitudes. In the Northern Hemisphere, it is called aurora borealis, or northern lights. We now know that the phenomenon is caused by the impact of charged particles entering the atmosphere and descending along magnetic lines, bombarding electrons and causing atmospheric gases to emit yellow-green or red light. In M.'s time, it was believed that auroras were sunlight reflected from *polar snow, or refracted light, like a rainbow's, the appearance of which would depend on the viewer's angle of vision.
M. 32; M.D. 56

NORTH POLE

See "Pole . . . . "
T. 21 and elsewhere

NORTHWEST PASSAGES

See "Pole . . . . "
M. 195 and elsewhere

NORWAY; NORWEGIAN

The kingdom of Norway (capital, Oslo) is a narrow mountainous strip on the west of the *Scandinavian peninsula, bordered by Skagerrak (S.), the North Sea and the Norwegian Sea of the *Atlantic (W.), Barents Sea of the *Arctic (N.), modern U.S.S.R. and *Finland (N.E.), and *Sweden (E.). It is a c. 1,000 mile strip of densely forested mountains and fjords, with some small islands.

Norway was originally composed of many small kingdoms. Harold I tried to unite the area in 872; with a strong sea-faring tradition, there were raids on *Normandy (accounting for the Norse duchy there), and by 1035 unity for the nation despite constant claims by *Denmark and Sweden. Norway was dominated by the *Hanse League in the fifteenth century. By the Treaty of Kiel (1814), Denmark ceded Norway to Sweden, and in the following year it achieved independence.

See also "King Canute"; "Maelstrom"; "Viking."
M. 36; R. 22; R. 33; M.D. 24; M.D. 36; I.P. 11; I.P. 15

NOR'-WEST COAST

Probably the Northwest Territories area, waters surrounding the area bounded by Davis Strait and *Baffin Bay, Hudson Strait and Hudson Bay: northern *Canada and the Yukon.
M. 1

NOR-WESTERS

Gales from a northwest direction.
M.D. 44

NOR'WEST PASSAGE

See "Pole . . . . "
M.D. 41

NO SUNDAYS OFF SOUNDINGS

Seven-day work week while at sea. See "Sabbath."
W. 38

"NO TRUST"

M.'s cynical publically posted slogan is probably a response to a phenomenon of his era. At a time of proliferating *Humane Societies, some agencies not directly involved in distribution of food and clothing posted similar notices. Robert H.

Bremner's *American Philanthropy* (Chap. 6) cites an example at the entrance to the Buffalo Charity Organization Society: "NO RELIEF GIVEN HERE."
C.M. 1; C.M. 42

NOVA SCOTIA
The east *Canadian province (capital, Halifax) is a peninsula 375 miles by fifty to 100 miles), connected to the mainland by the isthmus of Chignecto. It is bounded by the *Atlantic (E.,S.,W.), Bay of Fundy (N.W.), *New Brunswick and Northumberland Strait (N.), and the Gulf of *St. Lawrence (E.). The foggy peninsula has low hill ranges and a deeply indented coastline. Grand Pré village was the setting of *Longfellow's *Evangeline*. The *French called Nova Scotia "Acadia" (see "Arcadia"); the 1713 Treaty of Utrecht gave it to the *British (with the exception of Cape Breton Island, which remained French until 1820).
R. 20; R. 40

NOVA ZEMBLA
Novaya Zemlya Archipelago in the *Arctic Ocean (70°32' N. to 76°59' N, 54°46' E.). Although the *Russians were exploring it in the nineteenth century, parts remained unexplored because the surrounding water was always encumbered with ice.
R. 29; W. 25

NUBIA, --N
*Africa's Nubia is an ancient region dating from the Stone Age, extending from the Nile Valley's Aswan east to the Red Sea, west to the Libyan desert, and south to Khartoum. The *Pharoahs called it "Kush" and the Greeks "*Ethiopia," and its people are racially distinct from neighbors. The Egyptians built many temples in the area, later converted to Christianity and then conquered by the *Moslems. The *Romans brought into Nubia a black tribe which mixed in with the original population, forming a powerful kingdom. *Christianity was introduced in the sixth century and was supplanted by Islam in the fourteenth. Nubia had broken up into many separate states by the time of Mohammed Ali's conquest (1820-22).
In Nubian religion, Dedun (Greek "Tithonos") was the father of *Memnon. (In our century, many of the rich monuments of the area were salvaged when threatened by immersion at construction of the Aswan Dam.)
P. 8:1

NUKUHEVA

The largest (127 square miles) of the *Marquesas *Washington (northern) group, Nukahiva was explored by *Langsdorff in 1804, discussed by *Stewart, and visited by M.'s cousin, Pierre François Henry Thomas Wilson Melville (1806-1844) in 1829, all of which suggests that M. may have planned a visit long before it occurred.

He arrived at the "bay of Nukuheva" (properly Anna Maria Bay) on *Acushnet* (see "Pequod") on 23 June 1842. His desertion occurred on 9 July, and he signed on *Lucy Ann* (see "Julia") on 9 August, making his actual stay in the island's wilderness rather shorter than the four months "Tommo" spends with the *Typees in *T*.

Anderson's *Melville in the South Seas* is a careful comparison of contemporary history with M.'s fiction. The *French had taken formal possession on 2 June, having greatly empowered *Moana, the corrupt principal chief ridiculed in *T*. *London Missionaries had been poorly welcomed at Nukahiva and had departed for the southern Marquesas, but the French were protecting *Catholic missionaries. The "Typee/Happar" wars are fictionalized exaggerations of internecine strife, but in general *T*.'s descriptions of the natural habitat, customs, and institutions of the Marquesans agree with studies of the Bayard Domenick expedition of 1920.

See also "Dupetit-Thouars"; *"La Reine Blanche."*
T. Passim; O. Introduction

NULLI

M.'s fictional portrayal of John C. Calhoun of South *Carolina, who supported states' rights to nullification of Federal acts such as the Tariff of 1828.
M. 162

O

OAHU

One of the three largest *Hawaiian Islands, Oahu is forty miles long, twenty-six miles wide, located at 21°27' N., 158° W. Commercially the most important of the islands, Oahu contains *Honolulu, Pearl Harbor, Diamond Head, and Waikiki Beach. The diamond-shaped island was once two huge volcanoes which deposited the Koolau and Waianae mountain ranges.

M. arrived at Honolulu in May 1843.
T. 26; T. 34; O. 45; M. 68; M.D. 45

OATES, TITUS
     Oates's life (1648-1705) was a history of perjury and ex-
pulsion. Born in Oakham, *England, son of an Anabaptist
parson, he was expelled from his first school, eventually ordained without a degree, becoming curate to his father, who
had returned to Anglicanism. Both were jailed for perjury, but
Titus escaped and became a naval chaplain, then chaplain to
the Duke of Norfolk's Arundel *Protestants. Deciding to make
his fortune by discovering (actually inventing) *Catholic plots,
he persuaded *Jesuits that he wanted reconciliation with
*Rome, was admitted to a Spanish Jesuit college, expelled, but
claiming a D.D. degree then entered an English Catholic seminary in the *Netherlands, from which he was also expelled.
     His chief claim to infamy was the "Popish Plot" craze
(1678-9) that led to state trials of Catholics and at least thirty-
five executions. Oates had written forty-three articles detailing
Catholic plots to murder the King and Council, invade
*Ireland, massacre Protestants, and install the Duke of *York
on the throne. Although the articles were all false, strongly
anti-Catholic *London was swayed to give Oates increasing
power, despite his personal obnoxiousness. In 1679 he published his *True Narrative* of the plot, but the terror slackened
when lies were revealed, and with political events changing
rapidly, by 1684 Oates was arrested for calling the Duke of York
a traitor. When York assumed the throne in 1685, Oates was
tried and convicted. *Judge Jeffreys imposed a sentence including severe public whipping, followed by life imprisonment
if Oates survived. He spent James II's (see "Stuart") reign in
*Newgate, still writing anti-Catholic tracts, but was released
after the Revolution, with government financial help. He married a wealthy widow and became a *Baptist preacher, eventually expelled once more for hypocrisy and general disorderli-
ness.
O. 46

OB
     H. Bruce Franklin's notes to *C.M.* point out that
"*Guinea's" use of "ob" for "of" may be a play on words: a
covert reference to the land of the *Cossacks, at the northern-
most extremity of which flows the Ob River, into the *Arctic
Ocean.
C.M. 3

OBED MACY'S HISTORY OF NANTUCKET
See "Macy, Obed," and "Extracts" 53.
M.D. Extracts 53

O'BRIENS; O'REGANS
Prototype *Irishmen—fictional characters enabling M. to exercise his expertise in dialect.
0' is an Irish patronymic from the Gaelic *ogha*, Irish *oa*, meaning a descendant.
R. 53

OCCIDENT
The western world, as opposed to the *Orient.
M. 175

OCEANICA
In M.'s time, a collective name for the *Pacific islands correctly referred to as Oceania.
M.D. 71

OCEAN, OLD
*Milton so addresses the ocean in *Paradise Lost* IV, 165. (See "Quotations": "For many a league . . . ")
I.P. 25

OCHOTSH; OKOTSK
M. struggles to spell Okhotsk Sea, an inlet of the *Pacific, on the coast of Khabarovsk Krai, west of *Kamchatka Peninsula and the Kurile Islands, modern U.S.S.R. The area is known for its dense fogs and the Okhotsk Current, which brings cold from the Bering Sea.
R. 7; M.D. 45

O'CONNELL
Daniel O'Connell (1775-1847): "The Liberator" of *Ireland who spearheaded the popular movement to free Ireland from the *British. There are lives by his son (1846) and by W. Fagan (1847); his *Correspondence* was published in 1888.
R. 27

OCTAVO

A printers' term referring to the size of a book, based on the number of leaves made from a standard-sized piece of paper. Octavo books have eight leaves made from a sheet.
M.D. 32

"ODE ON THE INTIMATIONS OF DISTRUST IN MAN . . . "

Probably reaction to *Wordsworth's "Ode: Intimations of Immortality . . . "
C.M. 10

ODIN

The *Norse sky-father (corresponding to *Woden), supreme god, having supplanted Thor. God of wisdom, poetry, war, agriculture, he was an aloof figure with two ravens on his shoulder who brought him daily world news (Hugin—"Thought," and Munin—"Memory"). Responsible for postponing the end of the earth, Odin constantly sought wisdom, for which he sacrificed an eye (his remaining eye is the sun) and suffered further learning the mystery of the Runes (magical inscriptions; see "Runic"). He passed the knowledge to men, also stole mead from the Giants to start poetry. Attended by the Valkyries (maidens-Choosers of the Slain), he presided over banquets at *Valhalla for those slain in battle, as god of the dead. His father was perhaps Bör, and his doom was prophesied in the Elder *Edda. In art he is often represented as a one-eyed man wearing a hat and carrying a staff. Wednesday was named for him.
0. 7

OEDIPUS

There are many legends about the king of *Thebes, subject of the trilogy of *Sophocles (Sealts #147, Harper's Classical Library, vol. 14). Cast out and maimed (Oedipus means "swollen foot") by his father, King Laiüs, he was raised by a childless couple. When the oracle of *Delphi revealed that he would kill his father and marry his mother, he fled to Thebes, where he accidentally killed the king. After solving a riddle of the *Sphinx, he was made king and married Jocasta, Laiüs's widow and his mother. In Sophocles, the seer Teiresias reveals the truth; Jocasta kills herself and Oedipus jabs out his own eyes. There are many versions of his life afterwards: Sophocles has him exiled and guided by his daughter, Antigone; Euripides has him imprisoned by his sons; the

Iliad suggests he died in battle; legend says he cursed his sons.
W. 89; I.P. 25

OEDIPUS TYRANNUS
See "Oedipus" and "Sophocles."
W. 89

OFF-SHORE GROUND IN THE PACIFIC
The whaling ground southwest of the *Galapagos and east of the *Marquesas and *Tahiti.
M.D. 7

OF SPERMA CETI AND THE SPERMA CETI WHALE
See "Browne, Sir T . . . . "; "Extracts" 19.
M.D. Extracts 19

OGDOADS
An Ogdoad is the number eight or a group or a series of eight, especially for the *Gnostics, as a group of eight divine beings or aeons, or the heavenly region. Br. Mountagu's 1621 *Diatribuae* 258 attacks Gnosticism's "Ogdoades, Duodecads, Triacontads, Pleromaes, Bythos, Siges, and all the Aeones, blasphemous speculations."
M. 171

OHIO
The seventeenth state of the Union (admitted 1803) is bordered by *Michigan and Lake *Erie (N.), *Pennsylvania (N.E.), West *Virginia (S.E.), *Kentucky (S.W.), and Indiana (W.). The *French were established in the area in the 1670's, but continuous conflict with the *British ended in transfer to Britain of all French territory east of the *Mississippi in 1763. Ceded to the *United States after the *Revolution, Ohio became part of the Northwest Territory in 1787. *Cincinnati was founded in 1789. Construction of the *Erie Canal brought much development to the state in the 1840's, as the railroad did in the 1850's. Ohio played a large role in the "Underground Railroad" that brought *slaves to freedom at that time.
M. visited *Cleveland in 1840 and *lectured in Cleveland, Cincinnati, and Chillicothe, in 1858.
The "bandit of Ohio" (*C.M.* 1) is *Meason.
M. 28; W. 47; M.D. 83; C.M. 1; C.M. 22

OHIO RIVER; RIVER OHIO
The Ohio River begins as the confluence of the
*Allegheny and *Monongahela Rivers at Pittsburgh, flowing
over 980 miles to become the chief eastern tributary of the
*Mississippi. The Ohio forms several state boundaries; cities
grew up along its banks, especially after construction of a dam
and canal to circumvent the rapids at *Louisville, in 1830.
LaSalle discovered the Ohio in 1669; by the nineteenth century
it had become a major artery carrying settlers to the mid-west,
but this activity was slowed by construction of the *Erie Canal
in 1825 and the railroad in the 1850's.
M. 119; R. 33; R. 43; R. 61; W. 64; M.D. 42; C.M. 27

OHIO
The very fast seventy-four-gun warship *Ohio* was de-
signed by Henry Eckford and built 1817-20. M.'s cousin, Guert
*Gansevoort (1812-1868) was stationed on the ship, 1844-45.
Ohio's crew formed a *Temperance Society in the 1840's.
M. 28

OH-OH
Perhaps a parody of P.T. Barnum.
M. 122

OIL-JACKET
A garment waterproofed with linseed oil, as opposed to a
*Mackintosh, of rubber-coated fabric.
M.D. 49

OILY SANDWICH
See "Sandwiches."
M. 132

OKOTSK
See "Ochotsh; Okotsk."
R. 7

OLASSEN
Olafsen and Povelson's *Travels in *Iceland* (London,
1805) is mentioned in *Beale's work, which M. used as a
source for *M.D.*
M.D. 41

OLD BOY, THE
> The Devil (see "Satan"), especially in *Irish usage.
R. 27

"OLD CHURCH," THE
> See "St. Nicholas, Church of."
R. 36

OLD COMMONWEALTH'S HARBOR
> The *Boston harbor, scene of the Boston Tea Party, participated in by M.'s grandfather, Thomas Melville, on 16 December 1773.
M. 97

OLD CONSCIENCE
> *Job's comforter, Zophar.
C.M. 40

"OLD DOCK"
> *Liverpool: originally, four and three-quarter acre water area; opened 1715, adjacent to the *Customs House. It was filled in, in 1826.
R. 31; R. 32

"OLD FORTUNATUS"
> A comedy of 1600 by Thomas Dekker (?1570-1632). *Old Fortunatus* is a moralistic story in which magic talismans bring misfortune to those who seek riches rather than life's more meaningful treasures. It was based on a *German folk tale.
W. 41

OLD GUARD
> The generic term for stalwarts originated with the veterans of *Napoléon's Imperial Guard, who made the last *French charge at *Waterloo.
> Also, the ultraconservative members of a group or country.
T. 3; W. 3; W. 84; W. 85

OLD-HALL STREET
*Liverpool's Old Hall Street was developed in the 1670's. It runs roughly northwest to southeast, from Great Heward Street to *Chapel Street.
R. 31

OLD HONESTY
A sobriquet of *Charles Lamb, or perhaps merely an invention, parallel to nicknames for *Job's comforters.
C.M. 40

OLD HUNDRED
Also "Old Hundredth": familiar psalm tune named in Tate and Brady Psalter of 1696, indicating retention of position of Kethe's version of 100th psalm in 1563 Psalter. The tune had been set to 134th Psalm in 1551. In the *United States, the melody is most familiar as "Oh God, Our Help in Ages Past."
0. 45

"OLD IRONSIDES"
See "Constitution."
W. 3

"OLD MOTHER TOT"
"Old Mother--" and "Old Daddy--" are *Cockney prefixes of affection. The "tot" was originally the sailor's *grog ration: one-half pint of spirits or one quart of beer. But "tot" came to refer to any one small serving of alcohol.
O. 38

OLD NICK
A nickname for the Devil since the seventeenth century, perhaps derived from Ger. *Nickel*, a goblin.
See also "Satan."
M.D. Extracts 10

OLD PLAIN TALK
*Job's comforter, Eliphaz.
C.M. 40

OLD PRUDENCE
      *Job's comforter, *Bildad.
C.M. 40

OLD RED SANDSTONE
      See "Sandwiches."
M. 132

OLD ROWLEY
      See "Charles II, King of England."
M. 84

OLD TESTAMENT
      The Old Testament is the *Hebrew canon, finalized as
thirty-nine books c. 100 A.D. It covers the period of Patriarchs
(c. 2000 to 1700 B.C.), through that of the Hebrews in *Egypt
(1700 to 1290), the *Exodus and conquest of *Palestine (1290 to
1225), the period of the *Judges (1225 to 1025), the united Hebrew monarchy (1025 to 930), the divided kingdoms of Judah
(see "Judea") and *Israel (930 to 721), survival of Judah (721 to
586), the exile (586 to 538) and reestablishment of the Jewish
community as a *Persian province (538 to 333 B.C.).
      As Wright points out (Melville's Use of the Bible), M. ap-
pears to have identified more with the Old than with the *New
Testament which, as a nominal Christian, he should have preferred.
P. 7:4; C.M. 45 and elsewhere

OLMSTEAD
      Misspelling for Francis Allyn Olmsted (Incidents of a
Whaling Voyage, 1840).
M.D. 32

OLYMPIA
      See "Olympus."
M. 181

OLYMPIC THEATRE
      The Olympic Theatre existed from 1839 to 1849 (?) at 442
*Broadway, between Howard and Grand Streets, *New York
City. It was a tiny house that presented mainly comedy of the
burlesque-caricature type. If the "*Neversink's" *Purser was

a "stock actor" at the Olympic, he is probably even less respectable than M. paints him.
W. 47

OLYMPUS

Mount Olympus in Pieria (*Thessaly), almost 10,000 feet in elevation, was thought to be the home of the gods of mythology, as well as a haunt of the *Muses.

In *Greek mythology, the residence of the twelve great Olympic gods who succeeded the *Titans, it has been identified as the top of Greece's highest mountain, Mt. Olympus, in Thessaly. But the *Iliad suggests it is rather a mysterious region higher than the mountains, but not heaven. A gate of clouds guarded by the Seasons enclosed the gods' luxurious dwellings in perfect weather and perfect peace. The twelve Olympians are: Zeus (Roman *Jupiter), the chief; his brothers Poseidon (*Neptune) and *Hades (*Pluto); Hestia (Vesta), his sister; Hera (*Juno), his wife; Ares (*Mars), his son; his other children are *Athena (Minerva), *Apollo, *Aphrodite (Venus), Hermes (*Mercury), Artemis (*Diana), and Hera's (Possibly Zeus's) son, *Hephaestus (Vulcan).

M. saw Mt. Olympus several times in December of 1856.
M. 60

OMAI

Omai, from Ulietea rather than *Tahiti (as M. has it in O. 18), was taken to *London in 1775.
(Omai is "Mai" in Oliver's *Ancient Tahitian Society.*)
O. 18

OMBAY

Ombai Strait is a channel (twenty to fifty miles wide) connecting the Banda Sea (N.E.) and Savu Sea (S.E.) between *Timor (S.) and Alor (N.) islands. It is sometimes called Matua Strait. The "palmy beach of Ombay" (*M.D.* 45) is probably Alor.
M.D. 45

OMOO

The analogy of Omoo to "Taboo kannaker" in *O.* puts rather too glamorous a light on the word, which really signified "beachcomber," a derogatory term. For nine months after the 1842 mutiny on *Lucy Ann*, M. lived as a beachcomber, until joining the *Navy at the *Sandwich Islands, probably to escape prosecution as a deserter.

*Nathaniel Hawthorne's young son, Julian, referred to M. as "Mr. Omoo."

T. 29; O. Passim

ONTARIO; LAKE ONTARIO

In the *United States and *Canada, Lake Ontario is the smallest and most easterly of the *Great Lakes: 193 miles long, fifty-three miles wide, 788 feet deep. It receives the drainage of the entire Great Lakes system through the *Niagara River (by which it connects to Lake *Erie) and discharges through the *St. Lawrence River. Among its several barge connections, the New York State Barge Canal (see "Erie Canal") connects it with the *Hudson River. Lake Ontario was discovered in 1615 by Etienne Brulé and visited that same year by Champlain.

R. 32; W. 42; M.D. 54

"ON THE ABOLITION OF IMPRESSMENT"

As Philbrick shows, Captain *Marryat's *Suggestions for the Abolition of . . . Impressment* (1822) was mentioned in M.'s source for much W. 90 British Navy lore: an article by Thomas Hodgeskin, "Abolition of Impressment," in *Edinburgh Review* XLI [1824], 154-181.

W. 90

OOL

See "Sandwiches."

M. 132

OPHIR: OPHITES

Unidentified region (perhaps Sumatra) of the *Old Testament famous for gold (*Genesis 10:29; I *Kings 10:11), during *Solomon's time a far-off Eldorado, expeditions to which produced also sandalwood, ivory, and exotic fauna. Location was probably *Arabia or the East *African southern coast, although *Bombay, *India has also been considered.

The Ophites were a primitive *Gnostic sect who opposed the Old Testament God, glorifying and propitiating the serpent (Gr. *ophis*) as mankind's liberator.

W. 50; W. 75; M.D. 41; P. 7:4

OPORTO
*Portugal's second largest city, 175 miles north-north-east of *Lisbon, was settled long before the *Romans called it Portus Cale. It is renowned as the birthplace of Henry the Navigator and as the scene of historic battles of the Visigoths, *Moors, and *Wellington (against the *French). There was constitutional crisis during much of M.'s lifetime.
Oporto's main product is its port wine (see "Port; P.W.; Oporto").
R. 49; W. 37

OPS
In *Roman mythology, sister and wife to *Saturn (Gr. *Cronus), who was Protector of the Sowers and the Seed. She was a Harvest Helper and Sabine fertility goddess, later identified with (Gr.) Rhea—Queen of the Universe, mother of *Jupiter (Zeus), whom she saved from Cronus's devouring. She was also responsible for *Demeter's cooperation in bringing fertility back to earth. If M. paints her "black," he refers to her lifelong sadness and depression.
M. 184; P. 2:2

"OPTIMIST" SCHOOL
The reference in P. to the "Optimist" or "Compensation" school undoubtedly is directed at the teachings of *Ralph Waldo Emerson, especially to his essay, "Compensation."
Sealts #204 is Emerson's first series of essays, with M.'s autograph date of 1862. He is known to have read Emerson long before this acquisition, certainly before the end of the 1840's.
P. 20:1

ORATORIO OF THE CREATION
*Haydn's highly acclaimed Die Schöpfung was first performed on 29 and 30 April 1798.
W. 50

ORCHIS
H. Bruce Franklin's notes to C.M. discuss this word. The tuber of the plant, Orchis, is testicle-shaped, so the name adds to the book's sexual allegory. It also invokes Orcus, *Roman god of the underworld, mentioned in Clarel.
C.M. 40

OREGON

Oregon became the thirty-third state in 1859, bordered by the *Pacific, Washington and the *Columbia River (N.), Idaho (E.), Nevada and *California (S.). The *Spanish explored the area in the seventeenth century, and in 1792 the *American captain Robert Gray discovered the Columbia River, which was at first called the Oregon. Lewis and Clark explored, 1804-06, but John Jacob Astor's fur trade, beginning in 1811, was the impetus for real development. Oregon was jointly occupied by the *United States and *Britain from 1818 to 1846, becoming in 1848 a U.S. territory that included what is now the state of Washington (separated in 1853). The Oregon Trail brought some settlers starting in the 1840's, but Indian resistance hampered development; the railroad did not reach Oregon until the late nineteenth century, so in M.'s lifetime it remained rather a frontier area.
M. 44; W. 29; M.D. 42; P. 22:1

ORESTES

The *Oresteia* trilogy of *Aeschylus is the story of Orestes: The *Agamemnon* describes the return from the *Trojan war of Orestes's father, and his murder by his wife, Clytemnestra; the *Choephorae* describes Orestes's vengeance, taken with the help of his sister, Electra; the *Eumenides* shows the Furies in pursuit. Protected by *Apollo and *Athena, Orestes is saved and the *Furies transformed into the Kindly Ones.

There are other versions by *Sophocles and Euripides, as well as modern adaptations.
M. 33; P. 16:3

ORGAN MOUNTAINS

*Brazil's Serra dos Orgaos mountains include a landmark seen from *Rio de Janeiro: Dedo de Deus: the finger of *God (5,561 feet). Highest peaks are Pedra do Sino (7,365 feet) and Pedra Açu (7,323 feet).
W. 50

ORIENT, --S; ORIENTAL, --S; ORIENDA; OLD ORIENDA

As Finkelstein shows in *Melville's Orienda*, the Orient ("Old Orienda" of *M.* 168) meant for M. not only the Far East (of *China and *Japan), but the Near Eastern countries of *Egypt, *Assyria, *Babylonia, *Arabia, *Turkey, and *Palestine: the "Islamic" Orient, as well as the *Biblical one. In this respect, he followed contemporary preoccupation with then-emerging reading materials on the Near East. Horsford's edition of M.'s

Journal of a Visit to Europe and the Levant shows the focus on
the Near Eastern area that was to clothe *Clarel*. As China and
Japan were opened up to western inspection in the nineteenth
century, viewpoints (apparently shared by M.) emerged which
were to become stereotypes. "Arab" came to signify lush romantic wildness; countries father east represented cloaked
"dissipation" (*W*. 76) suggested by Opium use. "Fedallah"
(*M.D.*) seems to incorporate a mixture of Near and Far Eastern
stereotypes. Despite his participation in such narrow views,
M.'s final philosophy is perhaps best represented in his comment that "we shall know neither Orient nor Occident after
death" (*M*. 175).
Passim

ORIENTAL ISLES TO THE EAST OF THE CONTINENT
Perhaps the islands ranging southward from the
*Philippines to *Java.
M.D. 50

ORIENTAL STRAITS
M. seems to suggest straits of *Timor. Although there is
a Timor Sea, the straits in question must be Ombai (see
"Ombay") Strait.
M.D. 45

ORIFLAMME
Fr. "flame of gold": the ancient banner of the Kings of
*France, first used in 1124; standard of the Abbey of *St. Denys.
The banner is crimson on a gilded staff, with three points dec-
orated with green silk tassels. Legend grants it mystical pow-
ers, such as ability to blind infidels gazing upon it. It was last
used at Agincourt (1415) and was replaced by the blue Fleur de
Lis standard.
M. 60

ORIGEN
Origenes Adamantius (probably A.D. 185 or 186 to 254 or
255) was the official arbiter of the Eastern Church but was
eventually banished from his native *Alexandria because his
speculations aroused controversy.
Penny Cyclopaedia's characteristically humorless recounting (XVII, 1840) of his fate deserves quotation: "In his
twenty-first year, having taken up the opinion that the words of
our Saviour (Matthew, 19:12) ought to be understood literally,

he castrated himself; in later life he confessed his error in this matter."   *Matthew 19:12 mentions "eunuchs that made themselves eunuchs for the kingdom of heaven's sake," in its discussion on sexual continence.
W. 44

ORION
In *Greek myth, Orion is usually a Boeotian hunter/giant, son of Poseidon and lover of Artemis. She accidentally killed him, tricked by her brother, *Apollo. She placed him among the stars as the *constellation Orion, ill favored to mariners.
M. 3; M. 151; M. 169; M.D. 2

ORLEANS
See "New Orleans; Orleans."
M.D. 83

ORMUS, STRAITS OF
The Strait of Ormuz (or Hormuz) is a channel connecting the *Persian Gulf with the Gulf of Oman (of the *Arabian Sea), separating modern Iran and *Arabia. The strategically important waterway is forty- to sixty-miles-wide and has been known since ancient times. The island of Hormuz was visited by the forces of *Alexander the Great and in the thirteenth century by *Marco Polo. It was a center of trade by the fourteenth century, ruled by the *Portuguese early in the sixteenth, and under *Persian/*English rule from 1622.
M. 192

ORO
M.'s fictional god is modeled after the *Society Islands god, Oro, whose cult was dominant in the early nineteenth century, especially in *Tahiti, where the *Arioi sect promoted his worship. Oro is said to have arisen in Raiatea (see "Raiatair"), where the highest ranking humans were created. He appeared in many manifestations but came to be best known as god of war.
M. 112 and elsewhere

OROHENA
Mount Orohena, on *Tahiti, is the highest mountain of the *Society Islands: 7,618 feet.
O. 18

ORONOCO, --S

*Venezuela's Orinoco River is the third largest river system of *South America. The exact source is still not known, but it is presumed to rise in the Parima Mountains and empty into the *Atlantic Ocean south of Trinidad, a course of some 1,200 miles ending in a huge delta.
M. 119; M. 121; P. 16:1

ORPHEUS

In *Greek mythology, the *Thracian musician was the son of the *Muse Calliope by *Apollo, or by a Thracian king. There are many legends about him: he charmed even the beasts, rocks, and trees with the lyre Apollo gave him; he went to Hell to persuade *Hades to return his *Naïad nymph-wife, *Eurydice, but, disobeying an order not to look at her until daybreak, lost her again; he saved the *Argonauts from the *Syrens, he was torn apart by Maenads (female followers of *Dionysius, whom he perhaps worshipped as well); his head drifted to Lesbos, where it became an oracle; his lyre was placed among the stars by Apollo, as the *constellation, *Lyra.

The cult of Orphism gained strength in the sixth century B.C., influencing *Pythagorean philosophy, *Platonism and Neoplatonism. M. would have read about Orpheus in *Virgil, *Ovid, Boethius, *Burton, and in later writers.
R. 56; W. 2; W. 24; P. 3:3; C.M. 15

ORSAY, COUNT D'
See "D'Orsay."
W. 85

OSCEOLA

The able young chief of the *Seminole Indians led his people on the warpath in *Florida after they had been tricked by the *United States government into agreeing to migrate west. The war lasted from 1835 to 1838. He died a prisoner in Fort Moultrie, *Charleston Harbor.

M.'s fierce Osceola seems not related to the benignant figure Whitman wrote about in Leaves of Grass, and after whom many sites in the *Berkshires were named.
W. 15

OS INNOMINATUM

The "nameless bone" (Lat. in, "not"; nomino, "I name") bears "no resemblance to any known object," according to

Gray's. A pair of *os innominati* form the sides and wall of the pelvic cavity, by which the thigh is connected to the trunk. It originally consists of three separate parts, the *ilium*, the *ischium*, and the *os pubis*, which meet and form the cup-like *acetabulum.*
W. 63

OSSA, THE
     See "Pelion."
P. 25:4

OSSIAN; OSSIAN'S GHOSTS
     Ossian (Oisin) was a legendary Third Century Gaelic warrior/bard whose "works" were published by James Macpherson (1736-96) in the later eighteenth century. Macpherson, encouraged by John Home, a highly-placed court figure, and by *Hugh Blair, produced *Fragments of Ancient Poetry, Collected in the Highlands of Scotland, and Translated from the Galic or Erse Language.* Encouraged by its reception, he produced the 1762 *Fingal, an Ancient Epic Poem, in Six Books,* supposedly a translation of ancient writings of Ossian. *Temora* followed rapidly (1763), and the works were at first accepted and praised throughout Europe. *Samuel Johnson's enquiries spread suspicions, however, so that Macpherson was asked to produce physical evidence of his findings. After his death at least partial falsification was established, but the poems remained popular for their seemingly authentic primitivism, influencing *Goethe, Blake, and *Byron.
     Sealts #343 is M.'s annotated 1762 *Fingal...Together with Several Other Poems, Composed by Ossian....,* purchased in 1848. M. mentions Ossian's "admirable nature" and "pathos."
M. 119; R. 27

OTARD
     A fine brandy of Cognac (see "Cogniac"), *France.
M. 33; I.P. 9

OTHELLO'S
     *Shakespeare's *Othello, The Moor of Venice* had much to interest M. It is a story of emotional frailty in which the heroic protagonist's self-doubt leaves him open to malignity in the form of "Iago." The seeming ally's own denied ambitions prompt him to revenge himself by ruining the happy lives of

the black protagonist and his white wife, "Desdemona." A
chain of violence is set off in which all of the innocents are
killed and the evil "Iago" is under arrest. If "Pierre" feels
"Othello's" emotions, he is jealous because of a woman's possible perfidy—and therefore open to the fate which befalls
Shakespeare's hero: murder and suicide.
    On 3 April 1857, M. visited Palazzo Moro, *Venice—
home of Christoforo Moro, Shakespeare's supposed original for
Othello.
P. 15:1

OTHER OR OCTHER
    Othar of Helgeland was a mid-ninth century *Norseman
who discovered the North Cape, and proceeded into the White
Sea. He visited *Alfred the Great at court.
    (See also "Extracts" 9.)
M.D. Extracts 9; M.D. 24

OTIS
    An agricultural town of *Berkshire County, *Massa-
chusetts, nineteen miles south-southeast of *Pittsfield.
I.P. 1

"OTIUM CUM DIGNITATE"
    Lat.: leisure with dignity: Marcus Tullius *Cicero, De
Oratore II, 62.
T. 22

OTOO
    The name is Tu; M. follows *Ellis's error. Tu, king of
the larger peninsula of *Tahiti, was also called Mate, Vairaatoa, and Taina. He took the name of *Pomare, which became
the royal patronymic. There is much about him in Vol. I of
*Cook's Voyage of the Endeavor: 1768-1771.
O. 61; O. 80

OTTOMAN
    See "Turk . . . . "
W. 75; M.D. 88; I.P. 21

OVID
    Publius Ovidius Naso (43 B.C. - A.D. 18), *Roman poet of
immense popularity and influence, was born into a middle
class family and sent early to Rome, to be educated for the public service. He neglected his courses for verse writing and
eventually abandoned several minor offical posts to function as
the favorite writer on love and sexual intrigue in the sophisticated court society of the time. Banished by *Caesar Augustus
for an undisclosed infraction, he never returned to Rome, but
his works remained popular until *Christianization. A revival
in the eleventh century paved the way for almost unceasing future acclaim (except during *Puritan periods) and there are
few major writers in English since *Chaucer's time who have
not been influenced.
    Ovid's masterpiece, the *Metamorphoses*, uses *Greek
sources and original tales in innovative ways, in settings from
the *Creation to Ovid's time. Among his other works, in ele-
giac couplets: *Amores* (love poems), *Heroides* (fanciful letters), *Ars Amatoria* (a seduction manual), *Fasti* (Roman legends retold), *Tristia*, and *Epistulae ex Ponto* (nostalgic exile
pieces).
    Sealts #147, *Harper's Classical Library*, vols. 20 and 21,
contains various translations of the works.
W.l; W. 6; P. 17:2; C.M. 5; C.M. 31

OWEN
    Sir Richard Owen (1804-1892), *British biologist, was a
pioneer vertebrate paleontologist and comparative anatomist.
He catalogued parts of the *Hunterian Collection and helped
found the South Kensington natural history museum. Among
his many publications is a four-volume *History of British
Fossil Reptiles* (1849-84).
    See also "Creagh, Judge."
M.D. 32; M.D. 104

OWHYHEE IDOL
    This is a puzzling allusion. "Owhyhee" sounds as
though it indicates a *Sandwich Islands location, but I have
not been able to identify even an approximation of the name in
those or other islands. There is an "Owyhee" is Idaho, as well
as an Owyhee River, flowing from southwestern Idaho
through northern Nevada and southeastern *Oregon; if the allusion is an invention, these last might supply nomenclature.
The "idol" referred to does not resemble the totem-type idols described in *T.* and *M.* These depict character traits of the personage portrayed, so the *W.* 45 idol in Owhyhee may be tailor-

made by M. to punctuate "Lemsford's" point about the nature
of the reading public: "the head of a jackass, the body of a ba-
boon, and the tail of a scorpion"; that is, stubbornly deficient in
intellect, grossly slothful in demand for instant gratification,
and ultimately self-destructive, as is the scorpion's tail.
W. 45

OXFORD
England's Oxford University perhaps began in 1163.
Among its earliest colleges are University (1249), Balliol (1263)
and Merton (1264). The University expanded by confiscation of
town property, but much was returned at the time of the
*Protestant Reformation. Oxford's political sympathies have
had much effect on England's history and that of the Church of
England.
M. visited, 2--3 May 1857, viewing all of the colleges and
noting in his journal (2 May), "It was here I first confessed
with gratitude my mother land & hailed her with pride." He
comments at length on Oxford's unique buildings and gardens: "The picturesque never goes beyond this."
The city of Oxford is fifty miles west-northwest of
*London; it was a Royalist capital in the British Civil War.
W. 49; W. 55

P

PACIFIC OCEAN
Largest of Earth's oceans, the Pacific covers some
64,000,000 square miles (with adjoining seas, 70,000,000), many
of which M. sailed, as a sailor (see *United States), a
whaleman (see "Julia" and "Pequod"), or as a passenger on
his brother's ship, Meteor (see "California").
*Balboa had called the Pacific "South Sea" (or "Seas"),
which became an alternative name (often used by M.).
*Magellan called the ocean "Pacific."
The ocean is dotted with volcanic and coral islands,
especially in the south and west; it is the world's deepest, up to
14,000 feet. Pacific currents run counter clockwise south of the
*Equator and clockwise north of it. Prevailing winds are the
*Trades, blowing from the northeast in the north and from the
southeast in the south.
M. much preferred sailing on the colorfully picturesque
Pacific to the same on the cold and gray *Atlantic; his experi-

ences on the Pacific are detailed in Anderson's *Melville in the South Seas*.
Passim

PACIFIC SQUADRON
    See "Squadron."
W. Passim and elsewhere

PACTOLUS
    The Pactolus River, in Lydia (modern *Turkey), carried gold dust from Tmolus into the Hermes River and from thence into the sea, according to *Herodotus (V, 101). The river was the source of wealth of Croesus, last king of Lydia (560-546 B.C.). *Ovid says in *Metamorphosis* 11 that it became golden when *Midas washed his hands in it.
M.D. 99

PAGAN, --S; PAGANISM
    Non-*Christian heathenism. First English use (1433) John Lydgate, *St. Edmund and St. Fremund*, ii, 417.
Passim

PAIXHAN SHOT
    Eighty-pound paixhan guns were introduced into the *French navy, and used on French vessels blockading Vera Cruz in the 1830's. They were created for the horizontal firing of heavy, high calibre shells with proportionately less metal than solid-shot guns.
W. 11; W. 16; W. 75

PALACE OF ALADDIN
    See "Aladdin's Palace."
R. 46; R. 47

PALAIS DES BEAUX ARTS
    The modern (1900) Petit-Palais replaced the Musée des Beaux-Arts de la Ville de *Paris: off the *Champs Elysées.
I.P. 8

PALE ALE
Although it seems in W. 68 that M. may refer to water, pale ale was a mild light-colored *British ale first made in the eighteenth century: three- to five-percent alcohol.
W. 68

PALENQUE
The ruins of the Mayan city in Chiapas, southern *Mexico, were discovered in 1750. The Mayan center (some twenty miles long) had reached its peak of development by A.D. 700 and had been abandoned in the twelfth century. Among its ruins are many sculptures and palaces decorated with stucco and intricately carved stonework.
M. 132

PALERMO
*Sicily's largest city, the port of Palermo is the capital of Sicily and Palermo province, on the Gulf of Palermo, 200 miles south-southwest of *Naples. Traces of ancient structures give evidence of Palermo's stormy history. Founded by the *Phoenicians, it became a military base under the *Carthaginians. The *Romans moved in briefly in the third century B.C. The *Byzantines held it from the sixth to the ninth century, when they were replaced by the *Saracens; *Normans took over in 1072. Palermo was the scene of action of the tyrant *Phalaris and the site of the *Sicilian Vespers, after which it was under the rule of Aragon, Savoy, and the *Bourbon House of Naples. It was freed by Garibaldi in 1860.
O. 2; W. 8

PALE SHERRY
The expensive and fashionable dry fino *sherry wine, produced in Jerez de la Frontera province, *Spain. It is inbibed as an apéritif.
M.D. Extracts 7; P. 3:3

PALESTINE
Palestine (a name derived from "*Philistine"), the *Holy Land of Jews, *Christians, and *Moslems, is the *Canaan of the *Bible, located on the eastern shore of the *Mediterranean. Its only constant land mass has been the narrow (140 by 30-70 miles) strip between the Mediterranean and the *Jordan River, bordering southwest on *Egypt.

It was a *Hebrew kingdom after 1000 B.C. (under *Saul, *David, and *Solomon), becoming the separate states of Judah (see "Judea") and *Israel. Both were destroyed in the eighth and sixth centuries. The *Maccabees ruled for seventy years, starting 141 B.C. As a *Roman state, Palestine had the Herods as puppet kings: the Jews revolted in A.D. 66, and the Romans destroyed the Temple and expelled them. Under Constantine I (see "Constantinople"), it became the center for Christian pilgrimages; the Moslems arrived by the seventh century, and the *Crusaders entered in the eleventh. Palestine was also ruled by the Egyptians, the *Mamelukes, and the *Ottomans. European Jewish colonization started in the 1870's.

See also "Carmel"; "Galilee"; "Gilead"; "Haifa"; "Jaffa"; "Jerusalem"; "Moab"; "Samaria."
R. 56

PALESTINE, MELODIES OF
See "Hebrew captives."
R. 56

PALEY'S THEOLOGY
William Paley (1743-1805), Archdeacon of Carlisle (*Cumberland, *England), was a theological *Utilitarianist whose thinking influenced *Bentham's. Paley was an individualist from childhood, becoming the prototype clear-thinking but absent-minded and unkempt scholar. He was educated in mathematics at Christ's College, *Cambridge (ordained 1767) and became a teaching fellow whose lectures and textbooks reflected common-sense human values. He was a scholar who loved the theatre, horsemanship, whist, and fishing; he observed trials and took the side of *Epicureans in debate against proponents of the *Stoics. Paley was against *tithing, and against the slave trade; he took a liberal view of the *Thirty-Nine Articles, and advised his students to save time as ministers by writing one sermon and stealing five. He was finally prohibited from speaking in public.

Paley earned the nickname "Pigeon Paley" for comparing greedy property owners to a flock of pigeons, in his *Moral and Political Philosophy* (1785), which became a standard Cambridge textbook. "Paley's Theology" (*M.D.* Extracts 48) is his *Natural Theology* (1802), wherein he finds proof of *God's existence in natural phenomena, especially the human body. Paley also wrote *Evidences of Christianity* (1794). He was in 1793 Vicar of *Stanwix.

See also "Extracts" 48.
M.D. Extracts 48

PALISADES

The steep cliffs running some fifteen miles along the western bank of the *Hudson River, from Jersey City, *New Jersey, to Piermont, *New York. They range from 350 to 550 feet, and as depictions of the time show, were much more imposing looking in the nineteenth century, when buildings and greenery were lower.
R. 60

PALLAS

The *French frigate *La Pallas*, loaned to the *United States *Navy, captured *Countess of Scarborough* at *Flamborough Head, in the 1779 action of *John Paul Jones's forces. She was at the fall of *Charleston in 1780 and by the end of 1781 made part of the Continental Navy's four-ship fleet (with *Alliance, Deane*, and *Ariel*, which was also on loan).

In Greek mythology, the goddess Athena is called Pallas after she defeats a giant of the name. (Others called Pallas include a *Titan and an ally of Aeneas in *Virgil.)
I.P. 19

PALLID HORSE

*Revelation 6:8: "And I looked, and behold a pale horse: and his name that sat on him was Death, and Hell followed with him."
M.D. 42

PALM, --S

The family *Palmae* includes a number of species of tropical or sub-tropical trees with branchless trunks, and large evergreen feather- or fan-shaped leaves in a bunch at the top. *Cocoanut palm is the most important to South Sea islanders; there are also betel nut and date palms.

The palm leaf has long had importance as a symbol of victory or triumph and has been portrayed in many military decorations.
Passim

PALMER

The *English Dr. William Palmer (1824-1856) was the notorious poisoner of his wife, his brother, a friend, and others. Tried at the Old Bailey 14 May 1856, he was hanged one month later.
C.M. 26

PALMER LAND
Part of the South *Shetland Isles (57°55' W., 63°25' S.), 600 miles southeast of Cape Horn, the area is notorious for extreme cold and icebergs.
W. 70

PALMETTO
The fan-leafed *palm of the genus *Sabal*; the species of the southeastern *United States is *Sabal palmetto*; it has an edible terminal bud.
M. 99

PALMO'S
Originally "Palmo's Opera House," the theatre on Chambers Street east of *Broadway eventually became a comedy theatre. On 29 January 1847, M. heard Donizetti's *Lucia Di Lammermoor*, sung by Ferdinando Beneventano and Clotilde Barili at Palmo's. But like most *New York City opera houses of the time, it became (the following year) a popular house: leased by William E. Burton, leading an impressive company of comedy players which thrived until 1856.
R. 44

PALMYRA
See "Tadmor."
P. 1:2

PALOS
Palos, or Palos de la Frontera, or Palos de Moguer, in Huelva province of *Spain's *Andalusia (near *Cádiz) was a famous embarkation point. He "who stretched his van from Palos" (*M*. 169) is *Christopher Columbus, who sailed for the west from Palos in August of 1492 and returned in March of 1493. Cortés (see "Cortez") landed at Palos in 1528, after the conquest of *Mexico.
M. 169

PAMPAS
M. here refers to the winds of La Pampa, part of the Argentine *Pampas: the pampero, a name used in the coastal plains designating a strong, cool squall, often accompanied by thunderstorms.
M. 44

PAMPAS
The vast, treeless but fertile, plain of southern *South America (especially eastern Argentina) is bounded by the *Andes piedmont (W.), the Chaco region (N.), the *Atlantic (E.), and *Patagonia (S.): c. 293,000 square miles. There are two distinct zones, the fertile humid eastern and the barren dry western areas. Before the nineteenth century the land was undeveloped except for cattle-raising by the *Spanish *gauchos*, celebrated for their horsemanship. (See also entry above.)
M. 161

PAN
Pan's pipe is an ancient wind instrument: a series of graduated length pipes across the upper ends of which the player blows, producing thin, reedy notes. Legend has it that Pan, Greek god of pastures, forests, flocks and herds, who personified deity in all things, formed the pipe from a reed into which the nymph Syrinx was formed while fleeing his amorous overtures. Pan is represented with the lower part of a goat and the upper part of a man, wearing a leopard's skin. His lustful nature makes him a symbol of fecundity, but his character is pure.
M. 121; R. 49; M.D. 111

PANAMA
The Central American isthmus is the narrowest (c. 27 miles at the Canal) part of the Americas, between the *Caribbean *Atlantic and *Pacific Oceans, with a low depression where the Canal (1904-14) is located. It is bounded on the west by Costa Rica and on the east by *Colombia, of which it was a Department until 1830. It is an area of hardwood tropical forest mountains, with one inactive volcano (Chiriqui; 11, 410 feet).
*Columbus visited in 1502, and *Balboa crossed the isthmus in 1513; thereafter Panama became the route by which *Inca treasure was shipped to *Spain (encouraging many *pirates).
The *United States gained transit rights in 1846; the railroad crossed Panama by 1855. (Although Panama became a separate republic in 1903, the American-controlled Canal dominated the rest of its history.)
As M. points out (rather ungenerously) in *M.* 22, Panamanians are a mixture of races, with Spanish language and culture dominating. The "Panama hat" of *R.* 9 is a hand-plaited hat made from the leaves of the jipijapa plant (found elsewhere in Central and *South America, as well).
O. 1; O. 61; M. 22; R. 9

PANDANNUS

The "screw pine" of the genus *Pandanus* is found in southeastern *Asia, expecially in the *Malay Peninsula. It has dagger-like leaves.
M. 140

PANDECTS

(Gr. *pandektes*, all-receiving, all-containing).

Emperor *Justinian (reigned A.D. 527-565) ordered the fifty-book compendium of *Roman law superseding all previous laws and decisions, known as the Pandects of Justinian, or the Digest (*Digesta*). The Pandects replaced confused practice based on "old law" (*jus vetus*) and "new law" (*jus novum*). Justinian's commission gathered, condensed, and re-defined legal materials in a ten-volume work, which encouraged him to carry the project further, eventually repealing all other law and forbidding commentaries upon the Pandects, which were poorly arranged. Published in A.D. 533, the Pandects were the subject of much scholarly attention in nineteenth-century *Germany.
M. 65

PANDEMONIUM

*Milton's capital of Hell and abode of the demons: *Paradise Lost* 1. 756 (1667): "A solemn Council forthwith to be held at Pandaemonium, the high Capital of Satan and his Peers." Earliest use of the term as a place of "wild lawless violence, confusion and uproar": 1779, Swinburne's *Trav. Spain*, xlii. 367: "Every province would in turn appear a *Paradise, and a Pandaemonium."
T. 23; W. 25

PANDORA

In Greek mythology, a creation story tells that during the Golden Age only men lived on earth. To punish *Prometheus, Zeus (see "Jupiter" and "Jove") created the first woman, Pandora, "the gift of all." She was to become forerunner of all women, the evil ones of the world. The more familiar legend is of the infamous box which the gods filled with the evils of the earth and gave to Pandora. Despite Prometheus's warning never to accept things from Zeus, Epimetheus took Pandora as a gift. Her curiosity made her lift the lid of the forbidden box, releasing plagues, sorrow, and mischief upon the world. Only one good was contained in the box: hope.

Pandora and Epimetheus were the parents of Pyrrha, the only female left when the world flooded. (Pyrrha married the son of *Prometheus.)

The name Pandora has come to signify, especially to superstitious seamen, all of the evil and bad luck of the world.
M. 28; W. 11

PANDORA

The *British frigate *Pandora* (an unlucky name) was sent to *Tahiti to pick up the *Bounty* mutineers in 1787. Fourteen prisoners were kept in a small structure (called "*Pandora*'s Box") on deck. The apparently inept Captain Edward Edwards wrecked the ship attempting the crossing of Great Barrier Reef that *Captain Bligh had made. There was much loss of life, including some prisoners who remained chained in their little cell when *Pandora* sank.
M. 28

PANNANGIANS

Unidentified: perhaps an invention, as is its partner, "Brighggians"; perhaps such a corrupt phonetic spelling as to be unidentifiable.
M.D. 6

PANSA

Gaius Vibius Pansa, an enemy of Mark *Antony, shared the *Roman Consulship with Hirtius in 43 B.C., the year after *Caesar's assassination. Pansa died that year, as well. His mansion in *Pompeii is among that city's most celebrated ruins.

As Horsford's notes to the *Journal* (p. 258) point out, M. thought of the house when he was in *London, citing "Pansa" as "Pansi" in the entry of 29-30 April, 1 May 1857. The article on *Pompeii in *Penny Cyclopaedia* included description and illustration of the house.
R. 46

PANTHEIST, --S, --IC; PANTHEISM

Pantheism holds that *God is the totality of existence, present in all things, even the inanimate (Gr. *pan*, "all"; *Theos*, "God"), implying denial of the personality and the transcendence of God. The vaguely defined term came into common use in the eighteenth century, but various pantheistic beliefs existed long before, especially in *Stoicism, *Platonism,

and *Aristotelianism. There are elements also in Taoism, Buddhism, and Confucianism. Closer to M.'s time, *Goethe and *Emerson were considered pantheists.
M.D. 35; M.D. 66; P. 8:3; P. 17:2; P. 21:1; P. 22:3

PANTHEON, DOME OF THE
The principal surviving monument of *Rome, the Pantheon was first built in the time of *Augustus and reconstructed by *Hadrian. It is remarkable for the enormity of its dome, larger in diameter than *St. Peter's, and for its construction around a center oculus, the sole source of light.
As M.'s journal for February and March 1857 shows, he stayed in a hotel very close to the Pantheon.
M.D. 79

PAOLO
In Canto Five of *Dante's *Inferno*, "Paolo" is the brother of the deformed "Giovanni Malatesta" of Rimini, husband of "*Francesca." He falls in love with "Francesca" while the two are reading about "*Launcelot" and "Guinevere" and is killed with her by her husband. Dante confines them to the Second Circle of Hell where they whirl about together, forever blown by the wind.
P. 2:7

PAPEETE
Port and present-day capital of *Tahiti, on the northwest corner of the island. It was an important trade center from c. 1829, becoming the seat of the *French government.
O. Passim and elsewhere

PAPER JACKS
Sailors who are professed experts but limited to theoretical knowledge.
O. 2; W. 27

PAPOAR
Papaoa, *Tahiti, on the outskirts of Pare (*Paree). *Ellis (Chapter 15) devotes much space to description of the Royal Mission Chapel, or Cathedral of Tahiti, opened 11 May 1819. It was 712 feet long and 54 feet wide, with 133 windows; by the time of Ellis's visit in 1822, it had begun to decay.
O. 44

PAPUA

Papua is *New Guinea, "broiling" (*M*. 1) in an average daily temperature ranging from 72-95° F. The Gulf of Papua is an indent of southeastern New Guinea, on the Coral Sea. (The modern *Australian Territory of Papua was annexed in 1883.)
M. 1

PARACELSUS; PARACELSAN

Theophrast Bombast Von Hohenheim (1493-1541) probably invented his own pseudonym to show his equality with *Celcus. The Swiss-born physician/alchemist/astrologist, who established the importance of chemistry in medicine, quarrelled continually with colleagues at the University of Basle. As his bizarre interests developed, he publicly burned the works of earlier scholars and preached his own beliefs: man's body is an extract of all previously created beings—a compound of salt, sulfur, and mercury, the separation of which causes illness; the occult vital force is in the stomach; treatment should include mineral baths and the ingesting of opium, mercury, lead, sulfur, iron, *arsenic, copper sulfate and alcoholic beverages; the stars influence man's astral spirit; physicians must treat souls. He supported *Aristotle's idea of the four elements (earth, air, fire, water), which he believed inhabited by *nymphs, undines, gnomes, salamanders, *syrens, and other strange beings.

*Alexander Pope's *The Rape of the Lock* (1714; in Sealts #405) presents similar creatures; Robert Browning's fame began with his dramatic blank-verse poem, *Paracelsus* (1835); the *Rosicrucians were much influenced by his thinking.
M. 33; R. 49; M.D. 92; M.D. 94; I.P. 8

PARADISE; PARADISIAC

The word "Paradise" was used in Greek (*Xenaphon*) to signify an enclosed park, orchard, or pleasure ground; by the Septuagint it meant the Garden of *Eden, and in *New Testament and *Christian writers the abode of the blessed. In the rabbinic idea of seven heavens, the third heaven was "Paradise."

Its first use in English for garden of Eden occurs in 1175: *Cott. Hom.* 221.
T. 7; M. Passim; R. 2; R. 9; R. 29; W. 75; M.D. 113; P. 2:2; P. 2:4; P. 3:1 and elsewhere

PARADISE LOST

See "Milton . . . ."; "Extracts" 23, 24.
W. 7; M.D. Extracts 23; M.D. Extracts 24

PARAGUAY
The inland nation of south-central *South America is surrounded by rivers of the *Rio de la Plata system, bordering on Argentina (S.), *Brazil (E. and N.E.), and *Bolivia (N. and N.W.). It is divided into two halves by the Paraguay River, with the plains area (of *M*. 16) to the river's east. The Paraguay River was explored by Cabot in 1527; the capital city, Asunción, was founded in 1536 (?); separation from Argentina occurred in 1617. Paraguay was ruled by the Viceroyalty of *Peru until 1776 (with *Jesuits in control until 1767). There were three major ruling dictatorships in M.'s time (1814-70), and many minor dictatorships thereafter.
M. 16

PARAITA
The name remains untraced, but Paraita is perhaps one of the ambitious *Tahitian chiefs (along with *Kitoti) referred to by *Wilkes.
O. 32

PARCAE
See "Fate; the Fates; Three Fates."
I.P. 19

PARCHMENT BOILERS
Abdomens, or stomachs.
M.D. 101

PAREE
Pare, *Tahiti, south of *Matavai, is the hereditary district of the *Pomares; as *Ellis notes (Chapter 3), it was the scene of a rebellion in 1802.
O. 32; O. 49

PARIAHS
Outcasts. Pariah is the lowest Hindu (see "Hindoo") caste in *India. The word is from the word for "drummer," the pariah's role during some festivals.
I.P. 20

PARIS, MATTHEW

Matthew Paris (d. 1259), a monk at the monastery of St. Albans, compiled a vivid history of thirteenth-century *England, the *Chronica Majora* (M.'s *Historia Major*), as well as *Historia Minor* (or *Historia Anglorum*), numerous lives, and other documents. The *Chronica*, despite some errors, remains one of the most important sources of knowledge of European events of the time.

See also "Beards."

W. 87

PARIS, --IAN

M. spent ten days in the *French capital in 1849 (27 November-7 December), admiring much—grudgingly. The pervasiveness of his general dislike of all things French (especially Paris chic and the navy of "sea-Parisians" [*M.D.* 54]) must be seen as bias when we examine his praise of particulars. M. loved the cruelly blasphemous "Parisian wit" (*C.M.* 29) of *La Rochefoucauld and others. And although his journal closes with a grateful "Selah!" at his departure, there is much praise of Paris in earlier entries.

Of course he loved the food and wine, as well as the cafés and shops of the Palais Royale area. His room was on the left bank (12-14 Rue di Bussy; untraced in that spelling, but probably Rue de Buci, at Carrefour de Buci, the southern terminus of M.'s "*Rue Dauphiné"), and probably much like that described in *I.P.* He confessed, "I jabbered as well as I could" (30 November), in French. He was annoyed by the presence of uniformed troops and by the bureaucracy, but he was as thrilled by the sights as any American in Paris. Place de la Concorde was "magnificent" (27 November); Notre Dame (currently under repair) was "a noble old pile" (30 November); the *Louvre was better than the British Museum (30 November); Pére-Lachaise cemetery (1 December), the Madeleine, Hôtel des Invalides, and the *Luxembourg (12/2) were remarkable, as were the Arc de Triomphe and the Opéra Comique (12/3). The *Cluny (12/5) was "just the house I should like to live in."

Homesickness was beginning to haunt M. by this time; he had been away from wife and new baby for nearly two months. So the "Selah!" might well reflect not so much distaste for Paris as the wish to be finished traveling, with three weeks yet remaining before his return to *America.

Important Treaties of Paris up to M.'s time include that of 1763, ending the Seven Years War; 1783, ending the *American Revolution; 1814, 1815, ending the *Napoleonic Wars; 1856, ending the Crimean War.

See also: "Bourse, Paris"; "Catacombs, Paris"; "Champs Elysées"; "Henry IV statue"; "Latin Quarter"; "Morgue in Paris"; "Palais des Beaux Arts"; "Passy"; "Place-du-Carrousel"; "Pont Neuf"; "Seine"; "Sorbonne"; "Tuileries"; "Vendôme."
Passim

PARISIAN CASTS
As Howard Vincent shows (*The Tailoring of Melville's White-Jacket*, Chapter 11), plaster masks were on display when M. visited *Paris in 1849, but one of a *horned woman has not been traced. On 5 December, M. visited Museum Depuytren, recording in his journal: "Pathological. Rows of cracked skulls. Skeletons and things without a name."
See also "Anatomical Museums of Europe."
W. 61

PARKER
See "Nore."
W. 85

PARK, MUNGO
Park (1771-1806), *Scottish explorer of the *Niger, early became assistant surgeon on an East Indiaman, contributing materials on new species to the *Linnean Society. He explored *Africa from 1794 to 1797, writing about his adventures in the 1799 *Travels in the Interior of Africa*. He died on a second African expedition in 1805-06, drowned after attack by hostile natives.
M. 119; R. 43; M.D. 5

PARK, THE
In *C.M.*, probably a reference to *City Hall Park, *New York City, where *Gansevoort Melville had frequently orated about his (*Democrat) political party.
C.M. 19

PARKER, SIR PETER
Sir Peter Parker (the elder: 1721-1811) rose to become Admiral of the Fleet during the *American Revolution. *Nelson had served under him in his youth, and Parker was a chief mourner at Nelson's funeral (for reasons that *D.N.B.*

suggests were not totally noble). Parker participated in an isolated naval attack on *Charleston, 1776.

(Parker's son [1785-1814] became a Captain in the Navy. He wrote elegaic stanzas on his relative, *George Gordon Byron. He was killed at *Chesapeake Bay.)
W. 51

PARLIAMENT; PARLIAMENTARY

Originally, the *British Parliament was merely a periodic assembly of highly-placed friends of the crown, much an instrument of the monarch's wishes. Authority lay in the monarch; counselors and wealthy lay and spiritual associates who sat in the chamber eventually became the House of Lords. In the thirteenth century, British counties and boroughs were ordered to send local knights and burgesses empowered to represent constituencies to *Westminster. These first Commons (irregularly elected by freeholders) raised grievances which soon enabled them to achieve supremacy over the House of Lords, so that since at least 1395, Commons has been the more powerful house. It imposes taxes and delegates monies to public departments and services. The Prime Minister is now always a member of Commons.

W. 54 "Commons in Blue" is an ironic reference to the Navy.
Passim

PARLIAMENTARY ARMY
See "Cromwell's."
W. 55

PARNASSUS

The *Greek mountain connected with the *Muses as the seat of poetry and music, with the Oracle of *Delphi at its foot. It has two summits: one consecrated to *Apollo and the Muses, the other to *Bacchus. *Prometheus's son, Deucalion, along with Pyrrha, daughter of *Pandora, was saved from the Flood when his ark alighted on Parnassus.
R. 30; W. 11; P. 21:1

PARRY

Sir William Edward Parry (1790-1855), *English admiral, explored the *Artic region in a search for the *Northwest Passage. He had entered the Royal Navy at thirteen, and by 1810 was lieutenant in the *Spitsbergen whale fishery; he had

command of one ship in an Artic expedition of 1818. His own
successful expedition (1819) accomplished much of the journey
from *Greenland to *Bhering Strait and is described in *Journal of a Voyage to Discover a Northwest Passage* (1821). He attempted second and third expeditions in 1821 and 1824, and in
1827 reached 82°45' N. latitude, in an attempt at the *Pole, publishing *Narrative of the Attempt to Reach the North Pole*, on
his return. Knighted in 1829, he became Rear-Admiral and a
governor of *Greenwich Hospital after retirement.
M. 36

PARSEE
        Parsees in *India are followers of *Zoroaster—of
*Persian extraction (thus their designation). They migrated to
avoid *Moslem persecution between the eighth and tenth centuries A.D., and by M.'s time, they formed a large and wealthy
community of well-educated merchants in *Bombay. They
were somewhat split from the smaller number of Iranian
Zoroastrians (called Gabars) on some doctrine (notably the calendar specifying holy seasons and dates).
        Their group had been studied closely by western schol-
ars since the eighteenth century, so it is likely that M. knew
much about them. Parsees believe in helping good and fighting evil, obeying the *Zend-Avesta. Cultivation of the land and
procreation in consanguinous marriage are duties, as well as
participation in sacramental ceremony, prayer, and purification ritual. Central is a yearly sacrificial service before a perpetually burning sacred fire. In M.'s time, services for the
dead were held in the presence of a dog, who would expel
demons; the corpse was exposed to birds of prey and then the
bones collected to avoid defiling the earth or sea. (Thus, in
M.D., followers of Zoroaster are denied death ritual which
would atone for their sins.)
M.D. Passim

PARTHENON
        The chief temple of Athena, on the *Athens Acropolis,
was constructed between 447 and 432 B.C. Architects were Ict-
inus and Callicrates, supervised by the sculptor *Phidias. The
building measured over 100 by 228 feet and was surrounded by
*Doric columns curved so as to maximize light. A gold and
ivory statue of the fully armed Athena was removed in the fifth
century A.D., and the structure was used as a *Christian
church until the *Turks transformed it into a *mosque in the
fifteenth century. Further damage occurred as the result of a
fire magazine explosion and attempted removal of sculptures.

*Lord Elgin removed most of the remaining art work for the British Museum from 1801-03. M. undoubtedly saw these pieces when he visited London in 1849.

He visited the Parthenon in February 1857, commenting on it in his *lecture, "Statues in Rome," and composing a four-part poem, "The Parthenon," which praises the structure ("Seen aloft from afar," "Nearer viewed," "The frieze," "The last tile"). For M., it was "art's meridian."

See also "Phidias"; "Pisistratus."
M. 75; W. 91

PARTHIAN MAGI
        *Pliny's *Natural History* (xxx.vi. 16-17): King *Tiridates, as a Magus, would not cross the sea to visit *Nero because Magi hold it sinful to foul the sea by necessary human functions.

        See also "Parthians," "Chaldea," and "Magi; Magian."
W. 91

PARTHIANS
        Parthia was an ancient (c. third century B.C.) land occupying part of what is now Iran. Very little is known of its history as a *satrapy except that it revolted against *Darius I at the beginning of his reign and eventually became part of the Seleucid Empire. Parthian kings were known as Arsaces, after an early king.

        A Parthian shot or shaft is a parting shot that gives no chance for reply, after the Parthian horsemen's practice of turning in flight to discharge missiles at pursuers.
M. 119

PARTOOWYE
        M.'s "Partoowye" is Papetoai, a missionary station on the north of *Moreea.
O. 65; O. 81

PASCAL
        Blaise Pascal (1623-62), *French mathematician, physicist, and moralist, made important discoveries in the fields of geometry, hydrodynamics, and atmospheric pressure, and was an inventor of some importance. A Jansenist *Catholic, he was an active opponent of the *Jesuits and of *Montaigne. M.'s grouping him (*M.D.* 96) with *Cowper and *Rousseau

probably stems from Pascal's rather pessimistic vision of man's place in the world and in the universe.
M.D. 96

PASSED MIDSHIPMAN
See "Midshipmen."
P. 2:3

PASSEO PUBLICO
Passeio Público and Rua do Passeio, *Rio de Janeiro's public promenade and adjoining avenue, date from 1783. In M.'s time the promenade was probably on the waterfront facing the harbor entrance. Landfill and road construction have by now located it farther inland.
W. 39

"PASSING A GAMMONING"
Double entendre: passing the coil of rope used in lashing a bowsprit, or imposing on one's credulity.
W. 41

PASSION OF OUR LORD
The word "passion" is first used in *Acts 1:3 to designate the suffering and death of *Jesus.
M.D. 42

PASSY
The western residential district of *Paris (16th arrondissement), on the right bank of the *Seine.
I.P. 8

PASTILES
Deodorizing tablets.
M.D. 92

PAT
Synonym for an *Irishman from about 1825, Patrick then being the commonest Irish name.
See "Saint Patrick."
O. 37; R. 27

PATAGONIA, --N

Patagonia is in the southern parts of Argentina and
*Chile, although the name is usually used only for the Argen-
tine part (east of the *Andes). It extends c. 1,000 miles from
Rio Colorado to Cape *Horn, and includes M.'s *Terra del
Fuego and the *Isle of Desolation. The semi-arid grass and
scrub plateau where a dry wind blows constantly was discovered by *Magellan in 1520. The sheep-raising Tehuelche Indians made war against invading colonizers until c. 1880. The
boundary dispute between Argentina and Chile was settled by
a treaty of 1881.

See also "Staten Land."
W. 24; W. 30; W. 84; W. 85; M.D. 1; M.D. 7; M.D. 41; M.D.
56; M.D. 101; I.P. 21

PATCH, SAM

The leap of Sam Patch into *Niagara Falls was the subject of an 1836 play by E.H. Thompson.
R. 15; R. 24

PATER-NOSTERS

(Lat., Our Father)
The Lord's Prayer: *Pater noster* are the first two words
in Lat. version (*Matthew 6:9-14).

Also every eleventh bead of a rosary at which the Lord's
Prayer is repeated.
M. 175

PATHFINDER

See "Cooper, James Fenimore."
C.M. 26

PATROONS

See "Gansevoort."
P. 1:3 and elsewhere

PATTERSON, COLONEL JOHN; PATTERSON'S

M.'s decision to give *I.P.* a *Berkshire background necessitated his peopling the work with historical figures such as
John Patterson (or Paterson), who organized a local regiment
of *Lenox minutemen in 1774. After the battle of *Lexington,
the group went to *Boston.

M.'s source for this material was probably David Dudley Field's *A History of the County of Berkshire Massachusetts*. M.'s copy (Sealts #216) is heavily annotated and contains newspaper clippings which supply further background about Paterson's times.
I.P. 3

PAUL (AND PETER)
     "Peter and Paul" are theoretical persons, like *Tom, Dick and Harry.
O. 51

PAULET, LORD GEORGE
     Paulet (1722-1800) was a descendant of the ancient Paulet (Pawlet or Poulett) family which had held *British baronies, earldoms, and the dukedom of Bolton. Commanding HBM *Carysfort*, he arrived in *Honolulu in 1843, after departure of the British Consul, Charlton. Failing to be received by *King Kamehameha III (See "Kammahammaha"), he presented a list of demands to be enforced if not voluntarily complied with (adjustment of personal claims, acceptance of Alexander Simpson as successor, guarantees for British residents, communication without *G.P. Judd's interpretation).   The *Hawaiian king provisionally ceded the islands to Paulet, but intercession by American *President Tyler restored the Hawaiian flag.
     M. was present during much of this action: he arrived at *Lahaina on *Charles & Henry* in May 1843 and departed in August on *United States*. The full title of *T.* reflects his engagement: *Typee: A Peep at Polynesian Life. During a Four Months' Residence in a Valley of the Marquesas with Notices of the French Occupation of Tahiti and the Provisional Cession of the Sandwich Islands to Lord Paulet*.
T. Title; T. Appendix

PAUL PRY
     A busybody with no business of his own who meddles in other peoples': from John Poole's comedy of that name (1825).
T. Sequel; W. 42

PEACE CONGRESS; PEACE SOCIETY, --IES
     The Society for the Promotion of Permanent and Universal Peace was established in *London in 1816, some twelve years before the American Peace Society. As Franklin's notes

to *C.M.* point out (Chaper 26), four international Peace Congresses were held between 1848 and 1851. *The Book of Peace* (ed. George C. Beckwirth, Boston, 1845) reprinted a pamphlet of the American Peace Society, "Safety of Pacific Principles," which may include the "theory" referred to in *C.M.* 26.

Adler's *War in Melville's Imagination* posits M. as sympathetic to the aims of the Peace movement. But the general thrust of M's canon seems to hold out little hope for reform of a bellicose species.

R. 60; W. 83; I.P. 18; C.M. 26

PEACOCK

There were two U.S. *Navy sloops called *Peacock*. Commodore *Thomas ap Catesby Jones commanded the sloop-of-war *Peacock* on a *Sandwich Islands expedition of 1825 and might have been M.'s source for information about *Peacock*'s having been rammed by a whale. She made part of *Wilkes's fleet, and was wrecked on a bar off the *Columbia River, Oregon, July 1841; all hands were saved.

(A British brig *Peacock* was sunk by *Hornet* off British Guiana, 1813.)

M.D. 45

PEA-COFFEE

Made from chickpeas.

M.D. 1

PEARL SHELL ISLANDS

Probably fictional, but plausible islands, given the behavior of their inhabitants.

M. 22; M. 25; M. 32

PEARL STREET

M. was born in *New York City, at 6 Pearl Street. Pearl, which now terminates at Lafayette Street (at Customs Court) formerly extended westward to *Broadway. It is the oldest street in New York, and its numerous winding curves have had several incarnations: as the Strand, Great Dock, and Queen Street—when it faced the water's edge. Peter Stuyvesant built his home at *Whitehall and Pearl; Fraunces' Tavern is at the corner of Pearl and *Broad Street; the *Stadt Huys, New York's first *City Hall, stood at the juncture with *Coenties Slip; *Washington had temporary headquarters at Pearl and Cedar. Closer to M.'s time, DeWitt Clinton lived on

Pearl, as did Roosevelt forebears, Horace Greeley, Philip Freneau, and other noted Americans.

M.'s father was a "Pearl Street merchant" at a time when it was one of the most fashionable areas of the city. But *James Fenimore Cooper said that by 1849 Pearl Street was "chiefly occupied by the auction dealers, and the wholesale dry-good merchants, for ware-houses and counting rooms" (*The Spy*, Chapter 3).
W. 48

PEARSON, CAPTAIN

Sir Richard Pearson (1731-1806) already had a long and distinguished naval career behind him by the time he was given command of the fifty-four-gun *Serapis* in 1778. He was returning from the *Baltic with the hired ship *Countess of Scarborough* when engaged by *John Paul Jones, on *Bon Homme Richard*. After a lengthy struggle, Pearson surrendered to Jones. He was acquitted at a *pro forma* court-martial and (rather generously) knighted for his part in the battle. Pearson became Lieutenant-Governor of *Greenwich Hospital, where he died.

Pearson has gone down into history in *America as a result of his having asked Jones: "Do you ask for quarter?" Jones's response was: "I have not yet begun to fight."
I.P. 19

PECK SLIP

*Manhattan's Peck Slip ran from Gold Street east to the *East River. (It now starts at *Pearl Street.) The Peck Street ferry ran every ten minutes to Williamsburg, Brooklyn, in M.'s day.
R. 5; R. 9

PEDRO II, DON

Dom Pedro I (1798-1834) was first emperor of *Brazil, from 1822 until his 1831 abdication. His son, Dom Pedro II, was regent until 1840 and emperor from 1841 to 1889, when he was deposed and the monarchy replaced by the Republic of Brazil.

Pedro II (Dom Pedro de Alcántara; 1825-1891) died in self-exile. Although Pedro II ruled with partiality towards a narrow elite, he was rather a democratic ruler who is supposed to have said, "Were I not a monarch I should be a Republican." Among his accomplishments were ending of *African slave trade and abolition of slavery, as well as technological

progress and economic expansion. His interests in language, religion, education, and science made him a world traveler; he visited the United States Centennial Exposition in 1876. M.'s portrait of a slothful and imperialistic ruler seems fictional, although Pedro's corpulency is noted by such writers as Henry Augustus Wise.
W. 56

PEGU
Pegu, in Lower Burma (see "Burmese"), is a city of past glory, dating from the ninth century A.D. Situated on a river of the same name, it is still partially surrounded by ancient walls and moats. Pegu reached its greatest importance in the sixteenth-century, when it became the capital of a united Burma. It was visited by many Europeans in the seventeenth century but was annexed by the *British in 1852, its many glories making it even more M.'s "White Elephant."
R. 34; M.D. 42

PELEG, CAPTAIN
Peleg, pronounced "Pillick," was a common name in the *Nantucket of M.'s time and has come down to us as the classic sobriquet for the picturesque peg-legged sea captain. The name originates in the *Bible, notably in *Genesis 10:25, wherein we are told that the earth was "divided" in those days. This may refer to some geographical phenomenon or to the scattering of tribes after the *Babel incident. Peleg was fourth generation after *Noah's son, sixth generation before *Ishmael.
M.D. 16

PELEW
The Palau (or Pelew) island group of the Caroline Islands is in the western *Pacific, some 550 miles east of the *Philippines (at 7°30' N., 134°30' E.). The four volcanic and four coral islands were discovered by *Spaniards in 1526; they were ruled by Europeans from 1886 and were called the New Philippines.
(*Dana 24 mentions Pelew Islands: presumed to be Palau Islands: 7°15' N., 134°30' E.)
M. 149

PELEWS
See "Spenser."
W. 50

PELHAM
The popular 1828 novel, *Pelham*, by Bulwer Lytton, combined Gothic romance and the fashionable world.
W. 4; W. 6

PELION
In mythology, Mount Pelion, in *Thessaly, on the Aegean coast, played a part in the war between the gods and the giants. The giant Aloadae tried to reach heaven to overthrow the gods by piling Mount Ossa on Mount *Olympus and Mount Pelion on Mount Ossa.
M.'s journal for 6 and 8 December 1856 records his viewing of "Ossa and Pelion" off the shore of *Thessaly.
P. 25:4

PELISSE
A fur or fur-trimmed cloak.
M.D. 77

PELOPONNESIAN
The Peloponnesus is the (c. 140 miles N-S and E-W) peninsula of southern *Greece between the Ionian and Aegean Seas, separated from central Greece by the gulfs of Patras and *Corinth and the Saronic Gulf; it is linked to the mainland by the Isthmus of Corinth.
The mountainous area with deeply indented coastline was populated by Ionians and Achaens c. 1300 B.C. and by Dorians c. 1100 B.C. From the eighth to fifth centuries B.C., its city-states (including *Sparta) flourished. The Peloponnesians fought in the *Persian Wars (500-449 B.C.), and Sparta defeated *Athens in the Peloponnesian War of 431-404 B.C. After the third century the area passed to the *Macedonians. *Roman control began in 146 B.C.: the Peloponnesus then became part of the *Byzantine Empire. It was held from the sixth to eighth centuries A.D. by the Slavs: *French *Crusaders took control in the thirteenth century, and *Turkey annexed the area in 1460. The War of Independence was fought from 1821-28.
M.'s journal for 6 February 1857 records his cruise in the area.
See also "Thucydides," historian of the wars.
M. 32

PELTRY
Made from pelts.
M.D. 54

PENDENNIS CASTLE
A *Tudor fortress on the promontory of *Falmouth, *Cornwall, *England: a center of the Royalist cause in the British Civil War.

(Thackeray published *The History of Pendennis* [the hero's name], 1848-50.)
I.P. 21; I.P. 22

PENEM INTRANTEM FEMINAM MAMMIS LACTANTEM
Lat.: "A penis which enters the female, who suckles by means of teats."
M.D. 32

PENN
William Penn (1644-1718), son of the admiral Sir William Penn, was a *Quaker persecuted in *England and sent to the *Tower for publishing *The Sandy Foundation Shaken* (1668), an attack on orthodox doctrines. In the Tower, he wrote *No Cross, No Crown* (1669), a classic Quaker work on *Christian duty.

A refugee to *America, in 1682 he obtained land grants to form the new colony of *Pennsylvania (named after his father). He remained in America until 1684, organizing the colony, forming a liberal government, and making peace with the Indians. Accused of treason in England, he temporarily lost his colony and wrote *Some Fruits of Solitude* (1693), maxims of life, and *Essay Towards the Present and Future Peace of Europe* (1693), a confederation plan; a similar plan for America appeared in 1697.

His colony restored, Penn lingered from 1699 to 1701 to revise the charter, only to return to an English prison when the colony's affairs were judged mismanaged and he opposed the English plan for annexation of proprietary colonies.

Penn lost his memory in 1712. His wife, Hannah, assumed responsibility for the colony, as did her sons, after her death in 1727.
M. 28

PENNSYLVANIA
One of the original thirteen states of the Union, Pennsylvania is bordered by *New York and Lake *Erie (N.), New York and *New Jersey (E.), *Delaware, *Maryland, and West *Virginia (S.), West Virginia and *Ohio (W.); it is 312 miles wide (E.-W.) and 158 miles long; the *Appalachian mountains run throughout the state.

The *French explored the area in 1615, and the *Swedes made a 1643 settlement which was passed to the *Dutch. In 1681, *William Penn's property grant led to a settlement with constitutionally guaranteed religious freedom and universal suffrage, drawing the Welsh (see "Wales . . . .") *Quakers, the *English, the *Scottish-*Irish, and *French Huguenots, as well as the *Germans who later became known as the "Pennsylvania Dutch."

Indian resentment of the British led to the start of the French and Indian Wars in skirmishes at forks of the *Ohio River. The city of *Philadelphia became central to the *American Revolution as site of the first and second *Continental Congresses and signing of the *Declaration of Independence. The British occupied the Revolutionary capital (replaced by Harrisburg, 1800), and the battles of *Brandywine and Germantown, as well as *Washington's winter at Valley Forge (1777-78), focused attention on the colony; its present boundaries were established in 1792. The *Whisky Rebellion occurred here in 1794. Installation of the first successful oil well in 1859 (near Titusville), as well as the *Civil War battle of Gettysburg (July 1863), kept Pennsylvania prominent during M.'s lifetime.
M. 28; I.P. 9; C.M. 40

PENNSYLVANIA, --'S

The line-of-battle ship *Pennsylvania*, designed by Samuel Humphreys, was the most powerful warship of her time. She was fifteen years in the building, and was finally complete in 1837, patterned after *Santissima Trinidad. Pennsylvania* had 120 guns on four armed decks, including 32-pounders, but she was a very slow sailer, frustrating her officers. *Pennsylvania* was notorious for floggings, even when tied up as a receiving ship in the *United States.
M. 28

PENNY MAGAZINE

Charles Knight (1791-1873) was publisher to the "Society for the Diffusion of Useful Knowledge." He created The Penny Magazine, the Penny Cyclopaedia and numerous other works designed to make knowledge available to the poor. (Although not very "poor," M. used Knight's publications as regular sources.)
R. 41

PENSACOLA
The city of northwestern *Florida, on Pensacola Bay of the *Gulf of Mexico, is ten miles east of the *Alabama border. It was settled by the *Spanish in 1559, passed to *England in 1763, and was regained by Spain in 1783. *Jackson's forces captured the city in 1814, and it officially passed to the *United States in 1821. Pensacola has always been a center of shipbuilding and a naval station.
W. 58

PENTATEUCH
The first five books of the *Old Testament, attributed to *Moses (Gr. *penta*, five; *teuchos*, book or tool). *Genesis is the record of *Hebrew racial beginnings; *Exodus the story of enslavement and deliverance; *Leviticus, *Israel's religious laws; *Numbers, the story of life in the wilderness; *Deuteronymy, the legalization of the Covenant Code.
M. 13

PENTECOST
(Gr. *pentecoste*, fiftieth)
The festival held by *Jews on the fiftieth day after the second Sunday of Passover.
*Christian Whit Sunday commemorates (*Acts ii) the descent of the Holy Spirit on the *Apostles as tongues of fire, giving them the gift of languages with which to spread the Christian faith.
See "Whitsuntide."
M. 18; R. 33; C.M. 7

PENTHESILIAN
In the post-*Homeric legends of Pausanias, Penthesilea was Queen of the *Amazons, a nation of warring man-haters. She fought against *Greece for *Troy and was slain by *Achilles, who then mourned for her youth and beauty.
M. 28

PENZANCE
The seaport and resort borough of *Cornwall, England; departure point for the *Scilly Islands.
I.P. 14

"PEPPER BOX"
Presumably, one's head, or perhaps nose.
(Partridge: "a revolver.")
R. 27; W. 44

PEQUOD
The Pequod (or Pequot) Indian tribe of *Connecticut (not *Massachusetts, as M. has it) frequently battled the colonists near their fort in Mystic. When attacking colonists burned the fort in 1637, almost the entire tribe (500-800 individuals) were killed, and the few who escaped never reorganized. Early religious writers painted the Pequods as violent savages governed by a cruel chieftain, Sassacas, but Timothy Dwight in *Travels; in New-England and New-York* (New Haven, 1822) praised their statesmanship and bravery.

Roving solitary Pequods are characters in several works of M.'s time (including *Cooper's *The Wept of Wish-ton-Wish*, 1829), and M. is known to have discussed their plight at the dinner party (5 August 1850) at Stockbridge, Massachusetts where he first met *Hawthorne.

"Pequod" in *M.D.* (with "Dolly" in *T.*) is M.'s sobriquet for *Acushnet*, a whaler launched in December of 1840. When M. signed on at *New Bedford for her maiden voyage, he was twenty-one years old, five-foot nine and one-half inches tall, and dark-complexioned, having gained two years, one inch, and a sun tan since his service on *St. Lawrence* ("*Highlander"). *Acushnet*, captained by part-owner Valentine Pease, had been built at Rochester, *Massachusetts. She was square-sterned, 104'8 1/4" by 27'10", and 13'11" deep, with two decks and three masts, and a capacity of over 358 tons. She had cost $30,000 and had a library and other costly amenities.

Several of the twenty-six original crew members had already deserted *Acushnet* before she sailed on 3 January 1841, and M. undoubtedly endured a harsh existence on her, under an ill and tyrannical captain, before he and *Toby deserted in July of 1842. At the time of M.'s service, the tale of *Essex* and those of Mocha Dick (see "Moby-Dick") and other celebrated *cetaceans were much discussed by the crew: a relatively experienced group of white *Americans, free blacks, and *foreigners.

Before *Acushnet* reached *Rio de Janeiro in March, she had already encountered much whaling action and returned large quantities of oil, giving the appearance that she might set a record. She rounded Cape *Horn in April and by May had faced bad weather and was whaling off the coasts of *Chile and *Peru. She anchored at *Callao (headquarters of the American *Navy) for ten days, another crew member deserting there.

By June, *Acushnet* was cruising off the *Galapagos and then heading for the *equator, where her good fortune turned poor for the lack of catch. Pease turned south to zig-zag the *Off-Shore Ground, where there were whales but no luck in catching them. Intending to re-man his ship and replenish supplies before the onset of scurvy, he stopped at the *Marquesas, where M. and Toby deserted, as did at least four others at other ports. *Acushnet* then sailed for *Honolulu and *Japan. She returned to Massachusetts in May of 1845, heavily laden with sperm-oil, whale-oil, and bone.

In November (?) of 1850, M. made extensive notes on the fortunes of *Acushnet's* crew, reported to him by an ex-ship-mate who visited in *Pittsfield. Pease had retired, but the crew had left a trail of desertion, disease, suicide, and violence. *Acushnet* was wrecked on St. Lawrence Island 16 August 1851; her crew was saved, as was a large cargo of oil.

Leyda's *Log* I (p. 112) contains an illustration: "Plan of the Acushnet (drawn by Ansel Weeks, Jr., son of her builder)." M.D. (as ship) Passim; M.D. 16; I.P. 25

PERCHES
A "perch" is a unit of measurement which varies between sixteen and one-half and twenty-one feet.
M.D. 35

PERCY, --S
Percys are the Dukes of Northumberland in *England. Tradition is that when the *Scottish Malcolm III invaded England, Robert de Mowbray brought him the keys of Alnwick castle suspended on his lance, which he thrust into the Scottish king's eye, earning the name, "Pierce-eye." *Sir Walter Scott denies the legend in *Tales of a Grandfather* (iv), claiming the name originated in *Normandy.

Sir Henry Percy (Hotspur; 1364-1403), eldest son of Henry, first Earl of Northumberland, was the warrior immortalized in *Shakespeare's *Henry plays. He was killed outside Shrewsbury; his body was disinterred and his head fixed on one of the gates of *York.
M. 84; W. 65; M.D. 89

PEREGRINE!; PEREGRINE PICKLE
See "Smollett."
O. 77; W. 12

PERILOUS FLUID
Electricity, at first regarded as liquid.
M.D. 119

PERIS
Originally, in *Persian myth, beautiful but malevolent sprites responsible for natural catastrophes. Later amelioration made them fairies that direct the way to heaven. The *Koran* says they were under the rule of *Eblis and that *Mohammed was sent for their conversion as well as man's.

*Moore's *Lalla Rookh*'s second tale is "Paradise and the Peri," in which the Peri goes to heaven.

Later use refers to any fascinating or beautiful girl or woman.
R. 43

PERRY'S
Oliver Hazard Perry (1785-1819) was appointed U.S. *Navy *midshipman at the age of fourteen. He served in the *Mediterranean and in the *War of 1812, becoming a national hero as Master Commandant at the Battle of Lake *Erie (10 September 1813), when his nine vessels forced the surrender of the *British fleet of six. His message to Brigadier General *William Henry Harrison: "We have met the enemy and they are ours." Perry died at sea of yellow fever contracted in Venezuela.
W. 50

PERSEPOLIS
The ancient *Persian capital city (modern-day Takhte-E Jamshid, in southwest Iran), was the headquarters of *Darius the Great and his successors. Captured and partly destroyed by *Alexander the Great in 330 B.C., it was not wholly deserted. Ruins show the burial places of Darius, *Xerxes, *Artaxerxes II and III, and probably of *Cambyses.
M. 75

PERSEUS
In astronomy, Perseus is a northern *constellation.
See "Medusa," and "Guido."
M. 3; M. 18; M. 151; W. 84; M.D. 27; M.D. 55; M.D. 82

"PERSEUS DESCENDING"
     See "Hogarth" and "Medusa."
M.D. 55

'PERSEVERANCE, THE'
     Probably a fictional ship. M. might have borrowed the
name from a steam-powered craft of 1786.
T. 4

PERSIA; PERSIAN, --S
     Modern-day Iran was called Persia before 1935. A land
bridge between southern *Asia and approaches to Europe and
*Africa, it is currently bounded by the Gulf of Oman and
*Persian Gulf of the Arabian Sea (S.), Iraq and *Turkey (W.),
Azerbaijan and Armenian S.S.R.s, Caspian Sea and Turkmen
S.S.R. (N.), Afghanistan (see "Affghanistan") and Pakistan
(E.). Its mountain-surrounded central plateau was roamed by
ancient Persian nomads. In 1200 B.C. it was the state of Elam;
by 645 *Assyrians were in control. *Cyrus II (the Great) created the Achaemenian Persian Empire in 550 B.C., supplanting that of the *Medes (as noted in M. 3). The Achaemenids
were defeated by *Darius I (the Great) in 490 B.C. (M. 60).
From 521 to 485 B.C., the Persian Empire extended east to
northwestern *India and Afghanistan, northwest to the
Danube, and west to *Egypt, with capitals at *Persepolis,
*Susa, and the Ecbatana. *Xerxes I dominated the area from
480 B.C. Conquest by *Alexander the Great led to dissolution
of the empire after his death.
     The Persians converted to Islam under *Arab rule, and
the area flourished again under the Caliphate. But invasions,
including those of Genghis *Khan, the *Mongols, and
*Tamerlane, led to slow disintegration. By M.'s time, Persia
was ruled by a dynasty that lasted until 1925, all the while losing ground to European nations.
     There was an explosion of interest in Near-Eastern mat-
ters during M.'s time, at least partly inspired by contemporary
archaelogical study. As Finkelstein shows in *Melville's
Orienda*, M. was surrounded by popular and specialized books
on "Persian matter," many of them excerpted in reviews and
collections such as those of the Harpers. There was matter
about Persia in *Bayle and in *Harris's *Collection*, to supply
local color. Finkelstein's work is a trove of specific references
to materials M. might easily have seen. As she shows, interest
was especially high in Near-Eastern poetry, and M.'s works
are embroidered with Persian allegory, symbolism, imagery,
and language—particularly in *M.*, where the poet "Yoomy" is

certainly derived from M.'s conception of "the Persian poet."
The dualism of Persian creeds is important to *M.D.* and other
works, including *Clarel*.

The "Persian studs" of *R.* 49 are probably derived from
*Herodotus's reference to Xerxes's cavalry (3.403).

The claim in *M.D.* 1 that the Persians held the sea holy
is well documented in Herodotus. A source M. would likely
have seen is *Harper's Family Library* (Vol. 70, 1842): James B.
Fraser's *Historical and Descriptive Account of Persia*, which
notes that because the Persians would not defile the water, they
were prevented from being sailors.

Sealts #211 contains some unidentified volumes of the
"Family Library," many volumes of which were also on the
United States during M.'s navy service.

See also "Arab"; "Arabian Nights"; "Artaxerxes";
"Bactria"; "Bagdad"; "Cambyses"; "Chaldaic"; "Hafiz";
"Jones, Sir William"; "Leo, John"; "Parthia"; "Teheran";
"Xenophon"; "Zoroaster" (for "Persian fire worshippers," of
M.D. 42).
M. 3; M. 60; M. 97; M. 119; M. 121; M. 150; M. 168; M. 190;
R. 9; R. 43; R. 46; R. 49; R. 61; W. 50; W. 85; M.D. 1; M.D.
42; M.D. 44; M.D. 83; M.D. 86; M.D. 119; P. 2:2; C.M. 22

PERSIAN GULF, --SEA

A shallow arm of the *Arabian Sea between modern-day
Iran and Arabia, running from the mouth of the *Tigris and
*Euphrates Rivers to the Strait of *Ormuz, linking with the
Gulf of Oman to give a total length of some 600 miles.

See also "Salamis."
M.D. 44; P. 2:2

PERSIAN HOST WHO MURDERED HIS OWN GUESTS

In *Herodotus III, a Persian governor of Lydia lures a
tyrant of Samos to his death by crucifixion, c. 515 B.C.

(Sealts #147, *Harper Classical Library* vols. 29-31 contain
the works of Herodotus.)
M.D. 58

PERSIAN SHERBET

A dessert made with snow, scented with rose water; a
common referent in Persian and *Arabian tales and in *Scott's
The Talisman, at *Saladin's feast.
M.D. 29

PERSIUS

Aules Persius Flaccus (A.D. 44-62), Latin poet, wrote six satires: on decadent national morals; our relation to the gods; willful wrongdoing; public ethics; the *Stoic doctrine of freedom; the use of money.

The *W*. 84 reference to *Socrates as *Magister Barbatus* is found in *Penny Cyclopaedia*'s article on *beards.
W. 84

PERTH

M.D.'s smith takes his name from central *Scotland's locale for legends of *Ossian and *Scott and important historic battles: a picturesque area of lochs (including *Katrine), the Trossachs, castles, and cathedrals. In the city of Perth, *John Knox preached against idolatry in 1559. It is the site of the General Prison for Scotland, and of the murder of *James I in 1437.
M.D. 112

PERU; PERUVIAN

The third largest *South American country (after *Brazil and Argentina), modern-day Peru has a 1,400 mile *Pacific seacoast. It borders on Ecuador and *Colombia (N.), Brazil and *Bolivia (E.), and *Chile (S.), although these boundaries shifted considerably in the nineteenth century.

The area was settled as early as 8000 B.C. and had several advanced cultures by 1250 B.C., but the *Incas did not unify it until the fifteenth century A.D. *Pizarro and Diego de Almagro discovered Peru in 1524 and had conquered the Incas by 1533, but there was continuing rebellion, resulting in Pizarro's execution in 1548, and in constant struggle to maintain control by the *Spanish viceroyalty until the eighteenth century. *Lima was developed as the political, economic, and cultural capital. After struggles with the *Bourbon dynasty and the subsequent viceroyalties of New Granada and *Río de la Plata, Peru lost important cities such as *Guayaquil.

Independence was declared in 1821, and by 1826 Simon Bolivar had helped assure the break with Spain. But in M.'s time, war with Chile, civil wars, and other political disturbances were the rule. By the end of the nineteenth century, Peru was reduced in size (it had once held *Quito and Buenos Aires) but expanding economically, through rich agricultural and mineral resources.

Nineteenth-century North Americans (including M.) appear to have had great appetite for study of Peruvian culture. There are many articles expressing fascinated horror of its racial mix, rich Spanish *Catholic tradition, and liberal sexual mores.

In the 1830's, Peru was close to political anarchy. Attempting to slough off Spanish rule and establish independence, her problems were complicated by internal strife between her many racial and cultural types. The Battle of *Ayacucho finally freed her from Spanish rule. Although *Charles Wilkes (*Narrative*, Chap. XII) extensively discusses the disruptions, Prescott's *Conquest of Peru* was more likely on M.'s mind regarding this topic. Despite allusions in common, as well as mutual interest in the moral aspects of history, Prescott's and M.'s works in respect to the nature of command are diametrically opposed, Prescott being highly sympathetic to the conquistadores and to royalty in general.

See also: "Amazon"; "Andes"; "Callao"; "Cape Blanco"; "Chase, Jack"; "Pisco"; "Potosi"; "St. Dominic, --'s"; "Santa"; "Saya"; "Titicaca, lake"; "Tombez."
T. 4; T. 18; O. 52; M. 1; M. 38; M. 61; R. 56; W. Passim; M.D. 24; M.D. 42; M.D. 87; C.M. 30

PETER
The *Apostle and first *Pope. The reference in W. 15 is to *Matthew 26, *Mark 15, *Luke 22, *John 18.
W. 15

PETER
In low parlance, the name "Peter" means "penis."
W. 56

PETER AND PAUL
Theoretical persons, like *Tom, Dick, and Harry.
O. 51

PETER COFFIN
See "Charley Coffin."
M.D. 2; M.D. 15

PETER OF COLCHURCH
A bridgemaster in the *Southwark area of *London, Peter of Colechurch was chaplain of St. Mary Colechurch (destroyed in the *Great Fire). He had erected a structure at the site of *London Bridge in 1163, but by 1176 it needed to be replaced. He began work on a bridge modeled after the one at Av-

ignon but died in 1205 before it was completed. He was buried in the underpart of a chapel on the bridge dedicated to St. Thomas à *Becket, who had been baptized in St. Mary Colechurch. See also "Colchurch."
I.P. 24

PETER PENCE
P.'s "book designer" owes his name to Peter's Pence (Denarius of St. Peter, Peter's Farthings, Romescot, or Rome Penny), an annual contribution by Roman *Catholics for support of the Holy See. It was collected in Britain as early as the eighth century and well established by the time of *King Canute. It was abolished by *Henry VIII in 1534, by which time it had become in *England a tax supporting corruption.
P. 17:1

PETER THE GREAT
See "Tsar."
I.P. 16

PETER THE HERMIT
The First *Crusade preacher (c. 1050-1115) participated in the siege of Antioch (1092) and entered *Jerusalem with the crusaders. Later became Prior of Huy.
M. 19

PETER THE WILD BOY
The *French wild boy, called the "modern *Hairy Orson," was found in 1725 in a wood near Hameln, in Hanover, supposedly thirteen years old. He died in 1785.
W. 84; C.M. 21

PETRA
The ancient Rock City, or Red City, in modern-day Jordan, near the foot of Mount Hor, was the fortress-capital of Edom (Gr. Idumea), in the wasteland of the *Dead Sea. It is probably the "Sela" of the *Old Testament. Petra was once the center of the wealthy caravan trade: it declined and fell to the *Romans, becoming a seat of early *Christianity. It was taken by *Moslems in the seventh century and by *Crusaders in the twelfth.
The famous ruins include a theater, dwellings, temples, altars—all carved from stratified reddish rock. There are

mysterious inscriptions in several languages, thought in M.'s time to pre-date Christianity. The ruins were discovered in 1812 by the Swiss-born *Oriental scholar John Lewis Burckhardt (1784-1817), who disguised himself as a Moslem to facilitate his investigations. Burckhardt wrote many well-known books which M. might have seen, but it is generally thought that M.'s chapter, "Of Petra" (*Clarel* II, xxx), owes more to Arthur Penrhyn Stanley's *Sinai and Palestine in Connection with Their History . . . New Edition, with Maps and Plans* (New York: Widdleton, 1863; Sealts #488). M. owned and annotated this book.

M. did not visit Petra but mentions a "Petra Party" at *Jaffa, in his journal (20, 22 January 1857). He compares *Wall Street, deserted on Sunday, to Petra, in "Bartleby the Scrivener," and calls "New Petra" the home of a callous architect, in "I and My Chimney." In *Melville's Orienda*, Finkelstein limns M.'s assessment of "the petrified symbol of man's heavenly city which in its phosphorescent gloom and desolation strikes terror in man's heart" (I, 3, 74-75).
M. 132

PETRARCH, --S

Francesco Petrarca (1304-74), *Italian poet, is most famed for his "Rime Sparse," containing love poetry dedicated to a woman he called "Laura," whom he claimed to have seen in Provence in 1327. As poet laureate and most important humanist of Italy, he wa friend to Boccaccio and Cola di Rienzo (see "Rienzi"). He is credited with revival of the study of Greek and *Latin literature and mastery of the sonnet form, much emulated by major *British poets before the eighteenth century.
M. 119

PETRONIUS

Gaius (or? Titus Petronius) Petronius Arbiter (d. A.D. 66), reputed author of the first western European novel, the *Satyricon*, was a government official and pursuer of pleasure during the reign of *Nero. Excerpts of his pornographic picaresque romance, discovered in 1664, relate the wanderings of three low-life adventurers in a pure and elegant *Latin prose style interspersed with ribald colloquialisms. His verse and maxims have not gained the fame of the novel, which is remarkable as well for its character depiction, especially in the portion known as the *Cena Trimalchionis*, or "Banquet of Trimalchio."
R. 56; R. 58

PHAEDON
See "Plato . . . . "
W. 38; M.D. 35

PHALARIS
A cruel tyrant of Akragas in *Sicily, Phalaris (c. 570-554 B.C.) roasted his victims alive inside a bronze bull. He is said to have met his own end in this manner, after his overthrow by Telemachus. His reputation was laundered in later writings by *Lucian and other *sophists.
The story about him in *C.M.* has not been traced.
C.M. 29

PHARISAIC
The Pharisees, "those who have been set apart" (Heb. *perusim*, from *perash*, to separate), promulgated strict adherence to the Torah and were influential in the development of Orthodox Judaism. The *New Testament condemns them in several places: *Luke 18:9-14 tells of the Pharisee who exalts himself next to the truly humble Publican; *Matthew 23:13 quotes *Jesus's "Woe unto you, Scribes and Pharisees," hypocrites. Yet, *Paul (*Acts 23:6) boasts of his Pharasaic heritage.
M. 175

PHAROAH, --'S
Pharoah's "fat kine" alludes to Pharoah's dream in *Genesis 41:1-33, of "seven well favoured and fat kine" and seven "ill favoured and lean fleshed kine," interpreted by Joseph as prophesying seven years of plenty and seven years of famine.
M.D. 105

PHAROAH
"Pharoah" (without "the") in the *Bible is the *Egyptian royal title, rather than a personal name. None of those pharoahs mentioned in the Bible have been identified with certainty. M. appears to invoke the title to suggest ancientness as much as power.
M. 79; M. 84; M. 181; W. 19; M.D. 104; P. 1:4; C.M. 36

PHAROAH'S VAIN SORCERERS

In *Exodus 7-9, Pharoah's magicians cannot defeat *Moses and *Aaron, who bring plagues to *Egypt (except for the land of *Goshen).
C.M. 16

PHARPAR

The *Bible's Pharpar River of *Damascus is probably the A'waj, or perhaps a branch of the Barada (see "Abana").
O. 7

PHARSALIA

The battle of Pharsalus (near modern Farsala, in the *nomos* of Larissa, *Greece) was fought between the civil armies of *Pompey and *Caius Julius Caesar in 48 B.C. (August 9 in the Roman calendar, June 6 in the modern). *Bellum Civile*, Lucan's epic in *Latin hexameters, tells of Caesar's victory (Book vii), in which 24,000 Pompeians surrendered and the rest died or fled, while Caesar's casualties numbered about 250. Caesar probably exaggerated the difference in size of the opposing forces; it is now thought that Pompey started with 45,000 men to Caesar's 22,000.
M. 139

PHIDIAS, --'S

Active c. 475-430 B.C., Phidias (Pheidias) the *Athenian was the greatest of *Greek sculptors, originator of the idealistic classical style of the fifth and fourth centuries B.C. During Pericles's reign, Phidias was put in charge of all artistic undertakings of the great construction boom. His statue of Athena, forty feet high, in gold and ivory, stood inside the *Parthenon, the sculptures of which he probably designed.

His foremost work was the giant gold and ivory Zeus (see "Jupiter" and "Jove") for the temple at *Olympia. The figure, seven times life-size, sat on a throne, holding a Nike (winged victory goddess) and a sceptre. Phidias was also a painter, engraver, and metal embosser. Only parts of numerous copies of his works remain.
M. 84; M.D. 79

PHILADELPHIA, --n

The largest city of *Pennsylvania, and one of the nation's most historically important, Philadelphia is located in the southeastern part of the state, eighty miles southwest of *New

York City, on the Delaware River at the mouth of the Schuylkill River. The site was probably observed by both Verrazano (1524) and *Hudson (1609), but difficult navigation of the Delaware probably discouraged the idea of development. Settlers of the mid-seventeenth century stayed close to the Delaware; the first lasting settlement, by the *Swedes, took place in the 1640's. In 1682, William Penn established a *Quaker colony (leading to designation as "The City of Brotherly Love," or "The Quaker City").

*Benjamin Franklin helped make Philadelphia an early cultural center with establishment of the University of Pennsylvania in 1740. But there was no great growth of importance until *Revolutionary times. The first and second *Continental Congresses were held in Carpenters' Hall; Betsy Ross is said to have sewn the first Stars and Stripes American flag here; the *Declaration of Independence was signed in Philadelphia.

The British occupied the city, which was the Revolutionary capital, from October 1777 to June 1778; it was the capital of the nation from 1790 to 1800.

By M.'s time, Philadelphia had lost in political prestige but had begun rapid expansion in commerce and industry, at least in part because of construction of the Delaware Breakwater, which made the river more navigable. Philadelphia became the most important shipbuilding site of the nineteenth century, despite its location more than eighty miles from the ocean. There were Nativist (see "Foreigners") and anti-*Abolitionist riots during M.'s time. Philadelphia was probably the *Phrenology capital of America.

"Philadelphian regularity" (*C.M.* 15) refers to the city's streets, which meet at right angles.

See also "Chestnut Streets"; "Fairmount."
W. 16; W. 30; C.M. 4; C.M. 15; C.M. 21

PHILANTHROPOS
A play on the words of *Timon in *Shakespeare's *Timon of Athens*: "I am Misanthropos and hate mankind," Philanthropos signifying a lover of mankind.
C.M. 43

PHILIP OF MOUNT HOPE
King Philip (or Metacomet; d. 1676), son of *Massasoit, and chief of the Wampanoag Indians during King Philip's War (1675-76), at first lived in peace with the *Massachusetts colonists. Historians differ in ascribing blame for the war and in details of Philip's death. He may have been shot by a tribesman when his leadership faltered, or he may, along with

his entire tribe, have been killed by the colonists, his head exhibited at Plymouth, his wife and child sold into slavery. Various versions of his story have been written by Increase Mather, Washington Irving, *James Fenimore Cooper, and others.
M.D. 45; C.M. 25

PHILIPPINE
     The Philippines are made up of c. 7,000 islands and rocks in the southwest *Pacific, off southeastern *Asia in the *Malay Archipelago.   They extend some 1,152 miles north/south and 688 miles east/west: bounded by the Philippine Sea (E.), *Celebes Sea (S.), South China Sea (W.), Bashi (see "Bashee") Channel (N.).   The residents were *Malayans before European incursions of the early sixteenth century. (*Magellan was killed here.) The *Spanish conquered the islands late in that century, leading to conflicts with the *English and the *Dutch, and to much *pirate activity. During M.'s time, the Spanish were fighting the Moros (*Mohammedans).
M. 84; M.D. 87

"PHILIP'S RIGHT EYE, FOR"
     See "King of Macedon."
W. 16

PHILISTINE, --S
     Having failed in Asia Minor, *Cyprus, and *Syria, the Philistines ("Peoples of the [Aegean] Sea") tried in the twelfth century B.C. to invade *Egypt. They were driven back to the coastal plain of *Palestine (from *Joppa to the Wadi Ghazzeh), which became known as Philistia (forerunner of the *Greek name, "Palestine"). References in *Genesis are anachronistic, but the *Old Testament shows their constant conflict with the *Israelites (as in the *Samson story, *Judges, and I *Samuel). They were subjugated by *David but regained independence by the time of I *Kings 15.
     Despite their military prowess, there is much evidence showing them as oppressed. Their early monopoly on the use of iron (as opposed to the Israelites' softer copper or bronze) gave them an advantage.   They were subdued by the *Assyrians, and by the *Babylonian Nebuchadrezzar (see "Nebuchadnezzar"), eventually becoming part of the *Persian Empire.
     The Philistines left no written record, so the *Bible and Assyrian annals are the chief sources of information. Philis-

tine idols such as *Dagon, Ashtaroth, and *Beelzebub have
Semitic names, but little is known of their worship, despite
M.'s designation as "fowl" (*M.D.* 82). Not until the mid-nineteenth century did the term "Philistine" represent ignorance,
boorishness, and materialism. M.'s use follows the contemporary pejorative sense.
    See also "Temple of the Philistines."
M.D. 18; M.D. 82; M.D. 89; I.P. 21

PHILOMEL
    A nightingale, from the *Greek legend of Philomela
("lover of song"). Philomela had been raped by her brother-in-
law, King Tereus of *Thrace. To insure her silence, he cut out
her tongue, but she wove her story into a robe, and her sister,
Procne, seeking revenge, cut up their son and served him to
Tereus. When he pursued the two women, the gods changed
him into the hawk, Procne into the swallow, and Philomela
into the nightingale.
C.M. 10

PHILOSOPHICAL INTELLIGENCE OFFICE
    As Bruce Franklin points out, "Intelligence Office" was
a current term for domestic employment agency, and M.'s
embellishment is meant satirically.
C.M. 22

PHILOSOPHICAL NECESSITY
    See "Necessitarians."
M. 135

PHIL. TRANS.
    The *Royal Society of *London began publishing its pro-
ceedings in 1664/65, as *Philosophical Transactions: giving
some Accompt of the present undertakings, studies and
labours of the Ingenious in many considerable parts of the
world.* By 1832 it began *Abstracts of papers, printed in the
Philosophical Transactions from the year 1800*; it soon evolved
into *Proceedings of the Royal Society.*
    See also "Extracts 32."
M.D. Extracts 32

PHLEGETHON

One of the five rivers intersecting *Hades; the fiery one, with *Styx, Acheron, Cocytus, *Lethe. In *Dante, the red boiling river of blood in the first round of the seventh circle ("Inferno," XIV). In *Milton, "fierce Phlegethon/Whose waves of torrent fire inflame with rage (*Paradise Lost*, II, 580-1).

In M.'s "The Two Temples," Temple Second, the narrator longs to enter a crowded theatre: "Where else could I go for rest, unless I crawled into my cold and lonely bed far up in an attic of Craven Street, looking down upon the muddy Phlegethon of the *Thames." (M.'s *London address was Craven Street.)
W. 46; I.P. 24

PHOEBE, THE

The thirty-six-gun frigate H.B.M. *Phoebe* matched its captain, James Hillyar, with an old acquaintance, the *American *David Porter on *Essex, in the neutral port of *Valparaiso in 1813. Hillyar taunted Porter at first, bringing *Phoebe* within touching distance. A few weeks later, at sea, *Phoebe*'s powerful long guns brought about capture of *Essex* for the Royal Navy, and Hillyar permitted Porter and his crew to return home. The episode was a psychological letdown for the U.S., which had had great success in the first year of the *War of 1812.

The *Greek mythological Phoebe, a *Titan, was grandmother of Artemis (see "Diana) and *Apollo, sometimes identified with Artemis as goddess of the moon.
W. 74

PHOENICIAN

Phoenician is a vague name geographically, referring to places where the ancient Semitic-speaking Phoenician people established colonies, or to the heart of the territory of *Tyre and *Sidon (modern Saida), east of present-day *Lebanon (where they monopolized trade in cedars). In ancient times, Phoenicia was included in *Syria. The Phoenicians situated colonies along the coast of the eastern *Mediterranean about 2000 B.C. By 1250 B.C., they were skilled navigators and traders who had established the city of Tripoli, as well as colonies at *Carthage and Utica. They were much influenced by the *Egyptians. After withstanding many attacks by *Assyrian kings, they submitted to the *Persian Empire in the sixth century B.C. Originally worshippers of *Baal, they redeveloped their culture toward *Hellenism after *Alexander the Great took Tyre (333-332 B.C.).

Among Phoenician accomplishments is invention of an alphabet antedating that of the *Greeks. They were famous for Tyrian purple dyes (derived from shellfish). Phoenicians sailed as far north as the *British Isles, as well as down the coast of *Africa, perhaps going around the cape to the *East Indies.
W. 50

PHRENOLOGY; PHRENOLOGICAL, --LY; PHRENOLOGIST
Phrenology was a controversial new "science" which sought to predict human behavior through physiology. The brain was divided into areas, in each of which was located an abstract quality of human behavior: "benevolence," "combativeness," "acquisitiveness," etc. Exterior shaping of the head betokened these qualities. Although dismissed by many as quackery, phrenology had many exponents, including Whitman. M.'s frequent references suggest he did not utterly dismiss phrenology. Probably he saw the long, solemn, illustrated article in the 1840 *Penny Cyclopaedia* (XVIII). It is not known whether he visited Fowler and Wells's *New York center for phrenology (Nassau and Beekman Streets), where Whitman studied elaborate charts, busts, and books, especially *Johann Kaspar Spurzheim's *Phrenology*, the fundamental text in *America. Also available was a long illustrated article on phrenology in William and Robert Chambers, eds., *Information for the People. A Popular Encyclopedia* (Philadelphia, 1847), and other popular sources which analysed the heads of important people, among them many of M.'s referents.
In *M.D.* 80, M. plays with phrenology's vocabulary, with organs of "self-esteem," "veneration," and "firmness."
See also "Lavater, John Casper"; "Gall."
W. 44; M.D. 10; M.D. 79; M.D. 80; C.M. 22

PHYSIOGNOMY; PHYSIOGNOMIST
See "Phrenology."
M.D. 79; P. 4:4

PIAZZA, THE
*London's *Covent Garden Piazza, an arcade on the north and east sides, was designed by Inigo Jones; construction began in 1630.
C.M. 24

"PICTURE OF A PHYSETER....:
    See "Colnett, Captain."
M.D. 55

"PICTURE OF LONDON"
    M.'s father, Allan Melvill (see "Walter Redburn"), owned *The Picture of *London for 1818* . . . Nineteenth Edition. London, 1818 (Sealts #402), a standard guidebook of the day, by George Frederick Cruchley.
    *George Duyckinck supplied M. with an edition of this same book for M.'s 1849 excursion to *England.
    Thorp ("Redburn's Prosy Old Guidebook") compared editions of this work (one as early as 1803; London: Lewis and Co. Paternaster-row) but did not find pictures perfectly corresponding to the eight pictures M. mentions.
R. 30

PIERRE
    The French equivalent of "*Peter," the name Pierre has many associations for M. In *P.* he dramatizes the exploits of his grandfather, General Peter *Gansevoort; Pierre was the unused name of a cousin, Tom Melvill. A Pierre was said to have saved a woman from burning by Indians under the *Pittsfield elm.
    Pierre, or Peter, means "stone" or "rock" and M. also exploits this symbolic significance, especially in the work by that name. In light of the book's preoccupation with sexuality (or the lack thereof), M. may also be making a play on the name Peter, which has phallic connotations.
P. Passim

PIG-FISH
    See "Cetology" section.
M.D. 32

"PIG-TAIL"
    A tobacco twisted into thin rope and braided into sailors' hair, solving the pocketless problem addressed in *W.*: a fashion begun in seventeenth-century Europe.
M. 121; W. 86

PIKO
       Pico is in the *Azores Islands (38°16' N., 28°49' W.). Pico
Alto (7,613 feet) is the highest mountain in the group.
       Pico de Teyde (12,182 feet) is at the center of *Teneriffe,
*Canary Islands.
P. 22:4

PILATE
       Pontius Pilate (d. A.D. 36?), who condemned *Jesus to
death, was *Roman procurator of *Judea at a time when
*Jews were resisting the strangling Roman administration of
emperor *Tiberius and his favorite, Sejanus. Called upon to
explain cruel treatment of a *Samaritan revolt, Pilate perhaps
committed suicide in Rome
       In much of the *New Testament, Pilate seems driven by
politics to condemn Jesus. In *Matthew 27:19, he washes his
hands of responsibility. Only in *Luke is his cruelty mentioned
(13:1). Some *Christian history has painted Pilate as almost a
hero, or as a victim of the *Sanhedrin or Roman legal system.
For Jews, he is the prototype anti-Semite. Contemporaries
such as Philo and Josephus paint him as corrupt and cruel, as
well as inept.
       M.'s having *Pisistratus toast Pilate (M. 181) shows that
he believed the procurator a politically expedient tyrant.
       The "Hebrew governor" who "knew how to keep his
hands clean" in C.M. 7 is the Roman *pagan, Pilate.
       Nathalia Wright suggests in Melville's Use of the Bible
that Captain Vere, of Billy Budd, Sailor, is a type of Pilate.
M. 181

PILAU
       Meat prepared with boiled rice, raisins, spices ("pilaf").
M.D. 17

PILLGARLIC
       Pilgarlic, or Pill'd Garlic: a sixteenth-and seventeenth-
century term for a bald-headed man. Later use referred to
anyone avoided by his fellow man. *Rabelais uses in Pantagruel, V, viii.
R. 5

PINE BARRENS
       The only *New York Pine Barrens I have been able to
trace are on *Long Island. The *New Jersey Pine Barrens are

a coastal plain of sandy-soil swampland and streams in the southern and southeastern part of the state.
M.D. 53

PINNY
    An invented adjective, suggesting something thinlined or dainty.
M.D. 71

PINTADO PLUMES
    I have been unable to trace this reference. In Spanish, *pintado* means colorful. "*El mas pintado*" in colloquial usage means the best, or the bravest. There is an El Pintado village in Argentina; a Pintada Peak in Colorado, and a Salar de Pintados salt desert in *Chile, but I have not discovered any of these to be the source of plumes. Perhaps Pintado is another of *M*.'s fictional locales.
M. 74; M. 84

PINZELLA
    This allusion defies identification. It may refer to Martin Alonzo Pinzón, owner and master of the *Pinta*, which supposedly deserted *Christopher Columbus. Pinzón was a wealthy and erudite *Spaniard, highly placed in the society of Ferdinand and *Isabella. Although I have not found a record of his writings, the mysterious references to the figurehead Christopher Columbus in "Benito Cereno," and the presence of Prescott's *Ferdinand and Isabella* on board *United States* indicate M.'s possible knowledge of the theory that Pinzón and Alonzo Sanchez were the true discoverers of America.
    "Ella" is the diminutive ending in Spanish, which may add credence to Pinzón's being M.'s source.
W. 44

P.I.O.
    See "Philosophical Intelligence Office."
C.M. 22

PIOUS, THE
    See "Louis I of France."
M. 181

PIP; PIPPIN

A prototype of sorts exists for the fictional "Pip." M.'s former shipmate on *Acushnet* (see "Pequod"), Henry F. Hubbard, noted in his own copy of the *English edition of *M.D.* that Pip probably represented a young black boy called Backus who twice leaped overboard.

The name has interesting connections which M. might well have known. A pip or pippin is an apple while still but a seed, but "pip" in the pejorative sense stands for a miserably defeated or black-balled person, or, in the military, one suddenly promoted from lowly to high rank.
M.D. Passim

PIPE MY EYE

Cry, or snivel (Welsh *pipian*, to pule).
W. 23

PIRATE BLACK

One of the negative associations of the color black is with piracy; the Black Flag, the "Jolly Roger" is the pirate flag.
O. 27

PIRATE, --S

Piracy thrived from early times, as an almost respectable way for an otherwise unemployed mariner to get his living. There was a fine line between the "illegal" private vessel and the privateering ship commissioned by a government with a *letter of mart, or marque, authorizing the taking of "prizes." As noted in these pages, many "respectable" mariners mentioned by M. had been pirates (*Drake, *Cowley, *Dampier, *Wafer, etc.). *John Paul Jones aimed desperately for respectability while evincing most of the characteristics of a pirate. The notorious Jean Laffite was pardoned by the United States government for his contributions to the *New Orleans campaign of *Andrew Jackson.

Problems involving the *Barbary pirates probably brought about the beginning of the end of popular tolerance of piracy. But swashbuckling literature in pulp magazines memorialized the exploits of the *Captain Kidds. *Sir Walter Scott's *The Pirate* (1821) is a sentimental treatment. *The Pirates' Own* (R. 39) and other popular works made pirates romantic figures, so that it was not quite so outrageous in the nineteenth century that Gilbert and Sullivan had their hero "apprenticed to a pirate," in *The Pirates of Penzance* ((1879). Indeed, M. seems to have taken more offense at "pirate powers" (such as those of *M.D.* 89, "*Fast-Fish and Loose Fish") than at individuals attempting to earn a living in a difficult world—and doing it picturesquely.

(In "Benito Cereno," M. was to name the American captain's ship "Bachelor's Delight": the name of the pirate ship of Captain John Cook [1680's], on which *Cowley served.)
Passim

PISA; TOWER OF PISA
The capital city of Pisa province in Northwest *Tuscany, *Italy, is an ancient site of archeological importance for its *Roman baths and medieval buildings. Its greatest claim to fame is the campanile of the cathedral, the Leaning Tower, begun in 1174, of white marble inlaid with colors. The tower is one hundred and eighty-four and one half feet high on base walls thirteen feet thick at the foundation, which is only ten feet deep. Settling began early, as did straightening attempts. By 1829 the tower was fifteen and one half feet off perpendicular (seventeen feet off at the present time). Despite modern efforts, it will probably collapse.

M.'s journal for 23 March 1857 contemplates the tower: "Campanile like pine poised just ere snapping. You wait to hear crash . . . . There are houses in wake of fall."
M. 147; R. 27; W. 50; I.P. 18; I.P. 19

PISCATAQUA
The Piscataqua River of *Maine and *New Hampshire is formed by Salmon Falls and the Cocheco River at Dover, New Hampshire. It flows south-southeast to Portsmouth Harbor. The river was first sighted by the *English in 1603; it was explored by Captain John Smith in 1614.
I.P. 2

PISCES
See "Zodiac."
M. 13; M. 169; M.D. 99

PISCO
As M. notes (*O.* 1), Pisco (*muscat) brandy derives its name from the port town which shipped it. Pisco serves *Peru's Ica Valley, c. 160-180 miles south of *Lima (13°43' S., 76°07' W.). The *Spanish first produced the brandy after founding the city of Ica in 1563.
O. 1; O. 35; O. 41

PISGAH
A ridge of the Abarim mountains in ancient *Palestine, east of the north end of the *Dead Sea (now in Jordan). In Numbers 21, *Moses sees the *Promised Land from the top of Mount Pisgah (in *Deuteronomy 34:1: "Nebo").
W. 93

PISISTRATUS
Pisistratus (Peisistratus;   605?-528? B.C.) was an *Athenian statesman whose tyrannic rule imposed unification upon Attica and strengthened Athens.   His military feats, early "spoils system," taxation for public improvements, creation of a national religion, and purification of the island of *Apollo, Delos, brought him great popularity and lasting fame. To Pisistratus is sometimes ascribed creation of the *Parthenon, as well as collection of the poetry of *Homer.
M.'s having him toast *Pilate in *M*. 181 paints him as politically expedient, if not virtuously so.
M. 181

PISTAREENS
A pistareen was a *Spanish silver coin worth about twenty cents, widely used in colonial *America; the name is probably a corrupted diminutive of *peseta*. *C.M.* 20's "clipped" pistareens have been damaged to remove some of the silver; if they are "steamed," they have been heated to melt silver away. "Pistareen" came to describe any trifling thing.
C.M. 20

PISTOLES
*Spanish gold coins worth two *escudos*. An *escudo* contained c. 3.38 grams of gold.
See also "Doubloon"; "Joes."
M.D. 99

PITCAIRN'S ISLAND
The volcanic south-Pacific Island (25° S., 130°5' W.) is but two miles long and has only one village: Adamstown. The island was discovered by the *British in 1767 and was settled in 1790 by the *Bounty mutineers and Tahitian natives. The colony was discovered in 1808 by *Americans. The by-then crowded population was thinned out by removal of some inhabitants to *Tahiti, but some of those removed eventually returned.
M. 1

PITCH
A fictional character whose name follows *C.M.*'s pattern
of references to *whiteness and blackness.
C.M. 22

PITTI PALACE
See "Florence."
C.M. 36

PITTSFIELD
The capital of *Berkshire County, in western *Massachusetts, is located on the headstreams of the *Housatonic
River, forty-five miles northwest of Springfield. It was settled
in 1752, incorporated as a town in 1761, and as a city in 1889.
Pittsfield had become the main center of the *Berkshires even
before M. made his residence here (1850-1862). Leyda's *Log* (24
June 1857) reproduces an advertisement for M.'s Pittsfield
property which gives some sense of its character:

> For Sale. The place now occupied by the sub-
> scriber (two miles and a half from Pittsfield vil-
> lage by the east road to *Lenox,) being about sev-
> enty acres, embracing meadow, pasture, wood,
> and orchard, with a roomy and comfortable
> house. For situation and prospect, this place is
> among the pleasantest in Berkshire, and has
> other natural advantages desirable in a country
> residence.

M.'s reference (*W*. 18) to the large elm tree in Pittsfield
Park in 1841 suggests significance beyond its provenance or its
bulk. A Berkshire legend tells of a relative of M. saving a
young woman from burning by Indians at the base of the tree.
A case has been made for the tree as inspiration for "*Ahab's"
physique, both of them scarred from head to foot by lightning
strikes that did not destroy them.
It is ironic, given M.'s attraction to the elm's in-
domitability, that in the middle of the twentieth century all of
Pittsfield's elms were chopped down to prevent the spread of
elm blight.
W. 18

PIZARRO
The classic Conquistador, Francisco Pizarro (c. 1474-
1541) was born in Trujillo, *Spain. The poorly educated adven-

turer first crossed the *Atlantic shortly after *Columbus's discovery, enduring severe conditions even when stranded without provisions. Rumors of the *Peruvian Empire's existence convinced him to seek help from the Spanish sovereign, *Charles V. In 1531 he sailed with a small force, from *Panama along the western coast of *South America, crossing the mountains to contact the *Inca Atahualpa (see "Atahalpa"). He conquered the gold-rich empire, founding *Lima as the "City of the Kings," the eventual focus of Spanish colonization. The rapacious Pizarro was assassinated by followers of his former associate, Diego de Almagro.
M.D. 42; C.M. 30

PLACE-DU-CARROUSEL
Place du Carrousel, adjacent to the *Tuileries and the *Louvre in *Paris, derives its name from an equestrian show given by Louis XIV (see "Bourbon") in 1662. The area has its own reduced-scale Arc de Triomphe: a copy of the Arch of Septimius Severus, at *Rome.
It was possible for M. to breakfast "at a cheap place" in the Place du Carrousel on 5 December 1849; the area adjacent to the nearby palaces was still rather squalid at the time.
I.P. 12

PLAGUE
The word "plague" originally referred to any widespread mortal disease. The Great Plague of *London, referred to in *I.P.* 19, occurred from 1664-65 and killed at least 70,000 people in a population of about 460,000. The "*Great Fire" of 1666 was credited with halting further spread. Actually, the disease manifests itself in waves of infection that seem to subside naturally, so nineteenth-century efforts at control were often erroneously seen as effective. Rodent and human parasites were known to spread the disease, which had subsided in western Europe in M.'s time. But in the early and middle part of the century, *Indian and other mid-eastern and eastern populations were decimated. Not until 1894 was one causative organism (*Pasteurella pestis*) identified. Plague was not recognized in the United States until 1900.
Sealts #178 is Defoe's *History of the Plague in London, 1665; to Which Is Added The Great Fire of London, 1666, by an Anonymous Writer* . . . London, 1881. The purported narrative of a London resident is a graphic depiction of the plague. It was written in 1721, when another outbreak was anticipated in *Marseilles, occasioning the unpopular Quarantine Act. M.'s copy of Defoe's work is signed and annotated.
I.P. 19 and elsewhere

PLANTAGENETS

The Plantagenets were *England's royal family between 1154 and 1485. The name began as a nickname for Geoffrey, Count of Anjou (d. 1151), and despite use of surnames outside the royal family, the Plantagenets had none. Historians refer to them as the Angevin kings and, after 1399, kings of the House of *York (Henries) or of Lancaster (Edwards and Richard III). First Plantagenet king was Henry II (ruled 1154-89), son of the Count. Henry's first son became Richard I, *Coeur de Lion (1189-99), his second *King John (1199-1216). Other Plantagenet rulers were:

Henry III (1216-72)
Edward I (1272-1307)
Edward II (1307-27
*Edward III (1327-77)
Richard II (1377-99) (see "King Richard")
*Henry IV (1399-1413)
Henry V (1413-22)
Henry VI (1422-61, 1470-71)
Edward IV (1461-70, 1471-83)
Edward V (Apr. - June 1483)
*Richard III (1483-85)
Henry VII (1485-1509)

*Edward the Black Prince was father of Richard II; *John of Gaunt was father of Henry IV. Intermarried with Plantagenets were rulers of *France, *Scotland, *Spain, *Sicily, and *Norway, as well as members of the *Neville family
P. 1:3

PLATE, THE

See "Rio de la Plata."
M.D. 51

PLATO, --'S; PLATONIAN; PLATONIC; PLATONIST

The influential and prolific *Greek philosopher Plato (428/27--c. 348 B.C.), friend and admirer of *Socrates, was an aristocratic *Athenian who set up a school called the Academy c. 380 B.C. Most of Plato's early works were dialogues on ethics, with Socrates as the principal speaker; many demonstrate what has come to be known as the "Socratic method": posing questions that trap opponents into self-contradicton. These include the *Apology* and the *Crito*. *Phaedo* ("Phaedon," in *W.* 38 and *M.D.* 35), written between 371 and 367, which does not employ the Socratic method, concerns immortality. Later works show Plato's close study of the structure of nature and his deepening religious conviction (*Parmenides*, *Sophist*, *Statesman*, etc.).

"Platonic particles" (*P.* 2:2) refers to the *Symposium*, according to which humans were originally large, strong creatures with four arms and four legs who were about to dethrone the gods. *Jupiter cut them in two, creating love in order to reunite the parts. (*P.* 2:4, on love, owes much to Plato's ideas.) "Platonic love," one of the most influential ideas, is separate from and higher than "romantic" heterosexual attachment. (The idea came to be applied to non-carnal heterosexual relationship.) The idea of the "philosopher king," whose major work would be that of the informed mind, inspired many plans for its effecting. The Theory of Forms suggested a relationship between ideas (Forms), which are *real*, and the physical world, which is a copy. This belief heavily influenced the Cambridge Platonists, European Romantics, the American *Transcendentalists, and others. M. appears to examine the Theory of Forms at the end of *M.D.* 35, "The Masthead." The *Republic* posits an ideal type of state; it contains the allegory of the Cave, in which Socrates reveals the difference between enlightened and unenlightened men by reference to the misperception by men in a cave of shadows of real things.

(Sealts's 1942 dissertation examines M.'s response to philosophers such as Plato.) See also entries which follow.
M. 119; W. 38; M.D. 35; M.D. 75; M.D. 78; M.D. 85; M.D. 101; P. 2:2; P. 14:2; P. 17:2; P. 20:2; P. 21:1; P. 22:3; I.P. 7; I.P. 8; C.M. 36; C.M. 37

PLATONIAN LEVIATHAN
An "ideal" whale, in *Plato's terms.
M.D. 55

PLATONIC AFFECTON
Platonic love has generally been thought of as spiritual love between persons of opposite sexes, with no physical or sexual involvement. In the *Symposium* *Plato extols *Socrates' pure love for young men: the exception rather than the rule in ancient *Greece. Such love is "innocent of any hint of lewdness," and prefers "the more vigorous and intellectual bent" (*Symposium* 181).
T. 26

PLAY, THE
    See "Hamlet . . . . "
M.D. 127

"PLEASURES OF IMAGINATION"
    See "Akenside, Mark."
C.M. 5

PLEBEIAN
    In *Rome in about the fifth century B.C., a clear distinction developed between free citizens. The wealthy and highborn patrician class began excluding the lower-born common people, or plebeians, from high government office, even if they were land owners. As economic conditions worsened, poorer plebeians became *slaves or servants in exchange for protection. By the early fourth century, rich plebeians excluded from power began organizing strikes and secessions, becoming a state within a state. Legal conflicts ensued until the middle of the century, when the *plebiscita* (a law enacted by the assembly of tribes; not an election by the whole body of citizens) was passed and intermarriage began. But for almost another hundred years, examples of the separation remained in evidence in government.
I.P. 25

PLEIADES
    The nebulous star cluster in the *constellation *Taurus includes a third-magnitude star, Alcyone. The cluster is referred to in *Job 9:9 and 38:31. It was named for *Greek mythology's seven daughters of Atlas. One version makes them attendants of Artemis (*Diana), pursued by *Orion and changed by Zeus (*Jupiter) into pigeons and then into stars. Another myth makes them sisters of the *Hyades who grieved over their relatives' deaths and were changed into stars: Alcyone, Asterope, *Electra, Celaeno, Maia, Merope (see "Sisyphus"), and Taygeta.
    American Indian legend saw the Pleiades as little girls pursued onto a rock by bears; the gods raised the girls to the heavens to save them. (This legend is commemorated at Wyoming's Devil's Tower National Monument, established in 1906, but well known before, for its volcanic rock tower.)
M. 93; M. 169; M. 175

PLINNEE
     See "Pliny."
M. 121

PLINY; PLINY THE ELDER; "PLINNEE"
     Gaius Plinius Secundus (A.D. 23 or 24-79) was uncle to
Pliny the Younger (A.D. 61 or 62-c. 113), source of his biogra-
phy and bibliography. Pliny was born at Novum Comum
(Como), Transpadane *Gaul, coming to *Rome early to practice advocacy. He traveled widely with the military and as
procurator. As Prefect of the Roman fleet, he was stationed at
Misenum, Campania, where he died in the eruption of Mount
*Vesuvius. Pliny wrote on military procedures, history of
*German wars, biography, oratory, and politics. His only ex-
tant work, *Historiae Naturalis XXXVII* (*Natural History in
Thirty-Seven Books*) is a scholarly, if unscientific, description
of the world, the heavens, man, and animals (real and imaginary), colored by *pantheistic *Stoicism. Most interesting are
sections on human abnormalities (tales of reversed feet,
mouthlessness, exceptional powers), and on zoology (complete
with winged horses, unicorns, sympathetic dolphins). It is
valuable as a source of materials on ancient manners and art.
     (See also "Extracts" 7.)
M. 121; M.D. Extracts 7; M.D. 32; M.D. 56; M.D. 105

PLIOCENE
     The name bestowed on the geological age of the most re-
cent group of fossils by Sir Charles Lyell (1797-1875), along with
*Eocene and *Miocene, of earlier periods. All three names
were universally adopted. The Pliocene was the last epoch of
the *Tertiary Period in the Cenozoic Era (c. 65 million years
ago), during which modern plants and animals developed.
     See also "Sandwiches."
M. 132

PLOTINUS PLINLIMMON
     This fictitious character takes his first name from the
*Egyptian-born *Greek philosopher, Plotinus (c. 203-62), the
founder and chief exponent of Neoplatonism, which combined
*Platonic ideas with *Oriental mysticism, attempting to bring
together all systems of belief. His teachings had great impact
on Greek and *Christian philosophies, on the latter especially
during the *Middle Ages and the Renaissance (see "Revival of
Learning"). In the thinking of Plotinus, the One or the Good is
beyond the reach of the thought or language. He posited a

Great Chain of Being, with a "full" universe composed of an infinite series of forms sharing attributes with neighbors, thus linking the lowest forms to the highest, *God. His writings were collected by Porphyry.

Plinlimmon is a broad-domed *Welsh mountain (2,469 feet); it is mentioned in *Scott's *The Betrothed* and in Thomas Gray's poem, "The Bard."
P. 14:3

PLOWDEN

Edmund Plowden (1518-1585), who became one of *England's most eminent jurists, was born in Plowden, Shropshire. He qualified for the bar at Middle *Temple, and also studied at *Cambridge and *Oxford, at all three of which he was considered brilliant but excessively studious. Plowden attracted the attention of Queen *Elizabeth, who promised great honors to the member of *Parliament if he would renounce his Roman *Catholic faith. Plowden refused but had a distinguished career with many important defenses, despite encountering persistent bias against his religious inclination. His many publications were frequently quoted from by *Coke, *Hale, and others. One excerpt in particular, taken out of context and referred to in myriad situations, was often uttered: "The case is altered, quoth Plowden."
M.D. 90

PLUM-PUDDING VOYAGE

A brief (about six months) *Atlantic voyage.
M.D. 17

PLUNKET

William Conyngham Plunket, First Baron of Plunket (1764-1845), *Irish lawyer/orator/statesman, was Chancellor of Ireland from 1830-41. His two-volume *Life, Letters, and Speeches* was published in 1867.
R. 27

PLUTARCH; *PLUTARCH'S MORALS*

The widely admired prolific *Greek essayist/biographer lived from c. 46 to post-119. The son of philosopher/biographer Aristobolus traveled widely, lectured and perhaps held office in *Rome; in his life-long home at Chaeronea, in Boeotia, he taught and held office, married Timoxena and had at least four children.

His greatest work, *Bioi Paralleloi* (*Parallel Lives*), was a collection of forty-six (twenty-two extant) pairs of biographies of Greek and Roman statesmen, orators, and soldiers. It was designed to provide *exempla* and to promote respect between Greeks and Romans. The somewhat subjective "Lives" are modified Attic-style biographies peppered with anecdotes, quotations, and learned allusions. The other known writings are collected as the *Ethica* (*Moralia*), eclectic dialogues or diatribes on morality, philosophy, nature, medicine, politics, religion; influenced by the *Stoics, *Pythagoreans, Peripatetics, and *Platonists.

Until the nineteenth century, Plutarch's works influenced and were quoted by most great writers; by M.'s time, only *Emerson seemed a great admirer.

See also "Adrian, Emperor," regarding a misattribution in W. 85.

(See also "Extracts" 6 and "Beards.")
R. 14; W. 41; W. 85; M.D. Extracts 6

PLUTO; KING PLUTO
*Hades, in *Greek tradition, a brother (with *Neptune, or Poseidon) of Zeus (see "Jupiter" and "Jove"). He ruled over the dead and the underworld, with his wife *Proserpine, rarely visiting Earth.

As *Pluto, he is also God of Wealth, for the precious metals under the earth. His palace is said to have meadows of pale, ghostly flowers, many gates, and a crowd at all times. It is not otherwise described.

See also "Plutus."
M. 181; P. 2:2; P. 3:3; P. 22:4

PLUTUS
Plutus is a *Roman allegorical figure often confused with *Pluto, since both represent wealth. The wealth of Plutus comes from the cultivated earth; he is the son of Demeter, the corn-goddess. The wealth of Pluto comes from underground minerals. M.'s confusion is evident in *R.*: when Harry Bolton swears "by Plutus," he is talking about gold.
R. 61

PLYMOUTH
The seaport of Devon, *England, much used by the Royal Navy, was home port to *Drake and Grenville, departure point of *Raleigh's *Virginia colonists and of the fleet against the

*Spanish Armada, as well as stop-off point for the damaged
Mayflower.
R. 29

POCAHONTAS

The daughter of Indian chief *Powhattan, Matoaka (c.
1595-1617) was given the name "Pocahontas," which means
"sportive," to ward off the *English evil eye. She is the heroine
of Captain John Smith's legend in his *Generall Historie* (1624;
Book III, Chapter 2). The apocryphal story (which does not
appear in his earlier history) tells of Pocahontas's intervention
when Smith was to be put to death, in 1608. Pocahontas was
seized as a hostage in 1613 by *Virginia settler, Samuel Argall,
to force peace between her tribe and the colonists. She was
converted to *Christianity, taking the name "Rebecca," married colonist John Rolfe, was taken to England in 1616, where
she was received at court and lionized by the British. Her story
appears in many works of literature, and many *Americans
claim descent from her.
P. 1:3; C.M. 25

POE, EDGAR ALLAN

Although M. does not mention Poe (1809-49) in the novels, he could not escape Poe's presence. In addition to the
many poems (bringing *Emerson's sobriquet, "the jingle
man"), short stories (in the genre of which Poe is considered
the pioneer), his literary criticism and editing (especially for
Southern Literary Messenger) made him a figure that might
be mocked (as M. does in his romanticized ragged madman of
C.M. 36), but that was an unavoidable influence.

Although a study of Poe's influence on M. is not appropriate here, the reader should be aware of M.'s undoubted borrowings, especially from *The Narrative of Arthur Gordon Pym*
(1838). Moods, themes, and allusions in common show M.'s
close familiarity with the book (*Sydney, *Ariel, *Blackwood,
Bounty, *Coffin, *Owen Chase, *Gallipagoes, *Desolation,
*Cook, *Kreusenstern, *Enderby, *Petra, and many others ap-
pear in Poe's and in M.'s works.)

See also "Glendinning Stanly . . . " for a clear borrowing
from Poe's "William Wilson" (1839).

(Sealts #404a is the 1859 edition of *The Works*, containing
the notorious "Memoir" of Rufus Wilmot Griswold.)

POLAND

Polish history proper begins in the ninth century with resident "Polians": "dwellers in the field." *Christianity was accepted under the Piast dynasty in 966, and soon thereafter there were wars with *Germany, *Hungary, *Bohemia, *Denmark, and Kiev, with the crown going to Hungary in 1370. Wars were constant, especially with *Russia and *Sweden, so that Poland virtually ceased to be independent by the late seventeenth century. It was partitioned between *Prussia and Russia in the eighteenth century and by 1794 split again to include *Austria in the spoils. The *Congress of Vienna (1814-15) set up a marginally independent kingdom of Poland in union with what M. calls the "three pirate powers" (*M.D.* 14). An 1831 insurrection against Russia ended by virtual integration with Russia, with the Prussian portion becoming increasingly German.
M.D. 14; M.D. 89

POLE, --S; POLAR

The North Pole at the northern end of Earth's axis is located in the *Arctic regions, at 90° N., 00; the North Magnetic Pole is on Prince of Wales Island, at 73° N., 100° W.

The Polar Bear (*M.D.* 42), *Thalarctos maritimus*, is found only in the Arctic, and therefore M. is in error in calling it the "White bear of the Poles" in the same chapter. To all intents and purposes, M.'s many references to the Poles are based on early knowledge of the North Pole, the *Antarctic continent remaining a relative mystery even in the twentieth century. M. apparently presumed that what was true about geography of the north was true of that of the south.

The word "Arctic" is derived from the Greek *arktos*, "bear," referring to the northern *constellation. The area was much discussed in M.'s time, when "Arctic" referred to *Greenland, *Spitzbergen, and other islands, as well as northern parts of *Siberia, Alaska, and *Canada, *Labrador, *Iceland, and a strip of the northern coast of Europe. Arctic Europe was visited by ancient *Greeks, who called it *Thule, the end of the earth; the *Vikings settled portions in the ninth century. In the sixteenth century, *Dutch and *English explorers seeking a Northeast Passage to the Far East sailed into areas already known by *Russian seaman. Willem Barents and other Dutch explorers pushed north, but *Henry Hudson's crew mutinied, forcing his voyage west in 1609. Russia's Peter the Great (see "Tsar"), the Dane Vitus Bering, and *Captain James Cook, all accomplished further mapping, but it was not complete until Russian sledge journeys of 1820-24. There was no navigation of parts of the Northeast passage until the late 1870's.

The Northwest Passage was sought by Cartier and the Cabots after the discovery of the Americas, but *Sir Martin Frobisher was the first to enter the area, in 1576. A spurious map showing a country called *Friesland hampered mapping efforts. *John Davis made social contact with the *Eskimos in the late sixteenth century, and Hudson sailed *Discovery* into the area in 1610, suffering another mutiny in the process. Baffin and others sought a passage in the seventeenth century, but it was not until the nineteenth century that governments became involved. *Parry, *Beechey, and others made inroads, evidence of which was found in the 1850's, when existence of the passage was confirmed. The Northwest Passage was not navigated until the 1906 voyage of the *Norwegian Roald Amundsen; the North Pole was not reached until Richard E. Byrd's 1926 expedition.

Despite lack of success in navigation, early explorers contributed to geographical knowledge and paved the way for the Arctic whale trade, which was flourishing by the seventeenth century. By M.'s time, the Arctic whale population had been decimated except in East Greenland waters, *Baffin Bay, *Hudson Bay, and the Beaufort Sea (above Alaska). The *Scoresbys and others contributed much to mapping, which had previously been kept secret for fear of economic competition.

The South Pole (90° S, 00) is in Antarctica (from Greek *antarktikos*, "opposite the bear"); the South Magnetic Pole is on George V Coast, at 70° S., 148° E. The area, being almost completely unknown in M.'s time, gave rise to many myths, most important of which was based on theories of John Cleves Symmes, who believed the Earth hollow, with a hole at the South Pole (an idea *Poe plays with in *The Narrative of Arthur Gordon Pym*). Cook had crossed the Antarctic Circle in 1774, and Captain John Davis landed on the mainland in 1821. The American Antarctic Exploring Expedition of 1838, headed by *Wilkes, confirmed the existence of the land mass, seen also by *Bellinghausen. Wilkes charted whale migrations and mapped parts of the South Seas, but his findings were disputed until expeditions by Amundsen and R.F. Scott confirmed them in the early twentieth century. Until that time, myths such as that of Symmes retained some currency, despite the expeditions of "exploring whalers" such as the *Enderbys.

See also "Archangel"; "Crozetts"; "Nova Zembla"; "Ob."
Passim

POLAR CONSTELLATIONS
In the north, Ursa Minor, Cepheus, *Draco; in the south, *Argo, Canis Major.
See also "constellations."
M. 34

POLAR STAR
Probably a reference to Polaris, the North Star (not exactly true north), brightest in the *constellation Ursa Minor. Its closeness to the pole makes its apparent position remain nearly constant all night and all year. In actuality composed of three stars, Polaris is a convenient object for navigators.
M. 3

"POLITICS"
See "Aristotle."
C.M. 29

POLK, PRESIDENT
James Knox Polk (1795-1849), eleventh *President of the United States (1845-49), was born in North *Carolina and practiced law in *Tennessee, serving in the legislature and *Congress representing that state. A supporter of *Jackson, Polk was Speaker of the House and Governor of Tennessee (1839-41) before opposing Clay in the campaign of 1844. A militant nationalist, Polk was the foremost proponent of the annexation of *Texas and waging of the *Mexican War.
M. was in the Navy just before Polk's Presidency, which, with the help of *Secretary of the Navy *Bancroft, saw the opening of the Naval Academy at Annapolis and a general effort to raise Navy morale. M.'s elder brother, *Gansevoort Melville, worked actively in support of Polk.
W. 34

POLL, --'S
Partridge provides a long list of meanings for "Poll," including the two commonest, both of which M. probably intends. In *R*. 40, "Poll" is a parrot, used generically from the seventeenth century. In *W*. 90 the reference to "Poll" in a *Dibdin song signifies nautical use of the word for a woman, especially a harlot.
("Poll" also signifies a wig, a head, a decoy bitch for dog stealing. "Poll parrot" refers to a talkative or gossipy woman. As a verb, "poll" means "plunder," or "fleece.")
R. 40; W. 90

POLLARD, CAPTAIN

Captain George Pollard (1789-1870), in command of *Essex* when she was stove and sunk by a sperm whale, told his version of the story (slightly different from that of Owen Chase, or "*Chace," as M. has it) in *Tyerman and Bennett's *Journal of Voyages and Travels* (2 vols., 1831). Captain Pollard retired from the sea when, on his next voyage out, on *Two Brothers*, his ship hit a coral reef and sank, leaving him in an open boat at sea for several days more.

M.D. 45

POLO, MARCO

The patrician *Venetian Marco Polo (1254-1324) departed in 1271 with a relative on *Papal assignment to the court of Kublai, the Grand *Khan of *Tartary. His accounts of his twenty-four years of adventure (seventeen of them spent in service at court), though questioned in some quarters, were more reliable than most of the romantic "Eastern" romances of the day. They were frequently translated and were also published in *Hakluytus Posthumus, or *Purchas His Pilgrimes . . .* (1625), a collection of Hakluyt's unpublished materials.

M. 75

POLONIUS

The loquacious father of "Ophelia" and "*Laertes," in *Shakespeare's *Hamlet*. He is killed by "Hamlet" while spying on the Prince.

See also "The friends thou hast . . . ," in "Quotations" section.

C.M. 30

POLYNESIA;   POLYNESIAN, --S;   POLYNESIAN ARCHIPELAGO

The Greek word for "many islands," Polynesia refers to one of the three main divisions of isles of Oceania in the central and south-eastern *Pacific Ocean: an area of about 10,000 square miles. It includes the *Hawaiian, *Ellice, Phoenix and Tokelau groups, and *Samoa, *Tonga, the *Cook and Line Islands, French Polynesia (*Society, Windward, and Leeward Islands, Tuamotu Archipelago, Gambier Islands, Tubuai [Austral] Islands, *Marquesas and Clipperton Island), Easter Island and *New Zealand.

These are mostly summits of high volcanic mountains, with some low coral islands, all poor in mineral resources. Ethnologically, but not geographically, the area includes New

Zealand, whose Maori (see "*Mowree*") inhabitants come from the Polynesian stock, a mixture of Negroid, Mongoloid, and *Caucasian.

Parts of Polynesia, notably Tonga and Samoa, were settled soon after Fiji (see "Feegee . . . . "), around 1300 B.C. By A.D. 300, the Samoans had settled the Marquesas, which became between A.D. 400 and 850 a dispersal center for settlers, domesticated plants and animals, tools, fishing gear, and ornaments, to other islands in the area. The Hawaiian Islands are known to have been occupied around A.D. 400, the Society Islands by 800, the Southern Cooks and New Zealand by 850. All the other major islands were settled by 1300.

Early voyages of discovery include the 1721-22 circumnavigation of *Dutch admiral Jacob Roggeveen, which touched upon Easter Island and some of the Samoan group; the circumnavigation of *English navigator *Samuel Wallis, which discovered the Society Islands (*Tahiti), encouraging hopes of a habitable southern continent; *Cook's three voyages: 1768-71 circumnavigation which charted the coasts of New Zealand, explored the east coast of Australia, confirmed the existence of Torres Strait; 1772-75 circumnavigation which made the circuit of the southern oceans in high latitudes, charted *New Hebrides, discovered many islands, but ended the hope of a habitable continent; Cook/Clerke 1776-80 expedition's discovery of the *Sandwich Islands (Hawaii), explored much of the west coast of North America, and ended the hope of a navigable passage through the *Arctic to the *Atlantic.

The eighteenth century was the "Silver Age of Discovery," as much seeking scientific lore as commercial advantage. Voyages were now organized by governments, rather than by private interests, but the main aims remained discovery of a southern continent as suggested by *Ptolemy, Ortelius, and others, as well as a strait between northeast *Asia and northwest America. These were of course failures, and instead islands were discovered, New Zealand's insularity established and coasts charted, and the general configuration of American and Asian coasts of the North Pacific were revealed. Furthermore, these voyages eventually solved the problem of keeping mariners healthy.

Polynesian religious and cultural practices horrified nineteenth-century missionaries. Infanticide was commonly practiced in the Sandwich Islands. The Reverend Hiram Bingham describes a form of shark-worship involving the feeding of one's infant to a shark, which thereafter becomes a harmless friend.

T. Passim; O. Passim; M. Passim; R. 34; W. 28; W. 50; M.D. 24; M.D. 54; M.D. 115; C.M. 26 and elsewhere

POLYNESIA: OR AN HISTORICAL ACCOUNT OF THE
PRINCIPAL ISLANDS OF THE SOUTH SEA: BY THE
RIGHT REV. M. RUSSELL, L.L.D.
The *Harpers' Family Library* edition was published in
*Edinburgh in 1845.
O. 48

"POLYNESIAN RESEARCHES"
See "Ellis, --'s."
T. 1; O. Preface; O. 48

POLYP
A simple gelatinous sea animal with a tentacled mouth;
a zoophyte formerly thought of as a plant.
M. 155

POMARE, --S; POMAREE, --S
M. is basically correct in his comments about *Tahiti's
rulers, albeit with some anachronism and misassignment of
details about the Pomaré family. His information (or misinformation) came from *Beechey, *Cook, Lucett, *Olmsted,
*Stewart, *Wheeler, and *Wilkes.
"Otoo" (O. 61; O. 80) was really Tu (M. follows *Ellis's
error). The eighteenth-century king of Tahiti's larger peninsula was also called "Mate," "Taina," or "Vairaatoa." He had
his name changed to Pomaré, according to Ellis, when he had
a cold; in Tahitian, "po" means "night," and "mare" means
"cough." Tu liked the sound of the words and changed his
name to what became the royal patronymic. There is much
about Tu in Volume I of Cook's *Voyage of the Endeavor: 1768-
1771.* Tu is "the first Tahitian Pomaree" of *M.* 149, "the first
Pomaree" of *O.* 55 and *O.* 69.
"Pomaree II," of *O.* 49 and *O.* 80, reigned from 1803 to
1821 (or 1824). He became a *Christian in 1812. (M. makes his
father a convert, in *O.* 55). A regency of some years followed
his reign.
Pomaree III (*O.* 80) succeeded as an infant, reigning
nominally from 1824 to 1827.
Queen Pomaré IV is M.'s "Pomaree Vahinee I" (*O.* 80,
or "Queen Pomaree" (*O.* 80) or "Aimatá" (*O.* 80); most of M.'s
allusions to "Pomare" are to her. The queen was the sister of
Pomaré III. She was born in 1813 and "ruled" a licentious and
lawless court from 1827 to 1877. She was forced to cede Tahiti
to the French in 1842. The Queen's real name was Aimata,
which means "eye-eater" in Tahitian, the eye being the portion

offered to the ruler upon human sacrifice. She was nine years old when she married the son of the old chief of Taha'a (see "Tahar"); they divored and he became Tapoa II, of *Borabora and Taha'a. Her second husband's real name was Ariifaite, but as M. notes in *O.* 68, he was called "Pot Belly" (Aboo-rai, or "big belly," in Tahitian), or "*Pomaree-Tanee" (or merely "Tanee"), signifying a male ruler rather than "Pomaree's man" (*O.* 80). M. is in error about his background; he was chief of Huaheine and Raiatea (see "Raitair"). He was about sixteen years old at the time of his marriage to the Queen, who was at least ten years older. Although his submissiveness to Pomaré's violence is confirmed by M.'s sources, "Tanee" apparently became more dominant as he aged. The Queen's turning laundress to sailors is likewise confirmed.

(Pomaré V was the son of Queen Pomaré; he abdicated in 1880.)

T. 3; O. Passim; M. 149; W. 50

"POMAREE-TANEE"

In *Tahitian, "Pomare-tane" does not mean "Pomaree's man." It refers to a ruler of the masculine sex, as "Pomare-Vahine" refers to one of the feminine.

O. 80

POMONA

The *Roman, not *Greek, goddess of fruits and fruit trees (L. *pomum*—ruit, or fruit tree). Pomona did not love wild woods; she kept herself from men, perfecting the gardener's arts. Vertumnus, later god of seasons, gardens, and orchards, disguised himself as an old woman, kissed her passionately and, promising to work with her, dropped his disguise, whereupon Pomona yielded to his beauty and eloquence. They married and thereafter gardened together. Pomona and Vertumnus began as Numina, powers protecting orchards and gardens, and were later personified.

M. 181

POMOTU

The coral Paumotu (*Tahitian for "Submissive") Islands were so named by *Tahitians who visited them, having finally charted the Tuamotu ("Dangerous") archipelago of which they make a part.

O. 6; O. 17

POMPEII

The ancient city of southern *Italy's Campania lies in ruins near the southern foot of *Vesuvius, fourteen miles southeast of *Naples. It was founded in the late sixth or early fifth century B.C., by *Hercules, according to *Greek legend. It was a *Roman colony by 80 B.C. Earthquakes starting in A.D. 63 preceded the volcano's first recorded eruption in A.D. 79. The city was buried under twenty feet of pumice, cinders, and ashes. Some 2,000 people (perhaps 10% of the population) were killed, among them *Pliny.

The site was rediscovered in 1748; excavation starting in 1763 revealed well preserved ruins surrounded by two miles of walls enclosing wide lava-paved streets, two-storey houses, richly decorated mansions (including that of *Pansa), temples, a theater seating up to 5,000 persons and an amphitheater seating 20,000.

A depressed M. visited on 18 February 1857, when about one-quarter of the ruins had been cleared. He commented in his journal: "Pompeii like any other town. Same old humanity. All the same weather [whether] one be dead or alive." The volcano had erupted in 1855 and would do so again in 1858, so the crater might have been active when M. made the ascent.
R. 31; R. 46; I.P. 24

POMPEY, GREAT

Gnaeus Pompeius Magnus (106-48 B.C.), *Cicero's contemporary, rose to power from an originally *plebeian *Roman family. As a military commander, he conquered Mithradates VI, earning the title "Magnus" bestowed by Sulla (see "Sylla"), his step-father-in-law and later enemy. After defeating the last of *Spartacus's army, he was elected co-consul, with *Crassus. He made sweeping changes in the area of his conquests and later as consul was an isolated, unpopular, and suspected ruler. His fourth wife was the daughter of *Julius Caesar, but after her death they become enemies. He then married Cornelia, whose life was praised in a play of that name (pub. 1594), later known as *Pompey the Great, his faire Corneliaes Tragedie*. He fled to *Egypt and was murdered after Caesar's invasion of *Italy. Caesar Augustus later praised his adherence to constitutionality.
M. 181

POMPEY'S PILLAR

A mis-named red granite Corinthian column at *Alexandria, Egypt, recording its conquest in 296. There is no known connection with *Pompey.

M. saw the column on 27 December 1856, noting in his journal that the Pillar contributed to the panorama-like unreality of *Egypt.
M. 75; R. 41; M.D. 103

POMUM ADAMI

The familiar "Adam's apple," a vertical projection in the middle of the neck, most prominent in mature males, is the result of enlargement of the cartilages of the larynx, especially the thyroid.
W. 63

PONCE DE LEON'S

The *Spanish explorer Juan Ponce de León (1460-1521) sailed with *Columbus in 1493. He explored and settled Puerto Rico (see "Porto Rico") and was sent to search for a legendary Fountain of Youth on Bimini Island, Bahamas, in the process discovering *Florida in 1513. He became Governor of the area and crusaded against the Carib Indians of Trinidad, which he occupied. He was mortally wounded in an attack on Florida Indians and died in *Havana, never having discovered the fountain which was to restore youth.
M. 63

"PONCHO," --S

An article in *Harper's New Monthy Magazine*, "Lima and the Limanians," describes this garment:

> . . . a large fringed shawl with an opening in the centre, through which the head of the wearer passes; it then hangs gracefully over the shoulder, and falls nearly to the knee, leaving the hands and arms less embarrassed than any other species of cloak. These ponchos frequently display great brilliancy and variety; the color is often a snowy white, sometimes it is richly and fancifully embroidered; but the prevailing taste is for broad stripes of brilliant colors, such as orange, scarlet, blue, green, rose color, or combinations of all hues intermingled and diversified in every conceivable manner.

O. 61; M.D. 3

PONTIFF
        See "Pope . . . . "
M. 114; P. 14:1

PONT NEUF
        Despite its name ("New Bridge"), Pont Neuf is the oldest
bridge in *Paris, built in 1607: the first in the city that was
paved and without houses lining it. Pont Neuf runs from Quai
du *Louvre to Quai des Grands Augustins, crossing the western tip of Ile de la Cité to join the Right Bank to the Left. Running south from it is *Rue Dauphine. M. walked across Pont
Neuf on 3 December 1849, as his journal shows.
I.P. 7; I.P. 9

PONTOPPIDAN, BISHOP
        *John Knox, in *A New Collection of Voyages* (1767),
quotes Erik Pontoppidan's description in *Natural History of
Norway* (1752-1753) of a sea monster a mile and a half in circumference: *kraken, which at first glance appears to be a
group of sea-weedy islands.
M.D. 59

POOFAI
        Paofai was one of the *Tahitian chiefs whose forebears
had been dethroned by *Pomare I. *Wilkes (II, 18, 19) discusses their ambition and their vices, Paofai's being
"covetousness, and a propensity to intrigue."
O. 32; O. 45; O. 80

"POONJA"
        The oil referred to is "poon," from an East Indian tree of
the St. Johnswort family, genus *Calophyllum*. The seeds yield
the bitter oil used in ships and for cabinet work.
R. 34

POOR-HOUSE
        The *British Workhouse system for the poor was insti-
tuted in the early seventeenth century. In *America, the Plymouth colonists followed suit, putting able-bodied adults to
work, apprenticing children, and providing "humane" care in
"poor houses" for the disabled and the aged. The American
Workhouse system of poor laws passed into local administration, and by the nineteenth century a recipient had to have less

income than that provided by the lowest-paying job in the
community, but he was not to be paid so much as he could earn
at that job. The Poor Law Amendment Act of 1834 reordered
the British system severely in an attempt to force a multitude of
recipients onto the labor market; critics of the Act were accused of sentimentality.

(One of Will Carleton's [1845-1912] *Farm Ballads* [1873]
included the poem: "Over the Hill to the Poor House.")
P. 20:1

"POOROO"
    The large *Tahitian leaves referred to are "purau."
O. 68

'POOR RICHARD'; POOR RICHARD'S ALMANAC;
    See "Franklin, Benjamin . . . . "
I.P. 7; I.P. 8; I.P. 9; I.P. 11

POPAYAN
    Popayán is a city of southwestern Colombia, at the foot of
Puracé Volcano. Founded in 1536, it became a center of colonial trade and academic and religious life, as well as the site of
a mint, as noted in *M.D.* 99.
M.D. 99

POPE, --'S; PAPAL; PAPIST; PONTIFF; DIVINE PONTIFF
    The head of the Roman *Catholic Church, the Pope is
the Bishop of *Rome, in a line that has existed since the Roman Empire. First Pope was St. Peter. By M.'s time, the Papal throne had seated saintly and productive Popes, as well as
corrupt villains, in positions of great power and great vulnerability. Popes of M.'s time included Pius VII (1800-23), Leo XII
(1823-29), Pius VIII (1829-30), Gregory XVI (1831-46), Pius IX
(1846-78), Leo XII (1878-1903).
    Great strides were made during this time toward liber-
alization and democratization of the Church, but not such that
many Americans were willing to think fondly of the Pope.
    The allusion in *M.D.* 36 refers to the ceremony on Holy
Thursday (before Easter), at which the Pope imitates *Christ's
washing of the feet of the *Apostles (*John 13:1-17).
O. 32; M. 114; M. 149; R. 28; W. 31; W. 50; M.D. 36; M.D. 95;
P. 14:1; P. 18:2; C.M. 2; C.M. 26 and elsewhere

POPE, ALEXANDER

Alexander Pope (1688-1744) was born into a *London family of Roman *Catholic workers; he was a sickly child with permanently stunted growth, who educated himself (university being denied to Catholics) and who was writing serious poetry by his early teens. Association with poet/playwright William Wycherley (1641-1715), whose works Pope revised, led to entry into *Addison's and then Swift's circles. His *Essay on Criticism* (1711) and *The Rape of the Lock* (1711, 1714; quoted in *M.D.* "Extracts" 36), as well as his translation of the *Iliad* were much admired by *Coleridge and others; this translation, along with that of the *Odyssey* (1725-6), brought financial independence. Like many others who found Pope's work stiltedly Neo-Classic in style, M. preferred *Chapman's translations of *Homer.

Pope wrote only two poems about love, perhaps inspired by his "friendships" with Martha Blount (1690-1762), to whom he dedicated *Epistle . . . on the Characters of Women*, in *Moral Essays* (1731-5), and with lady Mary Wortley Montagu (1689-1762), with whom he later quarrelled. He wrote one play with John Gay (1685-1732), as well as numerous satires, including *Epistle to Dr. Arbuthnot* (1735) and the *Dunciad* (anonymously, starting in 1728; published in full in 1743). He wrote many minor works, as well as moral and philosophical poems in epistle form, frequently denying responsibility for his bad-tempered works directed at critics who (like M.) considered his work artificial. Pope was more a reflector of his times than a thinker, and more a stylist than a poet, producing compact and clear expression. A determined and independent craftsman of precise and vivid English, he was interested in "correctness," orthodoxy, and tradition.

The mock-heroic *The Rape of the Lock* remains the most popular of his writings; it is based on an actual event wherein two families overreacted to a youth's snipping of a lock of hair from the head of a young lady.

Sealts #405 is *The Poetical Works . . . with a Life*, by Rev. Alexander Dyce . . . Boston, Little, Brown, 1856; 3 vols. #147. *Harper Classical Library*, vols. 20, 21 (Ovid) and vols. 32-34 (Homer), contain Pope's translations.

See also "Extracts" 36, and "Quotations" section, "'Happy, thrice happy . . . '."
M.D. 99

POPE'S HEAD

A head of frizzled hair, like the large round brush called a Pope's head, used for washing windows.
O. 65; R. 17

POPINJAY
An old name for a parrot (originally Arabic, then Gr. *papagos*), popinjay came to signify a conceited and stupid fop. In *Britain, the Festival of the Popinjay occurred on the first Sunday in May. "Captain Popinjay" was the man who won the day's target practice at a parrot.
C.M. 24

POPOCATEPETL
The *Aztec "smoking mountain" is a (presumably) dormant volcano, 17,887 feet in altitude; it is located in central *Mexico, forty-five miles southeast of Mexico City. The snow-capped, symmetrically coned volcano last erupted in 1702; its huge crater still smokes. Popocatepetl was first ascended in 1519, by one of Cortés's (see "Cortez") men.
The "panthers" (*M*. 158) at the base are pumas: often called "Panthers," or "painters."
M. 158

PORPHEERO
M.'s fictional equivalent of Europe.   See "Porphyro-genitus."
M. 145

PORPHYROGENITUS
Lat. for "porphyrogenite": one born royal, "born to the purple." Originally, the word designated one born into the royal family of *Constantinople in a chamber called the *Porphyra*, the origin of which is disputed.
P. Dedication

PORT; P.W.; OPORTO
True port is a dessert wine produced in *Oporto, *Portugal, where it results from special grapes grown in special soil. It may have brandy added to the mash, but true vintage port is not blended or fortified. All port is very long in maturation.
Much inferior or bogus port wine was consumed during M.'s time, when it was, along with sherry, a highly popular and affordable drink (as shown in "the Cosmopolitan's" recognition of what "P.W." means, in *C.M.* 29).
O. 58; R. 29; R. 54; W. 2: W. 30; W. 37 (Oporto); W. 42; P. 3:3; P. 22:1; C.M. 29 (P.W.)

PORTER; CAPTAIN PORTER; COMMODORE PORTER; COMMODORE DAVID PORTER

David Porter (1780-43), commander of the frigate *Essex during the *War of 1812, was born in *Boston, *Massachusetts, son of an *American Revolutionary War naval officer. His adventures began before he entered the *Navy in 1798; accompanying his father on three voyages, he was impressed by the *British navy, but escaped. *Midshipman on Constellation at its defeat of Insurgente, he was promoted to lieutenant and saw much action against the *French. During the Tripoli war (see "Barbary"), as first lieutenant of Philadelphia, he was imprisoned after the ship grounded, was later made master commandant, then captain for his service against French privateers. On Essex's famous voyage, he captured the sloop, Alert, first British war vessel taken in the *War of 1812. Rounding Cape *Horn without orders, he took possession of *Nukahiva in 1813. Defeated by the British in 1814, he held administrative posts until 1823, when he commanded a West Indies squadron suppressing *piracy. After a misunderstanding with *Spanish authorities at Puerto Rico (see "Porto Rico"), he was court-martialed and suspended, after which he resigned (in 1826), becoming commander-in-chief of the Mexican navy against Spain. He later served as a diplomat for *President *Andrew Jackson. His writings include Journal of a Cruise Made to the Pacific Ocean in the U.S. Frigate Essex, in the Years 1812, 1813, and 1814 (2 vols., 1815), and Contantinople and Its Environs (1835). Memoir of Commodore David Porter (1875) was published by his son, Admiral David D. Porter.

The Journal is one of M.'s most important sources, especially in the early works. Despite disclaimer, M.'s descriptions of Porter's Nukahiva experience are relatively accurate transcriptions.

Porter, called "the first American imperialist" for his *Marquesan takeover, originally was to harass British shipping in the area. His violation of the islands was not sponsored by the United States. Seeking to force civilization on the natives, he devastated the "Typee" valley, despite his great admiration of Marquesan accomplishments in architecture, war, and navigation. An Enlightenment man, Porter wished to stimulate Marquesan rational capabilities rather than raise morals.

T. 1; T. 2; T. 4; T. 25; T. 27

"PORT FOR MEN..."

*Samuel Johnson: "*Claret is the liquor for boys; *port for men; but he who aspires to be a hero must drink brandy" (Boswell's *Life of Johnson*, April 7, 1779; Sealts #84).
W. 54

PORTIA

The heiress/heroine of *Shakespeare's *The Merchant of Venice*. (Another "Portia" is the wife of *Brutus, in *Julius Caesar*.)
See also "Belmont."
R. 46

PORTLAND

The Isle of Portland is a peninsula on the coast of Dorset, the source of the stone used in many of *England's most famous buildings. The area contains a famous prison, and castles of *Henry VIII and *William Penn. The southern tip, Portland Bill, is famous for its caves and for Pulpit Rock: "The *Gibralter of Wessex." M. visited on 2 November 1849, commenting in his journal: "Melancholy looking voyage, white cliffs indeed!" The famous breakwater was under construction at the time of his visit.
P. 1:3

PORT MAHON

See "Mahon."
W. 65

PORTMANTEAUS

Artificial words made of parts of others, espressing the denoted combination, as in Lewis Carroll's use of "Slithy" for "lithe and slimy" in *Through the Looking Glass* (1871).
M. 5

PORTO RICO

The *West Indies island is the smallest (100 by 35 miles) and easternmost of the Greater *Antilles. The *Arawak Indians called it "Boriquén," or "Borinquén," before *Columbus arrived in 1493. It was settled fifteen years later by Juan *Ponce de Léon, who named it Porto Rico ("Puerto" since 1932). San Juan became the capital in 1521. Black *slave labor was introduced when the native population was almost completely wiped out in the beginning of the sixteenth century.

The "Gibralter of the *Caribbean" was a *Spanish stronghold, attacked unsuccessfully by the *British (under *Drake), the *Dutch, and the *French. The independence movement began in the 1820's; slavery continued until 1873. (Porto Rico did not become free from Spain until 1898, at which time it was ceded to the *United States.)
I.P. 2

PORTSMOUTH

Portsmouth, in Hampshire, is the major naval base of *England. The area, which encompasses Portsea Island, has a harbor opening into *Spithead. It is heavily fortified and laden with museums, offices, and docks, including the Royal Dockyard (known colloquially as "*Pompey"), as well as *Lord Nelson's H.M.S. *Victory, and Dickens's (see "Hard Times") birthplace. M. visited on 25 December 1849, at a time when the outskirts of the area, "Point," was a rowdy sailor hangout.
O. 27; R. 9; R. 18; W. 92; I.P. 3; I.P. 13

PORTSMOUTH

*New Hampshire's only seaport is in the southeastern part of the state, at the mouth of the *Piscataqua River, opposite Kittery, *Maine. It was established in 1623, incorporated as Portsmouth Town in 1653, and as a city in 1849. Portsmouth was important as a port and in shipbuilding in the eighteenth and nineteenth centuries. *Ranger was built here in 1777; *John Paul Jones's residence is preserved. The Portsmouth Naval Base was established c. 1794.
W. 79; W. 82

PORTUGAL; PORTUGUESE

Portugal occupies the western part of the Iberian peninsula; it is bounded by the *Atlantic Ocean and by *Spain on the mainland, but it includes the *Azores and *Madeira islands, as well. The mainland portion is c. 360 miles long and 125 miles wide; the *Tagus River divides it into halves.

The *Romans settled Portugal in the second and first centuries B.C., combining it with parts of Spain to form "Lusitania." It was invaded later by *Germans, Visogoths (see "Goths"), and *Moors, but Ferdinand I of *Castile made inroads in the tenth century. Portuguese history proper begins with independence in 1140. After many dynastic wars, John I brought Portugal to its period of glory. His son, Henry the Navigator, explored the *African coast; *Diaz rounded the Cape of *Good hope, and da *Gama found a route to *India in the late fifteenth century. Pedro Alvares Cabral discovered *Brazil and other eventual possessions in *Asia, *Africa, and the Americas, and the nation enjoyed great commercial success until the late sixteenth century (when *Camöens was writing), when much was lost to the *Dutch and the Spanish. Under John IV, Portugal became allied to *England, in 1640. The eighteenth century brought wars and dictatorships, as well as a massive earthquake in the capital city of *Lisbon (1755).

The royal *Braganza family fled to Brazil after *Napoléon's conquest (1807), establishing *Rio de Janeiro. King Pedro I (elder son of John VI) returned in 1820; wars and dictatorships that followed lasted well beyond M.'s lifetime.

Among Portugueses colonies are parts of *India, *Guinea, and *Timor, as well as *Macao, *Cape Verde Islands, Angola, *Mozambique. See also "Cape St. Vincent," "Pedro II," "Oporto," "Serra da Estrêla."
O. 12; O. 22; O. 65; R. 12; R. 50; W. 12; W. 25; W. 50; W. 54; W. 56; W. 69; W. 71; M.D. 40; M.D. 41; M.D. 58; M.D. 83

"...PORTUGUESE DIAMOND"

I have not discovered reference to a particular diamond, but Williams's edition of *Anson's voyage (pp. 60-64) tells of the *Portuguese rape of *Brazilian diamonds, said to be so plentiful that they were sitting about in the dirt.
W. 56

PORUS, KING; KING PORUS'S ELEPHANTS

King Porus was defeated by *Alexander the Great at the river Hydaspes, 327 B.C. M. might have read William Mitford's *History of Greece* (London, 1838), which describes the rout in which the wounded elephants turned wild, injuring even their keepers, then withdrew completely, in unison.
M.D. 87; M.D. 105

POST-OFFICE; POSTMASTER

The Post Office Department of M.'s time was the center of the political patronage system of the *United States. The cabinet-level Postmaster was informal patronage chief. (The system was not reorganized into the U.S. Postal Service until 1970.) Thus, many of M.'s references to the Post Office or the Postmaster may have political implications. One of the ironies of M.'s short story, "Bartleby the Scrivener," is the fact that the narrator/employer has lost a patronage position (Master in

Chancery), and his erstwhile clerk, "Bartleby," has been re-moved from the *Washington Post Office's Dead Letter Office by a change in the administration; only one of the two men manages to survive the effects of political corruption.
Passim

POTIPHAR'S WIFE

The story of *Joseph and Potiphar's wife is contained in *Genesis 39. "Potiphar" is *Hebrew for "an *Egyptian."
R. 17

POTTERS' FIELDS

In *Matthew 27:6-10, the thirty pieces of siver that *Judas returned after his betrayal of Christ were used to buy a potter's field for burial of the poor: "The Field of Blood."
M.D. 111

POTTOWOTTAMIE SACHEM

The Pottowattamies, an Algonquin tribe related to the *Pequods, were originally from western *New York state. They were located on a Kansas reservation when Francis Parkman saw them in the 1840's. They wore scalp locks in-terwoven with feathers, pictures of which M. might have seen in periodicals of his day.
M.D. 16

POVELSON

Olafsen ("Olasson") and Povelson's Travels in *Iceland (London, 1805) is mentioned in *Beale's work, which M. used as a source for M.D.
M.D. 41

POVERTIRESQUE, --LY

Contemporary reviewers complained elaborately about such neologisms as "povertiresque" for "picturesque" poverty. Probably M. was attempting in this new word to articulate ironically the subject matter of painters such as *Gainsborough and poets such as *Wordsworth, and the Hud-son River School of art.
P. 20:1

POWHATTAN
The Powhatan Indians, an Algonquin confederacy, took their name from their great chief, the father of *Pocahontas and peace-maker with whites.   After Powhatan's death in 1618, his successor, Opechancanough, led the tribes in four- teen years of destruction of every white settlement except those around Jamestown.   The confederacy was broken up upon Opechancanough's execution in 1641, but a few thousand Powhatan people remain along the *Virginia coast today.
M. 181

PRAETORIANS
The household troops of the *Roman emperors came into existence in the second century B.C.   Their numbers were greatly increased after the Battle of Philippi, when 8,000 veter- ans refusing discharge were shared by Mark *Antony and Oc- tavian (later *Augustus Caesar).   *Tiberius concentrated their force and *Caligula increased their numbers further.   They were highly paid foot soldiers, often recruited from *Italy, who served at the imperial palace but not as personal bodyguards. They were used in foreign wars, as occasional policemen, and were involved in many sensational incidents.   *Diocletian re- duced their numbers, and Constantine (see "Constantinople") finally disbanded them in A.D. 312.
In *M.D.* M. errs in his claim that wealthy Praetorians could buy the Roman Empire.   But the powerful guard often chose the emperor and once even auctioned the office.
M.D. 108

PRAIRIES
In keeping with current fashion, M. visited *Illinois, "The Prairie State" in summer of 1840.   His uncle, Thomas Melville, formerly of Broadhall (*Pittsfield, Massachusetts), lived at Galena, at that time "the West."
M.D. 1; M.D. 42 and elsewhere

PRAISE-GOD-BAREBONES
See "Barbon, Praise-God."
C.M. 22

PRARIES
See "Prairies."
M.D. 42

PRATTICA   MANUALE   DELL'ARTIGLIERIA
Prattica Manuale di Artiglieria, by Luigi Colliado, 1606--
mentioned in *Penny Cyclopaedia*'s extensive article on gunnery (XI, 1838).
W. 83

PRAYA GRANDE
*Rev. Stewart was much taken with this place, which
was like *Oahu, except "in the charm, which the evidences of
taste and improvement ...threw over it" (Vol I, Letter 1, p. 51).
Always approving the blandishments of civilization, Stewart
adds, "It is less wild and lofty in its general features," by
virtue of the "plantation in all the luxuriance of artificial improvement."
W. 43

PRAYS DO FLAMINGO
Praia Flamengo lies on a broad sweep of Guanabara
Bay, *Rio de Janeiro; it is now taken up by a highway, a park,
and beach recreation area.
W. 39

PRE-ADAMITE
Before the time of *Adam.
M.D. 104

PREBLE
Edward Preble (1761-1807) commanded U.S. *Navy
*Mediterranean operations during the *Barbary Wars.
"Preble's Boys," including *Stephen Decatur, fired
Philadelphia when she ran aground off Tripoli (16 February
1804). Preble is credited with developing the esprit de corps of
the naval officer corps. He had served in the *American Revo-
lutionary War and spent fifteen years in the Merchant Service
before joining the Navy. He was Captain of *Essex* in the
*Pacific Command Third Squadron, with *Constitution* as
flagship. In 1805, he retired to shipbuilding in *Maine.
See also "*Commodore Preble*."
M.D. Extracts 20

PREDESTINARIANS
See "Predestination."
M. 123

PREDESTINATION

The doctrine that *God has chosen those whom he intends to save from damnation in hell has its origins in the words of *St. Paul:

> For those whom he foreknew he also predestined to be conformed to the image of his Son, in order that he might be the first-born among many brethren. And those whom he predestined he also called; and those whom he called he also justified; and those whom he justified he also glorified (Romans 8:29-30).

There are three basic strains of predestinarian doctrine. M.'s background would have taught the kind identified with *Calvin: "double" predestination, in which God will save whom he will regardless of men's acts or beliefs. The type associated with Semi-Pelagianism and Arminianism teaches that God saves those whose faith and merits he knew beforehand. The third, identified with *Saint Augustine and *Luther, ascribes salvation to God's unmerited grace but attributes divine reprobation to man's guilt.

See also "Determinism" and "Fatalism."
M. 145

PREFACE TO GONDIBERT

See "Davenant, Sir William," and "Extracts" 18.
M.D. Extracts 18

PREISSNITZ

According to *Nature in Disease, Vincent Preissnitz (1799-1851), Silesian water-cure operator, "died of premature disease at the age of fifty-two, in the midst of his own water-cure."
C.M. 16

PRESBYTERIAN

M.D.'s reference is to general theological doctrine derived from *Calvin. M. was baptized in the *Dutch Reformed church of his mother's family; his father was a Unitarian; M., his wife, and children belonged to the *Episcopal Church, and then the Unitarian. Of those faiths, only the Unitarian could be considered liberal, as opposed to "Presbyterian."
M.D. 10; M.D. 17

PRESIDENT, THE
   President, which started out as a forty-four-gun
*American frigate, proudly carried Commodore John Rodgers
in 1812 but was forced to surrender to the *British off the Cape
of *Good Hope in 1815. *President*, under *Stephen Decatur,
had bottomed out in the harbor and was so damaged that she
was overtaken by the British force and *Decatur finally surrendered.
   M. links her to *Macedonian*, a British ship turned-
American.
W. 64

PRESIDENT, THE
   The *President referred to in W. is John Tyler, Presi-
dent from 1841 to 1844. He was not the sailor's favorite.
Among his other gaffes, in 1842 Tyler reinstated Uriah Levy,
an Admiral dismissed for administering illegal punishment.
If he is "luffing up into the wind," Tyler is talking political hot
air.
W. 91

PRESIDENT OF THE UNITED STATES; PRESIDENT OF THE
UNION; PRESIDENCY
   The office of President of the United States was created to
resemble a monarchy in many respects. The President is the
"Chief of State," who presides over his Cabinet, manages the
Executive Branch, and exercises control over his political allies
in the *Congress. He has the power to make treaties, appoint
ambassadors and Cabinet officers, Judges of Federal Courts
(with the advice and consent of the *Senate); he is Commander
in Chief of the Armed Forces, and is removeable only by impeachment. By M.'s time, Congress had so exercised its powers that the Presidency often seemed honorary. (Even
*Washington's few attempts at direct contact with Congress
had ended in frustrated avowal never to appeal in person
again.) *Jackson broke the pattern somewhat.
   The President had little contact with the people and, until *Lincoln's time, almost never exerted supreme power. Few
beyond the earliest Presidents were re-elected. Many of them
were elected on the strength of their military feats. Among
M.'s unsigned works are satiric "Authentic Anecdotes" (in
Yankee Doodle) about *Mexican War hero Zachary Taylor (who
died after one year in office). M.'s family supported
*Democratic candidates for the Presidency. His contempo-
raries (such as *Hawthorne) secured political-plum positions
by writing flattering campaign biographies. But despite his

family's encouragement, M.'s political ambition appears to have been lukewarm at best, and his devotion to what he saw as "truth" kept him from pursuing plums through puffery.

Presidents during M.'s lifetime: (following Washington, Adams, *Jefferson, Madison):

James Monroe (1758-1831): Democratic-Republican, 1817-25.

John Quincy Adams (1767-1848): National Republican, 1825-29.

Andrew Jackson (1767-1845): Democrat, 1829-37.

Martin Van Buren (1782-1862): Democrat, 1837-41.

*William Henry Harrison (1773-1841): *Whig, 1841-41.

John Tyler (1790-1862): Whig, 1841-45.

*James K. Polk (1795-1849): Democrat, 1845-49.

Zachary Taylor (1784-1850): Whig, 1849-50.

Millard Fillmore (1800-1874): Whig, 1850-53.

Franklin Pierce (1804-69): Democrat, 1853-57.

James Buchanan (1791-1868): Democrat, 1857-61.

*Abraham Lincoln (1809-1865): *Republican (switched from Whig), 1861-65.

Andrew Johnson (1808-75): Republican, 1865-69.

Ulysses S. Grant (1822-85): Republican, 1869-77.

Rutherford B. Hayes (1822-93): Republican, 1877-81.

James A. Garfield (1831-81): Republican, 1881-81.

Chester A. Arthur (1830-86): Republican, 1881-85.

Grover Cleveland (1837-1908): Democrat, 1885-89.

Benjamin Harrison (1833-1901): Republican, 1889-93.

W. 27; W. 42; W. 44; W. 70; W. 91; P. 5:4; C.M. 21 and elsewhere

PRESTON

The port city of Lancashire, *England, is twenty-one miles south-southeast of Lancaster. A trade center and market since ancient times, it burgeoned as a result of the cotton industry. Preston was the site of Royalist headquarters during the English Civil War. By the eighteenth century, it had earned the epithet "proud," for its fashionable society.

M.'s father, Allan Melvill (see "Walter Redburn"), is known to have visited in 1811.
R. 30

PRIESTLEY ON NECESSITY

Joseph Priestley (1733-1804), chemist, dissenting British clergyman, and esteemed radical thinker, published extensively on the history of science, his own experiments, theology, grammar, biography, education, government, and psychology. His fame in *England arose from his contributions to the study of gases. Encouraged by *Benjamin Franklin, Antoine Lavoisier and others, he might have remained purely a respectable scientist in England, but his radical politics and philosophy, particularly his support of the French Revolution brought mob violence against him, so that in 1794 he fled to *America, to remain until death.   M.'s main interest is in Priestley's influence on *Bentham's development of *Utilitarianism. Priestley rejected the idea of free will, but saw the real goal of Christianity as encouragement of "virtuous living," patterned after the behavior of *Jesus, whose divinity he rejected.

Among his publications: *Essay on the First Principles of Government* (1768), defending laissez-faire theories; *The Doctrine of Philosophical Necessity* (1777); *Disquisitions Relating to Matter and Spirit* (1777); *History of the Corruptions of Christianity* (1782).
M. 2

PRIME MINISTER

First minister of the *British Crown; the Premier (From French *premier ministre*).
R. 29

PRIMROSE-HILL

The early nineteenth-century dueling place across from the Zoological Gardens north of Regent's Park in *London was commented upon in M.'s *Journal* entry for 15 November 1849. The view towards Hampstead was of green countryside, but "cityward it was like a view of hell from *Abraham's bosom," with "clouds of smoke."
C.M. 24

PRIMUM MOBILE

Lat.: the first moving thing. In the *Ptolemaic astronomy system, the *primum mobile* was the ninth or tenth sphere, revolving around the earth every twenty-four hours, drawing the other spheres with it. Beyond it was *God's seat, the empyrean. *Milton (*Paradise Lost*, iii, 483) and *Sir Thomas Browne (*Religio Medici*) refer to it.

In modern use, any machine, idea, or person which moves others.
R. 29

PRINCE OF THE POWERS OF THE AIR
*Ephesians 2:2 gives this title to the *Devil.
M.D. 27

PRINCE OF WALES
At the time of which M. speaks in R. (1839), no one held the title; Edward VII received it in 1841, at one month old. The eldest son of the British sovereign has been called Prince of Wales since 1301, when the future Edward II was so dubbed. The male heir apparent is at birth Duke of Cornwall and receives the Wales title later. The title lapses to the Crown and is renewed at the Sovereign's pleasure.
(A pun, in M.D.)
R. 27; M.D. 12

PRINCE REGENTS
*British princes ruling in place of the legal sovereigns-- sometimes vicariously. George, *Prince of Wales (later *George IV), acted as regent for his father, *George III from 1811 to 1820. In *France, from 1715-1723, the Duke of Orleans was regent for the minor Louis XV (see "Bourbon").
M. 181

PRINCE'S DOCK
*Liverpool's Prince's Dock opened its original eleven and three-quarter acre water area to shipping in 1816 (though not "completed" until 1821). The largest Liverpool dock built to date, it had two locks, each forty-five feet wide, and connection from its own four and one-half acre basin to *George's Dock basin to the south. Ships discharged on its west side and loaded on its east. Its landing stage was in construction at the time of M.'s visit in 1857.
Like most American trading ships to Liverpool, St. Lawrence (see "Highlander") had berthed at Prince's Dock during July of 1839. The Dock Gate area was the demarcation point between the regulated orderliness of the ship and the lawlessness and human degradation of the dock area painted throughout R.
O. 1; R. Passim

PRINCESS AMELIA'S
   See "George III; George the Third."
I.P. 4

PRIORS
   Matthew Prior (1664-1721) was an *English poet, diplomat, and Member of *Parliament. A converted *Tory, in 1718 he suffered imprisonment after the death of *Queen Anne, during which he wrote *Alma, or the Progress of the Mind*, a dialogue ridiculing various philosophies. The same year he published *Solomon on the Vanity of the World*. His earlier (1687) *The Hind and the Panther Transvers'd to the Story of the Country Mouse and the Town Mouse* is a mockery of *Dryden. He also wrote many soliloquies, narratives, burlesque ballads, and essays which were unpublished during M.'s time.
M. 119

PRITCHARD; MRS. PRITCHARD
   George Pritchard (1796-1883), missionary and British consul at *Tahiti, was born in Birmingham, *England and worked for his father, a journeyman brass founder. He became a local preacher and on 27 July 1824 left with his wife on a cargo ship bound for Tahiti, where he was welcomed by Queen *Pomare. In 1837 he was appointed consul for the Georgian, *Society, *Navigator's and Friendly Islands (see "Tonga"). The Tahitian queen's refusal to admit *French priests, *Laval and *Caret, started the quarrel which ended in the French protection (1842) and temporary annexation (1843). In 1838, *Du Petit-Thouars had demanded two thousand Spanish dollars, which Pritchard helped Pomare to pay. Incensed by her treatment and the outrages against the British, Pritchard returned again to England in 1841 to put the case before the government (in 1842 *Charles B. Wilson was acting consul) but returned in 1843 with no guarantees. In February of that year he offered Pomare protection in a British man-of-war, and in 1844 he was seized by French authorities, who claimed he encouraged dissatisfaction; his release was secured only on the condition he never return. At that point, the British government demanded apology and restitution of Pomare's property.
   Pritchard published *The Missionary's Reward, or the Success of the Gospel in the South Pacific* (1844) and *Queen Pomare and her Country* (1878). He left in manuscript "The Aggressions of the French at Tahiti and Other Islands in the Pacific."

Captain Robert Fitzroy's *Narrative of the Surveying Voyage of H.M.S. "Adventure" and "Beagle" ... 1826-1836* (London: 1839) speaks praisingly of Pritchard's stewardship, noting especially his fluency in the language.

Little is known about Mrs. George Pritchard, the former Miss Ayllen of West Meon, Hampshire, other than her constancy. M.'s tale of her intrepid defiance of French orders suggests she partook of her husband's spiritedness. She survived him, as did several children.
T. 3; O. 20; O. 51

PROCLUS

Proculus (A.D. 410-485): Neoplatonist; the principle source of knowledge of *Plato and *Plotinus for the *Middle Ages. He was born in *Constantinople, raised in Xanthas in Lycia, studied under *Plutarch and Syrianus and *Platonic *diadochi* (successors) at *Athens, where he was head of the Platonic Academy until his death.

Proculus represents passionate *paganism and elaborate metaphysical speculation; he was a great systematizer, expositor, and commentator through whose writings Neoplatonic ideas became diffused through the *Byzantine, Islamic, and medieval Latin western worlds. His writings were translated into *Latin, which later indirectly influenced *Christian thought. His most important Arabic work was *Liber de causis*, once thought to be *Aristotle's.
M. 119; C.M. 36

PROCOPIUS

An important *Byzantine historian during the time of *Justinian, Procopius was born at the end of the fifth century A.D. He had legal training and was adviser to *Belisarius, whom he criticized in his writings. He was perhaps prefect of *Constantinople. Procopius wrote prolifically on the wars, the constructions, and the politics of the time. M.'s knowledge of him probably comes from secondary sources: the whale anecdote in *M.D.* from the Kitto *Cyclopedia of Biblical Literature*.
M.D. 45

PROCRUSTEAN BEDS

In *Greek legend, Procrustes is an Attic robber who tortured his prisoners by stretching them or cutting off their legs, to fit his special bed. He was slain by Theseus.
C.M. 15

PRODIGAL, THE; --SON

In *Luke 15:11-32, *Jesus tells the parable of the son who leaves home, wasting his inheritance and his life. His father welcomes him back with feasting, answering the objection of the prodigal's brother: "It was meet that we should make merry, and be glad: for this thy brother was dead, and is alive again; and was lost, and is found."
M. 19; R. 44

PRODROMUS WHALES

This may be an error referring to the kind of whales discussed in Robert Sibbald's "prodromus" or "introduction" (1684) or illustrated in his 1692 book on whales.
See "Sibbald, Scotch."
M.D. 55

PROFANE AND HOLY STATE

See "Fuller, Thomas," and "Extracts" 25.
M.D. Extracts 25

"PROFESSOR, THE"

The actual "professor" of mathematics on *United States during M.'s service was Henry Hayes Lockwood. His brother, John A. Lockwood, wrote anonymous articles on *flogging for the United States Magazine and Democratic Review in 1849, upon one of which M. drew for W. 71 and W. 72.
W. Passim

PROMETHEUS

In *Greek mythology, son of the *Titan Iapetus and brother of Atlas, Prometheus is known as the savior of mankind. His name means "forethought," and he was wiser than the gods; his brother, Epimetheus, whose name means "afterthought," was dull-witted. When the time came to create men and beasts, Epimetheus began the process by giving animals all the superior physical attributes. Prometheus stepped in, making men upright, like the gods. He went to the sun in heaven and brought down fire—better than any animal asset. There were no women at this time, but Zeus (see "Jupiter" and "Jove") became so angry at Prometheus for his indulgence of men that he created the first woman: *Pandora, eventually wife to Epimetheus and bringer of evils to the world. Although Prometheus had aided Zeus in war against *Cronus, Zeus further punished him, binding him to a rock at *Caucasus, where

an eagle preyed on his body until *Hercules saved him. Drops of Prometheus's blood became a rare magical potion—protection from all harm. His son was Deucalion, saved with his wife, Pyrra, from the great flood.
M.75; R. 48; M.D. 44; M.D. 108; P. 26:5

PROMISED LAND

In *Genesis 17, *God promised *Abraham that he and his offspring would possess it:

> And I will establish my covenant between me and thee and thy seed after thee throughout their generations for an everlasting covenant, to be a God unto thee and to thy seed after thee. And I will give unto thee, and to thy seed after thee, the land of thy sojournings, all the land of *Canaan, for an everlasting possession; and I will be their God (7-9).

Figuratively: heaven, or place of fulfillment.
M. 166; I.P. 25

PROPHET, THE

See "Elijah."
M.D. 19

PROPONTIS

See "Marmora, Sea of."
M.D. 45; M.D. 87

PROSERPINE, --S

In *Roman myth, Persephone, the beautiful daughter of Demeter (or *Ceres), maiden of the spring and summer, was gathering flowers in the vale of *Enna, a meadow of grass and flowers. She was lured into picking one never seen before: a *narcissus created by Zeus (see "Jupiter" and "Jove") to secure her for his brother, *Hades (*Pluto), lord of the underworld. A chasm opened in the earth, and she was dragged below, scattering seeds that became the daffodil. Demeter eventually arranged for her return six months of the year (spring and summer), but Persephone was never again cheerful and came to be called "the maiden whose name may not be spoken," sometimes identified with the witch, *Hecate. She later became the goddess of sleep.
M. 167; P. 3:3

PROTEAN EASY-CHAIR
At the 1851 *London *World's Fair, a *Philadelphia manufacturer displayed reclining chairs for invalids, the position of which could be changed by leaning the body. M.'s adjective, "Protean," is probably inspired by the sea-god Proteus, who could change his shape at will.
C.M. 7

"PROTECTIONS"
Safe-conduct documents (such as passports), guaranteeing protection, exemption, or immunity.
W. 90

PROTECTORATE
Although the word "protectorate" was relatively new in the nineteenth century, the practice of a stronger nation's dominating a weaker without resorting to annexation was ancient. Establishment of protectorates had burgeoned since the sixteenth century, but by M.'s time, it became the accepted way to expand a colonial empire, especially for the *French, whose highly developed nation gained influence over less developed ones such as *Tahiti. International rules provided that peoples living in protectorates were not strictly subjects of the dominating state, but with the prohibition against intercourse with other foreign nations, that was a dubious distinction.
Tahiti remained a French Protectorate from 1842 until 1880, at which time it became a French colony.
O. 32 and elsewhere

PROTESTANT, --S
The western Christian sects which separated from the Roman *Catholic Church from the time of the Reformation begun by *Luther are called Protestant denominations. In contrast with Catholicism, Protestantism in general stresses the importance of Holy Scripture in matters of faith and order, grace justified through faith alone, and the priesthood of all believers.
Despite theoretical separation of *Church and State, America has considered itself a "Protestant country," founded for the most part by *Puritan Protestants who wished even farther separation from Catholicism than had been achieved by the Church of England.
M. considered himself a Protestant and was at the end of his life a member of the liberal All Souls Unitarian Church in *New York City.

See also "Baptist"; "Calvinist"; "Church of England"; "London Missionary Society"; "Mormon"; "Presbyterian"; "Quaker."
Passim

PROTESTANT BURIAL

Protestant sailors' graves were ignominious retreats in *Callao, where, of local inhabitants, bodies of the wealthy were cemented into a wall, while the poor were tossed over rear walls into a mass of earthquake ruins, according to *Rev. Stewart (*A Visit to the South Seas*, I). *Wilkes (*Narration of the United States Exploring Expedition*, I) also mentions the separate burying ground for *Englishmen and *Americans. This is in contrast to the beautiful *Protestant cemetery in *Rio, mentioned in *W*. 63.
W. 40

PROTESTANT CEMETERY

Rev. Stewart (Vol. I) discusses the *Rio "Protestant burial ground, situated on the bay between S. Cristovao and the city...a spot necessarily of interest to every *Protestant foreigner...said to surpass in loveliness almost every other locality on the shores of these charming waters."
W. 63

PROVERBS, BOOK OF

The Book of Proverbs, *Old Testament Wisdom Literature, is a collection (completed c. 200 B.C.) of didactic maxims, poems, and precepts reflecting the secular and religious lore of many civilizations and generally focusing on the inevitable prospering of the godly. Its ascription to *Solomon (accepted by M.) is now known to be erroneous.

Among those proverbs marked in M.'s *Bible: "Surely in vain the net is spread in the sight of any bird" (1:17); "The soul of the wicked desireth evil: his neighbor findeth no favour in his eyes" (21:10).

C.M.'s "*Charlie Noble" covertly alludes to the *utilitarian wisdom of Proverbs throughout the text; *Clarel* often falls into its style.

See also "Quotations" section: "*Jehovah shall be thy confidence"; "the man that wandereth out of the way of understanding . . . "; "Praise be unto the press . . . . "
C.M. 43

PROVIDENCE

The city of northern *Rhode Island's Providence county is forty miles south-southwest of *Boston, on a harbor at the head of Providence River. It was founded in 1636 by Roger Williams, who named it for "*God's merciful providence." The city grew slowly at first and was set back badly by *King Philip's War (1675-76), but by the eighteenth century it was a prosperous foreign commerce port. It was incorporated as a city in 1831.

I.P. 2

PROVIDE . . . PROVIDE

C.M.'s *Samaritan Pain Dissuader salesman plays on *Bible echoes in order to move merchandise. The "Happiness" and "Security" he suggests for the right and left hands are not scriptural aims, and Biblical admonitions to "provide" are always in contexts opposite the salesman's philosophy. In *Matthew 10:9, *Jesus says, *Provide neither gold, nor silver, nor brass in your purses"; in *Luke 12:33, "Provide yourselves bags which wax not old, a treasure in the heavens that faileth not, where no thief approacheth, neither moth corrupteth." In *Romans 12:7, *Paul says ". . . Provide things honest in the sight of all men."

(In the twentieth century, Robert Frost played with the same transmogrification of "higher" laws by a materialistic culture, in "Provide, Provide.")

C.M. 17

PRUSSIAN

Prussia was formerly the largest and most important state of *Germany, with *Berlin as its capital. In M.'s time, Prussia consisted of thirteen provinces occupying most of the northern part of Germany, from *Luxembourg, *Belgium and the *Netherlands (W.) to *Poland (E.), the North Sea, *Denmark, and the *Baltic (N.), to Czechoslovakia (S.).

"Old Prussia" refers to East Prussia which, from the thirteenth century, fought off superior Polish forces and struggled internally. By 1701, Frederick I was King of Prussia, independent of the *Holy Roman Empire, and Europe's leading military power. *Napoléon's 1806 victory led to loss of all lands west of *Elbe and most of the Polish holdings. But Prussian forces under *Blücher helped defeat Napoléon at *Leipzic (1815) and at *Waterloo (1815). After the *Congress of Vienna, Prussia regained all lost territory, as well as the *Rhine provinces, *Westphalia, and much of western Poland. With

Austria, it created the German Confederacy, pursuing the re-
actionary policies of Metternich.

By 1862, Bismarck achieved the expulsion of Austria and
Prussian hegemony over a unified Germany, but wars continued throughout the nineteenth century. (In 1918 the Kingdom
of Prussia joined the Weimar Republic as part of Germany.)
O. 81; O. 82

PRYNNE

William Prynne (1600-69) was a *British antiquar-
ian/barrister/*Puritan pamphleteer who struggled against
*Charles I, Archbishop William Laud, Arminianism, Roman
*Catholicism, *Presbyterianism, ceremonialism, the indepen-
dents, the army, the government, frivolous amusements such
as the stage (in *Histriomastix*), and various other targets. As a
result of his prolific publication, he was arrested, fined, imprisoned by the *Star Chamber, branded in the cheeks with the
letters S.L. (meaning "seditious libeler," but interpreted by
Prynne as "*stigmata Laudis*," "the marks of Laud"). He had
both ears cut off for his aspersion of Queen Henrietta Maria, a
performer in *masques.

A supporter of the Restoration, he eventually served in
*Parliament. As keeper of the national archives, Prynne pre-
served records of the *Tower, in which he had been imprisoned. The author of some 200 works, he is best known for *Bre-
via Parliamentaria Rediviva* (1662).

Referred to in *M.D.* 90 is *Aurum Reginae, or a Compen-
dious Tractate and Chronological Collection of Records in the
Tower and Court of Exchequer Concerning Queen-Gold* (1668),
a work about which M. might be said, were that possible, to
tweak Prynne's ears.
M.D. 90

PSALMS

The *Old Testament Book of Psalms consists of hymns,
songs of *Zion, songs of trust in *God, thanksgiving, sacred
history, royal psalms, wisdom psalms, and liturgies. They
were long ascribed to *David.

See also "Extracts" 4.
M.D. Extracts 4

PSYCHE GLASSES

Full-length mirrors. In a review of *J. Ross Browne's
Etchings of a Whaling Cruise (in *Literary World*, 6 March
1847), M. had hyperbolically examined the life of a sailor: "In a

ship's forecastle, alas! he will find no Psyche glass in which to
survey his picturesque attire."
W. 84

PTERICHTHYS
See "Sandwiches."
M. 132

PTOLEMY
The Ptolemy referred to in *M*. is Claudius Ptolemaeus,
the second-century A.D. *Alexandrian mathematician, astronomer, and geographer whose geocentric theory of astronomy was generally accepted until disproven by that of
*Copernicus. His encyclopedic book, known since the ninth
century as *Almagest* (from an Arab language superlative), has
thirteen parts, covering the geocentric system, mathematical
theory, motions of the sun and moon, eclipses, planetary
movement, and fixed stars. Other works are on geometry,
dating systems, optics, geography, and cartology.
Ptolemy's theories, even though full of error, bolstered
traditional *Christian concepts of an orderly hierarchical universe.
M. 151

PTOLEMY PHILOPATER
Ptolemy Philopater (M.'s spelling erroneous) was
Ptolemy XIII, brother of *Cleopatra VII, who ruled *Egypt
with her from 51 to 47 B.C. M.'s knowledge of him is probably
at several removes. Ptolemy is mentioned in *Montaigne (Vol.
2, Chap. 12), but the reference in *M.D.* probably shows him
using *Plutarch, who cites *Juba, who cites Ptolemy.
M.D. 86

PUCK
In *Shakespeare's *A Midsummer-Night's Dream*, a
mischievous sprite who mistakenly works magic on
"*Lysander."
C.M. 3

"PUDDINGING THE DOLPHIN"
A "pudding" is a padded fender used when harboring
against a "dolphin" (dock or other wooden structure). A double

meaning may be inferred from "pudding's" referring also to coition, the penis, or seminal fluid.
W. 41

PULPIT, THE
    See "Whaleman's Chapel."
M.D. 8

PUNCHBOWL HILL
    Punchbowl Hill is an extinct *Honolulu volcano some 500 feet in elevation, with heavily populated slopes; the crater now contains the National Memorial Cemetery of the Pacific.
T. Appendix.

PURCHAS; PURCHASS, SAMUEL
    Samuel Purchas (c. 1577-1626), vicar in Essex and *London, *England, compiled travel and discovery literature. An acquaintance of many seafarers, he attempted to popularize such literature and incurred the disapproval of scholars despite the inherent worth of many of his writings. They include: *Purchas, His Pilgrimage; or, Relations of the World and the Religions Observed in all Ages* (1613, -14, -17, -26); *Purchas, His Pilgrim. Microcosmus, or the Historie of Man* (1619); and *Hakluytus Posthumus or Purchas His Pilgrimes* (1625, 1905-07).
    See also "Extracts" 27.
M. 75; M.D. Extracts 27; M.D. 56; M.D. 75

PURITAN, --S; PURITANIC
    Puritanism arose within the *Church of England during the reign of Queen *Elizabeth. Puritans sought more reformation of the *Protestant church than had already occurred; the Puritan Revolution of 1640-60 politicized the conflict. American Puritans who founded the *Massachusetts Bay colony in 1620 were *Calvinist separatists. Their characteristics are thought to have colored at least *New England life for all time. M.'s references to Puritans and things Puritanic are generally not complimentary; for M., Puritans are self-righteous, excessively scrupulous, sententious, and militaristic.
    See also "Cromwell"; "Quaker"; "Shaker."
R. 44; M.D. 6; M.D. 27; I.P. 1; C.M. 30; C.M. 36 and elsewhere

PURITAN REPUBLIC
    See "Cromwell's."
W. 71

PURSER
    Until cessation of profits in 1847, the office of Purser was
a sinecure. The salary was $480 per year exclusive of rations,
but law allowed the purser a profit of from 10 to 50 per cent on
goods sold. McNally claimed that a purser on one frigate made
over $58,000 during a voyage.
W. 48 and elsewhere

"PURSER RIGGED AND PARISH DAMNED"
    A sailor who enlists in the *Navy because of poverty is
"*purser rigged"—that is clothed and supplied—and "parish
damned"—to all intents and purposes lost to the decent life he
left behind.
W. 90

PUSIE HALL
    The story of the sinking of the *English ship *Pusie Hall*
by a whale in 1835 is found in *Bennett II, p. 218.
M.D. 45

PUTNAM
    Major-General Israel Putnam (1718-1790) was sent
(along with William Prescott) by *George Washington to defend
*Bunker Hill. As M. notes in *I.P.* 2, he has gone down in history as having said, "Don't fire until you see the whites of their
eyes." Some sources, however, credit Prescott (1726-1795) with
the order. Frederick the Great (1712-1786) is said to have
ordered "No firing till you see the whites of their eyes" at
Prague, 6 May 1757.
I.P. 2; I.P. 3

P.W.
    See "Port; P.W.; Oporto."
C.M. 29

PYRAMIDS; PYRAMID OF CHEOPS
    See "Cheops."
T. 21; M. 75; M. 84; R. 31; R. 32

PYRRHO

Pyrrho of Elis (c. 365-275 B.C.), *Greek philosopher and ultimate sceptic, claimed that all perceptions and value judgements are relative, in a tangential system to one side of the thinking of *Democritus. Pyrrhonism evolved from Pyrrho's observations of *Indian placidity while he was traveling with *Alexander the Great. Most sceptics traced the origins of their beliefs to Pyrrho's ideas, which were incorporated into the poems of Timon of Phlius: we must be unperturbed by change in fortune; we must abstain from judgement and doubt even sense perception, in order to reach peaceful strength.

M. 119; M.D. 85

PYTHAGORAS; PYTHAGOREAN

Pythagoras, the sixth-century B.C. *Greek philosopher, migrated from Samos to Crotona, where he organized an influential ascetic brotherhood for the moral reformation of society which lasted until the fourth century. It consisted of mathematicians who studied the sciences and others who concentrated on moral precepts. Our picture of Pythagorean teachings is not based on the known beliefs of Pythagoras, no manuscripts surviving, but on those of his followers. Among the ideas: the transmigration of souls; the body as the soul's prison; the pure life centered on examination of conscience; the mathematical relation of all things (especially music); the relation of numbers to things and to concepts. Pythagoras is said to have discovered the earth's rotation on its axis; he is credited with the proof of the proposition that the square of the hypotenuse of a right triangle is equal to the sum of the square of the other two sides.

The reputation of Pythagoras has varied through the ages. He is seen by *Christian thinkers as a bridge between *Moses and *Plato; as a poet; as champion of the contemplative life. However, the post-first-century degrading of Pythagoreans into a cult has led him to be seen as a magician, and the father of the Cabala.

M. owned an 1853 edition (Sealts #183a) of Diogenes Laertius's *Lives of Eminent Philosophers*, which includes Pythagoras's advising his followers "to abstain from beans because they are flatulent and partake most of the breath of life" (VIII, 24).

M.D. 1; M.D. 98; P. 22:1

PYTHIAS
      See "Damon and Pythias."
W. 41; I.P. 22

QUAKER, --S; QUAKERISM; QUAKERISH
      The Society of Friends (Friends Church, in the *United States) is a *Christian religious group with no definite creed or ministery. It was founded in *Britain (1648-50) by George Fox (1624-91). The appellation "Quaker" was conferred when Fox bade a court justice quake at the word of *God. "Quaker" had previously applied to a religious sect whose adherents, like *Shakers, shook with religious fervor; it became an abusive term during *Cromwell's time, when there was much persecution of the left-wing *Puritan movement.
      By the mid-seventeenth century, meetings were established in America from *New England to *Virginia, as well as in the *West Indies. Except in *Rhode Island, Quakers were much persecuted here, as *Hawthorne notes in several works. By the nineteenth century, *Pennsylvania was a stronghold, but schisms between conservative and evangelical groups, westward migration, and conversions to Unitarianism and *Quietism sapped strength.
      Quakers hold regular meetings (rather than "services") under the presidency of Christ, with business presented by a clerk. There are no regular ministers, but recorded ministers and elders of both sexes. Meeting is open to the public; there are no sacraments, but "living silence," communal singing, and voluntary scripture-reading may take place in the (traditionally) plain rectangular building, with plain benches. Quaker belief holds scripture secondary to revelation of personal experience, collections of advice such as the *Book of Discipline* (or *Faith and Practice*), and "declarations of faith," reflecting "primitive Christianity revived." There are no sacraments and minimal observance of *Christmas, Easter, and *Pentecost, every day being "the Lord's Day."
      The Society has historically been a peace-movement church of noncombatants who pursue volunteer relief work: Quakers are traditionally against *slavery, capital punishment, and "worldly" clothing and furnishings. They have been for women's rights, penal reform, and *temperance. In M.'s time, their refusal to take oaths, or to bow or remove the hat out of respect, made for social problems.

As Tyrus Hillway pointed out ("Quaker Language in *Moby-Dick*"), the element of Quakerism most in question in *M.D.* is pacifism; M. saw incongruity in the attraction of peace-loving Quakers to the violent whaling business.

Quakers use "thee and thou" to equals, and "you" to superiors: what M. calls "Quaker idiom" (*M.D.* 16, *M.D.* 26) was a convention of romantic literature, rather than an exclusive Quaker attribute, as revealed in M.'s use of "thee and thou" throughout *P.*

The "Quaker" of *M.* 28 is of course an ironically named gun.

O. 48; M. 28 (gun); R. 23; W. 16; W. 75; W. 83; M.D. 16; M.D. 26; I.P. 15; I.P. 16; I.P. 18; C.M. 2 and elsewhere

QUAKER STYLE COAT; QUAKERISH

Nineteenth-century Quaker-style coats were made of coarse twilled cloth: usually brown, rather than blue. Coat tails were rather voluminous, in contrast to those of sailors' "monkey jackets," lacking in tails to enhance maneuverability.
W. 1; M.D. 16; I.P. 15

QUARRELER, THE

"Ludwig the Quarreler" is perhaps a reference to the Capetian Louis X *le Hutin,* or the Stubborn (1289-1316), king of *France from 1314. Inheriting a discontented nation from his father, Philip IV, in his short reign he dismissed and imprisoned ministers, attempted to ingratiate the clergy, and freed some serfs, in an effort at dramatic reversal.
M. 181

QUARTER JOES

See "Joes."
M.D. 99

QUARTERLY REVIEW

The literary journal founded by John Murray as a *Tory rival to the *Whig-leaning *Edinburgh Review* took conservative stances intended to preserve the established order, especially the Church of England. It enjoyed large circulation in the *United States and was a proponent of the *Scottish "common sense" school which M. mocked in reference to *Hugh Blair. *Sir Walter Scott was among important contributors, but *QR* was often charged with bias in choice of contributors and in critical attitudes. Its editors were forced to adapt some strangely liberal ideas so as to distinguish it from its rival, often condoning novel ideas in literature, provided that such ideas did not threaten the status quo. It supported *Wordsworth, *Coleridge, and *Byron, but condemned Keats, *Shelley, Tennyson, Dickens (see "Hard Times"), among others.

New Quarterly Review (First Quarter, 1852) dismissed M.D., erroneously claiming that there were no survivors of the "*Pequod" disaster, and therefore the work must be false: a position brought about when some editions omitted the "Epilogue."
W. 11

QUEBEC
The sometime-capital *Canadian city on the *St. Lawrence River, 150 miles northeast of *Montreal, is built on a 300-foot-high cliff. The center of *French Canadian culture had first been discovered by Jacques Cartier in 1535 and was flourishing by 1608. Quebec was much coveted by the *British. At the 1759 Battle of Quebec, the British under General Wolfe defeated the French under Montcalm; both men were killed in the action. The 1763 *Treaty of Paris ceded the city to the British, and in 1775 *Benedict Arnold attempted to take it. The Citadel was begun in 1823.

M. apparently shared the sentiments of his wife, Elizabeth Shaw Melville, regarding Quebec, which was a stop (20 August 1847) on their honeymoon trip. In a letter of 21 August to her stepmother, Hope Shaw, she writes: "Quebec looks so cold and forbidding and comfortless with its heavy walls and gates, and its huge citadel bristling with cannon . . . were it not for some scenes of interest in the vicinity we should have left here before this."
R. 40; W. 39; M.D. 8; M.D. 80

QUEEN, THE
See "La Reine."
R. 1

QUEEN ANNE'S FARTHING
A non-existent coin; no farthings were issued during the reign of *Queen Anne.
M.D. 89

QUEEN ANNE'S TIME
Anne (1665-1714), queen of *England and *Ireland from 1702-1714, was second daughter of *James II and Anne Hyde, daughter of the earl of *Clarendon. A *Protestant, she succeeded to the throne after the death of William, despite the claim of a half-brother. Married to Prince George of Denmark (1653-1708), she failed to produce heirs and so yielded the throne to the house of *Hanover.
The noted fashion of her time, referred to in *M.D.* 75, was the voluminous hoop skirt. See also *"Brandy-Nan."*
M.D. 75

QUEEN BESS
See "Elizabeth, Queen . . . . "
(A "Queen Bess" is also a lockpicking instrument.)
M. 139; M. 149; M.D. 32; P. 19:1; C.M. 21

QUEEN DOWAGERS
See "Dowagers."
M. 181

"QUEEN-GOLD"
See "Prynne."
M.D. 90

QUEEN MAACHAH
In *Kings I (15:13), Maachah is "removed from being queen, because she had made an idol in a grove; and Asa destroyed her idol, and burnt it by the brook Kidron."
(See "Kedron, Brook.")
M.D. 95

QUEEN MAB
A poem by *Shelley; or, in *Shakespeare's *Romeo and Juliet*, from "Mercutio's" comment on "Romeo's" dream (I, iv, 53-54, 58):

O, then, I see Queen Mab hath been with you.
She is the fairies' midwife, and she comes

.   .   .   .

Over men's noses as they lie asleep.

*Byron refers to "The ocean Mab" in *The Island* a poem
about the *Bounty mutiny.
W. 65; M.D. 31

QUEEN NATURE'S GRANITE-FOUNDED COLLEGE
   A frivolous reference to the *Manxman's head.
M.D. 125

QUEEN OF ENGLAND
   In *W.* 4, an indirect reference to *Victoria.
W. 4

QUEEN OF NUKUHEVA; ISLAND QUEEN
   See "Mowanna."
T. 1

QUEEN OF SCOTS
   See "Stuart, Mary."
P. 2:2

QUEEN-PINMONEY
   A play on "Queen Gold." See "Prynne."
M.D. 90

QUEEN'S DOCK
   *Liverpool: originally, six and one-half acre water area;
opened 1796. It was expanded to serve continental traders,
starting early in the nineteenth century, contributing to the
change of southern Liverpool from a residential area to an industrial and slum area.
R. 32

QUICKSILVER
   Mercury.
M.D. 107

QUIETIST
   Quietism, founded by Miguel de Molinos (1628-96), a
*Spanish priest, was a doctrine of *Christian perfection hold-
ing that perfection is possible if the soul is kept passively recep-

tive to divine action. Molinos advocated inactivity and contem-
plation which would invite the return of *God to the soul, a
mystic death similar to that of Eastern religions.

Quietism was heresy; it denied even good works or exercises of religious faith and suggested that immoral acts committed by the Quietist were not sins but acts of the *Devil, who
could master the contemplative's body. Molinos's *Spiritual
Guide* gained him converts in *Italy but was condemned by
Pope Innocent XI and caused Molinos to be sentenced to life
imprisonment. His work was carried on in *France, somewhat protected by *Mme. de Maintenon, by François de
Salignac de la Mothe Fénelon (1651-1715) and others, developing into a doctrine of pure love sometimes called Semi-Qui-
etism.
P. 15:2

QUILL-DRIVERS

The pejorative expression has various meanings; it
often refers to writing clerks. But *Dana uses it to describe the
unpopular agent who is a money-hungry businessman, in *Two
Years Before the Mast*. *Evert Duyckinck used it as an epithet
for a business writer, as opposed to a creative artist. In the
*Navy, a quill-driver was a member of the Supply and Secre-
tariat branch, with many clerical duties.
W. 18

QUINCUNXES

A quincunx is an arrangement of five objects so that four
occupy the corners of a square or rectangle and the fifth is in
the center, or a cruciform reliquary of five parts which can be
closed up by folding outer parts over the central one.

Probably M. got the term from *Sir Thomas Browne's
1658 *The Garden of Cyrus: or, The Quincunciall, Lozenge, or
Net-work Plantations of the Ancients, Artificially, Naturally,
Mystically Considered* (Sealts #89).
M. 170

QUIROS

A coal- and iron-mining area of northwest *Spain, eighteen miles south-southwest of Oviedo.
T. 25; O. 18

QUITO

The capital city of Ecuador is located in the north central part of the country at the southern foot of Pichincha volcano and is so high in the *Andes that its climate remains temperate despite proximity to the *Equator (0°17' S., 78°32' W.). It is an ancient city which was captured from the Quitu Indians by *Pizarro's forces in the fifteenth century. Under the *Peruvian vice-royalty, it became an administrative and cultural center, with picturesque cobbled streets and overhanging balconies on ornate buildings, and much valuable artwork in churches. Quito declared independence in 1830, with Juan José Flores its first President.

"Quito glow" (*M.D.* 99) refers to the precious metalwork of the area, as shown on the *doubloon.
M. 152; M.D. 29; M.D. 99

QUIXOTIC; QUIXOTISM

See "Don Quixote."
O. 65; W. 54

QUOHOG

(Quahaug) Indian word for thick-shelled American clam such as "Little Neck" and "Cherrystone."
M.D. 14; M.D. 18

R

RABBINICAL

The reference in W. to "Rabbinical" tradition is not to *Talmudic lore but rather to the *Jewish tradition of legends primarily for children. The "little boat" M. says followed *Noah's ark is probably confused with traditional Jewish legend that one animal, the "reëm," was so large that it could not fit in the ark, and Noah had to tie it onto the stern and tow it behind. (The giant, Og, king of Bashan, was also too large, according to legend, and had to ride on top of the ark.)
W. 65; M.D. 50

RABBINS, UNCANONICAL

*Jewish religious writers just before and after the inception of the *Christian era, writing under pseudonyms

("Pseudepigrapha") and outside the *Bible or the *Apocrypha:
for example, the Book of Enoch and the Book of Jubilees.
M.D. 50

RABELAIS, --'S
     The *French writer François Rabelais (c. 1494-c. 1553)
had been a Franciscan monk and secretary to a bishop, before
becoming a physician. His publications range from *Latin
treatises on medicine and archaeology to satires about the
giants *Gargantua* and *Pantagruel*. Rabelais was a true
"Renaissance man" with unbounded interests and skills tempered by humane objectives. His popular writings are an encyclopedic blend of burlesque obscenity and erudition, colored by
a basic optimism about mankind.
     Rabelais was first translated into English by Urquhart
(see "Urquhartian Club"). His works influenced such masters
as Swift and Sterne, and M.'s tribute to him, as "Rabeelee," a
laughing philosopher in *M.*, is clear.
     Sealts #417 is *The Works . . . Translated from the
French. With Explanatory Notes by Duchat, Ozell, and Others.*
. . . London, Smith, Miller, 1844. 4 vols.? M. borrowed this edition from *Duyckinck in 1848.
     See also "Extracts" 11.
M. 3; M.D. Extracts 11; M.D. 96; I.P. 13; C.M. 24

RACA
     Raca (rhaka) is a Greek epithet of *Chaldean origin sig-
nifying utter vilification: roughly, "Oh empty (or worthless)
one."
     In *Matthew 5:22 (the *Sermon on the Mount), *Jesus
says: ". . . whosoever is angry with his brother without a
cause shall be in danger of the judgement: and whosoever
shall say to his brother, Raca, shall be in danger of the council:
but whosoever shall say, Thou fool, shall be in danger of hell
fire."
R. 33

RACHEL
     In *Jeremiah 31:15, Rachel, wife of *Jacob and mother
of *Joseph and *Benjamin, mourns in her grave for the loss of
her exiled descendants: "Thus said the Lord, A voice was
heard in Ramah, lamentation, and bitter weeping: Rachel
weeping for her children refused to be comforted for her children because they were not." The passage is seen in *Matthew
2:18 as a prophecy of Herod's slaughter of the Innocents.

"Rachel" is an appropriate fictional name for the ship seeking a lost child and finding the "orphan" "*Ishmael," in *M.D.*
M.D. 128

RADACK
The Ratak chain of islands is the eastern row of parallel islands (with the Ralik) which together form the modern Marshall Islands, the easternmost group in Micronesia. They are coral caps of high dome volcanoes passed by in sixteenth-century *Spanish exploration but mapped by *Krusenstern (1803) and von *Kotzebue (1815, 1823).
M. 3; M. 12

RADCLIFFE HIGHWAY
Ratcliff (perhaps meaning "red cliff") is an outlying district of east *London in Stepney, and the site of a church dedicated to *St. Dunstan. M. "lounged on by . . . Ratcliffe Highway" on 10 November 1849, observing activities on the *Thames docks and undoubtedly unofficially tabulating the Highway's ale houses—of which there were reputedly more than in any London street of comparable length. The area was also famous for the 1811 Ratcliff-Highway murders; the murderer committed suicide and was buried locally with a stake through his heart. Trinity House, a fraternity of pilots, seamen, and other mariners, met in the area, in a building destroyed in the *Great Fire.
If *R.*'s "Jack Blunt" is a "graduate" of the area, he has attended a rough school.
R. 18

RAG FAIR
The expression has several meanings: an old-clothes market at *Houndsditch, *London; wool from torn rags: inspection of soldiers' kit bags, etc.
M. 23

RAIATAIR
Raiatea, *Society Islands: original location of the people who became *Tahitians, and center of *Polynesian cultural diffusion.
(*Raiatea* was a schooner owned by the American Consul at Tahiti, J.A. Moerenhout: M.'s "*Merenhout.")
O. 39; O. 45; O. 76

RAINBOW

The *French flag has blue, white, and red stripes. It was adopted officially after the Revolution of 1789, although it had been used unofficially before. (The white *Bourbon flag was used in France from 1815 to 1830.) The three colors were chosen for their association with the red-white-blue of the *Netherlands, representing that nation's long struggle for independence from *Spain.
W. 65

RAKE'S

"Rake" ("libertine," or "blackguard") is a contraction of "rakehell," used by *Milton and others.
O. 81

RALEIGH, SIR WALTER

Sir Walter Raleigh (or Ralegh; c. 1554-1618), English explorer and colonizer, author, soldier, and seaman, became a favorite of *Queen Elizabeth I. Born in South Devon, he attended Oriel College, *Oxford, for one year, and then fought with Huguenot forces in *France. After a brief association with the Middle *Temple, his action against *Irish rebels and desire for their rapid subjection brought him to the Queen's attention, and he was favored with estates and monopolies, knighted in 1585, and made captain of the Queen's guard in 1587. He is credited with establishing *Virginia's *Roanoke colony, and encouraging the planting of tobacco and potatoes, but he never visited the colony. A favorite at court for his own poetry, he introduced and encouraged *Spenser. Marriage to a maid of honor at court cast him into disfavor, and the two were banished to the *Tower, then released when Raleigh's services were needed to supervise the booty of privateers.

In 1595 he sailed on the expedition discussed in his *Discoverie of Guiana* (1596), encouraging belief in the existence of the gold of El dorado. In 1597, he joined an expedition to the *Azores.

In 1603, James I (see "Stuart"), suspecting him of treason, stripped him of goods and offices, and sent him to the Tower, from which he was not released for thirteen years. He worked on his *History of the World* until in 1616 he was returned to Guiana to secure gold without offending *Spain. The expedition was disastrous; convicted of conspiracy, he was beheaded.

The story of his spreading his cloak over a puddle for Elizabeth is probably *Fuller's invention, but in keeping with Raleigh's behavior with the Queen.
R. 23; W. 24

RAM, THE
See "Zodiac."
M.D. 99

RAMADAN
The ninth month of the *Moslem year, falling at various seasons, Ramadan (the "Scorcher") became the holy month of fasting for its connection with reception of the *Koran (Koran ii, 181). The period of atonement prescribes ritual prayer and proscribes food, drink, and sexual intercourse for precisely twenty-nine days, with some days of especial significance. It is followed by Shawwal, the festival of breaking fast.
Like most people of his time, M. tended to associate Ramadan with the *Christian period of Lent. In his poem, "The Rose Farmer," he uses a variant spelling: "Rhamadan."
M.D. 16; M.D. 17

RAMUSIO
Giovanni Battista Ramusio (1485-1557), Italian geographer and author of Delle Navigationi et Viaggi. Only two volumes were published in his lifetime: V. I (*Africa, 1550) and V. III (*America, 1557). V. II (*Asia) appeared in 1559, and all three went through later revisions. Most important sections of the regionally arranged work are Ramusio's version of *Marco Polo's travels and the description of Africa.
M. 75

RANDOLPH, JOHN; RANDOLPHS
The colorful John Randolph, self-styled "of *Roanoke" (his plantation), lived from 1773 to 1833, a lifelong proponent of States' rights. Descendant of a distinguished colonial family which included the Indian princess, *Pocahontas, Randolph included in his family one relative who was *George Washington's Attorney General (Edmund Randolph). His own career was dramatic and successful, despite lifelong ill health. He was elected to the House of Representatives in 1799 and was defeated for reelection only once—for his opposition to the *War of 1812. The skillful orator and feared debater was Chairman of the House Ways and Means Committee and leader of the House Republicans until he broke with them over *Jefferson's acquisition of *Florida. Thereafter he was an independent, elected to the Senate once, then defeated by John Tyler.
His denunciation of Henry Clay for supporting John Quincy Adams resulted in a duel (with no casualties). He broke with *Andrew Jackson over the South *Carolina nullifi-

cation ordinance. He defended the practice of *slavery despite freeing his own slaves and was altogether one of the most picturesque public figures of M.'s time.

On Randolph's 1831 trip to *Russia, a traditional navy disciplinarian, Master Commandant Matthew C. Perry, commanded the sloop-of-war *Concord.* Physically sickened by the persistent *flogging involved in breaking in new men, Randolph wrote to President Andrew Jackson that he would never again take passage on board a vessel of war, at least one with a newly-shipped crew, having seem more flogging in three weeks on the *Concord* than in seven years on his plantation with the same number of slaves. Were he in *Congress, he added, he would introduce a bill to abolish flogging.
W. 34; W. 90; M.D. 1; P. 1:3

RANGER
*John Paul Jones was appointed commander of the newly built eighteen-gun (?) ship-sloop *Ranger* on 14 June 1777, the day the Stars and Stripes became the *American emblem. *Ranger* received the first salute to the flag from the *French at *Quiberon Bay in 1778, before the treaty of alliance (America's first) was signed. After gathering numerous prizes in European waters, *Ranger* took the twenty-gun *British *Drake*, and Jones returned to *Brest hailed as a hero but with command of *Ranger* transferred to another man. *Ranger* fell into British hands at *Charleston, South *Carolina, in 1780, and was taken into the British Navy as *Halifax.*
See also "Serapis."
I.P. 14; I.P. 17

RAPE OF THE LOCK
See "Pope, Alexander"; "Extracts" 36.
M.D. Extracts 36

RAPHAEL
Raffaello Sanzio (1483-1520), *Italian High Renaissance painter and architect, was guided early into the study of art by his father, the minor painter Giovanni Santi. Raphael was a recognized master by the age of seventeen. Influenced by Pietro Perugino (c. 1445-1523), he produced *The Marriage of the Virgin* in 1504. Thereafter, the *Florentine art of *Leonardo and *Michelangelo affected the forms in his works.

He was called to *Rome by Pope Julius II in 1508 to decorate a series of *Vatican rooms. *The School of Athens* (1509-11) and a series of madonnas brought him such popularity that much of his subsequent work was done by assistants. His portraits of *Baldassare Castiglione* and *Cesare Borgia* show great voluptuousness and subtlety of characterization, the result of effective emulation of early masters.

Raphael was long considered the greatest of painters. M. seems to have concurred. He saw numerous Raphael works in Italy in 1857, holding them as standards, as indicated by his journal comments. A *Madonna* in *Naples is called "touchingly maternal" (21 February); he finds "faces, attitudes, expressions and groupings" reminiscent of Raphael throughout Italy (26 March).

Sealts #55 is Nancy R.E. Bell's *Raphael, by N. D'Anvers* (pseud.), 1880.
P. 26:1

RAPHAELS
The *archangel Raphael does not appear in canonical books of the *Bible. In Enoch 20:3, he is second in the order of the angels (with *Gabriel and *Michael). The *Apocryphal Book of Tobit makes him the angel of healing, who removes a film from Tobit's eyes and binds *Asmodeus to arrange the marriage of Tobit's son. Adding to confusion about Raphael is his changing places with Michael in much secular literature.

M.'s notion of a meek Raphael probably comes from *Milton's *Paradise Lost* VII, 217, in which the archangel is called "heavenly meek." In M.'s civil war poem, "The Conflict of Conviction" (1860-1), Raphael is a "white enthusiast."

(See also "Extracts 8.")
M.D. Extracts 8; C.M. 37

RARTOO
Perhaps a fictional chief, but the "hospitable" "Rartoo" is characteristic of the *Polynesian friendliness to strangers.
O. 62

RATTLER
The 880-ton *British steam sloop *Rattler* was one of the first screw propeller vessels to demonstrate the advantage over paddle drive. In a tug-of-war against the paddle-driven *Alecto* in April 1843, she matched her 200 horse-power engine against the equally powered paddle-drive *Alecto*, dragging her stern-first at a speed of 2.8 knots.

Rattler destroyed seventeen *pirate junks near *Hong Kong, in 1855.
M.D. 101

RAVAILLAC

François Ravaillac was the assassin hired (probably by Jean Louis de Nogaret de la Valette, Duc d'Epernon) to kill *France's Henry IV (see "Valois" and "Bourbon") in 1610. I.P. 5

RAVAVAI

Raivavae (Vavitu): one of Tubuai Islands (Austral Islands), south of *Society Islands. M. 1

RAVELINGS

Ungenerous or miserly sailors. W. 91

RAY

John Ray (Wray; 1627-1705), *English naturalist and developer of systems of natural classification, at first focused on flora. Turning to zoology after the death of his colleague, Francis Willughby (see "Willoughby"), he developed systems which greatly influenced *Peter Artedi and *Linnaeus. His basis for the natural classification of fishes was revealed in *Francisci Willughbeii . . . historia piscium* (1686). M.D. 32

REA

The daughter of *Coelus and *Terra, Rhea was the wife and sister of Cronus (*Saturn) and mother of Zeus (See "Jupiter" and "Jove"), Poseidon, *Pluto, Hestia, and Demeter. She is identified with the *Greek *Cybele and the Roman *Ops. M. 193

RED-CROSS STREET

In *London's *Southwark district (mentioned in *Israel Potter's autobiographical story). I.P. 25

RED-EYE

Fiery inexpensive *American brandy or whiskey which produced startling effects, especially if new. W. 43

RED-JACKET

Red-Jacket (c. 1756-1830), Chief of the Seneca Indians (Iroquois Confederacy, or *Five Nations) who supported the *Americans in the *War of 1812, was an ambiguously pacific figure, an orator and supporter of Indian cultural integrity.
C.M.25

REDOUBTABLES

Redoubtable was the *French ship at the battle of *Trafalgar from which a sharpshooter shot and killed *Nelson (21 October 1805), whose *Victory* lay alongside, in accordance with Nelson's belief in attempted boarding as the best route to capture. *Redoubtable* sank under tow on 24 October.
M. 28

RED-RAG BELAYED

"Red rag" is the tongue; to "belay" is to stop.
W. 56; W. 90

RED SEA

The name "Red" for the *Bible's "Sea of Reeds (or Rushes)" ("Tongue of the Sea of Egypt" in *Isaiah 11:15) is unclear. In Biblical times, it included the *Indian Ocean and the *Persian Gulf. In *Exodus, the *Jews cross the Red Sea somewhere between the *Mediterranean and the Gulf of Suez, pursued by the *Egyptians, who are destroyed by a disaster. Modern theory is that a strong easterly wind broke through a sand bar, causing the sea to pour into the shallows, inundating the Egyptian pursuers.

In I *Kings, the Red Sea is under the control of *Judea, and used by *Solomon's fleet in trade with *Ophir.
W. 22; M.D. 83; C.M. 2

REDUCTIO AD ABSURDUM

Proving a principle false by demonstrating that its logical consequence, carried to impractical lengths, is absurd. For example, saying that to be well-nourished humans should eat a great deal of food suggests that the more we eat the healthier we are.
W. 83; C.M. 36

REFORMATION, THE
The *Protestant Reformation was the sixteenth-century religious revolution which fractured western Europe's religious unity under the Roman *Catholic Church. It resulted in the establishment of Protestant Churches; its chief leaders were *Luther, *Calvin, and Zwingli.
Passim

REGENT STREET
M. walked along Regent Street to his *Craven Street lodging on 17 November 1849. Regent had been laid out in *Westminster in 1813 and was at the time one of *London's most beautiful streets, with a colonnade, balconied row houses, a riding academy, a *chapel of ease, memorials, and monuments.
M.D. 6

REGIFUGIUM
Lat. *regifugium*, describing the flight or expulsion of the *Roman kings. The word is common in works of Roman history, but its only proper usage is connected with the February 24 festival of *regifugium*, commemorating the flight (From *rex*, king; *fuga*, flight).
M. 161

REINE BLANCHE
The *French frigate *La Reine Blanche* may be seen as one of M.'s prime reasons to dislike the French navy. When he arrived at *Nukuhiva on "*Julia," probably in June, 1842, the French had just taken possession of the *Marquesas, and *Reine Blanche*, flagship of *Admiral Dupetit-Thouars, was in the harbor, in a squadron of perhaps six men-of-war. In Papeete in September, the ship was the scene of French demands for tribute from *Tahitian chiefs, and it was back at Nukuhiva early in October.

Max Radiquet, secretary to l'état-major général, and the log, *Le journal de bord de la Reine Blanche* (1841-1845), confirm the outline of M.'s details in *T.* and *O.*: M. was imprisoned on *Reine Blanche*, along with some nine other mutineers, spending from three to five days in the ship's brig in irons, given only poor food and watery wine for sustinence.
T. 3; T. 34; 0. 19; 0. 27; 0. 29

REPUBLIC, --S; REPUBLICAN, --S
     The *Latin root of "republic" means "the public thing."
It came to refer to a state and institutions controlled by the
*people who elect political decision-making agents as their
representatives.   Thus, a republic differs from a "pure"
democracy in that a middle-man makes the decisions rather
than a voter whose ballot directly expresses his wishes. There
are dangers inherent in the republican system, including limitations of suffrage, potential betrayal of interests, and para-
doxes such as that of the "Republican *slaves" of *M.D.* 89.
     The Republican Political Party is not referred to in M.'s
novels. *Jefferson's Democratic-Republican party was created
in opposition to the *Federalists, in 1791; it evolved into the
*Democratic Party, the main opposition to which (from 1836)
were the *Whigs (who opposed *Andrew Jackson). The Whigs
disintegrated by 1852; a coalition of Whigs and Jacksonian
Democrats was formed in 1856, calling itself the Republican
Party. (It won the *Presidency for *Abraham Lincoln in 1860
and thereafter dominated national politics until the 1930's.)
W. 51; W. 56; W. 71; M.D. 89

REPUBLICA DEL ECUADOR; QUITO
     See "Quito."
M.D. 99

RESACA DE LA PALMA
     A battle in the *Mexican War, near Matamoros, Mexico,
on 9 May 1846, won by U.S. troops under Zachary Taylor, four
days before *Congress declared war. In Spanish, "resaca"
means "undertow," or "dry river bed." "Palma" is "palm tree."
C.M. 19

RESACA DE LA *TOMBS*
     See "Tombs, the"; "Resaca de la Palma."
C.M. 19

REVENGE
     Revenge, a 500-ton galleon of great firepower, was
launched (1574-77?) when Queen *Elizabeth began rebuilding
her navy. *Revenge* became the model for many other *British
ships. With a crew of 190 men, she was commanded by *Drake
against the *Spanish Armada, and served on by Sir Richard
Grenville (1542-1591) in a 1591 battle lost to a huge *Spanish
fleet: commemorated in Tennyson's poem, "The Revenge."
M. 28

REVIVAL OF LEARNING
M. here refers to that which mid-nineteenth-century scholars began to call the Renaissance (Fr. for "rebirth," from Ital. *rinascenza*, or *rinascimento*): a sloughing-off of what was seen as the dark mind and spirit of the *Middle Ages.

Starting in *Italy in the mid-fourteenth century, and throughout Europe by the sixteenth, study of *Greek and *Latin classics spread, primarily through the efforts of *Petrarch and other humanists. Neoplatonic philosophy became the norm, through the thinking of Mirandola's disciples. In art, sculpture, and architecture, the aesthetic of *Michelangelo and his school turned to the natural—man and his earthly environment—rather than strictly to the superhuman. In politics, such thinkers as More and Erasmus were perhaps horrified by trends begun by the classically trained *Machiavelli, but efficiency and economy became the major concerns of statesmanship.

Correctly or not, the Renaissance is seen as the beginning of modern civilization.
M.D. 55

REVOLUTION; REVOLUTIONARY WAR
See "American Revolution."
Passim

RHAETIAN
The "Rhaetian heights above *Lombardy" are the Rhaetian *Alps, along the Italo-Swiss and Austro-Swiss border.
M. 168

RHEIMS
Rheims (or Reims) is in the Marne Département of northern *France, on the Vesle River and the Aisne-Marne Canal, eighty-five miles east-northeast of *Paris. It is the *champagne center of France. The allusion in *M*. 60 to the coronation of *Louis le Grand refers to the fact that Clovis I was crowned at Rheims, as were all subsequent French kings. (The present *Gothic cathedral at Rheims dates from 1211-1311.)
M. 60

RHENISH
Rhenish wines (or *hock) have been produced in *Germany along the *Rhine (and perhaps *Moselle) Rivers since *Roman times. They are generally fruity and flowery in bouquet: the favorite wines of Queen *Victoria, who once visited Rhine vineyards.
M.D. 77; P. 20:1

RHENISH
The "Rhenish baron" of *I.P.* 1 would originate from Rhenish Hesse: part of *Germany's *Rhineland area. (The post-World War II Rhenish Palatinate, formerly in *Bavaria, was historically part of the *Holy Roman Empire, from whence arise its titled nobility.)
I.P. 1

RHINE, --S; RHINELAND
The Rhine River of central and western Europe flows over 800 miles from the *Alps to the North Sea. It borders *Switzerland, Liechtenstein, *Austria, *France, *Germany, and the *Netherlands and connects with many canals.

The German portion, or Rhineland, is a picturesque region of ancient castles and forts, reflecting history from *Roman and *Holy Roman Empire times. It is dotted with *Rhenish wine vineyards, spas such as Mainz and Wiesbaden, and cultural centers such as *Cologne.

The formerly *Prussian Rhine Province was bounded by Luxembourg, *Belgium, the *Netherlands, the former province of *Westphalia and Hesse-Nassau, Hess, the Rhenish Palatinate, and France. Ongoing border controversy is too complex a topic to be treated in the present volume, but a dramatic example of the area's instability is seen in the first quarter of the nineteenth century: in 1801, all territories west of the Rhine were ceded to France, including what had previously been 100 independent principalities. The *Congress of Vienna returned most of them to Prussia in 1824, to form a Rhine Province with its capital at Coblenz.

When M. first visited the Rhineland (8-10 December 1849), he arrived at Cologne and was unable to obtain passage on a Rhine steamer. He wined, beered, and smoked his way to Coblenz by land. On his next trip, he visited *Strasbourg, *Heidelburgh, *Frankfurt am Main, and Mainz, where he boarded a Rhine cruise to Cologne that lasted some eight hours (20-24 April 1857).
M. 1; M. 84; M. 153; R. 33; C.M. 30

RHODE ISLAND
The smallest state (forty-seven miles N.-S., forty miles E.-W. along the *Atlantic) was one of the original thirteen states of the Union. It is bordered by *Massachusetts (N. and E.), the *Atlantic (S.), and *Connecticut (W.), and is indented by *Narragansett Bay, which runs north to *Providence. Verrazano explored the coastline in 1524, and the first settlement in 1636 brought victims of religious persecution seeking refuge in the haven Roger Williams had created on land purchased from the Indians. Boundary disputes with surrounding theocracies, *King Philip's War (1675-76), and privateering problems made development slow, but the city of Newport became important to the infamous "Triangular trade" of rum, *slaves, and molasses.

Rhode Island was the first colony to declare independence, as "The State of Rhode Island and Providence Plantations" (still its official name). It opposed the *War of 1812, which damaged its maritime profits. In the nineteenth century, a burgeoning textile industry brought *English, *Irish, and French *Canadian (and later *Polish and *Italian) immigrants, so that Rhode Island became the most densely populated state.

(Cranston, Rhode Island, was the birthplace of the historical *Israel Potter.)
I.P. 2

RHODES
The *Greek island in the Aegean, twelve miles off *Turkey, is forty-four miles long and twenty miles wide, with a top altitude of 3,986 feet. It was colonized c. 1000 B.C. by the Dorians and was independent until late sixth-century conquest by the *Persians. Rhodes was a member of the Delian League in the fifth century but separated during the *Peloponnesian Wars.

Its greatest prosperity (surpassing that of *Athens) came after the death of *Alexander (323 B.C.). The symbol of its greatness, the *Colossus in the harbor, fell in an earthquake in 224 B.C. Second-century involvement with *Rome weakened Rhodes, and its chief city was sacked in 43 B.C. It was part of the *Byzantine Empire until the Fourth *Crusade capture of *Constantinople, in 1204. Rhodes was neglected under *Suleiman I in the sixteenth century. The city of Rhodes remained walled and medieval and was barred to *Christians (until 1912).

M. must have been disappointed at the ship's failure to land at Rhodes on his cruise in February of 1857. His journal expresses that disappointment but adds, "One finds that, after

all, the most noted localities are made up of common elements of earth, air, & water" (4 February).
See also "Rhodian . . . . "
M.D. 35

RHODIAN OCEAN ORDINANCES

Penny Cyclopaedia (XIX, 1841) discusses the code of laws of the Rhodian navy, "adopted afterwards by other maritime states." But M. may have found the source of his comments also in *Democratic Review* XXV.
See also "Rhodes."
W. 72

RHONE, --S

The Rhone River of *Switzerland and southeastern *France flows for 505 miles (including its traverse of Lake Geneva: M.'s "*Lake Lemans"). The Rhone turns south in France, becoming the principal artery of northern France to the *Mediterranean.
M. 84; M. 153

RIBS AND TRUCKS

Vincent's *The Trying-Out of Moby-Dick* makes explicit M.'s debt to *Ribs and Trucks* (Boston, 1842).
See also "Extracts" 76.
M.D. Extracts 76

RICHARD

See "Coeur de Lion."
W. 39

RICHARD

See "*Bon Homme Richard.*"
I.P. 18

RICHARD III

Richard III (1452-1485), King of *England from 1483, was (Lancastrian) duke of Gloucester when he faithfully accompanied his brother, Edward IV, into exile and then fought at the battle of Tewkesbury.
Richard's deeds are shadowed in disapproval begun by *Tudor historians, spread by Sir Thomas More (in *Richard the*

Thirde, The History of King, 1543), and made generally accreditable by *Shakespeare's portrayal of him as a *Machiavellian tyrant.

Many of the cold-blooded acts ascribed to him (and undoubtedly credited by M.) have been proven false. He was probably involved in the murder of Henry VI (1471); he married Anne Neville to secure half the vast *Neville holdings; he beheaded Lord Hastings, defender of the validity of Edward IV's marriage and legitimacy of the minor Edward V, in order to have himself declared rightful king. It is not certain that he arranged for the murder of the child Edward and his brother in the *Tower, but contemporary credence in his guilt increased Richard's unpopularity.

Despite his numerous acts for the betterment of English life, alienation of the aristocracy, who supported Henry Tudor (later Henry VII), led to his death in battle against Henry's forces at Bosworth. His naked body was carried in public to burial without honor in Greyfriars Church.

There is little evidence that he was a hunchback.

The *R.* 30 allusion to "Wellingborough's" father's diary entry may refer to Allan Melvill's (see "Walter Redburn") notes of his 1808 *Liverpool visit and viewing of the play.
R. 30; M.D. 55

RICHARDSON'S DICTIONARY

Charles Richardson, *A New Dictionary of the English Language* (Philadelphia, 1851). All "etymology" quotations are accurate.
M.D. Etymology

RICHMOND

The ancient *British Richmond family appears to have originated in Brittany. Builder of the castle at Richmond, Yorkshire (Alan I, d. 1089), accompanied *William the Conqueror; first to hold the title Earl of Richmond formally was Alan III (d. 1146). Richmonds intermarried with royalty and were frequently a threat to British monarchs. *John of Gaunt (afterward Duke of Lancaster) surrendered the Earldom (in 1372) and it passed to John IV. Richmond lands (but not title) were at one time in *Neville hands.

Richmonds were characterized for posterity by *Shakespeare in *Richard III* (v, 4): the king refers to Henry of Richmond (by 1485, Henry VII):

> I think there be six Richmonds in the field;
> Five have I slain to-day, instead of him--
> A horse! a horse! my kingdom for a horse!

Intermarriage with *Stuarts in 1675 brought the Dukedom to Charles Lennox, illegitimate son of *Charles II (by Louise de Kéroualle). By M.'s time, the title was held by Gordon-Lennox (Charles, 1791-1860), nephew of *Lord George Gordon.

M. groups the Richmonds with other violent and ambitious "royal" families.
P. 1:3

"RIDDOUGH'S HOTEL"; RIDDOUGH'S ROYAL HOTEL
Riddough's Royal Hotel in *Liverpool (probably built in 1785, under another name) was at the bottom of *Lord Street (running at right angles to *Castle). The area had many shops and much traffic to the Exchange and the *Custom House. By the time of M.'s (1839) visit, fictionalized in *R*., it had been converted into shops, along with other area hotels. It is not shown on the map "Wellingborough" finds in *The Picture of Liverpool*. (Furthermore, M.'s father, Allan Melvill, fictionalized as "*Walter Redburn," was not in Liverpool on 20 March 1808, as "Walter" was.)
R. 30; R. 31

RIENZI
Nicolo Gabrini Rienzi (1313-1354) was a republican reformer upon whom Bulwer Lytton based his 1835 novel, *Rienzi*, the text for Wagner's opera of that name.
W. 54

RIGADIG
The rigadoon is a lively dance for two people, originating in the seventeenth century, in *France.
M.D. 27

RIGEL
A bright star, the blue supergiant at the heel of the *constellation *Orion.
M. 169

RIGHT HONORABLE
In *Britain, a courtesy title, without legal status. Right Honourable is prefixed to titles of *earls, viscounts, *barons, younger sons of dukes and marquesses, privy councillors,

some *lord mayors, Lords Justices, Justices of Appeal, some Commonwealth ministers.
R. 33

RIGHTS OF MAN
Seventeenth- and eighteenth-century philosophers posited certain inalienable rights expressed vividly by *Locke and embodied in the 1789 French Declaration of the Rights of Man, following the Declaration of Rights drawn up in 1774 by the First American *Continental Congress. Originally, the major trio of rights was expressed as "life, liberty, and property." The third item was changed to "the pursuit of happiness" in the 1776 *Declaration of Independence, presumably by *Thomas Jefferson.
W. 5; M.D. 89

RIGHT WHALE
See "Cetology" section.
M. 1; M. 13; M.D. 32 and elsewhere

"RILL"
M.'s use of the synonym for a small brook is a nod toward one of *Nathaniel Hawthorne's *Twice-Told Tales* (1837): "A Rill from the Town Pump" (Sealts #259).
W. 68

RINALDINI, RINALDO
Renaud (Rinaldo, or Rinaldino) was one of *Charlemagne's legendary knights, noted for his violence. In the cycle of legends, he was at first the eldest of the Four Sons of Aymon, and Charlemagne's enemy. Pardoned on condition he surrender his horse, Bayard, he became a hermit in *Palestine, but no other person could mount Bayard. Various other legends are recounted in *Orlando Furioso* and in *Tasso's *Gerusalemme Liberata*.
M.D. 45

". . . RING THE CHANGES"
In the underworld, replace good money with bad.
C.M. 4

RIO; RIO DE JANEIRO

M.'s decision in W. 50 to "yield and recant," providing the obligatory paean to "The Bay of all Beauties," keeps him in company with most other sea writers of the time, including *Wilkes (I, Chapter II, 74-75), and *Stewart, who devotes all of Chapter I, Letter 1 to it. Ammens (pp. 112-113) was to conclude: "whatever the differences of opinion to which sea-faring men are prone, they fairly agree that no other spot of intertropical grandeur and beauty that has met their vision is comparable to the Bay of Rio Janeiro."

Anderson (*Melville in the South Seas*, Chapter 14) shows that *United States* was in harbor for only one week, and that no shore leave was given. Most of the events of the W. chapters about Rio are imaginary, with the exception of the race (won by United States). M.'s letter of 1847 addressed to Augustus Platt van Schaick praises Rio (Davis and Gilman *Letters*, p. 62).

Rio de Janeiro is a state of south-eastern *Brazil, as well as a city. The name means "river of January," supposedly commemorating its "discovery" by André Goncalves and Amerigo Vespucci, 1 January 1502. Another claimant as discoverer was Goncalo Coelho (1504). *French Huguenots settled a colony, but the *Portuguese prevailed late in the 1560's, and the city was laid out as São Sebastiâo do Rio de Janeiro, in honor of King Sebastian of Portugal. Quarrels with the French continued throughout the eighteenth century, and the French influence is still much in evidence in modern Rio. The Portuguese court of *John VI moved to Rio in 1808, and the city was developed and thrown open to world commerce. Brazil was declared independent in 1822, and Rio became the capital (replaced by Brasilia in 1960), starting the process of turning a colonial town into an imperial city.

The seaport on the southwestern shore of Guanabara Bay has a deep landlocked harbor ringed by crescent-shaped beaches. In M.'s time, there were dangerous swamps which spread fever, and the city built on narrow valleys had narrow and picturesque streets, forerunners of the wide modern boulevards with names commemorating historical persons and events.

See also "Arcos de Carico"; "Benedictine"; "Botofogo, Bay of"; "Church de Candelaria"; "Church of Nossa Senora de Gloria"; "Court of the Brazils"; "Don Pedro II"; "Gloria Hill"; "Ilha das Cobras"; "Larangieros"; "Organ Mountains"; "Passeo Publico"; "Praya Grande"; "Prays do Flamingo"; "St. Christova"; "Santa Cruz"; "Sugar Loaf."

O. 1; W. 39; W. 50; C.M. 2 and elsewhere

RIO BELMONTE
A city in southeastern Bahia, *Brazil, famous for the production of gold and pink marble.
W. 56

RIO DE LA PLATA
The estuary of the Paraná and Uruguay Rivers, between Argentina and Uraguay, is the major indentation of the eastern coast of *South America: an estuary and an ocean gulf combined, with fresh water in the portions further inland. It was discovered in 1516 and explored by *Magellan in 1520; Europeans called it the "River of Silver" because of the ornate silver ornaments worn by the local Indians. The area was first settled by *Mendoza in 1536, at *Buenos Aires. The name is sometimes given to the whole river system of Paraná-Paraguay-Uruguay.
M.D. 51; M.D. 61

RIO SACRAMENTO
The Sacramento River is *California's largest, fed by *Sierra Nevada Streams and emptying into San Francisco Bay. It flows through the area where gold was discovered in 1848, giving rise to much development by the time of M.'s writing of *M*.
M. 119

RIVER HORSE
Hippopotamus.
M.D. 1

RIZZIO
David Rizzio (or Riccio) was the lowborn *Italian secretary of *Mary Stuart whose presumptuous behavior so offended *Scottish nobles that, with the complicity of Mary's husband, Henry Stewart, Lord Darnley, he was murdered at Holyrood palace on 9 March 1566. Rizzio was dragged from the queen's presence and stabbed fifty-six times. The pregnant queen fled from the conspirators, Darnley denying responsibility until his fellows produced his signed agreement to assist.
0. 65

ROANOKE

"Roanoke country" is a familiar designation for southwestern *Virginia's *Appalachian Valley and Blue Ridge Mountain area. The city of Roanoke (166 miles west-southwest of Richmond) was founded in 1834, as "Big Lick." It remained undeveloped until the 1880's. The Roanoke River runs from southwestern Virginia into North *Carolina.

(North Carolina's Roanoke Island, forty miles north of Cape *Hatteras, was the site of a lost colony of 1585-87: now found.)

See also "Randolph, John."
W. 34; W. 90; M.D. 64

ROBERT LONG

See "Whaleman's Chapel."
M.D. 7

ROBINSON CRUSOE

The hero of Daniel Defoe's (1661-1731) novel of 1719 is startled to discover that he is not the only inhabitant of the island that shelters him after a shipwreck. The *T*. reference is to a passage in the chapter, "I find the Print of a Man's Naked Foot."

Crusoe is presumed patterned after *Alexander Selkirk (or Selcraig; 1676-1721), who spent over four years (1704-1709?) on *Juan Fernández island, west of *Valparaiso, *Chile. He was discovered and rescued by Captain Woodes Rogers, of the *Duke*, the pilot of which was *Dampier.
T. 7; R. 17

ROBINS THE LONDONER

George Henry Robins (1778-1847), a highly persuasive auctioneer, was the son of an important auctioneer, entering his father's business at an early age. Through his wit, his command of glowingly descriptive language, and his ability to see the advantages of properties, Robins became the perfect auctioneer. He wrote his own often-exaggerated advertisements, but no purchases were ever rejected as misrepresented. Some important sales: 1840 lease of Olympic Theatre; 1842 sale of contents of Strawberry Hill, with *Horace Walpole's collections, drawing buyers from all over the world. A popular eccentric, Robins gave much of his wealth to charity. Just before his death, he was offered 2,000 guineas plus expenses to travel to the *United States.

In *O*., his protege, "*Stubbs," is probably fictional.
0. 9

ROB ROY
    See "Scott, Sir Walter."
W. 4

ROCHEFOUCAULT, --ITES
    See "La Rochefoucauld, François."
C.M. 29; C.M. 45

ROCKAWAY BEACH
    *New York's Rockaway peninsula is a c. twelve-mile
stretch parallel to and extending from the south shore of *Long
Island, between the *Atlantic Ocean and Jamaica Bay.
    (There is also a Rockaway Beach in *California.)
M.D. 1

ROCK OF GIBRALTER
    See "Gibralter . . . . "
W. 51 and elsewhere

ROCKY MOUNTAINS
    The major mountain system of North America extends
c. 3,000 miles from central northern *Mexico into western
*Canada and northern Alaska to *Bhering Strait, north of the
*Arctic Circle. The Rockies are at their highest elevation in
modern Colorado, with more than forty peaks over 14,000 feet
in elevation. (Mount Elbert is highest, at 14,431.) The mountain chain forms the Continental Divide, a formidable natural
barrier with rugged topography formed by stream and ice erosion. In M.'s day, it was simpler to reach *California in a ship
rounding Cape *Horn than to cross the Rockies.
M.D. 42; P. 21:1

RODNEY
    Sir George (later Lord) Brydges Rodney (1718-1792) was
an *English admiral who won important battles against
*French, *Spanish, and *Dutch forces. His most famous feat
was "breaking the line" of the French, under *DeGrasse in the
*West Indies: the "Battle of the Saints," opening negotiations
which led to the 1783 Treaty of *Versailles.
    Rodney's personality, vain and unscrupulous, blem-
ished his military image. He avidly sought to brace his financial position by booty-taking and pushed his family fortunes
openly; for example, he made his son a post captain at fifteen

years of age. In later years he was accused of sacrificing service interests to his own good.

Perhaps it is a comment on *Billy Budd*'s "Captain Vere" that he rose in the ranks on Rodney's coattails (chapter 6).

See also "Beards."

R. 29; W. 83; W. 84

RODNEY

*Liverpool's Rodney Street, site of the city's most beautiful Georgian houses, was one of *William Roscoe's projects. It was named for Lord George Brydges *Rodney, English Admiral.

R. 32

RODS

A rod equals 5 1/2 yards.

M.D. 73 and elsewhere

ROGERS'S BEST CUTLERY

Reference may be to the actual nineteenth-century master silvermakers or, in light of context in *W.*, to the priapean significance of "Roger," which had commonly known sexual connotations.

W. 42; M.D. 4

ROGUE'S MARCH

Played by trumpeters or fifers of a regiment to drum out disorderly persons in a military camp. Leech (*Thirty Years From Home*) notes that it was played during *flogging through the fleet.

W. 88

ROKOVOCO

See "Kokovoco."

M.D. 13

ROMAN ARCHES

See "Roman triumphal arch."

M.D. 54

ROMAN CATHOLIC
See "Catholic . . . . "
Passim

ROMAN CATHOLIC CHURCH
Discussion of Roman Catholic ceremonial vestments in
M.D. 42 is in error; the "alb," or long white linen robe of a
priest is traditionally worn outside the cassock. The liturgical
color of the last two weeks of Lent is not white, except for
Maundy Thursday's commemoration of the Last Supper.
Throughout the *Bible, white is the garment color associated
with the glory of *God, in some visions, and in baptismal gar-
ments. The liturgical color sequence (since changed) had
remained constant since the sixteenth century, although the
color symbolism was no longer quite clear.
M.D. 42

ROMAN GENERAL
The *Roman general alluded to in *M.D.* 24 is Marcus
Aemilius Scarus (Aedile, 58 B.C.), whom Kitto (*Cyclopaedia of
Biblical Literature*, article on "Whale") says brought the skele-
ton of a whale found in *Joppa to Rome.
M.D. 24

ROMAN HALLS OF THERMES
See "Cluny, Hôtel de."
M.D. 41

ROMAN TRIUMPHAL ARCH
From the second century B.C., the *Romans built round
segmental and flat arches of stone or, later, concrete faced
with stone or tile. The separate triumphal arch, which did not
always span a roadway, commemorated an event or campaign. It was decorated with columns, bas-reliefs, and sculpture. Among the most important were arches of *Titus, Septimius Severus, and *Trajan. By the time of *Augustus, there
were thirty-six triumphal arches. M. visited *Rome in February and March 1857, commenting on several specimens in
Journal of a Visit to Europe and the Levant.
M.D. 86

ROMAN VELLUM
    Strong parchment made from calfskin, lambskin, or kidskin: usually used in book-binding, or for high quality writing paper.
C.M. 5

ROMAN WALLS
    Roman walls have a middle layer covered by tiles.
M.D. 86

ROME; ROMAN, --S; ROMAN EMPIRE; ROMISH
    M. was bitterly disappointed at having to abbreviate his itinerary on the 1849 trip to Europe; he would have to miss Rome. That omission was corrected in 1857, when he spent almost a month (25 February—21 March) in the "Eternal City." "Rome," for M., meant ancient Rome, about which he knew a great deal, as other entries in the present work show. Despite the perils of "bare-bones" histories, M.'s allusions suggest one here, if only to situate other references.
    The capital of *Italy (and of *Latium and Roma provinces) is located on the west coast of the peninsula on both banks of the *Tiber, fifteen miles inland from the Tyrrhenian Sea. The site of the present-day *Vatican City, Rome traditionally owes its founding (via *Virgil and *Livy) to *Romulus in 753 B.C. (Actual founders were probably Latin settlers from the Alban Hills who mingled with neighboring *Sabines on the east bank of the river.) By the eighth century B.C., the *Etruscans had founded the legendary royal house of the *Tarquins, attaining hegemony over Latium. The Roman Republic lasted some four centuries, starting in 500 B.C., at first governed by patricians, with a senate and two consuls. Conquest of *Greece brought high culture to Rome, which became master of central Italy.
    Among military encounters, the Romans clashed with Pyrrhus over the Greek colonies in the south; with *Carthage in three *Punic Wars; with *Hannibal, whose defeat by *Scipio brought domination of *Spain, *Sicily, Sardinia, *Corsica, north *Africa, and surrounding waters. In 190 B.C., *Antiochus conquered Rome; in 168 *Macedonia became a province. The Greeks formed the Achaean League to counter Rome, but they were crushed, like others, because of centrally located Roman sea power. From 112 to 101 B.C., *Marius made conquests in Transalpine *Gaul; the slave revolt of *Spartacus was put down, 73-71, and in 70, *Pompey wiped out Sulla ("*Sylla"), becoming virtual master of Rome, having defeated Mithradates.

Pompey, *Crassus, and *Julius Caesar formed the First Triumvirate in 60 B.C.; in 58, Caesar began domination of Cisalpine Gaul, broke with Pompey, and seized power to end the Republic. At the time of his assassination (44), Roman power extended from Spain to *Palestine. The Second Triumvirate included Octavian (later *Augustus), *Antony, and Lepidus. Octavian defeated Antony and *Cleopatra at *Actium in 31 B.C., bringing about the Pax Romana and extension of the Empire, as far north as *Scotland. Other rulers mentioned by M. include *Tiberius, *Caligula, *Claudius I, and *Nero.

Most of the ancient Roman population lived on the right bank of the Tiber, with good sanitation, central heating and running water in their homes, and social services for the poor; many became *Christians very early. Later rulers mentioned by M. include *Vespasian, *Titus, *Domitian, *Trajan, *Hadrian, and *Aurelian. "Barbarian" invasions of the third century A.D. influenced *Diocletian's division of the Empire into east and west. Constantine I moved the capital to *Byzantium, naming it *Constantinople. Under *Julian the Apostate, there was a resurgence of *paganism; serious decline began with the permanent division of the Empire by Theodosius I. Alaric I took Rome in 410; it was also invaded by *Attila. Through all of this, the *Popes gained power; by 476, the last Emperor of the west was deposed by the *Goths, but the idea of Imperial Rome survived until the fall of Constantinople in 1453; it had been revived in the *Holy Roman Empire, with *Charlemagne first Holy Roman Emperor (800).

Cola di *Rienzi tried to revive ancient institutions in the fourteenth century, but Papal dominion was firmly in place within eighty years. The great Renaissance (see "Revival of Learning") Popes such as *Leo X made Rome a cultural haven. Papal rule was interrupted late in the eighteenth and early in the nineteenth century, as well as in 1849. Rome became the capital of Italy in 1871.

M.'s 1857 stay in Rome, during a prolonged period of mental depression, was a disappointment. He entered the city through the swampy *Campagna and, as his journal notes, Rome "fell flat" on his first day. The Tiber was a yellow "ditch"; *St. Peters was a let-down. Ruins such as the Coliseum, and art works such as the bust of Tiberius and statue of the "*Dying Gladiator" did little to alter his sense that there was "No place where [a] lonely man will feel more lonely" (26). He viewed the Baths of Caracalla, visited graves of Keats, *Shelley, and others; saw the *Cenci and Farnese palaces (with the latter's statue of *Hercules), and other "compulsory" museums, churches, and ruins, as well as the *Vatican and the outskirts of Rome, including *Tivoli. Much of his journal notation is occupied with small individual art works, rather than with grand buildings or other "large" features of Rome. He was to capitalize on this focus in his *lecture, "Statues in Rome." M. departed Rome in the rain, 21 March—having had his usual trouble with visas.

Livy is the source for the story of Tarquin and the eagle, in *M.D.* 130.

The "Roman nose" or "bill" of the *albatross (*M.D.* 32, *M.D.* 42) is the aquiline nose traditionally seen on Roman statues.

"Romish injunctions" (*M.D.* 54) is a slur on the *Catholic Church, "Rome" being a synonym for "Pope."

The "Roman story" of *W.* 89 is *Shelley's *Count Cenci.*

See also "Pilate"; "Plebian"; "Praetorians" (regarding the "auction" of the Roman Empire).
Passim

ROMEO
The comparison of "Pierre" with *Shakespeare's tragic lover, of *Romeo and Juliet,* sheds some light on interpretation of M.'s protagonist. "Poor Romeo!" . . . "Alas, Romeo!" echoes "Mercutio's" observations on how love has reduced "Romeo" to uselessness: "Alas, poor Romeo" (II, iv, 13).
P. 1:6

ROMISH FAITH
See "Catholic Church."
M.D. 42

ROMISH-PAINTED MADONNA
See "Raphael."
C.M. 17

ROMNEY
The *British fifty-gun ship *Romney* was launched in 1762. She was seized by John Hancock's sloop *Liberty* in a 1768 battle with *Customs, in *Boston Harbor.
W. 65

ROMULUS AND REMUS
Sons of *Mars, twin brothers, legendary founders of *Rome who were at birth cast into the wilderness to punish their Vestal Virgin mother, Rhea Silvia. Suckled by a she-wolf, they survived. Quarreling over plans for Rome, Romulus

slew Remus. Mars later took Romulus to the heavens in a fiery chariot, where he became the god Quirinus.
R. 30; R. 33

RONDELETIUS

Guillaume Rondelet (1507-66), *French biologist and friend to *Rabelais, investigated the fish species of the *Mediterranean.
M.D. 32

"ROORA"

I have not been able to trace "roora," which M. claims is the traditional *Tahitian *poncho. *Ellis describes what he calls the tiputa ("tiputo" in Oliver).
O. 61; O. 67

ROOROOTOO

Rurutu is a high island of the (French *Polynesian) Tubuai (Austral) group, some 400 miles south of the *Society Islands.
O. 33

ROPE'S END

A hangman's noose, or length of cordage used as a form of punishment: a "starter."
W. 90

ROPO

Roa-Pua, *Marquesas.
T. 2; T. 30

ROSAMUND THE FAIR

Rosamond Clifford (d. ?1176) was probably mistress to Henry II. Her legend is told in a ballad in Percy's *Reliques*; in a poem by Samuel Daniel (1592), "The Complaint of Rosamond"; in *Addison's opera, *Rosamond* (1707; music by Thomas Augustine Arne).

Supposedly, Henry kept Rosamond inside a maze at Woodstock, where only he could find her. The queen, Eleanor of Aquitaine, discovered her by following a thread, and Rosamond did not long survive.
R. 43

ROSCOE; MR. ROSCOE
William Roscoe (1753-1831) was a multi-talented scholar, bibliophile, and author. Skilled in the law, banking, botany, and languages, he was best known in *America for his opposition in *Parliament to the *slave trade. His principal work is *Life of Lorenzo de'*Medici*, but he also wrote poetry, children's literature, a life of *Pope Leo the Tenth, and an edition of *Pope.
R. 30; R. 31

ROSE-BUD
See "Bouton de Rose."
M.D. 91

ROSEMARY
The evergreen *Rosmarinus officinalis* is a member of the mint family, native to the *Mediterranean. It bears small light-blue flowers yielding a fragrant oil used for cooking and in perfumes. It is among the plants "Ophelia" offers in *Hamlet* IV, v, 173; as she notes, in "flower language," it stands for Remembrance.
P. 4:4

ROSICRUCIAN
Rosicrucian societies, fraternities, and orders probably originated before the seventeenth century. Their manifesto, *Fama Fraternitatis* (1614) traces the journey of the founder, one Christian Rosenkreuz (1378-1484), to the middle east, where he received the secret wisdom about nature and the spiritual world passed down through the orders since. The document demanded 100 years of secrecy, claiming that after 120 years Rosenkreuz's perfectly preserved body had been unearthed and hidden.
Some scholars relate the order, which somewhat resembles *freemasonry, to the Essenes of *Jesus's time, to early *Christians, to the *Jewish *cabala, and to the alchemy of *Paracelsus. The order supposedly emerges cyclically (every 108 years in a given locale).
The names of *Francis Bacon, *Isaac Newton, *Leibniz, *Benjamin Franklin, *Talleyrand, and many others have been associated with Rosicrucianism, which has been seen as a link between the Renaissance (see "Revival of Learning") and the "scientific revolution" of the seventeenth century.
C.M. 23

ROSSE

A nobleman of *Scotland who (along with "Angus") addresses "Macbeth" as the "*Thane of Cawdor," in *Shakespeare's *Macbeth I, iii.
W. 51

ROTHSCHILD, BARON

All five sons of Meyer Anshelm Rothschild (1743-1812), *German *Jewish founder of the European banking empire, were barons. The surname derives from a red shield on the Frankfurt ghetto house in which the family lived. The father established moneylending branches in Europe and *England, his sons acting as branch managers. The sons were made *Austrian barons in 1812, receiving the right to use "von" before their names.

Nathan Mayer, a grandson, gave the House of Rothschild historic eminence in raising $100,000,000 for European governments during the *Napoleonic Wars.

Many Rothschilds have entered politics and have been especially active in Jewish causes, and the family continues its influence today.

M. visited the Rothschild combination home and moneylending business in *Frankfurt am Main, *Germany, on 22 and 23 April 1857, commenting in his journal: "Eminent hard-ware merchant. Aspect of cash-room. kegs, barrels, rolls, presses, weights & scales, coopers, carmen & porters."
P. 2:2

ROTTERDAM

The port city of South *Holland, on the New Mass River, thirteen miles southeast of The Hague, was chartered in 1328. Its greatest growth occurred in the nineteenth century, after the separation of the *Netherlands and *Belgium.
R. 24

ROUND HOUSE

M.'s source, *Life and Remarkable Adventures of Israel R. Potter* (see "Israel Potter's autobiographical story"), provides a gloss: "a prison so called, appropriated to the confinement of run-aways, and those convicted of small offenses." (Undoubtedly constructed like a railroad roundhouse: circular, with pie-shaped sections.)
I.P. 24

ROUND ROBIN, THE

A petition or protest signed in circular form so that no name heads the list: used by sailors to make their grievances known, avoiding reprisal. A corruption of the French original: *rond ruban* (round ribbon).
0. 20; 0. 30

ROUSSEAU

Jean Jacques Rousseau (1712-1778), *French-*Swiss writer of fiction, political and social theory, and music, gives his *apologia pro vita sua* in *Confessions*, a copy of which M. purchased in 1849 (Sealts #429). Rousseau's concerns can be seen, however, even in the books M. wrote before that time. His main ideas, too complex to be explained briefly, are as follows: man is naturally good (there is no original sin); society (especially that of cities) is at fault for breaking bonds between men; unequal distribution of material goods and unequal rights are central problems of modern man. Rousseau's ideas have been greatly oversimplified so that we see him as exponent of the "natural" life in uncivilized places. His effect in his own time was ultimately revolutionary, although he did not preach revolution. Rather he was a great radical thinker who eloquently asked the right questions about modern society.

Early thrust into what became life-long poverty, Rousseau at first sought wealth and fame in *Paris. He received no positive recognition until his prize winning 1749 essay, *Discours sur les sciences et les arts*, after which he redirected his aims to less material matters, finding success in music, comedy writing, and such serious publications as *Discours sur l'origine de l'inegalité parmi les hommes*, *Discours sur l'économie politique*, and a novel, *Julie, ou la nouvelle Héloise*. By 1758, he had broken with philosophers; his writings such as *Du contrat social*, and *Emile* (a novelistic treatise on education) antagonized authority because of their skepticism and criticism of dogmatic religion. When a warrant was issued for his arrest, he fled to Switzerland, where he alienated Swiss religious leaders and then to England, with the help of *David Hume, with whom he quarreled. Returning to France, in 1767, still subject to arrest, he married and publicly read *Confessions*, the autobiographical work begun when *Voltaire denounced him. Toward the end of his life, he wrote *Dialogues: Rousseau juge de Jean Jacques*, which he attempted to place on the railed altar at Notre Dame, only to end feeling rejected even by *God. His *Rêveries du promeneur solitaire*, the final work, is a tribute to nature and its beauty.

Ex-schoolteacher M. was much taken by Rousseau's admission that when he was a school master he "could have killed his scholars sometimes."
T. 17; M.D. 96; C.M. 26

ROUSSEAU, THE

A *Rousseau* of *New Bedford (not *Nantucket, as M. has it in *M*. 32) spoke *Acushnet* (see "Pequod") off Albemarle island, 3 November 1841.
M. 32

ROWELS

Wheels with radiating sharp points, such as those on spurs.
M.D. 87

ROWLAND AND SON

The fictional compound that grows *beards may owe its name to the amusing work of the cartoonist Thomas Rowlandson (1756-1827), an admirer of *Hogarth who worked in caricature and political cartoons. He illustrated Sterne's works and *Munchausen's *Travels*.
P. 17:3

ROYAL COLLEGE OF SURGEONS

*London's diploma- and license-granting Royal College of Surgeons at Lincoln's Inn Fields (enlarged in 1848) was founded in 1745 when surgeons broke ranks with barbers in the three-hundred year-old Barber Surgeons' Company. Their first hall was in the Old Bailey, where they dissected murderers' bodies. In the early nineteenth century the Surgeons performed such experiments as attempted galvanization of a human body. By mid-century, they had a famous collection of skeletons (including those of dwarfs and giants), bones of anomalies (including the skulls of a two-headed child), and various mummies.

It was fashionable to visit the College's Museum (see "Hunter, William and John"), and M. did so on 14 December 1849. Although *W*. was "completed" and sold to publisher Richard Bentley, M. records (18 December): "Spent an hour or so looking over 'White Jacket' preparatory to sending it finally to Bentley—who, though he has paid his money, has not received his wares." Thus his visit of a few days earlier might

well have affected his characterization of the bizarre "Surgeon Cuticle."
W. 63

"ROYAL FISH, A"
*Scoresby (Vol II), claims that the whale was made royal property by Acts of Edward II in 1315 and 1324.
M.D. 24

ROYAL GEORGE
In one of the most dramatic sea tragedies, the *Royal George*, a classical three-decker ship called the greatest of her time, sank at *Spithead in 1782. The vessel had been heeled over for repairs, with guns run to one side and a large amount of rum being loaded, when water started entering the gun ports. The order to right ship was delayed, and many lives were lost when she fell on her side.
W. 54

ROYAL MISSION CHAPEL OF PAPOAR
See "Papoar."
O. 44

RUBENS
Sir Peter Paul Rubens (1577-1646) was the greatest *Flemish painter of his time. His youth was spent in *Westphalia and *Antwerp, but after 1600 he resided in *Genoa or *Rome, Italy, studying classical, Renaissance (see "Revival of Learning"), and contemporary artists. He developed his own sensuous and heroic style (using local folk as models) in the tryptychs, *The Raising of the Cross* (1610-11) and *The Descent from the Cross* (1611-14), which M. saw in *Cologne in 1849. The popular Rubens was a prolific artist whose studio employed 200 assistants to produce portraits, book illustrations, tapestries, and other decorations.
A skilled diplomat, Rubens was knighted by *Charles I. Among his other great works: *Hélène Fourment* (1631); *Rape of the Daughters of Leucippus* (c. 1618).
P. 26:1

RUBICON
To "cross the Rubicon" is to take a step from which there is no turning back. In ancient *Italy, the Rubicon was a small

stream flowing into the Adriatic and forming the boundary between Italy and Cisalpine *Gaul. Despite an edict forbidding
*Roman generals to cross, in 49 B.C. *Julius Caesar crossed in
pursuit of *Pompey, precipitating civil war.

(It is not certain that the modern Rubicone [formerly Fi-
umicino] River is the original.)
P. 11

RUE DAUPHINE

The only rue Dauphine (sans accent) in modern *Paris
runs a short distance from the south end of *Pont Neuf to Carrefour de Buci. M.'s claim in *M.D.* 104 that part of a whale
skull had been found in 1779 on "the Rue Dauphiné . . . , a
short street opening almost directly upon the palace of the
*Tuileries" seems to be in error. Vincent's *The Trying-Out of
Moby-Dick* (IV, 23) suggests several obscure sources for the
reference. But M. himself may have seen such an artifact at
the Dupuytren medical museum (visited 5 December 1849).
Kendra H. Gaines has provided M.'s probable source: the article "Whales," in *Penny Cyclopaedia*.
M.D. 104

RUHOOKA

A phonetic rendering of Ua Huka, *Marquesas,
*Washington Group.
T. 2

RULE OF THREE

See "Three, Rule of."
0. 17; W. 6

RUNIC

Runes (O.E. run, secret) are characters of the earliest
alphabet used by northern Europe's *Gothic tribes, most often
found in *Scandinavia and the *British Isles. They were supposedly magical inscriptions, employed for secrecy, divination,
and charms.

In Scandinavian mythology, *Odin won knowledge of the
Runes through suffering. In the *Elder Edda* he says he hung
"Nine whole nights on a wind-rocked tree/Wounded with a
spear" in order to pass the knowledge on to men who could in-
scribe runes on wood, metal, or stone for protection.
M. 109

RUPERT, PRINCE
The irascible Rupert of the *Rhine, or Rupert of the Palatinate (1619-1682), nephew of *Charles I of *England, was a hard and skilful commander in the English Civil War and was appointed general in 1644, to the dissatisfaction of several powerful factions and eventual displeasure even of the king. Transferred to ship command, he suffered a series of defeats and retired briefly to his native *Germany. After the Restoration, *Charles II rewarded him financially for his military services. He traded in shares, participated in the Hudson Bay Company, and dabbled in military scientific experiments in England, where he was created Duke of Cumberland and Earl of Holderness in 1644. Unmarried, he had two illegitimate children.
R. 36

RUSCHENBERGER
William S.W. Ruschenberger, a surgeon in the U.S. *Navy, visited *Honolulu five years before M., in 1838. His book, *A Voyage round the World, in the years 1835-1836-1837* (Philadelphia, 1838) is a valuable and impartial source of data on the *Sandwich Islands, somewhat corrective of missionary accounts.
O. 49

RUSSIA, --N
The name "Russia" applies to the Russian Empire which preceded the Union of Soviet Socialist Republics, with the capital at *St. Petersburg. The word originated as a designation for the tenth-century Kiev confederacy and gained western usage despite the fact that expansion by the *Cossacks encompassed not only Russian peoples. Ivan IV (the Terrible) first used the title *tsar, in 1547. Russian expansion was unabated during M.'s time.

"Russia leather," or Chamois (*P.* 17:1) is made from the flesh split of sheepskin, processed with fish oil.

See also "Cossacks, Cossacs"; "Kamschatka"; "Kremlin"; "Malakoff"; "Muscovite"; "Siberia."
O. 48; R. 7; R. 9; R. 44; R. 57; W. 34; W. 35; W. 46; W. 69; W. 72; W. 88; M.D. 45; M.D. 83; M.D. 89; P. 7:5; P. 17:1; I.P. 21; C.M. 36

RUSSIA, STATUTE BOOK OF THE DESPOTIC EMPIRE OF
See "Tsar."
W. 72

RYDAL MOUNT
    See "Wordsworth."
W. 11

S

SABAEAN, --S
    The Sabaeans were a Semitic nomad merchant people of
southwest *Arabia. "Sabaean odors," in poetic use, refers to
the renowned spices brought from Yemen, such as myrhh and
frankincense. The odors, although extravagantly lovely, au-
gur ill, and the Sabaean people, as represented in the book of
*Job, took hold of M.'s imagination. In Job 1:15, the messen-
ger first tells Job that the Sabaeans have taken his oxen and
slain his servants, adding "And I only am escaped alone to tell
thee" (the subtitle of the Epilogue to *M.D.*).
    The poetry in *W.* is misquoted from *Milton's *Paradise
Lost* (IV, 156-66):

> Now gentle gales
> Fanning their odoriferous wings dispense
> Native perfumes, and whisper whence they stole
> Those balmy spoils. As when to them who sail
> Beyond the Cape of Hope, and now are past
> Mozambick, off at sea north-east winds blow
> Sabaean odours from the spicy shore
> Of Araby the blest; with such delay
> Well pleas'd they slack their course, and many a
>   league
> Cheer'd with the grateful smell old Ocean smiles:
> So entertain'd those odorous sweets the Fiend.

W. 14

SABBATH
    The word is from the Hebrew *shabath*, to rest. The
fourth Commandment enjoined the *Hebrews to observe the
seventh day of the week as one of rest and worship (*Exodus
20:8-11), so *Christian and other holy "Sabbaths" are mis-
nomers. Christians observe Sunday (the first day of the week):
other traditions are: Monday—*Greeks; Tuesday—*Persians;
Wednesday—*Assyrians; Thursday—*Egyptians; Friday—
*Mohammedans.

The sanctimonious Captain Ringbolt, in "Sailors' Rights and Sailors' Wrongs," addresses himself to M.'s claim that there are "no Sundays off soundings" (W. 38): "Let us render obsolete the saying of 'no Sunday off soundings.' There *is* a Sabbath there as well as ashore, and we are as much bound to regard it as any men, to say the least, for none have more reason for gratitude to its Institutor than ourselves." (M. negatively reviewed Ringbolt's book in the 6 March 1847 *Literary World*, seeing its author as utterly supportive of the traditional tyrannical navy hierarchical system.)

*Reverend Stewart (I, p. 36) makes much of a Sunday conversation with a happy young sailor who has attended his services and exclaims, "I never expected such a sabbath at sea-earth can scarce know a better." M.'s argument in W. 38 is that true Christianity no more exists on a warship than it does off; services are a mere show and chaplains the servants of politics and war.

M. also refers to Sunday as the "Lord's Day" (passim).
Passim

SABINE
The Sabines were a politically disunited, superstitious people whose village was northeast of *Rome. After a long history of war, the Romans defeated them in 290 B.C.

The legend of the Sabine atrocity is not based on history: *Romulus could not provide his followers with wives, so he tricked the Sabine men, inviting them to participate in a day of games, during which the Roman youths carried off all the virgins they could find. The legend is frequently portrayed in art: most famous example, *Rubens' canvas: "The Rape of the Sabine Women."
T. 30

SABOTS
*French wooden shoes.
I.P. 25

SACO
The Saco River flows from the base of Mt. Washington, in *New Hampshire's *White Mountains, through the Notch area that *Hawthorne set several stories in, emptying finally into the *Atlantic in *Maine. M.'s 1847 wedding journey included the area.
M.D. 1

SADDLEBACK
See "Greylock."
I.P. 1

SADDLE-MEADOWS
P.'s fictional locale is no doubt modeled after the *Pittsfield, *Massachusetts area closely associated with the Melville family. Mount *Greylock is called "Saddleback," and neighboring places had "meadows" in their names (for example, Oliver Wendell Holmes's "Canoe Meadows"). "Pierre's" ancestral home resembles Broadhall, owned by M.'s grandfather, Major Thomas Melvill. There M. often visited his uncle, Major Thomas Melvill, Jr. The "Saddle Meadows Artillery Corps" (*P.* 1:4) hearkens back to the experiences of the military Melvills, as well as those of the military *Gansevoorts of New York State, M.'s maternal forebears.
The many biographical analogies are discussed fully in Murray's edition of *P.*
P. Passim

SAFETY-LAMP FOR COAL MINES
See "Davy, Sir Humphrey."
W. 31

SAGAS
"Saga" means "story" in Old Norse, particularly applied to narratives of the *Middle Ages from *Iceland and *Norway. There are three main types: family sagas, kings' sagas, and legendary heroic sagas. Most famous is *Njals saga*, a long, action-packed family chronicle which studies the social problems of a new community, as well as the emotional makeup of individuals.
Sealts #500 is *Frithiof's Saga, or the Legend of Frithiof,* by Esais Tegner (1835), a Norwegian saga translated from *Swedish.
M. 3

SAG HARBOR
A peninsula of southeastern *Long Island, on an inlet of Gardiners Bay, nine miles northeast of Southhampton. Sag Harbor was settled between 1720 and 1730 and incorporated in 1846. It was a very important whaling port in the nineteenth century, producing over a tenth of the nation's whale oil. Sag Harbor had the first *Custom House in *New York.
R. 23; M.D. 12; M.D. 13

SAGITTARIUS
See "Zodiac."
M.D. 99

SAHARA
The world's largest desert, covering 3,500,000 square
miles of northern *Africa, may indeed be called the "Fiery"
Desert (O. 73). With temperatures up to 136° F. and less than
ten inches of rain per year, the Sahara has no permanent
streams. It is a windswept, mountainous (some volcanic) region of denuded rocks such as Hammada el Hamra in southern Tripolitania, with the *Nile and *Niger rivers at its edges.
The 1,200 mile-wide Sahara, inhabited by only a few *Arabs,
was first traversed by Europeans in the nineteenth century.
O. 73; M. 12; M. 165; R. 30; W. 51; M.D. 96

SAILORS' MAGAZINE
Highly influential in the "*Christianizing" of seamen,
the original *Sailors' Magazine* was founded in *London in 1820
by the Reverend George C. Smith, mainstray of the *Bethel
movement. The *American counterpart started in 1825 as *The
Mariners' Magazine*, replaced in 1828 by *The Sailor's
Magazine and Naval Journal*, edited by the Reverend Joshua
Leavitt. The first issue set out an ambitious agenda (I, iii); the
magazine would include seafaring adventures and articles on
shipwrecks, religious experiences, churches and *Sunday
schools, nautical sciences, and the abuse of seamen. Ames
called it "an exceedingly silly periodical . . . too silly for children of five years old" (*Nautical Reminiscences*, Providence,
1832, pp. 47-48). But by 1847 *The Sailor's Magazine* was circulating 5,000 copies (many distributed free), and it later became
influential in the anti-*grog and anti-*flogging movements.
R. 9

SAILORS'-SNUG-HARBOR
At Alexander Hamilton's suggestion in 1801, twenty-
four acres of private land in *Manhattan were willed as the
site of a home for aged seamen, but economic realities forced
the transfer of the plan to *Staten Island land in 1831. Sailors'
Snug Harbor (no longer an asylum and now in the process of
becoming an historical landmark) is a combination of grand
Greek Revival edifices and Victorian cottages. Its columned
centerpiece edifice (1833) is flanked by symmetrical buildings
and columned porticoes overlooking Kill Van Kull near Upper
*New York Bay.

M.'s brother Thomas (1830-1884) was Governor of Sailors' Snug Harbor from 1867, and M. was a regular visitor to the institution, which often held grand annual dinners and other semi-public functions.
R. 24

ST. ALBANS

M. lumps the *Earl of St. Albans with other social-climbers. First Earl was Henry Jermyn (c. 1604-1684), lecherous courtier and favorite of *Charles I's Queen Henrietta Maria (whom he perhaps later married). A faithful Royalist, he was constantly rewarded, was assigned to the *French Court, and was finally made Earl by *Charles II, despite involvement in slander, seduction, and other scandals. A notorious gambler and glutton, he is castigated by Andrew Marvell as being "full of soup and gold," in "The Last Instructions to a Painter," 29 (1667).
P. 1:3

ST. ANTHONY

St. Anthony (or Antony) of *Egypt (c. A.D. 250-355). was the first *Christian monk, practicing a solitary ascetic life on a mountain near the *Nile. He emerged long enough to organize followers in a monastic life of poverty, chastity, and obedience and withdrew again to a mountain near the *Red Sea, site of the monastery bearing his name. He emerged once more at *Alexandria, just before his death. His feast day is January 17.
M. 94; W. 76

ST. AUGUSTINE

St. Augustine of Hippo (Numidia, in *Roman *Africa), the greatest thinker of *Christian antiquity, lived from 354 to 430. Brought up a Christian, he abandoned his religion but was converted in 387, as described in his *Confessions* (c. 400), a condemnation of his early life of sensuality. He renounced his profession of rhetorician, became bishop of Hippo in 396 and thereafter pursued theological controversies against *Manichaeans (whom he had followed), Donatists, and Pelagians.

For Augustine, original sin inherited from *Adam and Eve is man's basic flaw, but *God's grace is efficacious. Augustine's theology and self-hatred greatly influenced Franciscans and Cistercians of the *Middle Ages (while Dominicans followed Aquinas).

Other important works, heavily colored by the *Greek *Platonic tradition, are *De Civitate Dei (The City of God)*, a vindication of Christianity, and *De Doctrina Christiana*, which has influenced modern exegetical literary criticism. Augustine's feast is celebrated on August 28.

As Franklin points out (p. 174), the *P.I.O. man in *C.M.* tampers with Augustine's dates, for his own purposes.

M. 119; C.M. 22

ST. BEE'S HEAD

A sprit of land of *England's *Cumberland mountain lake area, extending into *Solway Firth (54°30' N., 3°40' W.). St. Bee's Head is the site of a twelfth-century *Benedictine priory and a New Stone Age site of c. 2500 B.C., discovered in 1870.

I.P. 16

ST. BERNARD; ST. BERNARD'S DOGS

St. Bernard dogs are large guard dogs of heavy coat, most noted for use at the Great St. Bernard Pass (8,100 feet) across the Pennine *Alps in *Switzerland. A hospice was founded on the site by St. Bernard of Menthon (d. c. 1081), and in M.'s time the dogs were employed in rescues, especially of Italian workmen.

M. 84; M.D. 81

ST. CHRISTINA

Santa Christina (Tauata or Tahuata) Island, in the southeastern *Marquesas, was a center of the *London Missionary Society's efforts in the early nineteenth century. As M. points out throughout *T.*, *Protestant proselytizers were repeatedly insulted and driven out. *Catholic missionaries, arriving somewhat later, were supported by the *French military contingent of *Dupetit-Thouars.

O. 3

ST. CHRISTOVA

São Cristovão, *Brazil, in the north of *Rio de Janeiro.

W. 39

ST. CLAIR

Lake St. Clair is located between southern *Ontario and southeastern *Michigan, just north of *Detroit. It is twenty-six miles long from north to south and twenty-four miles wide. It

is joined to Lake *Huron (N.) by the St. Clair River. It has always been important to *Great Lakes shipping. (Its islands
are now summer colonies, with present-day Grosse Pointe
along its shores.)

M. sailed Lake St. Clair in 1840, moving from Lake *Erie
to Huron.
R. 32

ST. DENIS
(Denys, or Dionysius)
First bishop of *Paris, Denis was sent to *Gaul to convert
the people under the emperor Decius. The patron saint of
*France, he was beheaded in 270. Legend tells that he was
over one hundred years old when martyred, and that he carried his head in his hands a considerable distance after the execution, depositing it on the site of the cathedral that was to
bear his name. In art, he is depicted this way. In 626 his
relics were placed in the new *Benedictine Abbey at St. Denis
(north of Paris).

St. Denis's banner is the *Oriflamme; the battlecry of
medieval France was "Montjoie St. Denis," from *Mons Jovis*, a
direction post.
0. 32; W. 65

ST. DOMINIC, --'S
The founder of the Dominican or *Black Friar preachers, Domingo de Guzmán (1170?-1221) was a noble *Castilian
*Spaniard. His order of barefoot mendicant *evangelical
preachers was organized partly in response to the increasing
power of the Albigenses, a *Manichaean group that denounced
the pleasures of the world. Following the rule of *St. Augustine, the Dominican order gained strength in monasteries and
convents in *Spain, *Italy, and *France. Dominic was a popular and inspiring leader. He was canonized in 1234; his feast
day is 4 August.

Dominic is the patron saint of the Cathedral of *Lima, a
city which M. saw as a prime symbol of corruption, in "Benito
Cereno" and throughout the canon.
M.D. 54; P. 8:2

ST. DUNSTAN'S
St. Dunstan (c. 909-988), *Archbishop of *Canterbury,
was a multitalented man who, as Abbot of Glastonbury, reformed monastic life along strict *Benedictine lines. A metal
worker and painter, he rebuilt churches, promoted education

and law, integrated the *Danes, and helped unify British politics, crowning Edward the Martyr in 975.

Legend says that when the *Devil tried to trick him by taking the form of a beautiful woman, St. Dunstan pinched him in the nose with a pair of red-hot tongs, refusing release until the Devil promised not to tempt him again.

He is the patron saint of goldsmiths. His image is often seen on *English pub signs, along with that of his tormentor, especially in the *Fleet Street area of *London.
P. 14: 1

ST. GEORGE

Patron saint of *England since the time of *Edward III (c. 1348); also patron of Aragon and *Portugal. Legend has it he slew a dragon that fed upon the people of Silene, *Libya—an allegory of *Christian triumph over evil. The actual original is in doubt; George may have been a *Roman officer or George of Cappodocia, *Arian Bishop of *Alexandria. He is said to have assisted the *Crusaders at Antioch (1089), so the *Normans took him as patron. Probably he was martyred under *Diocletian (c. 303).

Percy's *Reliques* ("St. George for England") says:

> St. George he was for England
> *St. Denis was for France;
> Sing, Honi soit qui mal y pense.

St. George's cross is red on a white field. M. uses "St. George" as a generic name for England.
0. 32; W. 64; W. 65; M.D. 55; M.D. 82

ST. GEORGE, ORDER OF

In *M.D.*, M. perhaps refers to the British Order of the Garter, patron saint of which is *St. George.

(There were Orders of St. George at the time in Bavaria, *Hanover, *Russia, a Constantinian Order of St. George in Parma and one in the *Two Sicilies.)
M.D. 82

ST. GEORGE'S

Built in the style of a huge Graeco-Roman temple, *Liverpool's St. George's Hall (completed in 1854) contains judicial offices and public areas including a large auditorium for banquets and presentations. M.'s journal (15 November 1849) records his visit and his wonder at the "grand organ," one of

the world's largest. In R,. M. suggests that things of the present world such as "St. George's spire" and his own "ship's mainmast" are surer guides than antiquities such as his father's guidebook and other wisdom of the past.
R. 31

ST. GEORGE'S PIER
Probably the *Liverpool pier on view from *St. George's Hall, at *George's Dock.
R. 44

ST. GEORGE'S-SQUARE
In *Liverpool: bounded by *Nelson Street on the north, St. Vincent Street on the South.
R. 41

ST. GILES'
The references to "Israel Potter's" "crawling into an abandoned doorless house in St. Giles'" (*I.P.* 25), which does not appear in the original (see "Israel Potter's autobiographical story"), is particularly apt. St. Giles is the patron saint of cripples, having been wounded himself by Childeric, King of *France. Churches dedicated to him were traditionally located outside city gates because it was forbidden for beggars and cripples to enter the city. *London's Cripplegate district (on the northwestern fringe of the ancient city) was so called for the adjacent St. Giles's (fourteenth century) Church, which attracted many indigents. St. Giles in the Fields, *Holborn, dating from the time of *Charles II, was famous for "Seven Dials": a *Doric pillar with six or seven sun dials facing streets rediating from it. M. visited the squalid area on 17 November 1849. (There is also a St. Giles's in *Southwark.)
I.P. 25

ST. HELENA
The *British island in the South *Atlantic, 1,200 miles west of the *African coast, was first sighted by the *Portuguese in 1502. The *Dutch annexed it in 1633, and through the eighteenth century struggled over it with the *East India Company. It passed to the British Crown in 1834.
St. Helena gained celebrity as the place of exile of *Napoléon: 1815-21.
M.D. 51

ST. JAGO, --'S

St. Jago's monkeys, denizens of the *Cape Verde Islands, are frequently sold to sailors as pets. "Jago" is also a nickname for a victualling paymaster," or synonym for "jacker," a name for a boy undergoing training on a ship.

The name is a corruption of the *Portuguese Sáo Tiago.
R. 24; W. 69; M.D. 40; M.D. 91

ST. JAMES

St. James's Palace, Pall Mall, *London, was built by *Henry VIII (1532-33), on the site of a hospital for lepers established before the *Norman Conquest. It has been the scene of much royal drama, some of it commemorated by initials and messages carved into walls and windows. Henry lived here with *Anne Boleyn; Edward VI, *Elizabeth I, and *Mary I were sometime residents. *Charles II, *James II, Mary II, Anne (see "Queen Anne"), and *George IV were born in the palace. *Charles I spent his last night alive here, and *Victoria and *Albert were married here, as were many others.

The building is a relatively unprepossessing structure containing official ceremonial rooms, private living quarters, and offices—"dingy" (*I.P.* 5) perhaps by Royal standards.

M. strolled in St. James's Park on 12 November and watched the changing of the *Horse Guards on 25 November 1849.
R. 28; I.P. 5; I.P. 25

ST. JAMES'; ST. JAMES'S PARK

St. James's Park makes up part of a three-mile park belt in *London: the Royal Parks. Originally a marshy area, its ninety-three acres were developed by *Henry VIII, formed into a garden by *Charles II, and rearranged by John Nash between 1827 and 1829. It includes a lake and grand Mall leading up to Buckingham Palace. M. visited on 12 and 25 November 1849, watching the changing of the mounted guard (see "Horse Guards").
W. 42; I.P. 25

ST. JAMES-STREET

*Liverpool's St. James's Street runs north-southwest in the southern part of the old city; it starts at Park Lane and culminates at St. James Church.
R. 31

ST. JOHN; ST. JOHN THE BAPTIST

The man called John the Baptist (not the *evangelist or the writer of *Revelation) is known to have been born before 4 B.C. and to have died c. 30 A.D. He is seen as a forerunner of the *Christian Messiah and to have influenced even the *Gnostics. *Luke follows his story from birth into a priestly family, but he is important also in the other *Gospels and in *Acts 19:1-7, showing his influence even several decades after his death. John's father was the priest Zechariah, and his mother was a relative of Mary, the mother of *Jesus. He lived as a hermit in the wilderness, wearing animal skins and eating "locusts and honey." There he received a call to preach and baptize, fulfilling the prophecy of *Isaiah 40:3 of a "voice . . . that crieth in the wilderness, Prepare ye the way of the Lord."

John ministered in the *Jordan valley, predicting catastrophic Divine judgement and the coming of a mightier baptizer, and demanding personal repentance. He is known to have baptized Jesus (*Matthew 3, *Mark 1). Luke says of him, "There is not a greater prophet than John the Baptist" (7:28).

John was beheaded by Herod Antipas (Matthew 14:1-11), his head presented on a charger to a woman not named in the *Bible but later called Salome.

The patron saint of missionaries, John has a feastday on June 24. He is represented wearing animal skins, holding a rude wooden *cross, or with a lamb.

In *Clarel*, M. refers to him as "The Essene" and "Teacher," as well as "Mad John."
M. 146; W. 68

ST. JOHNS CHURCH

St. John's Church, *Liverpool, was built in 1783, amid a clutter of industrial buildings, bounded by St. John's Lane, Shaws Place, Shaws Brow (now William Brown Street), and the sites of the *Haymarket and Liverpool Infirmary (Sick and Lame Hospital). By the nineteenth century the church was considered an eyesore not in harmony with the then-modern structures being erected in the area.
R. 30

ST. JOHN'S PARK

St. John's Park (or Hudson Square) covered the *New York City block bounded by Varick, Beach, Hudson, and Laight Streets. It was a private park adjacent to the elegant St. John's Chapel of Trinity Church, surrounded by the imposing red brick homes of families (such as Alexander Hamilton's) who were key-holders to the locked garden. By the 1850's, wealthy families were moving elsewhere; the park was sold in 1856, the elegant homes became unsightly tenements, and by 1869 the park was replaced by the freight depot of the Hudson River Railroad Company. (It is now circled by an exit artery of the Holland Tunnel.)

The Chapel stood until 1918-19, finally giving way to the widening of Varick Street and construction of the West Side Highway (dying a slow death in the late twentieth century). R. 3

ST. JOHN, VISION OF

The Revelation of John, or the *Apocalypse, is the last book of the *New Testament, thought to have been written about 96 A.D., at a time of *Roman persecution, when *Caesars were declaring themselves gods. The work calls *Christians to struggle passionately against evil forces and promises Christianity's triumph, even at the price of martyrdom. "John the Divine" is now known not to be the author of the *Gospels, a presumption of M.'s times. He was probably a *Jew by birth whose native language was Aramaic. He is thought to have lived in *Palestine and *Ephesus and was probably exiled to *Patmos, a penal colony. John called himself a prophet and received visions while in trance. In the "Vision" cited in *M.D.* 42, John sees *Christ: "His head and his hairs were white as wool, as white as snow" (Revelations 1:14). In Revelations 4:4, he sees "four and twenty elders sitting, clothed in white rainment." There are references to white robes elsewhere in the text.

When M. visited Patmos, he wrote in his journal (5 February 1857): "Was here again afflicted with the great curse of modern travel—skepticism. Could no more realize that St. John had ever had revelations here, than when off *Juan Fernandez, could believe in Robinson Crusoe according to De Foe."

See "Gospel; -s," "St. John, Vision of," and "Ephesian" (for M.'s use of the fabled undulations of the soil over John's grave).
M.D. 42; M.D. 111

ST. LAWRENCE

The St. Lawrence river flows some 2,350 miles from its most westerly connection, Lake *Superior, to the *Atlantic Ocean. The chief outlet of the *Great Lakes, it has many canals and tributaries. The St. Lawrence was ascended by Cartier in 1535; by 1608, Champlain had helped found the

*Quebec settlement on the river route for fur traders, explorers, and missionaries.
R. 40

ST. LOUIS

St. Louis is in eastern *Missouri, on the right bank of the *Mississippi, ten miles below the influx of the *Missouri River. It was the site of a fur trading post in 1763 and was founded as a town in 1764 (incorporated as a city in 1823). It was named for Louis IX of *France, patron saint of Louis XV (see "Bourbon").

Briefly held by the *Spanish, St. Louis made part of the *Louisiana Purchase of 1803 and was still predominantly French in culture in the nineteenth century, although many *Germans arrived in the 1850's. The "Gateway to the West" had much growth after the *War of 1812; the first steamer docked here in 1817. Although in M.'s time it was still the largest city of the Mississippi Valley and one of the greatest river ports, St. Louis's glory faded somewhat with the extension of the railroad in the mid-nineteenth century. It was Unionist in the *Civil War.

M. visited St. Louis in fall of 1840, gathering impressions later to be used in *C.M.*'s early chapters.
C.M. 1; C.M. 3; C.M. 6; C.M. 34; C.M. 45

ST. MARK

St. Mark was the *Gospel writer who died in prison (c. 68). He is represented in art in various ways: in the prime of life; dressed as a bishop with a lion at his feet and a scroll in his hand; with a pen in his right hand and Gospel in the left. His feast day is April 25; he is the patron saint of *Venice.
M. 149; M.D. 54

ST. MARY'S ISLE

St. Mary's Isle, in Kircudbright Bay, *Solway Firth, *Scotland, is a peninsula named for a twelfth-century priory there: site of the *Selkirk mansion. On 23 April 1778, *John Paul Jones landed on the isle intending to take the Earl of Selkirk hostage. The earl was absent, and instead, Jones's contingent made off with the family silver, and Jones later wrote a foolishly romantic letter to the Countess inspired by her noble behavior throughout the incursion.

(Among the less attractive and less credible legends about Jones is one which makes him a bastard member of the

Selkirk family, banished for attempting to rape a servant in the pantry.)
I.P. 17

ST. MARY'S, OLD CHURCH OF
See "Bury St. Edmunds."
R. 44

ST. MATTHEW
See "Gospel; -s."
P. 1:3

ST. NICHOLAS, CHURCH OF
In 1699, the *chapel of ease of Our Lady and St. Nicholas, at *Liverpool's pierhead, separated from its parent, becoming the first parish church.
R. 36

SAINT PATRICK
Despite the saint's official image as converter of *Ireland to *Christianity, there is no reliable information about his life or work, other than his flourishing in the 5th century A.D. His modest *Confessio*, written as a defense against *British ecclesiastics, tells the story of his capture from his British home by the Irish, trials and hardships endured in *slavery, "signs" received that his destiny was to save the Irish. At the end of the 9th century, two centuries after Patrick's death, the biographers Muirchú and Tírechán supplied much data that is spurious. Legends such as his banishment of the snakes from Ireland, blessing of the shamrock, and vision of purgatory, were much later additions to his story.
T. 7

ST. PAUL (CORINTHIAN'S CORRUPTION)
I *Corinthians xv, 42-43: "So also is the resurrection of the dead. It is sown in corruption; it is raised in incorruption; it is sown in dishonor; it is raised in glory; it is sown in weakness; it is raised in power."
M.D. 92

ST. PAUL; PAUL; SAUL OF TARSUS

Central to the spread of *Christianity was the work of Paul ("Saul" in *M.D.* 45) of *Tarsus, who was raised in *Jerusalem. Paul (Sha'ul in Hebrew, Paulus in Roman usage) was born into a *Pharasaic family of Jewish *Roman citizens. He pursued rabbinic studies and opposed the new faith of *Christianity until meeting *Jesus (described in *Acts and elsewhere). Sometimes called an *Apostle, Paul was a missionary in *Damascus, Tarsus, and *Syria, journeying to *Cyprus, Asia Minor, *Macedonia, and *Greece, before the voyage to Rome on which he was shipwrecked (Acts 27). He died a martyr c. A.D. 65.

Paul is credited with *New Testament works including epistles to the Thessalonians (see "Thessaly"), *Corinthians, Romans, *Ephesians. M.'s response to the writings is detailed in Wrights's *Melville's Use of the Bible*.

The *M.D.* 70 reference alludes to Paul's prophecy of safety despite contrary winds, in Acts 27. The *C.M.* 7 quotation, "scarcely for a righteous man . . . ," is from Romans 5:7.

See also "Euroclydon"; "Malta" (for "Paul's cave," of W. 65); references in "Quotations" section.

M. 97; M. 119; R. 27; R. 33; R. 35; W. 34; W. 65; M.D. 2; M.D. 9; M.D. 45; M.D. 70; C.M. 7; C.M. 29

ST. PAUL'S

The first St. Paul's Cathedral of *London was built in 604, with Mellitus as bishop. Inigo Jones restored it (1633-42), encasing it in masonry and fronting it with ten Corinthian columns fifty-six feet high. The present structure was reconstructed (1675-1710) in Baroque style by *Sir Christopher Wren after the *Great Fire of 1666. The famous three-shelled dome covers a Medieval-inspired long-aisled structure modelled in part on the *Sorbonne, the *Louvre, and *Italian churches. The cathedral is remarkable for its human-scale features, in contrast with *St. Peter's. *Nelson, John Donne, and *Wellington are buried in St. Paul's, along with Wren, whose epitaph reads, "*Si monumentum requiris, circumspice*": "If you seek a monument, look about you."

M. visited on 12 November 1849, noting in his journal: "Sat an hour in a dozing state listening to the chanting in the choir. Felt homesick and sentimentally unhappy. Rallied again . . . . " He attended services on 25 November, "a most foggy, melancholy, sepulchral day."

O. 79; R. 1; R. 30; R. 41; R. 43; R. 46; W. 8; W. 46

ST. PAUL'S

*New York City's gracefully colonnaded St. Paul's Chapel (still in existence) was built in 1764 on *Broadway (then "Great George Street") between Vesey and *Fulton Streets. (The *Astor House later stood directly across the street, on Broadway.) It has an old burying ground and plaques commemorating important early New Yorkers. St. Paul's was a prestigious church in M.'s time, but by the mid-nineteenth century it was too small for its congregation, which began deserting it for newer, more prestigious temples.

The Georgian chapel, influenced by the architecture of St. Martins-in-the Fields, *London, was constructed of local stone, with a metal-clad wooden steeple. Its interior decoration was by Pierre L'Enfant, who laid out the city of *Washington, D.C.

I.P. 16

ST. PETER'S

The Basilica of *St. Peter, the most famous *Vatican building, stands on the site of the previous St. Peter's, built by Constantine I (see "Constantinople"). It has never been the Cathedral of *Rome but has been closely associated with *Popes since the fourteenth century.

The area had been drained by the first century A.D., as the site of *Nero's circuses and gardens, as well as a burial ground. The mausoleum under the present structure holds a skeleton popularly accepted as Peter's. The new building was begun in 1506 by Pope Julius II and was completed in 1615, under Paul V. There were many architects and many plans changed—including that of *Michelangelo. The format is a triple-aisled Latin *cross with a dome at the crossing directly above the high altar covering the shrine of St. Peter. At 615 feet, it is the world's longest church. Four pilasters support the huge dome.

M. visited the chief pilgrimage site in Europe in 1857, commenting in his journal (25 February): "Front view disappointing. But grand approach. Interior comes up to expectations. But dome not so wonderful as St. Sophia's."

W. 20

ST. PETERSBURG; ST. PETERSBURGH

St. Petersburg (modern Leningrad) is a major *Baltic Sea port at the mouth of the Neva River, at the southern end of Karelian Isthmus, 400 miles northwest of Moscow. It was founded in 1703 by Peter the Great (see "Tsar") and replaced Moscow as capital of *Russia in 1713 (only to be replaced by

Moscow again in 1918). Despite only seasonal navigation, St. Petersburg became a major naval center in the 1820's. During M.'s time its many important buildings and churches (now mostly museums) included government offices, theaters, and fortresses. The baroque Winter Palace was built between 1754 and 1762, the Hermitage art museum between 1840 and 1852. It was a great cultural center and home to artists and writers (such as Pushkin) before becoming a major industrial center as a result of the 1848-51 rail link with Moscow. (The Russian Revolution started in St. Petersburg, which was called Petrograd from 1914 to 1924.)

The *Tsar's "Ice Palace" mentioned in *M.D.* 2 and *M.* 75 (wrongly ascribed to Moscow; see "Muscovite") was built annually and lit with torches for the accompanying festival.

See also "Granville, Dr."
R. 7; P. 22:2; P. 22:4

ST. PONS
Light blue St. Pons marble is mined from quarries in southern *France: Hérault département, in the Monts de l'Espinouse, twenty five miles west-northwest of Béziers.
M. 84; R. 46

ST. SHAKESPEARE
See "Shakespeare . . . . "
W. 41

ST. STYLITES
St. Simeon Stylites (390-459) of *Syria was the first of the Stylites or pillar saints of the fifth through twelfth centuries in Syria, *Mesopotamia, *Egypt, and *Greece. These ascetics lived atop pillars from which they never descended. St. Simeon started life as a shepherd, entered a monastery where he spent three years alone in a cell, then moved himself to the middle of a circular enclosure where crowds gathered to observe him. Eventually he built poles to escape from the public, spending between twenty and thirty years on various pillars, the last about fifty feet tall. He stood all the while, shelterless, eating little, praying and preaching for conversions. His most famous disciple, Daniel the Stylite of *Constantinople (409-493) spent thirty years on his pillar.

Tennyson wrote a poem, "St. Simeon Stylites," about the practice, which never spread to the west.
M. 116; M.D. 35

ST. VINCENT'S

The battle of Saint Vincent was fought by the *British and *Spanish off Cape St. Vincent, *Portugal, 14 February 1797. *Nelson and *Collingwood played important roles in the victory of fifteen British ships over twenty-seven Spanish ones. The huge *Santissima Trinidada escaped at Saint Vincent, only to be scuttled by her captain at *Trafalgar in 1805.

Admiral *Rodney had previously won a battle of Saint Vincent, in 1780.

W. 50

ST. VITUS' IMP, --HORNPIPE

St. Vitus Dance: disease confused with chorea when the Saint's aid was invoked against it. To secure good health the *Germans used to dance before St. Vitus's statue on his feast day, often to the point of mania.

St. Vitus was a *Sicilian youth martyred with his tutor and his nurse during the *Diocletian persecution, c. 303.

The hornpipe, associated with sailors, was originally danced to the pib-corn, or hornpipe, an obsolete instrument made from horn.

0. 50; M. 176; M.D. 36

SAIS

*J.C.F. von Schiller's poem, "The Veiled Statue at Sais" (contained in Sealts #439, Poems and Ballads, Bulwer Lytton trans.), tells of an innocent youth who went to *Egypt to study sacred lore. Entering the temple of Athena (or Isis or Nit or Demeter) at night, he lifted the statue's veil, seeking "Truth." Found by priests in the morning, he refused to tell what he had seen, but "his happiness in life had fled forever,/ and his deep sorrow soon conducted him/ to an untimely grave."

M. might also have read about the statue in *Herodotus II, 170-171 (Sealts # 147, Harper's Classical Library).

(First American edition of M.D. has typographical error: "Lais," for Sais.)

M.D. 76

SALADIN

The much-admired *Arabian leader of *Moslem armies against the *Crusaders, Saladin (Salah al-Din) founded the Ayyubid dynasty in *Egypt. In the First Crusade's "Battle of Egypt" (1164-68), he became *vizier and commander of troops. He reestablished Sunni Islam in Egypt, pacified it internally, and sponsored numerous public works projects, including defense structures.

After defeating the Franks in *Syria, he restored *Jerusalem to Islam. In the Third Crusade, he survived a two-year siege, only to be set back in 1191 by a naval blockade and the army of Richard I *Coeur de Lion. Although M. grants the victory to Richard, two of Saladin's biographers disagree, granting him at least a stalemate: Geoffrey Hindley, *Saladin*, and Sir Hamilton Gibb, *The Life of Saladin: From the Works of 'Imád ad-Din and Baha Ad-Din*. Certainly, Saladin weakened the Crusaders' holdings in the Near East.

Saladin is among the worthy unsaved in *Dante's *Inferno* and is a central character in *Scott's *The Talisman*.

M. saw Saladin's Cairo citadel in January of 1857.
M. 32; W. 39; M.D. 55

SALAMANCA
      Capital of Salamanca Province in west-central *Spain (6° W, 41° N), the ancient city has a dramatic history. *Hannibal conquered it in 220 B.C.; *Romans and *Moors contested it; *Christianity finally claimed it in the eleventh and twelfth centuries. It has long been a center of *Jesuit learning; St. Theresa of Avila founded a convent, Luis *Ponce de Léon lectured, and *Christopher Columbus was examined by the Council of Theologians here. In the legendary Cave of Salamanca, the writer, Enrique de Villene, practiced black magic. *French occupation forces destroyed many university buildings when *Wellington dislodged them in 1812. In modern times, Francisco Franco resided here during the Civil War (1936-39). At M.'s time, a great poetry revival was taking place, wherein Salamanca stood for content, *Seville for form.
M. 3

SALAMIS
      A ruined city in East *Cyprus, with remnants of a *Roman forum and aqueduct. Salamis was of Mycenaean origin, founded after the *Trojan War. The *Greek and *Persian war which M. refers to in *W*. 50 occurred throughout the fourth century B.C., when the former Greek stronghold revolted against Persian forces. It was also the scene of the naval victory of Demetrius Poliorcetes over Ptolemy I of *Egypt, in 306 B.C. *St. Paul and St. Barnabas are said to have visited. Salamis was finally destroyed after *Arab invasions of 647-648.
W. 30

SALEM

The city of northeastern *Massachusetts, fifteen miles northeast of *Boston was a leading port until the mid-nineteenth century. Settled in 1626, it was the site of the witchcraft trials of 1692, in which *Hawthorne's forebears had participated. Much of the old city has been preserved, including Hawthorne's "House of the Seven Gables," and the 1819 *Custom House which is the setting for the introduction to *The Scarlet Letter.* (Modern-day Salem has a silted-up harbor and is no longer a port.)
O. 21; W. 68; M.D. 6

SALIQUE LAW

Le Loi Salique, or Salic Law of Succession is named for the Salian Franks, ancestors of the *Merovingian kings. The law was essentially a penal code, prohibiting inheritance by a wife of her husband's property and limiting royal succession to males and descendents of royal males. It became *French monarchichal law in the fourteenth century but was invoked in other countries as well. When *Edward III used an interpretation of the law to make a claim to the French throne, the Hundred Years War resulted. (See also "Valois.")
P. 2:2

SALISBURY PLAIN

A chalk plateau in southern *England (51°15' N., 1°52' W.), east of the ancient Wiltshire cathedral city of Salisbury.
M.D. 53

SALT-HOUSE [DOCK]

*Liverpool: originally, four and three-quarter acre water area; opened 1753, to service the rock-salt refinery.
R. 32

SALVATOR

The major port of eastern *Brazil was founded in 1549 as São Salvador de *Bahia de Todos os Santos. It was the capital until 1763, a provincial capital from 1823, and state capital after the republic was declared in 1889.
R. 55

SAMARITAN, --S

In *Luke 10:30-35, a good man from Samaria aids the victim of thieves, becoming the prototypical charitable person.
M. 3; R. 40; C.M. 16; C.M. 17; C.M. 18; C.M. 39

SAMOA, --N

The Samoan archipelago (13°26' to 14°22' S.' 168°10' to 172°48' W.) is a rocky volcanic group of islands discovered by the *Dutch in 1722 and visited by De *Bougainville (who called them the *Navigator Islands; 1768) and von *Kotzebue (1824). The *London Missionary Society became established there in 1830, and *Wilkes surveyed the islands, in 1839. Nineteenth-century *British, *American, and *German claims divided the chain administratively.

Samoans are *Polynesians akin to *Hawaiians and Maoris (see "Mowree"), with an ancient language, a culture based on kinship ties, and a complex hierarchy of chieftain-ship based on heredity and oratorical ability.

See also "Saviian"; "Upolua . . . . "
M. 30 (Passim as character)

SAMPHIRE

Samphire, or glasswort (*crithmum maritinium*; Fr. *herbe de Saint Pierre*) is a succulent herb of the celery (apiacious) family. It grows in the clefts of rocks near the sea, especially the *Mediterranean, and was formerly burned for use in soap- and glass-making. In *Shakespeare's *King Lear* (IV, vi, 15), samphire-gathering is a "dreadful trade."

M.'s journal (26 January 1857) echoes Shakespeare regarding the monks of Mar Saba and repeats the allusion in *Clarel* II.
M.D. 47

SAMSON

Although the tribe of Dan's strong man, Samson, was to capture the world's imagination, he is a somewhat dubious hero in the early part of *Judges 13-16. An uninhibited local tribal warrior of *Jerusalem at a time of many invasions, in the latter part of his story he is enobled by his devotion to causes, his victimization by *Delilah, and his invincible spirit at death.

In Judges there are many tales of his exploits which shed light on contemporary culture. As a Nazarite, Samson was to abstain from alcohol, from cutting his hair, and from contact with the dead. The most famous episode concerns his love for the *Philistine Delilah, who is bribed to reveal to Philistine lords that Samson's great strength lies in his hair. They capture, shave, blind, and imprison him, but when his hair grows in, Samson is able to topple the Philistine temple at Gaza, killing all of those within and himself as well (16:4-21).

Samson's story has inspired many artistic works, including *Milton's *Samson Agonistes*, upon which is based *Handel's oratorio, *Samson*, probably heard by M. in *New York at the time he was writing *W*. M. mentions Samson also in *Clarel* II, 145.

W. 50; M.D. 132; I.P. 1; I.P. 21; C.M. 19

SAMUEL ENDERBY
See "Enderby, Samuel . . . "
M.D. 100; M.D. 106

SAMUEL GLEIG
See "Whaleman's Chapel."
M.D. 7

SANDWICH
Sandwich, in *Kent, *England, now two miles from the sea, was one of the original *Cinque Ports. Many of its streets and buildings date from the thirteenth century, and the outlying area was developed by the *Romans in the first century. White Friars was built on the site of a thirteenth-century *Carmelite priory; the 1539 *Barbican was one of a chain of block-houses along the coast.

M. visited on 5 November 1849, commenting in his journal on "Richboro' Castle," a Roman ruin in Rutupiae (Richborough).
M.D. 90; I.P. 14

SANDWICHES
The question of M.'s knowledge of geology was debated by Elizabeth S. Foster and Tyrus Hillway, in the pages of *American Literature*. The three articles supply possible sources for M.'s geological information (and misinformation), and the reader is directed thither for particulars and for discussion of contemporary theories about the earth's creation.

Following terminology of Sir Charles Lyell (1797-1875) in *Elements of Geology* (first published 1838) and other geologists, M. was generally correct in his description of the earth as a "sandwich" of various strata, adapting the "*Neptunian" view of an aqueous origin ("soup") with deposits ("dumplings") of primary fossils. As Foster shows, Lyell charted Primary Fossiliferous Strata of the Cambrian and Silurian periods, followed by a Secondary Period, which he called the Old Red Sandstone, supplying a name for M.'s "Old Red Sandstone sandwich." M.'s "New Red Sandstone sandwich" corresponds to Lyell's New Red Sandstone; his "Ool, or Oily sandwich" to Lyell's Oolite; his "Chalk or Coral sandwich" to Lyell's Cretaceous and Tertiary: *Eocene; his second and third "sidecourses" to Lyell's *Miocene and *Pliocene periods.

M. was somewhat less accurate in placing fossil types in their appropriate periods, but even here he does well for a nonspecialist. Among fossils mentioned in *M*. 132: zoophytes are plant-like animals such as coral or sponge, of Lyell's Primary Fossiliferous Age; cephalaspis is a lamprey-like cartilaginous fish with a huge head, of the "Old Red Sandstone" age; glytolepis is a sturgeon-like fish of the "Old Red Sandstone"; pterichthys is a shark-like cartilaginous fish of the "Old Red Sandstone"; cassowaries are large flightless birds of the Pliocene; mastodons (named by *Cuvier) are large elephant-like creatures (with different dentition) of the Pliocene; megatheriums are large sloth-like plant-eating animals of the Pliocene, similar also to the elephant.

M.'s theory of coral's emerging from great ocean depths is innacurate and might have been checked in many specialized and popular texts of the time.
M. 132

SANDWICH ISLANDS; --ISLANDERS

*Hawaii was first called the Sandwich Islands, after *Cook's patron, John Montagu, Fourth Earl of Sandwich (1718-1792). An important statesman and First Lord of the *British Admiralty, Sandwich was ruined during the *American Revolution, when his gambling failures and participation in corruption were most extreme. The sandwich was named for him when in 1762 he spent twenty-four hours in gambling and placed meat into bread rather than have interruption for a meal. His *Voyage . . . Round the Mediterranean in the Years 1738 and 1739* was published posthumously (1799).

The "Great Revival" (*O.* 45) at the Sandwich Islands which M. dates as "about the year 1836" actually occurred in 1837. The Reverend Hiram Bingham held week-long meetings involving 155 schools, 5,010 scholars, 5,000 *Sabbath School scholars, a singing school of eighty people, with 10,000 books distributed. He does not estimate how many souls were "born again."
T. Passim; O. Passim; M. 22; M.D. 45

SANDY HOOK

A narrow sandy peninsula of eastern *New Jersey, between Sandy Hook Bay and the Lower *New York Bay-*Atlantic area. It extends some five miles north toward *New York City, marking the southern side of the entrance to the Bay. *Hudson visited Sandy Hook in 1609, and the *British held it during the *Revolution. A lighthouse of 1763 is the oldest one still in use in the nation. (Sandy Hook is the modern-day Gateway National Recreation Area.)
R. 27

SANGRADOS

A dangerous quack doctor: from Le Sage's *Gil Blas (1715). Doctor Sangrados was a solemn, ignorant humbug medical practitioner whose prescriptions for every ailment were warm water and bleeding, his theory being that blood was not necessary for life.
M. 147; R. 40

SANHEDRIN

The supreme rabbinic legislative and judicial court of ancient *Jerusalem was instituted when a commonwealth supplanted the authority of kings and chieftains. Penalty for disobedience of the Great Sanhedrin's dogmatic edicts was excommunication.

*Christ was tried before the priestly state Synedrion sanctioned by *Pontius Pilate. There were many attempts to reinstitute the body after its dissolution in 66 A.D. Among leaders were Hillel and Simon ben Shetah. *Napoléon instituted a Sanhedrin in 1807, aiming to decide laws for *French *Jews.
P. 17:1; P. 22:1

SANSCRIT

Although the word Sanskrit remains the paradigm for "an impenetrable language," the eighteenth-century discovery that it was of the same family as western languages should have removed some of the mystery.

Sanscrit was the classical language of *India's Hindus (see "Hindoo), with records from c. 1500 B.C. (It is still written today.) The earliest *Vedas and *Brahmanas represent a spoken language; it is not clear when it ceased to be spoken, but Buddha requested his doctrines be preached in the vernacular, not in "Vedic."

With the Vedic language, Sanscrit is a dialect of Old
Indo-Aryan, belonging to our Indo-European family of languages; nearest realtive to Indo-Aryan is Iranian. Constant
migrations accounted for great diversity in dialects. It was
standardized in the fourth century B.C. by Panini, whose
grammar, *Astadhyayt* is considered by many the best grammar ever written, although it included no phonetic description.
Early use was for business writing; only in the last few centuries B.C. was Sanscrit used for literature. Studies of *Sir
William Jones, in 1786, gave impetus to modern Western lin-
guistic studies in identifying Sanscrit as one of the Indo-European languages.
    Sanscrit has a large, complex alphabet, complicated
grammar (despite relation to ours), but less complex syntax
than *Latin.
M. 40; W. 38

SANSOVINE
    Leigh Hunt, *Bacchus in Tuscany* (1825): "And drink of
the wine of the vine benign/That sparkles warm in Sansovine."
C.M. 28

SANTA
    A seaport and recruiting place in Ancash department of
west-central *Peru, on a coastal plain near the mouth of the
Santa River.
M.D. 19

SANTA CRUZ
    The suburb of *Rio de Janeiro is on the eastern side of
the entrance to Guanabara Bay, opposite the city. Since 1836 it
has been called Niterói, the Indian expression for "Hidden
Water." It was a favorite place of *Dom Pedro; a war memorial marks the fortress mentioned in W. 50.
W. 50

SANTA CRUZ, JUG OF
    The most likely referent is Santa Cruz de Graciosa, in
the central *Azores on Graciosa Island. Founded in 1485, it
became noted for whaling and wine. Among other possibilities
are a town of *Madeira island or Santa Cruz de Mudela, in
New Castile, *Spain, both of which are noted for alcohol distil-
lation.
C.M. 24

SANTA FE
The city in the north central part of modern-day New Mexico is fifty five miles northeast of Albuquerque and 290 miles south-southwest of Denver, Colorado. It is situated in the Sangre de Cristo range of the *Rocky Mountains, between the Pecos and Rio Grande rivers, at an altitude of c. 7,000 feet. Santa Fe was founded by the *Spanish on the site of an ancient Indian village; it became an important outpost for early Roman *Catholic missionaries. By M.'s time it was the terminus of the Santa Fe trail, the trade route between the *United States and *Mexico after Mexican independence from Spain (1821). By 1851 it was the capital of the Territory of New Mexico.
The "traders in striped blankets" of *C.M.* 2 still ply their trade in front of the three-hundred year-old Governor's Mansion in the center of Santa Fe's commercial district.
C.M. 2

SANTA FE DE BOGOTA
The capital city of modern *Colombia, Bogota is situated on a high (8,660 feet) plateau (4°36' N., 74°5' W.). It has been culturally important since colonial days, with many artistic and educational facilities: the "*Athens of *South America." It was founded in 1538 as Santa Fe de Bogotá, a name derived from a local chief's. It became the capital of the *Spanish viceroyalty of New Granada. Bolivar (see "Bolivia") took the city in 1815, lost it, then reentered in 1819.
P. 1:6

SANTISSIMA TRINIDADA
Santissima Trinidad (M.'s "Most Holy Trinity") was a huge (204 feet by 53 feet) *Spanish war ship upon which the *American *Pennsylvania* was modelled. She was sunk by her captain when Spanish forces faced defeat at *Trafalgar in 1805.
M. 28

SAPPHIRE THRONE OF GOD
*Ezekiel 1:26: "And above the firmament over their heads there was the likeness of a throne, in appearance like sapphire; and seated above the likeness of a throne was a likeness as it were of a human form."
P. 6:1

SARACENIC
Saracen is a word used by *Christians, starting in the *Middle Ages, to identify *Arab and *Turkish (Islamic) enemies. Use of the word was spread by the *Byzantines and the *Crusaders. M. uses it as a catch-all expression, as he does "Moorish." (See "Moor," "Alhambra," and "mosque," for discussion of the "Saracenic arch.")
R. 49

SARAH
In *Genesis 11-17, the wife of *Abraham is Sarai. When she is ninety years old and her husband ninety-nine (17), the Lord announces that she will bear her first child and will henceforth be called Sarah. She gives birth to *Isaac (21:3) and dies at the age of one hundred and seven (23:2). She is mentioned also in *Numbers, *Isaiah, *Romans. "Sarah" is from a *Hebrew word for a female noble.
C.M. 7

SARAH
See "Marlborough."
M. 23; M. 26

SARATOGA, --COUNTY
Eastern *New York State's Saratoga County was formed in 1791 around the Saratoga Springs spa, where local mineral springs provided therapeutic drinking water and curative baths. The village of Saratoga Springs (commonly referred to as "Saratoga") was incorporated in 1826. (It became a city in 1915.) It was *the* most fashionable resort in *America in the nineteenth century, its amenities including horse-racing (after 1850).

M.'s maternal forebears, the *Gansevoort family, played important roles in the county's history. M. visited the area in his youth and again in 1856, 1866, and 1877.

The battles of Saratoga in September and October, 1777, are considered turning points in the American Revolutionary War. The *British *General John Burgoyne, originally commanding a force of some 11,000 British and *German soldiers, was headed for Albany on 13 September, when he camped at Saratoga with a much smaller force and few supplies. Losses to *General Horatio Gates and *General Benedict Arnold further weakened his position, and by 7 October he was surrounded by an American force of 20,000. He surrendered on condition that his troops be freed to return to Great Britain, promising not to serve again in the war.

Arnold's behavior at Saratoga was severely criticized in William Leete Stone's *Life of Joseph Brant--Thayendanegea* (See "Brant, Joseph"). Without a command on 7 October, Arnold, it is charged, behaved strangely and was perhaps intoxicated: "more like a madman than a cool and discreet officer" (Appendix to Vol. 1, p. lvi), before being wounded and carried away.

See also   "Water-cure Establishment."
O. Dedication; M. 24; M.D. 37; M.D. 55; M.D. 87; I.P. 25

SARDANAPALUS
The *Greek historian Diodorus Siculus calls Sardanapalus the last of the line of thirty kings of *Assyria, but the sybaritic attributes assigned him are perhaps those of two other Assyrian kings, Ashurbanipal and his brother. Sardanapalus supposedly burned his palace, his concubines, and himself, when a *Median chief rebelled. *Byron published a play about the monarch in 1821, somewhat redeeming his reputation.
M. 73

SARVING OUT OF SLOPS
Usually, the administering of punishment at the gangway. But "slops" can also refer to ready-made clothing or to weak tea.
W. 90

SATAN, --'S; SATANIC
See "Devil."
M. 60; R. 12; M.D. 36; M.D. 86; M.D. 135; P. 10:2; I.P. 5; I.P. 19; C.M. 24; C.M. 29 and elsewhere

SATIN WOOD
Yellow-brown East *Indian mahogany.
M.D. 5

SATRAPS
Under the ancient *Persian monarchy, the governors of provinces; later any subordinate ruler, especially a despot.
M. 181

SATURN

The *Roman deity of Time is identified with the *Greek Kronos. A son of *Coelus, he castrated his father with a sickle. He devoured all of his children except *Jupiter (Air), *Neptune (Water), *Pluto (the Grave) and was finally banished by Jupiter. Despite all this, as god of the harvest, he reigned during what was considered a Golden Age.

The planet Saturn is traditionally an evil planet to be born under; to be "saturnine" is to be grave, dull, heavy, gloomy.

In astronomy, the yellowish planet sixth in order of distance from the sun is 744 times the volume of Earth. It is surrounded by a bright cloudy ring of ten satellite moons. Thought to be the most remote planet until the discovery of *Uranus in 1781, Saturn was studied closely from the late seventeenth century. *Galileo had discovered the rings in 1610, but their existence was not proven until 1785. Mathematicians studied their true nature starting in 1850, proving by 1857 that the rings consisted of myriads of discrete particles.

In *M.D.*, M. uses the adjective, saturnine. In *M.*, the character "Saturnina" is a parody of *Daniel Webster.

See also "Saturnalia"; "Zodiac."
O. 80; M. 58; M. 75; M. 175; M. 184; M.D. 104; M.D. 107; P. 2:2; P. 20:2; P. 21:3

SATURNALIA

*Saturn was also the *Roman god of sowing seed, whose cult owed much to the *Greek. His cult partner, the goddess Lua, was connected with *plague or destruction. The Saturnalia was the most popular Roman festival, during which all work was suspended and moral restrictions were eased. Madness reigned in the streets, in the fashion of Mardi Gras; gifts were exchanged and the statue of the god exposed. M.'s "saturnalia" refers to sexual licentiousness.
T. Appendix

SATURNINA

M.'s fictional portrait of *Daniel Webster.
M. 158

SAUL

See "Handel."
W. 50

SAUL OF TARSUS
    See "St. Paul."
M.D. 45

SAVAN
    Fr. *savant*: scholar.
I.P. 8

SAVANNAH
    The oldest city of *Georgia is in the southeastern part of
the state, on the Savannah River, seventeen miles from the
*Atlantic. It was founded in 1733 by James Oglethorpe and in-
corporated in 1789. Savannah was the seat of government of
the Royal Province in 1754; it was captured by the *British in
1778 and held until 1782, becoming the state capital until 1785.
Trade grew rapidly after the *War of 1812. In 1819 the first
steamship bound for *Liverpool, *The Savannah*, left from the
port. Savannah fell to the Union in 1864, after Sherman's
march across Georgia.
    In *M*. 11, M. associates Savannah with two other rich
ports, *Archangel and *Surat.
M. 11; R. 32; R. 39

SAVIIAN
    Savai'i is the largest of the *Samoa Islands.
M. 30

SAWNEY
    This pejorative term for a simpleton also refers to a
*Scot. *Smollett uses the term in *Roderick Random*.
W. 3

SAXON
    The Saxons, a Teutonic people from the southern part of
what is modern-day *Germany, began invading the southern
coast of *Britain in the fourth century A.D., according to *The
Anglo-Saxon Chronicle*. The Celts, original settlers of Britain,
used the name to designate other invaders (Jutes and Angles),
as well. Their legacy includes numerous castles in a rude
blend of wood and stone with carvings roughly imitative of the
*Roman, and place names such as Essex, Sussex, Middlesex,
Wessex, etc.

Old English derived much from the Saxon language, especially words for fundamental physical concepts. As "White-Jacket" points out, "afternoon" is a Saxon word: "after" is from Old English *aefter*, cognate with Old Saxon and Old High German *aftar-er*; "noon" is from Old Saxon nôn (noon, nuon).

M. frequently uses "Saxon" to refer to a physical type: blond, with clear ruddy complexion and blue eyes.
T. 25; 0. 53; 0. 73; R. 44; W. 7; W. 87; M.D. 101; C.M. 36 and elsewhere

SAYA

When he visited *Lima around January of 1844, M. saw women wearing the *saya y manta*: a petticoat-skirt-and-hooded-veil costume. His poem, "Crossing the Tropics," is subtitled "From 'The Saya-y-Manto'," suggesting that he planned a long poem or series of poems inspired by the costume.

Harper's New Monthly Magazine contains a disquisition on the garment and its uses in surreptitious activity, in "Lima and the Limanians."
P. 8:2

SCALDS

Scaldic (or Skaldic) verse, a form of Old Norse poetry, usually commemorated *Norwegian chieftains and families or told of Norse gods. The first known Scald was the ninth-century Bragi Boddason, but the distinctive Scaldic form flourished into the eleventh century. The third section of the *Edda is devoted to Skáldskaparmál (Speech of Poetry), in particular studying kennings: figures of speech based upon myth or nature. A ship might be a "horse of the sea"; the sea might be a "whale road."
M. 3

SCALES, THE

See "Zodiac."
M.D. 99

SCANDINAVIAN, --S

All of M.'s references to Scandinavia (*Sweden, *Norway, *Denmark, perhaps *Finland and *Iceland) betoken a stereotyped picture of the mass of peoples that is not necessarily present in his references to specific Scandinavian

groups. For M., to be "Scandinavian" is to be a wildly barbaric and piratical sea rover with a strong physiognomy and a grizzled beard: a frightening but picturesque spectre.
O. 33; W. 84; M.D. 16; M.D. 28

SCANDINAVIAN SEA-KING
Perhaps a *Viking hero of the *Sagas.
M.D. 16

SCARAMOUCH
A stock character in old *Italian farce, Scaramuccia was a bragging fool dressed in black like a *Spanish *don, introduced into *Britain in the late seventeenth century.
M.D. 91

SCARBOROUGH
See "Countess of Scarborough."
I.P. 19

"SCENES IN THE SOUTH SEAS"
See "Stewart."
T. 25

SCHILLER
Johann Christoph Friedrich von Schiller (1759-1805) was a *German poet, dramatist, essayist, and historian during the *Sturm and Drang* period of German literature. His dramas focus on themes such as authoritarianism vs. liberty, the despotism of the state, personal and moral responsibility. His poetry includes lyrics and ballads. He was a historian of the *Thirty Years War and of the revolt of the *Netherlands. A student of *Kant, he influenced German Romantics such as Schlegel and English Romantics such as *Coleridge.
Sealts #s 437-441 are M.'s numerous editions of Schiller's works, scored or annotated.
C.M. 36

SCHMERENBURGH
See "Smeerenberg."
M.D. 92

SCILLY
The Scilly Isles (numbering about 140) lie twenty or thirty miles off the coast of *Cornwall, *England. Only five islands are inhabited; they contain ruins of an abbey and fortresses from about the sixteenth century, but the isles have been known since ancient times. The others are small, rocky, and wild. Surrounding waters are a danger because of reefs and shoals in the area. In M.'s time, the Scillies were notorious *pirate lairs.
I.P. 14

SCONE
The *Scottish city of Scone (about two miles north of *Perth) is the site of the castle and abbey where ancient Scottish kings were crowned. In 1296, Edward I brought the coronation stone to *Westminster Abbey as part of *"Edward the Confessor's Chair," occupied by modern British monarchs at coronation.
There are numerous legends about the "Stone of Scone," or "Stone of Destiny," or "Tanist Stone" (in Gaelic tradition): it has been considered the original of *Jacob's stone or pillow in *Genesis (28:2); it is said that it was removed from Dunstaffnage, in Argyll, by Kenneth Mac Alpin in 843; tradition says that wherever the stone rests the Scottish race will reign.
M. 60

SCORESBY
M.'s "Captain Sleet" (M.D. 35) is Captain William Scoresby, Sr. (1760-1829), who made thirty successful *Arctic voyages without losing a ship. He invented numerous devices to improve nautical life and perfected the "crow's nest," inspiring much levity on M.'s part, especially in M.D. 35.
His son, William, Jr. (1789-1857), first sailed with his father at the age of ten. He was aboard *Resolution* when it reached what was then the highest latitude attained by a freely navigating ship, 81°30' N. (19° E.). After studying meteorology and *Polar natural history, he commanded *Resolution*, making discoveries that led to his election to the *Royal Societies of *Edinburgh and *London. In 1820, he published *An Account of the Arctic Regions and Northern Whale Fishery*, an important source for *M.D.* In 1825, he retired to become a clergyman, but he crossed the *Atlantic in 1848 and traveled to *Australia in 1856.
Gilman (*Melville's Early Life and Redburn*, 4) suggests that M. might have seen the younger Scoresby in *Liverpool in 1839 at the *Floating Chapel, of which he was minister.

Scoresby is also "Fogo Von Slack" in *M.D.* 92.
(See also "Extracts" 60.)
M.D. Passim

SCORPIO
     See "Zodiac."
M.D. 99

SCORPION, THE
     See "Zodiac."
M.D. 99

SCORPIONS
     Scorpion was a fast *American *Navy schooner with a
crew of thirty-five, one long thirty-two pound gun, and one
thirty-two pound carronade. She was part of *Oliver Hazard
Perry's squadron at Lake *Erie, in 1813.
M. 28

SCOTLAND; SCOTCH; SCOTS; SCOTTISH
     In light of M.'s Scottish ancestry and the importance of
the Melville family to Scotland, it is curious that his 1856 visit
is relatively unrecorded in the journal. M. briefly mentions
visits to *Edinburgh, *Glasgow, and Loch Lomond in entries
for 26-28 October, but then there is a gap of ten days before the
journal recommences in *Liverpool.
     References to Scotland in M.'s works are few, compared
to allusions to other European countries. The reader is directed to entries under: "Ailsa, Crag of"; "Bruce, the";
"Crokarty"; "Dunfermline"; "Fife"; "Forth, Firth of";
"Kirkaldy"; "Park, Mungo"; "Scott, Sir Walter"; "Stuart."
     Scotland's regions are often referred to as Highlands,
Lowlands, Uplands, dependent upon elevation of the ancient
mountain chain crossing Scotland from the Northwest Highlands to *Skye. M. is known to have visited Loch Lomond, located between the *Grampian Highlands and the Midlow-
lands, and possibly to have seen *Loch Katrine, in the Highlands.
     The "Scotch lords" (*M.* 57) and "Scotchmen" (*W.* 3) "in
*London in King James's time" were in a parlous position be-
cause the despised Catholic *Stuart James I had succeeded the
Protestant *Elizabeth as ruler of *England.
     The "Scotch traveller" of *M.D.* 5 is *Mungo Park.

The "Scotch jig" of *C.M.* 24 is a wildly energetic dance performed to music in six-eight or twelve-eight time. "Jig" is from *gigue*, referring to the music, rather than the dance.

The "Scottish Kirk" (*W.* 38) is a church.

The cloudy fog with drizzling rain common in Scotland is informally called "Scotch mist" (*W.* 1).

M. 57; R. 18; R. 28; W. 1; W. 3; W. 16; W. 38; W. 46; W. 83; M.D. 5; M.D. 104; P. 2:2; P. 14:2; I.P. 15; I.P. 17; C.M. 2; C.M. 24 and elsewhere

SCOTT, SIR WALTER

Walter Scott (1771-1832) was descended from a long line of swashbuckling adventurers. His father, first in the family to settle down, was an attorney in *Edinburgh. Paralysis in infancy left the young Scott with the permanently withered leg that dictated his writing adventure rather than living it. He was licensed in the law in 1792 and published his first poetry translations in 1796. A passion for collecting old ballads led to his *Minstrelsy of the Scottish Border* (3 vols., 1802-03). *The Lay of the Last Minstrel* (1805) was his first metrical romance. *The Lady of the Lake* (1810) and other romances of the time made him *Britain's most popular writer of the early nineteenth century, and a great favorite in the *United States, which had not yet produced comparable literature.

Scott married Margaret Charlotte Carpenter (or Charpentier), daughter of a *French royalist; he became Sheriff of Selkirkshire and was active with the local cavalry company. Silent partnership with the eventually bankrupt publishing firm of John Ballantyne ended in financial disaster for Scott, who assumed obligations he might have escaped, committing himself to overwork for the rest of his life.

Waverley was published in 1814, the first of the great historical novels (not avowed until 1827) which brought wealth and a title (in 1820): *The Heart of Midlothian* and *Rob Roy* (1818), *The Bride of Lammermoor* (1819), *The Monastery* (see "Avenel, White Lady of"; mentioned in *W.* 1) and *Ivanhoe* (1820), **Kenilworth* (1821), *Quentin Durward* (1823), *The *Talisman* (1825), and many others. Scott also wrote dramatic works, essays, and antiquarian material.

Scott was a politically conservative *Tory whose private liberality disarmed potential critics. His knowledge of history, taste for adventure, and love of country keep his works popular and fresh despite changing literary tastes. Seen as the father of the historical novel, he was widely imitated in the nineteenth century. His prevailing supremacy in the late 1840's may be illustrated by M.'s frustrated response to publisher John Murray's questioning: ". . . will you Britons not credit

that an American can be a gentleman, & have read the Waverly Novels, tho every digit may have been in the tar-bucket?—
You make miracles of what are commonplace to us" (25 March
1848, in Leyda *Log*).

Rob Roy (W. 4) is the story of an unfortunate outlaw at
the time of the Jacobite rising of 1715 who restores his family's
fortune and honor.

Kenilworth (*M*. 139, *W*. 65) follows the story of Amy
Robsart, secret wife of *Robert Leicester; she died tragically
during the time of Queen *Elizabeth.

Sealts #s 451a-454 are editions of *The Lay of the Last
Minstrel, Peveril of the Peak, Quentin Durward, Tales of a
Grandfather*; #359, *The Modern British Essayists*, includes an
unnumbered volume of *Critical and Miscellaneous Essays*.
W. 4; W. 50; W. 65

SCOTT'S [GENERAL]
   Winfield Scott (1786-1866) was a stickler for discipline
and formality even in his youth, leaving college in protest
against irreligious students, and court-martialed early in his
Army career for calling a superior officer a traitor. "Old Fuss
and Feathers" had a distinguished military career: he was
taken prisoner and wounded in the *War of 1812, was active in
the *Seminole and Creek campaigns in *Florida (1835-36), and
as General in Chief of the U.S. Army was much decorated for
his efforts in the *Mexican War in 1847. He captured Veracruz, attacked *Cerro Gordo and other strategic cities, and
entered Mexico City.

   Scott was the *Whig nominee for the *Presidency in 1852
but was defeated by Franklin Pierce (for whom *Hawthorne
worked). Although he served in the *Civil War, Scott was aged
and his methods outmoded by that time; he retired at his own
request in 1861.

   See also "Contreras."
C.M. 19

SCOUSE
   *Dana (Chap. 5) refers to this food as a "rare treat":
"biscuit pounded fine, salt beef cut into small pieces, and a few
potatoes, boiled up together, and seasoned with pepper."
W. 32

SCUTTLE-BUTT
   Cask holding daily fresh-water ration.
M.D. 43

SCYTHIAN

The Scythians were an ancient people of Europe and *Asiatic *Russia who thrived from the eighth century B.C. until their supplanting by the Sarmatians in the second century A.D. A nomadic group of horsemen, hunters, fishermen, metal workers, and farmers, they moved westward, wiping out the Cimmerians and settling in what is now Iran. The *Medes in *Persia resisted and pushed them back, and some Scythians blended into the *Parthian culture, while others went into *India. In the sixth century B.C. they successfully resisted *Darius, utilizing a scorched earth policy. The royal dynastic members had great wealth, as is evidenced in the elaborate art in tombs unearthed in the twentieth century. The kingdoms were divided into four districts, each with a governor; the people followed a tribal life style. The army was composed of freemen whose practice was to scalp their victims and then use the scalps in symbolic ceremonies. There was no organized religion; the Scythians venerated the graves of their ancestors and the elements: air, earth, water, fire, as well as the sun, moon, beasts, and war. There were no priests, but magicians and soothsayers. The Scythians had no written alphabet, so knowledge of them is limited to illustrations and artifacts preserved in tombs and buried structures.
M. 36; W. 86

SEA-FENCIBLES

Fencibles are men capable of making defense, fit to be called for defensive military service.
W. 47

SEA-LAWYERS

Nuisances who quote or misquote orders and regulations in support of their rights.
W. 90

SEALS AND VIALS

In *Revelation, the opening of seven seals of a book in *Heaven, bringing disasters to Earth.
M.D. 71

SEA OF TROUBLE

Hamlet III, i, 56-60:

To be, or not to be; that is the question:
Whether 'tis nobler in the mind to suffer

> The slings and arrows of outrageous fortune,
> Or to take arms against a sea of troubles,
> And by opposing end them . . . .

See also "Shakespeare."
P. 5:1

SEBASTIANO'S

Sebastiano Veneziano (c. 1485-1547) was a *Venetian painter active in *Rome. Using brilliant color and poetic feeling, he painted religious and mythological subjects, including *Polyphemus* (1511), a companion to *Raphael's *Galatea*. The association with the older master continued with *The Raising of *Lazarus* (1517-19). After the death of Raphael, Sebastiano was Rome's greatest portraitist. His nickname, "del Piombo," refers to the lead in papal seals, of which he became keeper in 1531.

(M.'s context in *M*. 140 suggests he had in mind Luca Signorelli's *Punishments of the Damned*.)
M. 140

SECRETARY OF THE NAVY

At the founding of the *American *Navy Department in 1798, the office of Secretary of the Navy was created: very much subject to *Presidential policies. First Secretary of the Navy was Benjamin Stoddert, who expanded the fleet from three vessels to fifty and who attempted to create a reserve and establish an admiralcy. His policies were altered by his successors, by the *Board of Navy Commissioners (1815), and by adoption of the Bureau system (1842). The U.S. Navy suffered a long and arduous development in the early nineteenth century, despite military conflicts that should have dictated otherwise. Navy Yards were established at *Portsmouth (*New Hampshire), *Boston, *New York, *Philadelphia, and Gosport (near *Norfolk), but the Monroe Doctrine discouraged formation of all *squadrons but small ones in response to immediate problems, and the *Jacksonians considered steam power to be overrated, keeping the United States too long in the age of sail.

By the time of M.'s Navy service, the *Whigs had come to power, bringing some development and reform. Secretary Abel Parker Upshur (1841-43) attempted to counter a recalcitrant system, but President John Tyler, in office during M.'s term (1843-44), was not the sailor's favorite. He appointed several short-term Secretaries (including Thomas W. Gilmer, who had been in office only ten days when he was killed in the explosion on *Stockton's *Princeton*). Not until the administra-

tion of Gideon Wells, beginning in 1861, did the Secretary of the Navy conduct a humane and organized office and the Navy become a valued and efficient force.
See also "Bancroft."
W. 7; W. 34; W. 55 and elsewhere

SECRETARY OF THE TREASURY
See "Treasury; Secretary of the Treasury."
W. 48

SEES
See "Archbishop."
W. 87

SEEVA
See "Shiva."
M.D. 40

SEIGNIOR SEIGNIORINI
A misspelling of "Signor Signoroni," credited in *Penny Cyclopaedia*'s "Tourniquets" article with invention to supersede the tourniquet.
See also "Senhor."
W. 63

SEINE
The Seine, *France's most navigable river, rises in the Plateau of Langres (1,545 feet above sea level), flowing generally northwest to the English *Channel at Le *Havre and Honfleur estuary: a course of over 480 miles. Its many tributaries and canals brought development to France's most important north-central cities, including *Paris, which makes of it a geographical reference distinguishing right and left banks.
I.P. 7; I.P. 8

SELKIRKS
Alexander Selkirk or Selcraig (1676-1721), prototype of *Robinson Crusoe, had a lifelong passion for the sea, despite family opposition. He was left on *Juan Fernandez island in September of 1704 and rescued in January of 1709 by one of *Dampier's ships. He next sailed with Dampier, meanwhile becoming the subject of many articles written about his long

experience. (Defoe's book did not appear until 1719.) When not at sea, he was involved in several notorious episodes, including assaults and desertion of his wife. Escaping again, he finally died at sea.

See "Jones, John Paul," regarding the "Countess of Selkirk" (*I.P.* 17).
I.P. 14; I.P. 17

SEMINOLE
The *Florida Seminole Indians, still under *Spanish rule, had been hostile to the *United States in the *War of 1812. In the first Seminole War (1817-18), their defeat by *Andrew Jackson led Spain to cede Florida. Forced off their fertile lands during Jackson's *Presidency, and tricked into an agreement to migrate to the west, as had other tribes (to their great decimation), some refused to move, and the U.S. government sent troops to oppose the braves led by *Osceola. The major war lasted (officially) from 1835 to 1838, costing some $14 million and over one thousand American lives and an unknown number of Indian lives.

Jackson's invasion of Florida constituted an act of war for which there was a failed movement for censure. The Seminole affair led to Jackson's break with John C. Calhoun, a former political ally.

Most Americans of the time would not have supported a "Seminole Widow and Orphan Asylum" (*C.M.* 6; *C.M.* 18), the tribe being seen as bloodthirsty ingrates, including in their ranks refugee Creeks who had refused removal to Mississippi, and former black *slaves seeking revenge.
R. 21; W. 15; C.M. 6; C.M. 7; C.M. 8; C.M. 18

SEMIRAMIS; SEMIRAMIAN
Semiramis is the *Greek name of a legendary heroic *Assyrian queen, probably the historical Sammuramat, mother of an Assyrian king of the eighth century B.C. Her reputed acts are mentioned in *Herodotus (i, 184) and in Diodorus Siculus (2, 13, 4). She is said to have reigned for many years after her husband's death, to have built the city of *Babylon, founded *Nineveh, and conquered many nations. Legend says she had many lovers killed and was finally killed herself, by her son, Ninyas. She appears in *Dante's Hell, in *Camoens's *Lusiad*, in *Byron's *Sardanapalus*, and she is the heroine of *Voltaire's *Semiramis* and of Rossini's opera, *Semiramide*.
M. 181; M.D. 105; P. 5:1

SENATE; SENATORS
See "Congress."
Passim

SENATOR WELLINGBOROUGH
The "Senator" who is "Redburn's" uncle, for whom "Redburn" is named, is probably patterned after M.'s uncle Leonard *Gansevoort (1751-1810), a member of the *Continental Congress, after whom M.'s brother Gansevoort was named.
R. 1

SENECA
Lucius Annaeus Seneca (c. 4 B.C.- 65 A.D.) rose from humble origins to become an important *Roman statesman, philosopher, satirist, and tragedian. Although we remember his idealism, cherished by early Church fathers and Renaissance writers, Seneca was himself a mixture of attributes: opportunistic and financially unscrupulous at the same time he practiced the self-government by reason promulgated by the *Stoics.
In the course of his life, he offended Emperors *Caligula and *Claudius, who exiled, then retrieved him to tutor young *Nero. Seneca at first had power during Nero's reign, but was finally ordered by the emperor to commit suicide; he did so philosophically.
His writings are about human vice, tyranny, corruption, psychology, science, literature, mythology.
(M. owned the *Workes . . . Both Morall and Naturall . . . Translated by Tho. Lodge* [London, 1614], Sealts # 457.)
R. 26; R. 56; W. 16; M.D. 1; C.M. 9; C.M. 37

SENEGAL
Senegal, on the *Atlantic Ocean in what was *French West *Africa, was explored by the *Portuguese in the fifteenth century. By the seventeenth, it was a French possession (lost to *Britain briefly during the *Napoleonic Wars), but it was not actually occupied until the 1850's and 1860's because of its unhealthful climate.
(In *R.* 34, "Cingalese" is probably "Senegalese.")
C.M. 26

SENHOR
Another exotic spelling (with *Seignior) of "Signor."
W. 61

SEPTEMBER, THREE DAYS OF
See "Three Days of September."
W. 3

SERAPIS
HMS *Serapis*, a fifty-four-gun (?) *British frigate, was leading the *Baltic merchant convoy (with *Countess of Scarborough*) when it was attacked and captured by *John Paul Jones, commander of *Bon Homme Richard*, 3 September 1779. *Serapis* commander Richard Pearson is said to have surrendered his sword to Jones while complimenting him on his incredible feat, while Jones expressed to Pearson the hope that next time the king might give him a better ship than *Serapis*. Serapis (pronounced Se-ray'pis) was actually a new copper-bottomed frigate, faster and better armed than Jones's.
I.P. 18; I.P. 19; I.P. 20

SERENE SUPERFLUITIES
Serene (Lat. *serenus*, clear, calm) was a royal designation formerly mainly in use by *German princes under the empire: Serene or Most Serene Highness. In modern times, Princess Grace of Monaco (née Grace Kelly) was called her Serene Highness.
"Superfluities" reflects M.'s estimation of royalty's worth.
M. 145

SERMON ON THE MOUNT
*Matthew 5-7 contains what is called the Sermon on the Mount (shorter version is in *Luke 6,11), actually a collection of various preachings of *Jesus. It has been called the *Magna Charta of *Christian ethics, for its new insights and eloquent reworking of traditional *Hebrew beliefs.
M. frequently quotes the sermon, which he heavily marked in his own *Bible, seeing in it an ideal of compassion. In his copy of *Emerson's *Essays*, he countered the *transcendentalist position on evil: "To annihilate all this nonsense read the Sermon on the Mount, and consider what it implies."
In a letter to *Duyckinck (24 February 1849) M. praised *Shakespeare as being "full of sermons-on-the-mount, & gentle, aye, almost as Jesus."
(See "Quotations" section for particular allusions.)
W. 70; W. 74; P. 14:2

SERPENT AND DOVE
P.'s Mr. Falsgrave refers to *Matthew 10:16: "Behold, I send you forth as sheep in the midst of wolves; so be wise as serpents and harmless as doves."
P. 5:4; I.P. 8

SERPENTINE
An oblong lake (1,500 yards long), separating *London's *Hyde Park from *Kensington Gardens.
P. 1:3

SERVING-MALLET BOAT
A serving mallet is used to beat joints flat when winding twine around spliced ropes. A canal boat, the blunt ends of which make it resemble a mallet head split lengthwise, is a "serving-mallet boat."
W. 91

SESOSTRIS
The *Greek name of a legendary *Egyptian king whom Diodorus Siculus called "Sesoosis." Perhaps one of three kings of the name (of the twelfth dynasty, ruling between 1971 and 1843 B.C.), he is said to have conquered *Asia, reorganized Egypt, reworked the legal and religious systems, and introduced the concept of caste.
M. 3

SETH MACY
See "Whaleman's Chapel."
M.D. 7

SEVENTH VIAL
In the *Revelation (16) of *St. John the Divine, seven vials of destruction are poured out by angels.
M.D. 71

SEVILLE
The province and major city of southwestern *Spain, in *Andalusia, has access to the *Atlantic Ocean through the *Guadalquiver River. The *Romans settled here in the second century B.C., and the *Vandals in the fifth century A.D. The *Moors arrived in 712, and the city flourished and took on the

"Moorish" character noted in *M*. 75. Important Moorish architecture includes the Alcázar, and the Torre del oro, a decagonal brick tower making up part of the city's wall, and an important landmark. Seville was captured in 1248 by Ferdinand III of *Castile. It declined rapidly under Spanish rule and by the eighteenth century was second to *Cádiz in importance. The picturesque city has been depicted in numerous paintings, literature, and music.
M. 75; W. 63

SEVRES
        The very delicate and expensive Sèvres china was originally manufactured at Vincennes, *France (starting in 1745). The factory moved to Sèvres in 1756, and Louis XV (see "Bourbon") became the proprietor in 1760, naming the works the *Manufacture National de Porcelaine*.
        Sèvres is located on the *Seine River, midway between *Paris and *Versailles. The modern city has the factory, a ceramics museum, a technical school of ceramics, and several ammunition factories.
M. 59

SEYCHELLE
        The Seychelles are a group of thirty islands, 700 miles northeast of *Madagascar, and 1,000 miles east of Zanzibar (3°40'-6°5' S., 53°55'-59°10 E.). The islands, of volcanic origin, were discovered by the *Portuguese in 1505. They were a center of *pirate activity until the *French occupation of the mid-eighteenth century. The Seychelles were part of the *British dependency of Mauritius by 1810 but were ceded to the French in 1814.
        The "Seychelle ground" was the rich surrounding whaling water.
M.D. 44

SHADRACH, MESHACH, AND ABEDNEGO
        In *Daniel 3, three faithful *Jews, Shadrach, Meshach, and Abednego, are saved by *God from death in a fiery furnace to which they are condemned for refusing to worship an idol. See also "Nebuchadnezzar."
M.D. 98

SHAKER

In 1776, Mother Anne Lee established the first *American community of Shakers (Millenial Church or the United Society of Believers in Christ's Second Appearing) at Niskayuna (M.'s "Neskyeuna," in *M.D.* 71), north of Albany, *New York.

The nickname "Shakers" was bestowed for the peculiar body movements made during services, the subject of some disapproval. Other Shaker communes known to M. were at Lebanon, N.Y., and at Hancock, Mass., near *Pittsfield, where it is known he visited.

The Shakers believed Mother Lee an incarnation of *Christ; they held property in common, and eventually became important agriculturists and craftsmen. Their movement died out because they practiced celibacy, but there are a few practicing Shakers even at this writing.

M. owned a copy of *A Summary View of the Millenial Church, or the United Society of Believers, Commonly Called Shakers. Comprising the Rise, Progress and Practical Order of the Society. Together With the General Principles of Their Faith and Testimony* (1848), which he purchased at Hancock 21 July 1850.

Although there is evidence of M.'s respect for the Shakers, he seems uneasy about their beliefs, particularly regarding Divine Revelation and charges made about their "*Manichaeism."

Sealts's "Melville and the Shakers" points out M.'s extensive annotation of *A Summary View* and demonstrates M.'s intense interest in the Shakers despite his failure to cite them by name in any fiction but *M.D.* 71. A comparison in his journal (14 December) of *Constantinople's *Dervishes with Shakers shows his continuing interest as late as 1856.
M.D. 71

SHAKESPEARE; SHAKSPEARE; ST. SHAKSPEARE

William Shakespeare (1564-1616) was born in Stratford-upon-Avon, *England: one of the large family of a businessman active in local civic affairs. In 1582, he married Anne Hathaway, with whom he was to have three children. Little is known of his fortunes before he became active in the theater in 1587, writing, acting, and directing for many years in Globe Theatre presentations. Performance *was* publication at the time, making it difficult in the nineteenth century to date, or to achieve precise editions of, the plays and poetry, which were first collected in the 1623 First *Folio.

By M.'s time, Shakespeare had been extolled by most of the great writers, but *American literati were holding up

Shakespeare as but one more British writer *not* to be emulated by Americans. In particular, the *Young America group, with which M. had contact (especially through the *Duyckincks), discouraged adulation of Shakespeare. So it is no surprise that M. spoke out against Shakespeare-worship in "Hawthorne and his Mosses" (1850), suggesting that *Hawthorne's work was almost comparable to that of "*St. Shakespeare." (In fact, M.'s original draft of the essay spoke out even more sharply against Shakespeare.)

Given M.'s canon, however, it is impossible not to see this negativism as a political pose of some kind. Certainly, Shakespeare was one of the greatest influences on M., who confessed to not having read the works closely until he purchased a large-print edition in 1849. (In terms of the present work, this explains the dearth of references prior to publication of *M.* in 1849.) In a letter to Duyckinck that same year (24 February), M. exclaimed about his recent reading and noted that Shakespeare was "gentle, aye, almost as *Jesus." Thereafter, the works are enriched throughout by direct citation and by covert allusion in such abundance as to fall outside the scope of this work. Most M. scholars have noted the influence of "*Shakspeare" (as M. sometimes spelled it), in imagery, verbal rhythms, and devices such as the stage directions and soliloquies of *M.D.* and the songs of *M.* More important are the focuses in common, especially on villainy in such "dark" characters as "Iago" and "*Goneril," and on the misguided greatness of such protagonists as "*Hamlet," "*Lear," "*Macbeth," and "*Timon." Olson's *Call Me Ishmael* is a prototype study which shows *King Lear* as inspiration for "*Ahab's" character. M. himself seems in his personal life to have consciously played the role of the melancholy "Jaques," or the clown "Touchstone," of *As You Like It.*

Sealts #s 460-465 are works by and about Shakespeare. #460 is the seven-volume 1837 edition which M. purchased in 1849. It is heavily annotated and, surprisingly, contains on the flyleaf of Volume VII what may be M.'s notes for *M.D.*, including "*Ego non baptizo . . . . "

M. visited Shakespeare's home, the recently renovated "New Place" at Stratford-Upon-Avon, as well as the Hathaway Cottage, on 3 May 1857. A picture M. saw at an 1865 exhibition evoked a poem, "The Coming Storm" (in *Battle-Pieces*), that examines the profound wisdom of art, especially as practiced by Shakespeare:

> . . . .
> No utter surprise can come to him
> Who reaches Shakespeare's core;
> That which we seek and shun is there--
> Man's final lore.

See also "Extracts" 15 and 16, and entries under: "Actium"; "Aeson"; "Angus"; "Antigonus"; "Antony, Mark"; "Apemantus' dog"; "Ariel"; "Autolycus"; "Belmont"; "Benedict"; "Brutus"; "Cade, Jack"; "Caesar, Julius Caesar"; "Calibans"; "Cambyses"; "Capulet"; "Cassandra"; "Clarence"; "Cleopatra"; "Cockney"; "Coriolanus, Caius Marcius"; "Davenant, Sir William"; "Fidele"; "Fletcher"; "Grave-digger"; "Hotspur"; "Jessica"; "John of Gaunt"; *"King Henry"*; "King Richard"; "Laertes"; "Lorenzo"; "Lysander"; "Malvolios"; "Montagues"; "Montaigne"; "Othello's"; "Percy; Percys"; "Polonius"; "Portia"; "Puck"; "Queen Mab"; "Richard III"; "Romeo"; "Rosse"; "Samphire"; "Shylock"; "The Tempest"; "Thane"; "Thersites." See also "Quotations" Section: "All the world's a stage . . . "; "bearer of evil tidings hath but a losing office"; "to consider the thing too curiously"; "et tu Brute!"; "in a fine frenzy rolling"; "The friends thou hast . . . "; "Greek to me"; "I turn the leaf to read . . . "; "A man may smile, and smile, and smile, and be a villain"; "nature . . . had meal and bran"; "Oh what a fool . . . "; "sea of trouble"; "The time is out of joint . . . "; "unkindest cut of all"; "the will of man is by his reason swayed."
M. 119; R. 30; R. 33; W. 9; W. 41; W. 51; W. 65; M.D. 87; P. 7:6; P. 9:2; C.M. 11; C.M. 30

SHAKSPEARE
See "Shakespeare . . . . "
R. 30; R. 33; W. 9; W. 41; W. 51; W. 65; P. 7:6; P. 9:2

SHARK-SYLLOGISM
A parody of a similar tale about a "Crocodile," in Chambers' *Cyclopaedia.*
M. 171

SHASTER
A general term for Hindu (see "Hindoo") sacred writings, such as the *vedas.
M.D. 82

SHAW, LEMUEL
M.'s father-in-law, Lemuel Shaw (1781-30 March 1861), was married in 1818 to Elizabeth Knapp (1784-1822), the mother of M.'s future wife, and of John Oakes (1820-1902). In 1827, he

married Hope Savage (1793-1879), mother of Lemuel (1828-1884) and Samuel Savage (1833-1915).

Shaw had been an old friend of M.'s father, Allan Melvill. M.'s marriage (in 1847) to Elizabeth Knapp Shaw (13 June 1822—31 July 1906) strengthened the bond. Throughout M.'s years of marriage, Shaw provided much financial support.

As Chief Justice of the Supreme Judicial Court of *Massachusetts (1830-1860), Shaw contributed much to the structure of American law.
T. Dedication

SHEFFIELD
Sheffield, in *Yorkshire, *England, has been famous for metalwork, especially cutlery, since the fourteenth century. By the late eighteenth and nineteenth centuries, the quality and variety of Sheffield products had reached a peak, after the introduction of crucible steel. By 1856, Henry Bessemer had set up works there, and a near-monopoly was established by metalworkers' groups descended from the early powerful craft guilds.

The safety razor, with a guard along one edge, first advertised in the Sheffield Directory for 1828, was the forerunner of modern razors.
R. 40; M.D. 107

SHELLEY; SHELLIAN
Percy Bysshe Shelley (1792-1822) was born in Sussex, *England and studied at *Oxford for a parliamentary career, following his father's pattern. From earlier school days, however, he had been known as "Mad Shelley"; in his teens he published Gothic stories and verse; at Oxford he was influenced by readings in radical authors such as Godwin. He behaved increasingly eccentrically, circulated a pamphlet on atheism, and was expelled. He eloped with sixteen year-old Harriet Westbrook (with whom he was to have two children) in 1811, forming an "open" marriage and attempting to set up a commune of those who also disapproved of standard marriage, religion, royalty, censorship, and the eating of meat. *Queen Mab (W. 65), published in 1813, expresses his political and poetic philosophies.

After his marriage ended (1814), Shelley lived for eight years with Mary Wollstonecroft, daughter of Godwin, and her stepsister; they traveled throughout Europe and together wrote History of a Six Weeks Tour (1817). Back in London in 1816, he published the poem Alastor; his son William was born that

year, the summer of which was spent with *Byron on Lake
Geneva (see "Lake Lemans"). While Mary wrote *Franken-
stein*, Shelley produced philosophic poems. When Harriet
drowned herself in the *Serpentine, Shelley married Mary
(1816) and got custody of his first two children. He developed
important friendships with other literati and wrote darkly
philosophical poetry and essays. Deeply in debt by 1818, Shelley
moved to *Italy, where he translated *Plato, wrote some of his
most important works, fathered a child by Mary (Percy, 1819),
registered another which was not Mary's, while two of his earlier children died and Mary had a breakdown. *Prometheus
Unbound* (1820) is a complex four-act lyrical drama focussed
on liberation (among other things). In addition to lyric poetry,
at this time Shelley wrote the verse melodrama *The Cenci*
(1819; mentioned in *W*. 89), which examined incest, atheism,
and the character of evil. In *Pisa, Shelley wrote *Defence of
Poetry* (1821) and *Adonais*, in response to the death of Keats.
His friendships with Byron, *Trelawney, and Leigh Hunt
turned his attention to the *Greek war of independence and its
implications in English history.

Shelley's last major poem, *The Truimph of Life*, was
written in an isolated house on the bay of Lerica, where Mary's
miscarriage, news of Byron's daughter's death, and mysterious occurrences involving the ghost of a child put him in an
omenous frame of mind. Shelley was drowned on the
*Mediterranean near *Leghorn, when his schooner, *Ariel*,
was taken in a squall. His body was cremated by Byron,
Trelawney, and Hunt.

"Shellian dietings" (*P*. 22:1) refers to the vegetarianism
practiced and promulgated by Shelley.

Works by and about Shelley are contained in Sealts
numbers 466, 467, 468, 469 (the *Works*), 520.
W. 65; W. 89; P. 22:1

SHEM
*Genesis 5:32: the eldest son of *Noah.
M.D. 104

SHERRY
True sherry wine comes from Jerez de la Frontera
province, *Spain, where local soil and grapes, the introduction
of special mildew-like flavorings, and blending of many vin-
tages, all produce apéritif and dessert wines considered superior to sherry-type wines of other areas. "Sherry" is a corruption of "Jerez."
W. 42; P. 22:1

SHETLAND ISLANDS; SHETLANDS
     *Scotland: 60°35' N; 2°10' W.
W. 4; M.D. Extracts 13; M.D. 27; I.P. 3; C.M. 26

SHIP OF FOOLS
     A much-used literary metaphor taking a ship and its
passengers as a microcosm of the world. Sebastian Brant's
Das Narrenschiff (1494) appears the source; it was adapted by
Alexander Barclay in 1509, as *The Shyp of Folys of the Worlde*,
which was in turn imitated by W.H. Ireland in *Modern Ship of
Fools* (1807), among others.
C.M. 3

SHIP'S NAVEL
     In *M.D.* 99, M. is toying with an aspect of primitive
*Greek religion. The shrine of *Apollo at *Delphi contained
the omphalos or navel-shaped stone, a cult object thought to
mark the center of the earth. *Mecca also claimed the honor,
for the "Kaaba," "navel of the world."
M.D. 99

'SHIPWRECK'
     See "Falconer."
W. 65

SHIPWRECKS AND DISASTERS AT SEA
     In "A Note on Melville's *Redburn*," Huntress suggests a
possible original for this book in *Interesting and Authentic
Narratives of the most Remarkable Shipwrecks, Fires,
Famines, Calamities, Providential Deliverances, and La-
mentable Disasters on the Seas, in most Parts of the World*, by
R. Thomas, A.M. He points out that the book, copyrighted in
Hartford, *Connecticut in 1835, was printed in separate vol-
umes, as "the second half of a book telling of noted *pirates and
piracies"; there were at least five editions.
R. 18

SHIRRA'S, REV. MR.
     The original for the dissenting clergyman is mentioned
in a footnote in Roberts C. Sand's compilation, *Life and Correspondence of John Paul Jones* (1830, pp. 176-77). Early editions
of *I.P.* use "Shirrer."
I.P. 18

SHIRRER'S, REV. MR.
   See "Shirra, Rev. Mr."
I.P. 18

SHIVA
   The caves of *Elephanta, near *Bombay, *India, are devoted to Saivism (or Shaivism), the Hindu (see "Hindoo") sect
that worships Shiva (or Siva), the Destroyer, as supreme power
in the trinity also containing *Brahma, the creator, and
*Vishnu, the preserver.
   Shiva's mission is to destroy the world prior to its recreation, an act of grace. In art, he is often represented
anthropomorphically as a dancer.
M.D. 40

SHYLOCK
   The *Jewish usurer, in *Shakespeare's The Merchant of
Venice.
   On 3 April 1857, M. saw what *Venetians called
"Shylock's" house, just off the *Grand Canal.
W. 88

SIAM, --ESE
   The modern-day Thailand ("Thailand" in 1939, "Siam"
in 1945, "Thailand" again in 1949), in the Indochinese and
*Malay peninsulas, was originally settled about A.D. 1000 and
was a Thai state by 1350. It expanded greatly until the fifteenth
century and began to have outside contact in the seventeenth.
   "Kings of Siam" in M.'s time were Rama II (1809-24),
who encouraged *British contact, Rama III (1824-51), who discouraged it, and Mongkut (1851-68), who opened the country up
to British and *French incursions.
   The "Siamese diphthong" of M. 13 alludes to the distinctive Thai language, with an alphabet and pronounciation radically different from English and indeed from most other languages, including those of neighboring peoples.
   See also "White elephants."
M. 13; M. 68; R. 34; R. 40; M.D. 42; M.D. 105

SIAMESE TWINS, --LIGATURE
   A "*Siamese" ligature is unbreakable. The "Siamese"
twins, Eng and Chang, were born in *China about 1814, discovered in 1829 at Mekong, *Siam, and exhibited as freaks by
P.T. Barnum. Their bodies were united at the breastbone.

They retired as farmers in North *Carolina in 1840, taking the
name "Bunker." They died within hours of each other on 17
January 1874, each leaving a wife and children.
M. 13; R. 17; M.D. 72; I.P. 19; C.M. 21

SIBBALD; SCOTCH SIBBALD; SIBBALD'S FIFE AND KIN-ROSS

Sir Robert Sibbald (1641-1722) was a physician and antiquary born and raised in *Edinburgh. He studied the history
and natural history of *Scotland and wrote numerous works,
including scientific treatises. Sibbald brought much serious-
ness and respectability to science in Scotland.

The reference to "Prodromus whales" is in error. In
1683, Sibbald published a natural history of Scotland, *Scotia il-
lustrata sive prodromus naturalis in quo regionis natura*,
which discusses whales but does not picture them. Illustrations were included in a later book, but both are quite rare and
seldom cited, so M.'s acquaintance with Sibbald remains a
mystery. The *blue whale is familiarly called "Sibbald's
rorqual." "Prodromus" means "introduction."

See also "Extracts" 31, for "Fife and Kinross."
M.D. Extracts 31; M.D. 32; M.D. 55

SIBERIA, --N

The vast *Asiatic portion of the modern U.S.S.R.: from
the *Ural Mountains to the *Pacific, and from the *Arctic
Ocean to Kazakhstan and the border with *China and
*Mongolia, conquered for *Russia by the *Cossacks, 1581-82.
There was no settlement of Siberia during M.'s time.
Although it is now known as a richly varied topographical
area, during the nineteenth century Siberia was known only as
the world's coldest place, with January mean temperatures
hovering about 60 or 65 degrees below zero f. in some areas.

M.'s knowledge of Siberia probably comes from
*Ledyard's account, rather than from *Marco Polo's.
M. 119; R. 43; R. 60; M.D. 5; M.D. 16; M.D. 45

SICILIAN VESPERS

The massacre of the *French by *Sicilians revolting
against Charles I began at vesper hour on Easter Monday, 30
March 1282. The riot began when the neglected and over-taxed
Sicilians came to the defense of a woman harassed by French
soldiers at the church of S. Spirito outside *Palermo; 2,000
French men, women, and children were killed and other Sicil-

ian cities arose, starting a war that lasted until the Treaty of Caltabellotta, 31 August 1302.
W. 85

SICILIES
See "Two Sicilies."
W. 4

SICILY; SICILIA; SICILIAN, --S
The triangular-shaped ancient Trinacria is the largest and most populated island in the *Mediterranean. With the islands of Pantelleria, Ustica, Lipari, and Egadi, it forms an autonomous region, separated from the mainland of *Italy by the Strait of *Messina (two to ten miles wide). A mountainous extension of the Apennines, Sicily has nine provinces: Catania (the site of Mt. *Etna, 10,705 feet high), Agrigento, Caltanissetta, *Enna, *Messina, *Palermo, Ragusa, Siracusa and Trapani.
It was settled by the *Phoenicians, followed by the *Carthaginians and *Greeks (eighth to sixth-century B.C.). The *Romans entered in 241 B.C. and the *Byzantines in A.D. 535, followed by *Arabs in the ninth century, *Normans in the eleventh, *Spanish in the fourteenth, and the *Bourbon house of *Naples in 1735. With the kingdom of Naples, it formed the Kingdom of the *Two Sicilies. Garibaldi freed Sicily in 1860, and it became part of Italy in 1861.
M. visited Messina 13-16 February 1857.
See also "Phalaris"; "Verres."
O. 33; M. 83; M. 119; R. 30; M.D. 40; P. 2:5; C.M. 29

SIC TRANSIT GLORIA MUNDI
*Thomas à Kempis (1380-1471), *Imitation of *Christ* (c. 1420), I, 3: *O quam cito transit gloria mundi*—How swiftly passes the glory of the world (words addressed to the *Pope at his elevation ceremony).
R. 23

SIDDON
The *American square-rigged packet ship *Siddons* was part of the Collins Line's *New York-to-Liverpool run. She was very fast and had elaborate facilities for first-class passengers. *Siddons* was named for the British actress in tragedy, Sarah Siddons (1755-1831).
R. 41

SIDNEY
    See "Sydney . . . . "
R. 33

SIDNEY, ALGERNON
    See "Jeffreys, Judge."
W. 71

SIDNEY, PHILIP
    *English poet Sir Philip Sidney (1554-86) was an acquaintance of Fulke Greville, *Hakluyt, and *Raleigh. He traveled extensively in Europe and was knighted for reasons of court protocol in 1582.
    His most famous work is *Astrophel and Stella* (pub. 1591), 108 sonnets and eleven songs based on his unhappy love affair with Penelope Devereux Rich. His *Defence of Poetry* (pub. 1595) is a vindication of literature, similar to contemporary Continental works.
    M.'s reference in *M*. 119 is to Sidney's seemingly useless gentility.
M. 119

SIDON
    Once the chief city of *Phoenicia, Sidon (Sayda, modern *Lebanon) was an ancient commercial state prophesied for destruction in the *Old Testament. It was founded in the third millenium B.C., ravaged, rebuilt, and ruled by many nations. In 1837, Sidon was badly damaged by an earthquake; a large necropolis was discovered in 1855.
W. 50; P. 7:4

SIENNA
    Red-mottled Siena marble from *Tuscany, *Italy, often brecciated (containing pieces of other rock), was used in the construction of many ancient edifices.
R. 46

SIERRAS
    Sierras are rugged mountains of a saw-toothed appearance. There are many peaks and mountain chains called Sierras throughout the world. Closest are the Sierra Nevada mountains of eastern *California, the site of Mount Whitney (14,495 feet). The Sierra Madres are *Mexico's chief mountain

system, with *Popocatepetl the most notable peak. Other Sierras include those of *Spain, the *Philippines, Wyoming, and Guatemala.
M. 161

SIKH
The name originally designated one from Sikkim (or Sikhim), *India, in the *Himalayan area of many Buddhist monasteries. Sikhism originated about A.D. 1500 among local Hindus (see "Hindoo") who rejected the caste system and idolatry.
R. 40

SIKOKE
Shikoku (or Sikoku) island is the smallest of the four major islands of *Japan: in M.'s time a sparsely populated fishing area.
M.D. 109

SILENUS
In *Greek mythology, sometimes said to be *Pan's son or brother, or Hermes's son, Silenus was a fat, drunken old man, usually riding an ass. He is associated mainly with *Bacchus, to whom he was early nurse or teacher, then devoted follower. In the story of King Midas, Silenus wanders into Midas's garden and is made sport of. Bacchus, eager to retaliate, grants Midas the tragic wish that everything he touch turn to gold. Silenus is referred to in Keats's *Endymion (IV, 209).
M. 66

SILLY MANSOUL
"Mansoul" (the soul of man) is the capital of the universe, which temporarily falls to the evil "Diabolus," in *Bunyan's allegory of the soul and the church, The Holy War (1682).
See also "Extracts" 22.
M.D. Extracts 22

SILVA, MARQUIS
*Rev. Charles R. Stewart (Vol. I) identifies Silva as the "private secretary and confidential friend of the emperor" of *Brazil.
W. 57

SILVER-HEADS
Fish similar in size to small carp; white with silver lines.
M. 48

SILVER-SPOONS
*Cervantes was the first to say, "Every man was not born with a silver spoon in his mouth" (*Don Quixote* IV, 73). Traditionally, to be born with a silver spoon in one's mouth is to be born wealthy or blessed—as though the usual gift from a godparent is inherited at birth.
M.D. 48

SIMEON
The reference in *C.M.* 45 is to the *New Testament figure, as opposed to the *Old Testament Levite Simeon, cursed by *Jacob in *Genesis 49. In *Luke 2:25-35, the seer Simeon recognizes the infant *Jesus as the Redeemer, fulfilling a prophecy that he should not die before seeing *God. Simeon's name became emblematic of the devout. As a saint, he is depicted carrying the infant Jesus or receiving him in the Temple. His feast-day is February 18. He is also called "Simon."
C.M. 45

SIMOON
Local name for a warm, dry desert wind of the sirocco variety, in *Arabia, northeast *Africa, and the Near East. It often damages vegetation.
M.D. 44

SIMPLICIUS, --'S
A sixth-century A.D. *Greek philosopher schooled by the Neoplatonists at a time when their teachings were forbidden, Simplicius sought temporary refuge in *Persia. After returning to Greece, he wrote commentaries on *Aristotle's *De coelo*, *Physica*, *De anima*, and *Categoriae* (as well as on the *Enchiridion* of *Epictetus), finding Aristotle's works in harmony with *Plato's.
W. 38

SIMPLON, THE
The Simplon Pass over the *Alps is in southern *Switzerland's Valois canton, a divide between the Pennine

(W.) and Lepontine (E.) Alps. *Napoléon built a road (1800-06) crossing the pass, one of the wildest in the Alps (tunneled through in 1906). *Wordsworth acclaimed it in "The Simplon Pass." (M. crossed the Alps in 1857 through the Saint Gotthard pass.)
M. 84

SIN; VIRTUE; VICE
   See "Bunyan."
W. 94

SINAI
   Musa, or Mt. Sinai (7,482 feet), thought of as the site of *Moses's reception of the law in *Exodus, is located on the Sinai Peninsula, between present-day *Egypt, *Israel, and Saudi Arabia. The area contains several higher peaks, and it is unclear to which Exodus refers.
   "Thunder like Sinai" (*M*. 28) refers to Exodus 19:16-19: Moses and his people are gathered on Mt. Sinai when there are "thunders and lightnings" and the Lord appears in fire and smoke.
M. 28; M. 60

SINBAD THE SAILOR
   See "Sindbad."
I.P. 25

SINDBAD
   In the *Arabian Nights story of Sinbad the Sailor, the Old Man of the Sea clung to the shoulders of Sinbad for many days; Sinbad finally released him by making him drunk. The Old Man of the Sea has come to signify any figurative or actual burden from which one cannot free oneself without great exertion.
T. 12; I.P. 25

SINGLE-STICK
   A fighting implement for serious games, owned by many *midshipmen, and mentioned in *Scott's The Monastery.
W. 66

SING-SING

New York State Prison at Sing Sing was founded in 1824, on the principle of using convict labor to work nearby marble quarries. It was named for the Sin Sinck Indians, a branch of the Mohicans, whose name means "stone upon stone."

The area, now called Ossining, is in Westchester County, *New York, on the east bank of the *Hudson River. It was privately purchased from the Sin Sincks in 1685 and seized by New York State in 1779 because of the owner's *Tory sympathies. It became incorporated as the village of Sing Sing in 1830, but the name was changed in 1901, in an attempt to disassociate from the prison.
W. 42; W. 58

SINKING PIT

Perhaps a play on the "Sinking Fund" established in *England in 1717 to pay off the national debt. It was reestablished by Pitt the Younger in 1786 but created a loss and was abandoned in 1828, only to be revived in 1875, 1923, and 1928.
M. 147

SINS OF THE FATHER

*Exodus 20:5,6: "I the Lord your *God am a jealous God, visiting the iniquity of the fathers upon the children unto the third and the fourth generation of those who hate me; And showing mercy unto them that love me, and keep my commandments."
P. 5:4

SIRACH, SON OF

The *Apocryphal Ecclesiasticus, or the Wisdom of Jesus the Son of Sirach, was composed by Joshua ben Sira (the *Hebrew form of the name), a teacher of *Old Testament law (c. 180 B.C.). It is a link between Old Testament wisdom literature and later rabbinical schools of the *Pharisees and Sadducees.

See also "Quotations" section, for M.'s specific allusions: "With much communication he will tempt thee . . . "; "An enemy speaketh sweetly with his lips . . . "; "Take heed of thy friends"; "There is a subtle man . . . "; "Who will pity the charmer . . . ?"

("Ecclesiasticus" means "The Church Book," a designation of the third century Latin *Church.)
C.M. 43; C.M. 45

SIREN; SYREN
In *Greek myth, an island-dwelling nymph with a woman's head and a bird's body whose melodious voice lured sailors to their deaths. There are various descriptions of Sirens, other than in *Homer's *Odyssey*: there were two or three; they had been transformed by Demeter as punishment; they played the lyre and the flute; their island was a mass of bleached bones of victims.
M. Passim; W. 45; W. 46; M.D. 101; P. 5:6

SIRIUS
Sirius, the Dog-star, is the brightest star of the *constellation Canis Major, and visually the brightest star. The *Egyptians believed that it caused the *Nile to flood; the *Romans thought it brought the year's hottest weather (thus the modern expression "dog days").
M. 175

SIR JOHNS AND SIR JOSHUAS
"Sir" is a title of honor prefixed to the *Christian name of *British baronets and knights. "John" is a generic name; Joshua is probably more common in Britain than in the *United States, because of its ancient *Biblical connection. Sir Johns and Sir Joshuas are Royal "John Does."
R. 8

SIR JOSHUAS
See "Sir Johns and Sir Joshuas."
R. 8

SIR PATRICK SPENS
The early *Scottish ballad is found in Percy's *Reliques*: despite a premonition, Sir Patrick goes on a sea mission for the king and dies with the rest of the ship's company. *Sir Walter Scott wrote a slightly altered version of the story.
W. 74

SIR T. HERBERT'S VOYAGES INTO ASIA AND AFRICA
Sir Thomas Herbert (1606-1682), traveller and author, was born into a family of wealthy *York merchants. He attended *Oxford and Trinity College, *Cambridge, and was in the diplomatic service in 1627, travelling on the East Indiaman *Rose* to the *Persian Gulf, the Cape of *Good Hope,

*Madagascar, *Surat, *Baghdad (and other important cities), *Ceylon, the *Coromandel Coast, Mauritius, and *St. Helena.

On the *Parliamentary side in the English Civil War, he became attendant to the captive *Charles I and later wrote memoirs of the experience. As a baronet, he became a writer and antiquarian.

Sir Thomas's digressive account of his eastern travels is *A Description of the Persian Monarchy now beinge: the Oriental Indyes Iles and other parts of the Greater Asia and Africk* (1634). In *M.D.* Extracts 28, the excerpt is from *Harris's *Collection* I, 406, rather than from the corresponding section (I, 13) of *Some Yeares Travels in Divers Parts of Asia and Afrique* (1638).

See also "Extracts" 28.
M.D. Extracts 28

SISTERS
In *P.*, the "six hands of the sisters" are those of the three *Fates.
P. 21:2

SISYPHUS
In Greek mythology, the crafty and avaricious Sisyphus, son of Aeolus (see "Aeloian") and father of *Ulysses and *Autolycus, is the founder of *Corinth. He outwits death, only to be forced by Hermes into *Hades, where *Pluto has him endlessly roll a huge stone up a hill. A "labor of Sisyphus" is a never-ending task.
I.P. 1

SIXTEENTH DAY OF DECEMBER, A.D. 1851
In the tradition of Southey, in *The Doctor* (Vol. 7, 1847), M. includes what is apparently the actual day of his composition (1850 in first English edition).
M.D. 85

SIXTY ROUND CENTURIES AGO
According to nineteenth-century *Biblical chronology, the time of the death of *Adam.
M.D. 7

SKILLAGALEE
Prison gruel: water in which meat has been cooked, thickened with oatmeal. "Galee" means "jaw," or "talk." W. 32

SKRIMSHANDER
Variously *scrimshaw, scrimshonting*: elaborate carving of whale-teeth or bone.
M.D. 3

SKULL-AND-CROSS-BONES
The *pirate's flag, showing a human skull and crossed thigh bones: the emblem of death.
(See "Ulna.")
M. 139; C.M. 23

SKULLS, SIGN OF THE
See "Golgotha."
M. 142

SKYE, ISLE OF; SKYEMAN
Skye is the largest island of *Scotland's Inner *Hebrides. Its 670-square-mile area is deeply indented so that all parts are relatively close to the sea. Its Cuillin Hills rise to over 3,000 feet; among its Red Hills stands the Old Man, a sea landmark. It is associated in history with Prince Charles Edward (the Young Pretender, grandson of *James II of England; 1720-1788). Skye is home to the Macdonald clan of chieftains and the MacCrimmons, hereditary pipers.
M. Passim

SLAVE, --S; SLAVERY
Slavery had been an issue long before the Colonies became the United States of *America. The Mason-Dixon line, drawn 1763-67 by surveyors Charles Mason (1728-86) and Jeremiah Dixon (d. 1777) runs west of *Pennsylvania, marking the boundary with *Delaware, *Maryland, and West *Virginia; it became the pre-*Civil War demarcation between slave and free states. *Jefferson had tried and failed to ban slavery in the *Constitution, and by the middle of the nineteenth century it was an issue touching almost every aspect of American life. Northern *Abolitionists were motivated partly by tarnished motives, slavery giving the southern part of the

nation an economic edge. Territorial acquisitions before and
after the *Mexican War raised the question of whether new
states would have slaves. The Missouri Compromise (1820)
provided that new states be admitted only in pairs, one slave,
and one free. The Fugitive Slave Law (1851) was declared constitutional and enforced by M.'s father-in-law, Massachusetts
Chief Justice *Lemuel Shaw, exacerbating an already dangerous disagreement between north and south. Only after a mas-
sively costly Civil War was slavery discontinued and attempts
made to rectify its aftermath, in the thirteenth, fourteenth, and
fifteenth amendments to the Constitution.

Although he was not a political activist, M. clearly
shows opposition to slavery, organized or not, throughout the
works, especially in *W.* and in the short story, "Benito Cereno."
Rogin's *Subversive Genealogy* examines the complexities of the
Melville family's positions regarding it.
Passim

SLEET'S CROW'S-NEST
        See "Scoresby."
M.D. 35

SLID!
        Archaic oath: "*God's lid."
M.D. 31

SMEERENBERG
        *Scoresby (Vol. 2, p. 52) gives the etymology: probably
derived from the *Dutch words *smeer*, signifying "fat," and
bergen, "to put up."
M.D. 92

SMELLS
        Part of a joke on *Scoresby, referred to as "Fogo Von-
Slack." Scoresby did not write a book on "Smells." He did dis-
cuss the "offensive smell" of whale oil in *An Account of the
Artic Regions (Vol. 2).
M.D. 92

SMITH, ELIZABETH OAKES
        Popular poet and writer (1806-93) of romantic and senti-
mental social, moral, and religious problem novels, Elizabeth
Oakes married Seba Smith (1792-1868), journalist and creator

of popular letters from "Major Jack Downing" which satirized
*Jacksonian *America.
        (See also "Extracts 59.")
M.D. Extracts 59

SMITHFIELD
        Smithfield, north of *London, *England, prefers to be
known for its meat market, in existence since the twelfth century. Charles Knight's *London* (Sealts # 312) says that 4,000
head of cattle were sold weekly at Smithfield, their average
weight 640 Pounds.
        During the Reformation and Counter-Reformation,
Smithfield was an execution site where hundreds of persons
perished at the stake for religious opinions (see "Mary,
Bloody"). Earlier (from the twelfth century), it had been the
scene of tournaments, jousts, and fairs. *William Wallace
was executed at Smithfield in 1305.
W. 75; M.D. 105; I.P. 25

SMITH'S
        Adam Smith (1723-90), *Scottish lecturer on literature at
*Edinburgh and professor of logic at *Glasgow, was a friend to
*Hume and *Johnson and acquaintance of *Voltaire, whom he
met while tutor to the Duke of *Buccleuch in *France.
        His *An Inquiry into the Nature and Causes of the
Wealth of Nations* (1776) revolutionized economic theory and
prophesied *American importance. Smith believed that a nation's labor, rather than its land, is the source of its substi-
nence; that increased capital means increased productive labor and decreased interest rates; that pursuit of self-good leads
to public good.
R. 18

SMOLLETT, --'S
        Tobias George Smollett (1721-71), satirical *Scottish au-
thor, was a navy surgeon's mate in the *West Indies and an
unsuccessful surgeon in *London before he began publishing.
His first large success was *The Adventures of Roderick Random* (1748). His European travels were made use of in *The Adventures of Peregrine Pickle* (1751), which M. refers to in *O.* 77.
The dubious hero's amour is "Emilia" (M.'s "Amelia"); her
love is gained when "Peregrine" finally repents of a lifetime of
sin and error. The libellous novel caricatures prominent persons including *Akenside; it was toned down for the second
edition (1758).

After several publications attacking his rival, the novelist Henry Fielding (1707-54), Smollett published *The Adventures of Ferdinand Count Fathom* (1753), referred to in *O*. 77 and *W*. 8. The monstrous "Count" benefits little morally from the assistance of "Count de Melvil," who is the focus of the later part of the novel.

Smollett translated *Cervantes, founded *Critical Review* (1756-1763), and wrote a *History of England* (1757-58), which finally brought financial security. He translated *Voltaire, wrote plays and novels, edited a short-lived *Tory journal, and wrote the epistolary *Travels Through France and Italy* (1766). Failure to secure a consulship in England, the death of his daughter, his own bad health, and attacks from those he had libelled, all drove him back to the Continent, where he wrote his greatest novel, *The Expedition of Humphry Clinker* (1771). He died near *Leghorn, having become a financial success but something of a pariah, his attempts to fight injustice and cruelty too deeply imbedded in his works in his own cruel humor.

Sealts #480 is the 1778 edition of *Roderick Random*.
O. 77; R. 29

SMUT

A smut is a furnace or iron or copper boiler. A secondary meaning is "witness," so the blacksmith's speech in *M.D.* 108 is doubly meaningful.
M.D. 108

SMYRNA

The western *Turkish city on the Aegean Sea is situated on a magnificent harbor framed by picturesque mountains. It is the chief export port for minerals, tobacco, figs, and other produce.

An early Ionian colony, Smyrna was captured by the *Romans, was an early seat of *Christianity under the *Byzantines, and was taken by *Tamerlane in 1402. *Mongol occupation was followed by *Ottoman Turkish control from 1424 (until 1919).

M. visited the cultural center, 20-23 December 1856, commenting at length in his journal on the city. He climbed Mt. Pagus, visited the ancient Acropolis, and made the obligatory tourist's stop at the Bazaar and the bustling Caravan Bridge across the Meles River. M. was a great lover of figs and stocked up even before leaving the ship, in Smyrna Harbor.
M. 14; M. 121

SNOWDON

Mt. Snowden, in *Wales, is one of the highest mountains on the island of *Britain (3,560 feet).
P. 1:3

SOAKITES

See "Water-cure Establishment."
P. 22:1

SOCIETY FOR THE SUPPRESSION OF CRUELTY TO GANDERS, SECRETARY OF

This is undoubtedly a joke on the multitude of special-interest *humane societies of M.'s time.
M.D. 65

SOCIETY ISLANDS; --GROUP; --ISLES

The largest island group of *French *Polynesia, the Society group (of volcanic and coral origins) is southwest of the *Marquesas. The islands were named by *Cook for Britain's *Royal Society, which sponsored his (1769) expedition to observe the *Transit of Venus. Society Islanders have contributed much to science through their memorized genealogies of migrations as early as the ninth century.

The higher-altitude Windward Group (Iles du vent), with an area of 455 square miles, includes *Tahiti and Moorea (see "Moreea"), site of Mt. Tohivea, the highest peak (3,960 feet). The Leeward Group (Iles sous le vent), about 150 miles northwest of Tahiti, have an area of 161 square miles. *Bora-Bora has the highest peak (Otemanu; 2,385 feet). Tahaa (M.'s "*Tahar") and Raiatea ("*Raiatair") are two miles apart within the same barrier reef.

M. arrived on *Lucy Ann* (see "Julia") c. January and returned on *United States*, staying for a week in October 1843 and passing the beautiful bay of *Taloo upon departure.

See also "Afrehitoo"; "Huwyenee"; "Martair"; "Partoowye"; "Tamai."
T. Preface; T. 29; O. Passim; W. 28

SOCIETY OF ANTIQUARIES

Sixteenth-century *England was much interested in the preservation of antiquities and in archeology. The Society of Antiquaries was founded about 1572 but abolished by *James I on political grounds. Revived in 1707, it was formally established as the Society of Antiquaries of *London in 1717 and chartered by *George II in 1751. Its elected membership by M.'s time had published *Vetusta Monumenta* (1747-1883), *Archaeologia* (1770-), and *Proceedings* (1843-1920).

Similar societies proliferated during M.'s time, in *Scotland, *France, *Ireland, *Denmark, and *Russia. The American Antiquarian Society was founded in 1812.
R. 31

SOCIETY OF FRIENDS
    See "Quaker . . . . "
C.M. 26

SOCRATES; SOCRATIC
    The *Athenian philosopher (469-399 B.C.) spent much of his life giving oral instruction in public places, in an effort to promulgate truth and expose error. *Plato's dialogues preserve the "Socratic Method" of seemingly simple questioning which traps the participant into self-contradiction leading to truth. *Xenophon's *Memorabilia* is another view of Socrates, who directed philosophy into the study of ethics by preaching that virtue is knowledge and wickedness ignorance.
    The *R*. 58 comment that Socrates died "the death of a *Christian" is puzzling. Socrates swallowed hemlock when he was sentenced to death for his teachings.
    The notion that the "soul is a harmony" (in *C.M.* 7) is expounded in Plato's *Republic, Phaedo*, and elsewhere.
    Socrates is *Magister Barbatus*, bearded master, in the works of *Stoic satirist *Persius (mentioned in *W*. 84; see also "Beards").
R. 58; W. 38; W. 84; M.D. 10; C.M. 7

SODOM
    One of the *Biblical "*Cities of the Plain," with *Gomorrah, Admah, Zeboim and Zoar (*Genesis 14:2 and *Deuteronomy 29:23), destroyed in Genesis 19:24 for the wickedness of its inhabitants, probably idolators. Probable location was north of the *Dead Sea near Gomorrah.
    Its proverbial wickedness is mentioned in Genesis 13:13 and 18:20; Lamentations 4:6; *Isaiah 3:9. Its story is an account of the coupling of divine judgment with natural disaster.
    There being no real evidence of the actual fruit intended in the Bible, "apples of Sodom" is probably a figurative allusion to the bitterness of *Israel's enemies. Modern usage identifies the fruit of the "Vine of Sodom" (see below) as "apple," referring to a tree and its fruit, the rendering of the Hebrew *tap-*

puah, akin to Arabian *tuffakh*, which means "apple." The reference might also be to apricot or citron. A student of *Linnaeus, visiting the Dead Sea in 1750, described *Poma Sodomica*, which fills with ashes after insect attack, the skin remaining beautiful and intact. Josephus Flavius (A.D. 37-95), the Jewish historian, describes the "apples of Sodom" (B.J. iv, viii, 4): "The ashes growing in their fruits, which fruits have color as if they were fit to be eaten, but if you pluck them with your hands they dissolve into smoke and ashes." There are two such fruits, neither of which grow on a vine: ushr, *Catotropis procera*, and colocynth, Arabian hondol, the bitter apple.

There is one direct reference to the "Vine of Sodom" (Deuteronomy 32:32):

> ...their vine is of the vine of Sodom,
> And of the fields of Gomorrah:
> Their grapes are grapes of gall,
> Their clusters are bitter.

M. mentions seeing the trees in the *Holy Land, in his journal for January 1857.
T. 8; R. 39; M.D. 9; I.P. 10; C.M. 29

SOFT-TACK
Bread, as distinct from ship's biscuit.
W. 32

SOFT-TOMMY
Soft bread.
W. 32

SOG; SOGGER
A "sogger" is anything large and heavy, in colloquial usage. In *Cheever, a "Sog" is a large whale.
M.D. 81

"SOGERS"
Malingerers.
W. 29

SOLANDER
*Swedish botanist Daniel Charles Solander (1736-1782), a friend of *Sir Joseph Banks, accompanied him as a naturalist on *Cook's circumnavigation, 1768-71.
M.D. 105

SOLDADOES
The "bloody-minded soldadoes" in *M.D.* are probably derived from the melodramatic *The Three Spaniards*, by George Walker.
M.D. 73

SOLDANS
See "Sultans."
M. 181

SOLEBY
H.M.S. *Solebay* frigate was in action off the *American coast in the 1770's and 1780's. On a privateering venture in 1776, *John Paul Jones on *Providence* narrowly escaped capture by *Solebay*.
I.P. 10

SOLOMON
Second king of Judah (see "Judea")—*Israel, Solomon (d. c. 934 [922] B.C.) succeeded his father, *David, and reigned for forty years, his mother, Bathsheba and her associates having convinced David that he should reign rather than Adonijah.

Solomon married the daughter of *Egypt's *Pharaoh and in other ways extended Israel's power, in a reign renowned for its wisdom and prosperity. He is celebrated in the first ten chapters of I *Kings; subsequent chapters show another side: Solomon's yielding to the heathen practices of his wives and concubines; loss of trade routes; internal strife and rebellion, caused by oppressive taxation, all of which damaged the kingdom his father had built.

It was long believed that Solomon was the writer of *Ecclesiastes and other *Bible books, and he is one of M.'s favorite "sources." In M.'s Bible, the apocryphal Wisdom of Solomon is heavily marked and annotated, as is Ecclesiastes (and I Kings). Also attributed is the Song of Solomon. Apparently, M. saw the rather pessimistic attributed material as the product of mature experience, as opposed to the more

"innocent" idealism expressed in the *Gospels. As Nathalia
Wright notes in *Melville's Use of the Bible*, "Solomonic" is his
synonym for "disillusioned."   In a June 1851 letter to
*Hawthorne, M. said: "I read Solomon more and more, and
. . . see deeper and deeper and unspeakable meanings in him."
But M. added the shrewd suspicion that the works were
"managed," with "corruptions and interpolations."

Among M.'s more specific allusions to Solomon are the
following:

M. 75: Solomon's elaborately decorated Temple (I Kings
6, ff; II *Chronicles 3-7) and his royal dwelling were thirteen
years in construction, in *Phoenician and other foreign style,
two gigantic pillars flanking the entrance. The Temple became the very center and symbol of Israel, and much of
Solomon's reputation for wisdom and magnificence arose because of it.

W. 50: Solomon's "annual squadron to *Ophir" refers to
the large fleet of ships the king used to travel to Ophir for treasure from King Hiram.

M.D. 45: "Nothing new under the sun" is from Ecclesiastes 1:9: "there is no new thing under the sun."

M.D. 88: "700 wives and 300 concubines" is from I Kings
11:3.

M.D. 96: "Vanity of vanities; all is vanity" is from Ecclesiastes 1:2. M. alluded to the saying also in his *lecture on
the "South Seas," in a reference to the *Solomon Islands,
thought to be Ophir, by early explorers.

C.M. 16: Solomon's knowledge of "all vegetables" is
from I Kings 33: "And he spake of trees, from the cedar tree
that is in *Lebanon even unto the hyssop that springeth out of
the wall."

See also "Cyclades"; "Handel"; "Solomon Islands."

See also "Quotations" section: "hyssop on the wall"
(*C.M*. 16) and "the man that wandereth out of the way of understanding . . . " (*M.D*. 96).
O. 44; M. 15; M. 75; M. 97; R. 14; R. 27; W. 50; M.D. 45; M.D.
52; M.D. 88; M.D. 96; M.D. 104; P. 4:1; P. 7:4; C.M. 16; C.M.
39; C.M. 40

SOLOMON ISLANDS

A 900-mile-long chain of Melanesian coral and volcanic
islands running northwest/southeast between 5° and 11° S.
and 154°40' and 162°30' E. The heavily forested islands were
discovered by Mendaña (see "Mendanna") in 1567, on his quest
for the site of *Ophir, presumed location of King *Solomon's
gold source. His attempt to colonize is discussed in Robert
Graves's *The Islands of Unwisdom* (1949). They were also ex-

plored by Carteret and de *Bougainville and others, and have been the seat of conflict throughout their history, claimed by the *British, *Germans, and *Japanese in World War II.
W. 76; M.D. 57

SOL'S RAYS
     See "Sun."
M. 77

SOLWAY FRITH
     Solway Firth (or Frith) is a twenty-two-mile-wide shallow *Irish Sea inlet between *England and *Scotland. The name derives from *sulwathe*, meaning "muddy ford": its character at low tide.
     See also "St. Bee's Head"; "Hadrian's Wall."
I.P. 17

SOLYMAN THE MAGNIFICENT
     Suleiman I (1494?-1566), the *Turkish Kanuni ("the law-giver"), is known in the west as "the Magnificent." Sultan of the *Ottoman Empire from 1520 to his death, Suleiman is most remembered for the splendor of his reign. The greatest Turkish statesmen and lawyers, artists, poets and architects contributed to the brilliance. Suleiman's military strength was formidable. His forces more or less controlled Belgrade, *Rhodes, *Hungary, *Austria, and much of *Persia. Under Barbarossa, the navy developed into controllers of the *Mediterranean until the Battle of *Lepanto (1571). Conflict between Suleiman's sons over succession brought about the execution of one. Suleiman himself was killed while besieging a Hungarian fortress.
     In *T.* 17, M. is in error; the Ottoman sultan Muhammad II successfully besieged *Constantinople in 1453. Suleiman failed in an attempted siege of *Vienna in 1529.
T. 17; M. 181

SOMNUS
     In *Ovid, god of sleep (Greek Hypnus). His abode was near the black country of the Cimmerians, where the sun never shined, the only sound was the stream of *Lethe (river of forgetfulness), the only flowers were poppies and other sleep-inducing herbs. He had three sons: *Morpheus, who could assume the form of any human being; Icelus, who gives

dreams of birds and beasts; Phantasus, who gives dreams of inanimate objects.
T. 20; C.M. 42

SONGS OF THE SIRENS
An invention; see "Siren."
W. 45

SON-OF-A-GENTLEMAN
In *Britain, a gentleman is historically a non-noble person above the social rank of yeoman, entitled to bear arms; one of some position in society, with appropriate manners, bearing, and behavior. In the *United States, he is a man of financial means to support a gentle lifestyle, with appropriate education. The son of a gentleman would expect to continue the rights and privileges accruing to his father's position. When M.'s "gentleman" father died in debt, he was denied these expectations. His hyphenation suggests a parallel with a common four-word epithet.
See "*My First Voyage*"; "Walter Redburn."
R. Title page

SOOLOO, --'S
Modern-day Sulu, which withstood *Spanish domination for centuries, is a *Moslem *Philippine Islands archipelago of c. 400 volcanic and coral islands, some of which remain unnamed. They extend 180 miles southwest from Basilan Island to *Borneo, separating the Sulu Sea from the *Celebes Sea. The Sulus were under *Spanish rule until the mid-nineteenth century. (They became officially part of the *Philippines in 1940.)
M. may owe much of his knowledge of the Sulus to *Wilkes, who describes "Sooloo" natives and discusses local *piracy, subsidized by Sulu princes.
M. could have read about the Sultan in *Penny Cyclopaedia*:

> The sultan is a mere cipher, and his orders are disputed by the meanest individual; he is unable to decide the most trivial points without the concurrence of his privy council . . . . The sultan seems to derive all his revenues from his own estates, as no taxes are paid by the noblemen or their subjects, and the only revenue, consisting of the customs on goods imported, is shared in unequal

proportions among the sultan and the members of
the Ruma Bechars (Council) according to their
rank.

(In 1915 the Sultan abdicated rights of sovereignty, retaining control of the Islamics. The sultanate was abolished in
1940, when Sulu became part of the Phillipines.)
M. 178; W. 46

SOPHIST
Use of this word as a pejorative belies its origin. The
sixth century *seven sages*, or Wise Men of *Greece were called
sophists (literally, "wise men") and until the fourth century
B.C. the term was applied to teachers. After *Pythagoras (fl. c.
540-c. 510 B.C.) humbly refused the title, preferring
"philosopher" ("wisdom-lover"), a split developed between followers of Pythagoras and those of Protagoras of Adera, who
called themselves "sophists." Their hypercritical tendencies
led to the downgrading of sophism as false "wisdom."
M. 125

SORBONNE
One of the oldest universities in Europe (with *Bologna),
the Sorbonne is part of the present-day decentralized University of *Paris (with the name "Sorbonne" still clinging to
branches III and IV, in the *Latin Quarter). It was founded c.
1252 by Robert de Sorbon, chaplain to Louis IV and rebuilt by
Richelieu in 1629. (Most of the buildings were replaced between 1885 and 1901.) The original faculty of theology colored
the Sorbonne's conservative philosophy. By M.'s time, it was
known for its condemnation of Joan of Arc, justification of the
*St. Bartholomew's massacre, and condemnation of the
philosophes. *Napoléon refounded the university, which became the center of the University of Paris in 1821.
M. "stumbled upon" the Sorbonne during a Paris perambulation of 1 December 1849. He entered the court and returned the following day to inspect the church (still standing),
Ste. Ursule de la Sorbonne, which holds Richelieu's tomb.
I.P. 8; C.M. 19

SOUP
See "Sandwiches."
M. 132

SOUTER JOHN
See "Tam O'Shanter.
C.M. 42

SOUTH AMERICA, --N
M.'s various voyages took him around the coast of the
continent several times and in both directions. He perhaps visited *Callao, *Lima, *Rio de Janeiro, *Santa, and *Valparaiso.
Passim

SOUTHERN CROSS
See "Crux-Australis."
W. 65

SOUTH POLE
See "Pole . . . . "
W. 26

SOUTH SEA, --S
*Balboa's name for the *Pacific Ocean (El Mar del Sur),
upon his discovery of it in 1513. Used in the plural, the name
came to refer to the waters of the Southern Hemisphere, especially of the Pacific.
Passim

SOUTH-STREET
The nineteenth-century "street of ships," South Street
was *Manhattan's major waterfront area, in the southern portion of the island, on the *East River. From the 1820's until
*Hudson steamships shifted activity, South Street was the cen-
ter of the city's commercial life, with trade of more importance
than that of *Broadway or *Wall Street.
Efforts at "gentrification" in the late twentieth century
have displaced the largely immigrant population of M.'s time
but preserved (as part of "South Street Seaport") such landmarks as the *Fulton Market and Sweets' Restaurant, the oldest seafood restaurant in *New York City; in M.'s time, illegal
*slave traders ("blackbirders") met at Sweets' to conduct their
nefarious business.
R. 18; R. 27; R. 61; R. 62

SOUTHWARK

*London's Southwark area is a meeting place of roads from the south approaching *London Bridge, with a busy dock area on the *Thames. *Chaucer's pilgrims start from the local Tabard Inn, and many of Dickens's (see "Hard Times") scenes are set there. A local church, St. Mary's at Rotherhite, contains memorials to seamen (including one to Captain Christopher Jones, of *Mayflower*), such as those in M.'s "*Whaleman's Chapel."

Southwark Cathedral (thirteenth century) was in the process of restoration when M. visited the *Elephant and Castle borough in November of 1849.

See also "Thames Tunnel," "Peter of Colchurch."
I.P. 24

SOW-FISH

See "Cetology" section.
M.D. 32

SPAIN; SPANIARD, --S; SPANISH; SPANISHLY

M.'s attitude toward Spain and things Spanish was not that of a "world citizen." Although he seems to have admired the uniquely picturesque Spanish culture for its clothing (*O.* 73), its horses (*O.* 30), its swords (*M.* 32), etc., in general his allusions to Spain are not complimentary. (The effete noble Spanish *slave-master of "Benito Cereno" seems paradigmatic of his impression.) Many of his references are to the conquistadors who took *South America, or to relatively minor faults such as contemporary use of stocks in jails (*O.* 31) or slaughter of cattle in *California (*O.* 54): quibbles.

Among more "neutral" references, the reader is directed to "Castilian"; "Malagas"; "Tagus"; "Toledo"; "Quiros"; "Spanish Armada." See also "Catholic."
Passim

SPANISH ARMADA

"Armada," the *Spanish word for "army," came to refer to a large fleet. The Spanish Armada was the fleet assembled by Philip II of Spain in 1588 for the invasion of Queen *Elizabeth's England. Her Navy under *Drake and others had 197 ships by which to counter Philip's 130 ships in the English *Channel. The first gun duel between ships propelled exclusively by sail, the battle against the Armada had great symbolic importance in its defense of *Protestant England against *Catholic incursions.

At least fifty Spanish ships were lost, as opposed to no British ships. There were few lives lost for the British, but both sides had severe losses due to typhus, food poisoning, and storms. The "sinking of the Spanish Armada" came to suggest any amazing victory against great odds.
W. 50

SPANISH DOLLARS
The Spanish dollar was a silver piece of eight, worth eight *reales* (it became the *peso*); the silver *reale* contained c. 3.43 grams of silver, worth half as much as an equal amount of gold.
T. Sequel

SPANISH OUNCE OF GOLD
The *doubloon, or *onza de oro* ("ounce of gold").
See also "Joes."
M.D. 36

SPANISH GRANDEE
Highest-ranking nobleman in *Spain, who need not uncover his head in the King's presence.
W. 93

SPANISH INQUISITION, --S
A 1478 *Papal bull set up the Inquisition to deal with supposed evil influences upon the conduct of *Christianity. Exempt from normal jurisdiction, the Inquisition, claiming the role of traditional defenders of the faith, employed cruel and unusual treatment in its examination of witnesses. *Tómas de Torquemada (1420-1498) was first inquisitor general. *Inigo de Loyola (1491-1556) founded the Society of *Jesus, a principal opponent of *Protestantism, and, secretive like *Freemasonry, an especial spectre for M. The year 1835 had brought the suppression of the *Jesuits in Spain, making the sect a current popular target.
M. 13; W. 31; W. 70; W. 72; M.D. 54; P. 4:5

"SPANISH LADIES"
Among the best known of sea songs, the lyrics to "Spanish Ladies" were altered by *American crews, who wrote ribald lyrics euphemistically called by the First *Nantucket sailor in *M.D.* 40 "Midnight, Forecastle") "sentimental."

Some of the more sedate verses:

--Farewell and adieu to you fine Spanish Ladies--
Farewell and adieu all you Ladies of Spain-
For we've received orders to sail for Old *England
And perhaps we shall never more see you again.

Chorus
We'll rant and we'll roar like true British Sailors,
We'll range and we'll roam over all the salt seas,
Until we strike soundings in the Channel of Old
    England-
From *Ushant to *Scilly 'tis thirty-five leagues.
We hove our ship to when the wind was sou'west,
    boys
We hove our ship to for to strike soundings clear,
Then we filled our main-tops'l and bore right
    away, boys,
And right up the *Channel our course we did
    steer.

Chorus
The first land we made it is known as the Dead-
    man,
Next Ram Head near *Plymouth, Start, *Portland
    and Wight;
We sailed past *Beachy, past Fairley and Dun-
    geness,
And then bore away for the South Foreland Light.

Chorus
Then the signal was made for the grand fleet to
    anchor
All all in the Downs that night for to meet,
So stand by your stoppers, see clear your shank-
    painters,
Haul all your clew-garnets, stick out tacks and
    sheets.

Chorus
Now let every man toss off a full bumper,
Now let every man toss off a full bowl,
For we will be jolly and drown melancholy
In a health to each jovial and true-hearted soul.

W. 74; M.D. 40

SPANISH MAIN; THE MAIN
Originally, Spanish Main referred to the coastal region of northern *South America between *Panama and the mouth of the Orinoco (see "Oronoco") River, where *English *pirates attacked *Spanish treasure ships. By M.'s time, it signified the entire *Caribbean area of pre-nineteenth century romantic pirate activity.

(In W. 53 and 85, "Jack Chase" errs in placing *Callao and *Coquimbo "on the Spanish Main.")
T. 6; O. 3; M. 22; W. 53; W. 85

SPANISH VICEROY
See "Mendoza, Marquess de."
T. 2

SPARKS
Jared Sparks (1789-1866), *Connecticut-born Unitarian minister, professor of history, and eventual president of *Harvard, was a prolific editor. He edited *The North American Review* and several multi-volume works. M.'s reference in *I.P.* is to his work on biographies, including lives of *John Ledyard (1828) and Gouverneur Morris (1832), and of *George Washington, in the first volume of the twelve-volume *Writings of George Washington* (1834-37). Sparks also edited *The Diplomatic Correspondence of the *American Revolution* (12 vols., 1829-30) and *The Works of *Benjamin Franklin* (10 vols., 1836-40). Today, his work is thought to be highly derivative.
I.P. Dedication

SPARTA; SPARTAN
See "Lacedemonian"; "Peloponnesian."
P. 18:1; C.M. 21

SPARTACUS
A *Thracian gladiator/slave celebrated for leading a slave revolt (73-71 B.C.) after his escape from a training school at Capua.
P. 16:2

"SPEARMAN'S BRITISH GUNNER"
James Martin Spearman's *The British Gunner* (1828) became a standard work on artillery.
W. 83

SPECKSYNDER

In Dutch, *Specksnijder*: "cutter of the fat," originally the man in charge of a vessel's fishery, as opposed to the commander, who navigated. "*Ahab" fills both roles on the "*Pequod."

See also "Chief Harpooneer."

M.D. 33

SPECTATOR, THE

1. *The Spectator*, a daily *British journal, established the vogue of the periodical essay and gave impetus to one of literature's best collaborations: that of *Joseph Addison and *Sir Richard Steele. *The Spectator* conducted by the two ran from March 1711 to December 1712, succeeding Steele's *The Tatler*. Addison conducted it alone for part of 1714, but the quality was not comparable to that of the collaborative effort. The publication posited the existence of a club of imaginary people, such as "Roger de Coverley," representing the landed gentry, and others of various types. "Mr. Spectator" was the observer/writer of apolitical essays on society, manners, morals, and literature which set new standards of quality for English prose and inspired many journals in imitation. (Sealts #5 is Addison's "Sir Roger de Coverley.")

2. A radical British weekly, starting in 1828.

R. 1

SPENCER

A waist-length jacket or outer coat without skirts: named for the second Earl Spencer (1758-1834).

C.M. 21

SPENCER, EARL

Earl George John Spencer was first lord of the *British admiralty from 1794 to 1801.

W. 85

SPENSER; SPENSERIAN

Edmund Spenser (c. 1552-99) was born in *London and educated at *Cambridge, where he began writing neoplatonist poetic works. In the households of *Leicester and other prominent persons, he met *Sir Philip Sidney, to whom he dedicated *The Shepheardes Calendar* (1579), which consists of dialogue modeled on classical eclogues and "complaints" by the author's representative, "Colin Clout."

The Faerie Queene (1589; cited in *M.D.* Extracts 17), his greatest work, is devoted to the glories of Queen *Elizabeth I. The work was projected as twelve books (six and a fragment were completed), in which twelve of her knights, representing twelve virtues, have adventures over twelve days. "Artegall" (M.'s "Artingall," in *W.* 50) is the hero of an allegorical rendering of Elizabeth's feats, in Book V. "Abba Thule" and the "Pelews" (also in *W.* 50) appear in the same book. ("Thule" is the ancient Greek and Roman name for the place considered the extreme northern limit of the world.) The quotation in Extracts 17 is from VI.X.xxxi. 5-9, accurately quoted.

Spenser's other works include *Astrophel and Stella* (written c. 1582) and *Epithalamion* (1595). Later works were supported in part by a small pension from the Queen, but Spenser died in poverty. History makes him "The Poet's Poet," for his rich use of language, and depth of philosophical, moral, and political content in pastorals, complaints, sonnets, and hymns. The much-imitated "Spenserian Stanza" is a work of eight iambic pentameter lines and a ninth of six iambic feet: rhyme scheme ababbcbcc.

Sealts #483 is the five-volume *Poetical Works* (1855). Carole Moses examines M.'s explicit debt to Spenser in "Melville's 'Cunning' Reading of Spenser."
W. 84; P. 1:2

SPHINX; SPHYNX, --'S, --ES
The traditional composite creature with a lion's body and a human head originated in *Greek legend as a wise, omniscient, threatening beast. Given a female head, in *Egypt (which M. visited in December and January 1856 and 1857) it came to symbolize the *Nile or the *Pharaoh as the sun-god Ra. The most famous representation is at Giza, Egypt: a colossal portrait statue of King Khafre (Chephren) of the fourth dynasty (c. 2550 B.C.), 140 feet long and 30 feet high.

The Greek Sphinx was said to be a daughter of Typhon and Chimaera; at *Thebes she set a riddle and devoured those who could not answer it. *Oedipus correctly guessed "man" to the question: "What goes on four feet, on two feet, and three, / But the more feet it goes on the weaker it be?"
M. 111; M.D. 70; M.D. 80; P. 19:1; P. 25:4

SPICE ISLANDS
See "Moluccas."
W. 29

SPINOZA, --'S; THE SPINOZAIST

The philosopher Benedictus (Hebrew "Baruch") de Spinoza (1632-1677) was born in *Holland of *Portuguese crypto-Jewish stock (descendants of Jews forced to convert under the *Spanish Inquisition). His wealthy merchant family had him educated in *Hebrew subjects, and he also learned Portuguese, Spanish, Dutch, Latin, and some Greek, French, and Italian, along with mathematics and the sciences.

Spinoza's views conflicted with Jewish scriptural teachings about *God's incorporality, the existence of angels, and the soul's immortality. Excommunicated, he was briefly banished from *Amsterdam and supported himself by making lenses.

In *Germany he studied *Descartes, developing his own philosophy countering Cartesians, to be presented as a major work defending the liberty to philosophize while remaining a believer. Upon his return to Holland, his *Tractatus theologico-politicus* became a *cause celebre*. His major work, *Ethica ordine geometrico demonstrata* remained umpublished while he wrote *Tractatus politicus*, still unfinished at his death from pulmonary disease caused by glass dust. His *Ethics* was published in 1677, but some work did not reach print until the nineteenth century, during which he was much discussed.

Spinoza disagreed with Descartes about the dualism that interfered with the world's intelligibility. He saw metaphysics as constructable logically, like mathematics; as capable of explaining the basic facts of human life; and as providing an object of worship and intellectual love—God. His was a rather *pantheistic and deterministic orderly universe, denying a transcendent distinction between good and evil and denying personal immortality, virtue being its own reward. His political doctrine defends the natural rights of man, especially freedom of thought, which should not be abrogated by the state despite conflicts between individuals and despite the necessary absolute power of the state.

Spinoza was denounced as an atheist by *Bayle and *Hume and defended by *Voltaire, *Goethe, and *Coleridge.

The journal, "The Spinozaist," in *P*. is apparently an invention, as is the "*Urquhartian Club."
M. 3; M.D. 75; P. 14:2; P. 20:2; P. 22:3

SPIRIT OF THE CAPE

In the *Lusiads* of *Camöens, the monster of natural forces who attempts to destroy Da *Gama and his men.
W. 26

SPITFIRE, THE
Spitfire was an *American (not *British, as M. has it in
M.) schooner. She made part of *Decatur's force at *Algiers,
in 1814. (See "Barbary coast.")
.M. 28

SPITHEAD
At the channel to England's *Portsmouth Harbor, between the Isle of Wight and the mainland, the Spithead anchorage was much used by *Channel fleets from the eighteenth century. It became the traditional spot for naval reviews
from Queen *Victoria's time.
The famous Spithead mutinies occurred in April and
May of 1797, when British sailors rebelled against poor conditions. They are cited also in *Billy Budd, Sailor* (3). Those of the
*Nore and Somers are also mentioned in the novella.
W. 54; W. 85; I.P. 3

SPITZBERGEN
The *Arctic Ocean archipelago (Svalbard) 400 miles
north of *Norway was discovered by the *Vikings in the twelfth
century and rediscovered late in the sixteenth. By 1607, *Henry
Hudson commented on the excellent whaling in the area, but it
was not mapped until the nineteenth century. Spitzbergen has
been claimed by *Russia and *Sweden, but has remained
mostly under Norwegian control. Surrounding waters are
navigable for about half of the year.
M.D. Extracts 30; M.D. 55; M.D. 101

"SPLICING THE MAIN-BRACE"
On board ship, "splicing the main brace" is taking an
alcoholic drink. The term is ironic because the actual "main
brace" (the rope by which the mainyard rope is positioned) is so
important that it would never be mended by splicing. When
damaged, it was replaced. Presumably, drinking on board
was equally rare: a falsehood.
W. 41

"SPREAD EAGLE, MAKING A"
Lashing a man to the rigging with outstretched arms
and legs—for *flogging.
R. 23

SPURM
Spurn Head is a sand spit on the *Humber River in *Yorkshire, *England. It is four miles long but only about 300 yards wide, and a few above sea level.
I.P. 19

SPURZHEIM
Johan Caspar Spurzheim (1776-1828), a *Viennese physician, worked with *Gall to localize the functions of the brain and develop the pseudo-science, *phrenology.
M. 158; M.D. 79

SQUADRON
After the Revolution, the *War of 1812, and the *Barbary Wars, the *United States recognized a need to control various waters, and the *Navy was ordered to form various semi-permanent squadrons. The *Mediterranean Squadron (associated with *Preble and *Decatur) dealt mostly with *piracy: it was organized in 1815. The *Pacific Squadron (1817) became most important during the *Mexican War; it was commanded in 1842 by Thomas ap Catesby Jones (see "Commodore . . . ") on *United States. (Jones was temporarily relieved of this command after he mistakenly invaded Mexico.) *Robert F. Stockton was also a commander of this squadron. The *West Indies Squadron (1822) was briefly commanded by *Porter; it was absorbed by the Home Squadron in 1841. Along with the East Indian (1817), *Brazilian (1826), and *African (associated with *Perry from 1820-23), these fleets controlled the *slave trade, guarded against piracy, and protected American vessels from search by foreign (usually *British) vessels.
Passim

SQUARE-TOED LUGGER
Small old-fashioned vessel with a lugsail (four sided) on an obliquely hung yard.
M.D. 16

SQUID
See "Cetology" section.
M.D. 59 (and elsewhere)

STADT HOUSE
See "City Hall"; "Haarlem; Harlem."
R. 30

STAGARITE, THE
    See "Aristotle."
M. 3

STAINES
    Staines, *England, is on the *Thames, eighteen miles
southwest of *Charing Cross. The site of the (1285) London
Mark Stone boundary, in M.'s time it was a part of *Middlesex:
the scene of a famous bridge (1832) and an annual fair established in the thirteenth century.
    (Reference to the city is made in the original work of
*Israel Potter.)
I.P. 4

STAMMERER, THE
    The sickly Carolingian Louis II *le Bèque*, or the Stam-
merer (846-879), son of Charles II the Bald, ruled *France from
877. He alienated the wealthy, the office-holders, and the *Pope
(John VIII).
M. 181

STANWIX, FORT
    The "rude but all-important stockaded fort" of *P*. 1:2 has
its original (not mentioned by name) in Fort Stanwix (Fort
Schuyler), near present-day Rome, *New York. M.'s maternal
grandfather, Peter *Gansevoort was the hero of the *Revolutionary War battle.
    M. apparently cared enough about the event to name his
second son "Stanwix."
P. 1:2

"STANZA TO BRAGANZA, A"
    Probably an invention. See "Braganza."
W. 56

STARBUCK
    A common name among *Nantucket *Quakers: Mary
Starbuck was an early spreader of the faith; William Starbuck
Mayo wrote *Kaloolah* (1849), the first chapter of which dis-
cusses the name.
M.D. Passim

STAR CHAMBER
    The Chamber evolved from the time of *Edward III
(fourteenth century), meeting in a room at Westminster Palace
that had stars painted on the ceiling. By the sixteenth century,
the room was used for councils' and judges' meetings. The
*Privy Council inherited jurisdiction from powerful medieval
kings. It was used for petitioners denied the use of other
courts and for civil cases. There were few forms to be observed,
no juries, and no common-law safeguards for subjects. The
*Tudors made much use of it, and by the sixteenth century,
under Chancellor Thomas Wolsey, it became more clearly defined in its power, met in private, and kept separate books. Arbitrary punishments were meted out to enforce unpopular
policies: imprisonment, fines, whipping, branding, and mutilation. Nevertheless, the Court of Star Chamber had great
popularity, except with opponents of *Charles I. It was abolished in 1641.
    Penny Cyclopaedia, with characteristic passion, calls it
a "mere engine of state . . . employed . . . for the assertion of
prerogative pretension and the enforcement of illegal taxation
. . . upon a mere oral proceeding, without hearing the accused,
without a written charge or record of any kind, and without
appeal."
W. 72

STATEN ISLAND
    The island in *New York Bay (consolidated as Richmond
Borough of *New York City, 1898) is five miles southwest of the
*Battery, and separated from adjacent *New Jersey by Kill Van
Kull and Arthur Kill. Lower New York Bay and the *Narrows
separate it from Brooklyn. The island is roughly fourteen
miles by seven miles and has several satellite islands. *Henry
Hudson discovered "Staaten Eylandt" in 1609; it was permanently settled in 1661, after the first settlement had been wiped
out by Indians.
    Staten Island is the site of several military facilities, as
well as of *Sailors' Snug Harbor, of which M.'s brother
Thomas (1830-1884) was Governor from 1867. M. was a regular
visitor to the bucolic island, reached by ferry from the Battery.
R. Passim

STATEN LAND
    Now known as Isla de los Estados, Staten Land (at the
tip of *South America: 55°05' S., 63°00' W.) represented for
*Dana the opposite of M.'s sparkling ice palace:

A more desolate-looking spot I never wish to set
eyes upon—bare, broken, and girt with rocks and
ice, with here and there, between the rocks and
broken hillocks, a little stunted vegetation of
shrubs. It was a place well suited to stand at the
junction of the two oceans, beyond the reach of
human cultivation, and encounter the blasts and
snows of a perpetual winter (Chapter 32).

W. 28

STATE OF NEW YORK
    See "New York, --State."
W. 35

STATE PRISON
    M. was probably in error in W. 90 regarding the manu-
facture of military clothing in State Prisons.
W. 90

STATE PRISON AT AUBURN
    See "Auburn, N.Y."
W. 58

STATES-GENERAL
    As Vincent's edition of *M.D.* shows, M. drew informa-
tion about the States-General, *Holland, A.D. 1695, "the only
formal whaling code," from *Scoresby (Vol. 2, pp. 312-332: an
extended discussion of whale-fishery laws).
M.D. 89

STEEL, FLINT & ASBESTOS
    An obvious invention, suggesting the hellfire that pub-
lishers can inflict.
P. 26:4

STETSON
    See "Astor House."
W. 15

STEWART

The Reverend Charles S. Stewart, an important source for M., was chaplain of the U.S. Ship *Vincennes*. Despite his optimistic Enlightenment mentality and apparent embrace of the conventional fruits and ceremony of civilization, Stewart was also a hardy and sympathetic person whose concern for the common sailor colors his books, which are worth reading for their own sakes, catching many physical details of natural history and politics recorded in the works which may not actually have been seen by M. but are cited by him. Stewart loves the sailor's character:

> Not the vulgarity and low vice too often found under the name, but the nobler traits which belong more distinctively to him than to any other order of men. I mean the warm heart and generous soul, the clan-like tie which leads him to hail every round jacket and tarpaulin hat, as if they were the features of a brother; the recklessness of danger and disregard to self; the humor, gay spirit, and credulity, tinctured with superstition, which are characteristically his own (*A Visit To the South Seas* . . . I, p. 19).

T. 1; T. 25

STIVER

*Dutch coin worth about two cents.
M.D. 16

STOCKHOLM

The capital city of *Sweden is a *Baltic Sea port built on islands and peninsulas with so many waterways and canals that it is called the "*Venice of the North." It was founded in 1255 and was long dominated by the *Hanse League.
R. 8

STOCKTON, COMMODORE

Robert Field Stockton (1795-1866), of Princeton, *New Jersey, grandson of a signer of the *Declaration of Independence, joined the *Navy as *midshipman in 1811. After brief service under strict discipline in the *War of 1812, he saw action against the *Barbary pirates in the *Mediterranean. As delegate of the American Colonization Society to *Africa, in 1821 he obtained the land which was to become Liberia.

He was active in New Jersey affairs during ten years of civilian life , after which he commanded the Mediterranean fleet. He helped design various military devices, including the first ironclad warship, *Princeton*, and was in command when his new gun exploded, killing the *Secretaries of State and of the Navy, and wounding numerous others.

In 1845, he delivered the U.S. government resolution for the *Texas annexation. He was in command of land and sea forces during the *Mexican War and served in the *Senate from 1851 to 1853.

Stockton crusaded against grog distribution and is considered a prime mover in the battle against *flogging (not abolished until 1862). He contributed libraries and other goods for the welfare of sailors.

W. 36

STOIC; THE STOICS

Stoicism originated with the philosopher *Zeno, who taught in the *stoa*, or colonnade of the marketplace. It flourished in *Athens from the third century B.C. and in *Rome from the first century B.C. until the third century A.D. In the Stoic ethic, all was material. Providence was a coherent force uniting men and governing their reason (*logos*), which was to be followed without regard to emotion, pain, or pleasure.

Among Stoic writers cited by M.: *Diogenes Laertius, *Cicero, *Seneca, *Epictetus, *Marcus Aurelius, *Petrarch, *Montaigne, *Addison. Their influence was especially felt in the nineteenth century.

M.D. 1; M.D. 75

STONEHENGE

Eight miles north of Salisbury, Wiltshire, *England, lies Stonehenge, an ancient circle of large standing stones (up to thirty feet long and fifty tons in weight) and ceremonial pits dating from the Late Neolithic and remodeled up to the Early Bronze Age (1800-1400 B.C.). Its sophisticated construction— stones cut to specific curves and pounded smooth with hammers, mortise-and-tenon and tongue-and-groove joints— remains a wonder, although much has been learned since M.'s time. Although we now presume Stonehenge the worship place and cemetery of a bellicose sect with advanced knowledge of the heavens, connection with the *Druids has been disproven, as has Geoffrey of Monmouth's claim in *Historia regum Britanniae* (c. A.D. 1136) that the stones were magically transported from *Ireland by Merlin the magician. M.'s connecting it with the Druids relies on the popular belief originat-

ing with John Aubrey (1626-97) and elaborated by William
Stukeley (1687-1765) in 1740. As Charles R. Anderson shows
(*Melville in the South Seas*, Chapter VII), Melville was
"drawing unnecessarily on his imagination" similarly in
ascribing the construction of Typee monuments to some early
race of "master builders."
T. 21; M. 75; R. 31

STOUT
    A dark, malty-flavored *ale often tasting strongly of hops
(see "Hop-Poles"), with alcohol content up to 6%. Stout is also
called "black porter," accounting for the pun in *P.* 23:4.
P. 23:4

STOWE
    Perhaps a reference to John Stow (1525-1605), bibliophile
said to have spent about £200 per year on books and
manuscripts. Originally a tailor, Stow became a chronicler,
transcriber, editor, and antiquary. Among his publications:
*The Workes of *Geoffrey Chaucer* (1561), editions of *English
chronicles (including Holinshed's, 1585-7), and a *Survey of
London (1598 and 1603) which is still in print.
M. 29

STOWELL
    William Scott, Baron Stowell (1745-1836), was an
*English admiralty judge who greatly influenced international
law. His decisions, guided by *Roman, canon, and international law, were accepted in the *United States, among them:
independence and equality of states, international law binding
even semi-barbarous states, etc.
    (See also "Tenterden.")
W. 66

STRAND, THE
    *London's Strand runs from St. Martin's in the Fields to
Somerset House. M.'s 1849 journal "commenced" at "25
Craven Street, Strand, at 6 1/2 P.M. on Wednesday November
7th." The centrally located address made much of London
easily accessible to the walker who wished to sample high culture while residing near the "American Bowling Saloon"
(visited 6 November) and the "Royal Lyceum Theatre"
(November 7), where a man went round with a "coffee-pot &
mugs, crying 'Porter, gents, porter!'"
R. 46

STRANGFORD, VISCOUNT
Percy Clinton Sydney (1780-1855), diplomat and poet, was sixth Baron Strangford. He was envoy-extrordinary to the *Portuguese Court in *Brazil from 1808 to 1815 and made a diplomatic mission to Brazil in 1838. In 1803 he had published *Poems from the Portuguese of *Camoens*. M. acquired a copy (1824 ed.) in 1867 (Sealts #116).
W. 56

STRASBOURG
The eastern *French city (two miles west of the *Rhine) has long been the cultural and economic center of Alsace. It was an important *Roman city and was destroyed by the *Huns in 455. By the thirteenth century it was a free imperial city, mainly *Protestant. Strasbourg belonged to France starting in 1681, taking on increasingly French characteristics. It passed to *Germany in 1871 (Treaty of Frankfurt), was recovered by France in 1919, only to be taken again by Germany in 1940 and restored after the war.
Among its claims to fame, it is said that Gutenberg invented the printing press here; *Goethe was a student at Strasbourg; in 1792 Rouget de Lisle here composed the *Marseillaise*.
The red Rhenish cathedral was constructed between 1015 and 1439 (making M.'s claim of 500 years rather an exaggeration, in *M*. 75). Its single spire is the highest in Europe (474 feet), and it has a large sixteenth-century astronomic clock, the animated figures and images of which go into action at 12 o'clock. M. visited Strasbourg on 21 April 1857, finding the cathedral "not fine as Milan."
M. 75; R. 27

STRELLA; STRELLO MOUNTAIN
Serra da Estrella is the highest mountain range of *Portugal, with numerous lakes near the top of its tallest peak, Malhoa (6532 ft.), source of the Mondego River, which flows to the *Atlantic. Legend has it that there are numerous wrecks in the lakes, as claimed in *Relation du Voyage d'Espagne* (1691) by Catherine Jumelle, Comtesse d'Aulnoy.
M.D. 41

... STRIPPED LIKE A SLAVE; SCOURGED WORSE THAN A HOUND
Paralleling the treatment of *Jesus.
W. 33

STUART

The *Catholic *Scottish royal family (also Stewart, or Steuart), inheritors of the *English crown, traced its ancestry to eleventh-century Brittany. The dynasty was an unfortunate one; of fourteen crowned sovereigns, four were murdered or beheaded, two died in combat, one died in exile, and seven ascended as minors.

First Stuart king was Robert II of Scotland (1316-1390). Direct male line of descent ended with James V (1512-42), father of Mary (see "Stuart, Mary"), Queen of Scots (1542-87), who was succeeded by her son, James VI (1566-1625) who, after the death of England's *Elizabeth I, became *King James I of England. His son, *Charles I (1600-1649), was executed by *Cromwell, and Stuarts were excluded until the Restoration crowning of *Charles II (1630-1685). His brother (1633-1701) became James VII of Scotland and therefore *James II of England. James's daughter, Mary (1662-1694), married William, Prince of Orange (1650-1703), who, it was hoped, would "rescue" England from the Stuarts; they became William III and Mary II. The 1701 Act of Settlement thereafter excluded Catholics from the throne. The legitimate male line of royal Stuarts ended with Henry (1725-1807), cardinal and titular Duke of *York.
W. 71

STUART, MARY

The daughter of James V of Scotland, Mary Stuart (1542-1587) inherited the crown in infancy. Brought up in *France, in 1558 she married the sickly dauphin who was Francois II for one year (See "Valois"). Scottish Catholics thought her rightful Queen of England, the future *Elizabeth I being illegitimate in their eyes. Mary's return to Scotland was made difficult by Elizabeth's resistance and by the shift of Scottish power to the nobles. Her second marriage, to Henry Stewart, Lord Darnley, was disastrous, and her friendship with *David Rizzio an affront. After the death of Darnley, her fondness for James Hepburn, Earl of Bothwell, cost her even more in popularity. Fleeing to England, hoping for Elizabeth's support, she eventually plotted again for the crown of England. She was tried (rather unfairly) and executed in the great hall at Fotheringhay Castle, a bold and romantic figure even at her beheading.

(See also "Stuart.")
P. 2:2

STUBB

"Stubbs" was a common name, according to the *Vital Records* of *New Bedford and *Nantucket.

The fictional character, "Stubb," need not have been from *Cape Cod to be called a "Cape-Cod man."
M.D. 27

STULTZ

Stultz was the leading tailor of early and mid nine-teenth-century *London, cited in works by Ruskin and Bulwer Lytton.
W. 8

STUMP THE STATE

A none-too-subtle analogy between political electioneering and contemporary evangelical religion.
P. 20:2

SUBDISJUNCTIVE

See "Disjunctive."
M. 171

SUBLIME SULTAN

See "Sultan."
W. 39

SUB-SUB

"Sub" was widely used in the mid-nineteenth century in reference to a subordinate or subaltern officer, as well as to a substitute. M.'s "Sub-Sub" is as low as one can get: a substitute subordinate.
M.D. Extracts

SUETONIUS

Gaius Suetonius Tranquillus (c. A.D. 70-c. A.D. 122) was a prolific *Roman writer, best known for his biographies, particularly *De vita Caesarum*, and *De viris illustribus*, both used as sources by later writers. Suetonius rose in Roman society with the help of his patron, Septicius Claras, a *praetorian prefect. In the service of *Hadrian, he controlled Roman libraries, was secretary of imperial correspondence, and privately pursued his own writings—mostly antiquarian works of

cultural importance, literary criticism, and natural history. His "Lives" of ten Caesars (From *Julius to *Domitian) are much responsible for the commonly accepted picture of decadent Roman society. They are vivid and provocative reading, with much scandalous gossip, written in informal and lucid periodic sentences.
R. 46

SUFFOLK

The county in eastern *England noted for its fine scenery was made famous in the paintings of John Constable. It was inhabited as early as 250,00 B.C. and has provided many artifacts from prehistoric, *Roman, *Saxon, *Danish, and *Norman civilizations. Suffolk has always been an important base of sea operations, but agriculture and cloth industries were important in M.'s time, as well.

See also "Bury St. Edmunds"; "Ickworth."
R. 44

SUFFREN, ADMIRAL

Pierre André de Suffren (1729-1788 or -89), *French Admiral, became a noted naval strategist by observation of errors made by the French fleet against *Admiral Edward Hawke at Cape Finistere in 1747 and at Minorca in 1756. Observing *Admiral C.H. d'Estaing in North America in 1778, Suffren developed a canon of rules regarding initiative, speed, and maximized strength against the enemy line, all of which d'Estaing violated. The engagement at *Coromandel and other *Indian waters, from which "Israel" escapes in *I.P.* 13, occurred between February 1782 and June 1783; Suffren gained great popularity in France as a result of these battles and was made Vice-Admiral in 1783. But he had little assistance from official quarters, which saw his policies as too daring and original. (Suffren is sometimes referred to as "Bailly de Suffren"; this may be a sobriquet derived from a French colloquial expression "baille," referring to an aged vessel.)
I.P. 13

SUGAR-LOAF MOUNTAIN

Páo de Acúcar, the 1,296-foot cone-shaped peak at the entrance to the Bay of *Rio de Janeiro, said by *Rev. Stewart to incline at an angle equal to that of the Tower of *Pisa.
W. 39; W. 50; W. 65

SULTAN, --S
Sultan is Arabian for king, the title of the ruler of the former *Turkish Empire and the former King of *Morocco, still used in some lesser *Mohammedan states. In medieval writings, sometimes *soldan* or *sowdan*.

The wife, mother, sister, or concubine of the sultan is the sultana.
M. 148; M. 150; M. 181; W. 39; W. 68; M.D. 13 and elsewhere

SULTAN OF MUSCAT
Said Ibn Sultan (1804-56) made Oman the most powerful *Arabian state. Senate Documents No. 448, first session of the twenty-sixth Congress (Vol. VII) is: "Correpondence concerning horses, pearls, etc. offered to the *President by the Imaum of Muscat, and declined by him, and afterwards tendered to United States Government; Also concerning a lion and lioness presented."
W. 44

SULTAN OF THE ISLES OF SOOLOO
See "Sooloo."
W. 46

SUMATRA
The second largest island of Indonesia, Sumatra is one of the Greater *Sundas, in the *Indian Ocean, southwest of the *Malay Peninsula and northwest of *Java. The volcanic island is 1,110 miles long and up to 280 miles wide. Its highest peak (over 12,480 feet) is Mt. Kerinchi, Indrapura.

Among the tribes in Sumatra's impenetrable forest are the Bataks: M.'s (*M*. 94) "blood-bibbing Battas." They were amongst the first to embrace *Christianity, although an equal number are *Moslems or animists. Bataks have a written language and build large elaborate residences and communal structures in the Lake Toba area.
M. 94; M.D. 2; M.D. 87

SUMPTION
M.'s "Doxodox" spouts the kind of diction used by supposed philosophers. M. probably found the word in Chambers's *Cyclopaedia*, in the definition of "Syllogism": the first part "is by way of eminence, called the *proposition* . . . the second is called the *assumption* . . . though they are both called *sumptiones*, because assumed for the sake of the third . . . . "
M. 171

SUN, THE

Among the smallest of visible stars (reckoned by *Ptolemy a planet), the Sun is about 109 times the size of Earth in diameter, with 300,000 times its mass. Its apparent hugeness, an illusion, gave rise from earliest times to numerous religions and myths attempting to explain its importance to man.

The ancient *Greeks called the Sun Phoebus and the sun-god Helios. The Sun-god/emperor of *Rome was *Heliogabalus, or Elagabalus. The Sun is also indentified with Hethras, Baal or Bel (see "Belial"), Osiris, *Adonis.

The sobriquet "Sol" is from the *Latin *sol, solis*; sun, sunshine, day.

Passim

SUNDA; STRAITS OF SUNDA

The Sunda Islands of Indonesia lie between the south China Sea and the *Indian Ocean, in the *Java, Flores, and Savu Seas. The Strait of Sunda lies between *Sumatra and Java.

M.D. 87

"SUNDAY"

A variation on Defoe's bestowal of the name "Friday" on his fellow island resident, whom the hero met on that day, in *Robinson Crusoe*.

O. 9; O. 38

SUPAAN

See "Burgoo."

R. 52

SUPERIOR

Lake Superior, of the *United States and *Canada, is the westernmost and largest of the *Great Lakes, as well as the largest fresh water lake in the world (350 miles long, 160 miles wide). It touches on Minnesota (N.W.), *Wisconsin and *Michigan (S.), *Ontario (N. and E.), and is connected to Lake *Huron at its southeastern end by St. Marys River. The *French first saw Lake Superior in the 1660's. It has many islands, river connections, and high rocky shores; it is navigable for only six or seven months per year.

R. 32; M.D. 54

SUPREME COURT

The *Constitution calls for and specifies the duties of the *United States Supreme Court (the highest court in the land), in Article III, Section 1, and Article VI. It does not specify the number of Justices, who are nominated by the *President (with the advice and consent of the *Senate), and the number has often varied from six members to ten, as Presidents have "packed" the Court to suit their political needs. (In *Civil War times, the number changed three times in six years, varying between seven and ten Justices.)
C.M. 26

SURAT

A port city on the Gulf of Cambay in Gujarat state, India, 160 miles north of *Bombay (21°08' N., 73°22' E.) with numerous historical buildings (mosques, tombs, a castle). Surat was developed under the *Moguls and by the seventeenth century was a rich trade center for staples and exotic handicrafts in silk, sandalwood carving, and gold and silver thread. Surat fell in importance in the mid-nineteenth century, its decay exacerbated by *British ascendency and ensuing politics, but it has revived in modern times.

Surat is connected in *M*. 11 to two other rich ports, *Archangel and *Savannah.
M. 11; R. 35

SURGEON PATELLA

The doctor is a fiction. The Patella (Lat. "small pan") is a flat triangular bone at the anterior part of the knee joint which protects the joint and increases its leverage. "Surgeon Patella" might be said to protect and increase the leverage of "Cuticle."
W. 62; W. 63

SURGEON'S ASTRONOMY

This may refer to a belief in astrological influence on body parts. (See "Zodiac.")
M.D. 99

SURGEON SAWYER

The fictional "Surgeon Sawyer's" name refers, of course, to one who saws: preparation for the amputation in *W*. 63. Ironically, "Sawyer" does not saw off the patient's leg.
W. 62; W. 63

SURREY

The county of *England directly southeast of *London was traditionally the site of royal country estates; thus the reference in *I.P.* 24 to "Israel's" entering London from the fashionable "Surrey side."
I.P. 24

SUSA'S

Susa (Shushan, or Shush) was capital of Susiana (Elam) in modern Iran, near the Karkheh (Choaspes) and Karun rivers. It was the chief residence of *Darius I and his successors from 521 B.C. The site was identified in 1850.

The Achaemenid empire had a history of conquests due to its able military leadership and fighting qualities of the army, despite separatist qualities of its peoples, all of whom were liable for military service. The main army troops were called the Immortals because their numbers were never allowed to drop below 10,000. There was also a large navy. Permanent garrisons were quartered in cities throughout the empire, their numbers including cavalrymen and mercenaries. The bow was the chief weapon, but spears and daggers were also employed by "Susa's bastions."
M. 75

SUSAN

See "Extracts" 54.
M.D. Extracts 54

SWALLOW-TAIL, MOUNT A

Put on a swallow-tail coat.
M.D. 121

SWEDENBORG

Emanuel Swedenborg (née Swedberg; 1688-1772), *Swedish philosopher, scientist, and theologian, attempted to provide a scientific explanation of the universe that would include a spiritual element.

The son of an important ecclesiastic in *Stockholm, Swedenborg was educated at Uppsala University and traveled widely in pursuit of mathematical and astronomical knowledge, which he applied to inventive plans for mechanical devices. His appointment at the Royal College of Mines spanned thirty years, during which he published widely in algebra, geometry, and other sciences, anticipating conclusions close to

those of modern nuclear scientists. He turned to anatomy and
physiology and the search for the soul, publishing numerous
theological works which gained his lasting reputation (notably
De Coelo et ejus mirabilibus, et de inferno, or *Heaven and
Hell*).

Swedenborg posited *God as Divine Man and scripture
as *Jehovah's attempt to heal God's separation from man. Despite his claims of divine visions, his followers in the still-
extant Church of the *New Jerusalem (including Blake) were
deeply influenced, as were Strindberg, the French Symbolists,
the elder Henry James, and the American *Transcendentalists. Especially accepted were Swedenborg's optimism,
his doctrine of correspondence, and his belief that natural
objects express spiritual causes.
C.M. 37

SWEDES
Sweden is a kingdom of northern Europe occupying the
eastern part of the *Scandinavian peninsula, bounded by the
Oresund, *Kattegat, and Skagerrak (S.W.), *Norway (1,030
mile land frontier, W.), *Finland (N.E.) and the *Baltic. It is
977 miles by 310 miles and is to the present time officially the
"Kingdom of the Swedes, *Goths and Wends." Scandinavian
tribes settled the area in Neolithic times, and by the tenth century A.D. it was a powerful force, especially at sea.
*Christianity was introduced c. 829, but *paganism survived
until well into the twelfth century. Activities of the *Hanse
League weakened it somewhat in the thirteenth century, and
by the fourteenth it was united with Norway and *Denmark
and governed from *Copenhagen. Independence was gained in
the sixteenth century, and Sweden reached its zenith of power
in the seventeenth, under Gustavius II (Adolphus).

It was a factor in the *Thirty Years' War and in conflicts
with *Poland and *Russia, and was torn by subsequent political factions and intrigues. Sweden's last involvement with
war cast it with the allies against *Napoléon in 1813. The ensuing *Congress of Vienna joined it again to Norway, and it
remained so until 1905. During M.'s time it was marked by political liberalization and industrialization. M. probably
thought of Swedes as a race instead of a distinct nation.

The "Growlands Walfish of the Swedes" (*M.D.* 32) is the
Grönlands Valfisk.
See also "Stockholm."
M.D. 32

"SWEET FIELDS BEYOND THE SWELLING FLOOD..."
    See "Watts."
M.D. 22

S.W.F.
    Sperm Whale Fishery.
M.D. 24

SWIG AT THE HALYARDS
    A nip or swig is a surreptitious drink; the prepositional
phrase denoted the locale of the act, as the loquacious
"Wellingborough Redburn" explains.
R. 9; W. 43

SWITZERLAND; SWISS
    The tiny country bounded by *Italy, *France, *Germany,
Liechtenstein, and *Austria is at least one-half covered by the
*Alps. The ancient Celtic Helvetii were conquered in 58 B.C. by
*Julius Caesar, and the area passed to the Franks in the sixth
century A.D., making part of the *Holy Roman Empire in 1033.
Thereafter, independent cantons were formed. Switzerland
was the important stronghold of *Calvin's Reformation, so the
*Catholic cantons were defeated and a new constitution in
place in 1847-48 (rewritten in 1874).
    M. traveled through Switzerland, 16-21 April 1857. He
went through the desolate St. Gothard pass, crossing lake
Lucerne, visiting *Berne and *Basle. M. was seemingly more
impressed by the scenery than by Swiss culture, about which
he laconically comments: "Thrift neatness &c." (18 April).
    The Swiss "mountain music" of I.P. 22 is undoubtedly
yodeling.
R. 58; W. 28; W. 75; M.D. 105; P. 21:1; I.P. 22

SWORD-MAT
    Sword-mats were used as chafing gear to absorb wear on
a ship or its parts. Olmsted (pp. 87-88) describes their construction from "spun yarn" by two men, one of whom wields a
"sword" of wood. (See also "Olmstead.")
M.D. 47

SYBIL, --S; SIBYLLIC
    A sibyl is a prophetess, the original a woman named Sy-
bylla who lived near *Troy. Inspired by *Apollo, she was fa-

mous for her babbling utterances. There were ten other sibyls, the most famous the Cumaean Sibyl, who guided *Aeneas to the Underworld.

M. visited the Cave of Sybil near *Avernus in February of 1857.

M. 58; C.M. 30

SYDNEY; SIDNEY

Sydney, *New South Wales, *Australia, on the south shore of Port Jackson, or Sydney Harbour, was founded in 1788 as the first British penal colony. (See also "Botany Bay.") Port Jackson, which encompasses Cockatoo Island, is a naval base.

Despite founding of a museum and several institutions of higher learning, Sydney retained its pejorative connotations in M.'s time. "Sydney gentry" (O. 82) are desperadoes. "Sydney Flash-Gorger" (O. 27) combines three insults: the association with crime made more specific with the addition of "*Flash" (or "flashy'), an Australian term for the proud, showy, vulgar fraud, and with the noun "gorger": a glutton (in nautical terms "a big haul of fish").

"Sydney Heads" (O. 2) refers to the projecting point of the coast, "Head" signifying a cape, promontory, sandbank, or other natural projection.

("Sidney" in R. 33.)

T. 18; O. Passim; R. 33

SYDNEY HEADS

See "Sydney."

O. 2

SYLLA

Lucius Cornelius Sulla (138-78 B.C.) was a *Roman dictator/general/reformer. In 107, as aide to Gaius *Marius, he attracted important attention, causing jealous rivalry with Marius which continued as the two rose in stature, finally precipitating the first great Roman civil war (in the 80's). After the death of Marius, Sulla became dictator under the *Lex Valeria*. He suddenly and mysteriously resigned the dictatorship in 79, having ruled for only three years. *Julius Caesar was much disturbed by this and by Sulla's son's marriage to the daughter of *Pompey and defection thereto.

M.D. 45

SYLPHIDES

A sylph is a slender, graceful female member of an imaginary race of beings inhabiting the air, in the works of *Paracelsus. Sylphides are small or young specimens.

Between 1839 and 1842, Filippo Taglioni's ballet *La Sylphide* was a great success in *New York.
T. 20

SYRACUSE

The port of southeastern *Sicily on the Ionian Sea was the chief *Greek city of ancient Sicily. It is connected to the small island of Ortygia, which has high archeological importance for its ruins dating from the fifth century B.C. The Foundation of *Arethusa, around which wild papyrus plants grow, and artistic ruins attract much interest from tourists and scholars.

The *Greeks founded "Syracusae" c. 743 B.C., ruling all of eastern Sicily. But Syracuse reached the peak of its power under *Dionysius the Elder, c. 406. The Second *Punic War led to *Roman occupation and the death of *Archimedes here. The *Saracens gained control in A.D. 878 and the *Normans in 1085. Among other legends, it is said that *Christianity began here, with a brief teaching visit of *St. Paul.
M.D. 41

SYREN

See "Siren."
M.D. 101; P. 5:6

"SYREN"

Syren was the 500-ton-burthen ship with a crew of thirty-six, fitted out by *Samuel Enderby in 1819. It was sent to *Japan to begin whaling operations. M.'s knowledge comes from *Beale (pp. 148-150).
M.D. 101

SYRIA, --N

The southwestern *Asian nation on the *Mediterranean is a mountainous desert area. Ancient Syria encompassed modern Syria and *Lebanon, as well as most of *Israel and *Jordan, and parts of northern *Arabia. Its location on the trade and military routes between the Mediterranean and *Mesopotamia made it prey to foreign powers throughout its history. From the nineteenth to the thirteenth centuries B.C.,

Syrians were probably *Hittites. Thereafter, Syria was included in all of the great empires: *Egyptian, *Phoenician, *Hebrew, *Assyrian, *Babylonian, *Persian, that of *Alexander the Great, the Seleucids, *Romans, *Byzantines, *Arabs. *St. Paul visited Syria, which turned to Islam during the *Arab period. It was entered by the *Crusaders in the eleventh century and was ruled by *Saladin in the twelfth, followed by the *Mamelukes and *Mongols. Syria became part of the *Ottoman Empire in 1516, was held by the *Egyptians from 1832 to 1839, and then returned to the *Turks for the rest of M.'s lifetime.

The area plays an important role in *Clarel*. The Druzes of Lebanon, offshoots of *Mohammedanism with their own scriptures, were much studied in the nineteenth century. M. includes a Druze in *Clarel*, as well as a wasted ascetic Syrian monk.

See also "Beirut"; "Damascus"; "Holy Land"; "Moab"; "Tadmor."
R. 12; M.D. 9; M.D. 24; M.D. 82

T

TABLE-LANDS
Broad, level elevated plateaus; in *M.D.* 120, "*Ahab" uses the expression figuratively to mean that nature's worst punishments have not yet reached his most elevated part, as the wind is often calm atop a mesa while its lower parts are continually eroded by it.
M.D. 120

TABOO GROVES
See "Marquesas."
T. 12; T. 160

TACITUS
Cornelius Tacitus (c. 56--c. 120) was the greatest historian of first-century Imperial *Rome. He probably belonged to a rising non-noble family, permitting a good education, marriage, and official career in public office and in the military. A celebrated orator, he turned to literature, producing a biography of his father-in-law, Julius Agricola; an ethnographical account of the German tribes; a work on oratory; all before his

major works, the twelve-book *Historiae* and the most celebrated eighteen-book *Annals*. These were designed to preserve for posterity the good and bad actions of men who live under tyranny. Tacitus was much read in the Renaissance, especially for his artistic prose style.
R. 55; C.M. 5; C.M. 9

TACONIC

The Taconic Mountains of *New England and *New York are part of the *Appalachian system, east of the *Hudson in New York and west of the *Green Mountains in *Vermont. They extend c. 150 miles south from southwest Brandon, Vermont, along the New York borders of *Massachusetts and *Connecticut, to north Putnam County, New York, where they meet the *Hudson Highlands. Highest of the Taconics is Mount Equinox (3,816 feet), near Manchester, Vermont.

In Massachusetts, the Taconics are called the *Berkshire Hills.
I.P. 1

TADMOR

Tadmor is the pre-Semitic name for the ancient city of modern *Syria, *Palmyra, which is the *Greek and *Latin form of Tadmor. Tadmor is mentioned on tablets and in letters from the nineteenth century B.C., and from the third century B.C. it was an important trade city of the Seleucids.

The Palmyrene written language was Aramaean; the earliest preserved inscription (from 44 B.C.) shows that it was a more highly developed language than the Judaeo-Aramaic of the Dead Sea Scrolls.

Two scripts existed, reflecting Palmyra's position between east and west: a monumental script and a *Mesopotamian cursive, both derived from Seleucid cursive. Inscriptions—most liturgical or honorific (there is no evidence of a literature)—often include a parallel text in Greek or Latin. Greek was the spoken language of the educated.

A common referent for poets, Tadmor was said to have been built by *Solomon. The network of ruins surrounds a principal street with a Great Colonnade, part of which still stands. Numerous structures (temples, houses, a theatre) have been unearthed, revealing a richly decorated Greco-Oriental art style and yielding much evidence of a thriving metropolis with highly evolved culture and complex early religions.
M. 75; M. 132; P. 1:2; P. 4:3; I.P. 19

TAGUS
     The Tagus River of *Spain and *Portugal rises in Teruel
province of eastern Spain (c. 100 miles from the *Mediterranean), flowing to its basin at *Lisbon, on the *Atlantic. The
Tagus flows some 600 miles through deep mountain gorges
and over plateaus, passing through such cities as *Madrid,
*Toledo, and *Abrantes. The reference to "steel of Tagus" in
M. 32 may be to the famous sword steel of Toledo, but it is
probably also a play on the Spanish name for the river: *Tajo*,
"cut."
M. 32

TAHAR
     Taha'a is one of the Leeward Group, *Society Islands.
O. 76

TAHAR, SON OF OLD KING OF
     Taha'a, the son of the old King, became Tapoa II of
*Borabora and Taha'a, He was reputedly impotent and of poor
character, and when he married *Pomaree Vahine I he refused to leave Borabora, and she refused to move from Tahiti,
so they were divorced.
O. 80

TAHITI, --AN
     Tahiti, *Society Islands, formerly called "Otaheite" (and,
briefly, "King *George III Island" and "Nouvelle Cythere"), is
the largest island of French Oceania: some thirty miles long.
It has four prominent peaks, the highest of which, *Orohena,
is 7,618 feet in altitude. Tahiti was discovered by the *British in
1767; *Bounty* visited in 1788. By the turn of the century, British and French missionaries were representing both nations'
claims, but Queen *Pomaree was forced into a French
*protectorate in 1843.
     As Forsythe notes in "Herman Melville's *Father Mur-
phy," M. is correct in noting in O. 42 that Tahitian missionaries' time system was one day in advance of that of the French
and other voyagers.
     See "*United States*," regarding M.'s visit; see also: "A
harree ta fow"; "Aorai"; "Aotooroo"; "Broom Road"; "Duff"
(ship);   "Du Petit Thouars";   "Fararer";   "Farnow";
"Hararparpi"; "Jim the Pilot"; "Kannakippers"; "'Lora Ta-
too'"; "Mahanar": "Narii"; "New Cytherea"; "Omai"; "Oro";
"Otoo"; "Papeete"; "Papoar"; "Paree"; "Pomotu"; "Pot Belly";

"Roora"; "Taiarboo"; "Tanee"; "Tararroa"; "Teearmoar"; "Townor"; "Whaiherea."
T. 1; T. 3; T. 26; T. Appendix; O. Passim; M.D. 40; M.D. 54; M.D. 58 and elsewhere

TAIARBOO
Tai'arapu, *Tahiti; "Taiarabu" in *Ellis Chapter 6.
O. 80

TALISMANIC
A talisman is a magical charm or *cabalistic word. It derives from the Arabic *tilasman* (from Greek *telesma*: mystery), and paper, wax, or metal talismans are still used in the middle east. The *Gnostics' "Abraxas," cut into metal or stone under astrological conditions conducive to good fortune, contained words denoting the Supreme Being and important mathematical formulas.
*Sir Walter Scott published a novel, *The Talisman*, in 1825.
P. 14:2

TALLEYRAND
Charles Maurice de Talleyrand-Périgord, Prince et Duc de Bénévent (1754-1838), *French statesman and diplomat extraordinaire, survived in political office from the French Revolution through the reign of Louis Philippe (see "Bourbon"). Born into an aristocratic but not wealthy family, he was lamed in childhood, ruling out a military career and directing him toward the seminary. Thereafter, his worldly existence as a priest led him to highly placed company. As a politically engagé bishop, he brought about many reforms, while remaining opposed to threatened mob rule. Excommunicated from the priesthood, he became secret counselor to Louis XVI (see "Bourbon"), beginning a diplomatic career in international affairs of high importance. Eventually denounced in France, he spent two years in the *United States, returning during the Directory, amassing a fortune, and finally resigning from public office. As *Napoléon's foreign minister he worked for the pacification of Europe but eventually lost favor with the Emperor. As foreign minister to Louis XVIII (see "Bourbon"), he used his diplomatic skills until retirement to write his memoirs, his greatest accomplishment being restoration of peace at the Congress of *Vienna.
C.M. 23

TALMUD
The compilation sacred to *Jews as divine in origin, like the Torah, until eighteenth-century reform movements questioned it (perhaps explaining the *M*. 57 reference to the Jew that "rejected" it). It is comprised of a law book (Mishna) and commentary (Gemara), along with miscellaneous matter. Composed at the time when *Jesus lived, the Talmud was long a source for Jewish history, religious practice, ethics, metaphysics, science, and folklore. It was continuously attacked by *Christians long before its questioning by some Jews.
M. 57

TALOO
The deep bay off *Moreea which is a partner to *Captain Cook Bay (Paopao) is mentioned by *Ellis and *Wheeler.
M. sailed past the bay on *United States* in October of 1843.
O. 61; O. 62; O. 65; O. 66; O. 79

TAMAI
A lake and village on the north-eastern side of *Moreea: described by *Ellis, who praises the beauty of its neat gardens and well-stocked lake. Ellis disagrees with M. in the matter of *Christianization of the natives, whom he suggests are devout. (Anderson believes that M. never visited the village.)
O. Passim

TAMARIND-TREES
Tamarindus indica, *Indian date, is a tropical leguminous tree with yellow flowers and brown acidic pulped pods used in foods and beverages.
M. 136

TAMARISK TREES
Trees or shrubs of the genus *Tamarix*. They have feathery flowers and grow best near salt water, where they are often cultivated as a windbreak.
M. 136

TAMERLANE, --'S
See "Marlow."
M. 18; M. 63; M. 181; M.D. 50

TAMMAHAMAHA; TAMMAHAMMAHA

References are to the renowned king and unifier of
*Hawaii, Kamehameha I (See "Kammahammaha") and to
Kamehameha III (*O.* 54's "present king of Hawaii").

The "T" spelling in some editions derives from the early
pre-literate Hawaiian language (as well as from M.'s idiosyncratic spelling). M.'s references to the kings alternate between
use of "T" and "K" and vary in their other letters, as well.
T. Passim; O. 54; M. 68; W. 50

TAM O'SHANTER

The farmer-hero of Robert Burns's 1791 narrative poem
spends market day drinking with "*souter Johnny," a teller of
the "queerest stories." Enroute home, Tam sees a witches'
gathering in a church and calls to a "winsome wench," which
sends "Old Nick, the Devil," Death, and other wicked beings in
pursuit. Tam arrives home safely, but his horse's tail is lost in
the process.
C.M. 42

TANAQUIL

See "Tarquin."
M.D. 130

TANEE

In *Tahitian, "Tane" means "husband," not "man," as
M. has it.
O. 80

TAPPA

In the *Marquesas and other islands of the South Pacific, *tapa* is a fabric women make from paper mulberry tree
bark, by beating it to desired thinness with grooved mallets.
Despite M.'s claim that "no description of its manufacture"
had ever been given (*T.* 19), *Ellis had written at length about it
in *Polynesian Researches*.
T. Passim

TAPPAN ZEE

*New York's *Hudson River swells for twelve miles be-
tween Grassy Point (near Haverstraw) to Piermont, just above
the *New Jersey border, forming Tappan Zee.
P. 18:1

TARAIBOO
Presqu'ile de Taiarapu, *Tahiti.
O. 32

TARARROA
Ta'aroa, in *Tahitian mythology, was the primal spirit who initiated the universe either by incantation, personification of himself, or sexual reproduction with beings he created. There are many legends about him. M.'s identification of him with *Saturn is unclear.
O. 80

TARO; TARA
"Taro" is a *Tahitian word referring to *Colocasia esulenta*, a plant with shield-shaped leaves and edible tuberous corms from which can be made poi ("poee-poee"), a paste-like staple food of the South Sea islanders. M.'s reference to "Indian turnip," or taro, in O. 52 is perhaps a play on words. Technically, "Indian turnip" is Jack-in-the pulpit, a member of the arum family, along with taro.
O. Passim; M. Passim

TARQUIN
M. would have read in *Livy (Sealts # 147, *Harper's Classical Library*, vols. 24-28) of Lucius (originally Lucomo) Tarquinus Priscus, seventh-century B.C. *Roman king married to the prophetess Tanaquil. Livy says that when Tarquin first set out to seek his fortune, an eagle circled his head three times, removing and replacing his cap. This was seen by Tanaquil as a great omen, verified when they reached Rome.
Tarquin built the Circus Maximus and the Roman sewers. He was assassinated c. 578 by the sons of Ancus Marcius, the king he had supplanted.
History paints Tanaquil as an ambitious woman who changed her name to Gaia Caecilia and, upon her husband's death, made her son-in-law, Servius Tullius, king. An expert spinner and weaver, she became a model for Roman brides.
M. 161; M.D. 130

TARSHISH
In M.'s time, Tarshish was identified with the *Spanish Tartessus, north of *Cádiz, near the mouth of the *Quadalquivir River.
M.D. 9

TARSUS

The birthplace (in *Acts 22:3) of *St. Paul, Tarsus is an ancient city on the Cydnus River on the plain of Cilicia, in *Turkey. It was prosperous from the fifth century B.C. until the seventh century A.D.: visited by *Xenophon and *Alexander the Great. It was occupied by the *Macedonians (who named it Antioch-on-the-Cydnus, in honor of *Antiochus Epiphanes). As a *Roman province, it was visited by *Caesar, Mark *Antony, and *Cleopatra. *Arab invaders laid it waste c. A.D. 660, and it was rebuilt a century later as a military base against the *Byzantines, who finally took it c. 965. The *Crusaders entered in 1097, and from the twelfth century until invasion by the *Mamelukes in the fourteenth, it was *Christian. The *Ottomans took Tarsus c. 1500.
R. 27; M.D. 45

TARTAN

Tartan is a chequered *Scottish fabric, with a unique tartan representing each clan. "Plaid," with which it is often confused, is not associated with a clan; it initially described twelve yards of cloth wrapped as a kilt.
R. 46

TARTAR, --S; TARTAREAN; TARTARIAN; TARTARY

Properly "Tatars," the Tartars are *Asiatic tribes associated with *Tartarus, or hell. Under Genghis *Khan they threatened thirteenth-century Europe with their savagery. The added "r" suggests the association with hell.

Tartar is also an expression for an adept, thief, or vagabond. Applied to a woman it denotes a shrew. Also, a short form for "Tartarus": Hell.
O. 80; M. 23; M. 119; M. 138; M. 150; M. 151; R. 35; W. 22; W. 65; W. 85; M.D. 13; M.D. 16; M.D. 32; M.D. 54; M.D. 87; M.D. 96; P. 3:1; P. 7:7; P. 9:1; I.P. 25; C.M. 2; C.M. 36

TARTAR

Tartar is the ship in which Potter is transported in leg irons from *Boston to *Portsmouth, *England, in "*Israel Potter's Autobiographical Story."
I.P. 3

TARTARUS

In *Greek mythology, a division (with *Erebus) of the underworld (sometimes called *Hades, after its ruler). Tar-

tarus is the deeper of the two sections, the prison of the Sons of
Earth, while Erebus is where the dead pass to as they die. The
name Tartarus is often used for the entire lower region, which
the *Iliad* says lies beneath the earth, while the *Odyssey* locates
it over the edge of the world across Ocean. Zeus (see "Jupiter"
and "Jove") confined the *Titans here.

M. visited *Italy's Laga de'Tartari (Lake Tartarus), near
*Tivoli, in March of 1857.

M. 9; C.M. 15

TASSO'S

Torquato Tasso (1544-1595), Italian Renaissance poet, is
most famous for the epic, *Jerusalem Delivered* (*Gerusalemme
liberata*, 1580-1). The son of Bernardo Tasso, epic-writer, he
followed his father into exile in 1552 and, after his mother's
mysterious death, traveled and studied law, philosophy, and
rhetoric. His first epic, *Rinaldo* (pub. 1562) was written under
the protection of highly placed sponsors at court and in the
Church. About 1575 he began publicly evincing behavior that
suggested psychotic persecution feelings. He was imprisoned
for seven years, beginning in 1579, according to legend, for his
love for Leonora, sister of the Duke of Ferrara. The real cause
was probably political. In prison he composed numerous
works, so that on his release he was acclaimed a great poet.
He disdained the attention and finished his life in poverty and
seclusion.

Tasso's legend has been the subject of numerous works:
*Byron's *The Lament of Tasso*, *Goethe's *Torquato Tasso*, and
Donizetti's opera of the same title. His influence on other poets
is too wide-ranging to particularize.

M.'s *Journal* entries for 9 and 31 March 1857 record visits to the site of Tasso's death and to his prison: a "mere cider-
cellar. Grated window, but not strong." In 1862 M. scored
lines by Mme. de Staël (*Germany*, p. 355) sympathetic to
Tasso's plight.

I.P. 22

TATI

The name remains untraced, but Tati is perhaps one of
the ambitious *Tahitian chiefs (along with *Kitoti) referred to
by *Wilkes.

O. 32

TATTOO LAND
*New Zealand, where the Maori (*Mowree) people were famous for tattooing.
M.D. 45

TAURUS
In astronomy, a *constellation of the *zodiac, pictorially represented as a bull, the "eye" of which is the red first-magnitude star, *Aldebaran; the location of the *Pleiades and *Hyades.
Also, the name of a mountain chain from *India to the Aegean Sea, the location of Armenia and *Media.
O. 57; M. 13; M. 149; M. 169; M.D. 99

TAYLOR, JEREMY
Born in humble *English surroundings, Taylor (1613-67) developed early preaching skills which enabled him to attend all Souls College, *Oxford and rise through church ranks to the bishopric of Dromore. His simple style is best exemplified in *The Rule and Exercises of Holy Living* (1650) and *The Rule and Exercises of Holy Dying* (1651; Sealts # 495a).
R. 41; C.M. 24

TEA-CADDY
A small container for storing loose tea. "Caddy" is derived from a *Malaysian word designating a weight of one pound, five ounces, two drams: used mostly in the east.
M.D. 72

TEAK
The large East Indian *Tectona grandis*, a member of the *verbena family, has white flowers and hard yellowish-brown wood used for shipbuilding and in furniture-making.
M. 37

TECUMSEH
The Shawnee Chief (1768?-1813), who established a confederacy of tribes from *Florida to the head of the *Missouri River, made war in 1811 on the *United States government in a dispute over common possession of Indian lands the government wished to acquire. The war ended when Tenskwatawa (1768?-1834), the "Shawnee Prophet," and perhaps Tecumseh's twin brother, went into the disastrous battle of Tippecanoe.

Joining the *British in the *War of 1812, Tecumseh, a brigadier general, was killed in battle, along with many of his warriors. He is memorialized in much literature, expecially for his humane treatment of prisoners.
C.M. 25

TEEARMOAR
Teihamoeroa i Matahihae, also called Hapai, or Teu, was born c. 1728. As *Vancouver noted (1801: I, 270-271), he was the father of the first *Pomare.
O. 49

TEES
*England's Tees River begins on the east side of the northern Pennine mountains and empties into the North Sea at Middlesbrough.
I.P. 19

TEHERAN
The city in modern-day Iran, seventy miles from the Caspian Sea, was founded in the twelfth century and gained its greatest reputation for an exotic *oriental flavor in the seventeenth. It was in the process of renovation from 1848 to 1896.
C.M. 24

TEJUCO
The *Brazilian city is the modern-day Diamantina, so called for the diamonds found in the local river since the eighteenth century. The city is built in the shape of an ampitheater.
W. 56

TELEOLOGICAL THEORISTS
Teleology is explanation by reference to some purpose or end (Greek *telos*, "end"; *teleios*, "complete"), or final causation. *Aristotle claimed that there could be no full explanation without taking into account not only "material," "formal," and "efficient" causes, but also a "final" cause. *Immanuel Kant and *George Berkeley were eighteenth-century teleological theorists, and *William Paley's late eighteenth-century biology was based on the organism as machine devised by an intelligent Creator. By M.'s time such mechanistic theories were being challenged.
P. 19:1

TELESTIC LORE
In philosophy, referring to an end.
M. 171

TEMPE
The Vale of Tempe (Gr. Tembi), in northeastern
*Thessaly between Mount *Olympus and Mount *Ossa, is for
its five-mile length the bed of the Peneus River. Tempe has
been important in art and in history. In mythology, it was sacred to *Apollo; laurel for wreaths of Pythian games victors
was gathered here. *Virgil acclaims the vale's beauties in *Georgics*. It has long been strategically important for its access
from *Macedonia. In 480 B.C. the *Greeks attempted to stop
*Xerxes's army here; in 336 B.C. *Alexander the Great moved
against the Greek cities using the vale.
O. 18

TEMPERANCE ASSOCIATION; TEMPERANCE SOCIETY; TEMPERANCE SOCIETIES
Temperance efforts began in *America in the last quarter of the eighteenth century. By the early 1840's, the American Seaman's Friend Society and other local temperance societies were flourishing, especially in the northeast. If statistics
can be credited, about one million people had signed abstinence
pledges by this time.
Kamehameha (see "Kammahammaha") III instituted
a temperance society in the *Sandwich Islands in 1842, and by
1843 missionaries were proclaiming its success. That year,
the *Maui Temperance Society reaffirmed its aim to restrict
alcohol to sailors such as M., who arrived in May on *Charles
and Henry*. But by July the *Temperance Advocate and Seaman's Friend* was again decrying local morals. By 1848, *The
Friend* would condemn M.'s ideas about morality, as expressed in *T*. Some of the crew of *United States* were to sign a
pledge, but it is doubtful that M. was among them.
Alcohol was a serious problem for sailors, and there is
no doubt that Temperance Societies were instrumental in ending the harmful *grog ration (in 1862). Yet M.'s frequent references to alcoholic beverages, and his comment to
*Hawthorne that he would not believe in a "Temperance
Heaven" (letter, 1? June 1851) suggest that he was not totally
approving of such societies.
See also "Humane Society."
R. 8; R. 29; M.D. 2; M.D. 72

TEMPERANCE MEN
See "Temperance Association; Temperance Society; Temperance Societies."
W. 43

TEMPLAR; TEMPLER
The Knights Templar, or Poor Knights of *Christ and the Temple of *Solomon, were formed with two other orders, the Order of the Hospital of St. John of *Jerusalem, and the Order of St. Lazarus, during the *Crusades; their duty was to protect pilgrims to the Holy Places from *Moslem attackers. Hugues de Payns of Champagne formed the protective religious community in 1119 or 1120, swearing obedience to the Patriarch of Jerusalem, and obeying *Augustinian vows of poverty and chastity, as well as later *Benedictine vows. The name derived from their quarters in the palace of Baldwin II, near the former Jewish Temple. Their controversial military nature was defended by St. Bernard of Clairvaux in *De laude novae militiae* (c. 1130-1135). Pope Innocent II's 1139 bull, *Omne datum optimum*, granted important privileges: exemption from *tithes; separate chapels and clergy; freedom from local bishops' jurisdictions, including that of the Patriarch of Jerusalem.

The Chapters were divided into four classes: combatant knights and sergeants (of non-noble birth), chaplains, and servants. Only knights wore the familiar white surcoat with red cross insignia. They were ruled by a self-chosen hierarchy, including a Grand Master who could make no important decisions without the chapter's assent.

By 1140, their original purpose no longer existing, the Templars had become the defenders of the Latin States, fighting for local rulers against the Muslims. The order was now large and wealthy, with men and materials from the western kingdoms. With numerous fortresses, they became a force almost equal to that of the sovereigns, and their political tendency was furthered by quarrels with the Hospitallers.

The end of the Latin States (c. 1290) forced their retreat to *Cyprus, where their wealth made them bankers; with resources throughout Christendom, they were used for safe deposit or as lenders, especially to the Kings of *France. Their great wealth and power led to Philip IV of France's decision to break the Order; denounced as heretics to Grand *Inquisitor William of *Paris, they were arrested, stripped of property, tortured, and burned at the stake—accused of crimes ranging from sodomy to secret Muslim treaties. Most important, however, were their secret ceremonies—allegedly denying *Christ and spitting upon a crucifix (c.f. *M.D.*, Chapter 19, "The

Prophet," in which "*Ahab" is accused of spitting into what is presumably a Holy Chalice). French harassment soon spread, and the order was officially suppressed in 1311, at the Council of Vienne; a papal bull transferred property to other orders maintaining Templar tradition.

The question of their guilt was a matter of dispute during M.'s time, when it was conjectured that the order had held *Gnostic beliefs, that a secret order had existed within the official one; that Templars were ancestors of *Freemasons.
T. 16; T. 24; I.P. 12

TEMPLE; TEMPLE-BAR

*London's Temple is the area between Fleet Street and the *Thames formerly occupied by buildings of the Knights *Templars. Since the fourteenth century, the area has been the domain of lawyers and law students forming the two Inns of Court (voluntary societies) known as the Inner and Middle Temples. (The other two Inns of Court are Lincoln's Inn and Gray's Inn). The present Inner Temple Hall dates from 1870; Middle Temple is from 1572.

Temple Bar is the old Fleet Street gateway into the city, formerly at the entrance into the Temple, where traitors' heads were exhibited.

M. visited the area on 10 November 1849; his journal mentions his "sauntering through the Temple courts & gardens." On 12 November, he visited Temple Church "to hear the music." He had numerous social engagements in the Temple area, including one dinner at Elm Court (19 December) which is presumed the model for the feast described in "The Paradise of Bachelors." Several dinners at the Erectheum Club probably provided details for the short sketch, as well. M. appears to have had mixed feelings about denizens of the Temple, probably arising from his ambivalence about the Knights Templars.

See also "London Club-houses."
R. 30

TEMPLE OF FREEDOM

M.'s fictional equivalent of the *United States *Senate.
M. 158

TEMPLE OF THE PHILISTINES

In *Judges 16:29, the temple at *Gaza destroyed by *Samson when he "took hold of the two middle pillars upon which the house stood, and on which it was borne up."

See also "Philistine . . . "
M.D. 89

TEMPLE OF THE YEAR
A reference to Simon Berington's *Memoirs of Sigr. Gaudentio di Lucca* (1737), which describes a similar structure. See also "Three-Hundred-And-Sixty-Five . . . "
M. 75

TENERIFFE
The largest of the *Canary Islands is located in the west-central part of the archipelago. It is a fifty-five mile-long, thirty-three mile-wide volcanic island, a *Spanish possession since the fifteenth century. The "Peak of Teneriffe" (*M.* 181) is Pico de Teide. It rises sharply to a jagged peak over 12,000 feet high: the natural "obelisk" of *M.* 75. *Nelson lost an arm in battle here in 1797 (*M.* 24).
M. 24; M. 75; M. 95; M. 181; M.D. 54

TENIERS; TENNIERS
David Teniers the Younger (1610-90), prolific *Flemish painter, produced some 2,000 pictures in *Antwerp and Brussels. He is best known for his peasant scenes, such as the humorous and crowded *Village Fete* (1643). As court painter to the Archduke Leopold Wilhelm, he did portraits, copies, and engravings.
Teniers was the sun of David Teniers the Elder (1582-1640; art dealer and guild master) and father to David (1638-1685), who imitated his father's work. He was married to Anna, a daughter of the artist, Jan Brueghel.
In 1857, M. saw Teniers tavern scenes with remarkable effects "produced by first dwarfing, then deforming humanity" (journal, 10 April).
M.'s first draft of *Timoleon* included a note: "A particular picture is here referred to." The painting was probably one by Teniers the Younger which he had seen in *Amsterdam: "L'heure du repos."
T. 29; W. 91

TENNESSEE; TENNESSEAN
The sixteenth state of the Union (admitted 1796) is bordered by *Kentucky and *Virginia (N.), North *Carolina (E.), *Georgia, *Alabama, and Mississippi (S.), *Arkansas and *Missouri (W.). The area was claimed by the *French but dominated by Indians until well into the eighteenth century and was lost to the *British in 1763. The first permanent settlement was made by Virginians in 1769, and even by M.'s time, population was only about 100,000.

Tennessee was to garner fame for its diversified scenery (still 50% forest), especially the *Great Smoky Mountains, Cumberland plateau tableland, and Tennessee River system (now dammed). Natives of the state include *Andrew Jackson, *Davy Crockett, and *James Polk.

Many important *Civil War battles were fought in Tennessee, including those of Stone River, Chattanooga, and Shiloh, about which M. was to write some of his finest poems.

"The poor poet of Tennesse" (*M.D.* 1) has not been identified. The "Tennessean by birth" of *C.M.* 3 is probably the bandit, *Murrell.
M.D. 1; P. 21:3; C.M. 3; C.M. 6

TEN-STROKE
A complete victory; among billiard players, ten is the highest stroke; in bowling, a ball that knocks down all the pins.
W. 23

TENTERDEN
Charles Abbott, first Lord Tenterden (1762-1832), became Lord Chief Justice of *England (despite a less-than-first-class mind). He published *Law Relative to Merchant Ships and Seamen* (1802).
W. 66

TERRA
In mythology, Terra is a *Roman name (with Tellus or Tithea) for the earth goddess called Ge, or Gaea, by the *Greeks. Mother and wife of *Coelus (Gr. Uranus), she also bore Oceanus, the *Titans, the *Cyclops, the Giants, and others.
P. 25:4; P. 25:5

TERRA DEL FUEGO; TERRA-DEL-FUEGO
Tierra del Fuego (Sp. "fire land") is an archipelago at the southern tip of *South America, separated from the mainland by the Strait of Magellan. There is one large island (called Tierra del Fuego, or Great Island), five smaller ones including *Desolation and *Staten Land, and numerous islets. At the southern extremity is Horn Island, for which Cape *Horn is named. It is a bleak, cold and desolate area inhabited by local tribes. Tierra del Fuego was discovered by *Magellan in 1520; it was not surveyed until the nineteenth century.
T. 17; W. 24; M.D. Extracts 22

TERRA FIRMA
Lat.: firm ground.
M. 54; C.M. 9 and elsewhere

TERRA INCOGNITA
Lat.: unknown, unexplored, or unidentified region.
M. 17; M.D. 58

TERROR STONE
See "Balance Rock."
P. 7:4; P. 7:5; P. 7:6

TERTIARY
In geology, the third period of the Cenozoic Era
(beginning some 65 million years ago), characterized by the development of many varieties of mammals.
M. 132; M.D. 104; M.D. 105

TERTULLIAN
Quintus Septimius Florens Tertullianus (c. 155-- after 220), great early *Christian writer, was born a pagan, in *Carthage. He was educated in Greek and Latin literature, philosophy, and the law. Converted to Christianity after witnessing much persecution, he became the great dogmatically orthodox defender of the faith against the pagan state, the *Jews, and the heretical sects, especially *Marcionites and *Gnostics. Among his writings are various apologetics, polemical-dogmatic treatises, and disciplinary, moral, and ascetic works, all in *Latin. His most famous work is the *Apologeticus* (197), addressed to *Roman governors. *De praescriptione haereticorum* (M.'s spelling incorrect) makes a legal objection aiming to end controversy between *Catholics and heretics.
W. 38

TETRADS
*Pythagoras called Deity a Tetrad or Tetracys, referring to the four sacred letters JHVH, the *Jewish name for the deity, probably pronounced Yahweh, later corrupted into *Jehovah.
M. 171

TEXAS; TEXAN; TEXIAN
The present state of Texas is bounded by *Mexico (along the Rio Grande, S.), New Mexico (W.), Oklahoma (N.), *Arkansas (N.E.), *Louisiana and the *Gulf of Mexico (E.). It was admitted to the Union as the twenty-eighth state in 1845, and was the largest state (roughly 770 miles east-to-west and north-to-south).
The *Spanish explored the area in 1519, and the *French attempted missionary colonies in the 1680's and 90's. Although the *United States officially renounced any claim in an 1819 treaty with Spain, American settlers were discontented with Mexican rule, and hostilities began to break out in 1835. In 1836, the Alamo (San Antonio) was lost (along with *Davy Crockett), but Sam Houston's victory at San Jacinto led to General Santa Anna's recognition of independence in that same year. Admission of Texas to the Union (as a *slave state) started the *Mexican War (1846-48).
The "Texian rangers" of *R*. 15 had been organized by the Republic of Texas to defend against Indians and Mexicans. They were mustered into Federal service in the Mexican War, where their distinctive independence and picturesque appearance made them paradigms of irregular troops.
"Texan Camanche" (*P*. 22:2) refers to the Comanches, a bellicose Indian tribe that uprose in Texas in 1840.
R. 15; M.D. 14; M.D. 89; P. 22:2

TEXEL, THE
Texel is the largest of the West Frisian Islands, off the northwestern *Netherlands. The sandy and gravelled island is fifteen miles long, six miles wide, and is dotted with dikes and dunes. It is inhabited mostly by sheep-raisers.
M.D. 101; I.P. 20

THALABA THE DESTROYER
Hero of Southey's 1800 poem of that name, "Thalaba" is a type of Joan of Arc who goes forth as a *God-appointed warrior against evil. He must destroy a race of magicians in their underwater palace.
W. 76

THAMES
*England's Thames River rises in the Cotswold Hills, Gloucester, flowing 210 miles to the *Nore and connected to several canals. It is naturally scenic until it reaches *London,

where it is crossed by fifteen bridges; thereafter, it is industrial.

M. took a steamer up the Thames to St. Katherine's wharf on 26 April 1857, noting in his journal the "many objects of interest." Among them was the hull of *Great Eastern*, a 692-foot-long iron super steamer. She remained unlaunched until 1858, despite completion in 1855. (*Great Eastern* became a white elephant for lack of engines large enough to run her efficiently. She was scrapped in 1887.)
M. 149; R. 5; R. 43; W. 73; M.D. 32; M.D. 55; M.D. 108; P. 1:3; P. 14:3; I.P. 1; I.P. 16; I.P. 24 and elsewhere

THAMES TUNNEL, --S
     The tunnel under *London's *Thames River, visited by M. in 1849 (journal 11 November), had opened in 1843, after twenty years of construction work. The shop-lined tourist attraction had walls decorated with paintings of British landscapes. It was 1,200 feet long, seventy-five feet below the ground, and connected Shadwell and Rotherkite. The tunnel never paid its way and eventually served the railways.
M.D. 105

THANE
     In ancient *Scotland, a person of high rank and holder of king's property. In *Shakespeare's *Macbeth, "Duncan" bestows the title "Thane of Cawdor" upon "Macbeth," and he is first addressed as such by noblemen "*Angus" and "Rosse."
W. 51

THANKSGIVING
     The first *American Thanksgiving occurred at Plymouth, *Massachusetts, in Fall of 1621, as noted by William Bradford. The occasion was irregularly scheduled until 26 November 1789, when *George Washington set aside a day of prayer for all denominations. It became a national holiday celebrated on the last Thursday in November in 1863 (since changed to the fourth Thursday).
     As M. notes in his journal (15 November 1849), Queen *Victoria scheduled a day of Thanksgiving for the end of the *cholera epidemic while M. was visiting *London.
P. 22:4

"THE ALCHYMIST"
     See "Jonson; Ben Jonson."
W. 41

THEATER ROYAL
        Erected in 1772 in Williamson Square, *Liverpool.
R. 30

THEBES; THEBAN
        (Greek Thebai; modern Greek Thívai) An ancient city
in Boeotia, *Greece; a citadel from the Early Bronze Age. Legend associates it with *Cadmus, *Hercules, and *Oedipus.
Theban history is of enmity with *Athens and *Sparta; a Theban attack on Plataea started a *Peloponnesian War. Thebes
was defeated by *Alexander the Great in 315, in the Middle
Ages fell under *Roman rule, then *Turkish.
        Thebes, *Egypt, was a royal residence, seat of the god
Ammon, location of the kings' necropolis.
O. 42; I.P. 23

"THE CITY MADAM"
        A comedy by Philip Massinger (1583-1640), a collaborator
of *Beaumont and *Fletcher. Acted in 1632, *The City Madam*
is a broad domestic comedy about the education of the proud
daughters of the wealthy Sir John Frugal and the hypocrisy of
his empoverished brother.
        (Sealts #358, *The Mermaid Series. The Best Plays of the
Old Dramatists*, is a late [1887-19?] collection which includes
some of Massinger's works in v. 6.)
W. 41

THE FAIRIE QUEEN
        See "Spenser"; "Extracts 17."
M.D. Extracts 17

*"THE GREAT ROADS, BOTH DIRECT AND CROSS,
THROUGHOUT ENGLAND AND WALES . . . ."*
        M.'s eight-line title for this work is actually a condensa-
tion of the full title, supplied by Thorp, in "Redburn's Prosy Old
Guidebook": *Cary's New Itinerary; or, an Accurate Delin-
eation of the Great Roads, Both Direct and Cross, Throughout
England and Wales; With many of the principal Roads in Scotland. From an Actual Admeasurement, made by Command of
His Majesty's Postmaster General, for Official Purposes; under the Direction and Inspection of Thomas Hasker, Esq. Surveyor of the Roads to the General Postoffice. To which are
added, at the end of each Route, the Names of those Inns
which supply Post Horses and Carriages; Accompanied with*

a most extensive Selection of Noblemen & Gentlemen's Seats; A List of the Packet Boats, and their Time of sailing; Copious Indexes, &c. &c. London: Printed for John Cary, N° 181 Strand, 1798 . . . Dedicated By Permission To the Right Honourable the Earls Chesterfield & Leicester The Liberal Patrons of this Work By Their Lordships' Much obliged and very obedient Servant London Feby 1 1798 John Cary.
R. 30

"THE HIDDEN WATER"
    "Hidden Water" is an old Indian name for Niterói (see "Santa Cruz"), rather than for *Rio de Janeiro, as M. has it in W. 50.
W. 50

"THE JEW OF MALTA"
    A blank-verse drama by Christopher Marlowe (see "Marlow"), performed about 1592. *The Jew of *Malta* is the story of Barabas, a rich *Jew persecuted by the *Turks who dies when he becomes a powerful *Machiavel cherishing "Infinite riches in a little roome."
W. 41

"THE KING OF THE OAKS"
    The (untraced) name for the *teak tree is puzzling. Oak is of the genus *Quercus* and belongs to the beech family; teak is of the *verbena family.
R. 34

"THE LATTER DAY COMING; OR NO TIME TO LOSE"
    See "Mormons."
M.D. 18

THE MESSIAH
    See "Handel."
W. 50

THEODOSIUS
    The reference in *M*. 35 cannot be to either *Roman Emperor of the name. Probably it is an error for "Theodora," in the *Belisarius story.
M. 35

"THE OLD WAGON PAID OFF"
   Although the theatricals aboard "Neversink" are fictional, "Old Wagon," her nickname, was the informal appellation of *United States* (sister ship to "Old Ironsides," *Constitution*).
W. 23

THE PEOPLE
   Throughout W. (and elsewhere), M. wrestles with the classic problem besetting the *United States in the nineteenth century: given a relatively young government supposedly controlled by the *Constitution's "We the people," complex questions of articulation and ethics arise.   Though the United States was to be a *democracy, it could not be a "pure" one, in which one man cast one vote, directly controlling affairs. Rather, it was made a *republic, in which leaders elected by "the people" theoretically enact the will of that people. The U.S. *Navy ship "*Neversink" is a microcosm of the United States (and indeed the world) in that a hierarchy of rather monarchical officers (themselves ranked invidiously) is set up for governance of a "mob" (W. 13) of underlings, creating all of the problems and questions extant in a republic. Who are "the people" at the bottom of the hierarchy? Are they *Jefferson's "natural aristocrats," who are "defrauded" (W. 44) by superiors? If so, the *Revolution and *Declaration of Independence are lies (W. 35). Are they the ignorant "mob" to whom "liberty" must be rationed, as in W. 54?
   These questions had troubled the U.S. government from its inception, as *Federalists countered Jefferson's Democratic-Republican belief in the inherent wisdom and dignity of "the people." The inauguration of *Andrew Jackson, wherein "the people," invited for the first time to a state occasion, tore public buildings apart, seemed by the 1830's to show that Jefferson's was a Pyrrhic victory, unleashing a monster unwilling to return to a cage.
   Apparently M. was a situational ethicist without resorting to virtuous expediency. Universalizing of suffrage had caused his own honorable *Dutch patroon forebears to lose office and power to unscrupulous leaders and political machines. Yet he seems to have felt strongly about the value of the "little" people and their right not to be abused. As an author, on the other hand, he resented the power of the mass of readers; the poet "*Lemsford" speaks to the dilemma for him in W. 45, making a distinction the boundaries of which are untraceable: "The public is one thing, . . . and the people another."
W. Passim

THE PICTURE OF LIVERPOOL . . .
    M.'s copy of of this book has not been located, but an edition with a slightly later date shows how heavily he drew upon the guide, despite disclaimers in *R*.   In "Redburn's Prosy Old Guidebook," Thorp reproduces the title page of the 1808 edition: *The Picture of *Liverpool; or Stranger's Guide. A New Edition, Considerably Enlarged. Embellished with Engravings on Wood By the First Artists.* Liverpool: Printed by Jones and Wright, Swift's Court;   and sold by Woodward and Alderson, 56, Castle Street, and the rest of the booksellers. 1808.
    This edition includes a map corresponding to M.'s "Plan of the Town," an illustration of the Town Hall, *Dr. Aiken's verse lines, quotations from the *Aeneid* and *Falconer's *Shipwreck*, the full anonymous poem which M. playfully rearranged, a toned-down reference to *Roscoe, a section on "Public Buildings" which M. drew on, as well as references to the Pool, *Birkenhead Abbey, the Earls of *Derby, *King's Dock, the Church of *St. Nicholas, *Walton, the "Institution for Restoring Drowned Persons," and the parrot whose commands backed a horse and wagon into the water. There is no account of *Prince's Dock, at which M. places "*Highlander."
R. 30

THERMES, ROMAN HALLS OF
    See "Cluny, Hôtel de."
M.D. 41

THERMOPYLAE
    The modern *Greek Thermopilai ("hot gates") is a narrow four-mile-long pass through hot springs, on the east coast of central Greece.   In 480 B.C., a small Greek force under the *Spartan king, Leonidas, defended the pass against a huge *Persian army.   It was also defended in 323, 279, and 191, the alternative mountain route inland being difficult.
M. 7

THERSITES
    In the *Iliad*, the loquacious Thersites is killed by *Achilles when he laughs over the hero's grief.   In *Shakespeare's *Troilus and Cressida* he is the ultimate cynic. He became a stock figure in *English drama as a boastful coward.
C.M. 42

"THE SHUTTLE"
     In *I.P.* 20, *John Paul Jones appears to play the same
role as "*Ishmael" in *M.D.* 47, "The Mat-Maker": an instrument or device mindlessly moving to and fro without regard to
effects or consequences. "Ishmael" finally reflects on the implications of his actions; Jones perhaps did not.
I.P. 20

THESSALY; THESSALIES
     A division of north-central *Greece, between *Epirus
(W.) and the Aegean Sea (E.), between *Macedonia (N.) and
central Greece (S.). It is an area roughly sixty miles square,
overlooked on the northeast by Mount *Olympus, with *Ossa
and Pelion barring access to the Aegean. Thessaly was settled
c. 2500 B.C., but the Thessalians, an Aeolian tribe, arrived at
least a thousand years later, forming an isolated, oligarchal
agricultural society. The area passed in 344 B.C. to *King
Philip II of Macedon and by 146 B.C. was incorporated into the
*Roman province of Macedonia, finally becoming a separate
province. The *Turks took control in 1400; Thessaly once more
became part of Greece in 1881.
     The "groves" of Thessaly are, despite low rainfall, abun-
dant producers of citrus fruit, olives, vegetables, wheat, and tobacco.
     M. was in the area 6 December 1856.
     See also "Tempe."
R. 50

"THE TEAR"
     Thackeray's "Arthur *Pendennis" writes a poem called
"To a Tear" (*Pendennis*, Ch. 3).
P. 18:1

THE TEMPEST
     The Tempest is *Shakespeare's romantic drama of
shipwreck, banishment, murder, magic, and solitude. The
first scene, alluded to by "*Jack Chase" in *W.* 65, takes place on
a ship at sea in a storm.
     M. underscored and annotated lines from the play in his
personal copy of *Dramatic Works* (Sealts #460). The markings
are reproduced in Leyda *Log* I, 289: *Tempest* V, 183-185: the
heroine, "Miranda," speaks of a "brave new world," and her
father, "Prospero," responds: "Tis new to thee."
W. 65

THETIS
   Thetis was the thirty-six-gun *British frigate sent to capture *John Paul Jones in the North Channel in 1778. (*Thetis* was nicknamed "Tea-chest," because she made a peculiar sound and because her captain ordered tea substituted for rum on board.)
   In mythology, Thetis is a nereid, daughter of Nereus and Doris, and the mother of *Achilles.
R. 40

"THE TROPICAL SUMMER"
   "The Tropical Summer" is probably self-parody. M.'s juvenilia is represented by "The Lansingburgh Fragments," reproduced in Gilman's *Melville's Early Life and Redburn*. The two pretentiously romantic fragments were published in *The Democratic Press and Lansingburgh Advertiser*, 4 and 18 may 1839.
   In the reproduced second piece, a narrator is conducted by a seductress calling herself (in a letter) "Inamorata" to a perfumed apartment straight out of the *Arabian Nights. (Perhaps the prototype for "*Aladdin's Palace" of *R*. 46.) Her satin-slippered, white-robed, Cupid-embroidered, diamond-bedecked, long-haired person beguiles our young hero, who plants "one long, long kiss upon her hot and glowing lips" and then gasps: "Does thy heart send forth vital fluid like my own? Am I loved,—even wildly, madly as I love?" The thrilling conclusion finds the young man bursting from the apartment in horror: "She was dumb! Great God, she was dumb! DUMB AND DEAF!"
P. 17:1; P. 18:1; P. 22:4

"THE TRUE HISTORY"
   See "Lucian"; "Extracts" 8.
M.D. Extracts 8

THEVENOT
   The *French Jean de Thèvenot travelled to the *Levant (1633-67) to see the *Ottoman court and household of the *sultan at first hand. M. owes many details to Thevènot's orthography, descriptions of clothing, furniture, etc. Thevènot's experiences were detailed in his *The Travels of Monsieur de Thèvenot into the Levant. In Three Parts*, 3 vols., London 1687 (parts of which were reprinted in *Harris's collection).

(*Benjamin Franklin's *Autobiography* mentions another Thèvenot, Melchisédeck de Thèvenot, whose "Motions and Positions" taught him to swim: *The Art of Swimming. Illustrated by Proper Figures* . . . was available in a 1699 *London translation.)
M. 75

THIBET
The central *Asian country of Tibet is in the highest region of the world (average elevation 13-15,000 feet), located on a plateau between the Kunlan (N.) and *Himalaya (S.) mountains. Numerous lakes and rivers dot the area populated by nomadic animal herders and other *Mongolians. Difficulty of access kept Tibet secluded through the nineteenth century, despite many attempts by foreigners to open up the area.
Before *Chinese suzerainty, the Grand, or Dalai, *Lama ruled Tibet. ("Dalai" means "sacred" or "all-embracing"; "Lama" is from the Tibetan *blama* [b is silent], meaning spiritual teacher, or lord.) Lamaism is derived from the Mahayana form of Buddhism. Some 10% of Tibet's population are (mainly celibate) lamas of c. 3,000 monasteries. There are three sects: Yellow Hat lamas follow direct reincarnation succession; Red Hat lamas are sons succeeding fathers; Bon Sect lamas follow pre-Buddhist, shamanistic, and Buddhist practices. From the seventeenth century, Tibet was a theocracy under the Dalai Lama, who is believed to be the reincarnaion of the deity Avalokita. Succession is by direct reincarnation; at the Dalai Lama's death, the country is searched for the proper boy who reveals himself by passing special tests, having received the dying Lama's soul at the moment of his birth.
W. 68

THIRTY-NINE ARTICLES
The Thirty-nine Articles of Religion, along with *The Book of Common Prayer, constitute the Anglican Church creed, adopted in 1563. They were based on the Forty-Two Articles "for the avoidance of controversy in opinion" codified by *Thomas Cranmer in 1553, primarily to rule out Roman *Catholic and Anabaptist doctrine. The articles are somewhat ambiguous, reflecting an *Elizabethan desire for comprehensiveness. They are also subscribed to by the *Episcopal Church in the *United States.
M.D. 16

THIRTY TYRANTS
At the end of the *Peloponnesian war, the thirty magistrates appointed by *Sparta over *Athens. In B.C. 403, Thrasybulos ended their one-year reign of terror.
M. 181; W. 91

THIRTY YEARS' WAR
In the seventeenth century, a series of wars between *German *Catholics and *Protestants, and skirmishes involving also *France, *Sweden, and the Habsburgs. It is usually thought of as beginning with the *Bohemian Revolt of 1618 and ending with the Peace of *Westphalia in 1648, but the struggle for the European balance of power really lasted for some fifty years. Popular history paints it as a struggle exploited by non-German peoples, wherein the German economy and culture were all but destroyed.
M.D. 3

THOMAS
The name of the *Apostle St. Thomas (Aramaic for "twin") came to stand for a skeptic. In *John 20, Thomas is not present when the risen *Jesus first appears to the Apostles. Eight days later he reappears, commanding Thomas: "Reach hither thy finger, and behold my hands; and reach hither thy hand, and thrust it into my side: and be not faithless, but believing" (27). Thomas explicitly acknowledges Christ's divinity, and Jesus then chastens him: "Thomas, because thou hast seen me, thou hast believed: blessed are they that have not seen, and yet have believed" (29).
Thomas, sometimes called "*Judas Thomas," was the evangelist of *Edessa. The *Apocryphal "Acts of St. Thomas," upon which much history of early Christianity in *India is based, tells of his enslavement in India, where he was martyred. A legend of his building a palace in heaven led to his designation as the patron saint of masons (see "freemason") and architects, his symbol a builder's square. His feast day is December 21.
M. 97

THOMAS A KEMPIS
Thomas Hämmerlein (or Hämmerken; 1380-1471), whose popular name means "of Kempen," the *German town of his birth, was a devout Augustinian (see "St. Augustine") monk to whom is attributed the mystical work, *De Imitatione*

Christi (*Of the Imitation of Christ*), which become one of the most popular and influential religious works ever written.
M. 119

THOMAS BEALE'S HISTORY OF THE SPERM WHALE
      See "Beale, Thomas"; "Extracts" 61.
M.D. Extracts 61

THOMAS EDGE'S TEN VOYAGES TO SPITZBERGEN
      See "Purchas, Samuel"; "Extracts" 27.
M.D. Extracts 27

THOMAS, REAR-ADMIRAL
      Richard Thomas (1777-1857) was born at Saltash, Cornwall, *England. He entered the navy in 1790 on *Cumberland* and thereafter served on numerous ships whose names might have inspired those in *Billy Budd*. On *Blanche* and *Nautilus* in the *West Indies, he returned to England on *Boyne* and survived her burning at *Spithead 1 May 1795, afterwards serving on *Glory*, *Commerce de Marseille*, *Barfleur*, and *Victory*. Promoted lieutenant of *Excellent* in 1797, he was with *Collingwood at the battle of Cape *St. Vincent, afterwards on *Thalia*, *Defence*, *Triumph* and again on *Barfleur*. Having been promoted to Commander in 1803, he was enroute to England on the *Lady Hobart* packet when she wrecked on an iceberg. After seven days at sea in a lifeboat, he escaped to an island near *Newfoundland. Back in England he serve on *Etna*, *Bellerophone*, and then on *Queen*, as Flag Lieutenant to Collingwood, with whom he served on *Ocean* and *Ville de Paris*. In 1811, on *Undaunted*, he assisted the *Spaniards along the coast of Catalonia. But poor health forced his return to England in 1813. From 1822-25 he was Captain of the Ordinary at *Portsmouth and the same at *Plymouth from 1834-37. Made Rear-Admiral in 1837, he was Commander-in-Chief of the Pacific from 1841 to 1844, during the revolutionary trouble. He arrived at *Honolulu on *Dublin* on 26 July 1843 and signed the agreement restoring the *Hawaiian flag after *Lord Paulet's act of seizure. He was made Vice-Admiral in 1848, and Admiral in 1854.
T. Appendix

THOMSON'S SEASONS
      Poet James Thomson (1700-48), son of a *Scottish minister, was educated at *Edinburgh University and moved to

*London, where friendship of *Pope, Gay,and Arbuthnot and patronage of influential persons (whose estates he was to write about) enabled him to begin publishing his topographical poem, *The Seasons*. It became a highly popular and influential work, praised by *Wordsworth as an example of the Sublime. *Coleridge led the school of less complimentary thought, and by the nineteenth century, the poem's artificial diction was criticized by Tennyson, although it was still being republished frequently.

Thomson's work was greatly influenced by landscape paintings of *Claude and Poussin, and J.M.W. Turner was in turn affected by it.

Thomson wrote other poems and a series of tragic plays and masques. He is thought to have composed "Rule, Brittania."

The four-book blank verse *Seasons* was published between 1726 and 1730. "Winter" (1726) describes the ravages of the elements on man and beast. "Summer" (1727) describes a pastoral day and concludes with a paean to Great Britain. "Spring" (1728) paints that season's effect on the natural world and on married love. "Autumn" (1730) focuses on hunting and harvesting and other outdoor pleasures. The poem concludes with a hymn.

Sealts #s 515 through 522 are various editions of the works. In the Boston (1854) edition, acquired in 1861, M. scored "Blessed is he who expecteth nothing, for he shall never be disappointed."

On 11 November 1849, M. visited Thomson's London neighborhood.
R. 30

THORKILL-HAKE
Thorkell Hákr of Lightwater, intemperate speaker of the eleventh-century *Icelandic *saga, *Njalssaga*, was called Thorkel foulmouth because he fought his enemies with his arms and his speech. He had his deeds memorialized in carvings on his shield, his bed, and his stepstool.
M.D. 16

THRACIAN
A native of Thrace, a region of southeastern Europe between the *Black and Aegean seas, east of *Macedonia—in ancient times ruled over by barbarians. The *Greeks mythologized it as the cold and barbaric home of *Boreas (the North Wind) and other cruel gods, as well as the place of origin of *Dionysius and *Orpheus.
See also "Philip's right eye."
W. 16

THRASEA

Publius Clodius Paetus Thrasea (d. A.D. 66), *Roman senator and *Stoic, opposed *Nero, finally retiring after an illustrious career, because of the Emperor's immorality. He was eventually put to death under suspicion of sedition.

The epigram, "he who hates vice, hates humanity," is preserved by *Pliny, Book VIII, Epistle 22.

C.M. 12

THREE, RULE OF

This allusion has a double meaning for sailors; navigation books define it as a method of finding a fourth number from three given numbers, of which the first is proportionate to the second as the third is to the unknown fourth. As such it is known as the "golden rule" of proportion.

Some readers of M.'s time would infer another meaning (especially in the unruly scene of its citation in *W.*). Slang usage refers to the penis and testes and to copulation. A waggish *Benjamin Franklin uses the expression in its secondary sense in a flirtatious letter to Miss Catherine Ray (16 October 1755). He has been advising young Katy on the conduct of marriage, especially as regards "multiplication": "I hope that you will become an expert in the *Rule of Three*; that when I have again the pleasure of seeing you, I may find you like my Grape Vine, surrounded with Clusters, plump, juicy, blushing, pretty little rogues, like their Mama."

Only one early reviewer noted *W.*'s double entendres: Frederick S. Cozzens, in *The Knickerbocker* for May 1850.

O. 17; W. 6

THREE DAYS OF SEPTEMBER

In September 1792 there were three days of wholesale murder as *Parisians, at the approach of the *Russian army, executed royalist and constitutionalist prisoners. There were twelve judges and jurors and even more executioners, who put to death approximately 1,500 people.

W. 3

THREE FATES

See "Fate."

M.D. 113

THREE-HUNDRED-AND-SIXTY-FIVE PILLARED TEMPLE OF THE YEAR
A reference to Simon Berington's *Memoirs of Sigr. Gaudentio di Lucca* (1737), which describes a temple with as many columns as the days of the year. (Some editions refer to ". . . seventy-five" pillars.)
M. 75

THREE KINGDOMS, THE
Probably *England, *Scotland, and *Ireland.
M.D. 90; I.P. 17

THREE PIRATE POWERS
*Russia, *Prussia, and *Austria partitioned *Poland in 1772, 1793, and 1795.
M.D. 14

THREE SEAS OFF
Three waves away.
M.D. 48

THREE SPANIARDS
Perhaps a reference to the 1800 novel by George Walker.
R. 17; M.D. 73

THREE WEIRD ONES, THAT TEND LIFE'S LOOM
See "Fate; the Fates; Three Fates."
M. uses the word "weird" here in the archaic sense of "prophetic," as he does in relation to the executed *Abolitionist John Brown, in the poem, "The Portent."
P. 4:2

THUCYDIDES
The greatest *Greek historian, who flourished during the second half of the fifth century B.C., wrote the incomplete *History of the *Peloponnesian War* (Sealts # 147, vols. 22-23). An early military career led the Athenian to a twenty-year exile which, he claimed, freed him to study the war between *Athens and *Sparta. His eight-book history ends at 411 B.C. (probably his death date), some years before the war's end. (The historian *Xenophon, takes up the task at this point.) The *History* is a speculative work which includes character stud-

ies, investigation of causality, and examination of technical matters, making it seem as much a classic tragedy as a record of events. It became popular as a result of several nineteenth-century translations.
M. 32; C.M. 5

THUGS, THE

Bands of vicious *Indian outlaws who worshipped Kali, Hindu (see "Hindoo") goddess of destruction and consort to *Shiva the Destroyer. They posed as travelers or pilgrims on their own riverboats, preying on innocent persons.

(As H. Bruce Franklin points out in his edition of *C.M.*, the Thugs believed it "a bad omen to meet . . . any person who has lost a limb.")
C.M. 1

THUMMIN

See Urim and Thummin.
O. 8

THUNDERER, THE

Thunderer was a *British radeau (flat-bottomed, square-ended "scow" or punt, variously rigged) in action against the *American fleet in 1776. She was strangely shaped: 91'9" long, with a 33'4" beam, a short, high quarterdeck, deep bulwarks, and nine gun ports.
M. 28

TI, THE

See "Marquesas" and "Bachelor."
T. 12

TIARBOO

Teahupoo, *Tahiti.
O. 30

TIBERIUS

*Roman emperor from A.D. 14, Tiberius Julius Caesar (42 B.C.-A.D. 37) was stepson of Octavian (*Augustus). His greatest skill was in military affairs, and early conquests reinforced ambitions that were at first frustrated by Augustus's preference for the sons of his daughter Julia, Tiberius's second wife, rather than for Tiberius and his son by a previous wife. Both sons conveniently died, as did the favorite nephew of Augustus, Germanicus, and Tiberius's fortunes rose. A series of intrigues, executions, and poisonings marked his reign, so that by his death, his popularity had reached its nadir.

*Tacitus, the main authority on Tiberius, paints him as a cruel and cunning tyrant. Stories of sexual excesses on the resort island of *Capreae (modern Capri) come from *Suetonius.

M. saw a bust of Tiberius in Rome in 1857; in his journal (26 February) he notes the bust's look of "sickly evil." However, in his *lecture, "Statues in Rome," he noted that Tiberius was "handsome, refined, and even pensive in expression." R. 46; R. 55

TIC-DOLLY-ROW

Fr. *tic douloureux*: neuralgia of the face which causes painful twitching. M.D. 29

TICKET-OF-LEAVE-MAN

A convict freed from prison on parole, with the obligation to report to authorities regularly until sentence is completed. The ticket was a warrant for liberty which came to be associated with any holiday or outing, then by the mid-nineteenth-century became a general term of abuse. O. 23

TICONDEROGA

The village of northeastern *New York on the falls at the Lake George outlet was settled in the seventeenth century and became important during the French and Indian Wars. Fort Ticonderoga was the *French Fort Carillon of 1755, renamed after *British capture in 1759. *Ethan Allen's *Green Mountain Boys, along with the troops of *Benedict Arnold, captured the fort 10 May 1775. It was occupied by *Burgoyne in the *Saratoga campaign, 1777, and held again by the British in 1780. I.P. 21; I.P. 22

TIDDERY-EYE

"Tiddly" is utter smartness and efficiency. "Tiddly bull" is excess "spit and polish," military ceremony. "Tiddery" is presumably a variation. W. 91

TIFFIN
In the north of *England, originally a short draught of liquor or late morning snack. In Anglo-Indian usage, a light lunch, especially of curry, chutney, and fruit.
M. 55; M. 123

TIGER-LILIES
Lilium tigrinum has orange flowers with purplish-black spots. In "flower language," it bears the message, "For once may pride befriend me."
M.D. 1

TIGRIS
The Tigris river begins as several mountain streams in *Turkey, flows southward almost 1,200 miles, then joins the *Euphrates and other rivers flowing through present-day *Syria, Iraq, and Iran. Its chief cities, *Baghdad and Basra, make it a busy channel.

First mention of the Tigris occurs in the third millenium B.C., in *Sumerian, *Babylonian, *Assyrian, and *Persian writings. *Nineveh, on the Tigris, was the locale of the *Jonah story, and a nearby *mosque is said to be his burial place.
M.D. 83

TILBURY
A two-wheeled carriage.
M.D. 81

TILLER
A bar of wood or iron, put into the head of the rudder, by which the ship's rudder is moved—serving the same purpose as a wheel.

As many readers have noticed, in two later chapters of *M.D.* (61, 118), the "*Pequod" is said to have a spoked helm wheel, as opposed to the tiller mentioned in *M.D.* 16.
Passim

TILLOTSON, --'S
John Tillotson (1630-94), popular latitudinarian preacher, was Archbishop of *Canterbury from 1691 to 1694. His plain, short sermons were a departure from the dramatic metaphysical style of John Donne and others.
R. 41; W. 41

TIMES, THE; *LONDON TIMES*

The Times of *London started on 1 January 1785, as *The Daily Universal Register*, a publicity outlet for its publisher, John Walter. It became *The Times* on 1 January 1788, and Walter used it so openly to criticize authority that he was repeatedly fined or imprisoned in *Newgate. Under the aegis of his son, John Walter II, after 1803, with improvements in news transmission and in printing, *The Times* grew in circulation, in size, and in respectability, so that by the mid-nineteenth century its influence was great and its competition faltered. Editor from 1817 to 1841 was Thomas Barnes; from 1841-77, John Thaddeus Delane (followed by Thomas Chenery and G.E. Buckle).

(In 1981, *The Times* came under control of Rupert Murdoch.)
R. 46; R. 51

TIMON; TIMONISM; TIMONIZED

The original Timon was a misanthrope in *Athens about the time of the *Peloponnesian Wars. He is mentioned in *Lucian's *Timon*, *Plutarch's *Life of Antony*, and Diogenes Laertius's *Lives of the Philosophers*. M.'s allusions are to *Shakespeare's portrayal in *The Life of Timon of Athens*, in which Timon goes to live alone in a cave, hating all men when his friends have abandoned him after he used all his money on them. His tomb by the sea bears on epitaph expressing hatred of all mankind:

> Here lies a wretched corse, of
>   wretched soul bereft:
> Seek not my name: a plague consume
>   you wicked caitiffs left!
> Here lie I, Timon; who, alive,
>   all living men did hate:
> Pass by and curse thy fill; but
>   pass and stay not here thy gait (V, iv, 70-73).

See also "Apemantus' dog."
M. 13; P. 17:3; C.M. 3; C.M. 24; C.M. 30; C.M. 42; C.M. 43

TIMOR

The largest and easternmost of the Lesser *Sundas is owned by Indonesia and *Portugal. It is located between the Savu and Banda Seas (N.) and Timor Sea (S.), 525 miles northwest of Darwin, *Australia (8°19'-10°22' S., 123°28'-127°18' E.). Timor is 300 miles long but only sixty miles wide at

its widest. It is an almost wholly mountainous area which has
been claimed variously by the Portuguese, the *Dutch, and the
*British. The border between its separately owned parts was
settled by a treaty of 1859.
M.D. 43; M.D. 87

TIMOR TOM
M.'s copy of *Beale's *Natural History of the Sperm
Whale* (Sealts # 52) underlines a reference to "Timor Jack," a
fighting whale. There are many references in other sources to
"Old Tom," "New Zealand Tom," etc.
M.D. 45

TIOR
See "Marquesans; Marquesas."
T. 4; T. 26; O. 81

TIRIDATES
Several *Parthian rulers were called by this name. The
reference in *W.* is probably to Tiridates III, a *Roman-
educated Magus who briefly reigned as king. *Pliny's *Natural
History* (XXX. vi. 16-17) says that Tiridates refused to cross the
sea to visit *Nero, it being sinful for *Magi to foul the ocean.
W. 91

TISBURY
A town on the northern coast of *Martha's Vineyard
(including Vineyard Haven Village), along with West Tisbury.
M.D. 27

TISTIG
A fictional character, perhaps inspired by a half-breed
squaw who prophesizes in *Joseph C. Hart's *Miriam Coffin, or
the Whale-Fishermen*.
M.D. 16; M.D. 19

TITAN; TITANIC; TITANISM
The primordial Titans, or Elder Gods, were one tribe of
the monstrous offspring of Heaven (Uranus) and Earth (Gaea,
or Ge). They became supreme because of their enormous size
and strength and were not purely destructive, but forceful and
lawless. *Hesiod's *Theogony* says there were twelve Titans.

Six were male (Oceanus, a river circling the earth; Colius; Crius; *Hyperion, father of the sun, moon, and dawn; Iapetus, father of Atlas and *Prometheus, and *Cronus, the most important). Six were female (Theia; Rhea; Themis, justice; *Mnemosyne, memory; *Phoebe; Tethys, wife of Ocean, who raised Hera).

Cronus (L. *Saturn) wounded his father, Heaven, for maltreating Heaven's children, becoming lord of the universe with his sister-queen, Rhea, the Roman *Ops. Cronus planned to devour Zeus (see "Jupiter" and "Jove"), who was to replace him, but Rhea tricked him into swallowing a stone. Zeus and his siblings made war against the Titans, dethroning Cronus who, as Saturn in Roman myth, went to Italy to start the Golden Age. In Greek myth the Titans are all finally hurled into *Tartarus and succeeded by the *Olympians.
M. 71; M.D. 86; M.D. 87; M.D. 127; P. 19:1; P. 25:3; P. 25:4; P. 25:5; I.P. 1; I.P. 22; C.M. 17

TITHE
        The word means "a tenth," in reference to a *Christian's obligation to give one tenth of his yearly income to the Church. The practice was voluntary in *Britain before the eighth century. "Great" tithes were those on major crops; "small" were those on lesser produce. An act of 1836 attempted to commute tithes to a single rent charge.

        Compulsory support of a religious institution was not original with Christians; the ancient *Hebrews had similar laws.
M.D. 44

TITICACA, LAKE
        The largest lake of *South America and the highest (c. 12,500 feet) large lake in the world, Lake Titicaca is located in southeastern *Peru and western *Bolivia. Titicaca Island, in the lake, is seven miles long and two miles wide; it is famous for its *Inca and pre-Inca ruins and is called Isla del Sol (Island of the Sun).
C.M. 1

TITLE PAGE
        See "My First Voyage."
R. 30

TITUS

Titus (A.D. 39-81) was son of the Roman emperor
*Vespasian, under whose rule his military career climaxed in
the capture of *Jerusalem (A.D. 70). He was made commander of the *praetorian guard, with tribunician power. His
popularity was tarnished by his relations with Berenice, sister
of Herod Agrippa II because the Romans wanted no marriage
with an Easterner for their prospective emperor, *Cleopatra
being fresh in their memory.

He was a popular ruler (79-81), attractive, cultivated,
and generous in private and in public works, and was deified
immediately upon his death. He was twice married and left
one daughter, Flavia Julia, who became mistress of Titus's
brother *Domitian, who is sometimes suspected in Titus's
death.

"Titus's amphitheater" is the Roman Colosseum, built
by Vespasian, Titus, and Domitian between 72 and 80. It is a
huge ellipse (about 620 by 510 feet) covering six acres. It seated
about 50,000 spectators and was built of concrete faced with
travertine marble, adorned with great sculptures.

Immediately upon Titus's death, Rome erected the Arch
of Titus, commemorating his triumph over Jerusalem.
M. 75

TIVOLI

Tivoli is situated in central *Italy, seventeen miles east-
northeast of *Rome. It is a picturesque area of olive groves and
waterfalls, with many ruins (from *Hadrian's time), a Temple
of Vesta, and the Villa d'Este.

M. visited Tivoli 20 March 1857. His journal comment,
"From *Tartarus to Tivoli," is cryptic, as is the reference to a
"Tivoli of wine" (M. 183).
M. 183

TOAD-STOOLS

Any fleshy, unbrella-shaped, spore-producing fungus or
mushroom considered poisonous.
M. 163

TOBY

M.'s "fictional" character in T. is based on Richard Tobias Greene (1819-1892), a *Buffalo house and sign painter who
announced in a local newspaper on 1 July 1846 that he was the
original. M. wrote to him and added "The Story of Toby" as a

sequel to subsequent editions. Greene later began a newspaper career.

M. grants Green a poetic name in his poem, "To Ned." T. Passim

TOKAY

The town of Tokaj, in modern *Hungary, has been renowned since the twelfth century for its Tokay wine, from grapes that thrive in the area of the fertile volcanic hills surrounding Mount Tokaj.
M. 84; W. 14; C.M. 24

TOLEDO

The capital of Toledo province of central *Spain, in New Castile, on the right bank of the *Tagus River, is forty miles south-southwest of *Madrid. Its medieval and *Moorish character make it architecturally important, as does its (continuing) manufacture of steel swords and other metal items. Toledo was settled by the *Romans, occupied by the Visogoths and Moors. It was the Spanish capital until 1561 and was occupied by the *French 1808-14.
M. 32

TOLLAND COUNTY

A manufacturing and agricultural area of northeastern *Connecticut, on the *Massachusetts border. Once part of *Pequod Indian holdings, it was constituted as a county in 1785.

If M.D.'s "*Pip" is from Tolland, he is a free person of color; if he is from *Alabama, he is not.

(The city of Tolland is on the Willimantic River, eighteen miles northeast of Hartford; founded 1715.)
M.D. 93; M.D. 99

TOM; TOMMO; TOMMA; TOMME

M.'s protagonist in T. is probably named for his cousin, Pierre François Henry Thomas Wilson Melville, called Thomas (1806-44). He entered the *Navy as *Midshipman in 1826, was with *Vincennes on its *Marquesas cruise, passing one day in the Typee valley. The manuscript journal of Thomas's commander, Captain William Bolton Finch, mentions the nobility and beauty of the Marquesans, sacrificial religious practices, and war between the natives of *Nukahiva (Taiohaë) Bay and the Typees (Taipis).
T. Passim

TOMBEZ
Tumbes is the northernmost department of *Peru; it was once an *Inca fortress and continued strategically important in the border conflict between Peru and Ecuador.
O. 51; W. 85

TOM BOWLING
See "Dibdin."
W. 3

TOMBS, THE
*New York City's "House of Justice" of M.'s time was The Tombs, built in 1838 at Leonard and Centre Streets, in *Manhattan. The nickname derived from the building's Egyptian-style architecture. It was constructed of white *Maine granite and stone retrieved from the demolished *bridewell near *City Hall. It cost $250,000 to build and remained, a dubious landmark, until 1902.

The Tombs was a quadrangle several stories high, with cells on the outer walls, courtrooms, and a yard with a gallows. Most of the cells were small and lit by slits in the wall through which prisoners were unable to see. There were separate prisons for men, women, and boys, as well as a busy "Bummers' Cell," where 200 alcoholic rowdies (including many sailors) would be detained on Saturday nights; children and hardened criminals were intermixed here.

M.'s short story, "Bartleby the Scrivener," gives a sense of the despair prisoners felt in an institution where food standards were so poor as to necessitate prisoners' purchase of special meals. The *Catholic Sisters of Mercy maintained a chapel on the premises, but *Protestant services were held in a noisy bare room where ministers like automatons recited set pieces of liturgy.

"Resaca de la *Tombs*" (*C.M.* 19) means, literally, "dry river bed (or undertow) of the Tombs." M.'s use here may have ironic overtones. The Tombs was built on the site of the old "Collect": a resort-like lake where fishing and ice skating were pleasant pursuits until its filling in with earth, brick, and mortar, early in the nineteenth century.

The hapless "Pierre" is undoubtedly in The Tombs, in *P.* 26:6 and 26:7.
W. 73; C.M. 19

TOM COXE'S TRAVERSE
There are various methods of performing this action, all of them elaborate "*sogering" or loafing. *Dana's *Two Years Before the Mast* (xii) says "every man who has been three months at sea knows how to work 'Tom Cox's travers'—'three turns round the longboat, and a pull at the scuttled butt.'" Sailors say: "Up one hatchway and down another; in everybody's mess and nobody's watch." By modern times the term applied to work which brought trouble.
Also "Tom Sawyer's Traverse."
W. 73

TOM, DICK, AND HARRY
Signifying the common run of persons (from about 1815, with variations occurring before that time).
P. 17:3

TOM-FOOL
The origination is unclear. Defoe is supposed to have said "More know Tom Fool than Tom Fool knows." It is a sarcastic response to one failing to recognize a salutation.
O. 71

TOM LEGARE
The undoubtedly fictional member of the "Juvenile Total Abstinence Association" may owe his name to Hugh Swinton Legaré (1797-1843), lawyer, vehement orator, and Attorney-General under Tyler; he established the *Southern Review*.
R. 8

TOMPKINS, GOVERNOR
Daniel D. Tompkins (1774-1825) had an active public career that ended in partial disfavor. In 1803 he served as member of the New York State Assembly; elected to the House of Representatives in 1804, he resigned for State Supreme Court justiceship; from 1807 to 1817, he was governor of *New York; from 1817 to 1825, he was Vice President of the *United States under James Monroe.
Tomkins distinguished himself in the *War of 1812, equipping the New York State militia with money he personally borrowed. Later charged mistakenly with a large debt to New York State, he performed inadequately as Monroe's Vice President, dispirited by the unjust charges against him.
R. 7

TONGA ISLANDS
The Tonga (also called "Friendly") Islands cover 270 square miles of Oceania (18°50' S., 175°20' W.). The 150 coral and volcanic islands are divided into three groups: Tongatapu, Vavau, and Haapai. The natives are *Polynesian. The Tongas were discovered by the *Dutch in 1616; *Cook visited in 1773, naming them the Friendly Islands.
See also "Tongatabooarrs."
O. 69

TONGATABOOARRS
M.'s "Tongatabooarrs" are from the largest island of *Tonga, Tongatapu, which is the site of the islands' capital city, Nukualofa.
M.D. 6

TOPHET
*Jeremiah 7:31-32: "And they have built the high places of Topheth, which is in the valley of the son of Hinnom, to burn their sons and their daughters in the fire . . . the days come . . . that it shall no more be called Topheth . . . but the valley of Slaughter." Here, apostate *Israelites of Hinnom forced their children to walk through fire to *Moloch, committing blasphemy.
(See also Jeremiah 19:6, 11-14; 2 *Kings 23:10.) The connection with blackness probably comes from *Milton's *Paradise Lost* (I, 403-405): "Black Gehenna." (See also "Gehenna.")
R. 33; W. 44; W. 90; M.D. 2; M.D. 15; I.P. 21

TOP-LIGHTS
Large signal lanterns in the afterpart of a top. Colloquially, eyes.
W. 53

TORNADO, --ES
The name for the violent funnel-shaped column of air descending from a cumulonimbus cloud to destroy everything in its path evolved from a *Spanish word for "thunder." Tornadoes are common in *Australia and the central *United States (as "twisters," or "cyclones"). The *Cuban tornado of *M.D.* 119 is more commonly referred to as a "hurricane," in English. Tornadoes rotate clockwise in the Southern Hemisphere and counter-clockwise in the Northern.

Such storms at sea are referred to as "typhoons"; they are common in the western *Pacific and South *China Sea.
Passim

TORQUEMADA

See "Spanish Inquisition."
W. 70; C.M. 11

TORTUGA

Tortuga (Sp. "Turtle") Island, off northwestern Haiti, is twenty-three miles long, but only three miles wide, making it a perfect (and notorious) rendezvous spot for *French and *English *pirates of the seventeenth century.
M. 89

TORY; TORIES

The name "Tory" was first applied to seventeenth-century *Irishmen who became outlaws after having been ejected from their holdings by English settlers. It was next applied to *Catholic supporters of *James II, and thereafter to those who supported the British Crown in general, the Church, and Constitutional authority, as opposed to *Whigs, who sought more democratic government. The term was replaced in the mid-nineteenth century by "Conservative," with only ultra-rightists still described as "Tory."

There was no *American Tory party, but Tory policies might best be seen in beliefs of supporters of *Federalism.
Passim

TOUCAN

M.'s castigation of the dishonest tropical bird was almost certainly inspired by *Penny Cyclopaedia*'s findings (XIX) about its propensity to prey upon other animals. The article includes a long and gory description of a toucan's attacking and finally devouring a gold finch, after first stripping it of its feathers, ripping it to shreds, relishing choice morsels, later regurgitating all, and eating it again. The toucans, according to *PC* were wont to perch in high trees looking innocent, while in fact waiting for parent birds to leave their eggs and babies unguarded.

The Grand National Museum at *Rio de Janeiro had a large collection of "*Ramphastos Tucanus*," the toucan.

M. calls the bird "imperial" because the clothing of South American royal personages was decorated with its feathers. Since he was no more generous in his descriptions of royal human behavior, the analogy is clear.

*Rev. Stewart notes the attire of Pedro I, father of *Don Pedro II: "in place of the ermine in other regal attire, a deep cope of the bright yellow feathers of the toucan" rested on his costume of green, white, yellow, gold, and diamonds (p. 59).
W. 56; C.M. 24

TOWER
        See "Tower of London."
M.D. 55

TOWER ARMORIES
        Most famous is probably the *Tower of London, the oldest part of which (The White Tower) was built by *William the Conqueror on the site of *Julius Caesar's fort constructed to intimidate local inhabitants.
M. 32

TOWER-HILL
        Rising ground on the north bank of the *Thames River, site of the *Tower of London.
T. 25; M.D. 57

TOWER OF LONDON
        The Tower of London, begun in 1078 by William I (the *Conqueror), is really a series of fortress towers surrounding the central White Tower. Many additions and changes have been made throughout the centuries, leading to the present eighteen-acre, thirteen-tower irregular quadrangle surrounded by moats and the *Thames River. Its buildings have been a fortress, a palace, a prison, a Royal Mint, a repository for Public Records, a Royal Observatory, a Royal Menagerie, an arsenal, and a series of modern museums.
        The central White Tower (Great Tower, or Keep), the oldest, is one of the largest keeps in western Europe: at one time whitewashed inside and out.
        The Bloody Tower on the south, originally The Garden Tower, covers a gateway built by Henry III and called by its present name since the late sixteenth century, perhaps because of the suicide in 1585 of Henry *Percy, the Eighth Earl of Northumberland. It was also the scene of the murder of the boy princes (Edward V and the Duke of York) in 1483, as well

as the prison of *Sir Walter Raleigh, *Judge Jeffreys, *Cranmer, Laud, and others.

The thirteenth-century Byward Tower on the southeast is the gatehouse of the Outer Ward and the main entrance to the complex.

Traitor's Gate (*M.D.* 55) is the water gate leading from the Thames on the south, covered by St. Thomas's Tower. Through it passed most of the prisoners lodged in the complex.

The Tower played an important role in the lives (and deaths) of many people mentioned by M., who visited in 1849 and commented in his journal (10 November) on the weapons and the "headsman's block."

See also references under "London."
M.D. 42

TOWN HALL [LIVERPOOL]

*Liverpool's Town Hall was built at the northern tip of *Castle Street: a rectangular Corinthian building designed by John Wood. Badly damaged in the fire of 1795, it was rebuilt as the domed structure M. would have seen in 1839 or 1857, which is still extant.

There is a picture of the hall in *The Picture of Liverpool* . . . .
R. 30; R. 31

TOWN-HO

M.D. 54, "The Town-Ho's Story," was published separately, in *Harper's New Monthly Magazine* (October 1851), with many differences in spelling, punctuation, and wording.
M.D. 54

TOWNOR

Taunoa, *Tahiti; east of *Papeete harbor.
O. 38

TOWSER, BOWSER, ROWSER, SNOWSER

A "towzer" is a swindler; a "bowser" is a drinker; a "rouser" is one who breaks wind. "Israel" himself is perhaps the "Snowser": a deceiver.
I.P. 20

TRADE WINDS; TRADES

Continuous winds toward the doldrums of the *Equator, blowing from the southeast in the southern hemisphere and the northeast, in the northern. They are steady in direction and speed, especially over the ocean, lending confidence to the sailor, as noted in "Benito Cereno."
Passim

TRAFALGAR

Cape Trafalgar is a headland on the *Atlantic coast of southwestern *Spain's *Cádiz province, at the west entrance to the Strait of *Gibralter.

The Battle of Trafalgar was fought on 21 October 1805. None of the twenty-seven *British ships under *Nelson and *Collingwood was lost, but the allied *French and *Spanish fleet of thirty-three ships was decimated; some twenty surrendered, but only four survived battle damage and an ensuing storm. Nelson was killed on *Victory by a sniper's shot from *Redoutable. The British victory frustrated *Napoléon's plan to invade England and secured long-lasting naval supremacy for Great Britain.

The victory is generally credited to Nelson's innovative tactics. Rather than forming the traditional single line of ships to move ahead into battle, Nelson attacked in several columns, with responsibility delegated to second-in-command officers. Because sinking a wooden ship was very difficult, Nelson believed in placing a ship alongside an enemy's, with an eye to boarding.

M. probably knew J.M.W. Turner's painting, *The Battle of Trafalgar* (1806-08), usually called "The Death of Nelson."

See also "Santissima Trinidada."
O. 29; M. 28; R. 18; R. 38; W. 16; W. 17; W. 35; W. 50; W. 68; I.P. 25

TRAFALGAR [DOCK]

*Liverpool: originally, eleven and three-quarter acre water area; opened 1836, as an addition to *Clarence Dock, for steamship use.
R. 32

TRAFALGAR SQUARE

*London's Trafalgar Square, commemorating *Nelson's victory at the Battle of *Trafalgar, was laid out by Sir Charles Barry (1795-1860). The central column by *Sir Edwin Landseer (1802-1873), is over 170 feet high, and is topped by a seventeen-

foot high statue of the Admiral. Landseer also designed the
four lions surrounding the large fountain. Around the
Square's periphery are the National Gallery (1838), National
Portrait Gallery (1896), and St. Martin-in-the-Fields (1726). M.
lodged near the Square in 1849.
M.D. 35

TRAIN OIL
        Right-whale oil, used like *Macassar oil.
M.D. 25; M.D. 65

TRAITOR'S GATE
        See "Tower of London."
M.D. 55

TRAJAN'S COLUMNS
        The 125-foot-high column in *Rome honored Marcus
Ulpius Traianus (A.D. 53-117), Roman emperor from A.D. 98.
His military and administrative skills earned him the title, *Op-
timus*. The column, at the base of which Trajan is buried, depicts incidents from the Dacian wars, the last major conquests
extending Roman borders. There is a spiral staircase inside
the column, revealing its use as a lookout place.
T. 1

TRANQUE
        See "Tranquo."
M.D. 102; M.D. 103

TRANQUO
        M.'s fictional king of a fictional island of the *Arsacides
probably derives from Gaius *Suetonius Tranquillus, *Roman
historian, secretary to *Hadrian, friend to *Pliny, and author
of *Lives of the Caesars*, who flourished at the end of the first
and the beginning of the second centuries A.D.
        There is an island called Tranque off the coast of *Chile
(43° S., 73°30' W.).
M.D. 102

TRANSCENDENTAL; TRANSCENDENTALIST, --S
        Transcendentalism, the philosophic and literary move-
ment flourishing in *New England in the mid-nineteenth cen-

tury, is best represented in the works of *Emerson, Thoreau, and other Concord, *Massachusetts residents. A reaction against eighteenth-century rationalism and skepticism and against puritan religious strictures, transcendentalism had no set credo, nor indeed, a formal membership. Taking ideas from *Plato, from Oriental thinkers, from *German mystic philosophers, and from *English romantic writers, *American transcendental leanings were optimistic, democratic, action-oriented, and eclectic. Among the most important of American transcendental publications: Emerson's "Nature," urging man's acceptance of his natural environment; "Self-Reliance," stressing independence from received opinion; "The Over-Soul," positing a Godhead of which man and nature make a part. Thoreau's *Walden* records the quotidien existence of a devoted transcendentalist. *The Dial* magazine (1840-44) was an organ of the movement, publishing works of Margaret Fuller, Elizabeth Peabody (sister-in-law of *Hawthorne), Bronson Alcott, and others, as well as contributions from members of a large fringe group. The Brook Farm and Fruitlands communes were experiments; Hawthorne's participation at the former probably helped move him from transcendental pilgrim to nay-sayer.

M.'s position on transcendentalist ideas was wavering but finally more negative than positive because of the danger he perceived in the almost unqualified optimism and the limited vision of otherwise brilliant thinkers.

P. 18:1; P. 20:2; C.M. 36

TRANSIT OF VENUS

The passage of the planet *Venus across the disc of the Sun.

*Captain Cook observed the Transit of Venus in *Tahiti, in 1769. Observations were to become a foundation for calculations which would determine the distance of the earth from the sun. The 1761 observations had been unsuccessful, and there was to be no other opportunity until 1874.

M. 179; O. 18; P. 2:5

TRANSYLVANIA

The name of the historic province of central Rumania is *Latin for "beyond the woods." The area was part of the Roman Dacia, established A.D. 107 by *Trajan. It was overrun by various tribes in the third century, was under *Hungarian rule by the eleventh, and was invaded by *Mongols and *Turks in the thirteenth. The seventeenth century was Transylvania's "Golden Age," with *Viennese rule and *Protestantism flour-

ishing. It was proclaimed a principality in 1765, was under the Hapsburgs from 1848 to 1851, but by 1867 was again part of Hungary.
R. 33

TREASURY; SECRETARY OF THE TREASURY

One of the first cabinet-level departments created during *Washington's *Presidency was the Treasury. As first Secretary of the Treasury, 1789-95, Alexander Hamilton amassed great power, which carried down with the position. Hamilton's policies established the *United States as a nation of manufacturers rather than agriculturalists (as *Jefferson would have preferred). The Treasury Department creates and recommends financial, tax, and fiscal policies, acts as financial agent for the government, manufactures coins and currency, and enforces laws: in a capitalistic nation, among the most important aspects of existence.

M. applied for a Treasury Department position in *Washington, in 1847. His efforts to secure government positions do not seem to have been whole-hearted. (See "Democrat, --ic.)
W. 44; W. 48

TREATISE UPON GUN-SHOT WOUNDS

See "Guthrie."
W. 63

TREES OF LIFE

The Tree of Life is first mentioned in *Genesis (1:9) as being planted in the Garden of *Eden, along with the tree of knowledge forbidden to *Adam and Eve: "And out of the ground made *Jehovah *God to grow every tree that is pleasant to the sight and good for food; the tree of life also in the midst of the garden, and the tree of the knowledge of good and evil." When Adam and Eve violate the latter tree, God ejects them from the Garden lest they partake of the tree of life as well, and become able to live forever (Gen. 3:22). In *Ezekiel (47:1-12) and *Revelation (2:7) the tree takes on new characteristics (perhaps more to the point in M.'s use of the reference in *M.*); it bears different fruit every month of the year, and is a symbol of fertility and fecundity. In Revelation (2:7) its fruit is promised to the faithful, representing eternal life. In general, the tree of life represents nourishment, healing, and immortal life.

Tree of life is sometimes another name for Tree of Knowledge, although, in *O.*, M. undoubtedly means that the bread-fruit tree is literally what sustains life in *Polynesia.
O. 69; M. 107

TRELAWNEY

When *Shelley drowned on the *Italian coast in 1822, Edward John Trelawney (1792-1881), writer and traveler, cremated his body, with the help of *Byron and Leigh Hunt. He later claimed he had snatched Shelley's heart from the flames.

Trelawney composed the epitaph for Shelley's grave in *Rome (near that of his friend, Keats). It is quoted in *Penny Cyclopaedia* (XXI, 1842):

> Percy Bysshe Shelley
>   Cor Corduum
> Natus IV Aug. MDCCXCII
> Obiit VIII Jul. MDCCCXXII
>
> (Nothing of him that doth fade
> But suffer a sea-change
> Into something rich and strange.)

> (*Tempest*)

(The verse is "*Ariel's" song, I, ii, 100-103.)
W. 65

TREMENDOUS, THE

Tremendous was a seventy-four-gun *British ship present at the battle of the "Glorious First of June," 1794, when Lord *Howe's *Channel fleet defeated a *French fleet.
M. 28

TRENCK'S MOUSE

Baron Friedrich von der Trenck (1726-94) tamed a mouse while in prison.
O. 10

TRENTON

The capital city of *New Jersey is in the western part of the state, on the Delaware River, thirty miles above Camden. It was settled by *Quakers in 1679 and was the site of much

*Revolutionary activity, including the 1776 battle of Trenton and *Washington's crossing of the Delaware (c. eight miles north). Trenton became the state capital in 1790 (incorporated as a city in 1792) and by the middle of the nineteenth century was an important industrial area.
I.P. 25

TREPANS
    In *M.*, "Krako," the "god of Trepans" has a cracked cocoanut for a head. The word "Trepan" is often wrongly used to represent the skull, but M. probably made capital of its real meaning: a surgical saw used at the time for sawing out pieces of bone, especially of the skull; to "trepan" is to cut out bone. Another "trepan" was used for boring shafts. In thieves' slang, a trepan is a person who traps or decoys, or the act of entrapment itself (*OED*).
M. 140

TRINITY
    See "Christ . . . . "
M.D. 99

TRISTRAM SHANDY
    The Life and Opinions of Tristram Shandy (1759-67) was written by Laurence Sterne (1713-68). It is considered a forerunner of modern novels in its self-conscious narrator, distortion of time, digression from plot, and erratic typography, all of which combine to provide an amusing if confusing novel. The serialized book inspired numerous forgeries and imitations.
    Sealts number 490 is an unidentified edition which M. is known to have begun reading for the first time in *London, 16 December 1849.
I.P. 13

TRITON
    In Greek and Roman mythology, the son of Poseidon and *Amphitrite or of *Neptune and Salacia. In art, usually a bearded man with the hindquarters of a fish, holding a trident and a shell-trumpet. "Triton" often refers to a strong seaman or a large ship: "A Triton among the minnows."
O. 11; W. 8; W. 39; W. 52; W. 74

TRIUMPHANT, THE
The *French frigate, *La Triomphante*, made part of the squadron with *La Reine Blanche* at *Nukuheva in 1842.
M. 28

TROCHANTER, GREATER AND LESSER
See *"femur."*
W. 62

TROGLODYTES; TROGLODITES
Prehistoric or ancient (Ethiopian, Syrian, or Arabian) cave dwellers. From the Greek words for "hole" and "go into." From the mid-nineteenth century, the word was used figuratively for a hermit living in seclusion or for a degraded person. One of M.'s favorite words, he used it in both figurative senses.
M. 75; W. 3; W. 12; W. 30 and elsewhere

TROPHONIUS
Trophonius was builder of the temple of *Apollo at *Delphi. Deified after his death, his oracle was located in a cave near Lebadeia, Boeotia, where those who consulted never smiled again. A chronically melancholy person was said to have "visited the cave of Trophonius."
M. 75

TROPIC OF CANCER
C. 23 1/2° north latitude.
O. 67; R. 34

TROPIC OF CAPRICORN
C. 23 1/2° south latitude.
M. 1; W. 65

TROY; TROJAN
The ancient (third millenium B.C.) Phrygian city (also called Ilium) near Mt. Ida, at the strategic southern entrance to the *Hellespont (Dardanelles, in modern *Turkey), has a lengthy mythical history. A group of tribes called Trojans defended their walled city (said to be the work of *Apollo and Poseidon) during a war with *Greece of confused mythological origin. The most picturesque legend has the handsome young Trojan prince Paris abducting *Helen, the beautiful wife of

Menelaüs. The most celebrated account of a part of the war is the *Iliad*; Appollodorus ("Epitome" 3-5) summarizes its main events.

*Priam, Troy's most important king, was defeated by *Agamemnon. Descendents of the most famous Trojan, *Aeneas, are said to have founded *Rome.

The Trojan war also figures in the *Odyssey* and in numerous medieval tales.

For the story of the Trojan horse, see "Laöcoon."
M. 39; M. 149; W. 51; P. 7:6

"TRUE YANKEE SAILOR"
        See "Dibdin."
W. 23

TRY POTS
        The inn is named for the large pots used for boiling or "trying out" oil from whale blubber.
M.D. 15

TSAR (CZAR)
        *Russia was for centuries a multi-national state before becoming a sovereign tsardom in 1480 and an empire in 1721. Russian history leading to the period of the tsars, whom M. always pictures as cruel despots, is of continual losing struggle of the various peoples against maltreatment. In the period immediately preceding the tsardom, there were areas of republicanism, with a developing aristocracy of wealthy capitalists. But in Central Russia, rulers became increasingly powerful, although subject to Tatar (see "Tartar") domination. The Tatars eventually helped Russian princes accumulate wealth, which led to their defeating the Tatars and calling themselves rulers "of all Russia," expanding her boundaries by the fifteenth century, with the problematic help of the Orthodox Church.

        Ivan IV (The Terrible; r. 1547-84), was first Tsar of the integrated Russian state, claiming divine right, breaking up the old aristocracy and the Church. Despite many improvements, he was strongly opposed and in retaliation made his own power absolute; he was free to pardon or condemn at will, destroying dissenters and separatists. When Ivan's son failed as Tsar, his son-in-law, Boris Godunov, continued and extended Ivan's policies and eventually had himself elected, establishing a force that held up against massive resistance. The Romanov dynasty which followed, leading to the Empire under Peter the Great (*I.P.* 16), was initially rather conservative, and by the eighteenth century, the only real displeasure lay with the peasants. In Peter's three-decade rule, Russia became militarily great, and peasant uprisings were contained. After Peter, who labored in the British Royal Navy Yard, court life flourished.

The initially liberal Catherine II The Great sought foreign respect and pursued an ambitious annexation policy and what has been called legislative mania, creating more regular courts and offices, eventually completely favoring the gentry and further alienating peasants in her reaction to the *French Revolution. Her son, Paul I, gave the peasants into serfdom, but so displeased the powerful that he was assassinated. The reign of Alexander I, Paul's son, was marked by wars and *Napoléon's 1812 invasion. Alexander was also initially liberal, attempting to undo some of the policies of his predecessors; some serfs were liberated, and public education was promoted. A resented early alliance with Napoléon had increased nationalism, and the situation was exacerbated by the Grand Army's retreat in the *Napoleonic wars.

Although the world saw Alexander as eventual savior of Europe, internal feelings were the reverse, and a period of reaction was beginning as Nicholas I (the "Iron Czar"), a martinet, ascended the throne in 1825, while idealist/students of Schelling, Fichte, and Hegel originated Russian socialism. Intellectuals were persecuted, universities were purged, and Nicholas, who saw himself as divinely inspired, sought to seize all of Europe with his famous manifesto: "Submit yourselves, ye peoples, for God is with us." His weak son, Alexander II, lost ground for the aristocracy by the 1861 emancipation of the serfs, leading to revolutionary movements which eventually culminated in the 1916 assassination of Nicholas II, the end of the Romanov dynasty, and the start of the Russian Revolution.

The Tsar's "Ice Palace," torch-illuminated, was built annually in *St. Petersburg.
M. 181; R. 52; R. 60; W. 6; W. 35; M.D. 2; M.D. 12; M.D. 89; P. 17:2; I.P. 10

TUCKER, ABRAHAM

Tucker (1705-74) was an early *English moralist *utilitarian writer who believed in the coincidence of self-satisfaction with the public good. His great work was *The Light of Nature Pursued* (six volumes: 1768-78). M. presented an inscribed copy to Richard Lathers, who recalled M., his relative by marriage, in *Reminiscences of Richard Lathers*.
P. 21:3

TUDOR

The *Welsh Tudor family rose from thirteenth-century royal stewards to rulers of *England from 1485 to 1603. Tudors became titled as a result of Owen Tudor's (1400-1461) fathering of five children by Catherine of *Valois, widow of the Lancastrian *King Henry V (1387-1422) and mother of Henry VI (1421-1471), who ruled from 1422 to 1461 and 1470 to 1471. Owen's grandson, the last male of Lancastrian descent at the time, became the first Tudor monarch, Henry VII (1457-1509), king from 1485. His second son became *Henry VIII (1491-1547), ruler from 1509 and father of three monarchs. By Jane Seymour, Henry was father of Edward VI (1537-53), king from 1547; by Catherine of Aragon, Mary I (1516-58) (see "Mary, Bloody"), Queen from 1553 to 58; by Anne Boleyn, *Elizabeth I (1533-1603), Queen from 1558, and the last Tudor monarch before the rise of the *Stuarts.
M. 75; M.D. 101

TUILLERIES; TUILERIES

In *Paris, *France, a public garden on the site (between the *Louvre and Place de la Concorde) of a palace burned down in 1871.

M. probably saw the palace in November or December of 1849.
O. 32; M.D. 104; M.D. 105; M.D. Extracts 7

TUN

Two-hundred-and-fifty-gallon cask.
See also "Heidelburgh Tun."
M.D. 16; M.D. 78

TUNICATA

Solitary or colonial sea chordates enclosed by a thick tunic-like sac: sea squirts and stockfish.
M. 163

TURK, --S; TURKEY; TURKISH

Modern-day Turkey has two separate sections, in southeastern Europe and Asia Minor. The European (western) sector is set off by the *Dardanelles, the *Sea of Marmora, and the *Bosporus, linking the *Black Sea with the Aegean (of the *Mediterranean); it borders on Bulgaria and *Greece. The (larger) eastern segment borders on the U.S.S.R., Iran, Iraq, and *Syria.

The Ottomans were the original (central *Asian) ancestors of the Turks; the *Hittites are known to have settled in the
area from c. 2000 to 1200 B.C. The *Ottoman Empire Sultanate
(*W*. 75; *M.D.* 88; *I.P.* 21), established in the thirteenth century
A.D., was heir to the *Byzantine Empire; at its zenith it held
the Balkans and southeastern Europe as far as *Vienna, and
the near east including present-day Syria, *Lebanon,
*Palestine, *Arabia, and parts of north *Africa, including
*Egypt. The Ottomans established Tripolitania, Tunis, and
*Algeria. The Empire declined after the eighteenth century
but was not finally ended until after World War II. It was opposed by many nationalist movements during the nineteenth
century.

Finkelstein points out the importance of M.'s reading to
his knowledge of Turkey, especially Thomas Hope's *Anastasius* and the multitude of materials on "*Solyman,"
"*Bajazet," and the *Mamelukes; she discusses irregular
spellings and usages traceable to sources such as *Thèvenot.
The near east was an important topic in the nineteenth century, with the weakening of the Ottoman Empire and European competition for eastern trade routes.

M. was in Turkey from 10 to 23 December 1856. His detailed journal (6 December) calls Salonica, Greece, "a walled
town on a hill side," with "minarets and cypress trees the most
conspicuous objects . . . . Turkish men of war in harbor." He
discusses the *mosques built by Greeks and changed by the
conquering Turks, as well as various ruins, and the "filthy"
bazaar: "aspect of streets like those of Five Points. Rotten
houses. Smell of rotten Wood." He was highly interested in
the people—Turks and those displaced of all nations, as well as
veiled harem women. On 10 December, from the Dardanelles
(ancient *Hellespont, near Ilium, the ancient *Troy), Asia
seemed, at his first glimpse of it, "a sort of used up—superannuated . . . . The sail up the Helespont [sic] is upon the whole
a very fine one. But I could not get up much enthusiasm;
though passing *Xerxes' bridge-piers . . . & the mouth of the
Granicus" [site of a victory of *Alexander the Great]. A thick
fog on the Sea of Marmora obscured his first view (12 December) of *Constantinople, Seraglio Point, and the Golden Horn.
He crossed to "Tophanna" (Top-Khaneh, on the Bosporus
shore), complaining of staying in at night for fear of assassins,
but he saw all of the tourist attractions, commenting at length
especially on the mosque of "*Solyman." He crossed to Stamboul (from which "Istanbul" is derived) on 14 December to observe the city walls, which seemed to him "the inexorable bar
between the mansions of the living and the dungeons of the
dead." He passed under an arch of the aqueduct of *Valens,
arrived at Pera (modern Beyoglu) too late to see the *Dervishes,

and was haunted "horribly" by the grief of a woman over a new grave. He was impressed by the beauty of the people, especially the women, with faces "which in *England or *America would be a cynosure in a ball room," despite the wretchedness of their houses and filth of their streets. He took a steamer up the Bosporus to Galata, praising the trip and the city and became bolder in walking about alone. He visited Scutari (üsküdar) and departed 19 December for *Smyrna (Izmir), leaving Turkey 23 December, having exhibited in his journal a kind of fascinated disgust with the juxtapositon of beauty and ugliness of the nation.

The "grand Turk" referred to in *M*. 20 is Ottoman Sultan Mohammed IV (ruled 1648-87), who succeeded as a minor. His Sultanate was marked by aggression in an attempt to restore the diminishing power of the Empire. *Austria was a major target, especially of Kara Mustafa, his ambitious grand vizier (see "Mustapha, Vizier"), whose loss of Vienna marked the beginning of the decline of the Ottoman Empire.

The "Turkish Mosque" honoring *Jonah, in *M.D.* 83, must be one *Bayle describes in a Turkish village of the tribe of Zabulon, which contains a lamp that burns continuously without oil. *Harris's *Voyages* places it "half a league from *Tigris," near *Nineveh. The lavishly decorated shrine is also mentioned in *Hakluyt.

The "Turkish seraglio" of *T*. 26 is the former Palace of the Sultans at Constantinople, on the Golden Horn, enclosed by walls. Chief entrance is the Sublime Gate; chief building is the Harem ("sacred" or "forbidden" spot), containing separate houses for the Sultan's wives and concubines—off limits to strangers. ("Seraglio" is the Italian word for "enclosure.")

The "Turkish code" of *W*. 71 is any violent, imperialistic, intolerant code with out-dated, sporadically enforced military service for an indefinite period.

Many of M.'s references are pejorative. Since the time of the Ottoman Empire inception, "Turk" has been an epithet signifying a barbarous and cruel person. It was in common use in the nineteenth century to designate an ill-natured and boorish person, or an unruly child.

For "Muezzin" (*M.D.* 78), see "mosque." See also "Beards"; "Emir"; "Euphrates"; "Mount Ararat"; "Navarino"; "Pergamum"; "Smyrna"; "Tarsus."
Passim; most important references are: T. 26; O. 68; M. 13; M. 20; M. 97; M. 149; R. 21; R. 35; R. 50; R. 58; W. 22; W. 31; W. 65; W. 69; W. 71; W. 74; W. 75; W. 78; W. 85; M.D. 41; M.D. 75; M.D. 78; M.D. 83; M.D. 88; M.D. 89; M.D. 92; M.D. 96; M.D. 133; M.D. 135; P. 2:2; I.P. 15; I.P. 21; C.M. 7

TURNBULL

John Turnbull, author of *A Voyage round the World, in the years 1800-1804,* visited *Tahiti in 1803. He said that the *London Society of Missionaries had not been successful in converting the natives and that indeed their morals had suffered as a result of the effort, simple charity yielding to selfish cleverness on their part.
O. 48

TURTLE REEF

If M's "Mondoldo" is a fiction in *M.,* then probably "Turtle Reef" is, as well. Although I have learned of Turtle bays, creeks, fords, islands, lakes, mountains, and rivers, I have been unable to trace Turtle Reef. If such did exist, it would probably be off the Turtle Islands of Sulu (*Sooloo) or of Sierra Leone, western *Africa. Or Turtle Reef might be a play on *Tortuga, (*M.* 89).
M. 99

TUSCAN

The Tuscany region of central Italy includes the capital, *Florence, as well as *Pisa, *Elba, and the Arno River. The area includes part of ancient *Etruria. The *Romans entered in the third century B.C. Tuscany later became a *Lombard duchy. It was tremendously important in the Renaissance (see "Revival of Learning"), especially to the "cool" policy of *Machiavelli (*P.* 15:1).

M. visited Tuscany in March of 1857.
P. 15:1

TUSCULAN DISPUTATIONS

See "Cicero, Marcus Tullius."
C.M. 22

TWENTY MILLIONS OF FREEMEN

U.S. population, according to offical census, was: in 1840—17,069,453 (with 6,100 serving on ships); in 1850—23,191,876 (including *Texas, *California, New Mexico, *Utah, Washington, *Oregon, and other acquisitions.
W. 40

"TWIGGING"
Appreciating, or understanding; from the *Irish *tuigim*: "I understand."
O. 37; M.D. 99

TWO AND TWO
*Genesis 7:9: "There went in two and two unto *Noah into the ark, the male and the female, as *God has commanded Noah."
M.D. 1

TWO SICILIES
M. could have read much about the Kingdom of the Two Sicilies in *Penny Cyclopaedia*, which abounds in references, including a long history (XXI). "Two Sicilies" refers to *Naples and the Mainland and to *Sicily, the kingdom proclaimed in 1816. Territory consisted of some 45,000 square miles, with close to eight million inhabitants by 1838. It was part of Philip II's inheritance at the abdication of his father, *Charles V.
W. 4

"TWO YEARS BEFORE THE MAST"
See "Dana's."
W. 24

TYBURN; TYBURN-TREES
The gallows. Tyburn was the place of public execution for *Middlesex, *England, until 1783. One who "preaches at Tyburn cross" is hanged.
W. 90; I.P. 22

TYERMAN
Daniel Tyerman (1773-1828), Congregationalist minister, was appointed by the *London Missionary Society to visit worldwide missions, in 1821. His associate was George Bennet (-t?), about whom little is known other than his residence: *Sheffield. The two sailed on the whaler *Tuscan* around Cape *Horn to *Tahiti, and the Leeward and *Sandwich Islands. In 1824, Tyerman traveled to *New South Wales through the *Torres Straits, to *Java, *Singapore, *Canton, *Calcutta, *Madras, and *Goa; in 1827 he visited Mauritius and *Madagascar. *Journal of Voyages and Travels by Tyerman*

and Bennet was first published by James Montgomery (London, 1831) the second edition appeared in 1841. The American edition (Boston) was published in 1832.

See also "Extracts" 65; "Montgomery's World before the Flood."
O. 49; M.D. Extracts 65

TYLER, WAT
Walter Tyler (d. 1381), an unattached soldier, led the 1381 English peasants' revolt against high taxation during the reign of *King Richard II. Tyler refused Richard's concessions, leading an anarchic mob through *London to St. Bartholomew's Hospital, where he was apprehended. He was beheaded at *Smithfield after "Tyler's Insurrection."
R. 24

TYPEE
The original *English title of this novel was *Narrative of a Four Months' Residence among the Natives of a Valley of the *Marquesas Islands; or, A Peep at *Polynesian Life.* The full title of the *American first edition was *Typee: A Peep at Polynesian Life. During a Four Months' Residence in a Valley of the Marquesas with Notices of the *French Occupation of *Tahiti and the Provisional Cession of the Sandwich Islands to *Lord Paulet.*

(M. is known to have been on the island for only about one month.)
T. Title page; O. Introduction

TYPEES
See "Marquesas; Marquesans."
T. Passim

TYPHOON, --S
See "Tornado, --es."
Passim (especially in M.D.)

TYRE
The peninsular seaport of Tyre (originally an island) in ancient *Phoenicia (modern *Lebanon) was an important trade center in ancient times. Its history is of great commercial success which drew various conquerors. In the fifteenth century, it was ruled by *Egypt; in the ninth century, Tyre

founded *Carthage; by the sixth century B.C., it was under
*Babylonian rule, then *Persian.

Tyrian *Baal was the religion of *Jezebel, and Tyre is
frequently mentioned in the Bible; *Jesus and *Paul were
there.

The siege of *Alexander the Great occurred in 332 B.C.
After the defeat of Darius III, Alexander demanded that
Phoenician cities surrender. Tyre refused and was besieged
for seven months and eventually demolished through Alexander's importation of great fleets and construction of elaborate
armed piers and towers from local rubble. Alexander might
have starved Tyre; instead he impatiently slaughtered 8,000 citizens, executed 2,000 and sold 30,000 into slavery.

The city later passed to the rule of the Seleucids and the
*Romans, under whose domain it became a center of the silk
trade and source of Tyrian purple dye, manufactured from local snails. By the second century A.D., it was a bishopric, the
grave site of *Origen. In the seventh century it was captured
by *Moslems, in the twelfth by the *Crusaders, in the thirteenth by Moslems again, at which time it was destroyed.
Modern Tyre is a small town, seemingly of no particular importance.
M. 97; W. 50; M.D. 2; P. 7:4

TYROL, THE
The beautiful *Bavarian Alpine province of western
*Austria is bordered by *Germany (N.), Salzburg and
Carinthia (E.), Italy (S.), and Vorarlberg (W.). It was a part of
the ancient *Rhaetia. The *Romans entered in 15 B.C. and the
Teuton invaders in the sixth century A.D. It was under Haps-
burg control from 1363, and although *Napoléon tampered
with its borders in the early nineteenth century, the *Congress
of Vienna (1815) restored the area to Austria.
W. 90

U

ULNA
Ulna is the bone of the forearm on the side opposite the
thumb (or the corresponding bone in the forelimb of other ver-
tebrates).

The Ulna, with the clavicle or collarbone, is not found on
the skull and crossbones, as M. has it in *M*.
M. 139

ULTRAMARINE
        See "lapis lazuli."
P. 2:5

ULYSSES
        Roman Ulixes, the equivalent of the Greek Odysseus, king of Ithaca, whose adventures after the *Trojan war comprise *Homer's *Odyssey*. He is husband of Penelope, father of Telemachus and others by *Circe and Calypso, inventor of the Trojan horse. Homer includes him also in the *Iliad*. Other writers see him variously as an unscrupulous adventurer or as a wise pilgrim/statesman.
        Sealts #s 277 and 278 are   *Chapman's *Iliad* and *Odyssey*.
W. 4; W. 24; W. 65

UNBEGOTTEN
        "The Father is made of none: neither created, nor begotten": *Athanasian Creed, in Anglican *Book of Common Prayer*.
M.D. 119

UNICAL HYPOSTASES
        The Hypostatic Union is the union of the three Persons in the Christian *Trinity and the union of the Divine and the Human in *Christ, in which elements retain their distinctness despite inseparable unity (Gr.: *hypo*, under; *stasis*, standing).
M. 170

UNICORN, --ISM
        The mythical animal on the *British coat of arms was represented by medieval writers as having the legs of a buck, tail of a lion, head and body of a horse, and a single red, white, and black horn. The body is white and the head red. The Unicorn could only be captured using a virgin as lure and became a symbol of *Christ.
        The old royal arms of *Scotland had two Unicorns, one of which James VI brought to the English coat of arms in 1603, supplanting the Red Dragon that represented *Wales, and joining the English lion on the coat.
R. 28; M.D. 32

UNION
M. is perhaps in error regarding the sinking of *Union* after collision with a whale in 1807. Details were available in *Obed Macy's *History of Nantucket* (Sealts #345, acquired after writing of *M.D.*), as well as in *Cheever and *Olmsted.
M.D. 45

UNION, THE
See "America . . . . "
Passim

UNITED STATES
"Neversink" was a readily decipherable pseudonym for the frigate *United States*. Launched in 1797, along with *Constitution* ("Old Ironsides"), the ship was destroyed with other Federal ships in *Norfolk Navy Yard, 20 April 1861, to prevent their falling into Confederate hands.
Designed by Josiah Humphreys, *United States* was 175 feet long, with a forty-three and one-half-foot beam and depth-hold of fourteen and one-half feet. Her highest moment occurred in her defeat of the *British ship *Macedonian*, 12 October 1812.
M. signed on *United States* at *Oahu, 17 August 1843, enlisting in the *Navy for three years or for the cruise. The ship's journal shows that M. witnessed *floggings the day after he signed on. Soon after, he heard the first monthly reading of the *Articles of War, witnessed a sea-burial, and the near-drowning of the cooper. *"Commodore J___," Thomas ap Catesby Jones, was aboard for part of the cruise, which touched on or passed the *Marquesas, *Tahiti, *Masafuera, *Juan Fernandez Island, *Valparaiso, *Callao, *Lima, *Mazatlan, Cape *Horn, *Rio de Janeiro, *Cape Cod, *Boston. M. was discharged 14 October 1844. The crew had included many greenhorns, so that ceremonies such as that of crossing the *Equator were foregone on *United States*.
See also "Captain Claret"; "Chase, Jack"; "The Old Wagon Paid Off."
W. Note

UNITED STATES
See "America . . . . "
Passim

UNITED STATES STATUTE BOOK; UNITED STATES STATUTES AT LARGE; AMERICAN STATUTE BOOK
The United States Statutes at Large is the precisely worded collection of statutes (signed by the *President or passed over his veto) passed by a particular *Congress and printed in order of passage.
W. 34; W. 44; W. 71

UNIVERSITY EDITION
See "Blair's Lectures."
W. 41

UNTAGGING THE POINTS OF HIS HOSE
In sixteenth- and seventeenth-century men's costume, loosening the laces fastening hose to the doublet.
M.D. 102

UPAS
The Javanese *Antiaris toxicarie* has poisonous juice used for tipping arrows. Legend holds that mere vapors from the tree can kill, that men or beasts who linger even within miles of the tree succumb.
Figuratively: any pernicious influence.
M. 192

UPOLUA, --N
Upolua is in what is now called Western *Samoa. It is a large (435 square miles) mountainous island with little level land.
M. Passim

UPPER MISSISSIPPI
See "Mississippi."
M.D. 68

URAL
The Ural mountains of modern U.S.S.R. (see "Russia") mark the border between Europe and Asia. They run north-south for 1,300 miles, from the *Arctic Ocean to the bend of the Ural River. Top elevation is c. 6,000 feet.
W. 50

URIM AND THUMMIN

Mysterious sacred lots on the breast-plates of *Hebrew high priests for divination to ascertain *God's will. They mean "light" and "perfection" and were probably jewels or stones (in *Exodus 28:30 and elsewhere in *Old Testament).
O. 8

"URQUHARTIAN CLUB"

P.'s fictional club, a parody of groups such as the modern Melville Society, probably honors Sir Thomas Urquhart (1611-1660), playful *Scottish author, linguist, and mathematician. He wrote undistinguished verse, impenetrable mathematical treatises using fantastic mnemonic devices, and a classic translation of the works of *Rabelais, as well as a "Vindication of the Honour of *Scotland," containing the story of the "Admirable Crichton." In 1834, his works were edited for the Maitland club.
See also "lecture"; "Literary and Scientific Societies."
P. 17:2

USHANT

M.'s fictional hero of the "massacre of the *Beards" is named for a small rocky island (Fr. Ouessant) twelve miles off the coast of Brittany: the scene of an indecisive battle related to the *American Revolution. On 27 July 1778, the forces of British Admiral Augustus Keppel met those of the *French Admiral d'Orvilliers and took no prizes. The French fleet thus kept their *British counterparts occupied, enabling *John Paul Jones to make raids on British coastal shipping.
W. Passim

U.S. EXPLORING EXPEDITION; U.S. EX. EX.

See "Wilkes"; "Extracts" 71.
O. 49; O. 54; M.D. Extracts 71

USHER

An assistant schoolmaster (derogatory). M. taught in the Sykes District, Richmond, *Massachusetts, 1837-38, and in Greenbush, New York, 1839-40.
M.D. Etymology

UTAH

The present state of Utah is bounded by Nevada (W.), Idaho (N.), Wyoming (N.E.), Colorado (E.), and Arizona (S.). The *Spanish explored the area in 1776, and from c. 1820 to 1840 it was a fur-trappers' post under *Mexican control. But it was not until Brigham Young (probably the "Green prophet" of *C.M.* 2) led his fellow *Mormons to Utah in July of 1847 that the area began permanent settlement, the capital, Salt Lake City, becoming established immediately.

Utah was ceded to the *United States in 1848 and organized in 1850 as a territory which the Mormons attempted to establish as the state of "Deseret." But *Congress refused recognition until the Mormon practice of polygamy was disavowed in 1890. Utah became the forty-fifth state in 1896.
C.M. 2

UTAMAI

The name remains untraced, but Utamai is perhaps one of the ambitious *Tahitian chiefs (along with *Kitoti) referred to by *Wilkes.
O. 32

UTILITARIANS

Utilitarianism became a central issue in nineteenth-century thought. In the eighteenth century, *Jeremy Bentham (1748-1832) named and developed the seventeenth-century theory of ethics that posits usefulness ("the greatest happiness for the greatest number") as man's most ethical aim. Contradicting the theories of the *French Revolution, he defended his ideas in *Principals of Morals and Legislation* (1789) and in the posthumously-published *Deontology* (1834). John Stuart Mill (1806-1873) interpreted Bentham's theory rather less hedonistically in *Utilitarianism* (1863). Dickens (see "Hard Times") and Carlyle, among others, attacked the ideas of the Utilitarians.
P. 18:1

UTOPIANISMS

"Utopia," a generic term derived from the works of Sir Thomas More, refers to an ideal or visionary community (Gr. *ou*, "not," and *topos*, "place"). Such communities have existed since ancient times, but they were much in evidence in *America during M.'s lifetime, following ideas of Robert Owen and *Charles Fourier. There was a thriving *Shaker commune near M.'s home in the *Berkshires, and secular Utopias flourishing elsewhere as well. In the 1840's, Brook Farm, near *Boston, boasted such denizens as *Hawthorne and Margaret Fuller, physically laboring in "phalanxes" during the day and creating art in the evening. The Oneida (N.Y.) Community mixed evangelical religion, communal marriage, and the manufacture of steel traps.

Utopianisms (*C.M.* 37) are, of course, high-minded, overly optimistic ideas or sayings.

C.M. 37

UZ

The homeland of *Job has not been identified with certainty, although Bezanson's notes to *Clarel* (571) call it "a deserted ancient region of the Edom wasteland." Perhaps like "*Queequeg's" "*Kokovoco" we must say "It is not down in any map; true places never are" (*M.D.* 12). Uz (from Uts, a son of Aram, progenitor of the *Aramaic people) is mentioned in *Genesis 10:23 and 36:28, in I *Chronicles, *Jeremiah, Lamentations.

R. 30; W. 7

VALE OF PAREE

See "Paree."

O. 32

VALENS'

Valens (c. 328-378), Eastern *Roman Emperor from 364 to 378, had been appointed as co-emperor by his brother, Valentinian I. During his reign, he encountered bloody revolts and conspiracies, as well as war with the Visigoths and the *Persians. He died in battle at Adrianople, and his body was never found.

A fervent *Arian, not tolerant of religious dissent as was his brother, Valens persecuted and executed *Catholics and banished bishops, while interfering little with *Pagans.

I have been unable to identify the "lorn widow" at *Edessa whom M. claims stopped the persecutions.

M. 9

VALHALLA

In *Scandinavian myth, the hall of the slain, where *Odin nightly feasted with resurrected men who had fallen in battle. The supply of *port and mead (intoxicating hart's milk), which never gave out, was distributed by the Valkyries, Odin's maids who decided the course of war and summoned to Valhalla fallen princely warriors and heroes who were faithful to the god.

M.'s reference to Valhalla as the land of "goblins and goblets" (*M.* 20) indicates his comprehension of the dual nature of the hall: in an endless cycle, men feasted and became drunk every night only to be returned to die in battle again.

M. 3; M. 20

VALLEY OF DEATH

*Psalms 23:4: "Yea, though I walk through the valley of the shadow of death, I will fear no evil; for thou art with me; thy rod and thy staff they comfort me."

M. 181

VALLEY OF THE ORANGES

Laranjeiras (M.'s "*Larangieros"), a suburb of *Rio de Janeiro, nestled at the base of the Serra de Carioca mountains.

W. 39

VALOIS

When the *French Capetian dynasty ended, Valois, a historic region of France, gave its name to a hereditary countship providing the first Valois king, Philippe VI (1328-50). The territory itself changed ownership often, and the power of the monarchy resided shakily in the family during the Hundred Years' War. Philippe's son, Jean II (*le Bon*; 1350-64), ascended a throne weakened by war and by *Black Death. His son Charles, *dauphin de Viennois, became Regent while Jean was imprisoned, facing insurrections by the bourgeoisie and losses to enemies. He became Charles V (*le Sage*; 1364-80), reestablishing France politically but leaving economic chaos to his son, Charles VI (*le Bien-Aim*; 1380-1422), who died mad. With the British controlling much territory after the victory of King Henry V at Agincourt (1415), the reign of Charles VII (*le Victorieux*; 1422-61) came about with the help of Jeanne d'arc, leaving the Valois dynasty undisputed and popular. Under Louis XI (1461-83), the nation was modernized and prospered, and the throne was strengthened. But Charles VIII (*l'Affable*; 1483-98) was a person of low intelligence whose incursions into *Italy set a pattern for his successor, Louis XII (le Père du Peuple; 1498-1515). Quarrels with the *Pope left the country further weakened. The cousin of Louis, François I (1515-47), was a popular king, despite problems with the *Holy Roman Emperor, *Charles V, whose possessions surrounded France. He strengthened the internal power of the throne, resisting threats from the *Reformation, but he left his son, Henri II (1547-59), unable to hold Italian territories. The brief reign (1559-60) of François II (married as dauphin to Mary Queen of Scots: see "Stuart") yielded to that of Charles IX (1560-74), whose mother, Catherine de *Médicis, as guardian and de facto ruler, was instrumental in destroying the very authority she attempted to reinforce. She persecuted Huguenots (see "St. Bartholomew's Day") and brought about constant civil war. The brother of Charles, Henri III (1574-89), was assassinated, leaving no heir to the throne but the Protestant cousin Henri de Navarre: as Henri IV (le Grand; 1589-1610), the first *Bourbon king.

It is not clear which women M. had in mind in claiming in P. that three "immortal flowers of the line of Valois" were excluded from the throne because of the *Salique Law. Women were excluded by custom from ancient times, and the law was often invoked for reasons other than female exclusion. Descendants of females were denied before and during the Valois accession (including Edward III of England and Charles II of Navarre). And attempts were made to clarify enforcements during the reign of Charles V. But there is much confusion about the law before its first clear invocation to exclude a female. (In 1593, it denied the Infanta Isabella.) The law was not invoked for the daughters of Louis X, Philip V, and Charles IV, although custom denied the throne. I suspect that M. is in error, presuming that Mary, Queen of Scots, Catherine de Médicis, and Marguerite Valois ("La Reine Margot," 1553-1615), Queen Consort to Henry IV, were victims of the Law. They were not.
P. 2:2

VALPARAISO
The city of central *Chile which is today that country's second largest was only developing in M.'s time from a picturesque village into the most important port of *South America's western coast. Valparaiso is sixty miles west-northwest of *Santiago and retains its picturesque amphitheatrical residential section of colonial homes overlooking the bay, which was an active whaling station and scene of many military confrontations. The site was discovered in 1536 and later developed by Pedro de Valdivia. *Pirate raids, earthquakes, and an

1866 naval bombardment by *Spain gave Valparaiso a stormy history. *United States anchored in the Bay of Valparaiso 21 November to 5 December 1843, but it is unlikely that M. spent much time ashore or that there would have been much to see if he had.
T. 3; T. Appendix; O. 25;; O. 27; O. 30; M. 22; R. 9; W. 74; W. 90

VANCOUVER

George Vancouver (1757-1798), *English navigator, entered the Navy at the age of 13 and was with *Cook on his voyages of 1772-75 and 1776-80. After long service with *Rodney in the *West Indies, where he earned a reputation as a harsh disciplinarian, in 1789 he was appointed commander of the expedition that disproved the existence of channels between the *Pacific Ocean and Hudson Bay. From 1791 to 1793, he surveyed the southwest coast of *Australia and sailed northeast to *New Zealand, *Tahiti, and the *Hawaiian Islands. He surveyed the west coast of North America from 30°27' N. to 56°44' N.

He was sent on a second visit to the Hawaiian Islands near the time of Cook's death (1794), but the annexation he was to implement was never ratified. Vancouver's four and one-half years of surveying constituted the most difficult exploring expedition accomplished at the time.

Vancouver, British Columbia is named for him; his exploits are recorded in the posthumously published A Voyage of Discovery to the North Pacific Ocean and Round the World . . . 1790-95, 3 vol. (1798).
T. 24; T. 25; T. 32; O. 18; O. 31; O. 45; O. 48; O. 54; M.D. 24

VANDALIC

The Vandals were a Teutonic race in northeastern *Germany that despoiled *Gaul, *Spain, North *Africa, and *Rome in the fifth century. The "Bande Noire" in the French Revolution performed similar wanton mutilation.
W. 76

VAN RENSSELAERS

The Van Rensselaers were descended from Kiliaen Van Rensselaer, an *Amsterdam diamond merchant whose *New York estate covered most of modern Albany and Rensselaer counties. His acquisition of land resulted from the patroonship system wherein after 1629 members of the Dutch West India Company could acquire land by peopling tracts with fifty adult

settlers. Van Rensselaer leased his land, encouraging the farm tenancy system later expanded by the British. His descendents constituted an American aristocracy in M.'s time.
See also "Gansevoort."
M.D. 1

VAPOR-BATHS; VAPORITES
See "Water-cure Establishment."
P. 22:1

VARRO
Marcus Terentius Varro (116 B.C.-27 B.C.) was *Rome's top scholar at the time of *Pompey. A prolific and learned writer of Menippean satires, he is thought to have written over 600 books, only one of which has survived complete: *Res rusticae*, a non-satirical study of country life.
R. 46

VARVOO
Given M.'s tendency to intrude "r's" into his orthography, the reference is probably to Vavau, an island group of northern *Tonga which includes Vavau island and c. thirty islets. Vavau is c. ten miles long and is noted for its caves. (I have not verified M.'s claim that warriors there amputate themselves.)
M. 24

VATICANS
Great libraries. At the time, "Vatican" meant the *Papal library, not the Holy See. M. visited the area in 1857, calling 2 March "Vatican Day."
(The sovereign Papal state was set up in 1929: 108.7 acres mostly on the west bank of the *Tiber River.)
M. 119; R. 41; M.D. Extracts 7

VATTEL
Emerich De Vattel (1714-1767) was a *Swiss jurist, a specialist in international law. His most famous work (not cited by M.) was the derivative *Jus gentium*. His own work, the 1758 *Le Droit des Gens* ("*Law of Nations") rejects the concept of a commonwealth of nations or world state, substituting the idea that had much influence on the *American *Declaration of Independence: the law of nature is to be followed where it is

clear, and where it is not, individual states must decide their own obligations. The most slippery aspect of Vattel's theory is, of course, defining the "law of nature," a code of conduct which reason deduces as consonant with justice.

Vattel's impractical idealism did not prevent his work's becoming a university text, a favorite citation of nineteenth-century authors.
W. 5

VAUXHALL BRIDGE

*London's Vauxhall Bridge was constructed between 1811 and 1816 (replaced in 1906) in what was a very fashionable area of Lambeth. Its name derives from Falkes (or Fulkes) de Breauté, thirteenth-century lord of the manor. M. took a penny steamer up the *Thames to Vauxhall on 14 November 1849.
R. 30

V.E.

See "Browne; Sir T. Brown; Sir Thomas Brown."
M.D. 91

VEDAS

The Vedas ("Books of Knowledge"), sacred hymns and verses of forebears of the Hindu (see "Hindoo") people, are traditionally a divine revelation to ancient seers who transmitted them orally. Vedic, an old form of *Sanskrit, was spoken by Aryan peoples who entered *India from the area of present-day Iran. Earliest of the Vedas (c. 1500 B.C.) were the *samhitas* (hymns); *brahmanas* (commentaries) appeared next, followed by *aranyakas* (c. 600 B.C.) and *upanishads* (c. 600-300 B.C.), summaries of the teachings.

Among deities of the Aryans, appearing in various *avatars, were Visnu the preserver (M.'s *Vishnu, or Vishnoo), an avatar of Krishna, and Siva the destroyer (see "Shiva").

During M.'s time, revelation that the Vedas were about as old as the *Old Testament, and rather similar to the *New, contributed to the general reassessment of *Christianity and much scrambling on the part of linguists and other scholars to provide justification for Christianity's preeminence.
M.D. 82

VEGA

Probably this reference is to the lower-case "vega": Sp. "fertile plain," rather than to a specific place called "Vega." La Vega is in northern *Venezuela, and Concepción de la Vega is in the Dominican Republic, both on M.'s misplaced *Spanish Main, but there is no Vega that I have discovered near *Coquimbo.
W. 85

VENDOME, COLUMN OF

The Vendôme Column, Place Vendôme, *Paris, honoring the Grande Armée, was modeled after *Trajan's Column in *Rome. It was in construction from 1806 to 1810, replacing a statue of Louis XIV (see "Bourbon") which had been torn down by a mob. The column stands in the center of an octagonal group of uniform houses dating from the seventeeth century (in one of which Chopin died six weeks before M. visited on 2 December 1849).

Place Vendôme was named for an illegitimate son of the Bourbon Henri IV.
M.D. 35

VENETIAN BLIND, --S

Horizontally slatted Venetian blinds were an eighteenth-century invention, much used in *English Georgian architecture. Probably M. was the first to see an analogy between Venetian blinds and *baleen, which hangs vertically (*M.D.* 58; *M.D.* 75; *M.D.* 81).
R. 25; W. 77; M.D. 58; M.D. 75; M.D. 81

VENICE

The capital of Veneto and Venezia provinces of northern Italy is located within the Lagoon of Venice, at the northwest corner of the Gulf of Venice (a northern part of the *Adriatic). Built on 118 small islands, Venice has some 160 canals and about 400 bridges, lined with Romanesque, *Gothic, and Renaissance palaces. First settled in the fifth century A.D., it was a strong maritime, commercial, and political power by the tenth, reaching the height of its world power in the fourteenth and fifteenth centuries. Venice lost most of its overseas possessions in the late sixteenth and seventeenth centuries and was occupied by *Napoléon in 1797. It was not politically united with the rest of the kingdom of Italy until 1866.

M. arrived in Venice on 1 April 1857, residing at the Hotel Luna, on the Piazza San Marco. He expressed disappointment with St. Mark's Cathedral, but enjoyed the "perfect deco-rum" (journal 2 April) of the square, with its musicians, fine ladies, and courtly soldiers. He visited the Palace of the *Doges, jewelry manufactories, and the dilapidated Arsenal (*M.* 32) of the Republic, a once-thriving ship-fitting facility. Traveling much on the *Grand Canal, he saw the Palazzo Moro (home of *Shakespeare's supposed original for "Othello"), as well as the residence of *Byron, the palace of the Duchesse de Berri, the Casa d'Oro, and the Hotel de la Ville, which he much admired (as Ruskin was to, later).

M.'s references to a "hired Venetian" (*M.D.* 41) and a "Venetianly corrupt" (*M.D.* 54) existence seem to have become manifest for him during this stay. His journal jottings include bits of rather threatening dialogue with a blind Venetian beg-gar (which he planned to use for *C.M.*).

M. saw Titians at the Accademia della Belle Arti, took gondolas to the Lido along the Adriatic, visited the *Bridge of Sighs, and summarized his stay in the journal entry of 5 April: "Rather be in Venice on rainy day then in other capital on fine one." He left the city the next day.
M. 32; W. 50; M.D. 41; M.D. 54; P. 4:4; I.P. 19

VENUS
Originally, minor *Roman goddess of garden fertility, Venus became identified with the Greek *Aphrodite, goddess of beauty, mother of love, and patroness of courtesans. A mys-terious girdle (Greek "zone," Roman "cestus") gave her ro-mantic power over *Vulcan, *Mars, *Mercury, *Bacchus, *Adonis, and others. "Venus rising from the sea" (W. 90) is probably a pun, referring to "Venus Anadyom'ene," a lost painting by Apelles, showing Venus accompanied by dolphins. Although it is not mentioned in his journal, M. probably saw Botticelli's version in the *Florence Accademia delle Belle Arti, in 1857.

In astronomy, the planet second closest to the sun, be-tween Mercury and Earth; as the evening star known to the ancients as *Hesperus or *Vesper; as the morning star, *Lucifer or Phosphorus. The second brightest object in the evening sky, Venus has phases, similar to those of the *Moon. The *Transit of Venus (M. 179; P. 2:5) refers to the passage of the planet across the disk of the sun, a phenomenon recorded by many important navigators.
T. 22; O. 18; O. 26; O. 43; M. 61; M. 88; M. 134; M. 179; W. 6; W. 90; W. 91; P. 1:5; P. 2:5; P. 15:1; C.M. 16

VENUS DE' MEDICI
The standard of female beauty, this Hellenistic-style statue in the Uffizzi Gallery in *Florence (since 1680), was dug up in pieces in the seventeenth century in the villa of *Hadrian, near *Tivoli and placed in the *Medici Palace at *Rome. It is the model for Botticelli's "Birth of *Venus."
T. 22

VERBENA
The (mostly tropical) verbena sends out spikes or clusters of showy flowers.
In "flower language," verbena expresses Sensibility; white means "pray for me"; scarlet means "united against evil"; pink means "family reunion."
*Vervain is another name for verbena.
M. 88

VERDANNA
M.'s fictional equivalent of *Ireland.
M. 152

VERMONT, --ER
Vermont was admitted to the Union as the fourteenth state, in 1791. It is bounded by *Quebec (N.), *New Hampshire (E.), *Massachusetts (S.), and *New York (W.) and is 156 miles from north to south and between thirty-seven and eighty-nine miles from east to west. It is the "*Green Mountain State"; Mount Mansfield is the highest peak, at 4,393 feet. The *Taconics and the *Connecticut River run through, and Lake Champlain makes part of its western border.
The *French had a military post in the area in 1666, but the first permanent settlement was made in 1724, near present Brattleboro. Vermont had many boundary conflicts with New Hampshire and New York, and resistance to New York authority (1770-1771) caused the creation of *Ethan Allen's "Green Mountain Boys."
Montpelier became the capital of Vermont in 1805. There was much smuggling activity in the *War of 1812 and later anti-*Masonry and anti-*slavery agitation in the state which embrace the *Republican Party at its inception in 1856 (and has voted Republican ever since).
M. and his wife returned from their honeymoon in *Canada by stagecoach through Vermont, in August 1847.
M. 28; M.D. 6; M.D. 42; I.P. 1; I.P. 21; I.P. 22

VERMONT
A seventy-four-gun *American warship launched in 1848.
M. 28

VERRES
Gaius Verres (C. 115-43 B.C. was an unscrupulous *Roman magistrate who had embezzled funds, plundered provincials, and bribed officials, even before becoming governor of *Sicily (73-71). *Cicero condemned his bribery, juggling of books, looting of art works, and arbitrary executions, and at his trial, Verres left before a verdict could be rendered. He was murdered in exile by order of Mark *Antony.
M. 83

VERSAILLES
The importance of the town of Versailles, *France (c. 15 miles west-wouthwest of *Paris), began when Louis XIII (see "Bourbon") had a hunting lodge there in 1624. Louis XIV began building the elaborate palace complex and gardens in 1661 (completed at great cost in 1710). Later additions were the *Grand Trianon* and under Louis XV the *Petit Trianon*. Versailles has been the residence of numerous monarchs and the scene of much history, including signing of the peace Treaty of Versailles officially ending the *American Revolution (1783), and the seizing of the king by the Paris mob in 1789.

By the time of M.'s day-long visit of 6 December 1849, it had been used much by the military and the government and rather badly redecorated by Louis-Philippe. Still, M. called it a "most magnificent & incredible affair altogether."
M. 121; R. 1; M.D. 56; P. 25:4

VERTU
A love of rare, curiously wrought art objects.
M.D. 102

VERULAM
See "Bacon, Lord."
M. 119

VERVAIN
"Vervain" is commonly used to signify *verbena. The European *Verbena officinalis* is used in folk medicine. In

"flower language," it means "Enchantment," rather different from the meaning of verbena.
M. 192

VESTRIS, MADAME

The Vestris (originally Vestri) were a famous *French theatrical family: Gaétan Vestris (Gaetano, 1729-1808), "the god of the dance"; Auguste Vestris (Marie Jean Augustin, 1760-1842), son of Gaétan and ballerina Marie Allard, famous for his leaps; Auguste Armand Vestris (1788-1825), son of Auguste and Catherine Augier, and ballet master at the King's Theatre, *London; his wife, Madame Vestris (Lucia Elizabeth Mathews, née Bartolozzi, 1797-1856), most celebrated of all as actress and opera singer who set standards in performance and visual arts. She later remarried and in 1838 visited the United States.

M.'s journal for 7 November 1849 refers to his seeing "The *Beauty and the Beast," starring Madame Vestris, at London's Royal Lyceum Theatre.
R. 44

VESUVIUS, --'

The only active volcano on the European mainland, Vesuvius is in Campania province of southern *Italy, on the eastern shore of the Bay of *Naples, eight miles east-southeast of the city. The mountain is c. 45 miles in circumference, with deeply scarred sides that rise sharply toward the cone, the height of which varies because of eruptions (c. 4,000 feet). The earliest recorded eruption occurred in A.D. 79: destroying *Pompeii, *Herculaneum, and Stabiae. Eruptions were also severe in 1631, 1779, 1794, 1822, 1872, and in the twentieth century.

M. went to Vesuvius on 18 February 1857, two years after a major eruption and one year before another. He ascended the mountain on horseback, and his already depressed state was exacerbated by haggling with his guide, physical discomfort from ashes, and sheer fear. He complains in his journal: "Modern crater like old abandoned quarry—burning . . . Red & yellow. Bellowing. Bellows, flare of flame. Went into crater. Frozen liquorice.—Came down with a rush."
M. 153; W. 68; M.D. 104; M.D. 135

VICAR-GENERAL

An ecclesiastical officer: representative of or assistant to a Bishop at official functions.

The *Pope is called "Christ's Vicar on Earth."
M.D. 71

VICE
The earliest use of the word as a synonym for depravity is 1297; the convention of capitalization appears from about 1400.
Passim

VICKSBURGH
Vicksburgh is in western Mississippi, located on bluffs above the *Mississippi River at the mouth of the Yazoo River, forty miles west of Jackson; it is the state's chief river port. The site of eighteenth-century *French and *Spanish forts, the town came to U.S. possession in 1798; it was incorporated in 1825. (Vicksburgh was besieged by General Grant in 1863; after the *Civil War it became the site of a national cemetery.)
C.M. 45

VICTORIA, QUEEN; VICTORIA'S
The *Hanover Victoria (1819-1901) was Queen of Great *Britain and *Ireland from 1837 and Empress of *India from 1876. She was the only child of Edward, Duke of Kent, fourth son of King *George III, and was raised simply. She acceded after disagreement over the Salic (see "Salique") law had split Britain and *Germany. It was a time of great political power in the throne, and it soon became urgent to secure a husband for Victoria, especially when she developed marked *Whig preferences. *Albert, her cousin, married her in 1840, leading to what has been called the "Albertine Monarchy," with Albert immersing himself in matters of state and questions of moral character (about which the Queen is said to have cared little, despite the pejorative "Victorian," which signifies moral primness). Victoria had nine children (and eventually thirty-seven grandchildren), to whom she was devoted while Albert saw England through the Whig crisis, the post Corn-Law crisis, accession of *Napoléon III, and the Crimean War. After his death (1861), she tended to retreat to Balmoral Castle, *Scotland, as her ministers retired or died. Benjamin Disraeli (1804-81) became an advisor; despite liberal minister William Ewart Gladstone's (1809-98) disagreements, a kind of peace in *Parliament and in *Ireland was achieved during her reign.
Victoria's mark on England is generally thought to be restoration of dignity to the monarchy that had preceded, in the unpopular person of William IV. Her voluminous letters and journals have been published in part.
On 22 November 1849, M. "met" Victoria at *Windsor. He and a friend saluted her carriage as it passed, and the salute was returned by the Queen but not by Albert. M.'s jour-

nal adds: "She is an amiable domestic woman . . . . I doubt
not, & God bless her, say I & long live the 'prince of whales'"
(see "Prince of Wales").
O. 45; O. 80; R. 23; R. 41; R. 43; W. 4; Covert references in R.
42; W. 4

VICTORY, THE; VICTORY'S

The *British ship of the line *Victory* was the scene of
*Nelson's death at the Battle of *Trafalgar, 21 October 1805. She
was a three-decker, 186 feet long, with guns on all decks. *Victory* is preserved at the naval dockyard, *Portsmouth, England.
A silver star marks the spot where Nelson fell. M. visited on 25
December 1849. In *Billy Budd, Sailor* (IV), he was to call *Victory* "a poetic reproach . . . to the *Monitors* and yet mightier
hulk of the European ironclads."
See also "Santissima Trinidada."
M. 28; R. 38; M.D. 8

VIDOCQ

François Eugène Vidocq (1775-1857) was a law-breaker
turned law-enforcer whose memoirs (4 vol., 1828) were widely
read. He became a friend to Hugo, Balzac, Dumas, and others,
and his more positive characteristics were borrowed by Sir
Arthur Conan Doyle for his "Sherlock Holmes."
M. probably had him in mind in creating "Billy Budd's"
"Claggart."
W. 6; M.D. 88

VIENNA

The capital of *Austria is an inland port on the Danube
River, 320 miles south-southeast of *Berlin. Originally a Celtic
settlement, Vienna became important early in its history as
the residence site of Marcus Aurelius. Among its many invaders were the Magyars in the tenth century. It was fortified
by the Babenbergs and chartered in 1221, coming under the
Hapsburgs in the thirteenth century. Vienna became a highly
respected cultural center, home to *Haydn, *Mozart, and
*Beethoven, as well as to many scientists.
*Napoléon entered in 1805 and 1809. The Revolution of
1848 forced the resignation of Metternich and the abdication of
Ferdinand I.
The Congress of Vienna (*P.* Dedication), meeting from
September 1814 to June 1815, reorganized Europe after the
*Napoleonic Wars. *Austria, *Prussia, *Russia, and *Britain
were included in the original plans; they were joined by

*Sweden, *Portugal, *Spain, and *France, but "the four" made
the real decisions. Europe's most important statesmen attended (including Metternich, the Duke of *Wellington, and
*Talleyrand). The then-unprecedented proceedings, the social
aspects of which caused great delay in producing action, almost resulted in war, given various promises made before the
Napoleonic Wars.

The settlement, which stood for forty years, brought
peace to Europe, but it involved numerous boundary, constitutional, and legal changes designed to balance power rather
than to respect nationality. (Until the Treaty of *Versailles
made even more drastic changes, the Congress of Vienna was
seen as an assembly that violated rights of many peoples.)

The "investment of Vienna" (*M*. 27) is untraced.

M. 20; M. 27; W. 50; P. Dedication

VIKING

The people we call Vikings are those *Scandinavian
conquerors whose military and naval prowess made them
powerful from roughly A.D. 800 to 1050. The term "Viking" is
unclear; close Scandinavian words are those for "sailor" and
"pirate." Ancient chronicles do not use the term. *Norwegian,
*Swedish, and *Danish Viking chiefs celebrated in music and
literature conquered *England, *Ireland, *France, the Baltics,
parts of *Russia, *Iceland, and other islands. Their ships
sailed as far west as North America. Theirs was a mercantile
culture rich in technology and mythologic literature deriving a
cosmography from common Indo-European sources.

The *Eddas tell of a giant, Ymir, a twin corresponding to
the *Roman *Janus, who was magically formed from the void.
Ymir reproduced creatures from parts of his own body. The
cow that fed him licked a man into life from a block of salty ice,
and *Odin and his brothers descended from this man. They
killed Ymir and created the world from the parts of his body
and the first man and woman from pieces of driftwood. The
world was seen as *M*.'s "*Jarl" envisions it: a central enclosure surrounded by sea ruled by a cosmic serpent.

Viking fighting ships, or longships, for local voyages in
calm waters, were narrow, shallow, single-sailed and oared
vessels over seventy-five feet long, pointed at both ends, with
elaborately decorated prows. They carried perhaps twenty
rowers and twice that number of warriors, whose shields
hung outside the bulwarks. They were steered by a starboard
oar. The *hafskip*, for peacetime use such as colonization, was
similar in length but wider in the beam, with a large square
sail and fewer rowers. It was steered by a starboard rudder.

The *hafskip* carried several boats and large numbers of people, animals, and supplies, sometimes under awnings.
See also "earl," for the original of "Jarl," of *M*.
M. Passim; W. 50

VINCENNES
The southwestern-Indiana city on the *Wabash River was a *French mission in 1702. It was fortified by and named for François Margane, sieur de Vincennes, c. 1730. Occupied by the *British in 1763, Vincennes was captured by the *Americans in 1779. By an *Indian treaty of 1805, it became an American possession, briefly the capital of Indiana Territory.
C.M. 27

VINCENNES
The eighteen-gun U.S. *Navy ship sloop *Vincennes*, launched in 1826, was important in its own right and of particular interest to the Melville family.   M.'s cousin, *Midshipman Pierre François Henry Thomas Wilson Melville (1806--26 September 1844), served on *Vincennes* on several cruises (1829--34). In one case he followed an itinerary that M. was later to duplicate, with stops at the *Marquesas, *Society, and *Sandwich Islands.   ("Tom" Melville had a brief and stormy life; he was suspended for fighting on *Vincennes* at least once and died near *Hawaii under irregular circumstances. As has been pointed out, he may be a partial model for "Tommo" of *T.*, as well as for the protagonist of *P*.)
        Vincennes was the first U.S. warship to navigate the world (September 1826--June 1830, commanded by William Bolton Finch). She was the first U.S. *Navy ship to visit Guam (1835), and was flagship of *Wilkes's fleet on the *United States Exploring Expedition (of August 1838-July 1842), departing *Norfolk, *Virginia for the Pacific and South *Polar regions. (A painting of *Vincennes* based on a sketch by Wilkes is contained in his *Narrative . . .*). In July of 1846, she was the first U.S. warship to visit Edo (Tokyo) Bay, in a failed attempt to open diplomatic relations. By 1854, she was delivering military personnel to Okinawa to enforce the Treaty of Naha.   *Vincennes* ran aground in *Civil War actions of October 1861, at Head of Passes, on the *Mississippi River.
        Chaplain of *Vincennes* was Reverend *Charles S. Stewart, whose *Visit to the South Seas*, an important source for M., is mentioned in *T.* 1.
T. 1; T. 25

VINEYARD, --ER
    See "Martha's Vineyard."
O. 82; W. 4; M.D. 16; M.D. 18; M.D. 54 and elsewhere

VING KING CHING
    See "Hang-Ho."
C.M. 2

VIRGIL
    (Vergil, Publius Vergilius Maro) The greatest *Roman
poet lived from 70 to 19 B.C. Born at Andes, near Mantua, he
was trained in the Roman and *Greek writers, in rhetoric and
philosophy. Among his works are the *Aeneid, the national
epic poem of the Romans. The poems of Eclogues relate historical events in pastoral settings. Georgics is a didactic poem on
farming, with social and political relevance. Juvenilia is attributed to him in Appendix Vergiliana. Virgil is *Dante's
guide in the Inferno.
    The reference in P. (15:3) to Virgil's eagerness at death
to burn the Aeneid comes from *Bayle: his friends Tucca and
Varius assured him that the Emperor *Augustus would not
permit the destruction, so Virgil left them his writings, forbidding changes in the works. Virgil is said to be buried at
*Pausilippo.
    Sealts #147, Harper Classical Library, Vols. 11 and 12,
contain The Eclogues, The Georgics, and The Aeneid.
O. 2; M. 119; R. 30; W. 11; W. 45; P. 2:7; P. 15:3; C.M. 16

VIRGIN
    See "Catholic . . . . "
O. 45

VIRGIN, THE
    See "Zodiac."
M.D. 99

VIRGINIA, --N
    Virginia was one of the original thirteen states of the
Union. Since 1792, when the county of *Kentucky became a
separate state, it has been bounded by the *Atlantic (E.),
*Maryland and *Washington, D.C. (N.E.), West Virginia
(N.W. and W.), Kentucky (S.W.), North *Carolina and
*Tennessee (S.). "Virginia" was at first the name for all North

American land not held by *France or *Spain. (Thus, *Jefferson's *Notes on the State of Virginia* refers not to the state alone.) The triangular-shaped state is 455 miles wide from E. to W. along its southern border and 200 miles N. to S. at its longest. It has c. 100 miles of coastal tide-water sandy plains along the *Chesapeake Bay with important maritime cities such as *Norfolk and Hampton Roads. The *Potomac River connects Virginia with the U.S. capital and points west.

The "Old Dominion" state has many important colonial sites as well as battlefields and monuments of the *Revolutionary War, *War of 1812, and *Civil War. Jamestown was North America's first permanent European settlement (1607); tobacco (*O.* 62) has been cultivated since 1619. The College of William and Mary was founded here in 1693.

Among Virginia's former residents are *George Washington (at Mount Vernon) and *Thomas Jefferson (at Monticello). The state is referred to as the "Mother of Presidents," including James Monroe, James Madison, John Tyler, William Henry Harrison, Zachary Taylor, Woodrow Wilson. Other "favorite sons" include *Patrick Henry, Meriwether Lewis, William Clark, Robert E. Lee, "Stonewall" Jackson, and *John Randolph.

At Yorktown, Virginia, *Cornwallis surrendered, ending the Revolutionary War. Virginia seceded from the Union in 1861; Richmond became the Confederate capital.

The "*Alleganian Ridge" of *M.D.* 3 is found in the 300 mile-long Blue Ridge (*M.D.* 42) mountains, upwards of 5,000 feet in altitude, hovering over the Great *Appalachian Valley.

M. visited Civil War troops in Virginia in April of 1864, perhaps stopping at General Ulysses S. Grant's headquarters. He accompanied a horseback scouting party from Vienna, Virginia, which inspired his long poem, "The Scout Toward Aldie."

See also "Dismal Swamp."

O. 62; M. 28; M. 75; R. 31; W. 29; W. 34; W. 66; W. 83; W. 90; W. 93; M.D. 3; M.D. 42; M.D. 96; M.D. 133; P. 1:3; P. 2:4; C.M. 26; C.M. 30

VIRGINIA
      The twenty-eight-gun frigate *Virginia* was captured when she ran aground in 1778. She became a *British thirty-two-gun ship of the same name.
M. 28

VIRGINIA'S NATURAL BRIDGE
The limestone arch in West Virginia is 215 feet high, 90 feet long.
M. 75; M.D. 133

VIRGO
See "Zodiac."
M.D. 99

VISCOUNTS
Viscount is a courtesy title granted by social custom, with no legal status, for a peer ranking below an *Earl and above a *Baron (esp. the eldest son of an Earl or *Marquis). Derivation is from L. *vice* and *comes*—deputy of a *count. An Earl was usually at court, and needed a deputy to tend his county affairs. First Viscount was John Lord Beaumont (1440). A Viscount is called the "Right Honorable"; he is addressed by the Sovereign as "Our right trusty and well-beloved Cousin."
W. 56

VISHNOO
See "Vedas" and "Avatar."
(Spelled "Vishnu" in *M.D.* 55.)
M.D. 82

VISHNU
See "Vedas" and "Avatar."
(Spelled "Vishnoo" in *M.D.* 82.)
M.D. 55

VIVENZA
M.'s fictional equivalent of the *United States.
M. 145 through M. 164

VIVIA
A fictional name derived from Latin *vivo*: to live.
P. 22:3

VIZIER; GRAND VIZIER
Arab *wazir*: bearer of the burden.

Chief minister or other official serving a caliph or other *Moslem ruler. Formerly *Turkish ministers and governors had the name. Chief minister until 1878 was the Grand Vizier.

See also "Mustapha . . . "
M. 20; M. 181; R. 29; W. 39; W. 68

VOLCANO BAY
Uchiura Bay, *Japan, a crescent-shaped expanse thirty-five miles long and thirty miles wide, at southwest Hokkaido. (Also called Iburi Bay.)
M.D. 44

"VOLPONE"
See "Jonson; Ben Jonson."
W. 41

VOLTAIC
The adjective denotes electricity produced by chemical action, or any electric current. The word is derived from the name of Alessandro Giuseppe Antonio Anastasio Volta (1745-1827), inventor of the electric battery.
P. 8:3

VOLTAIRE
François-Marie Arouet (1694-1778), born illegitimate and soon orphaned in *Paris, rose to become the Enlightenment's master satirist, historian, polemicist, correspondent, dramatist, and moralist. His freethinking godfather, Abbé de Châteauneuf, started him on the path with introductions to *Ninon (who made him an heir) and others. By the 1720's, he had taken the name of Voltaire, and his satires had made his place among intellectuals; they also cost him a stay in the *Bastille (1717-18) and exile to *England (1726-29), where he mastered English and studied English literature.

Voltaire's classically written, politically oriented, works include *La Henriade* (1723, 1728), a tribute to Henry of Navarre; *Lettres philosophiques* (in English, 1733; in French 1734), an attack on the *ancien régime* of Louis XIV (see "Bourbon"); *Zaïre* (1732), a comparison of the *crusaders and chivalrous *Moslems; *Le Siècle de Louis XIV* (1751), a history of French arts and sciences of the time; *Candide* (1759), which remains a popular critique of civil and ecclesiastical establishments.

By the time of his English exile he was close to literati including *Pope, Swift, and Congreve. The *Jesuit-educated Voltaire became an enemy of the Roman *Catholic Church, and created scandal through his life with mathematician-physicist-philosopher the Marquise du Châtelet (1706-1749) and other women. He contributed material to *Diderot's *Encyclopédie* so controversial as to stop its publication; he dramatically defended opponents of the Church, and was generally blamed for having almost single-handedly caused the French Revolution. Voltaire spent his last years in *Paris, writing and producing plays. He was surreptitiously buried in consecrated soil, but his remains were transferred to the Paris Pantheon in 1791. (M. visited 2 December 1849.)

In Schopenhauer's *The World as Will and Idea* (III, iv, 46; "The Vanity and Suffering of Life"; Sealts #448), M. scored references to Voltaire's ideas on the evil and misery of existence, the necessity of acts of will, and the reality of "*Locke's principle, that what thinks may also be material." In Schopenhauer's *The Wisdom of Life* (Introduction; Sealts #447), he scored Voltaire's "*We shall leave this world as foolish and as wicked as we found it on our arrival.*"

Sealts #537 is *Histoire de Charles XII. Roi de Suede* (Londres: 1808), which belonged to M.'s father (see "Walter Redburn").

As with other authors to whom M. was compared in his day, the paucity of direct citation belies the compatibility of philosophies.
P. 26:4

VON TROMP

The *Dutch Admiral Von Tromp to whom M. refers is Maarten Harpertszoon Tromp (1598-1653). Von Tromp had been captured at sea by *pirates when he was a child and imprisoned for two years before he was ten years old. His naval career began in 1622, and by 1637 he was Lieutenant-Admiral of *Holland. After amazing successes against privateers and against the combined fleets of *Spain and *Portugal, in 1652 he was sent with a large fleet to face England's *Robert Blake, but was forced to withdraw, beginning the first Anglo-Dutch War. After several engagements against the combined British fleets, Von Tromp was killed in battle when the British blockaded the Dutch coast.

Legend says that after his first defeat by Blake, Von Tromp sailed up the *Channel with a broom tied to his masthead, symbolizing his projected sweep of the seas.

(*W*. 50's reference to Von Tromp gives the impression that Admiral *Hawke defeated Von Tromp. Hawke's service occurred almost one hundred years after Von Tromp's death.)

Von Tromp's name is listed with naval leaders of "knightly valor" and "nobler qualities" in *Billy Budd, Sailor* (Chap. 4).
W. 50

VOYAGE DESCRIPTIF ET PHILOSOPHIQUE DE L'ANCIEN ET DU NOUVEAU PARIS: MIROIR FIDELE
This book by Louis Marie Prudhomme (Paris, 1815), originally published in 1814, was owned by M.'s father, Allan Melvill (Sealts #538). Presumably it is also the original of the "Guide to *Paris" mentioned in *I.P.* 7 and *I.P.* 9. (M. could not have had much expertise in French, but his father did. See "Walter Redburn.")

Thorp supplies the full title of the work, in "Redburn's Prosy Old Guidebook." M. omits *Qui indique aux étrangers et même aux Parisiens ce qui'ils doivent connaitre et éviter dans cette Capitale*; . . . Par L. P[rudhomme] A Paris. Chez l'Auteur, rue des Marais, F.S. Germain, N°18. 1814. Thorp adds that the book is "A fat, pink-covered duodecimo."
R. 30

VOYAGES AND TRAVELS ROUND THE WORLD
A theoretical book; travel literature had tremendous popularity during M.'s time.
R. 9

"VULGAR ERRORS"
See "Browne; Sir T. Brown; Sir Thomas Brown."
M. 13

WABASH RIVER
The Wabash rises in western *Ohio, gaining in size through Indiana and flowing some 475 miles to meet the *Ohio River at the southwestern corner of that state.
C.M. 25; C.M. 27

WAFER, LIONEL
    A *pirate who sailed with *Dampier, Lionel Wafer was
stranded on the Isthmus of *Panama for several months in the
seventeenth century. He wrote a valuable anthropological account of the experience, *A New Voyage* (1699). He was eventually apprehended, and the fine he paid for his activities was
used for the building of William and Mary College, Williamsburg, *Virginia.
    See also "Davis, Captain."
M.D. 45

WAGER, THE
    See "Anson, Lord."
W. 24

WAIURAR
    Vairara, in southwestern *Tahiti. ("Whaiherea," in *O.*
30.)
O. 67

WALDENSES
    This twelfth-century *French *Christian sect joined the
Reformation movement in the sixteenth century. It was
known for keeping separate from the Roman *Catholic church
from its inception. In the *Inquisition, the Waldenses, or
Vaudois, were accused of witchcraft and were persecuted.
W. 75

WALES; WELSH; WELSHMAN; WELSHWOMAN
    The ancient hill country of Britain (united with
*England in 1536) was never visited by M., but he sailed past it
on several occasions. In the nineteenth century, Wales was
thought to have been established by pre-Saxons driven westward by Anglo-Saxons; it was rapidly industrializing and
growing in population, and becoming increasingly radical
and nationalist in its nonconformist traditions, especially regarding its long-established language. The English word
"Wales" is from *Wealhas*, meaning "foreigners"; the Welsh
refer to their nation as Cymru.
    "*Prince of Wales" is a misnomer, developed from the
legend that Edward I promised the subdued Welsh people a
son who spoke no English.
    The "harpers of Wales" play the traditional triangular
Welsh harp common to other Celtic lands. It was a component

of folk-music performances, used by Welsh bards, who developed playing into an art form much in demand in royal circles. The nineteenth-century Welsh triple harp had three parallel rows of strings, in an attempt to chromaticize without mechanism.

See also "Snowdon."
O. 65; R. 27; R. 37; R. 49; M.D. 12; P. 3:3; P. 21:3; I.P. 15

WALLACE, WILLIAM

Sir William Wallace lived from c. 1270 to 1305. M.'s description of the death of the "convicted traitor" in "enlightened *England" probably comes from Penny Cyclopaedia's gory detailing of the *Scottish guerilla warrior's death: he was hanged at "the Elms in West *Smithfield . . . at the tails of horses . . . on the 23rd of August, 1305 . . . after which, his bowels having been taken out while he yet breathed, and burnt before his face, his head struck off, and his body hacked into quarters. His right arm was set up at *Newcastle, his left at Berwick, his right leg at *Perth, his left at Aberdeen, his head on *London Bridge" (XXVII, 1843).

A popular Scottish national hero as symbol of resistance to the English king, Edward I, Sir William Wallace was made "Guardian of the Kingdom." Later defeated by Edward's armies, he was arrested near *Glasgow, where no trial was deemed necessary for the confessed traitor. The many legends about his exploits were mostly apocryphal, ascribable to fifteenth-century minstrels.

M. saw Wallace's broadsword, a "great cleaver," on 28 October 1856, at Dumbarton Castle, Scotland.
T. 17; W. 76

WALLER, EDMUND

Edmund Waller (1606-87), *Cambridge graduate at the age of sixteen, entered *Parliament as a member of the opposition but later became a Royalist. Banished by *Cromwell, he was permitted to return to England in 1651. He had begun writing poetry at an early age and eventually produced a large number of sweetly simple poems dedicated to ladies or commemorating historical events; they were more valued in his own day than in ours.

The "Extracts" 20 quotation is slightly different from that of Poems London 1664, p. 66), Waller's "iron" becoming "modern" in some editions, and his feminine pronoun becoming masculine, to allow for M.'s omission.

See also "Extracts" 20.

(The quotation in *W.* 51 remains unidentified: testifying to the difficulty of researching the lines of an obscure but prolific poet.)
M. 119; W. 51; M.D. Extracts 20

WALLIS' ISLAND
Part of the *French *Protectorate Wallis and Futuna Islands, in the southwest *Pacific, 250 miles west of *Samoa (13°17' S., 176°10' W.). There is one volcanic island (Uvea) and several uninhabited coral islets in the group, which was discovered by the French in 1781, becoming a protectorate in 1842.
O. 32

WALL STREET; WALL-STREET
This important *Manhattan street dates from 1652, when Peter Stuyvesant ordered a wall built for protection from possible *British invasion. The wall was removed by 1699, but the street continued in significance. Immediately after the Revolution, city, state, and national governmental offices were located there. *Washington's first inaugural (1789) took place at the old Federal Building (on the site of the present Subtreasury Building); *Congress also met there.
By M.'s time, the street had attained its current character, location of the chief financial institutions of the *United States, its name synonymous with the stock market. Wall Street itself is a short (about seven blocks), narrow thoroughfare running from *Broadway to the *East River. The financial district surrounding it for several blocks in each direction houses offices of the international money market: major banks, insurance companies, large industries, and companies with securities listed on the New York Stock Exchange. Major structures house the New York Exchange, the American Stock Exchange, Cotton, Coffee, Metal, and Produce Exchanges, as well as private banking houses (J.P. Morgan's was formerly at Wall and *Broad Streets).
Because the Stock Exchange is closed on the weekends, the area is traditionally quiet on Saturdays and deserted on Sundays (although increasing tourist interest in downtown Manhattan in the late twentieth century has somewhat changed that). M. was to capitalize on the importance of Wall Street in "Bartleby, the Scrivener."
R. 14; R. 17; R. 32; R. 60; W. 22; C.M. 7

WALPOLE, HORACE; WALPOLE'S LETTERS

*English writer, connoisseur, and collector, Horace Walpole (1717-97), fourth earl of Orford, was educated at Eton and *Cambridge and traveled the Continent with Thomas Gray. After his father's death in 1745, Walpole began publishing poetry and articles on his own printing press at a *Gothic-style house he called Strawberry Hill. (His first publication was Gray's *Odes*.) His own Gothic novel, *The Castle of Otranto* (published pseudonymously in 1764), followed a book on painting. In 1768, he published a work attempting to clear the reputation of *Richard III, and his own verse tragedy, *The Mysterious Mother*. His memoirs were left ready for publication after his death, and his voluminous collection of letters began appearing in 1798.

The Gothic aspect of Walpole, to which M. alludes in *W*, gained attention in 1833, when Thomas Babbington Macauley's article in *Edinburgh Review* stimulated gossip about his involvement in Chatterton's suicide. Walpole's destruction of letters to a free-thinking *French lady, and the fact of his father's having married a long-time mistress after the death of Horace's mother, have intensified the aura of the forbidden around his dramas, "suppressed" for their suggestions of dark human passions such as torture and incest.

Sealts #s 544 and 545 are *The Castle of Otranto* and a Walpole letter.
W. 41; W. 89

WALTER CANNY
See "Whaleman's Chapel."
M.D. 7

WALTER REDBURN
"Walter Redburn," *R*.'s "French importer" is generally taken as signifying M.'s father, Allan Melvill ("e" added later; 7 April 1782—28 January 1832), an "importer of *French Goods and Commission Merchant." The son of Revolutionary fighter, Thomas Melvill, who was a participant in the "*Boston Tea Party," he was of *Scottish/*Dutch (and perhaps *Irish) descent. In 1814, he married Maria *Gansevoort (6 April 1791 —1 April 1872), daughter of the Revolutionary hero/defender of Fort *Stanwix, General Peter Gansevoort, fathering eight children, of which Herman was third.

The sophisticated but rather dour Allan spoke fluent French and traveled regularly to Europe, where he perhaps fathered a child out of wedlock (seen as pertinent to the plot of *P*.). He borrowed heavily in the *United States, from such creditors as Massachusetts Chief Justice *Lemuel Shaw, whose daughter Herman was to marry, and mortgaged his wife's inherited property. Business recession in 1830 contributed to the failure of his company, and he died in a delirious state which some biographers have called madness, leaving an impecunious family, accustomed to a high standard of living.

(See also "Son-of-a-Gentleman.")
R. 30

WALTON, PARISH OF

In 1699, *Liverpool separated from the Parish of Walton-on-the-Hill, forming its own Parish.
R. 36

WALTONIAN

Izaak Walton (1593-1683) was the son of an alehouse keeper. As a *London tradesman, he became a friend of highly placed Anglican churchmen, including John Donne, of whom he wrote a biography. The scholarly Walton is best known for *The Compleat Angler* (1653, 1655; later editions retitled), a much-praised compendium of practical and whimsical information about fishing. Its central character is "Piscator." "Waltonian prey" are, of course, fish.
M. 94

WALTZ OF DEATH

Dance, or Waltz, of Death (*danse macabre*, or *macabré*) probably arose in fourteenth-century *France in reaction to the plague. In an acted-out sermon, or morality play, people were carried off by their own corpses (later by a skeleton, Death), to the tune of eerie music. It is the subject of numerous paintings (notably by Holbein) and frequently alluded to in literature.
C.M. 36

WAPPING

*London's Wapping High Street, in the East-end dock area, was a traditional hang-out for sailors in M.'s time. Construction of docks such as St. Katharine's brought employment to poor local residents, but standards of living in the area remained very low until the twentieth century. M.'s journal for 10 November 1849 shows that he "lounged" in the area and

flung "a fourpenny piece to '*Poor Jack' in the mud" on the river bank. He was in the area again in April of 1857.
M.D. 6; M.D. 57

WARBECKS, PERKIN

The *Flemish-born (c. 1474) pretender to the *English throne was asserted by his supporters to be Richard, duke of York, the younger brother of Edward V, who had been supposed murdered with his brother in the *Tower of London in 1483. Warbeck's later confession revealed his humble origins in Flanders. In Cork, *Ireland, in 1491, he had been approached by the Irish to impersonate Richard. The French failed to support his efforts, but he found adherents in *Spain and the *Netherlands. The plot was eventually betrayed, but Warbeck persisted and was placed in the Tower in 1497. He was hanged at *Tyburn on 23 November 1499. His name has come to signify any pretender to a throne.
W. 56

WARD

In *Britain, a Ward is a unit of local government derived from the ancient practice of the Hundred, associated with and responsible to individual manors. In the *United States, the Ward is a subdivision of a city, used as a legislative district, administrative division, or political party unit (sometimes further divided into Precincts).
The "Watch-house of the Ward" is the local police precinct.
P. 16:3

WAR OF 1812

M. does not refer to the post-revolutionary conflict between *Britain and the *United States as the "War of 1812," but it is more convenient to do so in this volume. His "*Late War with England," or "*Last War with England," is the conflict of 18 June 1812—24 December 1814 (*Ghent treaty of peace; approved by the U.S. *Senate 16 February 1815). Early tension had arisen over American shipping of *French goods while England and France were at war. Potential paper blockades by both European powers left the United States in conflict over trade partners, but British impressment policies turned American sympathy to France as the lesser of two evils, especially after *Chesapeake* frigate was fired upon in 1807 to remove supposed British deserters. Various ineffective measures (including the Embargo Act of 1807 and the Non-Intercourse

Act of 1809) were taken by the United States, but it was not until *Napoléon appeared to ease his conditions that war with Britain appeared the only option.

The British enlisted the aid of *Tecumseh's Shawnee tribe, leading to slaughter of Governor *William Henry Harrison's troops at Tippecanoe (7 November 1811), motivating much of the nation (especially the south) for war. The surrender of Lake *Erie by *Hull, *Constitution's* capture of *Guerriere*, and *Perry's victory at Lake Erie opened hostilities dramatically in 1813. By 1814, British control of the *Great Lakes, invasion of *Chesapeake Bay, bombardment of *Baltimore's Fort McHenry, and the burning of *Washington gave the advantage to England. But *Jackson's January 1815 victory at *New Orleans (after the peace of Ghent), along with gains at Lake Champlain and in the *Hudson valley, put the U.S. in a better position.

Although maritime losses had been heavy, America was able to secure a favorable peace agreement, gaining in commerce and in morale. Continuance of the war might have brought open division between the "war hawk" south and *New England, which mostly opposed the war. M. probably sided with the latter, not so much out of politics as out of distaste for all wars (made manifestly clear throughout W.).

See also "Decatur"; "Scott's, General."

"WARS OF THE LORD, THE"
Mentioned in Numbers 21:14.
R. 31

WARWICK
See "Nevil, Richard."
T. 23; M. 160; W. 68

WASHINGTON
The capital city of the *United States (coextensive with the District of Columbia) is on the (eastern) *Maryland bank of the *Potomac River (the *Virginia border), thirty-five miles southwest of *Baltimore. *Congress established the district (1790-91) to end North-South rivalry for the capital (*slavery being an issue even then). Maryland and Virginia supplied the territory, but Virginia's land was later returned. *George Washington selected the actual site, and the city was designed by Pierre-Charles L'Enfant (1754-1825). There are gridiron streets with wheel-like patterns of wide avenues radiating from the Capitol and the White House.

*Congress met in Washington starting in 1800; *Presidential inaugurals were held there starting with *Jefferson's. The *British captured Washington in 1814, burning the White House, Capitol, and other buildings.

M. visited Washington in an attempt to secure a *Treasury Department position in 1847; he traveled through while on the *lecture circuit in 1858. On an extensive visit of 1860, while attempting to secure a Consulship, he met *Abraham Lincoln at the White House, observed a session of the Senate, and visited the (incomplete) Washington Monument. He was in Washington again in 1864 to obtain a pass to visit the Army of the Potomac.

Washington institutions and statesmen are satirized in M. 158's "Temple of Freedom."

A "Washington patent-office museum" (C.M. 22) would have been a crowded place indeed, even during M.'s time. Patents had been granted by individual states before establishment of the Federal government, and by 1790 Congress had centralized patents without search for originality. By 1836, a new act corrected that, out of necessity; patents were being granted at the rate of 600 per year. Many Congressional acts have modified the system since, but creation of the Department of the Interior (1849), which supervised patents, went far toward taming the chaos. Patents were not internationally recognized until the 1880's.
R. 51; C.M. 22

WASHINGTON

The brig *Washington* referred to in *I.P.* 10 was launched in 1837 as a revenue cutter. She was re-rigged as a brig and loaned to the Coast Survey from 1840 to 1852, when she was returned to revenue marine. *Washington* was seized by the state of *Louisiana at *New Orleans in 1860.

(Other *Washingtons* include a large galley of 1776 with 36 mismatched guns; a merchant schooner captured in the *Caribbean in 1799 and re-rigged by the *British as a brig; a revenue cutter of 1833 active in the *Seminole wars but ruined by dry rot incurred in southern waters.)
I.P. 3; I.P. 10

WASHINGTON, GEORGE; WASHINGTON'S

George Washington (1732-99), first *President of the United States (1789-97), gained fame as commander-in-chief of forces in the *American Revolution. He had served in both *Continental Congresses and was a *Federalist in politics. He was apotheosized after his death, when many legends sprang up and many adulatory biographies were written; he has been a main character in much American literature, which has continued to paint him larger than life.

Washington had appointed M.'s maternal grandfather, Peter *Gansevoort, commissioner to the *Iroquois at the war's close.

M.'s finest tribute is perhaps in his describing "Queequeg" as "George Washington cannibalistically developed," in *M.D.* 10.

The *Baltimore "Washington monument" of *M.D.* 35 is a Doric column of 1809-29.

W. 6; W. 76; W. 91; M.D. 10; M.D. 35; I.P. 3

WASHINGTON GROUP

Captain *Joseph Ingraham discovered the northern group of the *Marquesas in 1790, naming them the Washington Group: *Nuku-hiva; Ua Pu; Ua Huka; Eiao; Hatatu; Motu One (8°38' and 9°32' S. and 139°20' and 140°10' W.)
T. 2

WASPS

The eighteen-gun *American brig *Wasp*, sister ship of *Hornet*, itself owing much to *French *corvette design, became the model for a whole class of ships in 1813. One of the most noted men-of-war, she had been converted to a warship for use against the *Barbary *pirates but was lost at sea leaving no trace. The powerful and fast class of ships was used for commerce-raiding, privateer-hunting, and convey escort.
M. 28

WATCH-SEALS

Watch-fobs.
M.D. 91

WATER-BEARER, THE

See "Zodiac."
M.D. 99

WATER-CURE ESTABLISHMENT

Mineral-spring spas and baths have been popular since ancient times, especially in continental Europe. But the teachings of Vincent *Preissnitz made hydrotherapy a rage in the nineteenth century, with professorships established in

*Vienna and *England and spas such as Bath, Buxton, and Wildbad enjoying renewed popularity. As M. notes in *P.* 22:1, *Americans took up the practices with almost religious devotion. The claims made for the waters mentioned in that chapter are not exaggerated. The waters of various spas were said to contain therapeutic substances such as iodine, chlorine, magnesium, iron, inert gases, sulphur, and carbon dioxide. They were used in peat baths, mud packs, heart-failure treatments, and colonic irrigations by "*Vaporites" and "*Soakites." The *Romans had made an elaborate ritual of bathing, anointing in an "unctorium," in preparation for the "caldarium" (hot room) and the "sudatorium" or "laconium" (steam room). Afterwards, they visited the "tepidarium" (warm room) and the "frigidarium" (cold bath); M. saw ruins of these at Hôtel de *Cluny, in *Paris. England's Dr. Jonathan Green (1788?—1864) was a great proponent of "Fumigating Baths" to cure a multitude of diseases, during M.'s time.
W. 21

WATER-LILY
     The aquatic plants have large flat floating leaves and showy flowers of many colors: genera *Nymphaea*, *Nuphar*, *Nelumbo*.
M. 122

WATERLOO
     The Waterloo Campaign is the name given to battles of June 15-18, 1815 wherein the *French commander *Napoléon was defeated by a large mixed force of inexperienced *British, *German, and *Dutch-*Belgian soldiers under *Wellesley and a *Prussian group under *Blücher. It occurred in the area between the Franco-Belgian border and Waterloo (south of *Brussels). The defeat led to Napoléon's second abdication and exile on *St. Helena.
     "Waterloo game" of *O.* 29 appears to be wordplay suggesting that the French are not good fighters when "water" is involved.
     In Brussels in 1849, M. confessed in his journal (7 December): "Waterloo is some 8 miles off. Cannot visit it—& care not about it."
O. 29; M. 24; M. 90: M. 139; I.P. 25

WATERLOO PENSIONERS
     See "Greenwich."
M. 139

WATER STREET
         *Manhattan's Water Street runs N.-S. from *Fulton to
*Whitehall Streets, on the east side. In 1792, the Tontine Coffee
House on Water served as *New York's first stock exchange;
the first residential gas lights were installed at No. 286 in 1824
(and on the streets by the 1830's). But by M.'s day, Water Street
had denigrated into a district of low-rent laborers' shops and
cheap lodging houses, the rooms of which sometimes housed
wall-to-wall sleepers. An illustration in *Frank Leslie's Illustrated Newspaper* (1872) shows "Our Homeless Poor" on Water
Street, using the expression, "How the other half lives" eighteen years before Jacob Riis's exposé was published. Holt's
Hotel stood on the corner of Fulton and Water, next to the infamous Market Street dance house of John Allen. It was notorious in the 1860's for supporting prostitution while supplying
Bibles for every room. (Allen went out of business when his
more debauched customers deserted him for occasionally rent-
ing the premises for ministers' gatherings.)
         M. was well aware of his yolking of disparate Waters, in
M.D. 6; see *Liverpool's "*Water Street."
M.D. 6

WATER STREET
         *Liverpool's Water Street dates from at least the mid
1600's. It runs c. 100-feet from *Town Hall to *George's Dock.
The site of the first Liverpool *Customs House, it also contained Derby Tower, used at one time as a jail. At the time of
M.'s visits in 1839 and 1857, Water Street was lined with shops,
offices, and baths for the elite.
M.D. 6

WATTS
         Isaac Watts (1674-1748) was a prolific writer of
*Protestant hymns. The son of a Nonconformist English
tradesman, Watts was educated for the ministry but retired
early in ill health. He published verse, and theological and educational works, but is chiefly remembered for his hymns and
songs for children.
         In *M.D.*, Bildad's song, "Sweet fields beyond the
swelling flood," is Hymn 66, stanza 3 of a work usually denom-
inated by its first line, "There is a land of pure delight," as in
Hymns and Spiritual Songs (1707-1709), Book 2. There were
several collections of Watt's work containing this song which
were easily available to M., but church attendance probably accounts more for his familiarity with the hymns.
M.D. 22

'WAY TO WEALTH'
    See "Franklin, Benjamin . . . . "
I.P. 9

"WEALTH OF NATIONS"
    See "Smith's [Adam]."
R. 25

WEBSTER [DANIEL]; MR. WEBSTER
    Daniel Webster (1782-1852), famed lawyer, orator, and
statesman, was born in *New Hampshire and graduated from
Dartmouth. He was admitted to the bar in 1805 and elected to
*Congress in 1813 and 1823, gaining national recognition as a
lawyer and orator. In the Senate (1827-41), he opposed states'
rights and defended the Bank of the United States against
*Jackson's attack. He was Secretary of State for *Harrison and
Tyler but abandoned the latter because Tyler championed the
states.
    Returned to the Senate in 1845, he favored protective tar-
iffs, upheld the constitutional rights of slaveholders (M.'s point
in *M.*), and supported Clay's Compromise measures. He left
the Senate in 1850 to be Fillmore's Secretary of State, by then
considered a traitor to the *Whig spirit.
    Among his most famous speeches: the *Bunker Hill
oration, Discourse on the 200th Anniversary of the Pilgrims'
Landing (both 1825), and Discourse in Commemoration of
*Jefferson and Adams (1826).
    In the year of M.'s birth (1819), Webster's intercession
regarding the indebtedness of M.'s paternal uncle saved the
family from scandal that would have destroyed the careers of
family members in government posts. At the National
*Republican Convention of 1832, his speech extolled the virtues
of M.'s grandfather, Major Thomas Melvill (see "Walter Redburn.").
    See also "Extracts" 20 and "Extracts" 66.
M. 18; M.D. Extracts 20; M.D. Extracts 66

WEBSTER NOAH; WEBSTER'S; *WEBSTER'S DICTIONARY*
    Noah Webster (1758-1843), *Connecticut lexicographer
and philologist, gained lasting fame for *An American Dictionary of the English Language* (2 vols., 1828), his "*ark."
    An ardent Federalist, he sought national legislation on
the copyright question, a serious issue for a prolific writer.
Among his many works are *A Grammatical Institute of the
English Language* (forerunner of the *Dictionary*, 1783-85), the

first part of which became his famous spelling book; *Sketches of American Policy* was published in 1785, and *Dissertations on the English Language* in 1798. He was also editor of Federalist journals and books.

The *Dictionary* added some 5,000 American usages to existing works and based its definitions on American usage. It was almost doubled in size for the 1840 edition.

Sealts #s 550, 551, 552 are 1846 or later editions of the *Dictionary*. All "Etymology" quotations in *M.D.* are accurate.
M.D. Etymology; M.D. 53

"WEE-WEES"
    Dialectical references to the *French, not only in the *Marquesas but in *New Zealand, *Australia, and elsewhere.
T. Sequel; O. 32; O. 45

WELLINGTON; DUKE OF WELLINGTON
    Arthur Wellesley (1769-1852), first Duke of Wellington, was the *British hero of the battle of *Waterloo (1815). He had become a national figure by virtue of earlier military exploits and was created duke in 1814. By the 1830's, he was highly placed in politics, becoming Prime Minister and Secretary of State for Foreign Affairs.
    Called by two physically apt nicknames, "Old Nosey," or "The Iron Duke" (the latter used by M. in "The Paradise of Bachelors"), Wellington was not a personally attractive man. Caricaturists and satirists attacked his libertine behavior; living apart from his wife, he often indulged in drug-taking and gambling.
    Many writers (especially *Byron, in *Childe Harold's Pilgrimage*) praised Wellington, and Queen *Victoria granted him a magnificent state funeral, commemorated in Tennyson's "Ode on the Death of the Duke of Wellington."
    At *Christmas in 1871, M. presented his son, Stanwix, with a copy of *The Words of Wellington* (N.Y. 1869).
    M. had started giving titles to the chapters of "Billy Budd," when he left off work. One chapter about *Nelson was to bear the title, "Concerning the greatest sailor since the world began," from Tennyson's "Ode" on Wellington.
R. 46; W. 27; M.D. 90

WERTER'S CHARLOTTE
    The hero's beloved, in *Goethe's *The Sorrows of Young Werther*. The reference in *C.M.* 4, "bread and butter," alludes to "Werther's" first meeting "Charlotte" when she is serving

bread to her siblings. Thackery parodied the scene in his ballad, "Sorrows of Werther."
C.M. 4

WESLEY
John Wesley (1703-91), *English clergyman, founded
Methodism when he joined the study group of his brother,
Charles, at *Oxford. Becoming leader of the group, nicknamed "the Holy Club," or "the Methodists," Wesley turned its
attention from passive devotion to social action in prisons,
workhouses, and poverty-stricken areas.
Persuaded to carry his work to the Indians of *America,
Wesley visited *Georgia and became a member of the
*Moravian society. He was not popular in America but saw
the experience as "the second rise of Methodism," the task of
which was to spread belief in salvation by faith, good works,
and rejection of *predestination. He returned to England as
itinerant preacher, hoping to reinvigorate the *Church of England. He organized Methodism into evangelistic units, and by
the 1870's he declared his societies independent of Anglican
rule. By the time of his death, there were approximately one-
half million adherents, singing his popular hymns at services
and reading his many educational and practical works.
R. 41

WEST-BROADWAY
*New York City's West Broadway was formerly "Chapel
Street"; maps of the 1850's show both names. Both of M.'s references to West Broadway involve people of color ("Negro Mob,"
in W. 16; "mulatto," in R. 17), suggesting that the area was a
black neighborhood.
R. 17; W. 16

WEST-END
*London's West-End (between *Charing Cross and west-
ern *Hyde Park) was in M.'s time a fashionable area of fine
houses and squares patterned after *Covent Garden's Piazza.
Specialized luxury shops and wine stores, and fine tailors' and
gown-makers' establishments were interspersed with theatres. The area changed its character after 1870, when department stores sprang up and theatres were constructed in a
separate area.
R. 45

WESTERN ISLANDS
> The *Hebrides.

I.P. 2

WEST INDIA; WEST INDIES; WEST INDIAN
> M. follows contemporary practice of invoking "West Indies" to suggest swashbuckling adventures of rum-swigging *pirates. The name refers to the 2,500 mile-long crescent-shaped *Antilles archipelago, which runs from *Florida to the coast of *Venezuela, separating the *Atlantic from the *Caribbean. Its three units are the Bahama Islands, Greater Antilles, and Lesser Antilles.

Passim

WEST INDIA DOCKS
> The West India Docks on the Thames covered an area of 295 acres. M.'s interest in docks climaxes in *R.*, in which he devotes an entire chapter to the history, size, and nature of *England's docks (Chapter 32, "The Docks").

W. 73

WEST INDIA TRADE
> The West India trade constituted one leg of the triangular *slave trade, from the late seventeenth to the late eighteenth century. The *British were the largest participants, but the *French and *Dutch also took part. Ships would leave Europe bearing liquor (usually rum), firearms, and other goods to exchange for *Africans taken as slaves (most often from the Gulf of *Guinea: the Slave Coast). The "middle voyage" took the slaves to the West Indies or the *American colonies under horribly crowded and unsanitary conditions. (The mortality rate was over 20%.) The ship would return to Europe bearing molasses made in the West Indies, with which to make rum to trade for more slaves. Rum manufacture had begun probably in Barbados, where it was known first as "kill-devil," then "rum-bullion," and by 1667 "rum." (Sugar cane had been introduced by the *Spanish after *Columbus discovered *Cuba in 1492). From 1680 to 1786, 2,000,000 slaves were imported for British possessions and for the West Indies alone.

C.M. 37

WEST INDIES SQUADRON
> See "Squadron."

W. Passim

WESTMINSTER ABBEY

The abbey has been the coronation scene of every *British sovereign since *William the Conqueror, with the exceptions of Edward V and Edward II.

Westminster is one of the 32 boroughs constituting greater London: bounded on the west by the Royal Borough of Kensington and Chelsea, north by the boroughs of Brent and Camden, east by the City of *London, south by the *Thames River. As early as 785, near the present site, stood a *Benedictine monastery. In 1065, *Edward the Confessor built a new church, which Henry III pulled down in 1245 to build the present abbey church, which has retained its original appearance, despite frequent alteration.

M. visited on 14, 15, and 25 November 1849. He attended services several times and commented in his journal on the absence of seats.

See also "Plantagenets."
T. 22; M. 60; R. 43; W. 4; W. 16

WESTMORELAND

Correct spelling of the scenic Lake District county of *Wordsworth is "Westmorland."
W. 11

WESTPHALIA

A former *Prussian province of western *Germany, describing an area roughly bounded by the former Prussian *Rhine Province (S.W., W.), the *Netherlands (N.W.), and the former Prussian provinces of *Hanover (N.,E.) and Hesse-Nassau (S.E., S.). It was part of *Saxon lands from the *Elbe almost to the Rhine. Westphalia was a duchy in the twelfth century and later (c. 1500) a part of the *Holy Roman Empire. The Peace of Westphalia (1648) ended the *Thirty Years' War. From 1807 to 1813, it was a *Napoleonic kingdom; the boundaries established after the Congress of *Vienna remained in effect until 1945.
M. 40

WEST POINT

United States Military Academy, the army equivalent of Annapolis, located at West Point, *New York, on the *Hudson River about 50 miles north of *New York City. It was established as part of the Army Corps of Engineers in March of 1802, with a staff of five officers and ten cadets. West Point had been a key fortress during the *American Revolution, at which time was discovered a serious lack of leaders and technicians not provided for by practical and non-scientific colleges then in existence.

By 1812, it had reorganized and expanded to a class of 250, but most permanent changes came about between 1817 and 1833, under the guidance of Colonel Sylvanus Thayer, called the "father of the military academy." The modern West Point enrolls about 2,500 cadets in a four-year all-expense-paid college curriculum leading to a Bachelor of Science degree. There is much emphasis on military instruction aiming to produce leaders of great patriotism and mental and physical fitness. Appointments are made by *Congressmen, the *President, and the National Guard. Graduates are commissioned as Second Lieutenants in the Regular Army.
W. 83

WET DOCK
The first commercial wet dock in *Britain was opened as a private enterprise in *Liverpool in 1715 (completed in 1719). The original plan for *Old Dock became a model for future wet docks in that the facility was not carved out of the land but instead used the natural features of the water (the "Pool"), enclosed by means of a stone sea wall, with land reclaimed behind it. The designer was Thomas Steers, who had worked on *London's *Rotherhithe project.

"Wet Dock" is sometimes used to refer to locks.

See also "Dry Dock" with respect to M.'s "note" in *R*. 32.
R. 32

WHAIHEREA
Another phonetic spelling (with "Waiurar") of Vairara, *Tahiti's lake.
O. 30

"WHALE"
M.'s device of listing foreign translations of the word is perhaps borrowed from *J. Ross Browne's appendix to *Etchings From a Whaling Cruise*, which includes a chart and discussion of comparative language use.

There are several errors in M.'s list: the Danish adjective form is used, rather than the noun, *hval*. The correct Anglo-Saxon form is *hwael*. The closest Hebrew word is *tannin* (modern Hebrew: *walfish*). Greek is κγτος.
M.D. Etymology

WHALEMAN'S CHAPEL

*New Bedford's Seamen's Bethel on Johnny Cake Hill was built in 1830, dedicated in 1832 by "Father" Edward Taylor of *Boston (See "Father Mapple"). M. probably attended before sailing on *Acushnet*, 3 January 1841. The church burned down and was restored in the 1970's. None of the cenotaph names cited by *M.D.*'s "Ishmael" is that of a known real disaster victim in the area.

First Chaplain was Rev. Enoch Mudge (1832-1843,) another possible original for "Father Mapple."

The chapel's prow pulpit (*M.D.* 8) with a rope ladder is M.'s invention. But when a twentieth-century pastor was installing (to his congregation's dismay) a pulpit like M.'s, unearthed cement work showed supports for what might have been a similar one (which would have burned in a fire of 1866). M.D. 7

WHALE-TROVER

"Trover" is a legal term signifying court action to recover the value of illegally appropriated personal property. M.D. 89

WHALLEY

Regicide Edward Whalley (d. 1674 or 1675), a military and political hero of the English Civil War and the Commonwealth, was a relative of *Cromwell. In 1647, he was guard to the imprisoned *Charles I, a judge at his trial, and a signer of the death warrant. He became a member of the *House of Lords in 1657 but was dismissed at the Restoration, escaping under an assumed name to *Boston, *Massachusetts, with his son-in-law, Major General *William Goffe, before the return of *Charles II to England. Whalley lived in hiding for the rest of his life, in Cambridge, Massachusetts, in New Haven, *Connecticut, and in Hadley, Massachusetts. M. 97

WHEELER, DANIEL

The *Englishman Daniel Wheeler (1771-1840) went to sea at the age of twelve and was a *midshipman at fourteen. He left the Navy to serve in the Army, but after marriage to a *Quaker, he became a minister (1816). In 1818, Wheeler began managing the *Tsar's 3,000-acre farm in *St. Petersburg. After other adventurous pursuits, he sailed in 1833 on the large cutter *Henry Freeling*, which had been purchased by private members of the Society of Friends. The ship stopped at

*Norfolk enroute to *Tahiti where, in 1834, Queen *Pomaree welcomed Wheeler as a philanthropic, rather than an ecomomic, emissary from Europe. By 1835, he was enroute to the *Sandwich Islands, *Raratonga, the *Society Islands, and *Tongataboo. He was stranded at *Sydney when his ship was sold.

Wheeler visited *America in 1839 and 1840, dying on arrival on his second visit. He was buried at the Friends burial ground, Orchard Street, *Manhattan. His "Letters and Journals" were edited and published by his son Charles in 1835, -36, -38, and -39. They were published as one volume by his son Daniel: *Memoirs of the Life and Gospel Labours of Daniel Wheeler*. London 1842 (*O*. 46). M. probably used the simultaneously published *Philadelphia edition.
O. 46; O. 48; O. 49

WHIG, --S
*Britain's Whig political party arose in the seventeenth century, in favor of gradual change toward more democratic government by *Parliament, in opposition to the *Tories, who favored the Crown. "Whig" became synonymous with "Liberal." (The name came from *whiggamore*, a pejorative describing certain *Scots.)

The American Whig Party was established in 1836 by opponents of *Andrew Jackson. It elected *Harrison (1840) and Zachary Taylor (1848) and then split over the *slavery issue. See "Democrat."
Passim

WHIRLPOOLES
See "Descartes; Descartian"; "Equator . . . ."; "Extracts" 7.
M.D. Extracts 7 and elsewhere

WHISKY-PUNCH
The ingredients of whisky punch are lemon juice and rind, powdered sugar, boiling water, brandy, and Irish, Scotch, or *American whisky (probably the latter, if the barber in *C.M.* 43 were actually making whisky punch).
C.M. 43 and elsewhere

WHISTONIAN
William Whiston (1667-1752), *English clergyman and mathematician, revived the *Arian heresy in England. His *A*

New Theory of the Earth (1696) attempted to show that the biblical *creation, *deluge and conflagration myths could be scientifically explained; *The Accomplishment of Scripture Prophecies* (1708) claimed that *Bible prophecies can be interpreted
almost literally. Whiston interpreted early *Christian texts in
the five-volume *Primitive Christianity* (1711-12); he wrote an
emended Book of Common Prayer (1713), and a revision of the
*King James Version of the *New Testament (1745).

The "theory concerning the damned and the comets" is
from *Astronomical Principles of Religion* (1725), in which
Whiston conjectures that a comet is the Scriptural Hell.
(Franklin's *The Wake of the Gods* sees Whiston's thought as
central to the cosmography of *M.*, explaining the connection in
Chapter 2).
M. 1

WHITE-ASH
Oars were made of white-ash wood (*Fraxinus ameri-
cana*).
M.D. 81

WHITE BEAR OF THE POLES
See "Pole . . . . "
M.D. 42

WHITE BELT OF WAMPUM
The white belt of wampum of the *American Indian was
commonly written about, as an artifact of high symbolic importance, especially in the *Iroquois ceremony of the sacred White
Dog. In a "new year" ceremony in early February, a pure
white dog was strangled and his body decorated with painted
spots, ribbons, and feathers, and hung with a white belt of
wampum. He was then burned at a ceremonial fire with appropriate music and procession to an altar.
M.D. 42

WHITE DOG
See "White belt of wampum."
M.D. 42

WHITE ELEPHANTS, LORD OF THE
In the sixteenth century, there was continual struggle
between the rulers of *Siam, *Pegu, and Aracan for possession

of regal white elephants, which were venerated and somehow connected with the doctrine of Metempsychosis.

M.'s reference in *M.D.* to the king of Pegu as "Lord of the White Elephants" is also undoubtedly ironic, the city of Pegu by the nineteenth century being a prime example of a grand thing that has outlived its usefulness.
M.D. 42

WHITE FRIAR

In *England, mendicant Roman *Catholic *Carmelite monks are called White Friars. The order originated at *Palestine's Mt. Carmel early in the thirteenth century, taking as ideal the way of life of the prophet *Elijah, considered the founder of monasticism. Nineteenth-century liberal governments, especially the *French, suppressed the order, which had produced such mystics as St. John of the Cross. Their brown vestments are covered by a white robe, accounting for the sobriquet.
M.D. 42

WHITEHALL

The street leading from the lower *East River side of *Manhattan to *Broadway.
M.D. 1

WHITEHAVEN

A chief seaport of *Solway Firth and market town of *Cumberland, *England. The port for *St. Bees, Whitehaven was raided by *John Paul Jones in 1778.
I.P. 11; I.P. 14; I.P. 15; I.P. 17

WHITE HILLS

See "White Mountains."
W. 50

WHITE HOODS OF GHENT

See "Ghent."
M.D. 42

WHITE-LEAD

Used in making white paint.
M.D. 42

WHITE-MICE
    Master at arms' spies or informers.
W. 73

WHITE MOUNTAINS
        The granite mountains of *New Hampshire are a range
of the *Appalachians extending from the *Connecticut River
(W.) to western *Maine (E.). They have always been a popular
summer resort; the newly married Mr. and Mrs. Herman
Melville traveled through on their honeymoon trip of 1847 and
fled to the mountains in the 1870's and 80's to relieve Mrs.
Melville's allergies. Mount Washington and Crawford Notch
were frequent settings for literature of the time.
        "White Hills' (*W.* 50) is probably a reference to the White
Mountains; Whitehills is a town of East Hampshire,
*England, the state's namesake.
M.D. 42

"WHITENESS OF THE WHALE"
        Howard Vincent has suggested that M. was following a
trend in writing his treatise on whiteness. One starting point
may have been an article called the "The Doctrine of Colours,"
in the *American Magazine of Useful and Entertaining Knowledge* for May, 1836 (Vol. 2, p. 375), then edited by *Hawthorne.
*Newton's idea that colour is not inherent but is a property of
the light in which objects are placed was also debated by
*Goethe, and played with by *Poe in *The Narrative of Arthur
Gordon Pym* (1838). In *Pseudodoxia Epidemica* (Book 6),
*Browne had focused on Blackness.
M.D. 42

WHITE NUN
        In *England, "White Nuns," or "White Ladies" are Cis-
tercian Nuns, an order directed by the "White Monks" of the
Cistercians (later Bernardine) order. The group was founded
in *France before the close of the twelfth century, patterning
their lives on that of the Monks, whose monasteries thrived
under a mixed system of autonomy and dependence on central
governance.
M.D. 42

WHITE SEA
        In northern Russia.
R. 7; M.D. 42

WHITE STONE
     *Genesis 28: *Jacob marked the place of his ladder-vision with a stone, calling it Beth-el and promising to build a temple on the spot.
     *Revelation: 2:17: "To him that overcometh will I give to eat of the hidden manna, and will give him a white stone, and in the stone a new name written, which no man knoweth, saving he that receiveth it."
M.D. 42; C.M. 25

WHITE TOWER OF LONDON
     See "Tower of London."
M.D. 42

WHITE WALTHAM
     I.P.'s original (see "Israel Potter's autobiographical story") calls White Waltham "a country town about 30 miles from Brintford" (*Brentford): perhaps the present-day Great Waltham.
I.P. 6; I.P. 7

WHITE WHALE
     See "Moby Dick."
M.D. Passim

WHITIHOO
     Perhaps another exotic spelling (with "*Hytyhoo") of Vaitahu, *St. Christina Island, *Marquesas.
T. 1

WHITSUNTIDE
     In *Christian practice, the week beginning with Whitsunday, especially the first three days of the week. Whitsunday is the seventh Sunday after Easter, commemorating the descent of the Holy Spirit on *Pentecost, and formerly a day for baptism of converts.
M.D. 42

WHITTINGTON
     The legend surrounding Whittington and his cat: "Richard," a poor boy went to *London, hearing the streets were paved with gold. Serving in a rich merchant's house, he

shipped his cat to *Barbary, then ran away. The *Bow Bells of St. Mary-le-Bow in Cheapside summoned him back: "Turn again Whittington/Thrice Lord Mayor of London." The cat was purchased by the King of Barbary as a ratter, and "Dick" was able to marry his master's daughter, "Alice," then rose to be *Lord Mayor three times.

The actual Dick was the youngest son of Sir William de Whityngdon, born about 1358 in Gloucestershire. Unprovided for as the youngest, Dick rose on his own, becoming the owner of sailing vessels called "cats," with which he carried coal from *Newcastle to London. He became wealthy enough to make a large loan to Henry IV, and was mayor 1397-98; 1406-07; 1419-20. He died in 1423, leaving his wealth to charity. The epitaph on his grave (destroyed in the fire of London) read:

> Beneath this stone lies Wittington,
> Sir Richard rightly named,
> Who three times Lord Mayor served in London,
> In which he ne'er was blamed.
> He rose from indigence to wealth
> By industry and that,
> For lo! he scorned to gain by stealth
> What he got by a cat.

M. records seeing Whittington's house in his journal for 10 November 1849.
T. 29; R 36

WIDOW AND ORPHAN ASYLUM
        See "Humane Society."
C.M. 6; C.M. 8

WIDOW'S CURSE
        OED notes the use of "widow-cursed" as an adjective but fails to supply a definition.
W. 53

WILBURFORCE
        William Wilberforce (M.'s spelling in error; 1759-1833), *English statesman/philanthropist, played a large part in the abolition of Britain's *slave trade. Born into a landed Yorkshire family, he graduated from St. John's College, *Cambridge, and in 1870 began a career in *Parliament. An evangelical *Christian, and close associate of William Pitt, he soon became interested in the slavery question, in 1787 setting

up London's Committee for the Abolition of the Slave Trade and later speaking against the trade in the House of *Commons. After Pitt's death, Wilberforce became a vice-president of the Antislavery Society, founded in 1823, but the Emancipation Act was not passed until just after his death. C.M. 7

WILKES
    Charles Wilkes (1798-1877), best known today for his *Narrative of the United States Exploring Expedition*, was born in *New York into a wealthy Scottish-English-Dutch family of some historical importance. He attended private schools and worked in his father's office until wanderlust sent him to sea at an early age. A brutal merchant service cruise to *France did not dissuade him, and in 1818 he joined the *Navy as a *midshipman, becoming lieutenant in 1826. By 1834 he was head of the Navy Department Depot of Charts and Instruments, later the Naval Observatory and Hydrographics Office. After much political and bureaucratic delay and cancellations by projected participants, in 1838 *Congress finally authorized the United States Exploring Expedition, naming Wilkes commander despite personality problems that had already made him unpopular. "Father" of the Expedition had been Jeremiah N. Reynolds, advocate of the "Symmes Hole" theory that the Earth had entrances at the poles, and author of "Mocha-Dick; or the White Whale of the Pacific," published in *Knickerbocker Magazine* in 1839. *Nathaniel Hawthorne had originally applied to be historian of the cruise, and original commander was to have been *Thomas ap Catesby Jones, prototype for *W*.'s Commodore, assisted by James Armstrong, prototype for "*Captain Claret." A *Gansevoort relative, originally assigned, was reassigned before departure.
    The group left Hampton Roads, *Virginia on 18 August 1838: a fleet of small, ill-equipped ships: sloops of war *Vincennes* and *Peacock*; ship *Relief*; brig *Porpoise*; two tenders, *Flying Fish* and *Sea Gull* (lost off Cape *Horn). The primary aim was nationalistic; the United States was finally to compete with other nations in exploring. Equally important was securing of data that would promote the whaling industry: charts of undiscovered territory; whale routes; hydrographic and other research; studies to better relations with natives who hampered whaling efforts. Most of the scientists became famous; naturalists, botanists, minerologists, taxidermists, and a philologist participated in the east-to-west circumnavigation which crossed the *Pacific three times, finally returning to New York Harbor 10 June 1842, having sailed 87,000 miles. Many of the places M. focuses on were visited: *South

America, the *Paumotu Islands of the Low Archipelago, the *Samoan Islands, *New South Wales, *Sydney, the *Antarctic Continent (with Wilkesland named after the commander), the Fiji (*Feegee) Islands, *Hawaiian Islands, west coast of the United States (including the rivers of *Oregon, with an eye to the Oregon territory dispute with Britain), San Francisco Bay, the Sacramento River, the *Philippines, the *Sulu Archipelago, *Borneo, Singapore, *Polynesia, and the Cape of *Good Hope.

Although the Expedition accomplished much, it was as controversial at its conclusion as it had been originally. Wilkes no sooner returned than he was court-martialed and publicly reprimanded for infractions of discipline, earning the sobriquet "Stormy Petrel." He apparently behaved as autocratically as "*Ahab" in many respects, giving himelf the rank of captain during the Expedition, and largely revising its aims.

Wilkes served on the Coast Survey from 1842 to 1843, and wrote his Expedition report between 1844 and 1861. Twenty-eight volumes had been projected, but only nineteen were ever published. Wilkes contributed *Narrative* (1844), *Meteorology* (1851), and *Hydrography* (1861). *Narrative* appeared originally as five volumes with an atlas, lavishly illustrated; it was later reissued in six volumes and reprinted as recently as 1970. M. purchased the six-volume version in 1847 (Sealts # 532).

Wilkes's actions were controversial as late as the *Civil War. He was court-martialed again in 1864 and suspended this time for insubordination and conduct unbecoming an officer when, as commander of *San Jacinto*, he caused the famous *Trent* crisis. Wilkes removed from the British ship two Confederate commissioners to Europe, James M. Mason and John Slidell. The action was at first praised but then repudiated by President *Lincoln in order to save relations with Britain.

By 1866, Wilkes was a Rear-Admiral on the retired list, married to Jane Renwick. His miscellaneous publications include *Western America, Including California and Oregon* (1849), *Voyage Around the World* (1849), *Theory of the Winds* (1856), and various autobiographical pieces.

(See also "Moby-Dick," for discussion of "Mocha Dick.")
O. 49; O. 54

WILKIE
Sir David Wilkie (1785-1841) was a *Scottish genre, history, and portrait painter whose small-scale humorous domestic scenes reminiscent of *Teniers were highly popular in *London. Wilkie had less success when he later turned to

portrait painting in the style of *Murillo.   He died at sea
returning from a visit to the *Holy Land.
    Sealts #364 is John William Meisonnier's *Sir David
Wilkie* (1881).
W. 91

WILLIAM CREAM
    A fictional character whose name follows *C.M.*'s pattern
of references to whiteness.
C.M. 43

WILLIAM THE CONQUEROR
    William I of *England (c. 1028-1087), son of Duke Robert
I of *Normandy and his mistress, was called "the Bastard."
He earned his rights as heir through the support of the
*French king, Henry I, whose victories profited greatly from
William's military skill and bravery. William consolidated his
support in Normandy while Henry made an unsuccessful at-
tempt (1054) at an invasion of England. Henry's death in 1060
made possible the Norman annexation of Maine in 1062 and
the conquest of England in 1066. Supported by the *Papacy,
William was able to defeat Harold, successor to *Edward the
Confessor.   He had himself crowned king of England at
*Westminster Abbey on *Christmas Day 1066. Four years of
revolts were crushed, and Norman personnel infiltrated
English institutions.
    Married to Matilda of *Flanders (d. 1083), William had
four sons and five or six daughters, one of whom became the
mother of King Stephen of England. He died as a result of injuries incurred in a bizarre equestrian accident in *France,
where he was attempting to recover lost territories.
R. 30; W. 87

WILLIS ELLERY
    See "Whaleman's Chapel."
M.D. 7

WILLOUGHBY
    Francis Willughby (1635-72), *English biologist, under-
took a systematic description of the organic world, with his colleague, *John Ray. His early death left Ray to pursue the project upon which the system of *Linnaeus was based.
M.D. 32

WILL-O-WISPS

"Ignis Fatuus" ("foolish fire"), or "Friar's lantern," a flame-shaped phosphorescence on marshy ground, the result of spontaneous combustion of decaying vegetable matter. Figuratively an impracticable or misleading *Utopian scheme.
M. 173

WILSON

As Anderson shows in *Melville in the South Seas*, Charles B. Wilson, son of a missionary at Point Venus, was acting *English Consul of *Tahiti by 1842, during the *French occupation, having assumed the post some time after the departure of *Pritchard for England in February 1841. M.'s claim that he was a dissipated petty villain is corrobrated by *Wilkes and Wise.
O. Passim

WINDERMERE

The reference is probably to *England's largest lake, a ten and one-half by one-mile island-dotted lake between *Lancashire and *Westmorland. There is also a Lake Windermere resort in *Canada.
M. 165

WINDSOR

A town of *Berkshire County, western *Massachusetts: eleven miles east-northeast of *Pittsfield.
I.P. 1; I.P. 3

WINDSOR, --CASTLE

Windsor Castle, a *British Royal residence, is in the town of New Windsor, nineteen miles west of *London. The thirteen-acre castle is located on the site of a structure erected by *William the Conqueror. In 1180, Henry II began the Round Tower and outer walls, which were completed by Henry III. *Edward III made numerous additions, and the castle's original defensive purpose gradually yielded to its residential character, with changes made by *Henry VIII, *Elizabeth I, *Charles II, and *George IV. The various towers, chapels, tombs, ecclesiastical residences, parks, the "Hundred Steps" giving access to the north, along with art works by *Leonardo da Vinci, *Michelangelo, *Raphael, Holbein (the Younger), all make it a popular tourist stop. The Union Jack or Royal Standard is flown to signify the presence of the Royal family.

M. visited Windsor in 1849, commenting at length in his
journal (22 November). The view from the Round Tower was
noted, along with the "Cheerlessly damnatory fine" state
apartments of *Victoria, whom he saw on the premises. M.
saw the castle again in the distance on 2 May 1857, while enroute to *Oxford.
M.D. 32; M.D. 105; I.P. 24

WINNEBAGOES
    A Siouan Indian tribe of Wisconsin and Nebraska.
M. 68; W. 84; M.D. 54

WISBURY LAWS
    See "Hanse Towns."
W. 72

WISCONSIN
    The thirtieth state was admitted to the Union in 1848. It
is bordered by Lakes *Superior and *Michigan (N.), Lake
Michigan (E.), *Illinois (S.), Iowa and *Minnesota (W.). The
*French visited the area in 1634, settling in 1717 and establish-
ing Green Bay in 1745. The area was ceded to *Britain in 1763;
it made part of the Northwest Territory in 1787, part of Indiana
Territory in 1800, and Wisconsin Territory in 1836.
R. 33

WISDOM OF JESUS, THE SON OF SIRACH
    See "Sirach."
C.M. 45

WODEN
    The ancient Germanic war god and lord of the kingdom
of death, Woden is the god called Wodan (or Wotan) in English
usage. He is associated with the *Scandinavian *Odin and the
*Roman *Mercury, rather than *Mars. His name appears to
mean "one who makes mad," or "the bringer of ecstasy," for
his giving of fury and strength as the god of battle. Sacrifices to
him included ritual stabbing, strangulation, bloodletting to the
death. The name is preserved in the word "Wednesday."
    Woden was believed to be the founder of many royal dy-
nasties and was claimed as an ancestor by Germanic and
Anglo-Saxon kings. He is represented as bearer of the shield
and god of the wolf and raven.

Woden is said to have named the *Longobardi ("long beards").

See "Valhalla" with regard to the "suppers" of *M*. 181.
M. 181

WOEBEGONE
A theoretical person beset with misery.
M.D. 89

WONDER AND WEN
Murray's notes to *P*. suggest that M.'s fictional characters owe their names to "two pious hypocrites, Wenham and Wagg," in Thackeray's *Pendennis* (1850).
P. 17:1; P. 17:2

WOODCOCK, JOHN; SQUIRE WOODCOCK
In the *Life and Remarkable Adventures of Israel R. Potter* (see "Israel Potter's autobiographical story"), the historical "J. Woodcock Esq." introduces Israel to *Horne Tooke and *James Bridges and sends the letter through Israel to *Benjamin Franklin.
I.P. 6; I.P. 7; I.P. 12

WORDSWORTH
*Americans very grudgingly admired Wordsworth's poetry in the nineteenth century, and although M. probably shared in the grudging, it is a rare biographer who does not note the Wordsworthian echoes in M.'s works. Perhaps M.'s position can be likened to his feelings about *Emerson: respect for the "diver" conquering his particular aversions.

William Wordsworth (1770-1850) was a widely read romantic poet long before M. was born. His works celebrated the sublime simplicity of nature and psychologized about his own life, drawing to him the friendships of *Coleridge, *Scott, *Beaumont, DeQuincy, and others. Later romantic poets such as *Byron, *Shelley, and Keats were less impressed by his *transcendentalistic leanings, but Wordsworth's reputation was finally secured by the veneration of Matthew Arnold and John Stuart Mill. His personal life was a subject of some interest to the general public, involving as it did an illegitimate child, uncomfortable debt, lifelong bonding with his sister Dorothy, and early support of the *French Revolution.

Lyrical Ballads (1798, 1800, 1801, 1802), a collection with Coleridge, ushered in the age of English Romanticism. *Poems in Two Volumes* (1807) included the ode "Intimations of Immortality . . . . " *The Excursion* (1814) and other works extended his fame, as did the posthumously published *The Prelude* (1850), reflecting back on events of his life from childhood. Like many other English poets, he was named Poet Laureate long past the time of his greatest creativity, in 1843. His late work reflects his pursuit of travel and walking, as well as his love of England's Lakes District. His permanent reputation, however, rests on the innovative topics and forms demonstrated in works written before 1835.

Although M. overtly parodies the leech-gatherer of "Resolution and Independence" (1807; Stanza 7, lines 6-7) in his short story, "Cock-a-Doodle-Doo," and probably classed Wordsworth with the "*German mystics," his numerous references in the journal for March and April 1857 show his appreciative grasp of the earlier poet's contribution. As late as 1869, M. marked his own copy of Arnold's *Essays in Criticism* ("on Translating *Homer") so as to suggest the importance to him of lines from Book III of *The Prelude*:

> The marble index of a mind forever
> Voyaging through strange seas of
> Thought, alone.

"Rydal Mount" (*W.* 11), Ambleside, *Westmorland, was Wordsworth's home from 1813 until his death.
W. 11

WORLD'S FAIR
    The 1851 *London "Exposition of the Industry of All Nations" in the "Crystal Palace" (emulated in *New York in 1854) displayed almost nineteen acres of innovative devices.
C.M. 7

WOUVERMANS
    Philips Wouwerman (or Wouwermans; 1619-1668) was a *Dutch painter of military and hunting scenes. A pupil of Frans Hals, he is credited with more than 1,000 pictures. His favorite study was the horse, and most of his works portray a white one, perhaps suggesting M.'s study of *whiteness in *M.D.*
M. 13

WREN, SIR CHRISTOPHER

Renowned *English architect Sir Christopher Wren (1631-1723) studied anatomy, mathematics, and astronomy at *Oxford, along with other founders of the *Royal Society (of which he was President from 1681 to 1683). He was knighted in 1673. Wren's earliest major architectural work was the Chapel of Pembroke College, *Cambridge (1663-65). He designed some fifty London churches, including the rebuilt *St. Paul's (1675-1710). Wren created a great variety of church types, including *St. Bride's and St. Mary-le-Bow, and secular architecture including *Chelsea Hospital, *Greenwich Hospital and Observatory, *Temple Bar, *Hampton Court, and *Kensington Palace, all of which M. saw and admired in 1849 or 1857. Wren's epitaph in St. Paul's reads: *Si monumentum requiris, circumspice.* ("If you seek a monument, look about you.")
W. 41

WRIGGLE-TAILS

Probably not a proper species but any fish that moves in such character.
M. 48

X

XENOPHON

An *Athenian who lived from about 430 to 352 B.C., Xenophon is considered the world's first journalist. His most popular work, The *Cyropedia*, a fictionalized biography of king *Cyrus, is a forerunner of the modern novel. His other works are *Anabasis*, an account of a military expedition; *Hellenica*, a contemporary history; *Agesilaus*, about a monarch of the times; *Memorabilia and Symposium*, memoirs about *Socrates.

Sealts #147, *Harper Classical Library*, Vols. 1,2, are Edward Spelman's translation of *The Anabasis*.
M. 119

XERXES

Xerxes I, of the Achaemenid Dynasty, King of *Persia from 485 to 464 B.C. (between *Darius I, 521-485, and *Artaxerxes, 464-423), was the son of Darius I and Atossa,

daughter of *Cyrus II, the Great. Xerxes the Great invaded
*Greece during the Persian Wars by constructing a bridge of
boats across the *Hellespont; he cut a canal through the Isthmus of *Athos, overthrew the *Lacedaemions at
*Thermopylae, and sacked *Athens. Defeated at *Salamis, he
retreated into Asia. He was murdered by his *vizier, Arta-
banus, and succeeded by his son, Artaxerxes I. (Xerxes II,
son of Artaxerxes I, was also assassinated during his reign,
which followed his father's).

In the Bible, Xerxes is the banquet-prone *Ahasuerus
(Esther 1-10, Ezra 4:6, Dan. 9:1), ruler of twenty *satrapies
from *India to *Ethiopia, with a capital at *Persepolis and
quarters at *Susa, in *Elam. When his wife disobeys him,
Ahasuerus banishes her and marries the beautiful Esther,
unbeknownst to him, a Jew. Esther's cousin, *Mordecai,
warns Ahasuerus of plotters, and Esther's revelation to the
king of her kinship and Jewishness saves the Jewish population from the pogrom Ahasuerus has agreed to, after the
machinations of his wicked vizier, Haman, Mordecai's enemy.
Esther establishes the festival of Purim, and Ahasuerus
makes Mordecai second in command in the kingdom.

Ahasuerus is also the name of the Wandering Jew,
about whom *Goethe writes in *Truth and Poetry: From My
Own Life* (Sealts #228, Book 15). *Shelley made him a com-
plainer against deity in *Queen Mab* and an optimistic prophet
in *Hellas*.
M. 150; M. 164; M. 181; R. 49; M.D. 42; M.D. 81

"*XIPHIUS PLATYPTERUS*"
A *Pacific ocean fish called "Bill fish"; related to the
North *Atlantic swordfish, but larger.
M. 32

Y

YALE COLLEGE
Yale University was founded by Congregationalist min-
isters at Killingworth and Saybrook, *Connecticut, in 1701. It
was moved to New Haven in 1716 and then named in honor of
Elihu Yale, a contributor. Among main divisions extant in
M.'s time: Medical School (1813), Divinity School (1822), Law
School (1824), Sheffield Scientific School (1861), Fine Arts

School (1869). The first Ph.D. in the United States was conferred at Yale in 1861.
M.D. 24; M.D. 88

YANKEE
There are several theories about the derivation of the word, which M. appears to use naturally to designate "American." The earliest explanations arose in 1789: 1. Thomas Anburey, a *British officer, claims (*Travels* II. 50) it derives from the Cherokee work *eankke*, meaning "slave" or "coward," applied by the *Virginians to *New Englanders who would not help them in war against the Cherokees; 2. William Gordon in *History of the American War* notes its use about 1713 by a Cambridge, *Massachusetts, farmer, meaning "excellent." In 1822, Hecklewelder (*Indian Nations*) explained its derivation from Indian corruptions of "English," from "Yengees" to the modern form. One theory (from 1683) credits the Dutch "Janke," a derisive diminutive of "John."
By the nineteenth century, the word referred to a northern, as opposed to a southern, American. It was popularized in the song *"Yankee Doodle."
Passim

"YANKEE DOODLE"
The popular *American song was supposedly given lyrics by a British army surgeon during the French and Indian war of 1755. The tune is of disputed origin and was composed perhaps as early as Medieval times, as a church melody.
O. 29

YARMOUTH ROADS
The harbor of Great Yarmouth, *England, on the North Sea twenty miles east of *Norwich, is formed by the estuary of three rivers (Yare, Wavney, and Bure). It has been in use since ancient times, accommodating the largest of ships. "Roads" refers to a sheltering place for ships.
W. 90

YELLOW-BACK
A common tropical fish which often accompanies rays. It is many-finned, with a large head, and may be four feet long.
M. 48

YELLOW JACK
Yellow Fever.
C.M. 23

YELLOW LOTUS
A common sacred motif in *Egyptian and *Hindu art, signifying divine life.
M.D. 70

YELLOW SEA
Between mainland *China and the Korean peninsula.
M.D. 42

YERK
A lash, or smart blow, as of a whip or rod.
W. 2

YOJO
The name of "Queequeg's" idol possibly derives from the *Koran's equivalents of *Gog and Magog: Yâjooj and Majooj.
M.D. 16

YOKES
Pairs of whales.
M.D. 105

YORK
The York family is a branch of the British *Plantagenets. The name is derived from the Anglo-Saxon *Eure-wic* (pronounced Yorric), a town on the Ouse River, in *England. The Yorks boast three kings of England and many important historical personages, through their important marriages and political connections, and frequent usurpations. First Duke of York was the ineffectual Edmund Langley, son of Edward III. The Duke of York referred to in W. was created duke in 1634, later became *James II.
W. 71

YORK; YORK MINSTER, --'S
York, *England, 194 miles northwest of *London, has been strategically important since *Roman times. The first

minster was founded in 627, making York an important ecclesiastical capital, and later a center of learning under Alcuin.
The present minster was constructed between the thirteenth
and fifteenth centuries. At the time M. visited, it would have
shown damage from recent fires (1829 and 1840). A gap in
M.'s journal before it recommences on 8 November 1856 makes
it difficult to learn his precise impression of the massive
"West-front" (R. 49), which was completed in 1338, with towers
added in the fifteenth century.
R. 28; R. 49

YORKSHIRE
        The largest *English county covers almost the entire
northern part of the country, with towering chalk cliffs on the
eastern coast. The area's mountains, lowlands, and moors
show evidence of settlement since 10,000 B.C. *Roman, Germanic, early *Christian, *Scandinavian, and *Norman
strongholds preceded civil war activity in Yorkshire, where
*Percys and *Nevilles dominated. By M.'s time, the river sys-
tems and railroad connected its industrial (mining, textiles,
steels) areas and moved agricultural and fishery products. M.
traveled through Yorkshire in early November of 1856.
        See also "York"; "Tees"; "Humber"; "Hull";
"Sheffield"; "Leeds"; "Flamborough Head."
M.D. 102; I.P. 19

YOUNG
        Edward Young (1683-1765), poet of the popular *English
"graveyard" school, became a minister when his early literary
efforts were less acclaimed than those of *Pope and other contemporaries. His most famous work, *The Complaint, or Night
Thoughts on Life, Death and Immortality* ("Night Thoughts,"
1742-45), is a rambling didactic semi-autobiographical poem
focused on gloom and death. *Samuel Johnson praises him in
The Lives of the English Poets (1779-81).
M.D. 96

YOUNG AMERICA IN LITERATURE
        "Young America" originated in the "Tetractys Club": a
group of *New York-centered literati who banded together in
1836 through a common interest in works by Americans.
Among the most important members were *Evert Augustus
Duyckinck and Cornelius Mathews. By 1840, they were publishing a monthly magazine called *Arcturus* which at-

tempted to rival *Knickerbocker* but which failed within a year and one half.

The group represented a movement commendable for its attempt to support American genius but limited by some rather conventional attitudes and by politics. M. was at first assisted by the group, which came to see him as a renegade. Book 17 of *P.* is a satirical representation of such "assistance."

Young America's history is more fully discussed in Miller's *The Raven and the Whale*.
P. 17:1

YOUNG MEN'S ASSOCIATIONS
As members of a proper (if empoverished) family, M. and his brother *Gansevoort Melville belonged to the Albany Young Men's Association for Mutual Improvement (1835-38). Like its counterparts in other *American cities, the Albany YMA presented *lectures and debates on topics deemed important to the cultured young gentlemen who would eventually become prominent in statesmanship, business, and the arts. (One fellow member, Anthony Ten Eyck, scion of a renowned New York family, was to become in 1845 Commissioner of the *Sandwich Islands.) Gansevoort, ever the "straighter" of the brothers in his actions and ambitions, served on the Executive Committee and was President of the Debating Society. The more colorful M. was involved in 1837 in a personal conflict in the Philologos [Debating] Society which eventually became a public squabble aired in letters in a local publication.

When M. began receiving invitations to lecture, an early solicitation was from the Albany YMA. But if one may read M.'s personal beliefs into *P.*, it would seem that in his later, jaded perspective Young Men's Associations were lock-step cliques that one should outgrow if, indeed, one were not rejected by their members first. When he tried to eke out a living on the lecture circuit, such associations became M.'s less-than-generous employers.

On 27 January 1838, the *Albany Microscope* mockingly announced lectures at a "Young Men's Optimist Association For the Perfection of the Human Race."
P. 17:2

"YOUR GRACE"
*British courtesy title for dukes, duchesses, *archbishops.
R. 46

Z

ZADOCKPRATTSVILLE

A fictional representation of Prattsville, *New York, founded by Zadock Pratt (1790-1871) as the site of a tannery. M. was probably invited to *lecture at Prattsville.

This is otherwise perhaps another of M's none-too-subtly constructed inventions, which would have far more comprehensibility during his time. "Zadoc" is a parody of the Archbishop of *Canterbury, in *Dryden's *Absalom and Achitophel; "prat" (or "pratt") has long been slang for "buttocks"; "-ville" means town. So "Zadockprattsville" might be a town named after the buttocks of the Archbishop of Canterbury.
P. 17:2

ZANSOVINE

See "Sansovine."
C.M. 28

ZAUSOVINE

See "Sansovine."
C.M. 28

ZEALANDERS

These people might be from Zeeland, *Netherlands, or from Zealand, an island of *Denmark, or indeed from *New Zealand.
M.D. 101

ZEMBLA

See "Nova Zembla."
M. 148

ZEND-AVESTA

The Avesta is the most important *Zoroastrian scriptural work, called Zend-Avesta since its European introduction in the late eighteenth century. A scripture and prayer book for the *Parsees, it is unavailable in any single manuscript and presumed only a fragment of ancient Zoroastrian literature. *Herodotus and Pausanias discuss its use by the *Magi.
P. 21:3

ZENO

Probably M. refers to Zeno of Elea, *Greece (500 B.C.), a disciple of Parmenides and member of the Eleatic school which rejected polytheism and anthropomorphism. The inventer of "dialectic," Zeno strongly influenced *Plato, whose *Parmenides* relates a chronologically impossible conversation between Zeno and *Socrates (c. 470-399 B.C.).

Zeno the Stoic of Citium, *Cyprus (c. 334-261 B.C.), or Zeno the *Phoenician, founded the Stoic school at *Athens, making ethics central and teaching that happiness lies in conforming the will to the Divine wisdom governing the universe.

Zeno of *Tarsus was likewise a *Stoic, and Zeno of *Sidon was an *Epicurean.
M. 119

ZETLAND

*Shetland, *Scotland.
M. 149

ZEUGLODON

A sea-going mammal, "strap tooth," identified by *Sir Richard Owen in "Observations on the Basilosaurus of Dr. Harlan (*Zeuglodon cetoides*, Owen," *A Complete Collection of the Various Papers on Geology by Richard Owen, Selected from the Transactions of the Geological Society (1838-1845)*.

See "Creagh, Judge," for details of the Zeuglodon hoax.

M.'s source is undoubtedly the article "Whales," in *Penny Cyclopaedia* XXVII, which quotes Sir Richard Owen: "We cannot hesitate in pronouncing the colossal *Zeuglodon* to have been one of the most extraordinary of the *Mammalia* which the revolutions of the globe have blotted out of the number of existing beings."
M.D. 104

ZIMMERMAN

Johann Georg Ritter von Zimmerman (1728-95), *Swiss physician and writer on ethics, published the 1755 *Uber die Einsamkeit (On Solitude)*, revised 1784-85.
C.M. 11; C.M. 24

ZION, SONGS OF

The *German passengers of *R*. 33 sing songs with roots that go back as far as King *David, who first set *Jewish religious music to formalized ritual. The *Levites became custodians of ritual music, and by the time of the Book of *Psalms, musical terminology came into use, as well as named instruments; the *hazozra* was a shrill trumpet, the *shofar* a ram's or he-goat's horn used as a signal in the service even today. Secular music was played on the *kinnor* (a lyre), the 'ugab (a flute), the harp, the *tof* (drum) and cymbals.

The formulaic but improvised music was antiphonal and not so mournful in character as it was to become after the return from *Babylon, when the *shofar* became the only permitted instrument. The music of Zion greatly influenced western music (even to the use of notation). By the sixth and seventh centuries, foreign-influenced religious poetry was added to basic liturgical chant. By the *Middle Ages, the cantor (*hazzan*), a professional singer, had begun developing *Jewish singing into a stylized high, soft, nasal sound such as "Wellingborough" would have heard.
R. 33

ZODIAC

From early times, the zodiac (Gr. *zodiakos*, pertaining to animals), the imaginary belt of the heavens which the sun travels annually, has been divided into twelve equal parts of thirty degrees, proceeding from west to east, and originally corresponding to the zodiacal *constellations of the same names, but now coinciding with the constellations of the next-in-order names. The six northern are Aries (the ram), Taurus (the bull), Gemini (the twins), Cancer (the crab), Leo (the lion), Virgo (the virgin). The southern are Libra (the balance), Scorpio (the scorpion), Sagittarius (the archer), Capricornus (the goat), Aquarius (the water-bearer), and Pisces (the fish). Pictorial symbols designed for the zodiac signs appear in *Greek manuscripts from the *Middle Ages and have become conventional.

Astrology, the ancient art of forecasting human events by observation of the heavens, has influenced most religions. Casting of the horoscope depends on the positions of heavenly bodies at the moment of the subject's birth; the zodiacal sign under which he is born is said to affect his psychology and fortune throughout his life.

In astronomy, Aries is a small constellation with three visible stars; the vernal equinox is marked by the sun's passage into Aries: like the autumnal equinox (in Libra), a time of storm. Aries is denoted by a symbol like a ram's head, the original of which appears in the myth of Helle (see "Hellespont"). One born under the sign of Aries (March 20-April 20) is said to have leadership qualities: forcefulness, energy, resiliency, as well as headstrong impatience.

Taurus is an old constellation containing the *Pleiades and *Hyades, and the bright star, *Aldebaran. The bull symbol rises from the *Europa legend. One born under Taurus (April 20-May 21) is said to be unequalled in stubborness, patience, and resourcefulness, as well as in acquisitiveness.

Gemini, a constellation containing the bright stars, *Castor and Pollux, has a symbol with two vertical lines, which at first represented a pair of goats. The Greeks renamed the stars to fit their myth of the inseparable twins. Born under Gemini (May 21-June 21), one is insatiably curious, enthusiastic, aggressive, and talkative.

Cancer contains a large, loose cluster of stars. Its symbol represents the crab sent by *Juno to attack *Hercules during his battle against the *Hydra. Born under the sign of Cancer (June 21-July 23), one is tenacious—a sentimental homebody who is perhaps excessively caring.

Leo contains Regulus, a first-magnitude star. It is the source of the Leonid meteor showers which were spectacular at least twice in M.'s lifetime (1833 and 1866). Its symbol is like an upside-down horse-shoe (supposedly an evil omen). One born under Leo (July 23-August 23), as was M, is said to be a born leader: energetic, ambitious, perhaps domineering.

Virgo contains Spica, a blue star of the first magnitide. Its symbol probably honors *Astrea, the virgin daughter of *Jupiter by Themis. To be born under Virgo (August 23-September 23) is to be realistic, conscientious, and analytical, but overly critical and easily agitated.

Libra is a faint constellation which the sun enters at the autumnal equinox. Its symbol of the balance, or scales, refers to the equality of day and night at this time. The Libra-born (September 23-October 23) are said to be discriminating but tactful social creatures, rather indecisive and overly sensitive.

Scorpio's stars in the *Milky Way form a scorpion-like configuration. Its brightest star is the supergiant, Antares. One born under Scorpio (October 23-November 21) is bold and combative, intense and persistent.

Sagittarius is one of the brightest constellations of the Milky Way, containing the Big Dipper. It represents the centaur *Chiron, archer and instructor of *Achilles, *Jason, *Hercules, and *Aesculapius. One born under this sign (November 22-December 23) struggles with conflicting rational and animal instincts and is an extrovert who brooks no obstacles.

Capricornus is a faint constellation marking the sun's arrival by the winter solstice. In mythology, Capricorn was *Pan, who changed himself into a goat to escape Typhon, a monstrous *Titan. Born under Capricorn (December 23-January 20), one is a self-reliant, persevering and impassive realist who is at the same time cautious and disciplined: a lover of honors.

Aquarius is a faint constellation of third-magnitude stars. Its symbol represents part of a stream of water, reflecting the wet weather when the sun is in its range. Aquarians (January 20-February 19) are extreme individualists who resent authority. High-principled humanitarians, they are said to be too impersonal and permissive.

Pisces contains *Aphrodite and *Eros, changed into fishes when they jumped into the *Euphrates to escape Typhon, the monster. Pisceans (February 20-March 21) are self-sacrificing and sociallly responsible, but they are disorganized daydreamers.

M. 3; M. 75; M. 78; M. 79; M. 84; M. 181; M. 187; M.D. 44; M.D. 99; I.P. 7

ZOGRANDA
        An invention; another joke on *Scoresby.
M.D. 65

ZOOPHYTES
        See "Sandwiches."
M. 132

ZOPHAR
        One of the mistaken counsellors in the book of *Job.
C.M. 40

ZOROASTER; ZOROASTRIANISM
        Zoroaster (Greek form of Zarathushtra) was the reformer of ancient Iranian religion in the late seventh and early sixth centuries B.C. His teachings influenced the development of Judaism, *Christianity, Islam, and *Greek philosophy. Little is known of his life except that he opposed prevailing nomadic social conditions, encouraging agriculture. He was at first opposed for his attacks on priests and followers of ancient cults but became a legendary prophet after his death, credited with all the graces of priesthood, but not deified. He was eventually misindentified with astrology and magic, but by M.'s time a truer picture was emerging.

        The indo-Iranian religion (related to the *Vedic) was polytheistic, supporting a caste system reflecting the hierarchy of the gods. Zoroaster rejected all as demons, save one, Ahura Mazda. He explained evil as stemming from one of the sons of

Ahura Mazda, Angra Hainyu, or "Ahriman" (M.'s "*Arimanius," or Ariamanius). The other son was good: Spenta Mainyu. He saw the world as headed toward a conflagration from which only the good would emerge, establishing the good kingdom, Vohukhshathra. He condemned blood sacrifice but retained fire sacrifice, fire symbolizing truth, light, and order.

Many alterations occurred in Zoroastriaism over the centuries, but modern-day *Parsees, whose forebears emigrated from *Persia, keep it alive, with less emphasis on the evil principle, which they see as merely symbolic. The dualistic system which developed (similar to that of the *Magi) influenced the Jewish concept of the devil, as well as the language and symbolism of the *Bible (*Old and *New Testaments).

Zoroastrian literature falls into two parts: the Avesta (see "Zend-Avesta"), the original scriptural work, written in Avestan, and later works written in Pahlavi (Middle Persian) or in Persian (the *Denkart*, the *Bundahishn*, the *Gajastah Abdullah*, and minor works).

Bayle's *Dictionary* (Sealts #51) claims that Zoroaster died consumed by fire from heaven.
M. 119; M.D. 110

Extracts: Sources

The "Extracts" emulate Robert Southey's anonymous *The Doctor* (1834-47), which contains a "Prelude of Mottoes." They are from M.'s reading, secondary sources, and invention, as Luther Mansfield and Howard Vincent show in "Explanatory Notes" to Hendricks House edition.

They have been numbered for my purposes in this text, although that seems a desecration somehow, hampering their "browsability."

See also listings under individual names and titles, for explanatory material.

As the 1988 Northwestern-Newberry edition shows, M. made many minor wording changes or paraphrased in his adaption of the "Extracts" from sources. I have not indicated these changes except when they alter meaning dramatically or hamper location of the source. The reader is directed to N.N. for minute examination of M.'s practice.

1.
GENESIS
     1:21

2.
JOB
     41:32 ("Leviathan" for "he").

3.
JONAH
     1:17

4.
PSALMS
     104:26

5.
ISAIAH
       27:1

6.
HOLLAND'S PLUTARCH'S MORALS
       Philemon Holland 1603 trans., Sec. 31: "Which are the
Most Crafty, Water Animals or Those Creatures which Breed
upon the Land?"

7.
HOLLAND'S PLINY
       Holland 1604 trans. Pliny's *Natural History*, IX.ii.4.

8.
TOOKE'S LUCIAN. "THE TRUE HISTORY"
       William Tooke 1820 trans., II, 94.

9.
*OTHER OR OCTHER'S VERBAL NARRATIVE TAKEN
DOWN FROM HIS MOUTH BY KING ALFRED. A.D. 890.*
       Other . . . King Alfred, A.D. 890, in his trans. of Orosius,
History of the World, I, 1.
       (Quoted from J. Ross Browne.)

10.
MONTAIGNE - *APOLOGY FOR RAIMOND SEBOND*
       Michel Eyquem de Montaigne, *Apology for Raimond Se-
bond*, II, 12. (Sealts #366: title unidentified.) With minor
substitutions, from p. 219 of William Hazlitt's *The Complete
Works* . . . . (London, 1842).

11.
RABELAIS
       John Miller ed. of Rabelais. Sir Thomas Urquhart-Peter
Motteux trans. *Five Books of the Lives, Heroic Deeds and Sayings of Gargantua and his Son Pantagruel*, IV, 33, "How Pantagruel discovered a monstrous physeter, or whirlpool, near
the wild island."

12.
STOWE'S ANNALS
 The Annales, or General Chronicle of England, begun first by maister John Stowe (London, 1615), 9 July 1574 entry.

13.
LORD BACON'S VERSION OF THE PSALMS
 Francis Bacon, *Translation of Certain Psalms in English Verse* (London, 1625), Psalm 104:26.

14.
IBID. "HISTORY OF LIFE AND DEATH"
 Francis Bacon, *Historia Vitae et Mortis (1650), 3:48. History Naturall and Experimental of Life and Death* (London, 1638), with minor changes.

15.
KING HENRY
 William Shakespeare, *1 Henry IV*, I, iii, 57-58.

16.
HAMLET
 William Shakespeare, *The Tragedy of Hamlet, Prince of Denmark*, III, ii, 382.

17.
THE FAIRIE QUEEN
 Edmund Spenser, *The Fairie Queene*, Book 6, Canto 10, stanza 31, lines 5-9.

18.
SIR WILLIAM DAVENANT. PREFACE TO GONDIBERT
 Gondibert: an Heroick Poem (1651).

19.
SIR T. BROWNE. OF SPERMA CETI AND THE SPERMA CETI WHALE. VIDE HIS V.E.
 "Vulgar Errors," Sir Thomas Browne's *Pseudodoxia Epidemica, or Enquiries into Very Many Received Tenets and Commonly Presumed Truths* (1686), III, 26.
 (Sealts #90.)

20.
WALLER'S BATTLE OF THE SUMMER ISLANDS
    Edmund Waller, Canto III, lines 11-12, 53-54.

21.
OPENING SENTENCE OF HOBBES'S LEVIATHAN
    Thomas Hobbes, *Leviathan*, "Introduction," fifth sentence.

22.
PILGRIM'S PROGRESS
    "Extract" is not from *PP* but from John Bunyan, *The Holy War* (1682), Chapter 3.
    (Actually a paraphrase from Cheever.)

23.
PARADISE LOST
    John Milton, *P.L.* I, 200-202, with changes in some editions.

24.
IBID.
    John Milton, *Paradise Lost*, VII, 412-416.
    Quoted by Cheever, p. 52. (There are minor discrepancies in the phrasing which do not appear in M.'s edition: Hilliard, Gray, *The Poetical Works* [Boston, 1836; Sealts #358b], or in Cheever.)

25.
FULLER'S PROFANE AND HOLY STATE
    Thomas Fuller, *The Holy State and the Profane State*, Book 2, Chapter 21, "The Good Sea-Captain," Sec. 8.
    (Sealts # 221.)

26.
DRYDEN'S ANNUS MIRABILIS
    John Dryden, *Annus Mirabilis*, stanza 203.

27.

THOMAS EDGE'S TEN VOYAGES TO SPITZBERGEN, IN PURCHASS

Samuel Purchas, *Hakluytus Posthumus or Purchas His Pilgrims* (1625), Part II, Book 3, Chapter 2, Section 3.

(Actually a paraphrase from Harris I, 574. Only a few phrases correspond to the 1625 edition, III, 471.)

28.

SIR T. HERBERT'S VOYAGES INTO ASIA AND AFRICA. HARRIS COLL.

From Harris *Collection* I, 406, the wording of which differs from the corresponding section (I, 13) of Sir Thomas Herbert's *Some Years Travels in Divers Parts of Asia and Afrique* (1638).

29.

SCHOUTEN'S SIXTH CIRCUMNAVIGATION

William Cornelius Schouten's voyage described in *Navigantium atque Itinerantium Bibliotheca or, A Complete Collection of Voyages and Travels*, ed. John Harris (1705).

30.

A VOYAGE TO GREENLAND, A.D. 1671. HARRIS COLL.

Friedrich Martens, *Voyage into Spitzbergen and Greenland . . . anno 1671*, in Tancred Robinson, *Account of Several Late Voyages and Discoveries to the South and North . . .* (London, 1694). Plates in Harris. With minor changes, M. quotes from Harris I, 617, 632, 631, 630, 629). Corresponding sentences in the Robinson volume (1, 165, 158, 142, 135) are different.

31.

SIBBALD'S FIFE AND KINROSS

Sir Robert Sibbald, *The History, Ancient and Modern of the Sheriffdoms of Fife and Kinross* (1710; 1803), Part IV, Sec. 1- "Description of the Western Coast."

32.

RICHARD STRAFFORD'S LETTER FROM THE BERMUDAS PHIL. TRANS. A.D. 1668

Royal Society of London's *Philosophical Transactions*, Vol. III (19 October 1668). M.'s text differs from "An Extract of a Letter Written to the Publisher from the Bermudas by Mr. Richard Stafford," 16 July 1668. M. probably used Beale (137) or Browne (521).

33.
N.E. PRIMER
 The New England Primer For the More Easy Attaining the True Reading of English (Sealts #384).

34.
CAPTAIN COWLEY'S VOYAGE ROUND THE GLOBE. A.D. 1729
 Captain Ambrose Cowley, *A Collection of Voyages* (London, 1729), IV, Chapter 2. (Voyage occurred 1683-86.)
 (M.'s source actually William Hacke's *A Collection of Voyages*, in Dampier's 1699 or 1729 *A Collection of Voyages*, with changes and omissions.)

35.
ULLOA'S SOUTH AMERICA
 Don Antonio de Ulloa, *A Voyage to South America* (London 1758), II, p.332.
 (Except for the phrase "an insupportable smell," probably M.'s invention.)

36.
RAPE OF THE LOCK
 Alexander Pope, "The Rape of the Lock," Canto II, lines 117-120, with a minor change.

37.
GOLDSMITH, NAT. HIS.
 The almost-verbatim quotation is from "Of the Whale," in *Goldsmith's History of the Earth and Animated Nature*, Abridged . . . by Mrs. Pilkington (London: Vernor, Hood & Sharpe, 1807); Goldsmith's original was published in 1774.
 (Many of the works of Laetitia Van Lewin Pilkington [1712-1750], whom DNB calls an "adventuress," were published posthumously. Mrs. Pilkington was born in Dublin, the daughter of a male midwife. She married Matthew Pilkington, a penniless Irish parson/poet, who soon left her. She was then found in adultery, divorced, and went to London, where she was imprisoned for debt. Befriended by Colley Cibber and

others, she became known for her intelligence and wit.
Among her other publications: *Memoirs of Mrs. Laetitia Pilkington, wife to the Reverend Mr. Pilkington, written by herself*
[1748]; *Mrs. Pilkington's Jests, or the Cabinet of Wit and Humor* [1751, 1765]; *Poems* [1755].)

38.
GOLDSMITH TO JOHNSON
    James Boswell, *The Life of Samuel Johnson, LL.D*
(London 1839 or 1848). Purchased in London 19 December 1849
(Sealts #84).
    Actually, paraphrased from Boswell's *Life*.

39.
COOK'S VOYAGES
    Captain James Cook, *A Voyage to the Pacific . . . for
Making Discoveries in the Northern Hemisphere* (2nd ed.,
1785), II, 473.

40.
*UNO VON TROIL'S LETTERS ON BANKS'S AND SOLAN-
DER'S VOYAGE TO ICELAND 1772*
    Letters on Iceland (1780), Letter 12, with changes and
rearrangement.

41.
*THOMAS JEFFERSON'S WHALE MEMORIAL TO THE
FRENCH MINISTER IN 1778*
    With a large omission, the text is *Memoir, Correspon-
dence, and Miscellanies from the Papers of Thomas Jefferson*,
ed. Thomas Jefferson Randolph (Charlottesville, 1829; also
second ed., Boston, 1830), II, 398 (and II, 401 in the 1829 London edition). Early editions of *M.D.* misdated it.

42.
*EDMUND BURKE'S REFERENCE IN PARLIAMENT TO THE
NANTUCKET WHALE-FISHERY*
    *The Speech of Edmund Burke, Esq.; on Moving His Res-
olutions for Conciliation with the Colonies, March 22, 1775*
(London, 1775), p. 13.
    (Probably quoted from Browne or Beale.)

43.
EDMUND BURKE. (SOMEWHERE)
    Attributed by Burton Stevenson's 1944 *Home Book of Quotations* to a c. 1780 speech in the House of Commons, but the wording does not correspond to any known speech of Burke's.

44.
BLACKSTONE
    Sir William Blackstone, *Commentaries on the Laws of England* (1765-1769), Book I, Chapter 8.

45.
FALCONER'S SHIPWRECK
    William Falconer, *The Shipwreck* (1762), Canto II, lines 71-76, probably via Hart's *Miriam Coffin*.

46.
COWPER, ON THE QUEEN'S VISIT TO LONDON
    With changes, from Cowper's "On the Queen's Visit to London, the night of the 17th March, 1789" (Sealts #161).

47.
JOHN HUNTER'S ACCOUNT . . .
    Quoted in Beale's 1839 *Natural History of the Sperm Whale* (p. 104) and in William Paley, *Natural Theology: or Evidences of the Existence and Attributes of the Deity* (1802), Chapter 10, "Of the Vessels of Animal Bodies."

48.
PALEY'S THEOLOGY
    See previous "Extract" (Paley).

49.
BARON CUVIER
    Baron Georges Cuvier. *The Animal Kingdom Arranged in Conformity with its Organization, by the Baron Cuvier . . . With Additional Descriptions of All the Species Hitherto Named, and of Many Not Before Noticed, by Edward Griffith . . . and Others* (London, 1827-43). M. acquired Volume X on 1 January 1851 (Sealts # 171). (Or a paraphrase of *Penny Cyclopaedia* on "Whales," or of Cuvier's Volume IV, *The Class Mammalia*.)

50.
*COLNETT'S VOYAGE FOR THE PURPOSE OF EXTENDING
THE SPERMACETI WHALE FISHERY*
Capt. James Colnett,   *A Voyage to the South Atlantic
and Round Cape Horn . . . for the Purpose of Extending the
Spermaceti Whale Fisheries* (London, 1798), chapter 4, p. 28.

51.
MONTGOMERY'S WORLD BEFORE THE FLOOD
James Montgomery, *Pelican Island*, Canto 2, lines 22-42
(not *World before . . .*).

52.
CHARLES LAMB'S TRIUMPH OF THE WHALE
Charles Lamb, "The Triumph of the Whale" in 1848
Works (Sealts # 316).

53.
OBED MACY'S HISTORY OF NANTUCKET
History of Nantucket (1835).

54.
HAWTHORNE'S TWICE TOLD TALES
Nathaniel Hawthorne, "The Village Uncle," *Twice Told
Tales* (Sealts #s 258, 259, 260).

55.
IBID.
See previous "Extract": "Chippings with a Chisel."

56.
COOPER'S PILOT
James Fenimore Cooper, *The Pilot* (1823), Chapter 17.

57.
ECKERMANN'S CONVERSATIONS WITH GOETHE
J.P. Eckermann's *Conversations of Goethe* (1836), entry
for 31 January 1830, with minor differences.

58.
"NARRATIVE OF THE SHIPWRECK . . ."
     Owen Chase, *Narrative of the . . . Shipwreck of the
Whale-ship Essex* (1821), Chapter 2 (Sealts #s 133 and 134).

59.
ELIZABETH OAKES SMITH
     "The Drowned Mariner," lines 1-5, *The Poetical Writings of Elizabeth Oakes Smith* (1845).

60.
SCORESBY
     William Scoresby, *An Account of the Arctic Regions,
with a History and Description of the Northern Whale-Fishery*
(Edinburgh, 1820), II, Chapter 4, Section 9, and I, Chapter 6,
Section 1.
     (M. altered Scoresby's numbers and words somewhat.)

61.
THOMAS BEALE'S HISTORY OF THE SPERM WHALE
     Natural History of the Sperm Whale (1839), pp. 165 and
33.
     (Several words altered by M.)

62.
*FREDERICK DEBELL BENNETT'S WHALING VOYAGE
ROUND THE GLOBE. 1840*
     II, 213.

63.
*J. ROSS BROWNE'S ETCHINGS OF A WHALING CRUIZE.
1846*
     Page 115.

64.
*NARRATIVE OF THE GLOBE MUTINY, BY LAY AND
HUSSEY SURVIVORS. A.D. 1828*
     William Lay and Cyrus M. Hussey, *A Narrative of the
Mutiny, On Board the Ship Globe* (1828), Chapter 1. Sealts
#323.
     (M. substitutes "Whale-ship for "ship" in the original.)

65.
MISSIONARY JOURNAL OF TYERMAN AND BENNETT
Daniel Tyerman and George Bennett, *Journal of Voyages and Travels* (1832), I, 3. ("He" is whale-ship *Tuscan*'s captain; there are omissions.)

66.
"REPORT OF DANIEL WEBSTER'S SPEECH . . ."
U.S. Senate, 2 May 1828; regarding the Breakwater at Nantucket. With minor discrepancy, from *Speeches and Forensic Arguments* (Boston, 1830), p. 435.

67.
"THE WHALE AND HIS CAPTORS . . . "
Rev. Henry T. Cheever (1850), p. 151. Minor change in title.

68.
LIFE OF SAMUEL COMSTOCK
The Life of Samuel Comstock (Boston, 1840), p. 80. Abridged ed. 1845, p. 21.

69.
MCCULLOCH'S COMMERCIAL DICTIONARY
John Ramsay McCulloch, *A Dictionary, Practical, Theoretical, and Historical, of Commerce and Commercial Navigation* (London, 1832), p. 1110.
(Probably quoted from J. Ross Browne, p. 514.)

70.
FROM "SOMETHING" UNPUBLISHED
Not from any later M. work.

71.
CURRENTS AND WHALING. U.S. EX. EX.
United States Exploring Expedition, 1838-1842. United States Exploring Expedition. During the Years 1838, 1839, 1840, 1841, 1842. Under the Command of Charles Wilkes "Currents and Whaling" (Philadelphia, 1844, V, 526; 1845, V. 496), with minor changes. (Probably quoted from J. Ross Browne.)

72.
TALES OF A WHALE VOYAGER TO THE ARCTIC OCEAN
Robert Pearse Gillies, *Tales of a Voyager to the Arctic Ocean* (London, 1826), II, 316.

73.
NEWSPAPER ACCOUNT . . . HOBOMACK
There is disagreement regarding this extract. The 1988 Northwestern-Newberry edition (which prints "Hobomock") discusses (p. 828) the confusion. The reference is apparently to the Falmouth ship *Hobomok*, which did not suffer a native mutiny. M. may have meant the actions of Namorik Island natives on the Falmouth ship *Awashonks* (1835), or of Kingsmill Islanders on the Fairhaven ship *Sharon* (1842). The problem is exacerbated by M.'s idiosyncratic orthography (making the ship "Hobomak" in *T.* 4), and by his handwriting. (He might have intended "Hobomock.")
The referent is an evil deity of the Indians: variously "Hobomoko," "Hobbamock," "Abamacho."
Hobomok spoke *Acushnet* (see "Pequod") near Albemarle Island, 2 November 1841.

74.
CRUISE IN A WHALE BOAT
James A. Rhodes (1848).
(M. added the word "American.")

75.
MIRIAM COFFIN OR THE WHALE FISHERMAN
Joseph C. Hart, *Miriam Coffin, or the Whale Fisherman* (1834), II, 10, 156.

76.
A CHAPTER ON WHALING IN RIBS AND TRUCKS
W.A.G., *Ribs and Trucks, From Davy's Locker; being Magazine Matter Broke Loose, and Fragments of Sundry Things In-Edited* (1842), "A Chapter on Whaling," p. 13.
("Whale" substituted for "prize" in the original.)

77.
DARWIN'S VOYAGE OF A NATURALIST
Charles Darwin, *Journal of Researches into the Natural History and Geology of the Countries Visited during the Voy-*

age of H.M.S. Beagle round the World (1846), I, 10, 288, entry
for 28 January 1833 (Sealts #175).

78.
WHARTON THE WHALE KILLER
    Harry Halyard, *Wharton's the Killer! or, The Pride of
the Pacific; A Tale of the Ocean* (1848).

79.
NANTUCKET SONG
    As Frank shows in "'The King of the Southern Sea'
. . . ," this song is variously known as "Captain Bunker," "The
Bold Harpooneer," and "Nantucket Song." It is quoted by J.
Ross Browne (p. 17); M. cites the chorus in this Extract.

80.
WHALE SONG
    Title page, Henry T. Cheever, *The Whale and His Cap-
tors* (see "Extract" 67). As Frank shows in "'The King of the
Southern Sea' . . . ," the "Whale Song" was originally "The
King of the Southern Sea," a poem published anonymously in
The Sailors' Magazine (December 1843), ascribed "From the
Glasgow Chronicle."

Nautical Language

ABAFT THE . . . MAINMAST
Abaft means toward the stern; abaft the mainmast is the quarterdeck, domain of the officers.

ABLE SEAMAN
In the merchant and civil service, the rating above Ordinary Seaman: colloquially, "A.B."

AFT
Toward the rear of the ship.

AFTER-OAR
The oar farthest to the stern on the starboard side; "stroke oar."

ALOW AND ALOFT
Set all sails.
"Alow and aloft, and on both sides" refers to the studding sails (stun'sails), to be set on foremast and mainmast.

ANCHORS ARE WORKING
When anchors "work," they move.

BACKSTAYS
See "Stays."

"BACK THE MAINYARD"
To "back" a sail is to throw it aback. The main royal yard supports the royal.

BAND
The reef band is a narrow strip of canvas sewed to the top portion of a sail and containing reef points: ropes by which the sail is reefed.

BATTENED
A thing is battened, or fastened down, by strips of wood or iron; especially said of hatches, when tarpaulins are fastened. Batten is also put upon rigging, to keep it from chafing.

BELAYING PIN
Large wooden or metal peg set in the rail and to which running rig is secured. (See also main entry.)

BILLETED
Assigned to, or housed.

BILLY-TACKLES
Portable tackles, the smallest tackles.

BINNACLE
The binnacle is the box near the helm, containing the compass.

BLACK WATER
Still water.

BLOCK
A piece of wood with sheaves or wheels, through which ropes are rove.

BOARDING SWORD
M. glosses in *M.D.* 67: a "long, keen weapon" used to slice open a whale carcass.

BOATSWAIN'S MATE
In the Navy, a Petty Officer or Seaman classified as an apprentice ("striker"), who supervises the deck force in seamanship duties.

BOW
Front end of a ship.

BOWLINE
A knot tied so as to make a loop at the end of the rope; on sailing ships often used to keep the leach (edge) of a square sail out when sailing close-hauled, so as to get as much as possible to windward: "on a bowline."

BOWSMAN
On a whale boat, the handler of the second oar, next to the harpooneer.

BOWSPRIT
The large, strong spar projecting from the bow, to which jib sails are attached.

BREACHES
A whale breaches when she throws herself out of the water.

BRIDLE-BITTS
Bitts are perpendicular pieces of timber driven through the deck, for securing things, especially cables. Bridles are spans of rope attached to square sails.

BRIDLE-PORT
Opening in the bulwarks aft, for running out cable or hawser.

BRIG
A full-rigged brig is square-rigged on her two masts. Brigs were forerunners of modern-day destroyers.

BRIGANTINE
Also called hermaphrodite brig: two-masted with fore-mast square-rigged and aftermast fore-and-aft rigged.

BUCKLE-SCREW
Screw for buckle.

BULKHEADS
Temporary partitions separating parts of a vessel.

BULWARKS
A vessel's above-deck woodwork; boards fastened to stanchions (upright posts) and timber-heads that come above deck.

BURTON
A simple kind of hoisting tackle.

CABIN-SCUTTLE
Stairway from deck to cabin.

CABLE-TIER
The place in a hold or between decks where cables are coiled and stowed.

CAPSTAN-HEAD
The top of the deck machine used for strong purchase in hoisting or heaving. Men-of-war weigh anchor by capstans; merchant-men by a windlass.

CAPTAIN'S ROUND-HOUSE (*CABINET*)
A cabin built on the deck of a ship at the stern and roofed by the poop deck: used as a privy.

CARLINES
Carlings: short timbers running fore and aft between beams supporting the deck.

CARRICK-BEND
Single, double, and open carrick bend knots are used to bend two ropes together.

CHRONOMETER; PATENT CHRONOMETER; LONDON SEA-CHRONOMETERS
A highly accurate clock suspended within a gimbal to correct for ship's movement. The prototype of the modern chronometer was invented by Parisian Pierre Le Roy in 1765; it was perfected in England by 1785. Bowditch explains shipboard care of the chronometer, which must be protected from shocks and jars as well as extreme temperature change and magnetization. The ship's navigator is responsible for determining and correcting the daily rate of error (usually difference from Greenwich mean time).

COASTER; COASTING SMACK
A small fishing sloop or schooner.

COFFER-DAM
A large watertight box or chamber temporarily attached to a ship to facilitate below-waterline repairs. (Similar structures are used for repairs on dams, bridges, etc.)

COMMODORE'S PENNANT
On U.S. Navy ships there are many rules governing display of flags and personal pennants, and much hoop-la regarding them. The senior officer's pennant is displayed day and night; in the modern navy two lights are displayed from sunup to sundown, revealing the rank of the senior person aboard.

COMPANIONWAY
Stairway to a ship's cabin.

COOPER'S CLUB HAMMER
The barrelmaker's ax-like tool or adz.

COPPER
Sheathing on a ship's sides.

COPPER-PUMP
Used to pump whale oil from one cask to another.

CORVETTE
The French sloop of war by M.'s time had evolved into a large (over 110 feet) single-decked man-of-war with a flush, gunless deck: a powerful and fast ship used for commerce-raiding, privateer-hunting, and convoy escort. M.'s citation in *O.* of its "waspish" hull is a sly comparison with American sloops of the *Wasp* class—almost as effective as the French corvette.

Corvettes were fore-runners of modern-day destroyers and light cruisers.

CRAB
A rower is in a crab when he clumsily catches the oar in the water by a wave on the backstroke.

CROSS-TREES
Pieces of oak at the mast heads, supporting the tops on the lower mast and spreading the topgallant rigging at the topmast head.

CROWN
On an anchor, where the arms join the shank.

CRUPPERED
A ship is "cruppered" when finished off at the stern. "Crupper" literally refers to a horse's harness, or buttocks.

CUN
Steering or navigating a vessel by eye.

CUTTING STAGES
Platforms used in whale stripping.

DARBIES; DOUBLE DARBIES
Iron shackles; manacles; handcuffs.

DAVITS
Pieces of timber or iron with sheaves or blocks, projecting over a vessel's side for hoisting boats.

DINGY
The small extra boat in men-of-war and merchant ships was patterned after the "dinghy" or "dinghey" of Bombay, which was propelled by paddles and fitted with a sail on a mast pointed forwards.

DITTY BAY
The Ditty Bag or Ditty Box was a small container carrying a sailor's small personal articles. The name derives from "Dittis" or Manchester stuff: the name of which probably derives from the Saxon word "*dite*," meaning "tidy."

DOG-VANE
Small feather or bunting device to show wind direction; a wind-sock.
In *M*. 175, an insulting nickname.

"DOG-WATCHES"
Half watches of two hours each: from 4 to 6 and 6 to 8 P.M.

DOUGH-BOY
Boiled dumpling.

"DOWN HELM!"
Turn the tiller handle away from the wind (downward), bringing the ship away from the wind. (See "Up helm.")

"DUCKS"
"Duck" is a lighter and finer cloth than canvas, used for light or small sails, and, as M. uses it, for trousers.

ENSIGNS
Large national flags.

EUROPEAN CRUISERS
High-speed, lightly armed vessels such as the French single-decker corvette: too small for armed quarterdecks.

FATHOM
Six feet.

FELLUCAS
Small, narrow oar- or sail-driven ships used especially in the Mediterranean.

FERULE
Metal tip.

FID
Object used to support or steady something; an oakum plug for a gun vent, a piece of hard wood, metal bar, or pin. An iron fid is properly a marlin-spike.

FIRST LIEUTENANT
A Navy executive officer, responsible for the upkeep and cleanliness of the ship and its appurtenances and for deck seamanship: "First Luff."

FIRST LUFF
First Lieutenant.

FISHING
Strengthening or supporting with a "fish"—a flat plate or iron or wood laid upon a surface.

FLEMISH COILS
Rope coiled down into figure-of-eight coils for neat harbor stowage.

FORE, THE
The forward part of a vessel, especially the standing place near the foremast.

FORECASTLE
The part of the upper deck forward of a ship's foremast; below deck the domain of the sailors, in merchant vessels.

FORECASTLE DECK
Upper main deck, forward of the foremast, under which the sailors lived, on merchant vessels.

FORECASTLE SCUTTLE
The companionway or stair forward of the foremast, leading to the crew's quarters.

FORE HATCHWAY
Opening leading into storage space in the forecastle area.

FRIGATE
Traditionally, any man-or-war with a single gun deck, carrying a secondary battery on the quarterdeck, totalling about thirty guns. Frigates were small and built for speed needed in scouting, patrolling, convoying, etc.: forerunners of the modern cruisers.

FUSEE
Fuse.

GAFFS
A gaff is a short-handled hook, or a spar to which the head of a fore-and-aft sail is bent.

GALIOT; GALLIOT
A small, swift galley with sails and oars; a Dutch galliot is a single-masted, shallow-drafted merchant ship.

GAM
J.R. Browne (*Etchings*, Chap. VIII) defines a "gam" between whalers as a "mutual visit, for the purpose of interchanging the latest news, comparing reckoning, discussing the prospect of whales, and enjoying a general chit-chat." Specific "gams" are discussed in detail in the journal of Mary

Chipman Lawrence on the whaler *Addison* (Garner, *The Captain's Best Mate*).

GAMMON
Gammoning is lashing by which the bowsprit is secured to the cut-water, the foremost part of the prow.
See also "Passing a Gammoning," in main entries.

GIG
A light, narrow clinker-built galley or ship's boat, propelled by oars or by sail. The Captain's Gig is used exclusively for his transport; it seats from six to eight rowers.

GRAINS
Two-tined barbed spears on the ends of long poles.

GRAPNELS
Small four-pronged anchors used to secure boats or for dragging.

"GRIPE"
A vessel gripes when she tends to come up into the wind. A "gripe" is an underwater outside timber at the forefoot.

GROUND-TIER BUTTS
Large casks in the lowest tier of a ship's hold, always laid horizontally fore and aft.

GRUMMET
A ring of rope used to secure the upper edge of a sail to the stay; sometimes used as a substitute oarlock. Secondarily, a ship's boy, or cabin boy."
(Modern "grommet.")

HALF-STRANDED
A rope is stranded when it is unraveled, half-stranded when it is partway so.

HALYARD

Rope or tackle used to hoist or lower yards, gaffs, or sails.

HAMPER

A ship's "top-hamper" holds the upper spars, rigging, and sails.

HANDSPIKES

Heavy iron or wooden bars, used for levers when heaving at the windlass.

HARD UP (OF YARDS)

Turned as far as possible into the wind.

HAWSE-HOLE

Hole in the bow through which cable runs. See also main entry.

HAWSER

Heavy rope, at least five inches in diameter.

HEAD BOARDS

Bows.

HEAVER

Wooden staff or bar, for use as a lever or for twisting or tightening a rope or strap.

HEAVE TO

Stop a vessel's progress by heading into the wind or reducing sail; also "lie-to."

HEAVING DOWN

Tipping a ship on its side.

HERMAPHRODITE

See "brigantine."

HITCHING
    Jerking.

HOLD
    Interior part of a vessel, in which cargo is stowed.

HOLDERS
    Men stationed on the lowest deck or in the cargo area be-
low.

HOLDING THE SHIP IN THE WIND
    Catching wind on the front of the sails.

HOLY-STONING
    Holy-stone, soft sandstone used for scouring decks, is
probably so called because it came from St. Nicholas Church,
Great Yarmouth, England, associated with the Royal Navy.
Also called "ecclesiastical brick" or "hand bibles," the stones,
being porous, are "holey."

HORSE-PIECES
    Pieces of whale blubber about six inches by two or three
feet.

HOVE OVER
    Past tense of "heave over": to move alongside.

HOVE TO
    Past tense of "heave to": stop the vessel.

HULL HOVE OUT
    The hull, or body of the vessel is hove out when it is
tipped on its side.

JACKS
    Small flags designating nationality.

JIB-BOOM
A spar supported by and extending beyond the bowsprit, to which the rope of the jib sail (a triangular forward sail) is attached.

JIB-STAY
A supporting rope leading forward from the fore-top-mast to the jib sail, a triangular sail.

JOLLY-BOAT
Small boat, usually hoisted at the stern.

KEEL
The lowest and principal timber of a vessel, running fore and aft and supporting the entire frame. A "keelson" or "kelson" is a timber placed over the keel, parallel to it.

KENTLEDGE
Ballast, usually pig iron, laid on each side of the keelson, or board over the ship's lowest and principal timber.

KNEES
Crooked pieces of timber (usually live oak) with two arms: used to connect the vessel's beams with her timbers.

KNIGHT-HEADS
Timbers next to the stem on each side, forming a support for the bowsprit.

LANYARD
Rope rove through a "dead-eye" block of wood, for setting up rigging; a rope which secures something or provides a handle.

LARBOARD
Left ("port") side of a vessel.

LASH AND CARRY
    The order given to the watch below meaning that hammocks are to be lashed and stowed in the nettings. My father, an old World War I tar, used a variant: "Heave out and lash up!" to roust the family out of bed.

LAUNCH
    Long-boat of a ship of war.

LEAGUE
    About three nautical miles.

LEE
    The side of the ship away from the wind. See also main entry.

LEE-SCUPPERS
    Scuppers are openings in a ship's side, on a level with the decks, to allow water to run away. Lee scuppers run the most water.

LEEWARDINGS
    An invented word for prospects on the lee side of a ship.

LEEWAY
    The distance a vessel loses by drifing in a leeward direction. See "lee."

LIFT
    A lift is a rope or tackle supporting and moving a yard.

LINE TUBS
    Receptacles for coiled lines.

LOG AND LINE
    Glossed in *M.D.* 125: a "wooden reel and angular log" used to determine a ship's position and rate of progression.

LOGGERHEAD
Two-foot high post at the whaleboat stern.

LUBBER'S HOLE
A hole in the top, next to the mast, inside collars of rigging providing a safe route.

LUFF; LUFF UP
To move the helm so as to bring the ship up nearer to the wind. To luff "a point" is to turn the ship into the wind by about 11 degrees.

To luff up into the wind is to talk nonsense.

MAIN-CHAINS
The rigid links of iron on the ship's side beneath the bulwarks support the "channels," wide planks to which the lower ends of the shrouds are attached. The "Main-chains" serve the mainmast.

The chains area is often the scene of dramatic covert dialogue or action in M.'s works because it is one of the few secluded areas on a ship.

MAIN-ROYAL MAST HEAD
A look-out station aloft, near the royal sail, a light one next above a topgallant sail: the fourth from the deck.

MAIN ROYAL YARD
Piece of timber supporting the royal.

MAIN-TOPSAIL ABACK
Topsail is the second sail from the deck. When it is aback, its surface is pressed against the mast, tending to force the vessel astern.

MARLINE
A fine kind of spunyarn made into two-stranded tarred line for "marling," or twisting around another line.

MARLING-SPIKES; MARLINSPIKES
A marlingspike is an iron pin, sharpened at one end, with a hole in the other for a lanyard. "Marling-spikes" is also a nickname for a competent sailor.

MIDSHIPMAN'S NUTS
Small, hard pieces of broken biscuit; perhaps a double entendre.

MINCING KNIVES
Thirty-inch-long blubber-cutting instruments with wooden handles at both ends.

MIZEN RIGGING
Ropes of the aftermost mast.

MIZEN SHROUDS
Ropes supporting the mizzenmast, the aftermost mast.

MONKEY JACKET
The short, snug jacket worn by seamen: with "no more tail than a monkey."

NIPPERS
Nippers are a number of lines marled together to secure a cable to a messenger, or rope used for heaving. Also a strip of tendinous material from the whale's tail, used as a squilgee.

Also a nickname for cabin boys, or for top men who take the short rope binding the anchor, or for the rope itself.

OAKUM
Stuff made by picking rope-yarns to pieces; used for caulking.

OFFICER-OF-THE DECK
Officer on duty in charge of ship, representing the commanding officer.

OLY-COOKS
Doughnuts, or crullers.

ORDERLY SERGEANT
Messenger or personal attendant for a senior officer.

ORDINARY SEAMAN
An enlisted man with general deck and boat duties:
above a "boy" but beneath an "able seaman."

ORLOP
Vessel's lowest deck.

PAY-MASTER-GENERAL
Navy disbursing officer.

PAY OVER
Cover.

PIG-LEAD
Ballast pig-iron.

PILED-UP
A ship with all sails set is "piled-up."

PLUG-HOLE
A hole, sealed with a removable piece of wood, for keeping water out or for removing water from a raised boat.

POOP
A deck raised over the after part of the spar deck, at the
stern.

PORT
Left side of a ship ("larboard").

PORT-HOLES
Bulwark openings; on men-of-war for cannons.

POST-CAPTAIN
A full-grade captain, as distinguished from the courtesy title given the top man on a ship.

PROAS
Large outrigger canoes with sails.

QUARTER
A vessel's quarter is between the after part of the main chains and the stern. To be on someone's quarter is to be at a forty-five degree angle from the ship's stern.

QUARTER-BOAT
A boat suspended from the quarter deck.

QUARTERDECK
The part of the upper deck abaft the mainmast: domain of the officers.

QUOINS
Wooden wedges; on men-of-war to rest guns upon.

RACK
Rack is broken clouds. To rack is to seize two ropes together, with cross turns.

REEF
Reduce area of sail exposed to the wind; taking in its head if a square sail, or its foot if a fore-and-aft sail.
Reefing is described accurately in *R*. 24 and 59; sailors had to straddle the yard to perform the dangerous operation.

RINGROPE
Rope rove through the anchor ring in order to haul cable through to make it fast in bad weather, then run through the hawse-holes.

ROYAL

Fourth level of sail from the deck; a light sail.

ROYAL-MAST

Second topmost mast section.

ROYAL SHROUDS

Ropes supporting the royal sails, fourth level from the deck.

ROYAL YARD

The piece of timber supporting the fourth level of square sails above the deck.

SAIL

There are two basic kinds: square sails hang from yards lying across the line of the keel; fore-and-aft sails are set on gaffs or stays, parallel with the line of the keel.

"Sail" is also a generic term for a vessel.

"SAIL HO!"

Cry used when another vessel is spotted at sea.

SCUD

As a noun, scud means low thin clouds that move swiftly before the wind. As a verb, to scud is to drive before a gale with little or no sail, so as to keep a ship ahead of the sea. "Scudding under bare poles" occurs when a ship carries no sail.

SCUPPER-HOLE

Hole cut in the waterways to allow runoff.

SEIZINGS

Fastenings of ropes by numerous turns taken with smaller tarred yarns.

SEVENTY FOURS

Ships of the line carrying seventy-four guns.

SHALLOP
A nondescript class of small open or half-decked boats used in the shore fisheries or as household boats.

SHEARS
Spars raised at angles and lashed together near the upper end, used to take in masts.

SHEET-ANCHOR-MAN
Sheet-anchor, or forecastle, men were mature, reliable seamen rated as able, stationed on the forecastle near the anchors, bowsprit, and foreyard. They were among the best seamen on a ship.

SHEETED HOME
Sheets are ropes used in setting a sail; sheeted home means with sails spread out horizontally as far as possible.

SHIP
A ship has three or more masts, each with a complete set of square sails.

SHIP OF THE LINE
The expression for the fore-runner of the modern battleship was used until iron and steam replaced wood and sail. First "Ship of the Line" in the United States Navy was *Independence*: 190 feet long, with ninety-five guns and a crew of 790 officers and men.

SHIP'S RUN
The narrow, rising after-part of a ship's bottom, leading to the stern-post.

SHIVER HER
To shiver a sail is to take the wind out by bracing it so that the wind strikes upon the leach, or edge.

SICK-BAY
Infirmary or first-aid station.

SIDE-BOYS
Boys who take charge of the man-ropes and attend individuals boarding from or leaving on a boat.

SIGNALS
Communication flags.

SINNATE
Also sennet, or sinnit: a braid of plaited yarn. Also applied to braided hat straw.

SKIFF
Small rowboat.

SKYSAIL-POLES
The portion of the mast above the yards upon which the skysail (next above the royal) is spread.

SLIPPED . . . CABLE
To slip is to let a cable go and stand out to sea.

SLOOP
A ship with one mast, fore-and-aft rigged.

SLOOP OF WAR
See "corvette."

SOUSED
Pickled.

SPANKER-OUT-HAUL
A spanker is a fore and aft sail, set with a gaff and boom at the aftermost part; the out-haul is the rope used for hauling out the tack of a sail, as opposed to in-haul.

SPAR
Mast, yard, boom, gaff, etc.

SPLIT JIB
> A triangular sail set ahead of the foremast.

SQUARE IN!
> Bring the ship directly before the wind and set sails.

STAND BY TO STERN
> To be prepared for action at the stern, or to back water.

STARBOARD
> Right side of a ship.

STAR-BO-LEENS
> Starbowlines: familiar term for men in the starboard watch.

STATION BILL
> The Navy's listing of the crew's drill stations, on a given ship.

STAYS
> Ropes supporting the masts; those leading forward are fore-and-aft stays; those leading down to a vessel's sides are backstays.

STEEL-BITS
> Cutting edge of an axe or plane.

STEM-PIECE
> The foremost timber, rising from the keel to the bowsprit, to which the sides of the vessel are united.

STERN
> Rear of a ship.

STEWARD
> In charge of shipboard living accomodations upkeep, officers' or men's mess.

STRIKE; STRIKING . . . DOWN
Lowering, of sails or colors.

STUN' SAILS
Studdingsails: light sails carried only in moderate weather, set outside the square sails on booms rigged out for the purpose.

SWAYED
Hoisted, or raised.

T'GALLANT CROSS TREES
Pieces of oak at the mast heads to sustain the tops on the lower mast and to spread the topgallant rigging at the topmast head.

THOLE-PINS
On a boat's gunwale, pins between which an oar rests, when there is no rowlock.

THRUMMINGS
Matting made of small rope yarn.

THWART
Oarsman's seat.

TIERCE
Small cask.

TIERER
One stationed in the chain locker to stow chain.

TILLER
A bar of wood or iron, put into the head of the rudder, by which the ship's rudder is moved—serving the same purpose as a wheel.
(See also main entry.)

TOP
A platform placed over the head of a lower mast, to spread the rigging and for the convenience of men aloft.

TOP-BLOCKS
Large iron-bound blocks for the top-rope to reeve through in raising and lowering topmasts.

TOP-GALLANT SAILS
The third level of square sails above the deck.

TOPMAST
Second mast above the deck.

TOP-MAUL
Iron hammer used by riggers.

"TOT"
The origin of the word to denote a minute quantity is uncertain: *O.E.D.* lists its first use in this sense in the early eighteenth century. In nautical jargon, it is a sardonic reference to the grog ration: a half-pint of spirits (or a quart of beer).

TOW
As noun, broken rope fibers; as verb, to draw a vessel along by a rope, tow-line.

TRICED UP
Pulled up and secured by means of a lashing or "tricing line."

TRIM DISH
Obtain proper balance on the ship, by adjustment of ballast or sail.

TRUCK
Circular piece of wood at the head of the highest mast, with holes or sheaves for signal halyards. On a man-of-war, the wheel of a gun carriage.

TRY-POTS
Iron pots in which whale oil is boiled.

UP HELM!
"Helm" refers to the vessel's steering mechanisms: rudder, tiller, and wheel. To "Up helm" is to turn the tiller handle toward the wind (upward), to bring the ship before the wind.

VIERER
To "veer" is to pay out rope; a "vierer" presumably performs this menial task.

WAD
A wad is a piece of material rammed down upon the charge in a muzzle-loaded cannon.

WAIF-POLE
M. glosses in *M.D.* 87: "a pennoned pole, two or three of which are carried by every boat; and which, when additional game is at hand, are inserted upright into the floating body of a dead whale, both to mark its place on the sea, and also as token of prior possession."

WAIST
Area of the upper deck between the quarterdeck and the forecastle.

WAISTERS
The lowest-skilled and least necessary men of a crew.

WEATHER BOW
The side of the bow toward the wind. "Three points off the weather bow" means at an angle of some 33 degrees from the weather bow side.

WEATHER-SHEET

Windward-side rope controlling boom (spar along the bottom of the mainsail).

WHALE-PIKE

A single-pronged instrument for moving blubber about the deck.

WHITE SQUALLS

A squall of great violence, characterized by a low-lying white cloud in a dark sky, the white squall is described vividly by J. Ross Browne (*Etchings*, Chapter 9).

(*Knickerbocker* for Feb. 1939 contained "The White Squall," by Robert Burts.)

WINDLASS; WINDLASS-BITTS

Bitts, two upright timbers, support the windlass, the device by which merchant vessels weigh anchor.

YARD

Piece of timber supporting a sail.

Quotations

XIII OF 1ST CORINTHIANS

The "Charitable Lady" in *C.M.* 8 is reading the section that begins: "Though I speak with the tongues of men and of angels, and have not charity, I am become as sounding brass or a tinkling cymbal." It continues, "Charity suffereth long, and is kind; charity envieth not; charity vaunteth not itself, is not puffed up, . . . Beareth all things, believeth all things, hopeth all things, endureth all things," ending, "And now abideth faith, hope, charity, these three: but the greatest of these is charity."

C.M. 8

" . . . ALL BEFORE US WAS THE WIDE PACIFIC."

*Milton, *Paradise Lost* XII, 646-9: of *Adam and *Eve after the *Fall:

> The world was all before them, where to choose
> Their place of rest, and Providence their guide.
> They, hand in hand, with wandering steps and
>   slow,
> Through Eden took their solitary way.

O. 82

"ALL IS VANITY AND CLAY"

Ecclesiastes 1:2-5: "Vanity of vanities, saith the Preacher, vanity of vanities; all is vanity."

M.D. 96; I.P. 23

"ALL THE WORLD'S A STAGE . . . "

"Jaques," enlarging upon the banished "Duke's" suggestion, in *Shakespeare's *As You Like It*, II, vii, 141-42:

All the world's a stage,
And all the men and women merely players . . .

C.M. 41

"AND GOD HAD PREPARED A GREAT FISH . . . "
    *Jonah 1:17: "Now the Lord had prepared a great fish to
swallow up Jonah."
M.D. 9

"AND I ONLY AM ESCAPED ALONE TO TELL THEE"
    In *Job I: 14-19, four messengers announce to Job the
destruction of his family and his possessions, using similar
words.
    The "Epilogue" to *M.D.*, of which this expression is a
sub-title, was omitted in the first English edition of the book, so
that various *British reviewers proclaimed the impossibility of
a story with no survivors.
M.D. Epilogue

ANGELS CONSORTED WITH THE DAUGHTERS OF MEN
    *Genesis 6:2: "The sons of *God saw the daughters of
men that they were fair, and they took them wives of all which
they chose."
M.D. 50

"APPETITE FURNISHES THE BEST SAUCE"
    *Miguel de Cervantes: "There's no sauce in the world
like hunger" (*Don Quixote* III, 5).
T. 7

BAD ANGEL SHALL TEND THE GOOD
    As Murray's notes to *P.* show, *Burton quotes Ficinus
who, like *Plato, distinguishes between two necessary kinds of
angels: those who lead to the physical and those who lead to the
spiritual.
P. 23:3

... BEARER OF EVIL TIDINGS HATH BUT A LOSING OF-
FICE
      *Isaiah 52:7: "How beautiful upon the mountains are
the feet of him that bringeth good tidings, that publisheth
peace."
      *Shakespeare, *Henry IV*, 2 (I, 1, 100-104): "Northumber-
land" says:

            ... the first bringer of unwelcome news
            Hath but a losing office, and his tongue
            Sounds ever after as a sullen bell,
            Rememb'red tolling a departing friend.

T. 26

BE THOU, OLD PILOT, OUR GUIDE

            Lord, through this hour
            Be thou our Guide,
            So by Thy power
            No Foot shall slide.
                  Westminster Chimes

M. 4

"A BIRD IN THE HAND IS WORTH TWO IN THE BUSH."
      There are numerous possible originals:
      *Plutarch, *Morals of Garrulity*: "He is a fool who leaves
things close at hand to follow what is out of reach."
      John Heywood (c. 1497--c. 1580): *Proverbs* (1546), pt. 1,
ch. 11: "Better one bird in hand than ten in the wood."
      Thomas Lodge (c. 1558-1625), *Rosalyne* (1590): "One bird
in the hand is worth two in the wood."
      *Miguel de Cervantes, *Don Quixote*, Pt. I (1605), bk. IV,
ch. 4: "A bird in hand is worth two in the bush."
      [A sequel: *George Herbert, *Jacula Prudentum* (1640):
"A feather in hand is better than a bird in the air."]
T. 24

'BLESSED ARE THE POOR IN SPIRIT, AND BLESSED THEY
THAT MOURN'
      *Matthew 5:3-4 (*Sermon on the Mount): "Blessed are
the poor in spirit: for theirs is the kingdom of heaven. Blessed
are they that mourn, for they shall be comforted."
P. 5:1

... BLESSED, JACK GAVE UP HIS BEARD ...
    *Matthew 26:26-28:

> *Jesus took bread, and blessed it, and brake
> it, and gave it to the disciples, and said, Take, eat;
> this is my body.
> And he took the cup, and gave thanks, and
> gave it to them, saying, Drink ye all of it;
> For this is my blood of the new testament,
> which is shed for many for the remission of sins.

W. 85

"BORN UNDER A GUN, AND EDUCATED ON THE
BOWSPRIT"
    Lovett (p. 211) gives the "old definition of a man-of-war's
man . . . Begotten in the galley and born under a gun. Every
hair a rope yarn, every tooth a marline spike; every finger a
fish hook and in his blood right good *Stockholm tar."
W. 90

"BUT WHO CAN ALWAYS ON THE BILLOWS LIE? THE
WATERY WILDERNESS YIELDS NO SUPPLY."
    Edmund Waller, *Instructions to a Painter* (1666, on the
battle of Sole Bay).
W. 51

"CANST THOU FILL HIS SKIN WITH BARBED IRONS? . . . "
    *Job 41 is the meditation that begins "Can you draw out
*Leviathan with an hook? . . ." M.'s quotation is a variation of
41:7-29.
M.D. 81

"CHARITY BELIEVETH ALL THINGS"
    I Corinthians 13.
C.M. 1

"CHARITY ENDURETH ALL THINGS"
    I Corinthians 13.
C.M. 1

"CHARITY NEVER FAILETH"
    I Corinthians 13.
C.M. 1

"CHARITY THINKETH NO EVIL"
    I Corinthians 13.
C.M. 1

"CHARITY SUFFERETH LONG, AND IS KIND"
    I Corinthians 13.
C.M. 1

"`THE CHILD IS FATHER OF THE MAN . . .'"
    *Wordsworth: "My Heart Leaps Up."
C.M. 22

. . . CONFIDENCE . . . WERE GREAT GAIN
    I *Timothy 6:6: "Godliness with contentment is great
gain."
C.M. 15

"CONSISTENT, I SELDOM CARE TO BE . . ."
    In "Self-Reliance" (*Essays*, 1841), *Emerson wrote: A
foolish consistency is the hobgoblin of little minds, adored by
little statesmen and philosophers and divines. With consistency a great soul has simply nothing to do."
    (Sealts #204 is the 1847 edition.)
C.M. 36

"A DAGGER HANGING BY A LAS HADDE HE . . . "
    *Chaucer, *Canterbury Tales* Prologue, 11, 392-396.
W. 86

DEATH HIMSELF, ON THE PALE HORSE
    *Revelation 6:8: "and I looked, and behold, a pale horse;
and his name that sat on him was Death, and hell followed
with him."
C.M. 40

"DE BALENA VERO SUFFICIT, SI REX HABEAT CAPUT, ET REGINA CAUDAM."
"Concerning the whale, it really suffices that the king should have the head and the queen should have the tail" (*Henry de Bracton: *De Legibus et Consuetudinibus Angliae*, Tractus Secundus "De Corona," Book 3, Chapter 3: first printed 1569, but dated from the thirteenth century).
M.D. 90

... DEEPEST GLOOM PRECEDES THE DAY
*Thomas Fuller, *Pisgah Sight* II, 2: "It is always darkest just before the day dawneth."
P. 10:1

". . . DEVILS WHO, IN MAN'S FORM, HAUNTED THE TOMBS."
In *Genesis 19:5; *Matthew 8:28; *Mark 5:2.
C.M. 42

"DOWN TO [THE SEA] IN SHIPS"
*Psalm 107, 23-24: "They that go down to the sea in ships, that do business in great waters; These see the works of the Lord, and his wonders in the deep."
M.D. 14

"AN ENEMY SPEAKETH SWEETLY WITH HIS LIPS . . . I BELIEVED NOT HIS MANY WORDS."
Ecclesiasticus (see "Sirach") 12:16: "An enemy will speak sweetly with his lips,/ but in his mind he will plan to throw you into a pit."
Ecclesiasticus 13:11: "Do not try to treat him as an equal, / nor trust his abundance of words."
C.M. 43

_____ "FACILIS DESCENSUS AVERNI."
"Easy is the descent of Avernus": *Virgil, *Aeneid* VI, 126. Avernus is the opening to *Hades.
I.P. 25

... FEARFULLY AND WONDERFULLY MADE
*Psalms 139:14: "I will praise thee; for I am fearfully
and wonderfully made: marvellous are thy works; and that
my soul knoweth right well."
C.M. 14

"FOR MANY A LEAGUE,/ CHEERED WITH THE GRATE-
FUL SMELL, OLD OCEAN SMILED."
*Milton, *Paradise Lost* IV, 156-66:

> Now gentle gales
> Fanning their odoriferous wings dispense
> Native perfumes, and whisper whence they stole
> Those balmy spoils. As when to them who sail
> Beyond the Cape of Hope, and now are past
> Mozambick, off at sea north-east winds blow
> *Sabaen odours from the spicy shore
> Of Araby the blest; with such delay
> Well pleas'd they slack their course, and many a
> league
> Cheer'd with the grateful smell old Ocean smiles:
> So entertain'd those odorous sweets the Fiend.

W. 14

FORTITER IN RE ... SUAVITER IN MODO
"Strongly in deed, gently in method."
C.M. 24

"THE FRIENDS THOU HAST ... "
Part of "*Polonius's" advice to "*Laertes," in
*Shakespeare's *Hamlet*, I, iii, 62-63:

> The friends thou hast, and their adoption tried,
> Grapple them to thy soul with hoops of steel . . . .

C.M. 30

"HAPPY, THRICE HAPPY, WHO, IN BATTLE SLAIN,
PRESS'D IN ATRIDES' CAUSE THE *TROJAN PLAIN."
*Alexander Pope's translation of the *Odyssey*, Book V,
393-4.
W. 51

"A HARREE TA FOW . . . "
      The "prediction" of "Teearmoar," the "high priest of Pa-
ree" is nonsense verse, probably M.'s invention based on
sound.
O. 49

"HATE THE ONE AND CLEAVE TO THE OTHER"
      *Matthew 6:24 (*Sermon on the Mount): "No man can
serve two masters: for either he will hate the one, and love the
other; or else he will hold to one, and despise the other. Ye
cannot serve *God and *mammon."
W. 45

HE HOLDETH ALL OF US IN THE HOLLOW OF HIS HAND
      *Isaiah 40:12: "Who hath measured the waters in the
hollow of his hand . . . ?"
P. 7:8

"HERE A SHEER HULK LIES POOR TOM BOWLING"
      See "Dibdin."
W. 3

HE WHO DECLARED HE LOVED A GOOD HATER
      "He was a very good hater." (Quoted from *Samuel
Johnson, in *Anecdotes of Samuel Johnson* [1786], by Mrs. Pi-
ozzi).
M. 13

"HE WHO HATES VICE, HATES HUMANITY"
      Quoted from *Thrasea by *Pliny (Book VIII, Epistle 22).
C.M. 12

HE WHO IS ALREADY FULLY PROVIDED WITH WHAT IS
NECESSARY FOR HIM . . .
      *Matthew 25:29: ". . . For unto every one that hath shall
be given, and he shall have abundance: but from him that
hath not shall be taken away even that which he hath."
P. 18:2

"HE WHO SPEAKS FIVE LANGUAGES IS AS GOOD AS
FIVE MEN."
        See "Charles V."
W. 4

"HOW CALM THE WAVES, HOW MILD THE BALMY GALE!
. . . "
        M. has altered *Mickle's translation of *Lusiad* 1078-83,
the third line of which reads, "Old Ocean now appeased"; the
fourth, " . . . the bowsprit . . . your native shore"; the fifth,"
. . . the natal soil."
W. 93

HYSSOP ON THE WALL
        I *Kings 4:33: *Solomon "spake of trees, from the cedar
tree that is in *Lebanon even unto the hyssop that springeth
out of the wall."
C.M. 16

"I CONFIDE, I CONFIDE; HELP, FRIEND, MY DISTRUST."
        *Mark 9:24: *Christ casts a spirit out of a child whose
father pleads: "Lord, I believe; help thou mine unbelief."
C.M. 15

"I COULD DRINK A GREAT DEAL OF WINE, AND IT DID
ME A GREAT DEAL OF GOOD."
        See "Cyrus the Great."
P. 22:1

" . . . IN A FINE FRENZY ROLLING"
        *Shakespeare, *A Midsummer-Night's Dream*, V, i, 12-
17:

                The poet's eye, in a fine frenzy rolling,
                Doth glance from heaven to earth, from earth to
                        heaven;
                And, as imagination bodies forth
                The forms of things unknown, the poet's pen
                Turns them to shapes, and gives to airy nothing
                A local habitation and a name.

W. 11

... INCREASE AND MULTIPLY
    *Genesis 1:28: "Be fruitful, and multiply, and replenish
the earth, and subdue it: and have dominion over the fish of
the sea, and over the fowl of the air, and over every living thing
that moveth upon the earth."
T. 26

"IN JUDGING OF THAT TEMPESTUOUS WIND CALLED
*EUROCLYDON ... "
    The "old writer" is probably M. himself.
M.D. 2

"IN VAIN IT WAS TO RAKE FOR AMBERGRIESE IN THE
PAUNCH OF THIS LEVIATHAN, INSUFFERABLE FETOR
DENYING NOT INQUIRY."
    This quotation from *Browne is in error; the word "not"
should read "that."
M.D. 91

"I REJOICE THAT I HAVE CONFIDENCE IN YOU IN ALL
THINGS"
    II *Corinthians 7:16: *Paul, speaking to the *Apostles.
C.M. 8

"IS IT LAWFUL FOR YOU TO SCOURGE A MAN THAT IS A
ROMAN?"
    In *Acts 22:25, *Paul asks the centurion binding him as
a prisoner, "Is it lawful for you to scourge a man that is a
*Roman, and uncondemned," proclaiming his civil rights.
    *Stewart (I, pp. 30-31) claims that he never witnessed a
flogging without being reminded of the question. It was still on
M.'s mind while he wrote his *Battle Pieces*. In "The House-
Top," he notes the slur on the Republic that "holds that man is
naturally good,/and-more-is Nature's Roman, never to be
scourged."
W. 34

"I TURN THE LEAF TO READ"
    *Shakespeare, *Macbeth* (I, iii, 149-52). "Macbeth" ad-
dresses "Banquo" and the two noblemen who have called him
"*Thane of Cawdor":

> Kind gentlemen, your pains
> Are register'd where every day I turn
> The leaf to read them . . . .

W. 51

"JEHOVAH SHALL BE THY CONFIDENCE"

*Proverbs 3:26: "For the Lord shall be thy confidence, and shall keep thy foot from being taken."
C.M. 45

"JENNY! . . . GET YOUR HOE-CAKE DONE"

In *M.D.*, "Pip" sings bits of the minstrel song, "Old King Crow."
M.D. 99

"LAY NOT UP . . . "

*Matthew 6:19-21 (*Sermon on the Mount):

> Lay not up for yourselves treasures upon earth, where moth and rust doth corrupt, and where thieves break through and steal: But lay up for yourselves treasures in heaven. . . For where your treasure is, there will your heart be also.

M.D. 16

" . . . LEAVE ALL AND FOLLOW HIM"

*Matthew 19:21: *Jesus says: "If thou wilt be perfect, go and sell that thou hast, and give it to the poor, and thou shalt have treasure in heaven: and come and follow me."

*Mark 10:28: Peter says: "Lo, we have left all, and have followed thee."

*Luke 18:22: *Jesus says: ". . . Yet lackest thou one thing: sell all that thou hast, and distribute to the poor, and thou shalt have treasure in heaven."
O. 65

"LET US DRINK OF THE WINE OF THE VINE BENIGN"

A variation of Leigh Hunt, *Bacchus in Tuscany* (1825), 11.246: "And drink of the wine . . . . "
C.M. 28

... LEVELING UPWARD AND NOT DOWNWARD
    *Samuel Johnson: "Sir, your levelers wish to level down as far as themselves; but they cannot bear leveling *up* to themselves" (Boswell, *Life of Johnson*, July 21, 1763).
W. 40

THE LOVE DEEP AS DEATH
    Perhaps a reference to the Song of *Solomon 8:6: "Set me as a seal upon thine heart, as a seal upon thine ear: for love is strong as death; jealousy is cruel as the grave."
P. 23:1

" . . . A MAN MAY SMILE, AND SMILE, AND SMILE, AND BE A VILLAIN"
    *Shakespeare, *Hamlet* I,v,108: "That one may smile, and smile, and be a villain."
C.M. 29

"THE MAN THAT WANDERETH OUT OF THE WAY OF UNDERSTANDING SHALL REMAIN . . . IN THE CONGREGATION OF THE DEAD."
    *Proverbs 21:16 (attributed in M.'s time to *Solomon).
M.D. 96

"MAY THE RESURRECTION AND THE LIFE----"
    The order for burial of the dead, according to the Book of Common Prayer: "I am the resurrection and the life" (*John 11:25).
M.D. 131

MYSTERY OF INIQUITY
    2 Thessalonians 2:7: "the mystery of iniquity doth already work." M. double-checked the passage in his copy of the *Shaker *A Summary View* (p. 15). He uses the expression as well in *Clarel* II, xxxv, 23-24, and in *Billy Budd, Sailor*, Chapter 11.
    The phrase may well have been in his mind in "Isabel's" repetition of "Mystery! Mystery! . . . . Mystery of Isabel!" in *P.* 6:6 and 8:2.
M. 144

MY WISDOM (TIME) IS NOT OF THIS WORLD
     *John 18:36: *Jesus says, "My kingdom is not of this world."
P. 14:3

"NATURE . . . HAD MEAL AND BRAN"
     *Shakespeare's *Cymbeline* IV, ii, 26-27: "Cowards father cowards, and base things sire base; Nature hath meal, and bran; contempt, and grace."
C.M. 11

NEMO CONTRA DEUM NISI DEUS IPSE
     "No one against *God except God himself." *Goethe's *Autobiography, Truth and Poetry* (Bk. 20), which M. purchased in 1849 (Sealts #228), is probably the source.
P. 1:4

"OH WHAT A FOOL . . . "
     *Shakespeare's *The Winter's Tale* IV, iv, 593-594: "*Autolycus" is speaking: "Ha, ha! what a fool Honesty is! and Trust, his sworn brother, a very simple gentleman."
C.M. 30

"OUR CAPTAIN STOOD UPON THE DECK . . . "
     The lines given are from a song called "Captain Bunker," with lines from "The Mermaid" and "The Bonny Ship the Diamond," quoted from *J. Ross Browne (Chap. 8).
M.D. 40

PATIENT CONTINUANCE IN WELL-DOING
     *Romans 2:7: "To them who by patient continuance in well-doing, seek for glory, and honour, and immortality; eternal life."
C.M. 22

. . . POETRY IS ITS OWN EXCEEDING GREAT REWARD
     M. plays on the idea of virtue as its own reward, probably first expressed by Silius Italicus (A.D. c. 25-29) in *Punica* XIII, l. 663: *Ipsa quidem virtus sibimet pulcherrima merces.* There are many variations, including *Emerson's in "Friendship": "The only reward of virtue is virtue; the only way to have a

friend is to be one." *Sir Thomas Browne and Izaak Walton (see "Waltonian") offered their own renderings.

Ironically, by the twentieth century, instead of "poetry" being so honored, "success" was—by Robert Bontine Cunninghame-Grahame (1852-1936), in *Success* (1902).
W. 11

PORT FOR MEN, CLARET FOR BOYS
Quoted from *Samuel Johnson, in Boswell's *Life of Johnson*, 7 April 1779: "*Claret is the liquor for boys: *port for men; but who aspires to be a hero must drink brandy."

A variant in *P.* 3:3 is "Sherry for boys, and Port for men."
W. 54

POSSESSION IS HALF OF THE LAW
Colley Cibber, *Woman's Wit* (1697): "Possession is eleven points in the law."
M.D. 89

"POURING OUT HIS LAST PHILOSOPHY AND LIFE"
*Spenser *Faerie Queene*, II, vii, 52, line 8: drinking the hemlock, *Socrates "Pour'd out his life and last philosophy."
W. 84

"PRAISE BE UNTO THE PRESS ... "
A paragraph paraphrasing *Proverbs 23:29-31.
C.M. 30

PROVE ALL THE VIALS; TRUST THOSE WHICH ARE TRUE.
I Thessalonians 5:21: "Prove all things; hold fast that which is good."
C.M. 16

... RESIGNED HIS NOBLE BIRTHRIGHT TO A CUNNING KINSMEN FOR A MESS OF POTTAGE ...
*Genesis 25:33-34. See also "Esau."
P. 21:2

"THE RIBS AND TERRORS IN THE WHALE . . ."
        This hymn is probably M.'s invention, inspired by "The
Prayer of *Jonah," Song 30 in George Wither's *The Hymnes
and Songs of the Church* (1623), perhaps based on a version of
*Psalm 18, used in the Dutch Reformed Church.
M.D. 9

"ROLL ON, THOU DEEP AND DARK BLUE OCEAN, ROLL!
TEN THOUSAND BLUBBER-HUNTERS SWEEP OVER THEE
IN VAIN."
        A parody of *Byron's "Ten thousand fleets sweep over
thee in vain": *Childe Harold's Pilgrimage*, Canto IV, stanza
179, line 2.
M.D. 35

"THE ROOT OF ALL WAS A FRIENDLY LOAN."
        I *Timothy 6:10: "The love of money is the root of all
evil."
C.M. 40

RUN AND READ
        Habakkuk 2:2: "And the Lord answered me and said,
Write the vision, and make it plain upon tables, that he may
run that readeth it."
C.M. 14

"A SAD GOOD CHRISTIAN AT THE HEART--"
        *Alexander Pope's "Epistle to a Lady":

                A very heathen in the carnal part,
                Yet still a sad, good Christian at her heart.

O. 46

"SCARCELY FOR A RIGHTEOUS MAN WILL ONE DIE. . . . "
        Romans 5:7.
C.M. 7

"SELL ALL THOU HAST AND GIVE TO THE POOR"
        *Matthew 19:21: *Jesus says, "If thou wilt be perfect, go
and sell that thou hast, and give to the poor, and thou shalt
have treasure in heaven: and come and follow me."
C.M. 30

SHERRY FOR BOYS, AND PORT FOR MEN
    See "Port for men, claret for boys."
P. 3:3

SHIELD-LIKE, BEARING HIS SLATE BEFORE HIM
    *St. Paul's epistle to the Ephegians (6:14) talks of a
"breastplate of righteousness."
C.M. 1

SILENCE IS THE ONLY VOICE OF OUR GOD
    Menander, *Fragments*, No. 818: "In silence *God brings
all to pass."
    *Emerson, "Intellect" (*Essays*, First Series): "The an-
cient sentence said, Let us be silent for so are the gods."
    Carlyle used many variations on the idea.
P. 14:1

"THE SINS OF THE FATHER SHALL BE VISITED UPON
THE CHILDREN TO THE THIRD GENERATION"
    *Exodus 20:5: ". . . For I the Lord thy *God am a jealous
God, visiting the iniquity of the fathers upon the children unto
the third and fourth generation of them that hate me."
P. 5:4

"SIR, I DON'T BELIEVE IT."
    *Samuel Johnson, quoted in Hester Lynch Piozzi *Anec-
dotes of the Late Samuel Johnson*. Asked if he believed stories
of the *Lisbon earthquake, Johnson replied: "Oh! not for six
months   . . . at least. I *did* think that story too dreadful to be
credited."
    As Franklin ponts out in the notes to his edition of *C.M.*,
Johnson's remarks were made in the context of a universal
crisis of belief in *God's great plan for the world.
C.M. 28

" . . . SOUND MIND IN A SOUND BODY . . . "
    *Juvenal, *Satires* 10. 356: *Orandum est, ut sit mens
sana in corpore sano.* ("One should pray for a sound mind in a
sound body.")
C.M. 22

"SWEET FIELDS BEYOND THE SWELLING FLOOD . . ."
     Stanza three of *Isaac Watts's "A Prospect of Heaven
Makes Death Easy."
M.D. 22

SWEET IN THE ORATOR'S MOUTH, BITTER IN THE
THINKER'S BELLY
     *Revelation 10:9, of an angel's little book: ". . . Take it,
and eat it up; and it shall make thy belly bitter, but it shall be
in thy mouth sweet as honey."
P. 2:7

"TAKE HEED OF THY FRIENDS"
     Ecclesiasticus (see "Sirach") 6:13: "Separate thyself
from thine enemies, and take heed of thy friends."
C.M. 45

"THERE IS A SUBTLE MAN, AND THE SAME IS DE-
CEIVED."
     This is a summary of some verses from Chapters 19 and
20 of the apocryphal "The Wisdom of Jesus, the Son of *Sirach,
or Ecclesiasticus."
C.M. 5

"THERE'S A SWEET LITTLE CHERUB THAT SITS UP
ALOFT, TO LOOK OUT FOR THE LIFE OF POOR JACK."
     See "Dibdin."
T. 29

THEY DIVIDED HIS LACED HAT AND COAT AMONG
THEM.
     A parody of *John 19:24: "They parted my garments
among them / And upon my vesture did they cast lots."
W. 5

"THIS IS NO MORTAL . . ."
     *Dryden's translation of *Virgil's *Aeneid, XII, 632-633,
substituting "power" for the original "hands."
C.M. 16

"THIS IS THE BEARD OF OUR MATCHLESS JACK
CHASE ... "
    *Jesus, addressing his disciples (*Matthew 26:28): ". . .
this is my blood of the new testament, which is shed for many
for the remission of sins."
W. 85

"THIS YOUNG GENTLEMAN HAS PLEADED SO HU-
MANELY . . ."
    The anecdote concerning *Collingwood's psychologizing
was condensed from the May 1828 *Edinburgh Review:

> When a midshipman made a complaint, he would
> order the man for punishment the next day; and,
> in the interval, calling the boy down to him, would
> say, "In all probability the fault was yours; but
> whether it were or not, I am sure it would go to
> your heart to see a man old enough to be your fa-
> ther disgraced and punished on your account;
> and it will, therefore, give me a good opinion of
> your disposition, if when he is brought out, you
> ask for his pardon." Then this recommendation,
> acting as it did like an order, was complied with,
> and the lad interceded for the prisoner, Captain
> Collingwood would make great apparent difficulty
> in yielding, but at length would say, "This young
> gentleman has pleaded so humanely for you, that
> in the hope you will feel a due gratitude for him
> for his benevolence, I will for this time overlook
> your offence."

W. 52

"THOU ART AS A LION OF THE WATERS, AND AS A
DRAGON OF THE SEA."
    The reference from *Ezekiel 32:2 is quoted from the
Geneva Bible in the Penny Cyclopaedia article on whales,
which points out that the *King James Bible uses "whale":
"Son of man, take up a lamentation for *Pharoah king of
*Egypt, and say unto him, Thou art like a young lion of the na-
tions, and thou art as a whale in the seas . . . "
M.D. 82

"THOU SHALT NOT MAR THE CORNERS OF THY BEARD"
    *Leviticus 19:27.
W. 85

THOU SHALT SEE MY BACK PARTS.
In *Exodus 33:23, *God tells *Moses: "And I will take away mine hand, and thou shalt see my back parts; but my face shall not be seen."
M.D. 86

"THROUGH ME YOU PASS INTO THE CITY OF WOE; ... "
The four quoted lines are from the opening words of H.F. Cary's translation of Canto Three of *Dante's *Inferno*.
P. 9:2

"THE TIME IS OUT OF JOINT ... "
*Shakespeare's *Hamlet*, I, v, 188:

> The time is out of joint; o cursed spite,
> That ever I was born to set it right.

P. 9:2

"TO CONSIDER THE THING TOO CURIOUSLY"
In *Shakespeare's *Hamlet* V, i, 227, "Horatio" (not "Hamlet," as M. has it) is the speaker, replying to "Hamlet's": "Why may not imagination trace the noble dust of *Alexander till he find it stopping a bung hole?" "Horatio's" words: "'Twere to consider too curiously to consider so."
C.M. 18

... TURN THE LEFT CHEEK IF THE RIGHT BE SMITTEN
*Matthew 5:39: "... Resist not evil: but whosoever shall smite thee on thy right cheek, turn to him the other also."
P. 14:3

... UNKINDEST CUT OF ALL
*Shakespeare, *Julius Caesar* (II, ii, 188); *Antony, of *Brutus's part in the assassination of *Caesar: "This was the most unkindest cut of all."
W. 47

... "VAIL OF THE TEMPLE"
*Matthew 27:51: "And behold, the veil of the temple was rent in twain from the top to the bottom; and the earth did quake, and the rocks rent."
W. 26

VOICE CALLING THROUGH THE GARDEN
     In *Genesis 3:8-10.
C.M. 27

"WE'LL DRINK TONIGHT . . . "
     Lyrics from the third chorus of Charles Fenno Hoff-
man's "Sparkling and Bright," contained in various antholo-
gies of the time. The song was first published 8 May 1830 in the
New York American; it is reprinted in Hoffman's *The Vigil of
Faith and Other Poems* (1842).
M.D. 39

"A WET SHEET AND A FLOWING SEA!"
     Allan Cunningham (1784-1842): *The Songs of *Scotland*
(1825):

> A wet sheet and a flowing sea,
>   A wind that follows fast,
> And fills the white and rustling sail,
>   And bends the gallant mast.
>   ("A Wet Sheet and a
>   Flowing Sea," st.1)

C.M. 22

". . . WHAT IS MAN THAT HE SHOULD LIVE OUT THE
LIFETIME OF HIS GOD?"
     It is not clear which Bible passage, if any, M. has *M.D.*'s
"*Father Mapple" refer to in this question. The two closest are
the speech of *Zophar (marked in M.'s *Bible, Sealts #62, in
*Job 11: 7-8): "Canst thou by searching find out *God? canst
thou find out the Almighty unto perfection? It is as high as
heaven; what canst thou do? deeper than hell; what canst
thou know?" and the speech of Elihu in Job 36:26: "Behold God
is great, and we know him not; neither can the number of his
years be searched out."
     *Sir Thomas Browne (*Pseudodoxia Epidemica*, Book 7,
chap. 3) also treats of God's longevity:

> For unto God a thousand years are no more than a
> moment, and in his sight *Methuselah lived no
> nearer one day than *Abel, for all parts of time are
> alike unto him, unto whom none are referrible,
> and all things present unto whom nothing is past
> or to come; and therefore, although we be mea-

sured by the zone of time, and the flowing and continued instants thereof do leave at last a line and
circle about the eldest, yet can we not thus com-
mensurate the sphere of Trismegistus, or sum up
the unsuccessive and stable duration of God."

M.D. 9

WHEN AT ROME DO AS THE ROMANS DO

St. Ambrose (A.D. c. 340-397): "When you are at *Rome
live in the Roman style; when you are elsewhere live as they
live elsewhere" (*Advice to *St. Augustine*. From Jeremy Taylor, *Ductor Dubitantium* [1660] I, l, 5.)

["*Si Fueris Romae, Romano vivito more; Si fueris alibi,
vivito sicut ibi.*"]
T. 28

"WHO WILL PITY THE CHARMER THAT IS BITTEN WITH A SERPENT?"

Ecclesiasticus (see "Sirach") 12:13.
C.M. 36

"THE WILL OF MAN IS BY HIS REASON SWAYED . . . "

*Shakespeare, *A Midsummer Night's Dream*, II, ii, 115
and *Hamlet* III, iv, 82: " . . . reason panders will.
C.M. 3

"WITH MUCH COMMUNICATION HE WILL TEMPT THEE . . . "

Ecclesiasticus (see "Sirach") 13:11-13 (of a rich man):

> Do not try to treat him as an equal, nor trust his
> abundance of words; for he will test you through
> much talk, and while he smiles he will be exam-
> ining you. Cruel is he who does not keep words to
> himself; he will not hesitate to injure or to
> imprison. Keep words to yourself and be very
> watchful, for you are walking about with your own
> downfall.

C.M. 45

WRIT IN WATER

John Keats chose his own epitaph: "Here lies one whose name was writ in water."

Probably the earliest usage was by *Gaius Valerius Catullus (87- c. 54 B.C.), in *Carmina* LXX: "What a woman says to her ardent lover should be written in wind and running water." (*Sophocles had earlier said, "A woman's vows I write upon the wave.")

M.D. 134

" . . . YE KNOW HIM NOT"

In *Matthew 17:12, *Jesus says that Elias "is come already, and they knew him not." *John 1:10 says of *God: "He was in the world, and the world was made by him, and the world knew him not." Both echo *Genesis 28:16; *Jacob "awaked out of his sleep, and he said, Surely the Lord is in this place; and I knew it not."

P. 26:7

Bibliography

Account of the terrific and Fatal Riot at the New York Astor Place Opera House, On the night of May 10th, 1849; with the Quarrels of Forrest and Macready, Including all the Causes which led to that Awful Tragedy! . . . . New-York: H.M. Ranney, 1849.

Adler, Joyce Sparer. *War in Melville's Imagination.* New York: New York University Press, 1981.

Albion, Robert G. *Five Centuries of Famous Ships: From the Santa Maria to the Glomar Explorer.* New York: McGraw-Hill, 1978.

Ames, Nathaniel. *A Mariner's Sketches.* Providence: Cory, Marshall and Mammond, 1830.

Ammen, Rear-Admiral Daniel, U.S.N. *The Old Navy and the New.* Philadelphia: J.B. Lippincott, 1891.

Anderson, Charles R. "A Reply to Herman Melville's *White-Jacket* by Rear-Admiral Thomas O. Selfridge, Sr." *American Literature,* VII (May 1935), 123-44.

—. *Journal of a Cruise to the Pacific Ocean, 1842-1844, in the Frigate United States: With Notes on Herman Melville.* New York: AMS Press, 1966; rpt. Duke University Press, 1937.

—. *Melville in the South Seas.* New York: Columbia University Press, 1939.

Andrews, Deborah C. "Attacks of Whales on Ships: a Checklist." *Melville Society Extracts* 18 (May 1974), 3-17.

Arvin, Newton. *Herman Melville.* New York: The Viking Press, 1950. Compass Books Edition, 1957.

Bancroft, George. *The History of the United States of America from the Discovery of the Continent.* Abridged ed., Russel B. Nye, Editor. Chicago: University of Chicago Press, 1966.

Barraclough, Geoffrey, editor. *The Times Atlas of World History.* Maplewood, New Jersey: Hammond, 1978.

Bartlett, John. *Familiar Quotations: A Collection of passages, phrases and proverbs traced to their sources in ancient and modern literature.* 14th ed. Boston, Toronot: Little, Brown and Company, 1968.

Baugh, Albert C. *A History of the English Language.* Second Edition. New York: Appleton-Century-Crofts, 1957.

Bayle, Pierre. *A General Dictionary, Historical and Critical: in which a New and Accurate Translation of that of the Celebrated Mr. Bayle, with the Corrections and Observations printed in the late Edition at Paris is included; and interspersed with several thousand Lives never before published. By the Reverend Mr. John Peter Bernard; The Reverend Mr. Thomas Birch; Mr. John Lockman; and other Hands. And the articles relating to Oriental History By George Sale, Gent.* London: James Bettenham, MDCCXXXIV.

The Bay Psalm Book: Being a Facsimile Reprint of the First Edition, Printed by Stephen Daye At Cambridge, in New England in 1640. The New England Society, n.d.

Bazin, Germain. *The Louvre.* Trans. M.I. Martin. London: Thames and Hudson, Inc., 1957.

Beale, Thomas. *The Natural History of the Sperm Whale.* London: 1839.

Beechey, Frederick William. *Narrative of a Voyage to the Pacific and Bherring's Straits, under the command of Captain F.W. Beechey, R.N.* London, 1831.

—. *Narrative of a Voyage to the Pacific and Bering Straits.* Philadelphia: 1832. [Cited in Anderson.]

Benjamin Franklin. Editors, Chester E. Jorgenson and Frank Luther Mott. Revised Edition. New York: Hill and Wang, 1962.

Bennett, Frederick D. *Narrative of a Whaling Voyage round the Globe,...* 1833 to 1836. 2 volumes. London: 1840.

—. *Narrative of a Whaling Voyage round the World . . . 1836-1842.* 2 volumes. London: 1843.

Billington, Ray Allen. *The Protestant Crusade: 1800-1860: A Study of the Origins of American Nativism.* New York: Macmillan, 1938.

Bingham, Hiram. *A Residence of Twenty-One Years in the Sandwich Islands; or the Civil, Religious, and Political History of Those Islands: Comprising A Particular View of the Missionary Operations Connected with the Introduction and Progress of Christianity and Civilization among the Hawaiian People.* Second Edition. New York: Sherman Converse, 1848.

Bleyer, Willard Grosvenor. *Main Currents in the History of American Journalism.* Boston: Riverside Press Cambridge, 1927.

Bligh, William. *A Voyage to the South Sea, undertaken by command of His Majesty, for the purpose of conveying the bread-fruit tree to the West Indies, commanded by Lieutenant William Bligh. Including an account of the mutiny on board the said ship, and the subsequent voyage of part of the crew, in the ship's boat, from Tofoa, one of the Friendly Islands, to Timor, a Dutch settlement in the East Indies . . . .* Published by permission of the lords commissioners of the Admiralty. London: Printed for G. Nicol, 1792.

Bougainville, Louis Antoine de, Comte. *A Voyage round the World. Performed . . . in the Years 1766, 1767, 1768, and 1769 . . . Translated from the French by John Reinhold Forster, F.A.S.* London: Nourse [etc.], 1772.

Bowditch, Nathaniel. *New American Practical Navigator: Being an Epitome of Navigation.* 1802.

—. *American Practical Navigator: An Epitome of Navigation and Nautical Astronomy.* No. 9, United States Hydrographic Office. Washington: Government Printing Office, 1917.

Branch, Watson G., editor. *Melville: the Critical Heritage.* London and Boston: Routledge & Kegan Paul, 1974.

Bremner, Robert H. *American Philanthropy.* The Chicago History of American Civilization series. Chicago: University of Chicago Press, 1960.

Brewer, Rev. E. Cobham. *Brewer's Dictionary of Phrase and Fable.* New Edition. Philadelphia: J.B. Lippincott, 1930.

—. *Brewer's Dictionary of Phrase and Fable.* Centenary Edition. Revised by Ivor H. Evans. London: Cassell, 1970.

—. *Dictionary of Phrase and Fable: Giving the Derivation, Source or Origin of Common Phrases, Allusions and*

Words that have a Tale to Tell. 9th ed. Philadelphia: Claxton, Remsen, and Haffelfinger, 1917.

—. *Dictionary of Phrase and Fable.* 10th ed. London: J.B. Lippincott, 1894.

Briggs, Charles F. *The Adventures of Harry Franco.* New York: Garrett Press, 1969.

Briggs, Katherine M. *A Dictionary of British Folk Tales in the English Language: Incorporating the F.J. Norton Collection.* 2 volumes. Bloomington: Indiana University Press, 1970.

Brodhead, Richard H. *Hawthorne, Melville, and the Novel.* Chicago and London: University of Chicago Press, 1976.

Browne, J. Ross. *Etchings of a Whaling Cruise.* Ed. John Seelye. Cambridge: Belknap Press, 1968.

Bruce, James. *Interesting Narrative of the Travels of James Bruce, Esq. into Abyssinia, to Discover the Source of the Nile in the Years 1768-73.* 5 volumes. 1790.

Bryant, John, editor. *A Companion to Melville Studies.* New York: Greenwood Press, 1986.

Bulwer Lytton, Sir Edward. *Pelham or Adventures of a Gentleman.* Philadelphia: J.B. Lippincott, 1877.

Bunyan, John. *The Pilgrim's Progress.* Editor, Roger Sharrock. Harmondsworth, Middlesex, England: Penguin, 1965.

Burke, Edmund. *Reflections on the Revolution in France.* Editor, Thomas H.D. Mahoney. Indianapolis: Bobbs-Merrill, 1955.

Burke's Genealogical and Heraldic History of the Peerage Baronetage & Knightage. Founded 1826 by John Burke and Sir Bernard Burke. Ed. L. G. Pine. 101st Edition. MDMLVI. London: Burke's Peerage Limited.

Buttrick, George Arthur, editor. *The Interpreter's Dictionary of the Bible: An Illustrated Encyclopedia: Identifying and Explaining all Proper Names and Significant Terms and Subjects in the Holy Scriptures, Including the Apocrypha: With Attention to Archaelogical Discoveries and Researches into the Life and Faith of Ancient Times.* 4 volumes. New York: Abingdon Press, 1962, 1984.

Byron, John. *The Narrative of the Honourable John Byron . . . Containing an Account of the Great Distresses Suffered by Himself and His Companions on the Coast of Patagonia, from the Year 1740, till Their Arrival in England, 1746. With a Description of St. Jago de Chili, and the Manners and Customs of the Inhabitants. Also a Relation of The Loss of the Wager, Man of War, One of Admiral Anson's Squadron. Written by Himself.* Second Edition. London: Baker and Leigh, 1768.

Camoes, Luiz de. *Poems, from the Portuguese of Luis de Camoens. With Remarks on His Life and Writings. Notes, etc. etc.* By Lord Viscount Strangford . . . New Edition. London: Carpenter, 1824.

Chamberlin, Roy B. and Herman Feldman, editors. *The Dartmouth Bible: an Abridgement of the King James Version, With Aids To Its Understanding As History and Literature, and As a Source of Religious Experience.* Second Edition. Boston: Riverside Press, Houghton Mifflin, 1950, 1961.

Chambers, Ephraim. *Cyclopaedia: or, An Universal Dictionary of Arts and Sciences . . . .* London: Knapton, 1728. [Fifth Edition 1741, cited by Davis in *Melville's Mardi: A Chartless Voyage.*]

Chambers's Encyclopedia. New Revised Edition. 15 volumes. Pergamon Press, 1967. Aylesbury, Bucks, England: Hazell Watson and Viney Ltd.

Chambers, William and Robert. *Information for the People. A Popular Encyclopedia.* Philadelphia, 1847.

Chamier, Frederick. *Ben Brace: The Last of Nelson's Agamemnons.* London: George Routledge & Sons, n.d.

Chapelle, Howard I. *The History of American Sailing Ships.* New York: Bonanza Books, 1935.

Charvat, William. *The Origins of American Critical Thought 1810-1835.* New York: A.S. Barnes, 1961.

Chase, Owen. *Narrative of the Most Extraordinary and Distressing Shipwreck of the Whaleship Essex.* With supplementary accounts of survivors and Herman Melville's notes. Introduction by B.R. McElderry, Jr. The American Experience Series, Editor, Henry Bamford Parkes. New York: Corinth Books, 1963.

Cobban, Alfred. *A History of Modern France.* 3 volumes. Harmondsworth, Middlesex, England: Penguin, 1984-85 reprint.

Codman, John. *Sailors' Life and Sailors' Yarns, by Captain Ringbolt.* New York: C.S. Francis, 1847.

Coffler, Gail H., compiler. *Melville's Classical Allusions: A Comprehensive Index and Glossary.* Bibliographies and Indexes in American Literature, Number 2. Westport, Connecticut; London, England: Greenwood Press, 1985.

Cohen, Saul B., Geographic Editor. *Oxford World Atlas.* New York: Oxford, 1973.

Coletta, Paolo E. *The American Naval Heritage in Brief.* Second Edition. Washington, D.C.: University Press of America, 1980.

Colson, Percy. *The Strange History of Lord George Gordon.* London: Robert Hale & Company, MCMXXXVII.

Columbia Lippincott Gazetteer of the World. Morningside Heights: Columbia University Press, 1962.

The Compact Edition of the Oxford English Dictionary. Oxford University Press, 1971.

Cooper, James Fenimore. *The Sea Lions.* Editor, Warren S. Walker. Lincoln: University of Nebraska Press, 1965.

—. *The Spy.* New York: Popular Library, n.d.

Coulter, John M. *Adventures in the Pacific.* Dublin: 1845.

Coysh, A.W. *Historic English Inns.* New York: Drake Publishers Inc., 1972.

Cruden, Alexander. *Cruden's Complete Concordance to the Old and New Testaments.* Guildford and London: Lutterworth Press, 1941.

Dana, Richard Henry. *Two Years Before the Mast.* New York: Bantam, 1963.

Dante Alighieri. *The Divine Comedy.* Translator, Charles Eliot Norton. Revised Edition. Boston and New York: Houghton Mifflin Company, 1902.

The Dartmouth Bible: An Abridgement of the King James Version, With Aids to its Understanding as History and Literature, and as a Source of Religious Experience. Roy

B. Chamberlin and Herman Feldman, Editors. Boston: Houghton Mifflin Company, The Riverside Press Cambridge, 1961.

Davidson, H.R. Ellis. *Gods and Myths of Northern Europe.* New York: Penguin, 1984.

Davis, Merrell R. *Melville's Mardi: A Chartless Voyage.* New Haven: Yale University Press, 1952. Volume 119, Yale Studies in English, Benjamin Christie Nangle, Editor.

—. "The Flower Symbolism in *Mardi.*" *Modern Language Quarterly* 2 (1941), 625-38.

Debrett's Peerage and Baronetage With Her Majesty's Royal Warrant Holders. 1980. Debrett's Peerage Limited, London. Gale Research Company, Detroit. (Founded 1769; renamed Debrett 1802.)

Defoe, Daniel. *A Tour thro' the whole Island of Great Britain (1724-1727)*, Editor, G.D.H. Cole (1927). [Liverpool, Volume II, 665].

deKerchove, Rene. *International Maritime Dictionary: An Encyclopedic Dictionary of useful maritime terms and phrases, together with equivalents in French and German.* Toronto, New York, London: D. Van Nostrand, 1948.

A Descriptive Catalogue of the Government Publications of the United States, September 5, 1774--March 4, 1881. Compiled by Order of Congress by Ben: Perley Poore. Clerk of Printing Records. Washington: Government Printing Office, 1885. Misc. Documents No. 67 of *The Miscellaneous Documents of the Senate of the United States for the Second Session of the Forty-Eighth Congress, and the Special Session of the Senate Convened March 4, 1885*, in eight volumes. Vol. 4, No. 67. Washington: Government Printing Office, 1885, rpt. Ann Arbor: J.W. Edwards, 1953.

Dexter, Walter. *The England of Dickens*. Philadelphia: J.B. Lippincott Company, n.d.

Dictionary of International Biography. Cambridge, London and Dartmouth, England: Melrose Press Limited, 1973.

Dillingham, William B. *An Artist in the Rigging: The Early Work of Herman Melville*. Athens: University of Georgia Press, 1972.

Drabble, Margaret. *The Oxford Companion to English Literature*. Fifth Edition. Oxford: Oxford University Press, 1985.

Duban, James. *Melville's Major Fiction: Politics, Theology, and Imagination*. DeKalb: Northern Illinois University Press, 1983.

Dumont, H. *The Floral Offering, Comprising The Language and Poetry of Flowers*. Philadelphia, 1851.

The Edinburgh Review, or Critical Journal. October 1824, LXXXI and May 1928, XCIV.

Edinger, Edward F. *Melville's Moby-Dick: A Jungian Commentary*. New York: New Directions, 1975.

Efvergren, Carl. *Names of Places in a Transferred Sense in English*. Lund, 1909. Rpt. Detroit: Gale Research Company, 1969.

Eggleston, George T. *Tahiti: Voyage Through Paradise: The Story of a Small Boat Passage Through the Society Islands*. New York: The Devin-Adair Company, 1953.

Ellis, William. *Polynesian Researches*. 4 volumes. London: 1833.

—. *Polynesian Researches: Society Islands*. Rutland, Vermont: Charles E. Tuttle Company, 1969.

—. *The History of the London Missionary Society*. 1 volume. Printed London: 1844.

Emery, Allan Moore. "'Benito Cereno' and Manifest Destiny." *Nineteenth Century Fiction*. 39 (June 1984), 48-68.

The Encyclopedia Americana. International Edition. 30 volumes. Danbury, Connecticut: Grolier, 1988.

Encyclopaedia Britannica. Fourteenth Edition. Chicago: William Benton, 1970.

Espenshade, Edward B., Jr. and Joel L. Morrison, Editors. *Goode's World Atlas*. Fifteenth Edition. Chicago: Rand McNally, 1979.

Extracts, Melville Society Extracts. The Melville Society of America, 1969--.

Fairburn, John. *Fairburn's Edition of the Funeral of Admiral Lord Nelson Containing a Correct Account of His Body Laying in State at Greenwich, The Procession By Water and Land with the Funeral Service and Final interment of the Body in a Truly Magnificent State Coffin at St. Paul's Cathedral on Thursday, January 9, 1806*. London: John Fairburn, 1806.

Fanning, Edward. *Voyages round the World*. New York: 1833.

Farmer, J.S. and W.E. Henley. *Slang and its Analogues*. N.P.: Arno Press, 1970.

Feidelson, Charles Jr. *Symbolism and American Literature*. Chicago: University of Chicago Press, 1953.

Field, David Dudley. *A History of the County of Berkshire, Massachusetts; in Two Parts. The First Being a General View of the County; the Second, an Account of the Several Towns. By Gentlemen in the County, Clergymen and Laymen.* Pittsfield, 1829.

Forsythe, R.S. "Herman Melville's Father Murphy." *Notes and Queries.* CLXXII (April 10, 1937), 254-258; (April 17, 1937), 272-276.

Foster, Elizabeth S. "Another Note on Melville and Geology." *American Literature* XXII (January 1951), 478-87.

—. "Melville and Geology." *American Literature* XVII (March 1945), 50-65.

Fowler, William M., Jr. *Jack Tars and Commodores: The American Navy, 1783-1815.* Boston: Houghton Mifflin, 1984.

Frank, Stuart M. "'The King of the Southern Sea' and 'Captain Bunker': Two Songs in *Moby-Dick.*" *Melville Society Extracts* 63 (September 1985), 4-7.

Franklin, Benjamin. *The Autobiography of Benjamin Franklin.* Editors Leonard W. Labaree, Ralph L. Ketcham, Helen C. Boatfield, Helene H. Fineman. New Haven: Yale University Press, 1964.

Franklin, H. Bruce. *The Wake of the Gods: Melville's Mythology.* Stanford, California: Stanford University Press, 1963.

Franklin, S.R., Rear-Admiral U.S. Navy (Retired). *Memories of a Rear-Admiral: Who has Served for More than Half a Century in the Navy of the United States.* New York and London: Harper and Brothers, 1898.

Fraser, Edward. *Soldier and Sailor Words and Phrases.*
London: G. Routledge, 1925; rpt. Detroit: Gale
Research Co., 1968.

Fraser, Edward and John Gibbons. *Soldier and Sailor Words
and Phrases.* London, 1925.

Fuller, Thomas. *The Worthies of England.* Editor, John
Freeman, Ruskin House Museum Street London:
George Allen & Unwin Ltd., 1952.

Furnas, J.C. *The Americans: A Social History of the United
States: 1587-1914.* New York: G.P. Putnam's Sons,
1969.

Gaines, Kendra H. "A Consideration of an Additional Source
for Melville's *Moby-Dick*." *Melville Society Extracts* 29
(January 1977), 6-12.

Gale, Robert L. *Plots and Characters in the Fiction and
Narrative Poetry of Herman Melville.* Cambridge,
Massachusetts and London, England: The Massa-
chusetts Institute of Technology Press, 1969.

Garner, Stanton. "Melville in the Customhouse, 1881-1882: A
Rustic Beauty Among the Highborn Dames of Court."
Melville Society Extracts 35 (September 1978), 12-14.

—, Editor. *The Captain's Best Mate: The Journal of Mary
Chipman Lawrence on the Whaler Addison 1856-1860.*
Hanover: University Press of New England, 1966.

Gibb, Sir Hamilton. *The Life of Saladin: From the Works of
Imad ad-Din and Baha Ad-Din.* Oxford: Clarendon
Press, 1973.

Gidmark, Jill B. *A Melville Sea Dictionary.* Westport,
Connecticut: Greenwood, 1982.

Gilman, William H. *Melville's Early Life and Redburn*. New York: New York University Press, 1951.

Ginsberg, Robert, Editor. *A Casebook on The Declaration of Independence*. New York: Thomas Y. Crowell Company, 1967.

Ginzberg, Louis. *Legends of the Bible*. Philadelphia: The Jewish Publication Society of America, 1956.

Good, Dr. John Mason. *The Book of Nature*. Harper's Stereotype Edition. Hartford: Belknap and Hamersley, 1837.

Gorham, Maurice, and H. McG. Dunnett. *Inside the Pub*. London: The Architectural Press, 1950.

Granville, Augustus Bozzi. *St. Petersburg: A Journal of Travel* [1828].

Granville, Wilfred. *A Dictionary of Sailor's Slang*. London: Andre Deutsch, 1962.

Gray, Henry. *Anatomy: Descriptive and Surgical*. Revised American, from the Fifteenth English, Edition. Editors, T. Pickering Pick and Robert Howden. New York: Bounty Books, 1977.

Griggs, William N. *The Celebrated "Moon Story," its Origin Incidents; With a Memoir of the Author, and an Appendix, containing I. An Authentic Description of the Moon; II. A New Theory of the Lunar Surface, in Relation to That of the Earth*. New York: Bunnell and Price, 1852.

Gross, Seymour L., Editor. *A Benito Cereno Handbook*. Belmont, California: Wadsworth Publishing Co., 1965.

Hakluyt, Richard. *The Principal Navigations*. 1598.

Hall, James. *Sketches of History, Life, and Manners, in the West*. 1834 or 1835.

Hamilton, Alexander and James Madison, John Jay. *The Federalist Papers*. New York: New American Library Mentor Books, 1961.

Hamilton, Edith. *Mythology*. New York: New American Library, 1964.

Hammond, N.G.L. and H.H. Scullard, Editors. *The Oxford Classical Dictionary*. Second Edition. Oxford Clarendon Press, 1970.

Handy, E.S. Craighill. *Native Culture in the Marquesas*. Honolulu: 1923.

Harris, John. *Collection of Voyages and Travels (Navigantium atque Itinerantium Bibliotheca)*. 1705; 1748.

Harrison, Brian. *Drink and the Victorians: The Temperance Question in England 1815-1872*. N.P.: University of Pittsburgh Press, 1971.

Hart, James D. *The Oxford Companion to American Literature*, Fifth Edition. New York: Oxford University Press, 1983.

Harvey, Sir Paul. *The Oxford Companion to Classical Literature*. Oxford: Clarendon Press, 1937.

Heaps, Leo. *Log of the Centurion: Based on the Original Papers of Captain Philip Saumarez on Board HMS Centurion, Lord Anson's flagship during his circumnavigation 1740-44*. London: Hart Davis, MacGibbon, 1973.

Herbert, T. Walter, Jr. *Marquesan Encounters: Melville and the Meaning of Civilization*. Cambridge, Massachusetts: Harvard University Press, 1980.

—. *Moby-Dick and Calvinism: A World Dismantled*. New Brunswick, New Jersey: Rutgers University Press, 1977.

Hewett, Edward and W.F. Axton. *Convivial Dickens: The Drinks of Dickens and His Times*. Athens, Ohio: Ohio University Press, 1983.

Hillway, Tyrus. *Herman Melville*. Revised Edition. Twayne's United States Authors Series. Indianapolis: Bobbs-Merrill Educational Publishing, 1979.

—. "Melville's Geological Knowledge." *American Literature* XXI (May 1949), 232-8.

—. "Quaker Language in *Moby-Dick*?" [Melville Society] *Extracts* 23 (September 1975), 11, 12.

Hindley, Geoffrey, Editor. *The Larousse Encyclopedia of Music*, based on *La Musique: les hommes; les instruments; les oeuvres*. Editor, Norbert Dufourcq, 1965. New York: Crescent Books, 1971.

—. *Saladin*. New York: Harper and Row, 1976.

The History of Rome by Titus Livius. Volume I. Trans. Rev. Canon Roberts. New York: E.P. Dutton & Co., 1926 rpt. of 1912. #603, Everyman's Library.

Holloway, Mark. *Heavens on Earth: Utopian Communities in America 1680-1880*. Second Edition. New York: Dover Publications, 1966.

Holy Bible. Authorized King James Version. Wheaton, Illinois: Tyndale House Publishers, 1976, 1987.

The Holy Bible: Containing the Old and New Testments Translated out of the Original Tongues: Being the version set forth A.D. 1611: Compared with the most ancient authorities and revised A.D. 1881-1885. Editor, American Revision Committee A.D. 1901. New York: Thomas Nelson and Sons, 1901.

Howard, Leon. *Herman Melville: A Biography.* Berkeley: University of California Press, 1951.

—. *The Unfolding of Moby-Dick.* Glassboro, New Jersey: The Melville Society, 1987.

Hunt, Livingston. "Herman Melville as a Naval Historian." *Harvard Graduates' Magazine.* XXXIX (Sept. 1930), 22-30.

Huntress, Keith. "A Note on Melville's *Redburn.*" *New England Quarterly* XVIII (1945), 259-260.

—. "Melville's Use of a Source for *White-Jacket.*" *American Literature* XVII (March 1945), 66-74.

Hyamson, A.M. *Dictionary of Universal Biography.* Second Edition. Routledge, 1951.

Hyde, Francis E. *Liverpool and the Mersey: An Economic History of a Port: 1700-1970.* Newton Abbot, Devon: David & Charles, 1971.

Jaffé, David. *The Stormy Petrel and the Whale.* Baltimore: Port City Press, 1976.

Jane's Dictionary of Naval Terms. Compiled by Joseph Palmer. London: Macdonald and Jane's, 1975.

Janvier, Thomas A. *In Old New York.* New York: Harper & Brothers, 1922.

Jefferson, Thomas. *Notes on the State of Virginia.* Thomas Perkins Abernethy, Editor. New York: Harper & Row, 1964.

John Nichol, Mariner. Edinburgh: Blackwood, London: Cadell, 1822.

Johnson, Allen, Editor. *The Dictionary of American Biography.* 20 volumes plus *Index.* New York: Charles Scribner's Sons, 1928.

Jonas, Hans. *The Gnostic Religion: The Message of the Alien God and the Beginning of Christianity.* Boston: Beacon Hill Press 1958. Second Edition, Beacon Press, 1968.

Josephus, Flavius. *History of the Jewish War and Jewish Antiquities.* 77 or 78, 90's.

Karcher, Carolyn Lury. "The Story of Charlemont: A Dramatization of Melville's Concepts of Fiction in *The Confidence-Man: His Masquerade.*" *Nineteenth-Century Fiction* XXI (1966), 73-84.

Kenney, Alice P. *The Gansevoorts of Albany: Dutch Patricians in the Upper Hudson Valley.* Syracuse: Syracuse University Press, 1969.

Kent, William, Editor. *An Encyclopaedia of London.* New York: E.P. Dutton, 1937.

Kier, Kathleen E. "An Annotated Edition of Melville's *White-Jacket.*" Diss. Columbia University, 1980.

—. "'A Thing Most Momentous'? or 'Part of the General Joke'?" *Melville Society Extracts* 61 (February 1985), 11-13.

—. "'At Sea' in Port: Melville's Geophobia." *Melville Society Extracts* 60 (November 1984), 10-12.

Kitto, John, Editor. *Cyclopedia of Biblical Literature*. 1846.

Kobler, John. *Ardent Spirits: The Rise and Fall of Prohibition*. New York: G.P. Putnam's Sons, 1973.

Kotzebue, Otto von. *A New Voyage round the World, . . . 1823-1826*. 2 volumes. London: 1830.

Kouwenhoven, John A. *The Columbia Historical Portrait of New York: An Essay in Graphic History in Honor of the Tricentennial of New York City and the Bicentennial of Columbia University*. Garden City, New York: Doubleday and Company, 1953.

Lamb, Mrs. Martha, and Mrs. Burton Harrison. *History of the City of New York: Its Origin, Rise, and Progress*. 3 volumes. New York: A.S. Barnes Company, 1896.

Lamont, E.H. *Wild Life Among the Pacific Islanders*. London: 1867.

Landström, Björn. *The Ship: An Illustrated-History Written and illustrated by Björn Landström*. Garden City, New York: Doubleday & Company, 1961.

Lane, Edward William. *The Thousand and One Nights, Commonly Called, in England, The Arabian Nights' Entertainments. A New Translation from the Arabic, with Copious Notes. Illustrated by Many Hundred Engravings of Wood, from Original Designs by William Harvey*. 3 volumes. London: Charles Knight, 1841. [A series of articles by "Sahal-Ben-Haroun" commemorating a reprint of Lane's work ran in *Literary World*, 12 and 26 February, 18 and 25 March, 13 May, 14 October, 1848.]

Langley, Harold D. *Social Reform in the United States Navy, 1798-1862*. Urbana, Chicago, London: University of Illinois Press, 1967.

The Larousse Encyclopedia of Music. Hamlyn Publishing, 1971. Rpt. Crescent Books, Crown, 1987.

Leech, Samuel. *Thirty Years from Home, or A Voice from the Main Deck, being the Experience of Samuel Leech, who was for Six Years in the British and American Navies: Was Captured in The British Frigate Macedonian: Afterwards Entered the American Navy, and Was Taken in the United States Brig Syren, by the British Ship Medway*. Boston: Charles Tappan, 1843.

Lempriere, J. *Lempriere's Universal Biography; Containing a Critical and Historical Account of the Lives, Characters, and Labours of Eminent Persons in all ages and countries, Together with Selections of Foreign Biography from Watkins's Dictionary, Recently Published, and About Eight Hundred Original Articles of American Biography. By Eleazar Lord*. 2 volumes. New York: R. Lockwood, 1825.

Leo Africanus. *A Geographical Historie of Africa, Written in Arabicke and Italian by John Leo a More . . . Translated and Collected by John Pory*. London, 1600.

The Letters of Herman Melville. Editors, Merrell R. Davis and William H. Gilman. New Haven: Yale University Press, 1960.

Leyda, Jay, Editor. *The Complete Stories of Herman Melville*. New York: Random House, 1949.

—. *The Melville Log: A Documentary Life of Herman Melville 1819-1891.* 2 volumes. New York: Harcourt, Brace and Company, 1951.

"Lima and the Limanians." *Harper's New Monthly Magazine.* October 1851, pp. 598-609.

The Literary World. A Gazette for Authors, Readers and Publishers. I (March 6, 1847), 105-106.

London and Its Environs in the Nineteenth Century. Thomas H. Shepherd and James Elmes. New York: Benjamin Blom, 1968. First London pub. 1829.

Lovett, Richard. *The History of the London Missionary Society.* 2 volumes. London: 1899.

Lovette, Leland P., Vice Admiral United States Navy (Retired). *Naval Customs, Traditions and Usage.* Annapolis, Maryland: United States Naval Institute, 1959 (4th ed.).

[Lucett, Edward]. *Rovings in the Pacific, from 1837 to 1849 . . . by a Merchant Long Resident at Tahiti.* 2 volumes. London: 1851.

Macintyre, Captain Donald. *The Adventure of Sail 1520-1914.* New York: Random House, 1970.

Macy, Obed. *The History of Nantucket . . . Together with the Rise and Progress of the Whale Fishery.* Boston: 1835.

Madison, Mary K. *Books on Melville 1891-1981: A Checklist.* Evanston: Loose-Fish Books, No. 1, 1982.

Masefield, John. *Sea Life in Nelson's Time.* First pub. 1905; rpt. Freeport, N.Y. Books for Libraries Press, 1969.

Mathews, Cornelius. *Big Abel, and the Little Manhattan.* New York: Wiley & Putnam, 1845.

Matthews, Mitford M. *A Dictionary of Americanisms.* Chicago: University of Chicago Press, 1951.

Matthiessen, F.O. *American Renaissance: Art and Expression in the Age of Emerson and Whitman.* London: Oxford University Press, 1941.

Matz, B.W. *Dickensian Inns & Taverns.* New York: Charles Scribner's Sons, 1922.

—. *The Inns & Taverns of "Pickwick": With Some Observations on Their Other Associations.* New York: Charles Scribner's Sons, 1921.

Maurice, Thomas. *Indian Antiquities.* 2 volumes. London, 1800.

May, Herbert G., and Bruce M. Metzger, Editors. *The New Oxford Annotated Bible With the Apocrypha.* New York: Oxford University Press, 1977.

McCabe, James D., Jr. *Lights and Shadows of New York Life: or, the Sights and Sensations of the Great City.* A Facsimile Edition. New York: Farrar, Straus and Giroux, 1970. Rpt. of 1868 or 1872 edition.

McNally, William. *Evils and Abuses in the Naval and Merchant Service Exposed: With Proposals for Their Remedy and Redress.* Boston: 1839.

Melville, Herman. *The Battle-Pieces of Herman Melville.* Hennig Cohen, Editor. New York: Thomas Yoseloff, 1963.

—. *Billy Budd, Sailor (An Inside Narrative).* Editors, Harrison Hayford and Merton M. Sealts. Chicago: University of Chicago Press, 1962.

—. *Clarel: A Poem and Pilgrimage in the Holy Land.* Walter E. Bezanson, Editor. New York: Hendricks House, 1960. Rpt. 1973.

—. *The Confidence-Man: His Masquerade.* Harrison Hayford et al, Editors. Evanston and Chicago: Northwestern University Press and the Newberry Library, 1984

—. *The Confidence-Man: His Masquerade.* H. Bruce Franklin, Editor. Indianapolis: Bobbs-Merrill, 1967.

—. *The Confidence-Man: His Masquerade.* Hershel Parker, Editor. New York: W.W. Norton & Company, 1971.

—. "Fragments From a Writing Desk." *The Democratic Press and Lansingburgh Advertiser.* May 4 and 18, 1839. Rpt. in William H. Gilman, *Melville's Early Life and Redburn.* New York University Press, 1951.

—. *Israel Potter: His Fifty Years of Exile.* Alfred Kazin, Editor. New York: Warner, 1974.

—. *Israel Potter: His Fifty Years of Exile.* Harrison Hayford et. al., Editors. Evanston and Chicago: Northwestern University Press and The Newberry Library, 1982.

—. *Journal of a Visit to Europe and the Levant: October 11, 1856--May 6, 1857.* Howard C. Horsford, Editor. Princeton: Princeton University Press, 1955.

—. *Journal of a Visit to London and the Continent: 1849-1850.* Eleanor Melville Metcalf, Editor. Cambridge: Harvard University Press, 1948.

—. "Journal of Melville's Voyage in a Clipper Ship." *New England Quarterly*, II (1929), 120-25.

—. *Journal Up the Straits: October 11, 1856--May 5, 1857.* Raymond Weaver, Editor. New York: Cooper Square Publishers, 1971.

—. *The Letters of Herman Melville.* Merrell R. Davis and William H. Gilman, Editors. New Haven: Yale University Press, 1968.

—. *Mardi: and a Voyage Thither.* Harrison Hayford et al., Editors. Evanston and Chicago: Northwestern University Press and The Newberry Library, 1970.

—. *Moby-Dick: or, The Whale.* Charles Feidelson, Jr., Editor. New York: Bobbs-Merrill, 1964.

—. *Moby-Dick.* Harrison Hayford and Hershel Parker, Editors. New York: W.W. Norton, 1967.

—. *Moby-Dick: or, The Whale.* Luther S. Mansfield and Howard P. Vincent, Editors. New York: Hendricks House, 1962.

—. *Omoo.* In *Romances of Herman Melville.* New York: Tudor, 1931.

—. *Omoo: A Narrative of Adventures in the South Seas.* Harrison Hayford et al., Editors. Evanston and Chicago: Northwestern University Press and The Newberry Library, 1968.

—. *Piazza Tales.* Egbert S. Oliver, Editor. New York: Hendricks House, 1962.

—. *The Piazza Tales and Other Prose Pieces: 1839-1960.* Harrison Hayford et al., Editors. Evanston and Chicago:

Northwestern University Press and The Newberry Library, 1987.

—. *Pierre: or The Ambiguities*. Harrison Hayford et al., Editors. Evanston and Chicago: Northwestern University Press and The Newberry Library, 1971.

—. *Pierre, or the Ambiguities*. Editor, Henry A. Murray. New York: Hendricks House, Inc., 1962.

—. *Redburn: His First Voyage*. Editors, Harrison Hayford et al. Evanston and Chicago: Northwestern University Press and The Newberry Library, 1969.

—. "The Two Temples" in *Great Short Works of Herman Melville*. Editor, Warner Berthoff. New York: Harper & Row, 1970, 151-64.

—. *Typee: A Peep at Polynesian Life*. Harrison Hayford et al., Editors. Evanston and Chicago: Northwestern University Press and The Newberry Library, 1968.

—. *Weissjacke*. Deutsch von Walter Weber. Zurich: Conzett & Huber, 1948.

—. *White-Jacket*. Editor, A.R. Humphreys. London: Oxford University Press, 1966.

—. *White-Jacket: Or The World in a Man-of-War*. Hennig Cohen, Editor. New York: Holt, Rinehart and Winston, 1967.

—. *White-Jacket: Or the World in a Man-of-War*. Harrison Hayford et al, Editors. Evanston and Chicago: Northwestern University Press and The Newberry Library, 1970.

—. *Works*. 3 volumes. G. Thomas Tanselle, Editor. New York: Viking, Library of America, 1982, -83, -84.

Mercator, Gerardus (Gerhard Kremer). *Cosmographical meditationes de fabrica mundi et fabricati figura*. 1595.

Mercier, Henry James and William Gallop. *Life in a Man-of-War or Scenes in "Old Ironsides" During her Cruise in the Pacific*. By a Fore-Top-Man. Philadelphia: Lydia R. Bailey, Printer, 1841.

Metcalf, Eleanor Melville. *Herman Melville: Cycle and Epicycle*. Cambridge: Harvard University Press, 1953.

Meyers, Marvin. *The Jacksonian Persuasion: Politics & Belief*. Stanford, California: Stanford University Press, 1960.

Millar, John F. *American Ships of the Colonial and Revolutionary Periods*. New York: W.W. Norton & Company, 1978.

Miller, Perry. *The Raven and the Whale: The War of Words and Wits in the Era of Poe and Melville*. New York: Harcourt, Brace & World, Inc., 1956.

Mills, Gordon. "The Significance of 'Arcturus' in *Mardi*." *American Literature* (May 1942), 158-61.

Milton, John. *Paradise Lost and Selected Poetry and Prose*. Editor, Northrop Frye. New York: Holt, Rinehart and Winston, Inc., 1951.

Monteiro, George. "Melville and Camões: A Working Bibliography." *Melville Society Extracts* 64 (November 1985), 14, 15.

Mooney, James L., Editor. *Dictionary of American Naval Fighting Ships.* 8 volumes. Navy Department: Office of the Chief of Naval Operations, Naval History Division, Washington: U.S. Government Printing Office, 1959-1980.

Moore, Maxine. *That Lonely Game: Melville, Mardi, and the Almanac.* Columbia, Missouri: University of Missouri Press, 1975.

Moore, W.G. *A Dictionary of Geography: Definitions and Explanations of Terms Used in Physical Geography.* Baltimore, Maryland: Penguin Books, 1964. (Penguin Reference Books R 2).

Morgan, John. *A Complete History of Algiers.* London, 1731.

Morison, Samuel Eliot. *Admiral of the Ocean Sea: A Life of Christopher Columbus.* Boston: Little, Brown and Company: 1942.

—. *John Paul Jones: A Sailor's Biography.* Boston: Little, Brown and Company, 1959.

Moses, Carole. "Melville's 'Cunning' Reading of Spenser." *Melville Society Extracts* 68 (November 1986), 5-10.

Mushabac, Jane. *Melville's Humor: A Critical Study.* Hamden, Connecticut: Archon Books, The Shoe String Press, 1981.

Nash, William Giles. *America: The True History of its Discovery.* London: Grant Richards, 1924.

A Naval Encyclopedia: Comprising a Dictionary of Nautical Words and Phrases; Biographical Notices, and Records of Naval Officers; Special Articles on Naval Art and Science, Written Expressly for this Work by Officers and Others of Recognized Authority in the Branches Treated

*by Them. Together with Descriptions of the Principal
Naval Stations and Seaports of the World.* Philadelphia:
L.R. Hamersly & Co., 1884; rpt. Detroit: Gale Research
Co., 1971.

The New Oxford Annotated Bible With the Apocrypha.
Expanded Edition. Revised Standard Version. Herbert
G. May and Bruce M. Metzger, Editors. New York:
Oxford University Press, 1973, 1977.

Nicol, John. *The Life and Adventures of John Nicol, Mariner.*
Edinburgh: W. Blackwood, 1822.

Niebuhr, Carsten. *Travels through Arabia and Other
Countries in the East.* Translator, Robert Heron. 2
volumes. Edinburgh, 1792.

Noel, John V., Jr., and Edward L. Beach. *Naval Terms
Dictionary.* Fourth Edition. Annapolis, Maryland:
Naval Institute Press, 1978. (First Edition 1952).

Norton, Andrews. *The Evidences of the Genuineness of the
Gospels.* Cambridge, Massachusetts: John Owen, 1844.

Novarr, David, Editor. *Seventeenth-Century English Prose.*
Volume III, The Borzoi Anthology of 17th-Century
English Literature. New York: Alfred A. Knopf, 1967.

Odell, George C.D. *Annals of the New York Stage.* 15
volumes. New York: Columbia University Press,
1936.

Oliver, Douglas L. *Ancient Tahitian Society.* 3 volumes.
Honolulu: The University Press of Hawaii, 1974.

Olmsted, Francis A. *Incidents of a Whaling Voyage.* New
York: 1841.

Olson, Charles. *Call Me Ishmael.* San Francisco: City Lights Books, 1947.

The Oxford Classical Dictionary. Editors, N.G.L. Hammond and H.H. Sevllard. 2nd Edition. Oxford: Clarendon Press, 1970.

The Oxford Companion to Classical Literature. Editor, Sir Paul Harvey. Oxford: Clarendon Press, 1937.

Pagels, Elaine. *The Gnostic Gospels.* New York: Random House Vintage Books, 1981.

Parker, Hershel. *The Recognition of Herman Melville: Selected Criticism Since 1846.* Michigan: The University of Michigan Press Ann Arbor Paperbacks, 1970.

Parker, Hershel and Harrison Hayford, Editors. *Moby-Dick as Doubloon: Essays and Extracts (1851-1970).* New York: W.W. Norton & Company, 1970.

Partridge, Eric. *A Dictionary of Catch Phrases British and American, from the Sixteenth Century to the Present Day.* New York: Stein and Day, 1977.

—. *A Dictionary of Slang and Unconventional English: Colloquialisms and Catch-phrases, Solecisms and Catachreses, Nicknames, Vulgarisms, and such Americanisms as have been naturalized.* New York: Macmillan, 1961.

The Penny Cyclopaedia of the Society for the Diffusion of Useful Knowledge. 27 volumes. London: Charles Knight, 1833-1843.

The Penny Magazine of the Society for Useful Knowledge. London, 1843.

Perkins, Edward T. *Na Motu: or, Reef-Rovings in the South Seas*. New York: 1854.

Perry, Ralph Barton. *Puritanism and Democracy*. New York and Evanston: Harper Torchbooks, 1964.

Philbrick, Thomas. "Melville's 'Best Authorities.'" *Nineteenth Century Fiction* XV (September, 1960), 171-79.

Piper, David. *The Illustrated Dictionary of Art & Artists*. New York: Random House, 1984.

The Poetical Works of John Milton with Notes, and a Life of the Author. A New Edition. 2 volumes. 8 vo. Boston: Hilliard, Gray, and Company, 1836.

Pommer, Henry F. *Milton and Melville*. New York: Cooper Square Publishers, 1970.

Porter, David, Captain. *Journal of a Cruise Made to the Pacific Ocean, in the U.S. Frigate Essex, in the Years 1812, 1813, and 1814*. 2 volumes. Philadelphia: 1815.

Prescott, William H. *History of the Conquest of Peru*. New York: E.P. Dutton & Co. Inc., 1933.

—. *History of the Reign of Ferdinand and Isabella: The Catholic*. Philadelphia: J.B. Lippincott, 1904.

—. *History of the Reign of Philip the Second: King of Spain*. 3 volumes. London: George Routledge and Sons, n.d.

Pritchard, George. *The Missionary's Reward: or, The Success of the Gospel in the Pacific*. London: 1844.

Pritchard, William T. *Polynesian Reminiscences; or, Life in the Southern Pacific Islands*. London. 1866.

The Prose of Sir Thomas Browne. Editor, Norman Endicott. New York: W.W. Norton & Co. Inc., 1972.

Quirk, Tom. *Melville's Confidence Man: From Knave to Knight.* Columbia, University of Missouri Press, 1982.

The Recognition of Herman Melville. Editor, Hershel Parker. United States: University of Michigan Press, 1970.

Remini, Robert V., Editor. *The Age of Jackson.* New York: Harper & Row, 1972.

Reynolds, Larry J. "Antidemocratic Emphasis in *White-Jacket.*" *American Literature,* XLVIII (March 1976), No. 1, 13-28.

Robertson, Ian. *Blue Guide: Paris and Environs.* New York: Norton, 1985.

Rogin, Michael Paul. *Subversive Genealogy: The Politics and Art of Herman Melville.* Berkeley: University of California Press, 1985.

Rosenberry, Edward H. *Melville.* Boston: Routledge & Kegan Paul, 1979.

Routh, C.R.N., General Editor. *Who's Who in History.* 5 volumes. Oxford: Basil Blackwell, 1960-69.

Ruschenberger, William S.W. *A Voyage round the World.* Philadelphia: 1838.

Sachs, Viola. *The Game of Creation: The Primeval Unlettered Language of Moby-Dick; or, The Whale.* Paris: Editions de la Maison des sciences de l'homme Paris, 1982.

Sands, Robert C. *Life and Correspondence of John Paul Jones including his Narrative of the Campaign of the Liman.* New York, 1830.

Schlesinger, Arthur M., Jr. *The Age of Jackson.* Boston: Little, Brown and Company, 1945.

Scoresby, William. *An Account of the Arctic Regions, with a History and Description of the Northern Whale-Fishery.* Edinburgh: Constable, 1820. 2 volumes.

—. *Journal of a Voyage to the Northern Whale Fishery; Including Researches and Discoveries on the Eastern Coast of West Greenland . . . in . . . 1822. . . .* Edinburgh: Constable, 1823.

Scott, Sir Walter. *The Monastery.* 2 volumes. The Waverly Novels Vol. XVIII. Edinburgh: Adam and Charles Black, 1879. Vol. I.

Sealts, Merton M., Jr. "Melville and the Shakers." *Studies in Bibliography: Papers of the Bibliographical Society of the University of Virginia* 11 (1949-1950), 105-114.

—. *Melville as Lecturer.* Cambridge, Massachusetts: Harvard University Press, 1957.

—. *Melville's Reading: A Check-List of Books Owned and Borrowed.* Madison: University of Wisconsin Press, 1966.

Seltzer, Leon E., Editor. *The Columbia Lippincott Gazetteer of the World.* With the Geographical Research Staff of Columbia University Press and with the Cooperation of the American Geographical Society. With 1961 Supplement. Morningside Heights, New York: Columbia University Press by arrangement with J.B. Lippincott Company, 1962.

Sewall, Richard B. *The Life of Emily Dickinson.* 2 volumes. New York: Farrar, Straus and Giroux, 1974.

Shafritz, Jay M. *The Dorsey Dictionary of American Government and Politics.* Chicago: The Dorsey Press, 1988.

Shakespeare, William. *The Complete Works of William Shakespeare.* Cambridge Edition Text. Editor, William Aldis Wright. Garden City, New York: Garden City Publishing Co., 1936.

Shay, Frank. *A Sailor's Treasury: Being the Myths and Superstituions, Lore, Legends and Yarns, the Cries, Epithets and Salty Speech of the American Sailorman in the Days of Oak and Canvas.* New York: Norton, 1951.

Simons, Eric N. *The Devil of the Vault: A Life of Guy Fawkes.* London: Frederick Muller limited, 1963.

Slesser, Malcolm. *Brazil: Land Without Limit.* Cranbury, New Jersey: A.S. Barnes and Company, 1970.

Smith (Burleigh), Matthew Hale. *Sunshine and Shadow in New York.* Hartford: J.B. Burr and Company, 1868.

Smollett, Tobias. *The Adventures of Roderick Random.* London: Oxford University Press, 1930.

Smyth, Admiral W.H. *The Sailor's Word Book: An Alphabetical Digest of Nautical Terms Including Some More Especially Military and Scientific, but Useful to Seamen: As well as Archaisms of Early Voyages, etc.* London: Blackie and Son, 1867.

Solomon, Pearl Chesler. *Dickens and Melville in Their Time.* New York: Columbia University Press, 1975.

Southey, Robert. *History of Brazil*. 3 volumes. New York: Greenwood Press, 1969. Originally published 1819.

—. *The Life of Nelson* . . . . New York: Harper, 1855.

Spann, Edward K. *The New Metropolis: New York City, 1840-1857*. New York: Columbia University Press, 1981.

Spearman, James Martin. *The British Gunner*. 1828.

Stamp, Sir Dudley, Editor. *A Glossary of Geographical Terms*. London: Longman, 1966.

Stein, William Bysshe. *The Poetry of Melville's Late Years: Time, History, Myth, and Religion*. Albany: State University of New York Press, 1970.

Stephen, Leslie and Sidney Lee, Editors. *The Dictionary of National Biography*. 22 volumes. London, 1921.

Stewart, Charles S. *A Visit to the South Seas, in the U.S. Ship Vincennes, During the Years 1829 and 1830; with Scenes in Brazil, Peru, Manilla, the Cape of Good Hope, and St. Helena*. 2 volumes. New York: John P. Haven, 1831.

Stewart, Randall. *Nathaniel Hawthorne: A Biography*. New Haven: Yale University Press, 1948.

Stirling-Maxwell, Sir William. *The Cloister Life of the Emperor Charles V*. London: John C. Nemmo, 1891.

Strangford, Lord Viscount. *Poems, from the Portuguese of Luis de Camoens: With remarks on his Life and Writings*. 6th ed. London: Whittingham, and Rowland, 1810.

Strong, James. *Strong's Exhaustive Concordance.* Gordons-
ville, Tennessee: Dugan Publishers, Inc., n.d.

Sweeney, Gerard M. *Melville's Use of Classical Mythology.*
Volume 5 of *Melville Studies in American Culture.*
Editor, Robert Brainard Pearsall. Amsterdam: Rodopi,
N.V., 1975.

Sweetman, Jack. *American Naval History: An Illustrated
Chronology of the U.S. Navy and Marine Corps 1775-
Present.* Annapolis, Maryland: Naval Institute Press,
1984.

Taylor, John. *A Biographical Sketch of the Character of Caius
Cilnius Maecenas.* Liverpool: T. Bean, 1838.

Tharp, Louise Hall. *The Peabody Sisters of Salem.* Boston:
Little, Brown and Company, 1950.

Thomas, R. *Interesting and Authentic Narratives of the most
Remarkable Shipwrecks, Fires, Calamities, Providential
Deliverances, and Lamentable Disasters on the Seas, in
most Parts of the World.* (Cited in Huntress.)

Thompson, Lawrance. *Melville's Quarrel With God.* Princeton, New Jersey: Princeton University Press, 1952.

Thorp, Willard. "Redburn's Prosy Old Guidebook." *PMLA*
LIII (December 1938), 1146-1156.

Titus, David K. "Herman Melville at the Albany Academy."
Melville Society Extracts 42 (May 1980), 4-10.

The Tower of London. Publication of the Department of the
Environment, London: Her Majesty's Stationery Office,
1974.

Trilling, Lionel. *The Liberal Imagination: Essays on Literature and Society*. Garden City, New York: Anchor Doubleday, 1953.

Tripp, Edward. *The Meridian Handbook of Classical Mythology*. Originally published as *Crowell's Handbook of Classical Mythology*. New York: Meridian, New American Library, Signet, 1970.

Trollope, Frances. *Domestic Manners of the Americans*. Editor, Donald Smalley. New York: Vintage Books, 1960.

Trow Business Directory of New York City (Wilson's Business Directory) 1848/49. New York: H. Wilson, 1848.

Turnbull, John. *A Voyage round the World, in the years 1800-1804*. 3 volumes. London, 1805 (Philadelphia, 1810).

[Tyerman, Daniel, and George Bennett]. *Journal of Voyages and Travels* (Deputed by the London Missionary Society to Visit the South Seas, 1821-1825). James Montgomery, Editor. 2 volumes. Boston: 1832.

Uden, Grant, and Richard Cooper. *A Dictionary of British Ships and Seaman*. New York: St. Martin's Press, 1980.

Upjohn, Everard M. and Paul S. Wingert, Jane Gaston Mahler, Editors. *History of World Art*. New York: Oxford University Press, 1949.

Vaillant, George C. *Aztecs of Mexico: Origin, Rise, and Fall of the Aztec Nation*. Rev. by Suzannah B. Vaillant. Baltimore, Maryland: Penguin Books, 1965.

Vancouver, George. *A Voyage of Discovery to the North Pacific Ocean and Round the World in the Years 1790-1795 in the Discovery Sloop of War and Armed Tender*

Chatham, under the Command of Captain George Vancouver (3 volumes). 1798. With atlas of plates.

Van Deusen, Glyndon G. *The Jacksonian Era: 1828-1848.* New York: Harper & Row Harper Torchbooks, 1959.

Vigier, François. *Change and Apathy: Liverpool and Manchester during the Industrial Revolution.* Cambridge, Massachusetts and London, England: The M.I.T. Press, 1970.

Vincent, Howard P., Editor. *Melville and Hawthorne in the Berkshires: A Symposium: Melville Annual 1966.* Ohio: The Kent State University Press, 1968.

—. *The Tailoring of Melville's White-Jacket.* Evanston: Northwestern University Press, 1970.

—. *The Trying-Out of Moby-Dick.* Carbondale and Edwardsville: Southern Illinois University Press, 1949; rpt. N.P.: Arcturus Books, 1965.

Viney, Nigel. *A Dictionary of Toponyms.* London: The Library Association, 1986.

Wafer, Lionel. *A New Voyage and Description of the Isthmus of America.* 1699, 1704.

—. *A New Voyage and Description of the Isthmus of America.* 1699. New Edition by L.E. Elliott Joyce, 1934.

Walter, Richard and Benjamin Robins. *A Voyage Round the World in the years MDCCXL, I, II, II, IV by George Anson.* Editor, Glyndwr Williams. London: Oxford University Press, 1974.

Weales, Gerald, Editor. *Edwardian Plays.* New York: Hill and Wang, 1962.

Webster's New Geographical Dictionary. Springfield, Massachusetts: G. & C. Merriam Co., 1972, 1980.

Weidman, Bette. *"Typee and Omoo*: A Diverging Pair." *A Companion to Melville Studies.* John Bryant, Editor. New York: Greenwood Press, 1986.

Weissbuch, Ted N., "A Note on the Confidence-Man's Counterfeit Detector," *Emerson Society Quarterly*, 19 (1960), 16-18.

[Wheeler, Daniel]. *Memoirs of the Life and Gospel Labors of the Late Daniel Wheeler.* Philadelphia: [1842].

Whitman, Walt. *Leaves of Grass.* Editors, Harold W. Blodgett and   Sculley Bradley. New York: W.W. Norton, 1965.

Wilkes, Charles, U.S.N. *Narrative of the United States Exploring Expedition During the Years 1838, 1839, 1840, 1841, 1842 in Five Volumes, and an Atlas.* Philadelphia: Lea & Blanchard, 1845.

Wilkinson, George Theodore, Editor. *The Newgate Calendar I.* London: Panther, 1962.

Wilson, Rufus Rockwell. *New York: Old & New: Its Story, Streets, and Landmarks.* 2 volumes. Philadelphia: J.B. Lippincott Company, 1903.

Wines, Enoch C. *Two Years and a Half in the American Navy: Comprising a Journal of a Cruise to England, in the Mediterranean, and in the Levant, On Board of the U.S. Frigate Constellation, in the Years 1829, 1830, and 1831.* 2 volumes. London: Richard Bentley, 1833. Volume I.

Wise, Lieutenant [Henry A.] *Los Gringos: or an Inside View of . . . Polynesia.* New York: 1849.

Wolfe, Gerard R. *New York: A Guide to the Metropolis*. New
   York: New York University Press, 1975.

The Works of Geoffrey Chaucer. Editor, F.N. Robinson. 2nd
   Edition. Boston: Houghton Mifflin Co., 1957.

World Atlas. Maplewood: C.S. Hammond, 1964.

Wright, Nathalia. *Melville's Use of the Bible*. Durham, North
   Carolina: Duke University Press, 1949.

Yannella, Donald, and Hershel Parker, Editors. *The Endless,
   Winding Way in Melville: New Charts by Kring and
   Carey*. Glassboro, New Jersey: The Melville Society,
   1981.

DATE DUE

Demco, Inc. 38-293